2000

CHASE'S
SPORTS
CALENDAR OF EVENTS

Compiled by Steve Gietschier

CB
CONTEMPORARY BOOKS

— WARNING —

FOR PERMISSION TO REPRODUCE OR COPY ANY PORTION OF THE WORK, CONTACT THE PUBLISHER:

NTC/CONTEMPORARY PUBLISHING GROUP
A TRIBUNE COMPANY
4255 W TOUHY AVE
LINCOLNWOOD, ILLINOIS 60712-1975
FAX: (847) 679-6388
PHONE: (847) 679-5500

Printed in USA

— NOTICE —

Events listed herein are not necessarily endorsed by the editors or publisher. Every effort has been made to assure the correctness of all entries, but neither the authors nor the publisher can warrant their accuracy. IT IS IMPERATIVE, IF FINANCIAL PLANS ARE TO BE MADE IN CONNECTION WITH DATES OR EVENTS LISTED HEREIN, THAT PRINCIPALS BE CONSULTED FOR FINAL INFORMATION.

GRAPHIC IMAGES

The interior illustrations were created for this book by Dan Krovatin. The photographs in the interior are the property of *The Sporting News* and are used with its permission. Cover images copyright © 1997 PhotoDisc, Inc.

Gietschier, Steve
Chase's 2000 sports calendar of events,
Chicago, NTC/Contemporary Publishing Group   (c. 2000)

368 p., ill.
Includes index and tables.

ISBN: 0-8092-2600-6

ISSN: 1091-2959

The Library of Congress does not issue Cataloging in Publication information or a Library of Congress Number for publications classified as "Transitory."

TABLE OF CONTENTS

WELCOME TO *CHASE'S 2000 SPORTS CALENDAR OF EVENTS*

Welcome to the fourth edition of *Chase's Sports Calendar of Events*, a compilation of events from North America and around the world. The focus here is sports and recreational activities, covered in greater breadth and depth in this volume than in any other in print. *Chase's Sports Calendar of Events*, in fact, is the most thorough and detailed day-by-day record of notable events in the world of sports.

This fourth edition includes almost 6,000 entries for events and observances occurring in 2000. They have been compiled in the tradition and style of the widely respected *Chase's Calendar of Events*, the standard reference source for information about events, observances, birthdays, historical anniversaries and much more. *Chase's Sports Calendar of Events* provides information that sports enthusiasts, recreation seekers and vacation planners need to know in order to plan their leisure-time activities. For librarians, public relations firms, schools, retailers, the media and the general public, *Chase's Sports Calendar of Events* is an essential planning tool. It is:

- *the* book that sports broadcasters, writers, reporters and talk show hosts will consult to find program ideas, background material, filler copy and information about forthcoming events;
- *the* source that sports fans will devour for interesting and amusing information about both legendary and lesser-known sports organizations, teams, stadiums and players;
- *the* guide that recreational athletes and nonathletes will consult for fun and challenging activities in which they can participate;
- *the* directory that the public will check to find sports and recreational organizations of all kinds, at all levels and in all parts of the US and Canada;
- and *the* reference work that public relations and promotions people will scan when looking for a sport or recreational event, team or organization for their clients or companies to sponsor.

Attempting to be inclusive, we have defined sports and recreation rather broadly, listing a wide variety of local happenings from all across the US and Canada as well as some events in other countries. The selection of these items reflects our editorial opinion about the important, interesting and unusual events in the world of sports and recreation coming up in the new year.

Sports Throughout the Year
The sporting year has no beginning, and it has no end. To publish a calendar starting in January and ending in December does injustice to some sports. A number of leagues and sports organizations, some of which had not begun their 1999 seasons when this book went to press, could not supply their 2000 schedules for inclusion here. To alleviate this problem, readers should consult not only the Directory of Sports Organizations beginning on page 000 for addresses and phone numbers but also the website addresses located throughout the book and in a special chart on the inside front cover.

Featured for 2000
Besides the types of events described below, the 2000 edition of *Chase's Sports Calendar of Events* includes:

- Sportsquote of the Day: For various dates throughout the year, readers will find a quotation connected to a person or event commemorated on that date.
- Champions This Date: For certain events, like the Super Bowl or the World Series, that occur annually on or about the same date, readers will find past champions listed in special boxes on the appropriate dates.

2000 Spotlight
The sports spotlight in 2000 will shine on Sydney, New South Wales, Australia, site of the XXVIIth Summer Olympic Games. Through 1992, both the Winter Games and the Summer Games were held in the same year. Starting in 1994, the Winter Olympics moved to their own four-year cycle. Thus, the Summer Games were held in Atlanta in 1996 and will be held next in 2004 in Athens, Greece. The Winter Games began their own rotation in 1994 in Lillehammer, Norway, and continue with the Salt Lake City Games in 2002 and the Turin, Italy, Games in 2006.

The opening ceremony of the Sydney Games will begin on the morning of Friday, September 15, and the closing ceremony will commence on Sunday, October 1. Because of the time difference between Australia and the US—Sydney is 14 hours ahead of Eastern Time in the US—these ceremonies will seem to occur to Americans on Thursday, September 14, and Saturday, September 30, respectively. Since Americans will view most of the events of these Games on a tape-delayed basis on the NBC television network and its associated cable networks, events are listed in this book on the day they will happen in Australia.

Types of Events in *Chase's Sports Calendar of Events*
SPONSORED EVENTS: Sporting and recreational events sponsored by an individual or organization are listed with inclusive dates and places of observance, a brief description, the approximate attendance when provided and the sponsor's name and address—plus, if the sponsor agrees, phone number, fax number, E-mail address and website address.

HISTORIC ANNIVERSARIES, FOLKLORIC EVENTS AND BIRTHDAYS: Compiled from a wide variety of materials covering sporting and recreational events in virtually every part of the world, these entries are supported for accuracy whenever possible by two or more independent sources. Living persons are listed under "Birthdays Today."

HOLIDAYS AND SPECIAL OBSERVANCES: National holidays, traditional and religious observances and astronomical events, as well as special days, weeks and months related to the world of sports and recreation, are included.

Omissions/"Errors"
The omission of a sponsored event, particularly one listed in last year's edition, means that the date of the event was set too late for inclusion. Discrepancies in dating are most often the result of tentative information that is later changed by the sponsoring individual or organization.

Acknowledgments
Thanks to the many people who helped in a variety of ways to make this edition a reality: Martha Best, Gigi Grajdura, Pamela Juárez, Patricia Kirchberg, Richard Spears, Terry Stone, Kim Summers, Sandy Whiteley, Cindy Slater, Craig Boaden and James Meier. And, finally, to Donna, Katie, Sarah and Andy Gietschier.

And now we invite readers to join with us in celebrating sports and recreation in the coming year.

Steve Gietschier, Editor
July 1999

JANUARY 1 — SATURDAY
Day 1 — 365 Remaining

SATURDAY, JANUARY ONE, 2000. Jan 1. First day of the first month of the Gregorian calendar year, Anno Domini 2000, being a Leap Year, and (until July 4th) 224th year of American Independence. 2000 will be year 6713 of the Julian Period, a time frame consisting of 7,980 years, which began at noon, universal time, Jan 1, 4713 BC. Astronomers will note that Julian Day number 2,451,545 begins at noon, universal [Greenwich] time, Jan 1, 2000 (representing the number of days since the beginning of the Julian period). Jan 1 has been observed as the beginning of the year in most English-speaking countries since the British Calendar Act of 1751, prior to which the New Year began on Mar 25 (approximating the vernal equinox). New Year's Day has been called "Everyman's Birthday," and in some countries a year is added to everyone's age on Jan 1 rather than on the anniversary of each person's birth. New Year's Day is a public holiday in the US and in many other countries. Traditionally, it is a time for personal stocktaking, for making resolutions for the coming year, and sometimes for recovering from the festivities of New Year's Eve. In the world of sports, New Year's Day has special significance. It represents the beginning of the professional golf season, the climax of the college football season, even though some bowl games may be played on succeeding days, and play-off time in the National Football League. The basketball and hockey seasons are well underway on Jan 1, and baseball fans begin to count the days until the start of spring training and the regular season. For thoroughbred horses, Jan 1 is a universal birthday. Colts foaled in the spring of 1999 become yearlings. Colts foaled in 1997 are now 3-year-olds, eligible for the Triple Crown.

CHICAGO'S WINDY CITY JITTERBUG CLUB DANCE. Jan 1 (also Jan 15). Franklin Park, IL. First and third Saturdays of each month. Dance to the music of the '50s, '60s and more. Dances held twice a month at the Franklin Park American Legion Hall. Est attendance: 200. For info: CWCJC, PO Box 713, Franklin Park, IL 60131. Phone: (708) 456-6000. E-mail: ljtrbg2@aol.com.

CompUSA FLORIDA CITRUS BOWL. Jan 1. Orlando, FL. Postseason college football game matching the second-place teams from the Big Ten and the Southeastern Conferences. Sponsors: CompUSA and the Florida Department of Citrus. Est attendance: 70,000. For info: Florida Citrus Sports Assn, Inc, One Citrus Bowl Place, Orlando, FL 32805. Phone: (407) 423-2476. Fax: (407) 425-8451. E-mail: fcsports@psinet.com. Web: www.fx sports.com.

FEDEX ORANGE BOWL. Jan 1. Pro Player Stadium, Miami, FL. Postseason college football game matching two top teams in the Bowl Championship Series. Spon-

sored by FedEx. Est attendance: 75,000. For info: Orange Bowl Committee, 601 Brickell Key Dr, Ste 206, Miami, FL 33131. Phone: (305) 371-4600. Fax: (305) 371-4318. Web: www.orangebowl.com.

FIRST AMERICAN FOOTBALL LEAGUE CHAMPIONSHIP GAME: ANNIVERSARY. Jan 1, 1961. The Houston Oilers defeated the Los Angeles Chargers, 24–16, to win the first championship of the upstart American Football League. Houston quarterback George Blanda threw three touchdown passes, and Oilers receiver Billy Cannon was named the game's MVP. The championship was played at Houston's Jeppesen Stadium before 32,183 fans.

FIRST COTTON BOWL: ANNIVERSARY. Jan 1, 1937. Texas Christian University beat Marquette, 16–6, in the first Cotton Bowl football game played at Fair Park Stadium, Dallas, TX. The game was moved to the stadium called the Cotton Bowl in 1938.

FIRST ORANGE BOWL: 65th ANNIVERSARY. Jan 1, 1935. Bucknell beat the University of Miami, 26–0, in the first Orange Bowl football game played at Miami Field Stadium. The game was moved to the Orange Bowl in 1938 and to Joe Robbie Stadium (later called Pro Player Stadium) in 1996.

FIRST ROSE BOWL: ANNIVERSARY. Jan 1, 1902. Michigan defeated Stanford 49–0 in the first postseason football game, the Tournament of Roses Association Football Game. Known as the Rose Bowl since 1923, it is preceded each year by the Tournament of Roses Parade at Pasadena, CA.

FIRST SUGAR BOWL: 65th ANNIVERSARY. Jan 1, 1935. Tulane University beat Temple University, 20–14, in the first Sugar Bowl football game played at Tulane Stadium, New Orleans. The game was moved to the Louisiana Superdome in 1975.

FROZEN FOOT RENDEZVOUS. Jan 1–2. Oakwood Lakes State Park, White, SD. Features muzzle-loading shooting contest along with treasure hunting, outdoor camping and wild game cook-off. South Dakota State Park license required. Annually, the weekend after Christmas, beginning this time on Dec 31, 1999. For info: Dave and Julie Huebner, Frozen Foot Rendezvous, 47826 Main St, Bushnell, SD 57276. Phone: (605) 693-4589.

GREENBERG, HANK: BIRTH ANNIVERSARY. Jan 1, 1911. Henry Benjamin (Hank) Greenberg, Baseball Hall of Fame first baseman and outfielder, born at New York, NY. One of the game's most prodigious sluggers, Greenberg hit 331 home runs and drove in 1,276 runs in only nine full seasons. Baseball's first Jewish superstar, Greenberg entered the army after playing just 19 games in 1941 and did not return to the Detroit Tigers until midway through the 1945 season. His grand slam on that season's last day won the pennant for the Tigers and propelled them toward a World Series triumph. Inducted into the Hall of Fame in 1956. Died at Beverly Hills, CA, Sept 4, 1986.

HANGOVER HANDICAP RUN. Jan 1. Veteran's Park, Klamath Falls, OR. Two-mile fun run at 9 AM on New Year's Day morning. The 1st-place male and female finishers each take home a beer can trophy. Est attendance: 60. For info: Hangover Handicap, 1800 Fairmont, Klamath Falls, OR 97601. Phone: (541) 882-6922. Fax: (541) 883-6481.

KEEFE, TIM: BIRTH ANNIVERSARY. Jan 1, 1857. Timothy John (Tim) Keefe, Baseball Hall of Fame pitcher, born at Cambridge, MA. Keefe won 344 games in the 19th century. He pioneered a new pitch called the change of pace to complement his fastball and curveball. Inducted into the Hall of Fame in 1964. Died at Cambridge, MA, Apr 23, 1933.

McKINNEY, BONES: BIRTH ANNIVERSARY. Jan 1, 1919. Horace Albert ("Bones") McKinney, broadcaster, basketball coach and player, born at Lowland, NC. McKinney played at North Carolina State before World War II and North Carolina after the war. He was ordained a Baptist minister and then became basketball coach at Wake Forest, leading the Demon Deacons to a pair of ACC championships and a Final Four appearance in 1962. Died May 16, 1997.

January 2000

S	M	T	W	T	F	S
						1
2	3	4	5	6	7	8
9	10	11	12	13	14	15
16	17	18	19	20	21	22
23	24	25	26	27	28	29
30	31					

NEWPORT YACHT CLUB FROSTBITE FLEET RACE. Jan 1. Newport Yacht Club, Long Wharf, Newport, RI. Annual New Year's Day race. Sponsor: Newport Yacht Club. Est attendance: 5,000. For info: Newport Yacht Club, PO Box 488, Newport, RI 02840. Phone: (800) 326-6030. Fax: (401) 849-9060.

OUTBACK BOWL. Jan 1. Tampa Stadium, Tampa, FL. Postseason college football game matching the third-place teams from the Southeastern Conference and the Big Ten Conference. Sponsored by Outback Steakhouse. Est attendance: 65,000. For info: Mike Schulze, Tampa Bay Bowl Assn, Inc, 4511 N Himes Ave, Ste 260, Tampa, FL 33614. Phone: (813) 874-2695. Fax: (813) 873-1959.

PENGUIN PLUNGE. Jan 1. Mackeral Cove, Jamestown, RI. Annual plunge into the icy waters of Narragansett Bay to benefit Rhode Island Special Olympics. Annually, Jan 1. Est attendance: 2,000. For info: Rhode Island Special Olympics, 33 College Hill Rd, Bldg 31, Warwick, RI 02886. Phone: (401) 823-7411. Fax: (401) 823-7415.

POLAR BEAR SWIM. Jan 1. Sheboygan Armory, Sheboygan, WI. Each New Year's Day at 1 PM, more than 450 daring swimmers brave Lake Michigan's ice floes. Most are costumed, all are crazy. Refreshments and free live entertainment from 10–6. Sponsor: Sheboygan Polar Bear Club. Est attendance: 2,000. For info: Sheboygan CVB, 712 Riverfront Dr, Ste 101, Sheboygan, WI 53081. Phone: (920) 467-8436.

ROSE BOWL. Jan 1. Rose Bowl, Pasadena, CA. Postseason college football game matching two top teams in the Bowl Championship Series. Known familiarly as the "Grandaddy of Them All." Est attendance: 100,000. For info: Pasadena Tournament of Roses Assn, 391 S Orange Grove Blvd, Pasadena, CA 91184. Phone: (626) 449-4100. Fax: (626) 449-9066.

SNO'FLY: THE FIRST KITE FLY OF THE YEAR. Jan 1. Prairie View Park, Kalamazoo, MI. Keep the New Year's celebration in full flight at this high-flying alternative to (seemingly) endless football games. Sno'Fly takes off from the frozen lake at Prairie View Park. Est attendance: 500. For info: John Cosby, Mktg Coord, Kalamazoo County Parks Dept, 2900 Lake St, Kalamazoo, MI 49001. Phone: (616) 383-8778. Fax: (616) 383-8724. Web: www.kalcounty.com.

SOUTHWESTERN BELL COTTON BOWL CLASSIC. Jan 1. Cotton Bowl, Dallas, TX. 64th annual. Postseason college football game matching the second-place team from the Big 12 Conference and the third-place team from the SEC. Sponsored by Southwestern Bell. Est attendance: 68,000. For info: Cotton Bowl Athletic Assn, PO Box 569420, Dallas, TX 75356-9420. Phone: (214) 634-7525. Fax: (214) 634-7764. E-mail: mail@swbellcottonbowl.com. Web: www.cottonbowl.com.

TOYOTA GATOR BOWL. Jan 1. Gator Bowl, Jacksonville, FL. Postseason college football game matching the second-place team in the Atlantic Coast Conference and the second-place team from the Big East Conference or Notre Dame. Sponsored by Toyota Motor Sales USA, Inc. Est attendance: 77,000. For info: Gator Bowl Assn, Inc, One Gator Bowl Blvd, Jacksonville, FL 32202. Phone: (904) 798-1700. Fax: (904) 632-2080.

WALKER, DOAK: BIRTH ANNIVERSARY. Jan 1, 1927. Ewell Doak Walker, Jr, Pro Football Hall of Fame and Heisman Trophy running back, born at Dallas, TX. Walker won the Heisman Trophy in 1948, playing for SMU, and went on to an outstanding pro career with the Detroit Lions. He was a handsome, humble player during a time when football players could become national heroes. Inducted into the Hall of Fame in 1986. Died at Steamboat Springs, CO, Sept 27, 1998.

BIRTHDAYS TODAY

Robert (Bobby) Holik, 29, hockey player, born Jihlava, Czechoslovakia, Jan 1, 1971.

Fernando Tatis, 25, baseball player, born San Pedro de Macoris, Dominican Republic, Jan 1, 1975.

Derrick Vincent Thomas, 33, football player, born Miami, FL, Jan 1, 1967.

☆   ☆   ☆

JANUARY 2 — SUNDAY

Day 2 — 364 Remaining

CHASE'S SPORTSQUOTE OF THE DAY

"I can't wait until tomorrow 'cause I get better-lookin' every day." — Joe Namath

BELLOWS GETS 1,000th POINT: ANNIVERSARY. Jan 2, 1999. Right wing Brian Bellows of the Washington Capitals got the 1,000th point of his National Hockey League career, an assist in a 5–2 win over the Toronto Maple Leafs.

BOSSY SCORES 500th GOAL: ANNIVERSARY. Jan 2, 1986. Right wing Mike Bossy of the New York Islanders became the 11th player in National Hockey League history to score 500 regular-season goals when he scored into an empty net in a 7–5 victory over the Boston Bruins. Bossy ended his career with 647 goals and was inducted into the Hockey Hall of Fame in 1991.

JOE NAMATH SIGNS CONTRACT: 35th ANNIVERSARY. Jan 2, 1965. After finishing his college football career at the University of Alabama, quarterback Joe Namath signed a 3-year contract for an estimated $427,000 with the New York Jets of the American Football League. Namath was also drafted by the NFL's St. Louis Cardinals, but Jets owner Sonny Werblin won a bidding war for his services.

KURRI GETS 1,000th POINT: 10th ANNIVERSARY. Jan 2, 1990. Right wing Jari Kurri of the Edmonton Oilers got the 1,000th point of his National Hockey League career, an assist in a 6–4 win over the St. Louis Blues. Kurri finished his career with 1,398 points.

NEW ZEALAND: LOUIS VUITTON CUP SEMI-FINALS. Jan 2. Auckland, New Zealand. After three series of round-robin races, four yachts will compete in semi-final competition to decide the challenger yacht in the America's Cup races, which will commence on Feb 19.

RAMSAY WINS 800th GAME: ANNIVERSARY. Jan 2, 1987. The Indiana Pacers defeated the Los Angeles Clippers, 116–106, to give Pacers head coach Jack Ramsay the 800th victory of his NBA coaching career. Ramsay, the second coach to achieve this milestone, finished his career with a record of 864–783. He was inducted into the Basketball Hall of Fame in 1992.

RICKARD, TEX: BIRTH ANNIVERSARY. Jan 2, 1871. George Lewis ("Tex") Rickard, sports promoter, born at Leavenworth, KS. Rickard's promotion of boxing matches, especially involving Jack Dempsey, helped to make the sport a major attraction. Working with Madison Square Garden, he organized bicycle races and obtained an NHL franchise, nicknaming the team the Rangers as in "Tex's Rangers." Died at Miami, FL, Jan 6, 1929.

TOSTITOS FIESTA BOWL. Jan 2. Sun Devil Stadium, Tempe, AZ. Postseason college football game matching two top teams in the Bowl Championship Series. Est attendance: 73,000. For info: Arizona Sports Foundation, 120 S Ash Ave, Tempe, AZ 85281. Phone: (602) 350-0900. Fax: (602) 350-0915.

BIRTHDAYS TODAY

Royce Spencer Clayton, 30, baseball player, born Burbank, CA, Jan 2, 1970.

David Brian Cone, 37, baseball player, born Kansas City, MO, Jan 2, 1963.

Robert Brian (Robbie) Ftorek, 48, hockey coach and former player, born Needham, MA, Jan 2, 1952.

Calvin Hill, 53, former football player, born Baltimore, MD, Jan 2, 1947.

Jesse Craig James, 39, broadcaster and former football player, born Jacksonville, TX, Jan 2, 1961.

Gino Marchetti, 73, Pro Football Hall of Fame defensive end, born Smithers, WV, Jan 2, 1927.

Edgar Martinez, 37, baseball player, born New York, NY, Jan 2, 1963.

Mattias Norstrom, 28, hockey player, born Stockholm, Sweden, Jan 2, 1972.

Robert Svehla, 31, hockey player, born Martin, Czechoslovakia, Jan 2, 1969.

Forest Gregory (Greg) Swindell, 35, baseball player, born Ft Worth, TX, Jan 2, 1965.

Richard Stephen (Rick) Tabaracci, 31, hockey player, born Toronto, Ontario, Canada, Jan 2, 1969.

Pernell Whitaker, 36, boxer, born Norfolk, VA, Jan 2, 1964.

JANUARY 3 — MONDAY

Day 3 — 363 Remaining

BROWNS' 2OT PLAY-OFF WIN: ANNIVERSARY. Jan 3, 1987. Cleveland quarterback Bernie Kosar passed for 487 yards, an NFL playoff record, to lead the Browns to a double-overtime 23–20 victory over the New York Jets in an AFC divisional play-off game. The following week, Cleveland lost the AFC championship game, also in overtime, to the Denver Broncos by the identical score.

RUTH SOLD TO YANKEES: 80th ANNIVERSARY. Jan 3, 1920. Boston Red Sox owner and theatrical producer Harry Frazee sold pitcher–outfielder Babe Ruth to the New York Yankees for $125,000 and a $300,000 loan. Frazee used the loan several years later to produce *No, No, Nanette*, a hit musical.

STEINBRENNER BUYS YANKEES: ANNIVERSARY. Jan 3, 1973. A group headed by shipping executive George M. Steinbrenner, III, bought the New York Yankees from CBS for $10 million. "We plan absentee ownership," Steinbrenner said at the time of the purchase. "We're not going to pretend to be something we aren't. I'll stick to building ships."

BIRTHDAYS TODAY

Larry Robert Barnett, 55, baseball umpire, born Nitro, WV, Jan 3, 1945.

Stanley George ("Frenchy") Bordagaray, 90, former baseball player, born Coalinga, CA, Jan 3, 1910.

Darren Arthur Daulton, 38, former baseball player, born Arkansas City, KS, Jan 3, 1962.

Robert Marvin (Bobby) Hull, 61, Hockey Hall of Fame left wing, born Point Anne, Ontario, Canada, Jan 3, 1939.

Cheryl DeAnne Miller, 36, basketball coach and Basketball Hall of Fame forward, born Riverside, CA, Jan 3, 1964.

Luis Beltran Sojo, 34, baseball player, born Barquisimeto, Venezuela, Jan 3, 1966.

JANUARY 4 — TUESDAY
Day 4 — 362 Remaining

CELTICS RETIRE AUERBACH'S "NUMBER": 15th ANNIVERSARY. Jan 4, 1985. To honor team president and former coach Arnold ("Red") Auerbach, the Boston Celtics retired uniform number 2 in a ceremony prior to a game against the New York Knicks. Auerbach began coaching the Celtics in 1950–51 and led them to 16 NBA championships as coach, general manager and president.

FIRST NFL EXPANSION CHAMP: 30th ANNIVERSARY. Jan 4, 1970. The Minnesota Vikings became the first expansion team to win the NFL title when they defeated the Cleveland Browns, 27–7, at Minneapolis. The Vikings went on to lose Super Bowl IV to the Kansas City Chiefs.

GARTNER GETS 1,000th POINT: ANNIVERSARY. Jan 4, 1992. Right wing Mike Gartner of the New York Rangers got the 1,000th point of his National Hockey League career, a goal in a 6–4 loss to the New York Islanders. Gartner finished his career with 1,335 points.

LAST AFL CHAMPIONSHIP GAME: 30th ANNIVERSARY. Jan 4, 1970. The Kansas City Chiefs, aided by four interceptions, defeated the Oakland Raiders, 17–7, in the last American Football League championship game. The Chiefs went on to defeat the Minnesota Vikings in Super Bowl IV. For the 1970 season, the AFL became the American Football Conference within the National Football League.

NEELY, JESS: BIRTH ANNIVERSARY. Jan 4, 1898. Jess Claiborne Neely, football player, coach and administrator, born at Smyrna, TN. Neely played football at Vanderbilt and entered coaching after earning a law degree. He coached at Clemson and at Rice, winning six Southwest Conference titles. Died at Weslaco, TX, Apr 9, 1983.

NHL PUNCH LEADS TO INDICTMENT: 25th ANNIVERSARY. Jan 4, 1975. In an NHL game between the Boston Bruins and the Minnesota North Stars, Bruins winger Dave Forbes punched Henry Boucha, fracturing his cheekbone and opening a cut that required 30 stitches. Forbes was later indicted for using "excessive force," becoming the first professional athlete to be prosecuted for actions taken during a game. His trial that summer ended in a hung jury after which all charges were dropped.

NOKIA SUGAR BOWL. Jan 4. Louisiana Superdome, New Orleans, LA. Postseason college football game matching the top two teams in the Bowl Championship Series for the national championship. Sponsored by Nokia Mobile Telephones. Est attendance: 72,000. For info: Nokia Sugar Bowl, 1500 Sugar Bowl Dr, New Orleans, LA 70112. Phone: (504) 525-8573. Fax: (504) 525-4867. Web: www.nokiasugarbowl.com.

ONLY PRO BOWL IN NEW YORK: ANNIVERSARY. Jan 4, 1942. The Chicago Bears, NFL champions by virtue of their 37–9 victory over the New York Giants, defeated the NFL All-Stars, 35–24, in the only Pro Bowl game ever played in New York. The small Polo Grounds crowd, 17,725, led the league to abandon the Pro Bowl one year later until a new format, matching all-stars from one conference against all-stars from the other, was introduced in 1951.

PAUL, GABE: 90th BIRTH ANNIVERSARY. Jan 4, 1910. Gabriel Howard (Gabe) Paul, baseball executive, born at Rochester, NY. Paul began his baseball career as a minor league batboy and rose to run several major league teams, including the New York Yankees under owner George Steinbrenner. In all, he was responsible for trading, buying and selling more than 500 players. Died at Tampa, FL, Apr 26, 1998.

BIRTHDAYS TODAY

Gerald Garrison Hearst, 29, football player, born Lincolnton, GA, Jan 4, 1971.
Joseph William (Joe) Kleine, 38, basketball player, born Colorado Springs, CO, Jan 4, 1962.
John Christopher (Johnny) Lujack, Jr, 75, Heisman Trophy quarterback, born Connellsville, PA, Jan 4, 1925.
Floyd Patterson, 65, former heavyweight champion boxer, born Waco, NC, Jan 4, 1935.
Todd Sauerbrun, 27, football player, born Setauket, NY, Jan 4, 1973.
Donald Francis (Don) Shula, 70, Pro Football Hall of Fame coach and former player, born Painesville, OH, Jan 4, 1930.

JANUARY 5 — WEDNESDAY
Day 5 — 361 Remaining

CHASE'S SPORTSQUOTE OF THE DAY

"There is no single thing in a football game that turns the fortunes of the two teams more than a goal line stand."— Don Shula

ATLANTA BOAT SHOW. Jan 5–9. World Congress Center, Atlanta, GA. 38th annual show. The region's premiere nautical event offers the best selection of boats and marine accessories at the best prices. Informative boating and fishing seminars. For info: NMMA Boat Shows, 200 E Randolph Dr, Ste 5100, Chicago, IL 60601-6528. Phone: (312) 946-6262. Fax: (312) 946-0401. Web: www.boatshows.com.

BLOZIS, AL: BIRTH ANNIVERSARY. Jan 5, 1919. Albert C. (Al) Blozis, football player, born at Garfield, NJ. Blozis competed in track and field and played football at Georgetown University where he earned a degree in chemistry in 1942. At 6'6" and 240 pounds, he was initially rejected for military service because of his size and played for the New York Giants in the NFL. Finally

	S	M	T	W	T	F	S
January 2000							1
	2	3	4	5	6	7	8
	9	10	11	12	13	14	15
	16	17	18	19	20	21	22
	23	24	25	26	27	28	29
	30	31					

inducted into the army in late 1943, he went overseas in early 1945 and was killed in action when he ventured out in the snow to search for two missing soldiers in his command. Died in the Vosges Mountains, France, Jan 31, 1945.

GLOBETROTTERS LOSE: ANNIVERSARY. Jan 5, 1971. After posting victories in 2,495 straight games dating back to 1962, the Harlem Globetrotters suffered a rare defeat at the hands of their perennial opponents, the Washington Generals. In the closing seconds of a game at Martin, TN, a basket by Red Klotz gave the Generals a 100–99 win. (See also: "Globetrotters Lose: Anniversary" Sept 12.)

KAUFF, BENNY: 110th BIRTH ANNIVERSARY. Jan 5, 1890. Benjamin Michael (Benny) Kauff, baseball player, born at Pomeroy, OH. Kauff led the Federal League in batting in each of its two seasons, 1914 and 1915. He returned to the National League but a few years later was banned for life for alleged involvement in gambling. Died at Columbus, OH, Nov 17, 1961.

McKINLEY, CHUCK: BIRTH ANNIVERSARY. Jan 5, 1941. Charles Robert (Chuck) McKinley, tennis player, born at St. Louis, MO. McKinley was nationally ranked in the early 1960s. He won Wimbledon in 1963 and combined with Dennis Ralston to win the US National Doubles title three times and the 1963 Davis Cup Challenge Round, 3–2, over Australia. Died at Dallas, TX, Aug 11, 1986.

PICCARD, JEANNETTE RIDLON: 105th BIRTH ANNIVERSARY. Jan 5, 1895. Jeannette Ridlon Piccard, balloonist, born at Chicago, IL. Piccard became the first American woman to qualify as a free balloon pilot in 1934 and one of the first women to be ordained as an Episcopal priest in 1976. She set the record for a balloon ascent into the stratosphere (from Dearborn, MI) on Oct 23, 1934, at 57,579 ft with her husband, Jean Felix Piccard. She was an identical twin married to an identical twin. Died at Minneapolis, MN, May 17, 1981.

SAN ANTONIO SPORT, BOAT AND RV SHOW. Jan 5–9. San Antonio Convention Center, San Antonio, TX. Boating, travel, hunting, fishing, camping, RVs and recreation show. 43rd annual show. Sponsor: Boating Trades Assn of San Antonio, TX. For info: Mike Coffen, Double C Productions, Inc, PO Box 1678, Huntsville, TX 77342. Phone: (409) 295-9677. Fax: (409) 295-8859. E-mail: doublec @lcc.net. Web: lcc.net/~doublec.

SHULA RETIRES: ANNIVERSARY. Jan 5, 1996. After 33 seasons as a head coach, Don Shula retired from the helm of the Miami Dolphins to become part-owner and vice-chairman of the team. Shula left the game as the winningest professional coach of all time with a record, counting regular season and play-off games, of 347–173–6. His teams made the play-offs 20 times and won two Super Bowls.

David Tukatahi Dixon, 31, football player, born Auckland, New Zealand, Jan 5, 1969.

Warrick Dunn, 25, football player, born Baton Rouge, LA, Jan 5, 1975.

Jeffrey Joseph (Jeff) Fassero, 37, baseball player, born Springfield, IL, Jan 5, 1963.

Thomas Chandler (Chan) Gailey, 48, football coach, born Gainesville, GA, Jan 5, 1952.

Mike Grier, 25, hockey player, born Detroit, MI, Jan 5, 1975.

Joseph (Joe) Juneau, 32, hockey player, born Pont-Rouge, Quebec, Canada, Jan 5, 1968.

Charles Henry (Chuck) Noll, 68, Pro Football Hall of Fame coach, born Cleveland, OH, Jan 5, 1932.

James Edwin (Jim) Otto, 62, Pro Football Hall of Fame center, born Wausau, WI, Jan 5, 1938.

Felton LaFrance Spencer, 32, basketball player, born Louisville, KY, Jan 5, 1968.

JANUARY 6 — THURSDAY
Day 6 — 360 Remaining

ALL-CANADA SHOW. Jan 6–9. St. Charles Expo Hall, St. Charles, MO. This consumer show allows individuals an opportunity to talk face-to-face with Canadian lodge representatives and outfitters to plan their hunting, fishing and adventure trips to Canada. For info: Rodney Schlafer, Show Dir, All-Canada Show, Bay-Lakes Mktg, Inc, 1889 Commerce Dr, De Pere, WI 54115. Phone: (920) 983-9800. Fax: (920) 983-9985. Web: www.allcanada.com.

ENGLAND: LONDON INTERNATIONAL BOAT SHOW. Jan 6–16. Earls Court Exhibition Centre, London. One of the largest international boat shows in the world, displaying more than 600 craft, plus accessories for the marine enthusiast. Est attendance: 175,000. For info: British Marine Industries Federation/Natl Boat Shows Ltd, Meadlake Place, Thorpe Lea Road, Egham, Surrey, England TW20 8HE. Phone: (44) (178) 447-3377. Fax: (44) (178) 443-9678. Web: www.bigblue.org.uk.

FLYERS' RECORD STREAK: 20th ANNIVERSARY. Jan 6, 1980. The Philadelphia Flyers used two third-period goals to defeat the Buffalo Sabres, 4–2, and extend their NHL record for consecutive games without a loss to 35 (25–0–10). The streak came to an end on the following night when the Flyers lost to the Minnesota North Stars.

JOHNSON, BAN: BIRTH ANNIVERSARY. Jan 6, 1863. Byron Bancroft (Ban) Johnson, Baseball Hall of Fame executive, born at Cincinnati, OH. Johnson transformed the minor league Western League into the major league American League in 1901. He ruled as president with an iron hand and was eased out of power by the league's owners in 1927. Inducted into the Hall of Fame in 1937. Died at St. Louis, MO, Mar 28, 1931.

MIDDLECOFF, CARY: BIRTH ANNIVERSARY. Jan 6, 1921. Emmett Cary Middlecoff, golfer, born at Halls, TN. Middlecoff abandoned dentistry, his father's profession, to play professional golf, and he became the leading money winner of the 1950s. He won 40 tournaments including the US Open in 1949 and 1956 and the Masters in 1955. Died at Memphis, TN, Sept 1, 1998.

NANCY KERRIGAN ASSAULTED: ANNIVERSARY. Jan 6, 1994. American figure skater Nancy Kerrigan was struck on the knee with an iron rod at Cobo Arena at Detroit where she had been practicing for the upcoming US Championships. The contest winner was Tonya Harding, who was later accused, along with her ex-husband, Jeff Gillooly, and three others, of planning and carrying out the attack. Kerrigan recovered in time to participate in the Winter Olympics at Lillehammer, Norway, in February, winning a silver medal. Harding came in 8th, suffering a broken lace and later a fall. In plea bargaining Gillooly admitted his role in the attack and testified that Harding had been involved in the planning. Her bodyguard and two others were later indicted, and Harding was put on two years' probation. Harding also was stripped of her US title and banned from the US Figure Skating Association for life.

NASHVILLE FISHING EXPO. Jan 6-9. Tennessee State Fairgrounds, Nashville, TN. Annual event featuring the latest in fishing tackle, boats, boating equipment, guide services and other accessories. Top fishing pros will demonstrate their techniques. Est attendance: 10,000. For info: Cindy Crabtree, Esau, Inc, PO Box 50096, Knoxville, TN 37950. Phone: (423) 588-1233 or (800) 588-ESAU. Fax: (423) 588-6938.

PLANTE GETS 300th VICTORY: ANNIVERSARY. Jan 6, 1963. Jacques Plante of the Montreal Canadiens became the third goalie in National Hockey League history to win 300 games when the Canadiens defeated the New York Rangers, 6-0. Plante ended his career with 434 wins and was inducted into the Hockey Hall of Fame in 1978.

"PRO BOWLERS TOUR" TV PREMIERE: ANNIVERSARY. Jan 6, 1962. ABC's weekly coverage of professional bowling tournaments began with Chris Schenkel as the broadcast host. Over the years, he was assisted by Jack Buck (1962-64), Billy Welu (1964-74) and Nelson Burton, Jr (1974-97). The show made its last appearance on June 21, 1997.

SAN DIEGO BOAT SHOW. Jan 6-9. San Diego Convention Center and Marriott Marina, San Diego, CA. 12th annual show is largest one-stop nautical sports event on the West Coast. Features a wide selection of boats and accessories, plus informative boating and fishing seminars. For info: NMMA Boat Shows, 200 E Randolph Dr, Ste 5100, Chicago, IL 60601-6528. Phone: (312) 946-6262. Fax: (312) 946-0401. Web: www.boatshows.com.

WILKENS WINNINGEST COACH: 5th ANNIVERSARY. Jan 6, 1995. Lenny Wilkens became the winningest coach in professional basketball when his team, the Atlanta Hawks, defeated the Washington Bullets, 112-90. With this victory, Wilkens surpassed Arnold ("Red") Auerbach, who retired with 938 wins.

WYNN, EARLY: 80th BIRTH ANNIVERSARY. Jan 6, 1920. Early Wynn, Baseball Hall of Fame pitcher, born at Hartford, AL. A hard-throwing right-hander who never hesitated to whistle a pitch past a batter's ear, Wynn pitched in the major leagues from 1939 to 1963. He won 20 games five times and was a six-time all-star. He teamed with Bob Feller, Bob Lemon and Mike Garcia to give the Cleveland Indians one of baseball's greatest pitching rotations. Victimized by gout late in his career,

	S	M	T	W	T	F	S
January							1
2000	2	3	4	5	6	7	8
	9	10	11	12	13	14	15
	16	17	18	19	20	21	22
	23	24	25	26	27	28	29
	30	31					

he nevertheless hung on to record his 300th victory on May 31, 1963. Inducted into the Hall of Fame in 1972. Died at Venice, FL, Apr 4, 1999.

BIRTHDAYS TODAY

Paul William Azinger, 40, golfer, born Holyoke, MA, Jan 6, 1960.
Ralph Theodore Joseph Branca, 74, former baseball player, born Mt Vernon, NY, Jan 6, 1926.
Norman Wood (Norm) Charlton, III, 37, baseball player, born Ft Polk, LA, Jan 6, 1963.
Louis Leo (Lou) Holtz, 63, football coach, born Follansbee, WV, Jan 6, 1937.
Howard Michael (Howie) Long, 40, broadcaster and former football player, born Somerville, MA, Jan 6, 1960.
Nancy Lopez, 43, LPGA Hall of Fame golfer, born Torrance, CA, Jan 6, 1957.
Keenan Wayne McCardell, 30, football player, born Houston, TX, Jan 6, 1970.

JANUARY 7 — FRIDAY
Day 7 — 359 Remaining

CONIGLIARO, TONY: 55th BIRTH ANNIVERSARY. Jan 7, 1945. Anthony Richard (Tony) Conigliaro, baseball player, born at Revere, MA. Conigliaro led the American League in home runs in 1965 and was one of the most beloved Boston Red Sox players of his generation. He was beaned by Jack Hamilton on Aug 18, 1967, and after missing all of 1968, made a comeback. Died at Boston, Feb 24, 1990.

DIONNE GETS 1,000th POINT: ANNIVERSARY. Jan 7, 1981. Center Marcel Dionne of the Los Angeles Kings got the 1,000th point of his National Hockey League career, a goal in a 5-3 win over the Hartford Whalers. Dionne finished his career with 1,771 points.

FIRST BALLOON FLIGHT ACROSS ENGLISH CHANNEL: 215th ANNIVERSARY. Jan 7, 1785. Dr. John Jeffries, a Boston physician, and Jean-Pierre Blanchard, a French aeronaut, crossed the English Channel from Dover, England, to Calais, France, landing in a forest after being forced to throw overboard all ballast, equipment and even most of their clothing to avoid a forced landing in the icy waters of the English Channel. Blanchard's trousers are said to have been the last article thrown overboard.

GRAND AMERICAN COON HUNT. Jan 7-8. County Fairgrounds, Orangeburg, SC. Coon hunters and sportsmen from all over the US and Canada bring their dogs to compete for Grand American Champion. An ACHA qualifying hunt. Est attendance: 30,000. For info: Carol P. Whisenhunt, Orangeburg County Chamber of Commerce, PO Box 328, Orangeburg, SC 29116-0328. Phone: (803) 534-6821 or (800) 545-6153. Fax: (803) 531-9435. Web: www.sccsi.com/sc/ or www.orangeburgsc.com.

LAKERS SET VICTORY MARK: ANNIVERSARY. Jan 7, 1972. The Los Angeles Lakers defeated the Atlanta Hawks, 134-90, to win their 33rd game in a row, an NBA record.

MIZE, JOHNNY: BIRTH ANNIVERSARY. Jan 7, 1913. John Robert (Johnny) Mize, Baseball Hall of Fame first baseman, born at Demorest, GA. Known as the "Big Cat," Mize won the 1939 National League batting championship, four home run crowns and three RBI titles. He hit 51 homers in 1947, an NL record for left-handed batters. After playing with the St. Louis Cardinals and the New York Giants, Mize was sold to the New York Yankees in 1949. He played part-time and pinch hit through 1953. Inducted into the Hall of Fame in 1981. Died at Demorest, June 2, 1993.

MONTGOLFIER, JACQUES: 255th BIRTH ANNIVERSARY. Jan 7, 1745. Jacques Etienne Montgolfier, merchant and inventor, born at Vidalon-lez Annonay, Ardèche, France. With his older brother, Joseph Michel, in November 1782, he conducted experiments with paper and fabric bags filled with smoke and hot air, which led to invention of the hot-air balloon and the first flight by a human. Died at Serrieres, France, Aug 2, 1799.

NHL'S LEADING SCORER: 80th ANNIVERSARY. Jan 7, 1920. Joe Malone of the Quebec Bulldogs scored a pair of goals in a 4–3 victory over the Toronto Arenas to become the NHL's all-time scoring leader with 59 career goals.

ROBITAILLE SCORES 500th GOAL: ANNIVERSARY. Jan 7, 1999. Left wing Luc Robitaille of the Los Angeles Kings became the 27th player in the National Hockey League to score 500 regular-season goals. He tallied his 499th and 500th goals against the Buffalo Sabres in a 4–2 win.

US TROTTING ASSOCIATION FOUNDING: ANNIVERSARY. Jan 7, 1939. The US Trotting Association, the governing body for the sport of harness horse racing, was founded at Indianapolis, IN, at a meeting called by horseman Roland Harriman. The founding was actually a joining of several regional organizations resulting in uniform rules and regulations. This unification spurred the growth of harness racing, now followed by nearly 25 million fans in North America each year.

BIRTHDAYS TODAY

Donald Brashear, 28, hockey player, born Bedford, IN, Jan 7, 1972.
Randy Burridge, 34, hockey player, born Ft Erie, Ontario, Canada, Jan 7, 1966.
Alvin Ralph Dark, 78, former baseball manager and player, born Comanche, OK, Jan 7, 1922.
Simon ("Bobby") Engram, III, 27, football player, born Camden, SC, Jan 7, 1973.
Guy Andrew Hebert, 33, hockey player, born Troy, NY, Jan 7, 1967.
Jeffrey Thomas (Jeff) Montgomery, 38, baseball player, born Wellston, OH, Jan 7, 1962.
Erric Demont Pegram, 31, football player, born Dallas, TX, Jan 7, 1969.
Craig Barry Shipley, 37, baseball player, born Sydney, Australia, Jan 7, 1963.

JANUARY 8 — SATURDAY
Day 8 — 358 Remaining

CANADA: CANADIAN MIXED CURLING CHAMPIONSHIPS. Jan 8–16. Lethbridge, Alberta. National competition for men and women. For info: Media Relations, Canadian Curling Assn, 1600 James Naismith Dr, Ste 511, Gloucester, ON, Canada K1B 5N4. Phone: (613) 748-5628. Fax: (613) 748-5713. E-mail: cca@curling.ca. Web: www.curling.ca.

CICCARELLI SCORES 500th GOAL: ANNIVERSARY. Jan 8, 1994. Right wing Dino Ciccarelli of the Detroit Red Wings became the 19th player in the National Hockey League to score 500 regular-season goals. He tallied against goalie Kelly Hrudey of the Los Angeles Kings in a 6–3 victory.

FRESHMEN MADE ELIGIBLE: ANNIVERSARY. Jan 8, 1972. The NCAA announced that freshmen would be eligible to play varsity football and basketball starting in the fall of 1972.

JORDAN REACHES 20,000-POINT MARK: ANNIVERSARY. Jan 8, 1993. Michael Jordan scored 35 points to lead the Chicago Bulls to a 120–95 win over the Milwaukee Bucks. The points gave Jordan exactly 20,000 in the 620th game of his career and made him the second-fastest NBA player to reach that mark behind Wilt Chamberlin, who did it in 499 games.

KUCZYNSKI, BERT: 80th BIRTH ANNIVERSARY. Jan 8, 1920. Bernard Carl (Bert) Kuczynski, baseball and football player, born at Philadelphia, PA. Kuczynski was the first to play professional football and major league baseball in the same season. In 1943 he pitched for the Philadelphia Athletics and played football for the Detroit Lions. Died at Allentown, PA, Jan 19, 1997.

NATIONAL FOOTBALL LEAGUE WILDCARD PLAYOFFS. Jan 8–9. Sites TBA. Postseason play begins in the NFL with two games in the AFC and two games in the NFC. The three wildcard teams and the first-place team with the worst won-lost record in each conference square off in this first round. Winners advance to the divisional round next weekend. For info: NFL, 280 Park Ave, New York, NY 10017. Phone: (212) 450-2000. Fax: (212) 681-7573. Web: www.nfl.com.

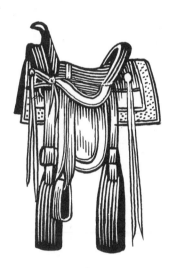

NATIONAL WESTERN STOCK SHOW AND RODEO. Jan 8–23. Denver, CO. One of the nation's largest livestock shows with more than 30 breeds of animals, 25 rodeo performances, 7 horse shows, 2 Mexican shows and cutting-horse and sheep-shearing contests. 94th annual. Est attendance: 625,000. For info: Natl Western Stock Show and Rodeo, 4655 Humboldt St, Denver, CO 80216. Phone: (303) 297-1166. Fax: (303) 292-1708.

NCAA CONVENTION. Jan 8–11. Marriott Marina Hotel, San Diego, CA. For info: NCAA, PO Box 6222, Indianapolis, IN 46206-6222. Phone: (317) 917-6222. Fax: (317) 917-6888. Web: www.ncaa.org.

NCAA EXPANDS FIELD TO 64: 15th ANNIVERSARY. Jan 8, 1985. The NCAA Executive Council decided to expand the field for its Division I Men's basketball tournament to 64 teams, arranged in four 16-team regional brackets.

NEW YORK NATIONAL BOAT SHOW. Jan 8–16. Jacob Javits Convention Center, New York, NY. 90th annual show. The world's longest running marine exhibition offers a wide selection of boats from entry-level inflatable to luxurious cruiser. Informative boating and fishing seminars. For info: NMMA Boat Shows, 200 E Randolph Dr, Ste 5100, Chicago, IL 60601-6528. Phone: (312) 946-6262. Fax: (312) 946-0401. Web: www.boatshows.com.

Dwight Edward Clark, 43, former football player, born Kinston, NC, Jan 8, 1957.

Jason Gilbert Giambi, 29, baseball player, born West Covina, CA, Jan 8, 1971.

Howard Bruce Sutter, 47, former baseball player, born Lancaster, PA, Jan 8, 1953.

Darryl Edwin Williams, 30, football player, born Miami, FL, Jan 8, 1970.

JANUARY 9 — SUNDAY
Day 9 — 357 Remaining

SUPERBOWL CHAMPIONS THIS DATE
1977   Oakland Raiders

BALLOONING IN AMERICA: ANNIVERSARY. Jan 9, 1793. A Frenchman, Jean Pierre Blanchard, made the first manned free-balloon flight in America's history at Philadelphia, PA. The event was watched by President George Washington and many other high government officials. The hydrogen-filled balloon rose to a height of about 5,800 feet, traveled some 15 miles and landed 46 minutes later. Reportedly Blanchard had one passenger on the flight, a little black dog.

BIRTH OF NEW YORK YANKEES: ANNIVERSARY. Jan 9, 1903. Frank Farrell and Bill Devery bought the Baltimore franchise in the American League for $18,000 and moved the team to New York to compete with the New York Giants. The team became known as the Highlanders and later the Yankees.

FIRST 40-POINT BAA GAME: ANNIVERSARY. Jan 9, 1947. Don Martin of the Providence Steamrollers became the first player in the Basketball Association of America to score 40 points in a game, accomplishing the feat against the Cleveland Rebels. The BAA merged with the National Basketball League after the 1948–49 season to form the National Basketball Association.

HIGH SCHOOL FREE THROW RECORD: ANNIVERSARY. Jan 9, 1979. New Orleans basketball player Daryl Moreau set a high school record by converting his 126th free throw in a row, a streak that lasted a year.

HUNTER GETS 1,000th POINT: ANNIVERSARY. Jan 9, 1998. Center Dale Hunter of the Washington Capitals got the 1,000th point of his National Hockey League career, an assist in a 4–1 win over the Philadelphia Flyers.

Tyrone Curtis ("Muggsy") Bogues, 35, basketball player, born Baltimore, MD, Jan 9, 1965.

Radek Bonk, 24, hockey player, born Kronov, Czechoslovakia, Jan 9, 1976.

Alan Marshall (Al) Clark, 52, baseball umpire, born Trenton, NJ, Jan 9, 1948.

Richard Allen (Dick) Enberg, 65, broadcaster, born Mt Clemens, MI, Jan 9, 1935.

Mark Martin, 41, auto racer, born Batesville, AR, Jan 9, 1959.

Otis Junior Nixon, 41, baseball player, born Evergreen, NC, Jan 9, 1959.

January **2000**

S	M	T	W	T	F	S
						1
2	3	4	5	6	7	8
9	10	11	12	13	14	15
16	17	18	19	20	21	22
23	24	25	26	27	28	29
30	31					

Bryan Bartlett (Bart) Starr, 66, Pro Football Hall of Fame quarterback and former coach, born Montgomery, AL, Jan 9, 1934.

JANUARY 10 — MONDAY
Day 10 — 356 Remaining

CHASE'S SPORTSQUOTE OF THE DAY
"It was over my head. I thought, Oh, oh, I can't get up that high. Something got me up there. It must have been God or something."—Dwight Clark on "The Catch"

ALL-CANADA SHOW. Jan 10–12. State Fair Grounds, Indianapolis, IN. This consumer show allows individuals an opportunity to talk face-to-face with Canadian lodge representatives and outfitters to plan their hunting, fishing and adventure trips to Canada. For info: Rodney Schlafer, Show Dir, All-Canada Show, Bay-Lakes Mktg, Inc, 1889 Commerce Dr, De Pere, WI 54115. Phone: (920) 983-9800. Fax: (920) 983-9985. Web: www.allcanada.com.

GOALIE'S ONE-NIGHT STAND: 20th ANNIVERSARY. Jan 10, 1980. The Boston Bruins gave goalie Jim Stewart his first and only start in the National Hockey League. Stewart surrendered three goals in the game's first four minutes and five in the first period. He was replaced and never played in the NHL again.

LAKERS' STREAK ENDS: ANNIVERSARY. Jan 10, 1972. The Milwaukee Bucks defeated the Los Angeles Lakers, 120–104, to snap the longest winning streak in major professional sports at 33 games. Milwaukee's Kareem Abdul-Jabbar, later to play for the Lakers, scored 39 points to hand Los Angeles its first loss since Oct 31, 1971.

PALMER DIAGNOSED WITH CANCER: ANNIVERSARY. Jan 10, 1997. Arnold Palmer, perhaps the most charismatic golfer of all time, was diagnosed with prostate cancer. Palmer underwent surgery at the Mayo Clinic on Jan 15, and on Mar 20 he returned to golf, carding an 81 in the first round of the Bay Hill Invitational. He also became a spokesman for the prevention of prostate cancer.

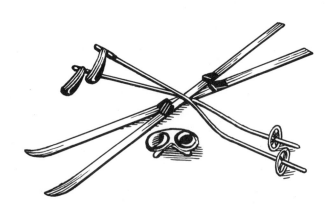

SPECIAL OLYMPICS VIRGINIA WINTER GAMES—SKIING. Jan 10–11. Wintergreen, VA. 120 athletes with mental disabilities compete in alpine skiing on the slopes of Wintergreen Resort. For info: Special Olympics Virginia, 3212 Skipwith Rd, Ste 100, Richmond, VA 23294. Phone: (804) 346-5544.

"THE CATCH": ANNIVERSARY. Jan 10, 1982. San Francisco 49ers wide receiver Dwight Clark jumped high in the Candlestick Park end zone to snare a touchdown pass from Joe Montana as the 49ers defeated the Dallas Cowboys, 28–27, in the NFC championship game. "The Catch," as the play came to be called, propelled San Francisco to Super Bowl XVI, which they won, 26–21, over the Cincinnati Bengals.

WRIGHT, HARRY: 165th BIRTH ANNIVERSARY. Jan 10, 1835. William Henry ("Harry") Wright, Baseball Hall of Fame player and manager born at Sheffield, England. Wright and his brother George were two of baseball's earliest pioneers. In 1869, he transformed the Red Stockings into the first openly professional club. He managed other teams and, after an eye disorder ended his career, he was named honorary Chief of Umpires in the National League. Inducted into the Hall of Fame in 1953. Died at Atlantic City, NJ, Oct 3, 1895.

BIRTHDAYS TODAY

Frank William Mahovlich, 62, Hockey Hall of Fame left wing, born Timmons, Ontario, Canada, Jan 10, 1938.
Willie Lee McCovey, 62, Baseball Hall of Fame first baseman, born Mobile, AL, Jan 10, 1938.
Glenn Allen Robinson, Jr, 27, basketball player, born Gary, IN, Jan 10, 1973.
William Anthony (Bill) Toomey, 61, Olympic gold medal decathlete, born Philadelphia, PA, Jan 10, 1939.

JANUARY 11 — TUESDAY
Day 11 — 355 Remaining

SUPERBOWL CHAMPIONS THIS DATE
1970   Kansas City Chiefs

CAREY, MAX: BIRTH ANNIVERSARY. Jan 11, 1890. Max George Carey, Baseball Hall of Fame outfielder, born Maximilian Carnarius at Terre Haute, IN. Carey left the seminary to play baseball where he was best known as a base stealer. He played 20 years with the Pittsburgh Pirates and the Brooklyn Dodgers. Inducted into the Hall of Fame in 1961. Died at Miami Beach, FL, May 30, 1976.

DESIGNATED HITTER RULE ADOPTED: ANNIVERSARY. Jan 11, 1973. The American League changed its playing rules to allow for the use of a designated hitter, one player to bat for the pitcher throughout the game without being required to play in the field. The rule was intended to boost offensive production and to allow better starting pitchers to remain in the game longer. (See also: "Designated Hitter Introduced: Anniversary" Apr 6.)

DRISCOLL, PADDY: 105th BIRTH ANNIVERSARY. Jan 11, 1895. John Leo ("Paddy") Driscoll, Pro Football Hall of Fame player and coach, born at Evanston, IL. Driscoll played at Northwestern, served in the Navy and then turned pro, playing with the Chicago Cardinals and the Chicago Bears. He coached high school and college football and then joined George Halas's Bears staff, taking over for Halas during a brief retirement in 1956 and losing the NFL title game. Inducted into the Hall of Fame in 1965. Died at Chicago, IL, June 29, 1968.

FLICK, ELMER: BIRTH ANNIVERSARY. Jan 11, 1876. Elmer Harrison Flick, Baseball Hall of Fame outfielder, born at Bedford, OH. Flick played 13 years in the major leagues and hit .315. After the 1907 season, the Detroit Tigers offered to trade Ty Cobb to the Cleveland Indians for Flick, but Cleveland refused. Inducted into the Hall of Fame in 1963. Died at Bedford, Jan 9, 1971.

NBA SILVER ANNIVERSARY TEAM: ANNIVERSARY. Jan 11, 1971. The National Basketball Association announced its Silver Anniversary team. Ten players were selected: Paul Arizin, Bob Cousy, Bob Davies, Joe Fulks, Sam Jones, George Mikan, Bob Pettit, Bill Russell, Dolph Schayes and Bill Sharman. The coach was Red Auerbach.

BIRTHDAYS TODAY

Tracy Caulkins, 37, Olympic gold medal swimmer, born Winona, MN, Jan 11, 1963.
Ben Daniel Crenshaw, 48, golfer, born Austin, TX, Jan 11, 1952.
Christopher Joseph (Chris) Ford, 51, basketball coach and former player, born Atlantic City, NJ, Jan 11, 1949.
Richmond Jewel Webb, 33, football player, born Dallas, TX, Jan 11, 1967.

JANUARY 12 — WEDNESDAY
Day 12 — 354 Remaining

SUPERBOWL CHAMPIONS THIS DATE
1969   New York Jets
1975   Pittsburgh Steelers

CLEVELAND RAMS MOVE TO LA: ANNIVERSARY. Jan 12, 1946. Less than a month after the Cleveland Rams won their first NFL title, the league gave owner Dan Reeves permission to move the team to Los Angeles. In approving this franchise shift, the NFL became the first major professional sports league to put a team on the West Coast. Fans at Cleveland quickly embraced a new team, the Browns in the new All-American Football Conference which lasted until the two leagues merged in 1950.

COLLEGE OF COACHES: ANNIVERSARY. Jan 12, 1961. The Chicago Cubs announced that they would forsake the traditional manager system and instead have a team of eight coaches lead the club, with several taking turns at the top. The experiment lasted two seasons during which the Cubs finished 64–90 and 59–103.

CRISLER, FRITZ: BIRTH ANNIVERSARY. Jan 12, 1899. Herbert Orrin ("Fritz") Crisler, college football coach and administrator, born at Earlsville, IL. Crisler played several sports at the University of Chicago and then coached three sports there after graduating. He moved to Minnesota, Princeton and then to Michigan in 1938. His Wolverine teams won 71 games and one national championship in ten years as Crisler became known as an innovative coach and a tireless athletic director. Died at Ann Arbor, MI, Aug 19, 1982.

GLOBETROTTERS PLAY 20,000th GAME: ANNIVERSARY. Jan 12, 1998. The Harlem Globetrotters, the most popular basketball attraction in the world, played their 20,000th game, defeating their perennial foils, the New York Nationals, 85–62, at Remington, IN. The victory brought the Trotters' overall record to 19,668 wins against only 332 defeats. The Globetrotters, originally known as the Savoy Five, were founded in 1926 by Abe Saperstein. They played before their first paying crowd in 1927, adopted their new name in 1930 and played their first game on foreign soil in 1939. In the nearly six decades since, they have played in 114 countries before an estimated total audience of 100 million.

HARROUN, RAY: BIRTH ANNIVERSARY. Jan 12, 1879. Raymond (Ray) Harroun, auto racer, born at Spartansburg, PA. Harroun began racing cars in 1905 and capped his career by winning the first Indianapolis 500 in 1911. His average speed was 74.59 mph. Instead of driving with a mechanic on board, he used his invention, the rear view mirror, to help him see his opponents. Harroun also invented the automobile bumper. Died at Anderson, IN, Jan 19, 1968.

HAUSER, JOE: BIRTH ANNIVERSARY. Jan 12, 1899. Joseph John (Joe) Hauser, baseball player, born at Milwaukee, WI. Hauser played six seasons in the major leagues, but he was most famous for twice surpassing the 60-home-run mark in the minor leagues. In 1930, he hit 63 homers for the Baltimore Orioles of the International League. Three years later, he hit 69 homers (still a record) for the Minneapolis Millers of the American Association. Died at Sheboygan, WI, July 11, 1997.

JETS WIN SUPER BOWL III: ANNIVERSARY. Jan 12, 1969. Overcoming their status as 17-point underdogs and living up to quarterback Joe Namath's bold prediction, the New York Jets upset the Baltimore Colts, 16–7, in Super Bowl III. The Jets got a touchdown from fullback Matt Snell and three field goals from Jim Turner to become the first American Football League team to snatch a championship from an NFL team.

NASHVILLE BOAT AND SPORTS SHOW. Jan 12–16. Nashville Convention Center, Nashville, TN. 14th annual show. The mid-South's largest selection of boats, accessories and fishing gear as well as numerous resort and travel exhibits. Informative boating and fishing seminars. For info: NMMA Boat Shows, 200 E Randolph Dr, Ste 5100, Chicago, IL 60601-6528. Phone: (312) 946-6262. Fax: (312) 946-0401. Web: www.boatshows.com.

SCHAYES SCORES 15,000 POINTS: 40th ANNIVERSARY. Jan 12, 1960. Two years to the day after he became the NBA's leading career scorer, Dolph Schayes of the Syracuse Nationals became the first NBA player to score 15,000 points. He finished his career in 1963–64 with 19,249 points.

TWO-POINT CONVERSION: ANNIVERSARY. Jan 12, 1958. The NCAA football rules committee made the first change in scoring rules since 1912 by introducing the optional two-point conversion. Under the rule, teams could kick for one point or run or pass for two points after touchdown.

BIRTHDAYS TODAY

Scott David Burrell, 29, basketball player and former minor league baseball player, born New Haven, CT, Jan 12, 1971.

Casey Todd Candaele, 39, former baseball player, born Lompoc, CA, Jan 12, 1961.

Thomas John (Tom) Dempsey, 59, former football player, born Milwaukee, WI, Jan 12, 1941.

Joe Frazier, 56, former heavyweight champion boxer, born Beaufort, SC, Jan 12, 1944.

Jocelyn Thibault, 25, hockey player, born Montreal, Quebec, Canada, Jan 12, 1975.

January 2000	S	M	T	W	T	F	S
							1
	2	3	4	5	6	7	8
	9	10	11	12	13	14	15
	16	17	18	19	20	21	22
	23	24	25	26	27	28	29
	30	31					

JANUARY 13 — THURSDAY
Day 13 — 353 Remaining

SUPERBOWL CHAMPIONS THIS DATE
1974   Miami Dolphins

ALL-CANADA SHOW. Jan 13–16. Pheasant Run Mega Center, St. Charles, IL. This consumer show allows individuals an opportunity to talk face-to-face with Canadian lodge representatives and outfitters to plan their hunting, fishing and adventure trips to Canada. For info: Rodney Schlafer, Show Dir, All-Canada Show, Bay-Lakes Mktg, Inc, 1889 Commerce Dr, De Pere, WI 54115. Phone: (920) 983-9800. Fax: (920) 983-9985. Web: www.allcanada.com.

ARKANSAS MARINE EXPO. Jan 13–16. Little Rock Expo Center, Little Rock, AR. 18th annual. For info: NMMA Boat Shows, 200 E Randolph Dr, Ste 5100, Chicago, IL 60601-6528. Phone: (312) 946-6262. Fax: (312) 946-0401. Web: www.boatshows.com.

CHAMBERLAIN TRADED: 35th ANNIVERSARY. Jan 13, 1965. After the NBA All-Star Game in which San Francisco Warriors center Wilt Chamberlain scored 20 points and grabbed 16 rebounds, the Warriors shocked the basketball world by announcing that they were trading Chamberlain to the Philadelphia 76ers for three minor leaguers and $150,000.

ICEBOX DAYS XX. Jan 13–16. International Falls, MN. Smoosh racing, "Freeze Yer Gizzard Blizzard Run," turkey bowling, ski races, mutt races and beach party. Est attendance: 5,000. For info: Kallie L. Briggs, Chamber of Commerce, 301 2nd Ave, International Falls, MN 56649. Phone: (800) 325-5766 or (218) 283-9400. Fax: (218) 283-3572. E-mail: intlfall@intlfalls.org. Web: www.intlfalls.org.

INTERNATIONAL FINALS RODEO. Jan 13–15. State Fair Arena, Oklahoma City, OK. The top 15 money-winning IPRA cowboys and cowgirls compete for world championships in seven events. Prize money more than $275,000. Trade show, dances, bucking stock sale. Est attendance: 40,000. For info: Jane Kirton, International Finals Rodeo, PO Box 83377, Oklahoma City, OK 73148. Phone: (405) 235-6540. Fax: (405) 235-6577. E-mail: iprainfo@intprorodeo.com.

JORDAN RETIRES: ANNIVERSARY. Jan 13, 1999. Michael Jordan, generally considered the greatest basketball player ever, announced his retirement after a career that saw him lead the Chicago Bulls to six NBA championships. Jordan had previously retired in October 1993, in order to play professional baseball, but he returned to the Bulls in March 1995. Jordan led the league in scoring 10 times and won 5 MVP awards. He averaged 31.5 points per game over 13 seasons, a record. His retirement came as the league and its players were settling a labor dispute that cut the 1998–99 season by about half.

MASTERTON FATALLY INJURED: ANNIVERSARY. Jan 13, 1968. In a game between the Minnesota North Stars and the Oakland Seals, Minnesota rookie center Bill Masterton was checked into the boards and fell heavily on his head. He suffered massive brain damage and died two days later, the only fatality in NHL history.

MESSIER GETS 1,000th POINT: ANNIVERSARY. Jan 13, 1991. Center Mark Messier of the Edmonton Oilers got the 1,000th point of his National Hockey League career, an assist in a 5–3 victory over the Philadelphia Flyers.

NCAA ADOPTS PROP 48: ANNIVERSARY. Jan 13, 1986. NCAA member schools voted overwhelmingly in convention to adopt Proposition 48, a controversial attempt to raise the academic performance of student-athletes. Prop 48 required incoming freshmen to score 700 or more on the Scholastic Aptitude Test (SAT) or 15 on the American College Testing (ACT) exam or graduate from high school with a 2.0 grade point average in order to be eligible for athletics during their freshman year.

OLDEST GOLFER TO GET HOLE-IN-ONE: 15th ANNIVERSARY. Jan 13, 1985. Otto Bucher of Switzerland became the oldest golfer to record a hole-in-one when he aced the 12th hole at a golf course in Spain. Bucher was 99 years old.

CHASE'S SPORTSQUOTE OF THE DAY

"Thank you for gracing our court for 13 seasons."— NBA Commissioner David Stern on the retirement of Michael Jordan

BIRTHDAYS TODAY

Robert Herbert (Bob) Forsch, 50, former baseball player, born Sacramento, CA, Jan 13, 1950.
Thomas Joseph (Tom) Gola, 67, Basketball Hall of Fame forward, born Philadelphia, PA, Jan 13, 1933.
Kelly Stephen Hrudey, 39, hockey player, born Edmonton, Alberta, Canada, Jan 13, 1961.
Ernie Irvan, 41, auto racer, born Salinas, CA, Jan 13, 1959.
Nikolai Khabibulin, 27, hockey player, born Sverdlovsk, USSR, Jan 13, 1973.
Mark Francis O'Meara, 43, golfer, born Goldsboro, NC, Jan 13, 1957.

JANUARY 14 — FRIDAY

Day 14 — 352 Remaining

SUPERBOWL CHAMPIONS THIS DATE

1968	Green Bay Packers
1973	Miami Dolphins

BREWER, CHET: BIRTH ANNIVERSARY. Jan 14, 1907. Chester Arthur (Chet) Brewer, baseball player and manager, born at Leavenworth, KS. Brewer pitched in the Negro Leagues, playing 14 seasons with the Kansas City Monarchs and five with the Cleveland Buckeyes. After retiring, he scouted for the Pittsburgh Pirates. Died at Los Angeles, CA, Mar 26, 1990.

MIAMI COMPLETES UNDEFEATED SEASON: ANNIVERSARY. Jan 14, 1973. The Miami Dolphins became the only team in NFL history to complete a season undefeated and untied by beating the Washington Redskins, 14–7, in Super Bowl VII. Miami finished the season 17–0.

NC RV AND CAMPING SHOW. Jan 14–16. Special Events Center, Greensboro Coliseum Complex, Greensboro, NC. A display of the latest in recreation vehicles and accessories by various dealers. Est attendance: 10,000. For info: Apple Rock Advertising & Promotion, 1200 Eastchester Dr, High Point, NC 27265. Phone: (336) 881-7100. Fax: (336) 883-7198.

NORTHERN EXPOSURE/MENOMINEE ICE CHALLENGE IN SHAWANO. Jan 14–16. Shawano, WI. Highlighted events include the Snowmobile Endurance Races on an oval track and ice carving exhibition in conjunction with the Menominee Casino International Ice Carving Competition. Time trials for the race will be held on Jan 14 with racing planned for Jan 15–16. This race could be considered a prelude to the World Championship Races to be held in Eagle River the following weekend. A family snowmobile ride is also scheduled for Jan 14.

Other events and competitions include a chainsaw exhibition and raffle, cross-cut saw competition, chili cook-off, large buckskinners' encampment, snow cave encampment, photography contest and several children's activities. Various vendors will be on site offering food, beverages and other items. A shuttle will be available between the casino and the fairgrounds, and sleigh rides will be offered at the fairgrounds. Est attendance: 6,000. For info: Shawano Area Chamber of Commerce, PO Box 38, Shawano, WI 54166. Phone: (715) 524-2139 or (800) 235-8528. Fax: (715) 524-3127. E-mail: chamber@shawano.com.

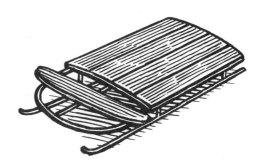

SEWARD POLAR BEAR JUMP FESTIVAL. Jan 14–16. Resurrection Bay, Seward, AK. Volunteers collect pledges to jump into bay in costumes. Festivities include goofy golf tournament, parade, dog weight pull, dogsled race, Polar Bear Arts and Crafts Fair, skijoring, ugly fish toss, Bachelor/Bachelorette Auction, ice bowling, talent show, Seafood Feed and much more. Benefits local nonprofit organizations and the American Cancer Society. The actual "Plunge" takes place on Saturday, Jan 15. Est attendance: 2,500. For info: Seward Polar Bear Jump Fest, PO Box 386, Seward, AK 99664. Phone: (907) 224-4049. Fax: (907) 224-4085.

SHIBE, BEN: DEATH ANNIVERSARY. Jan 14, 1922. Benjamin Franklin (Ben) Shibe, baseball executive, born at Philadelphia, PA, 1838. Shibe built the Reach Sporting Goods Company, inventing the two-piece baseball cover and the cork-center baseball. He joined Connie Mack to found the Philadelphia Athletics in 1901. Died at Philadelphia.

SPECIAL OLYMPICS OKLAHOMA WINTER GAMES. Jan 14–16. University of Oklahoma, Norman, OK. State-level competition in three sports, basketball, volleyball and bowling, for children and adults with mental retardation. For info: Special Olympics Oklahoma, 6835 S Canton Ave, Tulsa, OK 74136. Phone: (918) 481-1234. Fax: (918) 496-1515.

STONEHAM BUYS GIANTS: ANNIVERSARY. Jan 14, 1919. Charles Stoneham, John McGraw and Francis X. McQuade bought the New York Giants from Charles Hempstead. The Stoneham family controlled the Giants for the next 56 years and moved them to San Francisco after the 1957 season.

TIP-UP TOWN USA. Jan 14–23. Houghton Lake, MI. 50th anniversary. Ten straight days of fun. Michigan's largest winter festival featuring ice-fishing contests, softball on the ice, 3 Polar Bear Dips, 2 parades, carnival, vendors, monster truck rides, arts and crafts, fireworks, world's longest poker run and scavenger hunt, midweek MSDRA snowmobile drag races and more. Est attendance: 150,000. For info: Chamber of Commerce, 1625 W Houghton Lake Dr, Houghton Lake, MI 48629. Phone: (800) 248-5253. E-mail: hlcofc@freeway.net. Web: www.houghtonlakechamber.com.

BIRTHDAYS TODAY

David Wilson (Dave) Campbell, 58, broadcaster and former baseball player, born Manistee, MI, Jan 14, 1942.

Lethon Flowers, III, 27, football player, born Columbia, SC, Jan 14, 1973.

Sergei Nemchinov, 36, hockey player, born Moscow, USSR, Jan 14, 1964.

Carlos Perez, 29, baseball player, born Nigua, Dominican Republic, Jan 14, 1971.

JANUARY 15 — SATURDAY
Day 15 — 351 Remaining

SUPERBOWL CHAMPIONS THIS DATE

1967	Green Bay Packers
1978	Dallas Cowboys

AFRMA RAT AND MOUSE ANNUAL SHOW. Jan 15 or 22 (to be determined). Hacienda Heights, CA. Annual show where trophies are awarded to the winners. The American Fancy Rat and Mouse Association (AFRMA) was founded in 1983 to promote and encourage the breeding and exhibition of fancy rats and mice, to educate the public on their positive qualities as companion animals and to provide information on their proper care. For info: AFRMA (CAE), PO Box 2589, Winnetka, CA 91396-2589. Phone: (909) 685-2350. Fax: (818) 592-6590. E-mail: craigr@afrma.org. Web: www.afrma.org.

BAKER, HOBEY: BIRTH ANNIVERSARY. Jan 15, 1892. Hobart Amory Hare (Hobey) Baker, football and hockey player, born at Wissahickon, PA. Baker attended Princeton University and was proclaimed one of the greatest athletes of his time. He captained the hockey team for two years, playing the rover position, and the football team for one season. After graduation in 1914, he played amateur hockey until enlisting in the army in 1917. Died in an airplane crash at Toul, France, Dec 21, 1918. The DeCathalon Athletic Club of Bloomington, MN, annually presents the Hobey Baker Award to the country's top college hockey player.

CANADA: TORONTO INTERNATIONAL BOAT SHOW. Jan 15–23. Automotive and Coliseum Building, Exhibition Place, Toronto, Ontario. 42nd annual show. More than 1,000 new boats make this Canada's largest boat shopping spree. Special deals on a wide selection including inflatables, personal watercraft, fishing boats, cruisers and sailboats. Informative boating and fishing seminars. For info: NMMA Boat Shows, 200 E Randolph Dr, Ste 5100, Chicago, IL 60601-6528. Phone: (312) 946-6262. Fax: (312) 946-0401. Web: www.boatshows.com.

CHAPMAN, RAY: BIRTH ANNIVERSARY. Jan 15, 1891. Raymond Johnson (Ray) Chapman, baseball player, born at Beaver Dam, KY. The first major league baseball fatality, Chapman was beaned by New York Yankees pitcher Carl Mays on Aug 16, 1920, and died at New York, Aug 17, 1920.

DAVIES, BOB: 80th BIRTH ANNIVERSARY. Jan 15, 1920. Robert Edris (Bob) Davies, Basketball Hall of Fame guard, born at Harrisburg, PA. Davies was an outstanding player in the 1940s and early 1950s. He won the MVP award in the National Basketball League for the 1946–47 season. Inducted into the Hall of Fame in 1969. Died at Hilton Head, SC, Apr 22, 1990.

GENEWICH, JOE: BIRTH ANNIVERSARY. Jan 15, 1897. Joseph Edward (Joe) Genewich, baseball player, born at Elmira, NY. Genewich pitched nine seasons in the major leagues after playing neither in college nor the minor leagues. Died at Lockport, NY, Dec 21, 1985.

NATIONAL FOOTBALL LEAGUE DIVISIONAL PLAY-OFFS. Jan 15–16. Sites TBA. Postseason play in the NFL continues with the divisional round. In each conference the two winners from last weekend's wildcard round face off against the two first-place teams with the best won-lost records. Winners advance to the conference championships next weekend. For info: NFL, 280 Park Ave, New York, NY 10017. Phone: (212) 450-2000. Fax: (212) 681-7573. Web: www.nfl.com.

NATIONAL JUNIOR TEAM ORIENTEERING CHAMPIONSHIPS. Jan 15–16. Cartersville, GA. Students from high schools, middle schools and JROTC units from across the country compete for US championship team titles. For info: Jon Nash, Dir of Media Rel, US Orienteering, 20 Tenney Hill Rd, Kittery Point, ME 03905-5229. Phone: (207) 439-7096. Fax: (207) 439-7096. E-mail: jonnash@juno.com.

NORTHERN EXPOSURE/WOLF RIVER RENDEZVOUS. Jan 15–17. Shawano, WI. More than 6,000 spectators are expected to watch top sled dog racers from Europe, Canada and the US compete in four-, six- and 10-dog junior and amateur classes. The festival also features mutt sled dog races, skijoring (skiers pulled by dogs), snowshoe races, a buckskinners encampment, candlelight ski, moonlight snowmobile ride, horse-drawn sleigh rides, cross-cut saw competition and chain saw carving. Est attendance: 6,000. For info: Phone: (715) 524-2139 or (800) 235-8528.

PAUL BUNYAN SLED DOG RACES, SKIJORING AND MUTT RACES. Jan 15–16. Fair Grounds, Bemidji, MN. 28th annual competition. For info: Bemidji Area Chamber of Commerce, Carol Olson, Box 850, Bemidji, MN 56619-0850. Phone: (800) 458-2223 x100. Web: www.paulbunyan.net/paulbunyansleddograces.

RUCKER, JOHNNY: BIRTH ANNIVERSARY. Jan 15, 1917. John Joel (Johnny) Rucker, baseball player, born at Crabapple, GA. Rucker was the nephew of pitcher Nap Rucker and once graced the cover of *Life* magazine. Died at Moultrie, GA, Aug 7, 1985.

SNOW SHOVEL RIDING CONTEST. Jan 15. Economy Park, Economy, PA. Contest begins at 1 PM. Participants ride snow shovels downhill, handles extended, instead of sleds. Best time is the winner. For info: Beaver Co Tourist Promotion Agency, 215B Ninth St, Monaca, PA 15061-2028. Phone: (724) 728-0212. Fax: (724) 728-0456.

SUPER BOWL I: ANNIVERSARY. Jan 15, 1967. The Green Bay Packers won the first NFL–AFL World Championship Game, defeating the Kansas City Chiefs, 35–10, at the Los Angeles Memorial Coliseum. Packers quarterback Bart Starr completed 16 of 23 passes for 250 yards and was named the game's MVP. Pro football's title game later became known as the Super Bowl.

USA HOCKEY WINTER MEETING. Jan 15–17. Tampa, FL. For info: USA Hockey, 4965 N 30th St, Colorado Springs, CO 80919. Phone: (719) 599-5500.

USFTL NATIONAL FLAG AND TOUCH FOOTBALL CHAMPIONSHIPS. Jan 15–16. Orlando, FL. National championship for flag and touch football players in the USA. A double elimination tournament lasting two days. Adult men and women, youth, co-rec, and 35-and-over classifications. Annually, the weekend before Martin

	S	M	T	W	T	F	S
January							1
2000	2	3	4	5	6	7	8
	9	10	11	12	13	14	15
	16	17	18	19	20	21	22
	23	24	25	26	27	28	29
	30	31					

Luther King Day. Est attendance: 5,000. For info: US Flag/Touch Football League (USFTL), 7709 Ohio St, Mentor, OH 44060. Phone: (440) 974-8735. Fax: (440) 974-8441. E-mail: usftl@interax.com. Web: www.e-sports .com/USFTL.

USLA WINTER GAMES. Jan 15. Muskegon Luge Track, Muskegon Winter Sports Complex, Muskegon, MI. United States Luge Assn (USLA) competition. Open to the public. Lugers will have varying degrees of skill; competition will offer age groups. Race will take place on the upper track. Muskegon Luge is one of only two luges in the country. For info: Muskegon Sports Council, PO Box 5085, North Muskegon, MI 49445. Phone: (616) 755-6661. Luge Club phone: (616) 759-2201. Web: www.msports.org.

BIRTHDAYS TODAY

Corey Chavous, 24, football player, born Aiken, SC, Jan 15, 1976.

Delino Lamont DeShields, 31, baseball player, born Seaford, DE, Jan 15, 1969.

D'Tanyian Jacquez Green, 24, football player, born Ft Valley, GA, Jan 15, 1976.

Robert Anthony (Bobby) Grich, 51, former baseball player, born Muskegon, MI, Jan 15, 1949.

Mary Caroline Pierce, 25, tennis player, born Montreal, Quebec, Canada, Jan 15, 1975.

Randy Lee White, 47, Pro Football Hall of Fame defensive tackle, born Wilmington, DE, Jan 15, 1953.

JANUARY 16 — SUNDAY
Day 16 — 350 Remaining

SUPERBOWL CHAMPIONS THIS DATE
1972   Dallas Cowboys

BERMUDA: BANK OF BUTTERFIELD BERMUDA MARATHON. Jan 16. Hamilton, Bermuda. The course follows a 13-mile route showing the island's beauty as it follows shoreline and narrow winding coral and flower-lined roads. For info: Bermuda Marathon Committee, PO Box DV 397, Devonshire DV BX, Bermuda. Phone: (441) 236-6086.

CANADA: MINDEN SLED DOG DERBY. Jan 16–17. Minden, Ontario. World's largest limited-class speed sled-dog derby attracts top mushers from across North America. Est attendance: 7,000. For info: Minden Sled Dog Derby, Box 97, Minden, ON, Canada K0M 2K0. Phone: (705) 286-4768. Fax: (705) 286-4768. E-mail: mindentimes @halhinet.on.ca. Web: www.mindentimes.on.ca/sleddog .htm.

CAPITAL CITY MARATHON. Jan 16. Tallahassee, FL. For info: 3218 Albert Dr, Tallahassee, FL 32308. Phone: (904) 668-3839. E-mail: freddeck@juno.com.

COLLINS, JIMMY: BIRTH ANNIVERSARY. Jan 16, 1870. James Joseph (Jimmy) Collins, Baseball Hall of Fame third baseman, born at Buffalo, NY. Collins was an innovative fielder who modernized third base play. He shifted in or back depending on the situation and challenged bunters by fielding their bunts barehanded and throwing them out. Collins played in the majors for 14 years and became the first manager to win a World Series (Boston, 1903). Inducted into the Hall of Fame in 1945. Died at Buffalo, NY, Mar 6, 1943.

DEAN, DIZZY: BIRTH ANNIVERSARY. Jan 16, 1911. Jay Hanna ("Dizzy") Dean, Baseball Hall of Fame pitcher, born at Lucas, AR. Following his baseball career, Dean established himself as a radio and TV sports announcer and commentator, becoming famous for his innovative delivery. "He slud into third," reported Dizzy, who on another occasion explained that "Me and Paul [baseball player brother Paul "Daffy" Dean] . . . didn't get much education." Died at Reno, NV, July 17, 1974.

FIRST FIVE-ON-FIVE BASKETBALL GAME: ANNIVERSARY. Jan 16, 1896. The University of Chicago men's basketball team defeated an Iowa YMCA team, 15–12, in the first game played with five players on each side. Previously, games had been played with nine on each side.

METHODIST HEALTH CARE HOUSTON MARATHON. Jan 16. Houston, TX. 28th annual citywide race in conjunction with the Methodist Health Care Health & Fitness Exposition (Jan 14–15). Est attendance: 7,000. For info: Houston Marathon Committee, 720 N Post Oak Rd, Ste 335, Houston, TX 77024. Phone: (713) 957-3453. Fax: (713) 957-3406. E-mail: marathon@ghg.net. Web: www.houstonmarathon.com.

NO POINTS AFTER TOUCHDOWN?: ANNIVERSARY. Jan 16, 1952. The NFL Rules Committee voted 7–5 to eliminate points after touchdown and to make touchdowns worth an automatic seven points instead of six. Fortunately for traditionalists, a rules change required a vote of at least 10–2 for passage, so the proposal failed.

SAN DIEGO MARATHON. Jan 16. San Diego, CA. Marathon, half-marathon and marathon relay plus Clif Bar 5K Run/Walk and Keebler Kid's Marathon Mile and All About Fitness Expo. For info: In Motion, 511 S Cedros Ave, Ste B, Solana Beach, CA 92075. Phone: (888) 792-2900. Web: www.sdmarathon.com.

BIRTHDAYS TODAY

Stephen Charles (Steve) Balboni, 43, former baseball player, born Brockton, MA, Jan 16, 1957.

Sergi Bruguera, 29, tennis player, born Barcelona, Spain, Jan 16, 1971.

Anthony Joseph (A.J.) Foyt, Jr, 65, former auto racer, born Houston, TX, Jan 16, 1935.

Roy Jones, Jr, 31, boxer, born Pensacola, FL, Jan 16, 1969.

Donald James (Don) MacLean, 30, basketball player, born Palo Alto, CA, Jan 16, 1970.

Jack Burns McDowell, 34, baseball player, born Van Nuys, CA, Jan 16, 1966.

JANUARY 17 — MONDAY
Day 17 — 349 Remaining

SUPERBOWL CHAMPIONS THIS DATE
1971   Baltimore Colts

ALL-CANADA SHOW. Jan 17–19. Dane County Expo Center, Madison, WI. This consumer show allows individuals an opportunity to talk face-to-face with Canadian lodge representatives and outfitters to plan their hunting, fishing and adventure trips to Canada. For info: Rodney Schlafer, Show Dir, All-Canada Show, Bay-Lakes Mktg, Inc, 1889 Commerce Dr, De Pere, WI 54115. Phone: (920) 983-9800. Fax: (920) 983-9985. Web: www.allcanada.com.

AUSTRALIA: AUSTRALIAN OPEN (TENNIS). Jan 17–30. National Tennis Centre, Flinders Park, Melbourne. The national tennis championships of Australia with competition in men's and women's singles and men's, women's and mixed doubles. One of the sport's four Grand Slam events. For info: Ford Australian Open Office, Private Bag 6060, Richmond South 3141, Victoria, Australia. Phone: 61-3/92861175. Fax: 61-3/96501040.

BOB HOPE CHRYSLER CLASSIC. Jan 17–23. Bermuda Dunes, CA. A PGA Tour tournament played at 90 holes over four courses. Est attendance: 90,000. For info: Pat Bennett, PR and Production, Bob Hope Chrysler Classic, 39000 Bob Hope Dr, Rancho Mirage, CA 92270. Phone: (760) 346-8184. Fax: (760) 346-6329. E-mail: info@bhcc.com. Web: www.bhcc.com.

EARTHQUAKE DISRUPTS NBA: ANNIVERSARY. Jan 17, 1994. The Los Angeles (Northridge) earthquake forced postponement of a scheduled NBA game between the Lakers and the Sacramento Kings at the Great Western Forum. Earthquake damage forced the Clippers to move a pair of games from the Los Angeles Sports Arena. Their Jan 21 game against the Cleveland Cavaliers was played at the Forum, and their Jan 27 game against the New York Knicks was moved to The Pond at Anaheim.

FRANKLIN, BEN: BIRTH ANNIVERSARY. Jan 17, 1706. Benjamin (Ben) Franklin, swimmer, printer, diplomat and patriot, born at Boston, MA. Franklin taught himself to swim at an early age and swam most of his life for exercise. He was often called upon to demonstrate his skills and usually did so willingly. In 1968 the International Swimming Hall of Fame recognized Franklin as an Outstanding Contributor to the sport. Died at Philadelphia, PA, Apr 17, 1790.

MARTIN LUTHER KING DAY. Jan 17. Public Law 98-144 designates the third Monday in January as an annual legal public holiday observing the birth of Martin Luther King, Jr. First observed in 1986.

PLANTE, JACQUES: BIRTH ANNIVERSARY. Jan 17, 1929. Jacques Plante, Hockey Hall of Fame goaltender, born at Mont-Carmel, Quebec, Canada. Plante won five consecutive Vezina Trophies and led the Montreal Canadiens to five consecutive Stanley Cups (1956–60). He was the first goalie to wear a face mask in a game. Inducted into the Hall of Fame in 1978. Died at Geneva, Switzerland, Feb 26, 1986.

PRO GOLFERS MEET TO FORM ASSOCIATION: ANNIVERSARY. Jan 17, 1916. A group of 35 New York area golf professionals met for lunch at the Taplow Club, hosted by department store magnate Rodman Wanamaker. They discussed forming a national organization that promotes interest in the game and elevates the status of the professional golfer. The group appointed an organizing committee of seven to work on a constitution that was approved on Apr 16, forming the Professional Golfers' Association of America.

YZERMAN SCORES 500th GOAL: ANNIVERSARY. Jan 17, 1996. Center Steve Yzerman of the Detroit Red Wings became the 22nd player in National Hockey League history to score 500 regular-season goals as the Wings defeated the Colorado Avalanche, 3–2.

BIRTHDAYS TODAY

Muhammad Ali (born Cassius Marcellus Clay, Jr), 58, former heavyweight champion boxer, born Louisville, KY, Jan 17, 1942.

Charles Theodore ("Chili") Davis, 40, baseball player, born Kingston, Jamaica, Jan 17, 1960.

Howard Thomas Griffith, 33, football player, born Chicago, IL, Jan 17, 1967.

Kipchoge (Kip) Keino, 60, Olympic gold medal long distance runner, born Kipsamo, Kenya, Jan 17, 1940.

Jeremy Roenick, 30, hockey player, born Boston, MA, Jan 17, 1970.

Donald William (Don) Zimmer, 69, former baseball manager and player, born Cincinnati, OH, Jan 17, 1931.

JANUARY 18 — TUESDAY
Day 18 — 348 Remaining

SUPERBOWL CHAMPIONS THIS DATE
1976   Pittsburgh Steelers

CHAMPION RACE HORSE FOUND: ANNIVERSARY. Jan 18, 1941. The great thoroughbred racer Epinard was found by Paris police after being lost for several months during the Nazi occupation. Epinard was being used to make deliveries.

FIRST BLACK PLAYER IN NHL: ANNIVERSARY. Jan 18, 1958. Willie O'Ree became the first black player in the National Hockey League when he played for the Boston Bruins in a game against the Montreal Canadiens. Boston won, 3–0.

FLOOD, CURT: BIRTH ANNIVERSARY. Jan 18, 1938. Curtis Charles (Curt) Flood, baseball player, born at Houston, TX. Flood was one of baseball's best center fielders in the 1960s, batting .293 over 15 seasons and playing spectacular defense. After the 1969 season, he refused to accept a trade from the St. Louis Cardinals to the Philadelphia Phillies. "I am not a piece of property to be bought and sold irrespective of my wishes," he said in a letter to Commissioner Bowie Kuhn. The resulting lawsuit went to the Supreme Court where Flood lost. But his stand, taken because he did not want to switch teams, paved the way for the end of baseball's reserve clause

	S	M	T	W	T	F	S
							1
January	2	3	4	5	6	7	8
2000	9	10	11	12	13	14	15
	16	17	18	19	20	21	22
	23	24	25	26	27	28	29
	30	31					

and the advent of free agency. Died at Los Angeles, CA, Jan 20, 1997.

McGOWAN, BILL: BIRTH ANNIVERSARY. Jan 18, 1896. William Aloysius (Bill) McGowan, Baseball Hall of Fame umpire, born at Wilmington, DE. McGowan was arguably the best umpire in baseball history over his 30-year career, 1925 to 1954. He was selected to umpire the first All-Star Game in 1933 and the first-ever American League play-off in 1948, plus eight World Series. Inducted into the Hall of Fame in 1992. Died at Silver Springs, MD, Dec 9, 1954.

SOUTHWEST SENIOR INVITATIONAL GOLF CHAMPIONSHIP. Jan 18–21. Yuma Golf and Country Club, Yuma, AZ. A 36-hole medal play tournament, limited to 120 players 50 and older. For info: Caballeros de Yuma, Inc, Box 5987, Yuma, AZ 85366-5987. Phone: (520) 343-1715. Fax: (520) 783-1609. Web: www.caballeros.org.

SPECIAL OLYMPICS IOWA WINTER GAMES. Jan 18–20. Dubuque, IA. Olympic-style competition for children and adults with mental retardation. For info: Special Olympics Iowa, 3737 Woodland Ave, Ste 325, West Des Moines, IA 50266-1930. Phone: (515) 267-0131. Fax: (515) 267-0232. E-mail: iso@netihs.net.

BIRTHDAYS TODAY

Brady Kevin Anderson, 36, baseball player, born Silver Spring, MD, Jan 18, 1964.

Michael Scott (Mike) Lieberthal, 28, baseball player, born Glendale, CA, Jan 18, 1972.

Mark Douglas Messier, 39, hockey player, born Edmonton, Alberta, Canada, Jan 18, 1961.

Joseph Paul (Joe) Schmidt, 68, Pro Football Hall of Fame linebacker and former coach, born Mt Oliver, PA, Jan 18, 1932.

JANUARY 19 — WEDNESDAY
Day 19 — 347 Remaining

CHASE'S SPORTSQUOTE OF THE DAY

"I'm not afraid to fail. I'm afraid to be mediocre."—Junior Seau

COLLEGE BASKETBALL TRIPLEHEADER: ANNIVERSARY. Jan 19, 1931. Six college basketball teams played a tripleheader at New York's Madison Square Garden, the first time the sport was played in a large arena instead of a small gym. In the tripleheader, Columbia University beat Fordham University, 26–18, Manhattan College defeated New York University, 16–14, and St. John's University beat City College of New York, 17–8.

FIRST COLLEGE HOCKEY GAME: ANNIVERSARY. Jan 19, 1898. The first college ice hockey game ever played saw Brown University defeat Harvard University, 6–0. Fifty years later, the NCAA staged its first college hockey championship.

GANDIL, CHICK: BIRTH ANNIVERSARY. Jan 19, 1887. Arnold ("Chick") Gandil, baseball player, born at St. Paul, MN. Gandil played first base for the infamous Black Sox and was one of the eight players banned for their involvement in the conspiracy to fix the 1919 World Series. Died at Calistoga, CA, Dec 13, 1970.

HEARN BROADCASTS 3,000th STRAIGHT GAME: ANNIVERSARY. Jan 19, 1998. Francis Dayle ("Chick") Hearn, the only play-by-play announcer the Los Angeles Lakers have ever had, broadcast his 3,000th consecutive game when the Lakers hosted the Orlando Magic. Hearn's streak began after he missed a game on Nov 20, 1965, because bad weather kept him from making an airplane flight.

PGA ADMITS BLACKS: ANNIVERSARY. Jan 19, 1952. The Professional Golfers Association of America amended its rules to allow black golfers to participate in tournaments.

SANDPOINT WINTER CARNIVAL. Jan 19–23. Sandpoint, ID. Ten days of festivities celebrate winter in northern Idaho. Parade, snow sculptures, snowshoe softball, cross-country and telemark races, Schweitzer Day and more. Admission. Est attendance: 3,000. For info: Sandpoint Chamber of Commerce, Box 928, Sandpoint, ID 83864. Phone: (208) 263-0887. Fax: (208) 265-5289. E-mail: chamber@sandpoint.net. Web: www.sandpoint.org/chamber.

UCLA STREAK SNAPPED: ANNIVERSARY. Jan 19, 1974. The longest winning streak in college basketball history came to an end as Notre Dame defeated UCLA, 71–70, to snap the Bruins's 88-game reign. Down by 11 points with less than four minutes to play, the Irish took the lead at 0:29 on Dwight Clay's jump shot from the corner.

WILKENS DOUBLE MILESTONE: 15th ANNIVERSARY. Jan 19, 1985. Lenny Wilkens became the first person in NBA history to coach and play in 1,000 games as his Seattle SuperSonics defeated the Cleveland Cavaliers, 106–105. Wilkens had played in 1,077 games in a career that ended in 1975.

BIRTHDAYS TODAY

Ottis Jerome (O.J.) Anderson, 43, former football player, born West Palm Beach, FL, Jan 19, 1957.

Sylvain Cote, 34, hockey player, born Quebec City, Quebec, Canada, Jan 19, 1966.

Stefan Edberg, 34, former tennis player, born Vastervik, Sweden, Jan 19, 1966.

Walter Jones, 26, football player, born Aliceville, AL, Jan 19, 1974.

Jeffrey Daniel (Jeff) Juden, 29, baseball player, born Salem, MA, Jan 19, 1971.

Rick Michael Krivda, 30, baseball player, born McKeesport, PA, Jan 19, 1970.

Lucien James (Luc) Longley, 31, basketball player, born Melbourne, Australia, Jan 19, 1969.

Phillip Joseph (Phil) Nevin, 29, baseball player, born Fullerton, CA, Jan 19, 1971.

John Brian Patrick (Pat) Quinn, 57, hockey coach and former player, born Hamilton, Ontario, Canada, Jan 19, 1943.

Daniel Edward (Dan) Reeves, 56, football coach and former player, born Rome, GA, Jan 19, 1944.

Tiaina ("Junior") Seau, Jr, 31, football player, born San Diego, CA, Jan 19, 1969.

Amaury Regalado Telemaco, 26, baseball player, born Higuey, Dominican Republic, Jan 19, 1974.

Jeff Van Gundy, 38, basketball coach, born Hemet, CA, Jan 19, 1962.

Tyrone Wheatley, 28, football player, born Inkster, MI, Jan 19, 1972.

JANUARY 20 — THURSDAY
Day 20 — 346 Remaining

SUPERBOWL CHAMPIONS THIS DATE

| 1980 | Pittsburgh Steelers |
| 1985 | San Francisco 49ers |

ALL-CANADA SHOW. Jan 20–23. State Fair Park, West Allis, WI. This consumer show allows individuals an opportunity to talk face-to-face with Canadian lodge representatives and outfitters to plan their hunting, fishing and adventure trips to Canada. For info: Rodney Schlafer, Show Dir, All-Canada Show, Bay-Lakes Mktg, Inc, 1889 Commerce Drive, De Pere, WI 54115. Phone: (920) 983-9800. Fax: (920) 983-9985. Web: www.allcanada .com.

BILLS WIN FIRST OF FOUR AFC TITLES: ANNIVERSARY. Jan 20, 1991. The Buffalo Bills won the first of their record four consecutive AFC titles by overwhelming the Los Angeles Raiders, 51–3. Buffalo went on to lose Super Bowl XXV to the New York Giants, 20–19.

CHAMPIONSHIP SNOWMOBILE DERBY. Jan 20–23. Eagle River, WI. This annual event is the most recognized professional snowmobile race and one of the largest gatherings of sledders in the world. More than 300 pro snowmobile racers, some from as far away as Japan, will compete for the world championship and prizes. In addition to the high speed races, spectators can enjoy trail rides and carnival activities in town. Est attendance: 30,000. For info phone: (715) 479-4424.

ECKERT, SPIKE: BIRTH ANNIVERSARY. Jan 20, 1909. William Dole ("Spike") Eckert, baseball executive, born at Freeport, IL. A retired Air Force general, Eckert was elected Commissioner of Baseball in 1965. He was completely ineffectual in that role and was removed from office on Feb 3, 1969. Died at Freeport, Grand Bahamas, Apr 16, 1971.

FIRST BASKETBALL GAME: ANNIVERSARY. Jan 20, 1891. Under the direction of Dr. James Naismith, the first basketball game was played at the International YMCA at Springfield, MA. Peach baskets with the bottoms still in them were used as the goals. It wasn't until 1905 that someone had to bright idea to remove the baskets' bottoms, thereby eliminating a climb up a ladder after every goal.

KNOXVILLE FISHING EXPO. Jan 20–23. Jacob Building at Chilhowee Park, Knoxville, TN. Annual event featuring the latest in fishing tackle, boats, boating equipment, guide services and other accessories. Top fishing pros will demonstrate their techniques. Est attendance: 13,000. For info: Cindy Crabtree, Esau, Inc, PO Box 50096, Knoxville, TN 37950. Phone: (423) 588-1233 or (800) 588-ESAU. Fax: (423) 588-6938.

LONGHORN WORLD CHAMPIONSHIP RODEO. Jan 20–23. Tulsa Convention Center, Tulsa, OK. More than 450 cowboys and cowgirls compete in seven professional contests ranging from bronc riding to bull riding for top prize money and world championship points. Featuring colorful opening pageantry and Big, Bad BONUS Bulls. Major final weekend Centennial event for Tulsa's year-long Centennial Celebration. 10th annual. Est atten-

dance: 16,000. For info: W. Bruce Lehrke, Pres, Longhorn World Chmpshp Rodeo Inc, PO Box 70159, Nashville, TN 37207. Phone: (615) 876-1016. Fax: (615) 876-4685. E-mail: lhrodeo@idt.net. Web: www.longhornrodeo.com.

MULLANE, TONY: BIRTH ANNIVERSARY. Jan 20, 1859. Anthony John (Tony) Mullane, baseball player, born at Cork, Ireland. Mullane was a flashy, ambidextrous pitcher known as the "Apollo of the Box." He played without a glove and could pitch with either hand to the same batter. Died at Chicago, IL, Apr 25, 1944.

OLYMPIC BOYCOTT ANNOUNCED: 20th ANNIVERSARY. Jan 20, 1980. President Jimmy Carter announced that the US Olympic team would not compete in the 1980 Summer Games at Moscow as a protest against the Soviet Union's military intervention in Afghanistan in December 1979.

SAIL EXPO ATLANTIC CITY. Jan 20–23. The New Atlantic City Convention Center, Atlantic City, NJ. Largest indoor sailboat show in the nation with more than 100 sailboats available for inspection and boarding. Est attendance: 25,000. For info: Visitor Info, Atlantic City Conv & Visitors Authority, 2314 Pacific Ave, Atlantic City, NJ 08401. Phone: (609) 449-7130. For tickets and seminar info, call (800) 817-7245.

SITTLER GETS 1,000th POINT: ANNIVERSARY. Jan 20, 1983. Center Darryl Sittler of the Philadelphia Flyers got the 1,000th point of his National Hockey League career, a goal in a 5–2 win over the Calgary Flames. Sittler finished his career with 1,121 points.

SPECIAL OLYMPICS VIRGINIA WINTER GAMES— ICE SKATING. Jan 20–21. The Ice Palace, Yorktown, VA. More than 50 athletes with mental retardation will go for the gold in figure skating and speed skating at the Ice Palace. For info: Special Olympics Virginia, 3212 Skipwith Rd, Ste 100, Richmond, VA 23294. Phone: (804) 346-5544.

WINTER GRAVITY GAMES™. Jan 20–23. Mammoth Mountain, Mammoth Lakes, CA. The inaugural edition of an alternative sports, lifestyle and music festival. Sponsored by NBC Sports and EMAP Petersen, Inc. Competition in snowboarding, freeskiing, snow mountain biking, skiboarding and others. For info: Jen Faircloth, Advantage Intl, 1775 Pinnacle Dr, Ste 1500, McLean, VA 22102. Phone: (703) 905-3300. Fax: (703) 905-4335. E-mail: jfair@advantageintl.com. Web: www.gravitygames.com.

January 2000

S	M	T	W	T	F	S
						1
2	3	4	5	6	7	8
9	10	11	12	13	14	15
16	17	18	19	20	21	22
23	24	25	26	27	28	29
30	31					

BIRTHDAYS TODAY

Nelison ("Nick") Anderson, 32, basketball player, born Chicago, IL, Jan 20, 1968.

Marvin Larry Benard, 30, baseball player, born Bluefields, Nicaragua, Jan 20, 1970.

Brian Stephen Giles, 29, baseball player, born El Cajon, CA, Jan 20, 1971.

Oswaldo Jose (Ozzie) Guillen, 36, baseball player, born Oculare del Tuy, Venezuela, Jan 20, 1964.

Ronald (Ron) Harper, 36, basketball player, born Dayton, OH, Jan 20, 1964.

Carol Elizabeth Heiss, 60, Olympic gold medal figure skater, born New York, NY, Jan 20, 1940.

Eddie Joseph Kennison, III, 27, football player, born Lake Charles, LA, Jan 20, 1973.

Christopher Vernard (Chris) Morris, 34, basketball player, born Atlanta, GA, Jan 20, 1966.

John Phillips Naber, 44, broadcaster and Olympic gold medal swimmer, born Evanston, IL, Jan 20, 1956.

Jalen Rose, 27, basketball player, born Detroit, MI, Jan 20, 1973.

JANUARY 21 — FRIDAY
Day 21 — 345 Remaining

SUPERBOWL CHAMPIONS THIS DATE
1979   Pittsburgh Steelers

ASPEN/SNOWMASS WINTERSKOL. Jan 21–23. Snowmass Village, CO. A winter carnival–celebrating winter and having winter fun. Ski and snowshoe races, Mad Hatter's Ball, ski splash, sculpture contest and torchlight parade. Est attendance: 5,000. For info: Snowmass Resort Assn, Box 5566, Snowmass Village, CO 81615. Phone: (800) SNOW-MASS. Web: www.snowmassvillage.com.

AUGUSTA FUTURITY. Jan 21–29. Augusta, GA. Brings together the top cutting horses and riders in the world to compete for purse and awards of more than $700,000. Sponsors: Wrangler, John Deere, Manna Pro Feed Company, Ariat Boots, E-Z-GO Textron, Palmer & Cay Insurance, CellularOne, *Augusta Chronicle*, KMC Telecom, Gist Silversmiths, American Hat Company, CT Farm & Country, Jones Intercable, Area 18 CHA, Sedgwick of Georgia and March & McLennan Company. Est attendance: 42,000. For info: Skip Peterson, Dir of Mktg, PO Box 936, Augusta Futurity, Augusta, GA 30903. Phone: (706) 823-3370.

BROWNING, JOHN: BIRTH ANNIVERSARY. Jan 21, 1855. John Moses Browning, gunmaker and inventor, born at Ogden, UT. Browning was taught gunsmithing by his Mormon pioneer father, Jonathan Browning. Starting the J.M. & M.S. Browning Arms Company with his brother at Morgan, UT, he designed guns for Winchester, Remington, Stevens and Colt as well as American and European armies. Browning had more gun patents than any other gunsmith in the world. He is best known worldwide for inventing the machine gun in 1890 and the automatic pistol in 1896. The Browning Arms Company is still located at Morgan, UT. Died at Belgium, Nov 26, 1926.

CANADA: VANCOUVER INTERNATIONAL MOTORCYCLE SHOW. Jan 21–23. Tradex, Abbotsford, British Columbia. Major manufacturers, distributors and retailers, seminars and entertainment. Est attendance: 15,000. For info: Val Nogas, Mgr, Public Relations, Canadian Natl Sportsmen's Shows, 703 Evans Ave, Ste 202, Toronto, ON, Canada M9C 5E9. Phone: (416) 695-0311. Fax: (416) 695-0381. Web: www.sportsmensshows.com.

FEMALE REPORTERS IN NHL LOCKER ROOM: 25th ANNIVERSARY. Jan 21, 1975. Officials at the National Hockey League All-Star Game made history by allowing female reporters in the players' locker rooms, a first for American professional sports. The coaches of the two squads arranged for reporters to interview players before they took their showers.

FONSECA, LEW: BIRTH ANNIVERSARY. Jan 21, 1899. Lewis Albert (Lew) Fonseca, baseball player and manager, born at Oakland, CA. Fonseca played 12 years in the majors (1921–33) despite a tendency to get injured. He began taking movies of opposing players and turned this practice into the start of the annual All-Star Game and World Series highlights films. Died at Ely, IA, Nov 26, 1989.

McENROE TEMPER TANTRUM: 10th ANNIVERSARY. Jan 21, 1990. Tennis player John McEnroe's temper tantrum at the Australian Open got him disqualified from the tournament. McEnroe, leading his match against Mikael Pernfors, became the first player ever tossed from this tournament.

PURDUE'S NUDE OLYMPICS: ANNIVERSARY. Jan 21, 1986. More than 100 students from Purdue University ran naked through the streets of West Lafayette, IN, in the school's quite unofficial Nude Olympics. The runners were undeterred by a temperature just a few degrees above freezing.

SEATTLE BOAT SHOW. Jan 21–30. Exhibition Hall, Seattle, WA. Huge display of new boats, accessories and services. A second show, Seattle Boats Afloat, is scheduled for Aug 2000. Large boats (35 ft or longer) on display in Puget Sound with over 70 accessories dealers on land. Call NW Marine Trade Assn for specific dates. Est attendance: 90,000. For info: NW Marine Trade Assn, 1900 N Northlake Way, #233, Seattle, WA 98103. Phone: (206) 634-0911. Fax: (206) 632-0078.

SOUTHWESTERN EXPOSITION LIVESTOCK SHOW AND RODEO. Jan 21–Feb 6. Ft Worth, TX. Western-flavored extravaganza. Observed centennial in 1996. World's first indoor rodeo added in 1918 (45 acres under roof). Prize livestock displays, horse shows, midway, commercial exhibits and quality family-oriented entertainment. Est attendance: 815,000. For info: Delbert Bailey, PO Box 150, Ft Worth, TX 76101-0150. Phone: (817) 877-2400. Fax: (817) 877-2499. Web: www.fwstockshow rodeo.com.

WISCONSIN DELLS FLAKE OUT FESTIVAL. Jan 21–23. Tommy Bartlett Show Site, Wisconsin Dells, WI. Wisconsin-sanctioned snow sculpting competition. Winners will compete in the National Snow Sculpting Competition. Other activities include ice-carving competition, snowman making, snowmobile races, sleigh rides, ice skating, glowing hot-air balloons on Saturday evening and much more. Est attendance: 20,000. For info: Wisc Dells Visitor and Conv Bureau, PO Box 390, Wisconsin Dells, WI 53965. Phone: (800) 223-3557. Fax: (608) 254-4293. E-mail: info@wisdells.com. Web: www.wisdells.com.

BIRTHDAYS TODAY

Alan Paul Benes, 28, baseball player, born Evansville, IN, Jan 21, 1972.

Brian Walter Richard Bradley, 35, hockey player, born Kitchener, Ontario, Canada, Jan 21, 1965.

Thurman Clyde ("Rusty") Greer, III, 31, baseball player, born Ft Rucker, AL, Jan 21, 1969.

Christopher Andrew (Chris) Hammond, 34, baseball player, born Atlanta, GA, Jan 21, 1966.

Jack William Nicklaus, 60, golfer, born Columbus, OH, Jan 21, 1940.

Johnny Lane Oates, 54, baseball manager and former player, born Sylva, NC, Jan 21, 1946.

Hakeem Abdul Olajuwon (born Akeem Abdul Olajuwon), 37, basketball player, born Lagos, Nigeria, Jan 21, 1963.

Detlef Schrempf, 37, basketball player, born Leverkusen, West Germany, Jan 21, 1963.

Douglas D. (Doug) Weight, 29, hockey player, born Warren, MI, Jan 21, 1971.

JANUARY 22 — SATURDAY
Day 22 — 344 Remaining

SUPERBOWL CHAMPIONS THIS DATE

1984	Los Angeles Raiders
1989	San Francisco 49ers

CANADA: CIBC SENIOR CURLING CHAMPIONSHIP. Jan 22–30. Portage La Prairie, Manitoba. National competition for senior men and women. For info: Media Relations, Canadian Curling Assn, 1600 James Naismith Dr, Ste 511, Gloucester, ON, Canada K1B 5N4. Phone: (613) 748-5628. Fax: (613) 748-5713. E-mail: cca@curling.ca. Web: www.curling.ca.

DELCHAMPS SENIOR BOWL FOOTBALL GAME. Jan 22. Ladd Memorial Stadium, Mobile, AL. All-star football game featuring the nation's top collegiate seniors on teams coached by NFL coaching staffs. Proceeds go to charities. Est attendance: 40,700. For info: Vic Knight, PR Dir, Senior Bowl, 63 S Royal St, Ste 406, Mobile, AL 36602. Phone: (334) 438-2276. Fax: (334) 432-0409. E-mail: srbowl@seniorbowl.com. Web: www.seniorbowl.com.

FREEZE FOR FOOD 10K RACE AND 5K RUN/WALK. Jan 22. Vilas Park Shelter, Madison, WI. Fundraiser sponsored by the Returned Peace Corps Volunteers of Wisconsin-Madison. $10 registration fee for each event. Times posted; prizes awarded for top pledge raisers and event finishers. We will never cancel the race due to weather! Est attendance: 150. For info: Peter Joyce, 320 Russell St, Madison, WI 53704. Phone: (608) 249-8573.

January *2000*	S	M	T	W	T	F	S
							1
	2	3	4	5	6	7	8
	9	10	11	12	13	14	15
	16	17	18	19	20	21	22
	23	24	25	26	27	28	29
	30	31					

HOUSTON SHUT OUT IN OT: ANNIVERSARY. Jan 22, 1983. The Houston Rockets became the first team in NBA history to be shut out in overtime as the Portland Trail Blazers defeated them, 113–96. Portland outscored the Rockets in OT, 17–0.

LAFONTAINE SCORES 1,000th POINT: ANNIVERSARY. Jan 22, 1998. Center Pat LaFontaine of the New York Rangers became the 50th player in National Hockey League history to record 1,000 regular-season points. He scored a third-period goal in the Rangers' 4–2 loss to the Philadelphia Flyers.

NBA GRANTS FRANCHISES TO PHOENIX AND MILWAUKEE: ANNIVERSARY. Jan 22, 1968. The NBA Board of Governors awarded expansion franchises to Phoenix and Milwaukee. The Phoenix team adopted the nickname Suns, and the Milwaukee franchise became the Bucks.

SENIOR TOUR CREATED: 20th ANNIVERSARY. Jan 22, 1980. The Tournament Policy Board of the PGA approved a plan to create a Senior Tour for golfers over the age of 50. The idea grew out of a single tournament phenomenon called the Legends of Golf, held at Austin, TX. The first official Senior Tour event, the Atlantic City Senior Invitational, was played in June.

WIRTZ, ARTHUR: BIRTH ANNIVERSARY. Jan 22, 1901. Arthur Michael Wirtz, Sr, Hockey Hall of Fame executive and sports administrator, born at Chicago, IL. Wirtz prospered in Depression-era real estate and got involved in indoor sports arena ownership. He brought ice skater Sonja Henie to the US after the 1936 Olympics and launched the first ice show. He also owned the Chicago Blackhawks and was part-owner of the Chicago Bulls. Inducted into the Hockey Hall of Fame in 1971. Died at Chicago, July 21, 1983.

CHASE'S SPORTSQUOTE OF THE DAY

"One thing I do suffer from is over-confidence. It's something I'm working on."—George Foreman

BIRTHDAYS TODAY

Michel (Mike) Bossy, 43, Hockey Hall of Fame right wing, born Montreal, Quebec, Canada, Jan 22, 1957.

Louis (Lou) Creekmur, 73, Pro Football Hall of Fame defensive lineman, born Hopeland, NJ, Jan 22, 1927.

George Edward Foreman, 51, former heavyweight champion boxer, born Marshall, TX, Jan 22, 1949.

Fletcher Joseph (Joe) Perry, 73, Pro Football Hall of Fame fullback, born Stevens, AR, Jan 22, 1927.

George Gerald Seifert, 60, football coach, born San Francisco, CA, Jan 22, 1940.

☆ ☆ ☆

JANUARY 23 — SUNDAY
Day 23 — 343 Remaining

CHRIS STRATTON DART TOURNAMENT. Jan 23. Springbrook Golf Course, Battle Creek, MI. 8th annual benefit tournament dedicated to Chris Stratton, a great darter and well-liked person. Fifty percent of entry fees donated to American Cancer Society. Est attendance: 100. For info: Bill Buckner, Springbrook Golf Course, 1600 Ave A, Battle Creek, MI 49015. Phone: (616) 965-6512.

NATIONAL FOOTBALL LEAGUE CONFERENCE CHAMPIONSHIPS. Jan 23. Sites TBA. Play-offs in the NFL continue with championship games in the AFC and the NFC. Winners advance to the Super Bowl. For info: NFL, 280

Park Ave, New York, NY 10017. Phone: (212) 450-2000. Fax: (212) 681-7573. Web: www.nfl.com.

100-MILE SKATING RACE: ANNIVERSARY. Jan 23, 1893. Joe Donahue won a 100-mile ice skating race at Stamford, CT. His winning time was seven hours, 11 minutes, 38.2 seconds.

PERFECT GAME ON TV: ANNIVERSARY. Jan 23, 1988. For the first time ever, a bowler rolled a 300 game on television to win a professional tournament. Bob Benoit was the bowler. He won the Quaker State Open at Grand Prairie, TX, and earned a $100,000 bonus.

RED WINGS SCORE 15: ANNIVERSARY. Jan 23, 1944. The Detroit Red Wings set an NHL record for consecutive goals scored when they defeated the New York Rangers, 15–0.

ROBINSON ELECTED TO HALL OF FAME: ANNIVERSARY. Jan 23, 1962. Jackie Robinson became the first black ballplayer to be elected to the Baseball Hall of Fame. Robinson broke baseball's color line in 1947 and played for the Brooklyn Dodgers through 1956.

SPECIAL OLYMPICS KENTUCKY WINTER GAMES. Jan 23–25 (tentative). Lawrenceburg, IN. Olympic-style competition for children and adults with mental retardation. For info: Special Olympics Kentucky, 105 Lakeview Ct, Frankfort, KY 40601. Phone: (502) 695-8222. Fax: (502) 695-0496. Web: www.soky.org.

WINTER TRIATHLON. Jan 23. Muskegon Winter Sports Complex, Muskegon, MI. Contestants will compete in a 2.5K cross-country ski, two timed runs on the luge and four laps on the ice rink. Some instruction provided. For info: Muskegon Sports Council, PO Box 5085, North Muskegon, MI 49445. Phone: (616) 744-9629. Luge Club phone: (616) 759-2201. Web: www.msports.org.

BIRTHDAYS TODAY

Kurt Anthony Bevacqua, 53, former baseball player, born Miami Beach, FL, Jan 23, 1947.

Patrick Capper (Pat) Haden, 47, broadcaster and former football player, born Westbury, NY, Jan 23, 1953.

Larry Darnell Hughes, 21, basketball player, born St. Louis, MO, Jan 23, 1979.

Gerald Louis (Jerry) Kramer, 64, author (*Instant Replay*) and former football player, born Jordan, MT, Jan 23, 1936.

Kevin James Mawae, 29, football player, born Leesville, LA, Jan 23, 1971.

Brendan Frederick Shanahan, 31, hockey player, born Mimico, Ontario, Canada, Jan 23, 1969.

Richard Smehlik, 30, hockey player, born Ostrava, Czechoslovakia, Jan 23, 1970.

Mark Edward Wohlers, 30, baseball player, born Holyoke, MA, Jan 23, 1970.

JANUARY 24 — MONDAY
Day 24 — 342 Remaining

SUPERBOWL CHAMPIONS THIS DATE

1982	San Francisco 49ers

BOSSY GETS 1,000th POINT: ANNIVERSARY. Jan 24, 1986. Right wing Mike Bossy of the New York Islanders got the 1,000th point of his National Hockey League career, an assist in a 7–5 win over the Washington Capitals. Bossy finished his career with 1,126 points.

BOSSY NETS 50 IN 50: ANNIVERSARY. Jan 24, 1981. Right wing Mike Bossy of the New York Islanders scored his 50th goal in the season's 50th game as the Isles defeated the Quebec Nordiques, 7–3.

BRICKHOUSE, JACK: BIRTH ANNIVERSARY. Jan 24, 1916. John Beasley (Jack) Brickhouse, broadcaster, born at Peoria, IL. Brickhouse, a legend in Chicago broadcasting, was the play-by-play voice for the first baseball game televised by WGN, an exhibition between the Cubs and the White Sox on Apr 16, 1948. The dominant sports voice on Chicago radio and television, he broadcast Cubs games for 40 years, Chicago Bears football games for 24 years and did some games for the White Sox and the Chicago Bulls. Given the Ford Frick Award in 1983. Died at Chicago, IL, Aug 6, 1998.

COCHEMS, EDDIE: BIRTH ANNIVERSARY. Jan 24, 1877. Edward B. (Eddie) Cochems, football player and coach, born at Sturgeon Bay, WI. Although others are sometimes given credit for introducing the forward pass, Cochems, in fact, was the one. He served on the committee to rewrite the football rules after President Theodore Roosevelt called for the game's abolition because of excessive violence. The new rules allowed for passing. That fall, Cochems's team, St. Louis University, used the pass to great effect, winning all 11 games and outscoring its opponents, 407 to 11. Died at Madison, WI, Apr 9, 1953.

DUVAL SHOOTS 59: ANNIVERSARY. Jan 24, 1999. David Duval became the fifth professional golfer to shoot a 59 in a tour event. His record score came at Palm Springs, CA, in the final round of the Bob Hope Chrysler Classic, which Duval won by one shot over Steve Pate.

"THE FIGHT OF THE WEEK" TV PREMIERE: ANNIVERSARY. Jan 24, 1953. For 11 years, you could catch a boxing match every week on TV. Jack Drees announced the matches the first few seasons; Don Dunphy succeeded him.

GAINES WINS 800th GAME: 10th ANNIVERSARY. Jan 24, 1990. Winston-Salem State defeated Livingstone, 79–70, to give coach Clarence ("Big House") Gaines the 800th victory of his college basketball coaching career. Gaines coached from 1947 through 1993 and compiled a career record of 828–447.

BIRTHDAYS TODAY

Tshimanga ("Tim") Biakabutuka, 26, football player, born Kinshasa, Zaire, Jan 24, 1974.

Douglas Robert Zachariah (Doug) Brien, 30, football player, born Bloomfield, NJ, Jan 24, 1970.

Mary Lou Retton, 32, Olympic gold medal gymnast, born Fairmont, WV, Jan 24, 1968.

JANUARY 25 — TUESDAY
Day 25 — 341 Remaining

SUPERBOWL CHAMPIONS THIS DATE

1981	Oakland Raiders
1987	New York Giants
1998	Denver Broncos

DAY, JOHN: 75th DEATH ANNIVERSARY. Jan 25, 1925. John B. Day, baseball executive, born at Cliffside, NJ, 1848. Day was the founding owner of the New York Giants, one of baseball's historic franchises. Financial reverses in the 1890s forced Day to sell the team in 1895, after which he became supervisor of National League umpires. Died at Cliffside.

FIRST WINTER OLYMPICS: ANNIVERSARY. Jan 25, 1924. The first Winter Olympic Games opened at Chamonix, France, with 281 male and 13 female athletes from 16 nations competing in five sports. US athletes won four medals. The Canadian hockey team overwhelmed its opponents, scoring 85 goals in three games.

NBA'S 5,000,000th POINT: ANNIVERSARY. Jan 25, 1988. Guard Rickey Green of the Utah Jazz scored the 5,000,000th point in NBA history in a game against the Cleveland Cavaliers. Green made a three-point shot at the buzzer ending the third quarter. The Jazz won, 119–96.

NEW ZEALAND: LOUIS VUITTON CUP FINALS. Jan 25. Auckland, New Zealand. The two surviving yachts from semifinal races that began on Jan 2 will compete for the Louis Vuitton Cup and for the challenger's spot in the America's Cup race, set to start on Feb 19. For info: New Zealand Defense Committee, Royal New Zealand Yacht Squadron, PO Box 1927, Auckland, New Zealand. Phone: (011) 64-9-357-6712. Web: www.americascup2000.org.nz.

ONLY IHL DOUBLEHEADER: ANNIVERSARY. Jan 25, 1953. The Cincinnati Mohawks and the Troy (OH) Bruins played the only doubleheader in the history of the International Hockey League, with one game being played in each team's home city. The Bruins won the first game at Troy, 3–0. The Mohawks won the nightcap at Cincinnati, 2–1.

PREFONTAINE, STEVE: BIRTH ANNIVERSARY. Jan 25, 1951. Steve Roland ("Pre") Prefontaine, long-distance runner, born at Coos Bay, OR. Prefontaine was an outstanding athlete whose grit, determination and activism personified Americans' growing interest in physical fitness, jogging and running. Although never an Olympic champion or world record holder, he set 14 US records during his career cut short by a fatal automobile accident on a road where he often trained. Died at Eugene, OR, May 30, 1975.

SLOVAKIA: FIS NORDIC JUNIOR WORLD SKI CHAMPIONSHIPS. Jan 25–30. Strbske Pleso, Slovakia. For info: Intl Ski Federation, Blochstrasse 2, 3653 Oberhofen am Thunersee, Switzerland. Phone: (41) (33) 244-6161. Fax: (41) (33) 243-5353. E-mail: mail@fisski.org. Web: www.fisski.org.

BIRTHDAYS TODAY

Chris Chelios, 38, hockey player, born Chicago, IL, Jan 25, 1962.
Louis Roy (Lou) Groza, 76, Pro Football Hall of Fame tackle and placekicker, born Martins Ferry, OH, Jan 25, 1924.
William Earnest (Ernie) Harwell, 82, Ford Frick Award broadcaster, born Washington, GA, Jan 25, 1918.
Donald Rogers (Don) Maynard, 65, Pro Football Hall of Fame wide receiver, born Crosbyton, TX, Jan 25, 1935.
Richard Joseph (Dick) McGuire, 74, former basketball coach and Basketball Hall of Fame guard, born Huntington, NY, Jan 25, 1926.

January 2000

S	M	T	W	T	F	S
						1
2	3	4	5	6	7	8
9	10	11	12	13	14	15
16	17	18	19	20	21	22
23	24	25	26	27	28	29
30	31					

Christopher Lemonte (Chris) Mills, 30, basketball player, born Los Angeles, CA, Jan 25, 1970.
Paul Stephen Ranheim, 34, hockey player, born St. Louis, MO, Jan 25, 1966.
Mark Schlereth, 34, football player, born Anchorage, AK, Jan 25, 1966.
Jack Thomas Snow, 57, broadcaster and former football player, born Rock Springs, WY, Jan 25, 1943.
Esa Kalervo Tikkanen, 32, hockey player, born Helsinki, Finland, Jan 25, 1968.

JANUARY 26 — WEDNESDAY
Day 26 — 340 Remaining

SUPERBOWL CHAMPIONS THIS DATE	
1986	Chicago Bears
1992	Washington Redskins
1997	Green Bay Packers

BLAEHOLDER, GEORGE: BIRTH ANNIVERSARY. Jan 26, 1904. George Franklin Blaeholder, baseball player, born at Orange, CA. Blaeholder pitched in the major leagues from 1925 through 1936. He is credited with inventing the slider, a pitch that some liken to a cross between a fastball and a curve. Died at Garden Grove, CA, Dec 29, 1947.

CHICAGO WINS SUPER BOWL XX: ANNIVERSARY. Jan 26, 1986. In their first Super Bowl outing, the Chicago Bears romped over the New England Patriots to win Super Bowl XX, 46–10. Chicago spotted the Patriots a 3–0 lead but then scored the next 44 points while holding New England to seven yards rushing.

DESERT CIRCUIT. Jan 26–Mar 12. HITS Desert Horse Park, Indio, CA. Six weeks of hunter/jumper competition featuring Grand Prix show jumping every Friday and Sunday. The Desert Circuit began in 1992 at Indio, CA, and has rapidly grown into the largest horse show west of the Mississippi. The event attracts over 3,500 horses during its run. There are six Grand Prix events, four of which are World Cup qualifiers. The Desert Circuit draws both beginning and world class riders. Annually, late January through early March. Est attendance: 25,000. For info and exact dates of the Circuit events, contact: HITS, 13 Closs Dr, Rhinebeck, NY 12572. Phone: (914) 876-3666. Fax: (914) 876-5538. Web: www.equisearch.com.

GRETZKY SCORES 50 IN 49: 15th ANNIVERSARY. Jan 26, 1985. Center Wayne Gretzky of the Edmonton Oilers scored his 50th goal in the Oilers' 49th game, a 6–3 victory over the Pittsburgh Penguins.

HIGH SCHOOL SCORING RECORD: 40th ANNIVERSARY. Jan 26, 1960. Danny Heater of Burnsville, WV, set a national high school basketball record by scoring 135 points in a single game. Heater went on to play college ball at the University of Richmond.

JORDAN, HENRY: 65th BIRTH ANNIVERSARY. Jan 26, 1935. Henry Wendell Jordan, Pro Football Hall of Fame defensive tackle, born at Emporia, VA. Jordan played college football at the University of Virginia and starred with the great Green Bay Packers teams of the 1960s. He compensated for lack of size with quickness and agility and was known for his witty, gracious manner. Inducted into the Pro Football Hall of Fame in 1995. Died at Milwaukee, WI, Feb 21, 1977.

NEW CHICAGO BOAT, RV AND OUTDOORS SHOW. Jan 26–30. McCormick Place, Chicago, IL. The Midwest's largest selection under one roof, the 70th annual Chicago Boat, RV and Outdoors Show offers more than 900 boats and 300 recreational vehicles. Informative boating and fishing seminars. For info: Great Outdoors, 420 Lake

Cook Rd, Ste 108, Deerfield, IL 60015. Phone: (847) 914-0630 or (888) 462-7469. Fax: (847) 914-0333. E-mail: go2show@msn.com.

PALM BEACH CLASSIC. Jan 26–30. Palm Beach Polo Equestrian Club, Wellington, FL. The opening event of the 2000 Cosequin Winter Equestrian Festival. For info: Stadium Jumping, Inc, 3104 Cherry Palm Dr, Ste 220, Tampa, FL 33619. Phone: (800) 237-8924 or (813) 623-5801. Fax: (813) 626-5369. Web: www.stadiumjumping.com.

PONTIAC SILVERDOME CAMPER, TRAVEL AND RV SHOW. Jan 26–30. Pontiac Silverdome, Pontiac, MI. This event brings together buyers and sellers of RVs, motor homes, campers and camping accessories, as well as buyers and sellers of camping vacations and travel destinations. Est attendance: 28,000. For info: Mike Wilbraham, ShowSpan, Inc, 1400 28th St SW, Grand Rapids, MI 49509. Phone: (616) 530-1919. Fax: (616) 530-2122. Web: showspan.com.

US SYNCHRONIZED TEAM CHAMPIONSHIPS—MIDWESTERN SECTIONAL. Jan 26–30. Fraser, MI. For info: Media Relations, US Figure Skating Assn, 20 First St, Colorado Springs, CO 80906. Phone: (719) 635-5200. Fax: (719) 635-9548. E-mail: usfsa1@aol.com. Web: www.usfsa.org/events.

BIRTHDAYS TODAY

Jeffery Glenn (Jeff) Branson, 33, baseball player, born Waynesboro, MS, Jan 26, 1967.
Vincent Lamar (Vince) Carter, 23, basketball player, born Daytona Beach, FL, Jan 26, 1977.
Eric Wayne Davis, 32, football player, born Anniston, AL, Jan 26, 1968.
Wayne Douglas Gretzky, 39, former hockey player, born Brantford, Ontario, Canada, Jan 26, 1961.
Robert George (Bob) Uecker, 65, broadcaster, actor (*Major League*) and former baseball player, born Milwaukee, WI, Jan 26, 1935.

JANUARY 27 — THURSDAY
Day 27 — 339 Remaining

SUPERBOWL CHAMPIONS THIS DATE
1991   New York Giants

ALL-CANADA SHOW. Jan 27–30. Delta Plex, Grand Rapids, MI. This consumer show allows individuals an opportunity to talk face-to-face with Canadian lodge representatives and outfitters to plan their hunting, fishing and adventure trips to Canada. For info: Rodney Schlafer, Show Dir, All-Canada Show, Bay-Lakes Mktg, Inc, 1889 Commerce Dr, De Pere, WI 54115. Phone: (920) 983-9800. Fax: (920) 983-9985. Web: www.allcanada.com.

CHATTANOOGA BOAT SHOW. Jan 27–30. Chattanooga Convention Center, Chattanooga, TN. 15th annual show featuring thousands of square feet of boats from the area's largest marine dealers and booths displaying everything from water skis and marine equipment to fishing tackle and floating docks. Est attendance: 12,000. For info: Esau, Inc, PO Box 50096, Knoxville, TN 37950. Phone: (423) 588-1233 or (800) 588-ESAU. Fax: (423) 588-6938.

FALK, BIBB: BIRTH ANNIVERSARY. Jan 27, 1899. Bibb August Falk, baseball player, coach and manager, born at Austin, TX. Falk played football and baseball in college and enjoyed a fine career as a major league outfielder. After retiring, he coached baseball at the University of Texas, winning the national championship in 1949 and 1950. Died at Austin, June 8, 1989.

GLOBETROTTERS BORN: ANNIVERSARY. Jan 27, 1927. The Harlem Globetrotters opened their first tour with a game at Hinckley, IL. Founded by Abe Saperstein as a spin-off from the great Harlem Renaissance team, the Globetrotters quickly became fan favorites around the world.

GRETZKY'S SCORING STREAK: ANNIVERSARY. Jan 27, 1984. Center Wayne Gretzky of the Edmonton Oilers scored a goal against the New Jersey Devils to extend his streak of scoring either a goal or an assist to 51 games, an NHL record. The Great One was stopped by the Los Angeles Kings, a team he later played for, the next night.

POLLARD, FRITZ: BIRTH ANNIVERSARY. Jan 27, 1894. Frederick Douglas (Fritz) Pollard, football player and coach, born at Chicago, IL. In 1915, while playing for Brown, Pollard became the second black football player to be named a consensus All-American. He turned pro in the infant days of the NFL, playing for and coaching several teams. From 1927 to 1933, he organized and coached the Chicago Brown Bombers, an independent team. Died at Silver Spring, MD, May 11, 1986.

ROONEY, ART: BIRTH ANNIVERSARY. Jan 27, 1901. Art Rooney, Pro Football Hall of Fame executive, born at Coulterville, PA. As founder of the Pittsburgh Steelers, Rooney endured decades of futility on the field before the Steelers won their first NFL championship, a victory over the Minnesota Vikings in Super Bowl IX (1975). Inducted into the Hall of Fame in 1964. Died at Pittsburgh, PA, Aug 25, 1988.

STRICTLY SAIL—CHICAGO. Jan 27–31. Navy Pier, Chicago, IL. 5th annual show. The Midwest's largest and most comprehensive sail-only show features the latest sailboats, equipment and services as well as seminars and attractions for all levels of sailing ability. For info: NMMA Boat Shows, 200 E Randolph Dr, Ste 5100, Chicago, IL 60601-6528. Phone: (312) 946-6262. Fax: (312) 946-0401. Web: www.boatshows.com.

UCLA SETS RECORD: ANNIVERSARY. Jan 27, 1973. The UCLA Bruins, led by center Bill Walton, beat Notre Dame, 82–63, to set an NCAA record with their 61st consecutive victory. The Bruins broke the record set by the University of San Francisco in 1956 when Bill Russell played center for the Dons.

US SYNCHRONIZED TEAM CHAMPIONSHIPS—PACIFIC COAST SECTIONAL. Jan 27–29. Eugene, OR. For info: Media Relations, US Figure Skating Assn, 20 First St, Colorado Springs, CO 80906. Phone: (719) 635-5200. Fax: (719) 635-9548. E-mail: usfsa1@aol.com. Web: www.usfsa.org/events.

CHASE'S SPORTSQUOTE OF THE DAY

"Tomboy. All right, call me a tomboy. Tomboys get medals. Tomboys win championships. Tomboys can fly. Oh, and tomboys aren't boys."—soccer player Julie Foudy

BIRTHDAYS TODAY

Frank Cullen (Frankie) Albert, 80, former football coach and player, born Chicago, IL, Jan 27, 1920.
Patrice Brisebois, 29, hockey player, born Montreal, Quebec, Canada, Jan 27, 1971.
Anthony Cris Collinsworth, 41, broadcaster and former football player, born Dayton, OH, Jan 27, 1959.
Julie Foudy, 29, soccer player, born San Diego, CA, Jan 27, 1971.

JANUARY 28 — FRIDAY
Day 28 — 338 Remaining

SUPERBOWL CHAMPIONS THIS DATE
1990   San Francisco 49ers
1996   Dallas Cowboys

BLACK HILLS STOCK SHOW AND RODEO. Jan 28–Feb 6. Rapid City, SD. Events include PRCA rodeos, ranch rodeo, timed sheepdog trials, draft horse events, livestock shows and sales, buffalo show and sale, bucking horse and bull sale, stockman banquet and ball, world champion wild-horse races and commercial exhibits. Est attendance: 250,000. For info: Black Hills Stock Show & Rodeo, 800 San Francisco, Rapid City, SD 57701. Phone: (605) 355-3861.

CAMPANELLA INJURED: ANNIVERSARY. Jan 28, 1958. Catcher Roy Campanella of the Los Angeles Dodgers was severely injured in a car crash on an icy road in the early morning hours. Campanella was paralyzed from the waist down and spent the rest of his life in a wheelchair. His cheery disposition in the face of great adversity served as an inspiration.

CANADA: ONTARIO WINTER CARNIVAL BON SOO. Jan 28–Feb 6. Sault Ste Marie, Ontario. One of Canada's largest winter carnivals features more than 125 festive indoor and hearty outdoor events for all ages during a 10-day winter extravaganza. Annually, the last weekend in January through the first weekend in February. Est attendance: 100,000. For info: Donna Gregg, Bon Soo Winter Carnival Inc, PO Box 781, Sault Ste Marie, ON, Canada P6A 5N3. Phone: (705) 759-3000. Fax: (705) 759-6950.

DOAK, BILL: BIRTH ANNIVERSARY. Jan 28, 1891. William Leopold (Bill) Doak, baseball pitcher, born at Pittsburgh, PA. Doak was a pitcher who relied on the spitball and was one of those allowed to continue throwing the pitch after it was banned in 1920. He designed the "Bill Doak glove" in 1918, his royalties from which often added up to $25,000 a year. Died at Bradenton, FL, Nov 26, 1954.

McCALL WINTER CARNIVAL. Jan 28–Feb 6. McCall, ID. Come beat the winter blahs at this celebration of winter that includes ice sculptures, dances, food, snowmobile races, sled dog races, beard contest, parade and a sculpting contest. Est attendance: 20,000. For info: McCall Chamber of Commerce, PO Box D, McCall, ID 83638. Phone: (208) 634-7631 or (800) 260-5130. Fax: (208) 634-7752. E-mail: mccallcc@cyberhighway.net. Web: www.mccall-idchamber.org.

MESSENGER: DEATH ANNIVERSARY. Jan 28, 1808. Popularly known as "Imported Messenger," this horse was the "foundation" of the American Standardbred which compete in harness racing. Bred in England in 1780 and raced there, he was brought to the US to stud and was purchased by Henry Astor. Messenger died on Long Island, NY, and was buried near Oyster Bay in ground that is now part of the Piping Rock Golf Course. The spirited trotter's burial drew a crowd of horse lovers and race fans, and he was saluted with several volleys of rifle fire.

NC RV AND CAMPING SHOW. Jan 28–30. Charlotte Merchandise Mart, Charlotte, NC. A display of the latest in recreation vehicles and accessories by various dealers. Est attendance: 14,000. For info: Apple Rock Advertising & Promotion, 1200 Eastchester Dr, High Point, NC 27265. Phone: (336) 881-7100. Fax: (336) 883-7198.

OHIO INTERNATIONAL MOTORCYCLE SHOW. Jan 28–30. IX Center (West Hall) Cleveland, OH. Est attendance: 43,000. For info: Advanstar Communications, 201 E Sandpointe Ave, Ste 600, Santa Ana, CA 92707-5761. Phone: (800) 854-3112 or (714) 513-8400. Fax: (714) 513-8481. Web: www.motorcycleshows.com.

SAINT PAUL WINTER CARNIVAL. Jan 28–Feb 6. St. Paul, MN. Minnesota's largest tourist attraction and the nation's oldest and largest winter festival. The 114-year-old St. Paul Winter Carnival provides 10 fun-filled days with more than 100 indoor and outdoor events celebrating the thrills and chills of wintertime fun. Est attendance: 1,000,000. For info: Saint Paul Festival and Heritage Foundation, 429 Landmark Center, 75 W 5th St, St. Paul, MN 55102. Phone: (651) 223-4700. Fax: (651) 223-4707. Web: winter-carnival.com.

SPECIAL OLYMPICS FLORIDA STATE BASKETBALL CHAMPIONSHIPS. Jan 28–29. Gainesville, FL. Olympic-style tournament for children and adults with mental retardation. For info: Special Olympics Florida, 8 Broadway, Ste D, Kissimmee, FL 34741. Phone: (407) 870-2292. Fax: (407) 870-9810.

SPECIAL OLYMPICS HEARTLAND GAMES. Jan 28–29. St. Joseph and Weston, MO, and Atchison, KS. Olympic-style competition for athletes with mental retardation in cross country and alpine skiing, figure and speed skating and floor hockey. For info: Special Olympics Missouri, 520 Dix Rd, Ste C, Jefferson City, MO 65109. Phone: (573) 635-1660. Fax: (573) 635-8233. E-mail: hq@somo.org. Web: www.somo.org.

US SYNCHRONIZED TEAM CHAMPIONSHIPS—EASTERN SECTIONAL. Jan 28–30. West Acton, MA. For info: Media Relations, US Figure Skating Assn, 20 First St, Colorado Springs, CO 80906. Phone: (719) 635-5200. Fax: (719) 635-9548. E-mail: usfsa1@aol.com. Web: www.usfsa.org/events.

WRIGHT, GEORGE: BIRTH ANNIVERSARY. Jan 28, 1847. George Wright, Baseball Hall of Fame shortstop and sporting goods entrepreneur, born at New York, NY. Wright and his brother Harry were two of baseball's earliest pioneers. He played for the 1869 Red Stockings, was the first player signed by the Boston Red Stockings in 1871 and joined with Henry A. Ditson in 1879 to form the Wright & Ditson sporting goods company. Inducted into the Hall of Fame in 1937. Died at Boston, MA, Aug 21, 1937.

BIRTHDAYS TODAY
Michael Jerome Cage, 38, basketball player, born West Memphis, AR, Jan 28, 1962.
Tony Lorenzo Delk, 26, basketball player, born Covington, TN, Jan 28, 1974.
Michal Pivonka, 34, hockey player, born Kladno, Czechoslovakia, Jan 28, 1966.
Gregg Charles Popovich, 51, basketball coach, born East Chicago, IN, Jan 28, 1949.
Nicholas Raymond Leige (Nick) Price, 43, golfer, born Durban, South Africa, Jan 28, 1957.
William De Kova (Bill) White, 66, former baseball executive, broadcaster and player, born Lakewood, FL, Jan 28, 1934.

January 2000

S	M	T	W	T	F	S
						1
2	3	4	5	6	7	8
9	10	11	12	13	14	15
16	17	18	19	20	21	22
23	24	25	26	27	28	29
30	31					

JANUARY 29 — SATURDAY
Day 29 — 337 Remaining

SUPERBOWL CHAMPIONS THIS DATE
1995   San Francisco 49ers

DEMPSEY VOTED GREATEST: 50th ANNIVERSARY. Jan 29, 1950. Heavyweight Jack Dempsey was voted the greatest boxer of the first half of the 20th century in a poll of sportswriters and broadcasters conducted by the Associated Press. Dempsey polled 251 votes to runner-up Joe Louis's 104.

OLDFIELD, BARNEY: BIRTH ANNIVERSARY. Jan 29, 1878. Berna Eli ("Barney") Oldfield, auto racer, born at Wauseon, OH. Oldfield began racing bicycles in 1893 and switched to autos in 1902, almost immediately becoming a national hero for his exploits. On Memorial Day, 1903, he became the first American to drive one mile in one minute. He barnstormed across the country and in 1910 set a land speed record on the sand at Daytona Beach. He ran the first 100 mph lap at the Indianapolis Speedway and in his retirement was instrumental in forming a drivers' union, increasing insurance and improving safety regulations. Died at Beverly Hills, CA, Oct 4, 1946.

PRO FOOTBALL HALL OF FAME ELECTS CHARTER MEMBERS: ANNIVERSARY. Jan 29, 1963. The Pro Football Hall of Fame at Canton, OH, announced the election of its charter members, 11 players and six executives. The players selected were Sammy Baugh, Dutch Clark, Red Grange, Mel Hein, Pete Henry, Cal Hubbard, Don Hutson, Johnny McNally, Bronko Nagurski, Ernie Nevers and Jim Thorpe. They were joined by Bert Bell, Joe Carr, George Halas, Curly Lambeau, Tim Mara and George Preston Marshall.

ROBERTS, FIREBALL: BIRTH ANNIVERSARY. Jan 29, 1929. Glenn ("Fireball") Roberts, auto racer, born at Daytona Beach, FL. Roberts was one of the most popular stock car racers in NASCAR history. He won 35 races in 206 starts from 1950 to 1964 when he was critically injured in a fiery crash. Died at Charlotte, NC, July 7, 1964.

ROBITAILLE GETS 1,000th POINT: ANNIVERSARY. Jan 29, 1998. Left wing Luc Robitaille of the Los Angeles Kings got the 1,000th point of his National Hockey League career, an assist in a 5–3 win over the Calgary Flames.

SHOW OF WHEELS. Jan 29–30 (tentative). Lea County Fairgrounds, Lovington, NM. Car show presented by the Lovington Chamber of Commerce. Featuring antiques, classics, streetrods, motorcycles and minitrucks. A swap-meet, commercial exhibits and games will be an exciting part of the show. RV parking available. For info: Lovington Chamber of Commerce, PO Box 1347, Lovington, NM 88260. Phone: (505) 396-5311 or Ron Carson (505) 396-3661. Fax: (505) 396-2823.

TROTTIER GETS 1,000th POINT: 15th ANNIVERSARY. Jan 29, 1985. Center Bryan Trottier of the New York Islanders got the 1,000th point of his National Hockey League career, a goal in a 4–4 tie against the Minnesota North Stars. Trottier finished his career with 1,425 points.

CHASE'S SPORTSQUOTE OF THE DAY
"You have to be able to get off the floor when you can't." — Jack Dempsey

Dominik Hasek

BIRTHDAYS TODAY

Sean Burke, 33, hockey player, born Windsor, Ontario, Canada, Jan 29, 1967.

Dominik Hasek, 35, hockey player, born Pardubice, Czechoslovakia, Jan 29, 1965.

Gregory Efthimios (Greg) Louganis, 40, Olympic gold medal diver, born San Diego, CA, Jan 29, 1960.

William Joseph (Bill) Rigney, 82, former baseball manager and player, born Alameda, CA, Jan 29, 1918.

Aeneas Demetrius Williams, 32, football player, born New Orleans, LA, Jan 29, 1968.

JANUARY 30 — SUNDAY
Day 30 — 336 Remaining

SUPERBOWL CHAMPIONS THIS DATE
1983   Washington Redskins
1994   Dallas Cowboys

CELTICS RETIRE MCHALE'S NUMBER: ANNIVERSARY. Jan 30, 1994. The Boston Celtics retired No. 32, the jersey worn by forward Kevin McHale for 13 seasons, in a halftime ceremony. McHale scored 17,335 points, made seven All-Star teams and helped the Celtics win three NBA championships.

SUPER BOWL XXXIV. Jan 30. Georgia Dome, Atlanta, GA. The championship game of the National Football League between the NFC and AFC champions. Annually, the last Sunday in January. For info: PR Dept, Natl Football League, 280 Park Ave, New York, NY 10017. Phone: (212) 758-1500. Web: www.nfl.com.

BIRTHDAYS TODAY

Walter (Walt) Dropo, 77, former baseball player, born Moosup, CT, Jan 30, 1923.

David Allen (Davey) Johnson, 57, baseball manager and former player, born Orlando, FL, Jan 30, 1943.

Paul Maurice, 33, hockey coach, born Sault Ste. Marie, Ontario, Canada, Jan 30, 1967.

Chris Simon, 28, hockey player, born Wawa, Ontario, Canada, Jan 30, 1972.

Christopher Carroll (Chris) Slade, 29, football player, born Newport News, VA, Jan 30, 1971.

William Payne Stewart, 43, golfer, born Springfield, MO, Jan 30, 1957.

Curtis Northrop Strange, 45, broadcaster and golfer, born Norfolk, VA, Jan 30, 1955.

JANUARY 31 — MONDAY

Day 31 — 335 Remaining

SUPERBOWL CHAMPIONS THIS DATE

1988	Washington Redskins
1993	Dallas Cowboys
1999	Denver Broncos

FERGUSON, BOB: 155th BIRTH ANNIVERSARY. Jan 31, 1845. Robert V. (Bob) Ferguson, baseball player, manager and umpire, born at Brooklyn, NY. Ferguson was one of several early ballplayers to earn the nickname "Death to Flying Things" for his ability to catch fly balls. He played every position and was the game's first switch-hitter. Died at Brooklyn, May 3, 1894.

HAWERCHUK SCORES 500th GOAL: ANNIVERSARY. Jan 31, 1996. Center Dale Hawerchuk of the St. Louis Blues became the 23rd player in the National Hockey League to score 500 regular-season goals. He tallied against goalie Felix Potvin of the Toronto Maple Leafs in a 4–0 victory. Hawerchuk finished his career with 518 goals.

HENRY, CAMILLE: BIRTH ANNIVERSARY. Jan 31, 1933. Camille Joseph Wilfred Henry, hockey player, born at Quebec City, Quebec, Canada. Henry, nicknamed "The Eel," was a slight left wing with a deft scoring touch. He played for the New York Rangers, Chicago Blackhawks and St. Louis Blues from 1953 through 1970, scoring 279 goals. Died at Quebec City, Sept 11, 1997.

HUTSON, DON: BIRTH ANNIVERSARY. Jan 31, 1913. Donald Montgomery (Don) Hutson, Pro Football Hall of Fame end, born at Pine Bluff, AR. Hutson attended the University of Alabama where he starred on the team that won the 1935 Rose Bowl. He established himself as an outstanding pro with the Green Bay Packers, becoming the league's premier receiver. In 11 seasons, he led the league in receptions eight times and receiving yardage seven times. He caught 488 passes and 7,991 yards and 100 touchdowns. Most of his records lasted into the 1980s when each NFL season was much longer. Inducted as a charter member of the Hall of Fame in 1963. Died at Rancho Mirage, CA, June 26, 1997.

MIKAN CHOSEN GREATEST: 50th ANNIVERSARY. Jan 31, 1950. George Mikan, center for the Minneapolis Lakers, was chosen the greatest basketball player of the half-century by a national poll of sportswriters.

ROBINSON, JACKIE: BIRTH ANNIVERSARY. Jan 31, 1919. Jack Roosevelt Robinson, Baseball Hall of Fame infielder, born at Cairo, GA. Robinson was a star athlete at UCLA and an officer in the US Army during World War I. In October 1945, Branch Rickey of the Brooklyn Dodgers signed Robinson to a contract to play professional baseball, thereby breaking the sport's unofficial, but firm, color line. Robinson proved to be an outstanding player who endured unimaginable racial taunts and still excelled. He won Rookie of the Year honors in 1947 and was the National League's MVP in 1949. He led the Dodgers to six pennants and a World Series championship in 1955. Inducted into the Hall of Fame in 1962. Died at Stamford, CT, Oct 24, 1972.

WALCOTT, JERSEY JOE: BIRTH ANNIVERSARY. Jan 31, 1914. Jersey Joe Walcott, boxer, born Arnold Raymond Cream at Merchantville, NJ. Walcott lost a heavyweight title fight to Joe Louis in 1947, but then defeated Ezzard Charles to win the title in 1951 after losing to him twice before. At 37 years of age, he was the oldest man to win the heavyweight crown. Died at Camden, NJ, Feb 27, 1994.

BIRTHDAYS TODAY

Shirley Babashoff, 43, Olympic gold medal swimmer, born Vernon, CA, Jan 31, 1957.

Ernest (Ernie) Banks, 69, Baseball Hall of Fame shortstop and first baseman, born Dallas, TX, Jan 31, 1931.

Bobby Dollas, 35, hockey player, born Montreal, Quebec, Canada, Jan 31, 1965.

Othella Harrington, 26, basketball player, born Jackson, MS, Jan 31, 1974.

Kenard Lang, 25, football player, born Orlando, FL, Jan 31, 1975.

Lynn Nolan Ryan, 53, Baseball Hall of Fame player, born Refugio, TX, Jan 31, 1947.

Michael Glenn Sinclair, 32, football player, born Galveston, TX, Jan 31, 1968.

FEBRUARY 1 — TUESDAY
Day 32 — 334 Remaining

BIRMINGHAM SPORT AND BOAT SHOW. Feb 1–6. Birmingham/Jefferson Civic Center, Birmingham, AL. For info: Mike Coffen, Double C Productions, Inc, Box 1678, Huntsville, TX 77342. Phone: (409) 295-9677 or (800) 574-9650. Fax: (409) 295-8859. E-mail: doublec@lcc.net. Web: www.lcc.net/~doublec.

BIRTH OF ABA: ANNIVERSARY. Feb 1, 1967. The American Basketball Association (ABA) was born with 10 teams and George Mikan as commissioner in its first season. The ABA lasted nine years before four teams, the Denver Nuggets, the Indiana Pacers, the New Jersey Nets and the San Antonio Spurs, were absorbed into the NBA.

BOOTH, ALBIE: BIRTH ANNIVERSARY. Feb 1, 1908. Albert James (Albie) Booth, Jr, football player, coach and official, born at New Haven, CT. Booth captained five athletic teams at Yale and won eight varsity letters, becoming one of the nation's most exciting halfbacks (1929–31) during college football's heyday. In his sophomore season, he scored all of Yale's points in an epic 21–13 victory over Army. After graduation, he entered business but stayed close to sports, coaching part-time and holding a variety of official positions. Died at New York, NY, Mar 1, 1959.

FLAGSTAFF WINTERFEST. Feb 1–29. Flagstaff, AZ. This winter festival, now in its 14th year, showcases Flagstaff's mountain wonderland with more than 100 events including sled dog races, alpine and nordic ski activities, snow games, sleigh rides, snowmobile drag races, concerts, historic walking tours, Native American storytelling and a parade. Est attendance: 20,000. For info: Ann Dunlop, Winterfest Coord, Flagstaff Chamber of Commerce, 101 W Rte 66, Flagstaff, AZ 86001. Phone: (800) 842-7293. Fax: (520) 779-1209. E-mail: chamber@flagstaff.az.us. Web: www.flagstaff.az.us.

LANE, FRANK: BIRTH ANNIVERSARY. Feb 1, 1896. Frank Charles Lane, baseball executive, born at Cincinnati, OH. Lane served as general manager of four major league teams and earned the nickname "Trader Frank" for the more than 500 transactions he engineered. His teams never won a single pennant. Died at Richardson, TX, Mar 19, 1981.

SPECIAL OLYMPICS MICHIGAN STATE WINTER GAMES. Feb 1–4. Cedar, MI. Olympic-style competition for children and adults with mental retardation. For info: Special Olympics Michigan, Central Michigan Univ, Mt Pleasant, MI 48859. Phone: (800) 644-6404. Fax: (517) 774-3034. E-mail: M.K.Lindberg@cmich.edu. Web: www.somi.org.

THOMPSON, DANNY: BIRTH ANNIVERSARY. Feb 1, 1947. Danny Leon Thompson, baseball player, born at Wichita, KS. Thompson became the regular shortstop for the Minnesota Twins in 1972, but he was diagnosed with leukemia less than a year later. He played four more seasons before dying at Rochester, MN, Dec 10, 1976.

BIRTHDAYS TODAY

Michelle Anne Akers, 34, soccer player, born Santa Clara, CA, Feb 1, 1966.

Richard Goodhard (Rich) Becker, 28, baseball player, born Aurora, IL, Feb 1, 1972.

Paul L.D. Blair, 56, former baseball player, born Cushing, OK, Feb 1, 1944.

Kent Franklin Mercker, 32, baseball player, born Dublin, OH, Feb 1, 1968.

Timothy James (Tim) Naehring, 33, baseball player, born Cincinnati, OH, Feb 1, 1967.

Mark Recchi, 32, hockey player, born Kamloops, British Columbia, Canada, Feb 1, 1968.

Tommy Salo, 29, hockey player, born Surahammar, Sweden, Feb 1, 1971.

Geoff Sanderson, 28, hockey player, born Hay River, Northwest Territories, Canada, Feb 1, 1972.

Malik Sealy, 30, basketball player, born New York, NY, Feb 1, 1970.

Robert DeShaun Traylor, 23, basketball player, born Detroit, MI, Feb 1, 1977.

FEBRUARY 2 — WEDNESDAY
Day 33 — 333 Remaining

CHASE'S SPORTSQUOTE OF THE DAY

"Like most professional golfers, I have a tendency to remember my poor shots a shade more vividly than the good ones."—Ben Hogan

ATLANTIC CITY INTERNATIONAL POWER BOAT SHOW. Feb 2–6. The New Atlantic City Convention Center, Atlantic City, NJ. A Miami-style boat show offers a vessel for virtually every taste and pocketbook, and boating browsers can board the boats and explore the interiors. Est attendance: 25,000. For info: Atlantic City Conv & Visitors Authority, 2314 Pacific Ave, Atlantic City, NJ 08401. Phone: (609) 449-7130.

BEN HOGAN'S ACCIDENT: ANNIVERSARY. Feb 2, 1949. Golfer Ben Hogan was involved in a near-fatal automobile accident when the car he was driving was hit head-on by a bus. Hogan threw himself across the front seat to protect his wife, and this action saved his life. Despite serious injuries, Hogan recovered to win the 1950 US Open, beating Lloyd Mangrum and George Fazio in a play-off.

BEVO SCORES 113: ANNIVERSARY. Feb 2, 1954. Bevo Francis of Rio Grande College scored a small-college record 113 points in a 134–91 victory over Hillsdale. Francis broke his own record of 84 points, set two weeks previously against Alliance College.

FIRST ELECTION FOR BASEBALL HALL OF FAME: ANNIVERSARY. Feb 2, 1936. The brand-new Baseball Hall of Fame at Cooperstown, NY, announced the election of its five charter members. With 226 ballots cast, 170 votes were required to gain election. Ty Cobb was named on 222 ballots, Babe Ruth on 215, Honus Wagner on 215, Christy Mathewson on 205 and Walter Johnson on 189.

FORMATION OF NATIONAL LEAGUE: ANNIVERSARY. Feb 2, 1876. William Hulbert founded the National League of Professional Baseball Clubs at a meeting at Chicago. Original franchises were granted to Boston, Chicago, Cincinnati, Hartford, Louisville, New York, Philadelphia and St. Louis.

GOLD COAST JUMPER CLASSIC. Feb 2–6. Palm Beach Polo Equestrian Club, Wellington, FL. The 2nd event in the 2000 Cosequin Winter Equestrian Festival. For info: Stadium Jumping, Inc, 3104 Cherry Palm Dr, Ste 220, Tampa, FL 33619. Phone: (800) 237-8924 or (813) 623-5801. Fax: (813) 626-5369. Web: www.stadiumjumping.com.

HALAS, GEORGE: 105th BIRTH ANNIVERSARY. Feb 2, 1895. George ("Papa Bear") Halas, Pro Football Hall of Fame coach and owner, born at Chicago, IL. After playing football at the University of Illinois and baseball with the New York Yankees, Halas helped found the National Football League and the Chicago Bears in 1920. As coach of the Bears for 40 years, he compiled a record of 324 wins, 151 losses and 31 ties. Inducted into the Hall of Fame as a charter member in 1963. Died at Chicago, Oct 31, 1983.

STUDENT BOWLS 900 SERIES: ANNIVERSARY. Feb 2, 1997. Jeremy Sonnenfeld, 20, from Sioux Falls, SD, bowled a 900 series, three consecutive perfect games, in a tournament at Omaha, NE. Sonnenfeld, a sophomore at the University of Nebraska majoring in business, had the series sanctioned by the American Bowling Congress two days later. Two other bowlers had bowled three consecutive perfect games, but neither met the exacting standards required to qualify as a 900 series. In December 1993 Tony Ockerman bowled his games over two sets of competition. In April 1996 Norm Duke bowled his games in the middle of an eight-game block.

UELSES VAULTS 16 FEET: ANNIVERSARY. Feb 2, 1962. At the Millrose Games at Madison Square Garden, Marine Corps corporal John Uelses became the first man to pole vault higher than 16 feet, indoors or outdoors. Using a fiberglass pole, Uelses cleared 16 ft, ¼ in.

February 2000	S	M	T	W	T	F	S
			1	2	3	4	5
	6	7	8	9	10	11	12
	13	14	15	16	17	18	19
	20	21	22	23	24	25	26
	27	28	29				

Todd Bertuzzi, 25, hockey player, born Sudbury, Ontario, Canada, Feb 2, 1975.
Roland America ("Buddy") Biancalana, 40, former baseball player, born Larkspur, CA, Feb 2, 1960.
Christie Brinkley, 47, former *Sports Illustrated* swimsuit issue model, born Monroe, MI, Feb 2, 1953.
Kenneth Ray (Ken) Dilger, 29, football player, born Mariah Hill, IN, Feb 2, 1971.
Sean Michael Elliott, 32, basketball player, born Tucson, AZ, Feb 2, 1968.
Scott Gavin Erickson, 32, baseball player, born Long Beach, CA, Feb 2, 1968.
Arturs Irbe, 33, hockey player, born Riga, USSR, Feb 2, 1967.
Albert Fred ("Red") Schoendienst, 77, former manager and Baseball Hall of Fame second baseman, born Germantown, IL, Feb 2, 1923.

FEBRUARY 3 — THURSDAY
Day 34 — 332 Remaining

BINGAMAN, LES: BIRTH ANNIVERSARY. Feb 3, 1926. Lester (Les) Bingaman, football player, born at MacKenzie, TN. An enormous lineman, Bingaman starred at the University of Illinois and in the NFL with the Detroit Lions. Despite his size, 6'3" and 335 pounds, he was agile and quick as well as tough. After retirement, he was an assistant coach with the Lions and the Miami Dolphins. Died at Miami, FL, Nov 20, 1970.

MacPHAIL, LARRY: 110th BIRTH ANNIVERSARY. Feb 3, 1890. Leland Stanford ("Larry") MacPhail, Sr, Baseball Hall of Fame executive, born at Cass City, MI. MacPhail was one of baseball's most innovative general managers and owners. He introduced night baseball to the majors at Cincinnati and broke a boycott preventing radio broadcasts of games at New York City. Inducted into the Hall of Fame in 1978. Died at Miami, FL, Oct 1, 1975.

PYLE, CASH AND CARRY: DEATH ANNIVERSARY. Feb 3, 1939. Charles C. ("Cash and Carry") Pyle, sports promoter, born at Van Wert, OH, 1882. Pyle helped popularize the young sport of pro football in the 1920s by signing college star Red Grange to a contract that called for Grange to barnstorm in exhibition games and play for the Chicago Bears. Pyle put Grange in movies, worked a myriad of endorsement deals and even created a league to rival the NFL. Died at Los Angeles, CA.

SHOEMAKER'S FINAL FINISH: 10th ANNIVERSARY. Feb 3, 1990. Jockey Bill Shoemaker rode in the 40,350th and last race of his career, finishing fourth on a horse named Patchy Groundfog at Santa Anita. After 40 years of racing, Shoemaker's record stood at 8,833 wins, 6,136 places and 4,987 shows with $123,375,534 in earnings.

SPECIAL OLYMPICS SOUTH DAKOTA WINTER GAMES. Feb 3. Sioux Falls, SD. State-level Olympic style competition for children and adults with mental retardation in alpine skiing, nordic skiing, speed skating and figure skating. For info: Special Olympics South Dakota, 305 W 39th St, Sioux Falls, SD 57105. Phone: (605) 331-4117 or (605) 331-4326. E-mail: sosdak@aol.com.

STEPHENS, HELEN: BIRTH ANNIVERSARY. Feb 3, 1918. Helen Herring Stephens, Olympic gold medal sprinter, born at Fulton, MO. Known as the "Fulton Flash," Stephens earned the title "The World's Fastest Woman" by winning gold medals in the 100 meters and the 400-meter relay at the 1936 Olympics at Berlin. She held many scholastic and national records and also performed well in basketball, softball, bowling, fencing and swimming. Died at St. Louis, MO, Jan 17, 1994.

WINTER X GAMES. Feb 3–6. Mt Snow, VT. The signature winter alternative sports championship, featuring the world-class athletic talents of more than 200 international athletes competing in snowboarding, ice climbing, snowmobile snowcross, freeskiing and snow mountain bike racing, comes to Mt Snow for the first time. For info: Media Relations, ESPN, ESPN Plaza, Bristol, CT 06010-7464. Phone: (860) 766-2000.

BIRTHDAYS TODAY

James (Jim) Campbell, 27, hockey player, born Worcester, MA, Feb 3, 1973.

Keith Edward Carney, 30, hockey player, born Pawtucket, RI, Feb 3, 1970.

Jeffrey Alan (Jeff) Christy, 31, football player, born Natrona Heights, PA, Feb 3, 1969.

Vlade Divac, 32, basketball player, born Prijepolje, Yugoslavia, Feb 3, 1968.

Robert Allen (Bob) Griese, 55, broadcaster and Pro Football Hall of Fame quarterback, born Evansville, IN, Feb 3, 1945.

Fredric Michael (Fred) Lynn, 48, former baseball player, born Chicago, IL, Feb 3, 1952.

Carol Mann, 59, LPGA Hall of Fame golfer, born Buffalo, NY, Feb 3, 1941.

Dwayne Rudd, 24, football player, born Batesville, MS, Feb 3, 1976.

Francis Asbury (Fran) Tarkenton, 60, Pro Football Hall of Fame quarterback, born Richmond, VA, Feb 3, 1940.

FEBRUARY 4 — FRIDAY
Day 35 — 331 Remaining

ALL-CANADA SHOW. Feb 4–6. Polk County Convention Center, Des Moines, IA. This consumer show allows individuals an opportunity to talk face-to-face with Canadian lodge representatives and outfitters to plan their hunting, fishing and adventure trips to Canada. For info: Rodney Schlafer, Show Dir, All-Canada Show, Bay-Lakes Mktg, Inc, 1889 Commerce Dr, De Pere, WI 54115. Phone: (920) 983-9800. Fax: (920) 983-9985. Web: www.allcanada.com.

ARBITRATOR SEITZ'S DECISION UPHELD: ANNIVERSARY. Feb 4, 1976. US District Court Judge John W. Oliver upheld the ruling of baseball arbitrator Peter Seitz that had declared pitchers Andy Messersmith and Dave McNally to be free agents. The two had refused to sign contracts for 1974 as a test case and had argued that baseball's hallowed reserved clause bound them to their respective clubs not in perpetuity but for only one year beyond the expiration of their last signed contract.

AUERBACH WINS 800th GAME: ANNIVERSARY. Feb 4, 1964. Arnold ("Red") Auerbach became the first coach in professional basketball to win 800 games when his team, the Boston Celtics, defeated the St. Louis Hawks, 113–101. Auerbach coached for 20 years, compiling a

record of 938–479. He was inducted into the Basketball Hall of Fame in 1968.

BADGER STATE WINTER GAMES. Feb 4–6. Wausau and north central, WI. 12th annual Olympic-style competition for Wisconsin residents of all ages and abilities attracts more than 5,000 participants in 9 sports. Gold, silver and bronze to top three finishers and T-shirts to all participants. Approximately 5,000 athletes. Major sponsors: AT&T, Ameritech, Wisconsin Milk Marketing Board, Ministry Health Care, American Family Insurance. Member of the National Congress of State Games. Est attendance: 21,000. For info: Patrick Goss, Exec Dir, or Jack Eich, PR Dir, Badger State Games, PO Box 7788, Madison, WI 53707-7788. Phone: (608) 226-4780.

BOWIE KUHN ELECTED COMMISSIONER: ANNIVERSARY. Feb 4, 1969. Owners of the 24 major league baseball clubs elected attorney Bowie Kuhn commissioner for a one-year term at a salary of $100,000. Kuhn, who succeeded William D. Eckert, became baseball's fifth commissioner. He served until 1984 when he was replaced by Peter Ueberroth.

BROWN, JEROME: 35th BIRTH ANNIVERSARY. Feb 4, 1965. Jerome Brown, football player, born at Brooksville, FL. Brown was an All-American defensive tackle at the University of Miami and was drafted in 1987 by the Philadelphia Eagles. A two-time All-Pro, he was killed in a one-car accident that also took the life of his 12-year-old nephew. Died at Brooksville, FL, June 25, 1992.

BULLNANZA. Feb 4–5. Lazy E Arena, Guthrie, OK. Present and past champions in exciting competition in bull riding. Annually, the first Friday and Saturday in February. Est attendance: 14,000. For info: Lazy E Arena, Rte 5, Box 393, Guthrie, OK 73044. Phone: (800) 595-RIDE. Fax: (405) 282-3785. E-mail: arena@lazye.com.

CANADA: NORTHERN BC WINTER GAMES. Feb 4–6. Ft St. John, British Columbia. Olympic style competition in approximately two dozen sports. For info: BC Games Soc, Ste 200-990 Ft St, Victoria, BC, Canada V8V 3K2. Phone: (250) 387-1375. Fax: (250) 387-4489. E-mail: bcgames@bcgames.org. Web: www.bcgames.org.

CANADA: WINTERLUDE. Feb 4–6 (also Feb 11–13, 18–20). Ottawa, Ontario. 22nd annual celebration of Canadian winter and traditions for the whole family. Skating on Rideau Canal, the world's longest skating rink, snow and ice sculptures, world-class figure skating, North America's largest snow playground and exciting Winter Triathlon. Winterlude goes international this year and presents a "Gateway to Chile." Est attendance: 700,000. For info: Natl Capital Commission, 40 Elgin St, Ste 202, Ottawa, ON, Canada K1P 1C7. Phone: (613) 239-5000 or (800) 465-1867. Web: www.capcan.ca.

CORNHUSKER STATE WINTER GAMES. Feb 4–6. Omaha, NE. A multisport Olympic-style competition for athletes from the state of Nebraska. For info: Cornhusker State Games, PO Box 82411, Lincoln, NE 68501. Phone: (402) 471-2544. Fax: (402) 471-9712. E-mail: NEST GAMES@aol.com.

HOT AIR AFFAIR. Feb 4–6. Hudson, WI. More than 40 hot-air balloons from across the nation will launch and race over the St. Croix River Valley in northwest Wisconsin. A torchlight parade features balloon pilots and crews lighting up the night with blasts of fire from their balloon baskets. At an evening "moonglow," the balloonists fire their burners and "glow in the dark" as visitors stroll among them. Est attendance: 20,000. For info: (888) 247-2332.

IOWA GAMES WINTER SPORTS FESTIVAL. Feb 4–6. Dubuque, IA. A winter sports Olympic-style competition for athletes from the state of Iowa. For info: Iowa Games, PO Box 2350, Ames, IA 50010. Phone: (515) 292-3251. Fax: (515) 292-3254. E-mail: info@iowagames.org. Web: www.iowagames.org.

JOHNSTON, NEIL: BIRTH ANNIVERSARY. Feb 4, 1929. Donald Neil Johnston, Basketball Hall of Fame center, born at Chillicothe, OH. Johnston played basketball and baseball at Ohio State University and decided to forego finishing college to play pro baseball in the summer and pro basketball in the winter. After several seasons in the minor leagues, he quit baseball to concentrate on basketball where he became a standout with the Philadelphia Warriors. He led the NBA in scoring and field goal percentage three times and in rebounding once. He played in six All-Star Games and coached the Warriors as well. Inducted into the Hall of Fame in 1990. Died at Bedford, TX, Sept 27, 1978.

LONGHORN WORLD CHAMPIONSHIP RODEO. Feb 2–4. UTC Arena, Chattanooga, TN. More than 200 cowboys and cowgirls compete in six professional contests ranging from bronc riding to bull riding for top prize money and world championship points. Featuring colorful opening pageantry and Big, Bad BONUS Bulls. 18th annual. Est attendance: 15,000. For info: W. Bruce Lehrke, Pres, Longhorn World Championship Rodeo, Inc, PO Box 70159, Nashville, TN 37207. Phone: (615) 876-1016. Fax: (615) 876-4685. E-mail: lhrodeo@idt.net. Web: www.longhornrodeo.com.

MILLROSE GAMES. Feb 4 (tentative). Madison Square Garden, New York, NY. The oldest invitational track meet in the US, featuring the Wanamaker Mile. For info: Madison Square Garden, 4 Penn Plaza, New York, NY 10001. Phone: (212) 465-6000. Fax: (212) 465-6029. Web: thegarden.com.

MOOSE STOMPERS WEEKEND. Feb 4–6. Houlton, ME. Human curling, human dog sled racing, potato peeling contest, wiffle snow ball, giant sliding hill for children, snowmobiling activities, cross-country skiing, skating, bonfire, snowmobile light parade, snowshoe races, Moose Stompers ball, fireworks and much more. For info: Greater Houlton Chamber of Commerce, 109 Main St, Houlton, ME 04730. Phone: (207) 532-4216. E-mail: chamber@houlton.com. Web: www.mainerec.com/houlton.html.

1932 WINTER OLYMPICS OPEN: ANNIVERSARY. Feb 4, 1932. The third Winter Olympics opened at Lake Placid, NY, with 32 women and 274 men athletes representing 17 nations. This was the only edition of the Winter Games in which athletes from the US won more medals (six gold, four silver and two bronze) than athletes from any other country. The Games closed on Feb 15.

NRA RODEO FINALS. Feb 4–6. MetraPark Arena, Billings, MT. Rodeo action at its best. 24th annual finals. A fun-filled rodeo weekend in cowboy country! Est attendance: 16,000. For info: Northern Rodeo Assn, PO Box 1122, Billings, MT 59103. Phone: (406) 252-1122. Fax: (406) 252-0300.

PERCHVILLE USA. Feb 4–6. Tawas Bay, East Tawas, MI. A winter festival with ice-fishing contests, polar bear swims, IWPA dog weight pulls, softball tournaments and many children's activities. Annually, the first full weekend in February. Est attendance: 10,000. For info: Amy Dittenber, Program Dir, Tawas Area Chamber of Commerce, Box 608, Tawas City, MI 48764-0608. Phone: (517) 362-8643 or (800) 55-TAWAS.

STARS & STRIPES WINS AMERICA'S CUP: ANNIVERSARY. Feb 4, 1987. *Stars & Stripes*, skippered by Dennis Connor, defeated the Australian boat *Kookaburra III* for the fourth straight time to sweep the America's Cup challenge and return the prized trophy to the US. This was the last Cup defense to be contested by 12-meter yachts. It came four years after *Australia II*, with John Bertrand as skipper, wrested the Cup from the US for the first time ever.

WORLD SHOVEL RACE CHAMPIONSHIPS. Feb 4–6. Angel Fire, NM. This unique event highlights thrilling competition in production and modified divisions for several age groups. "Modified" competition reaches speeds of 75 mph. Spectator competition on stock grain scoop shovels. Est attendance: 3,000. For info: Angle Fire Resort, Attn: Spec Events, PO Drawer B, Angel Fire, NM 87710. Phone: (800) 633-7463 or (505) 377-4237. Fax: (505) 377-4395. E-mail: events@angelfireresort.com. Web: angelfireresort.com.

BIRTHDAYS TODAY

Oscar de la Hoya, 27, boxer, born Los Angeles, CA, Feb 4, 1973.

Dallas James Drake, 31, hockey player, born Trail, British Columbia, Canada, Feb 4, 1969.

Daniel Thomas (Dan) Plesac, 38, baseball player, born Gary, IN, Feb 4, 1962.

Joseph William (Joe) Sacco, 31, hockey player, born Medford, MA, Feb 4, 1969.

Lawrence Taylor, 41, Pro Football Hall of Fame linebacker, born Williamsburg, VA, Feb 4, 1959.

FEBRUARY 5 — SATURDAY
Day 36 — 330 Remaining

CHASE'S SPORTSQUOTE OF THE DAY

"I never want them to forget Babe Ruth. I just want them to remember Aaron."—Henry Aaron

---

ATLANTIC CITY CLASSIC CAR SHOW AND AUCTION. Feb 5–27. The New Atlantic City Convention Center, Atlantic City, NJ. Hundreds of antique and classic cars on display and on sale. Est attendance: 35,000. For info: Atlantic City Conv and Visitors Authority, 2314 Pacific Ave, Atlantic City, NJ 08401. Phone: (609) 449-7130.

AUSTRALIA: WORLD BOOMERANG CHAMPIONSHIPS. Feb 5–13. Melbourne, Victoria. For info: Rob Croll, Organizer, 5 Tyson Court, Wantirna South, Victoria, 3152 Australia. Phone: 61-03-9887-5085. E-mail: crolls@netwide.com.au. Web: www.fixaframe.com.au/worldcup/worldcup.htm.

BEARGREASE SLED DOG MARATHON. Feb 5–12. Duluth, MN. To commemorate John Beargrease, a Chippewa sled-dog mail carrier along the North Shore of Lake Superior from 1887–1900. A 400-mile endurance race with mushers and dogs from the US and Canada. Est attendance: 10,000. For info: Beargrease, Box 500, Duluth, MN 55801. Phone: (218) 722-7631. Fax: (218) 722-3675. Web: www.beargrease.com.

CANADA: KARCHER JUNIOR CURLING CHAMPIONSHIPS. Feb 5–13. Moncton, New Brunswick. National competition for young men and women. For info: Media Relations, Canadian Curling Assn, 1600 James Naismith Dr, Ste 511, Gloucester, ON, Canada K1B 5N4. Phone:

February 2000	S	M	T	W	T	F	S
			1	2	3	4	5
	6	7	8	9	10	11	12
	13	14	15	16	17	18	19
	20	21	22	23	24	25	26
	27	28	29				

(613) 748-5628. Fax: (613) 748-5713. E-mail: cca@curling.ca. Web: www.curling.ca.

CANADA: NATIONAL HOCKEY LEAGUE ALL-STAR WEEKEND. Feb 5–6. Toronto, Ontario. The National Hockey League's 50th All-Star Game on Feb 6 preceded by the NHL SuperSkills and Heroes of Hockey game on Feb 5. For info: Natl Hockey League, 1251 Ave of the Americas, 47th Floor, New York, NY 10020. Phone: (212) 789-2000. Fax: (212) 789-2080. Web: www.NHL.com.

CHESAPEAKE BAY BOAT SHOW. Feb 5–13. Baltimore Convention Center, Baltimore, MD. The 46th annual Chesapeake Bay Boat Show presents the latest boats and accessories at the lowest prices, plus informative boating and fishing seminars. For info: NNMA Boat Shows, 200 E Randolph Dr, Ste 5100, Chicago, IL 60601-6528. Phone: (312) 946-6262. Fax: (312)946-0401. Web: www.boat-shows.com.

CHRISTMAS MOUNTAIN VILLAGE WINTER CARNIVAL AND SLED DOG PULL. Feb 5. Christmas Mountain Village, Wisconsin Dells, WI. Nation's largest one-day event. Sled dog weight-pull, sleigh rides, chili cook-off, winter golf, craft fair, refreshments, children's activities, live entertainment and wood-splitting contests. Est attendance: 4,000. For info: Christmas Mountain Village, 5944 Christmas Mountain Rd, Wisconsin Dells, WI 53965. Phone: (608) 253-1000 or (608) 254-3991. Fax: (608) 254-3983. Web: www.wisdells.com.

DICK BUTTON WINS GOLD MEDAL: ANNIVERSARY. Feb 5, 1948. Dick Button became the first American to win a gold medal in figure skating when he triumphed at the Fifth Winter Olympics at St. Moritz, Switzerland. Button earned a second gold medal four years later at Oslo, Norway.

ENGLAND: BRISTOL CLASSIC CAR SHOW. Feb 5–6. Royal Bath and West Showground, Shepton Mallet, Somerset. Everything for the classic car enthusiast with club stands, trade stands and autojumble. Est attendance: 18,000. For info: Robert Ewin, Dir, Nationwide Exhibitions (UK) Ltd, PO Box 20, Fishponds, Bristol, England BS16 5QU. Phone: (44) (117) 970-1000. Fax: (44) (117) 970-1001. Web: www.nationwideexhibitions.co.uk.

FIRST SECURITY BOULDER MOUNTAIN TOUR. Feb 5. Galena Lodge, Sun Valley, ID. A 30K freestyle cross-country skiing race from Galena Lodge to the Sawtooth National Recreation Area (SNRA) headquarters. For info: Sun Valley/Ketchum Chamber of Commerce, Box 2420, Sun Valley, ID 83353. Phone: (800) 634-3347 or (208) 726-3423. Fax: (208) 726-4533. E-mail: sunval@micron.net. Web: www.visitsunvalley.com.

FIRST SECURITY WINTER GAMES OF IDAHO. Feb 5–27. Idaho Falls, Sun Valley, Boise, McCall and Kellogg, ID. Idaho's official winter sports competition: 10 days (four weekends) of competition in ice hockey, figure skating, alpine skiing, freestyle skiing, snowboarding and cross-country skiing with 3,000 participants. For info: Will Simons, Exec Dir, First Security Winter Games of Idaho, PO Box 15214, Boise, ID 83715. Phone: (208) 393-2257. Fax: (208) 393-2187.

HENDERSON, CAM: 110th BIRTH ANNIVERSARY. Feb 5, 1890. Eli Camden (Cam) Henderson, basketball player and coach, born at Marion County, WV. Lack of financial resources caused Henderson to cut short his education at Glenville State College (WV) where he played three sports. He began coaching at Bristol High School and invented the zone defense in a local YMCA game. He coached at several colleges including Marshall College where he pioneered an innovative, fast-break offense. Died at Cedar Hill, KY, May 3, 1956.

KLAMMER WINS DOWNHILL: ANNIVERSARY. Feb 5, 1976. Before a roaring crowd of fellow countrymen, Austrian Franz Klammer won the downhill ski race at the XIIth Winter Olympic Games at Innsbruck, Austria. Clad in bright yellow, Klammer electrified a worldwide television audience with his breathtaking run.

MACKINAW MUSH SLED DOG RACE. Feb 5–6. Old Railroad Depot, Mackinaw City, MI. Sanctioned ISDA event with purse and various classes. Races start at 9 each morning. Also children's events and weight pull. Annually, the first weekend in February. Est attendance: 4,000. For info: Mackinaw Area Tourist Bureau, PO Box 160, Mackinaw City, MI 49701. Phone: (800) 666-0160. Web: www.machinawcity.cok.

NOTRE DAME SIGNS WITH NBC: 10th ANNIVERSARY. Feb 5, 1990. The University of Notre Dame broke with the College Football Association and became the first college to sell the rights to televise its home football games to a major network. The Irish and NBC signed a 5-year contract to start in 1991.

PERRY'S "BRR" (BIKE RIDE TO RIPPEY). Feb 5. Perry, IA. Winter bike riding. Twenty-two miles of frigid fun. Annually, the first Saturday in February. Est attendance: 2,000. For info: John Doyle, Chamber of Commerce, 1226 Second St, Perry, IA 50220. Phone: (515) 465-4601. Fax: (515) 465-2256. E-mail: perrychmbr@aol.com. Web: www.perryia.org.

ROLEX 24 AT DAYTONA. Feb 5–6. Daytona International Speedway, Daytona Beach, FL. 38th annual running of the most prestigious endurance race in North America (exotic purpose-built race cars). Sponsor: Rolex Watch. For info: John Story, Dir of Public Relations, Daytona Intl Speedway, PO Box 2801, Daytona Beach, FL 32120-2801. Phone: (904) 947-6782. For tickets: (904) 253-RACE (7223). Fax: (904) 947-6791. Web: www.daytona.com.

SPORTSFEST. Feb 5–6. Held indoors at the Myriad Convention Center, Oklahoma City, OK. Oklahoma's amateur winter sports festival includes some 5,500 athletes competing in about 14 events, including gymnastics, basketball, tumbling, table tennis, volleyball and cheerleading plus a trade show and appearances by sports celebrities. Est attendance: 9,000. For info: Sooner State Games, 100 W Main, Ste 287, Oklahoma City, OK 73102. Phone: (405) 235-4222. Fax: (405) 232-7723. E-mail: snrstgms@aol.com.

TAYLOR GETS 1,000th POINT: ANNIVERSARY. Feb 5, 1991. Right wing Dave Taylor of the Los Angeles Kings got the 1,000th point of his National Hockey League career, an assist in a 3–2 win over the Philadelphia Flyers. Taylor finished his career with 1,069 points.

TOMS RIVER WILDFOWL ART & DECOY SHOW. Feb 5–6. Brick HS, Brick, NJ. 140 artists, carvers, suppliers, carving competitions, free seminars, kids paint a decoy, etc. Annually, the first weekend in February. Est attendance: 4,000. For info: Janet Sellitto, Show Coord, Ocean County YMCA, 1088 Whitty Rd, Toms River, NJ 08755. Phone: (732) 341-9622. Fax: (732) 341-1629. Web: www.ocymca.org.

USLA MICHIGAN STATE COMPETITION. Feb 5. Muskegon Luge Track, Muskegon Winter Sports Complex, Muskegon, MI. United States Luge Assn (USLA) competition. Open to the public. Competitors vary in skill; divisions by age group. Muskegon Luge is one of only two in country. For info: Muskegon Sports Council, PO Box 5085, North Muskegon, MI 49445. Phone: (616) 744-9629. Luge Club phone: (616) 759-2201. Web: www.msports.org.

BIRTHDAYS TODAY

Henry Louis (Hank) Aaron, 66, baseball executive and Baseball Hall of Fame outfielder, born Mobile, AL, Feb 5, 1934.

Roberto Alomar, 32, baseball player, born Ponce, Puerto Rico, Feb 5, 1968.

Richard Matvichuk, 27, hockey player, born Edmonton, Alberta, Canada, Feb 5, 1973.

Larry Craig Morton, 57, former football player, born Flint, MI, Feb 5, 1943.

Roger Thomas Staubach, 58, Pro Football Hall of Fame quarterback, born Cincinnati, OH, Feb 5, 1942.

Darrell Waltrip, 53, auto racer, born Owensboro, KY, Feb 5, 1947.

FEBRUARY 6 — SUNDAY
Day 37 — 329 Remaining

AUSTRIA: EUROPEAN FIGURE SKATING CHAMPIONSHIPS. Feb 6–13. Vienna, Austria. European championships in men's and women's singles, pairs and dance events. For info: Media Relations, US Figure Skating Assn, 20 First St, Colorado Springs, CO 80906. Phone: (719) 635-5200. Fax: (719) 635-9548. E-mail: usfsa1@aol.com. Web: www.usfsa.org/events.

BRETT HULL JOINS FATHER: 10th ANNIVERSARY. Feb 6, 1990. Brett Hull of the St. Louis Blues scored his 50th goal of the season to join his father, Hall of Fame left wing Bobby Hull, as the only father-son combination in NHL history to score 50 goals in a season.

DOG ARTISTS' REGISTRY AND EXHIBITION. Feb 6–May 7. The Dog Museum, St. Louis, MO. Want a painting of your champion hunting dog or obedience trials winner? The Dog Museum maintains a biographical listing of artists available by commission for dog portraits and dog-related art. Every other year the artists exhibit their work. Est attendance: 4,000. For info: Barbara Jedda, Curator, The Dog Museum, 1721 S Mason, St. Louis, MO 63131. Phone: (314) 821-3647. Fax: (314) 821-7381. E-mail: dogarts@aol.com.

GROUNDHOG RUN. Feb 6. Kansas City, MO. 18th annual. The only 5K and 10K underground races run in the world takes place at the Hunt Midwest Enterprises SubTropolis. More than 2,200 runners from all over the country participate in this event to benefit Children's TLC. Est attendance: 2,200. For info: Shannon O'Sullivan, Children's TLC, 3101 Main St, Kansas City, MO 64111. Phone: (816) 756-0780. Fax: (816) 756-1677.

LAS VEGAS INTERNATIONAL MARATHON. Feb 6. 34th annual. Marathon, half-marathon and 5K run. For info: Al Boka, PO Box 81262, Las Vegas, NV 89180. Phone: (702) 876-3870. Web: www.lvmarathon.com.

	S	M	T	W	T	F	S
February			1	2	3	4	5
2000	6	7	8	9	10	11	12
	13	14	15	16	17	18	19
	20	21	22	23	24	25	26
	27	28	29				

NFL PRO BOWL. Feb 6. Aloha Stadium, Honolulu, HI. The NFL's all-star game pitting the stars of the NFC versus the stars of the AFC. Est attendance: 50,000. For info: Aloha Stadium, PO Box 30666, Honolulu, HI 96820. Phone: (808) 486-9300.

NOKIA SUGAR BOWL MARDI GRAS MARATHON. Feb 6. New Orleans, LA. 35th annual. For info: New Orleans Track Club, PO Box 52003, New Orleans, LA 70152-2003. Phone: (504) 482-6682. Web: www.MardiGrasMarathon.com.

ROFFE WINS ALPINE MEDAL: 15th ANNIVERSARY. Feb 6, 1985. Skier Dianne Roffe, 17, took first place in a giant slalom race to become the first US woman to win a gold medal in a World Alpine Skiing Championship race.

RUTH, BABE: 105th BIRTH ANNIVERSARY. Feb 6, 1895. George Herman ("Babe") Ruth, Baseball Hall of Fame pitcher and outfielder, born at Baltimore, MD. One of baseball's greatest heroes, Ruth was raised at St. Mary's Industrial School for Boys. He was signed to a minor league baseball contract by Jack Dunn of the Baltimore Orioles and became known as "Dunn's Babe." An outstanding pitcher, Ruth began swatting home runs in record numbers and was converted to the outfield. He hit 714 home runs in 22 major league seasons of play (a record 60 in 1927) and played in 10 World Series. He was the game's greatest star and became an enduring legend. Inducted into the Hall of Fame in 1936. Died at New York, NY, on Aug 16, 1948.

US FIGURE SKATING CHAMPIONSHIPS. Feb 6–13. Gund Arena, Cleveland, OH. More than 300 skaters will compete in five categories: men's, ladies, pairs, dance and figures divisions. The results determine the skaters' national ranking and funding, along with international assignments for the upcoming year. The event determines who gets to go to the World Championships. Est attendance: 100,000. For info: Media Relations, US Figure Skating Assn, 20 First St, Colorado Springs, CO 80909. Phone: (719) 635-5200. Fax: (719) 635-9548. E-mail: usfsa1@aol.com. Web: www.usfsa.org/events.

BIRTHDAYS TODAY

Randy Hilliard, 33, football player, born Metairie, LA, Feb 6, 1967.

Mark Steven Hutton, 30, baseball player, born South Adelaide, Australia, Feb 6, 1970.

Shawn Christopher Respert, 28, basketball player, born Detroit, MI, Feb 6, 1972.

Thomas Joseph (Tom) Tupa, 34, football player, born Cleveland, OH, Feb 6, 1966.

Richard Walter (Richie) Zisk, 51, former baseball player, born New York, NY, Feb 6, 1949.

FEBRUARY 7 — MONDAY
Day 38 — 328 Remaining

ALL-CANADA SHOW. Feb 7–9. Aksarben, Omaha, NE. This consumer show allows individuals an opportunity to talk face-to-face with Canadian lodge representatives and outfitters to plan their hunting, fishing and adventure trips to Canada. For info: Rodney Schlafer, Show Dir, All-Canada Show, Bay-Lakes Mktg, Inc, 1889 Commerce Dr, De Pere, WI 54115. Phone: (920) 983-9800. Fax: (920) 983-9985. Web: www.allcanada.com.

BEANPOT TOURNAMENT. Feb 7 and 14. FleetCenter, Boston, MA. An annual college hockey tournament matching teams from Harvard, Boston College, Boston

University and Northeastern. Winners of the two games on Feb 7 meet for the championship on Feb 14. First-round losers play a consolation game. For info: Fleet-Center, 150 Causeway St, Boston, MA 02114. Phone: (617) 227-3206. Fax: (617) 227-8403.

BUTTS, WALLY: 95th BIRTH ANNIVERSARY. Feb 7, 1905. James Wallace (Wally) Butts, Jr, football player, coach and administrator, born at Milledgeville, GA. Butts played football at Mercer College, coached at the prep level and became head coach and athletic director at the University of Georgia in 1939. His teams compiled a record of 140–86–9 over 21 seasons and played in eight bowl games. He retired from coaching in 1960 and as athletic director in 1964. Died at Athens, GA, Dec 17, 1973

CRUMP FIRST WOMAN JOCKEY: ANNIVERSARY. Feb 7, 1969. Diana Crump became the first woman jockey to ride in a pari-mutuel race at a US track. Crump finished tenth in a field of 12 at Hialeah.

LESLIE SCORES 101: 10th ANNIVERSARY. Feb 7, 1990. Lisa Leslie of Morningside HS, Inglewood, CA, scored 101 points in the first half of a game against South Torrance HS. The game ended at the half with the score at 102–24 as the South Torrance coach refused to let his team finish the game.

MULLEN GETS 1,000th POINT: 5th ANNIVERSARY. Feb 7, 1995. Right wing Joey Mullen of the Pittsburgh Penguins got the 1,000th point of his National Hockey League career, an assist in a 7–3 win over the Florida Panthers. Mullen finished his career with 1,063 points.

QUISENBERRY, DAN: BIRTH ANNIVERSARY. Feb 7, 1953. Daniel Raymond (Dan) Quisenberry, baseball player, born at Santa Monica, CA. "Quiz," as he was known, was an outstanding relief pitcher for the Kansas City Royals. He was credited with 244 saves and made a major contribution to several championship Royals teams. Quisenberry used a submarine-style delivery and had a devastating sinker. He had an offbeat sense of humor and wrote poetry in his retirement. Died at Kansas City, MO, Sept 30, 1998.

SITTLER SETS POINTS RECORD: ANNIVERSARY. Feb 7, 1979. The Toronto Maple Leafs' Darryl Sittler set an NHL record for most points in a game when he scored six goals and earned four assists in an 11–4 victory over the Boston Bruins.

SULLIVAN WINS HEAVYWEIGHT CROWN: ANNIVERSARY. Feb 7, 1882. John L. Sullivan won the bare-knuckle heavyweight championship of the world by defeating Paddy Ryan in a nine-round fight at Mississippi City, MS. Sullivan was the last bare-knuckles champion. He held the title until 1892 when he lost to James J. Corbett in a fight conducted under the Marquess of Queensbury Rules.

BIRTHDAYS TODAY

Peter Bondra, 32, hockey player, born Luck, Ukraine, USSR, Feb 7, 1968.
Timothy L. (Tim) Bowens, 27, football player, born Okolona, MS, Feb 7, 1973.

Alexandre Daigle, 25, hockey player, born Montreal, Quebec, Canada, Feb 7, 1975.
Juwan Antonio Howard, 27, basketball player, born Chicago, IL, Feb 7, 1973.
Carney Ray Lansford, 43, former baseball player, born San Jose, CA, Feb 7, 1957.
Stephen John (Steve) Nash, 26, basketball player, born Johannesburg, South Africa, Feb 7, 1974.

FEBRUARY 8 — TUESDAY
Day 39 — 327 Remaining

BOWMAN EARNS 1,000th WIN: ANNIVERSARY. Feb 8, 1997. The Detroit Red Wings defeated the Pittsburgh Penguins, 6–5, in overtime, to make coach Scotty Bowman the first NHL coach to reach the 1,000-win plateau.

CLEVELAND BROWNS MOVE TO BALTIMORE: ANNIVERSARY. Feb 8, 1996. The National Football League approved the transfer of the Cleveland Browns to Baltimore. Owner Art Modell agreed to leave the team's nickname and colors in Cleveland and later decided to call his team the Ravens. The NFL awarded Cleveland an expansion franchise in 1998.

DALLAS TEXANS BECOME KANSAS CITY CHIEFS: ANNIVERSARY. Feb 8, 1963. Less than two months after defeating the Houston Oilers in the second championship game of the American Football League, the Dallas Texans, owned by Lamar Hunt, moved to Kansas City and were renamed the Chiefs.

GRAND CENTER BOAT SHOW. Feb 8–13. Grand Center, Grand Rapids, MI. This event brings together buyers and sellers of power and sail boats, boating accessories, docks, dockominiums and vacation properties. Est attendance: 32,000. For info: Mike Wilbraham, ShowSpan, Inc, 1400 28th St SW, Grand Rapids, MI 49509. Phone: (616) 530-1919. Fax: (616) 530-2122. Web: www.showspan .com.

KIDD AND HEUGA WIN MEDALS: ANNIVERSARY. Feb 8, 1964. Billy Kidd and Jim Heuga became the first American men to win Olympic medals in Alpine skiing when they captured the silver and bronze medals, respectively, in the slalom at the IXth Winter Olympics at Innsbruck, Austria.

LOPEZ MAKES HALL OF FAME: ANNIVERSARY. Feb 8, 1987. Nancy Lopez won the 35th LPGA tournament of her career, the $200,000 Sarasota Classic, and earned induction into the LPGA Hall of Fame.

MAN O' WAR VOTED THE GREATEST: 50th ANNIVERSARY. Feb 8, 1950. Man o' War was voted the greatest racehorse of the first half of the 20th century in a poll conducted by the Associated Press. Man o' War raced as a 2- and 3-year old, winning 20 of 21 races and setting five track records.

PULLIAM, HARRY: BIRTH ANNIVERSARY. Feb 8, 1869. Harry Clay Pulliam, baseball executive, born at Scottsville, KY. Pulliam was elected president of the National League in 1902 after being an official with the Pittsburgh Pirates. Intense controversies during his administration drove him to depression and suicide. Died at New York, NY, July 29, 1909.

ST. LOUIS BOAT AND SPORTS SHOW. Feb 8–13. America's Center and Trans World Dome, St. Louis, MO. The 46th annual St. Louis Boat and Sports Show presents hundreds of boats, engines and marine accessories, with fishing gear and vacation resort displays, seminars, personal appearances and special attractions all under one roof. For info: NMMA Boat Shows, 200 E Randolph Dr, Ste 5100, Chicago, IL 60601-6528. Phone: (312) 946-6262. Fax: (312) 946-0401. Web: www.boatshows.com.

Joseph (Joe) Black, 76, former baseball player, born Plainfield, NJ, Feb 8, 1924.

Cletis Leroy (Clete) Boyer, 63, former baseball player, born Cassville, MO, Feb 8, 1937.

Dino Ciccarelli, 40, hockey player, born Sarnia, Ontario, Canada, Feb 8, 1960.

Joy Lynn Fawcett, 32, soccer player, born Inglewood, CA, Feb 8, 1968.

Alonzo Mourning, 30, basketball player, born Chesapeake, VA, Feb 8, 1970.

Kirk Muller, 34, hockey player, born Kingston, Ontario, Canada, Feb 8, 1966.

FEBRUARY 9 — WEDNESDAY
Day 40 — 326 Remaining

CHASE'S SPORTSQUOTE OF THE DAY

"It isn't the high price of stars that is expensive, it's the high price of mediocrity."—Bill Veeck

CANADA: VANCOUVER INTERNATIONAL BOAT SHOW. Feb 9–13. BC Place Stadium and Coal Harbour Marina, Vancouver, British Columbia. Sail and powerboats, sailboards, inflatables, canoes, personal watercraft, marine electronics and accessories, marine services, charters, sailing schools, water skis, sporting goods, travel and resort destinations, fishing equipment and family entertainment. Est attendance: 45,000. For info: Val Nogas, Mgr, Public Relations, Canadian Natl Sportsmen's Shows, 703 Evans Ave, Ste 202, Toronto, ON, Canada M9C 5E9. Phone: (416) 695-0311. Fax: (416) 695-0381. Web: www.sportsmensshows.com.

HITS OCALA WINTER CIRCUIT. Feb 9–Mar 12. Golden Hills International Show Grounds, Ocala, FL. Five weeks of hunter/jumper competition. Riders from beginning levels to world class can be seen in competition all week long, with the featured Grand Prix show jumping event each Sunday. The shows attract more than 1,500 horses for each week of competition. Annually, February through early March. Est attendance: 10,000. For info and exact dates of circuit events: HITS, 13 Closs Dr, Rhinebeck, NY 12572. Phone: (914) 876-3666. Fax: (914) 876-5538. Web: www.equisearch.com.

KILKENNY–REDLAND NTERNATIONALE. Feb 9–13. Palm Beach Polo Equestrian Club, Wellington, FL. The third event in the 2000 Cosequin Winter Equestrian Festival. For info: Stadium Jumping, Inc, 3104 Cherry Palm Dr, Ste 220, Tampa, FL 33619. Phone: (800) 237-8924 or (813) 623-5801. Fax: (813) 626-5369. Web: www.stadiumjumping.com.

MAGIC'S ALL-STAR COMEBACK: ANNIVERSARY. Feb 9, 1992. Three months after announcing his retirement (on Nov 7, 1991) from the NBA because he had been infected with HIV, Magic Johnson led the West to a 153–113 victory over the East in the 42nd NBA All-Star Game. Magic was named All-Star Game MVP for the second time.

NATIONAL GIRLS AND WOMEN IN SPORTS DAY. Feb 9. Celebrates and honors all girls and women participating in sports. Recognizes the passage of Title IX (in 1972), the law that guarantees gender equity in federally-funded school programs, including athletics. Sponsored by Girls Inc, the Girl Scouts, the National Association for Girls and Women in Sports, the Women's Sports Foundation and the YWCA. For info: Natl Assn for Girls and Women in Sports, 1900 Association Dr, Reston, VA 20191. Phone: (703) 476-3452. E-mail: nagws@aahperd.org.

NEW ORLEANS BOAT SHOW. Feb 9–13. Louisiana Superdome, New Orleans, LA. 30th annual show of boat and marine products, fishing equipment and resort info. Informative boating and fishing seminars. For info: NMMA Boat Shows, 200 E Randolph Dr, Ste 5100, Chicago, IL 60601-6528. Phone: (312) 946-6262. Fax: (312) 946-0401. Web: www.boatshows.com.

TENNIS CHANGES THE RULES: ANNIVERSARY. Feb 9, 1912. The US Lawn Tennis Association amended the playing rules for its men's singles championship. The defending champion lost his bye directly into the final and was required to play through the tournament.

VEECK, BILL: BIRTH ANNIVERSARY. Feb 9, 1914. William Louis (Bill) Veeck, Jr, Baseball Hall of Fame executive, born at Chicago, IL. Veeck was baseball's premier promoter and showman as an owner of several teams. He integrated the American League, sent a midget to the plate to start a game and, in general, sought to provide fans with entertainment in addition to baseball. Inducted into the Hall of Fame in 1991. Died at Chicago, Jan 2, 1986.

Vladimir Alvino Guerrero, 24, baseball player, born Nizao Bani, Dominican Republic, Feb 9, 1976.

Todd William Lyght, 31, football player, born Kwajalein, Marshall Islands, Feb 9, 1969.

Bradley Alan (Brad) Maynard, 26, football player, born Tipton, IN, Feb 9, 1974.

Jimmy Lee Smith, Jr, 31, football player, born Detroit, MI, Feb 9, 1969.

John Wallace, 26, basketball player, born Rochester, NY, Feb 9, 1974.

William Hayward ("Mookie") Wilson, 44, former baseball player, born Bamberg, SC, Feb 9, 1956.

FEBRUARY 10 — THURSDAY
Day 41 — 325 Remaining

BEATTY BREAKS FOUR-MINUTE MARK: ANNIVERSARY. Feb 10, 1962. Jim Beatty became the first American to break the four-minute barrier for the indoor mile run with a 3:58.9 clocking at a meet at Los Angeles.

BOWE JOINS/LEAVES MARINES: ANNIVERSARY. Feb 10, 1997. Heavyweight Riddock Bowe announced that he had retired from boxing in order to join the US Marines. He had enlisted on Jan 27 and reported to Parris Island on this date. On Feb 21, Bowe announced that he had changed his mind and that the Marines had agreed to release him. "He could not," said the Corps, "handle the regulated lifestyle." In his Marines stint, he endured 36 hours of actual training. Bowe, 29, married and the father of five, had won the heavyweight championship in 1992 from Evander Holyfield only to surrender it to Holyfield in 1993.

BROWN, WALTER: 95th BIRTH ANNIVERSARY. Feb 10, 1905. Walter A. Brown, Basketball Hall of Fame executive, born at Hopkinton, MA. Brown became president of Boston Garden in 1937 upon his father's death and held that position until 1964. He helped to found the National Basketball Association and was president and co-owner of the Boston Celtics. He maintained a high

	S	M	T	W	T	F	S
February			1	2	3	4	5
2000	6	7	8	9	10	11	12
	13	14	15	16	17	18	19
	20	21	22	23	24	25	26
	27	28	29				

payroll to create the league's best franchise. Brown was also involved in international and Olympic hockey. Inducted into the Hall of Fame in 1965. Died at Hyannis, MA, Sept 7, 1964.

EVANS, BILLY: BIRTH ANNIVERSARY. Feb 10, 1884. William George (Billy) Evans, Baseball Hall of Fame umpire and executive, born at Chicago, IL. Evans was an American League umpire from 1906 to 1927, arguing successfully for using four umpires in the World Series. He wrote *Knotty Problems of Baseball*, a casebook. After retiring, he became general manager of the Cleveland Indians and, later, the Detroit Tigers. Inducted into the Hall of Fame in 1973. Died at Miami, FL, Jan 23, 1956.

FULKS NETS 63: ANNIVERSARY. Feb 10, 1949. Joe Fulks of the Philadelphia Warriors set an NBA record by scoring 63 points in a game against the Indianapolis Jets. Fulks' total was the largest recorded by an NBA player before the introduction of the 24-second clock in 1954. His record stood until Nov 8, 1959, when Elgin Baylor of the Minneapolis Lakers scored 64 points.

MEMPHIS SPORTFISHING, TRAVEL, HUNTING & OUTDOORS SHOW. Feb 10–13. Cook Convention Center, Memphis, TN. Travel and resort exhibits, hunting, fishing, boating and family travel and outdoor recreation. For info: Great Outdoors, 420 Lake Cook Road, Ste 108, Deerfield, IL 60015. Phone: (847) 914-0630 or (888) 462-7469. Fax: (847) 914-0333. E-mail: go2show@msn .com.

NORWAY: FIS SKIFLYING WORLD CHAMPIONSHIPS. Feb 10–13. Vikersund, Norway. For info: Intl Ski Federation, Blochstrasse 2, 3653 Oberhofen am Thunersee, Switzerland. Phone: (41) (33) 244-6161. Fax: (41) (33) 243-5353. E-mail: mail@fisski.org. Web: www.fisski.org.

PENNOCK, HERB: BIRTH ANNIVERSARY. Feb 10, 1894. Herbert Jeffries ("Herb") Pennock, Baseball Hall of Fame pitcher and general manager, born at Kennett Square, PA. Pennock was one of the best pitchers for the New York Yankees in the 1920s, a team that did not need a lot of good pitching but got it anyway. As general manager of the Philadelphia Phillies, he helped to build the "Whiz Kids," 1950 National League champions. Inducted into the Hall of Fame in 1948. Died at New York, NY, Jan 30, 1948.

TILDEN, BILL: BIRTH ANNIVERSARY. Feb 10, 1893. William Tatem (Bill) Tilden, Jr, tennis player, born at Philadelphia, PA. Generally considered one of the greatest players of all time, Tilden won more tournaments than the record books can count. A nearly flawless player, he was also an egotistical showman on the court with an interest in show business. He turned pro in 1930 and continued to win regularly. Died at Hollywood, CA, June 5, 1953.

BIRTHDAYS TODAY

Leonard Kyle (Lenny) Dykstra, 37, former baseball player, born Santa Ana, CA, Feb 10, 1963.

Robert Joseph (Bobby) Jones, 30, baseball player, born Fresno, CA, Feb 10, 1970.

Ty Law, 26, football player, born Aliquippa, PA, Feb 10, 1974.

Gregory John (Greg) Norman, 45, golfer, born Melbourne, Australia, Feb 10, 1955.

Alexander (Allie) Sherman, 77, former broadcaster, football coach and player, born New York, NY, Feb 10, 1923.

Mark Andrew Spitz, 50, Olympic gold medal swimmer, born Modesto, CA, Feb 10, 1950.

FEBRUARY 11 — FRIDAY
Day 42 — 324 Remaining

ANCHORAGE FUR RENDEZVOUS. Feb 11–20. Anchorage, AK. "Alaska's largest celebration." Features four world championships in three sled dog races and dog weight-pulling contest. Carnival, native dances, Eskimo blanket toss, fur auction, snow sculpture, snow sports and much more—more than 120 events. 65th anniversary. Annually, beginning the second Friday in February and running for 10 days. Est attendance: 250,000. For info: Greater Anchorage, Inc, 400 D St, Ste 200, Anchorage, AK 99501. Phone: (907) 274-1177. Fax: (907) 277-2199.

BAER, MAX: BIRTH ANNIVERSARY. Feb 11, 1909. Maximillian Adalbert (Max) Baer, boxer, born at Omaha, NE. Baer possessed awesome punching power and once knocked out a fighter who collapsed into a coma and died from his injuries. He won the heavyweight title from Primo Carnera on June 14, 1934, and lost it a year later to James Braddock, a severe underdog. Died at Hollywood, CA, Nov 21, 1959.

BELIVEAU SCORES 500th GOAL: ANNIVERSARY. Feb 11, 1971. Center Jean Beliveau of the Montreal Canadiens scored the 500th regular-season goal of his career in a 6–2 win over the Minnesota North Stars. "Big Jean," as he was known, thus became the 4th player in National Hockey League history to reach the 500-goal plateau. He finished his career with 507 goals and entered the Hockey Hall of Fame in 1972.

CANADA: BRACEBRIDGE WINTER CARNIVAL. Feb 11–13. Bracebridge, Ontario. Snowmobile activities and events, arts and crafts, children's ice and snow village, dances, winter baseball, broomball, helicopter rides, wreck 'm race, snow box derby, snow sculpture, turkey bowling, pancake breakfasts. More than 50 events—"The Best Family Winter Fun Under the Sun." Est attendance: 10,000. For info: Bracebridge Chamber of Commerce, 1-1 Manitoba St, Bracebridge, ON, Canada P1L 2A8. Phone: (705) 645-5231.

CANADA: CALGARY BOAT & SPORTSMEN'S SHOW. Feb 11–14. Roundup Centre, Corral, Stampede Park, Calgary, Alberta. Sail, power and fishing boats, hunting, fishing and camping supplies, resort destinations, outdoor recreation, outdoor groups, recreational vehicles, sport utility vehicles, mountain bikes, motorhomes, motorcycles and family entertainment. Est attendance: 25,000. For info: Val Nogas, Mgr, Public Relations, Canadian Natl Sportsmen's Shows, 703 Evans Ave, Ste 202, Toronto, ON, Canada M9C 5E9. Phone: (416) 695-0311. Fax: (416) 695-0381. Web: www.sportsmensshows.com.

CANADA: CALGARY WINTER FESTIVAL. Feb 11–21. Calgary, Alberta. 10-day festival includes feature events that celebrate winter, sport and entertainment of all sorts. Something for everyone. Est attendance: 170,000. For info: Calgary Winter Festival, 634 6th Ave SW, Ste 100, Calgary, AB, Canada T2P 0S4. Phone: (403) 543-5480. Fax: (403) 543-5490. E-mail: winfest@telusplanet.net. Web: www.discovercalgary.com/winterfest/events.html.

CANADA: FESTIVAL DU VOYAGEUR. Feb 11–20. Winnipeg, Manitoba. More than 400 shows, food and "joie de vivre" of the fur-trade era. Sled dog races, snow sculptures, costumed interpreters in historic Ft Gibraltar, arts and crafts display and sale, French-Canadian cuisine and much more at Western Canada's largest winter festival. Est attendance: 150,000. For info: Festival du Voyageur, 768 Tache Ave, Winnipeg, MB, Canada R2H 2C4. Phone: (204) 237-7692. Fax: (204) 233-7576. E-mail: voyageur@festivalvoyageur.mb.ca. Web:www.festivalvoyageur.mb.ca.

FRASER, GRETCHEN: BIRTH ANNIVERSARY. Feb 11, 1919. Gretchen Claudia Kunigk Fraser, Olympic gold medal skier, born at Tacoma, WA. Fraser became the first American to win an Olympic gold medal in Alpine skiing when she captured first place in the special slalom (now known as the giant slalom) at the 1948 Winter Olympics at St. Moritz. She added a silver medal in the Alpine combined. Died at Sun Valley, ID, Feb 17, 1994.

GOLFER WINS RIGHT TO RIDE: ANNIVERSARY. Feb 11, 1998. Professional golfer Casey Martin, who suffers from a circulatory ailment in his lower right leg that makes walking painful and difficult, won the right to use a golf cart during competition on the PGA Tour, according to a ruling by US Magistrate Thomas Coffin. Martin's victorious suit was the first judicial decision to apply the Americans with Disabilities Act to major sports. Coffin decided that the stamina expended and fatigue sustained by Martin exceeded those of non-disabled players. The PGA Tour announced that it would abide by Coffin's decision but would appeal it, too.

HITCHCOCK, TOMMY: 100th BIRTH ANNIVERSARY. Feb 11, 1900. Thomas (Tommy) Hitchcock, Jr, polo player, born at Aiken, SC. Hitchcock was one of the nation's great polo players, winning junior and senior honors and international competitions as well. He was rated a ten-goal player, the highest ranking, and captained the US team at the 1924 Olympics. During World War II, Hitchcock served in the Army Air Corps and crashed his Mustang fighter. Died at Salisbury, England, Apr 19, 1944.

HULMAN, TONY: BIRTH ANNIVERSARY. Feb 11, 1901. Anton (Tony) Hulman, Jr, auto racing executive, born at Terre Haute, IN. Hulman purchased the Indianapolis Motor Speedway from Captain Eddie Rickenbacker on Nov 14, 1945. He repaired and restored the facility and made the 500-mile race one of the premier events in sport. Hulman emphasized the human touch and became

famous for his intonation before the beginning of each race, "Gentlemen, start your engines." Died at Indianapolis, IN, Oct 28, 1977.

LONGHORN WORLD CHAMPIONSHIP RODEO. Feb 11–12. The Firstar Center, Cincinnati, OH. More than 200 cowboys and cowgirls compete in six professional contests ranging from bronc riding to bull riding for top prize money and world championship points. Featuring colorful opening pageantry and Big, Bad BONUS Bulls. 26th annual. Est attendance: 24,000. For info: W. Bruce Lehrke, Pres, Longhorn World Chmpshp Rodeo, Inc, PO Box 70159, Nashville, TN 37207. Phone: (615) 876-1016. Fax: (615) 876-4685. E-mail: lhrodeo@idt.net. Web: www.longhornrodeo.com.

NBA ALL-STAR WEEKEND. Feb 11–13. The Arena at Oakland, Oakland, CA. For info: Brian McIntyre, Sr VP, Comm, Natl Basketball Assn, Olympic Tower, 645 Fifth Ave, New York, NY 10022. Phone: (212) 407-8000.

NC RV AND CAMPING SHOW. Feb 11–13. Charlie Rose Expo Center, Fayetteville, NC. A display of the latest in recreation vehicles and accessories by various dealers. Est attendance: 5,000. For info: Apple Rock Advertising & Promotion, 1200 Eastchester Dr, High Point, NC 27265. Phone: (336) 881-7100. Fax: (336) 883-7198.

NHL PLAYERS ASSOCIATION FORMED: ANNIVERSARY. Feb 11, 1957. The National Hockey League Players Association was organized with Ted Lindsay of the Detroit Red Wings elected president.

RACE TO THE SKY—A GREAT MONTANA TRADITION SLED DOG RACE. Feb 11–17. 15th annual race starts near Helena, MT, ends at Missoula, MT. This 350-mile race along the Continental Divide is a beautiful and challenging trail. In what is known as the most beautiful dog sled race on earth, more than 30 teams compete from the US, Canada and Europe. Est attendance: 12,000. For info: Montana Sled Dog, Inc, PO Box 854, Helena, MT 59624. Phone: (406) 442-4008. Fax: (406) 442-4008.

BIRTHDAYS TODAY

Demetrius Antonio (Tony) Battie, 24, basketball player, born Dallas, TX, Feb 11, 1976.
Jacque Vaughn, 25, basketball player, born Los Angeles, CA, Feb 11, 1975.

FEBRUARY 12 — SATURDAY
Day 43 — 323 Remaining

CHASE'S SPORTSQUOTE OF THE DAY

"Young man, you have the question backwards."—Bill Russell when asked how he would have fared against Kareem Abdul-Jabbar

AMERICAN BOWLING CONGRESS/SANDIA CASINO CHAMPIONSHIPS TOURNAMENT. Feb 12–June 17. Albuquerque, NM. 97th annual. The largest participatory sporting event in the world features more than 50,000 bowlers from around the US and the world. Bowlers compete for titles in singles, doubles, five-player team and all-event categories in arena setting. Lanes are especially built for the tournament in convention centers around the US each year. Est attendance: 100,000. For info: Michael Deering, American Bowling Congress, 5301 S 76th St, Greendale, WI 53129. Phone: (414) 423-3309. Fax: (414) 421-7977.

CANADA: YUKON QUEST 1,000-MILE SLED DOG RACE. Feb 12–25. Fairbanks, AK, to Whitehorse, YT. The 17th annual "Challenge of the North" 1,000-mile dog sled race from Fairbanks, AK, to Whitehorse, YT. Top mushers from North America and around the world com-

February	S	M	T	W	T	F	S
2000			1	2	3	4	5
	6	7	8	9	10	11	12
	13	14	15	16	17	18	19
	20	21	22	23	24	25	26
	27	28	29				

pete for the $125,000 purse. Est attendance: 10,000. For info: Yukon Quest Intl Assn, Yukon Quest Intl Assn, Box 5555, Whitehorse, YT, Canada Y1A 5H4. Phone: (867) 668-4711. Info also from: Yukon Quest Intl, PO Box 75015, Fairbanks, AK 99707. Phone: (907) 452-7954. E-mail: yukonquest@polarcom.com. Web: www.yukon quest.yk.ca.

CORVETTE AND HIGH PERFORMANCE WINTER MEET. Feb 12–13. Puyallup, WA. Buy, sell and show cars and parts—new, used and reproductions. Est attendance: 10,000. For info: Larry Johnson, Show Organizer, PO Box 7753, Olympia, WA 98507. Phone: (360) 786-8844. Fax: (360) 754-1498.

ENGLAND: BRISTOL CLASSIC MOTORCYCLE SHOW. Feb 12–13. Royal Bath and West Showground, Shepton Mallet, Somerset, England. Everything for the motorcycle enthusiast with club stands, trade stands and autojumble. Est attendance: 17,000. For info: Robert Ewin, Dir, Nationwide Exhibitions (UK) Ltd, PO Box 20, Fishponds, Bristol, England BS16 5QU. Phone: (44) (117) 970-1000. Fax: (44) (117) 970-1001. Web: www.nationwide exhibitions.co.uk.

HAFEY, CHICK: BIRTH ANNIVERSARY. Feb 12, 1903. Charles James (Chick) Hafey, Baseball Hall of Fame outfielder, born at Berkeley, CA. Hafey started as a pitcher but switched to the outfield in 1922. He was one of the first ballplayers to wear eyeglasses and compiled a .317 batting average. Inducted into the Hall of Fame in 1971. Died at Calistoga, CA, July 2, 1973.

LAKE WINNEBAGO STURGEON SEASON. Feb 12–Mar 1. Fond du Lac, WI, at the foot of the lake is the Sturgeon Capital of the World. The sturgeon species have remained unchanged for more than 50 million years and the Lake Winnebago region has one of the major populations of them. Shanty and equipment rental available; sturgeon fishing tag required. Est attendance: 2,000. For info: Fond du Lac Area Conv Bureau, 19 W Scott St, Fond du Lac, WI 54935. Phone: (800) 937-9123 ext 95. Fax: (920) 929-6846. E-mail: visitor@fdl.com. Web: www.fdl.com.

Bill Russell

NEW YORK-TO-PARIS AUTO RACE BEGINS: ANNIVERSARY. Feb 12, 1908. Six automobiles left Times Square to begin a New York-to-Paris race that proved to be part sporting event and part expedition. The cars drove across the North American continent, took a boat across the Pacific and then raced across Siberia and Europe to the City of Lights. One car dropped out on the starting day; after a while, only two remained. A team of Americans reached Paris on July 31, four days after a German team, but the Americans were declared the winners because of a handicap imposed on the Germans. The Americans traveled 13,341 miles in 170 days.

SNOWFLAKE INTERNATIONAL SKI JUMP TOURNAMENT IN WESTBY. Feb 12–13 (tentative). Westby, WI. More than 150 participants—young and old, novice as well as Olympic caliber—compete on five different hills in this international tournament at the US home of ski jumping. World-class champions from more than 11 countries soar 300 feet through the air as they jump Timber Coulee, a 90-meter hill–the same size hill used in the Winter Olympics. For info: Eddie Lundy, Mgr, Snowflake Ski Club, Rt 1, PO Box 103A, Westby, WI 54667-9739. Phone: (608) 634-3211.

WALKER LAKE FISH DERBY. Feb 12–14. Walker Lake, NV. Fishing contest for cutthroat trout, hobo dinner and liars contest. Tagged fish worth $25,000 and many more prizes. Est attendance: 1,250. For local info: Mineral County Chamber of Commerce, PO Box 1635, Hawthorne, NV 89415. Phone: (775) 945-5896. Fax: (775) 945-1257.

BIRTHDAYS TODAY

Ruben Amaro, Jr, 35, baseball player, born Philadelphia, PA, Feb 12, 1965.
Dominic Paul (Dom) DiMaggio, 83, former baseball player, born San Francisco, CA, Feb 12, 1917.
Joseph Henry (Joe) Garagiola, 74, Ford Frick Award broadcaster and former baseball player, born St. Louis, MO, Feb 12, 1926.
Owen Nolan, 28, hockey player, born Belfast, Northern Ireland, Feb 12, 1972.
Michel Petit, 36, hockey player, born St. Malo, Quebec, Canada, Feb 12, 1964.
Scot Pollard, 25, basketball player, born Murray, UT, Feb 12, 1975.
William Felton (Bill) Russell, 66, former basketball coach and Basketball Hall of Fame center, sportscaster, born Monroe, LA, Feb 12, 1934.

FEBRUARY 13 — SUNDAY
Day 44 — 322 Remaining

BUD SHOOTOUT AT DAYTONA. Feb 13. Daytona International Speedway, Daytona Beach, FL. Preceded by Bud Pole Day on Feb 12. Winners of Bud Pole Awards for the '99 NASCAR Winston Cup season. Sponsor: Budweiser. For info: John Story, Dir of Public Relations, Daytona Intl Speedway, PO Box 2801, Daytona Beach, FL 32120-2801. Phone: (904) 947-6782. For tickets: (904) 253-RACE (7223). Fax: (904) 947-6791. Web: www.daytonausa.com.

CHASE, HAL: BIRTH ANNIVERSARY. Feb 13, 1883. Harold Harris (Hal) Chase, baseball player, born at Los Gatos, CA. Chase was a brilliant fielder as a first baseman whose reputation for dishonesty grew as his career lengthened. Accused more than once of throwing games, he was banned from several minor leagues but not the majors. Died at Colusa, CA, May 18, 1947.

FIRSTPLUS FINANCIAL 200 LATE MODEL STOCK CAR RACE. Feb 13. Daytona International Speedway, Daytona Beach, FL. 36th annual running. Season kick-off for the ARCA Bondo/Mar-Hyde Series. For info: John Story, Dir of Public Relations, Daytona Intl Speedway, PO Box 2801, Daytona Beach, FL 32120-2801. Phone: (904) 947-6782. For tickets: (904) 253-RACE (7223). Fax: (904) 947-6791. Web: www.daytonausa.com.

MOORE, DONNIE: BIRTH ANNIVERSARY. Feb 13, 1954. Donnie Ray Moore, baseball player, born at Lubbock, TX. Moore became an outstanding relief pitcher after developing a forkball in the mid-1980s. He gave up a key home run in the 1986 American League Championship Series to Dave Henderson of the Boston Red Sox and gradually grew despondent. Died of a self-inflicted gunshot wound at Anaheim, CA, July 18, 1989.

NICHOLLS GETS 1,000th POINT: ANNIVERSARY. Feb 13, 1994. Center Bernie Nicholls of the New Jersey Devils got the 1,000th point of his National Hockey League career, a goal in a 3–3 tie against the Tampa Bay Lightning.

SELVY SCORES 100: ANNIVERSARY. Feb 13, 1954. Frank Selvy of Furman University scored 100 points in a 149–95 victory over Newberry College. Selvy broke the record of 73 points set in 1951 by Temple's Bill Mlkvy. He made 41 field goals and 18 foul shots.

TROTTIER SCORES 500th GOAL: 10th ANNIVERSARY. Feb 13, 1990. Bryan Trottier of the New York Islanders scored the 500th regular-season goal of his career in a 4–2 loss to the Calgary Flames. Trottier, the 15th National Hockey League player to reach 500, finished his career with 524 goals and was inducted into the Hockey Hall of Fame in 1997.

BIRTHDAYS TODAY

Salvatore Leonard (Sal) Bando, 56, baseball executive and former player, born Cleveland, OH, Feb 13, 1944.

Patricia Jane (Patty) Berg, 82, LPGA Hall of Fame golfer, born Minneapolis, MN, Feb 13, 1918.

Ruben Pernell Brown, 28, football player, born Lynchburg, VA, Feb 13, 1972.

Marc Joseph John Crawford, 39, hockey coach and former player, born Belleville, Ontario, Canada, Feb 13, 1961.

Matthew Todd (Matt) Mieske, 32, baseball player, born Midland, MI, Feb 13, 1968.

Randy Moss, 23, football player, born Rand, WV, Feb 13, 1977.

Edward Gay (Eddie) Robinson, 81, former college football coach, born Jackson, LA, Feb 13, 1919.

Kevin Douglas Stocker, 30, baseball player, born Spokane, WA, Feb 13, 1970.

Mats Sundin, 29, hockey player, born Sollentuna, Sweden, Feb 13, 1971.

FEBRUARY 14 — MONDAY

Day 45 — 321 Remaining

ACE BAILEY BENEFIT GAME: ANNIVERSARY. Feb 14, 1934. The Toronto Maple Leafs played a team of stars from the other National Hockey League teams in a special game to benefit Ace Bailey, a Toronto player who had suffered a fractured skull on Dec 2, 1933. The Maple Leafs won, 7–3.

ALLEN, MEL: BIRTH ANNIVERSARY. Feb 14, 1913. Mel Allen, broadcaster, born Melvin Allen Israel at Birmingham, AL. Allen earned a law degree in 1936 from the University of Alabama, but his real love was sports. He left Alabama for the CBS radio network and was soon broadcasting New York Yankees and New York Giants baseball games as well as a host of other sporting events. He became the Yankees' lead announcer after World War II and became nationally famous for two phrases he used regularly: "How about that!" to describe a fine play and "Going, going, gone," his home run call. Years after being fired by the Yankees after the 1963 World Series, he attracted a new generation of listeners to his work on the weekly television show "This Week in Baseball." Received the Ford Frick Award in 1978. Died at Greenwich, CT, June 16, 1996.

BOBBY ALLISON WINS DAYTONA: ANNIVERSARY. Feb 14, 1988. Bobby Allison became the first 50-year-old driver to win the Daytona 500 when he outdueled his 26-year-old son Davey.

ESPY AWARDS. Feb 14. MGM Grand Hotel, Las Vegas, NV. Honoring the best athletic achievements of the previous year. 8th annual. For info: Media Relations, ESPN, ESPN Plaza, Bristol, CT 06010. Phone: (860) 585-2000.

HAYES, WOODY: BIRTH ANNIVERSARY. Feb 14, 1913. Wayne Woodrow (Woody) Hayes, football coach, born at Clifton, OH. Hayes became head coach at Ohio State in 1950 and remained there through the 1977 season. Known for an explosive temper and occasional sidelines antics, Hayes taught his teams ball-control offense epitomized by the phrase "three yards and a cloud of dust." During his tenure the Buckeyes won 205 games, lost 68 and tied 10. They won the national championship in 1968. Died at Upper Arlington, OH, Mar 12, 1987.

NATIONAL FIELD TRIAL CHAMPIONSHIP. Feb 14–18 (also Feb 21–25). Ames Plantation, Grand Junction, TN. To select the national champion all-age bird dog. Est attendance: 8,000. For info: Jim Anderson, Secy/Treas, Natl Field Trial Champion Assn, Box 389, Grand Junction, TN 38039. Phone: (901) 878-1067. Fax: (901) 878-1068. E-mail: amesplantation@lunaweb.net. Web: www.amesplantation.org.

SUGAR RAY WINS CROWN: ANNIVERSARY. Feb 14, 1951. Sugar Ray Robinson, often regarded as the greatest boxer of all time, won the world middleweight championship by knocking out Jake LaMotta in the 15th round of a fight at Chicago.

WESTMINSTER KENNEL CLUB DOG SHOW. Feb 14–15. Madison Square Garden, New York, NY. The 124th edition of the most prestigious dog show in America and the second oldest sporting event in the US, younger only than the Kentucky Derby. For info: Dog Show Committee, Westminster Kennel Club, 230 Park Ave, Ste 644, New York, NY 10169-0644. E-mail: write@westminsterkennelclub.org. Web: www.westminsterkennelclub.org.

February	S	M	T	W	T	F	S
2000			1	2	3	4	5
	6	7	8	9	10	11	12
	13	14	15	16	17	18	19
	20	21	22	23	24	25	26
	27	28	29				

Drew Bledsoe, 28, football player, born Ellensburg, WA, Feb 14, 1972.

David Francis (Dave) Dravecky, 44, former baseball player, born Youngstown, OH, Feb 14, 1956.

Tyus Dwayne Edney, 27, basketball player, born Gardena, CA, Feb 14, 1973.

Calle Johansson, 33, hockey player, born Goteborg, Sweden, Feb 14, 1967.

James Edward (Jim) Kelly, 40, former football player, born Pittsburgh, PA, Feb 14, 1960.

Steve McNair, 27, football player, born Mount Olive, MS, Feb 14, 1973.

Gheorghe Muresan, 29, basketball player, born Triteni, Romania, Feb 14, 1971.

Kelly Lee Stinnett, 30, baseball player, born Lawton, OK, Feb 14, 1970.

Petr Svoboda, 34, hockey player, born Most, Czechoslovakia, Feb 14, 1966.

Mary Kathryn ("Mickey") Wright, 65, LPGA Hall of Fame golfer, born San Diego, CA, Feb 14, 1935.

FEBRUARY 15 — TUESDAY

Day 46 — 320 Remaining

ALBRIGHT WINS WORLD TITLE: ANNIVERSARY. Feb 15, 1953. Tenley Albright made figure skating history by becoming the first American woman to win the world's championship. She also skated her way to a silver medal at the 1952 Winter Olympics and a gold medal at the 1956 Winter Olympics.

BLAIK, RED: BIRTH ANNIVERSARY. Feb 15, 1897. Earl Henry ("Red") Blaik, football player and coach, born at Detroit, MI. Blaik played three sports at Miami University (OH) and after graduation was appointed to the US Military Academy at West Point. In 1934 he was named head football coach at Dartmouth and moved to West Point in 1941. His teams won two national championships and seven Lambert Trophies, symbol of football supremacy in the East. He coached three Heisman Trophy winners and 35 All-Americans. Died at Colorado Springs, CO, May 6, 1989.

DOUBLE GOLD MEDAL WINNER: ANNIVERSARY. Feb 15, 1932. The US four-man bobsled team won the gold medal at the Winter Olympics at Lake Placid, NY. On the team was Edward F. Eagan, who had won a gold medal in boxing at the 1920 Summer Olympics. Eagan thus became the first person to win gold medals in both winter and summer games.

ESPOSITO GETS 1,000th POINT: ANNIVERSARY. Feb 15, 1974. Boston Bruins center Phil Esposito scored the 1,000th point of his National Hockey League career, an assist in Boston's 4–2 victory over the Vancouver Canucks. Esposito, the 10th player to reach 1,000 points, finished his career with 1,590 points.

FIRST NASCAR RACE: ANNIVERSARY. Feb 15, 1948. The newly-formed National Association of Stock Car Auto Racing (NASCAR) staged its first race on the Daytona Beach, FL, road/beach course. 14,000 fans watched driver Red Byron win the 150-mile event.

Kenneth Allan (Ken) Anderson, 51, former football player, born Batavia, IL, Feb 15, 1949.

Ronald Charles (Ron) Cey, 52, former baseball player, born Tacoma, WA, Feb 15, 1948.

Darrell Green, 40, football player, born Houston, TX, Feb 15, 1960.

John Willard Hadl, 60, former football player, born Lawrence, KS, Feb 15, 1940.

Jaromir Jagr, 28, hockey player, born Kladno, Czechoslovakia, Feb 15, 1972.

William Mark Price, 36, basketball player, born Bartlesville, OK, Feb 15, 1964.

Ugueth Urtain Urbina, 26, baseball player, born Caracas, Venezuela, Feb 15, 1974.

FEBRUARY 16 — WEDNESDAY

Day 47 — 319 Remaining

DELVECCHIO GETS 1,000th POINT: ANNIVERSARY. Feb 16, 1969. Center Alex Delvecchio of the Detroit Red Wings became the third player in the National Hockey League to accumulate 1,000 regular-season points. Delvecchio got an assist in a 6–3 win over the Los Angeles Kings. He finished his career with 1,281 points.

FLORIDA CLASSIC & WCHR SPECTACULAR. Feb 16–20. Palm Beach Polo Equestrian Club, Wellington, FL. The 4th event in the 2000 Cosequin Winter Equestrian Festival. For info: Stadium Jumping, Inc, 3104 Cherry Palm Dr, Ste 220, Tampa, FL 33619. Phone: (800) 237-8924 or (813) 623-5801. Fax: (813) 626-5369. Web: www.stadiumjumping.com.

GOULET SCORES 500th GOAL: ANNIVERSARY. Feb 16, 1992. Left wing Michel Goulet of the Chicago Blackhawks became the 17th player in the National Hockey League to score 500 regular-season goals. He tallied against goalie Jeff Reese of the Calgary Flames in a 5–5 tie. Goulet finished his career with 548 goals and was inducted into the Hockey Hall of Fame in 1998.

HAMILTON, SLIDING BILLY: BIRTH ANNIVERSARY. Feb 16, 1866. William Robert ("Sliding Billy") Hamilton, Baseball Hall of Fame outfielder, born at Newark, NJ. Hamilton was the leading base stealer of the 19th century, though recordkeeping was not then what it is now. With Ed Delahanty and Sam Thompson, he formed one of baseball's greatest outfields. Inducted into the Hall of Fame in 1961. Died at Worcester, MA, Dec 15, 1940.

JOHNSON WINS OLYMPIC DOWNHILL: ANNIVERSARY. Feb 16, 1984. Skier Bill Johnson became the first (and thus far, the only) American to win the Olympic downhill. Johnson's victory came at the 1984 Winter Olympics at Sarajevo, Yugoslavia.

LONGEST TENNIS MATCH: ANNIVERSARY. Feb 16, 1968. At the US Indoor Championships at Salisbury, MD, the longest match in US Tennis Association history pitted Englishmen Mark Cox and Bob Wilson against Americans Charlie Pasarell and Ron Holmberg. After six hours and 23 minutes, Cox and Wilson emerged victorious, 26–24, 17–19, 30–28.

MILWAUKEE BOAT SHOW AT THE MIDWEST EXPRESS CENTER. Feb 16–20. Midwest Express Center, Milwaukee, WI. This event brings together buyers and sellers of sail and power boats, including fishing boats, pontoons and boating accessories, as well as vacation property and travel destinations. Est attendance: 25,000. For info: Henri Boucher, ShowSpan, Inc, 1400 28th St SW, Grand Rapids, MI 49509. Phone: (616) 530-1919. Fax: (616) 530-2122.

MOUNTAIN WEST MEN'S AND WOMEN'S SWIMMING AND DIVING CHAMPIONSHIPS. Feb 16–19. Oklahoma City, OK. For info: Mountain West Conference, PO Box 35670, Colorado Springs, CO 80935-3567. Phone: (719) 533-9500. Fax: (719) 533-9512.

PONTIAC SILVERDOME BOAT, SPORT & FISHING SHOW. Feb 16–20. Pontiac Silverdome, Pontiac, MI. This event brings together buyers and sellers of boating, fishing and outdoor sporting products. US and Canadian hunting and fishing trips, as well as other vacation travel destinations, are featured. Est attendance: 30,000. For info: Henri Boucher, Show Span, Inc, 1400 28th St SW, Grand Rapids, MI 49509. Phone: (616) 530-1919. Fax: (616) 530-2122.

SEC MEN'S AND WOMEN'S SWIMMING AND DIVING CHAMPIONSHIPS. Feb 16–19. University of Alabama, Tuscaloosa, AL. For info: Southeastern Conference, 2201 Civic Center Blvd, Birmingham, AL 35203-1103. Phone: (205) 458-3010. Fax: (205) 458-3030. E-mail: twilson@sec.org. Web: www.secsports.com.

UP 200 SLED-DOG CHAMPIONSHIP. Feb 16–20. Upper Peninsula of MI. Race date is Feb 18. Intrepid mushers and their dog sled teams glide over white-carpeted fields, through snowy forests and across frozen lakes on a 240-mile round trip. The route extends across the middle of the Upper Peninsula from Lake Superior to Lake Michigan and back. Also kiddie mutt races, art show and snowball dances in Marquette and Escanaba. Est attendance: 15,000. For info: Marquette Country CVB. Phone: (800) 544-4321 or Travel Michigan (888) 784-7328.

BIRTHDAYS TODAY

Jerome Abram Bettis, 28, football player, born Detroit, MI, Feb 16, 1972.
John Patrick McEnroe, Jr, 41, broadcaster and former tennis player, born Wiesbaden, West Germany, Feb 16, 1959.
Amy Van Dyken, 27, Olympic gold medal swimmer, born Cherry Creek, CO, Feb 16, 1973.

FEBRUARY 17 — THURSDAY

Day 48 — 318 Remaining

CHASE'S SPORTSQUOTE OF THE DAY

"There are very few names that are even close to being associated with Michael Jordan in the sports world: Babe Ruth and Muhammad Ali."—Nike founder and CEO, Phil Knight

ACC WOMEN'S SWIMMING AND DIVING CHAMPIONSHIPS. Feb 17–19. University of North Carolina, Chapel Hill, NC. For info: Atlantic Coast Conference, PO Drawer ACC, Greensboro, NC 27417-6724. Phone: (336) 854-8787. Fax: (336) 854-8797.

ALL-CANADA SHOW. Feb 17–20. Brown County Expo, Green Bay, WI. This consumer show allows individuals an opportunity to talk face-to-face with Canadian lodge representatives and outfitters to plan their hunting, fishing and adventure trips to Canada. For info: Rodney Schlafer, Show Dir, All-Canada Show, Bay-Lakes Mktg, Inc, 1889 Commerce Drive, De Pere, WI 54115. Phone: (920) 983-9800. Fax: (920) 983-9985. Web: www.all-canada.com.

BARBER, RED: BIRTH ANNIVERSARY. Feb 17, 1908. Walter Lanier ("Red") Barber, broadcaster, born at Columbus, MS. Barber's first professional play-by-play job was announcing the Cincinnati Reds starting with Opening Day, 1934, the first major league baseball game he had ever seen. Barber switched to the Brooklyn Dodgers and later the New York Yankees and became one of the game's premiere announcers whose work was beloved by many. He broadcast the game in which Jackie Robinson broke baseball's color line and the game in which Roger Maris broke Babe Ruth's record for most home runs in a season. Well after he retired, he enjoyed a second career as a weekly commentator on National Public Radio. Given the Ford Frick Award in 1978. Died Oct 22, 1992, at Tallahassee, FL.

BIG TEN WOMEN'S SWIMMING AND DIVING CHAMPIONSHIPS. Feb 17–19. IUPUI, Indianapolis, IN. Est attendance: 600. For info: Big Ten Conference, 1500 W Higgins Rd, Park Ridge, IL 60068-6300. Phone: (847) 696-1010. Fax: (847) 696-1150. Web: www.bigten.org.

BIG 12 WOMEN'S SWIMMING AND DIVING CHAMPIONSHIPS. Feb 17–19. Texas A&M University, College Station, TX. For info: Big Twelve Conference, 2201 Stemmons Freeway, 28th Floor, Dallas, TX 75207. Phone: (214) 742-1212. Fax: (214) 742-2046.

CRABBE, BUSTER: BIRTH ANNIVERSARY. Feb 17, 1908. Clarence Lindon ("Buster") Crabbe, Olympic gold medal swimmer, born at Oakland, CA. Crabbe's first-place finish in the 400-meter freestyle was the only swimming medal won by an American at the 1932 Olympic Games at Los Angeles. After his swimming career was over, he played Tarzan, Flash Gordon and Buck Rogers in the movies. Died at Scottsdale, AZ, Apr 23, 1983.

FIRST SIX-DAY BIKE RACE: ANNIVERSARY. Feb 17, 1899. The first six-day bicycle race, featuring two-man teams, came to an end at New York's Madison Square Garden. The winning team of Charles Miller and Frank Waller rode a combined distance of 2,733 miles.

GATORADE 125-MILE QUALIFYING RACES (FOR DAYTONA 500). Feb 17. Daytona International Speedway, Daytona Beach, FL. 41st annual qualifying races for the Daytona 500; also to determine starting positions 3–30. Sponsor: Gatorade. For info: John Story, Dir of Public Relations, Daytona Intl Speedway, PO Box 2801, Daytona Beach, FL 32120-2801. Phone: (904) 947-6782. For tickets: (904) 253-RACE (7223). Fax: (904) 947-6791. Web: daytonausa.com.

GOLF AROUND CINCINNATI. Feb 17–27. Northgate Mall, Cincinnati, OH. 18-hole miniature golf course featuring replica Cincinnati landmarks at each hole built by local architects and building companies. Proceeds from the course benefit the Epilepsy Council of Greater Cincinnati. Events scheduled include a Celebrity Play, Senior's Day Out for golfers 55 and over and a Corporate Challenge Tournament. For info: Northgate Mall Information Center, 9501 Colerain Ave, Cincinnati, OH 45251. Phone: (513) 385-5600 or Mark Findlay, Epilepsy Council of Greater Cincinnati, 3 Centennial Plaza, 895 Central Ave, Ste 1000, Cincinnati, OH 45202. Phone: (513) 721-2905.

MAHOVLICH GETS 1,000th POINT: ANNIVERSARY. Feb 17, 1973. Left wing Frank Mahovlich of the Montreal Canadiens got the 1,000th point of his National Hockey League career, an assist in a 7–6 loss to the Philadelphia Flyers. Mahovlich finished his career with 1,103 points.

MIAMI INTERNATIONAL BOAT SHOW. Feb 17–23. Miami Beach Convention Center, Miami Beach, FL (Watson Island and Biscayne Bay Marriott). 59th annual boat show, the biggest in the US and considered the "main event" for product introductions. With more than 3,000 boats, this boat show offers an unparalleled opportunity to view the sport's latest products. For info: NMMA Boat Shows, 200 E Randolph Dr, Ste 5100, Chicago, IL 60601-6528. Phone: (312) 946-6262. Fax: (312) 946-0401. Web: www.boatshows.com.

NEYLAND, BOB: BIRTH ANNIVERSARY. Feb 17, 1892. Robert Reese (Bob) Neyland, Jr, football player, coach and administrator, born at Greenville, TN. Neyland played football at West Point and served in the American Expe-

February 2000	S	M	T	W	T	F	S
			1	2	3	4	5
	6	7	8	9	10	11	12
	13	14	15	16	17	18	19
	20	21	22	23	24	25	26
	27	28	29				

ditionary Forces in 1917. He moved to the University of Tennessee in 1925 to head the ROTC program and coach football. His Volunteers won 75 of 87 from 1926 to 1935. After a one-year hiatus, he returned to Tennessee where his teams won 33 straight games and held all opponents scoreless in 1939. After service in World War II, he returned to coaching again, with nearly equal success. His demeanor earned him the nickname, "The General." Died at New Orleans, LA, Mar 28, 1962.

PIPP, WALLY: BIRTH ANNIVERSARY. Feb 17, 1893. Walter Clement (Wally) Pipp, baseball player, born at Chicago, IL. Pipp was the New York Yankees' starting first baseman who, on June 1, 1925, took a day off, allegedly for a headache. Lou Gehrig played in his place and did not come out of the lineup for 2,130 games. Died at Grand Rapids, MI, Jan 11, 1965.

SIMPLOT GAMES. Feb 17–19. Holt Arena, Idaho State University, Pocatello, ID. One of the nation's largest indoor high school track and field events, featuring 2,500 top high school athletes from the US and Canada. Free admission. Est attendance: 20,000. For info: Carol Lish, Exec Dir, Simplot Games, PO Box 912, Pocatello, ID 83204. Phone: (208) 238-2777 or (800) 635-9444. Fax: (208) 238-2760. E-mail: clish@simplot.com. Web: www.simplot.com.

STRICTLY SAIL—MIAMI. Feb 17–23. Miami Yacht Club on Watson Island, Miami, FL. 15th annual show. Impressive sail-only show features the latest sailboats, equipment and services as well as seminars and attractions for all levels of sailing ability. For info: NMMA Boat Shows, 200 E Randolph Dr, Ste 5100, Chicago, IL 60601-6528. Phone: (312) 946-6262. Fax: (312) 946-0401. Web: www.boatshows.com.

US WINS FIRST WOMEN'S HOCKEY GOLD MEDAL: ANNIVERSARY. Feb 17, 1998. The US won the first Olympic gold medal ever awarded in women's hockey, defeating Canada in the final, 3–1, in the Nagano Winter Olympics. The American team was led by captain Cammi Granato and goalie Sarah Tueting.

WINTER GOODWILL GAMES. Feb 17–20. Lake Placid, NY. Inaugural event. International, multisport competition for athletes from around the winter sports world. Seven sports: bobsled, figure skating, luge, skiing, ski jumping, snowboarding and short track speed skating. Finals-only format. For info: Goodwill Games, One CNN Center, Box 105366, Atlanta, GA 30348-5366. Phone: (404) 827-3400. Fax: (494) 827-1394.

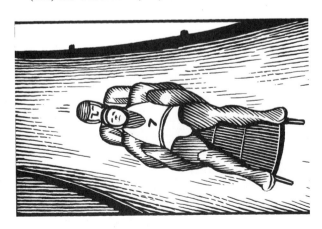

BIRTHDAYS TODAY

Drew William Barry, 27, basketball player, born Oakland, CA, Feb 17, 1973.

James Nathaniel (Jim) Brown, 64, Pro Football Hall of Fame fullback, born St. Simon's Island, GA, Feb 17, 1936.

Bryan Keith Cox, 32, football player, born St. Louis, MO, Feb 17, 1968.

Roger Lee Craig, 70, former baseball manager and player, born Durham, NC, Feb 17, 1930.

Dennis Green, 51, football coach, born Harrisburg, PA, Feb 17, 1949.

Todd Harvey, 25, hockey player, born Hamilton, Ontario, Canada, Feb 17, 1975.

Michael Jeffrey Jordan, 37, former basketball player, born New York, NY, Feb 17, 1963.

Lorenzo Levon Kirkland, 31, football player, born Lamar, SC, Feb 17, 1969.

David Klingler, 31, football player, born Stratford, TX, Feb 17, 1969.

Luc Robitaille, 34, hockey player, born Montreal, Quebec, Canada, Feb 17, 1966.

Lindy Cameron Ruff, 40, hockey coach and former player, born Warburg, Alberta, Canada, Feb 17, 1960.

Frank Vondel Sanders, 27, football player, born Ft Lauderdale, FL, Feb 17, 1973.

Joel Edward Steed, 31, football player, born Frankfurt, West Germany, Feb 17, 1969.

FEBRUARY 18 — FRIDAY
Day 49 — 317 Remaining

CHASE'S SPORTSQUOTE OF THE DAY

"Sometime, Rock, when the team is up against it, when things are wrong the breaks are beating the boys, tell them to go in there with all they've got and win just one for the Gipper."—Ronald Reagan as George Gipp in the movie, *Knute Rockne—All American*

ACC MEN'S AND WOMEN'S INDOOR TRACK AND FIELD CHAMPIONSHIPS. Feb 18–19. Virginia Tech University, Blacksburg, VA. For info: Atlantic Coast Conference, PO Drawer ACC, Greensboro, NC 27417-6724. Phone: (336) 854-8787. Fax: (336) 854-8797.

AMERICAN DOG DERBY. Feb 18–19. Ashton, ID. Premiere sled dog race. 10-dog teams race 120 miles in two days. Six-dog teams race 90 miles in two days. Weight pulls, mutt races, lots of fun. Est attendance: 3,500. For info: American Dog Derby, Ashton, ID 83420. Phone: (208) 652-3377.

CANADA: TREK OVER THE TOP DESTINATION TOK. Feb 18–20. Dawson City, Yukon. A 400-mile round trip snowmobile run that departs Dawson City, Yukon, and follows the Top of the World/Taylor Highway into Tok, AK. The weekend involves a number of planned snowmobile events, banquets, live entertainment and a casino. Annually, usually the third weekend in February. Est attendance: 50. For info: Trek Over the Top, Box 100, Dawson City, YT, Canada Y0B 1G0. Phone: (403) 993-5873. Fax: (403) 993-7423. E-mail: ezalitis@dawsoncity.net or pcayen@dawsoncity.net. Web: yukonweb.wis.net/special/trek.

COLLEGE BASKETBALL SCANDAL: ANNIVERSARY. Feb 18, 1951. New York County District Attorney Frank S. Hogan made the first arrests in a point-shaving scandal that rocked college basketball across the country. Hogan arrested players from the City College of New York, but before long the scandal spread to several other campuses, including Long Island University, New York University, Bradley and Kentucky.

COWBOY STATE GAMES WINTER SPORTS FESTIVAL. Feb 18–21. Casper, WY. The festival features a variety of winter sporting events for athletes of all ages. Est attendance: 1,600. For info: Eileen Ford, Cowboy State Games,

PO Box 3485, Casper, WY 82602. Phone: (307) 577-1125. Fax: (307) 577-8111. E-mail: csg@trib.com.

DISCOUNT AUTO PARTS 200. Feb 18. Daytona Beach, FL. 22nd annual race is season kickoff for the NASCAR Goody's Dash Series. Sponsor: Discount Auto Parts. For info: John Story, Dir of Public Relations, Daytona Intl Speedway, PO Box 2801, Daytona Beach, FL 32120-2801. Phone: (904) 947-6782. For tickets: (904) 253-RACE (7223). Fax: (904) 947-6791. Web: www.daytonausa.com.

GIPP, GEORGE: 105th BIRTH ANNIVERSARY. Feb 18, 1895. George Gipp, college football player, born at Laurium, MI. Gipp was a legendary halfback for Notre Dame and the school's first All-American. His lifestyle, however, was sharply at odds with Ronald Reagan's portrayal of him in a movie about Knute Rockne. Gipp rarely went to class, opting instead for pool, gambling and chasing girls. He never uttered the famous words, "Win one for the Gipper." Still, he was a dominant player who epitomized Notre Dame's underdog fighting spirit. Died at South Bend, IN, Dec 14, 1920.

HOUSTON LIVESTOCK SHOW AND RODEO. Feb 18–Mar 5. Astrodome Complex, Houston, TX. Livestock show with more than 30,000 entries. "Wild rodeo action" and top-name musical entertainment. For info: Mktg Dept, Houston Livestock Show and Rodeo Assn, Box 20070, Houston, TX 77225-0070. Phone: (713) 791-9000. Fax: (713) 794-9528. Web: www.hlsr.com. and for pay-per-view info: Web: www.rodeohouston.com.

INDIANAPOLIS BOAT, SPORT AND TRAVEL SHOW. Feb 18–27. Indiana State Fairgrounds, Indianapolis, IN. Est attendance: 200,000. For info: Kevin Renfro, VP, Ste E-2, Corporate Square East, 2511 E 46th St, Indianapolis, IN 46205. Phone: (317) 546-4344. Fax: (317) 546-3002. E-mail: insportshow@iquest.net.

IROC XXIV INTERNATIONAL RACE OF CHAMPIONS. Feb 18. Daytona International Speedway, Daytona Beach, FL. All-star race for the greatest drivers from different forms of racing in the US. Sponsor: True Value Hardware Stores. For info: John Story, Dir of Public Relations, Daytona Intl Speedway, PO Box 2801, Daytona Beach, FL 32120-2801. Phone: (904) 947-6782. For tickets: (904) 253-RACE (7223). Fax: (904) 947-6791. Web: www.datonausa.com.

JACKSON HOLE SHRINE CUTTER RACE. Feb 18–19. Melody Ranch, Jackson Hole, WY. Chariot racing Western-style as horse-drawn cutters vie in this 28th annual fundraiser. "The cutters run that a child may walk," spectators "bet" and the money goes to a hospital for crippled children at Salt Lake City. Annually, the Friday and Saturday before Presidents' Day. Est attendance: 7,000. For info: Jackson Hole Shrine Club, Box 2565, Jackson, WY 83001. Phone: (307) 733-1938.

JANSEN WINS GOLD: ANNIVERSARY. Feb 18, 1994. American speed skater Dan Jansen won a gold medal in the 1,000-meter race at the Winter Olympics at Lillehammer, Norway. Favored to win at 500 meters in three straight Olympics but unsuccessful each time, Jansen overcame a slip to break the jinx. Speed skating fans who had watched Jansen struggle on the ice and deal with family tragedy rejoiced.

LONGHORN WORLD CHAMPIONSHIP RODEO. Feb 18–19. The Palace of Auburn Hills, Auburn Hills, MI.

	S	M	T	W	T	F	S
February 2000			1	2	3	4	5
	6	7	8	9	10	11	12
	13	14	15	16	17	18	19
	20	21	22	23	24	25	26
	27	28	29				

More than 200 cowboys and cowgirls compete in six professional contests ranging from bronc riding to bull riding for top prize money and world championship points. Featuring colorful opening pageantry and Big, Bad BONUS Bulls. 36th annual. Est attendance: 35,000. For info: W. Bruce Lehrke, Pres, Longhorn World Chmpshp Rodeo, Inc, PO Box 70159, Nashville, TN 37207. Phone: (615) 876-1016. Fax: (615) 876-4685. E-mail: lhrodeo @idt.net. Web: www.longhornrodeo.com.

NJCAA MEN'S WRESTLING CHAMPIONSHIP. Feb 18–19. Rochester, MN. For info: John Grabko, Tourn Dir, Rochester Amateur Sports Commission, 150 W Broadway, Ste A, Rochester, MN 55904-6500. Phone: (507) 252-9914. Fax: (507) 288-9144. Web: www.njcaa.org.

RECREATIONAL VEHICLE SHOW. Feb 18–20 (also Feb 25–27). Timonium State Fairgrounds, Timonium, MD. Mid-Atlantic's oldest, largest and best-attended RV show with exhibitors to display all the latest in motor homes, camping and RV accessories. Est attendance: 20,000. For info: Maryland Recreational Vehicle Assn, 8332 Pulaski Hwy, Baltimore, MD 21237. Phone: (410) 687-7200. Fax: (410) 686-1486.

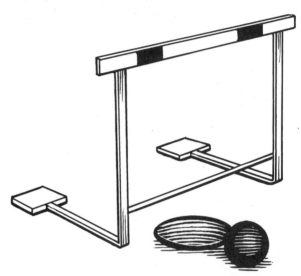

SEC MEN'S AND WOMEN'S INDOOR TRACK AND FIELD CHAMPIONSHIPS. Feb 18–20. University of Kentucky, Lexington, KY. For info: Southeastern Conference, 2201 Civic Center Blvd, Birmingham, AL 35203-1103. Phone: (205) 458-3010. Fax: (205) 458-3030. E-mail: twilson@sec.org. Web: www.secsports.com.

SPECIAL OLYMPICS NEW YORK WINTER GAMES. Feb 18–20. Schenectady, NY. Approximately 600 athletes with mental retardation compete in skiing, speed skating, figure skating, poly hockey, floor hockey and fitness. For info: New York Special Olympics, Inc, 504 Balltown Rd, Schenectady, NY 12304-2290. Phone: (518) 388-0790. Fax: (518) 388-0795. E-mail: bmosberg@nyso.org.

"THE KING" STRIKES OUT SIX: ANNIVERSARY. Feb 18, 1967. In a special exhibition of softball pitching versus baseball hitting, star softball hurler Eddie Feigner, known as "The King," struck out six of baseball's greatest hitters in a row: Willie Mays, Willie McCovey, Brooks Robinson, Roberto Clemente, Maury Wills and Harmon Killebrew.

BIRTHDAYS TODAY

Luis Enrique Arroyo, 73, former baseball player, born Penuelas, Puerto Rico, Feb 18, 1927.

Aaron Shawn Estes, 27, baseball player, born San Bernardino, CA, Feb 18, 1973.

Yevgeny Kafelnikov, 26, tennis player, born Sochi, USSR, Feb 18, 1974.

Charles Dallan (Dal) Maxvill, 61, former baseball executive and player, born Granite City, IL, Feb 18, 1939.

Alexander Mogilny, 31, hockey player, born Khabarovsk, USSR, Feb 18, 1969.

Robert Bruce (Bob) St. Clair, 69, Pro Football Hall of Fame tackle, born San Francisco, CA, Feb 18, 1931.

George Theo Teague, 29, football player, born Lansing, MI, Feb 18, 1971.

John William Valentin, 33, baseball player, born Mineola, NY, Feb 18, 1967.

FEBRUARY 19 — SATURDAY
Day 50 — 316 Remaining

CHASE'S SPORTSQUOTE OF THE DAY

"I consider football merely as just another extracurricular activity like debating, the band or anything else on campus."—Joe Paterno

ARCARO, EDDIE: BIRTH ANNIVERSARY. Feb 19, 1916. George Edward (Eddie) Arcaro, broadcaster and jockey, born at Cincinnati, OH. Arcaro is the only jockey to win racing's Triple Crown twice, triumphing with Whirlaway in 1941 and Citation in 1947. In all, he won five Kentucky Derbies, six Preakness Stakes and six Belmont Stakes. Died at Miami, FL, Nov 14, 1997.

BIG EAST MEN'S AND WOMEN'S INDOOR TRACK AND FIELD CHAMPIONSHIPS. Feb 19–20. Carrier Dome, Syracuse University, Syracuse, NY. For info: Big East Conference, 56 Exchange Terrace, Providence, RI 02903. Phone: (401) 272-9108. Fax: (401) 751-8540.

BLAIR WINS GOLD AGAIN: ANNIVERSARY. Feb 19, 1994. Olympian Bonnie Blair of Champaign, IL, became the first speed skater to win a gold medal in the same event in three consecutive Olympic Games when she won the 500 meters at Lillehammer, Norway. On Feb 23, she added a victory in the 1,000 meters to give her a total of five gold medals, more than any other American female athlete.

BRIGHTON FIELD DAY AND RODEO. Feb 19–20. Brighton Indian Reservation, Okeechobee, FL. Arts and crafts, alligator wrestling, PRCA rodeo, animal show, parade and beautiful Native American clothing. Sponsor: Seminole Tribe of Florida. Annually, the third weekend in February. Est attendance: 5,500. For info: Ellen Click, Field Day Contact Person, Rte 6, Box 666, Okeechobee, FL 34974. Phone: (941) 763-4128. Fax: (941) 763-5077.

CANADA: FIS ALPINE JUNIOR WORLD SKI CHAMPIONSHIPS. Feb 19–27. Le Relais, Stoneham and Mount Ste. Anne, Canada. For info: Intl Ski Federation, Blochstrasse 2, 3653 Oberhofen am Thunersee, Switzerland. Phone: (41) (33) 244-6161. Fax: (41) (33) 243-5353. E-mail: mail@fisski.org. Web: www.fisski.org.

CANADA: FROSTY FROLICS WINTER CARNIVAL. Feb 19–26. Bancroft, Ontario. Sled dog races, craft show and special attractions. National Natural Luge Championships. Est attendance: 5,000. For info: Bancroft and District Chamber of Commerce, PO Box 539, Bancroft, ON, Canada K0L 1C0. Phone: (613) 332-1513. Fax: (613) 332-2119. E-mail: chamber@commerce.bancroft.on.ca. Web: www.commerce.bancroft.on.ca.

CANADA: SCOTT TOURNAMENT OF HEARTS WOMEN'S CURLING CHAMPIONSHIP. Feb 19–27. Prince George, British Columbia. The Canadian Women's Curling Championship is the premiere women's sporting event in Canada showcasing the best female curlers from across the country. Weeklong activities include entertainment, artisans' show and sale, mini-spiels and tours. For info: Media Relations, Canadian Curling Assn, 1600 James Naismith Dr, Ste 511, Gloucester, ON, Canada K1B 5N4. Phone: (613) 748-5628. Fax: (613) 748-5713. E-mail: cca@curling.ca. Web: www.curling.ca.

GILBERT GETS 1,000th POINT: ANNIVERSARY. Feb 19, 1977. Right wing Rod Gilbert of the New York Rangers scored the 1,000th point of his National Hockey League career, a goal in a 5–2 loss to the New York Islanders. Gilbert finished his career with 1,021 points.

MAHRE BROTHERS WIN MEDALS: ANNIVERSARY. Feb 19, 1984. At the XIVth Winter Olympics at Sarajevo, Yugoslavia, skiers Phil and Steve Mahre of the US became the first brothers to finish first and second in the same Olympic event. Phil won the gold medal in the slalom, and Steve won the silver.

MYRTLE BEACH MARATHON. Feb 19. Myrtle Beach, SC. Marathon and marathon relay. For info: PO Box 8780, Myrtle Beach, SC 29578-8780. Phone: (843) 293-RACE. Web: coastal.edu/marathon.

NAPA AUTO PARTS 300 NASCAR BUSCH SERIES RACE. Feb 19. Daytona International Speedway, Daytona Beach, FL. 42nd annual race is season kickoff for the NASCAR Busch series. Sponsor: NAPA Auto Parts. For info: John Story, Dir of Pub Rel, Daytona Intl Speedway, PO Box 2801, Daytona Beach, FL 32120-2801. Phone: (904) 947-6782. For tickets: (904) 253-RACE (7223). Fax: (904) 947-6791. Web: www.daytonausa.com.

NEW ZEALAND: AMERICA'S CUP. Feb 19–26. Auckland, New Zealand. Best five-races-out-of-nine competition for sailing's most prestigious trophy, the America's Cup. New Zealand, as the defending champion, will host this competition. The challenger will emerge from a multination series of races that will culminate in the Louis Vuitton Cup Series. Races 6 through 9, if necessary, are scheduled for Feb 27, Feb 29, Mar 2 and Mar 4. For info: New Zealand Defense Committee, Royal New Zealand Yacht Squadron, PO Box 1927, Auckland, New Zealand. Phone: (011) 64-9-357-6712. Web: www.americascup2000.org.nz.

YARBOROUGH WINS CONSECUTIVE DAYTONAS: ANNIVERSARY. Feb 19, 1984. Cale Yarborough became only the second driver to win consecutive Daytona 500 races by sweeping into the lead just two turns from the finish and taking the checkered flag. Yarborough joined Richard Petty in this select circle.

BIRTHDAYS TODAY

Timothy Philip (Tim) Burke, 41, former baseball player, born Omaha, NE, Feb 19, 1959.

Robert (Rob) DiMaio, 32, hockey player, born Calgary, Alberta, Canada, Feb 19, 1968.

William Terrelle Henderson, 29, football player, born Chester, VA, Feb 19, 1971.

June Sheldon Jones, III, 47, former football coach and player, born Portland, OR, Feb 19, 1953.

Paul James Krause, 58, Pro Football Hall of Fame defensive back, born Flint, MI, Feb 19, 1942.

David Keith (Dave) Stewart, 43, former baseball player, born Oakland, CA, Feb 19, 1957.

Jahidi White, 24, basketball player, born St. Louis, MO, Feb 19, 1976.

Wally James Williams, Jr, 29, football player, born Tallahassee, FL, Feb 19, 1971.

FEBRUARY 20 — SUNDAY
Day 51 — 315 Remaining

APPLETON, SCOTT: BIRTH ANNIVERSARY. Feb 20, 1942. Gordon Scott Appleton, football player, born at Brady, TX. Appleton was a star defensive tackle at the University of Texas, winning several individual honors and awards, including the 1963 Outland Trophy. Drafted by both the Houston Oilers (AFL) and the Dallas Cowboys (NFL), he played five seasons as a pro. In retirement, Appleton struggled with alcoholism and then became a minister. Died of heart disease at Austin, TX, Mar 2, 1992.

BOITANO WINS "BATTLE OF THE BRIANS": ANNIVERSARY. Feb 20, 1988. Brian Boitano of the US won the gold medal in men's figure skating at the XVth Winter Olympic Games at Calgary, Alberta, Canada. Boitano skated a nearly flawless free program to edge Brian Orser of Canada. The Soviet Union's Viktor Petrenko took the bronze.

BUSCH BUYS CARDINALS: ANNIVERSARY. Feb 20, 1953. August A. Busch, president of Anheuser-Busch Brewery, purchased the St. Louis Cardinals Baseball Club from Fred Saigh, who was forced to sell the team by Commissioner Ford C. Frick after pleading no contest to tax evasion charges. Anheuser-Busch owned the Cardinals until 1995.

DAYTONA 500. Feb 20. Daytona International Speedway, Daytona Beach, FL. 42nd annual running of the "World's Greatest Race" is the season kickoff for the NASCAR Winston Cup Series season. For info: John Story, Dir of Public Relations, Daytona Intl Speedway, PO Box 2801, Daytona Beach, FL 32120-2801. Phone: (904) 947-6782. For tickets: (904) 253-RACE (7223). Fax: (904) 947-6791. Web: www.daytonausa.com.

ESA MID-WINTER SURFING CHAMPIONSHIP. Feb 20. Narragansett Town Beach, Narragansett, RI. Competition in all age categories and specialty events with prizes and trophies. Est attendance: 125. For info: Peter Pan, ESA Dir, 396 Main St, Wakefield, RI 02879. Phone: (401) 789-3399. Fax: (401) 782-0458.

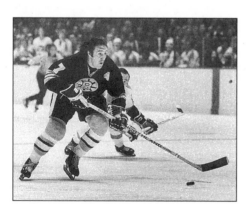

ESPOSITO SCORES 50th GOAL: ANNIVERSARY. Feb 20, 1971. Phil Esposito of the Boston Bruins became the first NHL player to score his 50th goal in February when he tallied in a 5–4 loss to the Los Angeles Kings. Esposito finished the season with 76 goals, a record.

HOWE SIGNS WITH AEROS: ANNIVERSARY. Feb 20, 1974. Gordie Howe, the oldest player in NHL history, came out of retirement at age 45 to play with his sons, Mark and Marty. He signed a four-year, $1 million contract with the Houston Aeros of the World Hockey Association.

LIPINSKI WINS GOLD MEDAL: ANNIVERSARY. Feb 20, 1998. Tara Lipinski, 15, performed a strong free skating routine to overcome Michelle Kwan and win the ladies' figure skating gold medal at the Winter Olympics at Nagano, Japan.

MOTOROLA AUSTIN MARATHON. Feb 20. Marathon and marathon relay. For info: Motorola Austin Marathon, PO Box 684587, Austin, TX 78768. Phone: (512) 505-8304. Web: www.motorolamarathon.com.

BIRTHDAYS TODAY

Charles Wade Barkley, 37, basketball player, born Leeds, AL, Feb 20, 1963.

Philip Anthony (Phil) Esposito, 58, former hockey coach and Hockey Hall of Fame center, born Sault Ste. Marie, Ontario, Canada, Feb 20, 1942.

Elroy Leon (Roy) Face, 72, former baseball player, born Stephentown, NY, Feb 20, 1928.

Thomas David (Tommy) Henrich, 87, former baseball player, born Massilon, OH, Feb 20, 1913.

Eisler ("Livan") Hernandez, 25, baseball player, born Villa Clara, Cuba, Feb 20, 1975.

Stephon Marbury, 23, basketball player, born New York, NY, Feb 20, 1977.

Michael Shane Spencer, 28, baseball player, born Key West, FL, Feb 20, 1972.

Robert William (Bobby) Unser, 66, former auto racer, born Albuquerque, NM, Feb 20, 1934.

FEBRUARY 21 — MONDAY
Day 52 — 314 Remaining

AFL MERGES WITH NFL: 30th ANNIVERSARY. Feb 21, 1970. After a protracted battle over players, fans and television ratings, the American Football League, founded in 1960, became part of the National Football League. Teams from the AFL were joined by the Cleveland Browns, the Pittsburgh Steelers and the Baltimore Colts to become the American Football Conference. Remaining NFL teams became the National Football Conference.

FIRST WOMEN'S 15-FOOT POLE VAULT: ANNIVERSARY. Feb 21, 1998. Australian Emma George became the first woman to pole vault 15 feet, doing so at the Robin Tait Classic at Auckland, New Zealand. George surpassed the previous record of 14 feet, 11 inches, on her first attempt.

JAPAN: FOUR CONTINENTS CHAMPIONSHIPS. Feb 21–27. Osaka, Japan. An international figure skating competition preceding the world championships in March. For info: Media Relations, US Figure Skating Assn, 20 First St, Colorado Springs, CO 80906. Phone: (719) 635-5200. Fax: (719) 635-9548. E-mail: usfsa1@aol.com. Web: www.usfsa.org/events.

NBA'S MILKMAN SPECIAL: ANNIVERSARY. Feb 21, 1952. Following a performance by the Ice Follies, Boston Garden hosted an unusual NBA game between the Celtics and the Ft Wayne Pistons. The game began at midnight and was billed as a "Milkman's Special." Bob Cousy scored 24 points to lead Boston to an 88–67 victory before 2,368 fans.

	S	M	T	W	T	F	S
February			1	2	3	4	5
2000	6	7	8	9	10	11	12
	13	14	15	16	17	18	19
	20	21	22	23	24	25	26
	27	28	29				

PRESIDENTS' DAY. Feb 21. The third Monday in February. Presidents' Day observes the birthdays of George Washington (Feb 22) and Abraham Lincoln (Feb 12). With the adoption of the Monday Holiday Law (which moved the observance of George Washington's birthday from Feb 22 each year to the third Monday in February), some of the specific significance of the event was lost, and added impetus was given to the popular description of that holiday as Presidents' Day. Present usage often regards Presidents' Day as a day to honor all former presidents of the US. Presidents' Day has statutory authority in Hawaii, Nebraska, Ohio and the Commonwealth of the Northern Mariana Islands, and popular recognition in most states.

YAWKEY, TOM: BIRTH ANNIVERSARY. Feb 21, 1903. Thomas Austin (Tom) Yawkey, Baseball Hall of Fame executive, born at Detroit, MI. Yawkey purchased the Boston Red Sox in 1933 and held the club until his death. His reputation was that of a sporting gentleman who treated his team as a public trust and not as a business. Inducted into the Hall of Fame in 1980. Died at Boston, MA, July 9, 1976.

BIRTHDAYS TODAY

John Eugene (Jack) Billingham, 57, former baseball player, born Orlando, FL, Feb 21, 1943.

John T. (Jack) Ramsay, 75, broadcaster and Basketball Hall of Fame coach, born Philadelphia, PA, Feb 21, 1925.

FEBRUARY 22 — TUESDAY
Day 53 — 313 Remaining

ANDERSON GETS 1,000th POINT: ANNIVERSARY. Feb 22, 1993. Right wing Glenn Anderson of the Toronto Maple Leafs got the 1,000th point of his National Hockey League career, a goal in an 8–1 victory over the Vancouver Canucks. Anderson finished his career with 1,099 points.

ATTELL, ABE: BIRTH ANNIVERSARY. Feb 22, 1884. Abe Attell, boxer, born Albert Knoehr at San Francisco, CA. Attell held the featherweight championship for 11 years in the early part of this century when boxing was not quite as organized as it could have been. A heavy gambler, he got involved in baseball's Black Sox scandal, actually delivering $10,000 to the player-conspirators. But he avoided prosecution, first by fleeing to Canada and then by convincing authorities that there were two Abe Attells and the other one was the guilty party. Died at Livingstone Manor, NY, Feb 6, 1970.

FINLEY, CHARLIE: BIRTH ANNIVERSARY. Feb 22, 1918. Charles O. (Charlie) Finley, baseball executive, born at Ensley, AL. Finley was the flamboyant and controversial owner who moved the Athletics from Kansas City to Oakland. He dressed his team in green and gold, had sheep grazing beyond the outfield wall, tangled often with Commissioner Bowie Kuhn, suggested that World Series games be played at night and put together a team that won three straight World Series (1972–74). Died at Chicago, IL, Feb 19, 1996.

FIRST DAYTONA 500: ANNIVERSARY. Feb 22, 1959. The first running of the Daytona 500, the race that has become the most important event on the NASCAR calendar, took place at the newly-opened Daytona International Speedway in Florida. Drivers Lee Petty and Johnny Beauchamp crossed the finish line in what appeared to be a dead heat, but photographs and film, examined later, showed Petty to be the winner.

FIRST RACE WON BY A WOMAN JOCKEY: ANNIVERSARY. Feb 22, 1969. Barbara Jo Rubin became the first woman jockey to win a thoroughbred horse race in the US. She rode Cohesion to victory by a neck over Reely Beeg in the ninth race at Charles Town Race Track in West Virginia.

KLEM, BILL: BIRTH ANNIVERSARY. Feb 22, 1874. William Joseph (Bill) Klem, Baseball Hall of Fame umpire, born at Rochester, NY. Klem umpired in the National League from 1905 to 1941 and is generally considered the greatest umpire ever. He worked 18 World Series and insisted that he never made a bad call. Inducted into the Hall of Fame in 1953. Died at Miami, FL, Sept 1, 1951.

LESNEVICH, GUS: 85th BIRTH ANNIVERSARY. Feb 22, 1915. Gus Lesnevich, boxer, born at Cliffside Park, NJ. Lesnevich rose from a Golden Gloves championship to the light heavyweight championship of the world. He won the title in 1941, had it "frozen" while he was in the Coast Guard during World War II and retained it after the war until being defeated in 1948. Died at Cliffside Park, Feb 28, 1964.

MIRACLE ON ICE: 20th ANNIVERSARY. Feb 22, 1980. The US Olympic hockey team upset the team from the Soviet Union, 4–3, at the Lake Placid Winter Games to earn a victory often called the "Miracle on Ice." The Americans went on to defeat Finland two days later and win the gold medal.

MORAN, UNCLE CHARLIE: BIRTH ANNIVERSARY. Feb 22, 1878. Charles Barthell ("Uncle Charlie") Moran, baseball and football player, baseball umpire and football coach, born at Nashville, TN. Moran played college and professional football and professional baseball and umpired in the National League for 24 seasons, including four World Series. He is most remembered, however, for coaching tiny Centre College (KY) to a 6–0 upset of mighty Harvard in 1924. Died at Horse Cave, KY, June 13, 1949.

BIRTHDAYS TODAY

Amy Strum Alcott, 44, LPGA Hall of Fame golfer, born Kansas City, MO, Feb 22, 1956.

George Lee ("Sparky") Anderson, 66, former baseball manager and player, born Bridgewater, SD, Feb 22, 1934.

Gilbert Jesse Brown, 29, football player, born Farmington, MI, Feb 22, 1971.

Michael Te Pei Chang, 28, tennis player, born Hoboken, NJ, Feb 22, 1972.

Mark William Chmura, 31, football player, born Deerfield, MA, Feb 22, 1969.

Gerald (Gerry) Davis, 47, baseball umpire, born St. Louis, MO, Feb 22, 1953.

Julius Winfield ("Dr. J") Erving, II, 50, Basketball Hall of Fame forward, born Roosevelt, NY, Feb 22, 1950.

Lisa Fernandez, 29, Olympic gold medal softball player, born Long Beach, CA, Feb 22, 1971.

Ricky Allen (Rick) Helling, 27, baseball player, born Atlantic, IA, Feb 22, 1973.

Adam Thomas Keefe, 30, basketball player, born Irvine, CA, Feb 22, 1970.

Vijay Singh, 37, golfer, born Lautoka, Fiji, Feb 22, 1963.

Jayson Williams, 32, basketball player, born Ritter, SC, Feb 22, 1968.

FEBRUARY 23 — WEDNESDAY
Day 54 — 312 Remaining

COSEQUIN PALM BEACH MASTERS. Feb 23–27. Palm Beach Polo Equestrian Club, Wellington, FL. The fifth event in the 2000 Cosequin Winter Equestrian Festival. For info: Stadium Jumping, Inc, 3104 Cherry Palm Dr, Ste 220, Tampa, FL 33619. Phone: (800) 237-8924 or (813)

623-5801. Fax: (813) 626-5369. Web: www.stadium jumping.com.

DREYFUSS, BARNEY: BIRTH ANNIVERSARY. Feb 23, 1865. Barney Dreyfuss, baseball executive, born at Freiburg, Germany. As owner of the Pittsburgh Pirates, Dreyfuss challenged the Boston Pilgrims to a postseason series in 1903, thereby creating the modern World Series. Died at New York, NY, Feb 5, 1932.

FIESTA DE LOS VAQUEROS. Feb 23–27. Tucson, AZ. 75th annual. Tucson celebrates its Old West heritage with parade, PRCA rodeo and other related rodeo events. Est attendance: 55,000. For info: Tucson Rodeo Committee, Inc, PO Box 11006, Tucson, AZ 85734. Phone: (520) 741-2233. Fax: (520) 741-7273.

GOULET GETS 1,000th POINT: ANNVERSARY. Feb 23, 1991. Left wing Michel Goulet of the Chicago Blackhawks got the 1,000th point of his National Hockey League career, a goal in a 3–3 tie against the Minnesota North Stars. Goulet finished his career with 1,152 points.

HEIDEN WINS FIFTH GOLD MEDAL: 20th ANNIVERSARY. Feb 23, 1980. US speedskater Eric Heiden won the 10,000 meters race to capture his fifth gold medal at the Lake Placid Winter Olympics. Heiden also won at 500 meters, 1,000 meters, 1,500 meters and 5,000 meters.

HEISS WINS GOLD MEDAL: 40th ANNIVERSARY. Feb 23, 1960. Carol Heiss won the gold medal in women's figure skating at the VIIIth Winter Olympic Games at Squaw Valley, CA.

HOWARD, ELSTON: BIRTH ANNIVERSARY. Feb 23, 1929. Elston Gene Howard, baseball player, born at St. Louis, MO. Howard was the first African-American to play for the New York Yankees. A catcher and an outfielder, he won the American League MVP award in 1963. Traded to the Boston Red Sox, he helped them win the 1967 AL pennant. Died at New York, NY, Dec 14, 1980.

KNIGHT THROWS CHAIR: 15th ANNIVERSARY. Feb 23, 1985. Indiana University basketball coach Bobby Knight was ejected from a game against Purdue for throwing a chair onto the court. Knight received his first technical foul for protesting two fouls called by the officials against his team. As Purdue shot the technical, Knight hurled a chair from the bench area onto the court, earning his second technical and automatic ejection. Purdue won, 72–63.

BIRTHDAYS TODAY

Frederick S. (Fred) Biletnikoff, 57, Pro Football Hall of Fame wide receiver, born Erie, PA, Feb 23, 1943.
Roberto Martin Antonio (Bobby) Bonilla, 37, baseball player, born New York, NY, Feb 23, 1963.
John Druce, 34, hockey player, born Peterborough, Ontario, Canada, Feb 23, 1966.
Dante Bert Joseph Lavelli, 77, Pro Football Hall of Fame end, born Hudson, OH, Feb 23, 1923.
Ed McDaniel, 31, football player, born Batesburg, SC, Feb 23, 1969.
Philip D. ("Flip") Saunders, 45, basketball coach, born Cleveland, OH, Feb 23, 1955.
Jackie Larue Smith, 60, Pro Football Hall of Fame tight end, born Columbia, MS, Feb 23, 1940.

February *2000*	S	M	T	W	T	F	S
			1	2	3	4	5
	6	7	8	9	10	11	12
	13	14	15	16	17	18	19
	20	21	22	23	24	25	26
	27	28	29				

Rondell Bernard White, 28, baseball player, born Milledgeville, GA, Feb 23, 1972.

FEBRUARY 24 — THURSDAY
Day 55 — 311 Remaining

CHASE'S SPORTSQUOTE OF THE DAY
"Wayne has done more for the game of hockey than any other person who has ever played or likely ever will."
—Bobby Hull on Wayne Gretzky

ACC MEN'S SWIMMING AND DIVING CHAMPIONSHIPS. Feb 24–26. University of North Carolina, Chapel Hill, NC. For info: Atlantic Coast Conference, PO Drawer ACC, Greensboro, NC 27417-6724. Phone: (336) 854-8787. Fax: (336) 854-8797.

ALL-CANADA SHOW. Feb 24–27. Canterbury Downs, Shakopee, MN. This consumer show allows individuals an opportunity to talk face-to-face with Canadian lodge representatives and outfitters to plan their hunting, fishing and adventure trips to Canada. For info: Rodney Schlafer, Show Dir, All-Canada Show, Bay-Lakes Mktg, Inc, 1889 Commerce Dr, De Pere, WI 54115. Phone: (920) 983-9800. Fax: (920) 983-9985. Web: www.allcanada.com.

BIG EAST MEN'S AND WOMEN'S SWIMMING AND DIVING CHAMPIONSHIPS. Feb 24–26. Goodwill Games Swimming Center, Uniondale, NY. For info: Big East Conference, 56 Exchange Terrace, Providence, RI 02903. Phone: (401) 272-9108. Fax: (401) 751-8540.

BIG TEN MEN'S SWIMMING AND DIVING CHAMPIONSHIPS. Feb 24–26. University of Michigan, Ann Arbor, MI. For info: Big Ten Conference, 1500 W Higgins Rd, Park Ridge, IL 60068-6300. Phone: (847) 696-1010. Fax: (847) 696-1110. Web: www.bigten.org.

CANADA: BC WINTER GAMES. Feb 24–27. Quesnel, British Columbia. Nearly 2,500 athletes competing in nearly 30 sports, indoors and outdoors. For info: BC Games Soc, Ste 200-990 Ft St, Victoria, BC, Canada V8V 3K2. Phone: (250) 387-1375. Fax: (250) 387-4489. E-mail: bcgames @bcgames.org. Web: www.bcgames.org.

CANADA: MONTREAL SPORTSMEN'S SHOW (SALON CAMPING, PLEIN AIR, CHASSE ET PECHE). Feb 24–27. Place Bonaventure, Montreal, Quebec. Major manufacturers, distributors and retailers of the outdoors, including camping, fishing and hunting, archery, tent trailers, fishing boats, canoes, kayaks and other crafts, tourism, campgrounds, outfitters, lodges, seminars and entertainment. For info: Val Nogas, Mgr, Public Relations, Canadian Natl Sportsmen's Shows, 703 Evans Ave, Ste 202, Toronto, ON, Canada M9C 5E9. Phone: (416) 695-0311. Fax: (416) 695-0381. Web: www.sportsmens shows.com.

CANADA: OTTAWA BOAT, SPORTSMEN'S & COTTAGE SHOW. Feb 24–27. Civic Centre, Coliseum & Aberdeen Pavilion, Landsdowne Park, Ottawa, Ontario. Brings the latest products and information in boating, fishing, hunting, archery, canoes, kayaks, camping, travel destinations, lodges and outfitters. Ottawa Cottage Show brings everything for cottage living. Est attendance: 30,000. For info: Val Nogas, Mgr, Public Relations, Canadian Natl Sportsmen's Shows, 703 Evans Ave, Ste 202, Toronto, ON, Canada M9C 5E9. Phone: (416) 695-0311. Fax: (416) 695-0381. Web: www.sportsmensshows.com.

CANADA: YUKON SOURDOUGH RENDEVOUS. Feb 24–27. Whitehorse, Yukon. Mad trapper competitions, bike races, flour packing, beard-growing contests, Old Time Fiddle show, sourdough pancake breakfasts, can-can girls, talent shows, etc. Also, many family-oriented activities. Visitors welcome to participate. Est attendance: 22,000. For info: Yukon Sourdough Rendezvous, Box 5108, Whitehorse, YT, Canada Y1A 4S3. Phone: (867) 667-2148 or (888) FUN-N-SNO. Fax: (867) 668-6755. E-mail: ysr@yukon.net. Web: rendezvous.yukon.net.

CHARRO DAYS. Feb 24–27. Brownsville, TX. Two Nations–Twin Cultures, a true example of international harmony and cooperation between Brownsville, Texas, and Matamoros, Mexico. Colorful celebration of the charro horseman of Mexico, a man of great riding skills. Dances, parades and carnival. Starts the last Thursday in February. Est attendance: 150,000. For info: Charro Days, Inc, PO Box 3247, Brownsville, TX 78523-3247. Phone: (956) 542-4245. Fax: (956) 542-6771.

FIRST SENIOR DAY: ANNIVERSARY. Feb 24, 1962. In his first season as head basketball coach at the University of North Carolina, Dean Smith inaugurated the practice of Senior Day, starting the seniors on his roster for their last regular-season home game. Smith remembered his own playing career at the University of Kansas when his coach, the legendary Phog Allen, said he had six starters but did not start Smith in his last home game. Senior Day has become a tradition at many colleges.

GRETZKY BREAKS ESPO'S RECORD: ANNIVERSARY. Feb 24, 1982. Wayne Gretzky, 21-year-old center for the Edmonton Oilers, scored his 77th goal of the season against the Buffalo Sabres to break Phil Esposito's single-season goal-scoring record. With Esposito, who had scored 76 goals in the 1970–71 season, in attendance, Gretzky stole the puck and broke a 3–3 tie with seven minutes to play. He added two more goals in the game's final two minutes and finished the season with 92 goals.

HOCKEY TEAM WINS GOLD MEDAL: 20th ANNIVERSARY. Feb 24, 1980. Two days after defeating the Soviet Union 4–3, the US hockey team won the gold medal at the XIIIth Winter Olympic Games by beating Finland, 4–2.

HOMER, WINSLOW: BIRTH ANNIVERSARY. Feb 24, 1836. Winslow Homer, artist, born at Boston, MA. Homer was noted for the realism of his work from Civil War reportage to highly regarded rugged outdoor scenes of hunting and fishing. Died at Prout's Neck, ME, Sept 29, 1910.

MATTI NYKANEN'S TRIPLE: ANNIVERSARY. Feb 24, 1988. Matti Nykanen of Finland, having already finished first in the 70- and 90-meter ski jumping events, won an unprecedented third gold medal in Nordic skiing when the Finnish team won the new 90-meter team jumping competition.

MIDDLE TENNESSEE BOAT SHOW. Feb 24–27. Nashville Convention Center, Nashville, TN. 2nd annual. For info: NMMA Boat Shows, 200 E Randolph Dr, Ste 5100, Chicago, IL 60601-6528. Phone: (312) 946-6262. Fax: (312) 946-0401. Web: www.boatshows.com.

MOUNTAIN WEST MEN'S AND WOMEN'S INDOOR TRACK AND FIELD CHAMPIONSHIPS. Feb 24–26. Air Force Academy, Colorado Springs, CO. For info: Mountain West Conference, PO Box 35670, Colorado Springs, CO 80935-3567. Phone: (719) 533-9500. Fax: (719) 533-9512.

OOSTERBAAN, BENNIE: BIRTH ANNIVERSARY. Feb 24, 1906. Benjamin Gaylord (Bennie) Oosterbaan, football player, coach and administrator, born at Muskegon, MI. Oosterbaan earned nine letters at the University of Michigan in baseball, basketball and football, winning All-American honors in 1925–27 at end. He remained at Michigan to be an assistant coach under Fielding Yost and became head coach in 1948. His Wolverines won

one national championship. Died at Ann Arbor, MI, Oct 25, 1990.

PAC-10 MEN'S AND WOMEN'S DIVING CHAMPIONSHIPS. Feb 24–26. University of Southern California, Los Angeles, CA. For info: PAC-10 Conference, 800 S Broadway, Ste 400, Walnut Creek, CA 94596. Phone: (510) 932-4411. Fax: (510) 932-4601.

PAC-10 WOMEN'S SWIMMING CHAMPIONSHIPS. Feb 24–26. Long Beach, CA. For info: PAC-10 Conference, 800 S Broadway, Ste 400, Walnut Creek, CA 94596. Phone: (510) 932-4411. Fax: (510) 932-4601.

SALOMON ELITE SPRINTS. Feb 24. Hayward, WI. Top world elite sprinters race head-to-head along Hayward's Main Street. For info: American Birkebeiner Ski Foundation, Inc, Box 911, Hayward, WI 54843. Phone: (715) 634-5025 or in WI (800) 722-3386. Fax: (715) 634-5663. E-mail: birkie@win.bright.net. Web: www.birkie.org.

SWISS MISS BARNEBIRKIE. Feb 24. Hayward, WI. Largest children's cross-country ski event in America, with more than 1,700 participants, ages 3–13. The courses, designed specifically for children, are based on age and experience with distances of 1, 2.5 and 5 kilometers. Each child receives a medal and cookies, juice and hot chocolate at the finish. For info: American Birkebeiner Ski Foundation, Inc, Box 911, Hayward, WI 54843. Phone: (715) 634-5025 or in WI (800) 722-3386. Fax: (715) 634-5663. E-mail: birkie@win.bright.net. Web: www.birkie.org.

WAGNER, HONUS: BIRTH ANNIVERSARY. Feb 24, 1874. John Peter ("Honus") Wagner, Baseball Hall of Fame shortstop, born at Chartiers, PA. Wagner, who played 21 years in the majors (1897–1917), is generally considered the greatest shortstop in baseball history. His nickname, pronounced "HA-nus," is a corruption of Johannes, the German translation of his first name. Inducted into the Hall of Fame as a charter member in 1936. Died at Carnegie, PA, Dec 6, 1955.

WORLD GOLF CHAMPIONSHIPS—MATCH PLAY. Feb 24–28. La Costa Resort & Spa, Carlsbad, CA. The inaugural event in the first World Golf Championships, a new initiative created by the PGA Tours International Federation composed of the world's five leading golf tours (the PGA Tour, the European Tour, the Southern Africa PGA Tour, the PGA Tour of Australasia and the PGA Tour of Japan). The World Golf Championships will consist of three events, this match play competition for 64 players, an invitational competition in August for all members of the last-named Presidents Cup and Ryder Cup teams and a stroke play competition in November for approximately 60 of the top players in the world. The Match Play event will begin on Wednesday, Feb 24, with 32 matches and will conclude on Sunday, Feb 28, with a 36-hole final. For info: PGA TOUR, 112 TPC Blvd, Ponte Vedra Beach, FL 32082. Phone: (904) 285-3700. Fax: (904) 285-2460.

YZERMAN GETS 1,000th POINT: ANNIVERSARY. Feb 24, 1993. Center Steve Yzerman of the Detroit Red Wings got the 1,000th point of his National Hockey League career, an assist in a 10–7 loss to the Buffalo Sabres.

BIRTHDAYS TODAY

Rene Arocha, 34, former baseball player, born Havana, Cuba, Feb 24, 1966.

Nicholas Andrew (Nick) Esasky, 40, former baseball player, born Hialeah, FL, Feb 24, 1960.

Alexei Kovalev, 27, hockey player, born Togliatti, USSR, Feb 24, 1973.

Eddie Clarence Murray, 44, former baseball player, born Los Angeles, CA, Feb 24, 1956.

Simeon Rice, 26, football player, born Chicago, IL, Feb 24, 1974.

Michael (Mike) Vernon, 37, hockey player, born Calgary, Alberta, Canada, Feb 24, 1963.

FEBRUARY 25 — FRIDAY
Day 56 — 310 Remaining

CHASE'S SPORTSQUOTE OF THE DAY

"Float like a butterfly, sting like a bee."—Cassius Clay on how he would defeat Sonny Liston

ALLISON, DAVEY: BIRTH ANNIVERSARY. Feb 25, 1961. Davey Allison, auto racer, born at Hueytown, AL. NASCAR's rookie of the year, Allison won 19 races in 191 starts, including one Daytona 500. The son of racer Bobby Allison, Davey was killed in a helicopter accident on the infield of the racetrack at Talladega, AL, July 13, 1993.

BASCOM, TEXAS ROSE: BIRTH ANNIVERSARY. Feb 25, 1922. Rose ("Texas Rose") Flynt Bascom, rodeo cowgirl, born at Covington County, MS. A Cherokee-Choctaw Indian, Flynt married a rodeo cowboy and learned trick roping, becoming known as the greatest female trick roper in the world. She appeared on stage, in movies and on early TV. She toured with the USO during WWII, performing at every military base and military hospital in the US. After the war she toured the world, entertaining servicemen stationed overseas. In 1981 she was inducted into the National Cowgirl Hall of Fame (Hereford, TX). Died Sept 23, 1993, at St. George, UT.

BIG 12 MEN'S AND WOMEN'S INDOOR TRACK AND FIELD CHAMPIONSHIPS. Feb 25–26. Iowa State University, Ames, IA. For info: Big Twelve Conference, 2201 Stemmons Freeway, 28th Floor, Dallas, TX 75207. Phone: (214) 774-2121. Fax: (214) 742-2046.

BISMARCK ALL-STATE INVITATIONAL VOLLEYBALL TOURNAMENT. Feb 25–27. Bismarck, ND. Watch more than 140 men's, women's and coed teams from several states and Canadian Provinces play. Or, recruit a team yourself! For info: Bismarck/Mandan CVB, PO Box 2274, Bismarck, ND 58502. Phone: (800) 767-3555. Fax: (701) 222-0647.

CLAY BECOMES HEAVYWEIGHT CHAMP: ANNIVERSARY. Feb 25, 1964. Twenty-two-year-old Cassius Clay (later Muhammed Ali) became world heavyweight boxing champion by defeating Sonny Liston when Liston was unable to answer the bell to start the seventh round of a fight at Convention Hall at Miami Beach. At the height of his athletic career Ali was well known for both his fighting ability and personal style. His most famous saying was, "I am the greatest!" In 1967 he was convicted of violating the Selective Service Act and was stripped of his title for refusing to be inducted into the armed services during the Vietnam War. Ali cited religious convictions as his reason for refusal. In 1971 the Supreme Court reversed the conviction. Ali is the first fighter to win the heavyweight fighting title three separate times. He defended that title nine times.

FIFTY STRAIGHT VICTORIES: ANNIVERSARY. Feb 25, 1993. The women's basketball team at the University of Vermont defeated Northeastern, 50–40, to earn its 50th consecutive regular-season victory, a record for Division I teams. Vermont extended its record to 52 wins before being beaten.

GIRLS' HIGH SCHOOL SCORING RECORD: ANNIVERSARY. Feb 25, 1924. Marie Boyd of Lonaconing (MD) High School made an incredible 77 field goals and a pair of foul shots in a game against Cumberland and Ursuline Academy. Her total points, 156, set a national girls' high school record that still stands. The final score: Lonaconing 162, Cumberland and Ursuline 3.

LONGHORN WORLD CHAMPIONSHIP RODEO. Feb 25–27. The Show Me Center, Cape Girardeau, MO. More than 200 cowboys and cowgirls compete in six professional contests ranging from bronc riding to bull riding for top prize money and world championship points. Featuring colorful opening pageantry and Big, Bad BONUS Bulls. 13th annual. Est attendance: 14,000. For info: W. Bruce Lehrke, Pres, Longhorn World Chmpshp Rodeo, Inc, PO Box 70159, Nashville, TN 37207. Phone: (615) 876-1016. Fax: (615) 876-4685. E-mail: lhrodeo@idt.net. Web: www.longhornrodeo.com.

LOST DUTCHMAN DAYS. Feb 25–27. Apache Junction, AZ. Three-day rodeo competition (senior pro rodeo), dance, carnival, parade, business vendors in celebration of the legend of the Superstition Mountains and the Lost Dutchman Mine. Annually, the last weekend in February. Est attendance: 30,000. For info: Apache Junction Chamber of Commerce, PO Box 1747, Apache Junction, AZ 85217-1747. Phone: (800) 252-3141. Fax: (602) 982-3234.

MOUNTAIN PACIFIC SPORTS FEDERATION MEN'S AND WOMEN'S INDOOR TRACK AND FIELD CHAMPIONSHIP. Feb 25–26. Reno, NV. Athletes from the PAC-10, Big West, WAC and Mountain West Conferences. For info: MPSF, 800 S Broadway, Ste 102, Walnut Creek, CA 94596-5218. Phone: (925) 296-0723. Fax: (925) 296-0724. E-mail: abeaird@psports.org. Web: www.pac-10.org/sports/mpsf.html.

NC RV AND CAMPING SHOW. Feb 25–27. NC State Fairgrounds, Raleigh, NC. A display of the latest in recre-

February 2000	S	M	T	W	T	F	S
			1	2	3	4	5
	6	7	8	9	10	11	12
	13	14	15	16	17	18	19
	20	21	22	23	24	25	26
	27	28	29				

ation vehicles and accessories by various dealers. Est attendance: 10,000. For info: Apple Rock Advertising & Promotions, 1200 Eastchester Dr, High Point, NC 27265. Phone: (336) 881-7100. Fax: (336) 883-7198.

RIGGS, BOBBY: BIRTH ANNIVERSARY. Feb 25, 1918. Robert Lorimer (Bobby) Riggs, tennis player, born at Los Angeles, CA. The crafty Riggs won the US National Singles championship in 1939 and 1941 and won three titles at Wimbledon in 1939. After World War II, he turned pro successfully but won his greatest fame for a pair of "battle of the sexes" matches in 1973. He won the first of these against Margaret Court and lost the second to Billie Jean King. Died at Leucadia, CA, Oct 25, 1995.

SMU GETS "DEATH PENALTY": ANNIVERSARY. Feb 25, 1987. After a series of NCAA violations over a period of years, the football program at Southern Methodist University was suspended for one year. The investigation leading to the "death penalty" uncovered payments of $61,000 to players from a booster slush fund.

BIRTHDAYS TODAY

Todd Alan Blackledge, 39, broadcaster and former football player, born Canton, OH, Feb 25, 1961.

Robert Earl (Bob) Brenly, 46, broadcaster and former baseball player, born Coshocton, OH, Feb 25, 1954.

Cesar Cedeno, 49, former baseball player, born Santo Domingo, Dominican Republic, Feb 25, 1951.

Byron Jaromir Dafoe, 29, hockey player, born Sussex, England, Feb 25, 1971.

Carl Lee Eller, 58, former football player, born Winston-Salem, NC, Feb 25, 1942.

Jeffrey Michael (Jeff) Fisher, 42, football coach and former player, born Culver City, CA, Feb 25, 1958.

Timothy Fitzpatrick (Tim) Floyd, 46, basketball coach, born Hattiesburg, MS, Feb 25, 1954.

Monford Merrill (Monte) Irvin, 81, Baseball Hall of Fame outfielder, born Columbia, AL, Feb 25, 1919.

Edward Francis (Ed) Lynch, 44, baseball executive and former player, born New York, NY, Feb 25, 1956.

Paul Andrew O'Neill, 37, baseball player, born Columbus, OH, Feb 25, 1963.

Ronald Edward (Ron) Santo, 60, broadcaster and former baseball player, born Seattle, WA, Feb 25, 1940.

Samaki Ijuma Walker, 24, basketball player, born Columbus, OH, Feb 25, 1976.

FEBRUARY 26 — SATURDAY

Day 57 — 309 Remaining

CHASE'S SPORTSQUOTE OF THE DAY

"Deplore it if you will, but Grover Cleveland Alexander drunk was a better pitcher than Grover Cleveland Alexander sober."—Bill Veeck

ALEXANDER, GROVER CLEVELAND: BIRTH ANNIVERSARY. Feb 26, 1887. Grover Cleveland ("Pete") Alexander, Baseball Hall of Fame pitcher, born at Elba, NE. Alexander won 373 games (tied for 3rd on the all-time list) pitching for 20 years with the Philadelphia Phillies, Chicago Cubs and St. Louis Cardinals. He won 30 or more games three times and won the National League earned run average title five times. In Game Seven of the 1926 World Series with St. Louis ahead, 3–2, he staggered in from the bullpen to strike out the New York Yankees' Tony Lazzeri with the bases loaded and held New York at bay for the last two innings. Ronald Reagan played Alexander in the movie, *The Winning Team.* Inducted into the Hall of Fame in 1938. Died at St. Paul, NE, Nov 4, 1950.

AMERICAN BIRKEBEINER. Feb 26. Cable to Hayward, WI. The largest and most prestigious cross-country ski marathon in North America attracts more than 8,000 participants for the 52K trek from Cable to Hayward. Preceded by a nordic festival of related ski events and activities. Est attendance: 8,000. For info: American Birkebeiner Ski Foundation, Inc, Box 911, Hayward, WI 54843. Phone: (715) 634-5025 or (800) 872-2953. Fax: (715) 634-5663. E-mail: birkie@win.bright.net. Web: www.birkie.org.

BIG TEN MEN'S INDOOR TRACK AND FIELD CHAMPIONSHIPS. Feb 26–27. Indiana University, Bloomington, IN. Est attendance: 2,000. For info: Big Ten Conference, 1500 W Higgins Rd, Park Ridge, IL 60068-6300. Phone: (847) 696-1010. Fax: (847) 696-1150. Web: www.bigten.org.

BIG TEN WOMEN'S INDOOR TRACK AND FIELD CHAMPIONSHIPS. Feb 26–27. University of Minnesota, Minneapolis, MN. Est attendance: 1,500. For info: Big Ten Conference, 1500 W Higgins Rd, Park Ridge, IL 60068-6300. Phone: (847) 696-1010. Fax: (847) 696-1150. Web: www.bigten.org.

CAROLINA MARATHON AND ASSOCIATED EVENTS. Feb 26. Columbia, SC. Marathon, 10K run/walk, wheelchair race and fun run for youths. This event will also serve as the 2000 US Olympic team trial for the women's marathon. For info: Carolina Marathon Assn, PO Box 5092, Columbia, SC 29250. Phone: (803) 929-1996. E-mail: cma@cyberstate.infi.net. Web: www.carolinamarathon.org.

CODY, BUFFALO BILL: BIRTH ANNIVERSARY. Feb 26, 1846. William Frederic ("Buffalo Bill") Cody, frontiersman, born at Scott County, IA. Cody claimed to have killed more than 4,000 buffalo. He was the subject of many heroic Wild West yarns, and he became successful as a showman, taking his acts across the US and to Europe. Died at Denver, CO, Jan 10, 1917.

DORAL-RYDER OPEN. Feb 26–Mar 5. Doral Resort & Spa, Miami, FL. A PGA Tour tournament with a full week of events, including a free outdoor pops concert, a skins game and three celebrity pro-ams. The Doral-Ryder Open is the nation's largest sports fund-raiser for the American Cancer Society. Est attendance: 150,000. For info: Mktg Dir, Doral-Ryder Open, 3600 NW 38th St, Ste 200, Miami, FL 33178. Phone: (305) 477-4653. Fax: (305) 477-4914.

JANOWICZ, VIC: 70th BIRTH ANNIVERSARY. Feb 26, 1930. Victor Felix (Vic) Janowicz, Heisman Trophy halfback and baseball player, born at Elyria, OH. Janowicz played several sports in high school and decided against signing a baseball contract in order to play football at Ohio State. His junior year was his best, earning him the 1950 Heisman. After graduation and a year in the military, he played both pro football and major league baseball. Died at Columbus, OH, Feb 27, 1996.

JENKINS WINS GOLD MEDAL: 40th ANNIVERSARY. Feb 26, 1960. David Jenkins of the US won the gold medal in men's figure skating at the VIIIth Winter Olympic Games at Squaw Valley, CA.

JOHNSON BANK OF HAYWARD KORTELOPET. Feb 26. Hayward, WI. This 25K race is sister to the American Birkebeiner. Participants begin with American Birkebeiner racers, but the finish line is at the half-way point of the longer race. Open to skiers ages 13 and over. 2,000 participants. Est attendance: 25,000. For info: American Birkebeiner Ski Foundation, Inc, Box 911, Hayward, WI 54843. Phone: (715) 634-5025 or in WI (800) 722-3386. Fax: (715) 634-5663. E-mail: birkie@win.bright.net. Web: www.birkie.org.

PAC-10 WRESTLING CHAMPIONSHIPS. Feb 26–27. University of California-Davis, Davis, CA. For info: PAC-10 Conference, 800 S Broadway, Ste 400, Walnut Creek, CA 94596. Phone: (510) 932-4411. Fax: (510) 932-4601.

RUTH SIGNS WITH BRAVES: 65th ANNIVERSARY. Feb 26, 1935. After being released by the New York Yankees, Babe Ruth signed a 3-year contract with the Boston Braves. He played in only 28 games before retiring in May.

SPECIAL OLYMPICS CONNECTICUT STATE WINTER GAMES. Feb 26–27. Hartford, CT. 600 athletes with mental retardation compete in speed skating, figure skating, alpine and cross-country skiing and floor hockey. For info: Special Olympics Connecticut, Inc, 2666-1 State St, Hamden, CT 06517-2232. Phone: (203) 230-1201. Fax: (203) 230-1202. Web: www.soct.org.

TRIG'S KLONDIKE DAYS. Feb 26–27. Eagle River Derby Track, Eagle River, WI. A re-creation of primitive camps used by early buckskinners, pioneers, trappers and traders, complete with tomahawk throwing and black powder musket shoot. Additional attractions include a 2-day horse weight-pull reminiscent of Wisconsin's logging days, a chain-saw carving competition, a Native American cultural presentation including a ceremonial dance exhibition, lumberjack competition, craft show, dog weight-pull, snow sculpting competition, Northwoods Wildlife Art & Amish Craft Show & Sale, and much more! Wisconsin's premier multifaceted winter festival. Est attendance: 12,000. For info: Eagle River Chamber of Commerce, PO Box 1917, Eagle River, WI 54521. Phone: (800) 359-6315.

USCA MEN'S AND WOMEN'S NATIONAL CHAMPIONSHIPS (CURLING). Feb 26–Mar 4. Ogden, UT. Curling national championship competition and USCA annual meeting. Est attendance: 8,000. For info: USA Curling, PO Box 866, Stevens Point, WI 54481. Phone: (715) 344-1199 or (888) CUR-LERS. Fax: (715) 344-2279. E-mail: usacurl@coredcs.com. Web: www.usacurl.org.

WERNER, BUDDY: BIRTH ANNIVERSARY. Feb 26, 1936. Wallace Jerold ("Buddy") Werner, skier, born at Steamboat Springs, CO. Werner skied on three US Olympic teams and was the first American to break into the sport's top rank by winning important races in Europe. While filming a ski movie, he was overtaken by an avalanche that he attempted to outrace. Died at St. Moritz, Switzerland, Apr 12, 1964.

☆   ☆   ☆

BIRTHDAYS TODAY

Marshall William Faulk, 27, football player, born New Orleans, LA, Feb 26, 1973.
Elwin Charles ("Preacher") Roe, 85, former baseball player, born Ashflat, AR, Feb 26, 1915.
David Scott Service, 33, baseball player, born Cincinnati, OH, Feb 26, 1967.
Jack Thomas (J.T.) Snow, Jr, 32, baseball player, born Long Beach, CA, Feb 26, 1968.
Charles Wesley Walls, 34, football player, born Batesville, MS, Feb 26, 1966.

February 2000	S	M	T	W	T	F	S
			1	2	3	4	5
	6	7	8	9	10	11	12
	13	14	15	16	17	18	19
	20	21	22	23	24	25	26
	27	28	29				

FEBRUARY 27 — SUNDAY
Day 58 — 308 Remaining

BRIGGS, SPIKE: BIRTH ANNIVERSARY. Feb 27, 1877. Walter Owen ("Spike") Briggs, baseball executive, born at Ypsilanti, MI. Briggs made a fortune in the automobile business and poured it into ownership of the Detroit Tigers. He bought the team in stages, securing the final piece in 1935. Died at Miami Beach, FL, Jan 17, 1952.

DANZIG, ALLISON: BIRTH ANNIVERSARY. Feb 27, 1898. Allison Danzig, sportswriter, born at Waco, TX. Danzig graduated from Cornell University in 1921, worked for the *Brooklyn Eagle* for two years and moved to the *New York Times* in 1923. From that date until his retirement in 1968, he served as the *Times's* leading sportswriter. Danzig covered five Olympic Games, wrote about all sports and specialized in tennis and college football. Died at New York, NY, Jan 27, 1987.

MIKITA SCORES 500th GOAL: ANNIVERSARY. Feb 27, 1977. Center Stan Mikita of the Chicago Blackhawks scored the 500th regular-season goal of his career in Chicago's 4–3 loss to the Vancouver Canucks. Mikita became the 8th player in National Hockey League history to reach 500. He finished his career with 541 goals and entered the Hockey Hall of Fame in 1983.

SARAZEN, GENE: BIRTH ANNIVERSARY. Feb 27, 1902. Gene Sarazen, golfer, born Eugenio Saraceni at Harrison, NY. Sarazen was one of the game's greatest players and in his later years one of its greatest goodwill ambassadors. The inventor of the sand wedge, Sarazen was also the first to win the modern grand slam (the Masters, US Open, British Open and PGA), although not in the same year. During the 1935 Masters, he hit one of golf's most famous shots, a four-wood for a double eagle on the par-5 fifteenth hole of the final round. The shot enabled him to tie Craig Wood for the lead and defeat him in a playoff. Sarazen's last shot was the traditional ceremonial tee shot to open the 1999 Masters. Died at Marco Island, FL, May 13, 1999.

SPECIAL OLYMPICS COLORADO WINTER GAMES. Feb 27–29. Copper Mountain Resort and Vail, CO. Multisport competition for athletes with mental retardation. For info: Colorado Special Olympics, 600 17th St, Ste 910, Denver, CO 80202. Phone: (303) 592-1361. Fax: (303) 592-1364.

SPECIAL OLYMPICS MONTANA WINTER GAMES. Feb 27–29. Big Mountain, Whitefish, MT. Competition for athletes with mental retardation in alpine and cross-country sports. For info: Special Olympics Montana, PO Box 3507, Great Falls, MT 59403. Phone: (406) 791-2368. Fax: (406) 454-9043. E-mail: MTSO@juno.com.

BIRTHDAYS TODAY

Willie Anthony Banks, 31, baseball player, born Jersey City, NJ, Feb 27, 1969.

Raymond Emmett Berry, 67, former football coach and Pro Football Hall of Fame end, born Corpus Christi, TX, Feb 27, 1933.

Tony Gonzalez, 24, football player, born Torrance, CA, Feb 27, 1976.

Matthew Wade (Matt) Stairs, 32, baseball player, born Fredericton, New Brunswick, Canada, Feb 27, 1968.

Loy Stephen Vaught, 33, basketball player, born Grand Rapids, MI, Feb 27, 1967.

James Ager Worthy, 39, broadcaster and former basketball player, born Gastonia, NC, Feb 27, 1961.

FEBRUARY 28 — MONDAY
Day 59 — 307 Remaining

BASKETBALL ON TV: 60th ANNIVERSARY. Feb 28, 1940. A basketball game between the University of Pittsburgh and Fordham University became the first game to be telecast live. Pitt won, 50–37, at Madison Square Garden.

BLONDIN, CHARLES: BIRTH ANNIVERSARY. Feb 28, 1824. Charles Blondin, daring French acrobat and aerialist, born Jean Francois Gravelet at St. Omer, France. He is especially remembered for walking across Niagara Falls on a tightrope, June 30, 1859, in front of a crowd estimated at more than 25,000. On other occasions, he repeated the trip blindfolded, pushing a wheelbarrow, carrying a man on his back and on stilts. Died at London, England, Feb 19, 1897.

HOCKEY TEAM WINS GOLD MEDAL: 40th ANNIVERSARY. Feb 28, 1960. The US hockey team defeated Czechoslovakia, 9–4, to win the gold medal at the VIIIth Winter Olympic Games at Squaw Valley, CA.

PETTY'S FIRST GRAND NATIONAL VICTORY: 40th ANNIVERSARY. Feb 28, 1960. Richard Petty won the first Grand National (later Winston Cup) stock car race of his career at Charlotte, NC. The victory earned him $800 and set him on the road toward 200 wins on the NASCAR circuit, including seven triumphs in the Daytona 500 and seven NASCAR driving titles.

BIRTHDAYS TODAY

Mario Gabrielle Andretti, 60, former auto racer, born Montona, Trieste, Italy, Feb 28, 1940.

Vincent Jerome Askew, 34, basketball player, born Memphis, TN, Feb 28, 1966.

Brian Harold Billick, 46, football coach, born Fairborn, OH, Feb 28, 1954.

Eric Lindros, 27, hockey player, born London, Ontario, Canada, Feb 28, 1973.

Shawn McEachern, 31, hockey player, born Waltham, MA, Feb 28, 1969.

Charles Aaron ("Bubba") Smith, 55, former football player, born Orange, TX, Feb 28, 1945.

FEBRUARY 29 — TUESDAY
Day 60 — 306 Remaining

BOURQUE GETS 1,000th POINT: ANNIVERSARY. Feb 29, 1992. Defenseman Raymond Bourque of the Boston Bruins got the 1,000th point of his National Hockey League career, an assist in a 5–5 tie with the Washington Capitals.

LEAP YEAR DAY. Feb 29. In 2000 we add one day, Feb 29, to bring our calendar more nearly into accord with the seasons. Under the Julian calendar of 46 BC every fourth year was a leap year, on the assumption that it took the Earth 365.25 days to orbit the sun. However, the Earth's orbital path is actually 365.23219 days. Over the more than 1,600 years that the Julian calendar was used, the calendar got out of sync with the seasons. The Gregorian calendar made just one small change: a leap day is added to the calendar once every four years except for century years which are not exactly divisible by 400. Since 2000 is divisible by 400, it is a leap year. 1900 was not. Traditionally leap year is a time during which women may propose marriage to men.

COMMON YEARS AND LEAP YEARS

A "common year" (any year that is not a leap year) comprises an exact number of weeks (52) plus one day. That extra day means that if a given date of the year, say, your birthday, falls on a Monday in one common year, it will fall on a Tuesday the next common year, and so on—one extra day per year as long as the years are common. However, the rule changes for leap years. A leap year is 52 weeks plus two days. So a date such as your birthday, that fell on a Monday the previous year, falls on a Wednesday, not a Tuesday, in a leap year. That is why the year is called a "leap year." The "leap" occurs throughout the year—the period from Mar 1 through the following Feb 28—in this instance, from Mar 1, 2000, to Feb 28, 2001.

BIRTHDAYS TODAY

Bryce Eric Paup, 32, football player, born Scranton, IA, Feb 29, 1968.

Henri Richard, 64, Hockey Hall of Fame center, born Montreal, Quebec, Canada, Feb 29, 1936.

Albert Leonard (Al) Rosen, 76, former baseball executive and player, born Spartanburg, SC, Feb 29, 1924.

MARCH 1 — WEDNESDAY

Day 61 — 305 Remaining

CELTICS' 2,000th VICTORY: ANNIVERSARY. Mar 1, 1987. The Boston Celtics defeated the Detroit Pistons, 112–102, to become the first NBA franchise to win 2,000 games.

GRETZKY ALL-TIME ASSIST LEADER: ANNIVERSARY. Mar 1, 1988. Center Wayne Gretzky of the Edmonton Oilers earned an assist in a game against the Los Angeles Kings to become the NHL's all-time career assist leader. It took Gretzky 681 games to garner 1,050 assists and surpass Gordie Howe who set the record in 1,767 games.

HOOSIER STATE GAMES. Mar 1. Various sites in Indiana from March through December. The Hoosier State Games is Indiana's only statewide amateur multisport festival. State champions will be crowned in more than a dozen sports throughout the spring and summer. For info: Indiana Sports Corp, 201 S Capitol Ave, Ste 1200, Indianapolis, IN 46225. Phone: (317) 237-5000 or (800) HI-FIVES. Fax: (317) 237-5041. E-mail: isc@indiana sportscorp.com. Web: www.indianasportscorp.com.

McKINNEY WINS WORLD CUP: ANNIVERSARY. Mar 1, 1983. Skier Tamara McKinney became the first American woman to win the overall World Cup championship.

NAIA MEN'S AND WOMEN'S SWIMMING AND DIVING CHAMPIONSHIPS. Mar 1–4. Site TBA. Individuals compete for All-America honors while teams compete for the national championship. 20th annual competition for women and 44th for men. Est attendance: 3,000. For info: Natl Assn of Intercollegiate Athletics, 6120 S Yale Ave, Ste 1450, Tulsa, OK 74136. Phone: (918) 494-8828. Fax: (918) 494-8841. E-mail: khenry@naia.org. Web: www.naia.org.

NJCAA MEN'S AND WOMEN'S SWIMMING AND DIVING CHAMPIONSHIP. Mar 1–4. San Antonio, TX. For info: Dennis Ryther, Tourn Dir, Palo Alto College, 1400 W Villaret, San Antonio, TX 78224. Phone: (210) 921-5234. Fax: (210) 921-5390. Web: www.njcaa.org.

PALM BEACH OPEN. Mar 1–5. Palm Beach Polo Equestrian Club, Wellington, FL. The sixth event in the 2000 Cosequin Winter Equestrian Festival. For info: Stadium Jumping, Inc, 3104 Cherry Palm Dr, Ste 220, Tampa, FL 33619. Phone: (800) 237-8924 or (813) 623-5801. Fax: (813) 626-5369. Web: www.stadiumjumping.com.

PHELAN WINS 800th GAME: ANNIVERSARY. Mar 1, 1999. The men's basketball team at Mount St. Mary's College at Emmittsburg, MD, defeated Central Connecticut State, 72–56, to give coach Jim Phelan the 800th victory of his coaching career. Phelan became the fourth coach to reach 800 wins. With the victory, the championship of the Northeast Conference, the Mounties clinched a berth in the NCAA tournament.

ROBYN SMITH WINS STAKES RACE: ANNIVERSARY. Mar 1, 1973. Robyn Smith rode North Star to victory in the Paumanok Handicap at Aqueduct Racetrack to become the first woman jockey to win a stakes race.

ROZELLE, PETE: BIRTH ANNIVERSARY. Mar 1, 1926. Alvin Ray ("Pete") Rozelle, Commissioner of the National Football League, born at South Gate, CA. Rozelle began his career in the public relations department of the Los Angeles Rams, became general manager and was elected commissioner in 1960. He built the NFL into a sporting power, uniting its development to television. He helped engineer the NFL's merger with the American Football League, created the Super Bowl as America's greatest sports extravaganza, conceived of the idea for Monday Night Football and persuaded NFL owners to accept revenue sharing. Died at Rancho Santa Fe, CA, Dec 6, 1996.

SHORE, DINAH: BIRTH ANNIVERSARY. Mar 1, 1917. Frances Rose ("Dinah") Shore, entertainer and honorary member of the LPGA Hall of Fame, born at Winchester, TN. Shore was a recording star in the 1930s and 1940s and one of the first women to be successful as a television host, beginning in the 1950s with the "Dinah Shore Chevy Show." In later life, she became enamored of golf and got seriously involved with the LPGA, including hosting a tournament bearing her name. Inducted into the Hall of Fame in 1994. Died at Beverly Hills, CA, Feb 24, 1994.

US SYNCHRONIZED SKATING CHAMPIONSHIPS. Mar 1–5. Plymouth Compuware Arena, Plymouth, MI. For info: Plymouth Compuware Arena, 14900 Beck Rd, Plymouth, MI 48170. Phone: (313) 459-6686.

WILKENS WINS 1,000th GAME: ANNIVERSARY. Mar 1, 1996. Lenny Wilkens became the first coach in professional basketball to win 1,000 games when his team, the Atlanta Hawks, defeated the Cleveland Cavaliers, 74–68.

March 2000	S	M	T	W	T	F	S
				1	2	3	4
	5	6	7	8	9	10	11
	12	13	14	15	16	17	18
	19	20	21	22	23	24	25
	26	27	28	29	30	31	

Omar Jose Cordaro Daal, 28, baseball player, born Maracaibo, Venezuela, Mar 1, 1972.

Ronald (Ron) Francis, 37, hockey player, born Sault Ste. Marie, Ontario, Canada, Mar 1, 1963.

Mayce Edward Christopher (Chris) Webber, III, 27, basketball player, born Detroit, MI, Mar 1, 1973.

MARCH 2 — THURSDAY
Day 62 — 304 Remaining

CHASE'S SPORTSQUOTE OF THE DAY

"He can speak ten languages, but he can't hit in any of them."—a teammate speaking of Moe Berg

BEE, CLAIR: BIRTH ANNIVERSARY. Mar 2, 1896. Clair Francis Bee, basketball player and Basketball Hall of Fame coach, born at Grafton, WV. Bee played basketball at several colleges but was much better known as one of the game's greatest innovators and promoters. He pioneered rules and strategy changes (including the three-second rule and the 1-3-1 zone defense) that helped make the sport a national attraction, and he also wrote the famous *Chip Hilton* stories for young people. Bee coached at Long Island University (1931–50), making the new school a power in the sport until the point-shaving scandals of the early 1950s. Many prominent coaches attended Bee's clinics and read his books. Inducted into the Hall of Fame in 1967. Died at Cleveland, OH, May 20, 1983.

BERG, MOE: BIRTH ANNIVERSARY. Mar 2, 1902. Morris (Moe) Berg, baseball player, born at New York, NY. Berg was a weak-hitting catcher more renowned for his intellect and linguistic abilities. He lived a secretive life and was long reputed to have been involved in espionage before and during World War II. Died at Belleville, NJ, May 29, 1972.

BIG 12 MEN'S SWIMMING AND DIVING CHAMPIONSHIPS. Mar 2–4. Texas A&M University, College Station, TX. For info: Big Twelve Conference, 2201 Stemmons Freeway, 28th Floor, Dallas, TX 75207. Phone: (214) 742-1212. Fax: (214) 742-2046.

BOBBY HULL GETS SECOND 50: ANNIVERSARY. Mar 2, 1966. Left wing Bobby Hull of the Chicago Blackhawks became the first NHL player to score 50 goals in a season twice when he scored his 50th goal of the 1965–66 season in a 5–4 win over the Detroit Red Wings.

COOPER, MORT: BIRTH ANNIVERSARY. Mar 2, 1914. Morton Cecil (Mort) Cooper, baseball player, born at Atherton, MO. Pitcher Mort and his brother, catcher Walker, formed a brother-brother battery for the St. Louis Cardinals. Mort won 22 games in 1942 and 1944 to lead the Cards to a pair of National League pennants and World Series titles. Died at Little Rock, AR, Nov 17, 1958.

ESPOSITO FIRST TO GET 100: ANNIVERSARY. Mar 2, 1969. Phil Esposito, center of the Boston Bruins, became the first player in National Hockey League history to score 100 points in a season when he scored a goal in Boston's 4–0 victory over the Pittsburgh Penguins.

KNOXVILLE BOAT SHOW. Mar 2–5. Knoxville Convention Center, Knoxville, TN. 17th annual show featuring more than 50,000 square feet of boats and 70 booths displaying scuba and marine equipment, water skis and much more. Est attendance: 14,000. For info: ESAU, Inc, PO Box 50096, Knoxville, TN 37950. Phone: (423) 588-1233 or (800) 588-ESAU. Fax: (423) 588-6938.

MILLER, DON: BIRTH ANNIVERSARY. Mar 2, 1902. Donald C. Miller, football player and coach, born at Defiance, OH. Miller, a halfback, was the only member of the famed Four Horsemen of Notre Dame to start every game over a three-year varsity career. After graduation, he played pro football and coached for a few years but devoted most of his life to a prominent legal career. Died at Cleveland, OH, July 28, 1979.

NAIA MEN'S AND WOMEN'S INDOOR TRACK AND FIELD CHAMPIONSHIPS. Mar 2–4. Devaney Sports Center, Lincoln, NE. Individuals compete for All-America honors while teams compete for the national championship. 35th men's and 20th women's annual competition. Est attendance: 2,500. For info: Natl Assn Intercollegiate Athletics, 6120 S Yale Ave, Ste 1450, Tulsa, OK 74136. Phone: (918) 494-8828. Fax: (918) 494-8841. E-mail: khenry@naia.org. Web: www.naia.org.

NORTH DAKOTA WINTER SHOW. Mar 2–12. Valley City, ND. 11-day agricultural expo featuring world's largest crop show, eight-breed cattle show, culinary arts show and competition, style and needlework show and competition, children's area, four-performance PRCA Rodeo, state team roping and penning championships, Draft horse pulls, Old-Time tractor pull (tractors built prior to 1955), 80 vendor farm toy show and single performance headliner country concert. Annually, beginning the first Thursday in March. Est attendance: 75,000. For info: Dale Hildebrant, Mgr, ND Winter Show, PO Box 846, Valley City, ND 58072. Phone: (701) 845-1401 or (800) 437-0218. Fax: (701) 845-3914. Web: www.fm-net.com/ndwintershow.

OTT, MEL: BIRTH ANNIVERSARY. Mar 2, 1909. Melvin Thomas (Mel) Ott, Baseball Hall of Fame outfielder, born at Gretna, LA. Playing for the New York Giants, Ott hit 511 home runs, 3rd on the all-time list when he retired and a National League record until Willie Mays surpassed it in 1966. Ott's swing was characterized by an unusual, high leg kick that helped him reach the short fences of the Polo Grounds for two-thirds of his homers. Inducted into the Hall of Fame in 1951. Died at New Orleans, LA, Nov 21, 1958.

PAC-10 MEN'S SWIMMING CHAMPIONSHIPS. Mar 2–4. Federal Way, WA. For info: PAC-10 Conference, 800 S Broadway, Ste 400, Walnut Creek, CA 94596. Phone: (510) 932-4411. Fax: (510) 932-4601.

WILT SCORES 100: ANNIVERSARY. Mar 2, 1962. Wilt Chamberlain poured in 100 points, an NBA record, as the Philadelphia Warriors defeated the New York Knicks, 169–147, at Hershey, PA. Chamberlain made 36 field goals and a record 28 foul shots and set yet another record by scoring 59 points in the second half.

Howard Albert ("Hopalong") Cassady, 66, Heisman Trophy halfback, born Columbus, OH, Mar 2, 1934.

Albert Louis (Al) Del Greco, Jr, 38, football player, born Providence, RI, Mar 2, 1962.

Ronald Edwin (Ron) Gant, 35, baseball player, born Victoria, TX, Mar 2, 1965.

Terry Lee Steinbach, 38, baseball player, born New Ulm, MN, Mar 2, 1962.

MARCH 3 — FRIDAY
Day 63 — 303 Remaining

ACC WOMEN'S BASKETBALL TOURNAMENT. Mar 3–6. Greensboro Coliseum, Greensboro, NC. For info: Atlantic Coast Conference, PO Drawer ACC, Greensboro, NC 27417-6724. Phone: (336) 854-8787. Fax: (336) 854-8797.

BELIVEAU GETS 1,000th POINT: ANNIVERSARY. Mar 3, 1968. Center Jean Beliveau of the Montreal Canadiens became the second player in the National Hockey League to accumulate 1,000 points. He scored a goal in a 5–2 loss to the Detroit Red Wings. Beliveau finished his career with 1,219 points.

BIG TEN WOMEN'S BASKETBALL TOURNAMENT. Mar 3–6. Conseco Fieldhouse, Indianapolis, IN. Big Ten Conference tournament for women's basketball. Winner of tournament receives automatic berth to NCAA Tournament. Est attendance: 18,000. For info: Big Ten Conference, 1500 W Higgins Rd, Park Ridge, IL 60068-6300. Phone: (847) 696-1010. Fax: (847) 696-1150. Web: www.bigten.org.

BILL MLKVY NETS 73: ANNIVERSARY. Mar 3, 1951. Bill Mlkvy of Temple University set an NCAA record by scoring 73 points in one game as Temple creamed Wilkes, 99–69.

BOROS, JULIUS: 80th BIRTH ANNIVERSARY. Mar 3, 1920. Julius Nicholas Boros, golfer, born at Fairfield, CT. Boros won the US Open in 1952 and 1963 and the PGA Championship in 1968. He had an easy, almost lazy swing that belied his ability to hit the ball hard and far. Died at Ft Lauderdale, FL, May 28, 1994.

BROWN WINS 800th GAME: ANNVERSARY. Mar 3, 1996. Larry Brown became the eighth coach in professional basketball to win 800 games when the Indiana Pacers defeated the Charlotte Hornets, 103–100.

CHALO NITKA. Mar 3–5. Moore Haven, FL. To promote Lake Okeechobee bass fishing and bring the Seminoles and the rest of the community together for a celebration. *Chalo Nitka* means "Day of the Big Bass" in the Seminole language. Annually, the first three-day weekend in March. Est attendance: 10,000. For info: Exec Dir, Glades County Chamber of Commerce, Box 490, Moore Haven, FL 33471. Phone: (941) 946-0440. Fax: (941) 946-2282.

KEELER, WEE WILLIE: BIRTH ANNIVERSARY. Mar 3, 1872. William Henry ("Wee Willie") Keeler, Baseball Hall of Fame outfielder, born at Brooklyn, NY. Despite his small stature, Keeler was one of the best hitters of all time. His 44-game hitting streak in 1897 is still the National League mark although it was later tied by Pete Rose. His aphorism, "Hit 'em where they ain't," is solid advice for all batters. Inducted into the Hall of Fame in 1939. Died at New York, NY, Jan 1, 1923.

LONGHORN WORLD CHAMPIONSHIP RODEO. Mar 3–5. Von Braun Civic Center, Huntsville, AL. More than 200 cowboys and cowgirls compete in six professional contests ranging from bronc riding to bull riding for top prize money and world championship points. Featuring colorful opening pageantry and Big, Bad BONUS Bulls. 21st annual. Est attendance: 16,000. For info: W. Bruce Lehrke, Pres, Longhorn World Chmpshp Rodeo, Inc, PO Box 70159, Nashville, TN 37207. Phone: (615) 876-1016. Fax: (615) 876-4685. E-mail: lhrodeo@idt.net. Web: www.longhornrodeo.com.

MISSOURI VALLEY CONFERENCE BASKETBALL TOURNAMENT. Mar 3–6. Kiel Center, St. Louis, MO. The MVC tournament returns to St. Louis for the 10th consecutive year with the winner earning an automatic berth in the NCAA tournament. Ten teams compete. For info: Missouri Valley Conf, 1000 St. Louis Union Station, Ste 105, St. Louis, MO 63103. Phone: (314) 421-0339. Fax: (314) 421-3505.

NCAA DIVISION III WRESTLING CHAMPIONSHIPS. Mar 3–4. Finals. Ohio Northern University, Ada, OH. For info: NCAA, PO Box 6222, Indianapolis, IN 46206-6222. Phone: (317) 917-6222. Fax: (317) 917-6888. Web: www.ncaa.org.

NJCAA MEN'S AND WOMEN'S INDOOR TRACK CHAMPIONSHIP. Mar 3–4. Manhattan, KS. For info: Cliff Rovelto, Kansas State Univ, Ahearn Fieldhouse, Manhattan, KS 66502-3308. Phone: (785) 532-6567. Fax: (785) 532-2340. Web: www.njcaa.org.

SHOEMAKER WINS $100 MILLION: 15th ANNIVERSARY. Mar 3, 1985. Willie Shoemaker became the first jockey to pass the $100 million mark in career earnings by riding Lord at War to victory in the Santa Anita Handicap.

SNOWFEST. Mar 3–12. North Lake Tahoe, CA and NV, and Truckee, CA. Snowfest is a fantastic vacation opportunity, showcasing America's largest concentration of skiing and outdoor recreation combined with the fun, sparkle and excitement of 10 full days of more than 100 special and unique events. Annually, beginning the Friday before the first Sunday in March. Est attendance: 100,000. For info: Festivals at Tahoe, PO Box 5, Crystal Bay, NV 89402. Phone: (775) 832-7625. Fax: (775) 832-2232.

UEBERROTH ELECTED COMMISSIONER: ANNIVERSARY. Mar 3, 1984. Major league baseball owners elected Peter V. Ueberroth, president of the Los Angeles Olympic Organizing Committee, to be Commissioner of Baseball to succeed Bowie Kuhn. Ueberroth assumed his duties after his responsibilities with the Olympics were finished, and he remained in office through Mar 31, 1989.

USA INDOOR TRACK & FIELD CHAMPIONSHIPS. Mar 3–4. Georgia Dome, Atlanta, GA. The US National Championships. Est attendance: 12,000. For info: Duffy Mahoney, Dir Op, USA Track & Field, PO Box 120, Indianapolis, IN 46225-0120. Phone: (317) 261-0500. Fax: (317) 261-0481. Web: www.usatf.org.

WARD, MONTE: 140th BIRTH ANNIVERSARY. Mar 3, 1860. John Montgomery (Monte) Ward, Baseball Hall of Fame infielder, born at Bellefonte, PA. Ward helped to organize the Brotherhood of Professional Base Ball Players, the original players' union that led to the creation of the Players League, a third major league that played only one season, 1890. Inducted into the Hall of Fame in 1964. Died at Augusta, GA, Mar 4, 1925.

WINTER CARNIVAL. Mar 3–4. Red Lodge, MT. Winter Carnival features parades, snow sculptures, King and Queen contest, Snow Ball, costume contest, Cardboard Classic Race (for which teams design crafts of cardboard for downhill race), live music and prizes. Torchlight parade and spaghetti dinner. Annually, the first weekend in March. Est attendance: 2,000. For info: Red Lodge Area Chamber of Commerce, PO Box 988, Red Lodge, MT 59068. Phone: (888) 281-0625. Fax: (406) 446-1718. E-mail: redlodge@wtp.net.

WINTER GAMES OF OREGON. Mar 3–5. Mt Hood, OR. Alpine and Nordic competition to be held at Timberline and Ski Bowl. For info: Oregon Amateur Sports Foundation, 4840 SW Western Ave, Ste 900, Beaverton, OR 97005. Phone: (503) 520-1319.

BIRTHDAYS TODAY

Jacqueline (Jackie) Joyner-Kersee, 38, Olympic gold medal heptathlete, born East St. Louis, IL, Mar 3, 1962.
Brian Joseph Leetch, 32, hockey player, born Corpus Christi, TX, Mar 3, 1968.

March 2000	S	M	T	W	T	F	S
				1	2	3	4
	5	6	7	8	9	10	11
	12	13	14	15	16	17	18
	19	20	21	22	23	24	25
	26	27	28	29	30	31	

Christopher John (C.J.) Nitkowski, 27, baseball player, born Suffern, NY, Mar 3, 1973.

Scott David Radinsky, 32, baseball player, born Glendale, CA, Mar 3, 1968.

Rick Alan Reed, 50, baseball umpire, born Detroit, MI, Mar 3, 1950.

Herschel Walker, Jr, 38, Heisman Trophy running back, born Wrightsville, GA, Mar 3, 1962.

MARCH 4 — SATURDAY
Day 64 — 302 Remaining

CHASE'S SPORTSQUOTE OF THE DAY

"When a pro hits it left to right, it's called a fade. When an amateur hits it left to right, it's called a slice."—Peter Jacobsen

ACC WRESTLING CHAMPIONSHIPS. Mar 4. University of Maryland, College Park, MD. For info: Atlantic Coast Conference, PO Drawer ACC, Greensboro, NC 27417-6724. Phone: (336) 854-8787. Fax: (336) 854-8797.

BIG EAST WOMEN'S BASKETBALL TOURNAMENT. Mar 4–7. University of Connecticut, Storrs, CT. For info: Big East Conference, 56 Exchange Terrace, Providence, RI 02903. Phone: (401) 272-9108. Fax: (401) 751-8540.

BIG TEN WRESTLING CHAMPIONSHIPS. Mar 4–5. Purdue University, West Lafayette, IN. For info: Big Ten Conference, 1500 W Higgins Rd, Park Ridge, IL 60068-6300. Phone: (847) 696-1010. Fax: (847) 696-1150. Web: www.bigten.org.

BIG 12 WRESTLING CHAMPIONSHIPS. Mar 4. University of Nebraska, Lincoln, NE. For info: Big Twelve Conference, 2201 Stemmons Freeway, 28th Floor, Dallas, TX 75207. Phone: (214) 742-1212. Fax: (214) 742-2046.

IDITAROD SLED DOG RACE. Mar 4. Anchorage to Nome, AK. The fabled 1,150-mile race with each sled drawn by 16 Northern Breed Dogs. For info: Iditarod Trail Committee, PO Box 870800, Wasilla, AK 99687. Phone: (907) 376-5155. Fax: (907) 373-6998. Web: www.iditarod.com.

JOHNSON, BOB: BIRTH ANNIVERSARY. Mar 4, 1931. Robert (Bob) Johnson, hockey player, coach and executive, born at Minneapolis, MN. Johnson played college hockey at the University of Minnesota and began coaching high school hockey in 1956. He moved to Colorado College in 1963 and to the University of Wisconsin in 1967. Johnson's Badgers won three NCAA titles. He coached four US National teams and the 1976 Olympic team. Johnson became head coach of the Calgary Flames in 1982 and led them to five straight Stanley Cup playoff appearances. He became executive director of the Amateur Hockey Association of the US in 1987 and coach of the Pittsburgh Penguins in 1990. They won the Stanley Cup a year later. Johnson was named coach of the US team for the 1991 Canada Cup, but surgery for a brain tumor prevented his participation. He was known throughout the hockey world for his favorite saying, "It's a good day for hockey." Died at Colorado Springs, CO, Nov 26, 1991.

LAFLEUR GETS 1,000th POINT: ANNIVERSARY. Mar 4, 1981. Forward Guy Lafleur of the Montreal Canadiens scored the 1,000th point of his National Hockey League career, a goal in a 9–3 victory over the Winnipeg Jets. Lafleur finished with 1,353 points.

NANTUCKET MARATHON. Mar 4. 11 AM start at Nantucket HS. Field limited to 500. Get application early. For info: Paul K. Daley, Nantucket Marathon, PO Box 401, Norton, MA 02766-0401. Phone: (508) 285-4544. E-mail: trghost@msn.com.

NEW ENGLAND SLED DOG RACES. Mar 4–5. Rangeley, ME. Unlimited eight-dog, six-dog, four-dog pro and junior classes race, 1–9 miles, depending on the size of the team. Annually, in March. Sponsor: New England Sled Dog Club. Est attendance: 500. For info: Gail Spaulding, Chamber of Commerce, PO Box 317, Rangeley, ME 04970. Phone: (207) 864-5364. E-mail: mtlakes@rangeley.org. Web: www.rangeleymaine.com.

O'DOUL, LEFTY: BIRTH ANNIVERSARY. Mar 4, 1897. Frank Joseph ("Lefty") O'Doul, baseball player, manager and executive, born at San Francisco, CA. O'Doul switched from pitching to the outfield and became one of the greatest players not in the Hall of Fame. His career batting average, .349, included hitting .398 in 1929 and .383 in 1930. After retiring, he helped to organize the major leagues in Japan. Died at San Francisco, Dec 7, 1969.

ROCKNE, KNUTE: BIRTH ANNIVERSARY. Mar 4, 1888. Knute Rockne, football coach, born at Voss, Norway. Rockne played end at the University of Notre Dame and then in 1918 was appointed head coach at his alma mater. Over 13 seasons, Rockne became a living legend, and Notre Dame football rose to a position of unprecedented prominence. His teams won 105 games (and three national championships) against only 12 losses and 5 ties. Rockne died in a plane crash at Bazaar, KS, Mar 31, 1931.

SOUTHEAST FLORIDA SCOTTISH FESTIVAL AND GAMES. Mar 4. Heritage Park, Plantation, FL. Est attendance: 8,000. For info: Scottish-American Soc of Southeast Florida, 5901 NE 21 Rd, Ft Lauderdale, FL 33308. Phone: (954) 776-5675. E-mail: mfcampbell@juno.com.

VANCE, DAZZY: BIRTH ANNIVERSARY. Mar 4, 1891. Arthur Charles ("Dazzy") Vance, Baseball Hall of Fame pitcher, born at Orient, IA. Vance "dazzled" opposing teams with his pitching prowess. He won 197 games over 16 years, mostly with inept Brooklyn Dodgers teams. Inducted into the Hall of Fame in 1955. Died at Homosassa Springs, FL, Feb 16, 1961.

BIRTHDAYS TODAY

Brian Scott Barber, 27, baseball player, born Hamilton, OH, Mar 4, 1973.

Thomas Alan (Tom) Grieve, 52, baseball executive and former player, born Pittsfield, MA, Mar 4, 1948.

Brian Ronald Hunter, 32, baseball player, born Torrance, CA, Mar 4, 1968.

Peter Erling Jacobsen, 46, golfer, born Portland, OR, Mar 4, 1954.

Kevin Maurice Johnson, 34, former basketball player, born Sacramento, CA, Mar 4, 1966.

Robert Scott Smith, 28, football player, born Euclid, OH, Mar 4, 1972.

MARCH 5 — SUNDAY
Day 65 — 301 Remaining

CHASE'S SPORTSQUOTE OF THE DAY

"He'll never be any good."—Baltimore Colts owner Robert Irsay on John Elway, whom Irsay traded to the Denver Broncos

AUTOGRAPH COLLECTING WEEK. Mar 5–11. Celebrating the fun of collecting autographs for love and money! Thousands of adults and children all over the world enjoy obtaining the signatures of the famous, infamous and nearly-famous and almost everyone has at least one special autograph tucked away somewhere. This week honors a hobby which can be started with little or no money and allows the hobbyist of any age to build an exciting and valuable collection. For a free brochure about how to get started in autograph collecting, send a SASE to the address below. ATTN: Autographs. For info: Cathy Stucker, On-Line Autograph Collectors Club, 4646 Hwy 6, Ste 123, Sugar Land, TX 77478. Phone: (281) 265-7342. Fax: (281) 265-9727. E-mail: cathy@idea lady.com. Web: www.idealady.com.

BOWLER ROLLS TWO PERFECT GAMES: ANNIVERSARY. Mar 5, 1924. Frank Carauna of Buffalo, NY, became the first bowler in history to roll two consecutive 300 games.

CHRISTMAN, PAUL: BIRTH ANNIVERSARY. Mar 5, 1918. Paul Joseph Christman, football player and broadcaster, born at St. Louis, MO. Christman played football at the University of Missouri under Coach Don Faurot. He excelled at quarterback and defensive halfback and led the Tigers to the 1939 Orange Bowl. Following military service during World War II, he played for the Chicago Cardinals, leading them to the NFL championship in 1947. In the 1960s, he was a color commentator on college football telecasts. Died at Lake Forest, IL, Mar 2, 1970.

CITY OF LOS ANGELES MARATHON. Mar 5. Los Angeles, CA. A multicultural athletic competition designed to foster community spirit as well as pride in one's physical well-being. Family Reunion Festival held in conjunction with marathon. Est attendance: 35,000. For info: Mike Gerlowski or John Wilson, Los Angeles Marathon, 11110 W Ohio Ave, Ste 100, Los Angeles, CA 90025. Phone: (310) 444-5544. Web: www.lamarathon.com.

March 2000	S	M	T	W	T	F	S
				1	2	3	4
	5	6	7	8	9	10	11
	12	13	14	15	16	17	18
	19	20	21	22	23	24	25
	26	27	28	29	30	31	

FIRST INTERCOLLEGIATE TRACK MEET: ANNIVERSARY. Mar 5, 1864. Track teams from two different universities, Oxford and Cambridge, met for the first time in an athletics match at Christ Church Ground, Oxford. The teams contested eight events with each school winning four.

GERMANY: WORLD JUNIOR FIGURE SKATING CHAMPIONSHIPS. Mar 5–12. Oberstdorf, Germany. For info: Media Relations, US Figure Skating Assn, 20 First St, Colorado Springs, CO 80906. Phone: (719) 635-5200. Fax: (719) 635-9548. E-mail: usfsa1@aol.com. Web: www.usfsa.org/events.

IRSAY, ROBERT: BIRTH ANNIVERSARY. Mar 5, 1923. Robert Irsay, football executive, born at Chicago, IL. After making his fortune in heating and air conditioning, Irsay bought the Los Angeles Rams in 1972 and soon thereafter traded the entire franchise for the Baltimore Colts. In one of the most infamous moves in American sport, the Colts slipped out of town in the middle of the night in 1984 and relocated at Indianapolis. Died at Indianapolis, IN, Jan 14, 1997.

NCAA MEN'S AND WOMEN'S DIVISION II INDOOR TRACK AND FIELD CHAMPIONSHIPS. Mar 5–6. Finals. Site TBA. For info: NCAA, PO Box 6222, Indianapolis, IN 46206-6222. Phone: (317) 917-6222. Fax: (317) 917-6888. Web: www.ncaa.org.

SEC WOMEN'S BASKETBALL TOURNAMENT. Mar 5–5. Chattanooga, TN. For info: Southeastern Conference, 2201 Civic Center Blvd, Birmingham, AL 35203-1103. Phone: (205) 458-3010. Fax: (205) 458-3030. E-mail: twilson@sec.org. Web: www.secsports.com.

"SEZ WHO?" FOURPLAY! MARCH(INETTI'S) MADNESS. Mar 5–27. Marchinetti's Restaurant, Winfield, IL. Two-player man-and-woman teams compete against one another, trying to complete humorous, provocative and otherwise memorable quotes made by basketball personalities. Annually, from the Sunday in March when NCAA Tournament field is announced through Monday, 22 days later, when the championship game is played. Est attendance: 250. For info: Rich Bysina, 853 Lorlyn Dr, #3D, W Chicago, IL 60185. Phone: (630) 876-9615.

SUTTER HOME NAPA VALLEY MARATHON. Mar 5. Calistoga, CA. 22nd annual. Est attendance: 2,000. For info: Dave Hill, PO Box 4307, Napa, CA 94558-0430. Phone: (707) 255-2609. E-mail: dahnkk@napanet.net.

BIRTHDAYS TODAY

Bryan Berard, 23, hockey player, born Woonsocket, RI, Mar 5, 1977.
Robert Patrick ("Rocky") Bleier, 54, former football player, born Appleton, WI, Mar 5, 1946.
Jeffrey Bryan Hammonds, 29, baseball player, born Plainfield, NJ, Mar 5, 1971.
Michael Jerome Irvin, 34, football player, born Ft Lauderdale, FL, Mar 5, 1966.
Paul Henry Konerko, 24, baseball player, born Providence, RI, Mar 5, 1976.
Roman Zubinsky Phifer, 32, football player, born Plattsburgh, NY, Mar 5, 1968.
Shjon Podein, 32, hockey player, born Rochester, MN, Mar 5, 1968.
Frederick Robert (Fred) Williamson, 62, former broadcaster and football player, born Gary, IN, Mar 5, 1938.

MARCH 6 — MONDAY
Day 66 — 300 Remaining

CLAY BECOMES ALI: ANNIVERSARY. Mar 6, 1964. Heavyweight champion Cassius Marcellus Clay announced that he had embraced the Nation of Islam and changed his name to Muhammad Ali. As Clay, he had won a gold medal in the 1960 Summer Olympic Games in Rome and captured the heavyweight crown with a stunning TKO of Sonny Liston at Miami Beach on Feb 25, 1964.

CONZELMAN, JIMMY: BIRTH ANNIVERSARY. Mar 6, 1898. James G. (Jimmy) Conzelman, Pro Football Hall of Fame player and coach, born at St. Louis, MO. Conzelman played at Washington University, St. Louis and at the Great Lakes Naval Training Station. He played for several pro teams in the 1920s and coached at his alma mater from 1934 to 1939. Returning to the pros in 1940 with the Chicago Cardinals, Conzelman coached them to the 1947 NFL title. Inducted into the Hall of Fame in 1964. Died at St. Louis, July 31, 1970.

FIRST WOMEN'S COLLEGIATE BASKETBALL GAME: ANNIVERSARY. Mar 6, 1892. The first women's collegiate basketball game was played at Smith College at Northampton, MA. Senda Berenson, then Smith's director of physical education and "mother of women's basketball," supervised the game, in which Smith's sophomore team beat the freshman team, 5–4.

GROVE, LEFTY: 100th BIRTH ANNIVERSARY. Mar 6, 1900. Robert Moses ("Lefty") Grove, Baseball Hall of Fame pitcher, born at Lonaconing, MD. Grove is generally considered one of the best left-handed pitchers of all time. He won 300 games even though he did not pitch in the major leagues until he was 25. Inducted into the Hall of Fame in 1947. Died at Norwalk, OH, May 22, 1975.

HAMILL WINS WORLD TITLE: ANNIVERSARY. Mar 6, 1976. Dorothy Hamill of the US completed women's figure skating celebrated double triumph by adding first place in the World's Championship, contested at Goteberg, Sweden, to the Olympic gold medal she won in February at Innsbruck, Austria.

KRONE SETS FEMALE JOCKEY RECORD: ANNIVERSARY. Mar 6, 1988. Julie Krone won the 1,205th victory of her career, thereby becoming the all-time winningest female jockey in history. Krone rode Squawter, a filly, to victory in the ninth race at Aqueduct Racetrack.

LARDNER, RING: 115th BIRTH ANNIVERSARY. Mar 6, 1885. Ringgold Wilmer (Ring) Lardner, sportswriter, born at Niles, MI. Lardner wrote about sports for a variety of newspapers, mostly in Chicago. In both his columns and his short stories, he reproduced ballplayers' vernacular speech patterns with great success, thereby laying the groundwork for generations of baseball fiction to come. Lardner abandoned baseball after the Black Sox scandal was exposed. He wrote songs, plays and magazine articles but never the novel that some of his friends thought he should. Taciturn and solemn with a biting sense of humor, Lardner drank and smoked to excess, even after contracting tuberculosis in 1926. Given the J.G. Taylor Spink Award in 1963. Died at East Hampton, NY, Sept 25, 1933.

OSGOOD SCORES GOAL: ANNIVERSARY. Mar 6, 1996. Chris Osgood of the Detroit Red Wings became the second goalie in NHL history to score a goal. He fired the puck into an empty net with 11 seconds remaining as Detroit beat the Hartford Whalers, 4–2.

SHAUGHNESSY, CLARK: BIRTH ANNIVERSARY. Mar 6, 1892. Clark Daniel Shaughnessy, football player and coach, born at St. Cloud, MN. After playing football at the University of Minnesota, Shaughnessy strung together a coaching career at several institutions: Tulane, Loyola of the South, Chicago, Stanford, Maryland and Pittsburgh. He coached the Los Angeles Rams and assisted George Halas with the Chicago Bears. Shaughnessy is known as the father of the modern T formation and played a key role in developing modern pro defensive football. Died at Santa Monica, CA, May 15, 1970.

USFL OPENS FIRST SEASON: ANNIVERSARY. Mar 6, 1983. The United States Football League opened its first season of play with five games. The USFL was designed to avoid competing with the NFL by playing in the spring, but it lasted only three years.

BIRTHDAYS TODAY

Peter (Pete) Gray (born Peter J. Wyshner), 85, former baseball player, born Nanticoke, PA, Mar 6, 1915.

Shaquille Rashaun O'Neal, 28, basketball player, born Newark, NJ, Mar 6, 1972.

Gregory Donovan (Greg) Ostertag, 27, basketball player, born Dallas, TX, Mar 6, 1973.

Wilver Dornel (Willie) Stargell, 60, Baseball Hall of Fame outfielder and first baseman, born Earlsboro, OK, Mar 6, 1940.

☆   ☆   ☆

MARCH 7 — TUESDAY
Day 67 — 299 Remaining

BIG 12 WOMEN'S BASKETBALL TOURNAMENT. Mar 7–11. Municipal Auditorium, Kansas City, MO. For info: Big Twelve Conference, 2201 Stemmons Freeway, 28th Floor, Dallas, TX 75207. Phone: (214) 742-1212. Fax: (214) 742-2046.

MAHRE WINS THIRD WORLD CUP: ANNIVERSARY. Mar 7, 1983. Skier Phil Mahre became the third man and the first American to win three overall Alpine World Cup championships in succession.

McDONALD GETS 1,000th POINT: ANNIVERSARY. Mar 7, 1989. Right wing Lanny McDonald of the Calgary Flames got the 1,000th point of his National Hockey League career, a goal in a 9–5 win over the Winnipeg Jets. McDonald finished his career with 1,006 points.

NAVIN, FRANK: BIRTH ANNIVERSARY. Mar 7, 1871. Frank Navin, baseball executive, born at Adrian, MI. Navin rose from an accountant's position with the Detroit Tigers to club ownership. He sold out gradually to Walter Briggs during the Great Depression. Died at Detroit, MI, Nov 13, 1935.

SHROVETIDE PANCAKE RACE. Mar 7. Olney, Buckinghamshire, England and Liberal, Kansas. The pancake race at Olney has been run since 1445. Competitors must be women over 16 years of age, wearing traditional housewife's costume, including apron and headcovering. With a toss and flip of the pancake on the griddle that each must carry, the women dash from marketplace to the parish church, where the winner receives a kiss from the ringer of the Pancake Bell. Shriving service follows. Starting time for the race is usually 11:45 AM. Annually, on Shrove Tuesday.

SOVIETS WIN WORLD HOCKEY CHAMPIONSHIP: ANNIVERSARY. Mar 7, 1954. The Soviet Union entered international ice hockey competition for the first time and came away with the world championship. The Soviets defeated Canada in the gold medal game, 7–2, played at Stockholm, Sweden.

12-FOOT BASKET EXPERIMENT: ANNIVERSARY. Mar 7, 1954. The Minneapolis Lakers defeated the Milwaukee Hawks, 65–63, in an NBA game for which the baskets were raised as an experiment from 10' to 12'.

BIRTHDAYS TODAY

Stephen Taylor (Steve) Beuerlein, 35, football player, born Hollywood, CA, Mar 7, 1965.

Jeffrey Alan (Jeff) Burroughs, 49, former baseball player, born Long Beach, CA, Mar 7, 1951.

Terry Carkner, 34, hockey player, born Smith Falls, Ontario, Canada, Mar 7, 1966.

Samuel Lee Gash, Jr, 31, football player, born Hendersonville, NC, Mar 7, 1969.

Janet Guthrie, 62, former auto racer, born Iowa City, IA, Mar 7, 1938.

Franco Harris, 50, Pro Football Hall of Fame running back, born Ft Dix, NJ, Mar 7, 1950.

Jeffrey Franklin (Jeff) Kent, 32, baseball player, born Bellflower, CA, Mar 7, 1968.

Ivan Lendl, 40, former tennis player, born Ostrava, Czechoslovakia, Mar 7, 1960.

Lynn Curtis Swann, 48, broadcaster and former football player, born Alcoa, TN, Mar 7, 1952.

MARCH 8 — WEDNESDAY
Day 68 — 298 Remaining

CHASE'S SPORTSQUOTE OF THE DAY

"I treat my horses better than the owners treat us."—Dick Allen

BIG EAST MEN'S BASKETBALL TOURNAMENT. Mar 8–11. Madison Square Garden, New York, NY. For info: Big East Conference, 56 Exchange Terrace, Providence, RI 02903. Phone: (401) 272-9108. Fax: (401) 751-8540.

DAYTONA INTERNATIONAL MOTORCYCLE SHOW. Mar 8–12. Daytona International Speedway, Daytona Beach, FL. Est attendance: 40,000. For info: Advanstar Communications, 201 E Sandpointe Ave, Ste 600, Santa Ana, CA 92707-5761. Phone: (800) 854-3112 or (714) 513-8400. Fax: (714) 513-8481. Web: www.motorcycleshows.com.

March	S	M	T	W	T	F	S
2000				1	2	3	4
	5	6	7	8	9	10	11
	12	13	14	15	16	17	18
	19	20	21	22	23	24	25
	26	27	28	29	30	31	

FRAZIER DECISIONS ALI: ANNIVERSARY. Mar 8, 1971. Joe Frazier won a 15-round unanimous decision over Muhammad Ali at New York's Madison Square Garden to become the heavyweight champion of the world.

HAWERCHUK GETS 1,000th POINT: ANNIVERSARY. Mar 8, 1991. Center Dale Hawerchuk of the Buffalo Sabres got the 1,000th point of his National Hockey League career, a goal in a 5–3 loss to the Chicago Blackhawks. Hawerchuk finished his career with 1,409 points.

LARMER GETS 1,000th POINT: 5th ANNIVERSARY. Mar 8, 1995. Right wing Steve Larmer of the New York Rangers got the 1,000th point of his National Hockey League career, an assist in a 6–4 win over the New Jersey Devils. Larmer finished his career with 1,012 points.

MARTINA PASSES $10 MILLION MARK: ANNIVERSARY. Mar 8, 1986. Martina Navratilova became the first woman tennis player to pass the $10 million mark in career earnings. She also set the single year record, $2,173,556, in 1984.

MOUNTAIN WEST MEN'S AND WOMEN'S BASKETBALL CHAMPIONSHIPS. Mar 8–11. UNLV, Las Vegas, NV. For info: Mountain West Conference, PO Box 35670, Colorado Springs, CO 80935-3567. Phone: (719) 533-9500. Fax: (719) 533-9512.

NAIA MEN'S DIVISION II BASKETBALL CHAMPIONSHIP TOURNAMENT. Mar 8–14. College of the Ozarks, Point Lookout, MO. 32-team field competes for the national championship. 9th annual. Est attendance: 30,000. For info: Natl Assn of Intercollegiate Athletics, 6120 S Yale Ave, Ste 1450, Tulsa, OK 74136. Phone: (918) 494-8828. Fax: (918) 494-8841. E-mail: khenry@naia.org. Web: www.naia.org.

NAIA WOMEN'S DIVISION II BASKETBALL CHAMPIONSHIP TOURNAMENT. Mar 8–14. Sioux City Auditorium, Sioux City, IA. 32-team field competes for the national championship. 9th annual. Est attendance: 12,500. For info: Natl Assn of Intercollegiate Athletics, 6120 S Yale Ave, Ste 1450, Tulsa, OK 74136. Phone: (918) 494-8828. Fax: (918) 494-8841. E-mail: khenry@naia.org. Web: www.naia.org.

NBA DOUBLEHEADER: ANNIVERSARY. Mar 8, 1954. The Milwaukee Hawks and the Baltimore Bullets played the only two-team doubleheader in NBA history. The Hawks won both games, 64–54 and 65–54.

NCAA MEN'S AND WOMEN'S DIVISION II SWIMMING AND DIVING CHAMPIONSHIPS. Mar 8–11. Finals. Flickinger Aquatic Center, Buffalo, NY. For info: NCAA, PO Box 6222, Indianapolis, IN 46206-6222. Phone: (317) 917-6222. Fax: (317) 917-6888. Web: www.ncaa.org.

NCAA MEN'S AND WOMEN'S SKIING CHAMPIONSHIPS. Mar 8–11. Park City, UT. For info: NCAA, PO Box 6222, Indianapolis, IN 46206-6222. Phone: (317) 917-6222. Fax: (317) 917-6888. Web: www.ncaa.org.

PALM BEACH FINALE. Mar 8–12. Palm Beach Polo Equestrian Club, Wellington, FL. The seventh event in the 2000 Cosequin Winter Equestrian Festival. For info: Stadium Jumping, Inc, 3104 Cherry Palm Dr, Ste 220, Tampa, FL 33619. Phone: (800) 237-8924 or (813) 623-5801. Fax: (813) 626-5369. Web: www.stadiumjumping.com.

SIX-YEAR-OLD MAKES HOLE-IN-ONE: ANNIVERSARY. Mar 8, 1968. Tommy Moore, 6 years old, made a hole-in-one at the Woodbrier Golf Course at Hagerstown, MD.

BIRTHDAYS TODAY

Richard Anthony (Dick) Allen, 58, former baseball player, born Wampum, PA, Mar 8, 1942.

James Alan (Jim) Bouton, 61, author (*Ball Four*) and former baseball player, born Newark, NJ, Mar 8, 1939.

Brent Fedyk, 33, hockey player, born Yorkton, Saskatchewan, Canada, Mar 8, 1967.

James Edward (Jim) Rice, 47, former baseball player, born Anderson, SC, Mar 8, 1953.

Charles Linwood ("Buck") Williams, 40, basketball player, born Rocky Mount, NC, Mar 8, 1960.

MARCH 9 — THURSDAY
Day 69 — 297 Remaining

ACC MEN'S BASKETBALL TOURNAMENT. Mar 9–12. Charlotte Coliseum, Charlotte, NC. For info: Atlantic Coast Conference, PO Drawer ACC, Greensboro, NC 27417-6724. Phone: (336) 854-8787. Fax: (336) 854-8797.

BIG TEN MEN'S BASKETBALL TOURNAMENT. Mar 9–12. United Center, Chicago, IL. For info: Big Ten Conference, 1500 W Higgins Rd, Park Ridge, IL 60068-6300. Phone: (847) 696-1010. Fax: (847) 696-1150. Web: www.bigten.org.

BIG 12 MEN'S BASKETBALL TOURNAMENT. Mar 9–12. Kemper Arena, Kansas City, MO. For info: Big Twelve Conference, 2201 Stemmons Freeway, 28th Floor, Dallas, TX 75207. Phone: (214) 742-1212. Fax: (214) 742-2046.

CANADA: EDMONTON'S BOAT & SPORTSMEN'S SHOW. Mar 9–12. Northlands, Agricom, Edmonton, Alberta. Fishing, sailing and powerboats, hunting, fishing and camping supplies, resort destinations, outdoor recreation, outdoor groups, RVs and motorhomes, sport utility vehicles, mountain bikes and family entertainment. Est attendance: 35,000. For info: Val Nogas, Mgr, Public Relations, Canadian Natl Sportsmen's Shows, 703 Evans Ave, Ste 202, Toronto, ON, Canada M9C 5E9. Phone: (416) 695-0311. Fax: (416) 695-0381. Web: www.sportsmensshows.com.

CANADA: QUEBEC CITY SPORTSMEN'S SHOW (SALON CAMPING, PLEIN AIR, CHASSE ET PECHE). Mar 9–12. Centre de Foires, Quebec City, Quebec. Major manufacturers, distributors and retailers of the outdoors, including camping, fishing, hunting and archery; fishing boats, canoes, kayaks and other crafts, tourism, outfitters, lodges and entertainment. For info: Val Nogas, Mgr, Public Relations, Canadian Natl Sportsmen's Shows, 703 Evans Ave, Ste 202, Toronto, ON, Canada M9C 5E9. Phone: (416) 695-0311. Fax: (416) 695-0381. Web: www.sportsmensshows.com.

CICCARELLI GETS 1,000th POINT: ANNIVERSARY. Mar 9, 1994. Right wing Dino Ciccarelli of the Detroit Red Wings got the 1,000th point of his National Hockey League career, a goal in a 5–1 win over the Calgary Flames.

ENGLAND: CRUFTS DOG SHOW. Mar 9–12. National Exhibition Centre, Birmingham, West Midlands. The world's greatest dog show in which more than 18,000 top pedigree dogs compete for the Best in Show title, the most prestigious award in the world of dogs. Est attendance: 110,000. For info: Crufts Office, The Kennel Club, 1 Clarges St, London, England W1Y 8AB. Phone: (44) (171) 493-7838. Fax: (44) (171) 518-1028. For ticket info: (44) (171) 518-1012. Web: www.crufts.org.uk.

JENSEN, JACKIE: BIRTH ANNIVERSARY. Mar 9, 1927. Jack Eugene (Jackie) Jensen, baseball player, born at San Francisco, CA. Jensen was an All-American at the University of California in both baseball and football. He starred in the outfield for the Boston Red Sox in the 1950s but retired prematurely, in part because of his fear of flying. Died at Charlottesville, VA, July 14, 1982.

NCAA MEN'S DIVISION II BASKETBALL TOURNAMENT. Mar 9–12. Regionals at sites TBA. For info: NCAA, PO Box 6222, Indianapolis, IN 46206-6222. Phone: (317) 917-6222. Fax: (317) 917-6888. Web: www.ncaa.org.

NCAA MEN'S AND WOMEN'S RIFLE CHAMPIONSHIPS. Mar 9–11. Virginia Military Institute, Lexington, VA. For info: NCAA, PO Box 6222, Indianapolis, IN 46206-6222. Phone: (317) 917-6222. Fax: (317) 917-6888. Web: www.ncaa.org.

NCAA WOMEN'S DIVISION III SWIMMING AND DIVING CHAMPIONSHIPS. Mar 9–11. Finals. Emory University, Atlanta, GA. For info: NCAA, PO Box 6222, Indianapolis, IN 46206-6222. Phone: (317) 917-6222. Fax: (317) 917-6888. Web: www.ncaa.org.

NCAA WOMEN'S DIVISION II BASKETBALL TOURNAMENT. Mar 9–12. Regionals at campus sites TBA. For info: NCAA, PO Box 6222, Indianapolis, IN 46206-6222. Phone: (317) 917-6222. Fax: (317) 917-6888. Web: www.ncaa.org.

NJCAA DIVISION III MEN'S BASKETBALL CHAMPIONSHIP. Mar 9–11. Delhi, NY. For info: Richard Coleman, Tourn Dir, SUNY at Delhi, Delhi, NY 13753-1190. Phone: (607) 746-4211. Fax: (607) 746-4119. Web: www.njcaa.org.

NJCAA DIVISION III WOMEN'S BASKETBALL CHAMPIONSHIP. Mar 9–11. Corning, NY. For info: Neil Bulkley, Tourn Dir, Corning Community College, One Academic Dr, Corning, NY 14830-3297. Phone: (607) 962-9399. Fax: (607) 962-9401. Web: www.njcaa.org.

NJCAA MEN'S AND WOMEN'S INVITATIONAL BOWLING CHAMPIONSHIP. Mar 9–11. Buffalo, NY. For info: Ralph Galanti, Tourn Dir, Eire Community College, 21 Oak St, Buffalo, NY 14203. Phone: (716) 851-1220. Fax: (716) 851-1219. Web: www.njcaa.org.

PERREAULT SCORES 500th GOAL: ANNIVERSARY. Mar 9, 1986. Center Gilbert Perreault of the Buffalo Sabres became the 12th player in the National Hockey League to score 500 regular-season goals. He tallied against goalie Alain Chevrier of the New Jersey Devils in a 4–3 win. Perreault finished his career with 512 goals and was inducted into the Hockey Hall of Fame in 1990.

SEC MEN'S BASKETBALL TOURNAMENT. Mar 9–12. Atlanta, GA. For info: Southeastern Conference, 2201 Civic Center Blvd, Birmingham, AL 35203-1103. Phone: (205) 458-3010. Fax: (205) 458-3030. E-mail: srodgers @sec.org. Web: www.secsports.com.

VAUGHAN, ARKY: BIRTH ANNIVERSARY. Mar 9, 1912. Joseph Floyd ("Arky") Vaughan, Baseball Hall of Fame shortstop, born at Clifty, AR. Vaughan was the Pittsburgh Pirates' regular shortstop during the 1930s. He won the National League MVP award in 1935 and finished his career with the Brooklyn Dodgers. Inducted into the Hall of Fame in 1985. Died at Eagleville, CA, Aug 30, 1952.

WILLIAMS, LEFTY: BIRTH ANNIVERSARY. Mar 9, 1893. Claude Preston ("Lefty") Williams, baseball player, born at Aurora, MO. Williams was one of two Chicago White Sox pitchers accused of conspiring to throw the 1919 World Series. He and seven teammates were banned for life. Died at Laguna Beach, CA, Nov 4, 1959.

YARDLEY SCORES 2,000: ANNIVERSARY. Mar 9, 1958. Forward George Yardley of the Detroit Pistons became the first NBA player to score 2,000 points in a season.

BIRTHDAYS TODAY

Mahmoud Abdul-Rauf (born Chris Wayne Jackson), 31, basketball player, born Gulfport, MS, Mar 9, 1969.

Paul Caliguiri, 36, soccer player, born Westminster, CA, Mar 9, 1964.

Dagoberto (Bert) Campaneris, 58, former baseball player, born Pueblo Nuevo, Cuba, Mar 9, 1942.

James Joseph (Jim) Colbert, 59, golfer, born Elizabeth, NJ, Mar 9, 1941.

Radek Dvorak, 23, hockey player, born Ceske Budejovice, Czechoslovakia, Mar 9, 1977.

Robert James (Bobby) Fischer, 57, former chess player, born Chicago, IL, Mar 9, 1943.

Adonal David Foyle, 25, basketball player, born Island of Canovan, Grenadines, Mar 9, 1975.

Phil Housley, 36, hockey player, born St. Paul, MN, Mar 9, 1964.

Terence John (Terry) Mulholland, 37, baseball player, born Uniontown, PA, Mar 9, 1963.

Benito Santiago, 35, baseball player, born Ponce, Puerto Rico, Mar 9, 1965.

MARCH 10 — FRIDAY

Day 70 — 296 Remaining

CHASE'S SPORTSQUOTE OF THE DAY

"Sports do not build character. They reveal it."—Heywood Hale Broun

ABRAMSON, JESSE: BIRTH ANNIVERSARY. Mar 10, 1904. Jesse Peter Abramson, sportswriter, born at Mountaindale, NY. One of the most knowledgeable reporters on track and field, Abramson covered every Summer Olympic Games from 1928 through 1976. His remarkable memory and concern for detail earned him the nickname, "The Book." Died at Mount Vernon, NY, June 11, 1979.

AMA NATIONAL HOT-SHOE DIRT TRACK RACE. Mar 10. Daytona Beach Municipal Stadium, Daytona Beach, FL. 10th annual. For info: John Story, Dir of Public Relations, Daytona Intl Speedway, PO Box 2801, Daytona Beach, FL 32120-2801. Phone: (904) 947-6782. For tickets: (904) 253-RACE (7223). Fax: (904) 947-6791. Web: www.daytonausa.com.

AMERICAN CROSSWORD PUZZLE TOURNAMENT AND CONVENTION. Mar 10–12. Stamford Marriott Hotel, Stamford, CT. 300 solvers from the US and Canada compete on eight puzzles during this 23rd annual event. Points are awarded for accuracy and speed. The final puzzle is played on giant white boards for everyone to watch. Prizes are awarded in 21 skill, age and geographical categories and the grand prize is $1,000. The weekend also includes group word games, guest speakers and appearances by celebrity crossword solvers. Solvers can compete at home for fun, either by mail or online, and receive a ranking in all their solving categories. Est attendance: 350. For info: Will Shortz, Dir, American Crossword Puzzle Tournament, 55 Great Oak Ln, Pleasantville, NY 10570. Phone: (732) 247-9848. Fax: (732) 247-9848. Web: www.crosswordtournament.com.

CANADA: TORONTO SPORTSMEN'S SHOW. Mar 10–19. National Trade Centre, Exhibition Place, Toronto, Ontario. Canada's oldest and largest sportsmen's show. Fishing manufacturers, retailers and seminars, travel/vacation/outfitter exhibits, camping products, boats and marine accessories, wildlife art, pet products and breeders, conservation, outdoor adventure equipment, outdoor organizations, sporting goods, clothing, indoor retrieval trials, arena show and family entertainment. Est attendance: 175,000. For info: Harley Austin, Show Mgr, Canadian Natl Sportsmen's Shows, 703 Evans Ave, Ste 202, Toronto, ON, Canada M9C 5E9. Phone: (416) 695-0311. Fax: (416) 695-0381. Web: www.sportsmensshows.com.

DRYDEN, CHARLIE: 140th BIRTH ANNIVERSARY. Mar 10, 1860. Charles (Charlie) Dryden, sportswriter, born at Monmouth, NH. Working for newspapers at Chicago and New York, Dryden wrote about sports with a sense of humor and gained fame for bestowing nicknames upon teams and players. He called the 1906 Chicago White Sox "The Hitless Wonders," White Sox owner Charles Comiskey "The Old Roman" and Chicago Cubs manager Frank Chance "The Peerless Leader." His most famous phrase captured the futility of the Washington Senators: "First in war, first in peace and last in the American League." Given the J.G. Taylor Spink Award in 1965. Died at Biloxi, MS, Feb 11, 1931.

FARR, HEATHER: 35th BIRTH ANNIVERSARY. Mar 10, 1965. Heather Farr, golfer, born at Phoenix, AZ. Farr was an outstanding amateur golfer and a promising member of the LPGA tour when she was stricken with breast cancer in 1988. Radical treatment allowed her to fight the disease with great courage for five years without losing her spirit or sense of humor. In Farr's honor, the LGPA annually presents the Heather Farr Player Award to the golfer, "who, through her hard work, dedication, and love of the game of golf, has demonstrated determination, perseverance, and spirit in fulfilling her goals as a player." Died Nov 20, 1993.

FLORIDA WILDLIFE AND WESTERN ART EXPO. Mar 10–12. The Lakeland Center, Lakeland, FL. Featuring more than 200 of the nation's finest wildlife artists, wood sculptors, conservation groups and live wildlife exhibits. Est attendance: 9,600. For info: Michael E. Kessler, Pres, Florida Wildlife Exposition Inc, PO Box 15693, Sarasota, FL 34277. Phone: (941) 364-9453. Fax: (941) 364-9453.

GIANTS HIRE WOMAN PA VOICE: ANNIVERSARY. Mar 10, 1993. The San Francisco Giants made baseball history by hiring Sherry Davis to be the team's public address announcer. Davis, a legal secretary, became the first woman PA voice in the major leagues after having done voice-over work since 1981.

GOLDENBERG, BUCKETS: BIRTH ANNIVERSARY. Mar 10, 1911. Charles R. ("Buckets") Goldenberg, football player, wrestler and restaurateur, born at Odessa, Russia. Goldenberg's family came to Milwaukee when he was four. He played football at the University of Wisconsin and for the Green Bay Packers, excelling as an offensive and defensive lineman. He wrestled in the off-season and entered the restaurant business when he tired of traveling. Died at Greendale, WI, Apr 16, 1986.

	S	M	T	W	T	F	S
March				1	2	3	4
2000	5	6	7	8	9	10	11
	12	13	14	15	16	17	18
	19	20	21	22	23	24	25
	26	27	28	29	30	31	

JACOBS, MIKE: 120th BIRTH ANNIVERSARY. Mar 10, 1880. Michael Strauss (Mike) Jacobs, sports promoter, born at New York, NY. Jacobs promoted boxing matches at Madison Square Garden and other venues, eventually exerting nearly monopolistic control over the sport at New York City. He signed the young Joe Louis and promoted all his fights, thereby opening up boxing to full integration. Died at Miami Beach, FL, Jan 24, 1953.

LONGHORN WORLD CHAMPIONSHIP RODEO. Mar 10–12. BI-LO Center, Greenville, SC. More than 200 cowboys and cowgirls compete in six professional contests ranging from bronc riding to bull riding for top prize money and world championship points. Featuring colorful opening pageantry and Big, Bad BONUS Bulls. 28th annual. Est attendance: 24,000. For info: W. Bruce Lehrke, Pres., Longhorn World Championship Rodeo, Inc, PO Box 70159, Nashville, TN 37207. Phone: (615) 876-1016. Fax: (615) 876-4685. E-mail: lhrodeo@idt.net. Web: www.longhornrodeo.com.

***MILWAUKEE JOURNAL SENTINEL* SPORTS SHOW.** Mar 10–19. The Milwaukee Center, Milwaukee, WI. Travel and resort exhibits, hunting, fishing, boating and family travel and outdoor recreation. Largest outdoor show in Wisconsin. 60th annual show. Est attendance: 115,000. For info: Great Outdoors, 420 Lake Cook Rd, Ste 108, Deerfield, IL 60015. Phone: (847) 914-0630 or (888) 462-7469. Fax: (847) 914-0333. E-mail: go2show@msn.com.

NAIA WRESTLING CHAMPIONSHIPS. Mar 10–11. Site TBA. Individuals compete for All-America honors in 12 weight divisions, while teams compete for the national championship. 43rd annual competition. Est attendance: 4,000. For info: Natl Assn of Intercollegiate Athletics, 6120 S Yale Ave, Ste 1450, Tulsa, OK 74136. Phone: (918) 494-8828. Fax: (918) 494-8841. E-mail: khenry@naia.org. Web: www.naia.org.

NCAA DIVISION II HOCKEY CHAMPIONSHIP. Mar 10–11. Finals. Site TBA. For info: NCAA, PO Box 6222, Indianapolis, IN 46206-6222. Phone: (317) 917-6222. Fax: (317) 917-6888. Web: www.ncaa.org.

NCAA DIVISION II WRESTLING CHAMPIONSHIPS. Mar 10–11. Finals. South Dakota State University, Brookings, SD. For info: NCAA, PO Box 6222, Indianapolis, IN 46206-6222. Phone: (317) 917-6222. Fax: (317) 917-6888. Web: www.ncaa.org.

NCAA DIVISION III HOCKEY CHAMPIONSHIP. Mar 10–12. Quarterfinals. Sites TBA. For info: NCAA, PO Box 6222, Indianapolis, IN 46206-6222. Phone: (317) 917-6222. Fax: (317) 917-6888. Web: www.ncaa.org.

NCAA MEN'S AND WOMEN'S DIVISION I INDOOR TRACK AND FIELD CHAMPIONSHIPS. Mar 10–11. Finals at site TBA For info: NCAA, PO Box 6222, Indianapolis, IN 46206-6222. Phone: (317) 917-6222. Fax: (317) 917-6888. Web: www.ncaa.org.

NCAA MEN'S AND WOMEN'S DIVISION III INDOOR TRACK AND FIELD CHAMPIONSHIPS. Mar 10–11. Finals. Illinois Wesleyan University, Bloomington, IL. For info: NCAA, PO Box 6222, Indianapolis, IN 46206-6222. Phone: (317) 917-6222. Fax: (317) 917-6888. Web: www.ncaa.org.

NCAA WOMEN'S DIVISION I SWIMMING AND DIVING CHAMPIONSHIPS. Mar 10–11. Regionals at US Naval Academy, Annapolis, MD; Auburn University, Auburn, AL; University of Minnesota, Minneapolis, MN; Texas A&M University, College Station, TX; and US Air Force Academy, Colorado Springs, CO. For info: NCAA, PO Box 6222, Indianapolis, IN 46206-6222. Phone: (317) 917-6222. Fax: (317) 917-6888. Web: www.ncaa.org.

NJCAA MEN'S ICE HOCKEY CHAMPIONSHIP. Mar 10–12. Buffalo, NY. For info: Ralph Galanti, Tourn Dir, Erie CC, 21 Oak St, Buffalo, NY 14203. Phone: (716) 851-1220. Fax: (716) 851-1219. Web: www.njcaa.org.

SPECIAL OLYMPICS KENTUCKY STATE BASKETBALL TOURNAMENT. Mar 10–12. Louisville, KY. Olympic-style tournament for children and adults with mental retardation. For info: Special Olympics Kentucky, 105 Lakeview Ct, Frankfort, KY 40601. Phone: (502) 695-8222. Fax: (502)695-0496. Web: www.soky.org.

SPECIAL OLYMPICS MICHIGAN JUNIOR AND SKILLS STATE BASKETBALL FINALS. Mar 10–11. Mt Pleasant, MI. Olympic-style tournament for athletes with mental retardation. For info: Special Olympics Michigan, Central Michigan University, Mt Pleasant, MI 48859. Phone: (800) 644-6404. Fax: (517) 774-3034. E-mail: M.K.Lindberg@cmich.edu. Web: www.somi.org.

SPECIAL OLYMPICS SOUTH DAKOTA BASKETBALL TOURNAMENT. Mar 10–11. Mitchell, SD. State-level Olympic style competition for adults and children with mental retardation. For info: Special Olympics South Dakota, 305 W 39th St, Sioux Falls, SD 57105. Phone: (605) 331-4117. Fax: (605) 331-4326. E-mail: sosdak @aol.com.

TIMED EVENT CHAMPIONSHIP OF THE WORLD. Mar 10–12. Lazy E Arena, Guthrie, OK. The top all-around cowboys in the world compete for $140,000 in all five timed events. Est attendance: 17,000. For info: Lazy E Arena, Rte 5, Box 393, Guthrie, Ok 73044-9205. Phone: (800) 595-RIDE. E-mail: arena@lazye.net. Web: www.lazye.com.

US JUNIOR FIGURE SKATING CHAMPIONSHIPS. Mar 10–12. Williamsville, NY. For info: Media Relations, US Figure Skating Assn, 20 First St, Colorado Springs, CO 80906. Phone: (719) 635-5200. Fax: (719) 635-9548. E-mail: usfsa1@aol.com. Web: www.usfsa.org/events.

BIRTHDAYS TODAY

Heywood Hale Broun, 82, former broadcaster, born New York, NY, Mar 10, 1918.

John Anthony Cangelosi, 37, baseball player, born New York, NY, Mar 10, 1963.

Steven Roy (Steve) Howe, 42, former baseball player, born Pontiac, MI, Mar 10, 1958.

Ronald Jack (Ron) Mix, 62, Pro Football Hall of Fame offensive tackle, born Los Angeles, CA, Mar 10, 1938.

Roderick Kevin (Rod) Woodson, 35, football player, born Ft Wayne, IN, Mar 10, 1965.

MARCH 11 — SATURDAY
Day 71 — 295 Remaining

AMA GRAND NATIONAL KICKOFF. Mar 11. Daytona Beach Municipal Stadium, Daytona Beach, FL. 12th annual. For info: John Story, Dir of Public Relations, Daytona Intl Speedway, Box 2801, Daytona Beach, FL 32120-2801. Phone: (904) 254-6782. For tickets: (904) 253-RACE (7223). Fax: (904) 947-6791. Web: www.daytonausa.com.

BIERMAN, BERNIE: BIRTH ANNIVERSARY. Mar 11, 1894. Bernard William (Bernie) Bierman, football coach, born at Springfield, MN. Bierman ran track and played football at the University of Minnesota and then began coaching at the high school level. After World War I, he moved to the University of Montana and then, after several stops as an assistant, became head coach at his alma mater in 1932. His Golden Gophers won four national championships before his retirement in 1950. Died at Laguna Hills, CA, Mar 8, 1977.

CANADIAN-AMERICAN DAYS FEST. Mar 11–19. Myrtle Beach, SC. Beach games and sporting events along with concerts, square dances and more. Est attendance: 100,000. For info: Holly Tanner, Fest Mgr, Myrtle Beach Chamber of Commerce, PO Box 2115, Myrtle Beach, SC 29578. Phone: (843) 626-7444. Web: www.myrtlebeach live.com.

DAYTONA SUPERCROSS BY HONDA. Mar 11. Daytona International Speedway, Daytona Beach, FL. 30th annual. One of the most famous and toughest Supercross races in the world. Sponsor: Honda. For info: John Story, Dir of Public Relations, Daytona Intl Speedway, PO Box 2801, Daytona Beach, FL 32120-2801. Phone: (904) 947-6782. For tickets: (904) 253-RACE (7223). Fax: (904) 947-6791. Web: www.daytonausa.com.

LOS ANGELES MARATHON QUALITY OF LIFE EXPO. Mar 11–13. Los Angeles Convention Center, Los Angeles, CA. Massive consumer show features health and fitness products and services, food and beverage sampling, financial institutions, travel, electronics, women's products and services, seminars and demonstrations. A bike section will also be featured. Est attendance: 74,000. For info: Mike Gerlowski, Dir Sales and Mktg, City of Los Angeles Marathon, Inc, 11110 W Ohio Ave, Ste 100, Los Angeles, CA 90025. Phone: (310) 444-5544 ext 17. Fax: (310) 473-8105. E-mail: raceinfo@lamarathon.com.

McGUIRE'S 5K ST. PATRICK'S DAY PREDICTION RUN. Mar 11 (tentative). Pensacola, FL. The largest, most popular 5K run in the history of Pensacola, "The Nation's Largest Prediction Run." 9 AM. Est attendance: 300. For info: Susi Lyon, McGuire's Irish Pub, 600 E Gregory St, Pensacola, FL 32501. Phone: (850) 433-6789. Fax: (850) 434-5400. E-mail: stpat5Krun@aol.com.

NATIONAL SKI-JORING FINALS. Mar 11–12. Red Lodge Rodeo Grounds, Red Lodge, MT. Horsemen and skiers provide action entertainment. Derived from the Scandinavian sport of pulling a skier behind a horse, Ski-Joring has evolved from a leisure winter diversion into lively, regulated competition. Annually, the second weekend in March. Est attendance: 3,000. For info: Red Lodge Chamber of Commerce, Box 988, Red Lodge, MT 59068. Phone: (888) 281-0625. Fax: (406) 446-1718. E-mail: information@redlodge.com. Web: www.redlodge.com.

NFL ADOPTS INSTANT REPLAY: ANNIVERSARY. Mar 11, 1986. After years of debate, NFL owners adopted a rules change allowing the limited use of televised replays to assist the officials on the field. This system was eliminated after the 1991 season. After several years of debate, a new system of instant replay was approved for the 1999 season.

NORTHWEST CRIBBAGE TOURNAMENT. Mar 11–12. Baker City, OR. Est attendance: 200. For info: Baker County VCB, 490 Campbell St, Baker City, OR 97814. Phone: (800) 523-1235.

PACIFIC NORTHWEST CRAB RACES. Mar 11–12. Lumberman's Park, Garibaldi, OR. Two days of elimination heats culminating in the Championship race at 4 PM Sunday. Children and adult divisions. Up to six people race at a time on the specially designed crab track at Mudflat Downs. Only male Dungeness Crabs are allowed. Losers are eaten. Winner gets $100 and an expense-paid trip to the World Championship at Westport, WA. Annually, the second weekend in March. Est attendance: 1,500. For info: Van Moe, Track Steward, KTIL/KMBD, PO Box 40, Tillamook, OR 97241. Phone: (503) 842-4422. Fax: (503) 842-4422.

QUEST WINS FIRST ABL TITLE: ANNIVERSARY. Mar 11, 1997. The Columbus Quest defeated the Richmond Rage, 77–64, to win the fifth and deciding game in the American Basketball League's first championship series. Columbus had trailed two games to one. The Quest were led by Valerie Still, who scored 14 points and was named MVP of the finals.

SAVARD GETS 1,000th POINT: 10th ANNIVERSARY. Mar 11, 1990. Center Denis Savard of the Chicago Blackhawks got the 1,000th point of his National Hockey League career, an assist in a 6–4 win over the St. Louis Blues. Savard finished his career with 1,338 points.

SPECIAL OLYMPICS COLORADO BASKETBALL TOURNAMENT. Mar 11. Greeley, CO. Competition for athletes with mental retardation. For info: Colorado Special Olympics, 600 17th St, Ste 910, Denver, CO 80202. Phone: (303) 592-1361. Fax: (303) 592-1364.

WOMEN'S INTERNATIONAL BOWLING CONGRESS CHAMPIONSHIP TOURNAMENT. Mar 11–June 30. Reno, NV. Est attendance: 150,000. For info: Bowling, Inc, 5301 S 76th St, Greendale, WI 53129. Phone: (414) 423-3356. Fax: (414) 421-3013.

BIRTHDAYS TODAY

Bob Kelly Abreu, 26, baseball player, born Aragua, Venezuela, Mar 11, 1974.
Ken James Baumgartner, 34, hockey player, born Flin Flon, Manitoba, Canada, Mar 11, 1966.
Dock Phillip Ellis, 55, former baseball player, born Los Angeles, CA, Mar 11, 1945.
Cesar Francisco Geronimo, 52, former baseball player, born El Seibo, Dominican Republic, Mar 11, 1948.
Martin Rucinsky, 29, hockey player, born Most, Czechoslovakia, Mar 11, 1971.
Shawn Springs, 25, football player, born Silver Spring, MD, Mar 11, 1975.

MARCH 12 — SUNDAY
Day 72 — 294 Remaining

DAYTONA 200. Mar 12. Daytona International Speedway, Daytona Beach, FL. 59th AMA Superbike Classic plus 14th 600 SuperSport International Challenge 100K AMA Race. For info: John Story, Dir of Public Relations, Daytona Intl Speedway, PO Box 2801, Daytona Beach, FL 32120-2801. Phone: (904) 947-6782. For tickets: (904) 253-RACE (7223) Fax: (904) 947-6791. Web: www.daytonausa.com.

DIDDLE, UNCLE ED: BIRTH ANNIVERSARY. Mar 12, 1895. Edgar Allen ("Uncle Ed") Diddle, Sr, basketball player and Basketball Hall of Fame coach, born at Gradyville, KY. Diddle played several sports at Centre College and coached at Western Kentucky from 1923 through 1964. His teams won 759 games and 32 conference titles. The colorful coach chewed on a red towel along the sidelines. Inducted into the Hall of Fame in 1971. Died at Bowling Green, KY, Jan 2, 1970.

FASTEST DISQUALIFICATION IN NBA HISTORY: ANNIVERSARY. Mar 12, 1956. Dick Farley of the Syracuse Nationals fouled out of an NBA game against the St. Louis Hawks after playing just five minutes, the fastest disqualification in league history.

March	S	M	T	W	T	F	S
2000				1	2	3	4
	5	6	7	8	9	10	11
	12	13	14	15	16	17	18
	19	20	21	22	23	24	25
	26	27	28	29	30	31	

HULL SCORES 51: ANNIVERSARY. Mar 12, 1966. Chicago Blackhawks left wing Bobby Hull became the first NHL player to score more than 50 goals in a season when he tallied his 51st goal of the year against the New York Rangers.

MILLS, ABRAHAM: BIRTH ANNIVERSARY. Mar 12, 1844. Abraham Gilbert Mills, baseball executive, born at New York, NY. Mills carried a bat and baseball with him during his service in the Civil War. He was president of the National League and, as chairman of the Mills Commission in 1905, helped to enshrine as fact the fanciful story that Abner Doubleday had invented baseball at Cooperstown, NY, in 1839. Died at Falmouth, MA, Aug 26, 1929.

TORVILL AND DEAN ACHIEVE PERFECTION: ANNIVERSARY. Mar 12, 1984. At the World Figure Skating Championships, Jayne Torvill and Christopher Dean of Great Britain became the first ice dancing team to earn nine perfect marks of 6.0.

BIRTHDAYS TODAY

John Andretti, 37, auto racer, born Bethlehem, PA, Mar 12, 1963.
Steven Allen (Steve) Finley, 35, baseball player, born Union City, TN, Mar 12, 1965.
Merton Edward Hanks, 32, football player, born Dallas, TX, Mar 12, 1968.
Vernon Sanders Law, 70, former baseball player, born Meridian, ID, Mar 12, 1930.
Edwin Durwood Merrill, 62, baseball umpire, born Cloud Chief, OK, Mar 12, 1938.
Raul Ramon Mondesi, 29, baseball player, born San Cristobal, Dominican Republic, Mar 12, 1971.
Dale Bryan Murphy, 44, former baseball player, born Portland, OR, Mar 12, 1956.
Isaiah Rider, Jr, 29, basketball player, born Oakland, CA, Mar 12, 1971.
Lawrence Lee (Larry) Rothschild, 46, baseball manager and former player, born Chicago, IL, Mar 12, 1954.
Rodney Marc Smith, 30, football player, born St. Paul, MN, Mar 12, 1970.
Darryl Eugene Strawberry, 38, baseball player, born Los Angeles, CA, Mar 12, 1962.
Rex Andrew Walters, 30, basketball player, born Omaha, NE, Mar 12, 1970.

MARCH 13 — MONDAY
Day 73 — 293 Remaining

AMERICAN BOWLING CONGRESS CONVENTION (WITH HALL OF FAME INDUCTION CEREMONIES). Mar 13–18. Albuquerque, NM. Local, state and national bowling leaders gather to decide the rules of the game in a democratic setting. The week features board of directors' meetings, special seminars, dinners honoring top leaders, Hall of Fame induction ceremonies and workshops. Est attendance: 5,000. For info: Michael Deering, American Bowling Congress, 5301 S 76th St, Greendale, WI 53129-0500. Phone: (414) 423-3309. Fax: (414) 421-3013.

BAKER, HOME RUN: BIRTH ANNIVERSARY. Mar 13, 1886. John Franklin ("Home Run") Baker, Baseball Hall of Fame third baseman, born at Trappe, MD. Baker earned his nickname for leading the American League in home runs from 1911 through 1914 and for hitting a pair of homers in the 1911 World Series. Yet, in baseball's dead ball era, he never hit more than 12 in a single season. Inducted into the Hall of Fame in 1955. Died at Trappe, June 28, 1963.

CALLAGHAN, HELEN: BIRTH ANNIVERSARY. Mar 13, 1929. Helen Callaghan, baseball player, born Helen St. Aubin at Vancouver, BC, Canada. St. Aubin and her sister, Margaret Maxwell, were recruited for the All-American Girls Professional Baseball League, which flourished in the 1940s when many major league players were off fighting World War II. She first played at age 15 for the Minneapolis Millerettes, an expansion team that moved to Indiana and became the Ft Wayne Daisies. The left-handed outfielder spent five years with the Daisies. For the 1945 season she led the league with a .299 average and 24 extra base hits. In 1946 she stole 114 bases in 111 games. She became known as the "Ted Williams of women's baseball." Her son Kelly Candaele's documentary on the women's 1940s baseball league inspired the film *A League of Their Own*. A second son, Casey Candaele, played major league baseball. Died at Santa Barbara, CA, Dec 8, 1992.

CHICAGO CARDINALS MOVE TO ST. LOUIS: 40th ANNIVERSARY. Mar 13, 1960. National Football League owners voted to allow the Chicago Cardinals to move to St. Louis. The Cardinals are generally regarded as the oldest continuing operation in pro football, having been founded as the Morgan Athletic Club, a neighborhood team, in 1899. The Cardinals remained at St. Louis through the 1987 season after which owner Bill Bidwill transferred the team to Phoenix, AZ.

DERBY. Mar 13. Biloxi, MS. Includes a 5K run and a 1K walk. Starts at 10 prior to the St. Patrick's Parade. For info: Hibernia Marching Soc of Mississippi, PO Box 707, Biloxi, MS 39533.

HULMAN, MARY: 95th BIRTH ANNIVERSARY. Mar 13, 1905. Mary Fendrich Hulman, auto racing executive, born at Evansville, IN. Married to Tony Hulman, who bought the Indianapolis Motor Speedway in 1945 and turned the Indianapolis 500 into the biggest spectacle in auto racing, Hulman chaired the Speedway's board of directors after her husband's death in 1977. Died at Indianapolis, IN, Apr 10, 1998.

NBA CONSECUTIVE-GAME STREAK ENDS: ANNIVERSARY. Mar 13, 1983. Randy Smith's NBA consecutive-game streak, a record, came to an end as he played in his 906th straight game. Smith played for Buffalo, San Diego, Cleveland, New York and San Diego (again).

STARTING GATE INVENTED: ANNIVERSARY. Mar 13, 1894. Englishman J. L. Johnstone invented the starting gate for horse racing.

BIRTHDAYS TODAY

Thomas Andrew (Andy) Bean, 47, golfer, born Lafayette, GA, Mar 13, 1953.

Joseph Michael (Joe) Bellino, 62, Heisman Trophy halfback, born Winchester, MA, Mar 13, 1938.

William Nuschler (Will) Clark, Jr, 36, baseball player, born New Orleans, LA, Mar 13, 1964.

Curtis LaMont Conway, 29, football player, born Los Angeles, CA, Mar 13, 1971.

Trent Farris Dilfer, 28, football player, born Santa Cruz, CA, Mar 13, 1972.

Mariano Duncan, 37, former baseball player, born San Pedro de Macoris, Dominican Republic, Mar 13, 1963.

Jorge Fabregas, 30, baseball player, born Miami, FL, Mar 13, 1970.

Dan Wilkinson, 27, football player, born Dayton, OH, Mar 13, 1973.

Christopher Robert (Chris) Zorich, 31, football player, born Chicago, IL, Mar 13, 1969.

MARCH 14 — TUESDAY
Day 74 — 292 Remaining

CARAY, HARRY: BIRTH ANNIVERSARY. Mar 14, 1914. Born Harry Christopher Carabina at St. Louis, MO. One of baseball's most beloved announcers, Caray enjoyed a long career at St. Louis, Oakland and Chicago. Some broadcasters are lucky to develop one trademark, but Caray had several: his oversized glasses, his home run call, "It might be, it could be, it is," his astonished "Holy Cow" and, most of all, his signature singing of "Take Me Out to the Ball Game" during the 7th-inning stretch. Given the Ford Frick Award in 1989. Died at Rancho Mirage, CA, Feb 18, 1998.

CHAMBERLAIN'S CONSECUTIVE COMPLETE GAME STREAK: ANNIVERSARY. Mar 14, 1962. Wilt Chamberlain of the Philadelphia Warriors completed a stretch of 47 consecutive games during which he played every minute. The streak, begun Jan 5 against the Syracuse Nationals and concluded against the Chicago Packers, still stands as an NBA record.

HOWE GETS 500th GOAL: ANNIVERSARY. Mar 14, 1962. Right wing Gordie Howe of the Detroit Red Wings became the second player in National Hockey League history to reach the 500-goal mark when he scored in a 3–2 loss to the New York Rangers. Howe wound up with 801 regular-season goals and entered the Hockey Hall of Fame in 1972.

MULLEN SCORES 500th GOAL: ANNIVERSARY. Mar 14, 1997. Right wing Joey Mullen of the Pittsburgh Penguins became the 25th player in the National Hockey League and the first American to score 500 regular-season goals. He tallied against goalie Patrick Roy in a 6–3 loss to the Colorado Avalanche. Mullen finished his career with 502 goals.

NAIA MEN'S DIVISION I BASKETBALL CHAMPIONSHIP. Mar 14–20. Tulsa Convention Center, Tulsa, OK. 63rd annual tournament. Est attendance: 35,000. For info: Natl Assn of Intercollegiate Athletics, 6120 S Yale Ave, Ste 1450, Tulsa, OK 74136. Phone: (918) 494-8828. Fax: (918) 494-8841. E-mail: khenry@naia.org. Web: www.naia.org.

NAIA WOMEN'S DIVISION I BASKETBALL CHAMPIONSHIP. Mar 14–20. Oman Arena, Jackson, TN. 32-team field competes for the national championship. 20th annual competition. Est attendance: 38,000. For info: Natl Assn of Intercollegiate Athletics, 6120 S Yale Ave, Ste 1450, Tulsa, OK 74136. Phone: (918) 494-8828. Fax: (918) 494-8841. E-mail: khenry@naia.org. Web: www.naia.org.

NJCAA DIVISION I MEN'S BASKETBALL CHAMPIONSHIP. Mar 14–18. Hutchinson, KS. For info: Tom Westfall, Tourn Dir, PO Box 625, 1101 N Halstead, Hutchinson, KS 67504-0625. Phone: (316) 663-5939. Fax: (316) 663-2764. Web: www.njcaa.org.

NJCAA DIVISION I WOMEN'S BASKETBALL CHAMPIONSHIP. Mar 14–18. Bicentennial Center, Salina, KS. For info: Tiffany Greene, Tourn Dir, PO Box 586, Salina, KS 67402-0586. Phone: (785) 827-9301. Fax: (785) 827-9758. Web: www.njcaa.org.

SHOEMAKER WINS 7,000th RACE: ANNIVERSARY. Mar 14, 1976. Jockey Bill Shoemaker won the 7,000th race of his career aboard Royal Derby II, a horse that hadn't won in three years. Shoemaker became the winningest jockey in history in 1970 when he surpassed Johnny Longden's total of 6,032. The Shoe retired in 1990 after having ridden 8,833 winners.

BIRTHDAYS TODAY

James Kevin Brown, 35, baseball player, born McIntyre, GA, Mar 14, 1965.

Larry Demetric Johnson, 31, basketball player, born Tyler, TX, Mar 14, 1969.

Lee Petty, 86, former auto racer, born Randleman, NC, Mar 14, 1914.

Kirby Puckett, 39, former baseball player, born Chicago, IL, Mar 14, 1961.

Antowain Smith, 28, football player, born Montgomery, AL, Mar 14, 1972.

Westley Sissel (Wes) Unseld, 54, basketball executive and Basketball Hall of Fame center and forward, born Louisville, KY, Mar 14, 1946.

March	S	M	T	W	T	F	S
2000				1	2	3	4
	5	6	7	8	9	10	11
	12	13	14	15	16	17	18
	19	20	21	22	23	24	25
	26	27	28	29	30	31	

MARCH 15 — WEDNESDAY

Day 75 — 291 Remaining

CHASE'S SPORTSQUOTE OF THE DAY

"I respect what Dean has done. He's a Hall of Famer. He has done a great deal for the game of basketball. He has just contributed so much."—Mike Krzyzewski on Dean Smith

ANDREYCHUK SCORES 500th GOAL: ANNIVERSARY. Mar 15, 1997. Dave Andreychuk of the New Jersey Devils became the 26th player in National Hockey League history and the second in two days to score 500 regular-season goals. Andreychuk's goal helped the Devils beat the Washington Capitals, 3–2.

LATHAM, ARLIE: 140th BIRTH ANNIVERSARY. Mar 15, 1860. Walter Arlington (Arlie) Latham, baseball player, born at West Lebanon, NH. Latham enjoyed a baseball career that spanned 76 years, starting as a professional player at age 15 in 1875 and concluding as custodian of the Yankee Stadium press box at age 92. Died at Garden City, NY, Nov 29, 1952.

LIEB, FRED: BIRTH ANNIVERSARY. Mar 15, 1888. Frederick George (Fred) Lieb, sportswriter, born at Philadelphia, PA. Lieb wanted nothing more from life than the opportunity to write about baseball, and he virtually got his wish. He began a monthly column in *Baseball Magazine* in 1909 and was still writing a few months before his death. Lieb was a close friend of Babe Ruth, Kenesaw Mountain Landis and hundreds of other baseball figures. He is credited with calling Yankee Stadium the "House That Ruth Built" and with writing 18 books, including his autobiography, *Baseball As I Have Known It*. Given the J.G. Taylor Spink Award in 1972. Died at Houston, TX, June 5, 1980.

LOUISIANA SPORTSMEN'S SHOW. Mar 15–19. New Orleans Superdome, New Orleans, LA. Louisiana's original sportfishing, hunting and boat show. Also covering Baton Rouge and the Gulf Coast. Est attendance: 80,000. For info: Louisiana Sportsmen's Show, PO Box 2116, Kenner, LA 70063. Phone: (504) 464-7363. Fax: (504) 835-8692. Web: www.delgiorno.com.

NATIONAL INVITATION TOURNAMENT. Mar 15 (tentative). First three rounds at campus sites TBA. Semifinals and final at Madison Square Garden, New York, NY. Postseason basketball tournament for 32 teams that do not qualify for the NCAA Tournament. For info: Media Relations, Natl Invitation Tourn, Madison Square Garden, 4 Penn Plaza, New York, NY 10001. Phone: (212) 465-6000. Fax: (212) 465-6029. Web: www.thegarden.com.

NJCAA DIVISION II MEN'S BASKETBALL NATIONAL CHAMPIONSHIP. Mar 15–18. Danville, IL. Est attendance: 8,000. For info: Jeanie Cooke, Exec Dir, Danville Area CVB, PO Box 992, Danville, IL 61834. Phone: (800) 383-4386. Web: www.njcaa.org.

NJCAA DIVISION II WOMEN'S BASKETBALL CHAMPIONSHIP. Mar 15–18. Hagerstown, MD. For info: James Brown, Tourn Dir, Hagerstown Jr College, 751 Robinwood Dr, Hagerstown, MD 21740-6590. Phone: (301) 790-2829, x366. Fax: (301) 739-0737. Web: www.njcaa.org.

SCHOLZ, JACKSON: BIRTH ANNIVERSARY. Mar 15, 1897. Jackson Volney Scholz, Olympic gold medal sprinter, born at Buchanan, MI. Scholz won a gold medal on the 400-meter relay team at the 1920 Olympics and another gold in the 200 meters at the Paris Olympics of 1924, the Games depicted in the movie, *Chariots of Fire*. Scholz worked as a freelance journalist and wrote 31 sport novels for boys. Died at Del Ray Beach, FL, Oct 26, 1986.

SMITH WINS 877th GAME: ANNIVERSARY. Mar 15, 1997. The University of North Carolina men's basketball team defeated Colorado, 73–56, in the second round of the NCAA tournament to give coach Dean Smith the 877th victory of his career, one more than Adolph Rupp. Smith's win, his 63rd in NCAA play, came in his 36th season as a head coach.

STICKUM OUTLAWED: ANNIVERSARY. Mar 15, 1981. The National Football League prohibited the use of any sticky substances on the body, uniform or equipment of any player. The rules change was largely aimed at the defensive unit of the Los Angeles Raiders, winners of the 1981 Super Bowl, and in particular at LA defensive back Lester Hayes, who coated his arms and chest with Stickum and intercepted 13 passes during the 1980 season.

VAN BROCKLIN, NORM: BIRTH ANNIVERSARY. Mar 15, 1926. Norman (Norm) Van Brocklin, Pro Football Hall of Fame quarterback and coach, born at Eagle Butte, SD. Van Brocklin played college football at Oregon and then signed with the Los Angeles Rams. He helped the Rams win their only NFL title in 1951. After finishing his playing career with the Philadelphia Eagles, he coached the Minnesota Vikings and the Atlanta Falcons. Inducted into the Hall of Fame in 1979. Died at Social Circle, GA, May 2, 1983.

WILKENS WINS 800th GAME: ANNIVERSARY. Mar 15, 1992. Lenny Wilkens became the fifth coach in professional basketball to win 800 games when his team, the Cleveland Cavaliers, defeated the Denver Nuggets, 100–91. Wilkens was inducted into the Basketball Hall of Fame as a player in 1988 and as a coach in 1998.

BIRTHDAYS TODAY

Harold Douglas Baines, 41, baseball player, born St. Michael's, MD, Mar 15, 1959.

Bobby Lee Bonds, 54, former baseball player, born Riverside, CA, Mar 15, 1946.

Robert Terrell (Terry) Cummings, 39, basketball player, born Chicago, IL, Mar 15, 1961.

Nelson Joseph (Nellie) King, 72, broadcaster and former baseball player, born Shenandoah, PA, Mar 15, 1928.

MARCH 16 — THURSDAY

Day 76 — 290 Remaining

FITCH WINS 800th GAME: ANNIVERSARY. Mar 16, 1991. Bill Fitch became the fourth coach in professional basketball to win 800 games when his team, the New Jersey Nets, defeated the Washington Bullets, 110–86. Fitch coached for 25 years and compiled a career record of 944–1,106.

FLORIDA STATE BOAT AND SPORTS SHOW. Mar 16–19. Florida Expo Park, Tampa, FL. Est attendance: 15,000. For info: NMMA Boat Shows, 200 E Randolph St, Ste 5100, Chicago, IL 60601-6528. Phone: (312) 946-6262. Fax: (312) 946-0401. Web: www.boatshows.com.

FOWLER, BUD: BIRTH ANNIVERSARY. Mar 16, 1858. John W. ("Bud") Fowler, baseball player, born at Ft Plain, NY. Fowler was the first black professional baseball player. Excelling as a second baseman, he played for many teams in black and white leagues over a 30-year career. Died at Frankfort, NY, Feb 26, 1913.

GRAND CENTER SPORT, FISHING & TRAVEL SHOW. Mar 16–19. Grand Center, Grand Rapids, MI. This event brings together buyers and sellers of fishing boats and equipment, campers and their accessories, as well as other outdoor sporting goods. US and Canadian hunting and fishing trips and other vacation travel destinations are featured. All aspects of fishing, including tackle boats, seminars, demonstrations and displays are emphasized. Est attendance: 45,000. For info: Henri Boucher, ShowSpan, Inc, 1400 28th St SW, Grand Rapids, MI 49509. Phone: (616) 530-1919. Fax: (616) 530-2122.

HUTCHESON BECOMES LEADING COLLEGIATE SCORER: 10th ANNIVERSARY. Mar 16, 1990. Phil Hutcheson of David Lipscomb University became the leading scorer in college basketball history when he reached 4,046 career points in an NAIA tournament game. Hutcheson, who scored in double figures in every college game he played, surpassed the mark set by Travis Grant of Kentucky State in 1969–72.

LONGEST SENIOR PGA PLAY-OFF: ANNIVERSARY. Mar 16, 1997. Bob Murphy sank an 80-foot birdie putt on the 9th sudden-death hole to win the longest play-off in Senior PGA history. Murphy defeated Jay Sigel to win the Toshiba Senior Classic at Newport Beach, CA. Sigel's own 22-foot putt for birdie just missed. The previous record, 8 play-off holes, was set at the 1992 Showdown Classic with Orville Moody besting Bob Bentley.

NCAA DIVISION I WRESTLING CHAMPIONSHIPS. Mar 16–18. Finals. University of Missouri-St. Louis, St. Louis, MO. For info: NCAA, PO Box 6222, Indianapolis, IN 46206-6222. Phone: (317) 917-6222. Fax: (317) 917-6888. Web: www.ncaa.org.

NCAA MEN'S DIVISION I BASKETBALL TOURNAMENT. Mar 16–19. First and second rounds at Marine Midland Arena, Buffalo, NY; Lawrence Joel Veterans Memorial Coliseum, Winston-Salem, NC; Nashville Arena, Nashville, TN; Birmingham-Jefferson Civic Center, Birmingham, AL; Cleveland State University Convocation Center, Cleveland, OH; Hubert H. Humphrey Metrodome, Minneapolis, MN; Jon M. Huntsman Center, Salt Lake City, UT; and McKale Center, Tucson, AZ. For info: NCAA, PO Box 6222, Indianapolis, IN 46206-6222. Phone: (317) 917-6222. Fax: (317) 917-6888. Web: www.ncaa.org.

NCAA MEN'S DIVISION III SWIMMING AND DIVING CHAMPIONSHIPS. Mar 16–18. Finals. Emory University, Atlanta, GA. For info: NCAA, PO Box 6222, Indianapolis, IN 46206-6222. Phone: (317) 917-6222. Fax: (317) 917-6888. Web: www.ncaa.org.

NCAA WOMEN'S DIVISION I SWIMMING AND DIVING CHAMPIONSHIPS. Mar 16–18. Finals. IU Natatorium, Indianapolis, IN. For info: NCAA, PO Box 6222, Indianapolis, IN 46206-6222. Phone: (317) 917-6222. Fax: (317) 917-6888. Web: www.ncaa.org.

NEBRASKA SETS SCORING RECORD: ANNIVERSARY. Mar 16, 1999. The Nebraska Cornhuskers baseball team set an NCAA scoring record, defeating Chicago State, 50–3, in the second game of a doubleheader. The game was 23–0 after three innings and was called after 6 ½ innings on the 10-run mercy rule. Nebraska had won the first game, 15–3.

SAINT PATRICK'S DAY DART TOURNAMENT. Mar 16–19. Battle Creek, MI. 16th annual tournament with seven separate contests to celebrate the luck of the Irish by encouraging the fast-growing interest in the US in the sport of darting. Annually, beginning the Thursday on or before St. Patrick's Day. Est attendance: 200. For info: Bill Buckner, Owner, Springbrook Golf Course, 1600 Ave A, Battle Creek, MI 49015. Phone: (616) 965-6512.

SPECIAL OLYMPICS KANSAS STATE BASKETBALL TOURNAMENT. Mar 16–18. Hays, KS. Olympic-style tournament for children and adults with mental retardation. For info: Special Olympics Kansas, 5280 Foxridge Dr, Mission, KS 66202. Phone: (913) 236-9290. Fax: (913) 236-9771. E-mail: rehdert@ksso.org. Web: www.ksso.org.

STRICTLY SAIL—NEW ENGLAND. Mar 16–19. Connecticut Expo Center, Hartford, CT. New England's only all-sail show. More than 150 exhibitors of sailboats, sailing equipment, charters and services will gather to break the ice and kick off a summer of sailing. Sailors from Boston to New York and all along the East Coast will be gearing up for the sailing season. Attendees will enjoy a wide variety of free seminars and attractions for all levels of sailing ability. For info: NNMA Boat Shows, 200 E Randolph Dr, Ste 5100, Chicago, IL 60601-6528. Phone: (312) 946-6262. Fax: (312) 946-0401. Web: www.boatshows.com.

TEMPLE WINS FIRST NIT: ANNIVERSARY. Mar 16, 1938. Temple University defeated Colorado, 60–36, to win the first National Invitation Tournament, played in New York's Madison Square Garden. The NIT was sponsored by the Metropolitan New York Basketball Writers Association and was the first postseason college basketball tournament. The NCAA tournament began one year later.

WANER, LLOYD: BIRTH ANNIVERSARY. Mar 16, 1906. Lloyd James Waner, Baseball Hall of Fame outfielder, born at Harrah, OK. Waner was "Little Poison" to his brother Paul's "Big Poison." He played 18 years in the majors, mainly with the Pittsburgh Pirates. Inducted into the Hall of Fame in 1967. Died at Oklahoma City, OK, July 22, 1982.

BIRTHDAYS TODAY

Don Lee Blasingame, 68, former baseball player, born Corinth, MS, Mar 16, 1932.
Hobert Neal (Hobie) Landrith, 70, former baseball player, born Decatur, IL, Mar 16, 1930.
Ozzie Newsome, Jr, 44, Pro Football Hall of Fame tight end, born Muscle Shoals, AL, Mar 16, 1956.
Rodney Peete, 34, football player, born Mesa, AZ, Mar 16, 1966.
Frederic Carl (Rick) Reichardt, 57, former baseball player, born Madison, WI, Mar 16, 1943.
Vivian Stringer, 52, basketball coach and former player, born Edenborn, PA, Mar 16, 1948.

MARCH 17 — FRIDAY
Day 77 — 289 Remaining

BIG TEN MEN'S GYMNASTICS CHAMPIONSHIPS. Mar 17–18. Michigan State University, East Lansing, MI. For info: Big Ten Conference, 1500 W Higgins Rd, Park Ridge, IL 60068-6300. Phone: (847) 696-1010. Fax: (847) 696-1150. Web: www.bigten.org.

March 2000

S	M	T	W	T	F	S
			1	2	3	4
5	6	7	8	9	10	11
12	13	14	15	16	17	18
19	20	21	22	23	24	25
26	27	28	29	30	31	

CANADA: NMI MOBILITY'S EXTREME MACHINE'S THUNDER ON ICE. Mar 17–19. Whitehorse, Yukon. Snowmachines, cars, dirt bikes and ATV's race on ice for a piece of the $100,000 in prize money. Includes the 500-mile Snowmachine Ice Enduro worth more than $50,000 in cash alone! Lots of kids' events to keep everyone entertained. For info: Extreme Alliances, Ste 308-204 Lambert St, Whitehorse, YT, Canada Y1A 4K8. Phone: (867) 393-8068. Fax: (867) 393-8072. E-mail: derekc@nmi.ca. Web: thunderonice.yukon.net.

FIRST ISSUE OF *THE SPORTING NEWS*: ANNIVERSARY. Mar 17, 1886. The first issue of *The Sporting News* was published at St. Louis at a price of two cents per copy. *The Sporting News*, long known as "The Bible of Baseball" and a multisport magazine since 1942, is the oldest continuously published sports publication in the country.

HOCKEY EAST TOURNAMENT. Mar 17–18. FleetCenter, Boston, MA. The post season tournament for the Hockey East Conference. For info: FleetCenter, 150 Causeway St, Boston, MA 02114. Phone: (617) 227-3206. Fax: (617) 227-8403.

JONES, BOBBY: BIRTH ANNIVERSARY. Mar 17, 1902. Robert Tyre (Bobby) Jones, Jr, golfer, born at Atlanta, GA. Jones was an outstanding amateur champion during the 1920s. He is the only golfer to win the sport's Grand Slam, a quartet of tournaments then consisting of the US Amateur, the US Open, the British Amateur and the British Open, doing so in 1930, after which he retired. Along with Alister Mackenzie, he designed the Augusta National Golf Club and created the tournament that soon became known as the Masters. Died at Atlanta, Dec 18, 1971.

LONGHORN WORLD CHAMPIONSHIP RODEO. Mar 17–19. Celeste Center, Ohio Expo Grounds, Columbus, OH. Held in conjunction with the Ohio Beef Expo and Ohio Deer & Turkey Expo. More than 300 cowboys and cowgirls compete in six professional contests ranging from bronc riding to bull riding for top prize money and world championship points. Featuring colorful opening pageantry and Big, Bad BONUS Bulls. 26th annual. Est attendance: 50,000. For info: W. Bruce Lehrke, Pres, Longhorn World Championship Rodeo, Inc, PO Box 70159, Nashville, TN 37207. Phone: (615) 876-1016. Fax: (615) 876-4685. E-mail: lhrodeo@idt.net. Web: www.longhornrodeo.com.

MOUNTAIN PACIFIC SPORTS FEDERATION MEN'S GYMNASTICS CHAMPIONSHIP. Mar 17–18. Air Force Academy, Colorado Springs, CO. Athletes from the PAC-10, Big West, WAC and Mountain West Conferences. For info: MPSF, 800 S Broadway, Ste 102, Walnut Creek, CA 94596-5218. Phone: (925) 296-0723. Fax: (925) 296-0724. E-mail: abeaird@mpsports.org. Web: www.pac-10.org/sports/mpsf.html.

NCAA MEN'S DIVISION III BASKETBALL TOURNAMENT. Mar 17–18. Finals. Salem Civic Center, Salem, VA. For info: NCAA, PO Box 6222, Indianapolis, IN 46206-6222. Phone: (317) 917-6222. Fax: (317) 917-6888. Web: www.ncaa.org.

NCAA WOMEN'S DIVISION I BASKETBALL TOURNAMENT. Mar 17–20. First and second rounds at campus sites. For info: NCAA, PO Box 6222, Indianapolis, IN 46206-6222. Phone: (317) 917-6222. Fax: (317) 917-6888. Web: www.ncaa.org.

NORTHEAST GREAT OUTDOORS SHOW. Mar 17–19. Empire State Plaza, Albany, NY. 14th annual expo with seminars by professional sportsmen, archery ranges, trout pond, flycasting pool, brew lodge, kid's adventure zone and lots more. Annually, the third full weekend in March. Est attendance: 20,000. For info: Tara Sullivan, Exec Dir, Ed Lewi Assoc, 6 Chelsea Pl, Clifton Park, NY 12065. Phone: (518) 383-6183. Fax: (518) 383-6755.

OPEN NORTH AMERICAN CHAMPIONSHIP SLED DOG RACE. Mar 17–19. Fairbanks, AK. World-famous test of skill as mushers from around the world gather in Fairbanks to compete. Oldest, continuously held sled dog race in the world. No limit to the number of dogs in each team—there have been as many as 24 dogs run in one team by one musher. Times from three heats of 20, 20 and 27.6 miles each are combined to determine the winner. Est attendance: 5,000. For info: Alaska Dog Mushers Assn, Box 662, Fairbanks, AK 99707. Phone: (907) 457-MUSH. E-mail: adma@polarnet.com. Web: www.sled-dog.org.

REISER, PETE: BIRTH ANNIVERSARY. Mar 17, 1919. Harold Patrick ("Pete") Reiser, baseball player, coach and manager, born at St. Louis, MO. Reiser saw an extremely promising career come up short after he fractured his skull crashing into an outfield wall in 1942. In all, he was carried off the field nine separate times. Died at Palm Springs, CA, Oct 25, 1981.

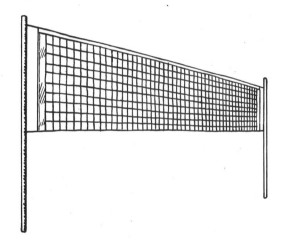

SHAMROCK SPORTSFEST MARATHON. Mar 17–18. Pavilion Convention Center, Virginia Beach, VA. 8K, Masters 8K, 5K walk, sports and fitness expo, runner's clinic and children's marathon. Friday night pasta party. Sat night party. Est attendance: 25,000. For info: Shamrock Sportsfest, 2308 Maple St, Virginia Beach, VA 23451-1310. Phone: (757) 481-5090. Fax: (757) 481-2942. E-mail: sportsfest@juno.com. Web: www.shamrocksportsfest.com.

SPECIAL OLYMPICS IOWA MID-WINTER TOURNAMENT. Mar 17–18. Iowa City, IA. Olympic-style competition for children and adults with mental retardation. For info: Special Olympics Iowa, 3737 Woodland Ave, Ste 325, W Des Moines, IA 50266-1930. Phone: (515) 267-0131. Fax: (515) 267-0232. E-mail: iso@netihs.net.

SPECIAL OLYMPICS MICHIGAN STATE SENIOR BASKETBALL FINALS. Mar 17–19. Grand Rapids, MI. State-level Olympic style competition for adults with mental retardation. For info: Special Olympics Michigan, Central Michigan Univ, Mt Pleasant, MI 48859. Phone: (800) 644-6404. Fax: (517) 774-3034. E-mail: M.K.Lindberg@cmich.edu. Web: www.somi.org.

SPECIAL OLYMPICS MISSOURI BASKETBALL CLASSIC. Mar 17–19. Blue Springs, MO. Olympic-style tournament for athletes with mental retardation. For info: Special Olympics Missouri, 520 Dix Rd, Ste C, Jefferson City, MO 65109. Phone: (573) 635-1660. Fax: (573) 635-8233. E-mail: hq@somo.org. Web: www.somo.org.

WERBLIN, SONNY: 90th BIRTH ANNIVERSARY. Mar 17, 1910. David Abraham ("Sonny") Werblin, sports executive, born at New York, NY. Werblin had several successful careers in radio, television and sports. After making a fortune in entertainment, he and several partners bought the New York Jets in 1963. He signed draft choice Joe Namath to a record contract for a football player and negotiated a large contract with NBC to televise AFL games. After selling his share of the Jets, he ran the New Jersey Sports and Exposition Authority and then became CEO of Madison Square Garden Corporation. Died at New York, Nov 21, 1991.

WHOOPERS AND HOOPERS INVITATIONAL BASKETBALL TOURNAMENT. Mar 17–19. Hastings, NE. 19th annual tournament in which more than 120 teams and 1,200 invited basketball participants—former professional, collegiate and high school—compete five-on-five. Divided into seven divisions including A (semipro or AAU caliber), B (upper intermediate), C (intermediate), D1 & D2 (small-town teams) and women's A (AAU caliber) and B (all others). Trophies awarded for top 4 places in each division. Est attendance: 3,000. For info: Whoopers and Hoopers, 606 W Fifth, Hastings, NE 68901. Phone: (402) 462-4159.

BIRTHDAYS TODAY

Daniel Ray (Danny) Ainge, 41, basketball coach, former basketball and baseball player, born Eugene, OR, Mar 17, 1959.

Samuel Adrian (Sammy) Baugh, 86, former football coach and Pro Football Hall of Fame quarterback, born Temple, TX, Mar 17, 1914.

William (Bill) Mueller, 29, baseball player, born Maryland Heights, MO, Mar 17, 1971.

John Patrick Smiley, 35, baseball player, born Phoenixville, PA, Mar 17, 1965.

Jerome Woods, 27, football player, born Memphis, TN, Mar 17, 1973.

MARCH 18 — SATURDAY

Day 78 — 288 Remaining

NCAA BASKETBALL CHAMPIONS THIS DATE

1953   Indiana

BERING SEA ICE GOLF CLASSIC. Mar 18. Nome, AK. A six-hole course played on the frozen Bering Sea. The object is to land the bright-orange ricocheting golf ball

March	S	M	T	W	T	F	S
2000				1	2	3	4
	5	6	7	8	9	10	11
	12	13	14	15	16	17	18
	19	20	21	22	23	24	25
	26	27	28	29	30	31	

into the sunken, flagged coffee cans before losing the ball among the built-up chunks of ice. Starts promptly at 10 AM at the Breakers Bar. Approximately 60 golfers. For info: Bering Sea Lions Club, Box 326, Nome, AK 99762.

BIG TEN WOMEN'S GYMNASTICS CHAMPIONSHIPS. Mar 18. Penn State University, State College, PA. For info: Big Ten Conference, 1500 W Higgins Rd, Park Ridge, IL 60068-6300. Phone: (847) 696-1010. Fax: (847) 696-1150. Web: www.bigten.org.

BRAVES ANNOUNCE SHIFT TO MILWAUKEE: ANNIVERSARY. Mar 18, 1953. In baseball's first franchise shift in half a century, the Boston Braves announced that they would become the Milwaukee Braves. The team remained at Milwaukee through the 1965 season after which it moved to Atlanta.

DONOHUE, MARK: BIRTH ANNIVERSARY. Mar 18, 1937. Mark Donohue, auto racing driver, born at Summit, NJ. Donohue became a professional race driver in 1966 and, after success in a variety of different kinds of racing, gravitated toward Indy cars. He finished seventh in his first Indianapolis 500 and won the race in 1972. He came out of retirement in 1974 and was killed in a crash practicing for the Austrian Grand Prix. Died near Graz, Austria, Aug 19, 1975.

ENGLAND: HEAD OF THE RIVER RACE. Mar 18. Mortlake to Putney, River Thames, London. At 3:30 PM. Processional race for 420 eight-oared crews, starting at 10-second intervals. Est attendance: 7,000. For info: Mr A.P. Ruddle, 59 Berkeley Ct, Oatlands Drive, Weybridge, Surrey, England KT13 9HY. Phone: (44) (193) 222-0401.

FRIEDMAN, BENNY: 95th BIRTH ANNIVERSARY. Mar 18, 1905. Benjamin (Benny) Friedman, football player, coach and administrator, born at Cleveland, OH. Friedman excelled at the University of Michigan, playing quarterback (1924–26) and earning All-American honors. As a pro, he played with the Cleveland Bulldogs, the Detroit Wolverines, the New York Giants and the Brooklyn Dodgers. He coached at CCNY and served as athletic director at Brandeis. Died at New York, NY, Nov 24, 1982.

JORDAN'S BACK: 5th ANNIVERSARY. Mar 18, 1995. Michael Jordan, easily considered one of the National Basketball Association's greatest all-time players, made history again when he announced that he was returning to professional play after a 17-month break. The 32-year-old star had retired just before the start of the 1993–94 season, following the murder of his beloved father, James Jordan. Jordan, who averaged 32.3 points a game during regular-season play, had led the Chicago Bulls to three successive NBA titles. While retired, he tried a baseball career, playing for a Chicago White Sox minor league team, the Birmingham Barons. After Jordan's return, the Bulls added a fourth NBA World Championship in the '95-'96 season, a fifth in '96-'97 and a sixth in '97-'98.

NCAA DIVISION III HOCKEY CHAMPIONSHIP. Mar 18–19. Finals. Site TBA. For info: NCAA, PO Box 6222, Indianapolis, IN 46206-6222. Phone: (317) 917-6222. Fax: (317) 917-6888. Web: www.ncaa.org.

PORTUGAL: WORLD CROSS-COUNTRY CHAMPIONSHIP. Mar 18–19. Vilamoura, Portugal. 28th competition. For info: Intl Amateur Athletic Federation, 17, rue Princesse Florestine, BP 359, 98007 Monte Carlo, Monaco. Phone: (377) 93-10-88-88. Fax: (377) 93-15-95-15. Web: www.iaaf.org.

ROCKET SCORES 50: 55th ANNIVERSARY. Mar 18, 1945. Right wing Maurice ("The Rocket") Richard of the Montreal Canadiens became the first player in the NHL to score 50 goals in a season when he tallied in a 4–2 win over the Boston Bruins.

SEC GYMNASTICS CHAMPIONSHIPS. Mar 18. Auburn University, Auburn, AL. For info: Southeastern Conference, 2201 Civic Center Blvd, Birmingham, AL 35203-1103. Phone: (205) 458-3010. Fax: (205) 458-3030. E-mail: twilson@sec.org. Web: www.secsports.com.

BIRTHDAYS TODAY

Geronimo Emiliano Berroa, 35, baseball player, born Santo Domingo, Dominican Republic, Mar 18, 1965.

Bonnie Blair, 36, Olympic gold medal speed skater, born Cornwall, NY, Mar 18, 1964.

Guy Carbonneau, 40, hockey player, born Sept-Iles, Quebec, Canada, Mar 18, 1960.

George Plimpton, 73, author (*Paper Lion, Out of My League, The Bogey Man*), born New York, NY, Mar 18, 1927.

Andre Previn Rison, 33, football player, born Flint, MI, Mar 18, 1967.

MARCH 19 — SUNDAY

Day 79 — 287 Remaining

NCAA BASKETBALL CHAMPIONS THIS DATE

1955	San Francisco
1960	Ohio State
1966	Texas Western

ASHBURN, RICHIE: BIRTH ANNIVERSARY. Mar 19, 1927. Don Richard (Richie) Ashburn, broadcaster and Baseball Hall of Fame outfielder, born at Tilden, NE. Ashburn won two National League batting titles and collected 2,574 hits over a 15-year career. He was a key member of the 1950 Philadelphia Phillies, known as the Whiz Kids. After retiring he broadcast Phillies games for 35 years. Inducted into the Hall of Fame in 1995. Died at New York, NY, Sept 9, 1997.

BERENSON, SENDA: BIRTH ANNIVERSARY. Mar 19, 1868. Senda Berenson Abbott, Basketball Hall of Fame physical educator and basketball innovator, born at Biturmansk, Lithuania. Berenson and her family came to Boston in 1875. She studied physical education at the Boston Normal School of Gymnastics and taught physical training at Smith College. After reading about James Naismith's new game of basketball, she introduced it to her students in 1892, adapting the rules for girls: no snatching the ball away from opponents, no holding the ball for more than three seconds and no more than three dribbles. She also divided the court into three areas and forbade players from crossing the lines. These rules, incorporated into a rule book that Berenson edited for 18 years, remained substantially in force until the 1960s. Inducted into the Hall of Fame in 1985. Died at Santa Barbara, CA, Feb 16, 1954.

CLARKE GETS 1,000th POINT: ANNIVERSARY. Mar 19, 1981. Center Bobby Clarke of the Philadelphia Flyers got the 1,000th point of his National Hockey League career, a goal in a 5–3 win over the Boston Bruins. Clarke finished his career with 1,210 points.

FEDERKO GETS 1,000th POINT: ANNIVERSARY. Mar 19, 1988. Center Bernie Federko of the St. Louis Blues got the 1,000th point of his National Hockey League career, an assist in a 5–3 loss to the Hartford Whalers. Federko finished his career with 1,130 points.

IMMACULATA WINS FIRST AIAW CROWN: ANNIVERSARY. Mar 19, 1972. Immaculata College defeated West Chester State, 52–48, to win the first Association of Intercollegiate Athletics for Women national basketball tournament. The AIAW crowned a champion for 11 years, but most Division I teams entered the new NCAA tournament starting in 1982.

MAUI MARATHON. Mar 19. Kahului, HI. For info: VIRR, PO Box 330099, Kahului, HI 96733. Phone: (808) 871-6441. E-mail: bark@maui.net. Web: www.mauimarathon.com.

McGINNITY, IRON JOE: BIRTH ANNIVERSARY. Mar 19, 1871. Joseph Jerome ("Iron Joe") McGinnity, Baseball Hall of Fame pitcher born at Rock Island, IL. McGinnity pitched 10 years in the major leagues at the turn of the 20th century and never had a losing season. He earned his nickname for his durability, such as pitching both ends of a doubleheader, which he did five times in 1903. Inducted into the Hall of Fame in 1946. Died at New York, NY, Nov 14, 1929.

MURDOCH BUYS DODGERS: ANNIVERSARY. Mar 19, 1998. Major league baseball owners gave final approval to the sale of the Los Angeles Dodgers from Peter O'Malley to media mogul Rupert Murdoch's Australian-based news conglomerate, News Corp. O'Malley had inherited the Dodgers from his father Walter who moved the team from Brooklyn to Los Angeles following the 1957 season. Critics of the $311 million sale bemoaned the extravagant price tag and the fact that the Dodgers would no longer be family-owned.

NATIONAL SPORTS TRIVIA WEEK. Mar 19–25. Discuss your favorite sports trivia question now! Super week of overlapping sports events: Final Four of college basketball is approaching, pro basketball and hockey still being played, spring training for baseball is underway. From the publishers of "Super Bowl Trivia" and "World Series Trivia." For info: Judy Colbert, Tuft Turtle Publishing, Box 3308, Crofton, MD 21114-0308. Phone: (301) 858-0196. E-mail: jmcolbert@aol.com.

PHILADELPHIA BOAT SHOW. Mar 19–23. Pennsylvania Convention Center, Philadelphia, PA. 64th annual show features more than 600 power boats, engines and accessories from all major manufacturers, plus informative boating and fishing seminars. Est attendance: 65,000. For info: NMMA Boat Shows, 200 E Randolph Dr, Ste 5100, Chicago, IL 60601-6528. Phone: (312) 946-6262. Fax: (312) 946-0401. Web: www.boatshows.com.

PROPP GETS 1,000th POINT: ANNIVERSARY. Mar 19, 1994. Left wing Brian Propp of the Hartford Whalers got the 1,000th point of his National Hockey League career, a goal in a 5–3 win over the Philadelphia Flyers. Propp finished his career with 1,004 points.

TEXAS WESTERN WINS NCAA CROWN: ANNIVERSARY. Mar 19, 1966. Texas Western University (later the University of Texas at El Paso) won the NCAA Men's Basketball Tournament by upsetting the University of Kentucky, 72–65. The game took on national significance as Texas Western, coached by Don Haskins, started five black players against Kentucky's all-white team at a time when race relations in the US was a major political and social issue.

BIRTHDAYS TODAY

Vladimir Konstantinov, 33, former hockey player, born Murmansk, USSR, Mar 19, 1967.
Janne Laukkanen, 30, hockey player, born Lahti, Finland, Mar 19, 1970.
Patrick Joseph (Pat) Leahy, 49, former football player, born St. Louis, MO, Mar 19, 1951.
Andrew Walter (Andy) Reid, 42, football coach, born Los Angeles, CA, Mar 19, 1958.

MARCH 20 — MONDAY
Day 80 — 286 Remaining

NCAA BASKETBALL CHAMPIONS THIS DATE	
1954	LaSalle
1965	UCLA

AUSTRALIA: WORLD FIGURE SKATING CHAMPIONSHIPS. Mar 20–26. Brisbane Entertainment Centre, Brisbane, Australia. World championship competition in men's, ladies, pairs and ice dancing divisions. Est attendance: 150,000. For info and tickets, E-mail: organ iser@skatingaus.com.au.

DIANE CRUMP WINS FIRST RACE: ANNIVERSARY. Mar 20, 1969. Jockey Diane Crump won the first race of her career less than two months after becoming the first woman to ride in a pari-mutuel race in the US. Her victory came at Gulfstream Park, FL.

FIRST COLLEGE BASKETBALL GAME: ANNIVERSARY. Mar 20, 1897. Yale beat Pennsylvania, 32–10, in the first men's intercollegiate basketball game, played at New Haven.

FIRST FIGURE SKATING CHAMPIONSHIPS: ANNIVERSARY. Mar 20, 1914. The first world's figure skating championships opened at New Haven, CT. Events included men's singles, women's singles, pairs and waltzing, later known as ice dancing.

FIRST NCAA HOCKEY CHAMPIONSHIP: ANNIVERSARY. Mar 20, 1948. The first NCAA ice hockey championship concluded at Colorado Springs, CO. The University of Michigan defeated Dartmouth College, 8–4, to win the title.

NABISCO DINAH SHORE CELEBRITY PRO-AM. Mar 20–26 (tentative). Mission Hills Country Club, Rancho Mirage, CA. The first of the year's four major championships in women's golf, held since 1972. For info: LPGA, 100 Intl Gold Dr, Daytona Beach, FL 32124. Phone: (904) 274-6200. Fax: (904) 274-1099. Web: www.lpga.org.

SPRING. Mar 20–June 20. In the Northern Hemisphere spring begins today with the vernal equinox, at 2:35 AM, EST. Note that in the Southern Hemisphere today is the beginning of autumn. Sun rises due east and sets due west everywhere on Earth (except near poles) and the daylight length (interval between sunrise and sunset) is virtually the same everywhere: 12 hours, 8 minutes.

SPRING FEVER GOLF TOURNAMENT. Mar 2 (tentative). Bay Oaks Country Club, Clear Lake Area, Houston, TX. Annual fundraiser sponsored by the Clear Lake Area Chamber of Commerce. For info: Clear Lake Area Chamber of Comm, 1201 NASA Rd 1, Houston, TX 77058. Phone: (281) 488-7676.

TAYLOR, FREDERICK: BIRTH ANNIVERSARY. Mar 20, 1856. Frederick Winslow Taylor, tennis player, born at Philadelphia, PA. Otherwise known as the "Father of Scientific Management," Taylor was an innovative athlete who played sports precisely and absolutely by the rules. He was a baseball pitcher when the ball was still pitched underhand, a tennis player who invented sturdier nets and a golfer who devised an irrigation method for greens and several unique golf clubs. Died at Philadelphia, Mar 21, 1915.

BIRTHDAYS TODAY

Daron Oshay ("Mookie") Blaylock, 33, basketball player, born Garland, TX, Mar 20, 1967.
Robert Gordon (Bobby) Orr, 52, Hockey Hall of Fame defenseman, born Parry Sound, Ontario, Canada, Mar 20, 1948.
Patrick James (Pat) Riley, 55, basketball coach and former player, born Schenectady, NY, Mar 20, 1945.

MARCH 21 — TUESDAY
Day 81 — 285 Remaining

NCAA BASKETBALL CHAMPIONS THIS DATE	
1959	California
1964	UCLA
1970	UCLA

BABE DIDRIKSON PITCHES FOR ATHLETICS: 65th ANNIVERSARY. Mar 21, 1934. Mildred ("Babe") Didriksen, perhaps the greatest woman athlete of all time, pitched one inning of baseball for the Philadelphia Athletics in an exhibition game against the Brooklyn Dodgers. Babe hit the first batter she faced and walked the next. The third hit into a triple play.

MAHOVLICH SCORES 500th GOAL: ANNIVERSARY. Mar 21, 1973. Frank Mahovlich of the Montreal Canadiens scored the 500th regular-season goal of his career in a 3–2 victory over the Vancouver Canucks, thus becoming the 5th player in National Hockey League history to reach 500. Mahovlich finished his career with 533 goals and entered the Hockey Hall of Fame in 1981.

McDONALD SCORES 500th GOAL: ANNIVERSARY. Mar 21, 1989. Right wing Lanny McDonald of the Calgary Flames scored the 500th and last regular-season goal of his National Hockey League career. He tallied against goalie Mark Fitzpatrick of the New York Islanders in a 4–1 win. McDonald, the 13th player to reach 500 goals, was inducted into the Hockey Hall of Fame in 1992.

March 2000	S	M	T	W	T	F	S
				1	2	3	4
	5	6	7	8	9	10	11
	12	13	14	15	16	17	18
	19	20	21	22	23	24	25
	26	27	28	29	30	31	

RAMS SIGN KENNY WASHINGTON: ANNIVERSARY.
Mar 21, 1946. One year before Jackie Robinson began playing major league baseball, Kenny Washington broke the NFL's color line. Washington signed a contract to play for the Los Angeles Rams.

SUTHERLAND, JOCK: BIRTH ANNIVERSARY.
Mar 21, 1889. John Bain ("Jock") Sutherland, football player and coach born at Coupar-Angus, Scotland. Sutherland came to the US at age 18, entering the University of Pittsburgh when he was 25. Despite never having played football, he became an All-American guard and studied dentistry. He coached at Lafayette and Pittsburgh. After World War II, his coaching success with the Pittsburgh Steelers was cut short by a fatal brain tumor. Died at Pittsburgh, PA, Apr 11, 1948.

BIRTHDAYS TODAY

Herman Thomas (Tommy) Davis, 61, former baseball player, born New York, NY, Mar 21, 1939.
Michael Joseph (Mike) Dunleavy, 46, basketball coach and former player, born New York, NY, Mar 21, 1954.
Shawon Donnell Dunston, 37, baseball player, born New York, NY, Mar 21, 1963.
Thomas Raymond (Tom) Flores, 63, former football coach and player, born Fresno, CA, Mar 21, 1937.
Johan Garpenlov, 32, hockey player, born Stockholm, Sweden, Mar 21, 1968.
Al Anthony Iafrate, 34, hockey player, born Dearborn, MI, Mar 21, 1966.
Vitaly Nikolaevich Potapenko, 25, basketball player, born Kiev, Ukraine, USSR, Mar 21, 1975.
Scott Christopher Williams, 32, basketball player, born Hacienda Heights, CA, Mar 21, 1968.

MARCH 22 — WEDNESDAY
Day 82 — 284 Remaining

NCAA BASKETBALL CHAMPIONS THIS DATE	
1958	Kentucky
1969	UCLA

BOATING ACCIDENT KILLS BALLPLAYERS: ANNIVERSARY.
Mar 22, 1993. Two members of the Cleveland Indians, Tim Crews and Steve Olin, were killed, and teammate Bob Ojeda was injured in a boating accident on Little Lake Nellie, FL. The trio, in Florida for spring training, hit a dock.

NCAA MEN'S DIVISION II BASKETBALL TOURNAMENT.
Mar 22–25. Finals. Commonwealth Convention Center, Louisville, KY. For info: NCAA, PO Box 6222, Indianapolis, IN 46206-6222. Phone: (317) 917-6222. Fax: (317) 917-6888. Web: www.ncaa.org.

NCAA WOMEN'S DIVISION II BASKETBALL TOURNAMENT.
Mar 22–25. Finals at campus site. For info: NCAA, PO Box 6222, Indianapolis, IN 46206-6222. Phone: (317) 917-6222. Fax: (317) 917-6888. Web: www.ncaa.org.

TAMPA BAY CLASSIC.
Mar 22–26. Bob Thomas Equestrian Center, Florida Expo Park, Tampa, FL. The eighth event in the 2000 Cosequin Winter Equestrian Festival. For info: Stadium Jumping, Inc, 3104 Cherry Palm Dr, Ste 220, Tampa, FL 33619. Phone: (800) 237-8924 or (813) 623-5801. Fax: (813) 626-5369. Web: www.stadiumjumping.com.

BIRTHDAYS TODAY

Sean Robert Berry, 34, baseball player, born Santa Monica, CA, Mar 22, 1966.

Shawn Paul Bradley, 28, basketball player, born Landstuhl, West Germany, Mar 22, 1972.
Marcus D. Camby, 26, basketball player, born Hartford, CT, Mar 22, 1974.
Robert Quinlan (Bob) Costas, 48, broadcaster, born New York, NY, Mar 22, 1952.
Luther Elliss, 27, football player, born Mancos, CO, Mar 22, 1973.
Glenallen Hill, 35, baseball player, born Santa Cruz, CA, Mar 22, 1965.
Charles Edward ("Easy Ed") Macauley, Jr, 72, Basketball Hall of Fame center and forward, born St. Louis, MO, Mar 22, 1928.
Ramon Jaime Martinez, 32, baseball player, born Santo Domingo, Dominican Republic, Mar 22, 1968.
Russell Maryland, 31, football player, born Chicago, IL, Mar 22, 1969.
Frank Victor Pulli, 65, baseball umpire, born Easton, PA, Mar 22, 1935.
Brian K. Shaw, 34, basketball player, born Oakland, CA, Mar 22, 1966.

MARCH 23 — THURSDAY
Day 83 — 283 Remaining

NCAA BASKETBALL CHAMPIONS THIS DATE	
1948	Kentucky
1957	North Carolina
1963	Loyola (IL)
1968	UCLA

CLEVELAND AWARDED NFL FRANCHISE: ANNIVERSARY.
Mar 23, 1998. The National Football League awarded an expansion franchise to the city of Cleveland to begin play in the 1999 season. The team, to be called the Browns, replaced Cleveland's former team, also the Browns and now the Baltimore Ravens.

CRAVATH, GAVVY: BIRTH ANNIVERSARY.
Mar 23, 1881. Clifford Clarence ("Gavvy") Cravath, baseball player, born at Escondido, CA. Cravath hit 24 home runs in 1915, the major league record until Babe Ruth came along. He led the National League in homers five times and tied for the league lead once. Died at Laguna Beach, CA, May 23, 1963.

FIRST ENGLISH TRACK AND FIELD CHAMPIONSHIPS: ANNIVERSARY.
Mar 23, 1866. The Amateur Athletic Club sponsored the inaugural English Athletics Championships at Walham Green, London. Eight events were contested.

NCAA MEN'S AND WOMEN'S FENCING CHAMPIONSHIPS.
Mar 23–26. Site TBA. For info: NCAA, PO Box 6222, Indianapolis, IN 46206-6222. Phone: (317) 917-6222. Fax: (317) 917-6888. Web: www.ncaa.org.

NCAA MEN'S DIVISION I BASKETBALL TOURNAMENT.
Mar 23–26. Regionals at Carrier Dome, Syracuse, NY; Frank Erwin Center, Austin, TX; The Palace of Auburn Hills, Auburn Hills, MI; and University Arena, Albuquerque, NM. For info: NCAA, PO Box 6222, Indianapolis, IN 46206-6222. Phone: (317) 917-6222. Fax: (317) 917-6888. Web: www.ncaa.org.

NCAA MEN'S DIVISION I SWIMMING AND DIVING CHAMPIONSHIPS. Mar 23–25. University of Minnesota, Minneapolis, MN. For info: NCAA, PO Box 6222, Indianapolis, IN 46206-6222. Phone: (317) 917-6222. Fax: (317) 917-6888. Web: www.ncaa.org.

QUICKEST THREE GOALS: ANNIVERSARY. Mar 23, 1952. Bill Mosienko of the Chicago Blackhawks set an NHL record by scoring three goals in 21 seconds in a game against the New York Rangers. Mosienko scored at 6:09, 6:20 and 6:30 of the third period against goalie Lorne Anderson. Chicago won, 7–6.

WLAF MAKES ITS DEBUT: ANNIVERSARY. Mar 23, 1991. The World League of American Football, part of a marketing attempt by the National Football League to extend the game's popularity in Europe, made its debut as the London Monarchs defeated the Frankfurt Galaxy, 24–11.

CHASE'S SPORTSQUOTE OF THE DAY

"I never thought I'd lead the NBA in rebounding, but I got a lot of help from my teammates. They did a lot of missing."—Moses Malone

---

BIRTHDAYS TODAY

Sir Roger Bannister, 71, physician and former track athlete, born Harrow, England, Mar 23, 1929.
Ronald Vincent (Ron) Jaworski, 49, broadcaster and former football player, born Lackawanna, NY, Mar 23, 1951.
Jason Frederick Kidd, 27, basketball player, born San Francisco, CA, Mar 23, 1973.
Moses Eugene Malone, 45, former basketball player, born Petersburg, VA, Mar 23, 1955.
Carl McNally Pickens, 30, football player, born Murphy, NC, Mar 23, 1970.
Daren James Puppa, 35, hockey player, born Kirkland Lake, Ontario, Canada, Mar 23, 1965.

☆ ☆ ☆

MARCH 24 — FRIDAY
Day 84 — 282 Remaining

NCAA BASKETBALL CHAMPIONS THIS DATE

1956	San Francisco
1962	Cincinnati
1980	Louisville

ASPEN/SNOWMASS BANANA SEASON. Mar 24–Apr 2. Snowmass Village, CO. Events: Banana Bonanza Hunt, High Altitude Beach Party and Chicken Legs contest for the whitest legs, Bartenders' Banana Brawl Drink Contest, Banana Sidewalk Sale. For the Banana Bonanza Hunt, hundreds of prize-filled plastic bananas are hidden on the ski slopes. Clues lead to one "Big Banana Prize." Est attendance: 3,000. For info: Snowmass Village Resort Assn, PO Box 5566, Snowmass Village, CO 81615. Phone: (970) 923-2000 or (800) SNOW-MASS.

March *2000*	S	M	T	W	T	F	S
				1	2	3	4
	5	6	7	8	9	10	11
	12	13	14	15	16	17	18
	19	20	21	22	23	24	25
	26	27	28	29	30	31	

DAYTONA BEACH SPRING '00 SPEEDWAY SPECTACULAR. Mar 24–26. Daytona International Speedway, Daytona Beach, FL. 11th annual car show of all makes and models of collector vehicles. Many car clubs make this their largest annual event. Show includes display of antiques, classics, sports cars, muscle cars, race cars, custom and special interest vehicles on the speedway infield with a large swap meet of auto parts and accessories. Collector car sales corral, vintage bicycle swap meet and crafts sale. Annually, the last or next to the last weekend in March. Est attendance: 30,000. For info: Rick D'Louhy, Exec Dir, Daytona Beach Racing and Recreational Facilities District, PO Box 1958, Daytona Beach, FL 32115-1958. Phone: (904) 255-7355. Web: www .carshows.org.

DUGAS, GUS: BIRTH ANNIVERSARY. Mar 24, 1907. Augustin Joseph (Gus) Dugas, baseball player, born at St.-Jean-de-Matha, Quebec, Canada. Dugas, an outfielder and first baseman, was the first Canadian-born player to appear in the major leagues. He played four seasons in the early 1930s and threw out the ceremonial first pitch at the first game at Montreal's Olympic Stadium in 1977. Died at Norwich, CT, Apr 14, 1997.

LEMIEUX GETS 1,000th POINT: ANNIVERSARY. Mar 24, 1992. Center Mario Lemieux of the Pittsburgh Penguins got the 1,000th point of his National Hockey League career, an assist in a 4–2 loss to the Detroit Red Wings. Lemieux finished his career with 1,494 points.

LENGLEN, SUZANNE: 100th BIRTH ANNIVERSARY. Mar 24, 1900. Suzanne Lenglen, tennis player, born at Compiegne, France. A dramatic tennis player with a temper she could not hide, Lenglen was one of the outstanding players in the post-World War I era. She won six singles titles at Wimbledon and another six French Opens. A daring woman, she appeared at Wimbledon in an outfit that exposed her arms, and she wore a headband that came to be known as the "Lenglen bandeaux." Died July 4, 1938.

LONGEST NHL GAME: ANNIVERSARY. Mar 24, 1936. Mud Bruneteau of the Detroit Red Wings scored at 16:30 of the sixth overtime period to end the longest game in National Hockey League history. The goal gave the Red Wings a 1–0 victory over the Montreal Maroons in a Stanley Cup semifinal game. Detroit won the series, three games to none, and went on to defeat the Toronto Maple Leafs in the finals.

LONGHORN WORLD CHAMPIONSHIP RODEO. Mar 24–26. ALLTEL Arena, Little Rock, AR. More than 200 cowboys and cowgirls compete in six professional contests ranging from bronc riding to bull riding for top prize money and world championship points. Featuring colorful opening pageantry and Big, Bad BONUS Bulls. 1st annual. Est attendance: 24,000. For info: W. Bruce Lehrke, Pres., Longhorn World Championship Rodeo, Inc, PO Box 70159, Nashville, TN 37207. Phone: (615) 876-1016. Fax: (615) 876-4685. E-mail: lhrodeo@idt.net. Web: www.longhornrodeo.com.

NCAA DIVISION I HOCKEY CHAMPIONSHIP. Mar 24–26. Regionals at the Pepsi Arena, Albany, NY, (Mar 25–26) and the Mariucci Arena, Minneapolis, MN (Mar 24–25). For info: NCAA, PO Box 6222, Indianapolis, IN 46206-6222. Phone: (317) 917-6222. Fax: (317) 917-6888. Web: www.ncaa.org.

SISLER, GEORGE: BIRTH ANNIVERSARY. Mar 24, 1893. George Harold Sisler, Baseball Hall of Fame first baseman, born at Manchester, OH. Sisler started out as a pitcher but was converted to a first baseman by Branch Rickey. He hit .407 in 1920 and .420 in 1922 and was a superb fielder. Inducted into the Hall of Fame in 1939. Died at St. Louis, MO, Mar 26, 1973.

SPECIAL OLYMPICS VIRGINIA BASKETBALL CHAMPIONSHIPS. Mar 24–25. Fredericksburg, VA. 600 athletes with mental disabilities hit the hoops in full-court, half-court and individual skills action. For info: Special Olympics Virginia, 3212 Skipwith Rd, Ste 100, Richmond, VA 23294. Phone: (804) 346-5544.

BIRTHDAYS TODAY

Jesus Maria (Jay) Alou, 58, former baseball player, born Haina, Dominican Republic, Mar 24, 1942.

Wilson Eduardo Alvarez, 30, baseball player, born Maracaibo, Venezuela, Mar 24, 1970.

Pat Bradley, 49, LPGA Hall of Fame golfer, born Westford, MA, Mar 24, 1951.

Stefan Andrew (Steve) Karsay, 28, baseball player, born New York, NY, Mar 24, 1972.

Peyton Williams Manning, 24, football player, born New Orleans, Mar 24, 1976.

Alejandro (Alex) Olmedo, 64, former tennis player, born Arequipa, Peru, Mar 24, 1936.

Patrick (Pat) Verbeek, 36, hockey player, born Sarnia, Ontario, Canada, Mar 24, 1964.

Lawrence Frank (Larry) Wilson, 62, Pro Football Hall of Fame defensive back, born Rigby, ID, Mar 24, 1938.

MARCH 25 — SATURDAY
Day 85 — 281 Remaining

NCAA BASKETBALL CHAMPIONS THIS DATE

1947	Holy Cross
1961	Cincinnati
1967	UCLA
1972	UCLA
1974	North Carolina State

BIG 12 WOMEN'S GYMNASTICS CHAMPIONSHIPS. Mar 25. Iowa State University, Ames, IA. For info: Big Twelve Conference, 2201 Stemmons Freeway, 28th Floor, Dallas, TX 75207. Phone: (214) 742-1212. Fax: (214) 742-2046.

COSELL, HOWARD: BIRTH ANNIVERSARY. Mar 25, 1918. Howard Cosell, broadcaster, born at New York, NY. After earning a law degree, Cosell began his broadcasting career as the host of "Howard Cosell Speaking of Sports." He achieved national prominence and a great deal of notoriety for his support of Muhammad Ali's stand against the Vietnam War and then as co-host of ABC's Monday Night Football. Died at New York, Apr 23, 1994.

CRUTCHFIELD, JIMMIE: 90th BIRTH ANNIVERSARY. Mar 25, 1910. John William ("Jimmie") Crutchfield, baseball player, born at Ardmore, MO. Crutchfield was an all-star outfielder for the Pittsburgh Crawfords, a Negro Leagues team in the 1930s. He was fast and hit .325 in his career. Died at Chicago, IL, Mar 31, 1993.

EAGLESON RESIGNS FROM HALL OF FAME: ANNIVERSARY. Mar 25, 1998. Following protests from other members, lawyer and former player agent Alan Eagleson resigned from the Hockey Hall of Fame, six days before the Hall's board was scheduled to vote on whether to expel him. Eagleson, in jail for fraud, thus became the first member of any of the major professional sports halls of fame to resign.

FIRST THREE-POINTER: ANNIVERSARY. Mar 25, 1979. Chris Ford of the Boston Celtics made the first three-point field goal in NBA history in a game against the Houston Rockets.

HORTON SMITH WINS FIRST MASTERS: ANNIVERSARY. Mar 25, 1934. Horton Smith shot four-under-par 284 to capture the first Masters golf tournament by one stroke over Craig Wood. Smith won again in 1936. Wood lost a play-off to Gene Sarazen in 1935 and won his own green jacket in 1941.

HOWARD, FRANK: BIRTH ANNIVERSARY. Mar 25, 1909. Frank James Howard, football player and coach, born at Barlow Bend, AL. Howard played guard at the University of Alabama where he was also named Phi Beta Kappa. He served as an assistant coach under Jess Neely at Clemson University and was named head coach in 1940. Howard's Tigers won eight conference crowns before his retirement in 1969. Died at Clemson, SC, Jan 26, 1996.

NCAA WOMEN'S DIVISION I BASKETBALL TOURNAMENT. Mar 25–27. Regionals at Stuart Siegel Center, Richmond, VA; The Pyramid, Memphis, TN; Municipal Auditorium, Kansas City, MO; and Memorial Coliseum, Portland, OR. For info: NCAA, PO Box 6222, Indianapolis, IN 46206-6222. Phone: (317) 917-6222. Fax: (317) 917-6888. Web: www.ncaa.org.

PAC-10 WOMEN'S GYMNASTICS CHAMPIONSHIPS. Mar 25. Stanford University, Palo Alto, CA. For info: PAC-10 Conference, 800 S Broadway, Ste 400, Walnut Creek, CA 94596. Phone: (510) 932-4411. Fax: (510) 932-4601.

POSSUM PEDAL 100 BICYCLE RIDE/RACE. Mar 25. Courthouse Square, Graham, TX. Bicycle fun ride with 1,000 participants through the rolling hills and around Graham. Sponsor: Rotary Club of Graham Scholarship Fund. Annually, the "Taste of Graham." Est attendance: 5,000. For info: Possum Pedal 100, PO Box 1240, Graham, TX 76450. Phone: (800) 256-4844 or (940) 549-3355. Fax: (940) 549-7405. E-mail: bbsinc@wf.net.

SMITHSONIAN KITE FESTIVAL. Mar 25. National Mall, Washington, DC. 34th annual. Rain date is Mar 26. For info: Smithsonian Institution, 900 Jefferson Dr SW, Washington, DC 20560. Phone: (202) 357-2700.

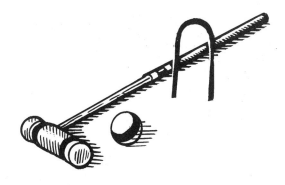

BIRTHDAYS TODAY

David Travis Fryman, 31, baseball player, born Lexington, KY, Mar 25, 1969.

Thomas Michael (Tom) Glavine, 34, baseball player, born Concord, MA, Mar 25, 1966.

Avery Johnson, 35, basketball player, born New Orleans, LA, Mar 25, 1965.

Lee Louis Mazzilli, 45, former baseball player, born New York, NY, Mar 25, 1955.

Robert (Bob) Sura, Jr, 27, basketball player, born Wilkes-Barre, PA, Mar 25, 1973.

Sheryl Swoopes, 29, basketball player, born Brownfield, TX, Mar 25, 1971.

Daniel Allen (Dan) Wilson, 31, baseball player, born Arlington Heights, IL, Mar 25, 1969.

Kenneth (Ken) Wregget, 36, hockey player, born Brandon, Manitoba, Canada, Mar 25, 1964.

MARCH 26 — SUNDAY
Day 86 — 280 Remaining

NCAA BASKETBALL CHAMPIONS THIS DATE

1946	Oklahoma A&M
1949	Kentucky
1952	Kansas
1973	UCLA
1979	Michigan State

ENGLE, RIP: BIRTH ANNIVERSARY. Mar 26, 1906. Charles Albert ("Rip") Engle, football player and coach, born at Elk Lick (now Salisbury), PA. Engle played college sports, including football, at Western Maryland and then began coaching at the high school level. He became head coach at Brown in 1944 and moved to Penn State in 1950. He coached the Nittany Lions to a 104–48–4 record and retired in 1966. Died at Bellefonte, PA, Mar 7, 1983.

SECOND-LARGEST TRADE IN NFL HISTORY: ANNIVERSARY. Mar 26, 1953. The Cleveland Browns and the Baltimore Colts completed the second-largest trade in National Football League history involving 15 players. The Browns sent Tom Catlin, Don Colo, Hershel Forester, Mike McCormack and John Petibon to Baltimore in exchange for Harry Agganis, Dick Batten, Gern Nagler, Bert Rechichar, Ed Sharkey, Don Shula, Art Spinney, Stu Sheets, Carl Taseff and Elmer Willhoite.

BIRTHDAYS TODAY

Marcus LeMarr Allen, 40, Heisman Trophy running back, born San Diego, CA, Mar 26, 1960.
Gino Raymond Michael Cappelletti, 66, former football player, born Keewatin, MN, Mar 26, 1934.
Ann Elizabeth Meyers, 45, broadcaster and Basketball Hall of Fame forward, born San Diego, CA, Mar 26, 1955.
Michael Peca, 26, hockey player, born Toronto, Ontario, Canada, Mar 26, 1974.
Michael John (Mike) Remlinger, 34, baseball player, born Middletown, NY, Mar 26, 1966.
Richard Shane Reynolds, 32, baseball player, born Bastrop, LA, Mar 26, 1968.
Ulf Samuelsson, 36, hockey player, born Fagersta, Sweden, Mar 26, 1964.
John Houston Stockton, 38, basketball player, born Spokane, WA, Mar 26, 1962.
Jose Luis Vizcaino, 32, baseball player, born San Cristobal, Dominican Republic, Mar 26, 1968.

MARCH 27 — MONDAY
Day 87 — 279 Remaining

NCAA BASKETBALL CHAMPIONS THIS DATE

1939	Oregon
1945	Oklahoma A&M
1951	Kentucky
1971	UCLA
1978	Kentucky

CUBS NICKNAME COINED: ANNIVERSARY. Mar 27, 1902. The *Chicago Daily News* began calling the city's

March *2000*	S	M	T	W	T	F	S
					1	2	3	4
	5	6	7	8	9	10	11
	12	13	14	15	16	17	18
	19	20	21	22	23	24	25
	26	27	28	29	30	31	

National League team the Cubs. Formed as the Chicago White Stockings, the team had also been known as the Colts and the Orphans.

FIRST NCAA TOURNAMENT: ANNIVERSARY. Mar 27, 1939. The Oregon Ducks defeated the Ohio State Buckeyes, 46–33, to win the first NCAA men's basketball tournament. Oregon beat Texas and Oklahoma to reach the final, held at Northwestern's Patten Gymnasium. Ohio State defeated Wake Forest and Villanova in the eastern half of the eight-team draw.

HUGGINS, MILLER: BIRTH ANNIVERSARY. Mar 27, 1879. Miller James Huggins, Baseball Hall of Fame manager, born at Cincinnati, OH. Huggins played major league baseball, but he made his mark as manager of the New York Yankees from 1918 to his death. It was his job to ride herd on Babe Ruth. Inducted into the Hall of Fame in 1964. Died at New York, NY, Sept 25, 1929.

MURPHY GETS 1,000th POINT: ANNIVERSARY. Mar 27, 1996. Defenseman Larry Murphy of the Toronto Maple Leafs got the 1,000th point of his National Hockey League career, a goal in a 6–2 win over the Vancouver Canucks.

BIRTHDAYS TODAY

Randall Cunningham, 37, football player, born Santa Barbara, CA, Mar 27, 1963.
Daniel Anthony (Danny) Fortson, 24, basketball player, born Philadelphia, PA, Mar 27, 1976.
Jaime Navarro, 32, baseball player, born Bayamon, Puerto Rico, Mar 27, 1968.
William Caleb (Cale) Yarborough, 60, former auto racer, born Timmonsville, SC, Mar 27, 1940.

MARCH 28 — TUESDAY
Day 88 — 278 Remaining

NCAA BASKETBALL CHAMPIONS THIS DATE

1942	Stanford
1944	Utah
1950	CCNY
1977	Marquette

BACK-TO-BACK PERFECT GAMES: ANNIVERSARY. Mar 28, 1989. Softball pitchers Cathy McAllister and Stefni Whitton of Southwestern Louisiana performed a feat unprecedented in NCAA history by throwing back-to-back perfect games against Southeastern Louisiana. McAllister won, 5–0, and Whitton struck out 14, winning 7–0.

BUSCH, GUSSIE: BIRTH ANNIVERSARY. Mar 28, 1899. August Adolphus (Gussie) Busch, Jr, baseball executive, born at St. Louis, MO. Busch bought the St. Louis Cardinals in 1953 and became one of the most influential team owners. He tied the success of the sport to the growth of his brewery's sales and took great pleasure in both. Died at St. Louis, Sept 29, 1989.

CCNY'S DOUBLE TITLES: 50th ANNIVERSARY. Mar 28, 1950. The City College of New York (CCNY) defeated Bradley, 71–68, in the title game of the NCAA basketball tournament, thereby becoming the only team to win both that championship and the NIT title in the same year. Ten days before, CCNY had beaten Bradley, 69–61, to win the NIT.

COLTS SNEAK OUT OF BALTIMORE: ANNIVERSARY. Mar 28, 1984. With little or no warning, the Baltimore Colts loaded moving vans in the dead of night and left for Indianapolis. Baltimore was left without an NFL team until 1996 when the Cleveland Browns moved there and were renamed the Ravens.

CONTINENTAL BASKETBALL ASSOCIATION PLAY-OFFS BEGIN. Mar 28 (tentative). Sites TBA. Following conclusion of the CBA regular season, play-offs begin to determine a league champion. The CBA, a developmental league for the NBA, will field nine teams in its 54th season: Connecticut, Ft Wayne, Grand Rapids, Idaho, La Crosse, Quad City, Rockford, Sioux Falls and Yakima. For info: Media Relations, Continental Basketball Assn, Two Arizona Center, 400 N 5th St, Ste 1425, Phoenix, AZ 85004. Phone: (602) 254-6677. Fax: (602) 258-9985. Web: www.cbahoops.com.

MOTTA WINS 800th GAME: ANNIVERSARY. Mar 28, 1987. Dick Motta became the third coach in professional basketball to win 800 games when his team, the Dallas Mavericks, defeated the Washington Bullets, 114–107. Motta coached for 25 years and finished his career with a record of 935–1,017.

WILT RETIRES WITHOUT FOULING OUT: ANNIVERSARY. Mar 28, 1973. Wilt Chamberlain retired from the NBA after playing in 1,045 games. During his entire 14-season career, Chamberlain never fouled out.

BIRTHDAYS TODAY

Richard Francis Dennis (Rick) Barry, III, 56, broadcaster and Basketball Hall of Fame forward, born Elizabeth, NJ, Mar 28, 1944.

Jeff Beukeboom, 35, hockey player, born Ajax, Ontario, Canada, Mar 28, 1965.

Shawn Kealoha Boskie, 33, baseball player, born Hawthorne, NV, Mar 28, 1967.

Craig Howard Paquette, 31, baseball player, born Long Beach, CA, Mar 28, 1969.

Gerald Eugene (Jerry) Sloan, 58, basketball coach and former player, born McLeansboro, IL, Mar 28, 1942.

Ernie Stewart, 31, soccer player, born Veghel, The Netherlands, Mar 28, 1969.

Keith Matthew Tkachuk, 28, hockey player, born Melrose, MA, Mar 28, 1972.

Paul Anthony Wilson, 27, baseball player, born Orlando, FL, Mar 28, 1973.

MARCH 29 — WEDNESDAY
Day 89 — 277 Remaining

NCAA BASKETBALL CHAMPIONS THIS DATE	
1941	Wisconsin
1976	Indiana
1982	North Carolina
1999	Connecticut

DUVAL FATHER AND SON SET RECORD: ANNIVERSARY. Mar 29, 1999. David Duval won the Players Championship, a PGA tournament, and his father Bob Duval won the Emerald Coast Classic, a Senior PGA tournament, to become the first father-son combination to win tour-sanctioned tournaments on the same day. Duval the younger closed with a 73 to defeat Scott Gump by two shots. Father Bob defeated Bruce Fleisher by the same margin.

TOURNAMENT OF CHAMPIONS. Mar 29–Apr 2. Bob Thomas Equestrian Center, Florida Expo Park, Tampa, FL. The ninth event in the 2000 Cosequin Winter Equestrian Festival. For info: Stadium Jumping, Inc, 3104 Cherry Palm Dr, Ste 220, Tampa, FL 33619. Phone: (800) 237-8924 or (813) 623-5801. Fax: (813) 626-5369. Web: www.stadiumjumping.com.

TUNNELL, EMLEN: 75th BIRTH ANNIVERSARY. Mar 29, 1925. Emlen Tunnell, Pro Football Hall of Fame defensive back born at Bryn Mawr, PA. After playing college football at Iowa, Tunnell played for the New York Giants from 1948 through 1958 and finished his career with three seasons at Green Bay. Inducted into the Hall of Fame in 1967. Died at Pleasantville, NY, July 22, 1975.

YOUNG, CY: BIRTH ANNIVERSARY. Mar 29, 1867. Denton True ("Cy") Young, Baseball Hall of Fame pitcher, born at Gilmore, OH. Young is baseball's all-time winningest pitcher, having accumulated 511 victories in his 22-year career. The Cy Young award is given each year in his honor to each major league's best pitcher. Inducted into the Hall of Fame in 1937. Died at Peoli, OH, Nov 4, 1955.

BIRTHDAYS TODAY

Earl Christian Campbell, 45, Heisman Trophy and Pro Football Hall of Fame running back, born Tyler, TX, Mar 29, 1955.

Jennifer Marie Capriati, 24, tennis player, born New York, NY, Mar 29, 1976.

Walter ("Clyde") Frazier, Jr, 55, Basketball Hall of Fame guard, born Atlanta, GA, Mar 29, 1945.

Thomas Francis (Tommy) Holmes, 83, former baseball player, born New York, NY, Mar 29, 1917.

Brian O'Neal Jordan, 33, baseball player, born Baltimore, MD, Mar 29, 1967.

Trevor Kidd, 28, hockey player, born Dugald, Manitoba, Canada, Mar 29, 1972.

Dennis Dale (Denny) McLain, 56, former baseball player, born Chicago, IL, Mar 29, 1944.

Alex Ochoa, 28, baseball player, born Miami Lakes, FL, Mar 29, 1972.

Kurt Thomas, 44, former gymnast, born Miami, FL, Mar 29, 1956.

MARCH 30 — THURSDAY
Day 90 — 276 Remaining

NCAA BASKETBALL CHAMPIONS THIS DATE	
1940	Indiana
1943	Wyoming
1981	Indiana
1987	Indiana
1998	Kentucky

DEBARTOLO BUYS 49ERS: ANNIVERSARY. Mar 30, 1977. A new era began in San Francisco football as Edward J. DeBartolo, Jr, bought the 49ers from the original owners. The 49ers never reached the NFL championship game while the Morabito family owned them, but they won five Super Bowls during the first 18 years of DeBartolo's tenure.

GALIMORE, WILLIE: 65th BIRTH ANNIVERSARY. Mar 30, 1935. Willie Lee Galimore, football player, born at St. Augustine, FL. Galimore was a star running back at Florida A&M and with the Chicago Bears from 1957 through 1963. He and teammate John Farrington died in an automobile accident at Rensselaer, IN, July 26, 1964.

KOUFAX AND DRYSDALE END HOLDOUT: ANNIVERSARY. Mar 30, 1966. Los Angeles Dodgers pitchers Sandy Koufax and Don Drysdale ended their joint month-long holdout by signing contracts for $130,000 and $105,000, respectively. Koufax (26–8 in 1965) and Drysdale (23–12) had shaken up the baseball establishment by joining forces and hiring lawyers to negotiate for them. Still, their contracts fell well short of their goal, a 3-year deal for $1.05 million.

BIRTHDAYS TODAY

Lomas Brown, Jr, 37, football player, born Miami, FL, Mar 30, 1963.
David (Dave) Ellett, 36, hockey player, born Cleveland, OH, Mar 30, 1964.
Jerry Ray Lucas, 60, Basketball Hall of Fame forward and center, born Middletown, OH, Mar 30, 1940.

MARCH 31 — FRIDAY
Day 91 — 275 Remaining

NCAA BASKETBALL CHAMPIONS THIS DATE	
1975	UCLA
1986	Louisville
1997	Arizona

ALM, JEFF: BIRTH ANNIVERSARY. Mar 31, 1968. Jeffrey Lawrence (Jeff) Alm, football player, born at New York, NY. Alm played on Notre Dame's 1988 national championship team and was drafted by the Houston Oilers in 1990. Died of gunshot wounds in an apparent suicide after a friend riding in his car was killed in a crash at Houston, TX, Dec 14, 1993.

DE PALMA, RALPH: DEATH ANNIVERSARY. Mar 31, 1956. Ralph De Palma, auto racer, born at Troia, Italy, Jan 23, 1884. De Palma came to the US in the 1890s and began racing in his youth. The greatest driver of racing's early era, he drove in 2,889 races and won 2,557 of them, including the Indianapolis 500 in 1915. Died at South Pasadena, CA.

DEVIL RAYS DEBUT: ANNIVERSARY. Mar 31, 1998. The Tampa Bay Devil Rays, an expansion team, made their debut in the American League, losing 11–6 to the Detroit Tigers at home. The team redeemed itself the next day, winning 11–8, also against Detroit. The Devil Rays finished with a record of 63–99, good for last place in the American League East.

DIAMONDBACKS DEBUT: ANNIVERSARY. Mar 31, 1998. The Arizona Diamondbacks, an expansion team, made their debut in the National League by losing at home to the Colorado Rockies, 9–2. Andy Benes was the losing pitcher. After losing four more games, the Diamondbacks won their first, 3–2, over the San Francisco Giants. Arizona finished the season with a record of 65–97, good for fifth place in the National League West.

FITZSIMMONS WINS 800th GAME: ANNIVERSARY. Mar 31, 1992. Cotton Fitzsimmons became the sixth coach in professional basketball to win 800 games when the Phoenix Suns defeated the Portland Trail Blazers, 128–111. Fitzsimmons compiled a career mark of 832–775.

JOHNSON, JACK: BIRTH ANNIVERSARY. Mar 31, 1878. Arthur John (Jack) Johnson, boxer, born at Galveston, TX. Johnson, an African-American, entered pro boxing at a time when the leading white fighters ignored black contenders. The dearth of good competition, though, after

the retirement of Jim Jeffries in 1905 gave Johnson a shot at the title, which he won on Dec 28, 1908, by defeating Tommy Burns. Johnson's flamboyant lifestyle and relationships with white women provoked the search for a "Great White Hope" to defeat him. A Mann Act conviction caused Johnson to flee to Europe. He eventually lost the title to Jess Willard in a 1915 fight at Havana, Cuba. Died at Raleigh, NC, June 10, 1946.

NCAA WOMEN'S DIVISION I BASKETBALL TOURNAMENT. Mar 31–Apr 2. Final Four. First Union Center, Philadelphia, PA. For info: NCAA, PO Box 6222, Indianapolis, IN 46206-6222. Phone: (317) 917-6222. Fax: (317) 917-6888. Web: www.ncaa.org.

VARIPAPA, ANDY: BIRTH ANNIVERSARY. Mar 31, 1891. Andrew (Andy) Varipapa, bowler, born at Carfizzi, Italy. Varipapa came to the US in 1902 and began bowling in 1907. He gained national prominence with an important tournament victory in 1930 and remained active in the sport more than 70 years. He gave clinics, made films and invented trick shot bowling. At age 78, unable to bowl right-handed because of wrist injuries, he began bowling left-handed and carried a 180 average within 18 months. Died at Hempstead, NY, Aug 25, 1984.

WOODEN'S LAST TITLE: 25th ANNIVERSARY. Mar 31, 1975. Two days after Coach John Wooden announced his intention to retire at season's end, the UCLA Bruins won their tenth NCAA title in 12 years, all under Wooden's tutelage. UCLA defeated Kentucky, 92–85, as Wooden closed his career with a 620–147 record.

BIRTHDAYS TODAY

Tom Barrasso, 35, hockey player, born Boston, MA, Mar 31, 1965.
Pavel Bure, 29, hockey player, born Moscow, USSR, Mar 31, 1971.
Gordon (Gordie) Howe, 72, Hockey Hall of Fame right wing, born Floral, Saskatchewan, Canada, Mar 31, 1928.
James Earl (Jimmy) Johnson, 62, Pro Football Hall of Fame defensive back, born Dallas, TX, Mar 31, 1938.
Herman ("J.R.") Reid, Jr, 32, basketball player, born Virginia Beach, VA, Mar 31, 1968.
Steven Delano (Steve) Smith, 31, basketball player, born Highland Park, MI, Mar 31, 1969.

APRIL 1 — SATURDAY
Day 92 — 274 Remaining

NCAA BASKETBALL CHAMPIONS THIS DATE

1985	Villanova
1991	Duke
1996	Kentucky

BUDWEISER AMERICAN INVITATIONAL. Apr 1. Raymond James Stadium, Tampa, FL. The 11th event in the 2000 Cosequin Winter Equestrian Festival. For info: Stadium Jumping, Inc, 3104 Cherry Palm Dr, Ste 220, Tampa, FL 33619. Phone: (800) 237-8924 or (813) 623-5801. Fax: (813) 626-5369. Web: www.stadiumjumping.com.

ENGLAND: OXFORD VS CAMBRIDGE UNIVERSITY BOAT RACE. Apr 1. Putney to Mortlake, River Thames, London. Popular amateur rowing event held since 1829 with crowds watching from towpaths along the river bank. For info: Alison Moor, Press Office, Scope Communications Management, Tower House, 8-14 Southampton St, London, England WC2E 7HA. Phone: (44) (171) 379-3234. Fax: (44) (171) 240-7729.

FIRST BASEBALL STRIKE BEGINS: ANNIVERSARY. Apr 1, 1972. The Major League Baseball Players Association went on strike for the first time, with the principal issue being contributions to the major league pension plan. The strike lasted 12 days and wiped out 86 regular season games.

GRAND STRAND FISHING RODEO. Apr 1–Oct 31. Myrtle Beach, SC. Awards for surf, inlet and deep-sea fish catches. For info: Chamber of Commerce, Box 2115, Myrtle Beach, SC 29578. Phone: (843) 626-7444. Fax: (843) 626-0009. Web: www.myrtlebeachlive.com.

KITE FLITE. Apr 1. Space Center, Alamogordo, NM. Annual event with kite flight. Est attendance: 300. For info: Jack Moore, Mktg Dir, Space Center, PO Box 533, Alamogordo, NM 88311. Phone: (800) 545-4021. Fax: (505) 437-7722. E-mail: spacepr@zianet.com. Web: www.spacefame.org.

NATIONAL KNUCKLES DOWN MONTH. Apr 1–30. To recognize and revive the American tradition of playing marbles and keep it rolling along. Please send SASE with inquiries. For info: Cathy C. Runyan-Svacina, The Marble Lady, 7812 NW Hampton Rd, Kansas City, MO 64152. Phone: (816) 587-8687.

NATIONAL YOUTH SPORTS SAFETY MONTH. Apr 1–30. Bringing public attention to the prevalent problem of injuries in youth sports. This event promotes safety in sport activities and is supported by more than 60 national sports and medical organizations. For info: Michelle Klein, Exec Dir, Natl Youth Sports Safety Foundation, 333 Longwood Ave, Ste 202, Boston, MA 02115. Phone: (617) 277-1171. Fax: (617) 277-2278. E-mail: nyssf@aol.com. Web: www.nyssf.org.

NCAA MEN'S DIVISION I BASKETBALL TOURNAMENT. Apr 1–3. Final Four. RCA Dome, Indianapolis, IN. For info: NCAA, PO Box 6222, Indianapolis, IN 46206-6222. Phone: (317) 917-6222. Fax: (317) 917-6888. Web: www.ncaa.org.

NCAA WOMEN'S GYMNASTICS CHAMPIONSHIPS. Apr 1. Regionals. Sites TBA. For info: NCAA, PO Box 6222, Indianapolis, IN 46206-6222. Phone: (317) 917-6222. Fax: (317) 917-6888. Web: www.ncaa.org.

NEW YORK LEGALIZES BETTING: 60th ANNIVERSARY. Apr 1, 1940. New York governor Herbert Lehman signed a bill legalizing pari-mutuel wagering at the state's racetracks and outlawing bookmaking.

PATRIOTS GO PUBLIC: 40th ANNIVERSARY. Apr 1, 1960. The Boston Patriots of the American Football League made Wall Street history by becoming the first professional sports team to issue public stock.

POLE, PEDAL, PADDLE. Apr 1. Jackson, WY. The original relay race of this kind. Alpine skiing, cross-country skiing, biking and boating from Teton Village to the Snake River. For info: Jackson Hole Ski Club, Box 461, Jackson, WY 83001. Phone: (307) 733-6433. Fax: (307) 733-2940.

PRO-AM SNIPE EXCURSION AND HUNT. Apr 1. Moultrie, GA. Celebrating the time-honored custom of snipe hunting. The denim snipe has come back from the brink of extinction and will be honored at the 2000 event which will include a Snipe Parade, a Snipe Ball and festivities at the Denim Wing of the Snipe Museum at New Elm, GA. New Snipe-O-Rama racing oval open! Annually, Apr 1. For info: Beth Gay, PO Box 2828, Moultrie, GA 31776. Phone: (912) 985-6540.

SEATTLE PILOTS BECOME MILWAUKEE BREWERS: 30th ANNIVERSARY. Apr 1, 1970. After one year as an American League expansion team, the Seattle Pilots moved to Milwaukee and became the Brewers. Automobile dealer Bud Selig purchased the team for $10.8 million.

TOUR de CURE. Apr 1–June 30. Thousands of cyclists participate in the American Diabetes Association's annual cycling event to raise money to help find a cure for diabetes and to provide information and resources to improve the lives of all people affected by diabetes. Tours are held in communities across America, combining fun and fitness with the chance to help people with diabetes.

Contact your local affiliate. For info: American Diabetes Assn, Natl HQ, 1660 Duke St, Alexandria, VA 22314. Phone: (800) TOUR-888.

TRAIL'S END MARATHON. Apr 1. Oregon coast. Local and regional runners and runners from across the nation are attracted to this officially sanctioned marathon run on Oregon's northern coast. The Northwest's oldest marathon. Also includes an 8K run and walk. Most of the course goes through Fort Stevens State Park, with the finish in Warrenton. Est attendance: 1,000. For info: Oregon Road Runners Club, 4840 SW Western Ave, #200, Beaverton, OR 97075. Phone: (503) 646-7867. Fax: (503) 520-0242. E-mail: orrc@orrc.net. Web: www.orrc.net.

VILLANOVA UPSETS GEORGETOWN: 15th ANNIVERSARY. Apr 1, 1985. In one of the greatest upsets in NCAA basketball tournament history, the Villanova University Wildcats upset the Hoyas of Georgetown University, 66–64, in the championship game. The Wildcats made 78.6 percent of their shots from the field and converted 22 of 27 free throws.

CHASE'S SPORTSQUOTE OF THE DAY

"Here's one thing I never say anymore: 'These people can't be that stupid, can they?'"—sportswriter George Vecsey on athletes and team owners

---

BIRTHDAYS TODAY

Richard Louis (Rich) Amaral, 38, baseball player, born Visalia, CA, Apr 1, 1962.

Frank Anthony Castillo, 31, baseball player, born El Paso, TX, Apr 1, 1969.

Mark A. Jackson, 35, basketball player, born New York, NY, Apr 1, 1965.

Philip Henry (Phil) Niekro, 61, Baseball Hall of Fame pitcher, born Blaine, OH, Apr 1, 1939.

Libby Riddles, 44, dogsled racer, born Madison, WI, Apr 1, 1956.

Glenn Edward ("Bo") Schembechler, Jr, 71, former baseball executive and college football coach, born Barberton, OH, Apr 1, 1929.

Daniel Joseph ("Rusty") Staub, 56, former baseball player, born New Orleans, LA, Apr 1, 1944.

Scott Stevens, 36, hockey player, born Kitchener, Ontario, Canada, Apr 1, 1964.

APRIL 2 — SUNDAY

Day 93 — 273 Remaining

NCAA BASKETBALL CHAMPIONS THIS DAY

1984	Georgetown
1990	UNLV

APPLING, LUKE: BIRTH ANNIVERSARY. Apr 2, 1909. Lucius Benjamin (Luke) Appling, Baseball Hall of Fame shortstop, born at High Point, NC. Appling won two American League batting titles, hitting .310 over 20 years with the Chicago White Sox. Inducted into the Hall of Fame in 1964. Died at Cumming, GA, Jan 3, 1991.

COLLEGE BASEBALL SLAUGHTER: ANNIVERSARY. Apr 2, 1996. In a Chicagoland Collegiate Athletic Conference baseball game, St. Francis of Illinois humiliated

	S	M	T	W	T	F	S
April							1
2000	2	3	4	5	6	7	8
	9	10	11	12	13	14	15
	16	17	18	19	20	21	22
	23	24	25	26	27	28	29
	30						

Robert Morris, 71–1, in a game that Robert Morris coach Gerald McNamara declared over after four innings. St. Francis scored 26 runs in the first inning, 22 in the second, 4 in the third and 19 in the fifth. The Fighting Saints broke a dozen NCAA Division II records and tied four others.

DAYLIGHT SAVING TIME BEGINS. Apr 2–Oct 29. Daylight Saving Time begins at 2 AM. The Uniform Time Act of 1966 (as amended in 1986 by Public Law 99–359), administered by the US Department of Transportation, provides that Standard Time in each zone be advanced one hour from 2 AM on the first Sunday in April until 2 AM on the last Sunday in October (except where state legislatures provide exemption). Many use the popular rule "spring forward, fall back" to remember which way to turn their clocks. The start of Daylight Saving Time marks the unofficial beginning of the summer recreation season, especially for children who revel in the opportunity to play outside after eating dinner. See also: "Daylight Saving Time Ends; Standard Time Resumes" (Oct 29).

JENNINGS, HUGH: BIRTH ANNIVERSARY. Apr 2, 1869. Hugh Ambrose Jennings, Baseball Hall of Fame player and manager, born at Pittston, PA. Jennings played for the great Baltimore Orioles teams of the 1890s and went on to become a colorful manager, especially with the Detroit Tigers. Inducted into the Hall of Fame in 1945. Died at Scranton, PA, Feb 1, 1928.

MAJOR LEAGUE BASEBALL REGULAR SEASON OPENS. Apr 2 (tentative). Major League Baseball opens a 26-week regular season leading to the play-offs and the World Series in October. The 14-team American League, established in 1901, begins its 100th season. The 16-team National League, established in 1876, begins its 125th season. Each team plays a 162-game schedule. For info: American League, 245 Park Ave, New York, NY 10167. Phone: (212) 931-7600. Fax: (212) 593-7138. National League, 245 Park Ave, New York, NY 10167. Phone: (212) 931-7700. Fax: (212) 935-5069. Web: www.majorleaguebaseball.com.

MITCHELL STRIKES OUT RUTH AND GEHRIG: ANNIVERSARY. Apr 2, 1931. Jackie Mitchell, 17, became the first woman to pitch in a professional baseball game after she was signed to a contract by the Chattanooga Lookouts of the Southern Association. In an exhibition game against the New York Yankees, Mitchell struck out Babe Ruth (who took strike three) and Lou Gehrig (who gallantly missed three straight pitches) before Tony Lazzeri walked.

THREE-POINT FIELD GOAL: ANNIVERSARY. Apr 2, 1986. The NCAA basketball rules committee adopted the three-point field goal, setting the arc at a distance of 19 feet, 9 inches, from the basket.

BIRTHDAYS TODAY

Roberto Francisco (Bobby) Avila, 76, former baseball player, born Veracruz, Mexico, Apr 2, 1924.

Carmen Basilio, 73, former boxer, born Canastota, NY, Apr 2, 1927.

Peter Joseph (Pete) Incaviglia, 36, baseball player, born Pebble Beach, CA, Apr 2, 1964.

Curtis John Leskanic, 32, baseball player, born Homestead, PA, Apr 2, 1968.

Ayako Okamoto, 49, golfer, born Hiroshima, Japan, Apr 2, 1951.

Walter William (Billy) Pierce, 73, former baseball player, born Detroit, MI, Apr 2, 1927.

Richard Raymond (Dick) Radatz, 63, former baseball player, born Detroit, MI, Apr 2, 1937.

William Thomas (Bill) Romanowski, 34, football player, born Vernon, CT, Apr 2, 1966.

Donald Howard (Don) Sutton, 55, broadcaster and Baseball Hall of Fame pitcher, born Clio, AL, Apr 2, 1945.

APRIL 3 — MONDAY
Day 94 — 272 Remaining

NCAA BASKETBALL CHAMPIONS THIS DATE

1989	Michigan
1995	UCLA

AGA NATIONAL CHAMPIONSHIP. Apr 3–9. Citrus Bowl, Orlando, FL. The 10th event in the 2000 Cosequin Winter Equestrian Festival. For info: Stadium Jumping, Inc, 3104 Cherry Palm Dr, Ste 220, Tampa, FL 33619. Phone: (800) 237-8924 or (813) 623-5801. Fax: (813) 626-5369. Web: www.stadiumjumping.com.

ALZADO, LYLE: BIRTH ANNIVERSARY. Apr 3, 1949. Lyle Martin Alzado, football player, born at New York, NY. Alzado grew up on Long Island and graduated from Yankton College in South Dakota with a bachelor's degree in special education. He played football, earning Little All-America honors, and was drafted in 1971 by the Denver Broncos. Alzado gained fame as part of Denver's "Orange Crush" defense and for his fierce demeanor. He was traded to the Cleveland Browns in 1979 and in 1982 to the Los Angeles Raiders. After retiring at the end of the 1985 season, Alzado acted in movies. He was diagnosed with brain cancer in 1991, which he attributed to a lifetime of steroid usage. He spent the last months of his life campaigning against steroids and human growth hormone. Died at Lake Oswego, OR, May 14, 1992.

CREWS, TIM: BIRTH ANNIVERSARY. Apr 3, 1961. Stanley Timothy (Tim) Crews, baseball player, born at Tampa, FL. Crews was a relief pitcher with the Dodgers and had signed as a free agent with the Cleveland Indians in January 1993. Died from injuries suffered in a boating accident at Orlando, FL, Mar 23, 1993.

DR. J'S NUMBER RETIRED: ANNIVERSARY. Apr 3, 1987. The New Jersey Nets honored former Net Julius ("Dr. J") Erving by retiring his number, 32. The ceremony occurred during a game against the Philadelphia 76ers, the team with whom Erving was finishing his 16-year career.

THE MASTERS. Apr 3–9. Augusta National Golf Club, Augusta, GA. The first of professional golf's four major championships. For info: Augusta Natl Golf Club, Augusta, GA 30904. Web: www.masters.org.

PERREAULT SCORES 1,000th POINT: ANNIVERSARY. Apr 3, 1982. Gilbert Perreault of the Buffalo Sabres scored the 1,000th point of his National Hockey League career, an assist in the Sabres' 5–4 win over the Montreal Canadiens. Perreault finished his career with 1,326 points.

RATELLE SCORES 1,000th POINT: ANNIVERSARY. Apr 3, 1977. Center Jean Ratelle of the Boston Bruins scored the 1,000th point of his NHL career, an assist in the Bruins' 7–4 victory over the Toronto Maple Leafs. Ratelle finished his career with 1,267 points.

STANLEY CUP CHAMPIONS THIS DATE

1930	Montreal Canadiens

BIRTHDAYS TODAY

Pervis Ellison, 33, basketball player, born Savannah, GA, Apr 3, 1967.

Michael Olowokandi, 25, basketball player, born Lagos, Nigeria, Apr 3, 1975.

James Thomas (Jim) Parker, 66, Pro Football Hall of Fame guard, born Macon, GA, Apr 3, 1934.

Picabo Street, 29, Olympic gold medal skier, born Sun Valley, ID, Apr 3, 1971.

Quilvio Alberto Perez Veras, 29, baseball player, born Santo Domingo, Dominican Republic, Apr 3, 1971.

APRIL 4 — TUESDAY
Day 95 — 271 Remaining

NCAA BASKETBALL CHAMPIONS THIS DATE

1983	North Carolina State
1988	Kansas
1994	Arkansas

GIAMATTI, BART: BIRTH ANNIVERSARY. Apr 4, 1938. Angelo Bartlett (Bart) Giamatti, Commissioner of Baseball and educator, born at Boston, MA. Giamatti received his education at Yale, taught classics there and became Yale's youngest president at the age of 39 in 1978. Following his tenure at Yale, he became the president of baseball's National League in 1986, serving in that capacity until he was appointed Commissioner of Baseball on Apr 1, 1989. An accomplished author, he moved freely between the worlds of literature and baseball, often linking the two in the many articles he wrote. One week prior to his death, he signed an agreement placing Pete Rose on the permanently ineligible list. Died at Martha's Vineyard, MA, Sept 1, 1989.

HODGES, GIL: BIRTH ANNIVERSARY. Apr 4, 1924. Gilbert Ray (Gil) Hodges, baseball player and manager, born at Princeton, IN. Hodges was the first baseman on the famous Brooklyn Dodgers "Boys of Summer" teams. He managed the New York Mets to the 1969 World Series title. Died at West Palm Beach, FL, Apr 2, 1972.

NJCAA ANNUAL MEETING. Apr 4–8. Doubletree Hotel, Colorado Springs, CO. For info: NJCAA, PO Box 7305, Colorado Springs, CO 80933. Phone: (719) 590-9788. Fax: (719) 590-7324. Web: www.njcaa.org.

POTVIN SCORES 1,000th POINT: ANNIVERSARY. Apr 4, 1987. Denis Potvin of the New York Islanders, the highest-scoring defenseman in NHL history at the time, scored the 1,000th point of his career. He ended his career with 1,052 points.

SPEAKER, TRIS: BIRTH ANNIVERSARY. Apr 4, 1888. Tristram E. (Tris) Speaker, Baseball Hall of Fame outfielder, born at Hubbard City, TX. Known as the "Gray Eagle," Speaker was one of the greatest center fielders of all time. He started his career with the Boston Red Sox, where he was part of the Hooper-Speaker-Lewis outfield, and then achieved stardom in a second city, playing for the Cleveland Indians. Inducted into the Hall of Fame in 1937. Died at Lake Whitney, TX, Dec 8, 1958.

BIRTHDAYS TODAY

Pat Burns, 48, hockey coach, born St.-Henri, Quebec, Canada, Apr 4, 1952.

JoAnne Gunderson Carner, 61, LPGA Hall of Fame golfer, born Kirkland, WA, Apr 4, 1939.

Michael Peter (Mike) Epstein, 57, former baseball player, born New York, NY, Apr 4, 1943.

Raymond Earl (Ray) Fosse, 53, former baseball player, born Marion, IL, Apr 4, 1947.

James Louis (Jim) Fregosi, 58, baseball manager and player, born San Francisco, CA, Apr 4, 1942.

John Allen Hannah, 49, Pro Football Hall of Fame guard, born Canton, GA, Apr 4, 1951.

Thomas Mitchell (Tommy) Herr, 44, former baseball player, born Lancaster, PA, Apr 4, 1956.

Allan Wade Houston, 29, basketball player, born Louisville, KY, Apr 4, 1971.

Arnold Malcolm ("Mickey") Owen, 84, former baseball player, born Nixa, MO, Apr 4, 1916.

Yanic Perreault, 29, hockey player, born Sherbrooke, Quebec, Canada, Apr 4, 1971.

Scott Bruce Rolen, 25, baseball player, born Evansville, IN, Apr 4, 1975.

Otis Jason (O.J.) Santiago, 26, football player, born Toronto, Ontario, Canada, Apr 4, 1974.

Jessie Lloyd Tuggle, 35, football player, born Spalding County, GA, Apr 4, 1965.

APRIL 5 — WEDNESDAY

Day 96 — 270 Remaining

NCAA BASKETBALL CHAMPIONS THIS DATE

1983	North Carolina

DEHNERT, DUTCH: BIRTH ANNIVERSARY. Apr 5, 1898. Henry ("Dutch") Dehnert, Basketball Hall of Fame center, born at New York, NY. Dehnert did not play basketball in either high school or college, but he was signed to play with the original Celtics because of his experience with early New York teams. He helped make the Celtics one of the game's greatest teams and was personally responsible for inventing the pivot play. He would back into his defender, take a pass from a guard, pick

April 2000	S	M	T	W	T	F	S
							1
	2	3	4	5	6	7	8
	9	10	11	12	13	14	15
	16	17	18	19	20	21	22
	23	24	25	26	27	28	29
	30						

the guard's defender and either give the ball off or roll and shoot. The original Celtics were inducted into the Hall of Fame as a team in 1959. Dehnert followed as an individual player in 1968. Died at Far Rockaway, NY, Apr 20, 1979.

DINNEEN, BILL: BIRTH ANNIVERSARY. Apr 5, 1876. William Henry (Bill) Dinneen, baseball player and umpire, born at Syracuse, NY. Dinneen pitched in the major leagues for 12 years and won three games in the 1903 World Series. In 1909 he broke in as an American League umpire less than two weeks after retiring as a player and enjoyed a 29-year career. He was known as an excellent balls-and-strikes umpire with a short temper. Died at Syracuse, Jan 13, 1955.

GREAT WHITE HOPE: 85th ANNIVERSARY. Apr 5, 1915. Towering Jess Willard beat Jack Johnson in the 26th round to win the heavyweight championship of the world at Havana, Cuba. Johnson, a black American who had held the title since defeating Tommy Burns in 1908, had been widely criticized for his flamboyant lifestyle. Willard, from Kansas, was touted as the "Great White Hope," whose goal it was to recapture the title for the "Caucasian race."

JULIAN, DOGGIE: BIRTH ANNIVERSARY. Apr 5, 1901. Alvin F. ("Doggie") Julian, Basketball Hall of Fame coach, born at Reading, PA. Julian played several sports at Bucknell University and played minor league baseball before beginning his coaching career. He coached at Muhlenberg, Holy Cross and Dartmouth plus two years with the Boston Celtics. Inducted into the Hall of Fame in 1968. Died at Hanover, NH, July 28, 1967.

KAREEM BECOMES NBA'S LEADING SCORER: ANNIVERSARY. Apr 5, 1984. Los Angeles Lakers center Kareem Abdul-Jabbar hit a sky hook, his signature shot, with 8:53 left to play against the Utah Jazz to bring his regular-season career point total to 31,420, one more than record holder Wilt Chamberlain. Abdul-Jabbar retired after the 1988–89 season, having scored 38,387 points.

MARLINS DEBUT: ANNIVERSARY. Apr 5, 1993. The Florida Marlins, a National League expansion team, made their regular season debut, beating the Los Angeles Dodgers, 6–3. Joe DiMaggio threw out the ceremonial first pitch. The Marlins finished the season with a record of 64–98, last in the National League East.

ROCKIES DEBUT: ANNIVERSARY. Apr 5, 1993. The Colorado Rockies, a National League expansion team, made their regular season debut, losing to the Mets in New York, 3–0. Dwight Gooden pitched a complete game for the Mets. David Nied took the loss. The Rockies finished the season with a record of 67–95, good for sixth place in the National League West.

SOBEK, JOE: BIRTH ANNIVERSARY. Apr 5, 1918. Joseph George (Joe) Sobek, inventor of racquetball, born at Greenwich, CT. In 1950, Sobek decided he needed more exercise. Such a good squash player that he was unable to find opponents and not interested in either handball or paddleball, Sobek invented racquetball. For the racquet, he added strings to a platform-tennis paddle. For the ball, he used the core of a tennis ball. By his death, his sport was being played by 8.5 million people in 91 nations. Died at Greenwich, Mar 27, 1998.

WARNER, POP: BIRTH ANNIVERSARY. Apr 5, 1871. Glenn Scobey ("Pop") Warner, football player and coach, born at Springville, NY. After playing several sports at Cornell, Warner began coaching football, most notably at the Carlisle Indian School where he coached Jim Thorpe. He coached three undefeated teams at the University of Pittsburgh and went to the Rose Bowl three times with Stanford. He ended a 44-year career at Temple. Died at Palo Alto, CA, Sept 7, 1954.

WORLD SYNCHRONIZED SKATING CHAMPIONSHIP.
Apr 5–8. Minneapolis, MN. The first-ever world championship in this new team event. For info: 2000 World SSC, PO Box 398046, Edina, MN 55439. Phone: (651) 455-4621. E-mail: tcfsa@usfamily.net. Web: www.tcfsa .org/2000wccs.htm.

BIRTHDAYS TODAY

Anthony Lamar (Tony) Banks, 27, football player, born San Diego, CA, Apr 5, 1973.
Isaac Jason (Ike) Hilliard, 24, football player, born Patterson, LA, Apr 5, 1976.

APRIL 6 — THURSDAY
Day 97 — 269 Remaining

NCAA BASKETBALL CHAMPIONS THIS DATE
1992	Duke

BIRTH OF MODERN OLYMPICS: ANNIVERSARY. Apr 6, 1896. The first modern Summer Olympic Games opened at Athens, Greece, with 311 competitors, all men, representing 13 nations. The very first race was the opening heat of the 100 meters, won by Francis Lane of the US. He finished fourth in the final, won by another American, Thomas Burke. The first Olympics were funded by the sale of commemorative stamps and medals and by a gift of one million drachmas from George Averoff, an architect.

COCHRANE, MICKEY: BIRTH ANNIVERSARY. Apr 6, 1903. Gordon Stanley ("Mickey") Cochrane, Baseball Hall of Fame catcher and manager, born at Bridgewater, MA. Cochrane was an outstanding catcher for the Philadelphia Athletics, winning the American League MVP Award in 1928, and the Detroit Tigers, for whom he also managed. His skull was fractured in 1937, effectively ending his career. Inducted into the Hall of Fame in 1947. Died at Lake Forest, IL, June 28, 1962.

DESIGNATED HITTER INTRODUCED: ANNIVERSARY. Apr 6, 1973. Following a rules change approved in January, Ron Blomberg of the New York Yankees became the first designated hitter in the American League in their opening day game against the Boston Red Sox. Blomberg came to bat for the first time with the bases loaded in the first inning and walked. The Red Sox won, 15–5. (See also: "Designated Hitter Rule Adopted: Anniversary" Jan 11.)

FIRST KOREAN VICTORY: ANNIVERSARY. Apr 6, 1996. Pitching in relief, Chan Ho Park of the Los Angeles Dodgers became the first Korean to win a major league baseball game. Park pitched four scoreless innings against the Chicago Cubs, allowed three hits and struck out four. The Dodgers won, 3–1.

LOMBARDI, ERNIE: BIRTH ANNIVERSARY. Apr 6, 1908. Ernest Natali (Ernie) Lombardi, Baseball Hall of Fame catcher, born at Oakland, CA. Lombardi was extremely slow afoot, but he was a powerful hitter who caught for 17 years in the National League. He won the NL MVP Award in 1938. Inducted into the Hall of Fame in 1986. Died at Santa Cruz, CA, Sept 26, 1977.

MAJOR LEAGUE SOCCER DEBUTS: ANNIVERSARY. Apr 6, 1996. Trying to capitalize on the momentum of the 1994 World Cup, held in the US, Major League Soccer, a new American professional league, made its debut. The San Jose Clash defeated DC United, 1–0, on a goal by Eric Wynalda. The game was played in San Jose before a capacity crowd of 31,683.

MARINERS DEBUT: ANNIVERSARY. Apr 6, 1977. The Seattle Mariners, an American League expansion team, made their regular season debut, losing to the California Angels, 7–0, at the Seattle Kingdome. Seattle's previous AL team, the Pilots, played only the 1969 season before moving to Milwaukee and becoming the Brewers. The Mariners won their first AL West division title in 1995.

CHASE'S SPORTSQUOTE OF THE DAY

"Duke is Duke. They're on TV more than *Leave It to Beaver* reruns."—Providence basketball coach Pete Gillen

BIRTHDAYS TODAY

Bret Robert Boone, 31, baseball player, born El Cajon, CA, Apr 6, 1969.
Gerald Diduck, 35, hockey player, born Edmonton, Alberta, Canada, Apr 6, 1965.
Donald Lewis (Donnie) Edwards, 27, football player, born San Diego, CA, Apr 6, 1973.
Randall Euralentris Godfrey, 27, football player, born Valdosta, GA, Apr 6, 1973.
John Gregory Huarte, 56, Heisman Trophy quarterback, born Anaheim, CA, Apr 6, 1944.
Olaf Kolzig, 30, hockey player, born Johannesburg, South Africa, Apr 6, 1970.
Oliver J. Miller, 30, basketball player, born Fort Worth, TX, Apr 6, 1970.
Sterling Sharpe, 35, broadcaster and former football player, born Chicago, IL, Apr 6, 1965.
LuBara Dixon ("Dickey") Simpkins, 28, basketball player, born Fort Washington, MD, Apr 6, 1972.

APRIL 7 — FRIDAY
Day 98 — 268 Remaining

NBA BASKETBALL CHAMPIONS THIS DATE
1956	Philadelphia Warriors

AFRMA RAT AND MOUSE DISPLAY. Apr 7–9. America's Family Pet Expo, Fairplex, Pomona, CA. American Fancy Rat and Mouse Association show exhibits rats and mice of "fancy" species that make good pets. For info: AFRMA (CAE), PO Box 2589, Winnetka, CA 91396-2589. Phone: (909) 685-2350. Fax: (818) 592-6590. E-mail: craigr@ afrma.org. Web: www.afrma.org.

ANDREYCHUK GETS 1,000th POINT: ANNIVERSARY. Apr 7, 1996. Center Dave Andreychuk of the New Jersey Devils scored a goal to record the 1,000th regular-season point of his NHL career as the Devils defeated the New York Rangers, 4–2.

BLUE JAYS DEBUT: ANNIVERSARY. Apr 7, 1977. The Toronto Blue Jays, an American League expansion team, played their first regular season game, beating the Chicago White Sox, 9–5, at Toronto's Exhibition Stadium. The Jays finished last in the AL East in 1977 with a record of 54–107. They won their first division title in 1985.

BREWERS DEBUT: 30th ANNIVERSARY. Apr 7, 1970. Three weeks after moving hurriedly from Seattle, where they were called the Pilots, the Milwaukee Brewers made their American League debut, losing to the California Angels, 12–0, at Milwaukee County Stadium. The Brewers finished fourth in the AL West in 1970 with a record of 65–97. They won their first division pennant in 1982 but lost the World Series to the St. Louis Cardinals.

CAMP, WALTER: BIRTH ANNIVERSARY. Apr 7, 1859. Walter Chauncey Camp, college athlete, coach and administrator, born at New Britain, CT. Camp played football and several other sports at Yale, but he gained prominence for helping to reshape the rules of rugby football into American football. Among his innovations were reducing the number of players on a side from 15 to 11, introducing the scrimmage, giving one team definite possession of the ball and proposing the downs system. He served as a volunteer coach at Yale and became a national figure as a promoter of football. He selected an All-American team from 1889 to his death. Died at New York, NY, Mar 14, 1925.

HOOSIER HORSE FAIR EXPO. Apr 7–9. Indiana State Fairground Event Center, Indianapolis, IN. All-breed gathering and informative exposition. Est attendance: 65,000. For info: Lucinda Davis, Exec Dir, Indiana Horse Council, 225 S East St, Ste 738, Indianapolis, IN 46202. Phone: (317) 692-7115. E-mail: indequine@aol.com. Web: www .indianahorsecouncil.org.

LEONARD, BENNY: BIRTH ANNIVERSARY. Apr 7, 1896. Benny Leonard, boxer, born at New York, NY. Leonard apprenticed as a printer but switched to fighting to survive in New York's rugged ethnic neighborhoods. He won the lightweight championship in 1917 and defended his title more than 80 times. He lost his wealth in the Great Crash. Died at New York, Apr 18, 1947.

MacINNIS GETS 1,000th POINT: ANNIVERSARY. Apr 7, 1998. Defenseman Al MacInnis of the St. Louis Blues got the 1,000th point of his National Hockey League career, an assist in a 5–3 loss to the Detroit Red Wings.

MANAGER TED WILLIAMS: ANNIVERSARY. Apr 7, 1969. Ted Williams made his debut as a major league manager as the New York Yankees defeated his Washington Senators, 8–4, in Washington's RFK Stadium before 45,000. The Senators finished the year in fourth place in the AL West with a record of 86–76. Williams's managerial career lasted four seasons. His teams won 273 games and lost 364.

McGRAW, JOHN: BIRTH ANNIVERSARY. Apr 7, 1873. John Joseph McGraw, Baseball Hall of Fame third baseman and manager, born at Truxton, NY. Generally regarded as the best manager ever or close to it, McGraw ran the New York Giants with an iron hand from 1902 to 1932. A scrappy ballplayer with the Baltimore Orioles in the 1890s, McGraw demanded and got total effort

from his players. Inducted into the Hall of Fame in 1937. Died at New Rochelle, NY, Feb 25, 1934.

MOUNTAIN PACIFIC SPORTS FEDERATION WOMEN'S WATER POLO CHAMPIONSHIP. Apr 7–9. San Jose State University, San Jose, CA. Athletes from the PAC-10, Big West, WAC and Mountain West Conferences. For info: MPSF, 800 S Broadway, Ste 102, Walnut Creek, CA 94596-5218. Phone: (925) 296-0723. Fax: (925) 296-0724. E-mail: abeaird@mpssports.org. Web: www .pac-10.org/sports/mpsf.html.

NCAA DIVISION I HOCKEY CHAMPIONSHIP. Apr 7–9. Finals. Providence Civic Center, Providence, RI. For info: NCAA, PO Box 6222, Indianapolis, IN 46206-6222. Phone: (317) 917-6222. Fax: (317) 917-6888. Web: www .ncaa.org.

SARAZEN'S DOUBLE EAGLE: 65th ANNIVERSARY. Apr 7, 1935. In the final round of the second Masters Tournament, Gene Sarazen reached the par-5 15th hole four shots out of the lead. His drive left him 220 yards short of the cup. Sarazen hit his 4-wood and knocked the ball over the pond protecting the green, onto the fringe and into the hole for a double-eagle 2. Sarazen tied Craig Wood at 282, 6 under par, and defeated him the next day in a play-off.

YOUTH HOCKEY TIER I NATIONAL CHAMPIONSHIP (12 and under). Apr 7–11. Washington, DC. For info: USA Hockey, 4965 N 30th St, Colorado Springs, CO 80919. Phone: (719) 599-5500.

YOUTH HOCKEY TIER I NATIONAL CHAMPIONSHIP (14 and under). Apr 7–11. Edina, MN. For info: USA Hockey, 4965 N 30th St, Colorado Springs, CO 80919. Phone: (719) 599-5500.

YOUTH HOCKEY TIER I NATIONAL CHAMPIONSHIP (17 and under). Apr 7–11. Washington, DC. For info: USA Hockey, 4965 N 30th St, Colorado Springs, CO 80919. Phone: (719) 599-5500.

BIRTHDAYS TODAY

Ricardo (Ricky) Bones, 31, baseball player, born Salinas, Puerto Rico, Apr 7, 1969.

Robert Pershing (Bobby) Doerr, 82, Baseball Hall of Fame second baseman, born Los Angeles, CA, Apr 7, 1918.

Anthony Drew (Tony) Dorsett, Sr, 46, Heisman Trophy and Pro Football Hall of Fame running back, born Rochester, PA, Apr 7, 1954.

Kevin Rey Smith, 30, football player, born Orange, TX, Apr 7, 1970.

Brett Daniel Tomko, 27, baseball player, born San Diego, CA, Apr 7, 1973.

Richard James (Ricky) Watters, 31, football player, born Harrisburg, PA, Apr 7, 1969.

Stephen Adam (Steve) Wisniewski, 33, football player, born Rutland, VT, Apr 7, 1967.

APRIL 8 — SATURDAY

Day 99 — 267 Remaining

STANLEY CUP CHAMPIONS THIS DATE

1943	Detroit Red Wings

AARON SETS HOME RUN RECORD: ANNIVERSARY. Apr 8, 1974. Henry (Hank) Aaron hit the 715th home run of his career, breaking the record set by Babe Ruth in 1935. Playing for the Atlanta Braves, Aaron broke the record in Atlanta in a game against the Los Angeles Dodgers. Al Downing was the pitcher who delivered the record breaker. Aaron finished his career in 1976 with a total of 755 home runs. At the time of his retirement,

	S	M	T	W	T	F	S
April							1
2000	2	3	4	5	6	7	8
	9	10	11	12	13	14	15
	16	17	18	19	20	21	22
	23	24	25	26	27	28	29
	30						

Aaron also stood first in career RBIs, second in at bats and runs scored and third in base hits.

BAY COUNTRY BOAT SHOW. Apr 8–9. Hollywood Volunteer Fire Department Grounds, Hollywood, MD. 11th annual Bay Country Boat Show includes more than 50 exhibitors of boats, trailers, accessories, nautical crafts, fishing tackle and refreshments. Both inside and outside exhibit areas. Est attendance: 3,000. For info: Bay Country Boat Show, Optimist Club of Hollywood, PO Box 369, Hollywood, MD 20636. Phone: (301) 373-5468. Fax: (301) 373-3501.

EXPOS DEBUT: ANNIVERSARY. Apr 8, 1969. The Montreal Expos, a National League expansion team, played their first regular season game, beating the New York Mets, 10–9, at New York's Shea Stadium. The Expos finished the year in sixth place in the NL East with a record of 52–110. They won their first division title in the strike-shortened 1994 season.

FIRST BLACK MANAGER: 25th ANNIVERSARY. Apr 8, 1975. Frank Robinson made his debut as playing manager of the Cleveland Indians and the first black manager in the major leagues. Robinson hit a home run in his first at bat as the Indians' designated hitter, and Cleveland beat the New York Yankees, 5–3.

FIRST INTERCOLLEGIATE RODEO: ANNIVERSARY. Apr 8, 1939. The first Intercollegiate Rodeo was held at historic Godshall Ranch, Apple Valley, CA. The student cowboys and cowgirls, who hailed from California and Arizona colleges, were assisted by world-champion professional cowboys including Harry Carey, Dick Foran, Curley Fletcher, Tex Ritter and Errol Flynn from Hollywood. Collegiate rodeos had been held since 1919 at Texas A&M University. College cowboys and cowgirls organized a national association in Texas in 1949 named the National Intercollegiate Rodeo Association, which continues today as the only national college rodeo organization.

HENIE, SONJA: BIRTH ANNIVERSARY. Apr 8, 1912. Sonja Henie, Olympic gold medal figure skater, born at Oslo, Norway. Henie competed in the 1924 Winter Olympics when she was just 11, but finished last in ladies' singles. She won gold medals at the Winter Games of 1928, 1932 and 1936. She became a professional skater and an actress and lived quite extravagantly. Died Oct 13, 1969.

HUNTER, CATFISH: BIRTH ANNIVERSARY. Apr 8, 1946. James Augustus ("Catfish") Hunter, Baseball Hall of Fame pitcher, born at Hertford, NC. Died Sept 9, 1999, at Hertford.

JACOBS, HIRSCH: BIRTH ANNIVERSARY. Apr 8, 1904. Hirsch Jacobs, Thoroughbred trainer and owner, born at New York, NY. Jacobs became a trainer in 1923 and was particularly adept at selecting horses in claiming races. He saddled 3,596 winners and earned $15,340,354. Died at Miami, FL, Feb 13, 1970.

KNIGHT, O. RAYMOND: BIRTH ANNIVERSARY. Apr 8, 1872. O. Raymond Knight, rodeo promoter, born at Payson, UT. In 1901, Knight's father, the Utah mining magnate Jesse Knight, founded the town of Raymond, Alberta, Canada. In 1902, young Raymond produced Canada's first rodeo, the "Raymond Stampede." He also built rodeo's first grandstand and first chute in 1903. He was known as the "Father of Canadian Rodeo." Died Feb 7, 1947. For info: John A. Bascom, Raymond Sports Hall of Fame, Max Court, Box 511, Raymond, AB, Canada T0K 2S0. Phone: (403) 752-3094.

OFF-TRACK BETTING BEGINS: ANNIVERSARY. Apr 8, 1971. New York City changed the "Sport of Kings" irrevocably by opening the nation's first off-track betting system. Horseplayers were now able to patronize OTB parlors instead of going to the track to place their wagers.

PADRES DEBUT: ANNIVERSARY. Apr 8, 1969. The San Diego Padres, a National League expansion team, made their regular season debut, defeating the Houston Astros, 2–1. The Padres finished the season with a record of 52–110, good for last place in the National League West.

ROYALS DEBUT: ANNIVERSARY. April 8, 1969. The Kansas City Royals, an American League expansion team, made their regular season debut, beating the Minnesota Twins, 4–3. The Royals finished the year with a record of 69–93, good for fourth place in the American League West.

TWO 300-GAME WINNERS: ANNIVERSARY. Apr 8, 1987. For the first time in modern major league history, two 300-game winners pitched for the same team in the same game. Phil Niekro and Steve Carlton combined their pitching talents to lead the Cleveland Indians to a 14–3 victory over the Toronto Blue Jays. Niekro started for the Indians and earned his 312th career victory. Carlton pitched four shutout innings of relief.

US INTERCOLLEGIATE ORIENTEERING CHAMPION-SHIPS. Apr 8–9. Lillington, NC. Individual and team champions determined in varsity, junior varsity and ROTC competition. For info: Joseph Huberman. Phone: (919) 828-6068. E-mail: joseph@treklite.com.

BIRTHDAYS TODAY

Gary Edmund Carter, 46, former baseball player, born Culver City, CA, Apr 8, 1954.

William D. Chase, 78, librarian and chronicler of contemporary civilization as cofounder and coeditor of *Chase's Annual Events*, born Lakeview, MI, Apr 8, 1922.

John J. Havlicek, 60, Basketball Hall of Fame forward, born Lansing, OH, Apr 8, 1940.

Randall Gilbert (Randy) Marsh, 51, baseball umpire, born Covington, KY, Apr 8, 1949.

Terry Porter, 37, basketball player, born Milwaukee, WI, Apr 8, 1963.

APRIL 9 — SUNDAY
Day 100 — 266 Remaining

STANLEY CUP CHAMPIONS THIS DATE	
1932	Toronto Maple Leafs
1935	Montreal Maroons
1946	Montreal Canadiens

ASTRODOME OPENS: 35th ANNIVERSARY. Apr 9, 1965. Dubbed the "Eighth Wonder of the World," the Houston Astrodome opened with an exhibition game between the Houston Astros and the New York Yankees. President Lyndon Johnson attended the game, and Texas governor John Connally threw out the ceremonial first pitch. Mickey Mantle hit a home run, but the Astros prevailed, 2–1, in 12 innings.

CHANDLER SUSPENDS DUROCHER: ANNIVERSARY. Apr 9, 1947. Baseball Commissioner A.B. ("Happy") Chandler suspended Brooklyn Dodgers manager Leo Durocher for one year because of Durocher's habit of consorting with unsavory characters, including gamblers. Burt Shotton took over for Durocher and managed the Dodgers to the National League pennant.

EBBETS FIELD OPENS: ANNIVERSARY. Apr 9, 1913. The Brooklyn Dodgers opened their new ballpark, Ebbets Field, but lost to the visiting Philadelphia Phillies, 1–0, before a crowd of 10,000. Ebbets Field was named for Charles Ebbets, the club's principal owner, and built at a cost of $750,000. It remained the Dodgers' home until they abandoned Brooklyn for Los Angeles after the 1957 season.

JIMMY STEWART RELAY MARATHON. Apr 9. Griffith Park, Los Angeles, CA. Team relay with five people, each running 5.2 miles. Funds raised go to benefit the St. John's Child and Family Development Center. 19th annual. Est attendance: 20,000. For info: Jimmy Stewart Relay Marathon, St. John's Health Ctr, 1328 22nd St, Santa Monica, CA 90404. Phone: (310) 829-8968. Fax: (310) 315-6167.

LAMBEAU, CURLY: BIRTH ANNIVERSARY. Apr 9, 1898. Earle Louis ("Curly") Lambeau, Pro Football Hall of Fame coach and executive, born at Green Bay, WI. Lambeau played college football at Notre Dame and then founded the Green Bay Packers in 1919. He played for the Packers from their inception through 1927 and coached them from 1919 through 1949. Inducted as a charter member of the Hall of Fame in 1963. Died at Sturgeon Bay, WI, June 1, 1965.

ROBESON, PAUL: BIRTH ANNIVERSARY. Apr 9, 1898. Paul Bustill Robeson, football player, born at Princeton, NJ. Robeson excelled academically and athletically and was a singer and an actor besides. Only the third black man to attend Rutgers, he earned 12 athletic letters, was a two-time All-American and made Phi Beta Kappa. He played pro football to finance attendance at law school and then gave up the bar for a career in entertainment and political activism. Died at Philadelphia, PA, Jan 23, 1976.

April	S	M	T	W	T	F	S
2000							1
	2	3	4	5	6	7	8
	9	10	11	12	13	14	15
	16	17	18	19	20	21	22
	23	24	25	26	27	28	29
	30						

ROCKIES HOME DEBUT: ANNIVERSARY. Apr 9, 1993. The Colorado Rockies played their first home game, defeating the Montreal Expos, 11–4, behind first-inning home runs from leadoff hitter Eric Young and Charlie Hayes. 80,227 fans packed Denver's Mile High Stadium to set a major league opening day attendance record, surpassing the 78,672 who saw the San Francisco Giants and the Los Angeles Dodgers open the 1958 season at the Los Angeles Coliseum.

YMCA SPRING HAS SPRUNG 5K. Apr 9. Kingston, NY. Begins and ends at the YMCA. 5K for runners and walkers on a moderate course. Kickoff for the YMCA scholarship campaign. For info: Dave Johnson, YMCA, 507 Broadway, Kingston, NY 12401. Phone: (914) 338-3810. Fax: (914) 338-0423.

NBA FINALS CHAMPIONS THIS DATE	
1959	Boston Celtics
1960	Boston Celtics

BIRTHDAYS TODAY

Helen Alfredsson, 35, golfer, born Goteborg, Sweden, Apr 9, 1965.

Paul Joseph Arizin, 72, Basketball Hall of Fame forward, born Philadelphia, PA, Apr 9, 1928.

Severiano (Seve) Ballesteros, 43, golfer, born Pedrena, Spain, Apr 9, 1957.

Joseph N. (Joe) Brinkman, 56, baseball umpire, born Little Falls, MN, Apr 9, 1944.

Graeme John Lloyd, 33, baseball player, born Geelong, Victoria, Australia, Apr 9, 1967.

William Harold (Hal) Morris, 35, baseball player, born Fort Rucker, AL, Apr 9, 1965.

Rick Tocchet, 36, hockey player, born Scarborough, Ontario, Canada, Apr 9, 1964.

Jacques Villeneuve, 26, auto racer, born St. Jean d'Iberville, Quebec, Canada, Apr 9, 1974.

APRIL 10 — MONDAY

Day 101 — 265 Remaining

NBA FINALS CHAMPIONS THIS DATE	
1953	Minneapolis Lakers
1955	Syracuse Nationals

CANNON, JIMMY: BIRTH ANNIVERSARY. Apr 10, 1909. Jimmy Cannon, sportswriter, born at New York, NY. Cannon covered the Lindbergh kidnapping case and then switched to sports, eventually being ranked as New York City's leading sportswriter. He specialized in baseball, boxing and horse racing and was particularly critical of baseball and other sports for their racism. Died at New York, Dec 5, 1973.

COLT .45s DEBUT: ANNIVERSARY. Apr 10, 1962. The Houston Colt .45s, a National League expansion team, hosted the first major league game ever played in Texas, beating the Chicago Cubs, 11–2, before 25,000 people. The Colt .45s finished the year in eighth place with a record of 64–96. Renamed the Astros in 1965, they won their first division title in 1980.

CONNORS, CHUCK: BIRTH ANNIVERSARY. Apr 10, 1921. Kevin Joseph ("Chuck") Connors, actor and baseball player, born at New York, NY. He played professional basketball and baseball before becoming an actor. "The Rifleman" of television fame, Chuck Connors played that role from 1958 to 1963. His portrayal of a slave owner in the miniseries *Roots* won him an Emmy nomination. Connors acted in more than 45 films and appeared on many TV series and specials. Died at Los Angeles, CA, Nov 10, 1992.

FIRST FOREIGNER TO WIN MASTERS: ANNIVER-SARY. Apr 10, 1961. South African Gary Player shot an 8 under par 280 to become the first foreign player to win the Masters. Player defeated Arnold Palmer and Charley Coe by one stroke. He won the tournament again in 1974 and 1978.

PGA FOUNDED: ANNIVERSARY. Apr 10, 1916. Following an organizational luncheon meeting in January, 82 charter members approved a constitution to create the Professional Golfers' Association of America. The members agreed to promote interest in the game of golf, elevate the standards of the golf professional's vocation, protect their mutual interests and establish a national professional championship.

SENATORS DEBUT: ANNIVERSARY. Apr 10, 1961. The Washington Senators, an American League expansion team, played their first regular seasson game, losing to the Chicago White Sox, 4–3. President John Kennedy threw out the ceremonial first pitch. The Senators were located in Washington to replace the original Senators who moved this same year to become the Minnesota Twins. The Senators finished with a record of 61–100, good for last place.

YOUNGS, ROSS: BIRTH ANNIVERSARY. Apr 10, 1897. Ross Middlebrook Youngs, Baseball Hall of Fame outfielder, born at Shiner, TX. Youngs played the outfield for the New York Giants in the years after World War I. He was exonerated of charges made in 1924 that he had taken money from gamblers to fix games. Inducted into the Hall of Fame in 1972. Died at San Antonio, TX, Oct 22, 1927.

STANLEY CUP CHAMPIONS THIS DATE	
1934	Chicago Blackhawks
1956	Montreal Canadiens

BIRTHDAYS TODAY

Melvin Cornell (Mel) Blount, 52, Pro Football Hall of Fame cornerback, born Vidalia, GA, Apr 10, 1948.

Enrico Ciccone, 30, hockey player, born Montreal, Quebec, Canada, Apr 10, 1970.

Michael (Mike) Devereaux, 37, baseball player, born Casper, WY, Apr 10, 1963.

Sean Gilbert, 30, football player, born Aliquippa, PA, Apr 10, 1970.

George Kenneth (Ken) Griffey, Sr, 50, former baseball player, born Donora, PA, Apr 10, 1950.

David Halberstam, 66, author (*October 64, The Summer of '49, The Breaks of the Game, The Amateurs*), born New York, NY, Apr 10, 1934.

Frank Strong Lary, 70, former baseball player, born Northport, AL, Apr 10, 1930.

John Earl Madden, 64, broadcaster and former football coach, born Austin, MN, Apr 10, 1936.

Joseph Donald (Don) Meredith, 62, former broadcaster and football player, born Mt Vernon, TX, Apr 10, 1938.

Robert Jose (Bob) Watson, 54, former baseball executive and player, born Los Angeles, CA, Apr 10, 1946.

APRIL 11 — TUESDAY
Day 102 — 264 Remaining

NBA FINALS CHAMPIONS THIS DATE	
1961	Boston Celtics

ANGELS DEBUT: ANNIVERSARY. Apr 11, 1961. The Los Angeles Angels, an American League expansion team, played their first regular season game, beating the Orioles at Baltimore, 7–2. The Angels finished the 1961 season in eighth place with a record of 70–91. Renamed the California Angels in 1966, they won their first division title in 1979.

GAITHER, JAKE: BIRTH ANNIVERSARY. Apr 11, 1903. Alonzo Smith ("Jake") Gaither, athlete, football coach and athletic director, born at Dayton, TN. Gaither was famed as the coach of Florida A&M's football team which he guided to a record of 203–36–4 from 1945 to 1960. He won six national black college championships and produced 36 All-Americans and 42 NFL players. Died at Tallahassee, FL, Feb 18, 1994.

GOALIE SCORES IN PLAY-OFFS: ANNIVERSARY. Apr 11, 1989. Goalie Ron Hextall of the Philadelphia Flyers scored an empty-net goal against the Washington Capitals as the Flyers won, 8–5. For Hextall it was the second goal of his career and the first scored by any goalie in a Stanley Cup play-off game.

HERSHEY'S KISSES FIGURE SKATING CHALLENGE. Apr 11. Utica, NY. For info: Media Relations, US Figure Skating Assn, 20 First St, Colorado Springs, CO 80906. Phone: (719) 635-5200. Fax: (719) 635-9548. E-mail: usfsa1@aol.com. Web: www.usfsa.org/events.

METS DEBUT: ANNIVERSARY. Apr 11, 1962. The New York Mets, a National League expansion team, played their first regular season game, losing, 11–4, to the Cardinals in St. Louis. The Mets lost eight more games before winning one, and they finished the year in 10th place with a record of 40–120. The Mets won their first division title in 1969 and went on to stun the Baltimore Orioles in the World Series.

MINNESOTA TWINS DEBUT: ANNIVERSARY. Apr 11, 1961. The Minnesota Twins, newly located from Washington, DC, where they were known as the Senators, won their first game, 6–0, over the Yankees in New York.

NICKLAUS WINS FIRST MASTERS: ANNIVERSARY. Apr 11, 1963. Jack Nicklaus, 23 years old, shot an even-par 72 in the final round to finish at 2-under-par 286 and win the Masters by one stroke over Tony Lema. Nicklaus's green jacket was his first of a record six, with his other victories coming in 1965, 1966, 1972, 1975 and 1986.

PILOTS DEBUT: ANNIVERSARY. Apr 11, 1969. The Seattle Pilots, an American League expansion team, played their first regular season game, defeating the Chicago White Sox, 7–0, at Seattle's Sicks' Stadium. The Pilots finished the year in sixth place in the AL West and left Seattle in 1970 to become the Milwaukee Brewers.

76ERS END CELTICS' SKEIN: ANNIVERSARY. Apr 11, 1967. The Philadelphia 76ers defeated the Boston Celtics in Game 5 of the Eastern Conference Finals, 140–116, to advance to the NBA Finals. Philadelphia thus ended Boston's eight-year streak of NBA titles and went on to beat the San Francisco Warriors for the championship, four games to two. The 76ers had won 68 games in the regular season and in 1980 were voted the greatest team in NBA history.

STANLEY CUP CHAMPIONS THIS DATE
1936   Detroit Red Wings

BIRTHDAYS TODAY

Sean Frederick Bergman, 30, baseball player, born Joliet, IL, Apr 11, 1970.
Blake Weeks Brockermeyer, 27, football player, born Fort Worth, TX, Apr 11, 1973.
Trevor Linden, 30, hockey player, born Medicine Hat, Alberta, Canada, Apr 11, 1970.
Bret William Saberhagen, 36, baseball player, born Chicago Heights, IL, Apr 11, 1964.
Reginald Clinton (Reggie) Tongue, 27, football player, born Baltimore, MD, Apr 11, 1973.
Jason A. Varitek, 28, baseball player, born Rochester, MN, Apr 11, 1972.

APRIL 12 — WEDNESDAY
Day 103 — 263 Remaining

NBA FINALS CHAMPIONS THIS DATE
1954   Minneapolis Lakers
1958   St. Louis Hawks

ATLANTA BRAVES DEBUT: ANNIVERSARY. Apr 12, 1966. The Atlanta Braves brought major league baseball to the South but lost their regular season opener, 3–2, to the Pittsburgh Pirates in 12 innings. The Braves, who moved from Milwaukee, finished the season in fifth place with a record of 85–77. They won their first division pennant in 1969.

JOSS, ADDIE: BIRTH ANNIVERSARY. Apr 12, 1880. Adrian ("Addie") Joss, Baseball Hall of Fame pitcher, born at Juneau, WI. Joss pitched a one-hitter in his major league debut and fashioned a spectacular career before being felled by tubercular meningitis. He threw two no-hitters and won 160 games in just nine years. Inducted into the Hall of Fame in 1978. Died at Toledo, OH, Apr 14, 1911.

KANSAS CITY ATHLETICS DEBUT: 45th ANNIVERSARY. Apr 12, 1955. The Kansas City Athletics, transplanted from Philadelphia, opened their first season in their new home by defeating the Detroit Tigers, 6–2, at Municipal Stadium. The A's finished the year in sixth place with a record of 63–91. They never won a pennant in Kansas City and moved to Oakland after the 1967 season.

LAPCHICK, JOE: 100th BIRTH ANNIVERSARY. Apr 12, 1900. Joseph Bohomiel (Joe) Lapchick, Basketball Hall of Fame player and coach, born at Yonkers, NY. Lapchick played basketball for pay from an early age. In 1923 he joined the original Celtics, one of the greatest pro teams of any era. The Celtics revolutionized the game with Lapchick as their great center. He began coaching at St. John's University in 1937, left for the New York Knicks in 1947 and returned to St. John's in 1957. The Celtics were inducted into the Hall of Fame in 1959, and Lapchick followed as an individual in 1966. Died at New York, NY, Aug 10, 1970.

April *2000*	S	M	T	W	T	F	S
							1
	2	3	4	5	6	7	8
	9	10	11	12	13	14	15
	16	17	18	19	20	21	22
	23	24	25	26	27	28	29
	30						

LAU, CHARLIE: BIRTH ANNIVERSARY. Apr 12, 1933. Charles Richard (Charlie) Lau, baseball player and coach, born at Romulus, MI. Lau was a major league catcher who gained fame as one of the game's most influential batting instructors. He taught his pupils, including George Brett, to hit line drives to the entire field. Died at Key Colony Beach, FL, Mar 18, 1984.

RED WINGS WIN RECORD GAME: ANNIVERSARY. Apr 12, 1996. The Detroit Red Wings set a National Hockey League record by winning their 61st regular season game, 5–3, over the Chicago Blackhawks. The previous record was held by the 1976–77 Montreal Canadiens. Detroit finished the season with 62 wins, 13 losses and 7 ties.

STANLEY CUP CHAMPIONS THIS DATE
1939   Chicago Blackhawks
1941   Boston Bruins

BIRTHDAYS TODAY

Donna Andrews, 33, golfer, born Lynchburg, VA, Apr 12, 1967.
John August (Johnny) Antonelli, 70, former baseball player, born Rochester, NY, Apr 12, 1930.
Michael Lockett (Mike) Garrett, 56, Heisman Trophy tailback, born Los Angeles, CA, Apr 12, 1944.
Adam Graves, 32, hockey player, born Toronto, Ontario, Canada, Apr 12, 1968.
Roman Hamrlik, 26, hockey player, born Gottwaldov, Czechoslovakia, Apr 12, 1974.
Michael Andrew (Mike) Macfarlane, 36, baseball player, born Stockton, CA, Apr 12, 1964.

APRIL 13 — THURSDAY
Day 104 — 262 Remaining

NBA FINALS CHAMPIONS THIS DATE
1949   Minneapolis Lakers
1957   Boston Celtics

BUTTS, ALFRED: BIRTH ANNIVERSARY. Apr 13, 1899. Alfred M. Butts, inventor of Scrabble, born at Poughkeepsie, NY. Butts was a jobless architect in the Depression when he invented the board game Scrabble. The game was just a fad for Butts's friends until a Macy's executive saw the game being played at a resort in 1952, and the world's largest store began carrying it. Manufacturing of the game was turned over to Selchow & Righter when 35 workers were producing 6,000 sets a week. Butts received three cents per set for years. He said, "One-third went to taxes. I gave one-third away, and the other third enabled me to have an enjoyable life." Died at Rhinebeck, NY, Apr 4, 1993.

DEVANEY, BOB: 85th BIRTH ANNIVERSARY. Apr 13, 1915. Robert S. (Bob) Devaney, football coach and athletic administrator, born at Saginaw, MI. Devaney was head coach at the University of Nebraska from 1962 through 1972, taking over a program that had enjoyed only three winning seasons in 21 years. He compiled a record of 101–20–2 and won national championships in 1970 and 1971. The latter team, with Heisman Trophy winner Johnny Rodgers and Outland Trophy winner Rich Glover on it, is often called the greatest college football team of all time. After the 1972 season, Devaney handed the coaching reins to Tom Osborne and concentrated on being Nebraska's athletic director, a position he held until January 1993. Died at Lincoln, NE, May 9, 1997.

FEDERAL LEAGUE OPENS: ANNIVERSARY. Apr 13, 1914. The Federal League opened its first season in Baltimore with the Terrapins defeating the Buffalo Buffeds, 3–2, before 27,140 fans. The Federal League challenged the American and National Leagues while accusing them of monopolistic practices and lasted only two seasons.

MILWAUKEE BRAVES DEBUT: ANNIVERSARY. Apr 13, 1953. The Milwaukee Braves, having moved from Boston after playing there every year since 1871, opened the season by losing to the Reds in Cincinnati, 2–0. The Braves were the first major league team to shift cities since the 1902 Baltimore Orioles became the 1903 New York Highlanders (later the Yankees).

NCAA MEN'S GYMNASTICS CHAMPIONSHIPS. Apr 13–15. University of Iowa, Iowa City, IA. For info: NCAA, PO Box 6222, Indianapolis, IN 46206-6222. Phone: (317) 917-6222. Fax: (317) 917-6888. Web: www.ncaa.org.

NCAA WOMEN'S GYMNASTICS CHAMPIONSHIPS. Apr 13–15. Finals. Site TBA. For info: NCAA, PO Box 6222, Indianapolis, IN 46206-6222. Phone: (317) 917-6222. Fax: (317) 917-6888. Web: www.ncaa.org.

NICKLAUS WINS SIXTH MASTERS: ANNIVERSARY. Apr 13, 1986. Jack Nicklaus, at age 46, won his sixth Masters, a record, and became the oldest player to win the tournament. Nicklaus shot 279, 9 under par, to defeat Greg Norman by one stroke.

ROSE GETS 4,000th HIT: ANNIVERSARY. Apr 13, 1984. Pete Rose of the Cincinnati Reds got the 4,000th hit of his major league career, a double off pitcher Jerry Koosman of the Philadelphia Phillies. Rose finished his career with 4,256 hits, the major league record.

THREE HOMERS TO LEAD OFF GAME: ANNIVERSARY. Apr 13, 1987. The San Diego Padres set a major league record when their first three batters—Marvell Wynne, Tony Gwynn and John Kruk—led off the first inning of a game against the San Francisco Giants with home runs. The Padres victimized pitcher Roger Mason, but the Giants won the game, 13–6.

TIGER WOODS WINS MASTERS: ANNIVERSARY. Apr 13, 1997. Tiger Woods, 21, became the youngest golfer to win the Masters. He did so with a record score of 270, 18 under par and 12 shots better than Tom Kite, who finished second. Woods broke the record of 271 held by Jack Nicklaus (1965) and Raymond Floyd (1976). He broke the margin-of-victory record by three shots. He was almost two years younger than Seve Ballesteros, who won the 1980 Masters at 23 years and 14 days of age.

US ADULT FIGURE SKATING CHAMPIONSHIPS. Apr 13–16. Lake Placid, NY. For info: Media Relations, US Figure Skating Assn, 20 First St, Colorado Springs, CO 80906. Phone: (719) 635-5200. Fax: (719) 635-9548. E-mail: usfsa1@aol.com. Web: www.usfsa.org/events.

STANLEY CUP CHAMPIONS THIS DATE	
1927	Ottawa Senators
1933	New York Rangers
1940	New York Rangers
1944	Montreal Canadiens

BIRTHDAYS TODAY

Dana Bruce Barros, 33, basketball player, born Boston, MA, Apr 13, 1967.

Sergei Gonchar, 26, hockey player, born Chelyabinsk, USSR, Apr 13, 1974.

Mark Edward Leiter, 37, baseball player, born Joliet, IL, Apr 13, 1963.

Davis Milton Love, III, 36, golfer, born Charlotte, NC, Apr 13, 1964.

John Ernest Muckler, 66, hockey coach, born Midland, Ontario, Canada, Apr 13, 1934.

John Douglas (Doug) Strange, 36, baseball player, born Greenville, SC, Apr 13, 1964.

Theodore (Ted) Washington, 32, football player, born Tampa, FL, Apr 13, 1968.

APRIL 14 — FRIDAY
Day 105 — 261 Remaining

STANLEY CUP CHAMPIONS THIS DATE	
1928	New York Rangers
1931	Montreal Canadiens
1948	Toronto Maple Leafs
1955	Detroit Red Wings
1960	Montreal Canadiens

ACC WOMEN'S GOLF CHAMPIONSHIP. Apr 14–16. Salem Glen Country Club, Clemmons, NC. For info: Atlantic Coast Conference, PO Drawer ACC, Greensboro, NC 27417-6724. Phone: (336) 854-8787. Fax: (336) 854-8797.

BASEBALL OUTSIDE THE US: ANNIVERSARY. Apr 14, 1969. The first major league baseball game played outside the US occurred as the Montreal Expos hosted the St. Louis Cardinals at Jarry Park. The Expos, an expansion team, won, 8–7.

DE VICENZO SIGNS INCORRECT CARD: ANNIVERSARY. Apr 14, 1968. After concluding the final round of the Masters with a magnificent 66, Argentinian Roberto de Vicenzo signed an incorrect scorecard that mistakenly recorded a par 4 on the 17th hole instead of a birdie 3. Under the rules of golf, de Vicenzo was disqualified, and Bob Goalby was declared the winner. Said de Vicenzo, "What a stupid I am."

RUTH PLAYS FIRST GAME FOR YANKEES: 80th ANNIVERSARY. Apr 14, 1920. After being sold by the Boston Red Sox, Babe Ruth played his first game for the New York Yankees. He got two singles against the Philadelphia Athletics but made an error in the outfield, giving the A's two runs and a 3–1 victory.

SWITZERLAND: WORLD JUNIOR (under 18) HOCKEY CHAMPIONSHIP. Apr 14–24. Various cities in Switzerland. For info: Intl Ice Hockey Fed, Parkring 11, 8002 Zurich, Switzerland. Phone: 411 289 86 00. Fax: 411 289 86 22. E-mail: iihf@iihf.com. Web: www.iihf.com.

**WORLD COW CHIP–THROWING CHAMPIONSHIP®
CONTEST.** Apr 14–16. Beaver, OK. 30th annual. A
highly specialized organic sporting event which draws
dung flingers from around the world. A special division
of this competition is held for politicians, who are known
to be highly practiced in this area. Est attendance: 2,500.
For info: Beth Elston, Secy, Beaver County Chamber of
Commerce, PO Box 878, Beaver, OK 73932-0878. Phone
and Fax: (580) 625-4726.

BIRTHDAYS TODAY

Bradley David (Brad) Ausmus, 31, baseball player, born
New Haven, CT, Apr 14, 1969.
Steven Thomas (Steve) Avery, 30, baseball player, born
Trenton, MI, Apr 14, 1970.
David Christopher Justice, 34, baseball player, born
Cincinnati, OH, Apr 14, 1966.
Gregory Alan (Greg) Maddux, 34, baseball player, born
San Angelo, TX, Apr 14, 1966.
Meg Mallon, 37, golfer, born Natick, MA, Apr 14, 1963.
Peter Edward (Pete) Rose, 59, former baseball player, born
Cincinnati, OH, Apr 14, 1941.

APRIL 15 — SATURDAY
Day 106 — 260 Remaining

STANLEY CUP CHAMPIONS THIS DATE
1937	Detroit Red Wings
1952	Detroit Red Wings

CHARLOTTE OBSERVER MARATHON FESTIVAL. Apr
15. Charlotte, NC. Marathon, 10K run, 10K walk and
other fitness activities. For info: Observer Marathon, Box
30294, Charlotte, NC 28230. Phone: (704) 358-5425. Fax:
(704) 358-5430. E-mail: donking@charlotte.com.

CITIBANK SPRING CUP REGATTA. Apr 15–16. San
Francisco, CA. Make way for the 2000 Citibank Spring
Cup Regatta, presented by KICU TV-36! Come on down
to Pier 39 and watch the world's finest sailors battle it
out in the exciting 11:Metre yachting action. America's
Cup participants, Olympic veterans and previous world
champions match wits in the longest-running, continuous, professional series in the Bay Area. Watch this
unique sporting event from the start/finish line at Pier
39, as the fleet combines strategy, skill and teamwork to
bring home the Citibank Cup. The stage is set as these
sleek racing vessels take to the demanding waters of San
Francisco Bay to grab their share of $10,000 in prize
money. Don't be left high and dry, set your sails for the
hottest sailing spectacle around. For info: Pier 39 Market
Development, PO Box 193730, San Francisco, CA 94119-
3730. Phone: (415) 705-5500. Fax: (415) 956-2911.
E-mail: jb@pier39.com. Web: www.pier39.com.

CREIGHTON, JIM: BIRTH ANNIVERSARY. Apr 15,
1841. James (Jim) Creighton, baseball player, born at
Brooklyn, NY. Baseball's first prominent pitcher,
Creighton stretched the rules of the day, which called for
underhand pitching with a straight arm and stiff wrist,
and put a little snap in his deliveries. His aggressive style
helped to revolutionize what had been a recreational
game. Died at Brooklyn, Oct 18, 1862.

April 2000	S	M	T	W	T	F	S
							1
	2	3	4	5	6	7	8
	9	10	11	12	13	14	15
	16	17	18	19	20	21	22
	23	24	25	26	27	28	29
	30						

DE PAOLO, PETER: BIRTH ANNIVERSARY. Apr 15,
1898. Peter De Paolo, auto racer, born at Roseland, NJ.
De Paolo started his racing career as riding mechanic for
his uncle, Ralph De Palma. He began driving in 1922 and
won the Indianapolis 500 and the national championship
three years later. After retirement, he became an unofficial ambassador for Indy, returning for the race every
year and singing its theme song, "Back Home Again in
Indiana," before the 1971 race. Died at Costa Mesa, CA,
Nov 26, 1980.

JEFFRIES, JIM: 125th BIRTH ANNIVERSARY. Apr 15,
1875. James Jackson (Jim) Jeffries, boxer, born at Carroll,
OH. Jeffries captured the world's heavyweight championship on June 9, 1899, defeating Bob Fitzsimmons in
only his 13th professional fight. He defended the crown
several times and retired in 1905, coming out of retirement in 1910 in an unsuccessful attempt to wrest the
title from Jack Johnson. Died at Burbank, CA, Mar 3,
1953.

KENDUSKEAG STREAM CANOE RACE. Apr 15. Bangor,
ME. 16.5-mile white-water open canoe race. Annually on
the third Saturday in April. Est attendance: 1,500. For
info: Bangor Parks and Rec Dept, 647 Main St, Bangor,
ME 04401. Phone: (207) 947-1018. Fax: (207) 947-1605.

NATIONAL ATLANTIC CITY ARCHERY CLASSIC. Apr
15–16. New Atlantic City Convention Center, Atlantic
City, NJ. Est attendance: 5,000. For info: Atlantic City
Conv and Visitors Authority, 2314 Pacific Ave, Atlantic
City, NJ 08401. Phone: (609) 449-7142.

NFL DRAFT. Apr 15–16. New York, NY. Teams in the
National Football League engage in their annual selection of college players. The draft has been an NFL institution since 1936 when University of Chicago
quarterback and Heisman Trophy winner Jay Berwanger,
the first player ever chosen, declined to play for the
Philadelphia Eagles and went into business instead. For
info: NFL, 280 Park Ave, New York, NY 10017. Phone:
(212) 450-2000. Fax: (212) 671-7573. Web: www.nfl.com.

ROBINSON'S NUMBER 42 RETIRED: ANNIVERSARY.
Apr 15, 1997. In ceremonies marking the 50th anniversary of the debut of Jackie Robinson in the major leagues,
Bud Selig, chairman of baseball's Executive Committee,
announced that Robinson's uniform number 42 would

be retired by all major league teams. Players then wearing 42 were allowed to continue to do so, but no team would ever assign 42 again.

ROBINSON BREAKS THE COLOR LINE: ANNIVERSARY. Apr 15, 1947. Jackie Robinson became the first black American to play in the major leagues in the 20th century when he made his debut for the Brooklyn Dodgers against the Boston Braves. Robinson went 0-for-3 but scored the deciding run as the Dodgers prevailed, 5–3.

SAN FRANCISCO GIANTS DEBUT: ANNIVERSARY. Apr 15, 1958. Major league baseball came to California as the San Francisco Giants, transplanted from New York, opened the season against the Los Angeles Dodgers, formerly of Brooklyn, at San Francisco's Seals Stadium. The Giants shut out their rivals, 8–0.

TAFT THROWS OUT FIRST BALL: 90th ANNIVERSARY. Apr 15, 1910. William Howard Taft began the tradition of the president throwing out a ceremonial first pitch when he did the honors before the Washington Senators' opening game against the Philadelphia Athletics. Washington won the game, 3–0, as Walter Johnson pitched a one-hitter.

TEXAS RANGERS DEBUT: ANNIVERSARY. Apr 15, 1972. The Texas Rangers, newly located from Washington, DC, where they were known as the Senators, began the season by losing to the California Angels in Anaheim, 1–0. Andy Messersmith was the winning pitcher, and Dick Bosman was the loser.

WORLD CHAMPIONSHIP GOLD PANNING COMPETITION. Apr 15–16. Consolidated Gold Mine, Dahlonega, GA. Competitions for the quickest gold panner. Annually, the third weekend in April. For info: Kate Brehe, Dahlonega-Lumpkin County Chamber of Commerce, 13 S Park St, Dahlonega, GA 30533. Phone: (706) 864-3513. Fax: (706) 864-7917. E-mail: dahlonegacoc @stc.net. Web: www.dahlonega.org.

YANKEES-METS DOUBLEHEADER AT SHEA: ANNIVERSARY. Apr 15, 1998. The New York Yankees and the New York Mets each played a home game at Shea Stadium, with the Yankees defeating the Anaheim Angels, 3–2, in the afternoon, and the Mets beating the Chicago Cubs, 2–1, at night. This unique doubleheader was occasioned by a structural accident at Yankee Stadium. A 500-pound steel beam fell from the upper deck on Apr 14, forcing New York City to close the park temporarily for inspection and repairs. The Yankees returned to their own home on Apr 25, beating the Detroit Tigers, 8–4.

CHASE'S SPORTSQUOTE OF THE DAY

"I believe in women. I believe in myself. I believe in my body."—sprinter Evelyn Ashford

BIRTHDAYS TODAY

Evelyn Ashford, 43, Olympic gold medal track athlete, born Shreveport, LA, Apr 15, 1957.
Jeromy Neal Burnitz, 31, baseball player, born Westminster, CA, Apr 15, 1969.
William Henry (Willie) Davis, 60, former baseball player, born Mineral Springs, AR, Apr 15, 1940.
Jason Sehorn, 29, football player, born Mt Shasta, CA, Apr 15, 1971.
Phillippi Dwaine Sparks, 31, football player, born Phoenix, AZ, Apr 15, 1969.
Kevin Michael Stevens, 35, hockey player, born Brockton, MA, Apr 15, 1965.

APRIL 16 — SUNDAY
Day 107 — 259 Remaining

STANLEY CUP CHAMPIONS THIS DATE	
1939	Boston Bruins
1949	Toronto Maple Leafs
1953	Montreal Canadiens
1954	Detroit Red Wings
1957	Montreal Canadiens
1961	Chicago Blackhawks

AVERILL'S DEBUT HOME RUN: ANNIVERSARY. Apr 16, 1929. Earl Averill of the Cleveland Indians became the first player in American League history to hit a home run in his first major league plate appearance. The Indians were playing the Detroit Tigers, and the homer came against pitcher Earl Whitehill. Cleveland won, 5–4, in 11 innings.

BULLS WIN 70 GAMES: ANNIVERSARY. Apr 16, 1996. The Chicago Bulls became the first NBA team to win 70 games in the regular season by defeating the Milwaukee Bucks, 86–80. After this game, Chicago's record stood at 70-9. The Bulls finished the year at 72-10 and won their fourth NBA title in six years.

GRETZKY ANNOUNCES RETIREMENT: ANNIVERSARY. Apr 16, 1999. Wayne Gretzky, the greatest hockey player of all time, announced his retirement from the New York Rangers. After one season in the WHA, Gretzky played nine seasons with the Edmonton Oilers, nearly eight with the Los Angeles Kings, 18 games with the St. Louis Blues and three years at New York. He ended his career with a multitude of records including most career points (2,857), most career goals (894), most career assists (1,963), most single-season points (215), most single-season goals (92) and most single-season assists (163). He won 10 Ross Trophies as the NHL's leading scorer, nine Hart Trophies as its MVP, four Lady Byng Trophies for gentlemanly play and four Stanley Cups. More than all this, he was universally recognized as the epitome of hockey excellence, an unrivaled exemplar of the beauty of the game, an unblemished role model and a Canadian national treasure who popularized hockey in the US as it never had been before. His retirement became effective on Apr 18 at the conclusion of the Rangers' last regular season game, a 2–1 overtime loss to the Pittsburgh Penguins.

MURPHY, ISAAC: BIRTH ANNIVERSARY. Apr 16, 1861. Isaac Murphy, jockey, born at Frankfort, KY. Murphy enjoyed great success in the 1880s and won the Kentucky Derby in 1884, 1890 and 1891. He rode Salvator to victory in a famous match race against Tenny in 1890. His career was cut short by the arrival of racial segregation in racing and by alcoholism. Died at Lexington, KY, Feb 12, 1896.

NATIONAL BOYS AND GIRLS CLUB WEEK. Apr 16–22. An annual event commemorating the founding of the first club 139 years ago. Every president since Herbert Hoover has served as Honorary Chairman of Boys and Girls Clubs of America. Today there are 1,700 clubs providing educational, arts and sports programs to 2.2 million young people in the US and the Virgin Islands. Annually, the third week in April. For info: Natl Boys and Girls Clubs of America, 1230 W Peachtree St NW, Atlanta, GA 30309. Phone: (404) 815-5700. Fax: (404) 815-5789.

NELSON WINS 800th GAME: ANNIVERSARY. Apr 16, 1994. Don Nelson became the seventh coach in professional basketball to win 800 games when his team, the Golden State Warriors, beat the Utah Jazz, 109–105.

OPENING DAY NO-HITTER: 60th ANNIVERSARY. Apr 16, 1940. Bob Feller of the Cleveland Indians pitched the only Opening Day no-hitter in major league history, beating the Chicago White Sox, 1–0. This was the first of three no-hitters for Feller, the others coming in 1946 and 1951.

TODD WINS FIRST POWER-LIFTING TITLE: ANNIVERSARY. Apr 16, 1978. At the first US power-lifting championships held at Nashua, NH, Jan Todd, a teacher from Nova Scotia, broke her own world record with a dead lift of 453¼ pounds. Cindy Reinhoudt won the award for best lifter after squatting 385 pounds, bench-pressing 205 pounds and dead lifting 385 pounds for a 975-pound total.

WANER, PAUL: BIRTH ANNIVERSARY. Apr 16, 1903. Paul Glee Waner, Baseball Hall of Fame outfielder, born at Harrah, OK. Waner was "Big Poison" to his brother Lloyd's "Little Poison." He played 20 years in the majors, mostly with the Pittsburgh Pirates, and won three National League batting titles. Inducted into the Hall of Fame in 1952. Died at Sarasota, FL, Aug 29, 1965.

BIRTHDAYS TODAY

Kareem Abdul-Jabbar (born Lewis Ferdinand Alcindor, Jr), 53, Basketball Hall of Fame center, born New York, NY, Apr 16, 1947.
Bruce Douglas Bochy, 45, baseball manager and former player, born Landes De Bussac, France, Apr 16, 1955.
Richard ("Night Train") Lane, 72, Pro Football Hall of Fame defensive back, born Austin, TX, Apr 16, 1928.
James Reynold (Jim) Lonborg, 58, former baseball player, born Santa Maria, CA, Apr 16, 1942.
Concepcion ("Conchita") Martinez, 28, tennis player, born Monzon, Spain, Apr 16, 1972.
Fernando Vina, 31, baseball player, born Sacramento, CA, Apr 16, 1969.

APRIL 17 — MONDAY
Day 108 — 258 Remaining

ANSON, CAP: BIRTH ANNIVERSARY. Apr 17, 1852. Adrian Constantine ("Cap") Anson, Baseball Hall of Fame player and manager, born at Marshalltown, IA. Anson played professional baseball from 1871 through 1897 and is considered one of the game's greatest first basemen. As a manager, he piloted the Chicago White Stockings (today's Cubs) to five National League pennants and a .575 winning percentage. Inducted into the Hall of Fame in 1939. Died at Chicago, IL, Apr 18, 1922.

April 2000	S	M	T	W	T	F	S
							1
	2	3	4	5	6	7	8
	9	10	11	12	13	14	15
	16	17	18	19	20	21	22
	23	24	25	26	27	28	29
	30						

BOSTON MARATHON. Apr 17. Boston, MA. The marathon begins in the rural New England town of Hopkinton, winds through cities and towns and finishes near downtown Boston. 2000 will be the 104th year of this historic running event. 15,000 participants. Est attendance: 2,000,000. For info: Boston Athletic Assn, Boston Marathon, PO Box 1998, Hopkinton, MA 01748. Phone: (508) 435-6905. E-mail: mile27@star.net. Web: www.bostonmarathon.org.

CARTWRIGHT, ALEXANDER: BIRTH ANNIVERSARY. Apr 17, 1820. Alexander Joy Cartwright, Jr, baseball innovator, born at New York, NY. Cartwright helped to organize the Knickerbocker Base Ball Club in 1845 and wrote the game's first rule book. He joined the California gold rush and eventually wound up in Hawaii, spreading the gospel of baseball all the way. Died at Honolulu, HI, July 12, 1892.

ERVING HITS 30,000-POINT MARK: ANNIVERSARY. Apr 17, 1987. Julius Erving of the Philadelphia 76ers scored 38 points to join Wilt Chamberlain and Kareem Abdul-Jabbar in pro basketball's 30,000-point club. Chamberlain and Abdul-Jabbar scored all their points in the NBA. Erving started his career in the ABA. He finished with 30,026 points.

MANTLE CLUBS LONG HOME RUNS: ANNIVERSARY. Apr 17, 1956. With President Dwight Eisenhower in attendance, Mickey Mantle of the New York Yankees opened the baseball season by hitting two massive home runs against the Washington Senators in Washington's Griffith Stadium. On this same date three years before, Mantle hit another homer, measured at 565 feet, one of the longest home runs ever.

MIKE SCHMIDT HITS FOUR HOME RUNS: ANNIVERSARY. Apr 17, 1976. Mike Schmidt of the Philadelphia Phillies became the first National League player since Bobby Lowe in 1894 to hit four home runs in consecutive at bats in the same game. Schmidt's feat came against the Chicago Cubs in an 18–16, 10-inning Phillies win. Schmidt connected twice off Rick Reuschel, once off Rick's brother Phil and once off Darold Knowles. He added a single and totaled eight RBIs as Philadelphia came back from a 13–2 deficit.

NATIONAL LEAGUE PLAYS ON SUNDAY: ANNIVERSARY. Apr 17, 1892. The National League ended its ban on Sunday baseball as the Cincinnati Reds defeated the St. Louis Browns (later the Cardinals), 5–1. From its start in 1876, the NL had prohibited Sunday play. The rival American Association (1882–91) allowed games on Sunday, and when the two leagues merged, the ban was lifted.

OAKLAND ATHLETICS DEBUT: ANNIVERSARY. Apr 17, 1968. The Oakland Athletics, having moved from Kansas City, made their debut in their new hometown, losing to the Baltimore Orioles, 4–1. Dave McNally pitched a two-hitter. Lew Krausse took the loss.

BIRTHDAYS TODAY

Don Anthony (Tony) Boselli, 28, football player, born Boulder, CO, Apr 17, 1972.
Kenneth (Ken) Daneyko, 36, hockey player, born Windsor, Ontario, Canada, Apr 17, 1964.
Norman Julius ("Boomer") Esiason, 39, broadcaster and former football player, born West Islip, NY, Apr 17, 1961.
Joseph (Joe) Foss, 85, first commissioner of the American Football League, born Sioux Falls, SD, Apr 17, 1915.

Marquis Deon Grissom, 33, baseball player, born Atlanta, GA, Apr 17, 1967.
Solomon Joseph (Solly) Hemus, 77, former baseball player and manager, born Phoenix, AZ, Apr 17, 1923.
Keith Allen Lyle, 28, football player, born Washington, DC, Apr 17, 1972.

APRIL 18 — TUESDAY
Day 109 — 257 Remaining

NBA FINALS CHAMPIONS THIS DATE
1962	Boston Celtics

COMEBACK FROM 0–3: ANNIVERSARY. Apr 18, 1942. The Toronto Maple Leafs completed the greatest comeback in Stanley Cup play-off history by defeating the Detroit Red Wings, 3–1, in Game 7 of the finals. The Leafs were down three games to none before they evened the series with 4–3, 9–3 and 3–0 victories.

CRAWFORD, SAM: BIRTH ANNIVERSARY. Apr 18, 1880. Samuel Earl (Sam) Crawford, Baseball Hall of Fame outfielder, born at Wahoo, NE. Crawford, known as "Wahoo Sam," played major league baseball for 19 years, mostly with the Detroit Tigers. He compiled a career batting average of .309 and hit 312 career triples, a record that still stands. Inducted into the Hall of Fame in 1957. Died at Hollywood, CA, June 15, 1968.

THE HOUSE THAT RUTH BUILT: ANNIVERSARY. Apr 18, 1923. More than 74,000 fans attended opening day festivities as the New York Yankees inaugurated their new stadium in the Bronx. Babe Ruth christened the park with a game-winning three-run homer into the right-field bleachers. In his coverage of the game for the *New York Evening Telegram*, sportswriter Fred Lieb described Yankee Stadium as "The House That Ruth Built," and the name stuck.

LOS ANGELES DODGERS HOME DEBUT: ANNIVERSARY. Apr 18, 1958. After having opened their first West Coast season in San Francisco, the Los Angeles Dodgers made their home debut. Playing before 78,672 in the Los Angeles Coliseum, the Dodgers beat the Giants, 6–5. Carl Erskine was the winning pitcher. The Giants could have tied the game in the ninth inning, but runner Jim Davenport was called out for failing to touch third base.

ONE-ARMED OUTFIELDER: 55th ANNIVERSARY. Apr 18, 1945. One-armed Pete Gray made his major league debut for the St. Louis Browns. Gray got one hit in four times at bat as the Browns beat the Detroit Tigers, 7–1. Gray hit .218 in 77 games.

SCHMIDT HITS 500th HOME RUN: ANNIVERSARY. Apr 18, 1987. The Philadelphia Phillies' Mike Schmidt hit the 500th home run of his career with two outs in the ninth inning of a game against the Pittsburgh Pirates. The Phillies rallied to win, 8–6. Schmidt finished his career with 548 homers, seventh on the all-time list.

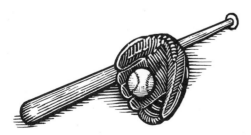

SEAVER STRIKES OUT 3,000th BATTER: ANNIVERSARY. Apr 18, 1981. Pitching for the Cincinnati Reds, Tom Seaver struck out the 3,000th batter in his career, Keith Hernandez of the St. Louis Cardinals. The Reds lost, 10–4. Seaver finished his career with 3,640 strikeouts and was inducted into the Baseball Hall of Fame in 1992.

STANLEY CUP CHAMPIONS THIS DATE
1942	Toronto Maple Leafs
1959	Montreal Canadiens
1963	Toronto Maple Leafs

BIRTHDAYS TODAY

Stephen Robert (Steve) Blass, 58, former baseball player, born Canaan, CT, Apr 18, 1942.
Geoff Bodine, 51, auto racer, born Elmira, NY, Apr 18, 1949.
Rico Joseph Brogna, 30, baseball player, born Turner Falls, MA, Apr 18, 1970.
Derrick Dewan Brooks, 27, football player, born Pensacola, FL, Apr 18, 1973.
James Michael (Jim) Eisenreich, 41, baseball player, born St. Cloud, MN, Apr 18, 1959.
Valeri Kamensky, 34, hockey player, born Voskresensk, USSR, Apr 18, 1966.
William Layton (Willie) Roaf, 30, football player, born Pine Bluff, AR, Apr 18, 1970.

APRIL 19 — WEDNESDAY
Day 110 — 256 Remaining

STANLEY CUP CHAMPIONS THIS DATE
1947	Toronto Maple Leafs

DODGERS PLAY IN NEW JERSEY: ANNIVERSARY. Apr 19, 1956. The Brooklyn Dodgers defeated the Philadelphia Phillies, 5–4, in 10 innings in a game played at Roosevelt Stadium at Jersey City. The game marked the first major league game played in New Jersey and was a prelude to the Dodgers' abandonment of Brooklyn after the 1957 season.

FIRST BOSTON MARATHON: ANNIVERSARY. Apr 19, 1897. John J. McDermott won the first running of the Boston Marathon with a time of 2:55:10.

FIRST WOMAN IN BOSTON MARATHON: ANNIVERSARY. Apr 19, 1967. Katherine Switzer defied organizers of the all-male Boston Marathon by submitting an entry under the name K. Switzer and having it accepted. She showed up at the starting line wearing heavy sweats and a hooded sweatshirt and peeled off these outer layers of clothing once the race began. Officials tried to force Switzer off the course, but her boyfriend, hammer thrower Thomas Miller, running with her, objected. She finished the race, but officials refused to record her time.

HITS CULPEPER. Apr 19–Oct 1. Commonwealth Park, Culpeper, VA. Seven weeks of hunter/jumper competition spread over the summer and the fall. Featuring Grand Prix jumping at Commonwealth Park. Draws both beginning and world-class riders. For info: HITS, 13 Closs Dr, Rhinebeck, NY 12572. Phone: (914) 876-3666. Fax: (914) 876-5538. Web: www.equisearch.com.

LONGEST BASEBALL GAME IN HISTORY: ANNIVERSARY. Apr 19, 1981. The Pawtucket Red Sox hosted the Rochester Red Wings in an International League game that turned into the longest contest in professional baseball history. It began on a cold Saturday night, Apr 18, and was suspended at 4:07 AM on Apr 19 with the teams tied, 2–2, after having played 32 innings. When the game resumed on June 23, Pawtucket pushed across the winning run in the bottom of the 33rd inning after only 18 minutes of play.

NATIONAL HOCKEY LEAGUE PLAY-OFFS BEGIN. Apr 19. Following the end of the regular season, play-offs begin in the National Hockey League. Eight teams from each of two conferences (three first-place teams plus five teams with the next-highest point totals) qualify for post-season play leading to the Stanley Cup Finals. For info: Natl Hockey League, 1251 Ave of the Americas, New York, NY 10020-1198. Phone: (212) 789-2000. Fax: (212) 789-2080. Web: www.NHL.com.

RACKING HORSE SPRING CELEBRATION. Apr 19–22. Decatur, AL. Racking horses from throughout the country are shown each night, culminating with the selection of award winners. Est attendance: 25,000. For info: Jacklyn Bailey, Decatur Conv and Visitors Bureau, 719 Sixth Ave SE, PO Box 2349, Decatur, AL 35602. Phone: (256) 350-2028 or (800) 524-6181.

RODMAN THE REBOUNDER: ANNIVERSARY. Apr 19, 1992. Dennis Rodman of the Detroit Pistons won the first rebounding title of his NBA career. He snared 1,530 rebounds, 42.1 percent of Detroit's total, for an average of 18.7 per game.

BIRTHDAYS TODAY

Alexis Arguello, 48, former boxer, born Managua, Nicaragua, Apr 19, 1952.
Micheal Calvin Barrow, 30, football player, born Homestead, PA, Apr 19, 1970.
Jose Cruz, Jr, 26, baseball player, born Arroyo, Puerto Rico, Apr 19, 1974.
Scott Andrew Kamieniecki, 36, baseball player, born Mt. Clemens, MI, Apr 19, 1964.
Brent Danem Mayne, 32, baseball player, born Loma Linda, CA, Apr 19, 1968.
Alfred (Al) Unser, Jr, 38, auto racer, born Albuquerque, NM, Apr 19, 1962.

APRIL 20 — THURSDAY

Day 111 — 255 Remaining

STANLEY CUP CHAMPIONS THIS DATE	
1958	Montreal Canadiens

ACC MEN'S AND WOMEN'S TENNIS CHAMPIONSHIPS. Apr 20–23. Racquet Club of the South, Atlanta, GA. For info: Atlantic Coast Conference, PO Drawer ACC, Greensboro, NC 27417-6724. Phone: (336) 854-8787. Fax: (336) 854-8797.

AGGANIS, HARRY: BIRTH ANNIVERSARY. Apr 20, 1929. Harry Agganis, baseball player, born at Lynn, MA. Agganis was a local favorite, playing football and baseball at Boston University and for the Red Sox before contracting leukemia. Died at Cambridge, MA, June 27, 1955.

BANCROFT, DAVE: BIRTH ANNIVERSARY. Apr 20, 1891. David James (Dave) Bancroft, Baseball Hall of Fame shortstop, born at Sioux City, IA. Bancroft was a superior fielder for four National League teams (1915–29). He managed the Boston Braves and several minor league teams. Inducted into the Hall of Fame in 1971. Died at Superior, WI, Oct 9, 1972.

April 2000	S	M	T	W	T	F	S
							1
	2	3	4	5	6	7	8
	9	10	11	12	13	14	15
	16	17	18	19	20	21	22
	23	24	25	26	27	28	29
	30						

BIG EAST MEN'S AND WOMEN'S TENNIS CHAMPIONSHIPS. Apr 20–23. Neil Schiff Tennis Complex, Coral Gables, FL. For info: Big East Conference, 56 Exchange Terrace, Providence, RI 02903. Phone: (401) 272-9108. Fax: (401) 751-8540.

CUBS OPEN IN WEEGHMAN PARK: ANNIVERSARY. Apr 20, 1916. The Chicago Cubs inherited Weeghman Park from the Chicago Whales of the defunct Federal League and used it as their home field starting with a game played against the Cincinnati Reds. The Cubs won, 7–6, in 11 innings. Weeghman Park was renamed Wrigley Field in 1926.

FENWAY PARK OPENS: ANNIVERSARY. Apr 20, 1912. The Boston Red Sox opened their new ballpark, Fenway Park, with a 7–6 win over the New York Yankees in 11 innings.

MOUNTAIN WEST MEN'S TENNIS CHAMPIONSHIP. Apr 20–22. University of New Mexico, Las Cruces, NM. For info: Mountain West Conference, PO Box 35670, Colorado Springs, CO 80935-3567. Phone: (719) 533-9500. Fax: (719) 533-9512.

NAVIN FIELD OPENS: ANNIVERSARY. Apr 20, 1912. The Detroit Tigers opened Navin Field (later Briggs Stadium and then Tiger Stadium) by defeating the Cleveland Naps (later the Indians), 6–5, in 11 innings. Tiger Stadium remained the Tigers' home through the 1999 season.

SEC MEN'S GOLF CHAMPIONSHIP. Apr 20–23. University of Mississippi, Oxford, MS. For info: Southeastern Conference, 2201 Civic Center Blvd, Birmingham, AL 35203-1103. Phone: (205) 458-3010. Fax: (205) 458-3030. E-mail: twilson@sec.org. Web: www.secsports.com.

SEC MEN'S TENNIS CHAMPIONSHIPS. Apr 20–23. University of Alabama, Tuscaloosa, AL. For info: Southeastern Conference, 2201 Civic Center Blvd, Birmingham, AL 35203-1103. Phone: (205) 458-3010. Fax: (205) 458-3030. E-mail: srodgers@sec.org. Web: www.secsports.com.

SEC WOMEN'S GOLF CHAMPIONSHIPS. Apr 20–23. University of Arkansas, Fayetteville, AR. For info: Southeastern Conference, 2201 Civic Center Blvd, Birmingham, AL 35203-1103. Phone: (205) 458-3010. Fax: (205) 458-3030. E-mail: srodgers@sec.org. Web: www.secsports.com.

SEC WOMEN'S TENNIS CHAMPIONSHIPS. Apr 20–23. University of Mississippi, Oxford, MS. For info: Southeastern Conference, 2201 Civic Center Blvd, Birmingham, AL 35203-1103. Phone: (205) 458-3010. Fax: (205) 458-3030. E-mail: srodgers@sec.org. Web: www.secsports.com.

TED WILLIAMS'S DEBUT: ANNIVERSARY. Apr 20, 1939. Ted Williams made his major league debut for the Boston Red Sox, getting one double in four at bats, as the Sox lost to the New York Yankees, 2–0.

CHASE'S SPORTSQUOTE OF THE DAY

"Man, what a pitcher's graveyard."—Satchel Paige on first seeing Fenway Park

BIRTHDAYS TODAY

Jon Dwayne Arnett, 66, former football player, born Los Angeles, CA, Apr 20, 1934.

Blair Atcheynum, 31, hockey player, born Estevan, Saskatchewan, Canada, Apr 20, 1969.

John Michael Carney, 36, football player, born Hartford, CT, Apr 20, 1964.

Todd Mathew Hollandsworth, 27, baseball player, born Dayton, OH, Apr 20, 1973.

Donald Arthur (Don) Mattingly, 39, former baseball player, born Evansville, IN, Apr 20, 1961.

Steven Orr (Steve) Spurrier, 55, football coach and Heisman Trophy quarterback, born Miami Beach, FL, Apr 20, 1945.

Ernest Alfred (Ernie) Stautner, 75, Pro Football Hall of Fame defensive tackle, born Prinzing-by-Cham, Bavaria, Germany, Apr 20, 1925.

Masato Yoshii, 35, baseball player, born Osaka, Japan, Apr 20, 1965.

APRIL 21 — FRIDAY

Day 112 — 254 Remaining

NBA FINALS CHAMPIONS THIS DATE

1948	Baltimore Bullets
1951	Rochester Royals

ACC MEN'S AND WOMEN'S OUTDOOR TRACK AND FIELD CHAMPIONSHIPS. Apr 21–22. Duke University, Durham, NC. For info: Atlantic Coast Conference, PO Drawer ACC, Greensboro, NC 27417-6724. Phone: (336) 854-8787. Fax: (336) 854-8797.

ACC MEN'S GOLF CHAMPIONSHIP. Apr 21–23. Old North State Club, Uwharrie Point, NC. For info: Atlantic Coast Conference, PO Drawer ACC, Greensboro, NC 27417-6724. Phone: (336) 854-8787. Fax: (336) 854-8797.

ACC MEN'S LACROSSE CHAMPIONSHIP. Apr 21–23. University of Maryland, College Park, MD. For info: Atlantic Coast Conference, PO Drawer ACC, Greensboro, NC 27417-6724. Phone: (336) 854-8787. Fax: (336) 854-8797.

BIG 12 WOMEN'S GOLF CHAMPIONSHIP. Apr 21–23. Lubbock Country Club, Lubbock, TX. For info: Big Twelve Conference, 2201 Stemmons Freeway, 28th Floor, Dallas, TX 75207. Phone: (214) 742-1212. Fax: (214) 742-2046.

CAJUNLAND VOLLEYBALL EASTER CLASSIC. Apr 21–23. Ernest N. Morial Convention Center, New Orleans, LA. Nearly 3,500 top female youth athletes will come to New Orleans for the third straight year to play in this three-day national volleyball tournament. For info: Dave Happoldt, Greater New Orleans Sports Foundation, 1400 Poydras St, Ste 918, New Orleans, LA 70112. Phone: (504) 619-6101. Fax: (504) 529-1622. E-mail: media@gnosports.com. Web: www.gnosports.com.

89ER DAYS PRCA RODEO. Apr 21–22. Lazy E Arena, Guthrie, OK. Celebrate the land run of 1889 at Oklahoma's largest rodeo, with more than 600 contestants competing. Est attendance: 17,000. For info: Lazy E Arena, Rte 5, Box 393, Guthrie, OK 73044. Phone: (405) 282-7433 or (800) 595-RIDE. E-mail: arena@lazye.net. Web: www.lazye.com.

ENGLAND: DEVIZES TO WESTMINSTER INTERNATIONAL CANOE RACE. Apr 21–24. Starts from Wharf Car Park, Wharf Street, Devizes, Wiltshire. Canoes race along 125 miles of the Kennet and Avon canals and the River Thames, ending at County Hall Steps, Westminster Bridge Road, London. Annually, Good Friday to Easter Monday. Est attendance: 6,000. For info: Competition Secy, Boscombe Forge, Church Road, Bookham, Surrey, England KT23 3JG. Phone: (44) (171) 401-8266. E-mail: dw@mackinlay.demon.co.uk. Web: www.mackinlay.demon.co.uk/dw.

FIRST RAINOUT AT LA: ANNIVERSARY. Apr 21, 1967. The scheduled game between the St. Louis Cardinals and the Dodgers at Los Angeles was rained out. This was the first Dodgers home game to be postponed since the team moved to Los Angeles in 1958.

KENTUCKY DERBY FESTIVAL. Apr 21–May 7. Louisville, KY. Civic celebration as Louisville warms up for the derby. About 70 events, two-thirds of which are free to the public. Est attendance: 1,500,000. For info: Kentucky Derby Festival, Inc, 1001 S Third St, Louisville, KY 40203. Phone: (502) 584-6383. Fax: (502) 589-4674. E-mail: kyderbyf@iglou.com. Web: www.kdf.org.

KGBX TYPEWRITER TOSS. Apr 21. KGBX-FM Radio, Springfield, MO. Participating secretaries toss a "typewriter," now a computer terminal, from a lift truck nearly 30 feet in the air. The "typewriter" landing closest to the bull's-eye wins an array of prizes. Definitely a "smashing" success! 11th annual toss. Est attendance: 250. For info: Teeg Stouffer, KGBX Radio, 1856 S Glenstone, Springfield, MO 65804. Phone: (417) 890-5555. Fax: (417) 890-5050. Web: www.kgbx.com.

LEAGUE PARK OPENS: 85th ANNIVERSARY. Apr 21, 1915. The Cleveland Indians opened their new ballpark, League Park, and lost to the Detroit Tigers, 5–0, before a crowd of 19,867. League Park, with its short right-field fence, remained the Indians' home until the 1940s when they moved their games to Municipal Stadium.

McCARTHY, JOE: BIRTH ANNIVERSARY. Apr 21, 1887. Joseph Vincent (Joe) McCarthy, Baseball Hall of Fame manager, born at Philadelphia, PA. McCarthy managed the Chicago Cubs (1926–30), the New York Yankees (1931–46) and the Boston Red Sox (1948–50). He was a strict disciplinarian whose career winning percentage was .614, the highest in major league history. Inducted into the Hall of Fame in 1957. Died at Buffalo, NY, Jan 13, 1978.

NEW ZEALAND: QUEENSTOWN GOLD RUSH INTERNATIONAL HILL CLIMB. Apr 21–23. Queenstown, New Zealand. 3rd annual. The Southern Hemisphere equivalent of the Pikes Peak International Hill Climb. Contested each year over Easter weekend, the Gold Rush course is 13.5 km long, zigzagging its way from 1,500 feet above sea level to 5,000 feet above sea level. The road surface is smooth, fine gravel with a large variety of corners. Sponsored by Silverstone. For info: Queenstown Gold Rush Ltd, PO Box 1160, Queenstown, New Zealand. E-mail: info@queenstowngoldrush.co.nz. Web: www.queenstowngoldrush.co.nz.

OWEN, STEVE: BIRTH ANNIVERSARY. Apr 21, 1898. Stephen Joseph (Steve) Owen, Pro Football Hall of Fame player, coach and executive, born at Cleo Springs, OK. Owens played football at Phillip University and wrestled professionally under an assumed name to preserve his amateur standing. He played tackle for the New York Giants and is ranked as one of the game's greatest defensive players. He coached the Giants for 23 years (1931–53) and won two NFL titles. Regarded as an innovator, he devised the umbrella defense, forerunner of the 4–3, to stop the Cleveland Browns' passing attack. Inducted into the Pro Football Hall of Fame in 1966. Died at New York, NY, May 17, 1964.

ROSIE RUIZ FRAUD: 20th ANNIVERSARY. Apr 21, 1980. Rosie Ruiz was the first woman to cross the finish line in the Boston Marathon, but she was soon disqualified after officials discovered that she had not run the entire course.

WILKINSON, J.L.: DEATH ANNIVERSARY. Apr 21, 1964. James L. Wilkinson, baseball executive, born at Perry, IA, 1874. Wilkinson was a key owner in the Negro Leagues. He assembled the Kansas City Monarchs in 1920 and kept them going through 1948. Starting in 1930, the Monarchs traveled with their own portable lights to play night games. Died at Kansas City, MO.

STANLEY CUP CHAMPIONS THIS DATE
1951	Toronto Maple Leafs

BIRTHDAYS TODAY

Ed Belfour, 35, hockey player, born Carmen, Manitoba, Canada, Apr 21, 1965.
Kenneth Gene (Ken) Caminiti, 37, baseball player, born Hanford, CA, Apr 21, 1963.
Jesse Russell Orosco, 43, baseball player, born Santa Barbara, CA, Apr 21, 1957.

APRIL 22 — SATURDAY
Day 113 — 253 Remaining

NBA FINALS CHAMPIONS THIS DATE
1947	Philadelphia Warriors

ACC WOMEN'S LACROSSE CHAMPIONSHIP. Apr 22–23. University of Maryland, College Park, MD. For info: Atlantic Coast Conference, PO Drawer ACC, Greensboro, NC 27417-6724. Phone: (336) 854-8787. Fax: (336) 854-8797.

BLOCK HOUSE STEEPLECHASE RACES. Apr 22. Foothills Equestrian Nature Center, Tryon, NC. 54th annual running of the Block House Steeplechase. Est attendance: 20,000. For info: Mitzi Lindsey, Tryon Riding & Hunt Club, PO Box 1095, Tryon, NC 28782. Phone: (800) 438-3681. Fax: (704) 859-5598. E-mail: trhc@tele plex.net. Web: www.teleplex.net/trhc.

FIRST NATIONAL LEAGUE GAME: ANNIVERSARY. Apr 22, 1876. In the first National League game ever played, the Boston Red Caps (later the Braves) defeated the hometown Philadelphia Athletics, 6–5. Jim O'Rourke got the first hit, and Joseph Borden, playing under the name of Josephs, was the winning pitcher.

	S	M	T	W	T	F	S
April							1
2000	2	3	4	5	6	7	8
	9	10	11	12	13	14	15
	16	17	18	19	20	21	22
	23	24	25	26	27	28	29
	30						

NBA EXPANDS BY FOUR: ANNIVERSARY. Apr 22, 1987. The NBA awarded expansion franchises to Charlotte, Miami, Minnesota and Orlando at a cost of $32.5 million per team. The Charlotte Hornets and the Miami Heat began play in the 1988–89 season. The Minnesota Timberwolves and the Orlando Magic followed a year later.

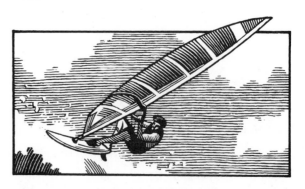

WARBIRDS IN ACTION AIR SHOW. Apr 22–23. Minter Field, Shafter, CA. 18th annual air show features flybys of up to 100 World War II trainers, fighters, bombers and reconnaissance aircraft. Also includes aerobatics, air racers and pilots' barbecue. Annually, the fourth weekend in April. Est attendance: 20,000. For info: Minter Field Air Museum, PO Box 445, Shafter, CA 93263-0445. Phone: (661) 393-0291. Fax: (661) 393-3296.

WHOOPING CRANE RUN. Apr 22. Fulton Navigation Park, Rockport, TX. 12th annual. 2-mile walk, 5K and 10K runs, plus ½K run for kids seven and under. For info: Rockport Fulton YMCA, PO Box 2272, Rockport, TX 78381. Phone: (361) 790-9622. E-mail: mysorski@dbs tech.com.

STANLEY CUP CHAMPIONS THIS DATE
1945	Toronto Maple Leafs
1962	Toronto Maple Leafs

BIRTHDAYS TODAY

Deane Beman, 62, golfer and former golf executive, born Washington, DC, Apr 22, 1938.
Vernell Eufaye ("Bimbo") Coles, 32, basketball player, born Covington, VA, Apr 22, 1968.
Terry Jon Francona, 41, baseball manager and former player, born Aberdeen, SD, Apr 22, 1959.
James Edward (Jimmy) Key, 39, former baseball player, born Huntsville, AL, Apr 22, 1961.
Michael Robert (Mickey) Morandini, 34, baseball player, born Kittanning, PA, Apr 22, 1966.
Peter Zezel, 35, hockey player, born Toronto, Ontario, Canada, Apr 22, 1965.

APRIL 23 — SUNDAY
Day 114 — 252 Remaining

NBA FINALS CHAMPIONS THIS DATE
1950	Minneapolis Lakers

AARON'S FIRST HOMER: ANNIVERSARY. Apr 23, 1954. Henry Aaron of the Milwaukee Braves hit the first home run of his major league career. It came against Vic Raschi of the St. Louis Cardinals in the Braves' 7–5 victory. Aaron went on to hit 754 more homers, more than any other player.

BOTTOMLEY, JIM: 100th BIRTH ANNIVERSARY. Apr 23, 1900. James LeRoy (Jim) Bottomley, Baseball Hall of Fame first baseman, born at Oglesby, IL. Bottomley played 16 seasons with the St. Louis Cardinals, Cincinnati Reds and St. Louis Browns. On Sept 16, 1924, he drove in 12 runs in one game to set a major league record. Inducted into the Hall of Fame in 1974. Died at St. Louis, MO, Dec 11, 1959.

CAMILLI, DOLF: BIRTH ANNIVERSARY. Apr 23, 1917. Adolf Louis (Dolf) Camilli, baseball player, born at San Francisco, CA. Camilli spent eight seasons in the minor leagues before getting a chance to play in the majors. A smooth fielder, he won the National League Most Valuable Player Award in 1941 while playing first base for the Brooklyn Dodgers. Camilli's son Doug also played major league baseball. Died at San Mateo, CA, Oct 21, 1997.

EASTER SUNDAY. Apr 23. Commemorates the Resurrection of Christ. Most joyous festival of the Christian year. The date of Easter, a movable feast, is derived from the lunar calendar (as prescribed by the Council of Nicaea, AD 325): the first Sunday following the first full moon on or after the vernal equinox (Mar 20)–always between Mar 22 and Apr 25. Many other dates in the Christian year are derived from the date of Easter.

EASTER BEACH RUN. Apr 23. Daytona Beach, FL. Annual beach run on "the world's most famous beach" includes a 4-mile run for 28 age divisions and a 2-mile run for youth 11 years old and younger. Est attendance: 2,000. For info: Easter Beach Run, Daytona Beach Leisure Services Dept, PO Box 2451, Daytona Beach, FL 32115-2451. Phone: (904) 258-3169. Fax: (904) 239-6550.

SODEN, ARTHUR: BIRTH ANNIVERSARY. Apr 23, 1843. Arthur Henry Soden, baseball executive, born at Framingham, MA. Soden was one of the original owners of the Boston Red Caps, the team that is now the Atlanta Braves. His legacy to the game includes the reserve clause that bound players to a team without their consent in perpetuity. Died at Lake Sunapee, NH, Aug 13, 1925.

TATIS HITS TWO GRAND SLAMS: ANNIVERSARY. Apr 23, 1999. Third baseman Fernando Tatis of the St. Louis Cardinals became the first player in major league history to hit two grand slams in the same inning of the same game. Playing against the Los Angeles Dodgers, Tatis hit both home runs in the third inning off pitcher Chan Ho Park. The first grand slam gave the Cardinals a 4–2 lead. The second extended their lead to 11–2. St. Louis won the game, 12–5. Only once before had a National League player, pitcher Tony Cloninger of the Atlanta Braves, hit two grand slams in the same game.

24-SECOND CLOCK: ANNIVERSARY. Apr 23, 1954. The NBA approved a proposal by Syracuse Nationals owner Danny Biasone to adopt a 24-second clock. The rule stated that "a team in control of the ball must make an attempt to score within 24 seconds after gaining possession of the ball." Biasone promoted the rule to boost the league's offensive output. He decided on 24 seconds by dividing the total number of shots taken in an average game by 48 minutes, the time played in a regulation game.

WILHELM'S ONLY HOMER: ANNIVERSARY. Apr 23, 1952. Hoyt Wilhelm of the New York Giants won the first game of his major league career (in relief), and he also hit a home run in his first major league at bat. Although Wilhelm appeared in 1,070 games, he never hit another homer.

WILKINSON, BUD: 85th BIRTH ANNIVERSARY. Apr 23, 1915. Charles ("Bud") Wilkinson, football player and coach and broadcaster, born at Minneapolis, MN. Wilkinson played football at the University of Minnesota and entered coaching immediately after graduation. He succeeded Jim Tatum as head coach at Oklahoma in 1947 and remained through 1964. During his tenure, the Sooners compiled a record 47-game winning streak. He headed the President's Physical Fitness Council and, after retiring from coaching, analyzed football games on ABC television. Died at Oklahoma City, OK, Feb 9, 1994.

STANLEY CUP CHAMPIONS THIS DATE

| 1950 | Detroit Red Wings |

BIRTHDAYS TODAY

Gail Charles Goodrich, Jr, 57, Basketball Hall of Fame guard, born Los Angeles, CA, Apr 23, 1943.
Rachel Hetherington, 28, golfer, born Port Macquarie, Australia, Apr 23, 1972.
Andruw Rudolf Jones, 23, baseball player, born Wellemstad, Curacao, Netherlands Antilles, Apr 23, 1977.
Samuel A. (Sam) Madison, 26, football player, born Thomasville, GA, Apr 23, 1974.
Warren Edward Spahn, 79, Baseball Hall of Fame pitcher, born Buffalo, NY, Apr 23, 1921.

APRIL 24 — MONDAY
Day 115 — 251 Remaining

NBA FINALS CHAMPIONS THIS DATE

| 1963 | Boston Celtics |
| 1967 | Philadelphia 76ers |

BIG 12 MEN'S GOLF CHAMPIONSHIP. Apr 24–25. Prairie Dunes Country Club, Hutchinson, KS. For info: Big Twelve Conference, 2201 Stemmons Freeway, 28th Floor, Dallas, TX 75207. Phone: (214) 742-1212. Fax: (214) 742-2046.

CHANDLER ELECTED COMMISSIONER: 55th ANNIVERSARY. Apr 24, 1945. Albert B. ("Happy") Chandler, US Senator from Kentucky, was elected Commissioner of Baseball by a unanimous vote of major league club owners. Chandler succeeded Kenesaw Mountain Landis who died in November 1944. He served one term and was replaced in 1951 by Ford C. Frick.

ENGLAND: HALLATON BOTTLE KICKING. Apr 24. Hallaton, Leicestershire. Perhaps the origin of soccer in England can be found in this ancient custom of kicking bottles around. Annually, on Easter Monday.

FIRST AMERICAN LEAGUE GAMES: ANNIVERSARY. Apr 24, 1901. The American League made its debut as a major league with a schedule of four games. Three were rained out, but the Chicago White Stockings beat the Cleveland Blues, 8–2, to get the season under way. 14,000 saw the game played at the Chicago Cricket Club.

MOUNTAIN WEST WOMEN'S GOLF CHAMPIONSHIP. Apr 24–26. Site TBA. For info: Mountain West Conference, PO Box 35670, Colorado Springs, CO 80935-3567. Phone: (719) 533-9500. Fax: (719) 533-9512.

PAC-10 MEN'S GOLF CHAMPIONSHIP. Apr 24–26. Arizona State University, Tempe, AZ. For info: PAC-10 Conference, 800 S Broadway, Ste 400, Walnut Creek, CA 94596. Phone: (510) 932-4411. Fax: (510) 932-4601.

PAC-10 WOMEN'S GOLF CHAMPIONSHIP. Apr 24–26. University of Oregon, Eugene, OR. For info: PAC-10 Conference, 800 S Broadway, Ste 400, Walnut Creek, CA 94596. Phone: (510) 932-4411. Fax: (510) 932-4601.

TAMPA AWARDED NFL FRANCHISE: ANNIVERSARY. Apr 24, 1974. The National Football League awarded a franchise for its 27th team to Tampa, FL. The team, called the Tampa Bay Buccaneers, began play in 1976.

WHITE HOUSE EASTER EGG ROLL. Apr 24. Traditionally held at executive mansion's south lawn on Easter Monday. Custom said to have started at Capitol grounds about 1810. Transferred to White House lawn in 1870s.

BIRTHDAYS TODAY

Michael Roy (Mike) Blowers, 35, baseball player, born Wurzburg, West Germany, Apr 24, 1965.
Larry Wayne ("Chipper") Jones, 28, baseball player, born De Land, FL, Apr 24, 1972.
Terry Anthony Tata, 60, baseball umpire, born Waterbury, CT, Apr 24, 1940.
Omar Enrique Vizquel, 33, baseball player, born Caracas, Venezuela, Apr 24, 1967.

APRIL 25 — TUESDAY
Day 116 — 250 Remaining

NBA FINALS CHAMPIONS THIS DATE	
1952	Minneapolis Lakers
1965	Boston Celtics

LLOYD, POP: BIRTH ANNIVERSARY. Apr 25, 1884. John Henry ("Pop") Lloyd, Baseball Hall of Fame shortstop, born at Palatka, FL. Lloyd was often compared to Honus Wagner and considered one of the best shortstops ever. He played and managed with black teams and made quite a career in Cuba where the fans nicknamed him "Cuchara" (scoop or shovel) for his big hands. Inducted into the Hall of Fame in 1977. Died at Atlantic City, NJ, Mar 19, 1965.

MONDAY RESCUES FLAG: ANNIVERSARY. Apr 25, 1976. Center fielder Rick Monday of the Chicago Cubs rescued an American flag from several fans who ran onto the field and attempted to set it on fire. The incident occurred in Dodger Stadium in the 4th inning of a 5–4, 10-inning victory by the Dodgers.

NBA DRAFTS FIRST BLACK PLAYER: 50th ANNIVERSARY. Apr 25, 1950. The Boston Celtics made Chuck Cooper, an All-American from Duquesne University playing with the Harlem Globetrotters, the first black player drafted by any NBA team when they selected him in the second round.

	S	M	T	W	T	F	S
April							1
2000	2	3	4	5	6	7	8
	9	10	11	12	13	14	15
	16	17	18	19	20	21	22
	23	24	25	26	27	28	29
	30						

NFL ADOPTS SUDDEN DEATH: ANNIVERSARY. Apr 25, 1974. The National Football League adopted a 15-minute, sudden-death quarter in an effort to reduce the number of tie games. The league also moved the goalposts from the goal line to the back line of the end zone to make it more difficult to kick field goals.

PALMER WINS FIRST MASTERS: ANNIVERSARY. Apr 25, 1958. Arnold Palmer struggled to a final-round 73, 1 over par, but still won the first of his four Masters championships. Palmer finished at 284, one shot better than Doug Ford and Fred Hawkins. He would win the tournament again in 1960, 1962 (in a play-off) and 1964.

STANLEY CUP CHAMPIONS THIS DATE	
1964	Toronto Maple Leafs

BIRTHDAYS TODAY

Timothy Theodore (Tim) Duncan, 24, basketball player, born St. Croix, Virgin Islands, Apr 25, 1976.
Darren Lee Holmes, 34, baseball player, born Asheville, NC, Apr 25, 1966.
Meadow George ("Meadowlark") Lemon III, 68, former basketball player, born Lexington, SC, Apr 25, 1932.
Keith Anthony (Tony) Phillips, 41, baseball player, born Atlanta, GA, Apr 25, 1959.
Darren Ray Woodson, 31, football player, born Phoenix, AZ, Apr 25, 1969.

APRIL 26 — WEDNESDAY
Day 117 — 249 Remaining

NBA FINALS CHAMPIONS THIS DATE	
1964	Boston Celtics

ALEXANDER, DALE: BIRTH ANNIVERSARY. Apr 26, 1903. David Dale Alexander, baseball player, born at Greeneville, TN. Alexander was an outstanding hitter from his rookie year, when he batted .343, to the end of his career. He won the American League batting title in 1932 with a .367 average despite being traded in June from the Detroit Tigers to the Boston Red Sox. Died at Greeneville, Mar 2, 1979.

BRUINS SNAP JINX: ANNIVERSARY. Apr 26, 1988. The Boston Bruins snapped a string of 18 straight Stanley Cup play-off series losses to the Montreal Canadiens, dating back to 1943, by ousting the Habs, four games to one. Boston used two goals each from Cam Neely and Steve Kasper and strong goaltending from Rejean Lemelin to defeat Montreal, 4–1.

FIRST BALLPARK ORGAN: ANNIVERSARY. Apr 26, 1941. The Chicago Cubs became the first major league team to install an organ in their ballpark. Roy Nelson played a pregame program.

RUNNING OF THE RODENTS. Apr 26. Louisville, KY. 28th annual. To celebrate the prefinals "Rat Race" that occurs each year, to develop community spirit and to unoffically kick off the Kentucky Derby festivities. Est attendance: 250. For info: Lauren Whalen, PR Dir, Spalding University, 851 S Fourth St, Louisville, KY 40203. Phone: (502) 585-7140 or (800) 896-8941, ext 140. Fax: (502) 585-7158. E-mail: pr2@spalding13.win.net. Web: www.spalding.edu.

TWINS DRAFTED: 35th ANNIVERSARY. Apr 26, 1965. In the third round of the NBA draft, the New York Knicks selected Dick Van Arsdale. With the next pick, the Detroit Pistons drafted Dick's twin brother, Tom. Both went on to distinguished careers.

WILSON, HACK: 100th BIRTH ANNIVERSARY. Apr 26, 1900. Lewis Robert ("Hack") Wilson, Baseball Hall of Fame outfielder, born at Ellwood City, PA. Wilson set the National League record for home runs in a season when he hit 56 in 1930. Short and squat, he got his nickname from his resemblance to George Hackenschmidt, a Russian wrestler and strongman. Inducted into the Hall of Fame in 1979. Died at Baltimore, MD, Nov 23, 1948.

CHASE'S SPORTSQUOTE OF THE DAY

"As a ballplayer, I would be delighted to do it again. As an individual, I doubt if I could possibly go through it again."—Roger Maris on breaking the home run record

---

BIRTHDAYS TODAY

Brian James Anderson, 28, baseball player, born Geneva, OH, Apr 26, 1972.
Fanny Blankers-Koen (born Francina Elsje Koen), 82, Olympic gold medal sprinter, born Amsterdam, Netherlands, Apr 26, 1918.
Donna de Varona, 53, women's sports executive, former broadcaster and Olympic gold medal swimmer, born San Diego, CA, Apr 26, 1947.
Natrone Jermaine Means, 28, football player, born Harrisburg, NC, Apr 26, 1972.
Michael Warren (Mike) Scott, 45, former baseball player, born Santa Monica, CA, Apr 26, 1955.

APRIL 27 — THURSDAY

Day 118 — 248 Remaining

BABE RUTH DAY: ANNIVERSARY. Apr 27, 1947. Babe Ruth Day was celebrated in every ballpark in organized baseball in the US as well as Japan. Ill with throat cancer that would claim his life 16 months later, Ruth appeared at Yankee Stadium to thank his former club for the honor.

BIG TEN MEN'S TENNIS CHAMPIONSHIPS. Apr 27–30. Indiana University, Bloomington, IN. Est attendance: 400. For info: Big Ten Conference, 1500 W Higgins Rd, Park Ridge, IL 60068-6300. Phone: (847) 696-1010. Fax: (847) 696-1150. Web: www.bigten.org.

BIG TEN WOMEN'S TENNIS CHAMPIONSHIPS. Apr 27–30. University of Michigan, Ann Arbor, MI. For info: Big Ten Conference, 1500 W Higgins Rd, Park Ridge, IL 60068-6300. Phone: (847) 696-1010. Fax: (847) 696-1150. Web: www.bigten.org.

BIG 12 MEN'S AND WOMEN'S TENNIS CHAMPIONSHIPS. Apr 27–30. Plaza Tennis Center, Kansas City, MO. For info: Big Twelve Conference, 2201 Stemmons Freeway, 28th Floor, Dallas, TX 75207. Phone: (214) 742-1212. Fax: (214) 742-2046.

FORT LAUDERDALE SPRING BOAT SHOW. Apr 27–30. Greater Fort Lauderdale/Broward County Convention Center. Everything from small boats to mega-yachts to boating equipment. For info: Greater Fort Lauderdale CVB, 1850 Eller Dr, Ste 303, Fort Lauderdale, FL 33316. Phone: (954) 765-4466.

HORNSBY, ROGERS: BIRTH ANNIVERSARY. Apr 27, 1896. Rogers Hornsby, Baseball Hall of Fame second baseman and manager, born at Winters, TX. Hornsby was baseball's greatest right handed hitter, winning six batting titles in a row, hitting .424 in 1924 and leading the National League in home runs and runs batted in several times. As a manager, Hornsby was tough and uncompromising, showing little feeling for players not as good as he was. Inducted into the Hall of Fame in 1942. Died at Chicago, IL, Jan 5, 1963.

MARCIANO RETIRES: ANNIVERSARY. Apr 27, 1956. Rocky Marciano retired as the only undefeated heavyweight champion. He finished his career with a record of 49–0 with 43 knockouts and six title defenses.

MOUNTAIN WEST WOMEN'S TENNIS CHAMPIONSHIP. Apr 27–29. UNLV, Las Vegas, NV. For info: Mountain West Conference, PO Box 35670, Colorado Springs, CO 80935-3567. Phone: (719) 533-9500. Fax: (719) 533-9512.

PAC-10 MEN'S AND WOMEN'S TENNIS CHAMPIONSHIPS. Apr 27–30. Ojai, CA. For info: PAC-10 Conference, 800 S Broadway, Ste 400, Walnut Creek, CA 94596. Phone: (510) 932-4411. Fax: (510) 932-4601.

PENN RELAY CARNIVAL. Apr 27–29 (tentative). Franklin Field, Philadelphia, PA. 106th running. The track meet that has provided competition for more athletes (high school, college and open) than any other in the world. 30 hours of competition over three days; more than 350 races. One of the great track and field experiences. For info: Penn Relay Carnival, Franklin Field, 235 S 33rd St, Philadelphia, PA 19104-6322. Phone: (215) 898-6145. Web: www.upenn.edu/relays.

VANCOUVER JOINS NBA: ANNIVERSARY. Apr 27, 1994. The NBA Board of Governors voted to grant an expansion franchise to the city of Vancouver, British Columbia. The Grizzlies, as the team was named, began play in the 1995–96 season.

BIRTHDAYS TODAY

George Gervin, 48, Basketball Hall of Fame guard, born Detroit, MI, Apr 27, 1952.
Lee Roy Jordan, 59, former football player, born Excel, AL, Apr 27, 1941.
Enos Bradsher Slaughter, 84, Baseball Hall of Fame outfielder, born Roxboro, NC, Apr 27, 1916.

APRIL 28 — FRIDAY

Day 119 — 247 Remaining

NBA FINALS CHAMPIONS THIS DATE

1966	Boston Celtics

BIG TEN WOMEN'S GOLF CHAMPIONSHIP. Apr 28–30. University of Wisconsin, Madison, WI. For info: Big Ten Conference, 1500 W Higgins Rd, Park Ridge, IL 60068-6300. Phone: (847) 696-1010. Fax: (847) 696-1150. Web: www.bigten.org.

BLUEBERRY HILL OPEN DART TOURNAMENT. Apr 28–30. St. Louis, MO. America's oldest and largest pub dart tournament open to everyone. 28th annual tournament. Est attendance: 400. For info: Joe Edwards, Blueberry Hill, 6504 Delmar, St. Louis, MO 63130. Phone: (314) 727-0880. Fax: (314) 727-1288. Web: www.blueberryhill.com.

CAVANAUGH, FRANK: BIRTH ANNIVERSARY. Apr 28, 1876. Francis W. (Frank) Cavanaugh, football coach, born at Worcester, MA. Cavanaugh earned the nickname the "Iron Major" for heroism in World War I. After the armistice, he developed Boston College and Fordham into national football powers. Died at Marshfield, MA, Aug 29, 1933.

DRAKE RELAYS. Apr 28–29. Des Moines, IA. Invitational track meet featuring nearly 100 events for high school, college and open competitors. For info: Drake Relays, Drake Fieldhouse, Des Moines, IA 50311. Phone: (515) 271-4268. Fax: (515) 271-3399. Web: www.drake relays.org.

NEWPORT TO ENSENADA INTERNATIONAL YACHT RACE. Apr 28–30. Newport, CA. One of the most prestigious and exciting yacht races of the year, preceded by a classic car and boat show and accompanied by some world-class partying. 53rd annual. For info: Newport Ocean Sailing Assn, PO Box 3546, Orange, CA 93857-0546. Phone: (714) 771-0691. Fax: (714) 771-2556. E-mail: nosa1@juno.com. Web: www.nosa.org.

RATTLESNAKE DERBY. Apr 28–30. Mangum, OK. Hunters stalk these wily reptiles and attempt to bring in the most snakes and the longest snake. Snakeskins and meat will be sold, and entertainment will include live music, a carnival and a flea market. A herpetologist will be on hand to educate festivalgoers. Est attendance: 40,000. For info: Chamber of Commerce, 222 W Jefferson, Mangum, OK 73554. Phone: (580) 782-2444 or (580) 782-2434.

RUSSIA: WORLD SENIOR HOCKEY CHAMPIONSHIP. Apr 28–May 14. St. Petersburg and Yaroslavl, Russia. For info: Intl Ice Hockey Fed, Parkring 11, 8002 Zurich, Switzerland. Phone: 411 280 86 00. Fax: 411 289 86 22. E-mail: iihf@iihf.com. Web: www.iihf.com.

SPECIAL OLYMPICS FLORIDA STATE SUMMER GAMES. Apr 28–30. Kissimmee, St. Cloud and Orlando, FL. Olympic-style competition for children and adults with mental retardation. For info: Special Olympics Florida State Summer Games, 8 Broadway, Ste D, Kissimmee, FL 34741. Phone: (407) 870-2292 or (800) 322-4376. Fax: (407) 870-9810.

☆   ☆   ☆

WHITE SOX GET 23 SINGLES: ANNIVERSARY. Apr 28, 1901. The Chicago White Sox set a record by getting 23 hits, all singles, defeating the Cleveland Indians, 13–1. Pitcher Bock Baker gave up all the hits.

BIRTHDAYS TODAY

Thomas Leo (Tom) Browning, 40, former baseball player, born Casper, WY, Apr 28, 1960.
Mark Anthony Carrier, 32, football player, born Lake Charles, LA, Apr 28, 1968.
John Patrick Daly, 34, golfer, born Carmichael, CA, Apr 28, 1966.
Edward Paul (Ted) Donato, 32, hockey player, born Dedham, MA, Apr 28, 1968.
Barry Louis Larkin, 36, baseball player, born Cincinnati, OH, Apr 28, 1964.

		S	M	T	W	T	F	S
April								1
		2	3	4	5	6	7	8
2000		9	10	11	12	13	14	15
		16	17	18	19	20	21	22
		23	24	25	26	27	28	29
		30						

Nicklas Lidstrom, 30, hockey player, born Vasteras, Sweden, Apr 28, 1970.
Pedro Ramos, 65, former baseball player, born Pinar del Rio, Cuba, Apr 28, 1935.

APRIL 29 — SATURDAY
Day 120 — 246 Remaining

ACC SOFTBALL TOURNAMENT. Apr 29–May 1. University of North Carolina, Chapel Hill, NC. For info: Atlantic Coast Conference, PO Drawer ACC, Greensboro, NC 27417-6724. Phone: (336) 854-8787. Fax: (336) 854-8797.

CARLTON STRIKES OUT 3,000th: ANNIVERSARY. Apr 29, 1981. Steve Carlton of the Philadelphia Phillies struck out Tim Wallach of the Montreal Expos in the first inning of the Phillies' 6–2 victory. Wallach was the 3,000th strikeout victim of Carlton's career. He finished with 4,136.

CLEMENS STRIKES OUT 20: ANNIVERSARY. Apr 29, 1986. Roger Clemens of the Boston Red Sox set a new American League and major league record for most strikeouts in a nine-inning game when he struck out 20 Seattle Mariners in a 3–1 Red Sox victory. The previous American League record, 19 strikeouts, was set by Nolan Ryan on Aug 12, 1974.

DERBY TRIAL. Apr 29. Churchill Downs, Louisville, KY. Held opening day of the Churchill Downs spring meeting on the Saturday before the Kentucky Derby. Est attendance: 20,000. For info: Churchill Downs, 700 Central Ave, Louisville, KY 40208. Phone: (502) 636-4400. Web: www.kentuckyderby.com.

FIRST NL EXTRA-INNING GAME: ANNIVERSARY. Apr 29, 1876. The Hartford and Boston clubs played the first extra-inning game in the National League. Hartford won, 3–2, in 10 innings.

FOXFIELD RACES. Apr 29 (also Sept 24). Charlottesville, VA. Steeplechase horse racing. Est attendance: 20,000. For info: W. Patrick Butterfield, Racing Mgr, Foxfield Racing Assn, PO Box 5187, Charlottesville, VA 22905. Phone: (804) 293-9501. Fax: (804) 293-8169.

GREAT PLAINS ROWING CHAMPIONSHIPS. Apr 29–30. Lake Shawnee, Topeka, KS. 16th annual 60-event rowing regatta for high school, college and master-age oarspeople. Sponsors: US Rowing and many other groups. Est attendance: 11,000. For info: Don Craig, 4336 SE 25th St Terrace, Topeka, KS 66605. Phone: (785) 233-9951. Fax: (785) 233-9952. E-mail: toprow@juno.com. Web: adams net.com/topekarowing.

HAWKS TRADE RUSSELL: ANNIVERSARY. Apr 29, 1956. The St. Louis Hawks traded their No. 1 draft choice, Bill Russell from the University of San Francisco, to the Boston Celtics for Cliff Hagan and Ed Macauley. Russell would lead the Celtics to 11 NBA titles in 13 seasons, but years later, Hawks owner Ben Kerner insisted he would make the trade again.

KITEFEST. Apr 29–30. River Oaks Park, Kalamazoo, MI. Family-oriented kite-flying event includes sport kite competition, children's kite-making workshop, kite competitions and lots of kite flying, including indoors. Est attendance: 5,000. For info: John D. Cosby, Mktg Coord, Kalamazoo County Parks Dept, 2900 Lake St, Kalamazoo, MI 49001. Phone: (616) 383-8778. Fax: (616) 383-8724. Web: www.kalcounty.com.

LAST HELMETLESS PLAYER RETIRES: ANNIVERSARY. Apr 29, 1997. Craig MacTavish, the last player to go without a helmet, retired from the National Hockey League. The NHL mandated helmets at the start of the 1979–80 season but allowed players then active to refrain by signing a waiver absolving the league of responsibility in case of head injury. MacTavish was the last remaining player of those who signed the waiver. He retired from the St. Louis Blues after a 16-year career during which he scored 213 goals. Despite his personal choice, he admitted, "Certainly, it's very dangerous out there without a helmet."

MARCH OF DIMES WALKAMERICA. Apr 29–30. The March of Dimes's largest fundraiser takes place in communities nationwide the last weekend in April with more than one million volunteers participating. Funds raised support research, education and community-based programs to prevent birth defects and to help lower the rate of premature births and infant mortality. Call your local chapter to learn how to participate. For info: March of Dimes Birth Defects Foundation, Natl HQ, 1275 Mamaroneck Ave, White Plains, NY 10605. Phone: (914) 997-4574.

MOUNTAIN PACIFIC SPORTS FEDERATION MEN'S VOLLEYBALL CHAMPIONSHIP. Apr 29. Final. Site TBA. For info: MPSF, 800 S Broadway, Ste 102, Walnut Creek, CA 94596. Phone: (925) 296-0723. Fax: (925) 296-0724. E-mail: abeaird@mpsports.org. Web: www.pac-10.org/sports/mpsf.html.

ONLY DERBY IN APRIL: ANNIVERSARY. Apr 29, 1901. For the first and only time, the Kentucky Derby was run in April instead of May. The winning colt was His Eminence, ridden by Jimmy Winkfield. Sannazarro finished second, a length and a half back.

ORIOLES END LOSING STREAK: ANNIVERSARY. Apr 29, 1988. The 1988 Baltimore Orioles finally won a game after losing the first 21 games of the season. They beat the Chicago White Sox, 9–0, on a combined four-hitter by pitchers Mark Williamson and Dave Schmidt. The Orioles' streak, lasting from Apr 4 to 28, set an American League record but fell two losses short of the National League mark.

PIONEER DAYS. Apr 29–May 7. Guymon, OK. One of the state's largest PRCA rodeos highlights Guymon's celebration of the community's pioneer spirit. Activities include a parade, chuckwagon breakfast, barbecue feed, arts and crafts fair and old-timers' reunion. Est attendance: 20,000. For info: Ron Biffel, Guymon Chamber of Commerce, Rte 3 Box 120, Guymon, OK 73942. Phone: (580) 338-3376.

BIRTHDAYS TODAY

Andre Kirk Agassi, 30, tennis player, born Las Vegas, NV, Apr 29, 1970.
George Herbert Allen, 78, former football coach, born Detroit, MI, Apr 29, 1922.
Luis Ernesto Aparicio, 66, Baseball Hall of Fame shortstop, born Maracaibo, Venezuela, Apr 29, 1934.
Joshua Gibson (Josh) Booty, 25, baseball player, born Starkville, MS, Apr 29, 1975.
Bruce Douglas Driver, 38, hockey player, born Toronto, Ontario, Canada, Apr 29, 1962.

Dale Earnhardt, 48, auto racer, born Kannapolis, NC, Apr 29, 1952.
James Warren (Jim) Hart, 56, former football player, born Evanston, IL, Apr 29, 1944.
Sterling Alex Hitchcock, 29, baseball player, born Fayetteville, NC, Apr 29, 1971.
Curtis Shayne Joseph, 33, hockey player, born Keswick, Ontario, Canada, Apr 29, 1967.
John Laurence (Johnny) Miller, 53, broadcaster and golfer, born San Francisco, CA, Apr 29, 1947.
God Shammgod, 24, basketball player, born New York, NY, Apr 29, 1976.
John Vander Wal, 34, baseball player, born Grand Rapids, MI, Apr 29, 1966.

APRIL 30 — SUNDAY
Day 121 — 245 Remaining

NBA FINALS CHAMPIONS THIS DATE

1971	Milwaukee Bucks

BIG SUR MARATHON. Apr 30. Carmel, CA. 15th annual. Marathon, half-marathon, marathon relay, 10.6- mile walk and 5K run/walk. Est attendance: 9,200. For info: Big Sur Marathon, PO Box 222620, Carmel, CA 93922. Phone: (831) 625-6226. Web: www.bsim.org.

HIGHLANDERS WIN HOME OPENER: ANNIVERSARY. Apr 30, 1903. The New York Highlanders won their home opener at Hilltop Park over the Washington Senators. The Highlanders had played the 1901 and 1902 American League seasons as the Baltimore Orioles. They changed their name to the New York Yankees in 1913.

MAYS HITS FOUR HOME RUNS: ANNIVERSARY. Apr 30, 1961. Willie Mays of the San Francisco Giants became the eighth player in major league history to hit four home runs in a single game. Mays performed the feat at Milwaukee County Stadium as the Giants beat the Braves, 14–4.

MUHAMMAD ALI STRIPPED OF TITLE: ANNIVERSARY. Apr 30, 1967. Muhammad Ali was stripped of the world heavyweight boxing championship when he refused to be inducted into military service. Said Ali, "I have searched my conscience, and I find I cannot be true to my belief in my religion by accepting such a call." He had claimed exemption as a minister of the Black Muslim religion. He was convicted of violating the Selective Service Act but the Supreme Court reversed this decision in 1971.

ROBERTSON'S PERFECT GAME: ANNIVERSARY. Apr 30, 1922. Charlie Robertson of the Chicago White Sox pitched major league baseball's fifth regular-season perfect game, beating the Detroit Tigers in Detroit, 2–0. Robertson pitched in the majors for eight years and had a 49–80 record.

RUN OF THE CHARLES CANOE AND KAYAK RACE. Apr 30. On the Charles River, Boston, MA. Amateur and professional canoe and kayak races with approximately 1,400 paddlers participating to help highlight improvements to the Charles River. For info: Classic Communications, 38 Mechanic St, #101, Foxboro, MA 02035. Phone: (508) 698-6810. Fax: (508) 698-6811. E-mail: crwarotc@aol.com.

YOST, FIELDING: BIRTH ANNIVERSARY. Apr 30, 1871. Fielding Harris ("Hurry Up") Yost, football player, coach and administrator, born at Fairview, WV. Yost developed the University of Michigan into one of college football's great early powers, winning a national championship in his first year, 1901, and the first Rose Bowl (1902) against Stanford. He remained at Michigan for 41 years as coach and/or athletic director. Died at Ann Arbor, MI, Aug 20, 1946.

CHASE'S SPORTSQUOTE OF THE DAY

"Winning is not everything. It is the only thing."
—Fielding Yost, 1905

BIRTHDAYS TODAY

Jeff Randall Brown, 34, hockey player, born Ottawa, Ontario, Canada, Apr 30, 1966.

Philip Mason (Phil) Garner, 52, baseball manager and former player, born Jefferson City, TN, Apr 30, 1948.

Raymond Roger (Ray) Miller, 55, baseball manager, born Takoma Park, MD, Apr 30, 1945.

Richard (Rich) Pilon, 32, hockey player, born Saskatoon, Saskatchewan, Canada, Apr 30, 1968.

Jeffrey Allen (Jeff) Reboulet, 36, baseball player, born Dayton, OH, Apr 30, 1964.

Isiah Lord Thomas, III, 39, former basketball player, born Chicago, IL, Apr 30, 1961.

MAY 1 — MONDAY
Day 122 — 244 Remaining

STANLEY CUP CHAMPIONS THIS DATE
1965   Montreal Canadiens

BATTLES, CLIFF: 90th BIRTH ANNIVERSARY. May 1, 1910. Clifford Franklin (Cliff) Battles, football coach and Pro Football Hall of Fame halfback, born at Akron, OH. Battles played football for West Virginia Wesleyan and then turned pro in 1932 with the Boston Redskins, soon to become the Washington Redskins. He helped Washington win the 1937 NFL title but retired at age 28 when owner George Preston Marshall would not offer him a raise. Inducted into the Pro Football Hall of Fame in 1968. Died at Akron, Apr 28, 1981.

BERARDINO, JOHNNY: BIRTH ANNIVERSARY. May 1, 1917. John (Johnny) Berardino, actor and baseball player, born at Los Angeles, CA. Berardino played 11 seasons in the major leagues and was on the World Champion 1948 Cleveland Indians. After retiring, he became a successful soap opera actor, spending more than three decades on "General Hospital." Died at Los Angeles, May 19, 1996.

CAGLE, CHRIS: 95th BIRTH ANNIVERSARY. May 1, 1905. Christian Keener (Chris) Cagle, football player, coach and executive, born at DeRidder, LA. Cagle was a three-time All-American at West Point in 1927, 1928 and 1929, but since he had played previously at Southwestern Louisiana Institute, a dispute over his eligibility resulted in a two-year cancellation of the Army-Navy game. He left West Point before graduating because he had violated academy rules by getting married. He played pro football for five years. Died after a fall down a stairway at New York, NY, Dec 23, 1942.

FLEMINGTON SPEEDWAY RACING SEASON. May 1–Oct 30 (Saturday nights). Flemington Fairgrounds, Flemington, NJ. Racing by various types of stock cars and other vehicles. 6 PM starting time. Est attendance: 5,000. For info: Paul Kuhl, Flemington Fairgrounds, PO Box 293, Rte 31, Flemington, NJ 08822. Phone: (908) 782-2413. Fax: (908) 806-8432.

GREAT CARDBOARD BOAT REGATTA. May 1. SIUC Campus Lake, Carbondale, IL. Teams and individuals design, build and race person-powered boats made of corrugated cardboard. "Titanic Award" for most spectacular sinking plus trophies for team spirit, most creative use of cardboard, best-dressed team, most spectacular-looking boat. Prizes for top finishers in three boat classes: Class I, propelled by oars or paddles; Class II, propelled by mechanical means such as paddle wheels or pro-

pellers; Class III, "Instant Boats" made from "Secret Kits" by spectators-turned-participants. Registration 10 AM; races begin at noon. 25th annual regatta. Additional competition at other locations across the country on various dates. Est attendance: 13,500. For info: Southern Illinois Univ, School of Art and Design, Carbondale, IL 62901. Phone: (618) 867-2346. Fax: (618) 453-7501. E-mail: commodore@gcbr.com. Web: www.gcbr.com.

KENNEDY NAMED NBA PRESIDENT: ANNIVERSARY. May 1, 1963. J. Walter Kennedy was named the second president of the NBA, succeeding Maurice Podoloff, who retired after the 1962–63 season.

LONGEST MAJOR LEAGUE GAME: 80th ANNIVERSARY. May 1, 1920. The Brooklyn Dodgers and the Boston Braves played the longest game in major league baseball history but did not finish it. After 26 innings, the game was halted because of darkness with the score tied, 1–1. Each team used just one pitcher, Leon Cadore for the Dodgers and Joe Oeschger for the Braves, who gave up 12 and 9 hits, respectively. Despite its 26 innings, the game took just 3 hours, 50 minutes. The next day, the Dodgers lost to the Philadelphia Phillies in 13 innings. The day after that, they returned to Boston and lost again in 19 innings.

MOUNTAIN WEST MEN'S GOLF CHAMPIONSHIP. May 1–3. Site TBA. For info: Mountain West Conference, PO Box 35670, Colorado Springs, CO 80935-3567. Phone: (719) 533-9500. Fax: (719) 533-9512.

NATIONAL BIKE MONTH. May 1–31. 42nd annual celebration of bicycling for recreation and transportation. Local activities sponsored by bicycling organizations, environmental groups, PTAs, police departments, health organizations and civic groups. About five million participants nationwide. Annually, the month of May. For info: League of American Bicyclists, 1612 K St NW, Ste 401, Washington, DC 20006. Phone: (202) 822-1333. Fax: (202) 822-1334. Web: www.bikeleague.org.

NATIONAL GOLDEN GLOVES TOURNAMENT OF CHAMPIONS. May 1–6. Detroit, MI. National Golden Gloves amateur boxing championship tournament. For info: Golden Gloves Assn of America Inc, 1503 Linda Lane, Hutchinson, KS 67502. Phone: (316) 663-6942.

NATIONAL PHYSICAL FITNESS AND SPORTS MONTH. May 1–31. Encourages individuals and organizations to promote fitness activities and programs. For info: President's Council on Physical Fitness and Sports, HHH Bldg, 200 Independence Ave SW, Room 738H, Washington, DC 20201-0004. Phone: (202) 690-9000. Fax: (202) 690-5211.

RICKEY HENDERSON STEALS BASE-THEFT CROWN: ANNIVERSARY. May 1, 1991. Rickey Henderson of the Oakland Athletics stole third base, the 939th steal of his career, to set a new major league record, surpassing Lou Brock. The A's beat the New York Yankees, 7–4.

RYAN PITCHES SEVENTH NO-HITTER: ANNIVERSARY. May 1, 1991. Nolan Ryan of the Texas Rangers pitched the seventh no-hitter of his career, extending his own major league record. Ryan struck out 16 as the Rangers beat the Toronto Blue Jays, 3–0.

STRIKE OUT STROKES MONTH. May 1–31. Dedicated to the prevention of strokes. Factors resulting from heredity or natural processes can't be changed, but with proper medical treatment and healthful lifestyle adjustments some risk factors can be changed. Kit materials available for $15. For info: Frederick S. Mayer, Pres, Pharmacy Council on Stroke Prevention, 101 Lucas Valley Rd, #210, San Rafael, CA 94903. Phone: (415) 479-8628. Fax: (415) 479-8608. E-mail: ppsi@aol.com.

WILLIAMS, ARCHIE: 85th BIRTH ANNIVERSARY. May 1, 1915. Archie Williams, Olympic gold medal sprinter, born at Oakland, CA. Along with Jesse Owens and others, Williams helped debunk Adolf Hitler's theory of Aryan superiority at the 1936 Summer Olympics at Berlin. As a member of the US track team, Williams, an African American, won a gold medal by running the 400-meters in 46.5 seconds. He earned a degree in mechanical engineering from the University of California–Berkeley in 1939 but had to dig ditches for a time because he couldn't find an engineering job. He joined the Army Air Corps in 1942 and later trained pilots at Tuskegee Institute. When asked during a 1981 interview about his treatment by the Nazis during the Olympics, he replied, "Well, over there at least we didn't have to ride in the back of the bus." Died at Fairfax, CA, June 24, 1993.

WOMEN'S INTERNATIONAL BOWLING CONGRESS ANNUAL MEETING. May 1–3. Reno, NV. Est attendance: 3,500. For info: Bowling, Inc, 5301 S 76th St, Greendale, WI 53129. Phone: (414) 423-3356. Fax: (414) 421-3013.

BIRTHDAYS TODAY

Charles Philip (Chuck) Bednarik, 75, Pro Football Hall of Fame center and linebacker, born Bethlehem, PA, May 1, 1925.
Steve Cauthen, 40, former jockey, born Walton, KY, May 1, 1960.
Bryan Marchment, 31, hockey player, born Scarborough, Ontario, Canada, May 1, 1969.

May *2000*	S	M	T	W	T	F	S
		1	2	3	4	5	6
	7	8	9	10	11	12	13
	14	15	16	17	18	19	20
	21	22	23	24	25	26	27
	28	29	30	31			

Oliver Genoa (Ollie) Matson, 70, Pro Football Hall of Fame halfback, born Trinity, TX, May 1, 1930.
Billy Eugene Owens, 31, basketball player, born Carlisle, PA, May 1, 1969.
Martin Armando Reynoso, 34, baseball player, born San Luis Potosi, Mexico, May 1, 1966.

MAY 2 — TUESDAY
Day 123 — 243 Remaining

NBA FINALS CHAMPIONS THIS DATE
1968   Boston Celtics

AMERICAN BOWLING CONGRESS MASTERS TOURNAMENT. May 2–6. Albuquerque, NM. Top professional and nonprofessional bowlers from across the US and the world compete for $250,000 in prize money and for one of bowling's most prestigious titles. The 2000 Masters will be part of the PBA Spring/Summer Tour, and the finals will be televised live on CBS. Each player rolls 10 qualifying games before a cut is made to the top ¼ of the field. Then another 5 qualifying games cut the field to 63, who join the defending champion in a unique 3-game, double-elimination match-play format. The second, third and fourth qualifiers then compete in a "shootout" format against each other for the opportunity to face the top qualifier for the title. Est attendance: 5,000. For info: Michael Deering, American Bowling Congress, 5301 S 76th St, Greendale, WI 53129-1127. Phone: (414) 423-3309. Fax: (414) 421-3013.

COLLINS, EDDIE: BIRTH ANNIVERSARY. May 2, 1887. Edward Trowbridge (Eddie) Collins, Sr, Baseball Hall of Fame second baseman and executive, born at Millerton, NY. Collins moved from Columbia University to the Philadelphia Athletics, leading the A's to three World Series triumphs (1910, 1911, 1913). He was sold to the Chicago White Sox where he played 12 years and put in a stint as manager. After retiring, he was an executive with the Boston Red Sox. Inducted into the Hall of Fame in 1939. Died at Boston, MA, Mar 25, 1951.

CROSBY, BING: BIRTH ANNIVERSARY. May 2, 1904. Harry Lillis ("Bing") Crosby, singer, actor and amateur golfer, born at Tacoma, WA. Crosby hosted an annual golf tournament that bore his name at Pebble Beach, CA, and also owned part of the Pittsburgh Pirates. Died after playing golf near Madrid, Spain, Oct 14, 1977.

DOUBLE NO-HITTER: ANNIVERSARY. May 2, 1917. Chicago Cubs left-hander James ("Hippo") Vaughn and Cincinnati Reds right-hander Fred Toney combined for baseball's only double no-hitter. After both pitchers threw nine innings of no-hit ball, the Reds scored a run on two hits in the top of the 10th inning. Toney set the Reds down in order in the bottom of the 10th to win the game.

FIRST NL HOME RUN: ANNIVERSARY. May 2, 1876. Second baseman Ross Barnes of the Chicago White Stockings hit the first home run in National League history. It was an inside-the-park homer hit off William ("Cherokee") Fisher of the Cincinnati Red Stockings.

GEHRIG'S STREAK ENDS: ANNIVERSARY. May 2, 1939. New York Yankees first baseman Lou Gehrig asked manager Joe McCarthy to take him out of the lineup for the game against the Detroit Tigers. By his sitting out, Gehrig's record streak of consecutive games played, begun May 25, 1925, stopped at 2,130. The slugger complained of fatigue, but he was really suffering from ALS, amyotrophic lateral sclerosis, a condition later known as Lou Gehrig's disease. Gehrig never played again.

MUSIAL HITS FIVE HOMERS: ANNIVERSARY. May 2, 1954. Stan Musial of the St. Louis Cardinals hit five home runs in a doubleheader against the New York Giants at St. Louis, setting a major league record. The Cardinals won the first game, 10–6, but fell to the Giants in the nightcap, 9–7.

STANLEY CUP CHAMPIONS THIS DATE

1967	Toronto Maple Leafs

BIRTHDAYS TODAY

Thomas Steven (Steve) Rippley, 46, baseball umpire, born St. Petersburg, FL, May 2, 1954.

Jamaal Abdul-Lateef Wilkes (born Jackson Keith Wilkes), 47, former basketball player, born Berkeley, CA, May 2, 1953.

MAY 3 — WEDNESDAY
Day 124 — 242 Remaining

FIRST TELEVISED DERBY: ANNIVERSARY. May 3, 1952. CBS became the first network to televise the Kentucky Derby. Eddie Arcaro rode Hill Gail to a two-length victory over Sub Fleet. Blue Man was third. For Arcaro, it was a record fifth Derby win. Trainer Ben A. Jones won for the sixth time, also a record.

GENUINE RISK SECOND FILLY TO WIN DERBY: 20th ANNIVERSARY. May 3, 1980. Genuine Risk, ridden by Jacinto Vasquez, became just the second filly to win the Kentucky Derby. She posted a one-length victory over Rumbo. The first filly to win the Derby was Regret in 1915.

NBA HAWKS MOVE TO ATLANTA: ANNIVERSARY. May 3, 1968. New owners Tom Cousins and Carl Sanders announced that the St. Louis Hawks of the NBA would move to Atlanta for the 1968–69 season. The team began as the Tri-Cities Blackhawks (1949–51), moved to Milwaukee and then to St. Louis in 1956.

PROJECT ACES DAY. May 3. 12th annual celebration of fitness and unity worldwide when All Children Exercise Simultaneously. "The World's Largest Exercise Class" takes place the first Wednesday in May as schools in all 50 states and 50 different countries hold fitness classes, assemblies and other fitness education events involving millions of children, parents and teachers. Conducted in cooperation with the President's Council on Physical Fitness and Sports during National Physical Fitness and Sports Month. For info send SASE to: Dept C, Youth Fitness Coalition, Inc, PO Box 6452, Jersey City, NJ 07306-0452. Phone: (201) 433-8993. Fax: (201) 332-3060. E-mail: yfcprojectaces@excite.com. Web: www.project aces.com.

ROBINSON, SUGAR RAY: BIRTH ANNIVERSARY. May 3, 1921. Ray ("Sugar Ray") Robinson, boxer, born Walker Smith, Jr, at Detroit, MI. Generally considered "pound for

pound the greatest boxer of all time," Robinson was a welterweight and middleweight champion who won 175 professional fights and lost only 19. A smooth and precise boxer, he fought until he was 45, dabbled in show business and established the Sugar Ray Robinson Youth Foundation to counter juvenile delinquency. To this day, his name connotes class, style and dignity. Died at Los Angeles, CA, Apr 12, 1989.

RUSSELL, HONEY: BIRTH ANNIVERSARY. May 3, 1903. John ("Honey") Russell, Basketball Hall of Fame player and coach, born at New York, NY. Russell played in more than 3,200 pro basketball games in the sport's early years. In 1936 he became coach at Seton Hall University, remaining there for 11 seasons. He was also a baseball scout, a football scout and a promoter. Inducted into the Hall of Fame in 1964. Died at Livingston, NJ, Nov 15, 1973.

TATUM, GOOSE: BIRTH ANNIVERSARY. May 3, 1921. Reece ("Goose") Tatum, basketball player, born at Calion, AR. Tatum played football and baseball and came into his own when Abe Saperstein asked him to play basketball with the Harlem Globetrotters. Tatum's best asset was his hands, big enough to allow him to hold the ball with one hand. He perfected the overhand hook shot later used by Wilt Chamberlain, Connie Hawkins and Kareem Abdul-Jabbar. Suspended by Saperstein in 1955, he formed his own team, the Harlem Magicians. Died at El Paso, TX, Jan 18, 1967.

BIRTHDAYS TODAY

Darren John Dreifort, 28, baseball player, born Wichita, KS, May 3, 1972.

Garfield (Gar) Heard, 52, basketball coach and former player, born Hogansville, GA, May 3, 1948.

Ron Hextall, 36, hockey player, born Winnipeg, Manitoba, Canada, May 3, 1964.

Jeffrey John (Jeff) Hornacek, 37, basketball player, born Elmhurst, IL, May 3, 1963.

Vyacheslav (Slava) Kozlov, 28, hockey player, born Voskresensk, USSR, May 3, 1972.

David Earl (Davey) Lopes, 55, former baseball player, born Providence, RI, May 3, 1945.

MAY 4 — THURSDAY
Day 125 — 241 Remaining

STANLEY CUP CHAMPIONS THIS DATE

1969	Montreal Canadiens

BASEBALL'S ONE-MILLIONTH RUN: 25th ANNIVERSARY. May 4, 1975. Bob Watson of the Houston Astros raced around the bases on Milt May's home run against the San Francisco Giants and crossed the plate with what was declared to be the one-millionth run scored in major league baseball history. Watson's hustle paid off. Dave Concepcion of the Cincinnati Reds scored another run in a different game in a different city seconds later.

DANCER'S IMAGE VS FORWARD PASS: ANNIVERSARY. May 4, 1968. Jockey Bob Ussery rode Dancer's Image to a 1½-length victory over Forward Pass in the Kentucky Derby. Three days later, Dancer's Image was disqualified when tests revealed the presence of an illegal painkilling drug in his system, and Forward Pass was declared the winner. Peter Fuller, owner of Dancer's Image, subsequently challenged the disqualification and the Kentucky Racing Commission split the difference, ruling that Dancer's Image won the race but Forward Pass could keep the purse.

ENGLAND: MITSUBISHI MOTORS BADMINTON HORSE TRIALS. May 4–7. Badminton, Gloucester. Famous international horse trials consisting of show jumping, cross-country and dressage. Est attendance: 200,000. For info: Box Office, Badminton Horse Trials, Badminton, Avon, England GL9 1DF. Phone: (44) (145) 421-8272. Fax: (44) (145) 421-8596. E-mail: info@bad minton-horse.co.uk.

FIRST PROFESSIONAL BASEBALL GAME: ANNIVERSARY. May 4, 1871. The first game in the new National Association, a full professional league, was played, pitting the Fort Wayne Kekiongas against the Forest City Club of Cleveland. Fort Wayne won, 2–0. James ("Deacon") White was the first man to bat; he got the first hit, a double, and was the first man erased in the first double play.

JOSEY'S WORLD CHAMPION JUNIOR BARREL RACE. May 4–7. Josey's Ranch, Marshall, TX. Youth barrel-racing competition. Annually, the first weekend in May. Est attendance: 4,000. For info: Pam Whisenant, Dir of Conv and Visitor Development, Marshall Chamber of Commerce, PO Box 520, Marshall, TX 75671. Phone: (903) 935-7868. Fax: (903) 935-9982. E-mail: cvb@internet work.net. Web: www.marshalltxchamber.com.

LAYDEN, ELMER: BIRTH ANNIVERSARY. May 4, 1903. Elmer F. Layden, football player, coach and executive, born at Davenport, IA. Layden was the fullback for Coach Knute Rockne's famous backfield, the Four Horsemen of Notre Dame. After graduating in 1925, he entered coaching and was appointed head coach at his alma mater in 1937. He left Notre Dame in 1941 to become NFL commissioner. Died at Chicago, IL, June 30, 1973.

SHOEMAKER STANDS UP IN THE SADDLE: ANNIVERSARY. May 4, 1957. Iron Liege, ridden by Bill Hartack, won the Kentucky Derby by a nose over Gallant Man, ridden by Bill Shoemaker. Gallant Man overtook Iron Liege in the stretch, but Shoemaker misjudged the finish line and stood up at the 1/16-pole, allowing Iron Liege to regain the lead and win the race.

TAFT SEES TWO BALL GAMES: 90th ANNIVERSARY. May 4, 1910. President William Howard Taft watched the St. Louis Cardinals play the Cincinnati Reds at Robison Field, but he didn't stay for the end of the game, won by the Cards, 12–3. Instead, he left for Sportsman's Park to see the St. Louis Browns and the New York Yankees play a 3–3, 14-inning tie, a game called by darkness.

CHASE'S SPORTSQUOTE OF THE DAY

"The game of baseball is a clean, straight game, and it summons to its presence everybody who enjoys clean, straight athletics."—William Howard Taft

---

BIRTHDAYS TODAY

Matthew Barnaby, 26, hockey player, born Belleville, Ontario, Canada, May 4, 1974.

Benjamin (Ben) Grieve, 24, baseball player, born Arlington, TX, May 4, 1976.

Rene George Lachemann, 55, former baseball manager and player, born Los Angeles, CA, May 4, 1945.

Eduardo Rafael (Eddie) Perez, 32, baseball player, born Cuidad Ojeda, Venezuela, May 4, 1968.

May *2000*	S	M	T	W	T	F	S
		1	2	3	4	5	6
	7	8	9	10	11	12	13
	14	15	16	17	18	19	20
	21	22	23	24	25	26	27
	28	29	30	31			

Elizabeth Earle (Betsy) Rawls, 72, LPGA Hall of Fame golfer, born Spartanburg, SC, May 4, 1928.

Dawn Staley, 30, basketball player, born Philadelphia, PA, May 4, 1970.

Cy Young

MAY 5 — FRIDAY
Day 126 — 240 Remaining

NBA FINALS CHAMPIONS THIS DATE	
1969	Boston Celtics

AMERICAN LEAGUE'S FIRST PERFECT GAME: ANNIVERSARY. May 5, 1904. Denton T. ("Cy") Young pitched the first perfect game in the American League, not allowing a single opposing player to reach first base. Young's outstanding performance led the Boston Americans in a 3–0 victory over Philadelphia. The Cy Young Award for pitching was named in his honor.

BENDER, CHIEF: BIRTH ANNIVERSARY. May 5, 1883. Charles Albert ("Chief") Bender, Baseball Hall of Fame pitcher, born at Crow Wing County, MN. Part Native American, Bender pitched for the Philadelphia Athletics from 1903 through 1914, winning 191 games. He played in the Federal League and then with the Philadelphia Phillies. Inducted into the Hall of Fame in 1953. Died at Philadelphia, PA, May 22, 1954.

BIG EAST MEN'S AND WOMEN'S OUTDOOR TRACK AND FIELD CHAMPIONSHIPS. May 5–7. Rutgers Track and Field Complex, Piscataway, NJ. For info: Big East Conference, 56 Exchange Terrace, Providence, RI 02903. Phone: (401) 272-9108. Fax: (401) 751-8540.

BIG EAST SOFTBALL TOURNAMENT. May 5–8. Boston College, Chestnut Hill, MA. For info: Big East Conference, 56 Exchange Terrace, Providence, RI 02903. Phone: (401) 272-9108. Fax: (401) 751-8540.

KENTUCKY OAKS. May 5. Churchill Downs, Louisville, KY. 126th running of the nation's premier race for 3-year-old fillies, held the day before the Kentucky Derby, run consecutively since 1875. Est attendance: 100,000. For info: Churchill Downs, 700 Central Ave, Louisville, KY 40208. Phone: (502) 636-4400. Web: kentuckyderby.com.

LOBSTER RACE AND OYSTER PARADE. May 5. Aiken, SC. The world's only thoroughbred lobster races and oyster party. The lobsters are raced in a unique sea-salt-water-filled track called "Lobster Downs." Beach music, gourmet seafood available. Oyster Parade at the "Mardi Claw" (our version of Mardi Gras) to highlight local land-locked maritime costumes will be held in Aiken's historical alley section. 16th annual Running of the Lobsters at Aiken. Est attendance: 6,000. For info: Greater Aiken Chamber of Commerce, Lobster Race/Oyster Parade, PO Box 892, Aiken, SC 29802. Phone: (803) 641-1111 or (803) 648-4981.

NCAA MEN'S DIVISION II TENNIS CHAMPIONSHIP. May 5–7. Regionals. Sites TBA. For info: NCAA, PO Box 6222, Indianapolis, IN 46206-6222. Phone: (317) 917-6222. Fax: (317) 917-6888. Web: www.ncaa.org.

ROSE GETS 3,000th HIT: ANNIVERSARY. May 5, 1978. Pete Rose of the Cincinnati Reds got the 3,000th hit of his career, a single off Steve Rogers of the Montreal Expos. Rose played in the majors from 1963 through 1986 and wound up with 4,256 hits, more than any other player.

SECRETARIAT WINS THE DERBY IN RECORD TIME: ANNIVERSARY. May 5, 1973. Secretariat, ridden by Ron Turcotte, won the Kentucky Derby in the record time of 1:59.2. "Big Red," as he was known, beat Sham by 2½ lengths and went on to win the Triple Crown.

WILDFLOWER TRIATHLONS FESTIVAL. May 5–7. Lake San Antonio, CA. Includes a long-course triathlon and a sprint-distance triathlon on May 6 and an Olympic-distance triathlon, which includes the USAT Collegiate National Championship, on May 7. For info: Event Mgt, Mktg, Promo, Tri-California Events, Inc, 1284 Adobe Ln, PO Box 51116, Pacific Grove, CA 93950. Phone: (831) 373-0678. Fax: (831) 373-7731. E-mail: events@tricalifornia.com. Web: www.tricalifornia.com.

WORLD CHAMPIONSHIP CRIBBAGE TOURNAMENT. May 5–7. Plumas County Fairgrounds, Quincy, CA. Founded in 1972, the country's oldest cribbage tournament now draws entrants from all over the country during the three-day event. Annually, the first weekend in May. Est attendance: 500. For info: Mike Taborski, Tournament Chair, PO Box B, Quincy, CA 95971. Phone: (530) 283-0800. Fax: (530) 283-3952. E-mail: featherpub@aol.com.

STANLEY CUP CHAMPIONS THIS DATE
1966   Montreal Canadiens

BIRTHDAYS TODAY

Juan Carlos Acevedo, 30, baseball player, born Juarez, Mexico, May 5, 1970.
Anthony Robert (Tony) Canadeo, 81, Pro Football Hall of Fame halfback, born Chicago, IL, May 5, 1919.
LaPhonso Darnell Ellis, 30, basketball player, born East St. Louis, IL, May 5, 1970.
Hideki Irabu, 31, baseball player, born Hyogo, Japan, May 5, 1969.
Charles Harrison Nagy, 33, baseball player, born Fairfield, CT, May 5, 1967.
Zigmund (Ziggy) Palffy, 28, hockey player, born Skalica, Czechoslovakia, May 5, 1972.
Mikael Renberg, 28, hockey player, born Pitea, Sweden, May 5, 1972.

MAY 6 — SATURDAY
Day 127 — 239 Remaining

BABE RUTH'S FIRST MAJOR LEAGUE HOME RUN: 85th ANNIVERSARY. May 6, 1915. George Herman ("Babe") Ruth of the Boston Red Sox hit his first major league home run in a game against the New York Yankees at New York. Over the course of his career, he hit 713 more.

BANNISTER SHATTERS FOUR-MINUTE-MILE BARRIER: ANNIVERSARY. May 6, 1954. Running the mile for the British Amateur Athletic Association team in a meet at Oxford University, Roger Bannister broke the four-minute barrier with a time of 3:59.4. Bannister shattered the existing record, set by Gunder Haag of Sweden in 1945, by a full two seconds. Four minutes (or one minute per quarter-mile) was at the time considered not only a physical barrier but also a psychological one. In this epic race, Bannister relied on two teammates to pace him. Chris Brasher helped Bannister for the first two laps with times of 57.5 and 1:58.2. Chris Chataway sprang to the lead for the third quarter (3:00.5). Bannister followed Chataway around the curve and started his kick on the backstretch. He sprinted past Chataway and, as he broke the tape, into track history. But his record lasted little more than a month, until John Landy of Australia ran 3:58.0 on June 21.

BARK IN THE PARK. May 6. Lincoln Park, Chicago, IL. In recognition of Be Kind to Animals Week, thousands of paws and feet will hit the ground running or walking for this 5K event. Entrance fee. Est attendance: 3,000. For info: The Anti-Cruelty Soc, 157 W Grand Ave, Chicago, IL 60610. Phone: (312) 644-8338. Web: www.anticruelty.org.

BOBO'S ONE AND ONLY: ANNIVERSARY. May 6, 1953. Alva ("Bobo") Holloman of the St. Louis Browns pitched a no-hitter in his first major league start, defeating the Philadelphia Athletics, 6–0. Holloman never pitched another complete game in his career which lasted just another 21 games.

EWBANK, WEEB: BIRTH ANNIVERSARY. May 6, 1907. Wilbur Charles ("Weeb") Ewbank, Pro Football Hall of Fame coach, born at Richmond, IN. Ewbank was the only coach to win titles in the National Football League and the American Football League. He led the Baltimore Colts to NFL titles in 1958 and 1959 and the New York Jets to the AFL title in 1968. Those same Jets became the first AFL team to win a Super Bowl, defeating the Colts on Jan 12, 1969, 16–7. Inducted into the Hall of Fame in 1978. Died at Oxford, OH, Nov 17, 1998.

"HAVE ANOTHER DOUGHNUT, YOU FAT PIG": ANNIVERSARY. May 6, 1988. After a 6–1 loss to the Boston Bruins in the Stanley Cup play-offs, New Jersey Devils coach Jim Schoenfeld confronted referee Don Koharski as the officials left the ice. In a scuffle, Koharski either fell or was pushed, causing Schoenfeld to mock him with the insult, "Have another doughnut, you fat pig." The league suspended Schoenfeld without a hearing, but a judge granted the Devils' request for an injunction. In response, regular officials chose not to work the next Devils-Bruins game. Instead, an amateur ref handled the game assisted by two off-ice officials acting as linesmen. The Devils won, 3–1.

IRISH, NED: 95th BIRTH ANNIVERSARY. May 6, 1905. Edward Simmons (Ned) Irish, Basketball Hall of Fame promoter, born at Lake George, NY. Irish attended the University of Pennsylvania and covered its sports teams for six New York and ten Philadelphia newspapers. In 1928 he began working for the *New York World-Telegram* and specializing in college basketball. He persuaded Madison Square Garden to host the first college basketball doubleheader in 1934 and soon left journalism to become the Garden's basketball director. He regularly brought top college teams to New York and founded the National Invitation Tournament. He also helped found the NBA and the New York Knicks. Inducted into the Hall of Fame in 1964. Died at New York, NY, Jan 2, 1982.

KBCO/BUDWEISER KINETIC SCULPTURE CHALLENGE. May 6. Boulder Reservoir, CO. Teams design kinetic sculptures that must be human-powered and able to travel over land and water. Each team has a theme and designs the sculpture and costumes to correspond. This all-day event includes a hot-air balloon classic, pancake breakfast to benefit a local charity, volleyball tournament and live music from world-class artists. Est attendance: 25,000. For info: KBCO 97.3 FM, 2500 Pearl St, Ste 315, Boulder, CO 80302. Phone: (303) 444-5600.

KENTUCKY DERBY. May 6. Churchill Downs, Louisville, KY. 126th running of America's premier Thoroughbred horse race, inaugurated in 1875. First jewel in the "Triple Crown," traditionally followed by the Preakness (the second Saturday after Derby) and the Belmont Stakes (the fifth Saturday after Derby). Annually, the first Saturday in May. Est attendance: 140,000. For info: Churchill Downs, 700 Central Ave, Louisville, KY 40208. Phone: (502) 636-4400. Web: kentuckyderby.com.

LEE-JACKSON LACROSSE CLASSIC. May 6. Virginia Military Institute, Lexington, VA. Communitywide event when the Washington and Lee University lacrosse team meets the Virginia Military Institute team. 2 PM. For info: Lexington Visitors Bureau, 106 E Washington St, Lexington, VA 24450. Phone: (540) 463-3777. Fax: (540) 463-1105. E-mail: lexington@rockbridge.net.

LONGEST FOOTRACE BEGINS: ANNIVERSARY. May 6, 1929. The longest footrace in history began at City Hall at New York City. It concluded on July 24 at San Francisco, 3,415 miles later. 60-year-old Abraham Lincoln Monteverde, a veteran of more than 100 marathons, not only won the race, but also was the only competitor to finish.

NEW ENGLAND VOLLEYBALL SERIES. May 6–7 (tentative). (Every weekend through the end of Sept.) Various locations. Amateur volleyball tour. Travels to all six New England states. For info: Bradley J. Van Dussen, Shot Block Promotions, 83 Withington Rd, Newtonville, MA 02160-2037. Phone: (508) 651-7900. E-mail: vball@shotblock.com. Web: www.shotblock.com.

NJCAA DIVISION I, II AND III WOMEN'S TENNIS CHAMPIONSHIP. May 6–12. Randolph Tennis Center, Tucson, AZ. For info: Hoyt Kinney, Tourn Dir, Pima Community College, 2202 W Anklam Rd, Tucson, AZ 85709. Phone: (520) 206-6005. Fax: (520) 884-6632. Web: www.njcaa.org.

NJCAA WOMEN'S SLOW PITCH SOFTBALL INVITATIONAL CHAMPIONSHIP. May 6. Site of Region XXII champion. For info: NJCAA, PO Box 7305, Colorado Springs, CO 80933. Phone: (719) 590-9788. Fax: (719) 590-7324. Web: www.njcaa.org.

PERRY WINS 300th GAME: ANNIVERSARY. May 6, 1982. Gaylord Perry of the Seattle Mariners defeated the New York Yankees, 7–3, to win the 300th game of his career. Long suspected of doctoring the baseball, Perry pitched for eight different teams over 22 years and won 314 games.

SCOTT'S STREAK STOPPED: 75th ANNIVERSARY. May 6, 1925. New York Yankees shortstop Everett Scott removed himself from the starting lineup and snapped his streak of 1,307 consecutive games played, started when he was a member of the Boston Red Sox. Scott gave way to Paul ("Pee Wee") Wanninger, whose major league career totaled 163 games. Scott's streak stood as the major league record until Lou Gehrig broke it.

VIRGINIA GOLD CUP. May 6. Great Meadow, The Plains, VA. Steeplechasing began in Ireland in 1762 when two horsemen held a cross-country match race to a faraway church steeple. Great Meadow is the largest steeplechase course in the country, with a spectacular hillside amphitheater. The Virginia Gold Cup race, sponsored by BMW and Land Rover, is run over a challenging 4-mile post-and-rail course of 23 fences. Advance tickets only. Benefits free year-round use of Great Meadow by nonprofit community organizations activities. Annually, the first Saturday in May. Est attendance: 50,000. For info: Virginia Gold Cup Assn, Box 840, Warrenton, VA 20188. Phone: (540) 347-2612. Fax: (540) 349-1829. Web: www.vagoldcup.com.

WHALERS WIN FIRST WHA CROWN: ANNIVERSARY. May 6, 1973. The New England Whalers won the first championship of the World Hockey Association. They defeated the Winnipeg Jets, 9–6, to win the final series, four games to one. Both teams later moved into the National Hockey League.

WOOD TIES STRIKEOUT RECORD: ANNIVERSARY. May 6, 1998. Chicago Cubs rookie pitcher Kerry Wood set the National League record and tied the major league record for most strikeouts in a 9-inning game when he fanned 20 Houston Astros in a 2–0 Chicago win. Roger Clemens set the major league record in 1986 and tied it in 1996. The former modern National League mark, 19, was held by three pitchers, Steve Carlton, Tom Seaver and David Cone.

BIRTHDAYS TODAY

Bob Bassen, 35, hockey player, born Calgary, Alberta, Canada, May 6, 1965.
Martin Brodeur, 28, hockey player, born Montreal, Quebec, Canada, May 6, 1972.
Willie Howard Mays, 69, Baseball Hall of Fame outfielder, born Westfield, AL, May 6, 1931.

MAY 7 — SUNDAY
Day 128 — 238 Remaining

NBA FINALS CHAMPIONS THIS DATE

1972	Los Angeles Lakers

CANADA: VANCOUVER INTERNATIONAL MARATHON. May 7. Vancouver, British Columbia. For info: Vancouver Intl Marathon, PO Box 3213, Vancouver, BC, Canada V6B 3X8. Phone: (604) 872-2928. Fax: (604) 872-2903. E-mail: vim@istar.ca. Web: www.wi.bc.ca.

FRANKENMUTH SKYFEST. May 7. Frankenmuth, MI. To encourage participation in a healthy outdoor sport that adapts to all age groups. 2000 will be the 19th annual Skyfest. Annually, the first Sunday in May. Est attendance: 4,500. For info: Audrey Fischer, Kite Kraft, 576 S Main St, Frankenmuth, MI 48734. Phone: (517) 652-2961.

GODFREE, KITTY: BIRTH ANNIVERSARY. May 7, 1896. Kathleen ("Kitty") McKane Godfree, tennis player, born at London, England. Godfree was one of the world's best tennis players in the years after World War I. She won four titles at Wimbledon, two at the US championships and five Olympic medals. In 1926 she and her husband, Leslie Godfree, became the first husband-and-wife team to win Wimbledon's mixed-doubles title. Died at London, June 19, 1992.

		S	M	T	W	T	F	S
May			1	2	3	4	5	6
2000		7	8	9	10	11	12	13
		14	15	16	17	18	19	20
		21	22	23	24	25	26	27
		28	29	30	31			

GOVERNOR'S BAY BRIDGE RUN. May 7. Sandy Point State Park, Annapolis, MD. "Maryland's Most Spectacular Run" 10K footrace across Chesapeake Bay Bridge, dramatic views of the bay and historic Annapolis, designer premium for all finishers, limited to 3,000 entries. Annually, the first Sunday in May. Since 1985. Est attendance: 3,000. For info: Annapolis Striders, Inc, PO Box 187, Annapolis, MD 21404-0187. Phone: (410) 268-1165.

NEW YORK GOLDEN ARMS TOURNAMENT. May 7. Belmont Stakes Fair, Belmont Race Track, Elmont, NY. Arm-wrestling competition held at fair determines winners who will compete in the Empire State Golden Arms Tournament of Champions on Oct 12. For info: New York Arm Wrestling Assn, Inc, 200-14 45th Dr, Bayside, NY 11361. Phone: (718) 544-4592. Web: www.nycarms.com.

RAIDERS WIN NFL SUIT: ANNIVERSARY. May 7, 1982. A federal jury decided that the National Football League was in violation of antitrust laws when it attempted to prohibit the Oakland Raiders from moving to Los Angeles. The Raiders, an original team in the American Football League, played at Oakland from 1960 through 1981 and at Los Angeles from 1982 through 1994, after which they returned to Oakland.

ROY CAMPANELLA NIGHT: ANNIVERSARY. May 7, 1959. 93,103 fans attended an exhibition game between the Los Angeles Dodgers and the New York Yankees at the Los Angeles Coliseum to show their support for injured Dodgers catcher Roy Campanella. A three-time MVP in the National League, Campanella was permanently paralyzed in an automobile accident in December 1958. The evening's ceremonies, dubbed "Roy Campanella Night," preceded the game, won by the Yankees, 6–2.

SCORE GETS HIT IN EYE: ANNIVERSARY. May 7, 1957. In a game between the New York Yankees and the Cleveland Indians, Yankees infielder Gil McDougald rifled a line drive at pitcher Herb Score, hitting him on the right eye. The ball broke Score's nose and damaged his eye. He missed the rest of the season but returned to pitch in 1958.

UPMC HEALTH SYSTEM/CITY OF PITTSBURGH MARATHON. May 7. Pittsburgh, PA. Marathon will also serve as the US Olympic team trial for the men's marathon. For info: UPMC Health System/City of Pittsburgh Marathon, 200 Lothrop St, Pittsburgh, PA 15213. Phone: (412) 647-7866. E-mail: grollmanlj@msx.upmc.edu. Web: www.upmc.edu/pghmarathon.

WINNING COLORS THIRD FILLY TO WIN DERBY: ANNIVERSARY. May 7, 1988. Winning Colors, ridden by Gary Stevens, became the third filly and the first roan to win the Kentucky Derby. Forty Niner finished second, and Risen Star was third. The first filly to win the Derby was Regret in 1915; the second was Genuine Risk in 1980.

WINTERTHUR POINT-TO-POINT. May 7. Wilmington, DE. Steeplechase races, antique carriage parade, canine agility competition, kids' activities, tailgating plus much more! Call for pricing. Rain or shine event. Est attendance: 20,000. For info: Greater Wilmington CVB, 100 W 10th St, Ste 20, Wilmington, DE 19801-1661. Phone: (800) 422-1181 or (302) 652-4088. E-mail: info@wilmcvb.org. Web: www.wilmcvb.org.

WRIGHT MAKES UNASSISTED TRIPLE PLAY: 75th ANNIVERSARY. May 7, 1925. Shortstop Glenn Wright of the Pittsburgh Pirates completed the fourth unassisted triple play in major league baseball history in the ninth inning of a game against the St. Louis Cardinals. Wright caught a line drive hit by Jim Bottomley, stepped on second to double off Jimmy Cooney and then tagged Rogers Hornsby before he could retreat to first.

BIRTHDAYS TODAY

Jean Claude Mark Raymond, 63, broadcaster and former baseball player, born St. Jean, Quebec, Canada, May 7, 1937.

John Constantine (Johnny) Unitas, 67, Pro Football Hall of Fame quarterback, born Pittsburgh, PA, May 7, 1933.

Richard Hirschfeld (Dick) Williams, 71, former baseball manager and player, born St. Louis, MO, May 7, 1929.

MAY 8 — MONDAY
Day 129 — 237 Remaining

NBA FINALS CHAMPIONS THIS DATE	
1970	New York Knicks

BROUTHERS, DAN: BIRTH ANNIVERSARY. May 8, 1858. Dennis Joseph ("Dan") Brouthers, baseball player, born at Sylvan Lake, NY. Brouthers (pronounced BROO-thers) was a slugging first baseman in the 1880s and 1890s. Allegedly he was the first to urge batters to "keep your eye on the ball." Died at East Orange, NJ, Aug 2, 1932.

FIRST 60-FOOT SHOT PUT: ANNIVERSARY. May 8, 1954. World-record holder William Parry O'Brien of the US became the first shot-putter to clear 60 feet with a throw of 60 feet, 5¼ inches, at a Los Angeles meet. O'Brien won gold medals at the 1952 and 1956 Olympics and a silver medal at the 1960 games.

HUNTER PITCHES PERFECT GAME: ANNIVERSARY. May 8, 1968. Jim ("Catfish") Hunter of the Oakland Athletics pitched a perfect game, defeating the Minnesota Twins, 4–0. This was the first regular-season perfect game in the American League since Charlie Robertson turned the trick in 1922.

LISTON, SONNY: BIRTH ANNIVERSARY. May 8, 1932. Charles ("Sonny") Liston, boxer, born at St. Francis County, AR. Liston rose above a record of criminal activity to defeat Floyd Patterson for the heavyweight title on Sept 25, 1962. He defeated Patterson in a rematch but then lost the title to Cassius Clay, who later changed his name to Muhammad Ali. In a rematch Ali knocked out Liston with a punch few observers saw. Died at Las Vegas, NV, Dec 30, 1970.

MARIUCCI, JOHN: BIRTH ANNIVERSARY. May 8, 1916. John P. Mariucci, hockey player, coach and executive, born at Eleventh, MN. Mariucci played hockey in high school and at the University of Minnesota where he earned All-American honors. He turned pro in 1940, played with the Chicago Blackhawks and became the first American-born player to captain an NHL team. After retiring, he coached at Minnesota and always sought out American players. Died at Minneapolis, MN, Mar 23, 1987.

OUIMET, FRANCIS: BIRTH ANNIVERSARY. May 8, 1893. Francis DeSales Ouimet, golfer, born at Brookline, MA. Ouimet is credited more than any other person with establishing the popularity of golf in the US. The son of a gardener, Ouimet began his golfing career as a caddy. In 1913, at age 20, he became a national hero and generated national enthusiasm for the game of golf when he became the first American and first amateur to win the US Open. He won the US Amateur in 1914 and 1931, and he was a member of the US Walker Cup team from its first tournament in 1922 until 1949, serving as its non-playing captain for six of those years. In 1949 he established the Francis Ouimet Caddy Scholarship Fund, and in 1951 he became the first American to be elected captain of the Royal and Ancient Golf Club of St. Andrews, Scotland. Died at Wellesley, MA, Sept 2, 1967.

REGRET, FIRST FILLY TO WIN DERBY: 85th ANNIVERSARY. May 8, 1915. Regret, ridden by Joe Notter, became the first filly to win the Kentucky Derby. She led wire-to-wire and finished the 1¼-mile race in 2:05.2. Pebbles was second, two lengths behind, and Sharpshooter was third.

SOVIETS BOYCOTT 1984 SUMMER OLYMPICS: ANNIVERSARY. May 8, 1984. The Soviet Union announced that it would not compete in the 1984 Summer Olympic Games, scheduled to open at Los Angeles on July 28. The Soviet National Olympic Committee's statement, issued on the day the Olympic torch relay began, declared that Soviet participation would be impossible because of "the gross flouting" of Olympic ideals by US authorities.

BIRTHDAYS TODAY

Douglas Leon (Doug) Atkins, 70, Pro Football Hall of Fame defensive end, born Humboldt, TN, May 8, 1930.

William Laird (Bill) Cowher, 43, football coach and former player, born Pittsburgh, PA, May 8, 1957.

Miguel Angel (Mike) Cuellar, 63, former baseball player, born Las Villas, Cuba, May 8, 1937.

John Broward ("Brad") Culpepper, 31, football player, born Tallahassee, FL, May 8, 1969.

Michael Andrew (Mike) D'Antoni, 49, basketball coach and former player, born Mullens, WV, May 8, 1951.

Dennis Patrick Leonard, 49, former baseball player, born New York, NY, May 8, 1951.

Ronald Mandel (Ronnie) Lott, 41, former football player, born Albuquerque, NM, May 8, 1959.

Korey Stringer, 26, football player, born Warren, OH, May 8, 1974.

	S	M	T	W	T	F	S
May		1	2	3	4	5	6
2000	7	8	9	10	11	12	13
	14	15	16	17	18	19	20
	21	22	23	24	25	26	27
	28	29	30	31			

MAY 9 — TUESDAY
Day 130 — 236 Remaining

EDDIE MURRAY'S DOUBLE DOUBLE: ANNIVERSARY. May 9, 1987. Switch-hitter Eddie Murray of the Baltimore Orioles became the first player in major league history to hit home runs from both sides of the plate in consecutive games.

GENTILE HITS CONSECUTIVE GRAND SLAMS: ANNIVERSARY. May 9, 1961. First baseman Jim Gentile of the Baltimore Orioles became the fourth player to hit grand slams in consecutive innings. Gentile hit his homers in the first and second innings of a game against the Minnesota Twins and added a sacrifice fly as the Orioles won, 13–5.

GONZALES, PANCHO: BIRTH ANNIVERSARY. May 9, 1928. Richard Alonzo ("Pancho") Gonzales, tennis player, born at Los Angeles, CA. A self-taught player, Gonzales won the 1948 US National Singles Championship and repeated in 1949. He turned pro and won the world's championship from 1954 through 1962. Gonzales was an aggressive, temperamental player who rarely trained. Died at Las Vegas, NV, July 3, 1994.

LONGEST EXTRA-INNING GAME: ANNIVERSARY. May 9, 1984. The Chicago White Sox defeated the Milwaukee Brewers, 7–6, on a Harold Baines home run in the 25th inning. The game, the first 17 innings of which were played the day before, was the longest extra-inning game by time, 8 hours, 6 minutes. The teams then played their regularly scheduled game of 9 innings, making a total of 34 innings in two days.

NCAA WOMEN'S DIVISION III TENNIS CHAMPIONSHIPS. May 9–15. Site TBA. For info: NCAA, PO Box 6222, Indianapolis, IN 46206-6222. Phone: (317) 917-6222. Fax: (317) 917-6888. Web: www.ncaa.org.

BIRTHDAYS TODAY

David Benoit, 32, basketball player, born Lafayette, LA, May 9, 1968.

Anthony Keith (Tony) Gwynn, 40, baseball player, born Los Angeles, CA, May 9, 1960.

Calvin Jerome Murphy, 52, Basketball Hall of Fame guard, born Norwalk, CT, May 9, 1948.

Mark Tinordi, 34, hockey player, born Red Deer, Alberta, Canada, May 9, 1966.

Stephane Yelle, 26, hockey player, born Ottawa, Ontario, Canada, May 9, 1974.

Steve Yzerman, 35, hockey player, born Cranbrook, British Columbia, Canada, May 9, 1965.

MAY 10 — WEDNESDAY
Day 131 — 235 Remaining

NBA FINALS CHAMPIONS THIS DATE

1973	New York Knicks

BARROW, ED: BIRTH ANNIVERSARY. May 10, 1868. Edward Grant (Ed) Barrow, Baseball Hall of Fame manager and executive, born at Springfield, IL. Barrow was a minor league executive when the Boston Red Sox named him field manager in 1918. In 1921 he became general manager of the New York Yankees and engineered their rise to decades of American League dominance. Inducted into the Hall of Fame in 1953. Died at Port Chester, NY, Dec 15, 1953.

BIG 12 SOFTBALL TOURNAMENT. May 10–13. Don Porter Hall of Fame Stadium, Oklahoma City, OK. For info: Big 12 Conference, 2201 Stemmons Freeway, 28th

Floor, Dallas, TX 75207. Phone: (214) 742-1212. Fax: (214) 742-2046.

BONNIE BLUE NATIONAL HORSE SHOW. May 10–13. Virginia Horse Center, Lexington, VA. Major all-breed event, "A"-rated show of the American Horse Show Association. For info: Lexington Visitors Bureau, 106 E Washington St, Lexington, VA 24450. Phone: (540) 463-3777. Fax: (540) 463-1105. E-mail: lexington@rockbridge.net.

GATLINBURG SCOTTISH FESTIVAL AND HIGHLAND GAMES. May 10–14 (tentative). Gatlinburg, TN. Celebration of Scotland, its people and traditions. Music, food and fun. Est attendance: 12,000. For info: Lanny Payne, PO Box 1487, Gatlinburg, TN 37738. Phone: (423) 966-9666. Fax: (423) 436-3704. Web: www.gatlinburg.com.

NCAA WOMEN'S DIVISION III LACROSSE CHAMPIONSHIP. May 10. First round. Sites TBA. For info: NCAA, PO Box 6222, Indianapolis, IN 46206-6222. Phone: (317) 917-6222. Fax: (317) 917-6888. Web: www.ncaa.org.

NCAA WOMEN'S LACROSSE CHAMPIONSHIP. May 10. First round. Sites TBA. For info: NCAA, PO Box 6222, Indianapolis, IN 46206-6222. Phone: (317) 917-6222. Fax: (317) 917-6888. Web: www.ncaa.org.

SIR BARTON WINS DERBY: ANNIVERSARY. May 10, 1919. Sir Barton, ridden by Johnny Loftus, won the Kentucky Derby by five lengths. Leading wire-to-wire, he went on to become the first horse to win the Triple Crown (the Derby, the Preakness Stakes and the Belmont Stakes).

SPECIAL OLYMPICS MONTANA STATE SUMMER GAMES. May 10–12. Billings, MT. Competition for athletes with mental retardation in gymnastics, track and field, aquatics, equestrian, cycling, golf, softball and other summer sports. For info: Special Olympics Montana, PO Box 3507, Great Falls, MT 59403. Phone: (406) 791-2368. Fax: (406) 454-9043. E-mail: MTSO@juno.com.

SPECIAL OLYMPICS OKLAHOMA SUMMER GAMES. May 10–12. Oklahoma State University, Stillwater, OK. State-level competition in six sports: aquatics, track and field, bowling, motor activities training (power lifting and softball) for children and adults with mental retardation. For info: Special Olympics Oklahoma, 6835 S Canton Ave, Tulsa, OK 74136. Phone: (918) 481-1234. Fax: (918) 496-1515.

WILHELM PITCHES IN 1,000th GAME: 30th ANNIVERSARY. May 10, 1970. Hoyt Wilhelm of the Atlanta Braves became the first major league pitcher to appear in 1,000 games when he was called in from the bullpen in a game against the St. Louis Cardinals. Wilhelm gave up three runs, and the Braves lost, 6–5.

STANLEY CUP CHAMPIONS THIS DATE	
1970	Boston Bruins
1973	Montreal Canadiens

BIRTHDAYS TODAY

Randolph William (Randy) Cunneyworth, 39, hockey player, born Etobicoke, Ontario, Canada, May 10, 1961.

Adam Deadmarsh, 25, hockey player, born Trail, British Columbia, Canada, May 10, 1975.

Daniel Leslie (Dan) Schayes, 41, basketball player, born Syracuse, NY, May 10, 1959.

Peter Alan (Pete) Schourek, 31, baseball player, born Austin, TX, May 10, 1969.

Ronald F. (Rony) Seikaly, 35, basketball player, born Beirut, Lebanon, May 10, 1965.

George Allen ("Pat") Summerall, 70, broadcaster and former football player, born Lake City, FL, May 10, 1930.

MAY 11 — THURSDAY
Day 132 — 234 Remaining

STANLEY CUP CHAMPIONS THIS DATE	
1968	Montreal Canadiens
1972	Boston Bruins

CHYLAK, NESTOR: BIRTH ANNIVERSARY. May 11, 1922. Nestor Chylak, Baseball Hall of Fame umpire, born at Peckville, PA. Chylak umpired in the American League from 1954 to 1978, working six All-Star games and five World Series. Most observers considered him the finest AL umpire of his generation. Inducted into the Hall of Fame in 1999. Died at Dunmore, PA, Feb 17, 1982.

ENGLAND: ROYAL WINDSOR HORSE SHOW. May 11–14. Home Park, Windsor, Berkshire. Major annual show-jumping event with royal pageantry and color. For bookings: Royal Windsor Horse Show Box Office, (44) (175) 341-9341. Est attendance: 60,000. For info: Penelope Henderson, Sec, Royal Windsor Horse Show, The Royal Mews, Windsor Castle, Windsor, Berkshire, England SL4 1NG. Phone: (44) (175) 386-0633 or (44) (175) 386-0633. Fax: (44) (175) 383-1074.

GEHRINGER, CHARLIE: BIRTH ANNIVERSARY. May 11, 1903. Charles Leonard (Charlie) Gehringer, Baseball Hall of Fame second baseman, born at Fowlerville, MI. Gehringer was known as the "Mechanical Man" for the methodical way he approached playing baseball. He hit .320 over 19 years with the Detroit Tigers. Inducted into the Hall of Fame in 1949. Died at Bloomfield Hills, MI, Jan 21, 1993.

MOUNTAIN WEST SOFTBALL CHAMPIONSHIP. May 11–13. University of Utah, Salt Lake City, UT. For info: Mountain West Conference, PO Box 35670, Colorado Springs, CO 80935-3567. Phone: (719) 533-9500. Fax: (719) 533-9512.

NJCAA DIVISION I MEN'S AND WOMEN'S OUTDOOR TRACK AND FIELD CHAMPIONSHIP. May 11–13. Southern Illinois University, Edwardsville, IL. For info: Lea Plarski, Tourn Dir, St. Louis Community College at Florissant Valley, 3400 Pershall Rd, St. Louis, MO 63135. Phone: (314) 595-4534. Fax: (314) 595-4544. Web: www.njcaa.org.

PITCHER DUNNING HITS LAST GRAND SLAM: ANNIVERSARY. May 11, 1971. Steve Dunning of the Cleveland Indians became the last pitcher in the American League to hit a grand slam prior to the inauguration of the designated-hitter rule in 1973. His homer, coming in a game against the Oakland A's pitcher Diego Segui, gave the Indians a 5–0 lead. They won the game, 7–5, but relief pitcher Phil Hennigan got the win.

SEC SOFTBALL TOURNAMENT. May 11–14. Columbus, GA. For info: Southeastern Conference, 2201 Civic Center Blvd, Birmingham, AL 35203-1103. Phone: (205) 458-3010. Fax: (205) 458-3030. E-mail: twilson@sec.org. Web: www.secsports.com.

Eugene Victor (Gene) Hermanski, 80, former baseball player, born Pittsfield, MA, May 11, 1920.

Kerry Dale Ligtenberg, 29, baseball player, born Rapid City, SD, May 11, 1971.

John Kennedy (Jack) Twyman, 66, Basketball Hall of Fame forward and guard, born Pittsburgh, PA, May 11, 1934.

Robert Andrew (Bobby) Witt, 36, baseball player, born Arlington, VA, May 11, 1964.

MAY 12 — FRIDAY

Day 133 — 233 Remaining

NBA FINALS CHAMPIONS THIS DATE

1974	Boston Celtics

BANKS HITS 500th HOME RUN: 30th ANNIVERSARY. May 12, 1970. Ernie Banks of the Chicago Cubs hit the 500th home run of his career off Pat Jarvis of the Atlanta Braves. The Cubs won the game, 4–3, at Wrigley Field. Banks played from 1953 through 1971 and wound up with 521 home runs.

BIG TEN MEN'S GOLF CHAMPIONSHIP. May 12–14. Purdue University, West Lafayette, IN. For info: Big Ten Conference, 1500 W Higgins Rd, Park Ridge, IL 60068-6300. Phone: (847) 696-1010. Fax: (847) 696-1150. Web: www.bigten.org.

BIG TEN SOFTBALL TOURNAMENT. May 12–13. Site of regular-season conference champion. For info: Big Ten Conference, 1500 W Higgins Rd, Park Ridge, IL 60068-6300. Phone: (847) 696-1010. Fax: (847) 696-1150. Web: www.bigten.org.

CARDINALS OPEN NEW BUSCH STADIUM: ANNIVERSARY. May 12, 1966. Four days after closing old Busch Stadium (formerly known as Sportsman's Park), the St. Louis Cardinals opened new Busch Stadium by defeating the Atlanta Braves, 4–3, in 12 innings. Felipe Alou hit a pair of homers for the Braves, but Lou Brock drove in the winning run with a single.

NCAA MEN'S DIVISION III TENNIS CHAMPIONSHIP. May 12–14. Regionals. Sites TBA. For info: NCAA, PO Box 6222, Indianapolis, IN 46206-6222. Phone: (317) 917-6222. Fax: (317) 917-6888. Web: www.ncaa.org.

NCAA MEN'S DIVISION I TENNIS CHAMPIONSHIP. May 12–14. Regionals. Sites TBA. For info: NCAA, PO Box 6222, Indianapolis, IN 46206-6222. Phone: (317) 917-6222. Fax: (317) 917-6888. Web: www.ncaa.org.

NCAA MEN'S DIVISION II TENNIS CHAMPIONSHIPS. May 12–15. Finals at a site TBA. For info: NCAA, PO Box 6222, Indianapolis, IN 46206-6222. Phone: (317) 917-6222. Fax: (317) 917-6888. Web: www.ncaa.org.

NCAA WOMEN'S DIVISION I TENNIS CHAMPIONSHIP. May 12–14. Regionals. Sites TBA. For info: NCAA, PO Box 6222, Indianapolis, IN 46206-6222. Phone: (317) 917-6222. Fax: (317) 917-6888. Web: www.ncaa.org.

NCAA WOMEN'S DIVISION II TENNIS CHAMPIONSHIPS. May 12–15. Site TBA. For info: NCAA, PO Box 6222, Indianapolis, IN 46206-6222. Phone: (317) 917-6222. Fax: (317) 917-6888. Web: www.ncaa.org.

May *2000*	S	M	T	W	T	F	S
		1	2	3	4	5	6
	7	8	9	10	11	12	13
	14	15	16	17	18	19	20
	21	22	23	24	25	26	27
	28	29	30	31			

SEC MEN'S AND WOMEN'S OUTDOOR TRACK AND FIELD CHAMPIONSHIPS. May 12–14. Louisiana State University, Baton Rouge, LA. For info: Southeastern Conference, 2201 Civic Center Blvd, Birmingham, AL 35203-1103. Phone: (205) 458-3010. Fax: (205) 458-3030. E-mail: jjames@sec.org. Web: www.secsports.com.

THIRTEEN ACES ON ONE HOLE: ANNIVERSARY. May 12, 1984. Golfer Joe Lucius of Tiffin, OH, recorded a hole-in-one on the 15th hole of the Mohawk Golf Course. It was the 13th time he had aced this same hole.

USFL FOUNDED: ANNIVERSARY. May 12, 1982. The United States Football League, a springtime alternative to the National Football League, was founded. The USFL played three seasons, 1983, 1984 and 1985, before going out of business.

Felipe Rojas Alou, 65, baseball manager and former player, born Santo Domingo, Dominican Republic, May 12, 1935.

Lawrence Peter ("Yogi") Berra, 75, former baseball manager and Baseball Hall of Fame catcher, born St. Louis, MO, May 12, 1925.

Mark Willard Clark, 32, baseball player, born Bath, IL, May 12, 1968.

Thomas Dooley, 39, soccer player, born Bechhofen, Germany, May 12, 1961.

James Michael (Jim) Furyk, 30, golfer, born West Chester, PA, May 12, 1970.

George Matthew Karl, 49, basketball coach and former player, born Penn Hills, PA, May 12, 1951.

Patricia Joan Keller (Patty) McCormick, 70, Olympic gold medal diver, born Seal Beach, CA, May 12, 1930.

Warren Stanley Rychel, 33, hockey player, born Tecumseh, Ontario, Canada, May 12, 1967.

MAY 13 — SATURDAY

Day 134 — 232 Remaining

BRAILLE INSTITUTE–OPTIMIST TRACK AND FIELD OLYMPICS. May 13. Braille Institute Youth Center, Los Angeles, CA. To offer athletic competition to blind and visually impaired youths. Annually, the second Saturday in May. Cosponsored by the Optimist Clubs of Southern California. Est attendance: 1,000. For info: Braille Institute, Communications Dept, 741 N Vermont Ave, Los Angeles, CA 90029. Phone: (323) 663-1111. Web: www.brailleinstitute.org.

CUBS WIN 8,000th GAME: ANNIVERSARY. May 13, 1982. The Chicago Cubs, charter members of the National League, won the 8,000th game in their history, beating the Houston Astros in the Astrodome, 5–0. The Cubs began their existence as the Chicago White Stockings in the National Association (1871, 1874–75) and moved to the National League in 1876. The team changed its name to the Colts in 1890, the Orphans in 1898 and the Cubs in 1902.

DELTA DEMOCRAT-TIMES GRAND PRIX CATFISH RACES. May 13. Greenville, MS. To recognize the noble racing heart of the thoroughbred pond-raised Mississippi catfish. 16th annual races. Annually, on the Saturday before Mother's Day. Est attendance: 10,000. For info:

Editor, *Delta Democrat-Times*, Box 1618, Greenville, MS 38701. Phone: (601) 335-1155. Fax: (601) 335-2860.

IROQUOIS STEEPLECHASE. May 13. Percy Warner Park, Nashville, TN. Nashville's original "Rite of Spring." This event is the oldest continuously run, weight-for-age steeplechase, held at Percy Warner Park. The steeplechase has a seven-race card with the featured Iroquois Memorial. Annually, the second Saturday in May. Est attendance: 30,000. For info: Steeplechase Office, 2424 Garland Ave, Nashville, TN 37212. Phone: (615) 332-7284. Fax: (615) 322-6453.

JOURNEYS MARATHON. May 13. Eagle River, WI. Annually, the second weekend in May. For info: Eagle River Area Chamber of Commerce, PO Box 1917, Eagle River, WI 54521. Phone: (715) 479-6400 or (800) 359-6315. E-mail: info@eagleriver.org. Web: www.journeysmarathon.org.

LOUIS, JOE: BIRTH ANNIVERSARY. May 13, 1914. Joe Louis, heavyweight boxing champion, born Joseph Louis Barrow near Lafayette, AL. Louis, nicknamed the Brown Bomber, is generally considered one of the greatest boxers of all time. He reigned as heavyweight champion from 1937 to 1949 and was immensely popular. Died at Las Vegas, NV, Apr 12, 1981. (Louis was buried at Arlington National Cemetery by presidential waiver, the 39th exception to the eligibility rules for burial there.)

MANTLE HITS 500th HOME RUN: ANNIVERSARY. May 13, 1967. Slugging outfielder Mickey Mantle of the New York Yankees hit the 500th home run of his career against Stu Miller of the Baltimore Orioles. The homer propelled the Yankees to a 6–5 victory. Mantle finished his career in 1968 with 536 home runs.

MUSIAL GETS 3,000th HIT: ANNIVERSARY. May 13, 1958. Stan Musial of the St. Louis Cardinals got the 3,000th hit of his career, a pinch-hit double off Moe Drabowsky of the Chicago Cubs. Musial finished his career in 1963 with 3,630 hits, 1,815 at home and an equal number on the road.

NCAA WOMEN'S LACROSSE CHAMPIONSHIP. May 13. Quarterfinals. Sites TBA. For info: NCAA, PO Box 6222, Indianapolis, IN 46206-6222. Phone: (317) 917-6222. Fax: (317) 917-6888. Web: www.ncaa.org.

NJCAA MEN'S INVITATIONAL LACROSSE CHAMPIONSHIP. May 13–14. Arnold, MD. For info: Bill Gorrow, Tourn Dir, Anne Arundel Community College, 101 College Pkwy, Arnold, MD 21012. Phone: (410) 541-2734. Fax: (410) 541-2489. Web: www.njcaa.org.

RON NECCIAI STRIKES OUT THE SIDE: ANNIVERSARY. May 13, 1952. Pittsburgh Pirates farmhand Ron Necciai, pitching for the Bristol Twins in the Class D Appalachian League, threw a perfect game against the Welch Miners. Incredibly, Necciai struck out all 27 batters he faced in the Twins' 7–0 victory. He made the major leagues later that year, pitching in 12 games but winning only 1. In 54.2 innings, he struck out 31 batters and walked 32.

SAVANNAH SCOTTISH GAMES AND HIGHLAND GATHERING. May 13. Old Ft Jackson, Savannah, GA. Clan tents, geological information, highland regimental pipe bands, Southeast Regional Scottish Highland Dancing Championship, single-malt Scotch whiskey tasting, kilted golf, entertainment by Scotland's finest musicians and children's games. Est attendance: 6,000. For info: Savannah Scottish Games and Highland Gathering, PO Box 13435, Savannah, GA 31416. Phone: (912) 897-5781 or (912) 961-1783. Fax: (912) 234-0447.

SMITH MOUNTAIN LAKE STATE PARK TRIATHLON. May 13. Smith Mountain Lake State Park, VA. An event combining a 1K swim, a 20K bike ride and a 5K run. For info: VA Amateur Sports, Inc., 305 First St, Ste 412, Roanoke, VA 24011. Phone: (540) 343-0987. Fax: (540) 343-7407.

BIRTHDAYS TODAY

Michael (Mike) Bibby, 22, basketball player, born Cherry Hill, NJ, May 13, 1978.

Jody Conradt, 59, basketball coach, born Goldwaithe, TX, May 13, 1941.

Douglas Edwards (Doug) Evans, 30, football player, born Shreveport, LA, May 13, 1970.

Lyle Joseph Mouton, 31, baseball player, born Lafayette, LA, May 13, 1969.

Thomas Andrew (Tom) Nalen, 29, football player, born Foxboro, MA, May 13, 1971.

James Lamar ("Dusty") Rhodes, 73, former baseball player, born Mathews, AL, May 13, 1927.

Jose Antonio Rijo, 35, former baseball player, born San Cristobal, Dominican Republic, May 13, 1965.

Dennis Keith Rodman, 39, basketball player, born Trenton, NJ, May 13, 1961.

John Junior Roseboro, 67, former baseball player, born Ashland, OH, May 13, 1933.

Darryl Marion Sydor, 28, hockey player, born Edmonton, Alberta, Canada, May 13, 1972.

Robert John (Bobby) Valentine, 50, baseball manager and former player, born Stamford, CT, May 13, 1950.

Leon Lamar Wagner, 66, former baseball player, born Chattanooga, TN, May 13, 1934.

MAY 14 — SUNDAY
Day 135 — 231 Remaining

NBA FINALS CHAMPIONS THIS DATE	
1981	Boston Celtics

COMBS, EARLE: BIRTH ANNIVERSARY. May 14, 1899. Earle Bryan Combs, Baseball Hall of Fame outfielder, born at Pebworth, KY. Combs abandoned a career in education to play baseball. He played with the great New York Yankees teams of the 1920s and 1930s, scoring more than 100 runs in eight consecutive years. Inducted into the Hall of Fame in 1970. Died at Richmond, KY, July 21, 1976.

JOHNSON WINS 300th GAME: 80th ANNIVERSARY. May 14, 1920. Pitcher Walter Johnson of the Washington Senators, considered by some to be the greatest pitcher of all time and the fastest, won the 300th game of his career, beating the Detroit Tigers, 9–8. Johnson played in the major leagues from 1907 through 1927. He compiled a record of 417 wins against 279 losses with an earned run average of 2.17.

KITEDAY. May 14. Charlottesville, VA. Fly a kite at Ash Lawn-Highland, home of President James Monroe. Est attendance: 300. For info: Ash Lawn-Highland, James Monroe Pkwy, Charlottesville, VA 22902. Phone: (804) 293-9539. Fax: (804) 293-8000. E-mail: ashlawnjm@aol .com. Web:monticello.avenue.gen.va.us/ashlawn.

LEFT-HANDED CATCHER: ANNIVERSARY. May 14, 1989. Benny DiStefano of the Pittsburgh Pirates became the first left-handed catcher in nine years when he played that position in the ninth inning of a 5–2 Pirates loss to the Atlanta Braves. The last left-hander to catch before DiStefano was Mike Squires of the Chicago White Sox in 1980.

MAGIC RETIRES AGAIN: ANNIVERSARY. May 14, 1996. Basketball player Earvin ("Magic") Johnson announced his retirement for the second time from the Los Angeles Lakers. Johnson had first retired before the start of the 1991–92 NBA season when he learned he was HIV-positive. Other players rebuffed his attempt to come back for the 1992–93 season, but he did play 32 games in 1995–96.

MOTHER'S DAY. May 14. Observed first in 1907 at the request of Anna Jarvis of Philadelphia, PA, who asked her church to hold service in memory of all mothers on the anniversary of her mother's death. Annually, the second Sunday in May.

MUDDER'S DAY OFF-ROAD CHALLENGE. May 14. Rhinelander, WI. 22K mountain bike race on the scenic Mudder's Day Trail at Holiday Acres Resort. Annually, on Mother's Day. For info: Rhinelander Area Chamber of Commerce, PO Box 795, Rhinelander, WI 54501. Phone: (800) 236-4386. Fax: (715) 365-7467. Web: www.rhine landerchamber.com.

NCAA WOMEN'S DIVISION III LACROSSE CHAMPI-ONSHIP. May 14. Quarterfinals. Sites TBA. For info: NCAA, PO Box 6222, Indianapolis, IN 46206-6222. Phone: (317) 917-6222. Fax: (317) 917-6888. Web: www .ncaa.org.

NEW YORK GOLDEN ARMS TOURNAMENT. May 14. Amsterdam Avenue Festival, Manhattan, NY. Arm-wrestling competition held at the festival determines winners who will compete in the Empire State Golden Arms Tournament of Champions on Oct 12. Est attendance: 7,000. For info: New York Arm Wrestling Assn, Inc, 200-14 45th Dr, Bayside, NY 11361. Phone: (718) 544-4592. Web: www.nycarms.com.

PAC-10 MEN'S AND WOMEN'S ROWING CHAMPI-ONSHIPS. May 14. Lake Natoma, CA. For info: PAC-10 Conference, 800 S Broadway, Ste 400, Walnut Creek, CA 94596. Phone: (510) 932-4411. Fax: (510) 932-4601.

RUNNING AND FITNESS WEEK. May 14–20. Educational campaign designed to introduce more Americans to the pleasures and benefits of participating in a regular exercise program. For info: Barbara Baldwin, American Running and Fitness Assn, 4405 East-West Hwy, Ste 405, Bethesda, MD 20814. Phone: (800) 776-2732. Fax: (301) 913-9520. E-mail: arfarun@aol.com. Web: www .arfa.org.

SIR BARTON WINS PREAKNESS: ANNIVERSARY. May 14, 1919. Just four days after winning the Kentucky Derby, Sir Barton, ridden by Johnny Loftus, won the Preakness Stakes. The colt went on to win the Belmont Stakes and became the first horse to win the Triple Crown.

WALSH, ED: BIRTH ANNIVERSARY. May 14, 1881. Edward Augustine (Ed) Walsh, Baseball Hall of Fame pitcher, born at Plains, PA. Walsh used a fastball and a spitball to become one of the best pitchers of the early 20th century. He won 195 games and hurled 57 shutouts. Inducted into the Hall of Fame in 1946. Died at Pompano Beach, FL, May 26, 1959.

STANLEY CUP CHAMPIONS THIS DATE	
1977	Montreal Canadiens

BIRTHDAYS TODAY

Jose Manuel (Joey) Cora, 35, former baseball player, born Caguas, Puerto Rico, May 14, 1965.

Voshon Kelan Lenard, 27, basketball player, born Detroit, MI, May 14, 1973.

Jose Dennis Martinez, 45, former baseball player, born Granada, Nicaragua, May 14, 1955.

Atanasio ("Tony") Perez, 58, former baseball manager and player, born Camaguey, Cuba, May 14, 1942.

Jerome ("Pooh") Richardson, Jr, 34, basketball player, born Philadelphia, PA, May 14, 1966.

Tony Siragusa, 33, football player, born Kenilworth, NJ, May 14, 1967.

Mike Sorber, 29, soccer player, born St. Louis, MO, May 14, 1971.

MAY 15 — MONDAY
Day 136 — 230 Remaining

GOLFER BEGAY FIRES RECORD 59: ANNIVERSARY. May 15, 1998. Golfer Notah Begay III, a college teammate of Tiger Woods, shot a 59 in the second round of the Nike Tour's Dominion Open at Richmond, VA. Begay thus became the third golfer to shoot a 59 in a US professional event after Al Geiberger and Chip Beck. Begay, however, did not go on to win the four-round tournament. Bob Burns did, shooting 14 under par 274. Begay tied for sixth place with a score of 277.

LEN BARKER PITCHES PERFECT GAME: ANNIVERSARY. May 15, 1981. Len Barker of the Cleveland Indians pitched a perfect game, the first in major league baseball in 13 years, defeating the Toronto Blue Jays, 3–0, at Cleveland. Barker finished the year at 8–7 and was traded to the Atlanta Braves during the 1983 season.

NAIA BASEBALL WORLD SERIES. May 15–31 (tentative). Lewiston, ID. 44th annual competition. Est attendance: 20,000. For info: Natl Assn of Intercollegiate Athletics, 6120 S Yale Ave, Ste 1450, Tulsa, OK 74136. Phone: (918) 494-8828. Fax: (918) 494-8841. E-mail: khenry@naia.com. Web: www.naia.org.

May 2000

S	M	T	W	T	F	S
	1	2	3	4	5	6
7	8	9	10	11	12	13
14	15	16	17	18	19	20
21	22	23	24	25	26	27
28	29	30	31			

NAIA MEN'S AND WOMEN'S OUTDOOR TRACK AND FIELD CHAMPIONSHIPS. May 15–31 (tentative). Site TBA. 49th annual men's and 20th annual women's competition. Est attendance: 2,500. For info: Natl Assn of Intercollegiate Athletics, 6120 S Yale Ave, Ste 1450, Tulsa, OK 74136. Phone: (918) 494-8828. Fax: (918) 494-8841. E-mail: khenry@naia.org. Web: www.naia.org.

NAIA MEN'S GOLF CHAMPIONSHIP. May 15–31 (tentative). Site TBA. 49th annual. Est attendance: 500. For info: Natl Assn of Intercollegiate Athletics, 6120 S Yale Ave, Ste 1450, Tulsa, OK 74136. Phone: (918) 494-8828. Fax: (918) 494-8841. E-mail: khenry@naia.org. Web: www .naia.org.

NAIA MEN'S TENNIS CHAMPIONSHIPS. May 15–31 (tentative). Site TBA. 49th annual competition. Est attendance: 1,500. For info: Natl Assn of Intercollegiate Athletics, 6120 S Yale Ave, Ste 1450, Tulsa, OK 74136. Phone: (918) 494-8828. Fax: (918) 494-8841. E-mail: khenry @naia.org. Web: www.naia.org.

NAIA SOFTBALL CHAMPIONSHIP. May 15–31 (tentative). Site TBA. 20th annual competition. Est attendance: 2,000. For info: Natl Assn of Intercollegiate Athletics, 6120 S Yale Ave, Ste 1450, Tulsa, OK 74136. Phone: (918) 494-8828. Fax: (918) 494-8841. E-mail: khenry@naia.org. Web: www.naia.org.

NAIA WOMEN'S GOLF CHAMPIONSHIP. May 15–31 (tentative). Site TBA. 6th annual competition. Est attendance: 300. For info: Natl Assn of Intercollegiate Athletics, 6120 S Yale Ave, Ste 1450, Tulsa, OK 74136. Phone: (918) 494-8828. Fax: (918) 494-8841. E-mail: khenry @naia.org. Web: www.naia.org.

NAIA WOMEN'S TENNIS CHAMPIONSHIPS. May 15–31. Site TBA. 20th annual tournament. Individuals compete for All-America honors, while teams compete for the national championship. Est attendance: 1,500. For info: Natl Assn of Intercollegiate Athletics, 6120 S Yale Ave, Ste 1450, Tulsa, OK 74136. Phone: (918) 494-8828. Fax: (918) 494-8841. E-mail: khenry@naia.org.

NCAA MEN'S DIVISION III GOLF CHAMPIONSHIPS. May 15–18. Bedford Valley Golf Course, Battle Creek, MI. For info: NCAA, PO Box 6222, Indianapolis, IN 46206-6222. Phone: (317) 917-6222. Fax: (317) 917-6888. Web: www.ncaa.org.

NJCAA DIVISION I, II AND III MEN'S TENNIS CHAMPIONSHIP. May 15–20. Tyler, TX. For info: John Peterson, Tourn Dir, Tyler Jr College, PO Box 9020, Tyler, TX 75711. Phone: (903) 510-2458. Fax: (903) 510-2434. Web: www.njcaa.org.

NJCAA WOMEN'S INVITATIONAL GOLF CHAMPIONSHIP. May 15–18. Seminole, OK. For info: Russell Beene, Seminole State College, PO Box 351, Seminole, OK 74818-0351. Phone: (405) 382-9201. Fax: (405) 382-9537. Web: www.njcaa.org.

BIRTHDAYS TODAY

George Howard Brett, 47, baseball executive and Baseball Hall of Fame third baseman, born Glen Dale, WV, May 15, 1953.

Leroy Hoard, 32, football player, born New Orleans, LA, May 15, 1968.

Desmond Kevin Howard, 30, Heisman Trophy wide receiver, born Cleveland, OH, May 15, 1970.

Ray Anthony Lewis, 25, football player, born Lakeland, FL, May 15, 1975.

Donald Arvid (Don) Nelson, 60, basketball coach and former player, born Muskegon, MI, May 15, 1940.

Emmitt James Smith, III, 31, football player, born Pensacola, FL, May 15, 1969.

John Andrew Smoltz, 33, baseball player, born Warren, MI, May 15, 1967.

Paul Robert Ysebaert, 34, hockey player, born Sarnia, Ontario, Canada, May 15, 1966.

☆ ☆ ☆

MAY 16 — TUESDAY
Day 137 — 229 Remaining

NBA FINALS CHAMPIONS THIS DATE
1980　　　　　Los Angeles Lakers

ACC BASEBALL TOURNAMENT. May 16–21. Knights Stadium, Ft Mill, SC. For info: Atlantic Coast Conference, PO Drawer ACC, Greensboro, NC 27417-6724. Phone: (336) 854-8787. Fax: (336) 854-8797.

AHPA FORMED: ANNIVERSARY. May 16, 1914. The Grand League of the American Horseshoe Pitchers Association was formed. The league set its first championship for Oct 23, 1915, at Kellerton, IA.

MARTIN, BILLY: BIRTH ANNIVERSARY. May 16, 1928. Alfred Henry ("Billy") Martin, baseball manager and player, born at Berkeley, CA. After a successful playing career mostly with the New York Yankees, the scrappy Martin managed five major league teams: the Yankees, Minnesota Twins, Detroit Tigers, Texas Rangers and Oakland Athletics. He compiled a record of 1,258 victories and 1,018 losses in his 16 seasons as a manager. His combative and fiery style both on and off the field kept him in the headlines, and he will long be remembered for his on-again/off-again relationship with Yankees owner George Steinbrenner, for whom he managed the Yankees five different times. Died in an auto accident at Johnson City, NY, Dec 25, 1989.

NATIONAL BIKE TO WORK DAY. May 16. At the state or local level, Bike to Work events are conducted by small and large businesses, city governments, bicycle clubs and environmental groups. About two million participants nationwide. Annually, the third Tuesday in May. For info: Donald Tighe, Program Dir, League of American Bicyclists, 1612 K St NW, Ste 401, Washington, DC 20006. Phone: 202822-1333. Fax: (202) 822-1334. E-mail: bikeleague@aol.com. Web: www.bikeleague.org.

NCAA MEN'S DIVISION II GOLF CHAMPIONSHIPS. May 16–19. Finals. Site TBA. For info: NCAA, PO Box 6222, Indianapolis, IN 46206-6222. Phone: (317) 917-6222. Fax: (317) 917-6888. Web: www.ncaa.org.

NCAA WOMEN'S DIVISION II AND III GOLF CHAMPIONSHIPS. May 16–19 or 17–20. Site TBA. For info: NCAA, PO Box 6222, Indianapolis, IN 46206-6222. Phone: (317) 917-6222. Fax: (317) 917-6888. Web: www.ncaa.org.

SNEAD CARDS A 59: ANNIVERSARY. May 16, 1959. Sam Snead shot an 11-under-par round of 59 at the Greenbrier at White Sulphur Springs, WV. Snead went out in 31, 4 under par, and came home in 28, 7 under par, but he was not playing in an official PGA event.

STANLEY CUP CHAMPIONS THIS DATE	
1976	Montreal Canadiens
1982	New York Islanders

BIRTHDAYS TODAY

Olga Korbut, 45, Olympic gold medal gymnast, born Grodno, USSR, May 16, 1955.

James John (Jim) Langer, 52, Pro Football Hall of Fame center, born Little Falls, MN, May 16, 1948.

John Scott (Jack) Morris, 45, former baseball player, born St. Paul, MN, May 16, 1955.

Gabriela Sabatini, 30, former tennis player, born Buenos Aires, Argentina, May 16, 1970.

Joan Benoit Samuelson, 43, Olympic gold medal marathoner, born Cape Elizabeth, ME, May 16, 1957.

Thurman Lee Thomas, 34, football player, born Houston, TX, May 16, 1966.

Alain Vigneault, 38, hockey coach and former player, born Quebec City, Quebec, Canada, May 16, 1962.

MAY 17 — WEDNESDAY
Day 138 — 228 Remaining

STANLEY CUP CHAMPIONS THIS DATE	
1983	New York Islanders

AARON GETS 3,000th HIT: 30th ANNIVERSARY. May 17, 1970. Henry Aaron of the Atlanta Braves, on his way to becoming baseball's all-time home run king, got the 3,000th hit of his career, a scratch single off Wayne Simpson of the Cincinnati Reds. Aaron finished his career in 1976 with a .305 batting average, 3,771 hits and 755 home runs.

BELL, COOL PAPA: BIRTH ANNIVERSARY. May 17, 1903. James Thomas ("Cool Papa") Bell, Baseball Hall of Fame outfielder, born at Starkville, MS. One of the preeminent stars of the Negro Leagues, Bell is generally considered one of the fastest players ever. Satchel Paige said Bell was so fast he could turn the light out at night and be in bed before the room got dark. Inducted into the Hall of Fame in 1974. Died at St. Louis, MO, Mar 7, 1991.

May 2000	S	M	T	W	T	F	S
		1	2	3	4	5	6
	7	8	9	10	11	12	13
	14	15	16	17	18	19	20
	21	22	23	24	25	26	27
	28	29	30	31			

BETSY KING WINS LPGA CHAMPIONSHIP: ANNIVERSARY. May 17, 1992. Betsy King shot 267 to win the LPGA Championship by 11 strokes over Karen Noble. King recorded rounds of 68, 66, 67 and 66, the first time that any LPGA player finished four rounds under 70 in a major championship. Her 267 was the lowest score ever recorded by any golfer, man or woman, in a major championship.

BIG EAST BASEBALL TOURNAMENT. May 17–20. Site TBA. For info: Big East Conference, 56 Exchange Terrace, Providence, RI 02903. Phone: (401) 272-9108. Fax: (401) 751-8540.

BIG 12 BASEBALL TOURNAMENT. May 17–21. SW Bell Bricktown Ballpark, Oklahoma City, OK. For info: Big 12 Conference, 2201 Stemmons Freeway, 28th Floor, Dallas, TX 75207. Phone: (214) 742-1212. Fax: (214) 742-2046.

BLUE JAYS' ATTENDANCE RECORD: ANNIVERSARY. May 17, 1992. The Toronto Blue Jays reached the one-million mark in home attendance faster than any other team in baseball history. The Blue Jays drew 1,006,294 fans in just 21 dates, surpassing the record held jointly by the 1981 Los Angeles Dodgers and the 1991 Blue Jays.

FIRST KENTUCKY DERBY: 125th ANNIVERSARY. May 17, 1875. The first running of the Kentucky Derby took place at Churchill Downs, Louisville, KY. Jockey Oliver Lewis rode the horse Aristides in a winning time of 2:37.25.

MOUNTAIN WEST BASEBALL CHAMPIONSHIP. May 17–20. UNLV, Las Vegas, NV. For info: Mountain West Conference, PO Box 35670, Colorado Springs, CO 80935-3567. Phone: (719) 533-9500. Fax: (719) 533-9512.

MOUNTAIN WEST MEN'S AND WOMEN'S OUTDOOR TRACK AND FIELD CHAMPIONSHIPS. May 17–20. Brigham Young University, Provo, UT. For info: Mountain West Conference, PO Box 35670, Colorado Springs, CO 80935-3567. Phone: (719) 533-9500. Fax: (719) 533-9512.

POLE SITTER DIES AT INDY: ANNIVERSARY. May 17, 1996. Scott Brayton, pole sitter for the Indianapolis 500 in both 1995 and 1996, died when the car he was driving in practice crashed into the Turn 2 wall. The crash was caused by a deflated tire. Brayton became the 40th driver to die at Indy, either in practice, qualifying or during the race, and the first since Jovy Marcelo in 1992.

SEC BASEBALL TOURNAMENT. May 17–21. Birmingham, AL. For info: Southeastern Conference, 2201 Civic Center Blvd, Birmingham, AL 35203-1103. Phone: (205) 458-3010. Fax: (205) 458-3030. E-mail: cbloom@sec.org. Web: www.secsports.com.

SPEAKER GETS 3,000th HIT: 75th ANNIVERSARY. May 17, 1925. Cleveland Indians center fielder Tris Speaker collected the 3,000th hit of his major league career off Tom Zachary of the Washington Senators. Speaker played from 1907 through 1928, got 3,515 hits and batted .344.

SPORTSCENTER'S 20,000th SHOW: ANNIVERSARY. May 17, 1998. ESPN's "Sportscenter," the cable network's signature program, broadcast its 20,000th edition with a special 90-minute show hosted by longtime anchors Chris Berman, Dan Patrick and Bob Ley. "Sportscenter" made its debut on Sept 7, 1979, ESPN's launch day, and was broadcast live three times each weekday and four times on Saturday and Sunday.

WELLS PITCHES PERFECT GAME: ANNIVERSARY. May 17, 1998. Left-hander David Wells of the New York Yankees pitched a perfect game (allowing no hits and no base runners of any kind) against the Minnesota Twins, winning 4–0. This was the first perfect game pitched in Yankee Stadium since Don Larsen's in Game 5 of the 1956

World Series. Oddly enough, Wells and Larsen attended the same high school, Point Loma at San Diego, CA. After the season, the Yankees traded Wells to the Toronto Blue Jays.

CHASE'S SPORTSQUOTE OF THE DAY

"What helped me develop my quickness was fear. I think the rougher the opponent, the quicker I am."—Sugar Ray Leonard

BIRTHDAYS TODAY

Hubert Ira Davis, Jr, 30, basketball player, born Winston-Salem, NC, May 17, 1970.

Mariel Margaret ("Mia") Hamm, 28, soccer player, born Selma, AL, Mar 17, 1972.

Ray Charles ("Sugar Ray") Leonard, 44, former boxer, born Wilmington, NC, May 17, 1956.

Daniel Ricardo (Danny) Manning, 34, basketball player, born Hattiesburg, MS, May 17, 1966.

Earl Edwin Morrall, 66, former football player, born Muskegon, MI, May 17, 1934.

Norval Eugene (Norv) Turner, 48, football coach, born LeJeune, NC, May 17, 1952.

MAY 18 — THURSDAY

Day 139 — 227 Remaining

STANLEY CUP CHAMPIONS THIS DATE
1971	Montreal Canadiens

ADAMS, BABE: BIRTH ANNIVERSARY. May 18, 1882. Charles Benjamin ("Babe") Adams, baseball player and sportswriter, born at Tipton, IN. Adams pitched for the Pittsburgh Pirates from 1909 through 1926. He won three complete games in the 1909 World Series against the Detroit Tigers. Died at Silver Spring, MD, July 27, 1968.

BIG TEN BASEBALL TOURNAMENT. May 18–21. Site of regular-season conference champion. For info: Big Ten Conference, 1500 W Higgins Rd, Park Ridge, IL 60068-6300. Phone: (847) 696-1010. Fax: (847) 696-1150. Web: www.bigten.org.

CALAVERAS COUNTY FAIR AND JUMPING FROG JUBILEE. May 18–21. Calaveras Fairgrounds, Angels Camp, CA. County fair and reenactment of Mark Twain's "Celebrated Jumping Frog of Calaveras County." This "Super Bowl" of the sport of frog jumping attracts more than 3,000 frogs annually from around the world. Est attendance: 45,000. For info: 39th District Agricultural Assn, S Hwy 49, PO Box 489, Angels Camp, CA 95222. Phone: (209) 736-2561. Fax: (209) 736-2476. E-mail: info@frogtown.org. Web: www.frogtown.org.

NCAA DIVISION III SOFTBALL TOURNAMENT. May 18–22. Finals. James I. Moyer Sports Complex, Salem, VA. For info: NCAA, PO Box 6222, Indianapolis, IN 46206-6222. Phone: (317) 917-6222. Fax: (317) 917-6888. Web: www.ncaa.org.

NCAA DIVISION II SOFTBALL TOURNAMENT. May 18–22. Finals. Site TBA. For info: NCAA, PO Box 6222, Indianapolis, IN 46206-6222. Phone: (317) 917-6222. Fax: (317) 917-6888. Web: www.ncaa.org.

NCAA MEN'S AND WOMEN'S DIVISION III OUTDOOR TRACK AND FIELD CHAMPIONSHIPS. May 18–20. Finals. North Central College, Naperville, IL. For info: NCAA, PO Box 6222, Indianapolis, IN 46206-6222. Phone: (317) 917-6222. Fax: (317) 917-6888. Web: www.ncaa.org.

NCAA WOMEN'S DIVISION I TENNIS CHAMPIONSHIP. May 18–26. Finals. Pepperdine University, Mal-

ibu, CA. For info: NCAA, PO Box 6222, Indianapolis, IN 46206-6222. Phone: (317) 917-6222. Fax: (317) 917-6888. Web: www.ncaa.org.

NJCAA DIVISION I WOMEN'S FAST PITCH SOFTBALL CHAMPIONSHIP. May 18–20. Osceola County Softball Complex, Kissimmee, FL. For info: Mickey Englett, Tourn Dir, Okaloosa-Walton CC, 100 College Blvd, Niceville, FL 32578. Phone: (850) 729-5371. Fax: (850) 729-5323. Web: www.njcaa.org.

NJCAA DIVISION III WOMEN'S FAST PITCH SOFTBALL CHAMPIONSHIP. May 18–20. Arnold, MD. For info: Bill Gorrow, Tourn Dir, Anne Arundel Community College, 101 College Pkwy, Arnold, MD 21012. Phone: (410) 541-2734. Fax: (410) 541-2489. Web: www.njcaa.org.

ROCK-A-THON. May 18. Houston, TX. Senior citizens and their friends and family and local businesses commit to rocking in rocking chairs to raise money for area children's hospitals and charities. Money raised is often used by the neonatal and pediatrics units of these hospitals to purchase rocking chairs to be used to rock and comfort sick children. For info: Rock-A-Thon/Mktg Dept, NGH Marriott, 8550 Katy Freeway, Ste 201, Houston, TX 77024. Phone: (713) 464-4884. Fax: (713) 827-7693.

SPECIAL OLYMPICS IOWA SUMMER GAMES. May 18–20. Ames, IA. Olympic-style competition for children and adults with mental retardation. For info: Special Olympics Iowa, 3737 Woodland Ave, Ste 325, W Des Moines, IA 50266-1930. Phone: (515) 267-0131. Fax: (515) 267-0232. E-mail: iso@netihs.net.

SPECIAL OLYMPICS SOUTH DAKOTA SUMMER GAMES. May 18–20. Sioux Falls, SD. State-level Olympic-style competition for children and adults with mental retardation in team volleyball, gymnastics, team soccer, individual soccer skills, aquatics, race walking, power lifting, and track and field. For info: Special Olympics South Dakota, 305 W 39th St, Sioux Falls, SD 57105. Phone: (605) 331-4117. Fax: (605) 331-4326. E-mail: sosdak@aol.com.

TIE GAME, TAKE TRAIN: ANNIVERSARY. May 18, 1957. The Chicago White Sox and the Baltimore Orioles played a 1–1 tie, a game called precisely at 10:20 PM so that the White Sox could catch a train out of Baltimore. The Orioles' Dick Williams hit a home run on the game's last pitch to tie the game and avoid defeat. The game was replayed from the beginning at a later date, and Baltimore won.

TIGERS ON STRIKE: ANNIVERSARY. May 18, 1912. Members of the Detroit Tigers protested a suspension of Ty Cobb, their star player, by refusing to play against the Philadelphia Athletics. Detroit manager Hugh Jennings recruited college players to avoid a forfeit, but his stop-gap team lost 24–2. Al Travers gave up all 24 runs and never pitched in the major leagues again. Cobb persuaded his teammates to return to work the next day.

Eric Eugene Gregg, 49, baseball umpire, born Philadelphia, PA, May 18, 1951.

Erik Brian Hanson, 35, baseball player, born Kinnelon, NJ, May 18, 1965.

Craig Anthony Hentrich, 29, football player, born Alton, IL, May 18, 1971.

Reginald Martinez (Reggie) Jackson, 54, Baseball Hall of Fame outfielder, born Wyncote, PA, May 18, 1946.

Donyell Lamar Marshall, 27, basketball player, born Reading, PA, May 18, 1973.

Ronald Eugene (Ron) Mercer, 24, basketball player, born Nashville, TN, May 18, 1976.

Yannick Simone Camille Noah, 40, former tennis player, born Sedan, France, May 18, 1960.

Brooks Calbert Robinson, 63, Baseball Hall of Fame third baseman, born Little Rock, AR, May 18, 1937.

Oleg Tverdovsky, 24, hockey player, born Donetsk, USSR, May 18, 1976.

Eric Orlando Young, 33, baseball player, born New Brunswick, NJ, May 18, 1967.

MAY 19 — FRIDAY
Day 140 — 226 Remaining

STANLEY CUP CHAMPIONS THIS DATE

1974	Philadelphia Flyers
1984	Edmonton Oilers

ATWOOD EARLY ROD RUN. May 19–21. Atwood, KS. Classic car show with several states represented. Includes downtown festival, remote-control car races, drag races, barbecue and '50s dance. Est attendance: 1,500. For info: Atwood Ambassadors, 410 N Fifth, PO Box 341, Atwood, KS 67730. Phone: (913) 626-3144. Web: www.quality-pro.com/rodrun.

BIG TEN MEN'S AND WOMEN'S OUTDOOR TRACK AND FIELD CHAMPIONSHIPS. May 19–21. University of Iowa, Iowa City, IA. For info: Big Ten Conference, 1500 W Higgins Rd, Park Ridge, IL 60068-6300. Phone: (847) 696-1010. Fax: (847) 696-1150. Web: www.big ten.org.

BIG 12 MEN'S AND WOMEN'S OUTDOOR TRACK AND FIELD CHAMPIONSHIPS. May 19–21. University of Missouri, Columbia, MO. For info: Big 12 Conference, 2201 Stemmons Freeway, 28th Floor, Dallas, TX 75207. Phone: (214) 742-1212. Fax: (214) 742-2046.

FISHING HAS NO BOUNDARIES—HAYWARD. May 19–21. Lake Chippewa Campgrounds, Hayward, WI. A three-day fishing experience for disabled persons. Any disability, age, sex, race, etc, eligible. Fishing with experienced guides on one of the best fishing waters in Wisconsin, attended by 200 participants and 500 volunteers. Advance registration before Mar 1 required. For info: Fishing Has No Boundaries, PO Box 375, Hayward, WI 54843. Phone: (715) 634-3185. Fax: (715) 634-1305.

KATE SMITH WINS STANLEY CUP: ANNIVERSARY. May 19, 1974. Singer Kate Smith made a personal appearance at the Spectrum at Philadelphia to sing "God Bless America" before the seventh game of the Stanley Cup finals, pitting the Philadelphia Flyers against the Boston Bruins. The Flyers had enjoyed remarkable success when they played Smith's recording of the Irving Berlin song. For the decisive game, the personal touch worked. The Flyers won, 1–0.

MILES CITY BUCKING HORSE SALE. May 19–21. Miles City, MT. Miles City is real "Lonesome Dove" country. Its annual bucking horse sale is where rodeo stock operators from around the West come to purchase their bucking horses for the coming rodeo season. As a festive event, the sale not only involves cowboys trying to ride some of the wildest horses in the country, but also Western artists displaying and creating works in a weekend art show, an antique show featuring guns and coins, a Western trade show featuring practical and gift items, a parade and Miles City's Western attractions such as the Range Riders Museum which chronicles the life of the cowboy on the northern Great Plains. (Miles City is the community featured in the novel and the two television miniseries about "Lonesome Dove.") Est attendance: 10,000. For info: Miles City Chamber of Commerce, 901 Main St, Miles City, MT 59301. Phone: (406) 232-2890.

MINT JULEP SCALE MEET. May 19–21. Rough River Dam State Resort Park, Falls of Rough, KY. A weekend for radio-controlled airplane enthusiasts. Annually, the third weekend in May. Est attendance: 450. For info: Tom DeHaven, Rec Supervisor, Rough River Dam State Resort Park, 450 Lodge Rd, Falls of Rough, KY 40119. Phone: (502) 257-2311.

NATIONAL EMPLOYEE HEALTH AND FITNESS DAY. May 19. To focus on the importance of fitness and healthy lifestyles at the work site. For info: Natl Assn of Governor's Councils on Physical Fitness/Sports, 201 S Capitol Ave, Ste 560, Indianapolis, IN 46225-1072. Phone: (317) 237-5630. Fax: (317) 237-5632. E-mail: govcouncil@aol.com. Web: fitnesslink.com/govcouncil.

NCAA DIVISION III BASEBALL TOURNAMENT. May 19–23. Regionals at sites TBA. For info: NCAA, PO Box 6222, Indianapolis, IN 46206-6222. Phone: (317) 917-6222. Fax: (317) 917-6888. Web: www.ncaa.org.

NCAA MEN'S DIVISION III TENNIS CHAMPIONSHIPS. May 19–24. Finals at a site TBA. For info: NCAA, PO Box 6222, Indianapolis, IN 46206-6222. Phone: (317) 917-6222. Fax: (317) 917-6888. Web: www.ncaa.org.

NCAA WOMEN'S LACROSSE CHAMPIONSHIPS. May 19–21. Finals. College of New Jersey, Ewing Township, NJ. For info: NCAA, PO Box 6222, Indianapolis, IN 46206-6222. Phone: (317) 917-6222. Fax: (317) 917-6888. Web: www.ncaa.org.

OCA RANGE ROUND-UP. May 19–20. Lazy E Arena, Guthrie, OK. Working cowboys from 12 of Oklahoma's

May 2000

S	M	T	W	T	F	S
	1	2	3	4	5	6
7	8	9	10	11	12	13
14	15	16	17	18	19	20
21	22	23	24	25	26	27
28	29	30	31			

largest ranches compete in six events, including wild cow milking and the hilarious wild horse race. Est attendance: 14,000. For info: Lazy E Promotions, Rte 5, PO Box 393, Guthrie, OK 73044. Phone: (405) 282-7433 or (800) 595-RIDE. E-mail: arena@lazye.net. Web: www.lazye.com.

SEASPACE. May 19–21. Hyatt Regency Downtown Hotel, Houston, TX. Scuba diving symposium featuring seminars, photo and video courses, photo contest and exhibit, film festival, environmental awareness area, free introduction to scuba and snorkeling, hall of exhibits and receptions. Sponsor: Houston Underwater Club. For more info send SASE. Est attendance: 10,000. For info: Seaspace, PO Box 3753, Houston, TX 77253-3753. Phone: (713) 467-6675. Web: www.seaspace.org.

SPECIAL OLYMPICS FLORIDA STATE EQUESTRIAN CHAMPIONSHIPS. May 19–20. Bob Thomas Equestrian Center, Florida State Fairgrounds, Tampa, FL. Olympic-style competition for children and adults with mental retardation. For info: Special Olympics Florida, 8 Broadway, Ste D, Kissimmee, FL 34741. Phone: (407) 870-2292. Fax: (407) 870-9810.

SPECIAL OLYMPICS MISSOURI SUMMER GAMES. May 19–21. Ft Leonard Wood, MO. Olympic-style competition for children and adults with mental retardation. For info: Special Olympics Missouri, 520 Dix Rd, Ste C, Jefferson City, MO 65109. Phone: (573) 635-1660. Fax: (573) 635-8223. E-mail: hq@somo.org. Web: www.somo.org.

WOMAN GOLFER GETS TWO ACES: ANNIVERSARY. May 19, 1942. Mrs W. Driver became the first golfer of either sex to get two holes in one in the same round. She aced the third hole and the eighth hole at Balgowlah Golf Club, Australia.

WORLD GOLF VILLAGE OPENS: ANNIVERSARY. May 19, 1998. The World Golf Village, an ambitious, 6,300-acre development supported by every major golf organization in the world and located at St. Augustine, FL, opened to the public. The complex includes three championship golf courses, a luxury hotel, vacation villas, retail stores, a convention center, a Mayo Clinic medical facility and the World Golf Hall of Fame with more than 70 exhibits arranged in an "18-hole" layout.

BIRTHDAYS TODAY

Kevin Garnett, 24, basketball player, born Mauldin, SC, May 19, 1976.
William (Bill) Laimbeer, Jr, 43, former basketball player, born Boston, MA, May 19, 1957.
Elisha Archie Manning, III, 51, former football player, born Cleveland, MS, May 19, 1949.
Gilbert James (Gil) McDougald, 72, former baseball player, born San Francisco, CA, May 19, 1928.
Adolph (Dolph) Schayes, 72, former basketball coach and Basketball Hall of Fame forward and center, born New York, NY, May 19, 1928.

MAY 20 — SATURDAY
Day 141 — 225 Remaining

AUTOMOTION. May 20–21. Wisconsin Dells, WI. More than 700 cars on display, including street machines, classics and antiques. Event includes swap meet, live entertainment, car corral, four $500 cash drawings, drawing for eight getaway packages valued at more than $400 each, sock hop and classic movie at Big Sky Drive-In Theatre, "Car Cruise" and other activities. Est attendance: 15,000. For info: Wisconsin Dells VCB, Box 390, Wisconsin Dells, WI 53965. Phone: (800) 223-3557. Fax: (608) 254-4293. Web: www.wisdells.com.

BASKETBALL HALL OF FAME AWARDS DINNER. May 20 (tentative). Springfield Marriott, Springfield, MA. National awards dinner hosted by the Basketball Hall of Fame. Est attendance: 500. For info: Craig Fink, Supervisor of Event Operations and Facility Mktg, Basketball Hall of Fame, 1150 W Columbus Ave, Box 179, Springfield, MA 01101-0179. Phone: (413) 781-6500.

BOYER, KEN: BIRTH ANNIVERSARY. May 20, 1931. Kenton Lloyd (Ken) Boyer, baseball player and manager, born at Liberty, MO. Boyer was an exceptional third baseman for the St. Louis Cardinals, winning the National League MVP Award in 1964. He managed the Cards from 1978 through June 8, 1980. Died at Ballwin, MO, Sept 7, 1982.

CANADA: SOUTHERN ONTARIO CYCLING RALLY. May 20–22. Southern Ontario. A three-day cycling festival held annually since 1988 over the Victoria Day weekend. This event has become a get-together of the cycling clans, attracting clubs and riders from Ontario, Quebec and the US border states. Riders stay on the campus of Trent University. Events include out-and-back tours on Saturday and Monday and a rally on Sunday in the scenic Kawartha Lakes district. For info: Veloforce, 145 King St W, Ste 1000, Toronto, ON, Canada M5H 1J8. Phone: (416) 484-8339. Fax: (416) 484-1613. Web: www.Cycle-Canada.com/ttt.html.

CUSTER STATE PARK SEASONAL VOLKSMARCH. May 20 (and various dates through Oct 31). Custer State Park, SD. Noncompetitive walks on a premarked trail. Walkers can earn awards or walk for free. Hike is 6.2 miles and begins at Peter Norbeck Visitors Center. South Dakota state park license is required. For info: Craig Pugsley, Custer State Park, HC 83, Box 70, Custer, SD 57730. Phone: (605) 255-4515. Fax: (605) 255-4460. E-mail: craigp@gfp-cu.state.sd.us.

FISHING HAS NO BOUNDARIES—MONTICELLO. May 20–21. Freeman Lake, Monticello, IN. A two-day event for disabled persons to experience fishing on the lake. Any disability, sex, age, race, etc, eligible. Est attendance: 50 participants and 130 volunteers. For info: FHNB, 7805 N Harrison, PO Box 325, Battleground, IN 47920. Phone: (765) 567-2567.

MILWAUKEE BRAVES SURPASS BOSTON ATTENDANCE: ANNIVERSARY. May 20, 1953. In just their 13th game of the season, the Braves, in their first year in Milwaukee, surpassed their total 1952 attendance of 281,278, their last year at Boston.

NATIONAL MUSHROOM HUNTING CHAMPIONSHIP. May 20. Boyne City, MI. Hunters are transported by school buses out to a secret hunting location where they are allowed to hunt for 90 minutes. The bags are collected from the hunters to count the number of morel mushrooms picked. In 1984, the grand champion picked 796 mushrooms in the allotted time. Carved wooden morel mushroom trophies and cash prizes awarded. Sponsored by the Boyne Valley Lions Club. Annually, the first Saturday after Mother's Day. Est attendance: 400. For info: Natl Mushroom Fest, 28 S Lake St, Boyne City, MI 49712. Phone: (616) 582-6222. Fax: (616) 582-6963.

★ **NATIONAL SAFE BOATING WEEK.** May 20–26. Presidential Proclamation issued since 1995 for a week in May. From 1958 through 1977, issued for a week including July 4 (PL85–445 of June 4, 1958). From 1981 through 1994, issued for the first week in June (PL96–376 of Oct 3, 1980). Not issued from 1978 through 1980. National Safe Boating Week activities, sponsored by the US Coast Guard, bring boating safety to the public's attention, decrease the number of boating fatalities and make the water safer for all boaters.

NCAA MEN'S DIVISION I TENNIS CHAMPIONSHIPS. May 20–28. Finals. University of Georgia, Athens, GA. For info: NCAA, PO Box 6222, Indianapolis, IN 46206-6222. Phone: (317) 917-6222. Fax: (317) 917-6888. Web: www.ncaa.org.

NCAA WOMEN'S DIVISION III LACROSSE CHAMPIONSHIP. May 20. Finals. Site TBA. For info: NCAA, PO Box 6222, Indianapolis, IN 46206-6222. Phone: (317) 917-6222. Fax: (317) 917-6888. Web: www.ncaa.org.

NEWHOUSER, HAL: BIRTH ANNIVERSARY. May 20, 1921. Harold (Hal) Newhouser, Baseball Hall of Fame pitcher, born at Detroit, MI. Newhouser was the American League's top left-handed pitcher during the 1940s. He compiled a lifetime record of 207–150 and became the only pitcher to win consecutive MVP Awards in 1944 and 1945. Inducted into the Hall of Fame in 1992. Died at Southfield, MI, Nov 10, 1998.

NJCAA DIVISION III BASEBALL CHAMPIONSHIP. May 20–26. Batavia, NY. For info: Bob Pacer, Tourn Dir, 214 Naramore Dr, Batavia, NY 14020. Phone: (716) 344-3938. Web: www.njcaa.org.

NO-RAINOUT RECORD: 15th ANNIVERSARY. May 20, 1985. The game between the Milwaukee Brewers and the Cleveland Indians at Cleveland was rained out. Remarkably, this was the first rainout of the season in either league after a major league-record 485 games had been played without a postponement.

PAC-10 MEN'S AND WOMEN'S OUTDOOR TRACK AND FIELD CHAMPIONSHIPS. May 20–21. University of Oregon, Eugene, OR. For info: PAC-10 Conference, 800 S Broadway, Ste 400, Walnut Creek, CA 94596. Phone: (510) 932-4411. Fax: (510) 932-4601.

POLE, PEDAL, PADDLE. May 20. Bend, OR. Five-stage iron man-type race for singles, teams and couples; includes downhill skiing, nordic skiing, biking, canoeing and running. Annually, the third Saturday in May. Sponsors: US Bank, Pepsi, Bud Light, Teva, Cellular One, Z21TV. Est attendance: 12,000. For info: Mt Bachelor Ski Education Foundation, PO Box 388, Bend, OR 97709. Phone: (541) 388-0002. Fax: (541) 388-7848. E-mail: mbsef@bendnet.com. Web: www.bendnet.com/ppp.

PREAKNESS STAKES. May 20. Pimlico Race Course, Baltimore, MD. 125th running of the Preakness Stakes, middle jewel in the Triple Crown, inaugurated in 1873. Annually, the third Saturday in May—two Saturdays after the Kentucky Derby—and followed, three Saturdays later, by the Belmont Stakes. Est attendance: 100,000. For info: Maryland Jockey Club, Pimlico Race Course, Baltimore, MD 21215. Phone: (410) 542-9400. Web: www.marylandracing.com.

WEBSTER COUNTY WOODCHOPPING FESTIVAL. May 20–28. Webster Springs, WV. South Eastern US World Championship Woodchopping Contest and State Championship Turkey-Calling Contest. Est attendance: 10,000. For info: Festival Committee, PO Box 227, Webster Springs, WV 26288. Phone: (304) 847-7666. Fax: (304) 847-5117.

BIRTHDAYS TODAY

Thomas Terrell Brandon, 30, basketball player, born Portland, OR, May 20, 1970.

	S	M	T	W	T	F	S
May		1	2	3	4	5	6
2000	7	8	9	10	11	12	13
	14	15	16	17	18	19	20
	21	22	23	24	25	26	27
	28	29	30	31			

Harold Peter ("Bud") Grant, 73, former basketball and football player and Pro Football Hall of Fame coach, born Superior, WI, May 20, 1927.
Stu Grimson, 35, hockey player, born Kamloops, British Columbia, Canada, May 20, 1965.
Dimetry Giovonni (Vonnie) Holliday, 24, football player, born Camden, SC, May 20, 1976.
Leroy Kelly, 58, Pro Football Hall of Fame running back, born Philadelphia, PA, May 20, 1942.
Bobby Ray Murcer, 54, broadcaster and former baseball player, born Oklahoma City, OK, May 20, 1946.
Liselotte Neumann, 34, golfer, born Finspang, Sweden, May 20, 1966.
Todd Vernon Stottlemyre, 35, baseball player, born Yakima, WA, May 20, 1965.
David Lee Wells, 37, baseball player, born Torrance, CA, May 20, 1963.

MAY 21 — SUNDAY
Day 142 — 224 Remaining

STANLEY CUP CHAMPIONS THIS DATE	
1979	Montreal Canadiens
1981	New York Islanders

AVERILL, EARL: BIRTH ANNIVERSARY. May 21, 1902. Howard Earl Averill, Baseball Hall of Fame outfielder, born at Snohomish, WA. Averill was the first future Hall of Fame member to hit a home run in his first major league at bat, doing so in 1929. He played for the Cleveland Indians, the Detroit Tigers and the Boston Braves and hit .318. Inducted into the Hall of Fame in 1975. Died at Everett, WA, Aug 16, 1983.

D.C. BOOTH DAY (WITH FISH CULTURE HALL OF FAME). May 21. D.C. Booth Historic National Fish Hatchery, Spearfish, SD. Antique auto show, musical entertainment, refreshments, free tours of the historic Booth home and installation of new members into the Fish Culture Hall of Fame. Est attendance: 1,200. For info: Molly Salcone, D.C. Booth Historic Natl Fish Hatchery, 423 Hatchery Circle, Spearfish, SD 57783. Phone: (605) 642-7730. Fax: (605) 642-2336.

EXAMINER BAY TO BREAKERS RACE. May 21. San Francisco, CA. Largest footrace in the world attracts 80,000 runners each year, from world-class athletes to fun runners, postrace festival, live concert, food and beverages. Annually, a Sunday in May. Est attendance: 200,000. For info: *Examiner* Bay to Breakers, PO Box 429200, San Francisco, CA 94142. Phone: (415) 808-5000 ext 2222. E-mail: breakers@examiner.com. Web: www.baytobreakers.com.

GRANT, EDDIE: BIRTH ANNIVERSARY. May 21, 1883. Edward Leslie (Eddie) Grant, baseball player, born at Franklin, MA. Grant played third base in the majors and retired in 1915 to practice law. In WWI, he led a mission to rescue the "Lost Battalion" and became the only major league ballplayer to be killed in action. Died at Argonne, France, Oct 5, 1918.

LUM PINCH-HITS FOR AARON: ANNIVERSARY. May 21, 1969. Henry Aaron of the Atlanta Braves was lifted for a pinch hitter for the first time in his career. Mike Lum batted for Aaron in the seventh inning of a game against the New York Mets after Aaron had come to the plate 9,015 times. Lum doubled, and the Braves won, 15–3.

PRCA PRO RODEO. May 21–23 (tentative). Payson Rodeo Grounds, Payson, AZ. Benefits the Gary Hardt Athletic Scholarship fund and underprivileged and needy children of Gila County. Est attendance: 3,500. For info: Rim Country Regional Chamber of Commerce, PO Box 1380,

Payson, AZ 85547. Phone: (800) 672-9766. Fax: (520) 474-8812. E-mail: pcoc@netzone.com. Web: www.net zone.com/~dggannon/payson.

SHORTEST NIGHT GAME: ANNIVERSARY. May 21, 1943. In the shortest night game in major league history, the Chicago White Sox defeated the Washington Senators, 1–0, in 1 hour, 29 minutes.

WALK & ROLL CHICAGO. May 21. Chicago, IL. 28th annual. The largest event of its kind in the US. More than 5,000 participants bike 15 miles, walk 5 miles or in line skate 10 miles along Chicago's lakefront and streets to raise more than $700,000 in the fight against cancer. Top fund raisers receive fabulous incentives. A huge celebration held in Grant Park includes entertainment, food, raffles and more! For info: American Cancer Soc, Chicago Area Office, 77 E Monroe, #1200, Chicago, IL 60603. Phone: (312) 372-0471. Fax: (312) 577-6058. E-mail: walkroll@cancer.org. Web: www.walkandrollchicago.org.

CHASE'S SPORTSQUOTE OF THE DAY

"To pronounce my name, you take 'par' as in golf, 'seag' as in Seagram's whiskey, and 'yen' as in Japanese money. Just think of a drunken Japanese golfer."—Ara Parseghian

---

BIRTHDAYS TODAY

Tommy Albelin, 36, hockey player, born Stockholm, Sweden, May 21, 1964.

Peter Andrew (Pete) Banaszak, 56, former football player, born Crivitz, WI, May 21, 1944.

Robert Joe (Bobby) Cox, 59, baseball manager and former executive and player, born Tulsa, OK, May 21, 1941.

Kent Alan Hrbek, 40, former baseball player, born Minneapolis, MN, May 21, 1960.

Herbert Dorsey Levens, 30, football player, born Syracuse, NY, May 21, 1970.

Ara Raoul Parseghian, 77, former broadcaster and college football coach, born Akron, OH, May 21, 1923.

Christopher Jon (Chris) Widger, 29, baseball player, born Wilmington, DE, May 21, 1971.

MAY 22 — MONDAY

Day 143 — 223 Remaining

FIRST WOMAN TO QUALIFY FOR INDY: ANNIVERSARY. May 22, 1977. Janet Guthrie became the first woman driver to qualify for the Indianapolis 500 with an average speed of more than 188 miles per hour. She lasted only 27 laps in the race, dropping out when her car broke a valve seal.

MANTLE NEARLY LEAVES THE BUILDING: ANNIVERSARY. May 22, 1963. Mickey Mantle of the New York Yankees hit a home run off Bill Fischer of the Kansas City Athletics as the Yankees beat the A's, 8–7. Mantle's blast caromed off the rooftop facade at Yankee Stadium and came within a few feet of becoming the only home run ever hit out of that park.

NATIONAL BACKYARD GAMES WEEK. May 22–29. Observance to celebrate the unofficial start of summer by fostering social interaction and family togetherness through backyard games. Get outside and be both physically active and mentally stimulated. Play classic games of the past while discovering and creating new ways to be active. For info: Frank Beres, Patch Products, PO Box 268, Beloit, WI 53511. Phone: (608) 362-6896. Fax: (608) 362-8178. E-mail: patch@patchproducts.com. Web: www.patchproducts.com.

SIMMONS, AL: BIRTH ANNIVERSARY. May 22, 1902. Aloysius Harry (Al) Simmons, Baseball Hall of Fame outfielder, born Aloysius Harry Syzmanski at Milwaukee, WI. Simmons was a right-handed hitter known for pointing his left foot straight down the third-base line. This unorthodox style worked for him as he accumulated 2,926 hits in his career. Inducted into the Hall of Fame in 1953. Died at Milwaukee, May 26, 1956.

SMITH, HORTON: BIRTH ANNIVERSARY. May 22, 1908. Horton Smith, golfer, born at Springfield, MO. Smith won the first Masters in 1934 and then won it again in 1936. He played on seven Ryder Cup teams and was undefeated. After WWII, Smith played an active role in golf administration, serving as president of the PGA and the PGA Seniors. Died at Detroit, MI, Oct 15, 1963.

WOMEN'S INTERNATIONAL BOWLING CONGRESS QUEEN'S TOURNAMENT. May 22–26. Reno, NV. For info: Bowling, Inc, 5301 S 76th St, Greendale, WI 53129. Phone: (414) 423-3356. Fax: (414) 421-3013.

BIRTHDAYS TODAY

Marcus L. Dupree, 36, former football player, born Philadelphia, MS, May 22, 1964.

Richard Paul (Richie) Garcia, 58, baseball umpire, born Key West, FL, May 22, 1942.

Thomas Edward (Tommy) John, 57, former baseball player, born Terre Haute, IN, May 22, 1943.

Jose Ramon Mesa, 34, baseball player, born Azua, Dominican Republic, May 22, 1966.

Janne Niinimaa, 25, hockey player, born Raahe, Finland, May 22, 1975.

Julian Tavarez, 27, baseball player, born Santiago, Dominican Republic, May 22, 1973.

MAY 23 — TUESDAY

Day 144 — 222 Remaining

FIRST NIGHT GAME RAINED OUT: 65th ANNIVERSARY. May 23, 1935. The first major league night game, scheduled to be played at Cincinnati, was rained out. History was made instead the following evening when the game was played.

HOY, DUMMY: BIRTH ANNIVERSARY. May 23, 1862. William Ellsworth ("Dummy") Hoy, baseball player, born at Houcktown, OH. Despite losing his hearing from childhood meningitis, Hoy played major league baseball from 1888 to 1902. He was a fine defensive outfielder who once threw out three runners at home plate in one game. Died at Cincinnati, OH, Dec 15, 1961.

NJCAA DIVISION I MEN'S GOLF CHAMPIONSHIP. May 23–26. Highland Oaks Golf Course, Dothan, AL. For info: Gene Dews, Tourn Dir, Wallace College, Rt 6, Box 62, Dothan, AL 36303. Phone: (334) 983-3521. Fax: (334) 983-4255. Web: www.njcaa.org.

WHALERS CHANGE NAME: ANNIVERSARY. May 23, 1979. The New England Whalers of the National Hockey League changed their name to the Hartford Whalers. The team was an original member of the World Hockey Association and won the first WHA championship, the Avco World Cup, in the 1972–73 season. When the WHA folded following the 1978–79 season, the Whalers were one of four WHA teams taken into the National Hockey League.

WHEAT, ZACK: BIRTH ANNIVERSARY. May 23, 1888. Zachariah David (Zack) Wheat, Baseball Hall of Fame outfielder, born at Hamilton, OH. Wheat played left field for the Brooklyn Dodgers from 1909 to 1926. He hit .317, won one batting title and was never ejected from a game. Inducted into the Hall of Fame in 1959. Died at Sedalia, MO, Mar 11, 1972.

BIRTHDAYS TODAY

David Michael (Dave) Babych, 39, hockey player, born Edmonton, Alberta, Canada, May 23, 1961.

Reginald Leslie (Reggie) Cleveland, 52, former baseball player, born Swift Current, Saskatchewan, Canada, May 23, 1948.

Ricardo (Ricky) Gutierrez, 30, baseball player, born Miami, FL, May 23, 1970.

Marvelous Marvin Hagler (born Marvin Hagler), 46, former boxer, born at Newark, NJ, May 23, 1954.

James Edward Hasty, 35, football player, born Seattle, WA, May 23, 1965.

John David Newcombe, 57, former tennis player, born Sydney, New South Wales, Australia, May 23, 1943.

William Nathaniel ("Buck") Showalter, III, 44, baseball manager, born DeFuniak Springs, FL, May 23, 1956.

MAY 24 — WEDNESDAY
Day 145 — 221 Remaining

STANLEY CUP CHAMPIONS THIS DATE

1980	New York Islanders
1986	Montreal Canadiens
1990	Edmonton Oilers

BASEBALL FIRST PLAYED UNDER THE LIGHTS: 65th ANNIVERSARY. May 24, 1935. After a rainout the night before, the Cincinnati Reds defeated the Philadelphia Phillies by a score of 2–1, as more than 20,000 fans enjoyed the first night baseball game in the major leagues. The game was played at Crosley Field, Cincinnati, OH.

CANADIENS WIN 23rd STANLEY CUP: ANNIVERSARY. May 24, 1986. The Montreal Canadiens defeated the Calgary Flames, 4–3, to win the Stanley Cup, four games to one. For the Canadiens, it was their 23rd title, putting them one major league championship ahead of the New York Yankees and their 22 World Series titles. Montreal won another Stanley Cup in 1993. The Yankees won their 23rd World Series in 1996 and their 24th in 1998.

DEMARET, JIMMY: 90th BIRTH ANNIVERSARY. May 24, 1910. James Newton (Jimmy) Demaret, golfer and broadcaster, born at Houston, TX. Demaret won the Masters three times and teamed successfully with Ben Hogan in the 1947 and 1951 Ryder Cup matches. He wore flamboyant clothes and played to the crowd. He worked on golf telecasts and founded the Legends of Golf tournament that grew into the Senior Tour. Died at Houston, Dec 28, 1983.

DISPUTED WIN AT INDIANAPOLIS: ANNIVERSARY. May 24, 1981. Bobby Unser finished first in the Indianapolis 500, but after the race was over, the stewards penalized him one lap for passing cars illegally under the yellow caution flag. The penalty vaulted Mario Andretti into first place, but Unser and Roger Penske, owner of Unser's car, appealed the stewards' decision to the US Auto Club. Four months later, the USAC ruled that Unser was guilty but that the punishment was too severe. The lap penalty was replaced by a $40,000 fine, and Unser recovered the championship.

HITS CATSKILLS. May 24–Sept 3. Ellenville, NY, in the heart of the Catskill Mountains. Five weeks of hunter/jumper competition throughout the summer. Riders from beginning levels to world class can be seen in competition all week long, with the featured Grand Prix show-jumping event each Sunday. The shows attract an average of 1,000 horses for each week of competition. Annually, spring and summer. Est attendance: 10,000. For info and exact dates of circuit events: HITS, 13 Closs Dr, Rhinebeck, NY 12572. Phone: (914) 876-3666. Fax: (914) 876-5538. Web: www.equisearch.com.

NCAA WOMEN'S DIVISION I GOLF CHAMPION-SHIPS. May 24–27. Finals. Sun River Resort, OR. For info: NCAA, PO Box 6222, Indianapolis, IN 46206-6222. Phone: (317) 917-6222. Fax: (317) 917-6888. Web: www.ncaa.org.

OUTRIGGER HOTELS ANNUAL HAWAIIAN OCEAN-FEST. May 24–June 4. Oahu, HI. A variety of events celebrating Hawaii's ocean sports. The Hawaiian International Ocean Challenge competition between six-person teams of the world's best lifeguards in kayak, surf rescue, paddleboard and outrigger canoe. Ocean Challenge includes a "World Team" selected from individual competition at the Waimea Open Ocean Challenge, an ocean iron man event with four continuous disciplines—run, kayak, swim and paddleboard. Est attendance: 50,000. For info: Team Unlimited, Pauahi Tower, 1001 Bishop St, Ste 880, Honolulu, HI 96813. Phone: (808) 521-4222. Fax: (808) 538-0314. E-mail: info@teamunlimited.com. Web: www.teamunlimited.com.

THIRTEEN HALL OF FAMERS IN SAME GAME: ANNIVERSARY. May 24, 1928. In a game between the Philadelphia Athletics and the New York Yankees, 13 future members of the Baseball Hall of Fame took the field. Ty Cobb, Tris Speaker, Mickey Cochrane, Al Simmons, Eddie Collins, Lefty Grove and Jimmie Foxx played for the Athletics. Earle Combs, Leo Durocher, Babe Ruth, Lou Gehrig, Tony Lazzeri and Waite Hoyt played for the Yankees. In addition, the two managers, Connie Mack and Miller Huggins, are also Hall of Famers.

CHASE'S SPORTSQUOTE OF THE DAY

"Golf is based on honesty. Where else would someone admit to a seven on an easy par three?"—Jimmy Demaret

BIRTHDAYS TODAY

Daniel (Danny) Bautista, 28, baseball player, born Santo Domingo, Dominican Republic, May 24, 1972.

Bartolo Colon, 25, baseball player, born Altamira, Dominican Republic, May 24, 1975.

Ricky Craven, 34, auto racer, born Newburgh, ME, May 24, 1966.

May 2000

S	M	T	W	T	F	S
	1	2	3	4	5	6
7	8	9	10	11	12	13
14	15	16	17	18	19	20
21	22	23	24	25	26	27
28	29	30	31			

Kris Bruce Draper, 29, hockey player, born Toronto, Ontario, Canada, May 24, 1971.

Joe Dumars, III, 37, basketball player, born Shreveport, LA, May 24, 1963.

Mitchell (Mitch) Kupchak, 46, former basketball player, born Hicksville, NY, May 24, 1954.

James Ernest (Jim) Mora, 65, football coach, born Los Angeles, CA, May 24, 1935.

MAY 25 — THURSDAY

Day 146 — 220 Remaining

NBA FINALS CHAMPIONS THIS DATE

1975   Golden State Warriors

ALI BEATS LISTON IN REMATCH: 35th ANNIVERSARY. May 25, 1965. Muhammad Ali knocked out Sonny Liston just one minute into the first round of a controversial rematch for the heavyweight championship at Lewiston, ME. Liston went down from a short right-hand punch that some swore never hit him.

BABE'S 714th BIG ONE: 65th ANNIVERSARY. May 25, 1935. George Herman Ruth could barely run and could no longer hit like he used to, but occasionally the Babe could still put on a show with his bat. On May 25, Ruth, playing for the Boston Braves, hit three home runs before a crowd of only 10,000 at Pittsburgh's Forbes Field. His last home run of the day—his 714th in regular-season play—proved to be Babe's last major league home run as well as his last big-league hit.

DIHIGO, MARTIN: 95th BIRTH ANNIVERSARY. May 25, 1905. Martin Dihigo, Baseball Hall of Fame player and manager, born at Mantanzas, Cuba. Dihigo was the most versatile player in the Negro Leagues and one of the best. He excelled as a pitcher and as a hitter and played all positions except catcher. Inducted into the Hall of Fame in 1977. Died at Cinefuegos, Cuba, May 20, 1971.

FILION WINS 10,000th RACE: ANNIVERSARY. May 25, 1987. Herve Filion drove Commander Bond to victory in the third race at Yonkers Raceway in New York to become the first harness racing driver to record 10,000 wins.

JENKINS STRIKES OUT 3,000th BATTER: ANNIVERSARY. May 25, 1982. Pitcher Ferguson Jenkins of the Chicago Cubs recorded the 3,000th strikeout in his major league career in a 2–1 loss to the San Diego Padres. Jenkins, the seventh pitcher to reach 3,000 strikeouts, wound up his career with 3,192 Ks, ninth on the all-time list.

KODIAK CRAB FESTIVAL. May 25–29. Kodiak, AK. A celebration of spring and the Emerald Isle. Featured are parades, carnival booths and midway, running events, a golf tournament, bicycle and survival suit races, a blessing-of-the-fleet ceremony and memorial services. Annually, Memorial Day weekend. Est attendance: 15,000. For info: Kodiak Chamber of Commerce, Box 1485, Kodiak, AK 99615. Phone: (907) 486-5557. Fax: (907) 486-7605. E-mail: chamber@kodiak.org. Web: www.kodiak.org/kodiak.

NATIONAL TAP DANCE DAY. May 25. To celebrate this unique American art form that represents a fusion of African and European cultures and to transmit tap to succeeding generations through documentation and archival and performance support. Held on the anniversary of the birth of Bill "Bojangles" Robinson to honor his outstanding contribution to the art of tap dancing on stage and in films through the unification of diverse stylistic and racial elements.

NCAA DIVISION I SOFTBALL WORLD SERIES. May 25–29. Finals. Don Porter Hall of Fame Stadium, Oklahoma City, OK. For info: NCAA, PO Box 6222, Indianapolis, IN 46206-6222. Phone: (317) 917-6222. Fax: (317) 917-6888. Web: www.ncaa.org.

NCAA MEN'S AND WOMEN'S DIVISION II OUTDOOR TRACK AND FIELD CHAMPIONSHIPS. May 25–27. Finals. Site TBA. For info: NCAA, PO Box 6222, Indianapolis, IN 46206-6222. Phone: (317) 917-6222. Fax: (317) 917-6888. Web: www.ncaa.org.

NELSON, LINDSEY: BIRTH ANNIVERSARY. May 25, 1919. Lindsey Nelson, broadcaster, born at Pulaski, TN. Nelson cut his broadcasting teeth at Knoxville, TN, and worked for the Liberty Radio Network in the early 1950s. For NBC television, he specialized in college football and gained an additional audience broadcasting Notre Dame games on a tape-delayed basis. In 1962 he joined Bob Murphy and Ralph Kiner as the original voices of the New York Mets. Given the Ford Frick Award in 1988. Died at Atlanta, GA, June 10, 1995.

NEW YORK GOLDEN ARMS TOURNAMENT. May 25. Fleet Week, *USS Intrepid*, New York, NY. Arm-wrestling competition held on the ship determines winners who will compete in the Empire State Golden Arms Tournament of Champions on Oct 12. For info: New York Arm Wrestling Assn, Inc, 200-14 45th Dr, Bayside, NY 11361. Phone: (718) 544-4592. Web: www.nycarms.com.

TUNNEY, GENE: BIRTH ANNIVERSARY. May 25, 1898. James Joseph ("Gene") Tunney, boxer, born at New York, NY. Tunney won the light heavyweight championship in 1922 and defeated Jack Dempsey for the heavyweight title on Sept 23, 1926. Their rematch at Soldier Field at Chicago on Sept 22, 1927, was the famous "Long Count" fight in which Tunney remained on the canvas more than 10 seconds after Dempsey hovered over him, a subject of controversy ever since. Died at New York, NY, Nov 7, 1978.

STANLEY CUP CHAMPIONS THIS DATE	
1978	Montreal Canadiens
1989	Calgary Flames
1991	Pittsburgh Penguins

BIRTHDAYS TODAY

Shawn Antoski, 30, hockey player, born Brantford, Ontario, Canada, May 25, 1970.

Carlton Chester ("Cookie") Gilchrist, 65, former football player, born Brackenridge, PA, May 25, 1935.

Kendall Cedric Gill, 32, basketball player, born Chicago, IL, May 25, 1968.

Keith Lamar Hamilton, 29, football player, born Paterson, NJ, May 25, 1971.

David Michael (Dave) Hollins, 34, baseball player, born Buffalo, NY, May 25, 1966.

K.C. Jones, 68, former basketball player, born Tyler, TX, May 25, 1932.

William Walton (Bill) Sharman, 74, former basketball coach, executive and Basketball Hall of Fame guard, born Abilene, TX, May 25, 1926.

MAY 26 — FRIDAY
Day 147 — 219 Remaining

STANLEY CUP CHAMPIONS THIS DATE	
1988	Edmonton Oilers

ALMA HIGHLAND FESTIVAL AND GAMES. May 26–28. Alma College, Alma, MI. Old World pageantry honoring Scottish traditions, including highland dancing, piping, drumming, athletic competitions, clan tents and grand parade. 33rd annual festival. Annually, Memorial Day weekend. Est attendance: 60,000. For info: Alma Highland Fest, 110 W Superior St, Alma, MI 48801. Phone: (517) 463-8979.

CANADA: NASSH CONVENTION. May 26–30. Banff, Alberta. 28th annual convention of the North American Society for Sport History whose purpose it is to promote, stimulate and encourage study, research and writing of the history of sport. Est attendance: 170. For info: Ronald A. Smith, Secy-Treas, NASSH, Box 1026, Lemont, PA 16851. Web: nassh.uwo.ca.

COAST-TO-COAST WALKING RACE: ANNIVERSARY. May 26, 1928. Andrew Payne of Claremore, OK, arrived at New York, NY, on foot and was declared the winner of the first coast-to-coast walking race. Payne had left Los Angeles 573 hours before. He beat 273 other walkers over the 3,422-mile route.

COLLEGE WORLD SERIES (NCAA DIVISION I BASEBALL TOURNAMENT). May 26–28. Regionals at campus sites TBA. For info: NCAA, 6201 College Blvd, Overland Park, KS 66211. Phone: (913) 339-1906.

GRUBSTAKE DAYS. May 26–29. Yucca Valley, CA. Includes parade, carnival, PCRA rodeo, dances, horseshoe tournament, food and community booths, arts and crafts booths and breakfasts offered by local service organizations. Annually, Memorial Day weekend. Est attendance: 20,000. For info: Yucca Valley Chamber of Commerce, 55569 29 Palms Hwy, Yucca Valley, CA 92284. Phone: (760) 365-6323. Fax: (760) 365-0763. E-mail: chamber@yuccavalley.org. Web: www.yuccavalley.org.

HADDIX'S NEAR-PERFECT GAME: ANNIVERSARY. May 26, 1959. Left-hander Harvey Haddix of the Pittsburgh Pirates pitched a perfect game for 12 innings before losing to the Milwaukee Braves, 1–0, in the 13th. In the decisive frame, Braves second baseman Felix Mantilla reached first on a throwing error by third baseman Don Hoak. Eddie Mathews sacrificed Mantilla to second, and Haddix walked Henry Aaron intentionally. Joe Adcock then hit a fly to deep right-center field that just cleared the fence for an apparent home run. Mantilla scored, but Aaron, who thought the ball landed on the field, touched second and headed for the dugout. Adcock kept running and was called out for passing Aaron, negating the home run. For the Braves, Lew Burdette pitched all 13 innings. He gave up 12 hits but got the victory.

MEMORIAL DAY GOLF TOURNAMENT. May 26–28. Pinehurst Golf Course, Pinehurst, ID. Invitational tournament that brings in people from all over the Northwest. Also, long drive competition and horse race. Annually, Memorial Day weekend. For info: Stan Edwards, Pro, Pinehurst Golf Course, PO Box 908/Country Club Ln, Pinehurst, ID 83850. Phone: (208) 682-2013.

NCAA ROWING CHAMPIONSHIPS. May 26–28. Site TBA. For info: NCAA, PO Box 6222, Indianapolis, IN 46206-6222. Phone: (317) 917-6222. Fax: (317) 917-6888. Web: www.ncaa.org.

PETERSBURG CHAMBER OF COMMERCE SALMON DERBY. May 26–29. Petersburg, AK. Four days of fishing with more than $30,000 in prizes awarded. Annually, Memorial Day weekend. Est attendance: 500. For info: Petersburg Chamber of Commerce, PO Box 649, Petersburg, AK 99833. Phone: (907) 772-4636. Fax: (907) 772-3646. Web: www.petersburg.org.

ROSE, MAURI: BIRTH ANNIVERSARY. May 26, 1906. Mauri Rose, auto racer, born at Columbus, OH. Rose ran in 15 straight Indianapolis 500s and won the race in 1941, 1947 and 1948. His success and consistency came despite the part-time nature of his career. His steady employment by a number of auto companies limited the time he could spend practicing and competing. Died at Detroit, MI, Jan 1, 1981.

SPECIAL OLYMPICS GEORGIA SUMMER GAMES. May 26–28. Atlanta, GA. More than 2,000 athletes with mental retardation compete at Emory University in track and field, aquatics, gymnastics, soccer, table tennis, tennis and volleyball. For info: Special Olympics Georgia, Inc, 3772 Pleasantdale Rd, Ste 195, Atlanta, GA 30340. Phone: (770) 414-9390, x114. Fax: (770) 414-9389.

SUMMER CELEBRATION. May 26–29. Florence, AL. Four days filled with sporting events for the entire family. All events focus on summer fun and safety and include ten-

	S	M	T	W	T	F	S
May		1	2	3	4	5	6
2000	7	8	9	10	11	12	13
	14	15	16	17	18	19	20
	21	22	23	24	25	26	27
	28	29	30	31			

nis, golf, Frisbee golf tournament, 5K run, century bike ride, mountain bike race, wave-runner races, BBQ cook-off and Veteran's Memorial Celebration complete with a fireworks show. Est attendance: 10,000. For info: Florence/Lauderdale Tourism, One Hightower Place, Florence, AL 35630. Phone: (256) 740-4141 or (888) FLO-TOUR. Fax: (256) 740-4142. E-mail: dwilson@flo web.com. Web: www.flo-tour.org.

BIRTHDAYS TODAY

Joseph Salvatore (Joe) Altobelli, 68, former baseball manager and player, born Detroit, MI, May 26, 1932.
Jason Phillip Bere, 29, baseball player, born Cambridge, MA, May 26, 1971.
Kevin Curtis Kennedy, 46, broadcaster and former baseball manager, born Los Angeles, CA, May 26, 1954.
Travis Reynolds Lee, 25, baseball player, born San Diego, CA, May 26, 1975.
James Gilbert (Jim) McKean, 55, baseball umpire, born Montreal, Quebec, Canada, May 26, 1945.
Brent Woody Musburger, 61, broadcaster, born Portland, OR, May 26, 1939.

MAY 27 — SATURDAY
Day 148 — 218 Remaining

STANLEY CUP CHAMPIONS THIS DATE
1975	Philadelphia Flyers

AERIAL GOLF: ANNIVERSARY. May 27, 1928. A unique golfing event transpired at the Old Westbury Golf Club at New York. Two-person teams competed in an aerial golf tournament. One member of each team flew above the course in an airplane and dropped a ball as close to each hole as possible. The other team member, on the ground, then putted out. The winning team was William Hammond and M.M. Merrill.

ALABAMA JUBILEE. May 27–29. Point Mallard, Decatur, AL. Hot-air balloon races, arts, crafts, antique cars, water and air shows. Annually, Memorial Day weekend. Est attendance: 100,000. For info: Jacklyn Bailey, Decatur CVB, Box 2349, 719 Sixth Ave SE, Decatur, AL 35602. Phone: (256) 350-2028 or (800) 524-6181. E-mail: dcvb@hiwaay.net.

AMERICAN BOWLING CONGRESS–WOMEN'S INTERNATIONAL BOWLING CONGRESS SENIOR CHAMPIONSHIPS. May 27–28. Reno, NV. For men and women 55 and over who qualify by winning their state and provincial championships in the four age divisions. For info: Bowling, Inc, 5301 S 76th St, Greendale, WI 53129-1127. Phone: (414) 423-3356. Fax: (414) 421-3013.

AMICALOLA FITNESS FESTIVAL. May 27. Dawsonville, GA. On the town square. First race begins at 8 AM. Featuring a fun/run/walk, a 30-mile recreational bicycle ride to Amicalola Falls, a 7K road race, a 7K/15 mile biathlon and a 15-mile bike ride. Ribbons to fun/run/walk and 30-mile bike finishers. Awards in all other categories. All participants receive an event T-shirt and a goody bag. Fees vary from $12 according to event chosen. Benefits the local Chamber of Commerce. Est attendance: 650. For info or an application: Dawson County Chamber of Commerce, PO Box 299, Dawsonville, GA 30534. Phone: (706) 265-6278. Fax: (706) 265-6279. E-mail: info@dawson.org. Web: www.dawson.org.

DEBUT OF OVERSIZED CATCHER'S MITT: ANNIVERSARY. May 27, 1960. Baltimore Orioles catcher Clint Courtney used an oversized mitt for the first time to catch knuckleballer Hoyt Wilhelm in a game against the New York Yankees. The mitt, designed by Orioles manager Paul Richards, was nearly 50 percent larger than a regular catcher's mitt. The Orioles won, 3–2.

ESCAPE FROM ALCATRAZ TRIATHLON. May 27 (tentative). San Francisco, CA. One of the most dramatic triathlons, encompassing a swim in treacherous San Francisco Bay. For info: Event Mgmt, Mktg, Promo, Tri-California Events, Inc, 1284 Adobe Ln, PO Box 51116, Pacific Grove, CA 93950. Phone: (831) 373-0678. Fax: (831) 373-7731. E-mail: events@tricalifornia.com. Web: www.tricalifornia.com.

FARMINGTON INVITATIONAL BALLOON FESTIVAL. May 27–28. Farmington, NM. Hot-air balloons launch off the banks of Farmington Lake. Famous Splash and Dash and Hare and Hound races included in the two-day event. Est attendance: 2,000. For info: Farmington CVB, 3041 E Main, Farmington, NM 87402. Phone: (800) 448-1240 or (505) 326-7602. Fax: (505) 327-0577. E-mail: fmncvb@cyberport.com. Web: www.farmingtonnm.org.

FIRST RUNNING OF PREAKNESS: ANNIVERSARY. May 27, 1873. The first running of the Preakness Stakes at Pimlico Race Track, MD, was won by Survivor with a time of 2:43. The winning jockey was G. Barbee, and the winning owner took one-year possession of the Woodlawn Vase, a trophy created in 1860 by Tiffany and Company. The Preakness was named for the colt that won the Dinner Party Stakes on the day the track opened in 1870. Preakness was shipped to Europe after being purchased by the Duke of Hamilton, who, some time later in a fit of pique, shot the horse dead.

HEAD-OF-THE-MON-RIVER HORSESHOE TOURNAMENT. May 27–29. Fairmont, WV. Open to horseshoe pitchers with a 2000 State/National Horseshoe Pitchers Association membership card. For info: Tri-County Horseshoe Club Dir, Davis "Catfish" Woodward, 1133 Sunset Dr, Fairmont, WV 26554. Phone: (304) 366-3819.

LITTLE 500. May 27. Anderson, IN. This 52nd annual "Granddaddy of all sprint car races" concludes a week-long festival of events in Anderson and serves as an appetizer for the Indianapolis 500 held the next day. Drivers compete for more than $100,000 in prize money in this 500-lap sprint car race. Annually, the day before the Indy 500. Est attendance: 9,000. For info: Anderson Speedway, 1311 Pendleton Ave, Anderson, IN 46011. Phone: (765) 642-0206.

LONE STAR PAPER CHASE. May 27. Amarillo, TX. Marathon, half-marathon, 10K and 10K three-person relay. For info: Lone Star Paper Chase, c/o Amarillo Globe-News, PO Box 2091, Amarillo, TX 79166. Phone: (806) 345-3451 or (800) 692-4052, x3451. E-mail: gtbagwell @amarillonet.com.

MANISTEE COUNTY SPORT FISHING SALMON DERBY. May 27–Sept 4. Manistee, MI. Cash prizes for trout and salmon in summerlong competition. For info: Fred MacDonald, Tournament Coord, Manistee County Sport Fishing Assn, PO Box 98, Manistee, MI 49660. Phone: (616) 723-7975.

MONTREAL AND SAN DIEGO AWARDED FRANCHISES: ANNIVERSARY. May 27, 1968. The National League voted to expand for the first time since 1962 and awarded franchises to Montreal (the first major league team outside the US) and San Diego. The Montreal club was called the Expos. San Diego named its team the Padres.

MORGAN HORSE OPEN BARN. May 27–29. McCulloch Farm, Old Lyme, CT. Newborn foals, young horses in training. Pet the horses. See historic and beautiful McCulloch Farm. 10 AM to 4 PM. Est attendance: 700. For info: McCulloch Farm Whippoorwill Morgans, 100 Whippoorwill Rd, Old Lyme, CT 06371. Phone: (860) 434-7355. Fax: (860) 434-1638.

NCAA DIVISION II BASEBALL TOURNAMENT. May 27–June 3. Finals. Paterson Field, Valdosta State University, Montgomery, AL. For info: NCAA, PO Box 6222, Indianapolis, IN 46206-6222. Phone: (317) 917-6222. Fax: (317) 917-6888. Web: www.ncaa.org.

NCAA MEN'S DIVISION I LACROSSE CHAMPIONSHIP. May 27–29. Finals. Byrd Stadium, University of Maryland, College Park, MD. For info: NCAA, PO Box 6222, Indianapolis, IN 46206-6222. Phone: (317) 917-6222. Fax: (317) 917-6888. Web: www.ncaa.org.

NJCAA DIVISION I BASEBALL CHAMPIONSHIP. May 27–June 3. Sam Suplizio Field, Grand Junction, CO. For info: Sam Suplizio, Tourn Dir, c/o Chamber of Commerce, Grand Junction, CO 81502. Phone: (303) 243-6600. Web: www.njcaa.org.

NJCAA DIVISION II BASEBALL CHAMPIONSHIP. May 27–June 3. Millington USA Stadium, Millington, TN. For info: John Diagle, Tourn Dir, PO Box 429, Millington, TN 38083-0429. Phone: (901) 872-9326. Web: www.njcaa.org.

ROC HILLCLIMB TIME TRAIL BIKE RACE. May 27. Roanoke, VA. 1.87 miles to top of scenic and historic Mill Mountain. Average gradient is 8 percent with 847-foot elevation gain. Sanctioned by USCF. $2,500 cash and omnium. For info: Wendi Schultz, CFE Exec Dir, Roanoke Festival in the Park, PO Box 8276, Roanoke, VA 24014. Phone: (540) 342-2640. Web: www.tourdfestival.com.

BIRTHDAYS TODAY

Jeffrey Robert (Jeff) Bagwell, 32, baseball player, born Boston, MA, May 27, 1968.

Pat Cash, 35, tennis player, born Melbourne, Australia, May 27, 1965.

Terry Lee Collins, 51, baseball manager, born Midland, MI, May 27, 1949.

Antonio Michael Freeman, 28, football player, born Baltimore, MD, May 27, 1972.

Todd Randolph Hundley, 31, baseball player, born Martinsville, VA, May 27, 1969.

John Emile Jaha, 34, baseball player, born Portland, OR, May 27, 1966.

Darrell A. Russell, 24, football player, born Pensacola, FL, May 27, 1976.

Ray Sheppard, 34, hockey player, born Pembroke, Ontario, Canada, May 27, 1966.

Samuel Jackson (Sam) Snead, 88, golfer, born Hot Springs, VA, May 27, 1912.

May 2000

S	M	T	W	T	F	S
	1	2	3	4	5	6
7	8	9	10	11	12	13
14	15	16	17	18	19	20
21	22	23	24	25	26	27
28	29	30	31			

Frank Edward Thomas, 32, baseball player, born Columbus, GA, May 27, 1968.

Jeffery Douglas (Doug) West, 33, basketball player, born Altoona, PA, May 27, 1967.

MAY 28 — SUNDAY
Day 149 — 217 Remaining

CHASE'S SPORTSQUOTE OF THE DAY
"Sir, you are the greatest athlete in the world."—King Gustav V of Sweden to Jim Thorpe

AMERICAN LEAGUE DIVIDES INTO TWO DIVISIONS: ANNIVERSARY. May 28, 1968. The American League announced that it would split into two divisions for the 1969 season. Teams in the AL East included the Baltimore Orioles, the Boston Red Sox, the Cleveland Indians, the Detroit Tigers, the New York Yankees and the Washington Senators. The AL West was made up of the California Angels, the Chicago White Sox, the Kansas City Royals, the Minnesota Twins, the Oakland Athletics and the Seattle Pilots.

CARDINAL BICYCLE ROAD RACE. May 28. Roanoke, VA. USCF sanctioned. 110 miles of rolling terrain with two climbs of 2,200 feet. $3,200 in cash prizes. For info: Roanoke Festival in the Park, PO Box 8276, Roanoke, VA 24014. Phone: (540) 342-2640. Web: www.rev.net/festival.

GILES, WARREN: BIRTH ANNIVERSARY. May 28, 1896. Warren Crandall Giles, Baseball Hall of Fame executive, born at Tiskilwa, IL. Giles began his baseball career as a minor league team executive. He became general manager of the Cincinnati Reds and president of the National League. Inducted into the Hall of Fame in 1979. Died at Cincinnati, OH, Feb 7, 1979.

HEROES MADISON MARATHON. May 28. Madison, WI. 5th annual. For info: Heroes Madison Marathon, 10 Birchwood Circle, Madison, WI 53704. Phone: (608) 256-9922. E-mail: info@madison-marathon.com. Web: madison-marathon.com.

HERSHBERGER, WILLARD: 90th BIRTH ANNIVERSARY. May 28, 1910. Willard McKee Hershberger, baseball player, born at Lemon Cave, CA. Hershberger, a catcher, committed suicide during the 1940 season. Died at Boston, MA, Aug 3, 1940.

INDIANAPOLIS 500. May 28. Indianapolis, IN. Recognized as the world's largest single-day sporting event. First race was in 1911. Annually, the Sunday of Memorial Day weekend. Est attendance: 400,000. For info: Indianapolis Motor Speedway Corp, 4790 W 16th St, Indianapolis, IN 46222. Phone: (317) 481-8500. Web: www.indy500.com.

ITALY: PALIO DEI BALESTRIERI. May 28. Gubbio, Italy. The last Sunday in May is set aside for a medieval crossbow contest between Gubbio and Saensepolcro; medieval costumes, arms.

KEY BANK VERMONT CITY MARATHON. May 28. Burlington, VT. Marathon and marathon relay. 12th annual. 5,000 runners. Annually, the Sunday before Memorial Day. For info: Andrea Riha, Key Bank Vermont City Marathon, PO Box 152, Burlington, VT 05402. Phone: (802) 863-8412. E-mail: runvt@together.net. Web: www.vcm.org.

NCAA MEN'S DIVISION III LACROSSE CHAMPIONSHIP. May 28. Byrd Stadium, University of Maryland, College Park, MD. For info: NCAA, PO Box 6222, Indianapolis, IN 46206-6222. Phone: (317) 917-6222. Fax: (317) 917-6888. Web: www.ncaa.org.

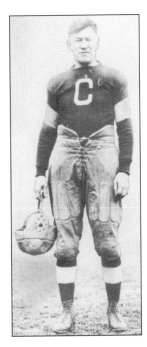

THORPE, JIM: BIRTH ANNIVERSARY. May 28, 1888. James Francis (Jim) Thorpe, Olympic gold medal track athlete, baseball player and football player, born at Prague, OK. Thorpe, a Native American, won the pentathlon and the decathlon at the 1912 Olympic games but later lost his medals when Olympic officials declared a stint as a minor league baseball player besmirched his amateur standing. He later played professional baseball and football and was acclaimed the greatest male athlete of the first half of the 20th century. Died at Lomita, CA, Mar 28, 1953. (Thorpe's medals were returned to his family many years after his death when the earlier decision was reversed.)

WYOMING MARATHON. May 28. Laramie, WY. Marathon and half-marathon plus the Rocky Mountain Double Marathon (52.4 miles). For info: Cheyenne Track Club, 402 W 31st St, Cheyenne, WY 82001. Phone: (307) 635-3316. Fax: (307) 635-5297. E-mail: RunWyo26point2 @compuserve.com.

BIRTHDAYS TODAY

Kirk Harold Gibson, 43, former baseball player, born Pontiac, MI, May 28, 1957.
Armen Louis Gilliam, 36, basketball player, born Pittsburgh, PA, May 28, 1964.
Damian G. Rhodes, 31, hockey player, born St. Paul, MN, May 28, 1969.
Glen Anthony Rice, 33, basketball player, born Flint, MI, May 28, 1967.
Eugene Keefe Robinson, 37, football player, born Hartford, CT, May 28, 1963.
Jerry Alan West, 62, basketball executive, former coach and Basketball Hall of Fame guard, born Cheylan, WV, May 28, 1938.
Ronald Lawrence (Ron) Wilson, 45, hockey coach, born Windsor, Ontario, Canada, May 28, 1955.

MAY 29 — MONDAY
Day 150 — 216 Remaining

BOLDER BOULDER 10K. May 29. Boulder, CO. A 10K race of runners, walkers and elite international teams through the streets of Boulder. Annually, on Memorial Day. Est attendance: 40,000. For info: Cliff Bosley, Bolder Boulder, PO Box 9125, Boulder, CO 80301-9125. Phone: (303) 444-7223. E-mail: cbosley@bolderboulder.com.

COURT DECLARES BASEBALL A SPORT: ANNIVERSARY. May 29, 1922. The Supreme Court, in a decision written by Justice Oliver Wendell Holmes, declared that baseball "would not be called trade or commerce in the commonly accepted use of those words." The court rejected the suit of the Baltimore Federal League club that wanted baseball made subject to federal antitrust legislation and interstate commerce regulation.

ENGLAND: ISLE OF MAN TT MOTORCYCLE RACES. May 29–June 9. Isle of Man. World-famous motorcycle road races held over a 38-mile course. Practice sessions precede the race days. Est attendance: 40,000. For info: Road Race Dept, Auto Cycle Union, Wood St, Rugby, Warwickshire, England, CV21 2YX.

FOYT WINS FOURTH INDY 500: ANNIVERSARY. May 29, 1977. A.J. Foyt became the first driver to win four Indianapolis 500s, but he had to share headlines with Janet Guthrie, the first woman to drive in the famous race. Foyt won his first Indy in 1961 and repeated in 1964 and 1967. Guthrie was forced out of the race after 27 laps because of mechanical problems.

HENDERSON BREAKS COBB'S RECORD: 10th ANNIVERSARY. May 29, 1990. Rickey Henderson of the Oakland A's stole the 893rd base of his career, thereby breaking Ty Cobb's American League record, in a game against the Toronto Blue Jays.

HORSES FLY COAST TO COAST: ANNIVERSARY. May 29, 1946. Chakoora and Uleta, a pair of two-year-old fillies, became the first Thoroughbreds to complete a transcontinental airplane trip. They flew from New York to California, a voyage that lasted 20 hours because of bad weather.

MEMORIAL DAY. May 29. Legal public holiday. (PL90–363 sets Memorial Day on the last Monday in May. Applicable to federal employees and District of Columbia.) Also known as Decoration Day. Most countries designate a day each year for decorating graves with flowers and for other memorial tributes to the dead. Especially an occasion for honoring those who have died in battle. (Observance dates from Civil War years in US: first documented observance at Waterloo, NY, May 5, 1865.) Memorial Day is a traditional day for picnics and recreational activities of all kinds.

☆   ☆   ☆

MOUNT EVEREST CONQUERED: ANNIVERSARY. May 29, 1953. Mt Everest, the highest mountain in the world, was conquered for the first time by New Zealander Edmund Hillary and Tenzing Norgay, a Sherpa guide.

NORTHERN LEAGUE INDEPENDENT PROFESSIONAL BASEBALL SEASON. May 29–Aug 31. An 86-games-per-team schedule that will be played in St. Paul, MN; Duluth, MN; Fargo, ND; Sioux City, IA; Madison, WI; Sioux Falls, SD; Winnipeg, MB and Schaumburg, IL. Est attendance: 1,000,000. For info: Northern League, Inc, PO Box 1282, Durham, NC 27702. Phone: (919) 956-8150. Fax: (919) 683-2693. E-mail: northernlg @earthlink.net. Web: www.northernleague.com.

SATURN FESTIVAL CUP BIKE RACE. May 29. Roanoke, VA. Sanctioned by USCF. $14,500 cash including prizes and omnium. Free race clinic available. Call for application. For info: Roanoke Festival in the Park, PO Box 8276, Roanoke, VA 24014. Phone: (540) 342-2640. Web: www.tourdfestival.com.

SOCCER TRAGEDY: 15th ANNIVERSARY. May 29, 1985. A riot at Heysel soccer stadium at Brussels, Belgium, killed 39 people. Fans attending the European Cup Final, between Liverpool and Juventus of Turin, clashed before the match started. Some 400 persons were injured in the riot. The incident was televised and viewed by millions throughout Europe. More than two years later, Sept 2, 1987, the British government announced that 26 British soccer fans (identified from television tapes) would be extradited to Belgium for trial. Hooliganism at soccer matches became the target of increased security measures for most of England's more than 90 professional teams following the tragedy.

TOUR OF SOMERVILLE. May 29. Somerville, NJ. The oldest continuously run major bicycle race in America. 2000 marks the 59th running. Attracts more than 600 top amateur cyclists for seven events. Annually, on Memorial Day. Est attendance: 40,000. For info: Dan Puntillo, Admin, 98 Grove St, Somerville, NJ 08876. Phone: (908) 725-7223. Fax: (908) 722-5411. E-mail: tourdeville@aol.com. Web: www.tourofsomerville.org.

ZALE, TONY: BIRTH ANNIVERSARY. May 29, 1913. Tony Zale, boxer, born Anthony Florian Zaleski at Gary, IN. Zale, known as the Man of Steel, won the middleweight title in 1941 from George Abrams. After WWII, he engaged in three classic bouts with Rocky Graziano, winning the first and the third and losing the second. He lost the title to Marcel Cerdan and was inducted into the International Boxing Hall of Fame in 1991. Died at Portage, IN, Mar 20, 1997.

BIRTHDAYS TODAY

Jason Allison, 25, hockey player, born Toronto, Ontario, Canada, May 29, 1975.

Eric Keith Davis, 38, baseball player, born Los Angeles, CA, May 29, 1962.

Ferris Roy Fain, 79, former baseball player, born San Antonio, TX, May 29, 1921.

Charles Dewayne (Charlie) Hayes, 35, baseball player, born Hattiesburg, MS, May 29, 1965.

Leslie Townes ("Bob") Hope, 97, golf tournament sponsor, born Eltham, England, May 29, 1903.

Mike Keane, 33, hockey player, born Winnipeg, Manitoba, Canada, May 29, 1967.

Raef Andrew LaFrentz, 24, basketball player, born Hampton, IA, May 29, 1976.

Bill Risley, 33, baseball player, born Chicago, IL, May 29, 1967.

Ken Schrader, 45, auto racer, born St. Louis, MO, May 29, 1955.

Alfred (Al) Unser, Sr, 61, former auto racer, born Albuquerque, NM, May 29, 1939.

Francis Thomas (Fay) Vincent, Jr, 62, former commissioner of baseball, born Waterbury, CT, May 29, 1938.

May *2000*	S	M	T	W	T	F	S
		1	2	3	4	5	6
	7	8	9	10	11	12	13
	14	15	16	17	18	19	20
	21	22	23	24	25	26	27
	28	29	30	31			

MAY 30 — TUESDAY
Day 151 — 215 Remaining

STANLEY CUP CHAMPIONS THIS DATE

1985	Edmonton Oilers

COONEY MAKES UNASSISTED TRIPLE PLAY: ANNIVERSARY. May 30, 1927. Shortstop Jimmy Cooney of the Chicago Cubs completed baseball's sixth unassisted triple play in a morning game against the Pittsburgh Pirates. In the fourth inning, Cooney caught Paul Waner's line drive, stepped on second to double off Lloyd Waner and tagged Clyde Barnhart, running from first to second.

DONLIN, TURKEY MIKE: BIRTH ANNIVERSARY. May 30, 1878. Michael Joseph ("Turkey Mike") Donlin, baseball player, born at Peoria, IL. Donlin enjoyed a 12-year career, checkered by injuries and controversies. He fancied himself a vaudeville star and made a few movies after his retirement. Died at Hollywood, CA, Sept 24, 1933.

LOWE HITS FOUR HOME RUNS: ANNIVERSARY. May 30, 1894. Bobby Lowe of the Boston Beaneaters became the first player in major league history to hit four home runs in a single game. Boston beat Cincinnati, 20–11, and all Lowe's homers came off Elton ("Icebox") Chamberlain.

METCALFE, RALPH: 90th BIRTH ANNIVERSARY. May 30, 1910. Ralph Harold Metcalfe, Olympic gold medal sprinter, born at Atlanta, GA. Metcalfe set world records in the 100 yards, 100 meters and 200 meters between 1932 and 1936. At the 1936 Berlin Olympics he finished second to Jesse Owens in the 100 meters and won a gold medal as a member of the 400-meter relay team. After WWII, Metcalfe was active in Chicago politics and served four terms in the US House of Representatives. Died at Chicago, IL, Oct 10, 1978.

NCAA MEN'S DIVISION I GOLF CHAMPIONSHIPS. May 30–June 2. Finals. Lake Course at the Grand National Golf Club, Opelika, AL. For info: NCAA, PO Box 6222, Indianapolis, IN 46206-6222. Phone: (317) 917-6222. Fax: (317) 917-6888. Web: www.ncaa.org.

RAY HARROUN WINS FIRST INDIANAPOLIS 500: ANNIVERSARY. May 30, 1911. Ray Harroun won the first running of the Indianapolis 500 in 6 hours, 42 minutes and 8 seconds. Harroun started from the 28th position and averaged 74.602 miles per hour.

STOPPING FOR CHICKEN: ANNIVERSARY. May 30, 1912. During the second running of the Indianapolis 500, driver Ralph Mulford was told he would have to finish the race to collect 10th-place money. Mulford did so, but it took him 8 hours, 53 minutes, more than 2½ hours longer than the winner. He stopped for fried chicken several times along the way, and the rule was changed the following year.

BIRTHDAYS TODAY

Allen Ray Aldridge, 28, football player, born Houston, TX, May 30, 1972.

Peter J. (P.J.) Carlesimo, 51, basketball coach and former player, born Scranton, PA, May 30, 1949.

Dana Andrew DeMuth, 44, baseball umpire, born Fremont, OH, May 30, 1956.

Omar Joseph ("Turk") Lown, 76, former baseball player, born New York, NY, May 30, 1924.

Michael Lee (Mike) Oquist, 32, baseball player, born La Junta, CO, May 30, 1968.

Manuel Aristides (Manny) Ramirez, 28, baseball player, born Santo Domingo, Dominican Republic, May 30, 1972.

Gale Eugene Sayers, 57, Pro Football Hall of Fame running back, born Wichita, KS, May 30, 1943.

Jiri Slegr, 29, hockey player, born Litvinov, Czechoslovakia, May 30, 1971.

MAY 31 — WEDNESDAY

Day 152 — 214 Remaining

NBA FINALS CHAMPIONS THIS DATE

1983   Philadelphia 76ers

CANADA: THE NATIONAL TOURNAMENT. May 31–June 4. Spruce Meadows, Calgary, Alberta. The National Tournament features the Canadian Show Jumping Championship, including the Canadian Pacific World Cup and the Shell Cup. Enjoy country atmosphere in the Spruce Meadows Marketplace on the Plaza. Live entertainment and activities daily. Est attendance: 85,000. For info: Spruce Meadows, RR #9, Calgary, AB, Canada T2J 5G5. Phone: (403) 974-4200. Fax: (403) 947-4270. E-mail: smeadows@telusplanet.net. Web: www.sprucemeadows.com.

COLLEGE FOOTBALL ASSOCIATION DISBANDED: ANNIVERSARY. May 31, 1996. The College Football Association (CFA), an organization and lobbying group that broke the NCAA's power to negotiate college football television contracts on an exclusive basis, voted itself out of existence. The CFA began in 1977 and ceased to exist on June 30, 1997.

HUBBELL'S STREAK ENDS: ANNIVERSARY. May 31, 1937. The Brooklyn Dodgers defeated pitcher Carl Hubbell and the New York Giants, 10–3, snapping Hubbell's winning streak at 24 games, a major league record. Hubbell's previous defeat had occurred on July 13, 1936. He finished that year with 16 straight wins and won 8 more in 1937 before losing to the Dodgers.

LONGEST DOUBLEHEADER: ANNIVERSARY. May 31, 1964. The New York Mets and the San Francisco Giants played the longest doubleheader by time in major league history, the two games consuming 9 hours, 52 minutes. The Giants won the first game in ordinary fashion, Juan Marichal beating the Mets, 5–3, in nine innings. But the second game went 23 innings and lasted 7:23 (a National League record) before the Giants emerged victorious, 8–6, on run-scoring hits by Del Crandall and Felipe Alou. 57,037 fans were on hand when the day began.

NATIONAL SENIOR HEALTH AND FITNESS DAY. May 31. Local sites in all 50 states. 7th annual event to promote the value of fitness and exercise for older adults. During this day—as part of Older Americans Month activities—seniors across the country are involved in organized health promotion activities. Annually, last Wednesday in May. For info: Tina Godin, Program Coord, Mature Market Resource Center, 621 E Park Ave, Libertyville, IL 60048. Phone: (800) 828-8225. Fax: (847) 816-8662. E-mail: maturemkt@aol.com. Web: www.fitnessday.com.

NCAA MEN'S AND WOMEN'S DIVISION I OUTDOOR TRACK AND FIELD CHAMPIONSHIPS. May 31–June 3. Finals. Duke University, Durham, NC. For info: NCAA, PO Box 6222, Indianapolis, IN 46206-6222. Phone: (317) 917-6222. Fax: (317) 917-6888. Web: www.ncaa.org.

NEUN MAKES UNASSISTED TRIPLE PLAY: ANNIVERSARY. May 31, 1927. One day after Jimmy Cooney made an unassisted triple play, Detroit Tigers first baseman Johnny Neun notched his own, the seventh in major league history. In the ninth inning of a game against the Cleveland Indians, Neun caught a line drive hit by Homer Summa, tagged Charlie Jamieson between first and second and then ran to second base to triple off Glenn Myatt. The triple play ended the game with the Tigers ahead, 1–0.

RUTH'S FINAL AT BAT: 65th ANNIVERSARY. May 30, 1935. Babe Ruth of the Boston Braves grounded out in his final major league at bat against pitcher Jim Bivin of the Philadelphia Phillies.

SPECIAL OLYMPICS NEBRASKA SUMMER GAMES. May 31–June 3. Omaha, NE. At Creighton University and other venues throughout Omaha. Events include speed skating, diving, aquatics, gymnastics, power lifting, bowling, volleyball and track and field. For info: Special Olympics Nebraska, 8801 F St, Omaha, NE 68127. Phone: (402) 331-5545. Fax: (402) 331-5964. E-mail: sonesn@aol.com. Web: www.sone.org.

WHITMAN, WALT: BIRTH ANNIVERSARY. May 31, 1819. Walter (Walt) Whitman, poet and journalist, born at West Hills, NY. Following a short-lived and largely unsuccessful career in journalism, Whitman in 1855 published the collection of poetry for which he is now most famous, *Leaves of Grass*. Among his many interests was baseball, of which he said, "I see great things in baseball. It's our game, the American game." Died at Camden, NJ, Mar 26, 1892.

STANLEY CUP CHAMPIONS THIS DATE

1987   Edmonton Oilers

BIRTHDAYS TODAY

Jim Carey, 26, hockey player, born Dorchester, MA, May 31, 1974.

Matthew Joseph (Matt) Harpring, 24, basketball player, born Cincinnati, OH, May 31, 1976.

Kenneth (Kenny) Lofton, 33, baseball player, born East Chicago, IL, May 31, 1967.

Felix Anthony ("Tippy") Martinez, 50, former baseball player, born La Junta, CO, May 31, 1950.

Joseph William (Joe) Namath, 57, Pro Football Hall of Fame quarterback, born Beaver Falls, PA, May 31, 1943.

Jeff Odgers, 31, hockey player, born Spy Hill, Saskatchewan, Canada, May 31, 1969.

Joseph Michael (Joe) Orsulak, 38, baseball player, born Glen Ridge, NJ, May 31, 1962.

Ray Clark Washburn, 62, former baseball player, born Pasco, WA, May 31, 1938.

JUNE 1 — THURSDAY
Day 153 — 213 Remaining

NBA FINALS CHAMPIONS THIS DATE
1979   Seattle Supersonics

AMECHE, ALAN: BIRTH ANNIVERSARY. June 1, 1933. Alan Dante ("The Horse") Ameche, Heisman Trophy fullback, born at Kenosha, WI. Ameche played at the University of Wisconsin and won the Heisman in 1954. He turned pro with the Baltimore Colts and was named NFL Rookie of the Year. His most famous moment occurred in the 1958 NFL title game against the New York Giants. The game went into overtime, and Ameche scored the winning touchdown. Died at Houston, TX, Aug 8, 1988.

ASSAULT WINS TRIPLE CROWN: ANNIVERSARY. June 1, 1946. Assault, ridden by Warren Mehrtens, won the Belmont Stakes to become the seventh horse to win the Triple Crown. Owned by the King Ranch, Assault covered the 1½ miles in 2:30.4, defeating Natchez.

BAILEY OUTRACES JOHNSON: ANNIVERSARY. June 1, 1997. Canadian sprinter Donovan Bailey won a special 150-meter match race against American Michael Johnson to reassert his claim to the title of the "World's Fastest Human." After Bailey had won the 100 meters at the 1996 Summer Olympics and Johnson had won the 200 meters and the 400 meters, the two engaged in a nasty bragging-rights battle. This special race was supposed to put an end to their flap. But the race at Toronto proved inconclusive as Johnson, well behind at the halfway point, pulled up short, claiming that he had injured his left quadriceps.

BRADLEY WINS ALL FOUR MAJORS: ANNIVERSARY. June 1, 1986. Pat Bradley won the LPGA Championship by one stroke over Patty Sheehan to become the first golfer to win all four women's major championships. Bradley won the du Maurier Classic in 1980 and 1986, the US Open in 1981 and the Dinah Shore in 1986. She was inducted into the LPGA Hall of Fame in 1991.

EVERETT SALTY SEA DAYS. June 1–4. Everett, WA. Family events to celebrate Everett's beauty, carnival, food, novelty and commercial booths, arts and crafts, live entertainment, fireworks, classic car show, limited hydro races, Hawaiian outrigger races, sanctioned soap box racing and various nautical events. Sponsor: City of Everett, Dwayne Lane. Est attendance: 100,000. For info: Marion Pope, Exec Dir, Salty Sea Days Assn, 2520 Colby Ave, Ste 101, Everett, WA 98201. Phone: (425) 339-1113. Fax: (425) 259-0131. E-mail: saltysea@aol.com. Web: www.saltyseadays.org.

GEHRIG BEGINS STREAK: 75th ANNIVERSARY. June 1, 1925. Lou Gehrig of the New York Yankees pinch-hit for Paul ("Pee Wee") Wanninger in the eighth inning to commence his streak of 2,130 consecutive games played. On the following day, Gehrig started at first base in place of Wally Pipp and remained in the lineup until May 2, 1939. Ironically, Wanninger had replaced Everett Scott as the Yankees regular shortstop on May 5, thereby ending Scott's string of 1,307 consecutive games played, the mark that Gehrig would surpass.

LICKING PRCA RODEO. June 1–3. Licking, MO. PRCA Rodeo. Annually, the weekend after Memorial Day. Est attendance: 9,000. For info: Vicki Peterson, Mktg, Licking Chamber of Commerce, PO Box 336, Licking, MO 65542. Phone: (573) 674-2510.

NIEKRO BROTHERS THE WINNINGEST: ANNIVERSARY. June 1, 1987. Phil Niekro pitched the Cleveland Indians to a 9–6 victory over the Detroit Tigers to put himself and his brother Joe into the lead as the winningest brothers in major league pitching history. Their 530 combined victories surpassed Gaylord and Jim Perry. The Niekros ended their careers with 539 wins, 318 by Phil and 221 by Joe.

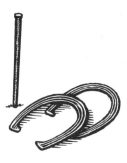

PORTLAND ROSE FESTIVAL. June 1–25. Portland, OR. Celebration includes more than 70 events featuring a grand floral parade, a top juried arts festival, auto races, a carnival, an air show and Navy ship visits. Est attendance: 2,000,000. For info: Portland Rose Festival Assn, 220 NW Second Ave, Portland, OR 97209. Phone: (503) 227-2681. Fax: (503) 227-6603. E-mail: info@rosefestival.org. Web: www.rosefestival.org.

June
2000

S	M	T	W	T	F	S
				1	2	3
4	5	6	7	8	9	10
11	12	13	14	15	16	17
18	19	20	21	22	23	24
25	26	27	28	29	30	

SPECIAL OLYMPICS MICHIGAN STATE SUMMER GAMES. June 1–4. Mt Pleasant, MI. Olympic-style competition for children and adults with mental retardation. For info: Special Olympics Michigan, Central Michigan Univ, Mt Pleasant, MI 48859. Phone: (800) 644-6404. Fax: (517) 774-3034. E-mail: M.K.Lindberg@cmich.edu. Web: www.somi.org.

STANLEY CUP CHAMPIONS THIS DATE

1992   Pittsburgh Penguins

BIRTHDAYS TODAY

Murray D. Baron, 33, hockey player, born Prince George, British Columbia, Canada, June 1, 1967.

Larry E. Centers, 32, football player, born Tatum, TX, June 1, 1968.

Paul Douglas Coffey, 39, hockey player, born Weston, Ontario, Canada, June 1, 1961.

Jeff Hackett, 32, hockey player, born London, Ontario, Canada, June 1, 1968.

Cecil Randolph (Randy) Hundley, 58, former baseball player, born Martinsville, VA, June 1, 1942.

Alexi Lalas, 30, soccer player, born Birmingham, MI, June 1, 1970.

JUNE 2 — FRIDAY

Day 154 — 212 Remaining

ACES ON THREE STRAIGHT DAYS: ANNIVERSARY. June 2, 1974. Golfer Robert Taylor, playing a course at Norfolk, England, aced the same hole for the third consecutive day.

BLACK HILLS BICYCLE TREK CLASSIC. June 2–4 (tentative). Black Hills, SD. Two-day organized ride in the Black Hills. Lodging and meals are provided, along with snacks and rest stops. Riders can pick options to meet their riding level. For info: Kathleen W. Sweere, American Lung Assn of South Dakota, 1212 W Elkhorn St, Ste 1, Sioux Falls, SD 57104. Phone: (800) 873-5864. Fax: (605) 336-7227. E-mail: lung@americanlungsd.org.

CALIFORNIA SENIOR GAMES SACRAMENTO. June 2–4. Sacramento, CA. Athletic competition for men and women age 50 and older. Compete in five-year age divisions. 21 sports. Est attendance: 1,000. For info: Kitty Esposto, Coord, 6005 Folsom Blvd, Sacramento, CA 95819. Phone: (916) 277-6094. Fax: (916) 277-6155.

CENTRALIA ANCHOR FESTIVAL. June 2–4. Centralia City Square, Centralia, MO. This family festival has special events which include a fun run, 3-on-3 basketball, archery shoot, crafts, car show and free entertainment. Annually, the first weekend after Memorial Day. Est attendance: 25,000. For info: Centralia Chamber of Commerce, PO Box 235, Centralia, MO 65240. Phone: (573) 682-2272. Fax: (573) 682-1111.

COLLEGE WORLD SERIES (NCAA DIVISION I BASEBALL TOURNAMENT). June 2–4. Super-regionals. Sites TBA. For info: NCAA, 6201 College Blvd, Overland Park, KS 66211. Phone: (913) 339-1906.

FESTIVAL SOFTBALL TOURNAMENT. June 2–4. Roanoke and Salem, VA. 8th annual USSSA-sanctioned tournament includes double-elimination competition for men's teams and round robin for women's teams. Divisional/state berths awarded in all divisions. Call for registration and fees. For info: Roanoke Festival in the Park, PO Box 8276, Roanoke, VA 24014. Phone: (540) 342-2640. Web: www.rev.net/festival.

GAME DELAYED BY GNATS: ANNIVERSARY. June 2, 1959. The game between the Baltimore Orioles and the Chicago White Sox at Comiskey Park was delayed for nearly half an hour as swarms of gnats invaded the field. Bug spray and torches did not disperse the gnats, but a smoke bomb, set to be used as part of a postgame fireworks display, did. The Orioles won, 3–2.

KENNETT KIWANIS RODEO. June 2–4. Delta Fairgrounds, Kennett, MO. Largest cash-paying rodeo in the area. For info: Kennett Kiwanis Club, 1704 Allison, Kennett, MO 63857.

KNIM RADIO'S BIG FISH. June 2–3. Nodaway Lake, Maryville, MO. The world's largest free fishing contest attracts hundreds of fishermen from a wide area. Participants in this 20th annual 18-hour contest compete for thousands of dollars in prizes, including a grand-prize boat, motor and trailer. Est attendance: 2,000. For info: KNIM Radio, 1618 S Main, PO Box 278, Maryville, MO 64468. Phone: (660) 582-2151. Fax: (660) 582-3211. E-mail: knim@maryville.heartland.net. Web: www.maryville.heartland.net/knim.

LAKE CHAMPLAIN BALLOON FESTIVAL. June 2–4. Addison County Field Days, New Haven, VT. Fifty hot-air balloons, including spectacular special shapes, will participate in five scheduled launches. Also a juried arts and crafts show, and an "evening Balloon Glow." 11th annual. Est attendance: 77,000. For info: Lake Champlain Balloon and Craft Festival, PO Box 115, Charlotte, VT 05445-0115. Phone: (802) 425-4884. Fax: (802) 425-4884. E-mail: lcbf@together.net. Web: www-balloonfest.together.com.

NJCAA MEN'S AND WOMEN'S INVITATIONAL MARATHON CHAMPIONSHIP. June 2. Lansing, MI. For info: Richard Mull, Tourn Dir, Lansing Community College, 419 N Capitol Ave, Lansing, MI 48901-7210. Phone: (517) 483-1625. Fax: (517) 483-1652. Web: www.njcaa.org.

ROBINSON, WILBERT: BIRTH ANNIVERSARY. June 2, 1863. Wilbert Robinson, Baseball Hall of Fame manager and catcher, born at Bolton, MA. Robinson was an outstanding catcher in the 19th century, especially for the great Baltimore Orioles teams of the 1890s. He managed the Brooklyn Dodgers during their inept 1920s. Inducted into the Hall of Fame in 1945. Died at Atlanta, GA, Aug 8, 1934.

RUTH RETIRES: 65th ANNIVERSARY. June 2, 1935. Three days after he benched himself from his last game (May 30), George Herman ("Babe") Ruth announced his retirement from major league baseball.

SPECIAL OLYMPICS COLORADO SUMMER GAMES. June 2–4. Site TBA. Multisport competition for athletes with mental retardation. For info: Colorado Special Olympics, 600 17th St, Ste 910, Denver, CO 80202. Phone: (303) 592-1361. Fax: (303) 592-1364.

SPECIAL OLYMPICS KANSAS STATE SUMMER GAMES. June 2–4. Wichita, KS. Olympic-style competition for children and adults with mental retardation in track and field, aquatics, cycling, gymnastics and power lifting. For info: Special Olympics Kansas, 5280 Foxridge Dr, Mission, KS 66202. Phone: (913) 236-9290. Fax: (913) 236-9771. E-mail: rehdert@ksso.org. Web: www.ksso.org.

WEISSMULLER, JOHNNY: BIRTH ANNIVERSARY.
June 2, 1904. Peter John (Johnny) Weissmuller, actor and Olympic gold medal swimmer, born at Windber, PA. Weissmuller won three gold medals at the 1924 Olympics and two more at the 1928 games. He set 24 world records and in 1950 was voted the best swimmer of the first half of the 20th century. After retiring from amateur competition, he appeared as Tarzan in a dozen movies and as "Jungle Jim" in the movies and on television. Died at Acapulco, Mexico, Jan 20, 1984.

BIRTHDAYS TODAY

Kurt Thomas Abbott, 31, baseball player, born Zanesville, OH, June 2, 1969.

Dontae' Antijuaine Jones, 25, basketball player, born Nashville, TN, June 2, 1975.

Michael Raymond (Mike) Kelly, 30, baseball player, born Los Angeles, CA, June 2, 1970.

Eugene Richard (Gene) Michael, 62, former baseball executive and player, born Kent, OH, June 2, 1938.

Kyle Petty, 40, auto racer, born Randleman, NC, June 2, 1960.

Larry Clark Robinson, 49, former hockey coach and Hockey Hall of Fame defenseman, born Winchester, Ontario, Canada, June 2, 1951.

Craig Robert Stadler, 47, golfer, born San Diego, CA, June 2, 1953.

William Michael (Mike) Stanton, 33, baseball player, born Houston, TX, June 2, 1967.

Garabed Sarkis (Garo) Yepremian, 56, former football player, born Larnaca, Cyprus, June 2, 1944.

JUNE 3 — SATURDAY
Day 155 — 211 Remaining

AEP/FESTIVAL CLASSIC RUN. June 3. Roanoke, VA. Annual festival 5K and 10K races. Call for registration fees and deadlines. Trophies and medals awarded at After Race celebration along with expo, food, beverages and music. T-shirt included in fee. For info: Roanoke Festival

	S	M	T	W	T	F	S
June					1	2	3
2000	4	5	6	7	8	9	10
	11	12	13	14	15	16	17
	18	19	20	21	22	23	24
	25	26	27	28	29	30	

in the Park, PO Box 8276, Roanoke, VA 24014. Phone: (540) 342-2640. Web: www.rev.net/festival.

BUFFALO DAYS CELEBRATION (WITH BUFFALO–CHIP THROWING). June 3. Luverne, MN. Parade, Arts in the Park and unique buffalo-chip throwing contest. Annually, the first Saturday in June. Est attendance: 8,000. For info: Dave Smith, Exec Dir, Luverne Area Chamber of Commerce, 102 E Main, Luverne, MN 56156. Phone: (507) 283-4061. Fax: (507) 283-4061. E-mail: chamber@rconnect.com.

COLLINS GETS 3,000th HIT: 75th ANNIVERSARY. June 3, 1925. Second baseman Eddie Collins of the Chicago White Sox got the 3,000th hit of his career, a single off Harry ("Rip") Collins of the Detroit Tigers. Chicago won the game, 12–7. Collins finished his career with 3,309 hits and was inducted into the Hall of Fame in 1939.

ENGLAND: VODAFONE DERBY AT EPSOM. June 3. Epsom Racecourse, Epsom, Surrey. "The most famous and prestigious horse race in the world was devised at a noble dinner party in 1779 and named after one of the diners—Lord Derby." Note: The Derby is followed by the Coronation Cup and the Vodafone Oaks Stakes, all at Epsom Racecourse. Est attendance: 100,000. For info: United Racecourses Ltd, Racecourse Paddock, Epsom Downs, Surrey, England KT18 5LQ. Web: www.epsom derby.co.uk.

FIRST BASEBALL UNIFORMS: ANNIVERSARY. June 3, 1851. The Knickerbocker Base Ball Club of New York City donned the sport's first uniforms: straw hats, blue full-length trousers and white shirts.

FISHING HAS NO BOUNDARIES—THERMOPOLIS. June 3–4. Boysen Reservoir, Thermopolis, WY. A three-day fishing experience for disabled persons. Any disability, age, sex, race, etc, eligible. Fishing with experienced guides, attended by 80 participants and 100 volunteers. Annually, the first full weekend in June. For info: Fishing Has No Boundaries, HSC Chamber of Commerce, Box 768, Thermopolis, WY 82443. Phone: (307) 864-3192 or (800) 786-6772. Fax: (307) 864-9463. E-mail: beutel@trib.com.

FOREST OF NISENE MARKS RUN. June 3. Aptos, CA. A marathon. Annually, the first Saturday in June. For info: Forest of Nisene Marks Run, PO Box 1676, Soquel, CA 97073. Phone: (408) 685-6700. E-mail: hooverthot @aol.com.

GEHRIG HITS FOUR HOME RUNS: ANNIVERSARY. June 3, 1932. Lou Gehrig became the first American League player to hit four home runs in one game, doing so in a 20–13 New York Yankees victory over the Philadelphia Athletics. Gehrig hit his homers in four straight at bats and narrowly missed a fifth. His teammate, Tony Lazzeri, hit for the cycle.

GOVERNOR'S CUP. June 3. Helena, MT. Montana's premier running event. Includes a marathon, marathon relay, 20K, 10K and 5K. Corporate entries. Approximately 7,000 runners. Annually, the first Saturday in June. Sponsor: Blue Cross/Blue Shield. Est attendance: 7,000. For info: Tracy L. Koder, Race Dir, Blue Cross & Blue Shield, Box 451, Helena, MT 59624. Phone: (406) 447-3414. Fax: (406) 447-8607. Web: www.govcup.bcbsmt.com.

GREAT WISCONSIN DELLS BALLOON RALLY. June 3–4. Wisconsin Dells, WI. More than 90 vividly colored balloons compete in this annual event. Live entertainment, clowns and an "Ask the Pilot" question-and-answer session. Est attendance: 100,000. For info: Wisc Dells Visitor and Conv Bureau, PO Box 390, Wisconsin Dells, WI 53965. Phone: (800) 223-3557. Web: www.wisdells.com.

HETTINGER ANNUAL RODEO. June 3–4. Adams County Fairgrounds, Hettinger, ND. Annual event with two days of action-packed rodeo events in conjunction with the Adams County Fair. Two nights of live bands entertain the rodeo crowd in the evenings after the rodeos. An ice cream social and beef giveaway at the rodeos are some of the added features to this weekend of fun. Annually, the first weekend in June. Sponsored by the Hettinger Area Chamber of Commerce. Est attendance: 2,500. For info: Wendy Hehn, Hettinger Chamber of Commerce, PO Box 1031, Hettinger, ND 58639. Phone: (701) 567-2531. Fax: (701) 567-2690. E-mail: adamsdv@hettinger.ctctel .com. Web: www.hettingernd.com.

HONG KONG: INTERNATIONAL DRAGON BOAT RACES. June 3–4. A day recognizing the death of Qu Yuan, 4th-century BC poet and former minister of state who threw himself into the river in protest of the corruption of the court. Local dragon boat races are held on the fifth day of the fifth lunar month, preceding the international races by several days. For info: Hong Kong Tourist Assn, 115 E 54th St, 2nd Floor, New York, NY 10022-4512. Phone: (212) 421-3382. Fax: (212) 421-8428. Web: www.hkta.org.

LONGEST NL NIGHT GAME: ANNIVERSARY. June 3, 1989. The Houston Astros defeated the Los Angeles Dodgers, 5–4, in 22 innings at the Astrodome. The longest night game by time in National League history, it lasted 7 hours, 22 minutes.

MARTINEZ'S NEAR-PERFECT GAME: 5th ANNIVERSARY. June 3, 1995. Pedro J. Martinez of the Montreal Expos pitched a near-perfect game against the San Diego Padres. He pitched nine perfect innings before Leon ("Bip") Roberts opened the 10th with a double. Mel Rojas then relieved Martinez and retired the game's final three batters. The Expos won, 1–0.

MIGHTY CASEY HAS STRUCK OUT: ANNIVERSARY. June 3, 1888. The famous comic baseball ballad "Casey at the Bat" was printed in the Sunday *San Francisco Examiner*. Appearing anonymously, it was written by Ernest L. Thayer. Recitation of "Casey at the Bat" became part of the repertoire of actor William DeWolf Hopper. The recitation took 5 minutes and 40 seconds. Hopper claimed to have recited it more than 10,000 times, the first being at Wallack's Theater at New York, NY, in 1888. (See also: "Thayer, Ernest Lawrence: Birth Anniversary" Aug 14.)

MISSOURI STATE CHAMPIONSHIP RACKING HORSE SHOW. June 3. Stoddard County Fair Grounds, Dexter, MO. At this 23rd annual event, elegant showmanship by both horse and rider provides an afternoon and evening of spectator pleasure. Annually, the first Saturday in June. Est attendance: 500. For info: Missouri State Chmpshp Racking Horse Show, PO Box 21, Dexter, MO 63841. Phone: (573) 624-7458 or (800) 332-8857. Fax: (573) 624-7459. E-mail: chamber@dexter.net.

NATIONAL FISHING WEEK. June 3–11. Annual celebration providing opportunities for youths to experience recreational fishing, learn about the environment first-hand and practice conservation ethics. We encourage all to take a friend fishing. Annually, the first week in June beginning on the first Saturday. For info: Natl Fishing Week Steering Committee, 1033 N Fairfax St, Ste 200, Alexandria, VA 22314-1540. Phone: (703) 684-3201. Fax: (703) 519-1872. Web: www.gofishing.org.

OUTLAWS BULL BUCK-OFF. June 3–4 (tentative). Macon County Park, Macon, MO. The wildest bulls and the toughest cowboys! Exciting action, good food and lots of souvenirs. Est attendance: 3,000. For info: Mary Beth Wyatt, Macon Area Chamber of Commerce, 218 N Rollins, Macon, MO 63552. Phone: (816) 385-5484. Fax: (816) 385-3972.

PEACHTREE JUNIOR. June 3. Atlanta, GA. A 3K non-competitive run for children ages 7–12. Entries limited to 2,500. Est attendance: 2,500. Send SASE for info: Atlanta Track Club, Peachtree Jr, 3097 E Shadowlawn Ave, Atlanta, GA 30305. Phone: (404) 231-9064. Web: www .atlantatrackclub.org.

ROGUE RIVER JET BOAT MARATHON. June 3–4. Gold Beach, OR. Watch jet boats ply the twisted, rushing whitewater rapids of the mighty Rogue at speeds faster than your eyes can focus, starting from Jot's Resort at the mouth of the Rogue in Gold Beach, about 30 miles upriver, to Agness, and back again. Other events include hydroplane racing and sprint-boat maneuvers. Est attendance: 4,000. For info: Gold Beach Chamber of Commerce, 29279 Ellensburg Ave, #3, Gold Beach, OR 97444. Phone: (800) 525-2334. Fax: (541) 247-0188. E-mail: gold beach@harborside.com.

RUN FOR JODI HUISENTRUIT. June 3. Iowa City, IA. 5th annual. 5K run/walk. For info: Iowa City Road Races, Inc, PO Box 3148, Iowa City, IA 52244. Phone: (319) 338-8108. Fax: (319) 338-6822. E-mail: runicrr@aol.com.

SMALL CRAFT WEEKEND. June 3–4. Mystic Seaport, Mystic, CT. The 30th annual weekend when small-craft enthusiasts gather at the museum with their boats. Traditional small boats of every type sail from docks of Mystic Seaport on the Mystic River. Annually, first weekend in June. Est attendance: 4,000. For info: Mystic Seaport, 75 Greenmanville Ave, Mystic, CT 06355. Phone: (860) 572-5315 or (888) 9-SEAPORT. Web: www.mysticsea port.org.

SOONER STATE SUMMER GAMES. June 3–4 (also June 10–11, 17–18 and 24–25). Oklahoma City, OK. Oklahoma amateur sports festival. More than 10,000 athletes of all ages from every county in the state. More than 34 sports competitions. Est attendance: 35,000. For info: Sooner State Games, 100 W Main, Ste 287, Oklahoma City, OK 73102. Phone: (405) 235-4222. Fax: (405) 232-7723. E-mail: snrstgms@aol.com.

SOUTH JERSEY CANOE AND KAYAK CLASSIC. June 3. Ocean County Park, Rte 88, Lakewood, NJ. Canoe and kayak vendors from around the country set up on a beach to show the public the thrill of water sports. You may test-paddle the boats of your choice and attend a clinic about canoeing or kayaking throughout the day. Event is free. Annually, the first Saturday in June. Est attendance: 3,000. For info: Cathy O'Leary, Coord, Wells Mills County Park, 905 Wells Mills Rd, Waretown, NJ 08758. Phone: (609) 971-3085. Fax: (609) 971-9540.

TURQUOISE LAKE 20K ROAD/TRAIL RUN. June 3. Leadville, CO. An accurate 20K race with elevations ranging from 9,870 to 10,200 feet. First 11K is on scenic, paved, hilly road and the last 9K is on rolling foot trail in trees next to a lake. Race is run no matter what the weather or snow conditions! Three-hour limit. This is one of many races held in the area. For info: Greater Leadville Area Chamber of Commerce, TL-20K, Leadville, CO 80461. Phone: (719) 486-3581 or (800) 933-3901. E-mail: leadville@leadvilleusa.com. Web: www.leadvilleusa.com.

TURTLE RACES. June 3. Knights of Columbus, Danville, IL. More than 100 turtles compete in the 35th annual races throughout the day. Concessions available. Food and fun. Proceeds go to help people in the area with disabilities. Annually, the first Saturday in June. Est attendance: 3,000. For info: Nadine Schramm, Turtle Club, 2932 Batestown Rd, Oakwood, IL 61858. Phone: (217) 446-5327 or (800) 383-4386.

WALL REGIONAL HIGH SCHOOL RODEO. June 3–4. Rodeo Grounds, Wall, SD. All rodeo events featuring area high-school students. Admission. Est attendance: 800. For info: Nola Price, Wall Badlands Area Chamber of Commerce, PO Box 527, Wall, SD 57790. Phone: (605) 279-2665 or (888) 852-9255. E-mail: wallchamber@gwtc .net. Web: ww.wall-badlands.com.

BIRTHDAYS TODAY

Russell (Russ) Courtnall, 35, hockey player, born Duncan, British Columbia, Canada, June 3, 1965.

William John (Billy) Cunningham, 57, former basketball coach and Basketball Hall of Fame forward, born New York, NY, June 3, 1943.

Carl Edward Everett, 29, baseball player, born Tampa, FL, June 3, 1971.

James Edward (Jim) Gentile, 66, former baseball player, born San Francisco, CA, June 3, 1934.

Hale S. Irwin, 55, golfer, born Joplin, MO, June 3, 1945.

Aaron David Ledesma, 29, baseball player, born Union City, CA, June 3, 1971.

Stephen John (Steve) Lyons, 40, broadcaster and former baseball player, born Tacoma, WA, June 3, 1960.

JUNE 4 — SUNDAY
Day 156 — 210 Remaining

CHASE'S SPORTSQUOTE OF THE DAY

"All the fat guys watch me and say to their wives, 'See, there's a fat guy doing okay. Bring me another beer.'"
—Mickey Lolich, Detroit Tigers pitcher

APPLEBEE, CONSTANCE: BIRTH ANNIVERSARY. June 4, 1873. Constance Mary Katherine Applebee, physical educator, born at Chigwall, Essex, England. While taking a summer course at Harvard in 1901, Applebee introduced field hockey to her classmates. Soon thereafter, she taught the game to students at Vassar and began teaching seminars and clinics to spread the game throughout the US. Died Jan 26, 1981, at Burley, England.

ASHMAN PLAYS 10 POSITIONS: ANNIVERSARY. June 4, 1983. Mike Ashman of the Albany-Colonie Athletics, a minor league team, became the first player in professional baseball history to play all 10 positions in a ball game. Ashman pitched, caught, played all infield and outfield positions and served as the team's designated hitter.

BEER NIGHT FORFEIT: ANNIVERSARY. June 4, 1974. The game between the Texas Rangers and the Indians at Cleveland's Municipal Stadium was forfeited to Texas when the Indians tied the score, 5–5, in the bottom of the 9th inning. Umpire Nestor Chylak awarded the game to Texas when carousing fans, enlivened by an evening of 10¢ beers, got out of hand.

EDWIN MOSES LOSES: ANNIVERSARY. June 4, 1987. The longest winning streak in track and field history came to an end as Danny Harris defeated Edwin Moses in the 400-meter hurdles at a meet at Madrid. Moses, who had won 122 races in a row dating back to Aug 26, 1977, finished .13 second behind.

FEMALE PITCHER IN MINOR LEAGUE GAME: ANNIVERSARY. June 4, 1996. Pamela Davis, a 21-year-old right-hander, pitched one inning of scoreless relief for the Jacksonville Suns and got credit for the win in an exhibition game against the Australian Olympic team. The Suns, a Class AA affiliate of the Detroit Tigers, thus became the first minor league team, under the current structure of minor league baseball, to employ a female player on its roster.

FIRST RYDER CUP: ANNIVERSARY. June 4, 1927. A team of American professional golfers beat a team of British professional golfers to win the first Ryder Cup competition, 9½ to 2½. The Ryder Cup was presented by British businessman Samuel Ryder. The first biennial competition was held at Worcester Country Club (MA).

FISHING HAS NO BOUNDARIES—EAGLE RIVER. June 4–6. "T" Docks, Dock Park, Eagle River, WI. A three-day fishing experience for disabled persons on the Eagle River Chain of 28 beautiful lakes. Any disability, age, sex, race, etc, eligible. Attended by 100 participants and 200 volunteers. For info: Wil Campbell, Fishing Has No Boundaries, PO Box 2200, Eagle River, WI 54521. Phone: (715) 479-9309. Fax: (715) 479-4782. E-mail: wbc1@newnorth .net.

NEW YORK GOLDEN ARMS TOURNAMENT. June 4. Fifth Avenue Spring Festival, Brooklyn, NY. Arm-wrestling competition held at the festival determines winners who will compete in the Empire State Golden Arms Tournament of Champions on Oct 12. Est attendance: 5,000. For info: New York Arm Wrestling Assn, Inc, 200-14 45th Dr, Bayside, NY 11361. Phone: (718) 544-4592. Web: www.nycarms.com.

STATE PARKS OPEN HOUSE AND FREE FISHING DAY. June 4. Wisconsin. Free admission to state parks and forests. No fishing license is required to fish in inland lakes and Lake Michigan accessed through Wisconsin. (Free to in-state as well as out-of-state residents.) Annually, the first Sunday of the first full weekend in June. Est attendance: 8,000. For info: Bureau of Parks and Recreation, Dept of Natural Resources, PO Box 7921, Madison, WI 53707-7921. Phone: (608) 266-2181. Fax: (608) 267-7474. E-mail: wiparks@dnr.state.wi.us. Web: www .dnr.state.wi.us.

TAOS MARATHON. June 4. Taos, NM. For info: PO Box 2245, Taos, NM 87571. Phone: (505) 776-1860. Web: www.emanuelli.com/emad/marathon-taos.

BIRTHDAYS TODAY

Derian Hatcher, 28, hockey player, born Sterling Heights, MI, June 4, 1972.

Sandra Jane Haynie, 57, LPGA Hall of Fame golfer, born Ft Worth, TX, June 4, 1943.

June 2000	S	M	T	W	T	F	S
					1	2	3
	4	5	6	7	8	9	10
	11	12	13	14	15	16	17
	18	19	20	21	22	23	24
	25	26	27	28	29	30	

Andrea Jaeger, 35, former tennis player, born Chicago, IL, June 4, 1965.
Scott Daniel Servais, 33, baseball player, born LaCrosse, WI, June 4, 1967.

JUNE 5 — MONDAY
Day 157 — 209 Remaining

NBA FINALS CHAMPIONS THIS DATE
1977   Portland Trail Blazers

ABL ADOPTS THREE-POINT FIELD GOAL: ANNIVERSARY. June 5, 1961. The American Basketball League, a short-lived challenger to the NBA, adopted a three-point field goal, an innovation that was later approved successively by the American Basketball Association, the NBA and the NCAA.

CHESBRO, JACK: BIRTH ANNIVERSARY. June 5, 1874. John Dwight (Jack) Chesbro, Baseball Hall of Fame pitcher, born at North Adams, MA. Chesbro pitched in both major leagues and won 41 games for the New York Highlanders in 1904. Nevertheless, his wild pitch on the last day of the season allowed the winning run to score in a game that gave the pennant to Boston. Inducted into the Hall of Fame in 1946. Died at Conway, MA, Nov 6, 1931.

COUNT FLEET WINS TRIPLE CROWN: ANNIVERSARY. June 5, 1943. Count Fleet, ridden by Johnny Longden, won the Belmont Stakes with a wire-to-wire performance. Fairy Manhurst was a distant second, 30 lengths behind. Count Fleet, the heavy favorite, thus became the sixth horse to win racing's Triple Crown—the Kentucky Derby, the Preakness and the Belmont.

ENGLAND: BRITISH AMATEUR (GOLF) CHAMPIONSHIP. June 5–10. Royal Liverpool and Wallasey Golf Clubs, Merseyside. Est attendance: 180,000. For info: Royal and Ancient Golf Club, St. Andrews, Fife, Scotland KY16 9JD. Phone: (44) (01334) 472112. Fax: (44) (01334) 477580.

GOLFER DUNAKEY SHOOTS 59: ANNIVERSARY. June 5, 1998. Just three weeks after Notah Begay III became the third professional golfer to shoot a record-low round of 59 in a professional tournament, Doug Dunakey became the fourth golfer to do so. Dunakey carded 10 birdies and an eagle in the second round of the Miami Valley Open, a Nike Tour event, at Springboro, OH. Needing only a par on the 18th hole to finish with 58, Dunakey three-putted from 25 feet for a bogey. He didn't win the tournament, though. Craig Bowden did, shooting 16 under par, two shots better than Dunakey.

NELSON, BATTLING: BIRTH ANNIVERSARY. June 5, 1882. Battling Nelson, boxer, born Oscar Nielson at Copenhagen, Denmark. Nelson fought three epic bouts against Joe Gans for the lightweight title. He was disqualified in the 42nd round on Sept 3, 1906; knocked Gans out in the 17th round on July 4, 1908; and knocked Gans out again in the 21st round two months later. Nelson was known for not bathing for weeks before a fight. Died at Chicago, IL, Feb 7, 1954.

SKYDOME DEBUT: ANNIVERSARY. June 5, 1989. The Toronto Blue Jays made their debut at their new home, SkyDome, by losing to the Milwaukee Brewers, 5–3. The state-of-the-art facility cost $375 million to construct and featured a four-section retractable roof.

UPPERVILLE COLT AND HORSE SHOW. June 5–11. Warrenton, VA. 147th annual, the oldest show in the US. A weeklong "A-rated" horse show involving hundreds of horse-and-rider combinations from 8- to 10-year-old children in the pony divisions to leading Olympic and World Cup riders and horses in the Hunter, Jumper and Grand Prix divisions. Sunday's highlight is the prestigious $50,000 Budweiser/Upperville Jumper Classic sponsored by Budweiser. Est attendance: 6,000. For info: Tommy L. Jones, Upperville Colt and Horse Show, PO Box 1288, Warrenton, VA 20188. Phone: (540) 592-3858. Fax: (540) 253-5761. Web: www.upperville.com.

WAR ADMIRAL WINS TRIPLE CROWN: ANNIVERSARY. June 5, 1937. War Admiral, a son of Man O'War, became the fourth horse to win the Triple Crown when he captured the Belmont Stakes by three lengths over Sceneshifter. Ridden by Charley Kurtsinger, War Admiral covered the 1½ miles in 2:28.3. Pompoon, second in the Kentucky Derby and the Preakness, finished out of the money.

BIRTHDAYS TODAY

Arthur James (Art) Donovan, Jr, 75, Pro Football Hall of Fame defensive tackle, born New York, NY, June 5, 1925.
Martin Gelinas, 30, hockey player, born Shawinigan, Quebec, Canada, June 5, 1970.
Edwin David (Eddie) Joost, 84, former baseball manager and player, born San Francisco, CA, June 5, 1916.
Raymond Lewis (Ray) Lankford, 33, baseball player, born Los Angeles, CA, June 5, 1967.
Bob Probert, 35, hockey player, born Windsor, Ontario, Canada, June 5, 1965.

JUNE 6 — TUESDAY
Day 158 — 208 Remaining

NBA FINALS CHAMPIONS THIS DATE
1976   Boston Celtics

BIRTH OF THE BAA: ANNIVERSARY. June 6, 1946. The Basketball Association of America was founded at a New York meeting of hockey team owners and arena managers interested in having their buildings used on open dates. The BAA played three seasons (1946–47, 1947–48 and 1948–49), after which it merged with the National Basketball League, founded in 1937, to form the National Basketball Association. Three original BAA teams remain: the Boston Celtics, the Golden State Warriors (originally the Philadelphia Warriors) and the New York Knicks.

CASEY FLIPS THE BIRD: ANNIVERSARY. June 6, 1918. Casey Stengel returned to Ebbets Field for the first time since being traded from the Brooklyn Dodgers to the Pittsburgh Pirates over the winter. Stengel celebrated the occasion by striding to the plate for his first at bat, calling time, doffing his cap and letting a live bird fly out. Fans broke into laughter.

DANIEL, DAN: 110th BIRTH ANNIVERSARY. June 6, 1890. Daniel (Dan) Daniel, sportswriter, born Daniel Markowitz at New York, NY. Daniel was regarded as one of the nation's finest and most authoritative baseball writers. He also helped Nat Fleischer found *The Ring*, boxing's most prestigious publication. Given the J.G. Taylor Spink Award in 1972. Died at Pompano Beach, FL, July 1, 1981.

DICKEY, BILL: BIRTH ANNIVERSARY. June 6, 1907. William Malcolm (Bill) Dickey, Baseball Hall of Fame catcher, born at Bastrop, LA. Dickey played 17 seasons with the New York Yankees and was a teammate of Babe Ruth, Lou Gehrig and Joe DiMaggio. He also helped improve the catching skills of Yogi Berra. Inducted into the Hall of Fame in 1954. Died at Little Rock, AR, Nov 12, 1993.

LADIES' DAY INITIATED IN BASEBALL: ANNIVERSARY. June 6, 1876. During a National League baseball game between the Cincinnati Red Stockings and the Louisville Grays, the Cincinnati owner noticed that a large number of women showed up in the park to watch handsome Tony Mullane pitch. Thereafter, he declared, Mullane would pitch every Tuesday, each occasion to be designated "Ladies' Day."

LET'S GO TO THE VIDEOTAPE: ANNIVERSARY. June 6, 1986. Manager Steve Boros of the San Diego Padres was ejected before the first pitch of a game with the Atlanta Braves when he attempted to give umpire Charlie Williams a videotape of a disputed play in the previous night's game, a 4–2 Braves victory.

MOKRAY, BILL: BIRTH ANNIVERSARY. June 6, 1907. William George (Bill) Mokray, Basketball Hall of Fame executive and historian, born at Passaic, NJ. Mokray was a journalist, a publicist and the first director of basketball at Boston Garden. While working as the Boston Celtics public relations director, he also compiled statistics and edited the annual Converse *Basketball Yearbook*. He founded the *NBA Guide* and wrote the 900-page *Ronald Basketball Encyclopedia*. Inducted into the Hall of Fame in 1965. Died at Revere, MA, Mar 22, 1974.

NEW YORK GOLDEN ARMS TOURNAMENT. June 6. Hicksville, NY. Arm-wrestling competition determines winners who will compete in the Empire State Golden Arms Tournament of Champions on Oct 14. For info: New York Arm Wrestling Assn, Inc, 200-14 45th Dr, Bayside, NY 11361.

BIRTHDAYS TODAY

Bjorn Rune Borg, 44, former tennis player, born Sodertalje, Sweden, June 6, 1956.

Anthony Joseph (Tony) Graffanino, 28, baseball player, born Amityville, NY, June 6, 1972.

Derrel McKinley ("Bud") Harrelson, 56, former baseball manager and player, born Niles, CA, June 6, 1944.

Robert Cornelius (Bobby) Mitchell, 65, Pro Football Hall of Fame running back and receiver, born Hot Springs, AR, June 6, 1935.

Mervin Weldon (Merv) Rettenmund, 57, former baseball player, born Flint, MI, June 6, 1943.

		S	M	T	W	T	F	S
June						1	2	3
		4	5	6	7	8	9	10
2000		11	12	13	14	15	16	17
		18	19	20	21	22	23	24
		25	26	27	28	29	30	

JUNE 7 — WEDNESDAY
Day 159 — 207 Remaining

NBA FINALS CHAMPIONS THIS DATE
1978	Washington Bullets

AFL VOTES TO EXPAND: ANNIVERSARY. June 7, 1965. The executive committee of the American Football League met in New Jersey and voted to expand the league from eight teams to nine. Two months later, the league awarded the expansion franchise to Miami for $7.5 million. The ownership group, headed by Joe Robbie and entertainer Danny Thomas, named its team the Dolphins.

ALLEN STOMPS OFF: ANNIVERSARY. June 7, 1938. Cleveland Indians pitcher Johnny Allen stomped off the mound and left the game when home plate umpire Bill McGowan ordered him to trim the dangling sleeve of his sweatshirt, saying it was a distraction. Cleveland manager Ossie Vitt fined Allen $250. The shirt ended up in the Hall of Fame.

BRADDOCK, JAMES: BIRTH ANNIVERSARY. June 7, 1906. James Walter Braddock, boxer, born at New York, NY. Braddock rose from the ranks of undistinguished fighters to win three key bouts in 1934 and 1935 that propelled him to a match for the heavyweight title. He upset the defending champion, Max Baer, on June 13, 1935, remained inactive for two years and then lost his first title defense to Joe Louis. Died at North Bergen, NJ, Nov 29, 1974.

GALLANT FOX WINS TRIPLE CROWN: 70th ANNIVERSARY. June 7, 1930. Gallant Fox, with jockey Earle Sande, became the second horse to win the Triple Crown. Trained by Sunny Jim Fitzsimmons, Gallant Fox won the Belmont Stakes by three lengths over Whichone in 2:31.3.

MUNSON, THURMAN: BIRTH ANNIVERSARY. June 7, 1947. Thurman Lee Munson, baseball player, born at Akron, OH. Munson played 11 years for the New York Yankees starting in 1970 and was regarded as one of the decade's top catchers. He won the Rookie of the Year Award, three Gold Gloves and was named American League MVP in 1976. His leadership helped the Yankees win pennants in 1976, 1977 and 1978. Died when a small plane he was flying crashed at Canton, OH, Aug 2, 1979.

OUTDOORS AND INDOORS: ANNIVERSARY. June 7, 1989. In the first game played both outdoors and indoors, the Toronto Blue Jays beat the Milwaukee Brewers, 4–2, at Toronto's SkyDome. The game began with the stadium's retractable roof open, but when thunder and dark clouds brought a threat of rain in the fifth inning, the roof was closed for the rest of the game.

RED RIVER RODEO. June 7–10. Wichita Falls, TX. Professional circuit rodeo held at the Wichita County Mounted Patrol Arena, this event features all of the traditional rodeo attractions. Est attendance: 20,000. For info: Kacey Gracy, Service and Mktg Asst, Wichita Falls CVB, 1000 Fifth St, Wichita Falls, TX 76301. Phone: (940) 716-5500 or (800) 799-6732. Fax: (800) 799-5509. Web: www.wichitafalls.org.

RICHMOND, TIM: 45th BIRTH ANNIVERSARY. June 7, 1955. Tim Richmond, auto racer, born at Ashland, OH. One of the most flamboyant racers on the NASCAR circuit, Richmond won 13 races in 185 starts between 1980 and 1987. Died of complications from AIDS, Aug 13, 1989.

WHIRLAWAY WINS TRIPLE CROWN: ANNIVERSARY. June 7, 1941. Whirlaway won the Belmont Stakes by 2½ lengths over Robert Morris to become the fifth horse to win the Triple Crown. Trained by Ben Jones for Calumet Farms and ridden by Eddie Arcaro, Whirlaway finished the Belmont in 2:31.

STANLEY CUP CHAMPIONS THIS DATE
1997	Detroit Red Wings

BIRTHDAYS TODAY

Jeffrey Lamar (Jeff) Burris, 28, football player, born York, SC, June 7, 1972.

Allen Iverson, 25, basketball player, born Hampton, VA, June 7, 1975.

Napoleon Kaufman, 27, football player, born Kansas City, MO, June 7, 1973.

Anna Kournikova, 19, tennis player, born Moscow, Russia, June 7, 1981.

Terance Mathis, 33, football player, born Detroit, MI, June 7, 1967.

Michael (Mike) Modano, 30, hockey player, born Livonia, MI, June 7, 1970.

Roberto Antonio Petagine, 29, baseball player, born Nueva Esparita, Venezuela, June 7, 1971.

Stephane Joseph Jean Richer, 34, hockey player, born Ripon, Quebec, Canada, June 7, 1966.

Herbert Jude (Herb) Score, 67, former broadcaster and baseball player, born Rosedale, NY, June 7, 1933.

Heathcliff Slocumb, 34, baseball player, born New York, NY, June 7, 1966.

JUNE 8 — THURSDAY
Day 160 — 206 Remaining

NBA FINALS CHAMPIONS THIS DATE
1982	Los Angeles Lakers
1986	Boston Celtics

BELANGER, MARK: BIRTH ANNIVERSARY. June 8, 1944. Mark Henry Belanger, baseball player and union executive, born at Pittsfield, MA. Belanger played shortstop for 18 years in the major leagues, 17 with the Baltimore Orioles. His slick fielding made a major contribution to championship Orioles teams in the 1960s. After retiring, he became an executive with the Major League Baseball Players Association. Died at New York, NY, Oct 6, 1998.

BRUNET, GEORGE: 65th BIRTH ANNIVERSARY. June 8, 1935. George Stuart Brunet, baseball player, born at Houghton, MI. Brunet pitched in professional baseball for 33 years, including 15 years in the majors. He finished his career with 13 years in the Mexican League where he pitched 55 shutouts. Died at Poza Rica, Mexico, Oct 25, 1991.

COWBOY STATE SUMMER GAMES. June 8–11. Casper, WY. The Summer Games feature more than 30 different events including everything from archery to wrestling, basketball to volleyball. Participation is open to Wyoming's amateur athletes of all ages. The Summer Games also feature a spectacular Opening Ceremony that will take place Friday evening, June 9. Est attendance: 4,000. For info: Eileen Ford, Cowboy State Games, PO Box 3485, Casper, WY 82602. Phone: (307) 577-1125. Fax: (307) 577-8111. E-mail: csg@trib.com.

KENNEDY, WALTER: BIRTH ANNIVERSARY. June 8, 1912. James Walter Kennedy, Basketball Hall of Fame executive, born at Stamford, CT. Kennedy used a Notre Dame degree in journalism and business administration to create a multifaceted career in and around sports. His public relations firm represented the Harlem Globetrotters in the 1950s, and in 1959 he was elected mayor of

Stamford. Four years later, he became commissioner of the NBA where he implemented an expansion program and developed the league's television package. He retired in 1975. Inducted into the Hall of Fame in 1980. Died at Stamford, June 26, 1977.

LOUDD, ROMMIE: BIRTH ANNIVERSARY. June 8, 1933. Rommie Lee Loudd, football coach and player, born at Madisonville, TX. Loudd played linebacker during the first four seasons of the American Football League and then became the AFL's first black assistant coach when he joined the staff of the New England Patriots in 1966. Died May 9, 1998, at Miami, FL.

McLENDON, GORDON: BIRTH ANNIVERSARY. June 8, 1921. Gordon Barton McLendon, broadcaster and executive, born at Paris, TX. McLendon graduated from Yale University where he began broadcasting baseball and basketball games. After buying radio station KLIF at Dallas, TX, McLendon began to create a network of stations dedicated to daily sports programming, including both live and re-created events. The Liberty Radio Network grew to well over 200 stations but collapsed rapidly in 1952 when major league owners, fearful of declining attendance, limited the number of games the network could broadcast. Died at Lake Dallas, TX, Sept 14, 1986.

MUNGO, VAN LINGLE: BIRTH ANNIVERSARY. June 8, 1911. Van Lingle Mungo, baseball player, born at Pageland, SC. Mungo was a colorful pitcher in the 1930s with the Brooklyn Dodgers. His lilting name was the title of a popular baseball song in the 1970s. Died at Pageland, Feb 12, 1985.

OMAHA WINS TRIPLE CROWN: 65th ANNIVERSARY. June 8, 1935. Omaha won the Belmont Stakes to become the third horse to win the Triple Crown. Ridden by Willie Saunders and trained by Sunny Jim Fitzsimmons, Omaha defeated Firethorn by 1½ lengths in a time of 2:30.3.

SCOTLAND: ROYAL SCOTTISH AUTOMOBILE CLUB INTERNATIONAL SCOTTISH RALLY. June 8–10. Throughout Scotland. Scotland's leading international rally attracts many of the world's leading drivers. Est attendance: 200,000. For info: Jonathan Lord, Royal Scottish Automobile Club (Motor Sport) Ltd, 11 Blythswood Square, Glasgow, Scotland G2 4AG.

YANKEES RETIRE NO. 7: ANNIVERSARY. June 8, 1969. The New York Yankees honored Mickey Mantle by retiring his number 7 in a ceremony preceding a doubleheader against the Chicago White Sox. 60,096 fans came out to salute Mantle and to watch the Yankees sweep the Sox, 3–1 and 11–2. The Yankees have retired 12 numbers in all, more than any other baseball team.

CHASE'S SPORTSQUOTE OF THE DAY

"The thing I miss the most is being around the clubhouse. I've got some guys on this team that are almost like brothers to me."—Mickey Mantle when the Yankees retired his number

BIRTHDAYS TODAY

Herbert A. (Herb) Adderley, 61, Pro Football Hall of Fame cornerback, born Philadelphia, PA, June 8, 1939.

Lindsay Davenport, 24, tennis player, born Palos Verdes, CA, June 8, 1976.

David John (Dave) Mlicki, 32, baseball player, born Cleveland, OH, June 8, 1968.

Bryant Reeves, 27, basketball player, born Ft Smith, AR, June 8, 1973.

Kevin D. Ritz, 35, baseball player, born Eatonstown, NJ, June 8, 1965.

Troy D. Vincent, 30, football player, born Trenton, NJ, June 8, 1970.

JUNE 9 — FRIDAY
Day 161 — 205 Remaining

NBA FINALS CHAMPIONS THIS DATE
1985   Los Angeles Lakers

BADGER STATE SUMMER GAMES. June 9–12. Regionals at eight statewide sites. (Finals in Madison area, June 22–25.) 16th annual Olympic-style competition for Wisconsin residents of all ages and abilities, featuring 26 sports and opening ceremonies. Major sponsors: AT&T, Ameritech, American Family Insurance, Wisconsin Milk Marketing Board and Ministry Health Care. Member of National Congress of State Games. Approximately 25,000 participants. Est attendance: 60,000. For info: Jack Eich, PR Dir, Badger State Games, PO Box 7788, Madison, WI 53707-7788. Phone: (608) 226-4780. Fax: (680) 226-9550. E-mail: badger@badgerstategames.org. Web: www.badgerstategames.org.

BULLNANZA. June 9–10. Municipal Auditorium, Nashville, TN. The Lazy E takes its most popular event on the road to the country music capital of the world. It's nothin' but bull ridin'! Est attendance: 17,000. For info: Lazy E Promotions, Rte 5, PO Box 393, Guthrie, OK 73044. Phone: (405) 282-7433 or (800) 595-RIDE. Fax: (405) 282-7433. E-mail: larena@lazye.com.

COLLEGE WORLD SERIES (NCAA DIVISION I BASEBALL TOURNAMENT). June 9–17. Finals. Johnny Rosenblatt Stadium, Omaha, NE. For info: NCAA, 6201 College Blvd, Overland Park, KS 66211. Phone: (913) 339-1906.

FIRST WLAF CHAMPIONSHIP: ANNIVERSARY. June 9, 1991. The London Monarchs defeated the Barcelona Dragons, 21–0, at Wembley Stadium at London to win the first championship of the World League of American Football.

McCRACKEN, BRANCH: BIRTH ANNIVERSARY. June 9, 1908. Emmett Branch McCracken, Basketball Hall of Fame player and coach, born at Monrovia, IN. McCracken played at Indiana University where he was a consensus All-American and then coached at Ball State University and his alma mater. His "Hurrying Hoosiers," so called for their fast-break offense and tenacious defense, won national titles in 1940 and 1953. Inducted into the Hall of Fame in 1960. Died at Bloomington, IN, June 4, 1970.

NEBRASKALAND DAYS AND BUFFALO BILL RODEO. June 9–20. North Platte, NE. To relive the Old West. Parades, contests, shoot-outs, art shows, frontier revue, top country and western stars. Est attendance: 100,000. For info: Nebraskaland Days, Box 706, North Platte, NE 69103. Phone: (308) 532-7939. Fax: (308) 532-3789. E-mail: nld@nebraskalanddays.com. Web: www.nebraskalanddays.com.

OLDSMOBILE BALLOON CLASSIC. June 9–11. Vermilion County Airport, Danville, IL. More than 100 hot-air balloons in five morning and evening races, continuous entertainment, familyland, Balloon Glo and activities all day long. Annually, the second weekend in June. Sponsor: Oldsmobile. Est attendance: 100,000. For info: Jeanie Cooke, Exec Dir, Danville Area CVB, 100 W Main St, Rm

146, PO Box 992, Danville, IL 61832. Phone: (217) 442-2096.

SECRETARIAT WINS TRIPLE CROWN: ANNIVERSARY. June 9, 1973. Secretariat, ridden by Ron Turcotte, won the Belmont Stakes in 2:24, a world-record time for 1½ miles. With his triumph, Secretariat became the ninth horse to win the Triple Crown. His margin of victory in the Belmont, an astounding 31 lengths, set a record for that race.

SPECIAL OLYMPICS CONNECTICUT STATE SUMMER GAMES. June 9–11 (tentative). Fairfield, CT. More than 2,000 athletes with mental retardation compete in track and field, aquatics, cycling, gymnastics, race walking, power lifting, soccer, tennis and masters sports. For info: Special Olympics Connecticut, Inc, 2666-1 State St, Hampen, CT 06517-2232. Phone: (203) 230-1201. Fax: (203) 230-1202. Web: www.soct.org.

SPECIAL OLYMPICS FLORIDA SENIOR SPORTS FESTIVAL. June 9–10. Lady Lake, FL. Olympic-style competition for athletes 35 years of age and older with mental retardation. For info: Special Olympics Florida, 8 Broadway, Ste D, Kissimmee, FL 34741. Phone: (407) 870-2292. Fax: (407) 870-9810.

STATE GAMES OF NORTH CAROLINA. June 9–25. Greensboro, NC. A multisport Olympic-style competition for athletes from the state of North Carolina. The State Games promotes health, physical fitness and personal development. For info: NC Amateur Sports, PO Box 12727, Research Triangle Park, NC 27709. Phone: (919) 361-1133. Fax: (919) 361-2559. E-mail: ncas@interpath.com. Web: www.ncsports.org.

USA HOCKEY ANNUAL CONGRESS. June 9–12. Colorado Springs, CO. For info: USA Hockey, 4965 N 30th St, Colorado Springs, CO 80919. Phone: (719) 599-5500.

UTAH SUMMER GAMES. June 9–24 (tentative). Cedar City, UT. A multisport Olympic-style competition for athletes from the state of Utah. For info: Utah Summer Games, 351 W Center St, Cedar City, UT 84720. Phone: (435) 865-8421 or (435) 865-8422. Fax: (801) 865-8420. E-mail: usg@suu.edu. Web: www.utahsummergames.org.

WAGNER GETS 3,000th HIT: ANNIVERSARY. June 9, 1914. Pittsburgh Pirates shortstop Honus Wagner, known as the "Flying Dutchman," became the first modern baseball player to get 3,000 hits in his career. Wagner played from 1897 through 1917 and finished with 3,418 hits.

STANLEY CUP CHAMPIONS THIS DATE
1993   Montreal Canadiens

BIRTHDAYS TODAY

John Raymond Cappelletti, 48, Heisman Trophy running back, born Philadelphia, PA, June 9, 1952.
D'Marco Marcellus Farr, 29, football player, born San Pablo, CA, June 9, 1971.
David Gene (Dave) Parker, 49, former baseball player, born Calhoun, MS, June 9, 1951.
Eric Wynalda, 31, soccer player, born Fullerton, CA, June 9, 1969.

JUNE 10 — SATURDAY
Day 162 — 204 Remaining

STANLEY CUP CHAMPIONS THIS DATE
1996   Colorado Avalanche

AFFIRMED WINS TRIPLE CROWN: ANNIVERSARY. June 10, 1978. Affirmed, ridden by Steve Cauthen, won the Belmont Stakes to become the 11th horse to win the

	S	M	T	W	T	F	S
June					1	2	3
	4	5	6	7	8	9	10
2000	11	12	13	14	15	16	17
	18	19	20	21	22	23	24
	25	26	27	28	29	30	

Triple Crown. In one of racing's greatest two-horse competitions, Affirmed edged Alydar in all three Triple Crown races.

ALOHA STATE GAMES. June 10–18. Honolulu, HI. A multisport Olympic-style competition for athletes from the state of Hawaii. Biennially in even-numbered years. For info: Aloha State Games, 1110 University Ave, #403, Honolulu, HI 96826-1508. Phone: (808) 947-4141. Fax: (808) 947-6648. E-mail: higames@aloha.net.

BELMONT STAKES. June 10. Belmont Park, Elmont, NY. Final race of the Triple Crown was inaugurated in 1867. Traditionally run on the fifth Saturday after the Kentucky Derby (third Saturday after the Preakness). Est attendance: 60,000. For info: Press Office, New York Racing Assn, PO Box 90, Jamaica, NY 11417. Phone: (718) 641-4700. Web: www.nyracing.com.

"BIG MAC" SHORELINE SPRING SCENIC TOUR. June 10–11 (also Sept 16–17). Mackinaw City and Harbor Springs, MI. Bike tours of 25-, 50-, 75- and 100-mile routes between Mackinaw City and Harbor Springs. Each scenic tour will take you along the Lake Michigan shoreline past sparkling water and windswept dunes, through the renowned "Tunnel of Trees," over rolling hills and through quaint resort towns and old Native American villages steeped in legend and charm. Registration fee. For info: Mackinaw Area Tourist Bureau, PO Box 160, Mackinaw City, MI 49701. Phone: (800) 666-0160. Web: www.mackinawcity.com.

CALIFORNIA FREE-FISHING DAY. June 10 (also Sept 23). As proclaimed by the governor, fishing is free today in all California public waters. Observed in conjunction with National Fishing Week (See also: "National Fishing Week" June 3). For info: Conservation Education, Dept of Fish and Game, 1416 Ninth St, Sacramento, CA 95814. Fax: (916) 653-1856. E-mail: smorris@hq.dfg.ca.gov.

COLAVITO HITS FOUR HOME RUNS: ANNIVERSARY. June 10, 1959. Rocky Colavito of the Cleveland Indians hit four home runs in consecutive at bats in a game against the Baltimore Orioles. Colavito homered in the 3rd, 5th, 6th and 9th innings. The Indians won, 11–8.

CUMBERLAND YMCA ROCKY GAP TRIATHLON. June 10. Rocky Gap State Park, Cumberland, MD. The adult and team event includes a ¼-mile swim, 10-mile bike and 2.8-mile run. Also youth event for kids 15 and under. Sponsored by Western Maryland Health System. Annually, the second Saturday of June. Est attendance: 300. For info: Jim Harris, Sr Program Dir, 601 Kelly Rd, Cumberland, MD 21502. Phone: (301) 777-9622. Fax: (301) 777-3467.

FORT WAYNE HOOSIER MARATHON. June 10. Ft Wayne, IN. 6th annual. For info: Ft Wayne Track Club, PO Box 11703, Ft Wayne, IN 46860. Phone: (219) 432-5998. E-mail: RRHRetired@aol.com. Web: members .aol.com/vernc3/marathon.htm.

GEIBERGER SHOOTS 59: ANNIVERSARY. June 10, 1977. Pro golfer Al Geiberger shot a PGA-record score of 59 in the second round of the Memphis Classic at the Colonial Country Club. Geiberger made 11 birdies, six pars and an eagle on the par-72 course.

LAST AMATEUR TO WIN OPEN: ANNIVERSARY. June 10, 1933. Golfer Johnny Goodman defeated Ralph Guldahl by one shot at North Shore Golf Club at Glenview, IL, to become the last amateur to win the US Open championship.

LEVINSKY, BATTLING: BIRTH ANNIVERSARY. June 10, 1891. Battling Levinsky, boxer, born Barney Lebrowitz at Philadelphia, PA. Levinsky, light heavyweight champ from 1916 to 1920, holds the distinction of having fought three main events in three different places on the same day. On Jan 1, 1915, he fought at Brooklyn, New York City, and Waterbury, CT, a total of 32 rounds ending in three no-decisions. Died at Philadelphia, Feb 12, 1949.

LUCY HARRIS DRAFTED: ANNIVERSARY. June 10, 1977. Lucy Harris of Delta State became the first woman basketball player selected in the NBA draft. She was selected in the seventh round by the New Orleans Jazz but chose not to try out for the team.

NUXHALL IS YOUNGEST PLAYER: ANNIVERSARY. June 10, 1944. With baseball's playing ranks depleted by World War II, Joe Nuxhall became the youngest person ever to play in a major league game. Nuxhall pitched ⅔ of an inning for the Cincinnati Reds in an 18–0 loss to the St. Louis Cardinals. Nuxhall was 15 years, 10 months and 11 days old.

STEPHEN FOSTER HANDICAP. June 10. Churchill Downs, Louisville, KY. One of the nation's top handicap races each summer. Est attendance: 25,000. For info: Churchill Downs, 700 Central Ave, Louisville, KY 40208. Phone: (502) 636-4400. Web: www.kentuckyderby.com.

SUNBURST MARATHON. June 10. South Bend, IN. Marathon, 10K, 5K, 5K race/walk, 5K fun/fitness walk and children's race. Races finish on the 50-yard line at Notre Dame Stadium. For info: Sunburst Marathon, 615 N Michigan St, South Bend, IN 46601. Phone: (219) 674-0090, category 6262. E-mail: ldperalta@aol.com. Web: sunburst.org.

TAKE A KID FISHING WEEKEND. June 10–11. St. Paul, MN. Resident adults may fish without a license on these days when fishing with a child under age 16. For info: Jack Skrypek, Fisheries Chief, DNR, Box 12, 500 Lafayette Rd, St. Paul, MN 55155-4012. Phone: (651) 296-0792. Fax: (651) 297-4916. Web: www.dnr.state.mn.us.

BIRTHDAYS TODAY

Floyd Franklin Bannister, 45, former baseball player, born Pierre, SD, June 10, 1955.

Kevin Thomas Donnalley, 32, football player, born St. Louis, MO, June 10, 1968.

Daniel Francis (Dan) Fouts, 49, Pro Football Hall of Fame quarterback, born San Francisco, CA, June 10, 1951.

Tara Lipinski, 18, Olympic gold medal figure skater, born Newark, DE, June 10, 1982.

Calvin ("Pokey") Reese, Jr, 27, baseball player, born Columbia, SC, June 10, 1973.

Kenneth Wayne (Ken) Singleton, 53, broadcaster and former baseball player, born New York, NY, June 10, 1947.

Brent Colin Sutter, 38, hockey player, born Viking, Alberta, Canada, June 10, 1962.

JUNE 11 — SUNDAY
Day 163 — 203 Remaining

CHASE'S SPORTSQUOTE OF THE DAY

"Some people try to find things in this game that don't exist. Football is two things: blocking and tackling."
—Vince Lombardi

BRESNAHAN, ROGER: BIRTH ANNIVERSARY. June 11, 1879. Roger Philip Bresnahan, Baseball Hall of Fame catcher, born at Toledo, OH. Bresnahan caught for John McGraw's New York Giants in the first decade of the 20th century. He introduced shin guards in 1907. Inducted into the Hall of Fame in 1945. Died at Toledo, Dec 4, 1944.

FIRST HALF OF DOUBLE NO-HITTER: ANNIVERSARY. June 11, 1938. Johnny Vander Meer of the Cincinnati Reds pitched a no-hitter against the Boston Braves, winning 2–0. Vander Meer returned to the mound four days later and no-hit the Brooklyn Dodgers, 6–0, to complete the only consecutive no-hitters in baseball history.

LOMBARDI, VINCE: BIRTH ANNIVERSARY. June 11, 1913. Vincent Thomas (Vince) Lombardi, Pro Football Hall of Fame coach, born at New York, NY. Lombardi played football for Fordham's famed "Seven Blocks of Granite" line in the mid-1930s, became a teacher and began to coach high school football. He became offensive line coach at West Point in 1949 and moved to the New York Giants in 1954. Five years later, he was named head coach of the Green Bay Packers, a position that lofted him to the peak of his profession. His Packers won five NFL titles and two Super Bowls in nine years, and Lombardi was generally regarded as the greatest coach and the finest motivator in pro football history. He retired in 1968 but was lured back into coaching the Washington Redskins a year later. He contracted cancer after coaching the Redskins only one season. Inducted into the Pro Football Hall of Fame in 1971. Died at Washington, DC, Sept 3, 1970.

June 2000	S	M	T	W	T	F	S
					1	2	3
	4	5	6	7	8	9	10
	11	12	13	14	15	16	17
	18	19	20	21	22	23	24
	25	26	27	28	29	30	

NEVERS, ERNIE: BIRTH ANNIVERSARY. June 11, 1903. Ernest Alonzo (Ernie) Nevers, Pro Football Hall of Fame player and coach, born at Willow Ridge, MN. Nevers played three sports at Stanford, including football under coach Glenn ("Pop") Warner. He is generally regarded as one of the greatest college football players of all time and as one of America's genuine sports heroes. He pitched for the St. Louis Browns and played pro football with the Duluth Eskimos and the Chicago Cardinals. Inducted into the Hall of Fame as a charter member in 1963. Died at San Rafael, CA, May 3, 1976.

SEATTLE SLEW WINS TRIPLE CROWN: ANNIVERSARY. June 11, 1977. Seattle Slew, ridden by Jean Cruguet, became the 10th horse to win the Triple Crown by triumphing in the Belmont Stakes. Slew led wire-to-wire and defeated Run Dusty Run by four lengths.

SIR BARTON WINS TRIPLE CROWN: ANNIVERSARY. June 11, 1919. Sir Barton became the first horse to win racing's Triple Crown by winning the Belmont Stakes. With Johnny Loftus in the saddle, Sir Barton pulled away from the only two other horses in the race coming down the stretch and won the 1⅜-mile race in 2:17.2, an American record.

BIRTHDAYS TODAY

Clarence Eugene ("Butch") Carter, 42, basketball coach and former player, born Middletown, OH, June 11, 1958.
Scott Edgar Mellanby, 34, hockey player, born Montreal, Quebec, Canada, June 11, 1966.
Lorne Russell Molleken, 44, hockey coach, born Regina, Saskatchewan, Canada, June 11, 1956.
Joseph Clifford (Joe) Montana, Jr, 44, former football player, born New Eagle, PA, June 11, 1956.
Jackie Stewart, 61, former auto racer, born Dunbartonshire, Scotland, June 11, 1939.
Frank Joseph Thomas, 71, former baseball player, born Pittsburgh, PA, June 11, 1929.

JUNE 12 — MONDAY
Day 164 — 202 Remaining

NBA FINALS CHAMPIONS THIS DATE

1984	Boston Celtics
1991	Chicago Bulls

BABE DIDRIKSON WINS BRITISH AMATEUR: ANNIVERSARY. June 12, 1947. Mildred ("Babe") Didrikson Zaharias became the first American-born golfer to win the British Ladies' Amateur championship. Didrikson began her remarkable athletic career playing basketball and then switched to track and field. After the 1932 Olympics, she picked up golf. In 1948, she turned professional and joined the new Ladies' Professional Golf Association.

BASEBALL HALL OF FAME OPENS: ANNIVERSARY. June 12, 1939. The National Baseball Hall of Fame and Museum, Inc, was dedicated at Cooperstown, NY. More than 200 individuals have been honored for their contributions to the game of baseball by induction into the Baseball Hall of Fame. The first players chosen for membership (1936) were Ty Cobb, Honus Wagner, Babe Ruth, Christy Mathewson and Walter Johnson. Memorabilia from the history of baseball are housed at this shrine of America's national sport.

CITATION WINS TRIPLE CROWN: ANNIVERSARY. June 12, 1948. Eddie Arcaro rode Citation to victory in the Belmont Stakes, making the colt the eighth horse to win the Triple Crown and the last until 1973.

HOGAN WINS OPEN WITH RECORD SCORE: ANNIVERSARY. June 12, 1948. Ben Hogan won the US Open at Riviera Country Club with a record score of 276, five strokes better than any previous Open score. For Hogan it was the first of four Open championships, the others coming in 1950, 1951 and 1953.

INTERLEAGUE PLAY BEGINS: ANNIVERSARY. June 12, 1997. Breaking with tradition, Major League Baseball inaugurated interleague play, regular-season games between National League teams and American League teams. At 7:07 PM CDT, Darren Oliver of the Texas Rangers threw Ball One to Darryl Hamilton of the San Francisco Giants to start the first interleague game, won by the Giants, 4–3. In other interleague games on this date, the Anaheim Angels beat the San Diego Padres, 8–4, the Oakland A's defeated the Los Angeles Dodgers, 5–4, and the Seattle Mariners outslugged the Colorado Rockies, 12–11.

★ **NATIONAL LITTLE LEAGUE BASEBALL WEEK.** June 12–18. Presidential Proclamation 3296, of June 4, 1959, covers all succeeding years. Always the week beginning with the second Monday in June. (H Con Res 17 of June 1, 1959.)

RICHMOND PITCHES PERFECT GAME: 120th ANNIVERSARY. June 12, 1880. Lee Richmond of the Worcester Ruby Legs (National League) pitched baseball's first perfect game, 1–0, against the Cleveland Blues.

WHITE, SOL: BIRTH ANNIVERSARY. June 12, 1868. King Solomon (Sol) White, baseball player and manager and sportswriter, born at Bellaire, OH. White played five seasons in white organized baseball and the balance of his career as a player and manager in black baseball. He wrote *The History of Colored Baseball* in 1907. Died at New York, NY, August 1955.

BIRTHDAYS TODAY

Marvin Philip (Marv) Albert (born Marvin Philip Aufrichtig), 57, broadcaster, born New York, NY, June 12, 1943.

Scott Phillip Aldred, 32, baseball player, born Flint, MI, June 12, 1968.

Damon Jackson Buford, 30, baseball player, born Baltimore, MD, June 12, 1970.

Antawn Cortez Jamison, 24, basketball player, born Shreveport, LA, June 12, 1976.

Kerry Kittles, 26, basketball player, born Dayton, OH, June 12, 1974.

Ryan Anthony Klesko, 29, baseball player, born Westminster, CA, June 12, 1971.

Mathieu Schneider, 31, hockey player, born New York, NY, June 12, 1969.

JUNE 13 — TUESDAY
Day 165 — 201 Remaining

NBA FINALS CHAMPIONS THIS DATE

1989	Detroit Pistons
1997	Chicago Bulls

DODGERS INFIELD PUT TOGETHER: ANNIVERSARY. June 13, 1973. The Los Angeles Dodgers started an infield of Steve Garvey at first base, Davey Lopes at second base, Bill Russell at shortstop and Ron Cey at third base for the first time. The quartet set a record by playing together for eight and a half years.

DOUBLE EAGLE IN US OPEN: 15th ANNIVERSARY. June 13, 1985. In the first round of the US Open played at the Oakland Hills Country Club at Birmingham, MI, golfer T.C. Chen recorded the first double eagle in Open history. On the par 5, 527-yard second hole, Chen's second shot from 255 yards away landed in the cup. But Chen did not win the championship; Andy North did. Chen and two others finished one shot back.

GRANGE, RED: BIRTH ANNIVERSARY. June 13, 1903. Harold Edward ("Red") Grange, Pro Football Hall of Fame halfback and broadcaster, born at Forskville, PA. Perhaps the most famous football player of all time, Grange had a spectacular college career at the University of Illinois, being named an All-American in 1923, 1924 and 1925. When Illinois dedicated its Memorial Stadium on Oct 18, 1924, against Michigan, Grange scored four touchdowns in the game's first 12 minutes. Known as the "Galloping Ghost," Grange joined the Chicago Bears in 1925 for what amounted to a barnstorming tour, the start of a professional career dictated by Grange and his manager, Charles C. ("Cash and Carry") Pyle. He retired in 1934 following a knee injury, having put pro football on the sports map. Grange entered business and did announcing work on radio and television. In retirement, he lived quietly and humbly. Inducted into the Hall of Fame as a charter member in 1963. Died at Lake Wales, FL, Jan 28, 1991.

MATHEWSON WINS 300th GAME: ANNIVERSARY. June 13, 1912. Christy Mathewson of the New York Giants defeated the Chicago Cubs, 3–2, to win the 300th game of his career. Mathewson pitched in the majors from 1900 through 1916 and finished with 373 victories, tied for third on the all-time list with Grover Cleveland Alexander, behind only Cy Young and Walter Johnson.

MUTRIE, JIM: BIRTH ANNIVERSARY. June 13, 1851. James (Jim) Mutrie, cricket player and baseball manager, born at Chelsea, MA. Mutrie made the transition from cricket to its American cousin, baseball. He managed the first incarnation of the New York Mets, a team in the American Association in 1883. As manager of the New York National League team in 1888, he lauded his big players as "my giants," giving the team its nickname. Died at New York, NY, Jan 24, 1938.

YANKEE STADIUM SILVER JUBILEE: ANNIVERSARY. June 13, 1948. The New York Yankees celebrated the 25th anniversary of the House That Ruth Built. Babe Ruth's famous uniform No. 3 became the first uniform number ever to be retired as Ruth made his final appearance at Yankee Stadium. He died just two months later.

CHASE'S SPORTSQUOTE OF THE DAY

"I can understand why a player would have an agent. I couldn't keep from laughing if I went in and demanded a million dollars from an owner."—Red Grange

BIRTHDAYS TODAY

Sam Aaron Adams, Jr, 27, football player, born Houston, TX, June 13, 1973.

John Donald (Don) Budge, 85, former tennis player, born Oakland, CA, June 13, 1915.

Valeri Bure, 26, hockey player, born Moscow, USSR, June 13, 1974.

Marcel Ernest Lachemann, 59, former baseball manager and player, born Los Angeles, CA, June 13, 1941.

JUNE 14 — WEDNESDAY
Day 166 — 200 Remaining

NBA FINALS CHAMPIONS THIS DATE

1987	Los Angeles Lakers
1990	Detroit Pistons
1992	Chicago Bulls
1995	Houston Rockets
1998	Chicago Bulls

BULLS WIN THREE STRAIGHT TITLES THE SECOND TIME: ANNIVERSARY. June 14, 1998. The Chicago Bulls defeated the Utah Jazz, 87–86, to win their third consecutive NBA championship, four games to two. For the Bulls, this was their second "three-peat." They had accomplished this feat for the first time in 1991, 1992 and 1993.

HALL HITS FOR CYCLE: ANNIVERSARY. June 14, 1876. Six years after playing center field for the Brooklyn Atlantics as they handed the famed Cincinnati Red Stockings their first loss ever, George Hall became the first major leaguer to hit for the cycle—that is, getting a single, a double, a triple and a home run in one game.

RANGERS END STANLEY CUP JINX: ANNIVERSARY. June 14, 1994. The New York Rangers defeated the Vancouver Canucks, 3–2, in Game 7 to win the Stanley Cup for the first time since 1940. The Rangers, led by Mark Messier, Brian Leetch and Mike Richter, ended a long drought that included defeats in the finals in 1950, 1972 and 1979.

RED STOCKINGS LOSE FIRST GAME: 130th ANNIVERSARY. June 14, 1870. The Cincinnati Red Stockings, baseball's first openly acknowledged professional team, lost to the Atlantics of Brooklyn, 8–7, in 11 innings. The Red Stockings were organized in 1869, toured the country and played the entire season without a loss. They began 1870 on the same note, winning 22 games straight before tasting defeat for the first time at the hands of the Atlantics. The team was disbanded at the end of the year, the owners claiming they had lost money.

REDSKINS TV CONTRACT: 50th ANNIVERSARY. June 14, 1950. American Oil Company announced plans to sponsor the telecast of every Washington Redskins football game during the upcoming season. The Redskins thus became the first pro football team to televise a complete slate of regular-season games.

STANLEY CUP CHAMPIONS THIS DATE

1994	New York Rangers

BIRTHDAYS TODAY

Benjamin Earl (Ben) Davidson, 60, former football player, born Los Angeles, CA, June 14, 1940.

Eric Desjardins, 31, hockey player, born Rouyn, Quebec, Canada, June 14, 1969.

Stephanie Maria (Steffi) Graf, 31, former tennis player, born Bruhl, West Germany, June 14, 1969.

Eric Arthur Heiden, 42, Olympic gold medal speed skater, born Madison, WI, June 14, 1958.

Eric Lloyd Murdock, 32, basketball player, born Somerville, NJ, June 14, 1968.

June 2000	S	M	T	W	T	F	S
					1	2	3
	4	5	6	7	8	9	10
	11	12	13	14	15	16	17
	18	19	20	21	22	23	24
	25	26	27	28	29	30	

Donald (Don) Newcombe, 74, former baseball player, born Madison, NJ, June 14, 1926.

James Patrick, 37, hockey player, born Winnipeg, Manitoba, Canada, June 14, 1963.

Samuel Bruce (Sam) Perkins, 39, basketball player, born New York, NY, June 14, 1961.

Patricia Sue (Pat) Head Summitt, 48, college basketball coach and former player, born Clarksville, TN, June 14, 1952.

Jack Nicklaus

JUNE 15 — THURSDAY
Day 167 — 199 Remaining

STANLEY CUP CHAMPIONS THIS DATE

1998	Detroit Red Wings

BASEBALL "RAIN IN" AT THE ASTRODOME: ANNIVERSARY. June 15, 1976. A 10-inch rainstorm caused the postponement of a regular-season baseball game between the Pittsburgh Pirates and the Houston Astros at the Astrodome, a domed stadium. The rain caused flash floods that prevented everyone except members of both teams from getting to the ballpark.

BRUSH, JOHN: BIRTH ANNIVERSARY. June 15, 1845. John Tomlinson Brush, Jr, baseball executive, born at Clintonville, NY. Brush moved from the clothing business to baseball, owning in turn the Indianapolis team in the National League, the Cincinnati Reds and the New York Giants. He designed the rules governing the World Series. Died at Louisiana, MO, Nov 26, 1912.

BUTCH CASSIDY OUTLAW TRAIL RIDE. June 15–18. Diamond Mountain, Vernal, UT. Father's Day weekend. Four days of historic trails, great food and programs around the campfire. Bring your own camper, tent, sleeping bag, horse and gear. Several rides of varying duration through beautiful scenery. What every horse lover wants to do on his horse. Sponsors: Dinosaur Travel Board, Utah Arts Council. Est attendance: 200. For info: Dinosaurland Travel Board, 25 E Main, Vernal, UT 84078. Phone: (800) 477-5558 or (801) 789-6932. Fax: (801) 789-7465. E-mail: dinoland@ubtanet.com.

CORSICANA 51, TEXARKANA 3: ANNIVERSARY. June 15, 1902. A Texas League baseball game between Corsicana and Texarkana was moved to a small ballpark at

Ennis, TX, because of the restrictions of the state's Sunday blue laws. Corsicana adjusted to the intimate facility rather well, defeating Texarkana, 51–3. Corsicana's catcher, Jay Clarke, hit eight home runs.

DAHLGREN, BABE: BIRTH ANNIVERSARY. June 15, 1912. Ellsworth Tenney ("Babe") Dahlgren, baseball player, born at San Francisco, CA. Dahlgren played 12 seasons in the majors, but he is best known for playing first base for the New York Yankees on May 2, 1939, the day Lou Gehrig took himself out of the lineup after 2,130 consecutive games. Died at Arcadia, CA, Sept 4, 1996.

NICKLAUS SETS US OPEN RECORD: 20th ANNIVERSARY. June 15, 1980. Jack Nicklaus won his fourth US Open, shooting a record score of 272 at Baltusrol Golf Club. The previous record score for the Open was 275, held by Nicklaus (1967) and Lee Trevino (1968).

SECOND HALF OF DOUBLE NO-HITTER: ANNIVERSARY. June 15, 1938. Johnny Vander Meer of the Cincinnati Reds pitched his second consecutive no-hitter, whitewashing the Brooklyn Dodgers, 6–0, in the first night game played at Ebbets Field. On June 11, Vander Meer had no-hit the Boston Braves. His double no-hitters have yet to be duplicated.

SPECIAL OLYMPICS NEW YORK SUMMER GAMES. June 15–18. Albany, NY. About 1,200 athletes with mental retardation compete in basketball, volleyball, track and field, swimming, tennis, power lifting, gymnastics, bowling and roller-skating. For info: New York Special Olympics, Inc, 504 Balltown Rd, Schenectady, NY 12304-2290. Phone: (518) 388-0790. Fax: (518) 388-0795. E-mail: bmosberg@nyso.org.

US OPEN (GOLF) CHAMPIONSHIP. June 15–18. Pebble Beach Golf Links, Pebble Beach, CA. The national golf championship of the US. For info: US Golf Assn, Golf House, Far Hills, NJ 07931. Phone: (908) 234-2300. Fax: (908) 234-9687. E-mail: usga@usga.org. Web: www.usga.org.

BIRTHDAYS TODAY

Johnnie B. ("Dusty") Baker, Jr, 51, baseball manager and former player, born Riverside, CA, June 15, 1949.

Wade Anthony Boggs, 42, baseball player, born Omaha, NE, June 15, 1958.

Anthony Christopher (Tony) Clark, 28, baseball player, born Newton, KS, June 15, 1972.

Michael Scott Doleac, 23, basketball player, born San Antonio, TX, June 15, 1977.

Michael George (Mike) Holmgren, 52, football coach, born San Francisco, CA, June 15, 1948.

Justin Charles Garret Leonard, 28, golfer, born Dallas, TX, June 15, 1972.

Andrew Eugene (Andy) Pettitte, 28, baseball player, born Baton Rouge, LA, June 15, 1972.

Cedric Pioline, 31, tennis player, born Neuilly/Seine, France, June 15, 1969.

Billy Leo Williams, 62, Baseball Hall of Fame outfielder, born Whistler, AL, June 15, 1938.

JUNE 16 — FRIDAY

Day 168 — 198 Remaining

NBA FINALS CHAMPIONS THIS DATE

1996	Chicago Bulls

ANTIQUES ON THE BAY. June 16–17. St. Ignace, MI. 4th annual show for antique and classic original vehicles, 25 years old or older. Special tours and awards plus auto world celebrities. For info: Edward K. Reavie, Pres, Nostalgia Productions, Inc, 268 Hillcrest Blvd, St. Ignace, MI 49781. Phone: (906) 643-8087. Fax: (906) 643-9784. E-mail: edreavie@nostalgia-prod.com. Web: www.auto-shows.com.

CADDIE KICKS TOURNAMENT: ANNIVERSARY. June 16, 1946. Byron Nelson lost the US Open in a play-off and probably had his caddie to blame. In the third round of the tournament, with Nelson's ball in the rough, his caddie, Eddie Martin, stumbled and accidentally kicked the ball. Nelson incurred a one-stroke penalty and wound up tied after regulation play with Vic Ghezzi and Lloyd Mangrum, who won the play-off.

SPECIAL OLYMPICS VIRGINIA SUMMER GAMES. June 16–18. Richmond, VA. More than 1,200 athletes will compete in track and field, aquatics, bowling, gymnastics, power lifting, softball and tennis at the University of Richmond and other venues. For info: Special Olympics Virginia, 3212 Skipwith Rd, Ste 100, Richmond, VA 23294. Phone: (804) 346-5544.

SQUEEZE PLAY FIRST USED: ANNIVERSARY. June 16, 1894. In a game against Princeton, two members of the Yale baseball team, George Case and Dutch Carter, executed baseball's first squeeze play. The squeeze play is executed with a runner on third with fewer than two outs. The batter bunts the ball, allowing the runner on third to score safely.

STATE GAMES OF MISSISSIPPI. June 16–18 and 22–25. Meridian, MS. A multisport Olympic-style competition for athletes in the state of Mississippi. Opening ceremony on June 18. Most competitions on the weekends. For info: State Games of Mississippi, PO Box 5866, Meridian, MS 39302. Phone: (601) 482-0205. Fax: (601) 483-0650. E-mail: stgamiss@aol.com.

WONAGO WORLD CHAMPIONSHIP RODEO. June 16–18. State Fair Coliseum, Milwaukee, WI. More than 200 cowboys and cowgirls compete in six professional contests ranging from bronc riding to bull riding for top prize money and world championship points. Featuring colorful opening pageantry and Big, Bad BONUS Bulls. 43rd annual. Est attendance: 10,000. For info: W. Bruce Lehrke, Pres, Longhorn World Championship Rodeo, Inc, PO Box 70159, Nashville, TN 37207. Phone: (615) 876-1016. Fax: (615) 876-4685. E-mail: lhrodeo@idt.net. Web: www.longhornrodeo.com.

WORLD RECORD IN 100: ANNIVERSARY. June 16, 1999. American sprinter Maurice Greene set a new world record in the 100 meters at a track meet in Athens, Greece. Greene was timed in 9.79 seconds, .05 second faster than the previous record, set by Canadian sprinter Donovan Bailey at the 1996 Summer Olympics at Atlanta.

BIRTHDAYS TODAY

Richard Leonard (Rick) Adelman, 54, basketball coach and former player, born Lynwood, CA, June 16, 1946.

Allen G. (Al) Cowlings, 53, former football player, born San Francisco, CA, June 16, 1947.

Roberto Duran, 49, former boxer, born Chorillo, Panama, June 16, 1951.

Ernest Thorwald (Ernie) Johnson, 76, former broadcaster and baseball player, born Brattleboro, VT, June 16, 1924.

Cobi Jones, 30, soccer player, born Detroit, MI, June 16, 1970.

Wallace Keith (Wally) Joyner, 38, baseball player, born Atlanta, GA, June 16, 1962.

Ronald LeFlore, 52, former baseball player, born Detroit, MI, June 16, 1948.

Philip Alfred (Phil) Mickelson, 30, golfer, born San Diego, CA, June 16, 1970.

Roger Neilson, 66, hockey coach, born Toronto, Ontario, Canada, June 16, 1934.

Matt Turk, 32, football player, born Greenfield, WI, June 16, 1968.

Kerry Lee Wood, 23, baseball player, born Irving, TX, June 16, 1977.

JUNE 17 — SATURDAY

Day 169 — 197 Remaining

CHASE'S SPORTSQUOTE OF THE DAY

"I think that God was on our side, but the referee was French."—Bulgarian soccer player Hristo Stoichkov on his team's loss to Italy in the 1994 World Cup

ABA TEAMS JOIN NBA: ANNIVERSARY. June 17, 1976. Four teams from the American Basketball Association joined the National Basketball Association as the ABA went out of business after nine years. The four teams, the Denver Nuggets, Indiana Pacers, New York Nets and San Antonio Spurs, brought the total number of teams in the NBA to 22.

BROWNING, PETE: BIRTH ANNIVERSARY. June 17, 1861. Louis R. ("Pete") Browning, baseball player, born at Louisville, KY. Partially deaf, Browning was one of baseball's early great hitters who was victimized by alcohol. Insisting on custom-made bats, he accepted an offer from John Hillerich to make the first "Louisville Slugger" for him. Died at Louisville, Sept 10, 1905.

CANADA: MIDNIGHT MADNESS. June 17. Inuvik, Northwest Territories. Celebrates the summer solstice (24 hours of sunlight) with a variety of community events including the Midnight Sun Fun Run, walk or jog, music, midnight swim and dancing at Jim Koe Park, late-night

sidewalk sales and other events. Annually, the Saturday closest to summer solstice. For info: Theresa Ross, Box 1160, Inuvik, NT, Canada X0E 0T0. Phone: (867) 777-4851. Fax: (867) 777-4764. E-mail: townrec1@inuvik .net. Web: www.inuvik.net.

COYOTE CHASE. June 17. Wellington, NV. Annual Beta Sigma Phi 10K and 5K runs and a 2-mile walk. Pancake breakfast, art, crafts and more. Annually, the third Saturday in June. For info: Mason Valley, Chamber of Commerce, 227 S Main St, Yerington, NV 89447. Phone: (702) 463-2245. Fax: (702) 463-3369.

ECKERSALL, WALTER: BIRTH ANNIVERSARY. June 17, 1886. Walter Herbert Eckersall, football player and official, born at Chicago, IL. Eckersall played quarterback at the University of Chicago and earned All-American honors in 1904, 1905 and 1906. He became a journalist and football referee, officiating many games involving Notre Dame. Died at Chicago, Mar 24, 1930.

GROTON TRIATHLON. June 17–18 (tentative). Groton, SD. Combines the best of the area's recreational activities into one great event. Four-man teams start by shooting 50 clay pigeons each at Swisher's Sporting Clay facility, advance to Olive Grove Golf Course to play nine holes of golf and then finish at Jungle Lanes & Lounge and bowl three games. Prize money goes to the top teams and individuals. Annually, Father's Day weekend. For info: Rick Schelle, Groton Chamber of Commerce, 107 E Ninth Ave, Groton, SD 57445. Phone: (605) 397-2361.

KALAMAZOO KITE THING-Y. June 17–18. River Oaks Park, Kalamazoo, MI. A family-oriented sport kite competition, with events for Junior, Novice, Intermediate, Experienced and Master classes. Competitions for Individuals, Teams and Pairs in Precision and Ballet. Sponsors: Kazoo Stringfellows Kite Club. Est attendance: 1,500. For info: John Cosby, Coord, PO Box 2241, Kalamazoo, MI 49003. Phone: (616) 345-5432. Fax: (616) 383-8778.

LAKESTRIDE HALF-MARATHON. June 17. Ludington, MI. Half-marathon race that begins at Lakeshore Drive and Tinkham (by the beach) takes runners along a scenic course through the wooded trails and sand dunes of Lake Michigan at Ludington State Park. Annually, the third Saturday in June. Est attendance: 10,000. For info: Sue Brillhart, Exec VP, Ludington Area CVB, 5827 W US 10, Ludington, MI 49431. Phone: (616) 845-0324. Fax: (616) 845-6857. Web: www.ludington.org.

MACKINAW CITY FUDGE CLASSIC. June 17–18. Mackinaw City, MI. 10th annual fun run and jog. Saturday's 5K and 10K runs start at Mackinaw City High School and continue toward Wilderness Park. Sunday's jog is across the Mackinac Bridge. For info: Mackinaw City Chamber of Commerce, PO Box 856, Mackinaw City, MI 49701. Phone: (616) 436-5574.

MAYOR'S MIDNIGHT SUN MARATHON. June 17. Anchorage, AK. Annually on the Saturday closest to the summer solstice. For info: Municipality of Anchorage Parks & Rec, PO Box 196650, Anchorage, AK 99519. Phone: (907) 343-4474. E-mail: mccleaji@anchorage.ak .us.

MIGHTY MO 5K RUN/WALK. June 17. Riverfront, South Sioux City, NE. 8th annual run/walk with open, masters, age group, 1-mile run. More than $2,000 in prizes awarded. Annually, usually the third weekend in June, during the Waterfest celebration. For info: South Sioux City CVB, 2700 Dakota Ave, South Sioux City, NE 68776. Phone: (800) 793-6327. Fax: (402) 494-5010.

NATIONAL HOLLERIN' CONTEST. June 17. Spivey's Corner, NC. 31st annual. To revive the almost lost art of hollerin' which was a means of communication in days gone by. Annually, the third Saturday in June. Est attendance:

	S	M	T	W	T	F	S
June					1	2	3
2000	4	5	6	7	8	9	10
	11	12	13	14	15	16	17
	18	19	20	21	22	23	24
	25	26	27	28	29	30	

3,000. For info: Ermon Godwin, Jr, Spivey's Corner Volunteer Fire Dept, PO Box 332, Spivey's Corner, NC 28335. Phone: (910) 567-2156.

NATIONAL JOUSTING HALL OF FAME JOUSTING TOURNAMENT. June 17. Natural Chimneys Regional Park, Mt Solon, VA. Ring jousting for novice, amateur, semiprofessional and professional jousters. Medieval jousting and Robin Hood skit. Annually, the third Saturday in June. Est attendance: 500. For info: Upper Valley Regional Park Authority, Box 478, Grottoes, VA 24441. Phone: (540) 350-2510. Fax: (540) 350-2140.

NATIONAL JUGGLING DAY. June 17. Juggling clubs affiliated with the International Jugglers Association in cities all over North America and the world hold local festivals to demonstrate, teach and celebrate their art. For info: Intl Jugglers Assn, PO Box 218, Montague, MA 01351. Phone: (413) 367-9398. Fax: (413) 367-0259. E-mail: ijugglersa@aol.com.

RENO RODEO. June 17–21. Reno, NV. World-class athletes compete in the "Wildest, Richest Rodeo in the West." 81st annual with associated activities. For info: Reno Rodeo Assn, Box 12335, Reno, NV 89510. Phone: (702) 329-3877 or for tickets: (800) 842-7633.

SOCCER'S WORLD CUP HELD IN US: ANNIVERSARY. June 17–July 17, 1994. The World Cup of soccer was played in the US for the first time. The international championship is held every four years. The 1994 games began at Chicago on June 17 with a match between Germany and Bolivia and ended at Los Angeles with a final between Brazil and Italy on July 17 with Brazil taking the Cup. Soccer, generally known as football outside the US, is the most popular spectator sport in the world, though it has never achieved great status in the US above the amateur level. The games were watched on television by billions of fans around the world.

STOKES, MAURICE: BIRTH ANNIVERSARY. June 17, 1933. Maurice (Mo) Stokes, basketball player, born at Pittsburgh, PA. Stokes played at St. Francis College (PA) and was drafted by the Rochester Royals of the NBA in 1955. He quickly became a top performer, winning the Rookie of the Year award in 1955–56 and making the All-Star team three years in a row. Following the 1957–58 season, Stokes collapsed and went into a coma. Encephalitis made him an invalid, but teammate Jack Twyman cared for him the rest of his life. Died at Cincinnati, OH, Apr 6, 1970.

USA WEIGHT LIFTING OLYMPIC TEAM TRIALS. June 17. Alario Center, New Orleans, LA. The nation's best men and women weight lifters will compete in this one-day event to decide who will represent the US at the Sydney Olympic Games. There will be at least 30 competitors, but only seven can advance to the Olympics. For info: Greater New Orleans Sports Foundation, 1400 Poyddras St, Ste 918, New Orleans, LA 70112. Phone: (504) 525-5678. Fax: (504) 529-1622. E-mail: media@gnosports.com. Web: www.gnosports.com.

WARD PITCHES PERFECT GAME: 120th ANNIVERSARY. June 17, 1880. John Montgomery Ward of the Providence Grays pitched a perfect game against the Buffalo Bisons, winning, 5–0. Ward's effort came just five days after John Richmond's perfect game.

WILLIAMS HITS 500th HOME RUN: 40th ANNIVERSARY. June 17, 1960. Ted Williams of the Boston Red Sox hit the 500th home run of his career against Wynn Hawkins of the Cleveland Indians. The ball cleared the left-field fence at Cleveland's Municipal Stadium. The Red Sox won, 3–1. Williams finished his career with 521 home runs and was inducted into the Hall of Fame in 1966.

BIRTHDAYS TODAY

Robert Lee (Bobby) Bell, 60, Pro Football Hall of Fame linebacker, born Shelby, NC, June 17, 1940.

Lawrence Donald (Don) Casey, 63, basketball coach, born Collingwood, NJ, June 17, 1937.

David Ismael (Dave) Concepcion, 52, former baseball player, born Aragua, Venezuela, June 17, 1948.

Dermontti Farra Dawson, 35, football player, born Lexington, KY, June 17, 1965.

Stephane Fiset, 30, hockey player, born Montreal, Quebec, Canada, June 17, 1970.

Jason Douglas Hanson, 30, football player, born Spokane, WA, June 17, 1970.

Elroy Leon ("Crazylegs") Hirsch, 77, Pro Football Hall of Fame end and halfback, born Wausau, WI, June 17, 1923.

Ronald Jerome ("Popeye") Jones, 30, basketball player, born Dresden, TN, June 17, 1970.

Venus Ebone Starr Williams, 20, tennis player, born Lynwood, CA, June 17, 1980.

JUNE 18 — SUNDAY
Day 170 — 196 Remaining

CHASE'S SPORTSQUOTE OF THE DAY

"I used to pitch, play golf, have fun, rest and pitch again. Now I pitch, recover, recover, recover, rest and pitch again."—Don Sutton

FATHER'S DAY. June 18. Recognition of the third Sunday in June as Father's Day occurred first at the request of Mrs John B. Dodd of Spokane, WA, on June 19, 1910. It was proclaimed for that date by the mayor of Spokane and recognized by the governor of Washington. The idea was publicly supported by President Calvin Coolidge in 1924 but not presidentially proclaimed until 1966. It was assured of annual recognition by Public Law 92–278 of April 1972.

FIBA FOUNDED: ANNIVERSARY. June 18, 1932. The International Amateur Basketball Federation (FIBA), the body that governs Olympic basketball and other international competitions, was founded at Geneva, Switzerland.

HODGES, RUSS: 90th BIRTH ANNIVERSARY. June 18, 1910. Russell Patrick (Russ) Hodges, broadcaster, born at Dayton, TN. Hodges was one of several Southerners (along with Mel Allen, Red Barber and Ernie Harwell) who prospered broadcasting baseball at New York City. His most famous call came on Oct 3, 1951, when Bobby Thomson of the New York Giants hit a home run to defeat the Brooklyn Dodgers in the third game of a National League play-off. Hodges yelled repeatedly, "The Giants win the pennant, the Giants win the pennant." Given the Ford Frick Award in 1980. Died at Mill Valley, CA, Apr 19, 1971.

OLDEST MANAGERIAL DEBUT: 40th ANNIVERSARY. June 18, 1960. The San Francisco Giants fired manager Bill Rigney and replaced him with Tom Sheehan. At 66 years, 2 months and 18 days of age, Sheehan was the oldest man to debut as a major league manager.

SUTTON WINS 300th GAME: ANNIVERSARY. June 18, 1986. Don Sutton of the California Angels pitched a three-hitter against the Texas Rangers to win the 300th game of his career by the score of 5–1. Sutton pitched in the majors from 1966 to 1988 and finished with 324 victories.

WHEEL TO WESTON. June 18. Downtown Weston, MO. 35- or 50-mile bike ride from Kansas City, MO, to Weston, MO, to benefit American Diabetes Assn. Est attendance: 1,000. For info: Weston Development Co, 502 Main, Weston, MO 64098. Phone: (816) 640-2909. Fax: (816) 640-2909. Web: ci.weston.mo.us.

BIRTHDAYS TODAY

Santos (Sandy) Alomar, Jr, 34, baseball player, born Salinas, Puerto Rico, June 18, 1966.

Doug Bodger, 34, hockey player, born Chemainus, British Columbia, Canada, June 18, 1966.

Louis Clark (Lou) Brock, 61, Baseball Hall of Fame outfielder, born El Dorado, AR, June 18, 1939.

Andres Jose Galarraga, 39, baseball player, born Caracas, Venezuela, June 18, 1961.

George Lawrence Mikan, Jr, 76, former basketball coach, executive and Basketball Hall of Fame center, born Joliet, IL, June 18, 1924.

Bruce Bernard Smith, 37, football player, born Norfolk, VA, June 18, 1963.

JUNE 19 — MONDAY

Day 171 — 195 Remaining

STANLEY CUP CHAMPIONS THIS DATE

1999	Dallas Stars

BIAS, LEN: DEATH ANNIVERSARY. June 19, 1986. Leonard Bias, basketball player, born at Washington, DC, Nov 18, 1963. Bias played at the University of Maryland and was drafted in the first round by the Boston Celtics on June 17, 1986. Two days later, he suffered a fatal heart attack induced by cocaine use. Died at Riverdale, MD.

CICOTTE, EDDIE: BIRTH ANNIVERSARY. June 19, 1884. Edward Victor (Eddie) Cicotte, baseball player, born at Detroit, MI. Pitching for the Chicago White Sox, Cicotte won 28 games in 1917 and 29 in 1919, using his knuckleball to great effectiveness. He was implicated in the Black Sox scandal of 1919 and banned from baseball for life. Died at Detroit, May 5, 1969.

FIRST NASCAR STRICTLY STOCK SERIES RACE: ANNIVERSARY. June 19, 1949. NASCAR staged the first race in its Strictly Stock series, using new model cars that fans could see at their favorite dealers. The 150-mile event around a dirt track at Charlotte, NC, was won by Glenn Dunnaway.

FIRST RUNNING OF THE BELMONT STAKES: ANNIVERSARY. June 19, 1867. The first running of the Belmont Stakes took place at Jerome Park, NY. Ruthless, ridden by J. Gilpatrick, finished first in a time of 3:05. The Belmont Stakes continued at Jerome Park until 1889, then moved to Morris Park, NY, during 1890–1905, and in 1906 settled at Belmont Park, NY, where it has continued to the present day (except for a short period when Belmont was being renovated). The Belmont Stakes is the oldest event of horse racing's Triple Crown.

GEHRIG, LOU: BIRTH ANNIVERSARY. June 19, 1903. Henry Louis (Lou) Gehrig, Baseball Hall of Fame first baseman, born Ludwig Heinrich Gehrig at New York, NY. Gehrig, known as the "Iron Horse," played in 2,130 consecutive games, a record not surpassed until Cal Ripken did so in 1995. He played 17 years with the Yankees, hit .340 and slugged 493 home runs, 23 of them grand slams. Gehrig retired abruptly in May 1939 and was diagnosed with the degenerative muscle disease amyotrophic lateral sclerosis, later known as Lou Gehrig's disease. Inducted into the Hall of Fame in 1939 by special election. Died at New York, June 2, 1941.

KNICKERBOCKERS PLAY NEW YORK CLUB: ANNIVERSARY. June 19, 1846. The Knickerbocker Club played a baseball game against the New York Club at the Elysian Fields at Hoboken, NJ. The New York Club, playing under rules devised by Alexander Cartwright of the Knickerbockers, won, 24–1. This game had been generally regarded as the first baseball match ever between two clubs, but recent research has unearthed earlier games in the fall of 1845.

WANER GETS 3,000th HIT: ANNIVERSARY. June 19, 1942. The Boston Braves' Paul Waner, known as "Big Poison," got the 3,000th hit of his major league career, but the Pittsburgh Pirates defeated Boston, 7–6. Waner played in the majors from 1926 to 1945, mostly with the Pirates, and finished with 3,152 hits.

BIRTHDAYS TODAY

Bruce Kastulo Chen, 23, baseball player, born Panama City, Panama, June 19, 1977.

Gunther Manfred Cunningham, 51, football coach, born Munich, West Germany, June 19, 1949.

Duane Eugene Kuiper, 50, broadcaster and former baseball player, born Racine, WI, June 19, 1950.

Brian McBride, 29, soccer player, born Arlington Heights, IL, June 19, 1971.

Shirley Roques ("Cha-Cha") Muldowney, 60, former drag racer, born Schenectady, NY, June 19, 1940.

Leo Joseph Nomellini, 76, Pro Football Hall of Fame defensive tackle, born Lucca, Italy, June 19, 1924.

JUNE 20 — TUESDAY

Day 172 — 194 Remaining

NBA FINALS CHAMPIONS THIS DATE

1993	Chicago Bulls

BROWNS IN TIGERS UNIFORMS: 85th ANNIVERSARY. June 20, 1915. The St. Louis Browns arrived at Detroit for a game against the Tigers without their uniforms. The Tigers lent the Browns spare uniforms and then beat them, 1–0.

	S	M	T	W	T	F	S
June 2000					1	2	3
	4	5	6	7	8	9	10
	11	12	13	14	15	16	17
	18	19	20	21	22	23	24
	25	26	27	28	29	30	

BULLS WIN THIRD STRAIGHT TITLE FOR THE FIRST TIME: ANNIVERSARY. June 20, 1993. The Chicago Bulls achieved a "three-peat," winning their third consecutive NBA championship, defeating the Phoenix Suns, 4 games to 2. The Bulls became the first team to "three-peat" since the Boston Celtics won their eighth straight title in 1966. Chicago went on to win a fourth championship in 1996, a fifth in 1997 and a sixth in 1998.

ENGLAND: ROYAL ASCOT. June 20–23. Ascot Racecourse, Ascot, Berkshire. World renowned as an international occasion of fashion and style. The Royal Procession takes place on each of the four days when the Royal Party enters the racecourse at the Golden Gates at 2 PM and drives up the course. The highlight of the first day is the St. James's Palace Stakes, first run in 1834, one of Europe's top mile races for three-year-old colts and geldings. The highlight of the second day is The Coronation Stakes, first run in 1840. This race, for three-year-old fillies, is the distaff equivalent of the St. James's Palace Stakes on Day One. The highlight of the third day is The Gold Cup, inaugurated in 1807. Run over 2 ½ miles, it is one of the longest flat races in the world and the ultimate prize for distance racers. The highlights of the fourth day are The King's Stand Stakes and The King Edward VII Stakes. The former, first run in 1862, is the first big sprint race of the season, while the latter is a popular race for horses who ran in the Derby. Indeed, from 1834 to 1925, it was called The Ascot Derby. Est attendance: 70,000. For info: The Secy, Grand Stand Office, Ascot Racecourse, Ascot, Berkshire, England SL5 7JN. E-mail: ascotraces@aol.com.

PATTERSON REGAINS HEAVYWEIGHT CROWN: 40th ANNIVERSARY. June 20, 1960. Floyd Patterson became the first boxer to regain the heavyweight championship when he knocked out Ingemar Johansson of Sweden at 1:51 of the fifth round. Patterson won the crown for the first time on Nov 30, 1956, defeating Archie Moore. Johansson scored a TKO over the champion on June 26, 1959. Johansson also lost a third fight on Mar 13, 1961.

POSEY, CUM: 110th BIRTH ANNIVERSARY. June 20, 1890. Cumberland Willis (Cum) Posey, Jr, baseball player, manager and executive, born at Homestead, PA. Posey was an exceptional baseball and basketball player at Penn State. He owned and managed the Homestead Grays, perhaps the greatest black baseball team of the late 1920s. Died at Pittsburgh, PA, Mar 28, 1946.

SENIOR TOUR INAUGURAL EVENT: 20th ANNIVERSARY. June 20, 1980. The new Senior PGA Tour began its first official event, the Atlantic City Senior International, contested at the Atlantic City Country Club at Northfield, NJ. The winner of the 54-hole event was Don January with a score of 205, 3 under par. Mike Souchak finished second, two shots back.

SUMMER. June 20–Sept 22. In the Northern Hemisphere summer begins today with the summer solstice, at 9:48 AM EDT. Note that in the Southern Hemisphere today is the beginning of winter. Anywhere between the Equator and the Arctic Circle, the sun rises and sets farthest north on the horizon for the year, and length of daylight is maximum (12 hours, 8 minutes at equator, increasing to 24 hours at the Arctic Circle).

BIRTHDAYS TODAY

Leonard Ray (Len) Dawson, 65, Pro Football Hall of Fame quarterback, born Alliance, OH, June 20, 1935.

Andrew Auguste (Andy) Etchebarren, 57, former baseball player, born Whittier, CA, June 20, 1943.

Jozef Stumpel, 28, hockey player, born Nitra, Czechoslovakia, June 20, 1972.

JUNE 21 — WEDNESDAY
Day 173 — 193 Remaining

NBA FINALS CHAMPIONS THIS DATE
1988   Los Angeles Lakers

BUNNING PITCHES PERFECT GAME: ANNIVERSARY. June 21, 1964. Jim Bunning of the Philadelphia Phillies pitched a perfect game against the New York Mets, winning, 6–0. Since Bunning had previously pitched a no-hitter for the Detroit Tigers, his effort against the Mets gave him a no-hitter in each league. Gus Triandos became the first catcher to handle a no-hitter in each league.

CASE, EVERETT: 100th BIRTH ANNIVERSARY. June 21, 1900. Everett Norris Case, Basketball Hall of Fame coach, born at Anderson, IN. Case coached high school basketball in Indiana and became head coach at North Carolina State University in 1946. His Wolfpack teams won 10 conference titles but had limited success in post-season play. He retired after the second game of the 1965–66 season, citing the pressures of coaching. Inducted into the Hall of Fame in 1981. Died at Raleigh, NC, Apr 30, 1966.

MIDNIGHT SUN BASEBALL GAME. June 21. Fairbanks, AK. To celebrate the summer solstice. Game is played without artificial lights at 10:35 PM. Est attendance: 4,000. For info: Alaska Goldpanners, Box 71154, Fairbanks, AK 99707. Phone: (907) 451-0095.

WNBA INAUGURAL SEASON: ANNIVERSARY. June 21, 1997. The Women's National Basketball Association opened its inaugural season with three games. The Houston Comets beat the Cleveland Rockers, 76–56, the New York Liberty defeated the Los Angeles Sparks, 67–57, and the Sacramento Monarchs beat the Utah Starzz, 70–60. Two teams, the Charlotte Sting and the Phoenix Mercury, began their season the following day with Phoenix defeating Charlotte, 76–59. Each team in the WNBA, a summer league operated by the NBA, played a 24-game schedule.

BIRTHDAYS TODAY

Thomas Doane (Tom) Chambers, 41, basketball player, born Ogden, UT, June 21, 1959.

Derrick D. Coleman, 33, basketball player, born Mobile, AL, June 21, 1967.

Michael Joseph (Mike) McCormack, Jr, 70, former football coach and Pro Football Hall of Fame tackle, born Chicago, IL, June 21, 1930.

Donovan Alan Osborne, 31, baseball player, born Roseville, CA, June 21, 1969.

Wade Phillips, 53, football coach, born Orange, TX, June 21, 1947.

Richard Lee (Rick) Sutcliffe, 44, former baseball player, born Independence, MO, June 21, 1956.

JUNE 22 — THURSDAY
Day 174 — 192 Remaining

NBA FINALS CHAMPIONS THIS DATE
1994   Houston Rockets

HUBBELL, CARL: BIRTH ANNIVERSARY. June 22, 1903. Carl Owen Hubbell, Baseball Hall of Fame pitcher, born at Carthage, MO. Known as the "Meal Ticket," Hubbell was one of the best pitchers of the 1930s. In the 1934 All-Star Game, he struck out five future Hall of Fame members consecutively. Inducted into the Hall of Fame in 1947. Died at Scottsdale, AZ, Nov 21, 1988.

JOE LOUIS WINS HEAVYWEIGHT TITLE: ANNIVERSARY. June 22, 1937. Joe Louis, the "Brown Bomber," knocked out James Braddock in the eighth round of a fight at Chicago's Comiskey Park to win the heavyweight championship of the world, a title he held for 11 years.

LOUIS AVENGES DEFEAT BY SCHMELING: ANNIVERSARY. June 22, 1938. Heavyweight champion Joe Louis knocked out challenger and former champion Max Schmeling in the first round of a fight at Yankee Stadium. Louis's stunning beating avenged a 1936 defeat to Schmeling, the only fight Louis lost between 1934 and 1949. Because Schmeling was German and Louis was black, the fight was viewed by some as a triumph of American democracy over Nazi racism.

MARAVICH, PISTOL PETE: BIRTH ANNIVERSARY. June 22, 1947. Peter Press ("Pistol Pete") Maravich, Basketball Hall of Fame guard born at Aliquippa, PA. Maravich was one of the greatest scorers and showmen in college basketball history, playing at Louisiana State University where his father, Press, was coach. As a pro with several teams, he was an all-star and led the NBA in scoring in 1976–77. Inducted into the Hall of Fame in 1987. He suffered a heart attack after a pickup game and died at Pasadena, CA, Jan 5, 1988.

O'BRIEN, DAVEY: BIRTH ANNIVERSARY. June 22, 1917. Robert David (Davey) O'Brien, football player, born at Dallas, TX. O'Brien backed up quarterback Sammy Baugh in his sophomore year at Texas Christian University and became a starter the next year. In 1937, his senior season, he led TCU to the national championship and won several awards, including the Heisman Trophy, as the nation's best player. He played pro football for two years and then retired to join the FBI. Each year, the Davey O'Brien Educational and Charitable Trust of Ft Worth presents the Davey O'Brien National Quarterback Award to the nation's top college quarterback. Died at Ft Worth, TX, Nov 18, 1977.

PGA CLUB PROFESSIONAL CHAMPIONSHIP. June 22–25. Oaktree Golf Club, Edmond, OK. The national championship for professional golfers who work as club professionals and not on the PGA Tour. For info: Kerry Haigh, Sr Dir of Tourn, PGA of America, Box 109601, Palm Beach Gardens, FL 33410-9601. Phone: (561) 624-8495. Fax: (561) 624-8429. Web: www.pga.org.

STRAITS AREA ANTIQUE AUTO SHOW. June 22–24. St. Ignace, MI. For info: Edward K. Reavie, Pres, Nostalgia Productions, Inc, 268 Hillcrest Blvd, St. Ignace, MI 49781. Phone: (906) 643-8087 or (906) 643-0313. Fax: (906) 643-9784. E-mail: edreavie@nostalgia-prod.com. Web: www.nostalgia-prod.com.

WATERMELON THUMP (WITH WORLD CHAMPION SEED-SPITTING CONTEST). June 22–25. Luling, TX. Features World Champion Seed-Spitting Contest, street dance each night, giant parade on Saturday, free live entertainment in the Beer Garden, car rally, champion melon auction, arts and crafts exhibit and sales, food, games, fun run and rides. Annually, the last weekend in June. Est attendance: 35,000. For info: Susan H. Ward, Secy, Luling Watermelon Thump Assn, Box 710, Luling, TX 78648. Phone: (830) 875-3214. Fax: (830) 875-2082. E-mail: lulingcc@bcsnet.net. Web: www.bcsnet.net/luling cc/thump.htm.

CHASE'S SPORTSQUOTE OF THE DAY
"The screwball's an unnatural pitch. Nature never intended a man to turn his hand like that throwing rocks at a bear."—Carl Hubbell

BIRTHDAYS TODAY
Darrell Armstrong, 32, basketball player, born Gastonia, NC, June 22, 1968.
Brant Michael Brown, 29, baseball player, born Porterville, CA, June 22, 1971.
Clyde Austin Drexler, 38, basketball coach and former player, born Houston, TX, June 22, 1962.
Maynard Faye Throneberry, 69, former baseball player, born Memphis, TN, June 22, 1931.

JUNE 23 — FRIDAY
Day 175 — 191 Remaining

CHASE'S SPORTSQUOTE OF THE DAY
"Believe me: the reward is not as great without the struggle."—Wilma Rudolph

AUDI MOUNT WASHINGTON HILLCLIMB–THE CLIMB TO THE CLOUDS. June 23–25. Gorham, NH. The "Climb to the Clouds" hillclimb is America's oldest motor-sports event, originating in 1904. An SCCA-sanctioned Sportscar Hillclimb. Preliminary events on Friday and Saturday with the race on Sunday. Est attendance: 8,000. For info: Paul Giblin, Dir, PO Box 278, Gorham, NH 03581. Phone: (603) 466-3988. E-mail: greatgln@mt-washington.com. Web: www.mt-washington.com.

BASEBALL'S GREATEST RELIEF EFFORT: ANNIVERSARY. June 23, 1917. Pitcher Ernie Shore of the Boston Red Sox retired all 26 men he faced in a game against the Washington Nationals. Babe Ruth, Boston's starting pitcher, walked the first batter and was ejected for arguing the call. Shore entered the game, the runner was caught stealing, and every other Washington batter was put out. The Red Sox won, 4–0.

	S	M	T	W	T	F	S
June					1	2	3
2000	4	5	6	7	8	9	10
	11	12	13	14	15	16	17
	18	19	20	21	22	23	24
	25	26	27	28	29	30	

CORVETTE AND HIGH PERFORMANCE SUMMER MEET. June 23–24. Puyallup, WA. Buy, sell and show cars and parts—new, used and reproductions. Friday night: cruise-in and sneak preview to swap meet. Saturday: show and swap meet. Est attendance: 3,500. For info: Larry W. Johnson, Show Organizer, PO Box 7753, Olympia, WA 98507. Phone: (360) 786-8844. Fax: (360) 754-1498.

FAUROT, DON: BIRTH ANNIVERSARY. June 23, 1902. Donald Burrows (Don) Faurot, football player, coach and administrator, born at Mountain Grove, MO. Faurot played at the University of Missouri, coached nine years at Northeast Missouri State Teachers College and then returned to his alma mater where he coached through 1956. He was an innovative and successful coach, introducing the split-T offense in 1941. After resigning as coach, he served as the Tigers' athletic director until 1967. Died at Columbia, MO, Oct 19, 1994.

IDAHO REGATTA. June 23–25. Burley, ID. A speedboat spectacular on the Snake River featuring 90 of the nation's fastest flat-bottom race boats. Annually, the last weekend in June. For info: Mini Cassia Chamber of Commerce, PO Box 640, 1177 7th St, Heyburn, ID 83336. Phone: (208) 679-4793. Fax: (208) 679-4794. E-mail: mcid@cyberhighway.net. Web: www.cyberhighway.net/~mcidcham.

KIVIAT, ABE: BIRTH ANNIVERSARY. June 23, 1892. Abel Richard (Abe) Kiviat, track athlete and official, born at New York, NY. Kiviat was the US's best middle-distance runner in the second decade of the 20th century. He won a silver medal in the 1,500 meters in the 1912 Olympics. After injuries cut short his career, he served as press steward for numerous track meets. At the 1984 Summer Olympics, he was recognized as the nation's oldest medalist, and also in 1984 he ran the Olympic flame across seven blocks of Manhattan. Died at Lakehurst, NJ, Aug 24, 1991.

MANISTEE COUNTY SPORT FISHING TOURNAMENT WEEK. June 23–25 (also July 22–23). Manistee County, MI. FMB Ladies Classic on June 23; Budweiser Pro-Am on June 24–25; MCSFA "10" Grand Open on July 22–25 ($20,000 guaranteed payout with 60-boat minimum). Est attendance: 2,500. For info: Captain Fred MacDonald, Tournament Coord, Manistee County Sport Fishing Assn, PO Box 98, Manistee, MI 49660. Phone: (616) 398-FISH. Fax: (616) 723-0603.

McQUADE BUDWEISER SOFTBALL TOURNAMENT. June 23–25. Bismarck/Mandan, ND. Challenge your team to the largest coed slow pitch softball tournament in the world, or watch one of the 400 teams from throughout the US compete. For info: Bismarck/Mandan CVB, PO Box 2274, Bismarck, ND 58502. Phone: (800) 767-3555. Fax: (701) 222-0647.

NIXON SIGNS TITLE IX: ANNIVERSARY. June 23, 1972. President Richard Nixon signed the Higher Education Act of 1972, including Title IX which barred gender discrimination in athletics and all other activities at colleges and universities receiving federal assistance.

RUDOLPH, WILMA: 60th BIRTH ANNIVERSARY. June 23, 1940. Wilma Glodean Rudolph, Olympic gold medal sprinter, born at Bethlehem, TN. Rudolph captured the hearts of America's Olympic fans when she won the 100 meters, the 200 meters and the 400-meter relay at the 1960 Rome games, thus becoming the first woman to win three gold medals at the same Olympics. She overcame polio as a child to star at Tennessee State University and won the Sullivan Award in 1961. Died at Brentwood, TN, Nov 12, 1994.

SHORTS AT WIMBLEDON: ANNIVERSARY. June 23, 1931. Spaniard Lili de Alvarez broke with tennis tradition by showing up for her match at the Wimbledon championships wearing not the customary skirt and stockings, but shorts! Actually, her outfit was more like trousers, quite baggy and falling to her calves. She didn't win the match, but her fashion statement opened the door for women athletes to dress more practically during competition.

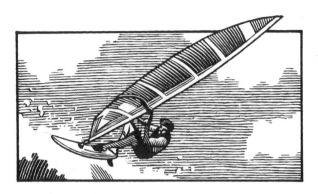

WATER SKI DAYS. June 23–25. Lake City, MN. Gala waterski shows, Grand Parade, Venetian sailboat parade, stage shows, arts and crafts show, classic car show, carnival, exotic-animal petting zoo, volleyball tournaments, Miss WSD pageant, teen tent, live bands, beer teen and penny hunt. Annually, the last weekend in June. Est attendance: 20,000. For info: Water Ski Days Chair, Lake City Area Chamber of Commerce, 212 S Washington St, Box 150, Lake City, MN 55041. Phone: (800) 369-4123 or (612) 345-4123. Fax: (612) 345-4123.

WORLD RECORD IN 200: ANNIVERSARY. June 23, 1996. Michael Johnson set a world record of 19.66 seconds in the 200 meters at the US Olympic Trials in Atlanta. Johnson erased the previous record of 19.72 seconds, set by Pietro Mennea of Italy on Sept 12, 1979.

BIRTHDAYS TODAY

Robert Darren Brooks, 30, football player, born Greenwood, SC, June 23, 1970.

James Joseph (Jim) Deshaies, 40, former baseball player, born Massena, NY, June 23, 1960.

Thomas Frank (Tom) Haller, 63, former baseball player, born Lockport, IL, June 23, 1937.

Hensley Filemon Acasio Meulens, 33, former baseball player, born Willemstad, Curacao, Netherlands Antilles, June 23, 1967.

Felix Potvin, 29, hockey player, born Anjou, Quebec, Canada, June 23, 1971.

Dontonio Wingfield, 26, basketball player, born Albany, GA, June 23, 1974.

JUNE 24 — SATURDAY
Day 176 — 190 Remaining

STANLEY CUP CHAMPIONS THIS DATE	
1995	New Jersey Devils

APFA BECOMES THE NFL: ANNIVERSARY. June 24, 1922. The American Professional Football Association, founded at Canton, OH, in 1920, voted to change its name to the National Football League. In the 1922 season, the league fielded 18 teams, down from 22 the previous year.

BEARTOOTH RUN. June 24. Red Lodge, MT. 8.2-mile or 4.4-mile footrace up scenic Beartooth Pass. Race will start at 7,000 feet and finish at 9,000 feet. Annually, the last Saturday in June. Est attendance: 350. For info: Joan Cline, Box 988, Red Lodge, MT 59068. Phone: (406) 446-1718. E-mail: redlodge@wtp.net. Web: www.wtp.net/redlodge.

DEMPSEY, JACK: BIRTH ANNIVERSARY. June 24, 1895. William Harrison ("Jack") Dempsey, boxer, born at Manassa, CO. Dempsey boxed under several pseudonyms in western mining camps, then came East and picked up Jack ("Doc") Kearns as his manager. After defeating all available heavyweights, Dempsey took on champion Jess Willard at Toledo, OH, July 4, 1919. Dempsey won when Willard failed to answer the bell for the fourth round. He reigned as champ for seven years but defended his title only six times, losing to Gene Tunney in 1926. Following his boxing career, he became a successful New York restaurateur. Died at New York, NY, May 31, 1983.

ENGLAND: CURTIS CUP. June 24–25. Ganton Golf Club, North Yorkshire, England. Biennial competition between teams of amateur women golfers from the US and the British Isles. Named after British golfing sisters Harriot and Margaret Curtis. Contested in even-numbered years since 1932 (except during World War II). For info: US Golf Assn, Golf House, Far Hills, NJ 07931. Phone: (908) 234-2300. Fax: (908) 234-9687. E-mail: usga@usga.org. Web: www.usga.org.

FISHING HAS NO BOUNDARIES—BEMIDJI. June 24–25. Lake Bemidji, MN. A two-day fishing experience for disabled persons. Any disability, age, sex, race, etc, eligible. Fishing with experienced guides attended by 75 participants and 130 volunteers. For info: Carol Olson, Bemidji Chamber of Commerce, Fishing Has No Boundaries, 300 Bemidji Ave, Bemidji, MN 56619-0850. Phone: (800) 458-2223, ext 100. Fax: (218) 759-0810. Web: www.paulbunyan.net/FHNB.

LONGEST DAM RUN. June 24. Glasgow, MT. 6th annual run across the face of Fort Peck Dam (largest hydraulic earth-filled dam in the world). 10K, 5K run or walk and 1-mile run. T-shirts for all entrants, prizes and lots of fun. Annually, the fourth weekend in June. Est attendance: 500. For info: Glasgow Area Chamber of Commerce & Agriculture, Inc, PO Box 832, Glasgow, MT 59230. Phone: (406) 228-2222. Fax: (406) 228-2244. E-mail: chamber@nemontel.com.

MORGAN HITS 256th HOMER: ANNIVERSARY. June 24, 1984. Joe Morgan of the Oakland A's hit the 256th home run of his career to break the record held by Rogers Hornsby for most home runs by a second baseman.

MUSCLECAR MANIA. June 24. Cheboygan County Fairgrounds, Cheboygan, MI. 5th annual event at the Cheboygan County Fairgrounds after the St. Ignace car show. Burnout contests, flame throwers, neon competition and muffler rapping. Program includes 18-mile muscle car cruise and contests. For info: Edward K. Reavie, Pres, Nostalgia Productions, Inc, 268 Hillcrest Blvd, St. Ignace, MI 49781. Phone: (906) 643-8087 or (906) 643-0313. Fax: (906) 643-9784. E-mail: edreavie@nostalgia-prod.com. Web: www.auto-shows.com.

SCOTLAND: WORLD SHOTGUN 2000. June 24. St. Andrews, Scotland. A unique celebration of golf, its traditions and values. More than 600 golfers will be teeing off in St. Andrews in four shotgun starts at midnight, 6 AM, noon and 6 PM. Golfers around the world are invited to join in by striking a ball at the same time. The aim is to create the biggest event in the history of golf with the maximum number of golfers linked together. For info: Royal and Ancient Golf Club, Fife, Scotland, KY16 9JD. Phone: (011) 44-1334-479555. E-mail: enquiries@worldshotgun2000.com. Web: worldshotgun2000.com.

SPOKANE BUS TRAGEDY: ANNIVERSARY. June 24, 1946. Nine members of the Spokane Indians baseball team in the Class B Western International League were killed when the team bus tumbled off a mountainside road on the way from Salem, OR, to Bremerton, WA.

SUTTON STRIKES OUT 3,000th BATTER: ANNIVERSARY. June 24, 1983. Pitcher Don Sutton of the Milwaukee Brewers struck out Alan Bannister of the Cleveland Indians, the 3,000th strikeout in his career. The Brewers won, 6–2. Sutton wound up his career with 3,574 strikeouts.

TAYLOR, CHUCK: BIRTH ANNIVERSARY. June 24, 1901. Charles B. (Chuck) Taylor, Basketball Hall of Fame contributor to the game, born at Brown County, IN. Taylor played professional basketball for 11 seasons, but he is better known for organizing the first basketball clinic and for "Chuck Taylor All-Stars," the best-selling Converse sneaker that he designed in 1931. Inducted into the Hall of Fame in 1958. Died at Port Charlotte, FL, June 23, 1969.

BIRTHDAYS TODAY

Juli Inkster, 40, golfer, born Santa Cruz, CA, June 24, 1960.

Samuel (Sam) Jones, 67, Basketball Hall of Fame guard, born Wilmington, NC, June 24, 1933.

Douglas Reid (Doug) Jones, 43, baseball player, born Covina, CA, June 24, 1957.

Jere Lehtinen, 27, hockey player, born Espoo, Finland, June 24, 1973.

Bernard Irvine (Bernie) Nicholls, 39, hockey player, born Haliburton, Ontario, Canada, June 24, 1961.

Predrag ("Preki") Radosavljevic, 37, soccer player, born Belgrade, Yugoslavia, June 24, 1963.

Loren Lloyd Roberts, 45, golfer, born San Luis Obispo, CA, June 24, 1955.

June 2000

S	M	T	W	T	F	S
				1	2	3
4	5	6	7	8	9	10
11	12	13	14	15	16	17
18	19	20	21	22	23	24
25	26	27	28	29	30	

JUNE 25 — SUNDAY

Day 177 — 189 Remaining

NBA FINALS CHAMPIONS THIS DATE
1999   San Antonio Spurs

FIRST AMERICAN TO WIN BRITISH OPEN: ANNIVERSARY. June 25, 1921. Golfer Jock Hutchinson became the first American to win the British Open by defeating Briton Roger Wethered by nine strokes in a 36-hole play-off. The Open Championship was played at St. Andrews, Scotland.

JOE LOUIS RETIRES: ANNIVERSARY. June 25, 1948. Joe Louis defended his heavyweight championship by knocking out Jersey Joe Walcott in the 11th round of a fight at Yankee Stadium. This was Louis's last title defense, after which he retired.

LONGEST WIMBLEDON MATCH: ANNIVERSARY. June 25, 1969. Pancho Gonzalez and Charlie Pasarell played the longest match in Wimbledon history. After 112 games and 5 hours, 12 minutes, Gonzales emerged triumphant.

NHL ANNOUNCES FOUR-TEAM EXPANSION: ANNIVERSARY. June 25, 1997. The National Hockey League announced that it had granted expansion franchises to four cities: Nashville (which began play in 1998–99), Atlanta (1999–2000), Minneapolis-St. Paul and Columbus (both 2000–2001). The Nashville team chose the nickname Predators. Atlanta will be known as the Thrashers, the Twin Cities as the Minnesota Wild and Columbus as the Blue Jackets. At the same time, the league's Board of Governors approved the move of the Hartford Whalers to North Carolina where they became known as the Hurricanes.

NOME RIVER RAFT RACE. June 25. Nome, AK. Homemade rafts paddle their way down the 1–2-mile course on the Nome River. The victorious team claims first-place recognition and the ownership of the fur-lined Honey-Bucket which is handed down from year to year. This event draws the entire town out for a fun afternoon at Nome's largest summer event. Annually, the Sunday closest to summer solstice. Est attendance: 300. For info: Bering Sea Lions Club, Box 326, Nome, AK 99762.

SPECIAL RECREATION DAY. June 25. To focus attention on the recreation abilities, aspirations, needs and rights of people with disabilities. (See also: "Special Recreation Week" June 25–July 1.) For info: John A. Nesbitt, Pres, SRDI, 362 Koser Ave, Iowa City, IA 52246-3038. Phone: (319) 337-7578. E-mail: john-nesbitt@uiowa.edu.

SPECIAL RECREATION WEEK. June 25–July 1. To focus attention on the recreation rights, needs, aspirations and abilities of people with disabilities—infants, children, youth, young adults, adults and seniors; living in the community, in residential services and in institutions; in 40 types of play, recreation and leisure pursuits. (See also: "Special Recreation Day" June 25.) For info: John A. Nesbitt, Pres, SRDI, 362 Koser Ave, Iowa City, IA 52246-3038. Phone: (319) 337-7578. E-mail: john-nesbitt@uiowa.edu.

USET FESTIVAL OF CHAMPIONS. June 25–27. USET Headquarters, Gladstone, NJ. Competitions in show jumping, dressage, endurance riding and combined driving. For info: Stadium Jumping, Inc, 3104 Cherry Palm Dr, Ste 220, Tampa, FL 33619. Phone: (813) 623-5801 or (800) 237-8924. Fax: (813) 626-5369. Web: www.stadium jumping.com.

BIRTHDAYS TODAY

Rene Corbet, 27, hockey player, born Victoriaville, Quebec, Canada, June 25, 1973.

Wardell Stephen (Dell) Curry, 36, basketball player, born Harrisonburg, VA, June 25, 1964.

Carlos Juan Delgado, 28, baseball player, born Aguadilla, Puerto Rico, June 25, 1972.

Douglas (Doug) Gilmour, 37, hockey player, born Kingston, Ontario, Canada, June 25, 1963.

Dikembe Mutombo Mpolondo Mukamba Jean Jacque Wamutombo, 34, basketball player, born Kinshasa, Zaire, June 25, 1966.

Willis Reed, Jr, 58, basketball executive, former coach and Basketball Hall of Fame center, born Hico, LA, June 25, 1942.

Aaron Helmer Sele, 30, baseball player, born Golden Valley, MN, June 25, 1970.

Robert Michael (Mike) Stanley, 37, baseball player, born Ft Lauderdale, FL, June 25, 1963.

William Edgar (Billy) Wagner, 29, baseball player, born Tannersville, VA, June 25, 1971.

JUNE 26 — MONDAY

Day 178 — 188 Remaining

BASKETBALL HALL OF FAME: CLASS OF 2000. June 26. Naismith Memorial Basketball Hall of Fame, Springfield, MA. The Hall of Fame announces its Class of 2000, selected from a group nominated in 1999. Enshrinement of the class will take place in November. For info: Craig Fink, Supervisor of Event Operations and Facility Mktg, Basketball Hall of Fame, 1150 W Columbus Ave, Box 179, Springfield, MA 01101-0179. Phone: (413) 781-6500.

BROWN, WILLARD: BIRTH ANNIVERSARY. June 26, 1913. Willard Jessie Brown, baseball player, born at Shreveport, LA. Brown played with the Kansas City Monarchs in the Negro National League and with the St. Louis Browns in 1947 when he was 34. He was the first African American to hit a home run in the American League. Died at Houston, TX, Aug 8, 1996.

DOUBLEDAY, ABNER: BIRTH ANNIVERSARY. June 26, 1819. Abner Doubleday, US Army officer, born at Ballston Spa, NY. Doubleday attended school at Auburn, NY, and Cooperstown, NY, and graduated from West Point in 1842. After service in the Mexican War and the Seminole War, he commanded gunners who fired the first Union shots from Ft Sumter in April 1861, and fought in several major battles. In 1907 a commission investigating the origins of baseball decided that Doubleday had invented the game at Cooperstown in the summer of 1839. Subsequent research has debunked the commission's finding thoroughly. Died at Mendham, NJ, Jan 26, 1893.

ENGLAND: ALL ENGLAND LAWN TENNIS CHAMPIONSHIPS AT WIMBLEDON. June 26–July 9. Wimbledon, London, England. Men's and women's singles and men's, women's and mixed doubles championships for the most coveted titles in tennis. One of the sport's four Grand Slam events. For info: All England Lawn Tennis and Croquet Club, Church Rd, Wimbledon, London, England SW19 5AE. Phone: (44) (181) 946-9122. Fax: (44) (181) 947-8752.

INDIANS DON NUMBERS: ANNIVERSARY. June 26, 1916. When the Cleveland Indians walked onto the field for their game against the Chicago White Sox, their home uniforms were adorned for the first time with numbers on the left sleeve. This innovation was abandoned after a short while, and uniform numbers did not appear again until the New York Yankees adopted them in 1929, not on the sleeves but on the backs of their jerseys.

TEXAS–OKLAHOMA JUNIOR GOLF TOURNAMENT. June 26–30. Wichita Falls, TX. More than 1,000 golfers 18 years old and under from 33 states and several foreign countries participate each year. Est attendance: 2,400. For info: Wichita Falls CVB, 1000 5th St, Wichita Falls, TX 76301. Phone: (940) 716-5500. Fax: (940) 716-5509. Web: www.wichitafalls.org.

WAR BOND FUND-RAISER: ANNIVERSARY. June 26, 1944. The Brooklyn Dodgers, New York Yankees and New York Giants played a special exhibition game at the Polo Grounds before 50,000 fans. In the six-inning contest, each team played successive innings against the other two and then sat out a frame. The combined final score was Dodgers 5, Yankees 1, Giants 0. The proceeds of the game went to purchase war bonds.

ZAHARIAS, BABE DIDRIKSON: BIRTH ANNIVERSARY. June 26, 1914. Mildred Ella ("Babe") Didrikson, golfer and Olympic gold medal track athlete, born at Port Arthur, TX. An athletic prodigy with enormous talent, Didrikson was named an All-American in basketball when she was only 16. At the 1932 Olympic games, she won two gold medals and also set world records in the javelin throw and the 80-meter high hurdles. Only a judging technicality prevented her from obtaining a third gold medal in the high jump. Didrikson married professional wrestler George Zaharias in 1938, six years after she began playing golf casually. In 1946 Babe won the US Women's Amateur, and in 1947 she won 17 straight golf championships and became the first American winner of the British Ladies' Amateur. Turning professional in 1948, she won the US Women's Open in 1950 and 1954, the same year she won the All-American Open. Babe also excelled in softball, baseball, swimming, figure skating, billiards—even football. In a 1950 Associated Press poll, she was named the top woman athlete of the first half of the 20th century. Died at Galveston, TX, Sept 27, 1956.

BIRTHDAYS TODAY

Harold Everett (Hal) Greer, 64, Basketball Hall of Fame guard, born Huntington, WV, June 26, 1936.

Derek Sanderson Jeter, 26, baseball player, born Pequannock, NJ, June 26, 1974.

Ed Jovanovski, 24, hockey player, born Windsor, Ontario, Canada, June 26, 1976.

Jason Daniel Kendall, 26, baseball player, born San Diego, CA, June 26, 1974.

Jerome Kersey, 38, basketball player, born Clarksville, VA, June 26, 1962.

Greg LeMond, 39, former cyclist, born Lakewood, CA, June 26, 1961.

Kirk McLean, 34, hockey player, born Willowdale, Ontario, Canada, June 26, 1966.

Shannon Sharpe, 32, football player, born Chicago, IL, June 26, 1968.

June 2000	S	M	T	W	T	F	S
					1	2	3
	4	5	6	7	8	9	10
	11	12	13	14	15	16	17
	18	19	20	21	22	23	24
	25	26	27	28	29	30	

JUNE 27 — TUESDAY
Day 179 — 187 Remaining

CANADA: TOUR DU CANADA. June 27–Sept 2. Vancouver, British Columbia, to St. John's, Newfoundland. The longest annual bicycle ride in the world, covering 4,500 miles through all 10 Canadian provinces. The tour is not a race. The route samples the flavor of the country with participants camping or staying in university dormitories and hostels and eating as a group. Organizers anticipate that four groups will leave Vancouver on June 27 and June 28 and will arrive at St. John's on Sept 2. For info: Veloforce, 1450 King St W, Ste 1000, Toronto, ON, Canada M5H 1J8. Phone: (416) 484-8339. Fax: (416) 484-1613. Web: www.CycleCanada.com/tdc.html.

CLYDE MAKES DEBUT: ANNIVERSARY. June 27, 1973. Eighteen-year-old David Clyde, recipient of a $125,000 bonus to sign with the Texas Rangers, made his major league debut against the Minnesota Twins. The Rangers won, 4–3, before 35,698 fans, the first sellout of the year at Arlington Stadium.

FIRST PLAYER TO GET SIX HITS: ANNIVERSARY. June 27, 1876. Davy Force, shortstop for the Philadelphia Athletics of the National League, became the first major league player to get six hits in one game. Force was nicknamed "Tom Thumb" because he stood only 5' 4" tall.

GOWDY ENLISTS: ANNIVERSARY. June 27, 1917. Catcher Hank Gowdy of the Boston Braves became the first major league baseball player to enlist in the military during World War I. He played 17 seasons in the majors and also served in the military during World War II.

INKSTER COMPLETES GRAND SLAM: ANNIVERSARY. June 27, 1999. Juli Inkster won the LPGA Championship at the DuPont Country Club at Wilmington, DE, to become the second golfer, after Pat Bradley, to complete the modern women's grand slam. Inkster won the Dinah Shore and the du Maurier in 1984, her first year on tour, and she added the US Women's Open earlier in 1999.

NBA DRAFT TELEVISED: ANNIVERSARY. June 27, 1989. The NBA draft was televised for the first time by WTBS. The Sacramento Kings selected center Pervis Ellison of Louisville with the first pick.

OLDEST PLAYER TO HIT HOME RUN: 70th ANNIVERSARY. June 27, 1930. John Quinn, 46, Philadelphia Athletics pitcher, became the oldest player in major league history to hit a home run when he connected in a game against the St. Louis Browns. Quinn was also the winning pitcher.

☆　☆　☆

BIRTHDAYS TODAY

Lester Milward Archambeau, 33, football player, born Montville, NJ, June 27, 1967.

Jeffrey Guy (Jeff) Conine, 34, baseball player, born Tacoma, WA, June 27, 1966.

James Patrick (Jim) Edmonds, 30, baseball player, born Fullerton, CA, June 27, 1970.

Tommy Tamio Kono, 70, Olympic gold medal weightlifter, born Sacramento, CA, June 27, 1930.

Chuck Connors Person, 36, basketball player, born Brantley, AL, June 27, 1964.

Frederick A. (Fred) Taylor, 24, football player, born Belle Glade, FL, June 27, 1976.

John Elway

JUNE 28 — WEDNESDAY
Day 180 — 186 Remaining

BRYAN, JIMMY: BIRTH ANNIVERSARY. June 28, 1926. James Ernest (Jimmy) Bryan, auto racer, born at Phoenix, AZ. Bryan was known as "Cowboy Jim" for his penchant for Western attire and his swaying, bucking-bronco style in the cockpit of his cars. He raced on dirt tracks, in Europe and at Indianapolis, winning the 500 in 1958. He won the USAC national championship in 1954, 1956 and 1957. Coming out of retirement, he returned to dirt-track racing in 1960 but crashed in his first race. Died at Langhorne, PA, June 19, 1960.

ENGLAND: HENLEY ROYAL REGATTA. June 28–July 2. Henley-on-Thames, Oxfordshire. International rowing event that is one of the big social events of the year. Est attendance: 100,000. For info: The Secy, Henley Royal Regatta, Regatta Headquarters, Henley-on-Thames, Oxfordshire, England RG9 2LY. Phone: (44) (149) 157-2153. Fax: (44) (149) 157-5509. Web: www.henley-on -thames.org.uk.

LAKE PLACID HORSE SHOW. June 28–July 2. Lake Placid Show Grounds, Lake Placid, NY. Hunter/jumper competition. For info: Stadium Jumping, Inc, 3104 Cherry Palm Dr, Ste 220, Tampa, FL 33619. Phone: (800) 237-8924 or (813) 623-5801. Fax: (813) 626-5369. Web: stadium jumping.com.

SUPREME COURT CLEARS ALI: ANNIVERSARY. June 28, 1971. The US Supreme Court voted 8–0 to overturn the 1967 conviction of Muhammad Ali for draft evasion.

TINKER STEALS HOME TWICE: 90th ANNIVERSARY. June 28, 1910. Shortstop Joe Tinker of the Chicago Cubs became the first major leaguer to steal home twice in the same game as the Cubs beat the Cincinnati Reds, 11–1. Tinker was part of the famous double-play combination, Tinker to Evers to Chance.

TWO 300-GAME WINNERS START: ANNIVERSARY. June 28, 1986. Don Sutton of the California Angels and Phil Niekro of the Cleveland Indians became the first pair of 300-game winners in the 20th century to start against each other. The Angels scored six runs in the bottom of the eighth inning to win the game, 9–3. Neither starter figured in the decision.

TYSON BITES HOLYFIELD'S EAR: ANNIVERSARY. June 28, 1997. In a fight for the WBA heavyweight championship at Las Vegas, challenger Mike Tyson was disqualified in the third round by referee Mills Lane for twice biting the ear of champion Evander Holyfield. After the fight, Tyson claimed that he had been upset that Holyfield head-butted him in the second round. The bites, which precipitated a near riot in and about the ring, were an attempt at retaliation. On July 9, the Nevada Boxing Commission fined Tyson $3 million and revoked his boxing license.

BIRTHDAYS TODAY

Karim Abdul-Jabbar (formerly known as Sharmon Shah), 26, football player, born Los Angeles, CA, June 28, 1974.
Don Edward Baylor, 51, former baseball manager and player, born Austin, TX, June 28, 1949.
Alphonso Erwin (Al) Downing, 59, former baseball player, born Trenton, NJ, June 28, 1941.
John Albert Elway, 40, former football player, born Port Angeles, WA, June 28, 1960.
Mark Eugene Grace, 36, baseball player, born Winston-Salem, NC, June 28, 1964.
Robert Matthew (Bobby) Hurley, 29, basketball player, born Jersey City, NJ, June 28, 1971.
Junior Johnson, 69, former auto racer, born Ronda, NC, June 28, 1931.
Matthew Dean (Matt) Karchner, 33, baseball player, born Berwick, PA, June 28, 1967.

JUNE 29 — THURSDAY
Day 181 — 185 Remaining

CHASE'S SPORTSQUOTE OF THE DAY

"Sometimes they write what I say and not what I mean."—Pedro Guerrero criticizing sportswriters

FIRST 7-FOOT HIGH JUMP: ANNIVERSARY. June 29, 1956. Charles Dumas of the US became the first high jumper to clear the 7-foot barrier when he reached 7 ft, 5/8 in, at the US Olympic Trials meet at Los Angeles. He won the gold medal at the Melbourne Olympics later that year at a height of 6 ft, 11½ in.

McCREARY, CONN: DEATH ANNIVERSARY. June 29, 1979. Conn McCreary, jockey and Thoroughbred trainer, born at St. Louis, MO, 1921. To be a successful jockey, McCreary had to overcome very short legs that made staying on a horse difficult. He won the Kentucky Derby and Preakness aboard Pensive in 1944, the 1951 Derby aboard Count Turf and the 1952 Preakness on Blue Man. After retiring, he trained horses for 10 years. Died at Ocala, FL.

"MOONLIGHT" GRAHAM PLAYS ONLY GAME: 95th ANNIVERSARY. June 29, 1905. Archibald Wright ("Moonlight") Graham, a real-life ballplayer made famous by his appearance in W.P. Kinsella's novel, *Shoeless Joe*, and the movie, *Field of Dreams*, played in his only major league game. A substitute outfielder for the New York Giants, Graham entered the game in the late innings, neither coming to bat nor making a fielding play. Poetic license in the book and film moved this game to 1922.

PORTSMOUTH SPARTANS BECOME DETROIT LIONS: ANNIVERSARY. June 29, 1934. After four years in the National Football League, the Portsmouth Spartans were sold to G.A. ("Dick") Richards. He moved the team to Detroit and changed its nickname from the Spartans to the Lions.

TWIN NO-HITTERS: 10th ANNIVERSARY. June 29, 1990. Dave Stewart of the Oakland Athletics pitched a 5–0 no-hitter against the Toronto Blue Jays at SkyDome. Later in the day, Fernando Valenzuela of the Los Angeles Dodgers pitched a 6–0 no-hitter against the St. Louis Cardinals. This marked the first time in major league history that no-hitters were recorded in each league on the same day and the first time in the 20th century that two pitchers hurled complete-game no-hitters on the same day.

US SENIOR OPEN (GOLF) CHAMPIONSHIP. June 29–July 3. Saucon Valley Country Club, Bethlehem, PA. For info: US Golf Assn, Golf House, Far Hills, NJ 07931. Phone: (908) 234-2300. Fax: (908) 234-9687. E-mail: usga@usga.org. Web: www.usga.org.

BIRTHDAYS TODAY

Jeff Burton, 33, auto racer, born South Boston, VA, June 29, 1967.

Daniel Lee (Dan) Dierdorf, 51, broadcaster and Pro Football Hall of Fame offensive tackle, born Canton, OH, June 29, 1949.

Theoren (Theo) Fleury, 32, hockey player, born Oxbow, Saskatchewan, Canada, June 29, 1968.

Craig Hartsburg, 41, hockey coach and former player, born Stratford, Ontario, Canada, June 29, 1959.

Frederick Wayne (Rick) Honeycutt, 46, former baseball player, born Chattanooga, TN, June 29, 1954.

Harmon Clayton Killebrew, 64, Baseball Hall of Fame third baseman, born Payette, ID, June 29, 1936.

Andrew Charles Lang, Jr, 34, basketball player, born Pine Bluff, AR, June 29, 1966.

JUNE 30 — FRIDAY
Day 182 — 184 Remaining

CANADA: RAYMOND STAMPEDE. June 30–July 1. Ray Knight Arena, Raymond, Alberta. Annual rodeo held at the home of Canada's first and oldest rodeo, started in 1902 by Ray Knight, founder of the town of Raymond. Annually, June 30 and July 1. Est attendance: 3,500. For info: Al Heggie, Raymond Stampede Committee Chair, PO Box 335, Raymond, AB, Canada T0K 2S0. Phone: (403) 752-3661.

LEWIS, STRANGLER: BIRTH ANNIVERSARY. June 30, 1891. Ed ("Strangler") Lewis, professional wrestler born Robert Friedricks at Nekoosa, WI. Lewis wrestled when wrestling was a genuine sport, winning the world's championship in 1920 over Joe Stetcher. He lost and regained the title several times over the next decade and retired after competing in more than 6,000 matches. Died at Muskogee, OK, Aug 7, 1966.

McCOVEY HITS 500th HOME RUN: ANNIVERSARY. June 30, 1978. Willie McCovey of the San Francisco Giants became the 12th player in major league history to hit 500 home runs. His milestone blast came off pitcher Jamie Easterly of the Atlanta Braves, but the Giants lost, 10–5.

MURRAY GETS 3,000th HIT: 5th ANNIVERSARY. June 30, 1995. Eddie Murray of the Cleveland Indians got the 3,000th hit of his career, a single to right in the 6th inning against Mike Trombley of the Minnesota Twins. The Indians won the game, 4–1. Murray ended his career with 3,255 hits.

REEVES, DAN: BIRTH ANNIVERSARY. June 30, 1912. Daniel Farrell (Dan) Reeves, Pro Football Hall of Fame executive, born at New York, NY. The heir to a chain of grocery stores, Reeves purchased the Cleveland Rams of the NFL in 1941. The team won the NFL title in 1945 but faltered financially. Reeves got the approval of his fellow owners to move the franchise to Los Angeles, the first major league team in any sport to play on the West Coast. The Rams survived a challenge from the AAFC while Reeves broke the league's color barrier and pioneered the use of television. Inducted into the Pro Football Hall of Fame in 1967. Died at New York, Apr 15, 1971.

RIVERFRONT STADIUM OPENS: 30th ANNIVERSARY. June 30, 1970. The Cincinnati Reds opened their new home, Riverfront Stadium, with a game against the Atlanta Braves. 51,050 fans packed the new park, but Henry Aaron hit a home run for Atlanta in the first inning, and the Braves won, 8–2. Riverfront Stadium later became known as Cinergy Field.

BIRTHDAYS TODAY

Louis Raymond (Louie) Aguiar, 34, football player, born Livermore, CA, June 30, 1966.

Garret Joseph Anderson, 28, baseball player, born Los Angeles, CA, June 30, 1972.

Steve Duchesne, 35, hockey player, born Sept-Iles, Quebec, Canada, June 30, 1965.

Octavio Antonio (Tony) Fernandez, 38, baseball player, born San Pedro de Macoris, Dominican Republic, June 30, 1962.

Mark James Grudzielanek, 30, baseball player, born Milwaukee, WI, June 30, 1970.

Sterling Marlin, 43, auto racer, born Franklin, TN, June 30, 1957.

William Mervin (Billy) Mills, 62, Olympic gold medal long distance runner, born Pine Ridge, SD, June 30, 1938.

Chan Ho Park, 27, baseball player, born Kong Ju City, Korea, June 30, 1973.

Mitchell James (Mitch) Richmond, 35, basketball player, born Ft Lauderdale, FL, June 30, 1965.

Ronald Alan (Ron) Swoboda, 56, broadcaster and former baseball player, born Baltimore, MD, June 30, 1944.

Michael Gerald (Mike) Tyson, 34, former heavyweight champion boxer, born New York, NY, June 30, 1966.

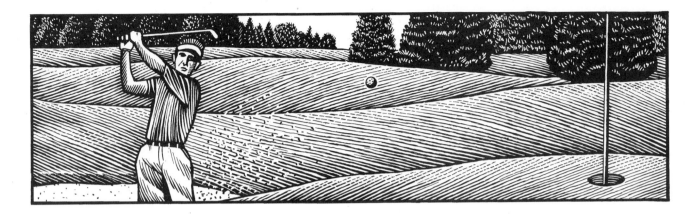

JULY 1 — SATURDAY
Day 183 — 183 Remaining

CANADA: CANADA DAY. July 1. National holiday. Canada's national day, formerly known as Dominion Day. Observed on following day when July 1 is a Sunday. Commemorates the confederation of Upper and Lower Canada and some of the Maritime Provinces into the Dominion of Canada on July 1, 1867.

CANADA: CANADA DAY CELEBRATION. July 1. Lucky Lake Waterslide Park, Watson Lake, Yukon. Outdoor concert, triathlon, canoe jousting, stick gambling, helicopter peanut drop, water slide, races and games, birthday cake and lots more. Est attendance: 900. For info: Watson Lake Canada Day Celebration, Box 590, Watson Lake, YT, Canada Y0A 1C0. Phone: (403) 536-2246. Fax: (403) 536-2498. E-mail: towl@watson.net. Web: www.yukon.net /northernlights.

CANADA: FRIENDSHIP FESTIVAL. July 1–4. Fort Erie, Ontario, and Buffalo, NY. Stage entertainment, highland games, horse show, air show, sports tournaments, arts and crafts, custom cars, fireworks, midway, food court and children's festival. Est attendance: 300,000. For info: Tracy Leblanc, Gen Mgr, Friendship Festival, PO Box 1241, Ft Erie, ON, Canada L2A 5Y2. Phone: (888) 333-1987 or (905) 871-6454. Fax: (905) 871-1266. E-mail: info@friendshipfestival.com. Web: www.friendshipfestival.com.

CANADA: NANISIVIK MIDNIGHT SUN MARATHON AND ROAD RACES. July 1–4 (tentative). Nanisivik, Northwest Territories. Runners challenge the treeless pass that links the Inuit Village of Arctic Bay to the mining community of Nanisivik north of the Arctic Circle on the northern shore of Baffin Island. 10K, 32K, 42K and 84K races at heights from 2m to 535m and in temperatures ranging from −5°C to +10°C in what is considered one of the toughest road races in the world. Entrants stay with miners' families or in government houses at Nanisivik. Limited to 100 runners. For info: Midnight Sun Marathon, c/o Nanisivik Mine, PO Box 225, Nanisivik, NT, Canada X0A 0X0. Phone: (867) 436-8000. Fax: (867) 436-7435.

CAPE FEAR 7s TOURNAMENT. July 1–2. UNCW, Wilmington, NC. 72-team Mid-Atlantic invitational rugby seven-men-a-side (and women) tournament. Annually, the weekend closest to the 4th of July. Est attendance: 1,200. For info: Bob Bogen, PO Box 5351, Wilmington, NC 28403. Phone: (910) 452-0543. Fax: (910) 452-9960. E-mail: bogen@wilmington.net.

CLARKSON, JOHN: BIRTH ANNIVERSARY. July 1, 1861. John Gibson Clarkson, Baseball Hall of Fame pitcher, born at Cambridge, MA. Clarkson won 326 games in a 12-year career. He pitched mainly for the Chicago White Stockings and the Boston Beaneaters, National League teams in the late 19th century. Inducted into the Hall of Fame in 1963. Died at Cambridge, Feb 4, 1909.

CONNOR, ROGER: BIRTH ANNIVERSARY. July 1, 1857. Roger Connor, Baseball Hall of Fame outfielder, born at Waterbury, CT. Connor was a powerful hitter in the 1880s and 1890s, compiling a .318 batting average over 18 seasons. He slugged more home runs (136) than any other 19th century player. Inducted into the Hall of Fame in 1976. Died at Waterbury, Jan 4, 1931.

FIRST INTERCOLLEGIATE BASEBALL GAME: ANNIVERSARY. July 1, 1859. Amherst and Williams played the first intercollegiate baseball game, with Amherst winning, 73–32. The next day, Williams evened the score by defeating Amherst in a chess match.

FIRST TRIPLE CHAMPION AT WIMBLEDON: 80th ANNIVERSARY. July 1, 1920. Suzanne Lenglen of France became the first woman tennis player to win three Wimbledon championships in the same year. She won the singles title, the doubles and the mixed doubles.

INTERNATIONAL CHERRY PIT SPITTING CONTEST. July 1. Tree-Mendus Fruit Farm, Eau Claire, MI. A nutritious sport—is there a better way to dispose of the pits once you have eaten the cherry? Entrants eat a cherry and then spit the pit as far as possible on a blacktop surface. The entrant who spits the pit the farthest including the roll is the champ. Annually, the first Saturday in July. Est attendance: 1,000. For info: Lynn Sage, Adv & Promo Mgr, Tree-Mendus Fruit Farm, 9351 E Eureka Rd, Eau Claire, MI 49111. Phone: (517) 782-7101. E-mail: treemendus@aol.com. Web: www.treemendus-fruit.com.

MACON COUNTY ANNUAL DEMOLITION DERBY. July 1. Macon County Park, Macon, MO. Enjoy the thrills and spills of north Missouri's #1 demolition derby. Lots of hard-hitting excitement. Est attendance: 3,000. For info: Mary Beth Wyatt, Macon Area Chamber of Commerce, 218 N Rollins, Macon, MO 63552. Phone: (816) 385-5484. Fax: (816) 385-3972.

MANDAN JAYCEE RODEO DAYS. July 1–4. Mandan, ND. Watch the region's top cowboys and cowgirls compete. In addition to the parade and the carnival midway, wander through local arts and crafts exhibits at Art in the Park. Est attendance: 50,000. For info: Bismarck/Mandan CVB, Box 2274, Bismarck, ND 58502. Phone: (800) 767-3555 or (701) 222-4308. Fax: (701) 222-0647.

MISSISSIPPI DEEP SEA FISHING RODEO. July 1–4. Gulfport, MS. Annual celebration, featuring fishing events, entertainment, rides, games and family fun. Sponsor: Mississippi Deep Sea Rodeo, Inc. Est attendance: 150,000. For info: Chuck Dedeaux, Mississippi Deep Sea Rodeo, PO Box 1289, Gulfport, MS 39502. Phone: (228) 863-2713.

NATIONAL RECREATION AND PARKS MONTH. July 1–31. To showcase and invite community participation in quality leisure activities for all segments of the population. For info: Natl Recreation and Parks Assn, 22377 Belmont Ridge Rd, Ashburn, VA 20148. Phone: (703) 858-0784. Fax: (703) 858-0794. E-mail: info@nrpa.org.

NATIONAL TENNIS MONTH. July 1–31. To promote tennis at the grassroots level. Players can participate in tournaments, clinics and special events at more than 2,000 tennis facilities nationwide. Presented by *Tennis Magazine* and World TeamTennis. For info: Natl Tennis Month, Attn: Lorraine Bloohm, 5520 Park Ave, Box 395, Trumbull, CT 06611. Phone: (203) 373-7123.

OLD COMISKEY PARK OPENS: 90th ANNIVERSARY. July 1, 1910. The Chicago White Sox opened their new home, originally called White Sox Park and later called Comiskey Park, losing to the St. Louis Browns, 2–0. Barney Pelty pitched the shutout for the Browns.

PEPSI 400. July 1. Daytona International Speedway, Daytona Beach, FL. 41st running of NASCAR Winston Cup's "Mid-Summer Classic." Sponsor: Pepsi. For info: John Story, Dir of Public Relations, Daytona Intl Speedway, PO Box 28014, Daytona Beach, FL 32120-2801. Phone: (904) 254-2700. For tickets: (904) 253-RACE (7223). Fax: (904) 947-6791. Web: www.daytonausa.com.

PLAY TACOMA DAYS. July 1–31. Tacoma, WA. A series of family events throughout the month of July celebrating Tacoma's recreation programs and opportunities, presented by Metro Parks Tacoma. These annual events include festivals, concerts, splash parties, salmon bakes, a golf tournament and much, much more. Est attendance: 280,000. For info: Metropolitan Park Dist, Rec Dept, 4702 S 19th St, Tacoma, WA 98405. Phone: (206) 305-1036. Fax: (206) 305-1014.

PRINCE, BOB: BIRTH ANNIVERSARY. July 1, 1916. Robert Ferris (Bob) Prince, broadcaster, born at Los Angeles, CA. Prince began broadcasting Pittsburgh Pirates games in 1947 and soon became fully identified with the fortunes of the team. Known as "the Gunner," Prince utilized a colorful style that endeared him to his listeners. His firing in 1975 occasioned protests by fans parading through downtown Pittsburgh. Given the Ford Frick Award in 1986. Died at Pittsburgh, PA, June 10, 1985.

STERN, BILL: BIRTH ANNIVERSARY. July 1, 1907. William (Bill) Stern, broadcaster, born at Rochester, NY. Stern worked as the chief sports announcer on the NBC radio network from 1939 to 1952 and rivaled Ted Husing as the nation's leading sports broadcaster. Stern's crit-

ics complained that he owed his success to his voice only and that his knowledge of sports was often shallow and faulty, but he was enormously popular. He did not make the transition to television well and, in addition, battled an addiction to prescription drugs in the 1950s. Died at New York, NY, Nov 19, 1971.

BIRTHDAYS TODAY

Frank Matt Baumann, 67, former baseball player, born St. Louis, MO, July 1, 1933.

Shawn Burr, 34, hockey player, born Sarnia, Ontario, Canada, July 1, 1966.

Rodrigue Gabriel (Rod) Gilbert, 59, Hockey Hall of Fame right wing, born Montreal, Quebec, Canada, July 1, 1941.

Jarome Iginla, 23, hockey player, born Edmonton, Alberta, Canada, July 1, 1977.

Frederick Carlton (Carl) Lewis, 39, Olympic gold medal sprinter and long jumper, born Birmingham, AL, July 1, 1961.

Nancy Lieberman-Cline, 42, broadcaster and Basketball Hall of Fame guard, born New York, NY, July 1, 1958.

JULY 2 — SUNDAY
Day 184 — 182 Remaining

BLACK HILLS ROUNDUP RODEO. July 2–4. Roundup Rodeo Grounds, Belle Fourche, SD. PRCA rodeo, carnival downtown, 4th of July parade, fireworks and the Miss South Dakota Rodeo pageant. Admission fee. Est attendance: 12,000. For info: Casey Hunter, Black Hills Roundup Committee, 41 5th Ave, Belle Fourche, SD 57717. Phone: (605) 892-2041.

BOXING'S FIRST MILLION-DOLLAR GATE: ANNIVERSARY. July 2, 1921. Jack Dempsey successfully defended his heavyweight championship against French contender Georges Carpentier. The challenger staggered Dempsey in the second round, but the "Manassa Mauler" recovered and knocked out Carpentier in the fifth round. The fight grossed $1,789,238, boxing's first million-dollar gate, as 80,000 fans took their seats in a specially-built outdoor arena at Jersey City, NJ.

CANADA: CALGARY HERALD STAMPEDE RUN-OFF. July 2. Calgary, Alberta. Marathon. For info: Calgary Herald Stampede Run-Off, PO Box 296, Station M, Calgary, AB, Canada T2P 2H9. Phone: (403) 264-2996. E-mail: stampede.run-off@home.com. Web: www.calgary herald.colm/runoff.

COLLIER, BLANTON: BIRTH ANNIVERSARY. July 2, 1906. Blanton Collier, football coach, born at Millersburg, KY. A high school coach before World War II, Collier joined the staff of Coach Paul Brown at the Great Lakes Naval Training Center and then with the Cleveland Browns. He moved to Kentucky in 1954 and returned to the Browns as head coach in 1963. His Browns reached the NFL title game four times. Died at Houston, TX, Mar 22, 1983.

DEATH OF ESCOBAR: ANNIVERSARY. July 2, 1994. Andres Escobar, 27, a defender on Colombia's 1994 World Cup soccer team, was shot 12 times and killed by an unknown assailant at Medellin, Colombia. The shooting

July 2000	S	M	T	W	T	F	S
							1
	2	3	4	5	6	7	8
	9	10	11	12	13	14	15
	16	17	18	19	20	21	22
	23	24	25	26	27	28	29
	30	31					

occurred ten days after Escobar had scored an "own goal," kicking the ball into his own net in a 2–1 opening round upset loss to the United States. Witnesses said the shooter shouted "Goal! Goal!" as he fired each shot.

DORAIS, GUS: BIRTH ANNIVERSARY. July 2, 1891. Charles Emile ("Gus") Dorais, football player, coach and administrator, born at Chippewa Falls, WI. Dorais made headlines in 1913 when he quarterbacked Notre Dame to a victory over Army, using forward passes to end Knute Rockne to engineer the upset. He coached at several colleges, most prominently the University of Detroit, and finished his career as coach of the Detroit Lions. Died at Birmingham, MI, Jan 4, 1954.

DUCKTONA 500. July 2. Riverview Park, Sheboygan Falls, WI. Plastic duck race in the park lagoon. "Kiss the Pig" contest, antique car show, games for children, five-mile run and live bands. Pancake breakfast, burgers, brats, beverages. Annually, the first Sunday in July. Est attendance: 3,000. For info: Lisa Wegener, Exec Dir, Sheboygan Falls Chamber Main Street Office, 641 Monroe, Ste 108, Sheboygan Falls, WI 53085. Phone: (414) 467-6206. Fax: (414) 467-9571.

LACOSTE, RENE: BIRTH ANNIVERSARY. July 2, 1904. Jean Rene Lacoste, tennis player and clothier, born at Paris, France. Lacoste, known as the Crocodile, was one quarter of the great French tennis players in the 1920s known at the Four Musketeers. He won Wimbledon and the US championship twice each, the French Open three times and was ranked No. 1 in the world in 1926–27. He designed the first shirt specifically for tennis, a loose-fitting cotton polo shirt that soon became the standard. He adorned the Lacoste shirt with a small crocodile, the first apparel logo. Died at St. Jean-de-Luz, France, Oct 12, 1996.

RED LODGE HOME OF CHAMPIONS RODEO AND PARADE. July 2–4. Red Lodge, MT. This rodeo is part of the Professional Rodeo Cowboys Association circuit and brings nearly all of the national champions to Red Lodge each year. At noon each day the Home of Champions Parade struts its way through downtown Red Lodge with colorful floats, antique cars, horses, dancing girls, wagons and more. Annually, July 2–4. Sponsor: Red Lodge Rodeo Association. Est attendance: 6,000. For info: Red Lodge Area Chamber of Commerce, Box 988, Red Lodge, MT 59068. Phone: (888) 281-0625. Fax: (406) 446-1718. E-mail: redlodge@wtp.net.

ZUPPKE, BOB: BIRTH ANNIVERSARY. July 2, 1879. Robert Carl (Bob) Zuppke, football coach and administrator, born at Berlin, Germany. After emigrating at age 2 to Milwaukee, Zuppke played basketball and studied art at the University of Wisconsin. He began coaching high school football and accepted the head job at the University of Illinois in 1913. His teams won four national championships, and Red Grange was the best player he coached. Zuppke retired after the 1941 season when the Illini went winless. Died at Champaign, IL, Dec 22, 1957.

BIRTHDAYS TODAY

Jose Canseco, Jr, 36, baseball player, born Havana, Cuba, July 2, 1964.
Sean Thomas Casey, 26, baseball player, born Willingsboro, NJ, July 2, 1974.
Eric Daze, 25, hockey player, born Montreal, Quebec, Canada, July 2, 1975.
Joseph David (Joe) Magrane, 36, former baseball player, born Des Moines, IA, July 2, 1964.
Richard Petty, 63, former auto racer, born Randleman, NC, July 2, 1937.

JULY 3 — MONDAY
Day 185 — 181 Remaining

ENNIS RODEO AND PARADE. July 3–4. Ennis, MT. Billed as the fastest two-day rodeo in Montana, this is a non-stop weekend of excitement. Parade with clowns, bucking broncos and everything imaginable. Annually, July 3–4. Est attendance: 4,000. For info: Pat Hamilton, PR, Ennis Rodeo Club, PO Box 236, Ennis, MT 59729. Phone: (406) 682-4700.

INDIANS PURCHASE DOBY: ANNIVERSARY. July 3, 1947. The Cleveland Indians purchased the contract of outfielder Larry Doby from the Newark Eagles of the Negro National League. Doby thus became the first black player in the American League. He made his debut as a player on July 5.

MARQUARD GOES TO 19–0: ANNIVERSARY. July 3, 1912. Rube Marquard of the New York Giants ran his season's record to 19–0 by defeating the Brooklyn Dodgers, 2–1. Marquard's 19 victories in a row in one season set a modern major league record. His streak came to an end on July 8 when he was beaten by the Chicago Cubs.

NUDE RECREATION WEEK. July 3–9 (tentative). "Body Acceptance Is the Idea, Nude Recreation Is the Way." Celebrate Nude Recreation Week at any of hundreds of nude beaches or resorts in the US and Canada. Skinny-dipping is an American tradition, wholesome, fun and family-oriented. For info: The Naturist Soc, PO Box 132, Oshkosh, WI 54902. Phone: (920) 231-9950. Fax: (920) 426-5184. E-mail: naturist@naturist.com. Web: www.naturist.com.

PITCHER HITS TWO GRAND SLAMS: ANNIVERSARY. July 3, 1966. Tony Cloninger of the Atlanta Braves became the first player in National League history to hit two grand slams in the same game. He added a single to drive in nine runs as the Braves beat the San Francisco Giants, 17–3.

BIRTHDAYS TODAY

Moises Rojas Alou, 34, baseball player, born Atlanta, GA, July 3, 1966.
Adrian Aucoin, 27, hockey player, born London, Ontario, Canada, July 3, 1973.
Tepo Kalevi Numminen, 32, hockey player, born Tampere, Finland, July 3, 1968.
Neil Kennedy O'Donnell, 34, football player, born Morristown, NJ, July 3, 1966.
Teemu Selanne, 30, hockey player, born Helsinki, Finland, July 3, 1970.
Gregory Lamont (Greg) Vaughn, 35, baseball player, born Sacramento, CA, July 3, 1965.

JULY 4 — TUESDAY
Day 186 — 180 Remaining

CHASE'S SPORTSQUOTE OF THE DAY

"I consider myself the luckiest man on the face of the earth."—Lou Gehrig

ANVIL MOUNTAIN RUN. July 4. Nome, AK. At 8 AM the day's activities start with the 17K run up 1,134-ft Anvil Mountain and back down to the city of Nome. Record time: 1 hr, 11 min, 23 sec. 22nd running. Annually, July 4. Est attendance: 1,000. For info: Rasmussen's Music Mart, PO Box 2, Nome, AK 99762-0002. Phone: (907) 443-2798. Fax: (907) 443-5777.

DEMPSEY WINS HEAVYWEIGHT TITLE: ANNIVERSARY. July 4, 1919. Jack Dempsey, the "Manassa Mauler," won the heavyweight championship of the world when Jess Willard failed to answer the bell for the start of the fourth round. The fight, which drew fans from as far away as New York, was held outdoors in a specially-built arena outside Toledo, OH.

GREAT CARDBOARD BOAT REGATTA. July 4 (tentative). Rock Island, IL. Teams and individuals design, build and race person-powered boats made of corrugated cardboard. See following entry for full description. Registration 7:30; races begin 9 AM. Est attendance: 2,000. For info: Jerry Tutskey, Rock Island Parks and Recreation, 1320 24th St, Rock Island, IL 61201. Phone: (309) 788-7275. Fax: (309) 788-7278.

GREAT CARDBOARD BOAT REGATTA. July 4. Rotary Riverview Park, Sheboygan, WI. The most spectacular and hilarious races of somewhat seaworthy craft ever launched in Wisconsin. Person-powered cardboard boats compete in various classes for prizes. Awards for the most spirited team, the most beautiful boats, boats following a theme and the most spectacular sinking (Titanic Award). Prizes for top finishers in three boat classes: propelled by oars or paddles, propelled by mechanical means such as paddle wheels or propellers and "Instant Boats" made from "Secret Kits" by spectators-turned-participants. Est attendance: 16,000. For info: John Michael Kohler Arts Center, 608 New York Ave, PO Box 489, Sheboygan, WI 53082-0489. Phone: (414) 458-6144. Fax: (414) 458-4473.

HARVARD WINS HENLEY: ANNIVERSARY. July 4, 1914. The eight-oared crew with coxswain from Harvard University became the first American crew to win the Grand Challenge Cup, the top event at the Royal Henley Regatta at England.

INDEPENDENCE DAY (FOURTH OF JULY). July 4. The US commemorates adoption of the Declaration of Independence by the Continental Congress. Celebrated as the nation's birthday. Legal holiday in all states and territories. The Fourth of July marks the unofficial halfway point of summer and of the baseball season. It is said, with only some accuracy, that teams in first place on the Fourth of July will go on to win the pennant. In 1914, the Boston Braves of the National League were in last place not only on the Fourth but also as late as July 18. Suddenly the team, managed by George Stallings, caught fire. The Braves reached first place on Sept 2 and went on to win the pennant. The team, known forever more as the "Miracle Braves," gives inspiration to any team seemingly out of the race at mid-season.

July 2000

S	M	T	W	T	F	S
						1
2	3	4	5	6	7	8
9	10	11	12	13	14	15
16	17	18	19	20	21	22
23	24	25	26	27	28	29
30	31					

LENEXA FREEDOM RUN. July 4. Old Town, Lenexa, KS. 22nd annual 10K and 5K runs. Est attendance: 1,500. For info: Lenexa Parks and Recreation, 13420 Oak, Lenexa, KS 66215-3652. Phone: (913) 541-8592. Fax: (913) 492-8118. E-mail: bnicks@ci.lenexa.ks.us. Web: www.ci.lenexa.ks.us.

LOU GEHRIG DAY: ANNIVERSARY. July 4, 1939. Having left the Yankees lineup and retired from baseball in May 1939, Lou Gehrig donned the New York uniform one more time for a special ceremony in his honor. His farewell speech of thanksgiving included the memorable words, "Today I consider myself the luckiest man on the face of the earth."

METS AND BRAVES WAKE UP THE NEIGHBORHOOD: ANNIVERSARY. July 4, 1984. The New York Mets defeated the Atlanta Braves, 16–13, in a 19-inning game at Atlanta-Fulton County Stadium. The game lasted until nearly 4 AM and was followed, as promised, by a fireworks show seen by approximately 10,000 fans who remained through the game. Residents of the neighborhood surrounding the stadium reportedly called the police when startled by the explosive noise.

MOUNT MARATHON RACE. July 4. Seward, AK. Grueling footrace begins in downtown Seward, then ascends and descends 3,022-ft Mt Marathon. Men, women and children. Race began as a wager between two sourdoughs. 73rd running. Est attendance: 20,000. For info: Seward Chamber of Commerce, PO Box 749, Seward, AK 99664. Phone: (907) 224-8051. Fax: (907) 224-5353. Web: www.seward.net/chamber.

NEW YORK GOLDEN ARMS TOURNAMENT. July 4. Orchard Beach Promenade, Orchard Beach, Bronx, NY. Arm wrestling competition held at promenade determines winners who will compete in the Empire State Golden Arms Tournament of Champions on Oct 12. For info: New York Arm Wrestling Assn, Inc, 200-14 45th Dr, Bayside, NY 11361. Phone: (718) 544-4592. Web: www.nycarms.com.

NIEKRO STRIKES OUT 3,000: ANNIVERSARY. July 4, 1984. Knuckleballing pitcher Phil Niekro of the New York Yankees struck out Larry Parrish of the Texas Rangers for the 3,000th strikeout in Niekro's career. He pitched in the majors from 1964 to 1987 and wound up with 3,342 strikeouts.

PEACHTREE ROAD RACE. July 4. Atlanta, GA. 10K run. 55,000-runner limit; advance registration only. For those with access to the *Atlanta Journal-Constitution*, application will appear on Mar 19. Others should send stamped envelope by Mar 1 to Peachtree 2000, c/o Atlanta Track Club. 45,000 entrants on first-come basis and 10,000 selected by lottery from other entries postmarked in March 2000. Annually, on July 4. Est attendance: 55,000. For info: Atlanta Track Club, 3097 E Shadowlawn Ave, Atlanta, GA 30305. Web: www.atlantatrackclub.org.

PIKES PEAK INTERNATIONAL HILL CLIMB. July 4. Pikes Peak, CO. "The Race to the Clouds." 77th Invitational. The second oldest auto race in the US (behind the Indianapolis 500), the Hill Climb is a speed contest for motorized vehicles that runs one vehicle at a time against the clock. The traditional starting line is Mile Post 7 at an altitude of 9,400 feet. The finish line, 12.42 miles away at the summit, is 14,110 feet altitude for a vertical rise of almost 5,000 feet. There are 156 separate curves, a maximum ascent of 10 percent and a minimum descent of 3 percent on the course. The road surface is well-maintained decomposed Pikes Peak granite. Annually, July 4. Est attendance: 6,000. For info: PPIHC, PO Box 67962, Colorado Springs, CO 80934. Phone: (719) 685-4400. Fax: (719) 685-5885. E-mail: ppihc@ppihc.com. Web: www.ppihc.com.

RYAN STRIKES OUT 3,000th BATTER: 20th ANNIVERSARY. July 4, 1980. Nolan Ryan of the Houston Astros struck out the 3,000th batter of his career, Cesar Geronimo of the Cincinnati Reds. Houston won the game, 8–1. Ryan finished his career with 5,714, more than anyone else, and was inducted into the Baseball Hall of Fame in 1999.

SAPERSTEIN, ABE: BIRTH ANNIVERSARY. July 4, 1902. Abraham Michael (Abe) Saperstein, Basketball Hall of Fame executive, born at London, England. Saperstein came to the US in 1905, played and coached basketball at Chicago and organized the Harlem Globetrotters in 1927. Originally an excellent and serious team, the Globetrotters evolved into the sport's premiere entertainment, playing thousands of games around the world and almost never losing. Inducted into the Hall of Fame in 1970. Died at Chicago, IL, Mar 15, 1966.

TOYOTA/ADT CHALLENGE OF CHAMPIONS. July 4. Pikes Peak, CO. 2nd annual. The official race-day kick-off event for the Pikes Peak International Hill Climb will feature racing greats Parnelli Jones, Roger Mears and Ivan Stewart racing in identical Toyota Racing Celicas. For info: PPIHC, PO Box 6962, Colorado Springs, CO 80934. Phone: (719) 685-4400. Fax: (719) 685-5885. E-mail: ppihc@ppihc.com. Web: www.ppihc.com.

US WOMEN'S AMATEUR PUBLIC LINKS (GOLF) CHAMPIONSHIP. July 4–9. Legacy Golf Links, Aberdeen, NC. For info: US Golf Assn, Golf House, Far Hills, NJ 07931. Phone: (908) 234-2300. Fax: (908) 234-9687. E-mail: usga@usga.org. Web: www.usga.org.

WORLD'S GREATEST LIZARD RACE. July 4. Chaparral Park, Lovington, NM. Participants and observers cheer as their lizards and iguanas race down a 16-ft ramp; winners are awarded trophies. Many other lizard events will be held throughout the day. Entertainment and other games are also featured. Annually, July 4. For info: Lovington Chamber of Commerce, PO Box 1347, Lovington, NM 88260. Phone: (505) 396-5311. Fax: (505) 396-2823.

WROK/WZOK/WXXQ ANYTHING THAT FLOATS ROCK RIVER RAFT RACE. July 4. Rock River, Rockford, IL. More than 100 rafts compete for prizes in speed and creativity. Est attendance: 60,000. For info: WROK/WZOK/WXXQ Radios, 3901 Brendenwood Rd, Rockford, IL 61107. Phone: (815) 399-2233. Fax: (815) 399-8148.

BIRTHDAYS TODAY

James Louis (Jim) Beattie, 46, baseball executive and former baseball player, born Hampton, VA, July 4, 1954.

Vinicio (Vinny) Castilla, 33, baseball player, born Oaxaca, Mexico, July 4, 1967.

Allen (Al) Davis, 71, football executive and former coach, born Brockton, MA, July 4, 1929.

La'Roi Damon Glover, 26, football player, born San Diego, CA, July 4, 1974.

Harvey Grant, 35, basketball player, born Augusta, GA, July 4, 1965.

Horace Grant, 35, basketball player, born Augusta, GA, July 4, 1965.

Pamela Howard (Pam) Shriver, 38, broadcaster and former tennis player, born Baltimore, MD, July 4, 1962.

George Michael Steinbrenner, III, 70, baseball executive, born Rocky River, OH, July 4, 1930.

JULY 5 — WEDNESDAY
Day 187 — 179 Remaining

BROTHERS HIT HOME RUNS: 65th ANNIVERSARY. July 5, 1935. Tony Cuccinello of the Brooklyn Dodgers and his brother, Al Cuccinello, of the New York Giants became the first brothers in major league history to hit home runs for opposing teams in the same game. The Dodgers won, 14–4.

CANADA: THE NORTH AMERICAN. July 5–9. Spruce Meadows, Calgary, Alberta. Show jumping tournament featuring the Nortel Queen Elizabeth II Cup and the Chrysler Classic. Enjoy country atmosphere in the Spruce Meadows Marketplace on the Plaza. Est attendance: 85,000. For info: Spruce Meadows, RR #9, Calgary, AB, Canada T2J 5G5. Phone: (403) 974-4200. Fax: (403) 974-4270. E-mail: smeadows@telusplanet.net. Web: www.sprucemeadows.com.

CLEMENS GETS 3,000th STRIKEOUT: ANNIVERSARY. July 5, 1998. Roger Clemens of the Toronto Blue Jays became the 11th pitcher in major league baseball history to reach the 3,000-mark in career strikeouts when he fanned Randy Winn of the Tampa Bay Devil Rays in the 3rd inning. The Blue Jays won, 2–1.

COLUMBIA WINS AT HENLEY: ANNIVERSARY. July 5, 1887. A four-oar crew from Columbia University became the first American entry to win an event at the Henley Regatta at London. Columbia defeated a crew from Hertford College to win the Visitors Challenge Cup. An American crew did not win Henley's greatest prize, the Grand Challenge Cup, until 1914 when a Harvard crew did so.

DAVIS, DWIGHT: BIRTH ANNIVERSARY. July 5, 1879. Dwight Filley Davis, tennis player, born at St. Louis, MO. Davis was a nationally prominent singles and doubles player, but his enduring contribution to the sport was his creation of the Davis Cup international competition. Davis purchased the cup from a Boston jeweler for $750 and helped win the first two competitions in 1900 and 1902. After retiring, he worked in government and was Secretary of War under President Calvin Coolidge. Died at Washington, DC, Nov 28, 1945.

DOBY BREAKS AL COLOR LINE: ANNIVERSARY. July 5, 1947. Larry Doby became the first African American to play in the American League when he appeared as a pinch hitter for the Cleveland Indians in a game against the Chicago White Sox. The Indians lost, 6–5.

I LOVE NEW YORK HORSE SHOW. July 5–9. North Elba Showgrounds, Lake Placid, NY. Hunter/Jumper competition. Featuring the $35,000 I Love New York Grandprix. For info: Classic Communications, 38 Mechanic St, Ste 101, Foxboro, MA 02035. Phone: (508) 698-6810.

76ERS TRADE WILT: ANNIVERSARY. July 5, 1968. The Philadelphia 76ers traded center Wilt Chamberlain to the Los Angeles Lakers for three players, Darrell Imhoff, Archie Clark and Jerry Chambers and an unannounced amount of cash.

BIRTHDAYS TODAY

BIRTHDAYS TODAY

David William (Dave) Eiland, 34, baseball player, born Dade City, FL, July 5, 1966.

Richard Michael ("Goose") Gossage, 49, former baseball player, born Colorado Springs, CO, July 5, 1951.

Chris Gratton, 25, hockey player, born Brantford, Ontario, Canada, July 5, 1975.

John Clark LeClair, 31, hockey player, born St. Albans, VT, July 5, 1969.

James David Lofton, 44, former football player, born Fort Ord, CA, July 5, 1956.

John Steven (Johnny) Rodgers, 49, Heisman Trophy running back, born Omaha, NE, July 5, 1951.

Timothy Howard (Tim) Worrell, 33, baseball player, born Pasadena, CA, July 5, 1967.

JULY 6 — THURSDAY
Day 188 — 178 Remaining

CHASE'S SPORTSQUOTE OF THE DAY

"No player overcame more obstacles to become a champion than Althea Gibson."—Bud Collins

AL ENDS NL ALL-STAR GAME STREAK: ANNIVERSARY. July 6, 1983. On the 50th anniversary of baseball's first All-Star Game, the American League defeated the National League, 13–3, to snap the NL's 11-game winning streak. Fred Lynn hit the first grand slam in All-Star competition off Attlee Hammaker in the third inning.

FIRST BASEBALL ALL-STAR GAME: ANNIVERSARY. July 6, 1933. Baseball's first official All-Star Game was held at Comiskey Park, Chicago, IL. Babe Ruth led the American League with a home run as they defeated the National League 4–2. Prior to the summer of 1933, All-Star contests consisted of pre- and post-season exhibitions that often found teams made up of a few stars playing beside journeymen and even minor leaguers.

FIRST BLACK TITLE AT WIMBLEDON: ANNIVERSARY. July 6, 1957. Althea Gibson of the US became the first African American to win a Wimbledon title when she beat Darlene Hard, also of the US, 6–3, 6–2, to win the women's singles championship.

HORNER HITS FOUR HOME RUNS: ANNIVERSARY. July 6, 1986. Bob Horner of the Atlanta Braves hit four runs against the Montreal Expos, but the Braves lost, 11–8. Horner hit three homers against Andy McGaffigan and one against Jeff Reardon.

O'NEILL, STEVE: BIRTH ANNIVERSARY. July 6, 1891. Stephen Francis (Steve) O'Neill, baseball player, coach and manager, born at Minooka, PA. O'Neill caught in the majors in the 1920s and 1930s, after which he coached and managed for several teams, including the 1945 Detroit Tigers, who won the World Series. Died at Cleveland, OH, Jan 26, 1962.

RUFFIAN INJURED IN MATCH RACE: 25th ANNIVERSARY. July 6, 1975. The filly Ruffian, undefeated in her career, met Kentucky Derby winner Foolish Pleasure in a special match race. On the backstretch, Ruffian sustained a severe leg injury and was pulled up by jockey Jacinto Vasquez. After a night of heroic medical and surgical efforts, she was humanely destroyed.

YOUNGEST OPEN CHAMP WINS IN SUDDEN DEATH: ANNIVERSARY. July 6, 1998. Korean Se Ri Pak rolled in an 18-foot birdie putt to defeat amateur Jenny Chuasiriporn on the second hole of sudden death and win the 1998 US Women's Open at Blackwolf Run GC at Kohler, WI. The two golfers had finished the regulation 72 holes tied at six over par and had battled evenly at two over par through an 18-hole play-off. Both parred the first extra hole, the first sudden-death hole in the history of the tournament. By winning, Pak became the youngest Open champ in history, at 20, and only the second golfer on the LPGA tour to win two major championships in her rookie year. Her earlier victory had come in the McDonald's LPGA Classic.

BIRTHDAYS TODAY

Kenneth Lance Johnson, 37, baseball player, born Lincoln Heights, IL, July 6, 1963.

Omar Olivares, 33, baseball player, born Mayaguez, Puerto Rico, July 6, 1967.

Douglas Bradford (Brad) Park, 52, Hockey Hall of Fame defenseman, born Toronto, Ontario, Canada, July 6, 1948.

Willie Larry Randolph, 46, former baseball player, born Holly Hill, SC, July 6, 1954.

Michael Joseph (Mike) Riley, 47, football coach, born Wallace, ID, July 6, 1953.

JULY 7 — FRIDAY
Day 189 — 177 Remaining

AFRMA RAT AND MOUSE DISPLAY ORANGE COUTY FAIR. July 7–23. Orange County Fair, Costa Mesa, CA. American Fancy Rat and Mice Association show exhibits rats and mice of "fancy" species that make good pets. For info: AFRMA, PO Box 2589, Winnetka, CA 91396-2589. Phone: (818) 992-5564 or (909) 685-2350. Fax: (818) 592-6590. E-mail: craigr@afrma.org. Web: www.afrma.org.

CANADA: CALGARY EXHIBITION AND STAMPEDE. July 7–16. Calgary, Alberta. Billed as the "Greatest Outdoor Show on Earth!" The world's top professional cowboys compete for supremacy during the Calgary Stampede Half-Million Dollar Rodeo. Each evening, nine heart-stopping chuckwagon races explode in an all-out dash to the finish. Outdoor stage spectaculars, International Stock Show, free pancake breakfasts, midway, casino and a city-wide celebration are what you can expect, jam-packed into 10 of the most varied and exciting days you'll ever experience. Est attendance: 1,200,000. For info: Calgary Stampede Assn, PO Box 1060 Station M, Calgary, AB, Canada, T2P 2K8. Phone: (800) 661-1260.

CHARLES, EZZARD: BIRTH ANNIVERSARY. July 7, 1921. Ezzard Mack Charles, boxer, born at Lawrenceville, GA. A precise boxer who liked to win on points, Charles lacked the killer instinct to be a truly great fighter. Nevertheless, he won the heavyweight championship on June 22, 1949, outpointing Jersey Joe Walcott after Joe Louis retired. Walcott took the crown from him in July 1951. Died at Chicago, IL, May 28, 1975.

ELKHART GRAND PRIX AND MOTOR SPORTS WEEKEND. July 7–9 (tentative). Elkhart, IN. The largest karting event race in the world follows a 4,900-ft course through downtown streets. More than 700 competitors from all over the world. Also features top-name race car drivers, antique and hot rod car show and swap meet, racing car displays, carnival and celebrity entertainment

	S	M	T	W	T	F	S
July 2000							1
	2	3	4	5	6	7	8
	9	10	11	12	13	14	15
	16	17	18	19	20	21	22
	23	24	25	26	27	28	29
	30	31					

at the 11th annual race. Est attendance: 70,000. For info: Curt Paluzzi, Natl Kart News, 51535 Bittersweet Rd, Granger, IN 46530. Phone: (219) 277-0033. Fax: (219) 277-4279. E-mail: nkartnews@aol.com. Web: www.nkn.com.

FERRIS, DAN: BIRTH ANNIVERSARY. July 7, 1889. Daniel Joseph (Dan) Ferris, amateur athletics administrator, born at Pawling, NY. Ferris became secretary to James E. Sullivan, secretary-treasurer of the Amateur Athletic Union of the US (AAU) in 1907. He succeeded Sullivan in 1927 and did not relinquish this position until 1957. Ferris worked long days with a small staff in defense of pure amateurism. He engaged in many public controversies, including the dismissal of swimmer Eleanor Holm from the 1936 Olympic team for drinking champagne and the protracted conflict between the AAU and the NCAA for control of amateur athletics. Died at Amityville, NY, May 2, 1977.

HERMAN, BILLY: BIRTH ANNIVERSARY. July 7, 1909. William Jennings Bryan (Billy) Herman, Baseball Hall of Fame second baseman, born at New Albany, IN. Herman played 15 seasons, participated in 10 All-Star Games and collected 2,345 hits. He later coached and managed. Inducted into the Hall of Fame in 1975. Died at West Palm Beach, FL, Sept 5, 1992.

MACY'S FISHING CONTEST IN PROSPECT PARK. July 7-15. Prospect Park, Brooklyn, NY. A contest for young anglers, 15 and under, with prizes for the largest or most fish. At the Rustic Shelter lakeside, near the Kate Wollman Rink parking lot. Groups must register ahead of time. Est attendance: 1,000. For info: Press Mgr, Public Info Office—Litchfield Villa, 95 Prospect Park W, Brooklyn, NY 11215. Phone: (718) 965-8954. Fax: (718) 965-8972. E-mail: prospect1@juno.com. Web: www.prospectpark.com.

NICKLAUS ENDS MAJORS' STREAK: ANNIVERSARY. July 7, 1998. Jack Nicklaus announced that he would not compete in either the 1998 British Open or the 1998 PGA Championship. Thus was ended a streak of unsurpassing durability and excellence. Going back to 1957, Nicklaus had played in the last 154 consecutive major championships for which he was eligible. Since he did not join the PGA Tour until 1962, he was not eligible to play in the PGA Championship until that year. Nor did he play in the British Open until 1962. But Nicklaus had not missed a major since the 1962 Masters, a streak of 146 straight that came to an end with the 1998 Masters and the 1998 US Open.

PAIGE, SATCHEL: BIRTH ANNIVERSARY. July 7, 1906. Leroy Robert ("Satchel") Paige, Baseball Hall of Fame pitcher, born at Mobile, AL. Paige was the greatest attrac-

tion in Negro Leagues baseball and one of black baseball's greatest players. He was also, at age 42, the first black pitcher in the American League. Inducted into the Hall of Fame in 1971. Died at Kansas City, MO, June 8, 1982.

PRAIRIE ROSE STATE GAMES. July 7-9. Bismarck, ND. A multisport Olympic-style competition for athletes from the state of North Dakota. For info: Prairie Rose State Games, 1835 Bismarck Expwy, Bismarck, ND 58504. Phone: (701) 328-5357. Fax: (701) 328-5363. E-mail: mwalth@pioneer.state.nd.us.

SACRAMENTO LOSES FIRST AMERICAN CFL GAME: ANNIVERSARY. July 7, 1993. The Ottawa Rough Riders defeated the Sacramento Gold Miners, 32–23, to spoil the debut of the first US team in the Canadian Football League. Ottawa quarterback Tom Burgess passed for three touchdowns.

SLOW-PITCH SOFTBALL TOURNAMENT. July 7-9. Elm Park, Williamsport, PA. 27th annual charitable tournament with 64 teams. Sponsor: Miller Lite. Est attendance: 8,500. For info: Don Phillips, Mid-State Beverage Co, Inc, 532 Sylvan Dr, South Williamsport, PA 17702. Phone: (570) 322-3331.

SPAIN: RUNNING OF THE BULLS. July 7-14. Pamplona, Spain. Every morning at 8 AM during the Fiesta of San Fermín daring young men run the streets of Pamplona, leading a herd of bulls from their pen into the bullring. The run lasts from two to three minutes and is about 800 meters long. On July 15 there is a parody of the run made by some diehards who refuse to face the fact that the Fiesta is over. They run in front of the early morning bus on Santo Domingo Street.

STATE GAMES OF OREGON. July 7-9. Portland, OR. Oregon's Olympic style amateur sports festival. Normally, the first weekend after July 4th. Est attendance: 20,000. For info: Kerry Duffy, Exec Dir, 4840 SW Western Ave, Ste 900, Beaverton, OR 97005. Phone: (503) 520-1319. Fax: (503) 520-9747.

UNSEEDED BECKER WINS WIMBLEDON TITLE: 15th ANNIVERSARY. July 7, 1985. 17-year-old Boris Becker of Germany became the youngest player and the first unseeded player to win the men's singles championship at Wimbledon. He defeated Kevin Curren, 6–3, 6–7, 7–6, 6–4, in the final.

BIRTHDAYS TODAY

David Allen (Dave) Burba, 34, baseball player, born Dayton, OH, July 7, 1966.

Jose Jimenez, 27, baseball player, born San Pedro de Macoris, Dominican Republic, July 7, 1973.

Edward Charles (Chuck) Knoblauch, 32, baseball player, born Houston, TX, July 7, 1968.

Michelle Kwan, 20, figure skater, born Torrance, CA, July 7, 1980.

Michael McCrary, 30, football player, born Vienna, VA, July 7, 1970.

Rumun Ndur, 25, hockey player, born Zaria, Nigeria, July 7, 1975.

Joseph Steve (Joe) Sakic, 31, hockey player, born Burnaby, British Columbia, Canada, July 7, 1969.

Ralph Lee Sampson, 40, former basketball player, born Harrisonburg, VA, July 7, 1960.

JULY 8 — SATURDAY
Day 190 — 176 Remaining

AVON RUNNING–HARTFORD. July 8. West Hartford, CT. 5K walk and 10K run for women and girls of all ages and abilities. For info: Beth Shluger, Avon Running–Hartford, 119 Hebron Ave, Glastonbury, CT 06033. Phone: (860) 652-8866. E-mail: eatnrun@erols.com. Web: www.avon running.com.

BILLIE JEAN WINS THREE TITLES: ANNIVERSARY. July 8, 1967. Tennis player Billie Jean King of the US won three titles at Wimbledon. She beat Ann Haydon Jones for the singles title, teamed with Rosie Casals for the women's doubles title and joined with Owen Davidson to capture the mixed doubles title.

BRAILLE RALLYE. July 8. Braille Institute Youth Center, Los Angeles, CA. Blind or visually impaired students from Braille Institute use braille or large-print instructions to navigate sighted drivers through more than 80 miles of LA streets. Celebrity drivers from television, radio and film help make this a special event. Annually, in July. For info: Braille Institute Communications Dept, 741 N Vermont Ave, Los Angeles, CA 90029. Phone: (213) 663-1111, ext 276. Fax: (213) 663-0867.

CANADA: THE BIQUE RIDE. July 8–15 (tentative). Toronto, Ontario, to Montreal, Quebec. 6th annual. The BiQue Ride is a weeklong cycling trip leaving from Old City Hall at Toronto and arriving at Old City Hall at Montreal. The route goes through historic communities along the scenic shores of Lake Ontario and the St. Lawrence River. Cyclists travel on side roads and country lanes to avoid traffic congestion. Total distance is 390 miles. For info: Veloforce, 145 King St West, Ste 1000, Toronto, ON, Canada M5H 1J8. Phone: (416) 484-8339. Fax: (416) 484-1613. Web: www.CycleCanada.com/bique .html.

CORNHUSKER STATE SUMMER GAMES. July 8–17. Site TBA. A multisport Olympic-style competition for athletes from the state of Nebraska. For info: Cornhusker State Games, PO Box 82411, Lincoln, NE 68501. Phone: (402) 471-2544. Fax: (402) 471-9712. E-mail: NESTGAMES@ aol.com.

ELLIOT, JUMBO: BIRTH ANNIVERSARY. July 8, 1914. James Francis ("Jumbo") Elliot, track athlete and coach, born at Philadelphia, PA. Elliot ran the quarter-mile at Villanova, but an injury prevented him from qualifying for the 1936 Summer Olympic team. He stayed at Vil-

lanova to become one of the most successful track coaches, specializing in middle-distance runners. His athletes won eight NCAA team championships and 63 individual titles. Elliot coached as a volunteer; his income came from a construction equipment leasing firm he founded. Died at Juno Beach, FL, Mar 22, 1981.

FISHING HAS NO BOUNDARIES—MADISON. July 8–9. Lake Mendota, Madison, WI. A two-day fishing experience for persons with disabilities. Expected attendance of 100 participants and 300 volunteers. For info: FHNB, 4923 Hammersley Rd, Madison, WI 53711. Phone: (608) 271-0440. Fax: (608) 271-1777.

MARQUARD'S STREAK ENDS: ANNIVERSARY. July 8, 1912. Pitcher Rube Marquard of the New York Giants was beaten by the Chicago Cubs, 7–2, ending his winning streak at 19 games, tying Tim Keefe's major league record for consecutive games won in a single season.

O'DAY, HANK: BIRTH ANNIVERSARY. July 8, 1862. Henry Francis (Hank) O'Day, baseball player, manager and umpire, born at Chicago, IL. O'Day pitched in the majors before the turn of the century and then worked as a National League umpire for 31 years. He handled the first World Series in 1903 plus nine others, called the only unassisted triple play in World Series history and ruled Fred Merkle out at second base in baseball's greatest dispute, Sept 23, 1908. Died at Chicago, July 2, 1935.

SHARK TOURNAMENT. July 8–9. Wakefield, RI. More than 100 boats and up to 400 anglers registered. 19th annual tournament. For info: Ellen Miller, Info Serv Coord, Rhode Island Tourism Division, 1 W Exchange St, Providence, RI 02903. Phone: (800) 556-2484 or (401) 277-2601. Fax: (401) 273-8270. E-mail: riedc@riedc.com. Web: www.algoma.org.

SULLIVAN DEFEATS KILRAIN: ANNIVERSARY. July 8, 1889. John L. Sullivan, heavyweight champion of the world, defeated Jake Kilrain in the 75th round of a fight at Richburg, MS. This was the last bare-knuckles title fight after which boxing was governed by the Marquess of Queensbury rules.

VALENTIN MAKES UNASSISTED TRIPLE PLAY: ANNIVERSARY. July 8, 1994. Shortstop John Valentin of the Boston Red Sox recorded the 11th triple play in major league history in a game against the Seattle Mariners. In the 6th inning, Valentin caught a line drive hit by Marc Newfield, stepped on second base to double Mike Blowers and tapped Keith Mitchell before he could return to first.

BIRTHDAYS TODAY

Roone Pinckney Arledge, 69, television executive, born New York, NY, July 8, 1931.

Robert Joseph (Bobby) Ayala, 31, baseball player, born Ventura, CA, July 8, 1969.

John David Crow, 65, Heisman Trophy halfback, born Marion, LA, July 8, 1935.

Karl Dykhuis, 28, hockey player, born Sept-Iles, Quebec, Canada, July 8, 1972.

John Harold (Jack) Lambert, 48, Pro Football Hall of Fame linebacker, born Mantua, OH, July 8, 1952.

July *2000*	S	M	T	W	T	F	S
							1
	2	3	4	5	6	7	8
	9	10	11	12	13	14	15
	16	17	18	19	20	21	22
	23	24	25	26	27	28	29
	30	31					

JULY 9 — SUNDAY
Day 191 — 175 Remaining

CHASE'S SPORTSQUOTE OF THE DAY

"No matter how hard I try, I just can't seem to break 64."—Jack Nicklaus

FIRST ALL-STAR GAME SHUTOUT: 60th ANNIVERSARY. July 9, 1940. The National League recorded the first shutout in All-Star Game history, defeating the American League, 4–0. Five National League pitchers held the Americans to three hits.

KINNICK, NILE: BIRTH ANNIVERSARY. July 9, 1918. Nile Clarke Kinnick, Jr, Heisman Trophy halfback, born at Adel, IA. Kinnick was the quintessential college football hero who excelled academically and athletically. He earned All-American honors as a sophomore and by his senior year was regarded as the nation's best back. After winning the Heisman Trophy and graduating Phi Beta Kappa, he entered law school. But World War II intervened, and he was killed in a plane crash at the Gulf of Paria, Venezuela, June 2, 1943.

MARSHALL GETS NFL FRANCHISE: ANNIVERSARY. July 9, 1932. The National Football League awarded its inactive Boston franchise to George Preston Marshall and a group of investors. The team used Braves Field in 1932 and was nicknamed the Braves. In 1933, the team played its home games at Fenway Park and changed its name to the Redskins. Four seasons later, the Redskins moved to Washington.

NATIONAL SPORTING ASSOCIATION WORLD SPORTS EXPO '00. July 9–11. McCormick Place, Chicago, IL. The international kickoff of the exposition where sporting goods retailers will see products for the year 2001. Est attendance: 70,000. For info: Larry Weindruch, Dir of Communications, Natl Sporting Goods Assn, 1699 Wall St, Mt Prospect, IL 60056-5780. Phone: (847) 439-4000. Fax: (847) 849-0111. E-mail: nsga1699@aol.com. Web: www.nsgachicagoshow.com.

NATIONAL THERAPEUTIC RECREATION WEEK. July 9–15. To increase awareness of therapeutic recreation programs and services, and to expand leisure opportunities for individuals with disabilities in their local communities. Annually, the second week in July. For info: Natl Therapeutic Recreation Soc, Ahren's NRPA Institute, 22377 Belmont Ridge Rd, Ashburn, VA 20148. Phone: (800) 626-NRPA. E-mail: ntrsnrpa@aol.com. Web: www.nrpa.org/branches/ntrs.htm.

NFL TRAINING CAMPS—"THE CHEESE LEAGUE." July 9–Aug 19 (approximate). Football fans can enjoy football in summer in Wisconsin's "Cheese League" towns where training camps hold scrimmages and exhibition games. Four teams will train in Wisconsin starting in mid-July—the Chicago Bears at the University of Wisconsin-Platteville, the New Orleans Saints at the University of Wisconsin-La Crosse, the Kansas City Chiefs at the University of Wisconsin-River Falls and the Green Bay Packers at Green Bay. For schedule info: (414) 270-6200. Web: www.wisports.com or www.travelwisconsin.com.

NICKLAUS WINS FIRST BRITISH OPEN: ANNIVERSARY. July 9, 1966. Jack Nicklaus shot 282 at Muirfield in Scotland to win his first British Open Championship. With this victory, Nicklaus joined Gene Sarazen, Ben Hogan and Gary Player as the only golfers to have won all four events comprising golf's modern Grand Slam: the Masters, the US Open, the British Open and the PGA Championship. Nicklaus won two other British Opens, in 1970 and 1978.

SELIG ELECTED COMMISSIONER: ANNIVERSARY. July 9, 1998. After serving nearly six years as interim commissioner, Allan H. ("Bud') Selig was elected to a five-year term as commissioner of baseball. Selig, owner of the Milwaukee Brewers, became interim commissioner upon the resignation of Fay Vincent in September 1992.

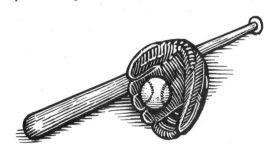

TRIPLE-A BASEBALL REALIGNS: ANNIVERSARY. July 9, 1997. Meeting at Des Moines, IA, for the annual Triple-A All-Star Game, owners of Triple-A minor league teams voted to realign from three leagues to two, effective with the start of the 1998 season. The vote kept teams of the International League and the Pacific Coast League together but split the American Association in two. The new International League included ten teams from the old International League, Buffalo, Indianapolis and Louisville from the American Association and an expansion team at Durham, NC. The new Pacific Coast League included ten teams from the old Pacific Coast League, Iowa, Nashville, New Orleans, Oklahoma City and Omaha from the American Association and an expansion team at Memphis.

BIRTHDAYS TODAY

Michael Jay (Mike) Andrews, 57, former baseball player, born Los Angeles, CA, July 9, 1943.

Peter Marcus (Pete) Kendall, 27, football player, born Weymouth, MA, July 9, 1973.

Hector Headley Lopez, 71, former baseball player, born Colon, Panama, July 9, 1929.

Orenthal James (O.J.) Simpson, 53, former broadcaster and Heisman Trophy and Pro Football Hall of Fame running back, born San Francisco, CA, July 9, 1947.

JULY 10 — MONDAY
Day 192 — 174 Remaining

ASHE, ARTHUR: BIRTH ANNIVERSARY. July 10, 1943. Arthur Robert Ashe, Jr, tennis player, born at Richmond, VA. Ashe became a legend for his list of firsts as a black tennis player. He was chosen for the US Davis Cup team in 1963 and became captain in 1980. He won the US men's singles championship and US Open in 1968 and in 1975 the men's singles at Wimbledon. Ashe won a total of 33 career titles. In 1985 he was inducted into the International Tennis Hall of Fame. A social activist, Ashe worked to eliminate racism and stereotyping and was arrested numerous times while protesting. He helped create inner-city tennis programs for youths and wrote the three-volume *A Hard Road to Glory: A History of the African-American Athlete*. Aware that *USA Today* intended to publish an article revealing that he was infected with the AIDS virus, Ashe announced on Apr 8, 1992, that he probably contracted HIV through a transfusion during bypass surgery in 1983. In September of 1992 he began a $5 million fundraising effort on behalf of the Arthur Ashe Foundation for the Defeat of AIDS and during his last year campaigned for public awareness regarding the AIDS epidemic. Died at New York, NY, Feb 6, 1993.

HEYDLER, JOHN: BIRTH ANNIVERSARY. July 10, 1869. John Arnold Heydler, baseball executive, born at Lafargeville, NY. Heydler was president of the National League from 1918 to 1934. He helped to found the Baseball Hall of Fame and, in 1929, suggested a rules change that became known as the designated hitter. Died at San Diego, CA, Apr 18, 1956.

HUBBELL STRIKES OUT FIVE HALL OF FAMERS: ANNIVERSARY. July 10, 1934. In baseball's second All-Star Game, National League pitcher Carl Hubbell of the New York Giants struck out Babe Ruth, Lou Gehrig, Jimmie Foxx, Al Simmons and Joe Cronin in succession. All five were later inducted into the Hall of Fame. Hubbell gave up only two hits in three innings, but the American League won the game, 9–7.

KLEIN HITS FOUR HOME RUNS: ANNIVERSARY. July 10, 1936. Outfielder Chuck Klein of the Philadelphia Phillies became the fourth player in major league history to hit four home runs in one game. He completed the feat in a 10-inning game against the Pittsburgh Pirates at Forbes Field. The Phillies won, 9–6.

LEAGUES APPROVE TWO DIVISIONS: ANNIVERSARY. July 10, 1968. After a long debate, the National League and the American League accepted a recommendation from baseball's Executive Council to operate in 1969 with two divisions of six teams each. The American League had approved a two-division alignment in May. Today the National League, in effect, agreed to go along.

McNAMEE, GRAHAM: BIRTH ANNIVERSARY. July 10, 1888. Graham McNamee, broadcaster, born at Washington, DC. McNamee began his radio career in 1923 and made his reputation calling that year's World Series between the New York Giants and the New York Yankees. His breezy and informal style suited both the sporting events he covered and other news stories as well. His motto was, "I tell it as it looks to me." Died at New York, NY, May 9, 1942.

SILVER HOOPS 3-ON-3 BASKETBALL TOURNAMENT. July 10. Teaters Field, Kellogg, ID. This is the sixth year of this chamber event designed to have fun while raising funds to support the Kellogg Chamber of Commerce. Est attendance: 200. For info: Silver Hoops 3-on-3 Basketball Tournament, Kellogg Chamber of Commerce, 608 Bunker Ave, Kellogg, ID 83837. Phone: (208) 784-0821. Fax: (208) 783-4343. E-mail: kellogg@nidlink.com. Web: www.nidlink.com/~kellogg/kellogg-id.org.

US AMATEUR PUBLIC LINKS (GOLF) CHAMPIONSHIP. July 10–15. Heron Lakes Golf Club, Portland, OR. For info: US Golf Assn, Golf House, Far Hills, NJ 07931. Phone: (908) 234-2300. Fax: (908) 234-9687. E-mail: usga@usga.org. Web: www.usga.org.

BIRTHDAYS TODAY

Martin Keevin (Marty) Cordova, 31, baseball player, born Las Vegas, NV, July 10, 1969.
Andre Nolan Dawson, 46, former baseball player, born Miami, FL, July 10, 1954.
Adam David Vernon Foote, 29, hockey player, born Toronto, Ontario, Canada, July 10, 1971.
Jake LaMotta (born Giacobe LaMotta), 79, former boxer, born New York, NY, July 10, 1921.

Harold Abraham (Hal) McRae, 55, former baseball manager and player, born Avon Park, FL, July 10, 1945.
DeWain Lee Stevens, 33, baseball player, born Kansas City, MO, July 10, 1967.
Sarah Virginia Wade, 55, former tennis player, born Bournemouth, England, July 10, 1945.

JULY 11 — TUESDAY
Day 193 — 173 Remaining

BABE'S DEBUT IN MAJORS: ANNIVERSARY. July 11, 1914. Babe Ruth made his debut in major league baseball when he took the mound at Fenway Park for the Boston Red Sox against the Cleveland Indians. Ruth was relieved for the last two innings but was the winning pitcher in a 4–3 game.

BASEBALL ALL-STAR GAME. July 11 (tentative). Turner Field, Atlanta, GA. All-Stars from the American League oppose All-Stars from the National League in Major League Baseball's 71st All-Star Game. The first All-Star Game, played in 1933 and planned as a one-time event, proved so popular that it immediately became an annual affair. No game was played in 1945 because of World War II. Two games were played in 1959, 1960, 1961 and 1962.

HAUGHTON, PERCY: BIRTH ANNIVERSARY. July 11, 1876. Percy Duncan Haughton, football player and coach and baseball executive, born at New York, NY. Haughton played football and baseball at Harvard, coached at Cornell and returned to Harvard in 1908. Over nine years, his teams won 71 games, lost 7 and tied 5. He dominated the Eastern football scene, emphasizing quick execution and deception over brute strength. He was briefly president of the Boston Braves and served in the army during World War I. Died at New York, Oct 27, 1924.

HOLMES'S HITTING STREAK ENDS: 55th ANNIVERSARY. July 11, 1945. Tommy Holmes of the Boston Braves went hitless, snapping his hitting streak at 37 games, then the National League record. Holmes's mark stood until 1978 when it was broken by Pete Rose.

RYAN STRIKES OUT 4,000: 15th ANNIVERSARY. July 11, 1985. Nolan Ryan of the Houston Astros became the first pitcher in baseball history to reach the 4,000 mark in career strikeouts when he made Danny Heep of the New York Mets his victim in the sixth inning. Ryan finished his career in 1993 with 5,714 strikeouts.

BIRTHDAYS TODAY

Andrew Jason (Andy) Ashby, 33, baseball player, born Kansas City, MO, July 11, 1967.
Billy Manual Ashley, 30, baseball player, born Taylor, MI, July 11, 1970.
Joe T. Johnson, 28, football player, born St. Louis, MO, July 11, 1972.
Allan (Al) MacInnis, 37, hockey player, born Inverness, Nova Scotia, Canada, July 11, 1963.
Leon Spinks, 47, former heavyweight champion boxer, born St. Louis, MO, July 11, 1953.
Rodney (Rod) Strickland, 34, basketball player, born New York, NY, July 11, 1966.

JULY 12 — WEDNESDAY
Day 194 — 172 Remaining

BOCA GRANDE TARPON TOURNAMENT ("WORLD'S RICHEST"). July 12–13. Boca Grande Pass, Boca Grande, FL. The world's richest tarpon tournament. Field limited to 60 boats with an entry fee of $3,500. First-place prize for the largest tarpon is $100,000. Annually, the week after the 4th of July. Est attendance: 1,000. For

	S	M	T	W	T	F	S
July 2000							1
	2	3	4	5	6	7	8
	9	10	11	12	13	14	15
	16	17	18	19	20	21	22
	23	24	25	26	27	28	29
	30	31					

info: Boca Grande Chamber of Commerce, PO Box 704, Boca Grande, FL 33921. Phone: (941) 964-0568. Fax: (941) 964-0620. E-mail: bgcc@ewol.com. Web: www .charlotte-online.com/bocagrande.

DISCO DEMOLITION NIGHT: ANNIVERSARY. July 12, 1979. The Chicago White Sox staged "Disco Demolition Night" as a promotion between games of a doubleheader against the Detroit Tigers. Fans, encouraged to bring disco records to the ballpark so that they could be destroyed, surged onto the field and caused such destruction that the second game had to be forfeited to the Tigers.

FIRST BLACKS IN ALL-STAR GAME: ANNIVERSARY. July 12, 1949. Jackie Robinson, Roy Campanella and Don Newcombe of the Brooklyn Dodgers and Larry Doby of the Cleveland Indians became the first black players to appear in baseball's All-Star Game. The American League won the game, played at Ebbets Field, 11–7.

JONES WINS GRAND SLAM: 70th ANNIVERSARY. July 12, 1930. Bobby Jones won the US Open golf championship by two strokes over Macdonald Smith at the Interlachen Country Club at Hopkins, MN. Having already won the British Open, the British Amateur and the US Amateur, Jones became the only golfer to win the Grand Slam.

TRIPLE-A BASEBALL ALL-STAR GAME. July 12 (tentative). Site TBA. All-Star game for players at the Triple-A minor league level. All-Stars from the Pacific Coast League play those from the International League. Annually, the day after the Major League All-Star Game. Est attendance: 10,000. For info: American Assn, 6801 Miami Ave #3, Cincinnati, OH 45243. Phone: (513) 271-4800. Fax: (513) 271-7887.

YOUNG WINS 300th GAME: ANNIVERSARY. July 12, 1901. Pitcher Denton True ("Cy") Young won the 300th game of his career, defeating the Philadelphia Athletics, 5–3. Young pitched in the major leagues from 1890 through 1911 and finished with 511 victories, more than anyone else.

BIRTHDAYS TODAY

Travis Eric Best, 28, basketball player, born Springfield, MA, July 12, 1972.

Chad Everett Brown, 30, football player, born Pasadena, CA, July 12, 1970.

Julio Cesar Chavez, 38, boxer, born Sonora, Mexico, July 12, 1962.

Ronald Ray (Ron) Fairly, 62, former baseball player, born Macon, GA, July 12, 1938.

Michael Anthony (Mike) Munoz, 35, baseball player, born Baldwin Park, CA, July 12, 1965.

Paul Theron Silas, 57, basketball coach and former player, born Prescott, AZ, July 12, 1943.

Richard Simmons, 52, TV personality, weight loss guru, author, born New Orleans, LA, July 12, 1948.

Mario Melvin Soto, 44, former baseball player, born Bani, Dominican Republic, July 12, 1956.

Kristi Tsuya Yamaguchi, 29, Olympic gold medal figure skater, born Hayward, CA, July 12, 1971.

JULY 13 — THURSDAY

Day 195 — 171 Remaining

CHASE'S SPORTSQUOTE OF THE DAY

"I don't play small. You have to go out and play with what you have. I admit I used to want to be tall. But I made it in high school, college and now the pros. So it doesn't matter."—Spud Webb, 5'7"

CALIFORNIA STATE GAMES. July 13–16. San Diego, CA. A multisport Olympic-style competition for athletes from the state of California. For info: California State Games, 3072 Palm St, San Diego, CA 92104. Phone: (619) 282-1360. Fax: (619) 282-1360. E-mail: calgames@sosinet .net. Web: www.sosinet.net/stategame.htm.

CANADA: EXPLOITS VALLEY SALMON FESTIVAL. July 13–17. Grand Falls–Windsor, Newfoundland. The Exploits Valley Salmon Festival is the largest festival at Newfoundland and Labrador and consists of five days of non-stop activities. A slow-pitch softball tournament, horse show, a fishing derby, major rock concert, dances, a salmon dinner, craft show, a major children's entertainer, carnival rides, games and food booths. For the past five years this event has been named by the American Bus Association as one of the top 100 events in North America. Annually, the third weekend in July. Est attendance: 30,000. For info: Exploits Valley Salmon Fest, PO Box 439, Grand Falls-Windsor, NF, Canada A2A 2J8. Phone: (709) 489-0450. Fax: (709) 489-0454.

COVALESKI, STANLEY: BIRTH ANNIVERSARY. July 13, 1889. Stanley Anthony Covaleski, Baseball Hall of Fame pitcher, born Stanislaus Kowalewski at Shamokin, PA. Covaleski won 215 games in his career including three for the Cleveland Indians in the 1920 World Series. A spitballer, he was one of those allowed to continue using that pitch after it was banned in 1920. Inducted into the Hall of Fame in 1969. Died at South Bend, IN, Mar 20, 1984.

DELAHANTY HITS FOUR HOME RUNS: ANNIVERSARY. July 13, 1896. Ed Delahanty of the Philadelphia Phillies hit four home runs, all of them inside-the-park, against Chicago's Adonis Terry. Delahanty added a single and drove in a total of 7 runs, but the Colts won, 9–8.

HANKS, SAM: BIRTH ANNIVERSARY. July 13, 1914. Samuel (Sam) Hanks, Jr, auto racer, born at Columbus, OH. Hanks enjoyed a successful career in midget cars, stock cars and Indy racing. He won the 1957 Indianapolis 500 at age 43, then the oldest driver to win that race. Died at Pacific Palisades, CA, June 27, 1994.

MONTANA GOVERNOR'S CUP WALLEYE TOURNAMENT. July 13–15. Fort Peck, MT. 13th annual. Two-person team event, limited to 200 teams. First place award of $10,000. There is an 80% payback of $260 entry fee. Kids' fishing event also. Annually, the second weekend in July. Est attendance: 2,000. For info: Glasgow Area Chamber of Commerce & Agriculture, Inc, Box 832, Glasgow, MT 59230. Phone: (406) 228-2222 or (887) 228-2223. Fax: (406) 228-2244.

NFL OWNERS TRADE TEAMS: ANNIVERSARY. July 13, 1972. Robert Irsay and Carroll Rosenbloom, NFL owners, swapped their teams in a professional sports first. Irsay paid $19 million to acquire the Los Angeles Rams from the estate of the late Dan Reeves. He then transferred ownership of the Rams to Carroll Rosenbloom in exchange for Rosenbloom's Baltimore Colts.

RUTH HITS 700th HOME RUN: ANNIVERSARY. July 13, 1934. Babe Ruth hit the 700th home run of his career against Tommy Bridges of the Detroit Tigers. The Yankees won the game, 4–2.

SHORTEST WIMBLEDON FINAL: ANNIVERSARY. July 13, 1881. William Renshaw won the first of his seven straight Wimbledon championships by defeating two-time defending champion John T. Hartley. Renshaw won, 6–0, 6–1, 6–1, in 37 minutes, the shortest Wimbledon men's final ever.

WYNN WINS 300th GAME: ANNIVERSARY. July 13, 1963. Pitcher Early Wynn, 43 years old, won the 300th and last game of his career, pitching the first five innings of the Cleveland Indians' 7–4 victory over the Kansas City A's.

BIRTHDAYS TODAY

Daniel Stanley (Danny) Abramowicz, 55, former football player, born Steubenville, OH, July 13, 1945.
Robert (Bob) Carpenter, 37, hockey player, born Beverly, MA, July 13, 1963.
Ruben Gomez, 73, former baseball player, born Arroyo, Puerto Rico, July 13, 1927.
Patrick Leland (Pat) Rapp, 33, baseball player, born Jennings, LA, July 13, 1967.
Erno Rubik, 56, inventor of the Rubik's Cube, born Budapest, Hungary, July 13, 1944.
Michael Spinks, 44, former heavyweight champion boxer, born St. Louis, MO, July 13, 1956.
David O'Neil Thompson, 46, Basketball Hall of Fame guard, born Shelby, NC, July 13, 1954.
Anthony Jerome ("Spud") Webb, 37, basketball player, born Dallas, TX, July 13, 1963.

JULY 14 — FRIDAY
Day 196 — 170 Remaining

AARON HITS 500th HOME RUN: ANNIVERSARY. July 14, 1968. Henry Aaron of the Atlanta Braves hit the 500th home run of his career, connecting off left-hander Mike McCormick of the San Francisco Giants. Aaron ended his career as baseball's all-time home run champ with 755 roundtrippers to his credit.

BASTILLE DAY MOONLIGHT GOLF TOURNAMENT. July 14. Greenleaf Point Golf Course, Fort McNair, Washington, DC. After a cookout, teams of four tee off wearing glow-in-the-dark necklaces and hitting glow-in-the-dark balls. Participants are given membership into the National Capital Moonlight Golf Association. Annually, July 14. For info: Fort McNair Sports Center, Bldg 17, 4th & P St SW, Washington, DC 20319-5050. Phone: (202) 685-3138.

BIG SKY STATE GAMES. July 14–16. Billings, MT. An Olympic-styled festival for Montana citizens. This statewide multisport program is designed to inspire people of all ages and skill levels to develop their physical and competitive abilities to the height of their potential through participation in fitness activities. Est attendance: 30,000. For info: Big Sky State Games, Box 7136, Billings, MT 59103-7136. Phone: (406) 254-7426. Fax: (406) 254-7439. E-mail: info@bigskygames.org. Web: www.bigsky games.org.

CANADA: CANADIAN TURTLE DERBY. July 14–16. Boissevain, Manitoba. A fun-filled family weekend, adjacent to the famous International Peace Garden. Live turtle races. Curling Bonspiel, ball and volleyball tourneys,

mini-triathlon, golf tournament, fireworks and children's entertainment. Outdoor Art Gallery with more than 17 murals! Ample camping available. 29th annual derby. Est attendance: 5,000. For info: Ivan Strain, Canadian Turtle Derby, PO Box 122, Boissevain, MB, Canada R0K 0E0. Phone: (204) 534-6000. Fax: (204) 534-6825.

CATCHER-UMP BROTHER DUO: ANNIVERSARY. July 14, 1972. In a first for major league baseball, Tom Haller was the catcher for the Detroit Tigers in a game for which his brother Bill was the home plate umpire.

CITATION PASSES $1 MILLION MARK: ANNIVERSARY. July 14, 1951. Citation, winner of the 1948 Triple Crown, became the first horse to pass the $1 million mark in career earnings by winning the Hollywood Gold Cup, after which the colt was retired. Citation raced 45 times, won $1,085,760 and finished out of the money only once.

COMMONWEALTH GAMES OF VIRGINIA. July 14–16. Roanoke, VA. A multisport Olympic-style competition for the people of Virginia. For info: Pete Lampman, Commonwealth Games of Virginia, 711-C 5th St NE, Roanoke, VA 24016. Phone: (540) 343-0987 or (800) 333-8274. Fax: (540) 343-7407. E-mail: pete@commonwealthgames.org. Web: www.commonwealthgames.org.

IOWA GAMES ANNUAL SPORTS FESTIVAL. July 14–16. Ames, IA. A multisport Olympic-style competition for athletes from the state of Iowa. For info: Iowa Games, PO Box 2350, Ames, IA 50010. Phone: (515) 292-3251. Fax: (515) 292-3254. E-mail: info@iowagames.org. Web: www .iowagames.org.

MATHEWS HITS 500th HOME RUN: ANNIVERSARY. July 14, 1967. Eddie Mathews of the Houston Astros hit the 500th home run of his career off Juan Marichal of the San Francisco Giants. Houston beat the Giants, 8–6. Mathews played in the majors from 1952 through 1968 and finished with 512 homers.

SPECIAL OLYMPICS KANSAS STATE SOFTBALL TOURNAMENT. July 14–16. Winfield, KS. Olympic-style tournament for children and adults with mental retardation. Competition in slow pitch, coach-pitch, individual skills and home run derby. For info: Special Olympics Kansas, 5280 Foxridge Dr, Mission, KS 66202. Phone: (913) 236-9290. Fax: (913) 236-9771. E-mail: rehdert@ ksso.org. Web: www.ksso.org.

USA OUTDOOR TRACK AND FIELD CHAMPIONSHIPS. July 14–23. Cal State University, Sacramento, CA. The US national championships and US World Championships team trials. For info: John McCasey, Sacramento CVB, 1421 K St, Sacramento, CA 95814. Phone: (916) 264-7777. Fax: (916) 264-7788. Web: www .usatf.org.

July **2000**

S	M	T	W	T	F	S
						1
2	3	4	5	6	7	8
9	10	11	12	13	14	15
16	17	18	19	20	21	22
23	24	25	26	27	28	29
30	31					

VERMONT 100-MILE ENDURANCE RUN. July 14–16. South Woodstock, VT. One of the oldest ultrarunning competitions in the country. 100 miles in less than 30 hours. For info: Vermont Adaptive Ski and Sports, PO Box 139, Leillington, VT 05751. Phone: (802) 484-3525. E-mail: vass@sover.net. Web: www.sover.net/~vass/vt100.

WORLD CHAMPIONSHIP SNOWMOBILE WATER-CROSS. July 14–16. Grantsburg, WI. 23rd annual. Snowmobilers from around the world will compete on open water in oval, sprint and drag competitions. Rated one of the 10 best racing events in the US. For info: Wisconsin Dept of Tourism, PO Box 7976, Madison, WI 53707. Phone: (715) 463-5466.

BIRTHDAYS TODAY

Lawrence Columbus ("Crash") Davis, 81, former baseball player, born Canon, GA, July 14, 1919.
Roosevelt (Rosey) Grier, 68, former football player, born Cuthbert, GA, July 14, 1932.
Derrick Brant May, 32, baseball player, born Rochester, NY, July 14, 1968.
Steven Michael (Steve) Stone, 53, broadcaster and former baseball player, born Euclid, OH, July 14, 1947.
Robin Mark Ventura, 33, baseball player, born Santa Maria, CA, July 14, 1967.

JULY 15 — SATURDAY
Day 197 — 169 Remaining

DROPO GETS TWELVE STRAIGHT HITS: ANNIVERSARY. July 15, 1952. Walt Dropo of the Detroit Tigers tripled, singled and doubled in his first three at bats in the second game of a doubleheader against the Washington Senators. The three hits gave him 12 in a row without making out, tying the major league record set by Mike ("Pinky") Higgins in 1938. Dropo went five-for-five the day before against the New York Yankees and four-for-four in the first game of the twin bill. His hit streak ended when he fouled out in his fourth at bat, but he finished the day with another single.

FIRST NL NO-HITTER: ANNIVERSARY. July 15, 1876. Pitcher George Washington Bradley of St. Louis hurled the first no-hitter in the National League, defeating the Hartford Blues, 2–0.

LEADVILLE MOSQUITO MARATHON. July 15. Leadville, CO. Two races—a 26.6-mile marathon leaving from downtown Leadville and traveling east to the top of North America's highest pass (Mosquito Pass), then back and a 15-mile run on the same course. For info: Greater Leadville Area Chamber of Commerce, PO Box 861, Leadville, CO 80461. Phone: (719) 486-3900 or (800) 933-3901. Fax: (719) 486-8478. E-mail: leadville@leadville usa.com. Web: www.leadvilleusa.com.

POVICH, SHIRLEY: 95th BIRTH ANNIVERSARY. July 15, 1905. Shirley Lewis Povich, sportswriter, born at Bar Harbor, ME. Povich worked for the *Washington Post* from 1922 until his death. He was a reporter, sports editor and a columnist who turned out "This Morning" six times a week. Even after his "retirement" in 1973, he wrote a column a week. Povich was highly regarded by the athletes he covered and was an early advocate of integration in sports. In 1962, in a classic case of gender confusion, he was included in *Who's Who of American Women*, an error that amused him. Given the J.G. Taylor Spink Award in 1976. Died at Washington, DC, June 4, 1998.

SAFECO FIELD OPENS: ANNIVERSARY. July 15, 1999. The Seattle Mariners opened their new ballpark, Safeco Field, with an interleague game against the San Diego Padres. Since coming into the American League in 1977, the Mariners had played in the Kingdome, an inside facil-

ity with artificial turf. Safeco Field seats 47,000 and has a grass surface.

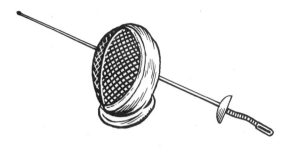

BIRTHDAYS TODAY

Kim Alexis, 40, former *Sports Illustrated* swimsuit issue model, born Lockport, NY, July 15, 1960.
Donn Alvin Clendenon, 65, former baseball player, born Neosho, MO, July 15, 1935.
Rickey Dudley, 28, football player, born Henderson, TX, July 15, 1972.
Alexander George (Alex) Karras, 65, former broadcaster and football player, born Gary, IN, July 15, 1935.
Carnell Augustino Lake, 33, football player, born Salt Lake City, UT, July 15, 1967.
Kirt Dean Manwaring, 35, baseball player, born Elmira, NY, July 15, 1965.
Khalid Reeves, 28, basketball player, born New York, NY, July 15, 1972.
Thomas Michael (Mike) Shannon, 61, broadcaster and former baseball player, born St. Louis, MO, July 15, 1939.
Barry Trotz, 38, hockey coach, born Winnipeg, Manitoba, Canada, July 15, 1962.

JULY 16 — SUNDAY
Day 198 — 168 Remaining

CHASE'S SPORTSQUOTE OF THE DAY
"Say it ain't so, Joe."—apocryphal

ADIOS BUTLER WINS CANE PACE: ANNIVERSARY. July 16, 1959. Adios Butler, driven by Clint Hodgins, won the Cane Pace, the first jewel in pacing's triple crown, at Yonkers Raceway. Adios Oregon finished second. Adios Butler went on to win the Messenger Stakes and the Little Brown Jug to become the first triple crown winner in pacing history.

CANADA: CANADIAN NORTH YELLOWKNIFE MIDNIGHT GOLF CLASSIC. June 16–17 (tentative). Yellowknife, Northwest Territories. Thieving ravens stealing well-placed shots off the sand fairways is one of the legendary hazards awaiting golfers at this all-night event. Nine new artificial greens await your best chip shot. Join local golf nuts and visiting celebrities in this rollicking social event that starts at 10 AM, Friday, and ends around noon, Saturday. Possible TSN coverage. Annually, the weekend closest to June 21. Est attendance: 300. For info: Yellowknife Golf Club, Box 388, Yellowknife, NT, Canada X1A 2N3. Phone: (867) 873-4326. Fax: (867) 873-4129.

JACKSON, SHOELESS JOE: BIRTH ANNIVERSARY. July 16, 1889. Joseph Jefferson ("Shoeless Joe") Jackson, baseball player, born at Brandon Mills, SC. Jackson's legendary excellence as one of the game's finest right-handed hitters is besmirched by his alleged involvement in the Black Sox scandal of 1919. Jackson stood accused of participating in the conspiracy to throw the World Series, and he, along with seven teammates, was banned for life. Died at Greenville, SC, Dec 5, 1951.

SCHWAN'S USA CUP 2000. July 16–22. Blaine, MN. Schwan's USA Cup attracts the top youth club soccer teams from across the US and around the world. The World Cup-style tournament strives to promote friendly competition, growth of character and international understanding. More than 13,000 youth athletes participate and stay in Blaine area homes. For info: USA Cup Registrar, Natl Sports Center, 1700 105th Ave NE, Blaine, MN 55449. Phone: (612) 785-5660. Fax: (612) 785-5699. E-mail: registrar@usacup.com. Web: www.usacup.com.

THREE RIVERS STADIUM OPENS: 30th ANNIVERSARY. July 16, 1970. The Cincinnati Reds defeated the Pittsburgh Pirates, 3–2, to spoil the Pirates' debut in their new ballpark, Three Rivers Stadium.

BIRTHDAYS TODAY

Gary Allan Anderson, 41, football player, born Parys, Orange Free State, South Africa, July 16, 1959.

Margaret Smith Court, 58, former tennis player, born Albury, New South Wales, Australia, July 16, 1942.

Aaron DeVon Glenn, 28, football player, born Humble, TX, July 16, 1972.

James William (Jimmy) Johnson, 57, football coach, born Port Arthur, TX, July 16, 1943.

Claude Lemieux, 35, hockey player, born Buckingham, Quebec, Canada, July 16, 1965.

Jyrki Lumme, 34, hockey player, born Tampere, Finland, July 16, 1966.

Barry David Sanders, 32, former football player, Heisman Trophy running back, born Wichita, KS, July 16, 1968.

William Joseph VanLandingham, 30, baseball player, born Columbia, TN, July 16, 1970.

JULY 17 — MONDAY
Day 199 — 167 Remaining

DAYS OF '47 WORLD CHAMPION RODEO. July 17–22 and 24. Delta Center, Salt Lake City, UT. One of the largest rodeos in the world, this PRCA-approved rodeo attracts world-champion competitors for seven days of the roughest, toughest rodeos around. Includes the largest all-horse parade in the nation with more than 1,200 horses from across the US (July 17). Est attendance: 50,000. For info: Days of '47 Rodeo Chair, PO Box 16507, Salt Lake City, UT 84116-0507. Phone: (801) 250-3890. Web: www.daysof47.com.

July *2000*	S	M	T	W	T	F	S
							1
	2	3	4	5	6	7	8
	9	10	11	12	13	14	15
	16	17	18	19	20	21	22
	23	24	25	26	27	28	29
	30	31					

DiMAGGIO'S HITTING STREAK ENDS: ANNIVERSARY. July 17, 1941. Joe DiMaggio's 56-game hitting streak came to an end as the Yankees center fielder was held hitless by pitchers Al Smith and Jim Bagby of the Cleveland Indians. The Yankees won, 4–3, but DiMaggio got no hits in four at bats.

DOC MEDICH TO THE RESCUE: ANNIVERSARY. July 17, 1978. Pitcher George ("Doc") Medich of the Texas Rangers saved the life of a fan suffering a heart attack before a game at Baltimore against the Orioles. Medich, a medical student, administered cardiac first aid until additional help arrived.

GIBSON STRIKES OUT 3,000: ANNIVERSARY. July 17, 1974. Bob Gibson of the St. Louis Cardinals struck out Cesar Geronimo of the Cincinnati Reds to become the second pitcher in baseball history, after Walter Johnson, to strike out 3,000 batters. Gibson pitched in the major leagues from 1959 through 1975 and finished with 3,117 strikeouts.

TWO TWINS TRIPLE PLAYS: 10th ANNIVERSARY. July 17, 1990. The Minnesota Twins became the first team in major league history to make two triple plays in the same game when they turned the trick against the Boston Red Sox. But the Red Sox won, 1–0.

BIRTHDAYS TODAY

Louis (Lou) Boudreau, 83, former broadcaster and Baseball Hall of Fame manager and shortstop, born Harvey, IL, July 17, 1917.

Calbert Nathaniel Cheaney, 29, basketball player, born Evansville, IN, July 17, 1971.

Donald Eulon (Don) Kessinger, 58, former baseball manager and player, born Forrest City, AR, July 17, 1942.

Daryle Patrick Lamonica, 59, former football player, born Fresno, CA, July 17, 1941.

Eric Shannon Moulds, 27, football player, born Lucdale, MS, July 17, 1973.

Tommy Soderstrom, 31, hockey player, born Stockholm, Sweden, July 17, 1969.

JULY 18 — TUESDAY
Day 200 — 166 Remaining

CHICAGO GOLF CLUB: ANNIVERSARY. July 18, 1893. The first 18-hole golf course in America, laid out by Charles Blair MacDonald, was incorporated at Wheaton, IL. MacDonald was the architect of many of the early US courses which he attempted to model on the best in Scotland and England. It was his belief that at each tee a golfer should face a hazard at the average distance of his shot.

EVANS, CHICK: 110th BIRTH ANNIVERSARY. July 18, 1890. Charles (Chick) Evans, Jr, golfer, born at Indianapolis, IN. Evans competed as an amateur against the best professionals in the early 20th century, winning the US Open in 1916. In the 1920s he established the Chick Evans Caddie Foundation, later called the Evans Scholarship Fund, that has helped send more than 4,000 people to college. Died at Chicago, IL, Nov 6, 1979.

FORBES TRIAL ENDS IN HUNG JURY: 25th ANNIVERSARY. July 18, 1975. The trial of Boston Bruins hockey player Dave Forbes, indicted for excessive force during a game on Jan 4 when he hit Henry Boucha of the Detroit Red Wings with his stick, ended in a hung jury. The prosecution decided not to seek a retrial.

MATTINGLY TIES LONG'S RECORD: ANNIVERSARY.
July 18, 1987. First baseman Don Mattingly of the New York Yankees hit a home run in his eighth consecutive game, thereby tying the major league record set in 1956 by first baseman Dale Long of the Pittsburgh Pirates.

MAYS GETS 3,000 HITS: 30th ANNIVERSARY. July 18, 1970. Willie Mays of the San Francisco Giants got the 3,000th hit of his career, a single off pitcher Mike Wegener of the Montreal Expos in a 10–1 Giants' victory. Mays played in the major leagues from 1951 through 1973 and finished with 3,283 hits.

SEEREY HITS FOUR HOME RUNS: ANNIVERSARY. July 18, 1948. Pat Seerey of the Chicago White Sox hit four home runs in an 11-inning game against the Philadelphia Athletics. Seerey connected in the 4th, 5th, 6th and 11th innings. The White Sox won this first game of a doubleheader, 12–11, and took the nightcap, 6–1.

SNAKE RIVER STAMPEDE. July 18–22. Nampa, ID. One of the top 15 rodeos in the nation featuring the world's top cowboys and cowgirls in action! Events include bareback bronc riding, saddle bronc riding, bull riding, calf roping, team roping, steer wrestling, barrel racing and the Wrangler bull fight. Admission. Est attendance: 40,000. For info: Snake River Stampede, Box 231, Nampa, ID 83653. Phone: (208) 466-8497. Fax: (208) 465-4438.

BIRTHDAYS TODAY

Tenley Albright, 65, Olympic gold medal figure skater, born Newton Center, MA, July 18, 1935.
Richard Totten (Dick) Button, 71, broadcaster and Olympic gold medal figure skater, born Englewood, NJ, July 18, 1929.
Nicholas Alexander (Nick) Faldo, 43, golfer, born Welwyn Garden City, England, July 18, 1957.
Michael Lewis (Mike) Greenwell, 37, former baseball player, born Louisville, KY, July 18, 1963.
Anfernee Deon ("Penny") Hardaway, 28, basketball player, born Memphis, TN, July 18, 1972.
Calvin Peete, 57, golfer, born Detroit, MI, July 18, 1943.
Joseph Paul (Joe) Torre, 60, baseball manager and former player, born New York, NY, July 18, 1940.

JULY 19 — WEDNESDAY
Day 201 — 165 Remaining

CHASE'S SPORTSQUOTE OF THE DAY

"Everybody on that team is dead but me. I guess I didn't get on base as often as the rest of them did. Those fellas tired themselves out."—Mark Koenig in 1990

APPLING HITS CRACKER JACK HOME RUN: ANNIVERSARY. July 19, 1982. In the first Oldtimers' All-Star Classic, sponsored by Cracker Jack and played at RFK Stadium at Washington, DC, 75-year-old Luke Appling led off the game with a home run against pitcher Warren Spahn.

BARR, GEORGE: BIRTH ANNIVERSARY. July 19, 1892. George McKinley Barr, baseball umpire and executive, born at Scammon, KS. Barr umpired in the National League from 1931 through 1949, working two All-Star games and four World Series. In 1935, he opened the first professional umpires school at Hot Springs, AR. Died at Tulsa, OK, July 26, 1974.

COBB GETS 4,000th HIT: ANNIVERSARY. July 19, 1927. Tyrus Raymond (Ty) Cobb of the Philadelphia Athletics doubled off the glove of outfielder Harry Heilman of the Detroit Tigers, Cobb's old team, to record the 4,000th hit of his career.

DAVIS, HARRY: BIRTH ANNIVERSARY. July 19, 1873. Harry H. Davis, baseball player and manager, born at Philadelphia, PA. Davis played for several teams around the turn of the century and once was traded between games of a doubleheader. As a member of the Philadelphia Athletics, he led the American League in home runs in 1904, 1905, 1906 and 1907. Died at Philadelphia, Aug 11, 1947.

DAYS OF '76. July 19–23 (tentative). Deadwood, SD. 77th anniversary of the Days of '76, with great events throughout the weekend. Three days of PRCA rodeo action and a Days of '76 parade featuring antique carriages and wagons. Admission. Est attendance: 13,000. For info: W.R. Davidson, Deadwood Visitors Bureau, 3 Siever St, Deadwood, SD 57732. Phone: (605) 578-1102.

FIRST UNASSISTED TRIPLE PLAY: ANNIVERSARY. July 19, 1909. Cleveland Blues shortstop Neal Ball recorded the first unassisted triple play in American League history in a game against the Boston Pilgrims. Ball caught a line drive hit by Amby McConnell, stepped on second base to double off Heine Wagner and tagged Jake Stahl before he could get back to first base. Ball also hit a home run as Cleveland won, 6–1.

GEORGIA GAMES. July 19–23. Augusta, GA. Multisport Olympic-style competition for amateur athletes in the state of Georgia. Est attendance: 15,000. For info: Georgia Games, 1415 Barclay Cir SE, Ste F, Marietta, GA 30060. Phone: (770) 528-3580. Fax: (770) 528-3590. E-mail: gagames@bellsouth.net. Web: www.georgiagames.org.

KOENIG, MARK: BIRTH ANNIVERSARY. July 19, 1902. Mark Anthony Koenig, baseball player, born at San Francisco, CA. Koenig was the last living member of the 1927 New York Yankees, considered by many to be baseball's greatest team. He also played for the Chicago Cubs and the New York Giants. Died at Willows, CA, Apr 22, 1993.

YOUNG WINS 500th GAME: 90th ANNIVERSARY. July 19, 1910. Denton True ("Cy") Young, player for the Cleveland Naps of the American League, won the 500th game of his pitching career, defeating the Washington Nationals, 5–4, in 11 innings. Young ended his career with 511 wins, more than any other pitcher.

BIRTHDAYS TODAY

LeRoy Butler, III, 32, football player, born Jacksonville, FL, July 19, 1968.
Philip Joseph (Phil) Cavaretta, 84, former baseball manager and player, born Chicago, IL, July 19, 1916.
Teresa Edwards, 36, basketball player, born Cairo, GA, July 19, 1964.
William Frederick (Billy) Gardner, 73, former manager and baseball player, born Waterford, CT, July 19, 1927.
Ilie Nastase, 54, former tennis player, born Bucharest, Romania, July 19, 1946.
David Vincent Segui, 34, baseball player, born Kansas City, MO, July 19, 1966.

JULY 20 — THURSDAY
Day 202 — 164 Remaining

BASEBALL DECLARED NONESSENTIAL OCCUPATION: ANNIVERSARY. July 20, 1918. Secretary of War Newton D. Baker declared baseball to be a nonessential occupation for the duration of World War I. He stated that all players of draft age should seek "employment to aid successful prosecution of the war or shoulder guns and fight." On July 26, Baker ruled further that baseball would be allowed to continue until Sept 1. The regular season was truncated and the World Series held immediately thereafter. Nearly 250 ballplayers entered the armed services.

CANADA: THE GREAT INTERNATIONAL WORLD CHAMPIONSHIP BATHTUB RACE & NANAIMO MARINE FESTIVAL. July 20–23. Nanaimo, British Columbia. The Great Race, which takes place on the last day of the Nanaimo Festival, involves 40–50 racing bathtubs from all over the world leaving Nanaimo harbor and traveling the Straits of Georgia (approximately 36 miles) and arriving back at Nanaimo at Departure Bay beach. The festival includes a variety of community and fun events, such as sabot race, parade, dances, Bavarian gardens, Marine Festival Food Fare, children's treasure hunt, arts and crafts and a large fireworks display. Est attendance: 75,000. For info: Loyal Nanaimo Bathtub Soc, 51A Commercial St, Nanaimo, BC, Canada V9R 5G3. Phone: (604) 753-RACE. Fax: (604) 753-7244. Web: www.bathtub.island.net.

FANS CHARGED TO SEE BASEBALL: ANNIVERSARY. July 20, 1858. Approximately 1,500 baseball fans were charged 50 cents each to watch a baseball game between the New York All-Stars and a Brooklyn team at Fashion Race Course on Long Island. The All-Stars won this first game with an admission charge, 22–18.

FIRST PGA MEDAL PLAY CHAMPIONSHIP: ANNIVERSARY. July 20, 1958. The PGA championship contested at match play since its inception in 1916 switched to medal or stroke play. Dow Finsterwald, runner-up in 1957 to Lionel Hebert, defeated Billy Casper by two strokes.

FIRST SPECIAL OLYMPICS: ANNIVERSARY. July 20, 1968. One thousand mentally retarded athletes competed in the first Special Olympics at Soldier Field, Chicago, IL. Today more than one million athletes from 146 countries compete at the local, national and international level.

LAST PITCHER TO THROW BOTH ENDS OF DOUBLEHEADER: ANNIVERSARY. July 20, 1973. Knuckleballer Wilbur Wood of the Chicago White Sox pitched both games of a doubleheader against the New York Yankees. No pitcher has done this since, but Wood lost both games.

MANUSH, HEINIE: BIRTH ANNIVERSARY. July 20, 1901. Henry Emmett ("Heinie") Manush, Baseball Hall of Fame outfielder, born at Tuscumbia, AL. Manush played for the Detroit Tigers and several other teams in a 17-year career. In 1933, he became the first player to be ejected from a World Series game. Inducted into the Hall of Fame in 1964. Died at Sarasota, FL, May 12, 1971.

SCOTLAND: BRITISH OPEN (GOLF) CHAMPIONSHIP. July 20–23. St. Andrews Golf Course, St. Andrews, Scotland. One of professional golf's four major championships, known in the US as the British Open and in Great Britain as the Open Championship. Est attendance: 170,000. For info: Royal and Ancient Golf Club, St. Andrews, Fife, Scotland KY16 9JD. Phone: (44) (01334) 472112. Fax: (44) (01334) 475483.

US WOMEN'S OPEN (GOLF) CHAMPIONSHIP. July 20–23. Merit Club, Libertyville, IL. The national women's golf championship of the US. For info: US Golf Assn, Golf House, Far Hills, NJ 07931. Phone: (908) 234-2300. Fax: (908) 234-9687. E-mail: usga@usga.org. Web: www.usga.org.

BIRTHDAYS TODAY

Walter Ray Allen, 25, basketball player, born Merced, CA, July 20, 1975.

Charles Joseph (Chuck) Daly, 70, Basketball Hall of Fame coach, born St. Mary's, PA, July 20, 1930.

Nelson Doubleday, 67, baseball executive, born Long Island, NY, July 20, 1933.

Peter Forsberg, 27, hockey player, born Ornskoldsvik, Sweden, July 20, 1973.

Sir Edmund Hillary, 81, explorer (first to climb Mt Everest), born Auckland, New Zealand, July 20, 1919.

Michael Ilitch, 71, sports executive and former minor league baseball player, born Detroit, MI, July 20, 1929.

Charles Edward Johnson, Jr, 29, baseball player, born Fort Pierce, FL, July 20, 1971.

Terrence Rodney (Terry) Murray, 50, hockey coach and former player, born Shawville, Ontario, Canada, July 20, 1950.

Pedro ("Tony") Oliva, 60, former baseball player, born Pinar del Rio, Cuba, July 20, 1940.

Claudio Reyna, 27, soccer player, born Livingston, NJ, July 20, 1973.

JULY 21 — FRIDAY
Day 203 — 163 Remaining

AARON HITS 700th HOME RUN: ANNIVERSARY. July 21, 1973. Henry Aaron of the Atlanta Braves hit the 700th home run of his career, a 3rd-inning drive against Ken Brett of the Philadelphia Phillies. The ball was retrieved by a fan who returned it to Aaron in exchange for 700 silver dollars. The Braves lost, 8–4. Aaron finished his career with 755 home runs, more than any other player, and was inducted into the Hall of Fame in 1982.

EVERS, JOHNNY: BIRTH ANNIVERSARY. July 21, 1881. John Joseph (Johnny) Evers, Baseball Hall of Fame second baseman, born at Troy, NY. Evers (pronounced EE-vers) was a member of the Tinker–to–Evers–to–Chance double play combination for the Chicago Cubs early in the 20th century. Evers was an aggressive player who never gave an inch. Inducted into the Hall of Fame in 1946. Died at Albany, NY, Mar 28, 1947.

FOUR HITS, FOUR DPS: 25th ANNIVERSARY. July 21, 1975. Felix Millan of the New York Mets got four singles, but each time he was erased from the basepaths as teammate Joe Torre grounded into four double plays. The Mets lost to the Houston Astros, 6–2.

JOHN HENRY RETIRES: 15th ANNIVERSARY. July 21, 1985. John Henry, the greatest money winner in thoroughbred racing history, retired after earning $6,597,947. John Henry started 83 races and won 39 times.

McSPADEN, JUG: BIRTH ANNIVERSARY. July 21, 1908. Harold ("Jug") McSpaden, golfer, born at Rosedale, KS. Known as one-half of the "Gold Dust Twins," McSpaden

	S	M	T	W	T	F	S
July							1
2000	2	3	4	5	6	7	8
	9	10	11	12	13	14	15
	16	17	18	19	20	21	22
	23	24	25	26	27	28	29
	30	31					

enjoyed success on the pro golf tour in the 1930s with his most prominent victory coming in the 1939 Canadian Open. In 1945, when Byron Nelson, the other "Gold Dust Twin," won 11 straight tournaments, McSpaden finished second 13 times. Found dead from carbon monoxide poisoning in his home at Kansas City, KS, Apr 22, 1996.

PALMER FIRST TO WIN $1 MILLION: ANNIVERSARY. July 21, 1968. Arnold Palmer became the first golfer to surpass the $1 million mark in career earnings despite losing the PGA championship to Julius Boros by one stroke.

SHOW ME STATE GAMES. July 21–23 (also July 28–30). Columbia, MO. An Olympic-style athletic festival for Missouri citizens. This statewide multisport program is designed to inspire Missourians of every age and skill level to develop their physical and competitive abilities to the height of their potential through participation in fitness activities. Annually, the last two full weekends in July. Est attendance: 48,000. For info: Gary Filbert, Exec Dir, Show Me State Games, 1105 Carrie Francke Dr, Columbia, MO 65211. Phone: (573) 882-2101. Fax: (573) 884-4004. E-mail: show4games@aol.com. Web: www.smsg.org.

SPECIAL OLYMPICS FLORIDA STATE AQUATICS TOURNAMENT. July 21–22. Pensacola, FL. Olympic-style competition for children and adults with mental retardation. For info: Special Olympics Florida, 8 Broadway, Ste D, Kissimmee, FL 34741. Phone: (407) 870-2292. Fax: (407) 870-9810.

SPECIAL OLYMPICS FLORIDA STATE SOFTBALL CHAMPIONSHIPS. July 21–22. Kissimmee, FL. Olympic-style tournament for children and adults with mental retardation. For info: Special Olympics Florida, 8 Broadway, Ste D, Kissimmee, FL 34741. Phone: (407) 870-2292. Fax: (407) 870-9810.

BIRTHDAYS TODAY

Michael Todd (Mike) Bordick, 35, baseball player, born Marquette, MI, July 21, 1965.
Brandi Denise Chastain, 32, soccer player, born San Jose, CA, July 21, 1968.
Steven Philip (Steve) Gietschier, 52, archivist, historian and compiler of *Chase's Sports Calendar of Events*, born New York, NY, July 21, 1948.
Alan Thomas (Al) Hrabosky, 51, broadcaster and former baseball player, born Oakland, CA, July 21, 1949.
Lyle Odelein, 32, hockey player, born Quill Lake, Saskatchewan, Canada, July 21, 1968.

JULY 22 — SATURDAY
Day 204 — 162 Remaining

HAINES, JESSE: BIRTH ANNIVERSARY. July 22, 1893. Jesse Joseph Haines, Baseball Hall of Fame pitcher, born at Clayton, OH. Between 1920 and 1937, Haines won 210 games for the St. Louis Cardinals. He pitched one no-hitter and won three World Series games. Inducted into the Hall of Fame in 1970. Died at Dayton, OH, Aug 5, 1978.

JOHNSON STRIKES OUT 3,000th BATTER: ANNIVERSARY. July 22, 1923. Walter Johnson of the Washington Senators became the first pitcher to strike out 3,000 batters in his career. He recorded five strikeouts in a 3–1 win over the Cleveland Indians. Johnson finished his career with 3,508 strikeouts and was inducted into the Baseball Hall of Fame in 1936.

PLAYER WINS PGA: ANNIVERSARY. July 22, 1962. Gary Player of South Africa became the first nonresident of the US to win the PGA championship. He defeated Bob Goalby by one stroke at Aronimink Golf Club at Newtown Square, PA.

PONY GIRLS SOFTBALL SLOW-PITCH NATIONAL CHAMPIONSHIPS. July 22–26. Burleson, TX. Slow-Pitch National Championships for girls ages 9–18. Est attendance: 2,000. For info: PONY Baseball/Softball, PO Box 225, Washington, PA 15301. Phone: (724) 225-1060. Fax: (724) 225-9852. E-mail: pony@pulsenet.com. Web: www.pony.org.

VIRGINIA SCOTTISH GAMES AND FESTIVAL. July 22–23. Alexandria, VA. Bagpipes, Highland dance, drumming, fiddling, celtic harp competition, animal trials, Scottish athletic games competition and British antique car show. Scottish food and gifts are sold. Annually, the fourth weekend in July. Est attendance: 30,000. For info: Virginia Scottish Games Assn, PO Box 1338, Alexandria, VA 22313. Phone: (703) 912-1943. Web: www.alex.org/homepages/vsg.

WHITWORTH BECOMES ALL-TIME WINNER: ANNIVERSARY. July 22, 1984. Kathy Whitworth won the Rochester Open to become the all-time winningest professional golfer. Her 85th victory surpassed the 84 tournament wins of Sam Snead.

BIRTHDAYS TODAY

Timothy Donell (Tim) Brown, 34, Heisman Trophy wide receiver, born Dallas, TX, July 22, 1966.
Keyshawn Johnson, 28, football player, born Los Angeles, CA, July 22, 1972.
Kristine Marie Lilly, 29, soccer player, born New York, NY, July 22, 1971.
Albert Walter ("Sparky") Lyle, 56, former baseball player, born DuBois, PA, July 22, 1944.
Manuel Joseph ("Jungle Jim") Rivera, 78, former baseball player, born New York, NY, July 22, 1922.
David Andrew (Dave) Stieb, 43, former baseball player, born Santa Ana, CA, July 22, 1957.
Sergei Zubov, 30, hockey player, born Moscow, USSR, July 22, 1970.

JULY 23 — SUNDAY
Day 205 — 161 Remaining

CHASE'S SPORTSQUOTE OF THE DAY

"My own little rule was two for one—if one of my team-mates got knocked down, then I knocked down two on the other team."—Don Drysdale

---

BEAUMONT, GINGER: BIRTH ANNIVERSARY. July 23, 1876. Clarence Howeth ("Ginger") Beaumont, baseball player, born at Rochester, WI. Beaumont won the National League batting title in 1902 and was the first player to bat in a World Series (1903). His nickname came from his red hair. Died at Burlington, WI, Apr 10, 1956.

DRYSDALE, DON: BIRTH ANNIVERSARY. July 23, 1936. Donald Scott Drysdale, broadcaster and Baseball Hall of Fame pitcher, born at Van Nuys, CA. Drysdale was an intimidating right-handed pitcher for the Brooklyn and Los Angeles Dodgers from 1956 to 1969, compiling a won-lost record of 209–166 with a career ERA of 2.95. Following his playing career he became a successful and popular broadcaster for the Chicago White Sox and then for the Dodgers. Inducted into the Hall of Fame in 1984. Died at Montreal, Quebec, Canada, July 3, 1993.

FIRST US SWIMMING SCHOOL OPENS: ANNIVERSARY. July 23, 1827. The first swimming school in the US opened at Boston, MA. Its pupils included John Quincy Adams and James Audubon.

FITZSIMMONS, SUNNY JIM: BIRTH ANNIVERSARY. July 23, 1874. James Edward ("Sunny Jim") Fitzsimmons, thoroughbred trainer, born at New York, NY. Fitzsimmons got his first job at a racetrack at age 11 and became a trainer in 1900. He saddled 2,428 winners in his 63-year career, including Triple Crown winners Gallant Fox and Omaha. "Mr Fitz," as he was known, was particularly noted for his ability to bring horses to peak performance in big races. Died at Miami, FL, Mar 11, 1966.

GEHRIG HITS FIRST GRAND SLAM: 75th ANNIVERSARY. July 23, 1925. Lou Gehrig of the New York Yankees hit the first grand slam of his career as the Yankees defeated the Washington Senators, 11–7. Gehrig hit 22 other grand slams and still holds the major league record.

RAWLS WINS FOURTH US OPEN: 40th ANNIVERSARY. July 23, 1960. Betsy Rawls became the first golfer to win the US Women's Open four times, adding the 1960 title to those won in 1951, 1953 and 1957.

REESE, PEE WEE: BIRTH ANNIVERSARY. July 23, 1918. Harold Henry ("Pee Wee") Reese, Hall of Fame shortstop, born at Ekron, KY. Died Aug 14, 1999, at Louisville, KY.

REGISTER'S ANNUAL GREAT BICYCLE RIDE ACROSS IOWA. July 23–29. A weeklong bicycle ride across Iowa with 7,500 riders from around the country. Annually, the last full week of July. After Nov 1 and before Mar 1 send a business-size SASE to address below. Sponsor: *Des Moines Register*. Est attendance: 7,500. For info: RAGBRAI Coord, PO Box 622, Des Moines, IA 50303-0622. Phone: (515) 284-8282. Fax: (515) 284-8138. Web: www.ragbrai.org.

July 2000

S	M	T	W	T	F	S
						1
2	3	4	5	6	7	8
9	10	11	12	13	14	15
16	17	18	19	20	21	22
23	24	25	26	27	28	29
30	31					

BIRTHDAYS TODAY

Elden Jerome Campbell, 32, basketball player, born Los Angeles, CA, July 23, 1968.
Anthony Nomar Garciaparra, 27, baseball player, born Whittier, CA, July 23, 1973.
Terry Glenn, 26, football player, born Columbus, OH, July 23, 1974.
Dimitri Khristich, 31, hockey player, born Kiev, USSR, July 23, 1969.
Gary Dwayne Payton, 32, basketball player, born Oakland, CA, July 23, 1968.

JULY 24 — MONDAY
Day 206 — 160 Remaining

ADDIE JOSS BENEFIT GAME: ANNIVERSARY. July 24, 1911. A group of American League all-stars played the Cleveland Indians in an exhibition game to benefit the widow of Addie Joss, Cleveland's star pitcher struck down by tubercular meningitis on Apr 14.

BRETT'S "PINE TAR" HOME RUN: ANNIVERSARY. July 24, 1983. In a game against the New York Yankees, George Brett of the Kansas City Royals hit a two-run home run with two out in the top of the ninth inning to give the Royals an apparent 5–4 lead. Yankees manager Billy Martin protested the excessive amount of pine tar on Brett's bat, and the umpires declared him out. The Royals protested this decision, and American League president Lee MacPhail overruled the umps. On Aug 18, the game was replayed from the point of the protest, and the Royals emerged triumphant.

CANADA: WORLD FOOTBAG CHAMPIONSHIPS. July 24–30. Vancouver, British Columbia. Seven-day sports event spotlights competition of footskills—the Super Bowl of footbag! Now in its 21st year, it attracts the world's top footbag competitors from the US and six other countries. Prize money exceeds $10,000. Sponsors: Wham-O, Sipa Sipa Footbags and The World Footbag Association. Est attendance: 5,000. For info: Bruce Guettich, Dir, World Footbag Assn, PO Box 775208, Steamboat Springs, CO 80477. Phone: (800) 878-8797. Fax: (970) 870-2846. E-mail: wfa@worldfootbag.com. Web: www.worldfootbag.com.

MARATHON DISTANCE SET: ANNIVERSARY. July 24, 1908. At the 1908 Olympic Games at London, the marathon was run from Windsor Castle to White City Stadium at Shepherd's Bush. At the request of Princess Mary, wife of the future King George V, the start took place directly beneath the windows of the nursery occupied by the royal princes so the boys could see the runners. The distance from this spot to the finish line in front of the royal box in the stadium measured 26 miles, 385 yards (42,195 meters). Heretofore, marathons had been run at a variety of distances, but the 1908 practice eventually became precedent. In 1924, the distance set to please the princes became official.

NATIONAL HIGH SCHOOL FINALS RODEO. July 24–30. Springfield, IL. More than 1,500 teenage contestants from North America will compete in rodeo events patterned after official Pro-Rodeo Association guidelines. Annually, the third week in July. Est attendance: 95,000. For info: Natl High School Rodeo Assn, 11178 N Huron, Ste 7, Denver, CO 80234. Phone: (303) 452-0820 or (800) 46-NHSRA. Fax: (303) 452-0912.

TENNIS ADOPTS TIEBREAKER: 30th ANNIVERSARY. July 24, 1970. The International Lawn Tennis Association changed tennis history by adopting a rule calling for sets tied 6–6 to be concluded by a nine-point tiebreaker.

WRONG WAY MARATHONER: ANNIVERSARY. July 24, 1908. Dorando Pietri of Italy led the marathon at the 1908 Olympics as he entered the stadium for the race's conclusion. Dazed and confused, he began to run the wrong way. Officials tried to correct him, but he fell four times. When they helped him to his feet, he was disqualified, and John Hayes of the US came on to win the race.

BIRTHDAYS TODAY

Walter Jones (Walt) Bellamy, 61, Basketball Hall of Fame center, born New Bern, NC, July 24, 1939.
Blaine Elwood Bishop, 30, football player, born Indianapolis, IN, July 24, 1970.
Barry Lamar Bonds, 36, baseball player, born Riverside, CA, July 24, 1964.
William Delford (Willie) Davis, 66, Pro Football Hall of Fame defensive end, born Lisbon, LA, July 24, 1934.
Kevin Lamont Hardy, 27, football player, born Evansville, IN, July 24, 1973.
Julieanne Louise (Julie) Krone, 37, former jockey, born Benton Harbor, MI, July 24, 1963.
Karl Malone, 37, basketball player, born Summerfield, LA, July 24, 1963.

JULY 25 — TUESDAY
Day 207 — 159 Remaining

ATLANTA HAWKS TOUR SOVIET UNION: ANNIVERSARY. July 25, 1988. The Atlanta Hawks began a 13-day trip through the Soviet Union, the first ever by an NBA team, beating a Soviet team, 85–84. The Hawks won the second game but then lost the third.

GROVE WINS 300th GAME: ANNIVERSARY. July 25, 1941. Robert ("Lefty") Grove of the Boston Red Sox won the 300th and last game of his major league career, defeating the Cleveland Indians, 10–6.

TENER, JOHN: BIRTH ANNIVERSARY. July 25, 1863. John Kinley Tener, baseball player and executive, born at County Tyrone, Ireland. Tener played amateur and professional baseball in the 19th century and retired to become a banker. He was president of the National League from 1913 to 1918. Died at Pittsburgh, PA, May 19, 1946.

TWO TRIPLE STEALS: 70th ANNIVERSARY. July 25, 1930. The Philadelphia Athletics executed a triple steal in the first inning of a game against the Cleveland Indians and another one in the fourth inning. This is the only game in which two triple steals have occurred.

BIRTHDAYS TODAY

Jon Allan Barry, 31, basketball player, born Oakland, CA, July 25, 1969.
Stanley F. Dancer, 73, former harness racer, born New Egypt, NY, July 25, 1927.
Anthony Lewis (Tony) Granato, 36, hockey player, born Downers Grove, IL, July 25, 1964.
Salvatore Anthony (Torey) Lovullo, 35, baseball player, born Santa Monica, CA, July 25, 1965.
Pedro Jaime Martinez, 29, baseball player, born Manoguayabo, Dominican Republic, July 25, 1971.
Walter Jerry Payton, 46, Pro Football Hall of Fame running back, born Columbia, MS, July 25, 1954.
Edward Nelson (Ed) Sprague, Jr, 33, baseball player, born Castro Valley, CA, July 25, 1967.
Nathaniel (Nate) Thurmond, 59, Basketball Hall of Fame center, born Akron, OH, July 25, 1941.

JULY 26 — WEDNESDAY
Day 208 — 158 Remaining

CHASE'S SPORTSQUOTE OF THE DAY

"It takes no effort at all to pitch a knuckleball. No windup is necessary. It's so simple that very little warmup in the bullpen is required. That's why I can pitch so often without being overworked."—Hoyt Wilhelm

BREADON, SAM: BIRTH ANNIVERSARY. July 26, 1876. Sam Breadon, baseball executive, born at New York, NY. Breadon was principal owner of the St. Louis Cardinals from 1917 to 1947. He supplied the financial backing as Branch Rickey built the Cards into the National League's dominant team. Died at St. Louis, MO, May 10, 1949.

DOUBLE DECATHLON WINNER: ANNIVERSARY. July 26, 1952. Bob Mathias of the US won the decathlon at the 1952 Summer Olympics at Helsinki, Finland, to become the first athlete to win the Olympic decathlon twice. His first victory came in the 1948 London Games. Daley Thompson of Great Britain equaled Mathias's feat in 1980 and 1984.

EAA AIRVENTURE OSHKOSH. July 26–Aug 1. Wittman Regional Airport, Oshkosh, WI. The world's largest and most significant aviation event features more than 11,000 airplanes—home-built, antique, aerobatic planes, military and general aviation aircraft. International visitors can attend more than 500 educational forums, seminars and workshops and view the displays of more than 700 exhibitors, including the National Aeronautics and Space Administration (NASA), the National Transportation Safety Board (NTSB) and the Federal Aviation Administration (FAA). Daily air shows showcase the talents of the world's top aerobatics performers. 48th annual. Est attendance: 830,000. For info: Dir, EAA Airventure Oshkosh, PO Box 3086, Oshkosh, WI 54903. Phone: (920) 426-4800. Fax: (920) 232-7772. E-mail: convention@eaa.org. Web: www.fly-in.org.

GALLICO, PAUL: BIRTH ANNIVERSARY. July 26, 1897. Paul William Gallico, sportswriter, born at New York, NY. Gallico put a twist on his career with the *New York Daily News* when he asked heavyweight champion Jack Dempsey to box a round with him in 1923. Thereafter, Gallico began to sample a wealth of other sports, competing against the very best. By 1936, Gallico was the highest-paid sportswriter in New York. He left the newspaper business to become a freelance writer and spent many years abroad attacking a variety of subjects. Died at Monte Carlo, Monaco, July 15, 1976.

JOHN HANCOCK US GYMNASTICS NATIONAL CHAMPIONSHIPS. July 26–29. St. Louis, MO. Includes men's, women's and rhythmic gymnastics as well as trampoline and tumbling. For info: USA Gymnastics, Pan American Plaza, 201 S Capitol Ave, Ste 300, Indianapolis, IN 46225. Phone: (317) 237-5050. Fax: (317) 237-5069. Web: www.usa-gymnastics.org.

WATERFIELD, BOB: 80th BIRTH ANNIVERSARY. July 26, 1920. Robert (Bob) Waterfield, Pro Football Hall of Fame quarterback, born at Elmira, NY. Waterfield competed in gymnastics and football at UCLA. After World War II, he joined the Cleveland Rams and became the first rookie quarterback to lead a team to the NFL title. Twice the league's MVP, Waterfield supplemented his passing skills with outstanding punting ability. Inducted into the Pro Football Hall of Fame in 1965. Died at Burbank, CA, Mar 25, 1983.

☆ ☆ ☆

BIRTHDAYS TODAY

Gregory Joseph (Greg) Colbrunn, 31, baseball player, born Fontana, CA, July 26, 1969.

Dorothy Hamill, 44, Olympic gold medal figure skater, born Riverside, CT, July 26, 1956.

Kenneth John (Ken) Kaiser, 55, baseball umpire, born Rochester, NY, July 26, 1945.

Maxine ("Mickey") King, 56, Olympic gold medal diver, born Pontiac, MI, July 26, 1944.

Robert Lewis (Bob) Lilly, 61, Pro Football Hall of Fame defensive tackle, born Olney, TX, July 26, 1939.

Thomas Franklin (Tommy) McDonald, 66, Pro Football Hall of Fame halfback and wide receiver, born Roy, NM, July 26, 1934.

Norman LeRoy (Norm) Siebern, 67, former baseball player, born St. Louis, MO, July 26, 1933.

James Hoyt Wilhelm, 77, Baseball Hall of Fame pitcher, born Huntersville, NC, July 26, 1923.

JULY 27 — THURSDAY

Day 209 — 157 Remaining

CHASE'S SPORTSQUOTE OF THE DAY

"If any of my players don't take a drink now and then they'll be gone. You don't play this game on gingersnaps."—Leo Durocher

ASA BOYS' FAST PITCH NATIONAL CHAMPIONSHIP. July 27–30. Sioux City, IA. For boys 10 and under, 12 and under, 14 and under and 16 and under. For info: ASA-USA Softball, 2801 NE 50th St, Oklahoma City, OK 73111. Phone: (405) 424-5266. Fax: (405) 424-3855. E-mail: info@softball.org. Web: www.softball.org.

BOMBING IN CENTENNIAL OLYMPIC PARK: ANNIVERSARY. July 27, 1996. A pipe bomb exploded in Centennial Olympic Park at Atlanta, GA, killing one person and injuring 111 others. The explosion occurred during the nightly free concert in the park, part of the celebrations surrounding the 1996 Summer Olympic Games.

July 2000	S	M	T	W	T	F	S
							1
	2	3	4	5	6	7	8
	9	10	11	12	13	14	15
	16	17	18	19	20	21	22
	23	24	25	26	27	28	29
	30	31					

CANADA: BC SUMMER GAMES. July 27–30. Victoria, British Columbia. 4,000 athletes competing in more than 30 sports. For info: BC Games Soc, Ste 200-990 Fort St, Victoria, BC, Canada V8V 3K2. Phone: (250) 387-1375. Fax: (250) 387-4489. E-mail: bcgames@bcgames.org. Web: www.bcgames.org.

CONTINENTAL LEAGUE FORMED: ANNIVERSARY. July 27, 1959. New York City attorney William A. Shea announced plans to establish the Continental League, a third major baseball league, with Branch Rickey as president. Shea awarded franchises to New York, Houston, Toronto, Denver and Minneapolis-St. Paul. The league never played a game, but all five cities eventually got major league teams: the New York Mets, the Houston Colt .45s, the Toronto Blue Jays, the Colorado Rockies and the Minnesota Twins.

CONTINENTAL AMATEUR BASEBALL ASSOCIATION TOURNAMENT. July 27–Aug 6. Tarkio, MO. This is the 15th year for the tournament for 11-year-olds. 32 teams from all over the US, including Hawaii, Puerto Rico and Mexico, compete. As the oldest continuous site for the CABA, Tarkio has received the Tournament of Excellence Award since 1989. Teams and fans attend a KC Royals game on "break day" and parade on the field before the game. Annually, beginning the last Thursday in July. Est attendance: 2,000. For info: Tarkio Chamber of Commerce, 222 Main, Tarkio, MO 64491. Phone: (660) 736-5772. Fax: (660) 736-5934. E-mail: tarkiocofc@maryville.heartland.net. Web: www.tarkio.org or www.cababaseball.com.

DUROCHER, LEO: 95th BIRTH ANNIVERSARY. July 27, 1905. Leo Ernest Durocher, baseball player and Baseball Hall of Fame manager, born at West Springfield, MA. He began his major league baseball career with the New York Yankees in 1925 and also played for the St. Louis Cardinals and the Brooklyn Dodgers, where he first served as player-manager in 1939. His trademark phrase was, "Nice guys finish last." As a manager, he guided the New York Giants to two World Series, defeating the Cleveland Indians in 1954. He later coached for the Los Angeles Dodgers and managed the Chicago Cubs and the Houston Astros. Inducted into the Hall of Fame in 1994. Died at Palm Springs, CA, Oct 7, 1991.

FOUL BALL SUIT: ANNIVERSARY. July 27, 1921. Baseball fan Reuben Berman brought suit in New York County Supreme Court against the New York Giants, alleging that on May 16 the Giants had "wrongfully and unlawfully imprisoned and detained" him and threatened him with arrest. Berman further alleged that he was "greatly humiliated before a large crowd of people . . . and thereby was caused mental and bodily distress and was thereby greatly injured in his character and reputation and in his physical health." Berman's crime? He refused to return a foul ball he had caught to a stadium attendant. Allowing fans to keep foul balls was not yet a general practice, but the court awarded Berman $100.

GREAT TEXAS MOSQUITO FESTIVAL COMPETITIONS. July 27–29. Clute Municipal Park, Clute, TX. Doubles horseshoe pitching tournament, doubles washer pitching contest, Century Buzz Bike and Skate Tour, Mosquito Chase with one-mile and 5K runs, both of which are certified by USA Track and Field and a host of other great festival doings. Est attendance: 30,000. For info: Great Texas Mosquito Festival, PO Box 997, Clute, TX 77531. Phone: (800) 371-2971. Fax: (409) 265-8767.

LEMOND WINS TOUR DE FRANCE: ANNIVERSARY. July 27, 1986. Cyclist Greg Lemond became the first American to win the Tour de France, the most important bicycle race in the world. In 1999 it was won by another American, Lance Armstrong.

MACKEY, BIZ: BIRTH ANNIVERSARY. July 27, 1897. Raleigh ("Biz") Mackey, baseball player and manager, born at Eagle Pass, TX. Mackey was one of the best catchers in the Negro Leagues. He was particularly adept at handling pitchers and grooming younger players, including Roy Campanella, for top-flight competition. Died at Los Angeles, CA, date unknown.

NEBRASKA'S BIG RODEO. July 27–29. Fairgrounds, Burwell, NE. Professional rodeo. Contestants compete in four exciting performances in historic, outdoor rodeo arena. Added thrills—chuckwagon races, wild horse races, Dinnerbell Derby, bull fighting-Burwell style. Also, quilt and art shows, parade, flea market, llama and longhorn cattle show, country and western music and dancing and Miss Burwell Rodeo Pageant. Est attendance: 10,000. For info: Peggy Haskell, Garfield County Frontier Fair Assn, Box 747, Burwell, NE 68823. Phone: (308) 346-5210 or (308) 346-5010 (July 10–29). Web: www.burwellnebr.com.

PITTSBURGH THREE RIVERS REGATTA. July 27–30 (tentative). Pittsburgh, PA. The country's largest inland river regatta featuring air, land and water events. Est attendance: 1,500,000. For info: Patrick J. DiCesare, 2825 Penn Ave, Pittsburgh, PA 15222. Phone: (412) 562-9900. Fax: (412) 562-9913.

SHORT MAJOR LEAGUE CAREER: ANNIVERSARY. July 27, 1918. Harry Heitman of the Brooklyn Dodgers made his major league debut as the starting pitcher against the St. Louis Cardinals. He got the first man out, but then the next four batters got hits. Heitman left the game and never played professional baseball again.

TINKER, JOE: 120th BIRTH ANNIVERSARY. July 27, 1880. Joseph Bert (Joe) Tinker, Baseball Hall of Fame shortstop, born at Muscotah, KS. Tinker was part of the Chicago Cubs' famous Tinker-to-Evers-to-Chance double play combination. He played with the Reds after the Cubs, played and managed in the Federal League and then managed the Cubs. Inducted into the Hall of Fame in 1946. Died at Orlando, FL, July 27, 1948.

TRAPPERS STREAK SNAPPED: ANNIVERSARY. July 27, 1987. The Salt Lake City Trappers of the Pioneer League, an independent team without a major league affiliation or working agreement, lost to Billings, 7–5, thereby bringing their record 29-game winning streak to an end.

BIRTHDAYS TODAY

Leonard Harold (Len) Barker, 45, former baseball player, born Fort Knox, KY, July 27, 1955.

Raymond Otis (Ray) Boone, 77, former baseball player, born San Diego, CA, July 27, 1923.

Peggy Gale Fleming, 52, broadcaster and Olympic gold medal figure skater, born San Jose, CA, July 27, 1948.

Alexander Emmanuel (Alex) Rodriguez, 25, baseball player, born New York, NY, July 27, 1975.

Elliott Taylor ("Bump") Wills, 48, former baseball player, born Washington, DC, July 27, 1952.

Craig Wolanin, 33, hockey player, born Grosse Pointe, MI, July 27, 1967.

Jason Douglas Woolley, 31, hockey player, born Toronto, Ontario, Canada, July 27, 1969.

JULY 28 — FRIDAY
Day 210 — 156 Remaining

DODGE CITY DAYS. July 28–Aug 6. Dodge City, KS. Western heritage celebration with concerts, arts and crafts, parades, PRCA rodeo, street dances, cookout, art show, antique car show. Est attendance: 75,000. For info: Dodge City CVB, 3rd and W Wyatt Earp Blvd, PO Box 1474, Dodge City, KS 67801. Phone: (800) OLD-WEST. Fax: (316) 225-8268. E-mail: dcvb@pld.com. Web: www.dodge city.org.

FOX, TERRY: BIRTH ANNIVERSARY. July 28, 1958. Terrence Stanley (Terry) Fox, inspirational athlete, born at Winnipeg, Manitoba, Canada. Fox captured the hearts and admiration of millions during his brief life. Stricken with cancer requiring amputation of the athlete's right leg at age 18, Fox was determined to devote his life to a fight against the disease. His "Marathon of Hope," a planned 5,200-mile run westward across Canada, started Apr 12, 1980, at St. John's, Newfoundland, and continued 3,328 miles to Thunder Bay, Ontario, Sept 1, 1980, when he was forced to stop by spread of the disease. During the run (on an artificial leg) he raised $24 million for cancer research and inspired millions with his courage. Died at New Westminster, British Columbia, Canada, June 28, 1981.

LUMBERJACK WORLD CHAMPIONSHIPS. July 28–30. Lumberjack Bowl, Hayward, WI. Professional male and female lumberjacks and logrollers from around the world compete in speed sawing, pole climbing, logrolling and chopping events in the Northwoods town of Hayward. Amateurs can also participate, there are logrolling events for kids and chopping and sawing competitions for adults. Visitors can also observe saw carving demonstrations and displays. Annually, the last full weekend in July. Est attendance: 12,000. For info: Exec Dir, Lumberjack World Chmpshps, PO Box 666, Hayward, WI 54843. Phone: (715) 634-2484.

MARTINEZ PITCHES PERFECT GAME: ANNIVERSARY. July 28, 1991. Dennis Martinez of the Montreal Expos pitched a perfect game, defeating the Los Angeles Dodgers, 2–0, at Dodgers Stadium.

NATIONAL BALLOON CLASSIC. July 28–Aug 5. Indianola, IA. A spectator-oriented balloon extravaganza involving fun events utilizing up to 100 balloons. It is held on the Classic's specially designed balloon field with a natural amphitheater for perfect viewing. Balloons fly morning and evening, weather permitting. The Classic stage features live local & regional entertainment. Est attendance: 75,000. For info: Gerald Knoll, PO Box 346, Indianola, IA 50125. Phone: (800) FLY-IOWA or (515) 961-8415. Fax: (515) 961-8415. E-mail: classicgk@aol.com. Web: www.nationalballoonclassic.com.

PRO FOOTBALL HALL OF FAME FESTIVAL. July 28–Aug 5 (tentative). Canton, OH. To honor the 2000 Class of Enshrinees inducted into the Pro Football Hall of Fame. Est attendance: 500,000. For info: Pro Football Hall of Fame Festival, Dennis P. Saunier, Exec Dir, 229 Wells Ave NW, Canton, OH 44703. Phone: (800) 533-4302.

ROGAN, BULLET JOE: BIRTH ANNIVERSARY. July 28, 1889. Wilbur ("Bullet Joe") Rogan, Baseball Hall of Fame pitcher, born at Oklahoma City, OK. Rogan starred as both a pitcher and a hitter in the Negro Leagues and is generally considered one of the best pitchers in black baseball history. Inducted into the Hall of Fame in 1998. Died at Kansas City, MO, Mar 4, 1964.

ROGERS PITCHES PERFECT GAME: ANNIVERSARY. July 28, 1994. Kenny Rogers of the Texas Rangers pitched a perfect game against the visiting California Angels, winning, 4–0. Rogers struck out 8 and retired the final batter, Gary DiSarcina, on a line drive to centerfield.

SPECIAL OLYMPICS MICHIGAN SUMMER SPORTS CLASSIC. July 28–29. Canton, MI. Olympic-style competition for children and adults with mental retardation. For info: Special Olympics Michigan, Central Michigan Univ, Mt Pleasant, MI 48859. Phone: (800) 644-6404. Fax: (517) 774-3034. E-mail: M.K.Lindberg@cmich.edu. Web: www.somi.org.

Bill Bradley

BIRTHDAYS TODAY

Vida Rochelle Blue, 51, former baseball player, born Mansfield, LA, July 28, 1949.

William Warren (Bill) Bradley, 57, former US Senator and Basketball Hall of Fame forward, born Crystal City, MO, July 28, 1943.

Paul Douglas (Doug) Collins, 49, broadcaster and former basketball coach and player, born Christopher, IL, July 28, 1951.

Robert (Bob) Milacki, 36, baseball player, born Trenton, NJ, July 28, 1964.

Garth Snow, 31, hockey player, born Wrentham, MA, July 28, 1969.

JULY 29 — SATURDAY
Day 211 — 155 Remaining

ALL-AMERICAN SOAP BOX DERBY. July 29. Derby Downs, Akron, OH. A weeklong festival culminating in world championship race by regional champs from US, Canada, Germany, Australia and Philippines. 63rd annual derby. Est attendance: 15,000. For info: Jeff Lula, General Mgr, Intl Soap Box Derby, Inc, PO Box 7225,

July 2000	S	M	T	W	T	F	S
							1
	2	3	4	5	6	7	8
	9	10	11	12	13	14	15
	16	17	18	19	20	21	22
	23	24	25	26	27	28	29
	30	31					

Akron, OH 44306. Phone: (330) 733-8723. Fax: (330) 733-1370. E-mail: 2077607@mcimail.com. Web: pages.prodigy.com/SOAPBOX.

ANTIQUE AUTO SHOW. July 29–30. Wheaton Village, Millville, NJ. 19th annual show, held rain or shine. Est attendance: 1,500. For info: Wheaton Village, 1501 Glasstown Rd, Millville, NJ 08332. Phone: (609) 825-6800 or (800) 998-4552. Fax: (609) 825-2410. E-mail: mail@wheatonvillage.org. Web: www.wheatonvillage.org.

AU SABLE CANOE MARATHON AND RIVER FESTIVALS. July 29–30. Grayling and Oscoda, MI. Gather at Grayling for the 9 PM start of North America's longest, toughest nonstop canoe race. Some 50 teams, carrying canoes atop their heads, run through the downtown streets and launch them into the Au Sable River. During the pre-race action at this 52nd annual event, you can frolic at a parade, county fair, arts and crafts show, ice cream social, antique car show, street dance and other festivities. While the hardy canoeists paddle for some 14 hours through the night, you can drive to Oscoda, stopping to cheer them on at bridges and dams along the 120-mile route. Annually, the last full weekend in July. For info: Grayling Area Visitors Council, (800) 937-8837 or Oscoda-Au Sable Chamber of Commerce, (800) 235-4625.

CANON GREATER HARTFORD OPEN. July 29–Aug 1. TPC at River Highlands, Cromwell, CT. A PGA Tour tournament, formerly known as the Insurance City Open and the Sammy Davis, Jr–Greater Hartford Open. Est attendance: 275,000. For info: Dir, Canon Greater Hartford Open, One Financial Plaza, Hartford, CT 06103. Phone: (860) 522-4171. Fax: (860) 278-5574.

ENGLAND: SKANDIA LIFE COWES WEEK. July 29–Aug 5. Cowes, Isle of Wight. Yachting festival covering all classes of yacht racing. Est attendance: 14,000. For info: Cowes Week Organizers, Cowes Combined Clubs, 18 Bath Rd, Cowes, Isle of Wight, England PO31 7QN. Phone: (44) (198) 329-5744. Fax: (44) (198) 329-5329.

FESLER, WES: BIRTH ANNIVERSARY. July 29, 1908. Wesley Eugene (Wes) Fesler, football player, coach and broadcaster, born at Youngstown, OH. Fesler was a three-time All-American end at Ohio State University and played baseball and basketball. He coached several sports at several schools before being named head football coach at Ohio State in 1947. His Buckeyes did well, but he resigned after the 1950 season, citing the intense pressure of coaching at Columbus. Six weeks later, he agreed to coach at the University of Minnesota where he stayed for three years. Died at Laguna Hills, CA, July 30, 1989.

FIRST 8-FOOT HIGH JUMP: ANNIVERSARY. July 29, 1989. Javier Sotomayor of Cuba became the first man to high jump 8 feet. He set the new world record at the Caribbean Championship meet at San Juan, Puerto Rico. Sotomayor held the previous record, 7 ft, 11½ in, set in 1988 in Spain.

FIRST WORLD HEAVYWEIGHT TITLE FIGHT: ANNIVERSARY. July 29, 1751. Jack Slack of England, the acknowledged champion, defeated challenger M. Petit of France, in the first International World Title Prize Fight at Harlston, Norfolk, England.

GARVEY'S STREAK ENDS: ANNIVERSARY. July 29, 1983. San Diego Padres first baseman Steve Garvey saw his consecutive game playing streak come to an end at 1,207 games, a National League record. He dislocated his left thumb in a collision at home plate with Atlanta Braves pitcher Pascual Perez and was unable to play in the second game of the doubleheader.

HAMBLETONIAN FESTIVAL. July 29–Aug 5. The Meadowlands, East Rutherford, NJ. A week of festive activities leading up to the 75th anniversary edition of the Hambletonian Stakes, the richest and most important race for trotting horses. First raced in 1926, this $1.2 million race, to be nationally televised, is the most coveted prize in trotting. Includes $1 million Breeders Crown Trot. For tickets call: (201) 935-8500. For info: Hambletonian Soc, 1200 Tices Ln, East Brunswick, NJ 08816. Phone: (732) 249-8500. Fax: (732) 294-3170. E-mail: moiHambS@aol.com. Web: www.hambletonian.org.

MARA, TIM: BIRTH ANNIVERSARY. July 29, 1887. Timothy James (Tim) Mara, Pro Football Hall of Fame executive, born at New York, NY. Mara was a successful bookmaker who bought the New York franchise in the NFL in 1925 for $500. His team, the Giants, became one of the most successful in the league, withstanding challenges from two early American Football Leagues, the All-America Football Conference of the late 1940s and the New York Jets of the AFL of the 1960s. Inducted into the Pro Football Hall of Fame as a charter member in 1963. Died at New York, Feb 16, 1959.

USFL WINS SUIT AGAINST NFL: ANNIVERSARY. July 29, 1986. The United States Football League won its antitrust suit against the National Football League, but the court awarded the upstart league only $1 (trebled to $3) instead of the $1.69 billion it sought. The jury deliberated five days before reaching its verdict.

BIRTHDAYS TODAY

Luis Rene Alicea, 35, baseball player, born Santurce, Puerto Rico, July 29, 1965.

Daniel (Danny) Driessen, 49, former baseball player, born Hilton Head, SC, July 29, 1951.

JULY 30 — SUNDAY
Day 212 — 154 Remaining

CHASE'S SPORTSQUOTE OF THE DAY

"They say some of my stars drink whiskey, but I have found that the ones who drink milkshakes don't win many ballgames."—Casey Stengel

BARE BUNS FUN RUN. July 30. Kaniksu Ranch, WA. 50 miles northwest of Spokane. Clothing is optional in this 5K road race. Cross the finish line nude and you'll get a T-shirt commemorating your achievement. Wear it proudly—on those days you choose to wear clothes. Annually, the last Sunday in July. For info: Bare Buns Fun Run, PO Box 5003, Spokane, WA 99205-0003. Phone: (509) 624-6777. Fax: (509) 624-4580. E-mail: BBFR5K@aol.com. Web: ontherun.com/barebuns.sht.

FORD, HENRY: BIRTH ANNIVERSARY. July 30, 1863. Henry Ford, automobile company executive, born at Dearborn, MI. Besides his role as founder of the Ford Motor Company, Henry Ford was also a racing pioneer, using the sport to garner publicity for his main business. He won the only race he entered, a 25-mile contest in 1901. In 1902, he organized the company that made racing cars for Barney Oldfield. Ford's Model T won the New York-to-Seattle race in 1909. Died at Detroit, MI, Apr 17, 1947.

HANSEN'S UNASSISTED TRIPLE PLAY: ANNIVERSARY. July 30, 1968. Washington Senators shortstop Ron Hansen completed the eighth regular-season unassisted triple play and the first one since 1927 in a game against the Cleveland Indians. In the first inning, Hansen snared a line drive hit by Jose Azcue, stepped on second base to double off Dave Nelson and then tagged Russ Snyder before he could get back to first. Hansen was traded to the Chicago White Sox three days later.

HIRSCH, MAX: 120th BIRTH ANNIVERSARY. July 30, 1880. Maximilian Justice (Max) Hirsch, thoroughbred trainer, born at Fredericksburg, TX. Hirsch was a jockey from age 14 to age 19 when he obtained his trainer's license. Closely associated with the King Ranch, he trained three winners of the Kentucky Derby, two of the Preakness Stakes and four of the Belmont Stakes. His most famous horse was Assault, winner of the 1946 Triple Crown. Died at New Hyde Park, NY, Apr 3, 1969.

ISUZU IRONMAN USA LAKE PLACID. July 30. Lake Placid, NY. One of the outstanding triathlons in the country. For info: Isuzu Ironman USA Lake Placid, PO Box 470, Lake Placid, NY 12946. Phone: (518) 523-2665. Fax: (518) 523-7542. E-mail: imanusa@capital.net. Web: www.ironmanusa.com.

STENGEL, CASEY: 110th BIRTH ANNIVERSARY. July 30, 1890. Charles Dillon ("Casey") Stengel, Baseball Hall of Fame outfielder and manager, born at Kansas City, MO. Stengel played the outfield for several teams and earned a reputation for goofiness. He carried this over into his career as a manager, but his success with the New York Yankees (ten pennants and seven World Series titles in 12 years) made him one of the game's enduring stars. Inducted into the Hall of Fame in 1966. Died at Glendale, CA, Sept 29, 1975.

BIRTHDAYS TODAY

Clinton Merrick (Clint) Hurdle, 43, former baseball player, born Big Rapids, MI, July 30, 1957.

Christopher Paul (Chris) Mullin, 37, basketball player, born New York, NY, July 30, 1963.

Markus Naslund, 27, hockey player, born Harnosand, Sweden, July 30, 1973.

Joseph Henry (Joe) Nuxhall, 72, broadcaster and former baseball player, born Hamilton, OH, July 30, 1928.

Thomas Alan (Tom) Pagnozzi, 38, former baseball player, born Tucson, AZ, July 30, 1962.

Robert Porcher, III, 31, football player, born Wando, SC, July 20, 1969.

Arnold Schwarzenegger, 53, actor and former bodybuilder, born Graz, Austria, July 30, 1947.

Allan Huber ("Bud") Selig, 66, Commissioner of Baseball, born Milwaukee, WI, July 30, 1934.

JULY 31 — MONDAY
Day 213 — 153 Remaining

ADCOCK HITS FOUR HOME RUNS: ANNIVERSARY. July 31, 1954. Joe Adcock of the Milwaukee Braves became the seventh player in major league history to hit four home runs in a single game. He added a double to lead the Braves to a 15–7 win over the Brooklyn Dodgers.

ASA GIRLS' GOLD 18-AND-UNDER FAST PITCH NATIONAL CHAMPIONSHIP. July 31–Aug 6. St. Louis, MO. For info: ASA-USA Softball, 2801 NE 50th St, Oklahoma City, OK 73111. Phone: (405) 424-5266. Fax: (405) 424-3855. E-mail: info@softball.org. Web: www.softball.org.

DALEY, ARTHUR: BIRTH ANNIVERSARY. July 31, 1904. Arthur John Daley, sportswriter, born at New York, NY. Daley played baseball at Fordham University but turned to sportswriting after injuring his thumb. He went to work for the *New York Times* in 1926 and became the first reporter to cover a sporting event overseas when he went to Berlin for the 1936 Summer Olympics. In 1942, he replaced John Kieran as writer of the "Sports of the Times" column, eventually producing more than 10,000 columns. He won the Pulitzer Prize in 1956. Died at New York, Jan 3, 1974.

MUNICIPAL STADIUM OPENS: ANNIVERSARY. July 31, 1932. The Cleveland Indians opened their new ballpark, Municipal Stadium, losing to the Philadelphia Athletics and pitcher Robert ("Lefty") Grove, 1–0, before 76,979. The Indians reserved their new home for Sunday and holiday games. They continued to play weekday games at League Park until the late 1940s.

ONLY ALL-STAR GAME TIE: ANNIVERSARY. July 31, 1961. The year's second All-Star Game ended in a 1–1 tie at Fenway Park as heavy rain caused the game to be called after nine innings. Baseball inaugurated the custom of two All-Star games in 1959 and abandoned the practice after 1962. The 1961 tie was the only one in All-Star history.

RYAN WINS 300th GAME: 10th ANNIVERSARY. July 31, 1990. Nolan Ryan of the Texas Rangers won the 300th game of his career, defeating the Milwaukee Brewers, 11–3. Ryan pitched in the major leagues from 1966 until 1993 and finished with 324 wins.

FIRST "UNTIL THERE'S A CURE" DAY: ANNIVERSARY. July 31, 1994. The San Francisco Giants joined the battle against AIDS by staging their first "Until There's a Cure" Day at Candlestick Park. The Giants wore red ribbons sewn on their uniforms. Together with the visiting Colorado Rockies, they joined 700 AIDS volunteers to form a giant human red ribbon on the field. One dollar from the price of every ticket sold went to Bay Area AIDS organizations. The Giants won the game, 9–4, behind home runs by Barry Bonds, Darryl Strawberry and Matt Williams, who hit two.

US GIRLS' JUNIOR (GOLF) CHAMPIONSHIP. July 31–Aug 5. Pumpkin Ridge Golf Club, Cornelius, OR. For info: US Golf Assn, Golf House, Far Hills, NJ 07931. Phone: (908) 234-2300. Fax: (908) 234-9687. E-mail: usga@usga.org. Web: www.usga.org.

US JUNIOR AMATEUR (GOLF) CHAMPIONSHIP. July 31–Aug 5. Pumpkin Ridge Golf Club, Cornelius, OR. For info: US Golf Assn, Golf House, Far Hills, NJ 07931. Phone: (908) 234-2300. Fax: (908) 234-9687. E-mail: usga@ix.netcom.com. Web: www.usga.org.

BIRTHDAYS TODAY

Henry Albert (Hank) Bauer, 78, former baseball manager and player, born East St. Louis, IL, July 31, 1922.

Evonne Fay Goolagong Cawley, 49, former tennis player, born Griffith, New South Wales, Australia, July 31, 1951.

Leon Durham, 43, former baseball player, born Cincinnati, OH, July 31, 1957.

Gustave Joseph (Gus) Frerotte, 29, football player, born Kittanning, PA, July 31, 1971.

Curtis (Curt) Gowdy, 81, Ford Frick Award broadcaster, born Green River, WY, July 31, 1919.

Kevin Darwin Greene, 38, football player, born New York, NY, July 31, 1962.

Jonathan Phillip Ogden, 26, football player, born Washington, DC, July 31, 1974.

Brian Skrudland, 37, hockey player, born Peace River, Alberta, Canada, July 31, 1963.

AUGUST 1 — TUESDAY
Day 214 — 152 Remaining

BLYLEVEN STRIKES OUT 3,000th BATTER: ANNIVERSARY. Aug 1, 1986. Pitcher Bert Blyleven of the Minnesota Twins became the tenth pitcher to pass the 3,000 mark in career strikeouts, beating the Oakland A's, 10–1. He ended his career with 3,701 strikeouts.

GORBOUS MAKES RECORD THROW: ANNIVERSARY. Aug 1, 1957. Minor league baseball player Glen Gorbous set a world record by throwing a baseball 445 ft, 10 inches, on the fly in a contest at Omaha Stadium, Omaha, NE. Gorbous used a six-step delivery to heave the ball from the right field corner to the left field corner. He retired from baseball two years later because of an arm injury.

KENWOOD CUP: HAWAII INTERNATIONAL OCEAN RACING SERIES. Aug 1–9. Oahu, HI. 13th biennial. The Kenwood Cup is series of 10 sailing races of varying distances and part of the Champagne Mumm World Cup international sailing series. 50 Grand Prix yachts, ranging in length from 35 to 82 feet, are expected from Australia, New Zealand, Canada, Europe and the US. There are four windward/leeward races (10–12 nautical miles each) and four ocean triangle races (22 nautical miles each) off Waikiki Beach, a 150-mile Honolulu-to-Maui race along Molokai's north shore, and a 390-mile race beginning and finishing off Oahu. Both long distance races finish off Diamond Head and can be viewed by spectators. Fun events include the Plymouth Cup team event with amateur boat construction to benefit charity. Est attendance: 2,000. For media info: Carol Hogan, (808) 325-7400. For race info: (808) 946-9061. E-mail: oceanpro@interpac.net. Web: www.worldvoyager.com.

McCOVEY HITS 18th GRAND SLAM: ANNIVERSARY. Aug 1, 1977. Willie McCovey of the San Francisco Giants hit the 18th and last grand slam of his career. His total still stands as the National League record. Lou Gehrig holds the major league record with 23.

McINTIRE'S ALMOST-NO-HITTER: ANNIVERSARY. Aug 1, 1906. Harry McIntire of the Brooklyn Superbas (later the Dodgers) pitched 10 ⅔ innings of no-hit baseball before Claude Ritchey of the Pittsburgh Pirates singled. McIntire stayed in the game but lost it in the 13th inning, 1–0. His effort stands as the longest "almost-no-hitter" in major league history.

NATIONAL BASEBALL CONGRESS WORLD SERIES. Aug 1–15. Lawrence-Dumont Stadium, Wichita, KS. 66th annual National Baseball Congress World Series. Est attendance: 100,000. For info: National Baseball Congress, PO Box 1420, Wichita, KS 67201. Phone: (316) 267-3372 or x 204. Fax: (316) 267-3382. E-mail: nbc@wichitawranglers.com. Web: www.wichitawranglers.com.

NFL ADMITS FIVE FRANCHISES: 75th ANNIVERSARY. Aug 1, 1925. The National Football League admitted five new franchises—a new Canton Bulldogs team, the Detroit Panthers, the New York Giants, the Pottsville Maroons and the Providence Steam Rollers. The Bulldogs and the Panthers lasted two seasons, the Maroons four and the Steam Rollers seven. The Giants still exist although they play in New Jersey.

OTT HITS 500th HOME RUN: 55th ANNIVERSARY. Aug 1, 1945. Outfielder Mel Ott of the New York Giants hit the 500th home run of his career in a 9–2 win over the Boston Braves at the Polo Grounds. At this point in baseball history, Ott stood third on the all-time home run list behind Babe Ruth with 714 and Jimmie Foxx with 531. Ott finished with 511 homers.

ROSE'S HITTING STREAK ENDS: ANNIVERSARY. Aug 1, 1978. Pete Rose of the Cincinnati Reds saw his 44-game hitting streak come to an end as he went 0-for-4 against Larry McWilliams and Gene Garber of the Atlanta Braves in a 16–4 Braves win. Rose's streak tied Willie Keeler's mark, set in 1897, as the longest in National League history.

US WOMEN WIN FIRST OLYMPIC SOCCER TITLE: ANNIVERSARY. Aug 1, 1996. The US defeated China, 2–1, to win the first Olympic gold medal awarded in women's soccer. The game was played at Sanford Stadium at Athens, GA, as part of the 1996 Summer Olympics. Tiffeny Milbrett scored the winning goal, assisted by Joy Fawcett.

BIRTHDAYS TODAY

Greg Adams, 37, hockey player, born Nelson, British Columbia, Canada, Aug 1, 1963.

Stacey Orlando Augmon, 32, basketball player, born Pasadena, CA, Aug 1, 1968.

Brian Edward Bohanon, Jr, 32, baseball player, born Denton, TX, Aug 1, 1968.

Gregory Scott (Gregg) Jefferies, 33, baseball player, born Burlingame, CA, Aug 1, 1967.

John Albert (Jack) Kramer, 79, former tennis player, born Las Vegas, NV, Aug 1, 1921.

Samuel (Sammy) Lee, 80, Olympic gold medal diver, born Fresno, CA, Aug 1, 1920.

Anthony Joseph (Tony) Muser, 53, baseball manager and former player, born Van Nuys, CA, Aug 1, 1947.

AUGUST 2 — WEDNESDAY
Day 215 — 151 Remaining

CHASE'S SPORTSQUOTE OF THE DAY

"Heigh-ho! What a life!"—John Kieran on spring training

ASA BOYS' SLOW PITCH NATIONAL CHAMPIONSHIP. Aug 2–6. Ft Payne, AL. For boys 16-and-under and 18-and-under. For info: ASA-USA Softball, 2801 NE 50th St, Oklahoma City, OK 73111. Phone: (405) 424-5266. Fax: (405) 424-3855. E-mail: info@softball.org. Web: www.softball.org.

COLLEGE ALL-STARS UPSET PACKERS: ANNIVERSARY. Aug 2, 1963. In the annual tilt between the defending NFL champions and a team of college all-stars on their way to their rookie pro seasons, the collegians upset the Green Bay Packers, 20–17. The College All-Star Game was contested from 1934 through 1977 with the collegians winning nine times and earning one tie (in the inaugural game).

KIERAN, JOHN: BIRTH ANNIVERSARY. Aug 2, 1892. John Francis Kieran, sportswriter, born at New York, NY. Kieran graduated from Fordham University and earned two advanced degrees. His wide knowledge made his writing for the *New York Times* different from other sportswriters and merited the first by-lined column in the *Times.* Kieran also served as a panelist for ten years on the radio quiz show, "Information Please." Given the J.G. Taylor Spink Award in 1973. Died at Rockport, MA, Dec 10, 1981.

US WINS OLYMPIC BOXING TITLE: ANNIVERSARY. Aug 2, 1952. Five American boxers won gold medals at the Summer Olympics at Helsinki, Finland, giving the US the unofficial team championship for the first time. The gold medalists were flyweight Nate Brooks, light welterweight Charley Adkins, middleweight Floyd Patterson, light heavyweight Norvell Lee and heavyweight Eddie Sanders.

YELLOW BASEBALLS USED: ANNIVERSARY. Aug 2, 1938. The Brooklyn Dodgers and the St. Louis Cardinals played a doubleheader in which they experimented with a yellow baseball in the first game. They went back to the traditional white ball for the second game, and the Dodgers won both contests, 6–2 and 9–3.

BIRTHDAYS TODAY

Anthony Lewis (Tony) Amonte, 30, hockey player, born Hingham, MA, Aug 2, 1970.
Cedric Z. Ceballos, 31, basketball player, born Maui, HI, Aug 2, 1969.
Lamar Hunt, 68, Pro Football Hall of Fame executive, born El Dorado, AR, Aug 2, 1932.
Timothy Stephen (Tim) Wakefield, 34, baseball player, born Melbourne, FL, Aug 2, 1966.

August **2000**	S	M	T	W	T	F	S
			1	2	3	4	5
	6	7	8	9	10	11	12
	13	14	15	16	17	18	19
	20	21	22	23	24	25	26
	27	28	29	30	31		

AUGUST 3 — THURSDAY
Day 216 — 150 Remaining

BRONCO LEAGUE WORLD SERIES. Aug 3–9. Monterey, CA. International youth baseball World Series for players of league ages 11 and 12. Est attendance: 10,000. For info: Pony Baseball/Softball, PO Box 225, Washington, PA 15301. Phone: (724) 225-1060. Fax: (724) 225-9852. E-mail: pony@pulsenet.com. Web: www.pony.org.

CANADA: SQUAMISH DAYS LOGGERS SPORTS FESTIVAL. Aug 3–6. Squamish, British Columbia. A four-day festival including two days of competitive loggers sports and an RV rally as well as dances and lullabe festival. Annually, the first weekend in August (the BC Day long weekend). For info: Squamish and Howe Sound District Chamber of Commerce, Box 1009, Squamish, BC, Canada V0N 3G0. Phone: (604) 892-9244. Fax: (604) 892-2034. E-mail: information@squamishchamber.bc.ca.

CANADA: WORLD JUNIOR BASEBALL CHAMPIONSHIP. Aug 3–14. Edmonton, Alberta. XIXth competition. For info: Ron Rice, Pres, Canadian Baseball Fed, 1600 James Naismith Dr, Ottawa, ON, Canada K1B 5N4. Phone: (613) 748-5606. Fax: (613) 748-5767. E-mail: info@baseball.ca. Web: www.baseball.ca.

COLT LEAGUE WORLD SERIES. Aug 3–10. Lafayette, IN. International young adult baseball World Series for players of league ages 15 and 16. Est attendance: 10,000. For info: Pony Baseball/Softball, PO Box 225, Washington, PA 15301. Phone: (724) 225-1060. Fax: (724) 225-9852. E-mail: pony@pulsenet.com. Web: www.pony.org.

FIRST INTERCOLLEGIATE ROWING RACE: ANNIVERSARY. Aug 3, 1852. The first intercollegiate athletic competition, a rowing race between Harvard and Yale, took place on Lake Winnipesaukee, NH. Over a two-mile course, Harvard beat Yale by four lengths.

FORMATION OF NBA: ANNIVERSARY. Aug 3, 1949. The National Basketball Association (NBA) was established from the merger of the National Basketball League (NBL) and the Basketball Association of America (BAA).

HEILMANN, HARRY: BIRTH ANNIVERSARY. Aug 3, 1894. Harry Edwin Heilmann, Baseball Hall of Fame outfielder and broadcaster, born at San Francisco, CA. Heilmann hit .394 for the Detroit Tigers in 1921 and went on to win three American League batting titles. After retiring, he became a broadcaster for the Tigers. Inducted into the Hall of Fame in 1952. Died at Detroit, MI, July 9, 1951.

JOKL, ERNST: BIRTH ANNIVERSARY. Aug 3, 1907. Ernest Jokl, sports medicine pioneer, born at Breslau, Germany. Jokl received his medical education in Germany, moved to South Africa in 1933 and later to the US. An early student of sports physiology, he was the first US physician to hold a degree in sports medicine and was a founder of the American College of Sports Medicine. Died at Lexington, KY, Dec 13, 1997.

TRADE OF MANAGERS: 40th ANNIVERSARY. Aug 3, 1960. In an unprecedented baseball transaction, two teams traded managers. The Cleveland Indians sent Joe Gordon to the Detroit Tigers for Jimmy Dykes.

BIRTHDAYS TODAY

Lance Dwight Alworth, 60, Pro Football Hall of Fame wide receiver, born Houston, TX, Aug 3, 1940.
Rodney Roy (Rod) Beck, 32, baseball player, born Burbank, CA, Aug 3, 1968.
Sidney Eugene (Sid) Bream, 40, former baseball player, born Carlisle, PA, Aug 3, 1960.
Travis Hall, 28, football player, born Kenai, AK, Aug 3, 1972.

Nathaniel (Nate) McMillan, 36, basketball player, born Raleigh, NC, Aug 3, 1964.
Sandis Ozolinsh, 28, hockey player, born Riga, USSR, Aug 3, 1972.
Trevor Pryce, 25, football player, born Winter Park, FL, Aug 3, 1975.

AUGUST 4 — FRIDAY
Day 217 — 149 Remaining

ASA MEN'S 23-AND-UNDER FAST PITCH NATIONAL CHAMPIONSHIP. Aug 4–7. Oviedo, FL. For info: ASA-USA Softball, 2801 NE 50th St, Oklahoma City, OK 73111. Phone: (405) 424-5266. Fax: (405) 424-3855. E-mail: info@softball.org. Web: www.softball.org.

BECKLEY, JAKE: BIRTH ANNIVERSARY. Aug 4, 1867. Jacob Peter (Jake) Beckley, Baseball Hall of Fame first baseman, born at Hannibal, MO. He played first base in the majors from 1888 to 1907. He is said to have invented the hidden ball trick. Inducted into the Hall of Fame in 1971. Died at Kansas City, MO, June 25, 1918.

BOOM DAYS. Aug 4–6. Leadville, CO. The city's oldest annual celebration features a large parade, street races, mining events, pack burro race and arts and crafts. Fun for the whole family. Est attendance: 35,000. For info: Chamber of Commerce, PO Box 861, Leadville, CO 80461. Phone: (719) 486-3900 or (800) 933-3901. Fax: (719) 486-8478. E-mail: leadville@leadvilleusa.com. Web: www.leadvilleusa.com.

CAREW GETS 3,000th HIT: 15th ANNIVERSARY. Aug 4, 1985. Rod Carew of the California Angels got the 3,000th hit of his career, a single in the third inning off Frank Viola of the Minnesota Twins. The Angels won, 6–5. Carew finished his career with 3,053 hits and was inducted into the Hall of Fame in 1991.

CUNNINGHAM, GLENN: BIRTH ANNIVERSARY. Aug 4, 1909. Glenn V. Cunningham, track and field athlete, born at Atlanta, KS. Cunningham overcame severe burns to his legs in a schoolhouse fire to become a great middle-distance runner. He won the Sullivan Award for 1933 and starred in the mile run as it became the premier track event. He set a world record, 4:06.7, in 1934 that lasted three years. After World War II, he and his wife opened a youth ranch and cared for more than 10,000 foster children plus ten of their own. Died at Menifee, AR, Mar 10, 1988.

LUQUE, ADOLFO: 110th BIRTH ANNIVERSARY. Aug 4, 1890. Adolfo Luque, baseball player, born at Havana, Cuba. Luque was the first Latin player to appear in the World Series, with the 1919 Cincinnati Reds. Near the end of his career, he became a relief pitcher exclusively, a prototype for players to come. Died at Havana, July 3, 1957.

MOLYNEUX, TOM: DEATH ANNIVERSARY. Aug 4, 1818. Tom Molyneux, boxer, born at Virginia or Maryland, 1784. Molyneux was a slave who won his freedom by winning a fight on which his owner had wagered. He made his way to New York and then to England where he narrowly lost a fight against Tom Cribb on Dec 18, 1810, for the heavyweight title. Died at Dublin, Ireland.

MUSTANG LEAGUE WORLD SERIES. Aug 4–8. Irving, TX. International youth baseball World Series for players league ages 9 and 10. Est attendance: 5,000. For info: Pony Baseball/Softball, Inc, PO Box 225, Washington, PA 15301. Phone: (724) 225-1060. Fax: (724) 225-9852. E-mail: pony@pulsenet.com. Web: www.pony.org.

SEAVER WINS 300th GAME: 15th ANNIVERSARY. Aug 4, 1985. Tom Seaver, pitching for the Chicago White Sox against the Yankees at New York, won the 300th game of his career. He gave up seven hits, walked one and struck out seven as the Sox won, 4–1. Seaver pitched in the majors from 1967 through 1986, mostly for the New York Mets, and won 311 games.

WORLD FREEFALL CONVENTION. Aug 4–13. Quincy, IL. More than 4,600 skydivers converge in Quincy and fill the skies with their brilliant colored parachutes. Spectators can enjoy the sights and take part in helicopter rides, biplane rides and hot-air balloon rides. Those wishing to skydive may purchase a tandem skydive or take lessons and skydive on their own. Est attendance: 60,000. For info: World Freefall Convention, RR 1, Box 123, Quincy, IL 62301. Phone: (217) 222-5867. Fax: (217) 221-9999. E-mail: wffc@freefall.com.

YOUNGBLOOD HITS FOR TWO TEAMS: ANNIVERSARY. Aug 4, 1982. Joel Youngblood became the first major leaguer to play and get a hit for two different teams in two different cities in the same day. In an afternoon game, Youngblood drove in the winning run for the New York Mets as they beat the Cubs at Chicago, 7–4. After the game, he was traded to the Montreal Expos, who played at Philadelphia that night. Youngblood flew there, entered the game in the fourth inning and got a single.

BIRTHDAYS TODAY

William Roger Clemens, 38, baseball player, born Dayton, OH, Aug 4, 1962.
Jeff Gordon, 29, auto racer, born Vallejo, CA, Aug 4, 1971.
George Dallas Green, 66, former baseball manager and player, born Newport, DE, Aug 4, 1934.
Cleon Joseph Jones, 58, former baseball player, born Plateau, AL, Aug 4, 1942.
Troy Franklin O'Leary, 31, baseball player, born Compton, CA, Aug 4, 1969.
Joseph Henri Maurice ("Rocket") Richard, 79, Hockey Hall of Fame right wing, born Montreal, Quebec, Canada, Aug 4, 1921.
Robert John Riggins, 51, Pro Football Hall of Fame fullback, born Centralia, KS, Aug 4, 1949.
Mary Decker Slaney, 42, middle distance runner, born Bunnvale, NJ, Aug 4, 1958.

AUGUST 5 — SATURDAY
Day 218 — 148 Remaining

AARON, TOMMIE: BIRTH ANNIVERSARY. Aug 5, 1939. Tommie Lee Aaron, baseball player, born at Mobile, AL. The brother of home-run king Henry Aaron hit 13 homers in a seven-year major league career. Died at Atlanta, GA, Aug 16, 1984.

CANADA: KIN SLO-PITCH TOURNAMENT. Aug 5–7. Edson, Alberta. Canada's, perhaps North America's, largest coed slo-pitch tournament. 256 teams ranging from very competitive to very awful descend on Edson every year for some fun-soaked days of competition and camaraderie. Annually, on Canada's Civic Holiday, August Long Weekend, the first full weekend in August. Est attendance: 12,000. For info: David Miller, Miller Sports, Box 8012, 218 Main St, Edson, AB, Canada T7E 1W28. Phone: (403) 723-2289. Fax: (403) 712-7339.

E.P. "TOM" SAWYER STATE PARK/LOUISVILLE LAND SHARK TRIATHLON XVIII. Aug 5. Tom Sawyer State Park, Louisville, KY. Participants swim ½ mile, bicycle 16 miles and run 5K cross-country. Est attendance: 500. For info: Tim Curtis, Recreation Dir, E.P. Tom Sawyer Park, 3000 Freys Hill Rd, Louisville, KY 40241-2172. Phone: (502) 426-8950.

FIRST BASEBALL BROADCAST: ANNIVERSARY. Aug 5, 1921. Radio station KDKA at Pittsburgh broadcast a baseball game for the first time as the Pirates beat the Philadelphia Phillies, 8–5. Announcer Harold Arlin called the game.

FIRST HAMBLETONIAN DEAD HEAT: ANNIVERSARY. Aug 5, 1989. For the first time, the race off in the Hambletonian, harness racing's most prestigious race, ended in a dead heat with Park Avenue Joe being declared the winner over Probe. Park Avenue Joe finished second in the first heat and won the second heat. Probe won the first heat but broke stride and finished ninth in the second heat.

NATIONAL SCRABBLE CHAMPIONSHIP. Aug 5–10. Providence, RI. Players compete for the national championship in the popular game invented by unemployed architect Alfred Butts in 1931. Est attendance: 500. For info: John D. Williams, Jr, Exec Dir, Natl Scrabble Assn, PO Box 700, Greenport, NY 11944. Phone: (516) 477-0033. Fax: (516) 477-0294. E-mail: info@scrabble-assoc .com. Web: www.scrabble-assoc.com.

PINCH-HIT HOME RUN RECORD: ANNIVERSARY. Aug 5, 1984. Cliff Johnson of the Toronto Blue Jays hit the 19th pinch-hit home run of his career to set the major league record as the Blue Jays beat the Baltimore Orioles, 4–3. Johnson hit an additional pinch homer in 1986 to extend his record to 20.

RUPPERT, JACOB: BIRTH ANNIVERSARY. Aug 5, 1867. Jacob Ruppert, Jr, baseball executive, born at New York, NY. Ruppert was the son of a brewery owner who purchased the New York Yankees in 1914 with Tillinghast Huston for $450,000. Ruppert bought Babe Ruth from the Boston Red Sox, built Yankee Stadium and made his team the best in baseball. Died at New York, Jan 13, 1939.

TALL TIMBER DAYS FESTIVAL. Aug 5–6. Grand Rapids, MN. Festival features the Sheer Brothers Lumberjack Show, chainsaw carvers, arts and crafts, Applecords Quartet, competitions, YMCA run, canoeing and bed racing. Families welcome. Annually, the first full weekend in August. Est attendance: 30,000. For info: Tall Timber Days, PO Box 134, Grand Rapids, MN 55744. Phone: (218) 326-5618. E-mail: mojo@uslink.net.

BIRTHDAYS TODAY

Nelson Kelley (Nellie) Briles, 57, broadcaster and former baseball player, born Dorris, CA, Aug 5, 1943.

Bernard (Bernie) Carbo, 53, former baseball player, born Detroit, MI, Aug 5, 1947.

Bruce Noel Coslet, 54, football coach, born Oakdale, CA, Aug 5, 1946.

Patrick Aloysius Ewing, 38, basketball player, born Kingston, Jamaica, Aug 5, 1962.

Roman Ildonzo Gabriel, Jr, 60, former football player, born Wilmington, NC, Aug 5, 1940.

August	S	M	T	W	T	F	S
2000			1	2	3	4	5
	6	7	8	9	10	11	12
	13	14	15	16	17	18	19
	20	21	22	23	24	25	26
	27	28	29	30	31		

John Garrett Olerud, 32, baseball player, born Seattle, WA, Aug 5, 1968.

Otis Henry Thorpe, 38, basketball player, born Boynton Beach, FL, Aug 5, 1962.

AUGUST 6 — SUNDAY
Day 219 — 147 Remaining

AMERICAN QUARTER HORSE ASSOCIATION YOUTH WORLD CHAMPIONSHIP SHOW AND CONVENTION. Aug 6–14. Ft Worth, TX. World's largest, single-breed youth world championship horse show. For info: AQHA, PO Box 200, Amarillo, TX 79168. Phone: (806) 376-4811. Fax: (806) 349-6409. Web: aqha.com.

EDERLE SWIMS ENGLISH CHANNEL: ANNIVERSARY. Aug 6, 1926. American Gertrude Ederle became the first woman to swim the English Channel, completing the trip in 14 hours, 31 minutes. Ederle, an Olympic gold medal winner in 1924, entered the water early in the morning on the French side of the Channel. Despite a storm that added 14 miles to her 21-mile route, she completed the swim in the best time ever for a woman or a man.

SPLIT SEASON APPROVED: ANNIVERSARY. Aug 6, 1981. After a seven-week strike that cut the heart out of the regular baseball season, major league players approved a plan for a split season with the post-strike games to constitute the second half. The New York Yankees, Oakland Athletics, Philadelphia Phillies and Los Angeles Dodgers were declared first-half champions, automatically qualifying for special divisional play-offs.

STRONG, KEN: BIRTH ANNIVERSARY. Aug 6, 1906. Elmer Kenneth (Ken) Strong, Jr, Pro Football Hall of Fame halfback and placekicker, born at West Haven, CT. Strong played baseball and football at New York University and then played both sports professionally. His placekicking skills several times put him among the NFL's leading scorers. He coached kicking after he retired and wrote a book that incorporated motion picture studies. Inducted into the Pro Football Hall of Fame in 1967. Died at New York, NY, Oct 5, 1979.

BIRTHDAYS TODAY

Stanley Peter (Stan) Belinda, 34, baseball player, born Huntingdon, PA, Aug 6, 1966.

Dale Ellis, 40, basketball player, born Marietta, GA, Aug 6, 1960.

Clement Walter (Clem) Labine, 74, former baseball player, born Lincoln, RI, Aug 6, 1926.

David Maurice Robinson, 35, basketball player, born Key West, FL, Aug 6, 1965.

AUGUST 7 — MONDAY
Day 220 — 146 Remaining

ASA BOYS' 18-AND-UNDER FAST PITCH NATIONAL CHAMPIONSHIP. Aug 7. Oviedo, FL. For info: ASA-USA Softball, 2801 NE 50th St, Oklahoma City, OK 73111. Phone: (405) 424-5266. Fax: (405) 424-3855. E-mail: info@softball.org. Web: www.softball.org.

DALY WINS PGA: ANNIVERSARY. Aug 7, 1991. A last-minute entry who didn't have the opportunity to play a practice round, John Daly won the PGA Championship at Crooked Stick Golf Club in Indiana by three strokes over Bruce Lietzke. Daly endured a wealth of personal problems in the ensuing years, including marital difficulties and alcoholism. But he continued to thrill tournament crowds with his prodigious drives and his "grip it and rip it" approach to the game.

DIDRIKSON DISQUALIFIED: ANNIVERSARY. Aug 7, 1932. Mildred ("Babe") Didrikson, perhaps the greatest American women athlete ever, was disqualified in the high jump at the 1932 Summer Olympics at Los Angeles. Didrikson had already won gold medals in the javelin and the 80-meter hurdles when she faced off with Jean Shiley, another American, in the high jump. Both cleared 5 feet, 5 ¼ inches, and then 5 feet, 5¾ inches, in a jump-off. Officials then correctly ruled that Didrikson's technique, clearing the bar head first, was illegal. Shiley won the gold medal and Didrikson had to settle for the silver.

FRANCE: WORLD AEROBATIC CHAMPIONSHIPS. Aug 7–19. Site TBA. At least 20 countries will compete for team and individual world titles. Biannual event.

LARGEST MINOR LEAGUE CROWD: ANNIVERSARY. Aug 7, 1956. 57,000 people, the largest minor league baseball crowd in history, watched former Negro Leagues star and major leaguer Satchel Paige pitch for the Miami Marlins in an International League game against the Columbus Jets. The game was played at the Orange Bowl, and Miami won.

McKECHNIE, BILL: BIRTH ANNIVERSARY. Aug 7, 1886. William Boyd (Bill) McKechnie, Baseball Hall of Fame manager, born at Wilkinsburg, PA. McKechnie is generally recognized as one of greatest strategic managers in history. He took three National League teams to the pennant, the Pittsburgh Pirates in 1925, the St. Louis Cardinals in 1928 and the Cincinnati Reds in 1939 and 1940. Inducted into the Hall of Fame in 1962. Died at Bradenton, FL, Oct 29, 1965.

STURGIS RALLY AND RACES. Aug 7–13. Sturgis, SD. The granddaddy of all motorcycle rallies and races. For 59 years the small community of Sturgis has welcomed motorcycle enthusiasts from around the world to a week of varied cycle racing, tours of the beautiful Black Hills, old and new cycles at the National Motorcycle Museum, trade shows and thousands of bikes on display. Annually, beginning the Monday after the first full weekend in August. Est attendance: 215,000. For info: Sturgis Rally & Races, Inc, PO Box 189, Sturgis, SD 57785. Phone: (605) 347-6570. Fax: (605) 347-3245. E-mail: srr@rally.sturgis.sd.us. Web: www.rally.sturgis.sd.us.

US WOMEN'S AMATEUR (GOLF) CHAMPIONSHIP. Aug 7–12. Waverly Country Club, Portland, OR. For info: US Golf Assn, Golf House, Far Hills, NJ 07931. Phone: (908) 234-2300. Fax: (908) 234-9687. E-mail: usga@usga.org. Web: www.usga.org.

WAITZ WINS MARATHON: ANNIVERSARY. Aug 7, 1983. At the first World Track and Field Championships at Helsinki, Finland, Grete Waitz of Norway won the women's marathon, an event for many years thought beyond the capability of women.

BIRTHDAYS TODAY

Don James Larsen, 71, former baseball player, born Michigan City, IN, Aug 7, 1929.
Alan Cedric Page, 55, Pro Football Hall of Fame defensive tackle, born Canton, OH, Aug 7, 1945.
Edgar Enrique Renteria, 25, baseball player, born Barranquilla, Colombia, Aug 7, 1975.
Alberto Salazar, 43, marathon runner, born Havana, Cuba, Aug 7, 1957.

AUGUST 8 — TUESDAY
Day 221 — 145 Remaining

ASA GIRLS' 10-AND-UNDER FAST PITCH NATIONAL CHAMPIONSHIP. Aug 8–13. Stockton, CA. For info: ASA-USA Softball, 2801 NE 50th St, Oklahoma City, OK 73111. Phone: (405) 424-5266. Fax: (405) 424-3855. E-mail: info@softball.org. Web: www.softball.org.

ASA GIRLS' 18-AND-UNDER A FAST PITCH NATIONAL CHAMPIONSHIP. Aug 8–13. Normal, IL. For info: ASA-USA Softball, 2801 NE 50th St, Oklahoma City, OK 73111. Phone: (405) 424-5266. Fax: (405) 424-3855. E-mail: info@softball.org. Web: www.softball.org.

Karl Malone

DREAM TEAM WINS GOLD MEDAL: ANNIVERSARY. Aug 8, 1992. The Dream Team, a specially-assembled team of NBA all-stars, defeated Croatia, 117–85, to win the gold medal at the 1992 Summer Olympics at Barcelona. The Dream Team, coached by Chuck Daly, included Charles Barkley, Larry Bird, Clyde Drexler, Patrick Ewing, Magic Johnson, Michael Jordan, Christian Laettner, Karl Malone, Chris Mullin, Scottie Pippen, David Robinson and John Stockton.

FIRST HAMBLETONIAN AT THE MEADOWLANDS: ANNIVERSARY. Aug 8, 1981. Shiaway St. Pat, driven by Ray Remmen, won the Hambletonian, the most important race for three-year-old trotters, contested for the first time at the Meadowlands in New Jersey after moving from DuQuoin, Illinois.

FIRST WRIGLEY FIELD NIGHT GAME POSTPONED: ANNIVERSARY. Aug 8, 1988. The first night game at Chicago's Wrigley Field was postponed by rain with the Cubs leading the Philadelphia Phillies, 3–1, in the bottom of the fourth inning. The Phillies' Phil Bradley led off the game with a home run, but in a postponed game all statistics were washed out.

JACOBS, HELEN: BIRTH ANNIVERSARY. Aug 8, 1908. Helen Hull Jacobs, tennis player born at Globe, AZ. Jacobs won the US Women's singles championship at Forest Hills four times (1932–35) and finished second four other times. She was named Associated Press Female Athlete of the Year for 1933. Jacobs engaged in a storied rivalry with Helen Wills Moody, but she defeated Moody only once in their 11 meetings and that when Moody retired in the third set because of an injury. Died at Easthampton, NY, June 2, 1997.

TEMPLE, JOHNNY: BIRTH ANNIVERSARY. Aug 8, 1928. John Ellis Temple, baseball player, born at Lexington, NC. Temple teamed with shortstop Roy McMillan to form a wonderful double play combination for the Cincinnati Reds in the 1950s. He was a six-time all-star, four times with the Reds and twice with the Cleveland Indians. Died at White Rock, SC, Jan 9, 1994.

WHITE SOX DON SHORTS: ANNIVERSARY. Aug 8, 1976. The Chicago White Sox made baseball sartorial history by donning shorts for a game against the Kansas City Royals. The Sox won, 5–2, but the shorts, a novelty thought up by owner Bill Veeck, lasted only a while.

☆　☆　☆

BIRTHDAYS TODAY

Elijah Alfred Alexander, III, 30, football player, born Ft Worth, TX, Aug 8, 1970.
Marcelo Balboa, 33, soccer player, born Chicago, IL, Aug 8, 1967.
Frank Oliver Howard, 64, former baseball manager and player, born Columbus, OH, Aug 8, 1936.
John Raymond Hudek, 34, baseball player, born Tampa, FL, Aug 8, 1966.
Bruce Rankin Matthews, 39, football player, born Arcadia, CA, Aug 8, 1961.
Esther Williams, 77, swimmer and actress (*Take Me Out to the Ball Game*), born Los Angeles, CA, Aug 8, 1923.

AUGUST 9 — WEDNESDAY
Day 222 — 144 Remaining

CHASE'S SPORTSQUOTE OF THE DAY

"Baseball fans have been forced to endure countless indignities by those who just cannot leave well enough alone: Designated hitters, plastic grass, uniforms that look like pajamas, . . . and of course the most heinous sacrilege, lights in Wrigley Field."—Congressman Dick Durbin

ASA GIRLS' 14-AND-UNDER A FAST PITCH NATIONAL CHAMPIONSHIP. Aug 9–13. Panama City, FL. For info: ASA-USA Softball, 2801 NE 50th St, Oklahoma City, OK 73111. Phone: (405) 424-5266. Fax: (405) 424-5266. E-mail: info@softball.org. Web: www.softball.org.

ASA GIRLS' 12-AND-UNDER SLOW PITCH NATIONAL CHAMPIONSHIP. Aug 9–13. Gadsden, AL. For info: ASA-USA Softball, 2801 NE 50th St, Oklahoma City, OK

August 2000	S	M	T	W	T	F	S
			1	2	3	4	5
	6	7	8	9	10	11	12
	13	14	15	16	17	18	19
	20	21	22	23	24	25	26
	27	28	29	30	31		

73111. Phone: (405) 424-5266. Fax: (405) 424-3855. E-mail: info@softball.org. Web: www.softball.org.

COMPLETE GAMES STREAK: ANNIVERSARY. Aug 9, 1906. Jack Taylor of the St. Louis Cardinals pitched his 187th complete game in a row, not counting 15 relief appearances in which he needed no help. Taylor's incredible streak, begun June 13, 1901, was snapped in his next start, Aug 13, 1906.

FIRST TENNIS ON TELEVISION: ANNIVERSARY. Aug 9, 1939. New York's experimental television station, W2XBS, broadcast tennis for the first time ever. Cameras were set up at the Eastern Grass Court championships at Rye, NY.

FIRST WRIGLEY FIELD NIGHT GAME: ANNIVERSARY. Aug 9, 1988. After a postponement the night before, the first night game in Wrigley Field saw the Chicago Cubs defeat the New York Mets, 6–4.

MARRIED AND DISQUALIFIED: ANNIVERSARY. Aug 9, 1957. The Amateur Athletic Union, governing body for amateur sports in the US, ruled that Lee Calhoun, gold medal winner in the 1956 Olympics in the 110-meter hurdles, had sacrificed his amateur standing. Calhoun had gotten married on the television show *Bride and Groom* and had accepted gifts from the show.

SEASON RESUMES WITH ALL-STAR GAME: ANNIVERSARY. Aug 9, 1981. The 1981 baseball season, interrupted by a players' strike, resumed with the All-Star Game played at Cleveland's Municipal Stadium. 72,086 fans watched the National League defeat the American League, 5–4.

WALTON, ISAAC: BIRTH ANNIVERSARY. Aug 9, 1593. Isaac Walton, English author of classic treatise on fishing, *The Compleat Angler*, born at Stafford, England. He published his famous book in 1653. "Angling," Walton wrote, "may be said to be so like the mathematics, that it can never be fully learnt." Walton's first name, often given as "Isaak," is spelled "Isaac" on his church birth record and on his tombstone. Died at Winchester, England, Dec 15, 1683.

BIRTHDAYS TODAY

Tommie Lee Agee, 58, former baseball player, born Magnolia, AL, Aug 9, 1942.
Rod Jean Brind'Amour, 30, hockey player, born Ottawa, Ontario, Canada, Aug 9, 1970.
Robert Joseph (Bob) Cousy, 72, former soccer executive, former basketball coach and Basketball Hall of Fame guard, born New York, NY, Aug 9, 1928.
Vincent Joseph (Vinny) Del Negro, 34, basketball player, born Springfield, MA, Aug 9, 1966.
Ralph George Houk, 81, former baseball manager and player, born Lawrence, KS, Aug 9, 1919.
Brett Hull, 36, hockey player, born Belleville, Ontario, Canada, Aug 9, 1964.
Rodney George (Rod) Laver, 62, former tennis player, born Rockhampton, Australia, Aug 9, 1938.
Patrick Lavon (Pat) Mahomes, 30, baseball player, born Bryan, TX, Aug 9, 1970.
Kenneth Howard (Ken) Norton, Sr, 55, former heavyweight champion boxer, born Jacksonville, IL, Aug 9, 1945.
Troy Eugene Percival, 31, baseball player, born Fontana, CA, Aug 9, 1969.
Deion Luwynn Sanders, 33, football and baseball player, born Ft Myers, FL, Aug 9, 1967.
Robert Guy (Bob) Scanlan, Jr, 34, baseball player, born Los Angeles, CA, Aug 9, 1966.
John ("Hot Rod") Williams, 38, basketball player, born Sorrento, LA, Aug 9, 1962.

AUGUST 10 — THURSDAY
Day 223 — 143 Remaining

ASA BOYS' SLOW PITCH NATIONAL CHAMPIONSHIP. Aug 10–13. Anniston, AL. Competition for boys 10-and-under, 12-and-under and 14- and-under. For info: ASA-USA Softball, 2801 NE 50th St, Oklahoma City, OK 73111. Phone: (405) 424-5266. Fax: (405) 424-3855. E-mail: info@softball.org. Web: www.softball.org.

ASA GIRLS' 18-AND-UNDER SLOW PITCH NATIONAL CHAMPIONSHIP. Aug 10–13. Albany, GA. For info: ASA-USA Softball, 2801 NE 50th St, Oklahoma City, OK 73111. Phone: (405) 424-5266. Fax: (405) 424-3855. E-mail: info@softball.org. Web: www.softball.org.

ASA GIRLS' 14-AND-UNDER SLOW PITCH NATIONAL CHAMPIONSHIP. Aug 10–13. Hattiesburg, MS. For info: ASA-USA Softball, 2801 NE 50th St, Oklahoma City, OK 73111. Phone: (405) 424-5266. Fax: (405) 424-3855. E-mail: info@softball.org. Web: www.softball.org.

ASA GIRLS' 16-AND-UNDER A FAST PITCH NATIONAL CHAMPIONSHIP. Aug 10–13. Garland, TX. For info: ASA-USA Softball, 2801 NE 50th St, Oklahoma City, OK 73111. Phone: (405) 424-5266. Fax: (405) 424-3855. E-mail: info@softball.org. Web: www.softball.org.

ASA GIRLS' 16-AND-UNDER SLOW PITCH NATIONAL CHAMPIONSHIP. Aug 10–13. Tupelo, MS. For info: ASA-USA Softball, 2801 NE 50th St, Oklahoma City, OK 73111. Phone: (405) 424-5266. Fax: (405) 424-3855. E-mail: info@softball.org. Web: www.softball.org.

ASA GIRLS' 10-AND-UNDER SLOW PITCH NATIONAL CHAMPIONSHIP. Aug 10–13. Columbus, GA. For info: ASA-USA Softball, 2801 NE 50th St, Oklahoma City, OK 73111. Phone: (405) 424-5266. Fax: (405) 424-3855. E-mail: info@softball.org. Web: www.softball.org.

ASA GIRLS' 12-AND-UNDER A FAST PITCH NATIONAL CHAMPIONSHIP. Aug 10–15. Bloomington, IN. For info: ASA-USA Softball, 2801 NE 50th St, Oklahoma City, OK 73111. Phone: (405) 424-5266. Fax: (405) 424-3855. E-mail: info@softball.org. Web: www.softball.org.

ASA WOMEN'S CLASS A FAST PITCH NATIONAL CHAMPIONSHIP. Aug 10–13. Portland, OR. For info: ASA-USA Softball, 2801 NE 50th St, Oklahoma City, OK 73111. Phone: (405) 424-5266. Fax: (405) 424-3855. E-mail: info@softball.org. Web: www.softball.org.

ASA WOMEN'S CLASS B FAST PITCH NATIONAL CHAMPIONSHIP. Aug 10–13. Memphis, TN. For info: ASA-USA Softball, 2801 NE 50th St, Oklahoma City, OK 73111. Phone: (405) 424-5266. Fax: (405) 424-3855. E-mail: info@softball.org. Web: www.softball.org.

ASA WOMEN'S MAJOR FAST PITCH NATIONAL CHAMPIONSHIP. Aug 10–13. Clearwater, FL. For info: ASA-USA Softball, 2801 NE 50th St, Oklahoma City, OK

73111. Phone: (405) 424-5266. Fax: (405) 424-3855. E-mail: info@softball.org. Web: www.softball.org.

BALLOONFEST/LEWIS AND CLARK HERITAGE FAIR. Aug 10–12. Salmon, ID. 9th annual balloonfest with more than 20 hot-air balloons. Est attendance: 6,500. For info: Salmon Valley Chamber of Commerce, 200 Main St, Ste 1, Salmon, ID 83467. Phone: (208) 756-2100. Fax: (208) 756-4840.

BIRTH OF SABR: ANNIVERSARY. Aug 10, 1971. The Society for American Baseball Research, an organization of baseball historians, statisticians, researchers and fans, was founded at a meeting at Cooperstown, NY. SABR members number more than 7,000.

CLOSE BUT NO CIGAR: ANNIVERSARY. Aug 10, 1996. The attempt of the thoroughbred Cigar to set a modern North American record for consecutive races won at 17 came up one victory short as Dare and Go scored an upset in the Pacific Classic at Del Mar Race Track at San Diego, CA. Dare and Go, ridden by Alex Solis, came from off the pace to win by 3½ lengths. Cigar, tied with Citation at 16 straight wins, finished second. He had last lost on Oct 7, 1994, at Belmont Park, NY.

FEWEST PITCHES: ANNIVERSARY. Aug 10, 1944. Charles ("Red") Barrett of the Boston Braves pitched a 2–0 shutout against the Cincinnati Reds and threw only 58 pitches to complete the nine-inning game, a major league record for the fewest pitches in a complete game.

FIRST DAVIS CUP: 100th ANNIVERSARY. Aug 10, 1900. The Davis Cup, an international team tennis competition established by American player Dwight Davis, was held for the first time with the US defeating Great Britain, 3–0, at Boston.

GRAND AMERICAN TRAP SHOOTING. Aug 10–19. Vandalia, OH. 101st annual. The largest trap shooting event in the world. Est attendance: 30,000. For info: Amateur Trapshooting Assn, 601 W National Rd, Vandalia, OH 45377. Phone: (513) 898-4638. Fax: (513) 898-5472.

KILLEBREW HITS 500th HOME RUN: ANNIVERSARY. Aug 10, 1971. Harmon Killebrew of the Minnesota Twins became the tenth player in major league history to reach the 500-mark in career home runs when he hit Nos. 500 and 501 off Mike Cuellar of the Baltimore Orioles in a 4–3 Orioles victory.

NAGY, STEVE: BIRTH ANNIVERSARY. Aug 10, 1913. Steve Joseph Nagy, bowler, born at Shoaf, Fayette County, PA. Nagy helped organize the Professional Bowlers Association and was elected Bowler of the Year in 1952 and 1955. Died at Cleveland, OH, Nov 10, 1966.

NORTH AMERICAN YOUNG RIDERS' CHAMPIONSHIP. Aug 10–15. Tempel Farm, Wadsworth, IL. The premier equestrian competition in North America for young riders, ages 16–21, who come from the US, Canada, Mexico, Puerto Rico and the Caribbean islands. Riders compete in the three Olympic disciplines of show jumping, dressage and eventing. For info: Classic Communications, 38 Mechanic St, #101, Foxboro, MA 02035. Phone: (508) 698-6810. Fax: (508) 698-6811.

SLOAN, TOD: BIRTH ANNIVERSARY. Aug 10, 1873. James Forman ("Tod") Sloan, jockey, born at Kokomo, IN. Sloan invented the "monkey crouch" style of racing, tucking his knees under his chin and laying along the horse's neck. He won races in the US and England and became one of the world's big spenders, going through $1 million in two years. Died at Los Angeles, CA, Dec 21, 1933.

BIRTHDAYS TODAY

Rocco Domenico (Rocky) Colavito, 67, former baseball player, born New York, NY, Aug 10, 1933.
Walter Lee (Walt) Harris, 26, football player, born LaGrange, GA, Aug 10, 1974.
Bret Michael Hedican, 30, hockey player, born St. Paul, MN, Aug 10, 1970.
Andrew Neal (Andy) Stankiewicz, 36, baseball player, born Inglewood, CA, Aug 10, 1964.
John Levell Starks, 35, basketball player, born Aug 10, 1965.

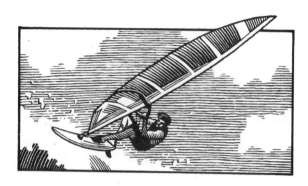

AUGUST 11 — FRIDAY

Day 224 — 142 Remaining

ALABAMA PRO NATIONAL TRUCK AND TRACTOR PULL. Aug 11–12. Lexington, AL. Six different classes compete: Pro National 7500 Superstock, Pro National 6200 2-Wheel Drive Trucks, Pro National 7200 Modified Tractors (multiengine), State Level 6200 4-Wheel Drive Truck, Local Level 4x4 Street Class and Local Level 15,200 Farm Class. Est attendance: 25,000. For info: Debbie Wilson, Dir, Florence/Lauderdale Tourism, One Hightower Pl, Florence, AL 35630. Phone: (256) 740-4141 or (888) FLO-TOUR. Fax: (256) 740-4142. E-mail: dwilson@floweb.com. Web: www.flo-tour.org.

ASA WOMEN'S CLASS C FAST PITCH NATIONAL CHAMPIONSHIP. Aug 11–13. Salem, VA. For info: ASA-USA Softball, 2801 NE 50th St, Oklahoma City, OK 73111. Phone: (405) 424-5266. Fax: (405) 424-3855. E-mail: info@softball.org. Web: www.softball.org.

BULLNANZA–OKLAHOMA CITY. Aug 11–12. Lazy E Arena, Guthrie, OK. Patterned after Bullnanza, the top bull riders in the world compete for $65,000. It's nothin' but bull ridin'! Est attendance: 20,000. For info: Lazy E Promotions, Rte 5, Box 393, Guthrie, OK 73044. Phone: (800) 595-RIDE or (405) 282-RIDE. Web: www.lazye.com.

CANADA: ABBOTSFORD INTERNATIONAL AIRSHOW. Aug 11–13. Abbotsford Airport, Abbotsford, British Columbia. Leading air show in North America attracts the world's top aeronautical performers. Thrill to the grace of the Canadian Snowbirds, the raw power of the international air demonstration squadrons, dramatic teams of daring performers and soloists. Static displays and food booths. Open daily 8–5; aerial show 11–5. Airshow camping facilities. Est attendance: 250,000. For info: Abbotsford Intl Airshow, Unit 4, 1276 Tower St,

Abbotsford, BC, Canada V2T 6H5. Phone: (604) 852-8511. E-mail: info@abbotsfordairshow.com. Web: abbotsford airshow.com.

HUNDRED WINS IN BOTH LEAGUES: 30th ANNIVERSARY. Aug 11, 1970. Jim Bunning of the Philadelphia Phillies defeated the Houston Astros, 6–5, to become the first pitcher to win 100 games in each major league. Bunning, who started his career with the Detroit Tigers, became a Congressman from Kentucky after retiring from baseball and was inducted into the Baseball Hall of Fame in 1996.

INTERNATIONAL SOFTBALL CONGRESS WORLD FAST-PITCH TOURNAMENT. Aug 11–20. Phil Welch Stadium, St. Joseph, MO. Premier event in the sport features 48 of the top teams in the world competing for the coveted ISC World Championship in a double-elimination, 10-day tournament. Leading pitchers throw balls in excess of 100 mph from 46 feet, yet the best hitters consistently post averages well over .300. Annually, starting the second Friday in August. Est attendance: 100,000. For info: Intl Softball Congress, 6007 E Hillcrest Circle, Anaheim Hills, CA 92807. Phone: (714) 998-5694. Fax: (714) 282-7902. Web: www.fastpitch-softball.com.

PADDOCK, CHARLIE: 100th BIRTH ANNIVERSARY. Aug 11, 1900. Charles William (Charlie) Paddock, Olympic gold medal sprinter, born at Gainesville, TX. Paddock set or tied world records in about 25 events, ranging from 50 yards to 250 meters, in a career that ran from 1913 to 1929. He won the 100 meters at the 1920 Olympics and gloried in his nickname, the "World's Fastest Human." Died in a military air crash at Sitka, AK, July 21, 1943.

PALOMINO LEAGUE WORLD SERIES. Aug 11–14. Site TBA. International young adult baseball World Series for players of league ages 17 and 18. Est attendance: 6,650. For info: Pony Baseball/Softball, Inc, Box 225, Washington, PA 15301. Phone: (724) 225-1060. Fax: (724) 225-9852. E-mail: pony@pulse.net.com. Web: www.pony.org.

RUTH HITS 500th HOME RUN: ANNIVERSARY. Aug 11, 1929. Babe Ruth of the New York Yankees became the first player to hit 500 career home runs when he connected off Willis Hudlin as the Cleveland Indians defeated the Yankees, 6–5. The homer was also the 30th of the year for the Bambino.

SCHEFFING, BOB: BIRTH ANNIVERSARY. Aug 11, 1913. Robert Boden (Bob) Scheffing, baseball player, manager and executive, born at Overland, MO. Scheffing was a major league catcher, manager of the Detroit Tigers and general manager of the New York Mets. Died at Phoenix, AZ, Oct 26, 1985.

SPAHN WINS 300th GAME: ANNIVERSARY. Aug 11, 1961. Warren Spahn of the Milwaukee Braves won the 300th game of his career, a 2–1 victory over the Chicago Cubs at Milwaukee. Spahn pitched a complete game and struck out 5 batters. He finished his career with 363, more than any other left-hander, and was inducted into the Hall of Fame in 1973.

SPECIAL OLYMPICS MISSOURI OUTDOOR CLASSIC. Aug 11–13. Jefferson City, MO. Olympic-style competition for children and adults with mental retardation. For info: Special Olympics Missouri, 520 Dix Rd, Ste C, Jefferson City, MO 65109. Phone: (573) 635-1660. Fax: (573) 635-8233. E-mail: hq@somo.org. Web: www.somo.org.

BIRTHDAYS TODAY

Joel Craig Ehlo, 39, former basketball player, born Lubbock, TX, Aug 11, 1961.
Hulk Hogan (born Terry Gene Bollea), 47, wrestler, born Augusta, GA, Aug 11, 1953.

	S	M	T	W	T	F	S
August			1	2	3	4	5
2000	6	7	8	9	10	11	12
	13	14	15	16	17	18	19
	20	21	22	23	24	25	26
	27	28	29	30	31		

AUGUST 12 — SATURDAY
Day 225 — 141 Remaining

CONNECTICUT RIVER RIDE. Aug 12–13. Hartford, CT. A 150-mile scenic bicycle journey along the Connecticut River. For info: Carole Phelan, CT Cycle Tours, PO Box 368, Woodbury, CT 06798. Phone: (860) 274-4166. E-mail: ctcycle.tours@eudoramail.com. Web: www.ct cycle.com.

CRATER LAKE RIM RUNS AND MARATHON. Aug 12. Crater Lake National Park, OR. One of the toughest and most spectacular races you'll ever run! Race routes are around Crater Lake, the deepest lake in the US. Included are 6.7-mile and 13-mile races and a full marathon. Est attendance: 500. For info: Crater Lake Rim Runs, 5830 Mack Ave, Klamath Falls, OR 97603. Phone: (541) 884-6939.

DOWN WITH THE RATS: ANNIVERSARY. Aug 12, 1996. National Hockey League general managers agreed upon a rule change taking effect at the start of the 1996–97 season. If fans litter the ice during the game, the referee is empowered to give a warning and then, if the offense is repeated, to penalize the home team for delay of game. The rule was a response to fans of the Detroit Red Wings, whose tradition called for throwing octapi on the ice, and more particularly to fans of the Florida Panthers, who littered the ice with plastic rats after Panther goals during the 1995–96 season.

FIRST NFL TEAM TO PLAY OUTSIDE US: 50th ANNIVERSARY. Aug 12, 1950. The New York Giants defeated the Ottawa Rough Riders of the Canadian Football League, 27–6, in an exhibition game played at Ottawa. The Giants thus became the first NFL team to play outside the US.

HUTCHINSON, FRED: BIRTH ANNIVERSARY. Aug 12, 1919. Frederick Charles (Fred) Hutchinson, baseball player and manager, born at Seattle, WA. Hutchinson was a major league pitcher who started managing the Detroit Tigers before he stopped playing. Known as the "Big Bear" for his physique and his demeanor, Hutchinson struggled courageously against cancer. Died at Bradenton, FL, Nov 12, 1964.

INTER-STATE FAIR AND RODEO. Aug 12–20. Coffeyville, KS. Largest outdoor fair and rodeo event in southeast Kansas and northeast Oklahoma plus concerts, demolition derby and livestock shows. Est attendance: 75,000. For info: Montgomery County Fair Assn, Box 457, Coffeyville, KS 67337. Phone: (316) 251-2550. Fax: (316) 251-5448. E-mail: chamber@coffeyville.com. Web: www .coffeyville.com.

LEADVILLE TRAIL 100 BIKE RACE. Aug 12. Leadville, CO. Some 600 cyclists compete in this 100-mile off-road bike race over Colorado's high peaks—out 50 miles to a peak above Twin Lakes and back to Leadville. Sponsor: Leadville Trail 100, Inc. Est attendance: 1,000. For info: Greater Leadville Area Chamber of Commerce, PO Box 861, Leadville, CO 80461. Phone: (719) 486-3900 or (800) 933-3901. Fax: (719) 486-8478. E-mail: leadville@lead villeusa.com. Web: www.leadvilleusa.com.

☆　☆　☆

MATHEWSON, CHRISTY: 120th BIRTH ANNIVERSARY. Aug 12, 1880. Christopher (Christy) Mathewson, Baseball Hall of Fame pitcher, born at Factoryville, PA. Mathewson, a college graduate, was one of baseball's first clean-cut stars. A pitcher, he hurled three shutouts in the 1905 World Series and ended his career with 373 wins. Inducted into the Hall of Fame in 1936. Died at Saranac Lake, NY, Oct 7, 1925.

PAAVO NURMI MARATHON. Aug 12. Upson, WI. Annually, the second Saturday in August. For info: Hurley Area Chamber of Commerce, 316 Silver St, Hurley, WI 54534. Phone: (715) 561-4334. E-mail: hurley@hurleywi.com. Web: www.hurleywi.com.

SCHALK, RAY: BIRTH ANNIVERSARY. Aug 12, 1892. Raymond William (Ray) Schalk, Baseball Hall of Fame catcher, born at Harvey, IL. Schalk played on the 1919 Chicago White Sox, but he did not participate in the conspiracy to fix the outcome. Inducted into the Hall of Fame in 1955. Died at Chicago, IL, May 19, 1970.

SEWARD SILVER SALMON DERBY. Aug 12–20. Seward, AK. Alaska's largest salmon derby. Fishermen vie for cash prizes, including tagged fish and daily top fish awards. 45th annual. Est attendance: 10,000. For info: Seward Chamber of Commerce, PO Box 749, Seward, AK 99664. Phone: (907) 224-8051. Fax: (907) 224-5353. Web: www.seward.net/chamber.

SILVER VALLEY CLASSIC HORSESHOE TOURNAMENT. Aug 12–13. City Park, Kellogg, ID. Annually, the second weekend of August. Saturday, sanctioned National Horseshoe Association singles tournament. Sunday, doubles fun tournament. For info: Don Heidt, 13555 S Hwy 3, Cataldo, ID 83810-9695. Phone: (208) 556-0406.

SPECIAL OLYMPICS COLORADO SUMMER CLASSIC. Aug 12–13. Colorado Academy, Colorado Springs, CO. Multisport competition for athletes with mental retardation. For info: Colorado Special Olympics, 600 17th St, Ste 910, Denver, CO 80202. Phone: (303) 592-1361. Fax: (303) 592-1364.

WOJCIECHOWICZ, ALEX: 85th BIRTH ANNIVERSARY. Aug 12, 1915. Alexander Francis (Alex) Wojciechowicz, Pro Football Hall of Fame center and linebacker, born at South River, NJ. Wojciechowicz played for Fordham's legendary line, the "Seven Blocks of Granite," in the late 1930s. He was drafted by the Detroit Lions and later played for the Philadelphia Eagles, earning All-Pro honors four times. Inducted into the Pro Football Hall of Fame in 1968. Died at South River, July 13, 1992.

BIRTHDAYS TODAY

Robert Ray (Bob) Buhl, 72, former baseball player, born Saginaw, MI, Aug 12, 1928.

George F. McGinnis, 50, former basketball player, born Indianapolis, IN, Aug 12, 1950.

Pete Sampras, 29, tennis player, born Washington, DC, Aug 12, 1971.

Regan Charles Upshaw, 25, football player, born Detroit, MI, Aug 12, 1975.

Antoine Devon Walker, 24, basketball player, born Chicago, IL, Aug 12, 1976.

AUGUST 13 — SUNDAY
Day 226 — 140 Remaining

CHASE'S SPORTSQUOTE OF THE DAY
"I couldn't wait for the sun to come up the next morning so that I could get out on the course again."—Ben Hogan

BROCK GETS 3,000th HIT: ANNIVERSARY. Aug 13, 1979. Outfielder Lou Brock of the St. Louis Cardinals got the 3,000th hit of his career, an infield single against Dennis Lamp and the Chicago Cubs. St. Louis won the game, 3–2. Brock finished his career that season with 3,023 hits.

CATALINA WATER SKI RACE. Aug 13. Long Beach, CA. International water-ski racing teams race 62 miles across open seas, round-trip from Long Beach to Catalina Island and back. Est attendance: 9,000. For info: Rick Lemmon, Long Beach Boat and Ski Club, PO Box 2370, Long Beach, CA 90801. Phone: (714) 894-3498. Fax: (714) 893-2363.

EXETER ROAD RALLY. Aug 13. Exeter City Park, Exeter, NE. Participants decipher clues which take them throughout the countryside and into neighboring communities. Evening meal served. Registration 1 PM. 14th annual rally. Annually, the second Sunday in August. Est attendance: 150. For info: Norene Fitzgerald, Box 368, Exeter, NE 68351. Phone: (402) 759-4910. Fax: (402) 759-4455.

HOGAN, BEN: BIRTH ANNIVERSARY. Aug 13, 1912. William Benjamin (Ben) Hogan, golfer, born at Dublin, TX. One of only four players to win all four major professional championships, his 63 career victories rank third behind Sam Snead and Jack Nicklaus. Hogan won nine major championships and was known for his precise swing and stoic demeanor that earned him the nickname the "Wee Ice Mon" in Scotland. He survived a serious automobile accident in 1949 and came back barely more than 14 months later to win the US Open in a play-off over Lloyd Mangrum and George Fazio. Died at Ft Worth, TX, July 25, 1997.

ITALY: PALIO DEL GOLFO. Aug 13. La Spezia. A rowing contest over a 2,000-meter course. Annually, the second Sunday in August.

LEADVILLE TRAIL 100—10K. Aug 13. Leadville, CO. Out and back course using the first 3.1 miles and the last 3.1 miles of the famous Leadville Trail 100 Ultramarathon course. Starting elevation: 10,152 feet! Paved and dirt roads. Small entry fee. This is one of many races held in the area. For info: Gloria Cheshier, Greater Leadville Area Chamber of Commerce, PO Box 861, Leadville, CO 80461. Phone: (719) 486-3502 or (800) 933-3901. E-mail: leadville@leadvilleusa.com. Web: www.leadvilleusa.com.

MIZELL, VINEGAR BEND: 70th BIRTH ANNIVERSARY. Aug 13, 1930. Wilmer David ("Vinegar Bend") Mizell, baseball player and US Congressman, born at Leakesville, MS. Mizell got his nickname from the town where he grew up, Vinegar Bend, AL. He pitched in the major leagues for nine years, finishing his career with the 1962 New York Mets. He became a Republican congressman from North Carolina. Died at Kerrville, TX, Feb 21, 1999.

	S	M	T	W	T	F	S
August 2000			1	2	3	4	5
	6	7	8	9	10	11	12
	13	14	15	16	17	18	19
	20	21	22	23	24	25	26
	27	28	29	30	31		

NEUDECKER, JERRY: 70th BIRTH ANNIVERSARY. Aug 13, 1930. Jerome A. (Jerry) Neudecker, baseball umpire, born at Marine, IL. Neudecker, who umpired in the American League from 1965 through 1986, was the last major league umpire to use an outside or balloon chest protector. Died at Ft Walton Beach, FL, Jan 11, 1997.

NEW YORK GOLDEN ARMS TOURNAMENT. Aug 13. Staten Island, NY. Arm wrestling competition held at fair determines winners who will compete in Empire State Golden Arms Tournament of Champions on Oct 12. For info: New York Arm Wrestling Assn, Inc, 200-14 45th Dr, Bayside, NY 11361. Phone: (718) 544-4592. Web: www.nycarms.com.

ROLLER DERBY BEGINS: 65th ANNIVERSARY. Aug 13, 1935. The first roller derby competition, staged by promoter Leo Seltzer, took place at Chicago.

TIED AND TIED AGAIN: 90th ANNIVERSARY. Aug 13, 1910. The Brooklyn Dodgers and the Pittsburgh Pirates played an unusual tie game, finishing at 8–8. Each team had 38 at bats, 13 hits, 12 assists, two errors, five strikeouts, three walks, one hit batter and one passed ball.

UPSET DEFEATS MAN O'WAR: ANNIVERSARY. Aug 13, 1919. The aptly-named Upset defeated Man O'War to win the Sanford Memorial Stakes at Saratoga. The race marked Man O'War's only loss in 21 races.

BIRTHDAYS TODAY

Jay Campbell Buhner, 36, baseball player, born Louisville, KY, Aug 13, 1964.

Fidel Castro, 73, President of Cuba and former amateur baseball player, born Mayari, Oriente Province, Cuba, Aug 13, 1927.

Robert Earle (Bobby) Clarke, 51, hockey executive and Hockey Hall of Fame center, born Flin Flon, Manitoba, Canada, Aug 13, 1949.

Shayne Corson, 34, hockey player, born Barrie, Ontario, Canada, Aug 13, 1966.

Gerald Joseph (Jerry) Crawford, 53, baseball umpire, born Philadelphia, PA, Aug 13, 1947.

Cris Edward Dishman, 35, football player, born Louisville, KY, Aug 13, 1965.

Alexander (Alex) Fernandez, 31, baseball player, born Miami Beach, FL, Aug 13, 1969.

James Timothy ("Mudcat") Grant, 65, former baseball player, born Lacoochee, FL, Aug 13, 1935.

Elvis Grbac, 30, football player, born Cleveland, OH, Aug 13, 1970.

Elizabeth (Betsy) King, 45, LPGA Hall of Fame golfer, born Reading, PA, Aug 13, 1955.

Thomas Albert (Tom) Prince, 36, baseball player, born Kankakee, IL, Aug 13, 1964.

William Harrison Thomas, Jr, 32, football player, born Amarillo, TX, Aug 13, 1968.

AUGUST 14 — MONDAY
Day 227 — 139 Remaining

CHASE'S SPORTSQUOTE OF THE DAY

"I don't think there will ever be another 6'9" point guard who smiles while he humiliates you."—James Worthy on Magic Johnson

---

DEAN, DAFFY: BIRTH ANNIVERSARY. Aug 14, 1913. Paul Dee ("Daffy") Dean, baseball player, born at Lucas, AR. Dizzy Dean's less-famous brother won 19 games in 1934 and 1935 for the St. Louis Cardinals before hurting his arm. Died at Springdale, AR, Mar 17, 1981.

FORMATION OF AFL: ANNIVERSARY. Aug 14, 1959. The formation of the American Football League was announced at a press conference at Chicago. Play was set to begin in 1960 with at least six and possibly eight franchises.

OLDEST PITCHER TO WIN GAME: ANNIVERSARY. Aug 14, 1932. John Quinn, 49, became the oldest winning pitcher in baseball history as a member of the Brooklyn Dodgers. Quinn relieved Van Mungo in the ninth inning of a game against the New York Giants with the score tied, 1–1. The Dodgers won it in the 10th, and Quinn got credit for the victory.

PONY LEAGUE WORLD SERIES. Aug 14–21. Washington, PA. International youth baseball World Series for teams of players ages 13 and 14. Est attendance: 16,700. For info: Pony Baseball/Softball, PO Box 225, Washington, PA 15301. Phone: (724) 225-1060. Fax: (724) 225-9852. E-mail: pony@pulsenet.com. Web: www.pony.org.

THAYER, ERNEST LAWRENCE: BIRTH ANNIVERSARY. Aug 14, 1863. Ernest Lawrence Thayer, poet and journalist, born at Lawrence, MA. He wrote a series of comic ballads for the *San Francisco Examiner*, of which "Casey at the Bat" was the last. It was published on Sunday, June 3, 1888, and Thayer received $5 in payment for it. Recitations of the ballad by the actor William DeWolf Hopper greatly increased its popularity. It is said that by 1900 there were few Americans who had not heard of "Casey at the Bat." Died at Santa Barbara, CA, Aug 21, 1940. (See also: "Might Casey Has Struck Out: Anniversary" June 3.)

365-INNING SOFTBALL GAME: ANNIVERSARY. Aug 14–15, 1976. The Gager's Diner softball team played the Bend'n Elbow Tavern in a 365-inning softball game in 1976. Starting at 10 AM Aug 14, the game was called because of rain and fog at 4 PM, Aug 15. The 70 players, including 20 women, raised $4,000 for construction of a new softball field and for the Monticello, NY, Community General Hospital. The Gagers beat the Elbows 491–467. To date, this remains the longest softball game on record.

BIRTHDAYS TODAY

John Riley Brodie, 65, former football player, born Menlo Park, CA, Aug 14, 1935.

Wayne Chrebet, 27, football player, born Garfield, NJ, Aug 14, 1973.

Gregory Lemont (Greg) Ellis, 25, football player, born Wendell, NC, Aug 14, 1975.

Marty Glickman, 83, former broadcaster and track athlete, born New York, NY, Aug 14, 1917.

Earvin ("Magic") Johnson, Jr, 41, former basketball player and coach, born Lansing, MI, Aug 14, 1959.

Mark David Loretta, 29, baseball player, born Santa Monica, CA, Aug 14, 1971.

Adam Larry Timmerman, 29, football player, born Cherokee, IA, Aug 14, 1971.

Rusty Wallace, 44, auto racer, born St. Louis, MO, Aug 14, 1956.

AUGUST 15 — TUESDAY
Day 228 — 138 Remaining

COMISKEY, CHARLES: BIRTH ANNIVERSARY. Aug 15, 1859. Charles Albert Comiskey, Baseball Hall of Fame first baseman, manager and executive, born at Chicago, IL. Comiskey's career spanned 50 years, 30 of them as founding owner of the Chicago White Sox. But before that, he was an outstanding and innovative player and a tough, successful manager. Inducted into the Hall of Fame in 1939. Died at Eagle River, WI, Oct 26, 1931.

FIRST WOMAN IN PRO FOOTBALL: 30th ANNIVERSARY. Aug 15, 1970. Patricia Palinkas became the first woman to play in a professional football game when she held the ball for the point after a touchdown kick by her husband, Steve, placekicker for the Orlando Panthers of the Atlantic Coast League. The snap was off-target, and Palinkas was tackled when she attempted to run with the errant ball.

FORFEIT BY GROUND CREW: ANNIVERSARY. Aug 15, 1941. The Washington Senators lost a game by forfeit when the umpires ruled that the ground crew at Griffith Stadium put the tarpaulin on the field too slowly during a rain storm. The Senators were beating the Boston Red Sox, 6–3, when the rain came in the eighth inning. The umpires decided that the ground crew deliberately moved much too slowly, hoping that the game would have to be called. It was, but because of the forfeit, the Red Sox won.

PITCHER HITS HOMER IN EVERY PARK: 45th ANNIVERSARY. Aug 15, 1955. Pitcher Warren Spahn of the Milwaukee Braves hit a home run off Mel Wright of the St. Louis Cardinals at Sportsman's Park, St. Louis, to give him at least one homer in every National League ballpark.

THREE MEN ON THIRD: ANNIVERSARY. Aug 15, 1926. Babe Herman of the Brooklyn Dodgers doubled with the bases loaded in a game against the Boston Braves. The hit drove in the winning run, but the runner on second, the runner on first and Herman all wound up on or near third base. Two of them were called out, so that Herman, in effect, doubled into a double play.

TWICE TOSSED: 25th ANNIVERSARY. Aug 15, 1975. Manager Earl Weaver of the Baltimore Orioles, a frequent antagonist of umpires, was ejected during the first game of a doubleheader by Ron Luciano and then was ejected again by Luciano before the start of the second game.

BIRTHDAYS TODAY

Walter Andrew ("Bubby") Brister, III, 38, football player, born Alexandria, LA, Aug 15, 1962.

Scott David Brosius, 34, baseball player, born Hillsboro, OR, Aug 15, 1966.

Jeffrey Kent (Jeff) Huson, 36, baseball player, born Scottsdale, AZ, Aug 15, 1964.

Jay Thomas (Tom) Kelly, 50, baseball manager and former player, born Graceville, MN, Aug 15, 1950.

Yancey Dirk Thigpen, 31, football player, born Tarboro, NC, Aug 15, 1969.

Eugene T. (Gene) Upshaw, Jr, 55, Players' Association executive and former football player, born Robstown, TX, Aug 15, 1945.

Amos Alonzo Stagg

AUGUST 16 — WEDNESDAY
Day 229 — 137 Remaining

CHASE'S SPORTSQUOTE OF THE DAY

"Coach Stagg was the Babe Ruth of college football. To me, he is on a pedestal."—Paul ("Bear") Bryant

BASEBALL IN MEXICO: ANNIVERSARY. Aug 16, 1996. The San Diego Padres and the New York Mets made baseball history by playing the first major league game ever in Mexico. The two teams agreed to move their three-game series from San Diego to Monterrey in order to avoid a potential conflict with the Republican National Convention. The Padres won, 15–10, behind the starting pitching of Fernando Valenzuela, a native Mexican who also threw out the ceremonial first pitch.

FIRST ISSUE OF *SPORTS ILLUSTRATED*: ANNIVERSARY. Aug 16, 1954. The first issue of *Sports Illustrated* was published. The cover photograph showed Eddie Mathews of the Milwaukee Braves batting at Milwaukee County Stadium. The cover price was 25 cents.

NATIONAL COLLEGIATE FIGURE SKATING CHAMPIONSHIPS. Aug 16–19. Site TBA. For info: Media Relations, US Figure Skating Assn, 20 First St, Colorado Springs, CO 80906. Phone: (719) 635-5200. Fax: (719) 635-9548. E-mail: usfsa1@aol.com. Web: www.usfsa.org/events.

RAY CHAPMAN BEANED: 80th ANNIVERSARY. Aug 16, 1920. Cleveland Indians shortstop Ray Chapman was hit in the head by a pitch thrown by Carl Mays of the New York Yankees. Chapman collapsed with a fractured skull and died the next day. His death stands as the only on-field fatality in major league history.

RUTH, BABE: DEATH ANNIVERSARY. Aug 16, 1948. George Herman ("Babe") Ruth, Baseball Hall of Fame pitcher and outfielder, born at Baltimore, MD, Feb 6, 1895. The left-handed pitcher and "Sultan of Swat" hit 714 home runs in 22 major league seasons of play and played in 10 World Series. Baseball fans mourned when

he died of throat cancer. His body lay in state at the main entrance of Yankee Stadium where people waited in line for hours to march past the coffin. On Aug 19, countless numbers of people surrounded St. Patrick's Cathedral for the funeral mass and lined the streets along the route to the cemetery as America bade farewell to one of baseball's greatest legends. Died at New York, NY.

STAGG, AMOS ALONZO: BIRTH ANNIVERSARY. Aug 16, 1862. Amos Alonzo Stagg, football player and coach, born at West Orange, NJ. Stagg played baseball and football at Yale and then forsook the ministry for physical education. He built the football program at the University of Chicago as an integral part of William Rainey Harper's plan to build a great university. Over 40 years at Chicago, he became the game's greatest innovator and master strategist. When Chicago de-emphasized football, he moved to the College of the Pacific, finishing his career with a record of 314–181–15. Died at Stockton, CA, Mar 17, 1965.

BIRTHDAYS TODAY

Roger Leandro Cedeno, 26, baseball player, born Valencia, Venezuela, Aug 16, 1974.
Ben Terrence Coates, 31, football player, born Greenwood, SC, Aug 16, 1969.
Frank Newton Gifford, 70, Pro Football Hall of Fame halfback and end, born Santa Monica, CA, Aug 16, 1930.
Richard Allen (Rick) Reed, 36, baseball player, born Huntington, WV, Aug 16, 1964.
John ("Rocky") Roe, 50, baseball umpire, born Detroit, MI, Aug 16, 1950.
Eric Jerrod Swann, 30, football player, born Pinehurst, NC, Aug 16, 1970.
Marion Anthony (Tony) Trabert, 70, former tennis player, born Cincinnati, OH, Aug 16, 1930.
Zach Allan Wiegert, 28, football player, born Fremont, NE, Aug 16, 1972.

AUGUST 17 — THURSDAY
Day 230 — 136 Remaining

ASA WOMEN'S MASTERS (35-AND-OVER) SLOW PITCH NATIONAL CHAMPIONSHIP. Aug 17–20. Minto, ND. For info: ASA-USA Softball, 2801 NE 50th St, Oklahoma City, OK 73111. Phone: (405) 424-5266. Fax: (405) 424-3855. E-mail: info@softball.org. Web: www.softball.org.

BOSTON-MONTREAL-BOSTON 2000. Aug 17–20. Boston, MA, to Montreal, Quebec, and back again. The American Randonee. Skilled endurance amateur cyclists gather from around the world to participate in the BMB. This endurance challenge originated in 1988. The distance is 750 miles with a strict time limit of 90 hours. BMB is a randonneur event. Randonneuring is a hybrid of racing and touring, less a race than a test in which one competes against oneself. Ordinary cyclists can compete in BMB. Recent participants have ranged in age from 14 to 70 years old. Qualifying events called brevets are held around the world prior to BMB. For info: Jennifer Wise, 10 Bliss Mine Rd, Middletown, RI 02842. Phone: (401) 847-1715. Fax: (401) 847-1718. E-mail: wise@edgenet.net.

FISK HITS 328th HOME RUN: 10th ANNIVERSARY. Aug 17, 1990. Carlton Fisk of the Chicago White Sox hit the 328th home run of his career as a catcher, surpassing the major league record set by Johnny Bench. The White Sox beat the Texas Rangers, 4–2. Fisk ended his career with 376 homers, 351 as a catcher.

GEHRIG BREAKS SCOTT'S RECORD: ANNIVERSARY. Aug 17, 1933. Lou Gehrig of the New York Yankees played

August 2000	S	M	T	W	T	F	S
			1	2	3	4	5
	6	7	8	9	10	11	12
	13	14	15	16	17	18	19
	20	21	22	23	24	25	26
	27	28	29	30	31		

in his 1,308th consecutive game to break the record held by Everett Scott. Gehrig went on to extend his streak to 2,130 games before leaving the Yankees lineup.

KEARNS, DOC: BIRTH ANNIVERSARY. Aug 17, 1882. Jack ("Doc") Kearns, born John Leo McKernan at Waterloo, MI. Kearns lived a wild life in the American West and finally settled on being a boxing promoter. His most famous fighter was Jack Dempsey, who won the heavyweight title in 1919, but he continued managing and promoting until his death. Died at Miami, FL, July 7, 1963.

PGA CHAMPIONSHIP. Aug 17–20. Valhalla Golf Club, Louisville, KY. The 82nd national professional championship conducted by the Professional Golfers' Association of America. Est attendance: 150,000. For info: Kerry Haigh, Senior Dir of Tourn, PGA of America, Box 109601, Palm Beach Gardens, FL 33410-9601. Phone: (561) 624-8495. Fax: (561) 624-8429.

RACINE IN-WATER BOAT SHOW. Aug 17–20. Reefpoint Marina, Racine, WI. 15th annual. For info: NMMA Boat Shows, 600 Third Ave, 23rd Floor, New York, NY 10016. Phone: (212) 922-1212 or (312) 946-6262. Fax: (312) 946-0401. Web: www.boatshows.com.

SPECIAL OLYMPICS SOUTH DAKOTA EQUESTRIAN COMPETITION. Aug 17–18. Huron, SD. State-level Olympic style competition for adults and children with mental retardation in English equitation, stock seat equitation, working trials, barrel racing and showmanship at halter/bridle. For info: Special Olympics South Dakota, 305 W 39th St, Sioux Falls, SD 57105. Phone: (605) 331-4117. Fax: (605) 331-4326. E-mail: sosdak@aol.com.

TWO PITCHING RECORDS: ANNIVERSARY. Aug 17, 1894. Pitcher John Wadsworth of the Louisville club in the National League set two unfortunate records in the same game. He gave up 28 singles and 36 hits overall. Both marks still stand.

WORLD'S OLDEST CONTINUOUS PRCA RODEO. Aug 17–20. Payson, AZ. The Payson Rodeo has been held continuously since 1884. Named number one small outdoor rodeo in America! Est attendance: 20,000. For info: Rim Country Regional Chamber of Commerce, Box 1380, Payson, AZ 85547. Phone: (800) 672-9766. Fax: (520) 474-8812. E-mail: pcoc@netzone.com.

BIRTHDAYS TODAY

Harrison V. Chase, 87, associate professor emeritus (Florida State University–Tallahassee), cofounder and coeditor of *Chase's Annual Events* (1957–70), born Big Rapids, MI, Aug 17, 1913.

James Spencer (Jim) Courier, 30, tennis player, born Samford, FL, Aug 17, 1970.

Nelson Donald Emerson, 33, hockey player, born Hamilton, Ontario, Canada, Aug 17, 1967.

Jon Gruden, 37, football coach, born Sandusky, OH, Aug 17, 1963.

Christian Donald Laettner, 31, basketball player, born Angola, NY, Aug 17, 1969.

Jamie Macoun, 39, hockey player, born Newmarket, Ontario, Canada, Aug 17, 1961.

Ed McCaffrey, 32, football player, born Allentown, PA, Aug 17, 1968.

Dottie Pepper, 35, golfer, born Saratoga Springs, NY, Aug 17, 1965.

Nelson Piquet, 48, former auto racer, born Brasilia, Brazil, Aug 17, 1952.

Jorge Rafael Posada, Jr, 29, baseball player, born Santurce, Puerto Rico, Aug 17, 1971.

John Wesley ("Boog") Powell, 59, former baseball player, born Lakeland, FL, Aug 17, 1941.

Guillermo Vilas, 48, former tennis player, born Mar del Plata, Argentina, Aug 17, 1952.

AUGUST 18 — FRIDAY
Day 231 — 135 Remaining

CHASE'S SPORTSQUOTE OF THE DAY

"Only one thing could ever really stop Roberto Clemente, and it did."—sportswriter Milton Richman

ASA WOMEN'S MAJOR MODIFIED PITCH NATIONAL CHAMPIONSHIP. Aug 18–22. Worton, MD. For info: ASA-USA Softball, 2801 NE 50th St, Oklahoma City, OK 73111. Phone: (405) 424-5266. Fax: (405) 424-3855. E-mail: info@softball.org. Web: www.softball.org.

BRAVES FIELD OPENS: 85th ANNIVERSARY. Aug 18, 1915. The Boston Braves opened their new ballpark, Braves Field, with a 3–1 victory over the St. Louis Cardinals. The Braves called this park home through the 1952 season after which they moved to Milwaukee.

CLEMENTE, ROBERTO: BIRTH ANNIVERSARY. Aug 18, 1934. Roberto Walker Clemente, Baseball Hall of Fame outfielder, born at Carolina, Puerto Rico. Clemente, one of the game's best and most exciting outfielders, played his entire career with the Pittsburgh Pirates, leading them to a World Series in 1971 and collecting 3,000 hits. While on a mission of mercy to deliver supplies to victims of a Nicaraguan earthquake, he perished in a plane crash. Inducted into the Hall of Fame in 1973 after the mandatory five-year waiting period was waived. Died near Carolina, Dec 31, 1972.

GEORGIA BOAT & SPORTS SHOW. Aug 18–20. Cobb Galleria Centre, Atlanta, GA. For info: NMMA Boat Shows, 600 Third Ave, 23rd Floor, 10016. Phone: (212) 922-1212 or (305) 531-8410. Fax: (305) 534-3139. Web: www.boatshows.com.

GRIMES, BURLEIGH: BIRTH ANNIVERSARY. Aug 18, 1893. Burleigh Arland Grimes, Baseball Hall of Fame pitcher and manager, born at Emerald, WI. Grimes was the last legal spitball pitcher, a gritty performer who won 270 games in 19 years. He coached and managed after retiring as a player. Inducted into the Hall of Fame in 1964. Died at Clear Lake, WI, Dec 6, 1985.

JETS BEAT GIANTS: ANNIVERSARY. Aug 18, 1969. The New York Jets played their crosstown rivals, the Giants, for the first time and came away winners, 37–14, in this preseason game. Joe Namath threw three touchdown passes for the Jets.

MT WHITNEY SCALED: ANNIVERSARY. Aug 18, 1873. Mt Whitney, the second highest peak in the US, was conquered for the first time by a trio of American climbers, Charles D. Begole, A.H. Johnson and John Lucas.

PODOLOFF, MAURICE: 110th BIRTH ANNIVERSARY. Aug 18, 1890. Maurice Podoloff, Basketball Hall of Fame executive, born at Elisabethgrad, Russia. Podoloff entered basketball through hockey and served as the first president of the Basketball Association of America, one of the NBA's two predecessor leagues. When the BAA merged with the National Basketball League in 1949, Podoloff was named the NBA's first president. He governed the league through its uneasy early years and secured its first national television contract. Inducted into the Hall of Fame in 1974. Died at New Haven, CT, Nov 24, 1985.

TEXAS RANCH ROUNDUP. Aug 18–19. Wichita Falls, TX. Cowboys from prestigious ranches in Texas compete in the events that make up their daily work. Cattle roping and penning and other rodeo-type events plus ranch cooking contests, ranch talent contests. Est attendance: 18,000. For info: Kacey Gray, Mktg Asst, Wichita Falls CVB, 1000 5th St, Wichita Falls, TX 76301. Phone: (940) 716-5500 or (800) 799-6732. Fax: (940) 716-5509. Web: www.wichitafalls.org.

WEAVER, BUCK: 110th BIRTH ANNIVERSARY. Aug 18, 1890. George Daniel ("Buck") Weaver, baseball player, born at Pottstown, PA. Weaver was one of eight Chicago White Sox players suspended and later banned for life for conspiring to fix the 1919 World Series. He did not participate in the plot but knew of it and declined to report it. Died at Chicago, IL, Jan 31, 1956.

BIRTHDAYS TODAY

Geoff Courtnall, 38, hockey player, born Victoria, British Columbia, Canada, Aug 18, 1962.
Robert Leigh (Bobby) Higginson, 30, baseball player, born Philadelphia, PA, Aug 18, 1970.
Rafer Lewis Johnson, 65, Olympic gold medal decathlete, born Hillsboro, TX, Aug 18, 1935.
Matthews (Matt) Snell, 59, former football player, born Garfield, GA, Aug 18, 1941.

AUGUST 19 — SATURDAY

Day 232 — 134 Remaining

BIKE VAN BUREN XIII. Aug 19–20. Van Buren County, IA. A laid-back bicycle tour of the villages, landmarks and landscape of this rural Iowa county. The "red carpet of hospitality" is rolled out for the bikers as they pass through. Annually, third full weekend in August. For info: Stacey Gladon, Exec Dir, Villages of Van Buren, Inc, PO Box 9, Keosauqua, IA 52565. Phone: (800) 868-7822. Fax: (319) 293-6250. E-mail: bike@800-tourvbc.com. Web: www.800-tourvbc.com.

BLUE CLAW CRAB CRAFT SHOW & CRAB RACE. Aug 19. Harvey Cedars, NJ. Crafters display their goods at Sunset Park. Crab race determines fastest crab on Long Beach Island. For info: Harvey Cedars Activity Committee, PO Box 3185, Harvey Cedars, NJ 08008. Phone: (609) 494-6905. Fax: (609) 494-2335. E-mail: hcboro@cyber comm.net.

COBB GETS 3,000th HIT: ANNIVERSARY. Aug 19, 1921. Outfielder Ty Cobb of the Detroit Tigers, at age 34, became the youngest player ever to get 3,000 hits in his career. Cobb finished his career with 4,191 hits, a total later revised in some record books to 4,189, and was inducted into the Hall of Fame in 1936.

EDDIE GAEDEL AT BAT: ANNIVERSARY. Aug 19, 1951. In one of owner Bill Veeck's most outrageous promotions, the St. Louis Browns sent Eddie Gaedel, a midget, to the plate as the first batter in the second game of a doubleheader against the Detroit Tigers. Gaedel walked on four pitches and was lifted for a pinch-runner. Two days later, the American League banned Gaedel from further competition.

GIANTS TO MOVE TO SAN FRANCISCO: ANNIVERSARY. Aug 19, 1957. Horace Stoneham, principal owner of the New York Giants baseball team, announced that the board of directors had voted, 9–1, to move the franchise to San Francisco for the start of the 1958 season. The Giants were accompanied to the West Coast by the Dodgers who moved from Brooklyn to Los Angeles.

GIANTS RIDGE MOUNTAIN BIKE FESTIVAL. Aug 19. Biwabik, MN. Trail rides, uphill-downhill, cross-country. Est attendance: 400. For info: John Filander, Events Program Dir, PO Box 190, Biwabik, MN 55708. Phone: (800) 688-7669 or (218) 865-4143. Fax: (218) 865-4733.

GREAT AMERICAN DUCK RACE. Aug 19–20. Deming, NM. "World's richest duck race." Also Duck Queen and Darling Duckling contests, Tortilla Toss, parade and other festivities. Est attendance: 24,000. For info: The Great American Duck Race of Deming, Inc, 101 N Copper, Deming, NM 88030. Phone: (888) 345-1125.

LEADVILLE TRAIL 100 ULTRAMARATHON. Aug 19–20. Leadville, CO. One of the toughest 100-mile foot races in the country, the course goes through the Rocky Mountains 50 miles to the ghost town of Winfield and back. Runners begin at 4 AM and must complete race in 30 hours. All race applications mailed Jan 2. Race fills within 2 weeks. Contact prior to Jan 2 for packet. Sponsor: Leadville Trail 100, Inc. Est attendance: 2,000. For info: Greater Leadville Chamber of Commerce, PO Box 861, Leadville, CO 80461. Phone: (719) 486-3900 or (800) 933-3901. Fax: (719) 486-8478. E-mail: leadville@lead villeusa.com. Web: www.leadvilleusa.com.

MAINE HIGHLAND GAMES. Aug 19. Thomas Point Beach, Brunswick, ME. Presented by the Saint Andrew's Society of Maine. Adult athletics including tossing of the caber, wheat sheaf toss and putting of the stone, border collie herding demonstrations, Highland cattle and individual piping contests. Bagpipe bands, Highland and Scottish dancing, Scottish arts and crafts fair, folksingers, Scottish fiddling, children's games, American and Scottish foods galore. The only Scottish event of its kind held in Maine! Scots and non-Scots will enjoy the color, pageantry and friendly atmosphere. 22nd annual games. Admission fees charge. Est attendance: 6,000. For info: Thomas Point Beach, 29 Meadow Rd, Brunswick, ME 04011. Phone: (207) 725-6009. Web: www.thomaspoint beach.com.

★ **NATIONAL AVIATION DAY.** Aug 19. Presidential Proclamation 2343, of July 25, 1939, covers all succeeding years. Always Aug 19 of each year since 1939. Observed annually on anniversary of the birth of Orville Wright, who piloted "first self-powered flight in history," Dec 17, 1903. First proclaimed by President Franklin D. Roosevelt.

NATURAL CHIMNEYS JOUSTING TOURNAMENT. Aug 19. Natural Chimneys Regional Park, Mt Solon, VA. A modern version of a medieval contest, believed to be the oldest continuously held sporting event in America.

	S	M	T	W	T	F	S
August 2000			1	2	3	4	5
	6	7	8	9	10	11	12
	13	14	15	16	17	18	19
	20	21	22	23	24	25	26
	27	28	29	30	31		

Annually, the third Saturday in August. Est attendance: 500. For info: Upper Valley Regional Park Authority, Box 478, Grottoes, VA 24441. Phone: (540) 350-2510. Fax: (540) 350-2140.

YOUNGEST 300 BOWLER: ANNIVERSARY. Aug 19, 1971. Matt Throne, 12, of Millbrae, CA, rolled a 300 game in sanctioned league competition, thus becoming the youngest bowler to do so.

BIRTHDAYS TODAY

Morten Andersen, 40, football player, born Struer, Denmark, Aug 19, 1960.

John Egan Boles, Jr, 52, baseball manager, born Chicago, IL, Aug 19, 1948.

Mary Joe Fernandez, 29, tennis player, born Dominican Republic, Aug 19, 1971.

Gary Joseph Gaetti, 42, baseball player, born Centralia, IL, Aug 19, 1958.

Bobby Joseph Hebert, Jr, 40, football player, born Baton Rouge, LA, Aug 19, 1960.

Michael Anthony Munoz, 42, Pro Football Hall of Fame offensive tackle, born Ontario, CA, Aug 19, 1958.

Cindy Nelson, 45, former alpine skier, born Lutsen, MN, Aug 19, 1955.

Robert Clinton (Bobby) Richardson, 65, former baseball player, born Sumter, SC, Aug 19, 1935.

William Lee (Willie) Shoemaker, 69, former jockey, born Fabens, TX, Aug 19, 1931.

Darryl John Sutter, 42, hockey coach and former player, born Viking, Alberta, Canada, Aug 19, 1958.

AUGUST 20 — SUNDAY

Day 233 — 133 Remaining

CHASE'S SPORTSQUOTE OF THE DAY

"My life is a living testimony and is an incongruity and a contradiction to what America has hitherto asked for success."—Don King

CANADA: MARATHON BY THE SEA. Aug 20. St. John, New Brunswick, Canada. Associated with the Festival by the Sea, Canada's Musical and Cultural Showpiece. For info: Canada Games Aquatic Centre, 50 Union St, St. John, NB, Canada E2L 1A1. Phone: (506) 696-4922. E-mail: aquatics@nbnet.nb.ca. Web: www.aquatics.nb.ca.

FEATHERS, BEATTIE: BIRTH ANNIVERSARY. Aug 20, 1908. William Beattie Feathers, football player and coach, born at Bristol, VA. Feathers was an All-American back at the University of Tennessee in 1932. He starred in the first College All-Star Game and, playing for the Chicago Bears, became the first NFL back to rush for more than 1,000 yards in one season. He coached at Appalachian State and North Carolina State. Died at Winston-Salem, NC, Mar 11, 1979.

FIRST MILLIONAIRE THREE-YEAR-OLD: ANNIVERSARY. Aug 20, 1966. The thoroughbred Buckpasser, owned by Ogden Phipps, won the Travers Stakes at Saratoga to become the first three-year-old to pass the $1 million mark in career earnings.

HARRISON, LES: BIRTH ANNIVERSARY. Aug 20, 1904. Lester (Les) Harrison, Basketball Hall of Fame contributor, born at Rochester, NY. Harrison founded and coached the Rochester Royals, who played first in the National Basketball League, then in the Basketball Association and then in the National Basketball Association. He integrated the NBL in 1946 by signing Dolly King and Pop Gates. Inducted into the Hall of Fame in 1979. Died at Rochester, Dec 23, 1997.

NEW YORK GOLDEN ARMS TOURNAMENT. Aug 20. Belmont Festival, Belmont Race Track, Elmont, NY. Arm wrestling competition held at the festival determines winners who will compete in the Empire State Golden Arms Tournament of Champions on Oct 12. Est attendance: 1,200. For info: New York Arm Wrestling Assn, Inc, 200-14 45th Dr, Bayside, NY 11361. Phone: (718) 544-4592. Web: www.nycarms.com.

SOAP BOX DERBY WINNER DISQUALIFIED: ANNIVERSARY. Aug 20, 1973. James Gronen was disqualified as champion, two days after winning the Soap Box Derby at Akron, OH. Officials discovered that Gronen's car was equipped with an illegal magnetic system that gave it an unfair advantage.

YOUNGEST PLAYER TO HIT HOME RUN: 55th ANNIVERSARY. Aug 20, 1945. Tommy Brown of the Brooklyn Dodgers became the youngest player in major league history to hit a home run when he connected against pitcher Preacher Roe of the Pittsburgh Pirates. Brown was 17 years, eight months and 14 days old.

BIRTHDAYS TODAY

Andrew Charles (Andy) Benes, 33, baseball player, born Evansville, IN, Aug 20, 1967.

Thomas Andrew (Tom) Brunansky, 40, former baseball player, born Covina, CA, Aug 20, 1960.

Chris Drury, 24, hockey player, born Trumbull, CT, Aug 20, 1976.

Donald (Don) King, 69, boxing promoter, born Cleveland, OH, Aug 20, 1931.

Mark Edward Langston, 40, baseball player, born San Diego, CA, Aug 20, 1960.

Alfonso Raymon (Al) Lopez, 92, Baseball Hall of Fame manager and catcher, born Tampa, FL, Aug 20, 1908.

AUGUST 21 — MONDAY

Day 234 — 132 Remaining

BLANCHARD, THERESA WELD: BIRTH ANNIVERSARY. Aug 21, 1893. Theresa Weld Blanchard, figure skater, born at Brookline, MA. Blanchard began competitive figure skating at age 21 and quickly established herself as one of the best. She won six US titles as a singles skater and nine as a pairs skater. At the 1920 Winter Olympics at Antwerp, she skated wonderfully and athletically but had to settle for a bronze medal. Her style of skating, incorporating jumps into her routine, was viewed by the judges as too "unladylike." Died Mar 12, 1978.

FINGERS RECORDS 300th SAVE: ANNIVERSARY. Aug 21, 1982. Relief pitcher Rollie Fingers of the Milwaukee Brewers became the first pitcher to record 300 saves in his career as the Brewers beat the Seattle Mariners, 3–2.

LARNED WINS USLTA TITLE: ANNIVERSARY. Aug 21, 1901. William Larned won the first of his seven men's singles titles at the US Lawn Tennis Association championships. Larned followed this victory with wins in 1902, 1907, 1908, 1909, 1910 and 1911.

LITTLE LEAGUE BASEBALL WORLD SERIES. Aug 21–27. Williamsport, PA. Eight teams from the US and foreign countries compete for the World Championship. Est attendance: 200,000. For info: Little League Baseball HQ, Box 3485, Williamsport, PA 17701. Phone: (570) 326-1921. Fax: (570) 326-1074. Web: www.littleleague.org.

RUTH HITS 600th HOME RUN: ANNIVERSARY. Aug 21, 1931. Babe Ruth hit the 600th home run of his career, a prodigious drive in St. Louis off George Blaeholder of the Browns. The homer bounced off a car parked on Grand Avenue beyond the rightfield wall of Sportsman's Park. The ball was retrieved by a fan who gave it to Ruth in exchange for an autographed ball and cash. The Yankees won, 11–7. Ruth finished his career with 714 home runs and was inducted into the Hall of Fame in 1936.

SKOWHEGAN LOG DAYS. Aug 21–27. Skowhegan, ME. Golf, horseshoe, darts and bass tournaments, logging events, moonlight madness and whacky water race, bingo, megaducks and pub night, pancake breakfast, lobster bake and chicken BBQ, parade, fireworks, teen night and craft fair. Annually, the last full week in August. Est attendance: 50,000. For info: Skowhegan Chamber of Commerce, PO Box 326, Skowhegan, ME 04976. Phone: (207) 474-3621.

US AMATEUR (GOLF) CHAMPIONSHIP. Aug 21–27. Baltusrol Golf Club, Springfield, NJ. For info: US Golf Assn, Golf House, Far Hills, NJ 07931. Phone: (908) 234-2300. Fax: (908) 234-9687. E-mail: usga@usga.org. Web: www.usga.org.

BIRTHDAYS TODAY

James Eric (Jim) Bullinger, 35, baseball player, born New Orleans, LA, Aug 21, 1965.
Wilton Norman (Wilt) Chamberlain, 64, former basketball coach and Basketball Hall of Fame center, born Philadelphia, PA, Aug 21, 1936.
Craig John Counsell, 30, baseball player, born South Bend, IN, Aug 21, 1970.
Steven Michael (Steve) Everitt, 30, football player, born Miami, FL, Aug 21, 1970.

August	S	M	T	W	T	F	S
2000			1	2	3	4	5
	6	7	8	9	10	11	12
	13	14	15	16	17	18	19
	20	21	22	23	24	25	26
	27	28	29	30	31		

Willie Edward Lanier, 55, Pro Football Hall of Fame linebacker, born Clover, VA, Aug 21, 1945.
James Robert (Jim) McMahon, 41, former football player, born Jersey City, NJ, Aug 21, 1959.
Ismael Valdes, 27, baseball player, born Victoria, Mexico, Aug 21, 1973.
John Karl Wetteland, 34, baseball player, born San Mateo, CA, Aug 21, 1966.

AUGUST 22 — TUESDAY
Day 235 — 131 Remaining

AMERICA'S CUP: ANNIVERSARY. Aug 22, 1851. A silver trophy (then known as the "Hundred Guinea Cup" and offered by the Royal Yacht Squadron) was won in a race around the Isle of Wight by the US yacht *America*. The trophy, later turned over to the New York Yacht Club, became known as the America's Cup.

DONATELLI, AUGIE: BIRTH ANNIVERSARY. Aug 22, 1914. August Joseph (Augie) Donatelli, baseball umpire, born at Heilwood, PA. Donatelli advanced to the National League in 1950 after only four years as a minor league umpire. He was the principal organizer of the umpires' union in 1964. Died at St. Petersburg, FL, May 24, 1990.

HEIN, MEL: BIRTH ANNIVERSARY. Aug 22, 1909. Melvin J. (Mel) Hein, Pro Football Hall of Fame center, born at Redding, CA. Hein played football at Washington State and captained the first Cougar team to go to the Rose Bowl (1931). He joined the New York Giants and garnered All-Pro honors eight years in a row. His 15-year career earned him the nickname "Old Indestructible." Inducted into the Hall of Fame as a charter member in 1963. Died at San Clemente, CA, Jan 31, 1992.

MARICHAL CLUBS ROSEBORO: 35th ANNIVERSARY. Aug 22, 1965. While at bat against the Los Angeles Dodgers, pitcher Juan Marichal of the San Francisco Giants turned on catcher John Roseboro and clubbed him with his bat. Marichal took exception to a couple of return throws from Roseboro to the pitcher that he deemed too close to his head. Roseboro was cut on the head by the bat, and a brawl ensued. Marichal was later suspended eight playing days and fined a then-record $1,750.

RYAN STRIKES OUT 5,000: ANNIVERSARY. Aug 22, 1989. Nolan Ryan of the Texas Rangers became the first pitcher to strike out 5,000 batters when he fanned Rickey Henderson of the Oakland A's in the fifth inning of a 2–0 Oakland win. Henderson went down on a 3–2 count, swinging at a fastball. Ryan ended his career with 5,714 strikeouts.

TATUM, BIG JIM: BIRTH ANNIVERSARY. Aug 22, 1913. James Moore ("Big Jim") Tatum, football player and coach, born at McColl, SC. Tatum played baseball and football at the University of North Carolina before becoming one of the most successful football coaches in Atlantic Coast Conference history. After his 1946 Oklahoma team went to the Gator Bowl, Tatum moved to the University of Maryland. In nine years, his Terps won one national championship and finished undefeated three times. Died at Chapel Hill, NC, July 12, 1959.

BIRTHDAYS TODAY

Stephen Gerard Boyd, 28, football player, born Valley Stream, NY, Aug 22, 1972.
Darrin Jay Jackson, 37, baseball player, born Los Angeles, CA, Aug 22, 1963.
Paul Leo Maguire, 62, broadcaster and former football player, born Youngstown, OH, Aug 22, 1938.
Paul Leo Molitor, 44, former baseball player, born St. Paul, MN, Aug 22, 1956.

Duane Charles ("Bill") Parcells, 59, football coach, born Englewood, NJ, Aug 22, 1941.

Hipolito Antonio Pichardo, 31, baseball player, born Jicome Esperanza, Dominican Republic, Aug 22, 1969.

Carl Michael Yastrzemski, 61, Baseball Hall of Fame outfielder, born Southampton, NY, Aug 22, 1939.

AUGUST 23 — WEDNESDAY

Day 236 — 130 Remaining

ASA MEN'S MASTERS (40-AND-OVER) FAST PITCH NATIONAL CHAMPIONSHIP. Aug 23–27. Decatur, IL. For info: ASA-USA Softball, 2801 NE 50th St, Oklahoma City, OK 73111. Phone: (405) 424-5266. Fax: (405) 424-3855. E-mail: info@softball.org. Web: www.softball.org.

DAVIS, GEORGE: 130th BIRTH ANNIVERSARY. Aug 23, 1870. George Stacey Davis, Baseball Hall of Fame shortstop and manager, born at Cohoes, NY. Davis played for the New York Giants in the 1890s and for the Chicago White Sox after the turn of the century. He was involved in the contract controversies surrounding the creation of the American League in 1901. Inducted into the Hall of Fame in 1998. Died at Philadelphia, PA, Oct 17, 1940.

FIRST BOXING MATCH TELEVISED: ANNIVERSARY. Aug 23, 1933. Boxers Archie Sexton and Laurie Raiteri fought an exhibition at Broadcasting House at London. The fight was the first boxing match ever televised, if only on an experimental basis.

FIRST GAME BETWEEN AFL AND NFL: ANNIVERSARY. Aug 23, 1966. Following announcement of a planned merger between the American Football League and the National Football League, the Kansas City Chiefs of the AFL and the Chicago Bears of the NFL played the first exhibition game between teams from the rival leagues. The Chiefs won, 66–24.

INTERNATIONAL MARINE TRADES EXHIBIT & CONFERENCE (IMTEC). Aug 23–25. McCormick Place, Chicago, IL. 42nd annual. For info: NMMA Boat Shows, 600 Third Ave, 23rd Floor, New York, NY 10016. Phone: (212) 922-1212 or (312) 946-6262. Fax: (312) 946-0401. Web: www.boatshows.com.

MITCHELL, DALE: BIRTH ANNIVERSARY. Aug 23, 1921. Loren Dale Mitchell, baseball player, born at Colony, OK. With two out in the top of the ninth inning in Game 5 of the 1956 World Series, Dale Mitchell of the Brooklyn Dodgers pinch-hit for pitcher Sal Maglie. New York Yankees pitcher Don Larsen struck Mitchell out, thereby completing the only perfect game in World Series history. Died at Tulsa, OK, Jan 5, 1987.

UMPIRE TOSSES TWO: ANNIVERSARY. Aug 23, 1952. In a game against the St. Louis Cardinals at New York, Giants infielder Bob Elliott objected to a called strike by kicking dirt and was ejected from the game by home plate umpire Augie Donatelli. Bobby Hofmann pinch-hit for Elliott and was called out on strikes. He objected and was also ejected.

Ronald Mark (Ron) Blomberg, 52, former baseball player, born Atlanta, GA, Aug 23, 1948.

Allan Mercer Bristow, Jr, 49, former basketball coach and player, born Richmond, VA, Aug 23, 1951.

Kobe B. Bryant, 22, basketball player, born Philadelphia, PA, Aug 23, 1978.

Hugh Douglas, 29, football player, born Mansfield, OH, Aug 23, 1971.

George Davis ("Pete") Gent, 58, author (*North Dallas Forty*) and former football player, born Bangor, MI, Aug 23, 1942.

Glenn Healy, 38, hockey player, born Pickering, Ontario, Canada, Aug 23, 1962.

Christian Adolph ("Sonny") Jurgensen, III, 66, Pro Football Hall of Fame quarterback, born Wilmington, NC, Aug 23, 1934.

George Clyde Kell, 78, former broadcaster and Baseball Hall of Fame third baseman, born Swifton, AR, Aug 23, 1922.

Cortez Kennedy, 32, football player, born Osceola, AR, Aug 23, 1968.

Jeffrey Paul (Jeff) Manto, 36, baseball player, born Bristol, PA, Aug 23, 1964.

Rik Smits, 34, basketball player, born Eindhoven, The Netherlands, Aug 23, 1966.

AUGUST 24 — THURSDAY

Day 237 — 129 Remaining

CHASE'S SPORTSQUOTE OF THE DAY

"In 1951, in a moment of madness, I became owner and operator of a collection of old rags and tags known to baseball historians as the St. Louis Browns."—Bill Veeck

ASA COED CLASS A SLOW PITCH NATIONAL CHAMPIONSHIP. Aug 24–27. Midland, TX. For info: ASA-USA Softball, 2801 NE 50th St, Oklahoma City, OK 73111. Phone: (405) 424-5266. Fax: (405) 424-3855. E-mail: info@softball.org. Web: www.softball.org.

BROWNS FANS VOTE ON DECISIONS: ANNIVERSARY. Aug 24, 1951. St. Louis Browns owner Bill Veeck, one of baseball's greatest showmen, allowed fans attending a game against the Philadelphia Athletics to participate in the strategy decisions normally made by the team's manager. More than 1,000 fans were given placards reading "YES" and "NO" and were asked to vote on what the Browns should do at various points in the game. It worked; St. Louis won, 5–3.

CICCARELLI SENTENCED TO JAIL: ANNIVERSARY. Aug 24, 1988. Minnesota North Stars winger Dino Ciccarelli was sentenced to one day in jail and fined $1,000 for hitting Luke Richardson of the Toronto Maple Leafs during a game played Jan 8. The referee gave Ciccarelli a match penalty, and the league suspended him for 10 games. The fine and jail term were the first given to a hockey player for an on-ice incident.

CRIM FESTIVAL OF RACES. Aug 24–26. Flint, MI. Festival includes 24th-anniversary celebration, international 10-mile road race, 5K and 8K runs, 8K racewalk, 5K and 8K walks, one-mile run and teddy bear trot for children ages 4–12. Sports and fitness expo on Aug 24–26, Pasta Party on Aug 25 at University Pavilion Rink and food festival on Aug 24–26. Est attendance: 30,000. For info: Crim Festival of Races, 503 S Saginaw St, Ste 110, Flint, MI 48502. Phone: (810) 235-7131. Fax: (810) 235-5130. Web: www.doitsports.com/crim.

HOOPER, HARRY: BIRTH ANNIVERSARY. Aug 24, 1887. Harry Bartholomew Hooper, Baseball Hall of Fame outfielder, born at Elephant Head Homestead, CA. Hooper was one-third of the famous Boston Red Sox outfield that also included Tris Speaker and Duffy Lewis. He suggested to manager Ed Barrow that pitcher Babe Ruth should play every day in the outfield. Inducted into the Hall of Fame in 1971. Died at Santa Cruz, CA, Dec 18, 1974.

KAHANAMOKU, DUKE: 110th BIRTH ANNIVERSARY. Aug 24, 1890. Duke Paoa Kahanamoku, Olympic gold medal swimmer, born at Honolulu, HI. Kahanamoku won gold medals in the 100-meter freestyle in the 1912 Olympics and at the 1920 Olympics. He enjoyed a long career, not retiring from competition until age 42. Credited with inventing the flutter kick, Kahanamoku acted in movies and served as sheriff of Honolulu, running alternately on the Republican and Democratic tickets. Died at Honolulu, Jan 22, 1968.

OHIO TOBACCO FESTIVAL WITH TOBACCO WORM RACE. Aug 24–27. Ripley, OH. Celebration in honor of southern Ohio's cash crop of white burley tobacco. 19th annual festival activities include tobacco worm race, five-mile run, arm wrestling, cow chip throw, pipe smoking, clogging competition, antique car show, continuous country music, queen contest, arts and crafts, quilt show and more. Est attendance: 50,000. For info: Ohio Tobacco Festival, Box 91, Ripley, OH 45167. Phone: (937) 392-4369. Fax: (937) 392-4299.

PENNEL VAULTS 17 FEET: ANNIVERSARY. Aug 24, 1963. John Pennel of the US became the first pole vaulter to clear 17 feet when he vaulted 17', 3/4", at a meet in Miami.

ROSE MADE INELIGIBLE: ANNIVERSARY. Aug 24, 1989. Former baseball player and manager Pete Rose signed a five-page agreement with Major League Baseball placing his name on the permanently ineligible list. Rose did not admit to gambling on baseball although a report made to Commissioner Bart Giamatti concluded that he had. The agreement barred Rose from being considered for the Hall of Fame.

TENNESSEE WALKING HORSE NATIONAL CELEBRATION. Aug 24–Sept 2. Celebration Grounds, Shelbyville, TN. More than 3,800 entries compete for more than $650,000 in prizes and awards and the World Grand Championship titles. Trade show also. A 10-day festival for the whole family. Est attendance: 250,000. For info: Barbara Simmons, Public Relations Dir, Tennessee Walking Horse Natl Celebration, Calhoun and Evans, Shelbyville, TN 37160. Phone: (931) 684-5915. Fax: (931) 684-5949.

BIRTHDAYS TODAY

Benoit Brunet, 32, hockey player, born Pointe-Claire, Quebec, Canada, Aug 24, 1968.

Gerry Cooney, 44, former boxer, born New York, NY, Aug 24, 1956.

Archie Mason Griffin, 46, two-time Heisman Trophy running back, born Columbus, OH, Aug 24, 1954.

Reginald Wayne (Reggie) Miller, 35, basketball player, born Riverside, CA, Aug 24, 1965.

Calvin Edwin (Cal) Ripken, Jr, 40, baseball player, born Havre de Grace, MD, Aug 24, 1960.

		S	M	T	W	T	F	S
August				1	2	3	4	5
2000		6	7	8	9	10	11	12
		13	14	15	16	17	18	19
		20	21	22	23	24	25	26
		27	28	29	30	31		

Timothy James (Tim) Salmon, 32, baseball player, born Long Beach, CA, Aug 24, 1968.

Michael Edward (Mike) Shanahan, 48, football coach, born Oak Park, IL, Aug 24, 1952.

AUGUST 25 — FRIDAY
Day 238 — 128 Remaining

ASA MEN'S MASTERS (40-AND-OVER) SLOW PITCH NATIONAL CHAMPIONSHIP. Aug 25–27. Valdosta, GA. For info: ASA-USA Softball, 2801 NE 50th St, Oklahoma City, OK 73111. Phone: (405) 424-5266. Fax: (405) 424-3855. E-mail: info@softball.org. Web: www.softball.org.

BALLUNAR LIFTOFF. Aug 25–27. Clear Lake Area, Houston, TX. Come and enjoy a festive weekend with more than 100 hot-air balloons, sky diving competitions and other aerial demonstrations on site at NASA/Johnson Space Center. Sponsored by Space Center Houston/Clear Lake Area Chamber of Commerce and Re/Max. For info: Clear Lake Area Chamber of Commerce, 1201 Nasa Rd One, Houston, TX 77058. Phone: (281) 488-7676. Fax: (281) 488-8981.

CORVETTE SHOW. Aug 25–27. State Dock, Mackinaw City, MI. Parade of Corvettes on Friday at 7 PM. Show and visitor viewing, awards and Sunset Boat Cruise on Saturday. Est attendance: 3,000. For info: Corvette Show, 706 S Huron, PO Box 856, Mackinaw City, MI 49701. Phone: (616) 436-5574 or (800) 666-0160. Fax: (616) 436-7989. E-mail: pvance@freeway.net. Web: mackinawcity.com.

HOTTER-N-HELL HUNDRED. Aug 25–27. Wichita Falls, TX. Thousands of cyclists of all ages participate in the largest sanctioned century bicycle ride in the US. Aug 25—Criterium racing. Aug 26—Hotter-N-Hell ride. Aug 27–Criterium racing and time trials. Est attendance: 27,500. For info: Joe Schalling, Wichita Falls CVB, 1000 5th St, Wichita Falls, TX 76301. Phone: (817) 723-5800. E-mail: HH100@WF.net. Web: www.wtr.com/hhh.

MANTLE MONUMENT DEDICATED: ANNIVERSARY. Aug 25, 1996. The New York Yankees dedicated a monument to the late Mickey Mantle at Monument Park in Yankee Stadium. The new monument joined three others honoring Babe Ruth, Lou Gehrig and Miller Huggins. Mantle died Aug 13, 1995.

YOUNGEST 20-GAME WINNER: 15th ANNIVERSARY. Aug 25, 1985. Dwight Gooden of the New York Mets became the youngest pitcher to win 20 games in a season. Gooden defeated the San Diego Padres, 9–3. He was 20 years, nine months and nine days old.

BIRTHDAYS TODAY

Albert Jojuan Belle, 34, baseball player, born Shreveport, LA, Aug 25, 1966.

Cornelius O'landa Bennett, 35, football player, born Birmingham, AL, Aug 25, 1965.

Jacques Demers, 56, hockey coach, born Montreal, Quebec, Canada, Aug 25, 1944.

Roland Glen (Rollie) Fingers, 54, Baseball Hall of Fame pitcher, born Steubenville, OH, Aug 25, 1946.

Althea Gibson, 73, former tennis player, born Silver, SC, Aug 25, 1927.

Marvin Daniel Harrison, 28, football player, born Philadelphia, PA, Aug 25, 1972.

Robert Keith Horry, 30, basketball player, born Andalusia, AL, Aug 25, 1970.

AUGUST 26 — SATURDAY
Day 239 — 127 Remaining

CHASE'S SPORTSQUOTE OF THE DAY

"If I was going to get beat up, I wanted it to be indoors where it was warm."—Tom Heinsohn on why he played basketball instead of football

AFRMA RAT AND MOUSE SHOW. Aug 26. Hosted by the West Coast Model Horse Collector's Jamboree, Pomona, CA. American Fancy Rat and Mouse Association show exhibits rats and mice of "fancy" species that make good pets. For info: AFRMA, PO Box 2589, Winnetka, CA 91396-2589. Phone: (818) 992-5564 or (909) 685-2350. Fax: (818) 592-6590. E-mail: craigr@afrma.org. Web: www.afrma.org.

CALVERT COUNTY JOUSTING TOURNAMENT. Aug 26. Christ Church grounds, Port Republic, MD. The 134th annual tournament of Maryland's official state sport, steeped in colorful pageantry. Country supper, bazaar, organ recitals, children's activities, one-room schoolhouse, colonial church. Admission fee. Est attendance: 1,500. For info: Christ Church, 3100 Broomes Island Rd, Port Republic, MD 20676. Phone: (410) 586-0565.

CHAPTICO CLASSIC. Aug 26. Chaptico, MD. 17th annual Chaptico Classic for the benefit of Alternatives for Youth. 5K and 10K road race and walk. Annually, the last Saturday in August. For info: Michael J. Whitson, Race Dir, PO Box 746, Hughesville, MD 20637. Phone: (301) 475-2886. Fax: (301) 475-3157.

CHILI CHALLENGE OFF-ROAD BIKE RACE. Aug 26–27. Angel Fire, NM. Annual bike race held on the ski mountain in this beautiful alpine setting. All skill levels. Est attendance: 400. For info: Special Events, Angel Fire Resort, PO Drawer B, Angel Fire, NM 87710. Phone: (800) 633-7463 or (505) 377-4237. Fax: (505) 377-4395. E-mail: events@angelfireresort.com. Web: www.angelfireresort.com.

FIRST BASEBALL GAMES TELEVISED: ANNIVERSARY. Aug 26, 1939. WXBS television at New York City broadcast major league baseball for the first time, a doubleheader between the Cincinnati Reds and the Brooklyn Dodgers at Ebbets Field. Announcer Red Barber interviewed Leo Durocher, manager of the Dodgers, and Bill McKechnie, manager of the Reds, between games.

WICC GREATEST BLUEFISH TOURNAMENT ON EARTH. Aug 26–27. Long Island Sound, CT and NY. One of the nation's largest fishing tournaments of its kind. More than $45,000 in prizes for the biggest fish at this 17th annual tourney. Annually, the last weekend in August. Est attendance: 7,000. For info: Jill Dotlo, Tourn Dir, Bluefish Tournament, 2 Lafayette Square, Bridgeport, CT 06604. Phone: (203) 366-6000.

WORLD GOLF CHAMPIONSHIPS—INVITATIONAL. Aug 26–29. Firestone Country Club, Akron, OH. The second event in the first World Golf Championships, a new initiative created by the PGA Tours International Federation composed of the world's five leading golf tours (the PGA Tour, the European Tour, the Southern Africa PGA Tour, the PGA Tour of Australasia and the PGA Tour of Japan). The World Golf Championships will consist of three events, a match play competition in February for 64 players, this invitational event for all members of the last-named Presidents Cup and Ryder Cup teams and a stroke play competition in November for approximately 60 of the top players in the world. The Invitational Event will be contested at 72 holes of stroke play with no cut, Thursday, Aug 26, through Sunday, Aug 29. For info: PGA Tour, 112 TPC Blvd, Ponte Vedra Beach, FL 32082. Phone: (904) 285-3700. Fax: (904) 285-2460.

BIRTHDAYS TODAY

Ricky Paul Bottalico, 31, baseball player, born New Britain, CT, Aug 26, 1969.

Thomas William (Tommy) Heinsohn, 66, former coach and Basketball Hall of Fame forward, born Jersey City, NJ, Aug 26, 1934.

Chadden Michael (Chad) Kreuter, 36, baseball player, born Greenbrae, CA, Aug 26, 1964.

AUGUST 27 — SUNDAY
Day 240 — 126 Remaining

ANNAPOLIS RUN. Aug 27. Navy-Marine Corps Memorial Stadium, Annapolis, MD. Maryland's premiere 10-mile foot race, through historic Annapolis and along Naval Academy seawalls; designer premium for all finishers; entries limited to 4,000. Annually, the last Sunday of August since 1976. (Non-Labor Day weekend.) Est attendance: 4,000. For info: Annapolis Striders, Inc, PO Box 187, Annapolis, MD 21404-0187. Phone: (410) 268-1165.

CANADA: IRONMAN CANADA TRIATHLON. Aug 27. Penticton, British Columbia. 1,700 athletes testing themselves on one of the most difficult challenges in sport: a 2.4-mile swim, a 112-mile bike ride and a 26.2-mile marathon run. Sponsored by Subaru. For info: Subaru Ironman Canada, 104-197 Warren Ave E, Penticton, BC, Canada V2A 8N8. Phone: (250) 490-8787. Fax: (250) 490-8788. E-mail: ironman@vip.net. Web: www.ironman.ca.

HAMPTON CLASSIC HORSE SHOW. Aug 27–Sept 2. Bridgehampton, NY. 24th annual. The nation's top horses and riders showcase their talents at one of the finest horse shows in the country. Total prize money of $425,000. Est attendance: 45,000. For info: Classic Communications, 348 Mechanic St, #101, Foxboro, MA 02035. Phone: (508) 698-6810. Fax: (508) 698-6811. E-mail: classic@peconic.net. Web: www.hamptonclassic.com.

HANLON, NED: BIRTH ANNIVERSARY. Aug 27, 1857. Edward Hugh (Ned) Hanlon, Baseball Hall of Fame player and manager, born at Montville, CT. Hanlon managed the great Baltimore Orioles teams of the 1890s, the teams that devised an aggressive style of play called "inside baseball." Inducted into the Hall of Fame in 1996. Died at Baltimore, MD, Apr 14, 1937.

HENDERSON BREAKS BROCK'S SINGLE-SEASON RECORD: ANNIVERSARY. Aug 27, 1982. Oakland Athletics outfielder Rickey Henderson stole his 119th base of the season in a game against the Milwaukee Brewers, thereby breaking Lou Brock's major league record for most stolen bases in one season, set in 1974. Henderson added three more steals in the game, which Oakland lost, 5–4.

LEAHY, FRANK: BIRTH ANNIVERSARY. Aug 27, 1908. Francis William (Frank) Leahy, football player and coach, born at O'Neill, NE. Leahy played at Notre Dame and then commenced an outstanding coaching career at Boston College and his alma mater. His career winning percentage stands second to Knute Rockne among coaches with ten years' service and was highlighted by the 37–0–2 mark achieved by Notre Dame from 1946 through 1949. Died at Portland, OR, June 21, 1973.

RICHARDS BARRED FROM US OPEN: ANNIVERSARY. Aug 27, 1976. Transexual tennis player Renee Richards, who had formerly competed as Dr. Richard Raskind, was barred from competing in the US Open Women's championship after refusing to submit to a chromosome qualification test.

VOYAGE OF THE *GYPSY MOTH*: ANNIVERSARY. Aug 27, 1966. Sir Francis Charles Chichester, 65-year-old British yachtsman and aviator, began his around-the-world voyage in a 53-foot ketch named *Gypsy Moth*. He left Plymouth, England, and took 107 days to reach Sydney, Australia. He returned by way of Cape Horn in 119 days.

BIRTHDAYS TODAY

David Gus ("Buddy") Bell, 49, former baseball manager and player, born Pittsburgh, PA, Aug 27, 1951.
Ernest Gilbert (Ernie) Broglio, 65, former baseball player, born Berkeley, CA, Aug 27, 1935.
James Michael (Jim) Flanigan, 29, football player, born Green Bay, WI, Aug 27, 1971.
Brian Wesley McRae, 33, baseball player, born Bradenton, FL, Aug 27, 1967.
Adam Oates, 38, hockey player, born Weston, Ontario, Canada, Aug 27, 1962.
Michael Dean Perry, 35, football player, born Aiken, SC, Aug 27, 1965.
James Howard (Jim) Thome, 30, baseball player, born Peoria, IL, Aug 27, 1970.

AUGUST 28 — MONDAY
Day 241 — 125 Remaining

US OPEN (TENNIS). Aug 28–Sept 10. US National Tennis Center, Flushing Meadows, NY. The national tennis championships of the US with competitions in men's and women's singles, women's and mixed doubles. One of the sport's four Grand Slam events. For info: USTA, 70 W Red Oak Ln, White Plains, NY 10604. Phone: (914) 696-7000. Fax: (904) 696-7167.

US WINS FIRST WALKER CUP: ANNIVERSARY. Aug 28, 1922. A team of amateur golfers from the US defeated a team of amateur golfers from Great Britain, 8–4, to win the first Walker Cup competition. The Walker Cup was presented by American businessman George Walker and has generally been put in competition every two years.

BIRTHDAYS TODAY

Janet Evans, 29, Olympic gold medal swimmer, born Placentia, CA, Aug 28, 1971.
Ronald Ames (Ron) Guidry, 50, former baseball player, born Lafayette, LA, Aug 28, 1950.

August *2000*	S	M	T	W	T	F	S
			1	2	3	4	5
	6	7	8	9	10	11	12
	13	14	15	16	17	18	19
	20	21	22	23	24	25	26
	27	28	29	30	31		

Scott Hamilton, 42, Olympic gold medal figure skater, born Toledo, OH, Aug 28, 1958.
Lee MacLeod Janzen, 36, golfer, born Austin, MN, Aug 28, 1964.
Darren Joel Lewis, 33, baseball player, born Berkeley, CA, Aug 28, 1967.
Louis Victor (Lou) Piniella, 57, baseball manager and former player, born Tampa, FL, Aug 28, 1943.
Mark Anthony Smith, 26, football player, born Vicksburg, MS, Aug 28, 1974.

Moses Malone

AUGUST 29 — TUESDAY
Day 242 — 124 Remaining

BROCK BREAKS COBB'S RECORD: ANNIVERSARY. Aug 29, 1977. Lou Brock stole the 893rd base of his career, surpassing Ty Cobb's modern record for career stolen bases. He finished his career with 983 stolen bases, a total that was later surpassed by Rickey Henderson.

GLADSTONE DRIVING EVENT. Aug 29–Sept 5. Hamilton Farm, Gladstone, NJ. Equestrian combined driving competition in singles, pairs and four-in-hands. For info: Gladstone Equestrian Assn, PO Box 119, Gladstone, NJ 07934. Phone: (908) 234-0151.

HOYLE, EDMOND: DEATH ANNIVERSARY. Aug 29, 1769. Edmond Hoyle, games authority, born place unknown, ca. 1672. Today is a day to remember Hoyle and a day for fun and games *according to the rules*. Little is known about Hoyle. He is believed to have studied law. For many years he lived at London and gave instructions in the playing of games. His "Short Treatise" on the game of whist (published in 1742) became a model guide to the rules of the game. Hoyle's name became synonymous with the idea of correct play according to the rules, and the phrase "according to Hoyle" became a part of the English language. Died at London, Aug 29, 1769.

HYMAN, FLO: BIRTH ANNIVERSARY. Aug 29, 1954. Flora (Flo) Hyman, volleyball player, born at Inglewood, CA. Hyman stood 6'5" and was regarded as the best player in the US, starring on the 1984 Olympic team that won the silver medal. She suffered from Marfan's syndrome, a hidden congenital aorta disorder. Died at Matsue, Japan, Jan 24, 1986.

MOSES MALONE SKIPS COLLEGE: ANNIVERSARY. Aug 29, 1974. Moses Malone became the first basketball player to jump from high school to professional basketball, skipping college to sign a contract with the Utah Stars of the ABA.

BIRTHDAYS TODAY

Douglas Vernon (Doug) DeCinces, 50, former baseball player, born Burbank, CA, Aug 29, 1950.
William Edward (Will) Perdue, III, 35, basketball player, born Melbourne, FL, Aug 29, 1965.
Pierre Turgeon, 31, hockey player, born Rouyn, Quebec, Canada, Aug 29, 1969.
Wyomia Tyus, 55, Olympic gold medal sprinter, born Griffin, GA, Aug 29, 1945.

AUGUST 30 — WEDNESDAY

Day 243 — 123 Remaining

CHASE'S SPORTSQUOTE OF THE DAY

"There goes Ted Williams, the greatest hitter who ever lived."—Ted Williams on what he wanted people to say about him

ASA MEN'S CLASS A FAST PITCH NATIONAL CHAMPIONSHIP. Aug 30–Sept 4. College Station, TX. For info: ASA-USA Softball, 2801 NE 50th St, Oklahoma City, OK 73111. Phone: (405) 424-5266. Fax: (405) 424-3855. E-mail: info@softball.org. Web: www.softball.org.

ASA MEN'S CLASS B FAST PITCH NATIONAL CHAMPIONSHIP. Aug 30–Sept 4. Springfield, MO. For info: ASA-USA Softball, 2801 NE 50th St, Oklahoma City, OK 73111. Phone: (405) 424-5266. Fax: (405) 424-3855. E-mail: info@softball.org. Web: www.softball.org.

ASA MEN'S CLASS C FAST PITCH NATIONAL CHAMPIONSHIP. Aug 30–Sept 4. Aurora, CO. For info: ASA-USA Softball, 2801 NE 50th St, Oklahoma City, OK 73111. Phone: (405) 424-5266. Fax: (405) 424-3855. E-mail: info@softball.org. Web: www.softball.org.

CANADA: GRAND FORKS INTERNATIONAL BASEBALL TOURNAMENT. Aug 30–Sept 4. James Donalson Park, Grand Forks, British Columbia. 12-team invitational tournament draws from the four corners of North America and from the Pacific Rim. Annually, Labor Day weekend, beginning Wednesday. Est attendance: 35,000. For info: Larry Seminoff, Box 1214, Grand Forks, BC, Canada V0H 1H0. Phone: (250) 442-2110. Fax: (250)442-3788.

COOPER, TARZAN: BIRTH ANNIVERSARY. Aug 30, 1907. Charles Theodore ("Tarzan") Cooper, Basketball Hall of Fame center, born at Newark, DE. Four years after graduating from high school at Philadelphia in 1925, Cooper signed to play basketball with the New York Renaissance. He starred for the Rens for 11 years and helped make them one of the two greatest teams (along with the Original Celtics) of the era. The Rens were inducted into the Hall of Fame as a team in 1963. Cooper followed as an individual player in 1976. Died at Philadelphia, Dec 19, 1980.

CUYLER, KIKI: BIRTH ANNIVERSARY. Aug 30, 1899. Hazen Shirley ("Kiki") Cuyler, Baseball Hall of Fame outfielder, born at Harrisville, MI. Cuyler was an outfielder in the 1920s and 1930s, primarily with the Pittsburgh Pirates. He was an outstanding hitter with good speed and fine defensive skills. Inducted into the Hall of Fame in 1968. Died at Ann Arbor, MI, Feb 11, 1950.

FIRST $1 MILLION HORSE RACE: ANNIVERSARY. Aug 30, 1981. Jockey Bill Shoemaker rode John Henry to a nose victory to win the inaugural running of the Arlington Million, the first $1 million horse race, at Arlington Park in Illinois.

HOUSTON COMETS WIN FIRST WNBA TITLE: ANNIVERSARY. Aug 30, 1997. The Houston Comets defeated the New York Liberty, 65–51, to win the first WNBA title. Houston was led by the new league's MVP, Cynthia Cooper, who scored 25 points.

TWIN FALLS COUNTY FAIR AND RODEO. Aug 30–Sept 4. Filer, ID. County fair features PRCA rodeo, demolition derby, draft horse show, team sorting, livestock show, competitive exhibits (culinary arts, horticulture and fine arts), country music concerts and more. Annually since 1916, on Labor Day weekend beginning on Wednesday. Est attendance: 100,000. For info: Idaho Dept of Commerce, PO Box 83720, Boise, ID 83721-0093. Phone: (208) 326-4396. Fax: (208) 334-2631.

BIRTHDAYS TODAY

Jean-Claude Killy, 57, Olympic gold medal alpine skier, born Saint Cloud, France, Aug 30, 1943.
Vladimir Malakhov, 32, hockey player, born Sverdlovsk, USSR, Aug 30, 1968.
Frank Edwin ("Tug") McGraw, 56, former baseball player, born Martinez, CA, Aug 30, 1944.
Robert Lee Parish, 47, former basketball player, born Shreveport, LA, Aug 30, 1953.
Theodore Samuel (Ted) Williams, 82, Baseball Hall of Fame outfielder, born San Diego, CA, Aug 30, 1918.

AUGUST 31 — THURSDAY

Day 244 — 122 Remaining

CHASE'S SPORTSQUOTE OF THE DAY

"I had a friend with a lifetime contract. After two bad years the university president called him into his office and pronounced him dead."—Dob Devaney, football coach

ASA MEN'S CLASS A MODIFIED PITCH NATIONAL CHAMPIONSHIP. Aug 31–Sept 4. Fond du Lac, WI. For info: ASA-USA Softball, 2801 NE 50th St, Oklahoma City, OK 73111. Phone: (405) 424-5266. Fax: (405) 424-3855. E-mail: info@softball.org. Web: www.softball.org.

BIRTH OF PROFESSIONAL FOOTBALL: 105th ANNIVERSARY. Aug 31, 1895. A football team from Latrobe, PA, defeated a squad from Jeanette, PA, 12–0, in what could be regarded as the first professional football game. Latrobe quarterback John Brallier was paid $10 expense money.

DANDRIDGE, RAY: BIRTH ANNIVERSARY. Aug 31, 1913. Raymond Emmett (Ray) Dandridge, Baseball Hall of Fame third baseman, born at Richmond, VA. Dandridge was a standout third baseman in the Negro Leagues. He was 35 years old when Organized Baseball called, but he never played a day in the major leagues. Inducted into the Hall of Fame in 1987. Died at Palm Beach, FL, Feb 12, 1994.

FIRST COLLEGE ALL-STAR FOOTBALL GAME: ANNIVERSARY. Aug 31, 1934. The first College All-Star Football Game, matching the defending NFL champion against a team of college seniors from the previous season, was played at Chicago's Soldier Field. Organized by sportswriter Arch Ward, the game was an annual charity affair played through 1976. In the first game, the Chicago Bears and the All-Stars played to a 0–0 tie before a crowd of 79,432.

FIRST MAJOR COLLEGE FOOTBALL OVERTIME: ANNIVERSARY. Aug 31, 1996. Oklahoma State University defeated Southwest Missouri State University, 23–20, in the first Division I-A college football game to be decided in overtime. The game was tied, 17–17, at the end of regulation time. Under new rules effective that year, Southwest Missouri State got the ball first in overtime and kicked a 47-yard field goal. Oklahoma State then got the ball and answered with a 13-yard touchdown run.

GREAT PERSHING BALLOON DERBY. Aug 31–Sept 4. Brookfield, MO. Hot-air balloon flights, Balloon Glow, fly-in breakfast at Pershing Memorial Airport. Queen/Princess/Little Miss contest, craft fair in downtown Brookfield. All flights are subject to weather. Various admission fees and requirements for balloon flights. Annually, Labor Day weekend. Est attendance: 10,000. For info: Green Hills Ballooning, PO Box 451, Brookfield, MO 64628. Phone: (660) 376-3543 or (660) 258-5290.

GRIFFEYS' FATHER-SON ACT: 10th ANNIVERSARY. Aug 31, 1990. Ken Griffey, Jr, 20, and Ken Griffey, Sr, 40, made major league history by becoming the first father and son to play together in the same game. They played for the Seattle Mariners in a game against the Kansas City Royals.

HODGES HITS FOUR HOME RUNS: 50th ANNIVERSARY. Aug 31, 1950. First baseman Gil Hodges of the Brooklyn Dodgers became the sixth player in major league history to hit four home runs in one game. He added a single as the Dodgers beat the Boston Braves, 19–3.

NETHERLANDS: FIS ROLLER SKIING WORLD CHAMPIONSHIPS. Aug 31–Sept 3. Rotterdam, The Netherlands. For info: Intl Ski Federation, Blochstrasse 2, 3653 Oberhofen am Thunersee, Switzerland. Phone: (41) (33) 244-6161. Fax: (41) (33) 243-5353. E-mail: mail@fisski .org. Web: www.fisski.org.

PLANK, EDDIE: 125th BIRTH ANNIVERSARY. Aug 31, 1875. Edward Stewart (Eddie) Plank, Baseball Hall of Fame pitcher, born at Gettysburg, PA. Plank won more games than any other left-handed pitcher in American League history during a 17-year career. His victory total, including those achieved in the Federal League, is 327. Inducted into the Hall of Fame in 1946. Died at Gettysburg, Feb 24, 1926.

POTATO BALL: ANNIVERSARY. Aug 31, 1987. Catcher Dave Bresnahan of Williamsport in the Class AA Eastern League introduced some humor into a game when he attempted to throw out a baserunner with a potato instead of the ball. He had concealed the potato in his shirt waiting for the proper moment. To punish his indiscretion, the team released Bresnahan but later retired his number, 59.

WASHINGTON, KENNY: BIRTH ANNIVERSARY. Aug 31, 1918. Kenneth S. (Kenny) Washington, football player, born at Los Angeles, CA. After gaining All-American honors at UCLA where he was a teammate of Jackie Robinson, Washington and Woody Strode became the first blacks to play in the NFL after World War II, breaking the league's color barrier with the Los Angeles Rams. He played three seasons and then retired to a career in business. Died at Los Angeles, June 24, 1971.

YOUNG, DICK: DEATH ANNIVERSARY. Aug 31, 1987. Dick Young, sportswriter, born at New York, NY, 1917 or 1918. Young's career spanned nearly half a century. While covering the Brooklyn Dodgers, he pioneered an aggressive reporting style in which he interviewed players before and after games to gather quotations he incorporated into his stories. His column, "Young Ideas," provided a forum for his increasingly acerbic and conservative views that he believed represented the viewpoint of the average fan. Given the J.G. Taylor Spink Award in 1978. Died at New York.

BIRTHDAYS TODAY

Thomas Caesar (Tom) Candiotti, 43, baseball player, born Walnut Creek, CA, Aug 31, 1957.

Thomas (Tom) Coughlin, 54, football coach, born Waterloo, NY, Aug 31, 1946.

James (Jim) Fassel, 51, football coach, born Anaheim, CA, Aug 31, 1949.

Edwin Corley Moses, 45, Olympic gold medal hurdler, born Dayton, OH, Aug 31, 1955.

Scott Niedermayer, 27, hockey player, born Edmonton, Alberta, Canada, Aug 31, 1973.

Hideo Nomo, 32, baseball player, born Osaka, Japan, Aug 31, 1968.

Frank Robinson, 65, baseball executive, former manager and Baseball Hall of Fame outfielder, born Beaumont, TX, Aug 31, 1935.

Andrei Trefilov, 31, hockey player, born Moscow, USSR, Aug 31, 1969.

SEPTEMBER 1 — FRIDAY
Day 245 — 121 Remaining

ASA COED MAJOR SLOW PITCH NATIONAL CHAMPIONSHIP. Sept 1–4. Phoenix, AZ. For info: ASA-USA Softball, 2801 NE 50th St, Oklahoma City, OK 73111. Phone: (405) 424-5266. Fax: (405) 424-3855. E-mail: info@softball.org. Web: www.softball.org.

ASA MEN'S CLASS A CHURCH SLOW PITCH NATIONAL CHAMPIONSHIP. Sept 1–4. Mobile, AL. For info: ASA-USA Softball, 2801 NE 50th St, Oklahoma City, OK 73111. Phone: (405) 424-5266. Fax: (405) 424-3855. E-mail: info@softball.org. Web: www.softball.org.

ASA MEN'S CLASS A INDUSTRIAL SLOW PITCH NATIONAL CHAMPIONSHIP. Sept 1–4. Dothan, AL. For info: ASA-USA Softball, 2801 NE 50th St, Oklahoma City, OK 73111. Phone: (405) 424-5266. Fax: (405) 424-3855. E-mail: info@softball.org. Web: www.softball.org.

ASA MEN'S CLASS A 16-INCH SLOW PITCH NATIONAL CHAMPIONSHIP. Sept 1–4. Chandler, AZ. For info: ASA-USA Softball, 2801 NE 50th St, Oklahoma City, OK 73111. Phone: (405) 424-5266. Fax: (405) 424-3855. E-mail: info@softball.org. Web: www.softball.org.

ASA MEN'S CLASS A SLOW PITCH NATIONAL CHAMPIONSHIP. Sept 1–4. Lancaster, CA. For info: ASA-USA Softball, 2801 NE 50th St, Oklahoma City, OK 73111. Phone: (405) 424-5266. Fax: (405) 424-3855. E-mail: info @softball.org. Web: www.softball.org.

ASA MEN'S MAJOR CHURCH SLOW PITCH NATIONAL CHAMPIONSHIP. Sept 1–4. Dothan, AL. For info: ASA-USA Softball, 2801 NE 50th St, Oklahoma City, OK 73111. Phone: (405) 424-5266. Fax: (405) 424-3855. E-mail: info@softball.org. Web: www.softball.org.

ASA MEN'S MAJOR INDUSTRIAL SLOW PITCH NATIONAL CHAMPIONSHIP. Sept 1–4. Stratford, CT. For info: ASA-USA Softball, 2801 NE 50th St, Oklahoma City, OK 73111. Phone: (405) 424-5266. Fax: (405) 424-3855. E-mail: info@softball.org. Web: www.softball .org.

ASA MEN'S MAJOR MODIFIED PITCH NATIONAL CHAMPIONSHIP. Sept 1–4. Decatur, AL. For info: ASA-USA Softball, 2801 NE 50th St, Oklahoma City, OK 73111. Phone: (405) 424-5266. Fax: (405) 424-3855. E-mail: info@softball.org. Web: www.softball.org.

ASA MEN'S MAJOR 16-INCH SLOW PITCH NATIONAL CHAMPIONSHIP. Sept 1–4. Joliet, IL. For info: ASA-USA Softball, 2801 NE 50th St, Oklahoma City, OK 73111. Phone: (405) 424-5266. Fax: (405) 424-3855. E-mail: info@softball.org. Web: www.softball.org.

ASA MEN'S MAJOR SLOW PITCH NATIONAL CHAMPIONSHIP. Sept 1–4. Lawton, OK. For info: ASA-USA Softball, 2801 NE 50th St, Oklahoma City, OK 73111. Phone: (405) 424-5266. Fax: (405) 424-3855. E-mail: info@softball.org. Web: www.softball.org.

ASA MEN'S MASTERS (35-AND-OVER) SLOW PITCH NATIONAL CHAMPIONSHIP. Sept 1–4. Bismarck, ND. For info: ASA-USA Softball, 2801 NE 50th St, Oklahoma City, OK 73111. Phone: (405) 424-5266. Fax: (405) 424-3855. E-mail: info@softball.org. Web: www.softball.org.

ASA MEN'S SENIOR SLOW PITCH NATIONAL CHAMPIONSHIP. Sept 1–4. Jacksonville, FL. For men 75 and over, 70 and over, 65 and over, 60 and over, 55 and over and 50 and over. For info: ASA-USA Softball, 2801 NE 50th St, Oklahoma City, OK 73111. Phone: (405) 424-5266. Fax: (405) 424-3855. E-mail: info@softball.org. Web: www.softball.org.

ASA WOMEN'S CHURCH SLOW PITCH NATIONAL CHAMPIONSHIP. Sept 1–4. Altamonte Springs, FL. For info: ASA-USA Softball, 2801 NE 50th St, Oklahoma City, OK 73111. Phone: (405) 424-5266. Fax: (405) 424-3855. E-mail: info@softball.org. Web: www.softball.org.

ASA WOMEN'S CLASS A SLOW PITCH NATIONAL CHAMPIONSHIP. Sept 1–4. Auburn, AL. For info: ASA-USA Softball, 2801 NE 50th St, Oklahoma City, OK 73111. Phone: (405) 424-5266. Fax: (405) 424-3855. E-mail: info @softball.org. Web: www.softball.org.

BRITT DRAFT HORSE SHOW. Sept 1–3. Hancock County Fairgrounds, Britt, IA. Largest draft horse hitch show in North America, featuring 16 draft six-horse hitches from the US and Canada representing the very best of the Belgian, Percheron and Clydesdale performance horses. Annually, Labor Day weekend. Est attendance: 10,000. For info: Randel or Melodie Hiscocks, Britt Draft Horse Assn, PO Box 312, Britt, IA 50423. Phone: (515) 843-4181.

BROWN, JOHNNY MACK: BIRTH ANNIVERSARY. Sept 1, 1904. Johnny Mack Brown, football player and actor, born at Dothan, AL. Brown played at the University of Alabama and starred on Coach Wallace Wade's undefeated 1925 team that defeated Washington in the 1926 Rose Bowl, 20–19. Brown took a screen test and acted in several dramatic films before appearing in the first of more than 300 westerns. Died at Woodland Hills, CA, Nov 14, 1974.

CANADA: CLASSIC BOAT FESTIVAL. Sept 1–3. Victoria, British Columbia. Classic sail and power vessels from all over the west coast of the US, Canada and beyond gather in Victoria's Inner Harbour. View these lovingly restored and maintained boats with their polished brass fittings and rich teak and oak decks and hulls. Schooner races, sailpast, steamboat parade. Sponsored by Victoria Real Estate Board and *Times Colonist*. For info: Victoria Real Estate Board, 3035 Nanaimo St, Victoria, BC, Canada V8T 4W2. Phone: (250) 385-7766. Fax: (250) 385-8773. E-mail: vreb@vreb.org.

CORBETT, GENTLEMAN JIM: BIRTH ANNIVERSARY. Sept 1, 1866. James John ("Gentleman Jim") Corbett, boxer, born at San Francisco, CA. Corbett boxed 61 rounds against Peter Jackson on May 21, 1891, to no decision, but the fight got him a match with heavyweight champion John L. Sullivan. This fight, on Sept 7, 1892, was the first governed by the Marquess of Queensbury Rules and the first in which the fighters used gloves. Corbett decisioned Sullivan in 21 rounds, using the jab, the punch he invented. Died at Bayside, NY, Feb 18, 1933.

EVERT WINS 100th MATCH: ANNIVERSARY. Sept 1, 1989. Chris Evert defeated Patricia Tarabini, 6–2, 6–4, in an early round of the US Open tennis tournament. The victory made Evert, playing in her final US Open, the first 100-match winner in the 108 years of US national tennis championship competition.

FREEDMAN, ANDREW: 140th BIRTH ANNIVERSARY. Sept 1, 1860. Andrew Freedman, baseball executive, born at New York, NY. Freedman purchased controlling interest of the New York Giants in 1895, but he was an extremely unpopular owner. He sold the team in 1902 because he was not making as much money as he had anticipated. Died at New York, Dec 4, 1915.

HOG CAPITAL OF THE WORLD FESTIVAL. Sept 1–4. Kewanee, IL. World's largest pork chop BBQ. Also features Model T races, four-mile run (Hog Stampede) and the Hogatta Regatta, plus professional entertainment, carnival, flea market, parade and more. Annually, Labor Day weekend. Est attendance: 60,000. For info: Mark Mikenas, Exec VP, Kewanee Chamber of Commerce, 113 East 2nd St, Kewanee, IL 61443. Phone: (309) 852-2175. Fax: (309) 852-2176. E-mail: chamber@kewanee-il.com. Web: www.kewanee-il.com.

INTERNATIONAL GAY SQUARE DANCE MONTH. Sept 1–30. Emphasis on square dancing as a healthy, fun, recreational activity. For info: Intl Assn of Gay Square Dance Clubs (IAGSDC), PO Box 15428, Crystal City, VA 22215-0428. Phone: (800) 835-6462. E-mail: information@iagsdc.org. Web: www.iagsdc.org.

MARCIANO, ROCKY: BIRTH ANNIVERSARY. Sept 1, 1923. Rocky Marciano, boxer, born Rocco Francis Marchegiano at Brockton, MA. Marciano used superb conditioning to fashion an impressive record that propelled him to a fight against Jersey Joe Walcott for the heavyweight title on Sept 23, 1952. Marciano knocked Walcott out, and in 1956 he retired as the only undefeated heavyweight champion. Died in a plane crash at Newton, IA, Aug 31, 1969.

NATIONAL CHAMPIONSHIP CHUCKWAGON RACES. Sept 1–3. Clinton, AR. Five divisions of chuckwagon races, bronc fanning race, Snowy River race, live entertainment, barn dance, western show, western art, plus saddle, tack and clothing vendors. 15th annual races. Annually, Labor Day weekend. Est attendance: 20,000. For info: Dan Eoff, Rt 6, Box 187-1, Clinton, AR 72031. Phone: (501) 745-8407. Fax: (501) 745-4416. E-mail: chuckwag@ar telco.com.

PIRATES LOSE THREE GAMES: 110th ANNIVERSARY. Sept 1, 1890. The Pittsburgh Pirates lost three games in the same day to the Brooklyn Bridegrooms (later known as the Dodgers). In the morning, the Pirates scored nine runs in the ninth inning but lost 10–9. In the afternoon, Pittsburgh dropped a doubleheader, 3–2 and 8–4.

SMOKY JOE BESTS THE BIG TRAIN: ANNIVERSARY. Sept 1, 1912. In a specially-arranged pitching matchup, Smoky Joe Wood of the Boston Red Sox outdueled Walter Johnson, the "Big Train," of the Washington Senators, 1–0. The victory was the 14th straight for Wood. Johnson had a 16-game winning streak earlier in the year.

WISCONSIN STATE COW CHIP THROW. Sept 1–2. Prairie du Sac, WI. Cow Chip Throw. Anyone can participate; however, it takes a powerful toss to win. Also, chip chucking for children, a corporate throw, National Tug of War competition, 5K and 10K runs, an arts and crafts fair and bovine bingo (where a bet is placed on the location of a wandering cow's fresh pie). Est attendance: 50,000. For info: Wisconsin State Cow Chip Throw, PO Box 3, Prairie du Sac, WI 53578. Phone: (608) 643-4317. Fax: (608) 643-5421. E-mail: toolsmkt@bank pds.com.

BIRTHDAYS TODAY

Brian Bellows, 36, hockey player, born St. Catherines, Ontario, Canada, Sept 1, 1964.

Ricardo Adolfo (Rico) Carty, 61, former baseball player, born San Pedro de Macoris, Dominican Republic, Sept 1, 1939.

Timothy Duane (Tim) Hardaway, 34, basketball player, born Chicago, IL, Sept 1, 1966.

Hardy Otto Nickerson, 35, football player, born Los Angeles, CA, Sept 1, 1965.

Jason Paul Taylor, 26, football player, born Pittsburgh, PA, Sept 1, 1974.

Zach Michael Thomas, 27, football player, born Lubbock, TX, Sept 1, 1973.

David Lee West, 36, baseball player, born Memphis, TN, Sept 1, 1964.

September 2000

S	M	T	W	T	F	S
					1	2
3	4	5	6	7	8	9
10	11	12	13	14	15	16
17	18	19	20	21	22	23
24	25	26	27	28	29	30

SEPTEMBER 2 — SATURDAY

Day 246 — 120 Remaining

ASA MEN'S MAJOR FAST PITCH NATIONAL CHAM-PIONSHIP. Sept 2-6. Prescott, AZ. For info: ASA-USA Softball, 2801 NE 50th St, Oklahoma City, OK 73111. Phone: (405) 424-5266. Fax: (405) 424-3855. E-mail: info@softball.org. Web: www.softball.org.

CAPITAL DISTRICT SCOTTISH GAMES. Sept 2-3 (tentative). Altamont, NY. Celtic festival features the Northeastern US Pipe Band and Open Highland Dancing Championships, Highland athletics, Scottish dogs, country dancers, Celtic goods, Scottish and American food and beverages. Est attendance: 10,000. For info: Donald Martin, Capital District Scottish Games, 7 Lori Ln, Latham, NY 12110. Phone: (518) 785-5951.

CHARLESTON DISTANCE RUN. Sept 2. Charleston, WV. To provide an amateur 15-mile race of professional quality for residents and visitors to Charleston. A 5K (3.1 miles) race also will be held. Est attendance: 1,500. For info: Danny Wells, Race Dir, Charleston Festival Commission, Inc, PO Box 2749, Charleston, WV 25330. Phone: (304) 348-6419 or (304) 348-5122. Fax: (304) 348-1740.

FIRST MARATHON: ANNIVERSARY. Sept 2-9, 490 BC. Anniversary of the events from which the marathon race is derived. Phidippides, "an Athenian and by profession and practice a trained runner," according to Herodotus, was dispatched from Marathon to Sparta (26 miles), Sept 2 (Metageitnion 28), to seek help in repelling the invading Persian army. Help being unavailable by religious law until after the next full moon, Phidippides ran the 26 miles back to Marathon on Sept 4. Under the leadership of Miltiades, and without Spartan aid, the Athenians defeated the Persians at the Battle of Marathon on Sept 9. According to legend Phidippides carried the news of the battle to Athens and died as he spoke the words "Rejoice, we are victorious." The marathon race was revived at the 1896 Olympic Games at Athens to commemorate Phidippides' heroism. Course distance, since 1924, is 26 miles, 385 yards. Oldest in the US is the Boston Marathon, an annual event since 1897.

LIKE FATHER, LIKE SON: 40th ANNIVERSARY. Sept 2, 1960. Nearing the end of his career, Ted Williams of the Boston Red Sox hit a home run against Don Lee, a pitcher for the Washington Senators. In 1939, Williams's rookie year, he had homered against Thornton Lee, Don's father.

MAGIC CIRCLE BIKE CHALLENGE. Sept 2. Willcox, AZ. A 109-mile bicycle challenge with a 66-mile loop and 33-mile bike challenges. Annually, the Saturday of Labor Day weekend. Sponsor: Rex Allen Days, Inc. Est attendance: 500. For info: Willcox Chamber of Commerce and Agriculture, 1500 N Circle I Rd, Willcox, AZ 85643. Phone: (520) 384-2272. Fax: (520) 384-0293.

OREGON TRAIL RODEO. Sept 2-4. Hastings, NE. PRCA-sanctioned rodeo. Annually, Saturday–Monday of Labor Day weekend. Est attendance: 7,000. For info: Sandy Himmelberg, General Mgr, Oregon Trail Rodeo, 947 S Baltimore, Hastings, NE 68901. Phone: (402) 462-3247. Fax: (402) 462-4731. Web: www.adamscountyfairgrounds.com.

RUPP, ADOLPH: BIRTH ANNIVERSARY. Sept 2, 1901. Adolph Frederick Rupp, Basketball Hall of Fame coach, born at Halstead, KS. Rupp played basketball in high school and at the University of Kansas where his coach was Forrest ("Phog") Allen. He became coach at the University of Kentucky in 1930 and remained there until he was forced to retire after the 1972 season. Rupp's teams won 874 games, ranking him first among college coaches, and four NCAA titles (1948, 1949, 1951 and 1958) and lost the final game twice. Inducted into the Hall of Fame in 1968. Died at Lexington, KY, Dec 10, 1977.

SPALDING, ALBERT: 150th BIRTH ANNIVERSARY. Sept 2, 1850. Albert Goodwill Spalding, Baseball Hall of Fame pitcher and executive, born at Byron, IL. Spalding was a star pitcher in the 1870s and retired to run his sporting goods business, help administer the National League and attempt to popularize baseball throughout the world. Inducted into the Hall of Fame in 1939. Died at Point Loma, CA, Sept 9, 1915.

STA-BIL NATIONALS CHAMPIONSHIP LAWN MOWER RACE. Sept 2. Tri-County Fair, Mendota, IL. Three classes of races for winners of regional races held across the US. Mowers will travel at speeds ranging from 10 mph to more than 50 mph. Held in conjunction with the Tri-County Fair. Est attendance: 2,000. For info: US Lawn Mower Racing Assn, 1812 Glenview Rd, Glenview, IL 60025. Phone: (847) 729-7363. E-mail: letsmow@aol.com. Web: www.letsmow.com.

THRONEBERRY, MARV: BIRTH ANNIVERSARY. Sept 2, 1933. Marvin Eugene (Marv) Throneberry, baseball player, born at Collierville, TN. Throneberry parlayed modest talent into status as a fan favorite when he played for the New York Mets in 1962 and 1963. His fame was later reinforced when he appeared in a television beer commercial. Died at Fisherville, TN, June 23, 1994.

BIRTHDAYS TODAY

Nathaniel ("Tiny") Archibald, 52, Basketball Hall of Fame guard, born New York, NY, Sept 2, 1948.

Eldon LeRoy Auker, 90, former baseball player, born Norcatur, KS, Sept 2, 1910.

Terry Paxton Bradshaw, 52, broadcaster and Pro Football Hall of Fame quarterback, born Shreveport, LA, Sept 2, 1948.

James Scott (Jimmy) Connors, 48, former tennis player, born East St. Louis, IL, Sept 2, 1952.

Eric Demetric Dickerson, 40, Pro Football Hall of Fame running back, born Sealy, TX, Sept 2, 1960.

John Thompson, 59, former college basketball coach and player, born Washington, DC, Sept 2, 1941.

Peter Victor Ueberroth, 63, former commissioner of baseball and Olympics executive, born Evanston, IL, Sept 2, 1937.

SEPTEMBER 3 — SUNDAY

Day 247 — 119 Remaining

CHASE'S SPORTSQUOTE OF THE DAY

"I don't think these people at Wrigley Field ever saw but two players they liked—Billy Williams and Ernie Banks. Billy never said anything, and Ernie always said the right thing."—Ferguson Jenkins, Cubs pitcher

BILLY WILLIAMS'S STREAK ENDS: 30th ANNIVERSARY. Sept 3, 1970. Outfielder Billy Williams of the Chicago Cubs asked to be taken out of the starting lineup, breaking his consecutive games played streak at 1,117, a National League record until Steve Garvey broke it in 1983.

CHEETAH RUN. Sept 3. Cincinnati Zoo. The Cheetah Run is a 2.5-mile course throughout the beautiful zoo grounds. The race is followed by a Fun Run for children around Swan Lake. An awards ceremony follows the race. Est attendance: 1,500. For info: Events and Promotions Dept, Cincinnati Zoo and Botanical Garden, 3400 Vine St, Cincinnati, OH 45220. Phone: (513) 281-4701. Fax: (513) 559-7790. Web: www.cincyzoo.org.

ITALY: HISTORICAL REGATTA. Sept 3. Venice. Traditional competition among two-oar racing gondolas, preceded by a procession of Venetian ceremonial boats of the epoch of the Venetian Republic. Annually, the first Sunday in September.

ITALY: JOUST OF THE SARACEN. Sept 3. Arezzo. The first Sunday in September is set aside for the Giostra del Saracino, a tilting contest of the 13th century, with knights in armor.

NATIONAL FOOTBALL LEAGUE REGULAR SEASON. Sept 3–Dec 24 (tentative). The National Football League opens a 17-week regular season leading to Super Bowl XXXV, Jan 28, 2001, at Tampa, FL. Each of the league's 30 teams plays a 16-game schedule with one bye week. Six teams from the American Football Conference and six from the National Football Conference will qualify for the play-offs commencing Dec 30–31. For info: NFL, 280 Park Ave, New York, NY 10017. Phone: (212) 450-2000. Fax: (212) 681-7573. Web: www.nfl.com.

THIGPEN SETS SAVE RECORD: 10th ANNIVERSARY. Sept 3, 1990. Relief pitcher Bobby Thigpen of the Chicago White Sox set a major league record for most saves in a season when he chalked up his 47th save in a 4–2 White Sox victory over the Kansas City Royals. Thigpen finished the season with 57 saves.

TROPICAL TRIATHLON. Sept 3 (tentative). Lake Worth, FL. Sprint triathlon includes a ¼-mile swim, an 11-mile bike ride and a 3.1-mile run. Sanctioned by the USAT. For info: Star Group Intl, Inc, 777 S Flagler Dr, West Tower, West Palm Beach, FL 33401. Phone: (561) 547-0667. Fax: (561) 586-7928. E-mail: info@stargroup.net. Web: www.stargroup.net.

BIRTHDAYS TODAY

David Earl (Dave) Clark, 38, baseball player, born Tupelo, MS, Sept 3, 1962.
Luis Emilio Gonzalez, 33, baseball player, born Tampa, FL, Sept 3, 1967.
Damon Lamon Stoudamire, 27, basketball player, born Portland, OR, Sept 3, 1973.
Martin Straka, 28, hockey player, born Pizen, Czechoslovakia, Sept 3, 1972.
Byron Keith Traylor, 31, football player, born Malvern, AR, Sept 3, 1969.
Renaldo Lavalle Wynn, 26, football player, born Chicago, IL, Sept 3, 1974.

September 2000

S	M	T	W	T	F	S
					1	2
3	4	5	6	7	8	9
10	11	12	13	14	15	16
17	18	19	20	21	22	23
24	25	26	27	28	29	30

SEPTEMBER 4 — MONDAY
Day 248 — 118 Remaining

BRAVES PLAY TWO NINE TIMES: ANNIVERSARY. Sept 4, 1928. The Boston Braves began an unprecedented and grueling string of nine doubleheaders played on nine straight days, a major league record.

CANADA: GREAT KLONDIKE INTERNATIONAL OUTHOUSE RACE AND BATHROOM WALL LIMERICK CONTEST. Sept 4. Dawson City, Yukon. Crazy race of outhouses on wheels over a 1.5-mile course through the streets of downtown Dawson City. Awards presentation at Diamond Tooth Gertie's gambling hall following the race. Est attendance: 3,000. For info: Klondike Visitors Assn, Box 389W, Dawson City, YT, Canada Y0B 1G0. Phone: (867) 993-5575. Fax: (867) 993-6415. E-mail: kva@dawson.net. Web: www.hyperborean-web.com/kva.

COLUMBIA RIVER CROSS CHANNEL SWIM. Sept 4. Hood River, OR. The annual swim across the mighty Columbia River draws 550 contestants each year to swim the approximately one mile distance for fun. Est attendance: 550. For info: Hood River County Chamber of Commerce, Columbia River Cross Channel Swim, 405 Portway Ave, Hood River, OR 97031. Phone: (800) 366-3530. Fax: (541) 386-2057. E-mail: hrccc@gorge.net.

DODGERS ATTENDANCE RECORD: ANNIVERSARY. Sept 4, 1966. The Los Angeles Dodgers became the first team in major league history to draw two million fans at home and two million on the road in the same season when they played the Reds at Cincinnati before a crowd of 18,670.

GREAT BATHTUB RACE. Sept 4. Nome, AK. 23rd annual. Lets people know that participants bathe at least once a year. Further, when politicians participate, they can let their constituents know that they clean up their act yearly. Bathtubs mounted on wheels are raced down Front Street. Each team has five members, one in the tub, with bubbles apparent in the bath water. Tub must be full of water at beginning and have at least 10 gallons at the finish line. The other four team members must wear large-brim hats and suspenders and carry either a bar of soap, washcloth, towel or bath mat for the entire race. Winning team claims trophy, a statue of Miss Piggy and Kermit taking a bath, which is handed down from year to year. Annually, at noon on Labor Day. Est attendance: 1,000. For info: Rasmussen's Music Mart, PO Box 2, Nome, AK 99762-0002. Phone: (907) 443-2798 or (907) 443-2219. Fax: (907) 443-5777.

LABOR DAY. Sept 4. Legal public holiday. Public Law 90–363 sets Labor Day on the first Monday in September. Observed on this day in all states and in Canada. First observance believed to have been a parade at 10 AM, on Tuesday, Sept 5, 1882, at New York, NY, probably organized by Peter J. McGuire, a Carpenters and Joiners Union secretary. In 1883, a union resolution declared "the first Monday in September of each year a Labor Day." By 1893, more than half of the states were observing Labor Day on one or another day, and a bill to establish Labor Day as a federal holiday was introduced in Congress. On June 28, 1894, President Grover Cleveland signed into law an act making the first Monday in September a legal holiday for federal employees and the District of Columbia. Labor Day traditionally represents the end of the summer recreation season.

LITTLE MO WINS FIRST TITLE: ANNIVERSARY. Sept 4, 1951. Maureen Connolly, known as "Little Mo," won the first of her three straight US Lawn Tennis Association national championships at the age of 16. She defeated Shirley Fry, 6–3, 1–6, 6–4.

MACKINAC BRIDGE WALK. Sept 4. St. Ignace, MI. Labor Day is the only day of the year pedestrians are permitted to walk across the five-mile-long span, one of the world's longest suspension bridges, connecting Michigan's two peninsulas. Walk is from St. Ignace to Mackinaw City. Est attendance: 55,000. For info: Mackinac Bridge Authority, 333 Interstate 75, St. Ignace, MI 49781. Phone: (906) 643-7600. Fax: (906) 643-7668. E-mail: i:rossj @state.mi.us.

MATHEWSON VERSUS BROWN: ANNIVERSARY. Sept 4, 1916. In a specially arranged pitching matchup, Christy Mathewson of the Cincinnati Reds and Mordecai Brown of the Chicago Cubs hurled the final games of their careers against one another. The Reds won, 10–8.

NEW HAVEN LABOR DAY ROAD RACE. Sept 4. New Haven Green, New Haven, CT. Men's 20K national championship, 5K race and ½-mile children's fun run. Annually, on Labor Day. For info: New Haven Labor Day Road Race, (203) 481-5933 or, Greater New Haven CVB, 59 Elm St, New Haven, CT 06510. Phone: (203) 777-8550 or (800) 332-STAY. Fax: (203) 782-7755. Web: www.newhaven cvb.org. or www.newhavenroadrace.org.

SEDGMAN WINS USLTA CHAMPIONSHIP: ANNIVERSARY. Sept 4, 1951. Frank Sedgman became the first Australian to win the men's singles title at the US Lawn Tennis Association national championships at Forest Hills, NY. Sedgman defeated American Vic Seixas in straight sets.

STEARMAN FLY-IN DAYS. Sept 4–10. Galesburg, IL. The largest gathering of Stearman airplanes—the biplane trainers that gave wings to more military pilots than any other series of aircraft in the world. Annually, Labor Day through the following Sunday. Est attendance: 7,500. For info: Galesburg Area CVB, PO Box 749, Galesburg, IL 61402-0749. Phone: (309) 343-1194. Fax: (309) 343-1195. E-mail: visitors@galesburg.org. Web: www.galesburg .org/visitors.

TALBERT, BILL: BIRTH ANNIVERSARY. Sept 4, 1918. William Franklin Talbert, III, tennis player, born at Cincinnati, OH. Talbert overcame the limitations enforced by diabetes to become an exceptional player. With his partner, Gardnar Mulloy, Talbert won eight US national doubles titles and succeeded in the Davis Cup as well. He became the US Open's tournament director and was instrumental in the adoption of the sudden-death tiebreaker. Died at New York, NY, Feb 28, 1999.

WAIKIKI ROUGHWATER SWIM. Sept 4. Waikiki Beach, Honolulu, HI. The 30th annual swim is 2.4 miles from Sans Souci Beach to Duke Kahanamoku Beach. "The World's Largest Open Water Swimming Event." Preregistration is required. Annually, Labor Day. Est attendance: 1,200. For info: Jim Anderson, One Keahole Place #1607, Honolulu, HI 96825-3414. Fax: (808) 396-8868. E-mail: waikikijim@aol.com.

YANKEES WIN FIFTH PENNANT IN A ROW: ANNIVERSARY. Sept 4, 1953. The New York Yankees clinched their fifth consecutive American League pennant, a feat then unprecedented in baseball history. The Yankees went on to defeat the Brooklyn Dodgers in the World Series for their fifth Series crown in a row.

BIRTHDAYS TODAY

Raymond Loran Floyd, 58, golfer, born Ft Bragg, NC, Sept 4, 1942.

Dawn Fraser, 63, Olympic gold medal swimmer, born Balmain, Australia, Sept 4, 1937.

Kenneth Smith (Ken) Harrelson, 59, broadcaster, former baseball executive and player, born Woodruff, SC, Sept 4, 1941.

Michael Joseph (Mike) Piazza, 32, baseball player, born Norristown, PA, Sept 4, 1968.

Tomas Sandstrom, 36, hockey player, born Jakobstad, Finland, Sept 4, 1964.

John Vanbiesbrouck, 37, hockey player, born Detroit, MI, Sept 4, 1963.

Thomas Sturges (Tom) Watson, 51, golfer, born Kansas City, MO, Sept 4, 1949.

SEPTEMBER 5 — TUESDAY
Day 249 — 117 Remaining

CHASE'S SPORTSQUOTE OF THE DAY

"If I helped at all, I helped the notion that it's okay for a woman to be an athlete, to be competitive, to be tough."—Chris Evert

ANNE MEYERS SIGNS WITH PACERS: ANNIVERSARY. Sept 5, 1979. Anne Meyers, All-American basketball player from UCLA, made history by signing a contract with the Indiana Pacers of the NBA, the first woman to do so. Meyers worked out with the team throughout training camp but was cut before the season began.

BAUMAN HITS 72: ANNIVERSARY. Sept 5, 1954. Joe Bauman of the Roswell team in the Longhorn League hit three home runs to bring his season total to 72, a record for any level of professional play. Bauman was a poor defensive player and never made the major leagues.

EVERT'S CAREER ENDS: ANNIVERSARY. Sept 5, 1989. Chris Evert's tennis career came to an end in the quarterfinals of the US Open when she was defeated, 7–6, 6–2, by Zina Garrison.

ISRAELI OLYMPIC MASSACRE: ANNIVERSARY. Sept 5–6, 1972. Eleven members of the Israeli Olympic team were killed following an attack on the Olympic Village at Munich, Germany, by members of the Black September faction of the Palestinian Liberation Army. The Palestinians kidnapped athletes and coaches and made their way to the Munich airport where German forces, with the approval of the Israeli government, counterattacked. Four of the seven guerrillas were also killed. In retaliation, Israeli jets bombed Palestinian positions at Lebanon and Syria on Sept 8, 1972.

LAJOIE, NAP: 125th BIRTH ANNIVERSARY. Sept 5, 1875. Napoleon (Nap) Lajoie, Baseball Hall of Fame second baseman, born at Woonsocket, RI. Lajoie was a good enough player to have his team, the Cleveland Naps (later the Indians), named in his honor. He played 21 years in the major leagues and hit .338. Inducted into the Hall of Fame in 1937. Died at Daytona Beach, FL, Feb 7, 1959.

LUCAS, HENRY: BIRTH ANNIVERSARY. Sept 5, 1857. Henry Van Noye Lucas, baseball executive, born at St. Louis, MO. Lucas used his family fortune to organize the Union Association, a third major league that played only one year, 1884. He lost more than $250,000 in the venture. Died at St. Louis, Nov 15, 1910.

SHEPPARD, MEL: BIRTH ANNIVERSARY. Sept 5, 1883. Melvin Winfield (Mel) Sheppard, Olympic gold medal middle distance runner, born at Almenesson, NJ. Sheppard achieved fame for his frontrunning style of racing. He won three gold medals at the 1908 Olympics and one at the 1912 Stockholm Games. Died at New York, NY, Jan 4, 1942.

BIRTHDAYS TODAY

Henry Eugene (Gene) Bearden, 80, former baseball player, born Lexa, AR, Sept 5, 1920.
Jeffrey Hoke (Jeff) Brantley, 37, baseball player, born Florence, AL, Sept 5, 1963.
Bradley D. Hopkins, 30, football player, born Columbia, SC, Sept 5, 1970.
William Orland (Billy) Kilmer, Jr, 61, former football player, born Topeka, KS, Sept 5, 1939.
Tony Derrick Martin, 35, football player, born Miami, FL, Sept 5, 1965.
William Stanley (Bill) Mazeroski, 64, former baseball player, born Wheeling, WV, Sept 5, 1936.
Nazr Tahiru Mohammed, 23, basketball player, born Chicago, IL, Sept 5, 1977.
Dennis Eugene Scott, 32, basketball player, born Hagerstown, MD, Sept 5, 1968.

SEPTEMBER 6 — WEDNESDAY
Day 250 — 116 Remaining

CANADA: BC SENIORS GAMES. Sept 6–9. Kelowna, British Columbia. Olympic-style competition in a variety of sports for senior athletes. For info: BC Games Soc, Ste 200-990 Fort St, Victoria, BC, Canada V8V 3K2. Phone: (250) 387-1375. Fax: (250) 387-4489. E-mail: bcgames @bcgames.org. Web: www.bcgames.org.

CANADA: THE MASTERS. Sept 6–10. Spruce Meadows, Calgary, Alberta. World-class show jumping competition, along with Equi-Fair, Breeds for the World and Festival of Nations. Feature events are the Bank of Montreal Nations' Cup and the $725,000 du Maurier International, the world's most prestigious Grand Prix. Est attendance: 150,000. For info: Spruce Meadows, RR #9, Calgary, AB, Canada T2J 5G5. Phone: (403) 974-4200. Fax: (403) 974-4270. E-mail: smeadows@telusplanet.net. Web: www .sprucemeadows.com.

DiMAGGIO, VINCE: BIRTH ANNIVERSARY. Sept 6, 1912. Vincent Paul DiMaggio, baseball player, born at Martinez, CA. The oldest of the three major league

	S	M	T	W	T	F	S
September						1	2
2000	3	4	5	6	7	8	9
	10	11	12	13	14	15	16
	17	18	19	20	21	22	23
	24	25	26	27	28	29	30

DiMaggio brothers played ten years in the National League. Died at North Hollywood, CA, Oct 3, 1966.

FABER, RED: BIRTH ANNIVERSARY. Sept 6, 1888. Urban Clarence ("Red") Faber, Baseball Hall of Fame pitcher, born at Cascade, IA. One of the last of the legal spitball pitchers, Faber starred for the Chicago White Sox from 1914 through 1933. He once threw only 67 pitches in a complete game. Inducted into the Hall of Fame in 1964. Died at Chicago, IL, Sept 25, 1976.

MURRAY HITS 500th HOME RUN: ANNIVERSARY. Sept 6, 1996. Eddie Murray of the Baltimore Orioles hit the 500th home run of his career, joining Willie Mays and Henry Aaron as the only ballplayers to retire with at least 500 homers and 3,000 hits. Murray homered in the 7th inning against Felipe Lira of the Detroit Tigers. The Orioles lost the game, 5–4, in 12 innings.

RIPKEN SETS RECORD: 5th ANNIVERSARY. Sept 6, 1995. Cal Ripken, Jr, of the Baltimore Orioles played in his 2,131st consecutive game, thus breaking Lou Gehrig's mark. Ripken hit a home run as the O's defeated the California Angels, 4–2.

ROSENBLOOM, SLAPSIE MAXIE: BIRTH ANNIVERSARY. Sept 6, 1904. Maxie ("Slapsie Maxie") Rosenbloom, boxer, born at Leonard's Bridge, CT. Rosenbloom fought nearly 300 times and held the light heavyweight championship from 1930 to 1934. He used a defensive style and hit his opponents with open gloves, giving rise to his nickname. Died at South Pasadena, CA, Mar 6, 1976.

YEAGER INJURED: ANNIVERSARY. Sept 6, 1976. Los Angeles Dodgers catcher Steve Yeager, waiting in the on-deck circle, was seriously injured when he was struck in the neck by a shattered bat. The injury caused Yeager to introduce a new piece of baseball equipment, the neck protector, a flap attached to his catcher's mask.

BIRTHDAYS TODAY

John Patrick Dockery, 56, broadcaster and former football player, born New York, NY, Sept 6, 1944.
Dow Finsterwald, 71, golfer, born Athens, OH, Sept 6, 1929.
Derrek Leon Lee, 25, baseball player, born Sacramento, CA, Sept 6, 1975.
Patrick James (Pat) Meares, 32, baseball player, born Salina, KS, Sept 6, 1968.
Chad Oliver Scott, 26, football player, born Washington, DC, Sept 6, 1974.
Kevin Alvin Willis, 38, basketball player, born Los Angeles, CA, Sept 6, 1962.

SEPTEMBER 7 — THURSDAY
Day 251 — 115 Remaining

ASA MEN'S MASTERS (45-AND-OVER) FAST PITCH NATIONAL CHAMPIONSHIP. Sept 7–10. Cullman, AL. For info: ASA-USA Softball, 2801 NE 50th St, Oklahoma City, OK 73111. Phone: (405) 424-5266. Fax: (405) 424-3855. E-mail: info@softball.org. Web: www.softball.org.

CONNOLLY WINS GRAND SLAM: ANNIVERSARY. Sept 7, 1953. American tennis great Maureen ("Little Mo") Connolly became the first woman to win the Grand Slam, the four major tournaments in the same year. She began with the Australian Open, then the French Open and then Wimbledon. At the US championships at Forest Hills, NY, she defeated Doris Hart in the final, 6–2, 6–4. Connolly was so dominating that the match lasted only 43 minutes.

CORBETT–SULLIVAN PRIZE FIGHT: ANNIVERSARY. Sept 7, 1892. John L. Sullivan was knocked out by James J. Corbett in the 21st round of a prize fight at New Orleans, LA. It was the first major fight under the Marquess of Queensberry Rules.

GREAT PEANUT TOUR. Sept 7–10. Skippers, VA. Assorted bicycle rides from 13 to 125 miles. Special peanut tour ride to examine peanuts growing, method of harvesting and a sampling of more than 40 peanut goodies. Unique water stops, nature walks, music, campfires with marshmallow roast. Annually, the weekend following Labor Day. Est attendance: 1,500. For info: Robert C. Wrenn, Emporia Bicycle Club, PO Box 631, Emporia, VA 23847. Phone: (804) 348-4215. Fax: (804) 348-4020. E-mail: gpt@3rddoor.com. Web: www.3rddoor.com/gpt.html.

KASS KOUNTY KING KORN KARNIVAL AND MUD DRAGS. Sept 7–10. Plattsmouth, NE. Krowning of a King and Queen of Kornland, three large parades. Free street entertainment, including fire department Wall of Water, flower show, Korn Palace, museum exhibits, Hauf Brau Garten, Ugly Pickup Contest, Cow Chip Bingo, fun run, scarecrow contest, flea market, go cart, two-wheel bicycle race, Mud Drag races and horseshoe tournament on Sunday and much more. Annually, the second weekend in September. Est attendance: 30,000. For info: Patricia Baburek, Coord, 141 S 3rd St, PO Box 40, Plattsmouth, NE 68048. Phone: (402) 296-4155. Fax: (402) 296-4082.

LONGS PEAK SCOTTISH HIGHLAND FESTIVAL. Sept 7–10. Estes Park, CO. Scottish-Irish celebration with athletic championships, pipe bands, Highland and Irish dancing and gathering of the clans. Annually, the first weekend after Labor Day. Est attendance: 30,000. For info: Longs Peak Scottish Highland Festival Inc, Box 1820, Estes Park, CO 80517. Phone: (970) 586-6308. Fax: (970) 586-6308.

McGWIRE HITS 61st HOME RUN: ANNIVERSARY. Sept 7, 1998. Mark McGwire of the St. Louis Cardinals hit his 61st home run of the year, tying the record set by Roger Maris in 1961. McGwire's homer came off pitcher Mike Morgan of the Chicago Cubs in a 3–2 Cardinals victory.

ONLY SENATORS' HOME RUN AT HOME: 55th ANNIVERSARY. Sept 7, 1945. The Washington Senators defeated the St. Louis Browns, 3–2, to stay a game-and-a-half behind the first-place Detroit Tigers. Roger Wolff pitched a four-hitter, and Joe Kuhel hit an inside-the-park home run that was the only home run the Senators hit that year at their spacious home, Griffith Stadium.

ROCKFORD AREA SENIOR GAMES. Sept 7–10. Rockford, IL. Athletic and social events for adults ages 50 and up, including archery, baseball hit, basketball three-on-three, basketball free throw, billiards, bowling, casting, croquet, cycling, darts, golf, horseshoes, miniature golf, shuffleboard, swimming, table tennis, tennis, track and field and volleyball. Sponsored by the Rockford Park District. Annually, the first weekend after Labor Day. Est attendance: 800. For info: Rockford Park District, 1401 N Second St, Rockford, IL 61107-3086. Phone: (815) 987-8844 or TTD: (815) 963-DEAF. Fax: (815) 987-1631. E-mail: PHayes707@aol.com.

RYAN'S EXPRESS: ANNIVERSARY. Sept 7, 1974. A pitch thrown by Nolan Ryan of the California Angels in a game against the Chicago White Sox was clocked at 100.8 mph, the first time a pitch had ever been timed more than 100 mph.

SHOEMAKER BREAKS LONGDEN'S RECORD: 30th ANNIVERSARY. Sept 7, 1970. Jockey Willie Shoemaker won the 6,033rd race of his career at Del Mar race track in California, surpassing the record for career wins previously held by Johnny Longden.

US MEN'S STATE TEAM (GOLF) CHAMPIONSHIP. Sept 7–9. Golden Horseshoe Golf Course, Williamsburg, VA. For info: US Golf Assn, Golf House, Far Hills, NJ 07931. Phone: (908) 234-2300. Fax: (908) 234-9687. E-mail: usga@usga.org. Web: www.usga.org.

WHITEN HITS FOUR HOME RUNS AND TIES RBI RECORD: ANNIVERSARY. Sept 7, 1993. Mark Whiten of the St. Louis Cardinals hit four home runs in the second game of a doubleheader against the Cincinnati Reds. The Cardinals won, 15–2. Whiten hit a grand slam off Larry Luebbers, two 3-run homers against Mike Anderson and a 2-run homer off Rob Dibble. His 12 runs batted in tied the major league record set by Jim Bottomley in 1924.

BIRTHDAYS TODAY

Bruce Charles Armstrong, 35, football player, born Miami, FL, Sept 7, 1965.

Darren William Bragg, 31, baseball player, born Waterbury, CT, Sept 7, 1969.

Jeffrey Allen (Jeff) Hartings, 28, football player, born Henry, OH, Sept 7, 1972.

Robert William (Bob) Hartley, 40, hockey coach, born Hawkesburg, Ontario, Canada, Sept 7, 1960.

John F. Hirschbeck, 46, baseball umpire, born Bridgeport, CT, Sept 7, 1954.

Jason Derek Isringhausen, 28, baseball player, born Brighton, IL, Sept 7, 1972.

Jacques Gerard Lemaire, 55, former hockey coach and Hockey Hall of Fame center, born Ville LaSalle, Quebec, Canada, Sept 7, 1945.

Antonio Keithflen McDyess, 26, basketball player, born Quitman, MS, Sept 7, 1974.

Gino Odjick, 30, hockey player, born Maniwaki, Quebec, Canada, Sept 7, 1970.

Briana Collette Scurry, 29, soccer player, born Minneapolis, MN, Sept 7, 1971.

Mae Louise Suggs, 77, LPGA Hall of Fame golfer, born Atlanta, GA, Sept 7, 1923.

Erik George Williams, 32, football player, born Philadelphia, PA, Sept 7, 1968.

SEPTEMBER 8 — FRIDAY
Day 252 — 114 Remaining

CHASE'S SPORTSQUOTE OF THE DAY
"Losing hurts me. I was always determined to be the best."—Chris Evert

ASA MEN'S MASTERS (45-AND-OVER) SLOW PITCH NATIONAL CHAMPIONSHIP. Sept 8–10. Boaz, AL. For info: ASA-USA Softball, 2801 NE 50th St, Oklahoma City, OK 73111. Phone: (405) 424-5266. Fax: (405) 424-3855. E-mail: info@softball.org. Web: www.softball.org.

AUSTIN YOUNGEST OPEN CHAMPION: ANNIVERSARY. Sept 8, 1979. Tracy Austin, 16, became the youngest woman to win the US Open tennis championship when she upset Chris Evert Lloyd, 6–4, 6–3.

BULLNANZA. Sept 8–9. Reno Livestock Events Center, Reno, NV. The Lazy E takes its most popular event on the road to Reno. It's nothin' but bull ridin'! Est attendance: 15,000. For info: Lazy E Arena, Rte 5, Box 393, Guthrie, OK 73044. Phone: (405) 282-7433 or (800) 595-RIDE (7433). Fax: (405) 282-3785. E-mail: arena@lazye.com.

CAMPANERIS PLAYS ALL NINE POSITIONS: 35th ANNIVERSARY. Sept 8, 1965. Bert Campaneris of the Oakland A's became the first player in major league history to play all nine positions in the same game. He performed the feat against the California Angels, but he had to leave the game after 8⅔ innings because of a collision with catcher Ed Kirkpatrick. The Angels won, 5–3, in 13 innings.

DAUGHERTY, DUFFY: 85th BIRTH ANNIVERSARY. Sept 8, 1915. Hugh Duffy Daugherty, football player and coach, born at Emeigh, PA. Daugherty played the line at Syracuse University and began coaching after World War II. He became head coach at Michigan State University in 1949 and retired 19 years later with his best teams playing in 1965 and 1966. He was a popular banquet speaker and, after retirement, a television commentator. Died at Santa Barbara, CA, Sept 25, 1987.

GIAMATTI ELECTED COMMISSIONER: ANNIVERSARY. Sept 8, 1988. At a meeting of major league owners, A. Bartlett Giamatti, president of the National League and former president of Yale University, was elected to a five-year term as commissioner of baseball. Giamatti took office on Apr 1, 1989, upon the retirement of Peter Ueberroth, but he served only until Sept 1, when he died of a heart attack.

LAVER COMPLETES SECOND GRAND SLAM: ANNIVERSARY. Sept 8, 1969. Australian Rod Laver won the US Open by defeating fellow countryman Tony Roche in four sets to complete the second grand slam of his tennis career. Laver had previously won the Australian Open, the French Open and Wimbledon. His first grand slam occurred in 1962.

LEONARD, BUCK: BIRTH ANNIVERSARY. Sept 8, 1907. Walter Fenner ("Buck") Leonard, Baseball Hall of Fame first baseman, born at Rocky Mount, NC, Sept 8, 1907. Known sometimes as the "Black Lou Gehrig," Leonard was the preeminent first baseman in the Negro Leagues. With catcher Josh Gibson, he led the Homestead Grays to nine consecutive Negro National League pennants,

	S	M	T	W	T	F	S
September						1	2
2000	3	4	5	6	7	8	9
	10	11	12	13	14	15	16
	17	18	19	20	21	22	23
	24	25	26	27	28	29	30

1937–45. Smooth in the field and at the plate, he hit for consistent high averages while slugging home runs as well. Inducted in the Hall of Fame in 1972. Died at Rocky Mount, Nov 27, 1997.

McGWIRE HITS 62nd HOME RUN: ANNIVERSARY. Sept 8, 1998. Mark McGwire of the St. Louis Cardinals set a new single-season home run record when he hit his 62nd homer against pitcher Steve Trachsel of the Chicago Cubs. The homer came on the first pitch when McGwire came to bat with 2 out and nobody on base in the 4th inning. The Cardinals won, 6–3.

MUSKIES INC INTERNATIONAL MUSKIE TOURNAMENT. Sept 8–10. North Central, MN. 32nd annual fundraiser for nonprofit sportsmen's organization. Proceeds go toward muskie stocking, rearing and research projects along with Department of Natural Resources fisheries improvements. This tournament strongly encourages "catch and release." Annually, the Friday, Saturday and Sunday after Labor Day. The $50 entry fee entitles the contestant to participate in the Sunday banquet and compete for thousands of dollars in prizes. Grand Prize in the "Release Division" is a boat, motor and trailer with a retail value of approximately $28,000. We welcome corporate sponsorship inquiries. Est attendance: 600. For info: Dave Griffin, Twin Cities Chapter of Muskies, Inc, 4434 Dorchester Rd, Mound, MN 55364.

USA INTERNATIONAL DRAGON BOAT FESTIVAL. Sept 8–10. Riverview Park, Dubuque, IA. Teams of 25 enthusiastic paddlers race ornately carved and painted dragon boats on the Mississippi River. Pageantry, competition, international fellowship. Held in conjunction with River Fest. Sponsor: Dubuque Chapter of the American Dragon Boat Association. Est attendance: 6,000. For info: Dubuque Area Chamber of Commerce, 770 Town Clock Plaza, PO Box 705, Dubuque, IA 52004-0705. Phone: (319) 582-5406 or (800) 798-8844. Fax: (319) 557-1591. Web: www.dubuque.org.

Lemuel Jackson (Lem) Barney, 55, Pro Football Hall of Fame cornerback, born Gulfport, MS, Sept 8, 1945.

Latrell Fontaine Sprewell, 30, basketball player, born Milwaukee, WI, Sept 8, 1970.

Rogatien Rosaire (Rogie) Vachon, 55, former hockey executive and player, born Palmarolle, Quebec, Canada, Sept 8, 1945.

Clarence Weatherspoon, 30, basketball player, born Crawford, MS, Sept 8, 1970.

SEPTEMBER 9 — SATURDAY

Day 253 — 113 Remaining

AMERICAN BOWLING CONGRESS FOUNDED: 105th ANNIVERSARY. Sept 9, 1895. A group of bowling enthusiasts met at New York City's Beethoven Hall and founded the ABC. Since then the Congress has grown to become the world's largest sports membership organization with more than 2.4 million members.

CHANCE, FRANK: BIRTH ANNIVERSARY. Sept 9, 1877. Frank Leroy Chance, Baseball Hall of Fame first baseman and manager, born at Fresno, CA. Chance was part of the legendary Tinker–to–Evers–to–Chance double-play combination. As manager of the Chicago Cubs, his teams won four National League pennants and two World Series titles. Inducted into the Hall of Fame in 1946. Died at Los Angeles, CA, Sept 15, 1924.

ENCHANTED CIRCLE CENTURY BIKE TOUR. Sept 9–10. Red River, NM. 100-mile scenic ride and one of the longest and most difficult bicycle tours in the Southwest. Est attendance: 1,000. For info: Red River Chamber of Commerce, PO Box 870, Red River, NM 87558. Phone: (800) 348-6444. Fax: (505) 754-3104. E-mail: rrinfo @newmex.com. Web: redrivernewmex.com.

FIRST AFL GAME: 40th ANNIVERSARY. Sept 9, 1960. The American Football League opened its inaugural season with a game between the Boston Patriots and the Denver Broncos. Denver won, 13–10, before 21,597 fans at Boston University Field.

FRISCH, FRANKIE: BIRTH ANNIVERSARY. Sept 9, 1898. Frank Francis (Frankie) Frisch, Baseball Hall of Fame second baseman and manager and broadcaster, born at New York, NY. In one of baseball's epic trades, the New York Giants sent Frisch to the St. Louis Cardinals for Rogers Hornsby in 1926 after the Cards, with Hornsby as manager, had won the World Series. Frisch led the Cards to pennants in 1928, 1930, 1931 and 1934. Inducted into the Hall of Fame in 1947. Died at Wilmington, DE, Mar 12, 1973.

HOYT, WAITE: BIRTH ANNIVERSARY. Sept 9, 1899. Waite Charles Hoyt, broadcaster and Baseball Hall of Fame pitcher, born at New York, NY. Hoyt pitched excellent baseball for the New York Yankees from 1921 to 1929 and finished his career with several other teams. In retirement, he became a much beloved radio announcer for the Cincinnati Reds. Inducted into the Hall of Fame in 1969. Died at Cincinnati, OH, Aug 25, 1984.

KOUFAX PITCHES PERFECT GAME: 35th ANNIVERSARY. Sept 9, 1965. Sandy Koufax pitched the fourth no-hitter of his career, a perfect game against the Chicago Cubs. Koufax struck out 14 batters, but the Dodgers won by only 1–0 as Cubs pitcher Bob Hendley gave up only one hit.

LEAVENWORTH RIVER FEST. Sept 9–10. Leavenworth, KS. Antique car exhibits, parade, aircraft display and rides, arts and crafts and children's carnival. Plenty of entertainment, food and competitions and several feature attractions. Annually, the second weekend in September. Est attendance: 25,000. For info: Connie Hachenburg, Dir, Leavenworth CVB, 518 Shawnee, Box 44, Leavenworth, KS 66048. Phone: (913) 682-3924. Fax: (913) 682-8170.

MARYLAND RECREATIONAL VEHICLE SHOW. Sept 9–10 (also Sept 15–17). Timonium State Fairgrounds, Timonium, MD. 8th annual outdoor show of motor homes, trailers, five-wheel trailers and pickup campers, campground booths, accessories and related items. Annually, beginning the first Saturday after Labor Day. Est attendance: 8,000. For info: Richard T. Albright, Pres, Maryland Rec Vehicle Dealers Assn, Inc, 8332 Pulaski Hwy, Baltimore, MD 21237. Phone: (410) 687-7200. Fax: (410) 686-1486.

McCARTHY, CLEM: BIRTH ANNIVERSARY. Sept 9, 1882. Charles Louis ("Clem") McCarthy, broadcaster, born at East Bloomfield, NY. McCarthy virtually invented calling horse races on the radio. His distinctive voice and staccato delivery endeared him to listeners. He called every Kentucky Derby from 1928 to 1950. Died at New York, NY, June 5, 1962.

MONSTER MOPAR WEEKEND XIV. Sept 9–10. Gateway International Raceway, Madison, IL. More than 500 restored Chrysler muscle cars and 400 race cars converge for a car show, race and swap meet. Est attendance: 9,000. For info: Scott Sieveking, Pres, S.S. Promotions, PO Box 686, Eureka, MO 63025. Phone: (314) 938-6629. E-mail: rbtrainman@aol.com.

MORGAN HORSE VERSATILITY EVENT. Sept 9. McCulloch Farm, Old Lyme, CT. Demonstrations of all the different sports and activities that America's first breed of horse perform. Est attendance: 450. For info: McCulloch Farm Whippoorwill Morgans, 100 Whippoorwill Rd, Old Lyme, CT 06371. Phone: (860) 434-7355. Fax: (860) 434-1638.

SELIG NAMED ACTING COMMISSIONER: ANNIVERSARY. Sept 9, 1992. Following the resignation of Commissioner Francis T. ("Fay") Vincent, Milwaukee Brewers owner Bud Selig assumed the commissioner's duties as chairman of the owners' executive committee. Insisting that a new labor agreement with the Major League Baseball Players' Association must precede the election of a new commissioner, the owners endured a players' strike in 1994 and the cancellation of that year's World Series with Selig in charge.

UNDERHAND FREE-THROW SHOOTING TOURNAMENT. Sept 9–10. Downtown area, Winfield, IL. Men, women, boys and girls are invited to test their skill at shooting free throws the old-fashioned way—underhand! Those who qualify (at least 6 out of 10) compete in the finals on Sunday afternoon. Highest scorer wins a complete basketball apparatus donated by Target Greatland at Wheaton. Runners-up win basketballs donated by Wheaton Sport Center. Believed to be the only tournament of its kind in the US. Annually, the weekend after Labor Day during Winfield's Good Old Days. For info: Winfield Chamber of Commerce, PO Box 209, Winfield, IL 60190. Phone: (630) 682-3712. Fax: (630) 682-3726. E-mail: bysina@winfield-chamber.com.

US MID-AMATEUR (GOLF) CHAMPIONSHIP. Sept 9–14. The Homestead, Hot Springs, VA. For info: US Golf Assn, Golf House, Far Hills, NJ 07931. Phone: (908) 234-2300. Fax: (908) 234-9687. E-mail: usga@usga.org. Web: www.usga.org.

YOUNT GETS 3,000th HIT: ANNIVERSARY. Sept 9, 1992. Robin Yount of the Milwaukee Brewers got the 3,000th hit of his career, a single to right against Jose Mesa of the Cleveland Indians. Cleveland won, 5–4. Yount finished his career with 3,142 hits and was inducted into the Hall of Fame in 1999.

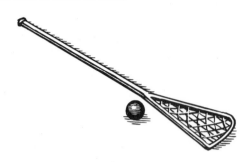

BIRTHDAYS TODAY

Benjamin Roy ("B.J.") Armstrong, 33, basketball player, born Detroit, MI, Sept 9, 1967.

Earl Douglas Averill, 69, former baseball player, born Cleveland, OH, Sept 9, 1931.

James Bernard (Jim) Corsi, 39, baseball player, born Newton, MA, Sept 9, 1961.

Johns Joseph (Joey) Hamilton, 30, baseball player, born Statesboro, GA, Sept 9, 1970.

Michael Joseph (Mike) Hampton, 28, baseball player, born Brooksville, FL, Sept 9, 1972.

Kevin John Hatcher, 34, hockey player, born Detroit, MI, Sept 9, 1966.

Daniel Lewis (Dan) Majerle, 35, basketball player, born Traverse City, MI, Sept 9, 1965.

Joseph Robert (Joe) Theismann, 51, broadcaster and Pro Football Hall of Fame quarterback, born New Brunswick, NJ, Sept 9, 1949.

Todd Edward Zeile, 35, baseball player, born Van Nuys, CA, Sept 9, 1965.

SEPTEMBER 10 — SUNDAY

Day 254 — 112 Remaining

BUCHANAN, BUCK: 60th BIRTH ANNIVERSARY. Sept 10, 1940. Junious ("Buck") Buchanan, Pro Football Hall of Fame defensive tackle, born at Gainesville, AL. Buchanan played offensive and defensive tackle at Grambling and was rated one of the greatest small college athletes of all time. He signed with the Dallas Texans (later the Kansas City Chiefs) and played a key role on the team that lost Super Bowl I and won Super Bowl IV. A six-time All-Pro, he coached defensive linemen after retirement. Inducted into the Hall of Fame in 1990. Died at Kansas City, MO, July 16, 1992.

CANADA: INTERNATIONAL TEXAS HOLDEM POKER TOURNAMENT. Sept 10. Dawson City, Yukon. Most northern Holdem Tournament hosted by White Ram Bed and Breakfast. Annually, the Sunday after Labor Day. For info: White Ram, Bag 5000, Dawson City, YT, Canada Y0B 1G0. Phone: (867) 993-6789. Fax: (867) 993-6777. E-mail: accommodations@dawsoncity.net.

September 2000

S	M	T	W	T	F	S
					1	2
3	4	5	6	7	8	9
10	11	12	13	14	15	16
17	18	19	20	21	22	23
24	25	26	27	28	29	30

CORVETTE SHOW. Sept 10 (rain date Sept 17). Wheaton Village, Millville, NJ. Presented by Corvettes Unlimited Corvette Club. Est attendance: 1,500. For info: Wheaton Village, 1501 Glasstown Rd, Millville, NJ 08332. Phone: (609) 825-6800 or (800) 998-4552. Fax: (609) 825-2410. E-mail: mail@wheatonvillage.org. Web: www.wheaton village.org.

CROWLEY, JIM: BIRTH ANNIVERSARY. Sept 10, 1902. James H. (Jim) Crowley, football player and coach, born at Chicago, IL. One of Notre Dame's famed Four Horsemen, Crowley played halfback for Knute Rockne's legendary backfield. He played pro football, coached at Michigan State and Fordham and served as commissioner of the All-America Football Conference. Died at Scranton, PA, Jan 15, 1986.

FULLERTON, HUGH: BIRTH ANNIVERSARY. Sept 10, 1873. Hugh Stuart Fullerton, sportswriter, born at Hillsboro, OH. Fullerton wrote mostly for Chicago newspapers and became famous for using statistics to predict the winner of each year's World Series. His accusations about the 1919 World Series, published in the New York *Evening World*, led to the investigation that uncovered the Black Sox Scandal. Given the J.G. Taylor Spink Award in 1963. Died at Dunedin, FL, Dec 27, 1945.

ITALY: GIOSTRA DELLA QUINTANA. Sept 10. Foligno. A revival of a 17th-century joust of the Quintana, featuring 600 knights in full costume. Annually, the second Sunday in September.

JCBC CENTURY RIDE. Sept 10. Junction City, Milford Lake, Ft Riley, KS. 100-mile bicycle ride (in loops) of various course routes and optional stopping points. Annually, the second Sunday in September. Sponsor: Bicycle Club. Est attendance: 200. For info: Casey Thomas, 2206 Prospect Circle, Junction City, KS 66441. Phone: (913) 762-3310. Fax: (913) 238-8351. E-mail: kspetdr@kansas .net.

KELLY, HIGH POCKETS: 105th BIRTH ANNIVERSARY. Sept 10, 1895. George Lange ("High Pockets") Kelly, Baseball Hall of Fame first baseman, born at San Francisco, CA. Kelly played 16 years in the majors and anchored the infield for the New York Giants in the early 1920s. He was brilliant defensively and hit for power as well. Inducted into the Hall of Fame in 1973. Died at Burlingame, CA, Oct 13, 1984.

MARIS, ROGER: BIRTH ANNIVERSARY. Sept 10, 1934. Roger Eugene Maris, baseball player, born Roger Eugene Maras at Hibbing, MN. In 1961, Maris broke one of baseball's sacred records, hitting 61 home runs to surpass the mark of 60 set by Babe Ruth in 1927. He won the American League MVP award in 1960 and 1961 and finished his career with the St. Louis Cardinals. Died at Houston, TX, Dec 14, 1985.

NORTHEAST MISSOURI TRIATHLON CHAMPIONSHIP. Sept 10. Thousand Hills State Park, Kirksville, MO. Swim 3/4 mile, bike 18 miles, run five miles. USA Triathlon Federation certified. Qualifier for International Course Nationals. Annually, the Sunday after Labor Day. Est attendance: 800. For info: KRXL Radio, Box 130, Kirksville, MO 63501. Phone: (816) 626-2213. Fax: (816) 626-2483.

US LOSES OLYMPIC BASKETBALL GAME: ANNIVERSARY. Sept 10, 1972. The US lost its first basketball game in Olympic history, snapping a streak going back to 1936, when the Soviet Union won the gold medal game at the Munich Summer Games, 51–50. The game was quite controversial. After the clock expired with the US ahead, International Amateur Basketball Federation officials intervened and required the referees to replay the last three seconds. This time, the Soviets scored to eke out the victory. US officials protested in vain. The American team refused to accept the silver medals.

WATERMELON SEED-SPITTING AND SPEED-EATING CHAMPIONSHIP IN PARDEEVILLE.
Sept 10. Pardeeville, WI. Annual national competition with visitors from as far as New York and Australia. The current speed-eating record is 2.5 pounds of watermelon in 2.98 seconds. Included are the championships, free watermelon and much more. Annually, the Sunday after Labor Day. Est attendance: 5,000. For info: Pardeeville Area Business Assn (PABA), PO Box 337, Pardeeville, WI 53954. Phone: (608) 429-3121.

BIRTHDAYS TODAY

Matthew Allen (Matt) Geiger, 31, basketball player, born Salem, MA, Sept 10, 1969.
Randall David (Randy) Johnson, 37, baseball player, born Walnut Creek, CA, Sept 10, 1963.
Robert Jerry (Bob) Lanier, Jr, 52, Basketball Hall of Fame center, born Buffalo, NY, Sept 10, 1948.
Joe Nieuwendyk, 34, hockey player, born Oshawa, Ontario, Canada, Sept 10, 1966.
Arnold Daniel Palmer, 71, golfer, born Latrobe, PA, Sept 10, 1929.

Bear Bryant

SEPTEMBER 11 — MONDAY
Day 255 — 111 Remaining

CHASE'S SPORTSQUOTE OF THE DAY
"He's a perfectionist. If he was married to Racquel Welch, he'd expect her to cook."—Don Meredith on Tom Landry

BRYANT, BEAR: BIRTH ANNIVERSARY.
Sept 11, 1913. Paul William ("Bear") Bryant, college football player and coach, born at Moro Bottoms, AR. Bryant earned his nickname by wrestling a bear for money as a young man. He played football at the University of Alabama with All-Americans Don Hutson and Dixie Howell and began coaching in 1940. After World War II, he was named head coach at Maryland. He later coached at Kentucky, Texas A&M and Alabama (1958–82). His career was legendary. His Alabama teams appeared in bowl games 24 consecutive years and won six national championships. He won coach-of-the-year honors three times and finished his career with 325 wins, then a record. Died at Tuscaloosa, AL, Jan 26, 1983.

HUSBAND RACES AGAINST WIFE: ANNIVERSARY.
Sept 11, 1976. In the third race at Latonia, jockeys John Oldham and Suzanne Picou became the first husband and wife to ride against each other in a US pari-mutuel race. Oldham finished second riding Harvey's Hope. Picou finished 11th aboard My Girl Carla.

McSHERRY, JOHN: BIRTH ANNIVERSARY.
Sept 11, 1944. John Patrick McSherry, umpire, born at New York, NY. McSherry umpired his first National League game in 1971 and was, by the time of his death, a crew chief who was respected by players and colleagues alike. Severely overweight, McSherry suffered a fatal heart attack on the field at Cincinnati's Riverfront Stadium just prior to the start of the opening game of the season. Died at Cincinnati, OH, Apr 1, 1996.

MUNN, BIGGIE: BIRTH ANNIVERSARY.
Sept 11, 1908. Clarence L. ("Biggie") Munn, football player and coach and athletic administrator, born at Grow Township, MN. Munn ran track and played football at the University of Minnesota. He coached at several institutions before being hired by Michigan State in 1947. His Spartans won 28 straight games over four seasons (1950–53) and one national championship. Died at Lansing, MI, Mar 18, 1975.

ROSE BECOMES ALL-TIME HIT LEADER: 15th ANNIVERSARY.
Sept 11, 1985. Pete Rose of the Cincinnati Reds became baseball's all-time career hit leader when he singled in the first inning of a game against Eric Show of the San Diego Padres. The hit, coming on a 2–1 count, was Rose's 4,192nd, surpassing the mark previously held by Ty Cobb.

BIRTHDAYS TODAY

Lawrence Donald (Larry) Bearnarth, 59, former baseball player, born New York, NY, Sept 11, 1941.
Ellis Rena Burks, 36, baseball player, born Vicksburg, MS, Sept 11, 1964.
Thomas Wade (Tom) Landry, 76, Pro Football Hall of Fame coach and former player, born Mission, TX, Sept 11, 1924.
Donna A. Lopiano, 54, women's sports executive and former softball player, born Stamford, CT, Sept 11, 1946.

SEPTEMBER 12 — TUESDAY
Day 256 — 110 Remaining

BETTENHAUSEN, TONY: BIRTH ANNIVERSARY.
Sept 12, 1916. Melvin Eugene ("Tony") Bettenhausen, auto racer, born at Tinley Park, IL. Bettenhausen began racing at 22 and competed in 14 Indianapolis 500s. He won the USAC national championship in 1951. Died in a crash at Indianapolis, IN, May 12, 1961.

BULLS SIGN JORDAN: ANNIVERSARY. Sept 12, 1984. The Chicago Bulls signed their No. 1 draft choice, Michael Jordan, a guard from the University of North Carolina. Jordan was the No. 3 choice overall behind Akeem (later Hakeem) Olajuwon, taken by Houston, and Sam Bowie, selected by Portland.

CHENEY STRIKES OUT 21: ANNIVERSARY. Sept 12, 1962. Tom Cheney of the Washington Senators set a major league record for most strikeouts in an extra-inning game when he fanned 21 Baltimore Orioles in a 16-inning game that he won 2–1.

GLOBETROTTERS LOSE: 5th ANNIVERSARY. Sept 12, 1995. The Harlem Globetrotters lost to a team led by former NBA great Kareem Abdul-Jabbar, 91–85, thus bringing the Trotters' 24-year, 8,829-game winning streak to a halt. Playing serious basketball for a change, the Globetrotters had defeated Abdul-Jabbar's team in two previous games. (See also: "Globetrotters Lose: Anniversary" Jan 5.)

HORVATH, LES: BIRTH ANNIVERSARY. Sept 12, 1921. Leslie (Les) Horvath, Heisman Trophy halfback, born at South Bend, IN. Horvath played college football at Ohio State for coach Paul Brown and won the Heisman in 1944. After three years as a pro, he went to dental school, opening a practice in 1950. Died at Glendale, CA, Nov 15, 1995.

OWENS, JESSE: BIRTH ANNIVERSARY. Sept 12, 1913. James Cleveland (Jesse) Owens, Olympic gold medal track athlete, born at Oakville, AL. Owens won four gold medals at the 1936 Summer Olympic Games at Berlin, Germany, putting the lie to Hitler's theories of Aryan superiority. In his career, Owens set 11 world records. During a Big Ten meet at the University of Michigan at Ann Arbor on May 23, 1935, Owens, representing Ohio State University, broke five world records and tied a sixth in the space of 45 minutes. Died at Tucson, AZ, Mar 31, 1980.

YASTRZEMSKI GETS 3,000th HIT: ANNIVERSARY. Sept 12, 1979. Carl Yastrzemski of the Boston Red Sox got the 3,000th hit of his career, a single to right against Jim Beattie of the New York Yankees. Boston won the game, 9–2, as Yastrzemski became the first American Leaguer to record 3,000 hits and 400 home runs. He ended his career with 3,419 hits and was inducted into the Hall of Fame in 1989.

BIRTHDAYS TODAY

Wilfred Benitez, 42, former boxer, born New York, NY, Sept 12, 1958.

Kenneth Leonard ("Ki-Jana") Carter, 27, football player, born Westerville, OH, Sept 12, 1973.

Lennox Dominique ("Terry") Dehere, 29, basketball player, born New York, NY, Sept 12, 1971.

Patrick Alan (Pat) Listach, 33, baseball player, born Natchitoches, LA, Sept 12, 1967.

Vernon Maxwell, 35, basketball player, born Gainesville, FL, Sept 12, 1965.

Ricky Rudd, 44, auto racer, born Chesapeake, VA, Sept 12, 1956.

SEPTEMBER 13 — WEDNESDAY
Day 257 — 109 Remaining

AUSTRALIA: SUMMER OLYMPICS: PRE-COMPETITION. Sept 13–14. Sydney, New South Wales. Preliminary competition in soccer. For info: Sydney Org Committee for the XXVII Olympic Games, Level 14, Maritime Centre, 207 Kent St, Sydney, NSW 2000, Australia. Phone: (61.2) 9297.2000. Fax: (61.2) 9297.2020. Web: www.sydney.olympic.org.

DAY RIDES EIGHT WINNERS: ANNIVERSARY. Sept 13, 1989. Jockey Pat Day rode eight winners in nine races at Arlington Park in Illinois, breaking the record for most winners in a single day of racing at one track. Day finished second in his sole loss.

FIRST NEW YORK CITY MARATHON: 30th ANNIVERSARY. Sept 13, 1970. The first New York City marathon drew 126 runners, 55 of whom finished the course. Gary Muhrcke won the race with a time of 2:31:38.2.

FRANK, CLINT: 85th BIRTH ANNIVERSARY. Sept 13, 1915. Clinton Edward (Clint) Frank, Heisman Trophy halfback, born at St. Louis, MO. Frank, an All-American at Yale, won the Heisman in 1937. He declined to play pro football, opting instead for a career in advertising. Died at Evanston, IL, July 7, 1992.

MAYS HITS 500th HOME RUN: 35th ANNIVERSARY. Sept 13, 1965. Willie Mays of the San Francisco Giants hit the 500th home run of his career against Don Nottebart of the Houston Astros. The Giants won, 5–1. Mays finished his career with 660 homers and was inducted into the Hall of Fame in 1979.

PATRIOTS BROADCAST IN FRENCH: ANNIVERSARY. Sept 13, 1987. The New England Patriots became the first NFL team to broadcast its games on a regular basis on a French-Canadian radio network. Pierre Donais handled the play-by-play with radio station KCLM, a 50,000-watt station at Laval, Quebec, serving as the flagship.

ROBINSON HITS 500th HOME RUN: ANNIVERSARY. Sept 13, 1971. Frank Robinson of the Baltimore Orioles hit the 499th home run of his career in the first game of

September 2000	S	M	T	W	T	F	S
						1	2
	3	4	5	6	7	8	9
	10	11	12	13	14	15	16
	17	18	19	20	21	22	23
	24	25	26	27	28	29	30

a doubleheader against the Detroit Tigers and the 500th in the nightcap. Baltimore won the first game, 9–1, but lost the second, 10–5. Robinson finished his career with 586 homers and was inducted into the Hall of Fame in 1982.

SOSA HITS 61st AND 62nd HOME RUNS: ANNIVERSARY. Sept 13, 1998. Sammy Sosa hit the 61st and 62nd home runs of the season, tying Mark McGwire for the league lead and becoming only the third player to surpass 60 homers in a season. Sosa's homers came against pitchers Bronswell Patrick and Eric Plunk of the Milwaukee Brewers in a game won by the Cubs, 11–10. He finished the season with 66 homers, four behind McGwire, but more than any other player except the Cardinals first baseman.

SULLIVAN, BILLY: 85th BIRTH ANNIVERSARY. Sept 13, 1915. William Hallissey (Billy) Sullivan, Jr, sports executive, born at Lowell, MA. Sullivan was the founding owner of the Boston (later New England) Patriots. Rebuffed by the NFL, he helped establish the American Football League in 1960 and later helped it merge with the older league. In 1988, he sold the Patriots to Victor Kiam for $83 million. Died at Atlantis, FL, Feb 23, 1998.

VINCENT ELECTED COMMISSIONER: ANNIVERSARY. Sept 13, 1989. Following the sudden death of A. Bartlett Giamatti, Major League Baseball's Executive Committee appointed Francis T. (Fay) Vincent acting commissioner on Sept 2. At an owners meeting 11 days later, Vincent was elected unanimously to serve out Giamatti's term, due to end Mar 31, 1994. Disputes with the owners, however, caused Vincent to resign in 1992.

BIRTHDAYS TODAY

John Rikard (Rick) Dempsey, 51, former baseball player, born Fayetteville, TN, Sept 13, 1949.

Goran Ivanisevic, 29, tennis player, born Split, Croatia, Yugoslavia, Sept 13, 1971.

James Bradley (Brad) Johnson, 32, football player, born Marietta, GA, Sept 13, 1968.

Travis James Knight, 26, basketball player, born Salt Lake City, UT, Sept 13, 1974.

Igor Kravchuk, 34, hockey player, born Ufa, USSR, Sept 13, 1966.

Dennis Edward (Denny) Neagle, Jr, 32, baseball player, born Gambrills, MD, Sept 13, 1968.

Bernabe Figueroa (Bernie) Williams, 32, baseball player, born San Juan, Puerto Rico, Sept 13, 1968.

SEPTEMBER 14 — THURSDAY
Day 258 — 108 Remaining

CHASE'S SPORTSQUOTE OF THE DAY

"McCovey swings and misses, and it's fouled back."—Jerry Coleman, known for his "Colemanisms"

ANVIL MOUNTAIN 59-MINUTE, 37-SECOND CHALLENGE. Sept 14. Nome, AK. A running event that starts at the base of Anvil Mountain. Runners must run 834 ft up the face of the mountain and return in less than 59 minutes and 37 seconds or be disqualified from the competition. Trophies awarded for first–third finishers, first woman finisher and first finisher 16 years of age or under. Annually, the second Thursday in September. Est attendance: 1,000. For info: Anvil Mountain Challenge, Rasmussen's Music Mart, PO Box 2, Nome, AK 99762-0002. Phone: (907) 443-2798 or (907) 443-2919. Fax: (907) 443-5777.

AUSTRALIA: SUMMER OLYMPICS: OPENING CEREMONY. Sept 14. Sydney, New South Wales. Sydney is 14 hours ahead of the Eastern time zone in the US. The schedules of Olympic events will be listed in this book as they occur in the host city. (See also: "Australia: Summer Olympics: Opening Ceremony" Sept 15.)

BURNS MAKES UNASSISTED TRIPLE PLAY: ANNIVERSARY. Sept 14, 1923. First baseman George Burns of the Boston Red Sox made the third unassisted triple play in major league history in the second inning of a game against Cleveland. Burns caught a line drive hit by Frank Brower, tagged Rube Lutzke before he could return to first and stepped on second before Riggs Stephenson could return.

DICKINSON, GARDNER: BIRTH ANNIVERSARY. Sept 14, 1927. Gardner Dickinson, golfer, born at Dothan, AL. Dickinson was a seven-time winner on the PGA Tour and an outstanding competitor in the Ryder Cup. He helped to organize the Senior PGA Tour in 1980 and was a respected teacher of the game. He was married to Judy Dickinson, a player herself and president of the LPGA. Died at Tequesta, FL, Apr 19, 1998.

GRIFFEYS HIT BACK-TO-BACK HOMERS: 10th ANNIVERSARY. Sept 14, 1990. Ken Griffey, Sr, and Ken Griffey, Jr, father and son, hit unprecedented back-to-back home runs for the Seattle Mariners in a game against the California Angels. Kirk McCaskill was the pitcher. The Mariners lost, 7–5.

HORSE RACING AT FAIRPLEX PARK. Sept 14–Oct 1. Fairplex Park, Pomona, CA. Thoroughbred, quarter horse, Arabian and Appaloosa horse racing during the Los Angeles County Fair. The Fairplex Park racing season ranks only behind the other major Southern California racetracks for average daily handle among all tracks in North America. Annually, beginning on the second Thursday after Labor Day, traditionally held between the Del Mar and Oak Tree seasons. Presented by the Los Angeles County Fair Association. Est attendance: 100,000. For info: Communications Mgr, Fairplex, PO Box 2250, Pomona, CA 91769. Phone: (909) 623-3111. Fax: (909) 629-2067. E-mail: Robinson@fairplex.com. Web: www.fairplex.com.

HUNDLEY SET HOMER MARK: ANNIVERSARY. Sept 14, 1996. Catcher Todd Hundley of the New York Mets hit his 41st home run of the year to set a major league record for most home runs in a season by a catcher. Roy Campanella hit 41 homers for the Brooklyn Dodgers in 1953, but one of these came when he pinch-hit on the last day of the season.

KETCHEL, STANLEY: BIRTH ANNIVERSARY. Sept 14, 1886. Stanley Ketchel, boxer, born Stanislaus Kiecal at Grand Rapids, MI. Ketchel became a fighter after both his parents were murdered. He won the middleweight title in 1908 and proved to be one of the sport's most popular champions. In 1909 he took on heavyweight champ Jack Johnson and lasted 12 rounds despite giving away 35 pounds. Embroiled in a love triangle, he was fatally shot by Walter A. Dipley, a hired hand on the farm where Ketchel was training. Died at Conway, MO, Oct 15, 1910.

LUMBERJACK DAYS. Sept 14–17. Orofino, ID. An international event which attracts loggers from all over the world. Competitions include burling, axe throwing, tree race, two-person hand saw races and power saw events. Est attendance: 2,000. For info: Orofino Chamber of Commerce, Box 2346, Orofino, ID 83544. Phone: (208) 476-4335. Fax: (208) 476-3634.

McLAIN WINS 30 GAMES: ANNIVERSARY. Sept 14, 1968. Denny McLain of the Detroit Tigers defeated the Oakland A's, 5–4, to become the first pitcher since Dizzy Dean in 1934 to win 30 games in a season.

NICHOLS, KID: BIRTH ANNIVERSARY. Sept 14, 1869. Charles Augustus ("Kid") Nichols, Baseball Hall of Fame pitcher, born at Madison, WI. Nichols was one of the greatest pitchers of the 19th century. In the 1890s, he led the Boston National League team to five championships in nine seasons, winning 30 or more games seven years in a row. Inducted into the Hall of Fame in 1949. Died at Kansas City, MO, Apr 11, 1953.

SOLO TRANSATLANTIC BALLOON CROSSING: ANNIVERSARY. Sept 14–18, 1984. Joe W. Kittinger, 56-year-old balloonist left Caribou, ME, in a 10-story-tall helium-filled balloon named *Rosie O'Grady's Balloon of Peace* on Sept 14, 1984, crossed the Atlantic Ocean and reached the French coast, above the town of Capbreton, in bad weather on Sept 17 at 4:29 PM EDT. He crash-landed amid wind and rain near Savone, Italy, at 8:08 AM EDT, Sept 18. Kittinger suffered a broken ankle when he was thrown from the balloon's gondola during the landing. His nearly 84-hour flight, covering about 3,535 miles, was the first solo balloon crossing of the Atlantic Ocean and a record distance for a solo balloon flight.

TAMPA BOAT SHOW. Sept 14–17. Tampa Convention Center and adjacent marina, Tampa, FL. 35th annual show is Gulf Coast's premier nautical event, showcasing hundreds of new boats and accessories, plus informative boating and fishing seminars. Est attendance: 22,000. For info: Carolyn Luis, 400 Arthur Godfrey Rd, Ste 310, Miami Beach, FL 33140. Phone: (305) 531-8410. Fax: (305) 534-3139. Web: www.boatshows.com.

TEAM USA WINS WORLD CUP: ANNIVERSARY. Sept 14, 1996. Team USA defeated Team Canada, 5–2, in Game 3 of the best-of-three final series to win hockey's World Cup. This competition matched teams of professionals from eight teams in a pair of round robins followed a single elimination bracket for the top four teams. Team Canada won the first game of the finals, 4–3, in overtime. Team USA won Game 2, 5–2, to even the series. Other teams represented Sweden, Finland, Russia, Germany, Slovakia and the Czech Republic.

US SENIOR WOMEN'S AMATEUR (GOLF) CHAMPIONSHIP. Sept 14–19. Sea Island Golf Club, St. Simons Island, GA. For info: US Golf Assn, Golf House, Far Hills, NJ 07931. Phone: (908) 234-2300. Fax: (908) 234-9687. E-mail: usga@usga.org. Web: www.usga.org.

September 2000

S	M	T	W	T	F	S
					1	2
3	4	5	6	7	8	9
10	11	12	13	14	15	16
17	18	19	20	21	22	23
24	25	26	27	28	29	30

David Michael Bell, 28, baseball player, born Cincinnati, OH, Sept 14, 1972.
Lawrence Harvey (Larry) Brown, 60, basketball coach and former player, born New York, NY, Sept 14, 1940.
Gerald Francis (Jerry) Coleman, 76, broadcaster and former baseball manager and player, born San Jose, CA, Sept 14, 1924.
Kurt Keola Gouveia, 36, football player, born Honolulu, HI, Sept 14, 1964.

SEPTEMBER 15 — FRIDAY
Day 259 — 107 Remaining

ALI WINS TITLE FOR THIRD TIME: ANNIVERSARY. Sept 15, 1978. Muhammad Ali became the first fighter to win the heavyweight championship for a third time when he scored a unanimous 15-round decision over Leon Spinks at the Louisiana Superdome. Ali, then known as Cassius Clay, won the title for the first time on Feb 25, 1964, over Sonny Liston. He regained the crown the first time on Oct 30, 1974, by knocking out George Foreman.

ANTIQUE AND CLASSIC CAR SHOW. Sept 15–17. Willow Park, Bennington, VT. Brass cars, Woodies, costume judging and events of skill and dexterity in handling these wonderful machines of yesteryear are all part of this car show. A flea market with auto-related parts and memorabilia entices collectors seeking that elusive fender or gas running lamp. A display and demonstration of antique motorcycles, tractor and farm machinery are also featured. Est attendance: 10,000. For info: Michael Williams, Bennington Area Chamber of Commerce, Veterans Memorial Dr, Bennington, VT 05201. Phone: (802) 447-3311. Fax: (802) 447-1163. E-mail: benncham@sover.net. Web: www.bennington.com.

AUSTRALIA: SUMMER OLYMPICS: OPENING CEREMONY. Sept 15. Sydney, New South Wales. The Opening Ceremony of the XXVIIth Summer Olympic Games. Approximately 10,200 athletes from 198 countries will compete in 296 events in 28 sports. Three women's sports have been added to these games: modern pentathlon, water polo and weightlifting. (Since Sydney is 14 hours ahead of the Eastern time zone in the US, Americans will watch the Opening Ceremony on the evening of Thursday, Sept 14.) For info: Sydney Org Committee for the XXVII Olympic Games, Level 14, Maritime Centre, 207 Kent St, Sydney, NSW 2000, Australia. Phone: (61.2) 9297.2000. Fax: (61.2) 9297.2020. Web: www.sydney.olympic.org.

DODGERS PASS THREE-MILLION MARK: ANNIVERSARY. Sept 15, 1978. The Los Angeles Dodgers became the first major league baseball team to pass the three-million mark in home attendance in a 5–0 victory over the Atlanta Braves.

GOTTLIEB, EDDIE: BIRTH ANNIVERSARY. Sept 15, 1898. Edward (Eddie) Gottlieb, Basketball Hall of Fame executive, born at Kiev, Russia. Barely 20 years old, Gottlieb organized the Philadelphia SPHAS, one of the best early professional basketball teams. He also promoted Negro Leagues baseball and wrestling. Gottlieb owned and coached the Philadelphia Warriors and helped to engineer the merger of the BAA and NBL in 1949. His innovative ideas to improve the game included double-headers involving four teams, outlawing zone defenses and awarding bonus foul shots. He also arranged the NBA's schedule for years. Inducted into the Hall of Fame in 1971. Died at Philadelphia, PA, Dec 7, 1979.

HALL OF FAME CATCH AND RELEASE. Sept 15–17. Lake Chippewa Flowage, Hayward, WI. 5th annual Catch & Release Walleye Tournament, held on the famous

Chippewa Flowage. Fund raiser for Hall's building fund. Entry fee. Cash prizes based on number of entries. Annually, the second weekend after Labor Day. For info: Natl Fresh Water Fishing Hall of Fame, PO Box 33, Hayward, WI 54843. Phone: (715) 634-4440. Fax: (715) 634-4440.

HARLEY, CHIC: 105th BIRTH ANNIVERSARY. Sept 15, 1895. Charles Wesley ("Chic") Harley, football player, born at Chicago, IL. Harley was a three-time All-American at Ohio State (1916–17, 1919) where he set a career scoring record that lasted 36 years. The Buckeyes won every game but one while Harley played. Ohio State constructed massive Ohio Stadium in 1922, nicknaming the structure the "House That Chic Built." Died at Danville, IL, Apr 21, 1974.

JAFFEE, IRVING: BIRTH ANNIVERSARY. Sept 15, 1906. Irving W. Jaffee, Olympic gold medal speed skater, born at New York, NY. Jaffee began skating at the famous Roseland Ballroom and soon developed Olympic aspirations. At the 1928 Games at St. Moritz, he finished fourth in the 5,000 meters and had the best time in the 10,000 when the race was voided because of high temperatures. After retiring for a while to care for his mother, he began competing again and won both races at the 1932 Games at Lake Placid. Died at San Diego, CA, Mar 20, 1981.

JEANNETTE, BUDDY: BIRTH ANNIVERSARY. Sept 15, 1917. Harry Edward ("Buddy") Jeannette, basketball coach and executive and Basketball Hall of Fame guard, born at New Kensington, PA. Jeannette played in three early pro leagues in the 1930s and 1940s and was player-coach of the Baltimore Bullets, 1948 champions in the Basketball Association of America. Inducted into the Hall of Fame in 1994. Died at Nashua, NH, Mar 11, 1998.

NEW HAMPSHIRE HIGHLAND GAMES. Sept 15–17. Loon Mountain, Lincoln, NH. From the tossing of the caber to the lilting melodies of the clarsach plus massed pipe bands on parade, there's something for everyone at New Hampshire's Highland Games: a three-day Scottish festival crammed with music, dance, crafts, athletic events, Scottish food and more. For those of Scottish heritage, there's also a chance to look up one's clan connection, as more than 60 Scottish clans and societies have tents with displays. Admission charged. Est attendance: 35,000. For info: New Hampshire Highland Games, PO Box 4197, Concord, NH 03302-4197. Phone: (603) 229-1975. Fax: (603) 229-7644. E-mail: nhscot @aol.com. Web: www.nhscot.org.

ON THE WATERFRONT SWAP MEET AND CAR SHOW. Sept 15–17. St. Ignace, MI. 10th anniversary. Car show, Corvette and Chevy judging. Plus toy show, truck display and swamp meet. Est attendance: 5,500. For info: Edward K. Reavie, Nostalgia Productions, Inc, 268 Hillcrest Blvd, St. Ignace, MI 49781. Phone: (906) 643-8087. Fax: (906) 643-9784. E-mail: edreavie@nostalgia prod.com. Web: www.autoshows.com.

ORIOLES SET NEW HOME RUN MARK: ANNIVERSARY. Sept 15, 1996. The Baltimore Orioles hit five home runs as they beat the Detroit Tigers, 16–6, to set a new major league record for most home runs in a season by a team. Mark Parent's three-run homer in the 3rd inning wins the record-breaker, the teams's 241st home run of the year, breaking the mark set by the 1961 New York Yankees. The Orioles ended the year with 257 homers.

RICHARD CRANE MEMORIAL TRUCK SHOW. Sept 15–17. St. Ignace, MI. 5th annual show featuring 18-wheeler competition. $2,000 cash Best of Show, Parade of Lights across the Mackinac Bridge. Est attendance: 5,000. For info: Edward K. Reavie, Pres, Nostalgia Productions, Inc, 268 Hillcrest Blvd, St. Ignace, MI 49781. Phone: (906) 643-8087. Fax: (906) 643-9784. E-mail: edreavie@nostalgia-prod.com. Web: www.autoshows.com.

SEPTEMBER 16 — SATURDAY

Day 260 — 106 Remaining

AUSTRALIA: SUMMER OLYMPICS: DAY 2. Sept 16. Sydney, New South Wales. Competition in swimming, water polo, badminton, basketball, boxing, cycling, equestrian, fencing, soccer, gymnastics, team handball, field hockey, judo, shooting, table tennis, triathlon, volleyball, beach volleyball and weight lifting. For info: Sydney Org Committee for the XXVII Olympic Games, Level 14, Maritime Centre, 207 Kent St, Sydney, NSW 2000, Australia. Phone: (61.2) 9297.2000. Fax: (61.2) 9297.2020. Web: www .sydney.olympic.org.

BIDWILL, CHARLES: BIRTH ANNIVERSARY. Sept 16, 1895. Charles W. Bidwill, Sr, Pro Football Hall of Fame executive, born at Chicago, IL. A lawyer, Bidwill purchased the Chicago Cardinals of the NFL in 1933 and served as president of the team until his death. He kept a low profile as an owner but helped build the team that won the 1947 NFL championship several months after his death. Inducted into the Hall of Fame in 1967. Died at Chicago, Apr 19, 1947.

BIRTH OF USAC: 45th ANNIVERSARY. Sept 16, 1955. The United States Auto Club (USAC) was formed to supervise four major categories of auto racing.

BOTTOMLEY DRIVES IN 12 RUNS: ANNIVERSARY. Sept 16, 1924. First baseman Jim Bottomley of the St. Louis Cardinals set a major league record by driving in 12 runs in a single game against the Brooklyn Dodgers. Bottomley got three singles, a double and a pair of home runs as the Cardinals won, 17–3.

BROWNING PITCHES PERFECT GAME: ANNIVERSARY. Sept 16, 1988. Tom Browning of the Cincinnati Reds pitched the 11th perfect game in regular-season major league play, defeating the Los Angeles Dodgers, 1–0.

BROWNS UPSET EAGLES: 50th ANNIVERSARY. Sept 16, 1950. Playing in their first National Football League game, the Cleveland Browns defeated the NFL's defending champs, the Philadelphia Eagles, 35–10. The Browns had joined the NFL after four sterling years in the All-America Football Conference during which they won 47 games, lost four, tied one and captured all four championships. Cleveland carried its success into the NFL, finishing first in the American Conference and winning the league title, 30–28, over the Los Angeles Rams.

BUD LIGHT 2-DAY OPEN BUDDY BASS TOURNAMENT. Sept 16–17. Mark Twain Lake, Blackjack Marina, Perry, MO. This 16th annual event is the largest bass tournament in the state of Missouri. With 500 entries, first place is $10,000. Sponsored by the Golden Eagle District of Hannibal, MO, and the Mark Twain Lake Chamber of Commerce. Annually, the third weekend in September. For info: Mark Twain Lake Chamber of Commerce, PO Box 59, Perry, MO 63462. Phone: (573) 565-2228. Fax: (573) 565-3241.

EQUINOX MARATHON. Sept 16. Fairbanks, AK. 8 AM start. For info: Steve Bainbridge, c/o Running Club North, PO Box 84237, Fairbanks, AK 99708. Phone: (907) 452-8351. E-mail: runner49@ptialaska.net.

HODAG MUSKIE CHALLENGE. Sept 16–17. Rhinelander, WI. $15,000 catch and release Muskie Tournament. Annually, the third weekend in September. Est attendance: 200 Teams. For info: Rhinelander Area Chamber of Commerce, PO Box 795, Rhinelander, WI 54501. Phone: (800) 236-4386. Fax: (715) 365-7467. E-mail: info@ci.rhinelander.wi.us. Web: www.rhinelanderchamber.com.

KING TURKEY DAYS (WITH TURKEY RACE). Sept 16. Worthington, MN. Festival includes parade, speaker, family activities, free pancake breakfast and live turkey race. Est attendance: 15,000. For info: King Turkey Days, Inc, 1121 Third Ave, Worthington, MN 56187. Phone: (800) 279-2919 or (507) 372-2919. Fax: (507) 372-2827.

MOLITOR GETS 3,000th HIT: ANNIVERSARY. Sept 16, 1996. Paul Molitor of the Minnesota Twins got the 3,000th hit of his career, a triple against Jose Rosado of the Kansas City Royals. The Twins lost, 6–5. Molitor became either the 20th or 21st player to reach the 3,000-hit plateau (depending on whether the list includes Adrian ("Cap") Anson, whose statistics are in dispute). He was the first to triple for No. 3,000.

MR TROUT FISHERMAN TOURNAMENT. Sept 16–17. Bennett Springs State Park, Lebanon, MO. 9th annual. Attendees (by invitation only) compete for the coveted Mr Trout trophy presented to the sportsman catching the longest trout. No shavin', no showerin' and lots of guy things. For info on setting up your own Mr Trout competition: PO Box 217, Madison, IL 62060.

SAN DIEGO BAYFAIR PRESENTS THE WORLD SERIES OF POWER BOAT RACING ON MISSION BAY. Sept 16–17. Mission Bay, San Diego, CA. Featured are the Bill Muncey Cup on Mission Bay, Thunderboats (Unlimited Hydroplanes), Formula One PROP Series, International Hot Boat Association Drag Boats, NASBOAT (Unlimited Lights) and more! Only event in the world with all the top motor sport and boating competitions all on the same body of water, all in the same week! Indy

on water! Family festival, vendors, displays, interactive rides, concert and fireworks show. Coverage and advertising on ESPN TV and live radio. Annually, the third weekend of September. Est attendance: 160,000. For info: Thunderboats Unlimited, Inc, 1500 Quivira Way, San Diego, CA 93109. Phone: (619) 225-9160. Fax: (619) 225-9230. E-mail: buff@bayfair.com. Web: www.bayfair.com.

SOUTHWEST IOWA PROFESSIONAL HOT-AIR BALLOON RACES. Sept 16–17. Creston, IA. Hare-and-hound races held at sunrise and sunset, night glow, bathtub races, parade and marching band contest, craft show, flea market and much more. Annually, the third weekend in September. Est attendance: 7,000. For info: Chamber of Commerce, Box 471, Creston, IA 50801. Phone: (515) 782-7021. Fax: (515) 782-9927.

300 OAKS RACE. Sept 16. Bankston School campus, Greenwood, MS. 18th year of 10K run, 5K walk, 1-mile fun run. Trophies and medallions given to winners in age groups of five-year increments in 10K and 5K. Pre-race party on Sept 15 and post-race party including food and drink, after which prizes are awarded. This is a Grand Prix event of the Mississippi Track Club. Outstanding hospitality from the organizers, great race course over flat territory in historic residential area. Annually, the third Saturday in September. Est attendance: 1,000. For info: Janice H. Moor, Exec VP, Greenwood-Leflore County Chamber of Commerce, PO Box 848, Greenwood, MS 38935-0848. Phone: (662) 453-4152. Fax: (662) 453-8003.

TRIATHLON AT PACIFIC GROVE. Sept 16. Pacific Grove, CA. Includes an Olympic-length triathlon and a sprint triathlon. For info: Event Management, Mktg, Promo, Tri-California Events, Inc, 1284 Adobe Ln, PO Box 51116, Pacific Grove, CA 93950. Phone: (831) 373-0678. Fax: (831) 373-7731. E-mail: events@tricalifornia.com. Web: www.tricalifornia.com.

WINFIELD GETS 3,000th HIT: ANNIVERSARY. Sept 16, 1993. Dave Winfield of the Minnesota Twins got the 3,000th hit of his career, a 9th-inning single to left that drove in a run against Dennis Eckersley of the Oakland A's. The Twins won the game, 5–4, in 13 innings. Winfield finished his career with 3,110 hits.

BIRTHDAYS TODAY

Elgin Gay Baylor, 66, former coach and Basketball Hall of Fame forward, born Washington, DC, Sept 16, 1934.

Rosemary (Rosie) Casals, 52, former tennis player, born San Francisco, CA, Sept 16, 1948.

Orel Leonard Quinton Hershiser, IV, 42, baseball player, born Buffalo, NY, Sept 16, 1958.

Chester McGlockton, 31, football player, born Whiteville, NC, Sept 16, 1969.

Mark Alan Parent, 39, baseball player, born Ashland, OR, Sept 16, 1961.

Timothy (Tim) Raines, 41, baseball player, born Sanford, FL, Sept 16, 1959.

Amos Tom Wargo, 58, golfer, born Marlette, MI, Sept 16, 1942.

Robin R. Yount, 45, Baseball Hall of Fame shortstop and outfielder, born Danville, IL, Sept 16, 1955.

SEPTEMBER 17 — SUNDAY
Day 261 — 105 Remaining

AUSTRALIA: SUMMER OLYMPICS: DAY 3. Sept 17. Sydney, New South Wales. Competition in swimming, water polo, archery, badminton, baseball, basketball, boxing, canoe/kayak, cycling, equestrian, fencing, soccer, gymnastics, team handball, field hockey, judo, rowing, sailing, shooting, softball, table tennis, triathlon, volleyball,

September 2000

S	M	T	W	T	F	S
					1	2
3	4	5	6	7	8	9
10	11	12	13	14	15	16
17	18	19	20	21	22	23
24	25	26	27	28	29	30

beach volleyball and weight lifting. For info: Sydney Org Committee for the XXVII Olympic Games, Level 14, Maritime Centre, 207 Kent St, Sydney, NSW 2000, Australia. Phone: (61.2) 9297.2000. Fax: (61.2) 9297.2020. Web: www.sydney.olympic.org.

CAMINITI SETS SWITCH-HIT HOMER RECORD: 5th ANNIVERSARY. Sept 17, 1995. Ken Caminiti of the San Diego Padres, a switch-hitter, hit home runs from both sides of the plate for the second game in a row, an unprecedented feat, as the Padres beat the Chicago Cubs, 11–3. Caminiti did it again on Sept 19. Only 12 players have hit same-game switch-hit homers three times in their entire careers.

CHICHESTER, SIR FRANCIS: BIRTH ANNIVERSARY. Sept 17, 1901. Francis George Chichester, yachtsman and aviator, born at North Devon, England. After graduating from Marlborough College, Chichester piloted airplanes. He flew solo from England to Australia in 1929 and was a navigation officer in the RAF during World War II. He turned to sailing later in life, making a record solo crossing of the Atlantic in 1962 and sailing the *Gypsy Moth* around the world in 1966–67. Knighted in 1967. Died at Plymouth, England, Aug 26, 1972.

CONNOLLY, MAUREEN: BIRTH ANNIVERSARY. Sept 17, 1934. Maureen ("Little Mo") Catherine Connolly Brinker, tennis player, born at San Diego, CA. Connolly became the second-youngest woman to win the US National championship at Forest Hills, NY, when she captured that title in 1951. She repeated in 1952 and won Wimbledon, too. In 1953, she became the first woman to win the Grand Slam, taking the US, French, Australian and Wimbledon championships. After winning a second straight French title and a third straight Wimbledon, she suffered a crushed leg in a horseback riding accident and never competed again. Died at Dallas, TX, June 21, 1969.

FIRST BLACK WOMAN IN USGA EVENT: ANNIVERSARY. Sept 17, 1956. Ann Gregory became the first black woman golfer to play in a USGA national championship when she participated in the Women's Amateur. Marlene Stewart won the championship, contested at Meridian Hills Country Club at Indianapolis, IN, defeating JoAnne Gunderson, 2 and 1.

FOSTER, RUBE: BIRTH ANNIVERSARY. Sept 17, 1879. Andrew ("Rube") Foster, baseball player and Baseball Hall of Fame executive, born at Calvert, TX. The son of a minister, Foster is known as the "Father of Negro Baseball." He was a manager and star pitcher, earning 51 victories in one year. After playing for the Chicago Lelands in 1907 and leading that team to a record of 110 wins and 10 losses, in 1908 he formed the Chicago American Giants who won 129 games and lost only 6 in their first season. In 1919, he called a meeting of black baseball owners and organized the first black baseball league, the Negro National League. He served as its president until his death. Inducted into the Hall of Fame in 1981. Died at Kankakee, IL, Dec 9, 1930.

"HEY RUBE GET A TUBE." Sept 17. Ocean Avenue and Atlantic Ocean, Pt Pleasant Beach, NJ. A parade featuring zany floats, bands, clowns and more, followed by an Ocean Inner Tube Race. Contestants dash into the ocean and paddle backward from one beach to another. Annually, the third Sunday in September. Est attendance: 20,000. For info: Lions Club, PO Box 444, Pt Pleasant, NJ 08742. Phone: (732) 899-3306 or (732) 892-5200. Fax: (732) 892-5505.

JACKSON HITS 500th HOME RUN: ANNIVERSARY. Sept 17, 1984. Reggie Jackson of the New York Yankees became the 13th player to hit 500 home runs in his career when he connected off Bud Black of the Kansas City Royals.

KELLY, DAN: BIRTH ANNIVERSARY. Sept 17, 1936. Daniel (Dan) Kelly, broadcaster, born at Ottawa, Ontario, Canada. Kelly began his broadcasting career at several small radio stations and eventually graduated to covering the Canadian Football League and the Montreal Canadiens. In 1968, he began a 21-year association with the St. Louis Blues and KMOX. His trademark slogan, "He shoots, he scores," made him famous in two countries. Died at Chesterfield, MO, Feb 10, 1989.

NATIONAL FOOTBALL LEAGUE FORMED: 80th ANNIVERSARY. Sept 17, 1920. After a preliminary meeting on Aug 20, at which the owners of four teams formed the American Professional Football Conference, a second meeting at Canton, OH, brought together these teams and others, and the APFC changed its name to the American Professional Football Conference. This league, which played its first games in the fall, later became the National Football League.

YARBROUGH, LEEROY: BIRTH ANNIVERSARY. Sept 17, 1938. Leeroy Yarbrough, auto racer, born at Jacksonville, FL. Yarbrough won 14 races, including 7 in 1969, in 198 career NASCAR starts. Died Dec 7, 1984.

BIRTHDAYS TODAY

George Frederick Blanda, 73, Pro Football Hall of Fame quarterback and placekicker, born Youngwood, PA, Sept 17, 1927.

Mark Allen Brunell, 30, football player, born Los Angeles, CA, Sept 17, 1970.

Orlando Manuel Cepeda, 63, Baseball Hall of Fame first baseman, born Ponce, Puerto Rico, Sept 17, 1937.

John Anthony Franco, 40, baseball player, born New York, NY, Sept 17, 1960.

Philip D. (Phil) Jackson, 55, basketball coach and former player, born Deer Lodge, MT, Sept 17, 1945.

Scott William Simpson, 45, golfer, born San Diego, CA, Sept 17, 1955.

Rasheed Abdul Wallace, 26, basketball player, born Philadelphia, PA, Sept 17, 1974.

Rob Zamuner, 31, hockey player, born Oakville, Ontario, Canada, Sept 17, 1969.

SEPTEMBER 18 — MONDAY
Day 262 — 104 Remaining

AUSTRALIA: SUMMER OLYMPICS: DAY 4. Sept 18. Sydney, New South Wales. Competition in swimming, water polo, archery, badminton, baseball, basketball, boxing, canoe/kayak, cycling, equestrian, fencing, gymnastics, team handball, field hockey, judo, rowing, sailing, shooting, softball, table tennis, volleyball and beach volleyball. For info: Sydney Org Committee for the XXVII Olympic Games, Level 14, Maritime Centre, 207 Kent St, Sydney, NSW 2000, Australia. Phone: (61.2) 9297.2000. Fax: (61.2) 9297.2020. Web: www.sydney.olympic.org.

BANKHEAD, SAM: 90th BIRTH ANNIVERSARY. Sept 18, 1910. Samuel (Sam) Bankhead, baseball player and manager, born at Empire, AL. Bankhead starred for several teams in the Negro Leagues from 1930 to 1950. In 1951 he became organized baseball's first black manager, handling the Farnham team in the Provincial League. Died at Pittsburgh, PA, July 24, 1976.

CLEMENS STRIKES OUT 20 AGAIN: ANNIVERSARY. Sept 18, 1996. Pitcher Roger Clemens of the Boston Red Sox tied his own record for most strikeouts in a nine-inning game when he struck out 20 Detroit Tigers in a 4–0 Red Sox victory. Clemens set the record on Apr 29, 1986, against the Seattle Mariners.

CROSLEY, POWEL: BIRTH ANNIVERSARY. Sept 18, 1886. Powel Crosley, Jr, baseball executive, born at Cincinnati, OH. Crosley took a fortune made in the radio and appliance businesses and bought the Cincinnati Reds. He introduced night baseball to the majors in 1935 and generally let baseball men run his club. Died at Cincinnati, Mar 28, 1961.

IRON HORSE OUTRACED BY HORSE: 170th ANNIVERSARY. Sept 18, 1830. In a widely celebrated race, the first locomotive built in America, the Tom Thumb, lost to a horse. Mechanical difficulties plagued the steam engine over the nine-mile course between Riley's Tavern and Baltimore, MD, and a boiler leak prevented the locomotive from finishing the race. In the early days of trains, engines were nicknamed "Iron Horses."

TWO DAYS, TWO NO-HITTERS: ANNIVERSARY. Sept 18, 1968. Ray Washburn of the St. Louis Cardinals pitched a no-hitter against the San Francisco Giants one day after the Giants' Gaylord Perry no-hit the Cardinals.

BIRTHDAYS TODAY

William Scott (Scotty) Bowman, 67, Hockey Hall of Fame coach, born Montreal, Quebec, Canada, Sept 18, 1933.
Tom Chorske, 34, hockey player, born Minneapolis, MN, Sept 18, 1966.
Toni Kukoc, 32, basketball player, born Split, Croatia, Sept 18, 1968.
Everett Eric Lindsay, 30, football player, born Burlington, IA, Sept 18, 1970.
Richard (Rick) Pitino, 48, basketball coach, born New York, NY, Sept 18, 1952.
Ryne Dee Sandberg, 41, former baseball player, born Spokane, WA, Sept 18, 1959.

SEPTEMBER 19 — TUESDAY

Day 263 — 103 Remaining

AUSTRALIA: SUMMER OLYMPICS: DAY 5. Sept 19. Sydney, New South Wales. Competition in swimming, water polo, archery, badminton, baseball, basketball, boxing, canoe/kayak, cycling, equestrian, fencing, soccer, gymnastics, team handball, field hockey, judo, rowing, sailing, shooting, softball, table tennis, tennis, volleyball, beach volleyball and weight lifting. For info: Sydney Org Committee for the XXVII Olympic Games, Level 14, Maritime Centre, 207 Kent St, Sydney, NSW 2000, Australia. Phone: (61.2) 9297.2000. Fax: (61.2) 9297.2020. Web: www.sydney.olympic.org.

September 2000

S	M	T	W	T	F	S
					1	2
3	4	5	6	7	8	9
10	11	12	13	14	15	16
17	18	19	20	21	22	23
24	25	26	27	28	29	30

CONERLY, CHARLIE: BIRTH ANNIVERSARY. Sept 19, 1921. Charles Albert (Charlie) Conerly, Jr, football player, born at Clarksdale, MS. Conerly played halfback at the University of Mississippi for two years before entering the Marine Corps during World War II. He returned to Ole Miss in 1946, switched to quarterback and became an All-American a year later. He played 14 years with the New York Giants, won the Rookie of the Year Award in 1948 and was named MVP in 1959. He is often considered one of the greatest players not in the Pro Football Hall of Fame. Died at Memphis, TN, Feb 13, 1996.

FRICK ELECTED COMMISSIONER: ANNIVERSARY. Sept 19, 1951. National League President Ford C. Frick was elected the third Commissioner of Baseball, replacing Albert B. ("Happy") Chandler. Frick, a former sportswriter, served until 1965.

KINER HITS 50 FOR THE SECOND TIME: ANNIVERSARY. Sept 19, 1949. Ralph Kiner of the Pittsburgh Pirates hit his 50th home run of the season to become the first player in National League history to reach the 50 mark twice. After hitting 51 homers in 1947, Kiner finished the year with 54.

PORSCHE, FERRY: BIRTH ANNIVERSARY. Sept 19, 1909. Ferdinand (Ferry) Porsche, auto maker, born at Wiener-Neustadt, Austria. Porsche ran Porsche AG, the company founded by his father, and in the wake of World War II, turned the company toward producing a luxury sports car. The result was an auto of surpassing excellence that succeeds both in the luxury car market and in racing. Died at Zell am See, Austria, Mar 27, 1998.

RODRIGUEZ JOINS 40-40 CLUB: ANNIVERSARY. Sept 19, 1998. Shortstop Alex Rodriguez of the Seattle Mariners hit his 40th home run of the season to become the third player ever to hit 40 homers and steal 40 bases in the same season. The homer came in a game against the Anaheim Angels. "A-Rod" finished the year with 42 home runs and 46 steals.

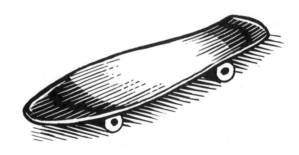

BIRTHDAYS TODAY

James Anthony (Jim) Abbott, 33, baseball player, born Flint, MI, Sept 19, 1967.
Roger Angell, 80, sportswriter, born New York, NY, Sept 19, 1920.
Jim Druckenmiller, 28, football player, born Allentown, PA, Sept 19, 1972.
Brian Alfred Hill, 53, basketball coach, born East Orange, NJ, Sept 19, 1947.
Katrina McClain, 35, basketball player, born Washington, DC, Sept 19, 1965.
Joe Leonard Morgan, 57, broadcaster and Baseball Hall of Fame second baseman, born Bonham, TX, Sept 19, 1943.
Randall Kirk (Randy) Myers, 38, baseball player, born Vancouver, WA, Sept 19, 1962.
Alfred Adolph (Al) Oerter, Jr, 64, Olympic gold medal discus thrower, born New York, NY, Sept 19, 1936.
Edwin Donald ("Duke") Snider, 74, Baseball Hall of Fame outfielder, born Los Angeles, CA, Sept 19, 1926.

SEPTEMBER 20 — WEDNESDAY
Day 264 — 102 Remaining

CHASE'S SPORTSQUOTE OF THE DAY

"I was sure I could beat any woman player in the world." —Bobby Riggs

ALEXANDER WINS 300th GAME: ANNIVERSARY. Sept 20, 1924. Pitcher Grover Cleveland Alexander of the Chicago Cubs won the 300th game of his career, defeating the New York Giants, 7–3, in 12 innings. Alexander finished his career with 373 wins.

AUSTRALIA: SUMMER OLYMPICS: DAY 6. Sept 20. Sydney, New South Wales. Competition in swimming, water polo, archery, badminton, baseball, basketball, boxing, canoe/kayak, cycling, equestrian, fencing, soccer, gymnastics, team handball, field hockey, judo, rowing, sailing, shooting, softball, table tennis, tennis, volleyball and weight lifting. For info: Sydney Org Committee for the XXVII Olympic Games, Level 14, Maritime Centre, 207 Kent St, Sydney, NSW 2000, Australia. Phone: (61.2) 9297 .2000. Fax: (61.2) 9297.2020. Web: www.sydney.olympic .org.

BILLIE JEAN KING WINS THE "BATTLE OF THE SEXES": ANNIVERSARY. Sept 20, 1973. Billie Jean King defeated Bobby Riggs in the nationally televised "Battle of the Sexes" tennis match in three straight sets.

DRESSEN, CHARLIE: BIRTH ANNIVERSARY. Sept 20, 1898. Charles Walter (Charlie) Dressen, baseball player and manager, born at Decatur, IL. Dressen played infield in the major leagues with several teams, but made his mark as manager of the Brooklyn Dodgers from 1951 through 1953 and three other teams. He was at the Dodgers' helm when they lost the 1951 National League play-off to the New York Giants. Died at Detroit, MI, Aug 10, 1966.

GOLDEN ASPEN MOTORCYCLE RALLY. Sept 20–24. Ruidoso, NM. Trade show, bike shows, riding tours, skill events, parade, awards banquet, stunt shows and thousands in prizes. Est attendance: 20,000. For info: Golden Aspen Rally Assn, PO Box 1458, Ruidoso, NM 88355. Phone: (800) 452-8045. Web: www.motorcyclerally.com.

MORANDINI MAKES UNASSISTED TRIPLE PLAY: ANNIVERSARY. Sept 20, 1992. Second baseman Mickey Morandini of the Philadelphia Phillies recorded the 10th unassisted triple play in major league history in a game against the Pittsburgh Pirates. In the 6th inning, Morandini caught a line drive hit by Jeff King, stepped on second base to retire Andy Van Slyke and tagged Barry Bonds before he could return to first.

RIPKEN'S STREAK ENDS: ANNIVERSARY. Sept 20, 1998. Cal Ripken of the Baltimore Orioles removed himself from the starting lineup, thereby snapping his streak of consecutive games played at a record 2,632. Ripken approached manager Ray Miller before a game against the New York Yankees and announced that it was time for him to take a day off. The game, won by New York, 5–4, was the Orioles' final home game of the season. Ripken's streak had begun on May 30, 1982.

ST. LOUIS NATIONAL CHARITY HORSE SHOW. Sept 20–30. American Exposition Park, Lake St. Louis, MO. 22nd annual. More than 800 horses, 4,000 owners and families, trainers and groomers from more than 40 states will participate in this two-week event. The Hunter/Jumper Show will be held Sept 20–24 followed by the Saddlebred/Arabian/Road Ponies/Western Show Sept 27–30. Est attendance: 20,000. For info: President, St. Louis National Charity Horse Show, 16419 Village Plaza View, Wildwood, MO 63011-4913. Phone: (636) 458-7994. Fax: (636) 458-8511.

BIRTHDAYS TODAY

Arnold Jacob ("Red") Auerbach, 83, Basketball Hall of Fame coach, born New York, NY, Sept 20, 1917.
Donald A. Hall, 72, author (*Fathers Playing Catch with Sons*), born New Haven, CT, Sept 20, 1928.
Bobby Hoying, 28, football player, born St. Henry, OH, Sept 20, 1972.
Guy Damien Lafleur, 49, Hockey Hall of Fame right wing, born Thurso, Quebec, Canada, Sept 20, 1951.
Ronald McKinnon, 27, football player, born Ft Rucker Army Base, AL, Sept 20, 1973.
James Charles (Jim) Taylor, 65, Pro Football Hall of Fame fullback, born Baton Rouge, LA, Sept 20, 1935.
Gawen Deangelo ("Bonzi") Wells, 24, basketball player, born Muncie, IN, Sept 20, 1976.

SEPTEMBER 21 — THURSDAY
Day 265 — 101 Remaining

ASA WOMEN'S CLASS D SLOW PITCH NATIONAL CHAMPIONSHIP. Sept 21–24. Shreveport, LA. For info: ASA-USA Softball, 2801 NE 50th St, Oklahoma City, OK 73111. Phone: (405) 424-5266. Fax: (405) 424-3855. E-mail: info@softball.org. Web: www.softball.org.

AUSTRALIA: SUMMER OLYMPICS: DAY 7. Sept 21. Sydney, New South Wales. Competition in swimming, archery, badminton, baseball, basketball, boxing, cycling, equestrian, fencing, gymnastics, team handball, field hockey, judo, rowing, sailing, shooting, softball, table tennis, tennis, volleyball and beach volleyball. For info: Sydney Org Committee for the XXVII Olympic Games, Level 14, Maritime Centre, 207 Kent St, Sydney, NSW 2000, Australia. Phone: (61.2) 9297.2000. Fax: (61.2) 9297.2020. Web: www.sydney.olympic.org.

BIRTH OF MONDAY NIGHT FOOTBALL: 30th ANNIVERSARY. Sept 21, 1970. Following the complete merger of the American Football League and the National Football League, ABC joined CBS and NBC in televising weekly games with the debut of "Monday Night Football." The show began as an experiment but soon became an institution. Announcers Howard Cosell, Keith Jackson and Don Meredith called the first game, a 31–21 victory by the Cleveland Browns over the New York Jets.

FIRST NOTABLE INTERNATIONAL TRACK AND FIELD MEET: 105th ANNIVERSARY. Sept 21, 1895. The first international track and field competition of notable significance was held at Manhattan Field, New York, between the New York Athletic Club and the London Athletic Club. Eleven events were contested, and Americans won all of them. Bernard Wefers ran the 100-yard dash in 9.8 seconds, and Thomas Conneff won both the mile run in 4:18.2 and the three-mile run in 15:36.2.

JETS AND DOLPHINS PASS FOR 884 YARDS: ANNIVERSARY. Sept 21, 1986. The New York Jets and Miami Dolphins combined for a record 884 passing yards and scored 96 points between them, including 13 touchdowns and a pair of field goals. Quarterback Ken O'Brien completed four touchdown passes to wide receiver Wesley Walker, including the game-winner in overtime. The final score: New York 51, Miami 45.

LITTLE BROWN JUG. Sept 21. Delaware County Fairgrounds, Delaware, OH. The Little Brown Jug brings together the best pacing horses in the world to race for more than $500,000. The contest will draw racing fans from three continents, swelling the small but picturesque town's population from 16,000 to 60,000 in a single day! Est attendance: 55,000. For info: US Trotting Assn, 750 Michigan Ave, Columbus, OH 43215. Phone: (614) 224-2291. Fax: (614) 224-4575. E-mail: jpawlak@ustrotting.com. Web: www.ustrotting.com.

MICHAEL SPINKS WINS HEAVYWEIGHT TITLE: ANNIVERSARY. Sept 21, 1985. Michael Spinks won the heavyweight championship by taking a unanimous 15-round decision over Larry Holmes at Las Vegas. Spinks held the title until June 27, 1988, when he was knocked out by Mike Tyson in the first round.

NORWALK INTERNATIONAL IN-WATER BOAT SHOW. Sept 21–24. Norwalk Cove Marina, Norwalk, CT. 25th annual. For info: NMMA Boat Shows, 600 Third Ave, 23rd Floor, New York, NY 10016. Phone: (212) 922-1212. Fax: (212) 922-9607. Web: www.boatshows.com.

RAY, SHORTY: BIRTH ANNIVERSARY. Sept 21, 1884. Hugh L. ("Shorty") Ray, Pro Football Hall of Fame official, born at Highland Park, IL. Ray was the NFL Supervisor of Officials from 1938 through 1952. He wrote the high school rule book that became the basis for all football rule books. He raised the quality of officiating by conducting seminars and requiring officials to take written exams. Inducted into the Hall of Fame in 1966. Died Sept 16, 1956.

BIRTHDAYS TODAY

Kevin Louis Carter, 27, football player, born Tallahassee, FL, Sept 21, 1973.

Danny Bradford Cox, 41, former baseball player, born Northampton, England, Sept 21, 1959.

Bob Errey, 36, hockey player, born Montreal, Quebec, Canada, Sept 21, 1964.

Cecil Grant Fielder, 37, former baseball player, born Los Angeles, CA, Sept 21, 1963.

Artis Gilmore, 51, former basketball player, born Chipley, FL, Sept 21, 1949.

Curtis Michael Leschyshyn, 31, hockey player, born Thompson, Manitoba, Canada, Sept 21, 1969.

Tab Ramos, 34, soccer player, born Montevideo, Uruguay, Sept 21, 1966.

Scott Edward Spezio, 28, baseball player, born Joliet, IL, Sept 21, 1972.

SEPTEMBER 22 — FRIDAY
Day 266 — 100 Remaining

CHASE'S SPORTSQUOTE OF THE DAY

"A pitcher's got to be good, and he's got to be lucky to get a no-hit game."—Cy Young

ANDERSON, HUNK: BIRTH ANNIVERSARY. Sept 22, 1898. Heartley William ("Hunk") Anderson, football player and coach, born at Tamarack, MI. Anderson played at Notre Dame under Knute Rockne and then with the Chicago Bears. In 1926, he became Rockne's full-time assistant and was named head coach after Rockne was

killed in a 1931 plane crash. After three seasons he moved to North Carolina State University and then served as line coach for several college and pro teams. Died at West Palm Beach, FL, Apr 24, 1978.

ASA MEN'S CLASS B SLOW PITCH NATIONAL CHAMPIONSHIP. Sept 22–24. Lakeland, FL. For info: ASA-USA Softball, 2801 NE 50th St, Oklahoma City, OK 73111. Phone: (405) 424-5266. Fax: (405) 424-3855. E-mail: info@softball.org. Web: www.softball.org.

ASA MEN'S CLASS C SLOW PITCH NATIONAL CHAMPIONSHIP. Sept 22–24. Marietta, GA. For info: ASA-USA Softball, 2801 NE 50th St, Oklahoma City, OK 73111. Phone: (405) 424-5266. Fax: (405) 424-3855. E-mail: info@softball.org. Web: www.softball.org.

ASA MEN'S CLASS D SLOW PITCH NATIONAL CHAMPIONSHIP. Sept 22–24. Montgomery, AL. For info: ASA-USA Softball, 2801 NE 50th St, Oklahoma City, OK 73111. Phone: (405) 424-5266. Fax: (405) 424-3855. E-mail: info@softball.org. Web: www.softball.org.

ASA WOMEN'S CLASS B SLOW PITCH NATIONAL CHAMPIONSHIP. Sept 22–24. Gadsden, AL. For info: ASA-USA Softball, 2801 NE 50th St, Oklahoma City, OK 73111. Phone: (405) 424-5266. Fax: (405) 424-3855. E-mail: info@softball.org. Web: www.softball.org.

AUSTRALIA: SUMMER OLYMPICS: DAY 8. Sept 22. Sydney, New South Wales. Competition in swimming, diving, water polo, archery, track & field, badminton, baseball, basketball, boxing, equestrian, fencing, trampoline, team handball, field hockey, judo, rowing, sailing, shooting, softball, table tennis, tennis, volleyball, beach volleyball and weight lifting. For info: Sydney Org Committee for the XXVII Olympic Games, Level 14, Maritime Centre, 207 Kent St, Sydney, NSW 2000, Australia. Phone: (61.2) 9297.2000. Fax: (61.2) 9297.2020. Web: www.sydney.olympic.org.

AUTUMN. Sept 22–Dec 21. In the Northern Hemisphere, autumn begins today with the autumnal equinox, at 1:27 PM, EDT. Note that in the Southern Hemisphere today is the beginning of spring. Everywhere on Earth (except near the poles) the sun rises due east and sets due west, and daylight length is nearly identical—about 12 hours, 8 minutes.

BOXING'S LONG COUNT: ANNIVERSARY. Sept 22, 1927. In a heavyweight title fight between champion Gene Tunney and former champ Jack Dempsey, Tunney was knocked down in the 7th round. Following the rules, referee Dave Barry refused to begin the count until the hovering Dempsey moved to a neutral corner. The extra few seconds allowed Tunney time to recover and get up at the count of nine. He won the fight and retained the title. The fight, held at Soldier Field at Chicago, grossed $990,446, the largest fight purse to that time. Nearly half the population of the US is believed to have listened to the radio broadcast. Dempsey's appeal of the decision was denied, and he never fought again. Tunney retired the following year after one more (successful) fight.

FLATLANDERS FALL FESTIVAL. Sept 22–24. Goodland, KS. Classic on Friday and Saturday features mini-sprint stock car races, Fall Festival on Saturday on Main Street is a street festival featuring crafts, food, entertainment, also on Saturday, the Motorcycle Show features Harleys, Hondas, Kawasakis, all brands, all accessories, Saturday and Sunday, the Early Iron Car Club Rod Run on Highways 24 and 27. Est attendance: 9,000. For other info: Goodland Chamber of Commerce, 104 W 11th, PO Box 628, Goodland, KS 67735. Phone: (913) 899-7130. Fax: (913) 899-3061.

MAYS HITS 600th HOME RUN: ANNIVERSARY. Sept 22, 1969. Willie Mays of the San Francisco Giants hit the

September 2000	S	M	T	W	T	F	S
						1	2
	3	4	5	6	7	8	9
	10	11	12	13	14	15	16
	17	18	19	20	21	22	23
	24	25	26	27	28	29	30

600th home run of his career, a pinch-hit homer against Mike Corkins of the San Diego Padres. Mays broke a 2–2 tie, and the Giants won, 4–2. He finished his career with 660 homers and was inducted into the Hall of Fame in 1979.

RACKING WORLD CELEBRATION. Sept 22–30. Decatur, AL. Weeklong event featuring racking horses from across the nation. The highlight of the 75-class event is the crowning of the World Grand Racking Horse Champion on the last night. Annually, the last full week in September. Est attendance: 25,000. For info: Jacklyn Bailey, Decatur CVB, 719 6th Ave SE, Decatur, AL 35602. Phone: (256) 350-2028 or (800) 524-6181. E-mail: dcvb@hi waay.net.

RIVER CITY ROUNDUP AND RODEO. Sept 22–27. Omaha, NE. Take a moment to reflect on the Midwest's proud past. A celebration of Omaha's agricultural and western heritage, including PRCA rodeo, barbecue and chili contests, trail rides, the world's largest 4-H Livestock Expo and a downtown parade. Est attendance: 300,000. For info: Christy Aegerter, Program Mgr, River City Roundup and Rodeo, 6800 Mercy Rd, Ste 206, Omaha, NE 68106. Phone: (402) 554-9610 or (402) 554-9611. Fax: (402) 554-9609. E-mail: knights@aksarben.org. Web: www.aksarben.org.

SPECIAL OLYMPICS FLORIDA STATE GOLF CHAM-PIONSHIPS. Sept 22–23. Gainesville, FL. Olympic-style competition for children and adults with mental retardation. For info: Special Olympics Florida, 8 Broadway, Ste D, Kissimmee, FL 34741. Phone: (407) 870-2292. Fax: (407) 870-9810.

TOVAR PLAYS ALL NINE POSITIONS: ANNIVERSARY. Sept 22, 1968. Cesar Tovar of the Minnesota Twins played all nine positions in a single game, one inning at each position. Tovar became the second player to perform this feat. Bert Campaneris did it on Sept 8, 1965.

YOUNG'S FINAL WIN: ANNIVERSARY. Sept 22, 1911. Cy Young, pitching for the Boston Braves, won the 511th and last game of his career, a 1–0 shutout against the Pittsburgh Pirates. Young holds the record for most games won in a career.

BIRTHDAYS TODAY

Vincent Maurice (Vince) Coleman, 39, former baseball player, born Jacksonville, FL, Sept 22, 1961.
Lawrence Edward (Larry) Dierker, 54, baseball manager, former broadcaster and player, born Hollywood, CA, Sept 22, 1946.
Pat Falloon, 28, hockey player, born Foxwarren, Manitoba, Canada, Sept 22, 1972.
Mark Hirschbeck, 40, baseball umpire, born Bridgeport, CT, Sept 22, 1960.

Thomas Charles (Tommy) Lasorda, 73, Baseball Hall of Fame manager, born Norristown, PA, Sept 22, 1927.
Robert Granville (Bob) Lemon, 80, former baseball manager and Baseball Hall of Fame pitcher, born San Bernardino, CA, Sept 22, 1920.
Michael Scott (Mike) Matheny, 30, baseball player, born Reynoldsburg, OH, Sept 22, 1970.
Michael Thomas (Mike) Richter, 34, hockey player, born Philadelphia, PA, Sept 22, 1966.
Gary Dajaun Trent, 26, basketball player, born Columbus, OH, Sept 22, 1974.

SEPTEMBER 23 — SATURDAY
Day 267 — 99 Remaining

ALOU TRIFECTA: ANNIVERSARY. Sept 23, 1996. Montreal Expos outfielder Moises Alou flied out to right field against the Atlanta Braves to make the final out in the final regular-season game ever played at Atlanta-Fulton County Stadium. The Braves won, 3–1. Alou's out completed an unusual family coincidence. In the first game played at the same park on Apr 12, 1966, Moises's uncle, Matty Alou, was the first batter for the visiting Pittsburgh Pirates. His father, Felipe Alou, was the Braves' first batter. Pittsburgh won that game, 3–2, in 13 innings.

AT&T WIRELESS SERVICES KOKOPELLI TRAIL MAR-ATHON. Sept 23. Grand Junction, CO. On the beautiful Kokopelli Trail. Marathon, half-marathon, 10K and 50K ultra. For info: Event Mktg Group, PO Box 60217, Grand Junction, CO 81506. Phone: (970) 242-7802. E-mail: emgmh@gj.net.

AUSTRALIA: SUMMER OLYMPICS: DAY 9. Sept 23. Sydney, New South Wales. Competition in swimming, water polo, track & field, badminton, baseball, basketball, boxing, cycling, fencing, soccer, trampoline, team handball, field hockey, rowing, sailing, shooting, softball, table tennis, tennis, volleyball, beach volleyball and weight lifting. For info: Sydney Org Committee for the XXVII Olympic Games, Level 14, Maritime Centre, 207 Kent St, Sydney, NSW 2000, Australia. Phone: (61.2) 9297.2000. Fax: (61.2) 9297.2020. Web: www.sydney.olympic.org.

BASEBALL'S GREATEST DISPUTE: ANNIVERSARY. Sept 23, 1908. In an important game between the Chicago Cubs and the New York Giants, the National League pennant race erupted in controversy during the bottom of the ninth with the score tied, 1–1, at the Polo Grounds, New York, NY. New York was at bat with two men on. The batter hit safely to center field, apparently scoring the winning run. But Chicago claimed that the runner on first, Fred Merkle, seeing the run score, headed toward the clubhouse without touching second base. Chicago second baseman Johnny Evers attempted to get the ball and force Merkle at second, but he was prevented from doing so by the fans streaming onto the field. Harry C. Pulliam, NL president, upheld Evers's position and called the game a tie. When the game was replayed, the Cubs won 4–2. Fairly or not, the disputed play quickly became known as "Merkle's Boner."

BRIGGS AND STRATTON/AL'S RUN AND WALK FOR CHILDREN'S HOSPITAL OF WISCONSIN. Sept 23. Milwaukee, WI. Choose from an 8K run, 4-mile walk or 2.5-mile walk along the lake and through the streets. Benefit fundraiser named after Al McGuire, network basketball announcer. Finish line party on Summerfest grounds with free entertainment and fitness expo. Est attendance: 18,000. For info: Children's Hospital Foundation, Briggs & Stratton/Al's Run & Walk, PO Box 1997 MS#3050, Milwaukee, WI 53201. Fax: (414) 266-6139. E-mail: alsrun@execpc.com. Web: www.alsrun.execpc .com.

CANSECO REACHES 40-40 CLUB: ANNIVERSARY. Sept 23, 1988. Jose Canseco of the Oakland A's became the first player ever to hit 40 home runs and steal 40 bases in the same season. In a game against the Milwaukee Brewers, he hit his 41st homer of the season and stole two bases, Nos. 39 and 40. The A's won, 9–8, in 14 innings.

CARLTON WINS 300th GAME: ANNIVERSARY. Sept 23, 1983. Steve Carlton of the Philadelphia Phillies won the 300th game of his career, 6–2 over the St. Louis Cardinals, the team that traded him to the Phillies in 1972. Carlton finished his career with 329 victories and was inducted into the Hall of Fame in 1994.

CITIBANK FALL CUP REGATTA. Sept 23–24. San Francisco, CA. Make way for the 2000 Citibank Fall Cup Regatta, presented by KICU TV-36! Come on down to Pier 39 and watch the world's finest sailors battle it out in the exciting 11:Metre yachting action. America's Cup participants, Olympic veterans and previous world champions match wits in the longest running, continuous, professional series in the Bay Area. Watch this unique sporting event from the start/finish line at Pier 39, as the fleet combines strategy, skill and teamwork to bring home the Citibank Cup. The stage is set as these sleek racing vessels take to the demanding waters of San Francisco Bay to grab their share of $10,000 in prize money. Don't be left high and dry, set your sails for the hottest sailing spectacle around. For info: Pier 39 Market Development, PO Box 193730, San Francisco, CA 94119-3730. Phone: (415) 705-5500. Fax: (415) 956-2911. E-mail: jb@pier39 .com. Web: www.pier39.com.

FAMILY HEALTH AND FITNESS DAYS—USA. Sept 23–24. 3rd annual event promoting family health and fitness. During these days families across the country will be involved in locally organized health promotion activities at more than 800 locations. Annually, the last weekend in September. For info: Maria Tuthill, Program Coord, Health Information Resource Center, 621 E Park Ave, Libertyville, IL 60048. Phone: (800) 828-8225. Fax: (847) 816-8662. E-mail: hlthinfo@aol.com. Web: www.fitness day.com.

FIRST FRONTIER DAYS: ANNIVERSARY. Sept 23, 1897. The city of Cheyenne, WY, held its first Frontier Days celebration, a one-day rodeo featuring a competition roping horses that had never been roped before. Frontier Days has grown to be the largest rodeo in the world.

		S	**M**	**T**	**W**	**T**	**F**	**S**
September							1	2
2000		3	4	5	6	7	8	9
		10	11	12	13	14	15	16
		17	18	19	20	21	22	23
		24	25	26	27	28	29	30

★ **NATIONAL HUNTING AND FISHING DAY.** Sept 23. Presidential Proclamation 4682, of Sept 11, 1979, covers all succeeding years. Annually, the fourth Saturday of September.

OCEAN COUNTY DECOY AND GUNNING SHOW. Sept 23–24. Pinelands High & Middle Schools and Tip Seaman County Park, Tuckerton, NJ. Gathering to celebrate the local waterfowling heritage. Emphasizes traditional skills such as decoy carving, working decoy rigs, sneakbox building, gunning, retrieving and goose calling contests. More than 500 vendors. Est attendance: 50,000. For info: Lillian Hoey, Asst Show Coord, Wells Mills County Park, 905 Wells Mills Rd, Waretown, NJ 08758. Phone: (609) 971-3085. Fax: (609) 971-9540.

QUICKEST BOXING MATCH: ANNIVERSARY. Sept 23, 1946. Al Couture recorded the quickest knockout in boxing history, flooring Ralph Walton with only half a second gone in the first round. Couture threw the knockout punch while Walton was still sitting in his corner adjusting his mouthpiece.

RHEAUME FIRST FEMALE IN NHL: ANNIVERSARY. Sept 23, 1992. 20-year-old Manon Rheaume became the first woman to play in an NHL game when the Tampa Bay Lightning took on the St. Louis Blues in an exhibition. Rheaume led the Lightning onto the ice, made seven saves in one period of action and left with the game tied, 2–2.

TRIPLE PICKOFF: ANNIVERSARY. Sept 23, 1886. Pittsburgh pitcher Pud Galvin walked the bases loaded in a game against Brooklyn. He then picked George Smith off first, Bill McClellan off second and Jim McTamany off third.

US SENIOR AMATEUR (GOLF) CHAMPIONSHIP. Sept 23–28. Charlotte Country Club, Charlotte, NC. For info: US Golf Assn, Golf House, Far Hills, NJ 07931. Phone: (908) 234-2300. Fax: (908) 234-9687. E-mail: usga@usga .org. Web: www.usga.org.

WILLS BREAKS COBB'S RECORD: ANNIVERSARY. Sept 23, 1962. Maury Wills of the Los Angeles Dodgers stole his 96th and 97th bases of the season to tie and then break Ty Cobb's record for most stolen bases in a season, set in 1915. Wills finished the year with 104 stolen bases and won the National League's MVP award.

BIRTHDAYS TODAY

Donald Audette, 31, hockey player, born Laval, Quebec, Canada, Sept 23, 1969.

Jeffrey Howard (Jeff) Cirillo, 31, baseball player, born Pasadena, CA, Sept 23, 1969.

Emilion Antonio (Tony) Fossas, 43, baseball player, born Havana, Cuba, Sept 23, 1957.

Peter Thomas (Pete) Harnisch, 34, baseball player, born Commack, NY, Sept 23, 1966.

Tony Joseph Mandarich (born Ante Josip Mandarich), 34, football player, born Oakville, Ontario, Canada, Sept 23, 1966.

Larry Hogan Mize, 42, golfer, born Augusta, GA, Sept 23, 1958.

Eric Scott Montross, 29, basketball player, born Indianapolis, IN, Sept 23, 1971.

Christopher J. (Chris) Palmer, 51, football coach, born Brewster, NY, Sept 23, 1949.

SEPTEMBER 24 — SUNDAY

Day 268 — 98 Remaining

CHASE'S SPORTSQUOTE OF THE DAY

"Golf is an awkward set of bodily contortions designed to produce a graceful result."—Tommy Armour

ARMOUR, TOMMY: BIRTH ANNIVERSARY. Sept 24, 1895. Thomas Dickson (Tommy) Armour, golfer, born at Edinburgh, Scotland. Blinded in one eye during World War I, Armour became one of the great golfers of the 1920s. He won every important tournament and, after retiring, became a prominent teaching pro. He improved the games of the likes of Bobby Jones and Babe Didrikson Zaharias. Died at Larchmont, NY, Sept 11, 1968.

AUSTRALIA: SUMMER OLYMPICS: DAY 10. Sept 24. Sydney, New South Wales. Competition in diving, synchronized swimming, water polo, track & field, baseball, basketball, boxing, cycling, fencing, soccer, gymnastics, team handball, field hockey, rowing, sailing, table tennis, tennis, volleyball, beach volleyball, weight lifting and wrestling. For info: Sydney Org Committee for the XXVII Olympic Games, Level 14, Maritime Centre, 207 Kent St, Sydney, NSW 2000, Australia. Phone: (61.2) 9297 .2000. Fax: (61.2) 9297.2020. Web: www.sydney.olympic .org.

BANKOH NA WAHINE O KE KAI. Sept 24. Molokai to Oahu, HI. 22nd annual. Women's 40.8-mile, six-person championship outrigger canoe race. More than 75 teams of the best female outrigger canoe paddlers in the world compete for the championship title. Competitors come from Australia, New Zealand, mainland US, Canada, Tahiti and other countries. Traditionally, the Aloha Festivals Court is waiting to formally welcome the finishers when they arrive on the beach. Est attendance: 4,000. For media info: Carol Hogan, Ocean Promotion, (808) 325-7400 or Linda Chinn, Bank of Hawaii, (808) 537-8658. For race info: Hannie Anderson, (808) 262-7567.

CANADA: CHARLOTTETOWN PARKS & RECREATION/ATLANTIC SUPERSTORE ISLAND MARATHON. Sept 24 (tentative). Charlottetown, Prince Edward Island. For info: Wayne Long and Dave Campbell, 1 Kirkdale Rd, Charlottetown, PE, Canada C1E 1R3. Phone: (902) 368-1025. E-mail: wlong@city.charlottetown.pe.ca.

FOXX HITS 500th HOME RUN: 60th ANNIVERSARY. Sept 24, 1940. Jimmie Foxx of the Boston Red Sox hit the 500th home run of his career against pitcher George Caster of the Philadelphia Athletics, Foxx's former team. Ted Williams hit three homers in the same game, the first half of a doubleheader. Foxx played in the majors from 1925 through 1945 and hit a total of 534 homers.

KALINE GETS 3,000th HIT: ANNIVERSARY. Sept 24, 1974. Al Kaline of the Detroit Tigers doubled off Dave McNally of the Baltimore Orioles in the fourth inning of a 5–4 Orioles win. The hit was the 3,000th of Kaline's career which began in 1953 and ended in 1974.

NEW YORK GOLDEN ARMS TOURNAMENT. Sept 24. Columbus Avenue Festival, Manhattan, NY. Arm wrestling competition determines winners who will compete in the New York Golden Arms Tournament of Champions on Oct 12. For info: New York Arm Wrestling Assn, Inc, 300-14 45th Dr, Bayside, NY 11361. Phone: (718) 544-4592. Web: www.nycarms.com.

SIX GAP CENTURY & THREE GAP FIFTY BIKE RIDE. Sept 24. Dahlonega, GA. Begins and ends at North Georgia College & State University. 100- and 50-mile rides through north Georgia mountains. For info: Kate Brehe, Dahlonega-Lumpkin County Chamber of Commerce, 13 S Park St, Dahlonega, GA 30533. Phone: (706) 864-3513.

Fax: (706) 864-7917. E-mail: dahlonega@stc.net. Web: www.dahlonega.org.

WORLD HOCKEY ASSOCIATION FORMED: ANNIVERSARY. Sept 24, 1971. The World Hockey Association announced its formation with 12 teams scheduled to begin play in 1972. The WHA lasted seven seasons after which four surviving teams entered the National Hockey League.

BIRTHDAYS TODAY

Edward Nathan (Eddie) George, 27, football player, born Philadelphia, PA, Sept 24, 1973.

Otis Bernard Gilkey, 34, baseball player, born St. Louis, MO, Sept 24, 1966.

Charles Edward ("Mean Joe") Greene, 54, Pro Football Hall of Fame defensive tackle, born Temple, TX, Sept 24, 1946.

John Mackey, 59, Pro Football Hall of Fame tight end, born New York, NY, Sept 24, 1941.

James Kenneth (Jim) McKay (born James Kenneth McManus), 79, broadcaster, born at Philadelphia, PA, Sept 24, 1921.

Rafael Palmeiro, 36, baseball player, born Havana, Cuba, Sept 24, 1964.

Paul Nikola Spoljaric, 30, baseball player, born Kelowna, British Columbia, Canada, Sept 24, 1970.

Winfred O'Neal Tubbs, 30, football player, born Hollywood, FL, Sept 24, 1970.

☆　☆　☆

SEPTEMBER 25 — MONDAY

Day 269 — 97 Remaining

AUSTRALIA: SUMMER OLYMPICS: DAY 11. Sept 25. Sydney, New South Wales. Competition in diving, synchronized swimming, water polo, track & field, basketball, equestrian, gymnastics, team handball, field hockey, sailing, softball, table tennis, tennis, volleyball, beach volleyball, weight lifting and wrestling. For info: Sydney Org Committee for the XXVII Olympic Games, Level 14, Maritime Centre, 207 Kent St, Sydney, NSW 2000, Australia. Phone: (61.2) 9297.2000. Fax: (61.2) 9297.2020. Web: www.sydney.olympic.org.

BROADCASTER ALBERT PLEADS GUILTY: ANNIVERSARY. Sept 25, 1997. Broadcaster Marv Albert, renowned for his expertise handling basketball, hockey and football games, pled guilty to a charge of assault and battery in a case involving a relationship with a woman. In exchange for his guilty plea, prosecutors dropped more serious charges. On Oct 24, the judge in the case delayed sentencing for a year, provided that Albert stay out of further legal troubles and continue a program of mental health counseling. He resumed his broadcasting career about a year later.

JORDAN, SHUG: 90th BIRTH ANNIVERSARY. Sept 25, 1910. James Ralph ("Shug") Jordan, football coach, born at Selma, AL. Jordan played several sports at Auburn (then Alabama Polytechnic Institute) and after graduation became an assistant football coach and head basketball coach. He served in the army during World War II and then coached briefly at the University of Georgia. He returned to Auburn as football coach in 1951, won the national championship in 1957 and retired after the 1975 season with a record of 175–83–7. The football stadium at Auburn is named Jordan-Hare Stadium. Died at Auburn, AL, July 17, 1980.

SATCHEL PAIGE'S LAST GAME: 35th ANNIVERSARY.
Sept 25, 1965. Satchel Paige, the oldest player in major league history at an estimated 59 years, 8 months, 5 days, pitched the last game of his career. He hurled three scoreless innings for the Kansas City Athletics against the Boston Red Sox. Paige gave up only one hit to Carl Yastrzemski.

SMITH, RED: 95th BIRTH ANNIVERSARY. Sept 25, 1905. Walter Wellesley ("Red") Smith, sportswriter, born at Green Bay, WI. Following the death of Grantland Rice in 1954, Smith became the most widely syndicated sports columnist in the country. He wrote for the *New York Herald–Tribune* and later the *New York Times* and won the Pulitzer Prize in 1976. Smith shunned cliches and overblown prose and was generally considered one of the most literate sportswriters. Given the J.G. Taylor Spink Award in 1976. Died at Stamford, CT, Jan 15, 1982.

BIRTHDAYS TODAY

Chauncey Ray Billups, 24, basketball player, born Denver, CO, Sept 25, 1976.
John Terrence Lynch, 29, football player, born Hinsdale, IL, Sept 25, 1971.
Scottie Pippen, 35, basketball player, born Hamburg, AR, Sept 25, 1965.
Philip Francis (Phil) Rizzuto (born Fiero Francis Rizzuto), 83, former broadcaster and Baseball Hall of Fame shortstop, born New York, NY, Sept 25, 1917.
John Franklin (Johnny) Sain, 83, former baseball player, born Havana, AR, Sept 25, 1917.
Anthony Darrell (Tony) Womack, 31, baseball player, born Danville, VA, Sept 25, 1969.

September 2000	S	M	T	W	T	F	S
						1	2
	3	4	5	6	7	8	9
	10	11	12	13	14	15	16
	17	18	19	20	21	22	23
	24	25	26	27	28	29	30

SEPTEMBER 26 — TUESDAY
Day 270 — 96 Remaining

AUSTRALIA: SUMMER OLYMPICS: DAY 12. Sept 26. Sydney, New South Wales. Competition in diving, synchronized swimming, water polo, baseball, basketball, boxing, canoe/kayak, cycling, equestrian, soccer, gymnastics, team handball, field hockey, sailing, softball, tennis, volleyball, beach volleyball, weight lifting and wrestling. For info: Sydney Org Committee for the XXVII Olympic Games, Level 14, Maritime Centre, 207 Kent St, Sydney, NSW 2000, Australia. Phone: (61.2) 9297.2000. Fax: (61.2) 9297.2020. Web: www.sydney.olympic.org.

FRANCE, BILL: BIRTH ANNIVERSARY. Sept 26, 1909. William Henry Getty (Bill) France, Sr, stock car racing executive, born at Washington, DC. While running a service station at Daytona Beach, FL, France took an interest in the auto races contested on the beach. He got involved in race promotion and organization and founded NASCAR in 1948. He remained at the helm long enough to see the once-primitive sport evolve into a series of fantastic spectator events. Died at Ormond Beach, FL, June 7, 1992.

MARIS TIES RUTH: ANNIVERSARY. Sept 26, 1961. Roger Maris hit his 60th home run of the season to tie Babe Ruth's record. Maris's homer came off pitcher Jack Fisher of the Baltimore Orioles in the Yankees' 159th game.

RYAN PITCHES FIFTH NO-HITTER: ANNIVERSARY.
Sept 26, 1981. Nolan Ryan of the Houston Astros became the first pitcher to throw five career no-hitters. He blanked the Los Angeles Dodgers, 5–0, at the Astrodome. Ryan ended his career with seven no-hitters.

STEWART, BILL: BIRTH ANNIVERSARY. Sept 26, 1894. William J. (Bill) Stewart, hockey coach and referee and baseball umpire, born at Fitchburg, MA. Stewart was an NHL referee from 1928 to 1941 except for a short period when he coached the Chicago Blackhawks. In that position for the 1937–38 season and part of the 1938–39 season, he became the first American to coach a team to the Stanley Cup. He also served as a National League umpire from 1933 to 1954. Died at Boston, MA, Feb 14, 1964.

BIRTHDAYS TODAY

David Edwin (Dave) Duncan, 55, former baseball player, born Dallas, TX, Sept 26, 1945.
Craig Harlan Janney, 33, hockey player, born Hartford, CT, Sept 26, 1967.
David (Dave) Martinez, 36, baseball player, born New York, NY, Sept 26, 1964.
Serena Williams, 19, tennis player, born Saginaw, MI, Sept 26, 1981.

SEPTEMBER 27 — WEDNESDAY
Day 271 — 95 Remaining

ALSTON'S ONLY GAME: ANNIVERSARY. Sept 27, 1936. Walter Alston played in the only major league game of his career as a member of the St. Louis Cardinals. He entered the game as a substitute for first baseman Johnny Mize, made one error in two chances and struck out in his only plate appearance. Alston was inducted into the Hall of Fame in 1983, but as a manager, not a player.

AUSTRALIA: SUMMER OLYMPICS: DAY 13. Sept 27. Sydney, New South Wales. Competition in diving, track & field, baseball, basketball, boxing, canoe/kayak, cycling, equestrian, field hockey, sailing, taekwondo, tennis, volleyball and wrestling. For info: Sydney Org Committee for the XXVII Olympic Games, Level 14, Maritime Centre, 207 Kent St, Sydney, NSW 2000, Australia. Phone: (61.2) 9297.2000. Fax: (61.2) 9297.2020. Web: www. sydney.olympic.org.

BONDS JOINS 40–40 CLUB: ANNIVERSARY. Sept 27, 1996. Barry Bonds of the San Francisco Giants stole his 40th base of the year in a game against the Colorado Rockies to become the second player in major league history to hit 40 home runs and steal 40 bases in the same season. Jose Canseco, the original member of the 40–40 club, achieved the feat in 1988. Bonds finished the year with 42 home runs and 40 steals.

FIRST $100G WINNER-TAKE-ALL HORSE RACE: ANNIVERSARY. Sept 27, 1947. Belmont Park hosted the first $100,000 winner-take-all thoroughbred race between Armed, then the leading money winner, and Assault, the 1946 Triple Crown winner. Armed won an easy victory.

LAJOIE GETS 3,000th HIT: ANNIVERSARY. Sept 27, 1914. Napoleon Lajoie of the Cleveland Indians got the 3,000th hit of his career, a double in the first game of a doubleheader against the New York Yankees. Cleveland lost, 5–3. Lajoie finished his career with 3,252 hits and was inducted into the Hall of Fame in 1937.

McGWIRE HITS 69th AND 70th HOME RUNS: ANNIVERSARY. Sept 27, 1998. Mark McGwire of the St. Louis Cardinals finished the season by hitting his 69th and 70th home runs in a game against the Montreal Expos. McGwire hit No. 69 in the 3rd inning against Mike Thurman. No. 70 came in the 7th inning against Carl Pavano. The Cardinals won, 6–3.

WILSON HITS 56th HOME RUN: 70th ANNIVERSARY. Sept 27, 1930. Hack Wilson of the Chicago Cubs hit two home runs, giving him 56 for the year. This total stood as a National League record until 1998 when Mark McGwire hit 70 and Sammy Sosa hit 66.

BIRTHDAYS TODAY

Stephen Douglas (Steve) Kerr, 35, basketball player, born Beirut, Lebanon, Sept 27, 1965.

Robert S. (Rob) Moore, 32, football player, born New York, NY, Sept 27, 1968.

John Michael (Johnny) Pesky (born John Michael Paveskovich), 81, former baseball manager and player, born Portland, OR, Sept 27, 1919.

Michael Jack (Mike) Schmidt, 51, Baseball Hall of Fame third baseman, born Dayton, OH, Sept 27, 1949.

Kathrynne Ann (Kathy) Whitworth, 61, LPGA Hall of Fame golfer, born Monahans, TX, Sept 27, 1939.

SEPTEMBER 28 — THURSDAY
Day 272 — 94 Remaining

CHASE'S SPORTSQUOTE OF THE DAY

"I done it for the wife and kiddies."—Eddie Cicotte on throwing the World Series

AUSTRALIA: SUMMER OLYMPICS: DAY 14. Sept 28. Sydney, New South Wales. Competition in diving, synchronized swimming, track & field, basketball, boxing, canoe/kayak, equestrian, soccer, rhythmic gymnastics, team handball, field hockey, sailing, taekwondo, tennis, volleyball and wrestling. For info: Sydney Org Committee for the XXVII Olympic Games, Level 14, Maritime Centre, 207 Kent St, Sydney, NSW 2000, Australia. Phone: (61.2) 9297.2000. Fax: (61.2) 9297.2020. Web: www. sydney.olympic.org.

BLACK SOX INDICTED: 80th ANNIVERSARY. Sept 28, 1920. Eight members of the 1919 Chicago White Sox were indicted by a grand jury at Chicago on charges that they conspired to fix the 1919 World Series and allowed the Cincinnati Reds to win. The eight players were Eddie Cicotte, Oscar ("Hap") Felsch, Charles ("Chick") Gandil, ("Shoeless") Joe Jackson, Fred McMullin, Charles ("Swede") Risberg, George ("Buck") Weaver and Claude ("Lefty") Williams. White Sox owner Charles Comiskey immediately suspended the eight. They were acquitted but were nevertheless banned from baseball for life.

BRUNDAGE, AVERY: BIRTH ANNIVERSARY. Sept 28, 1887. Avery Brundage, sports administrator, born at Detroit, MI. Brundage was a track and field athlete in high school and at the University of Illinois. He made a fortune in the construction of buildings at Chicago and dedicated his life to the administration of amateur sports. He was elected to the International Olympic Committee in 1936 and served as president from 1952 to 1972. It was his controversial decision to continue the 1972 Munich Summer Games after the murder of 11 Israeli athletes by Palestinian terrorists. Died at Garmisch-Partenkirchen, West Germany, May 5, 1975.

FIRST NIGHT FOOTBALL GAME: ANNIVERSARY. Sept 28, 1892. The first night football game in America was played between Mansfield State Normal School (now Mansfield University) and Wyoming Seminary.

HARMON, TOM: BIRTH ANNIVERSARY. Sept 28, 1919. Thomas D. (Tom) Harmon, Heisman Trophy halfback and broadcaster, born at Gary, IN. Harmon became a national figure by his exploits in the backfield for the University of Michigan. Known as "Old 98," his uniform number, he won many awards, including the Heisman in 1940. After service in World War II, during which he bailed out twice from destroyed planes, Harmon played two years with the Los Angeles Rams. After retiring, he worked as a sportscaster. Died at Los Angeles, CA, Mar 15, 1990.

"HOMER IN THE GLOAMIN'": ANNIVERSARY. Sept 28, 1938. Chicago Cubs catcher Gabby Hartnett hit his famous ninth-inning "homer in the gloamin'" to give the Cubs a 6–5 victory over the Pittsburgh Pirates. The win was the ninth in a row for the Cubs and a key triumph on their way to the National League pennant.

SHORTEST GAME IN HISTORY: ANNIVERSARY. Sept 28, 1919. The shortest game in major league history saw the New York Giants defeat the Philadelphia Phillies, 6–1, in only 51 minutes. The game was the first half of a doubleheader.

TED WILLIAMS FINISHES AT .406: ANNIVERSARY. Sept 28, 1941. Ted Williams of the Boston Red Sox, starting the day with a batting average of .3995, went six-for-eight in a doubleheader against the Philadelphia Athletics to finish the season with a batting average of .406. Williams rejected manager Joe Cronin's suggestion to sit out the day and have his average rounded up to .400. He went four-for-five in the first game to raise his average to .404 and got two hits in three at bats in the nightcap.

BIRTHDAYS TODAY

Bruce Neal Froemming, 61, baseball umpire, born Milwaukee, WI, Sept 28, 1933.

Grant Fuhr, 38, hockey player, born Spruce Grove, Alberta, Canada, Sept 28, 1962.

Stephen Michael (Steve) Largent, 46, US Congressman and Pro Football Hall of Fame wide receiver, born at Tulsa, OK, Sept 28, 1954.

Max Schmeling, 95, former heavyweight champion boxer, born Brandenburg, Germany, Sept 28, 1905.

Charles Robert (Charley) Taylor, 59, Pro Football Hall of Fame wide receiver, born Grand Prairie, TX, Sept 28, 1941.

SEPTEMBER 29 — FRIDAY
Day 273 — 93 Remaining

ASTROS RETIRE RYAN'S NUMBER: ANNIVERSARY. Sept 29, 1996. The Houston Astros retired uniform number 34 in honor of their former pitcher, Nolan Ryan, who played for Houston for nine seasons (1980–88). The ceremony made Ryan the only player to have his number retired by three teams, the California Angels and the Texas Rangers having previously accorded him the honor.

AUSTRALIA: SUMMER OLYMPICS: DAY 15. Sept 29. Sydney, New South Wales. Competition in diving, synchronized swimming, water polo, track & field, basketball, boxing, canoe/kayak, equestrian, soccer, rhythmic gymnastics, team handball, field hockey, sailing, taekwondo, volleyball and wrestling. For info: Sydney Org Committee for the XXVII Olympic Games, Level 14, Maritime Centre, 207 Kent St, Sydney, NSW 2000, Australia. Phone: (61.2) 9297.2000. Fax: (61.2) 9297.2020. Web: www.sydney.olympic.org.

AUTRY, GENE: BIRTH ANNIVERSARY. Sept 29, 1907. Orvon Gene Autry, movie star cowboy and baseball executive, born at Tioga, TX. After a career as one of Hollywood's most famous singing cowboys, the success from which he parlayed into businesses worth millions of dollars, Autry acquired the American League's expansion franchise that became the Los Angeles (later the California and then the Anaheim) Angels. Autry spent lavishly over the years but never saw his team reach the World Series. Died at Los Angeles, CA, Oct 2, 1998.

OFFICE OLYMPICS. Sept 29. Downtown Shreveport, LA. A one-day event that spotlights the office employee! 100 teams of five (men and women) office workers compete in such zany events as The Water Break Relay, Beat the Clock, Carpool Chaos, The Office Chair Roll-off, Toss the Boss, Memo Mania, The Human Post-it-Note and Musical Office Chairs. Sponsor: KVKI Radio. Est attendance: 6,000. For info: Melinda R. Coyer, Office Olympics Founder, KVKI Radio, PO Box 31130, Shreveport, LA 71130-1130. Phone: (318) 688-1130. Fax: (318) 687-8574.

PACIOREK GOES 3-FOR-3: ANNIVERSARY. Sept 29, 1963. John Paciorek of the Houston Colt .45s played the only major league game of his career and got three hits in three times at bat with two walks, three RBIs and four runs scored. A back injury prevented his playing ever again. He is the only player to finish his career with a 1.000 batting average and as many as three hits.

PATTON, JIMMY: BIRTH ANNIVERSARY. Sept 29, 1933. James Russel Patton, Jr, football player, born at Greenville, MS. Despite his slight stature (5'11", 175 pounds), Patton played quarterback in high school, offensive and defensive halfback at the University of Mississippi and safety for the New York Giants. In his eight pro seasons, the Giants reached the NFL title game six times, and he made five Pro Bowls. Died in an automobile accident at Villa Rica, GA, Dec 26, 1972.

TOLAN, EDDIE: BIRTH ANNIVERSARY. Sept 29, 1908. Thomas Edward (Eddie) Tolan, Olympic gold medal sprinter, born at Denver, CO. Tolan was the first black American athlete to win two gold medals, triumphing in the 100 meters and the 200 meters at the 1932 Olympics at Los Angeles. At his death, he still held the Michigan high school record of 9.8 seconds in the 100-yard dash. Died at Detroit, MI, Jan 31, 1967.

WILLIE MAKES "THE CATCH": ANNIVERSARY. Sept 29, 1954. Willie Mays made a fabulous over-the-shoulder catch that many regard as the most famous in baseball history. It came in the first game of the World Series as the New York Giants were playing the Cleveland Indians. Vic Wertz of the Indians hit a long drive to deep center field in the Polo Grounds. Mays turned on the ball, caught it running full stride about 475 feet from home plate, wheeled and threw. The Giants won the game, 3–0, in 10 innings on Dusty Rhodes's pinch-hit home run and swept the Indians in the Series.

BIRTHDAYS TODAY

David (Dave) Andreychuk, 37, hockey player, born Hamilton, Ontario, Canada, Sept 29, 1963.

Carol Blazejowski, 44, Basketball Hall of Fame center, born Elizabeth, NJ, Sept 29, 1956.

Raymond Louis (Ray) Buchanan, 29, football player, born Chicago, IL, Sept 29, 1971.

Warren Livingston Cromartie, 47, former baseball player, born Miami Beach, FL, Sept 29, 1953.

Bryant Gumbel, 52, broadcaster and amateur golfer, born New Orleans, LA, Sept 29, 1948.

Hersey R. Hawkins, Jr, 34, basketball player, born Chicago, IL, Sept 29, 1966.

Brad Allen Lohaus, 36, basketball player, born New Ulm, MN, Sept 29, 1964.

Kenneth Howard (Ken) Norton, Jr, 34, football player, born Jacksonville, IL, Sept 29, 1966.

Kelly Robbins, 31, golfer, born Mt. Pleasant, MI, Sept 29, 1969.

Vince Tobin, 57, football coach, born Burlington Junction, MO, Sept 29, 1943.

SEPTEMBER 30 — SATURDAY
Day 274 — 92 Remaining

AUSTRALIA: SUMMER OLYMPICS: DAY 16. Sept 30. Sydney, New South Wales. Competition in diving, water polo, track & field, basketball, boxing, canoe/kayak, cycling, equestrian, soccer, rhythmic gymnastics, team handball, field hockey, modern pentathlon, sailing, taekwondo, volleyball and wrestling. For info: Sydney Org Committee for the XXVII Olympic Games, Level 14, Maritime Centre, 207 Kent St, Sydney, NSW 2000, Australia. Phone: (61.2) 9297.2000. Fax: (61.2) 9297.2020. Web: www.sydney.olympic.org.

BABE SETS HOME RUN RECORD: ANNIVERSARY. Sept 30, 1927. George Herman ("Babe") Ruth hit his 60th home run of the season off Tom Zachary of the Washington Senators. Ruth's record for the most homers in a single season stood for 34 years, until Roger Maris hit 61 in 1961.

	S	M	T	W	T	F	S
September 2000						1	2
	3	4	5	6	7	8	9
	10	11	12	13	14	15	16
	17	18	19	20	21	22	23
	24	25	26	27	28	29	30

BABE'S LAST GAME AS YANKEE: ANNIVERSARY. Sept 30, 1934. Babe played his last game for the New York Yankees. Soon after, while watching the fifth game of the World Series (between the St. Louis Cardinals and Detroit Tigers) and angry that he was not to be named Yankees manager, Ruth told Joe Williams, sports editor of the Scripp-Howard newspapers, that after 15 seasons he would no longer be playing for the Yankees.

BRETT GETS 3,000th HIT: ANNIVERSARY. Sept 30, 1992. George Brett of the Kansas City Royals singled off Tom Fortugno of the California Angels in the 7th inning, thus recording the 3,000th hit of his major league career. The single gave Brett four hits in a game for the 59th time. He was accorded a standing ovation and became so distracted that he was picked off first.

CLEMENTE'S LAST HIT: ANNIVERSARY. Sept 30, 1972. Roberto Clemente of the Pittsburgh Pirates doubled against New York Mets pitcher Jon Matlack as the Pirates defeated the Mets, 5–0. It was Clemente's 3,000th career hit and his last one as he was killed in a plane crash on Dec 31, delivering relief supplies to earthquake victims in Nicaragua.

FIRST TELEVISED WORLD SERIES: ANNIVERSARY. Sept 30, 1947. The first World Series to be televised opened with the New York Yankees beating the Brooklyn Dodgers, 5–3. The Yankees won the Series, four games to three.

HERSHISER'S SCORELESS STREAK: ANNIVERSARY. Sept 30, 1988. Pitcher Orel Hershiser of the Los Angeles Dodgers extended his streak of consecutive scoreless innings to 59, thereby breaking Don Drysdale's mark by one inning. Hershiser shut out the San Diego Padres for 10 innings, but the Padres won the game, 2–1, in 16 innings.

OUIMET WINS OPEN: ANNIVERSARY. Sept 30, 1913. 20-year-old amateur Francis Ouimet shocked the golf world by winning the US Open, contested at The Country Club at Brookline, MA. Ouimet defeated seasoned professionals Harry Vardon and Ted Ray in a play-off, shooting 72 to Vardon's 77 and Ray's 78.

WITT PITCHES PERFECT GAME: ANNIVERSARY. Sept 30, 1984. Mike Witt of the California Angels pitched a perfect game against the Texas Rangers, winning, 1–0, on an unearned run. Witt struck out 10 and retired the last batter, pinch-hitter Marvis Foley, on a groundout. He threw only 94 pitches.

BIRTHDAYS TODAY

Jamal Sharif Anderson, 28, football player, born Woodland Hills, CA, Sept 30, 1972.

Martina Hingis, 20, tennis player, born Kosice, Slovakia, Sept 30, 1980.

Jose D. Lima, 28, baseball player, born Santiago, Dominican Republic, Sept 30, 1972.

David Joseph (Dave) Magadan, 38, baseball player, born Tampa, FL, Sept 30, 1962.

John Joseph (Johnny) Podres, 68, former baseball player, born Witherbee, NY, Sept 30, 1932.

Robin Evan Roberts, 74, Baseball Hall of Fame pitcher, born Springfield, IL, Sept 30, 1926.

OCTOBER 1 — SUNDAY
Day 275 — 91 Remaining

AUSTRALIA: SUMMER OLYMPICS: DAY 17. Oct 1. Sydney, New South Wales. Competition in water polo, basketball, boxing, canoe/kayak, equestrian, rhythmic gymnastics, team handball, modern pentathlon, volleyball and wrestling plus the Closing Ceremony. For info: Sydney Org Committee for the XXVII Olympic Games, Level 14, Maritime Centre, 207 Kent St, Sydney, NSW 2000, Australia. Phone: (61.2) 9297.2000. Fax: (61.2) 9297.2020. Web: www.sydney.olympic.org.

BABE CALLS HIS SHOT: ANNIVERSARY. Oct 1, 1932. In the fifth inning of Game 3 of the World Series, with a count of two balls and two strikes and with hostile Cubs fans shouting epithets at him, Babe Ruth gestured and then hit a home run. The Yankees won the game and went on to sweep the Series. For more than half a century, baseball fans have debated whether Ruth pointed toward the bleachers and then, in effect, called his shot. Even eyewitnesses disagreed. Joe Williams of the *New York Times* wrote, "In no mistaken motions, the Babe notified the crowd that the nature of his retaliation would be a wallop right out of the confines of the park." But Cubs pitcher Charlie Root said, "Ruth did *not* point at the fence before he swung. If he'd made a gesture like that, I'd have put one in his ear and knocked him on his ass." Ruth's daughter has said that he denied it. But the Babe himself also claimed he had. Fact or folklore? Either way, legend!

BIRTH OF ESPN2: ANNIVERSARY. Oct 1, 1993. ESPN2, designed to supplement the coverage of sports broadcast on ESPN, began broadcasting to approximately 10 million cable households. Originally positioned as an alternative network for a younger, hipper audience, "the Deuce," as it became known, soon evolved into a full partner with ESPN in the telecast of mainstream sports.

BROWNS WIN ONLY PENNANT: ANNIVERSARY. Oct 1, 1944. Emil ("Dutch") Leonard defeated the Detroit Tigers, 4–1, to pitch the St. Louis Browns to the only American League pennant in their history. The Browns went on to lose the World Series to the St. Louis Cardinals, four games to two.

October	S	M	T	W	T	F	S
2000	1	2	3	4	5	6	7
	8	9	10	11	12	13	14
	15	16	17	18	19	20	21
	22	23	24	25	26	27	28
	29	30	31				

FIRST MODERN WORLD SERIES GAME: ANNIVERSARY. Oct 1, 1903. The Pittsburgh Pirates defeated the Boston Pilgrims (later the Red Sox), 7–3, in the first game of the 1903 World Series, the first postseason series matching the champions of the National League and the American League. Jimmy Sebring of Pittsburgh hit the first World Series home run. Deacon Phillippe was the winning pitcher, Cy Young the loser.

FIRST NL PLAY-OFF GAME: ANNIVERSARY. Oct 1, 1946. For the first time in National League history, two teams wound up tied for first place at the end of the regular season. The St. Louis Cardinals and the Brooklyn Dodgers compiled a record of 96–58, necessitating a three-game play-off. The Cards took the first game, 4–2, and won the second on Oct 3, 8–4.

HICKMAN, HERMAN: BIRTH ANNIVERSARY. Oct 1, 1911. Herman Michael Hickman, Jr, football player and coach, wrestler and broadcaster, born at Johnson City, TN. Hickman played college football at the University of Tennessee under Coach Bob Neyland and three seasons of pro football with the Brooklyn Dodgers. He wrestled under the nickname the "Tennessee Terror" and coached at several colleges, including Yale. In 1952, he resigned to concentrate on television and radio. Died at Washington, DC, Apr 25, 1958.

MARIS HITS 61st HOME RUN: ANNIVERSARY. Oct 1, 1961. Roger Maris of the New York Yankees hit his 61st home run, breaking Babe Ruth's record for most home runs in a season. Maris hit his homer against pitcher Tracy Stallard of the Boston Red Sox as the Yankees won, 1–0. Controversy over the record arose because the American League had adopted a 162-game schedule in 1961. The Yankees actually played 163 games, with one tie, and Maris played in 161. In 1927, when Ruth set his record, the schedule called for 154 games. The Yankees played 155 games (again, a tie), and Ruth played in 151. On Sept 8, 1998, Mark McGwire of the St. Louis Cardinals broke Maris's record.

NATIONAL PHYSICAL THERAPY MONTH. Oct 1–31. To increase awareness of the role of physical therapy in health care, physical therapists celebrate by hosting special activities such as fitness clinics, open houses, hot lines, athletic events, health seminars and exhibits. Annually, the month of October. For info: American Physical Therapy Assn, 1111 N Fairfax St, Alexandria, VA 22314. Phone: (800) 999-2782 or (703) 706-3248.

NATIONAL ROLLER SKATING MONTH. Oct 1–31. A monthlong celebration recognizing the health benefits and recreational pleasure of roller skating and in-line skating. Also includes an emphasis on safe skating. For info: Roller Skating Assn, 6905 Corporate Dr, Indianapolis, IN 46278. Phone: (317) 347-2626. Fax: (317) 347-2636. E-mail: rsa@oninternet.com. Web: www.roller skating.org.

PELE PLAYS FINAL GAME: ANNIVERSARY. Oct 1, 1977. Pele, generally considered the greatest soccer player ever, played the last game of his career before 75,646 fans at Giants Stadium. Pele played the first half for the New York Cosmos and the second for Santos of Brazil, his original team.

PERRY STRIKES OUT 3,000th BATTER: ANNIVERSARY. Oct 1, 1978. Gaylord Perry of the San Diego Padres struck out the 3,000th batter of his career in a game against the Los Angeles Dodgers that the Padres won, 4–3, in 11 innings. Perry finished the season with 3,001 strikeouts and ended his career with 3,534. He was inducted into the Baseball Hall of Fame in 1991.

ST. GEORGE MARATHON. Oct 1. St. George, UT. For info: Leisure Services, 85 S Main St, St. George, UT 84770. Phone: (801) 634-5850. E-mail: leisure@infowest.com. Web: www.infowest.com/stgeorgemarathon.

THRILLER IN MANILA: 25th ANNIVERSARY. Oct 1, 1975. Muhammad Ali scored a 15th-round TKO against Joe Frazier to retain the heavyweight championship in a fight billed as the "Thriller in Manila."

VERMONT 50–MILE MOUNTAIN BIKE AND RUN. Oct 1 (tentative). Brownsville, VT. Fifty miles of trails and back roads through the hills of central Vermont at the height of the foliage season. 7,300 vertical feet, moderately technical. For info: Vermont Adaptive Ski and Sports, PO Box 261, Brownsville, VT 05037. Phone: (802) 484-3630. E-mail: vass@sover.net. Web: www.sover.net~vass/vt100.

BIRTHDAYS TODAY

Rodney Cline (Rod) Carew, 55, Baseball Hall of Fame infielder, born Gatun, Canal Zone, Oct 1, 1945.
Conrad Francis Dobler, 50, former football player, born Chicago, IL, Oct 1, 1950.
Roberto Conrado Kelly, 36, baseball player, born Panama City, Panama, Oct 1, 1964.
Anthonia Wayne ("Amp") Lee, 29, football player, born Chipley, FL, Oct 1, 1971.
Alton Lavelle Lister, 42, basketball player, born Dallas, TX, Oct 1, 1958.
Jacques Martin, 48, hockey coach, born Rockland, Ontario, Canada, Oct 1, 1952.
Charles Dwayne (Chuck) McElroy, 33, baseball player, born Port Arthur, TX, Oct 1, 1967.

Mark David McGwire, 37, baseball player, born Pomona, CA, Oct 1, 1963.
Grete Andersen Waitz, 47, former marathoner, born Oslo, Norway, Oct 1, 1953.
Alexei Zhamnov, 30, hockey player, born Moscow, USSR, Oct 1, 1970.

OCTOBER 2 — MONDAY
Day 276 — 90 Remaining

WORLD SERIES CHAMPIONS THIS DATE	
1932	New York Yankees
1954	New York Giants

DENT'S HOMER WINS PLAY-OFF: ANNIVERSARY. Oct 2, 1978. Bucky Dent hit a three-run home run in the seventh inning off pitcher Mike Torrez to propel the New York Yankees to a 5–4 victory over the Boston Red Sox in a one-game play-off to decide the pennant in the American League East. The Yankees went on to defeat the Kansas City Royals for the AL pennant and the Los Angeles Dodgers in the World Series.

GIBSON STRIKES OUT 17: ANNIVERSARY. Oct 2, 1968. Bob Gibson of the St. Louis Cardinals struck out 17 Detroit Tigers, a record, in the first game of the World Series. The Tigers recovered to win the Series in seven games.

JOSS PITCHES PERFECT GAME: ANNIVERSARY. Oct 2, 1908. Addie Joss of the Cleveland Naps (later the Indians) pitched the fourth perfect game in major league history. He defeated the Chicago White Sox, 1–0. Joss pitched a second no-hitter in 1910, also against Chicago.

ONLY 20TH-CENTURY TRIPLEHEADER: 80th ANNIVERSARY. Oct 2, 1920. In the only major league tripleheader played in the 20th century, the Cincinnati Reds took two games from the Pittsburgh Pirates before the Pirates won the nightcap, called by darkness after six innings.

WICHITA STATE PLANE CRASH: 30th ANNIVERSARY. Oct 2, 1970. Fourteen members of the football team at Wichita State University were killed when their plane crashed in the Rocky Mountains.

YOUNGEST AMERICAN LEAGUE PLAYER: ANNIVERSARY. Oct 2, 1909. The youngest player in American League history, Jim Curry, made his major league debut for the Philadelphia Athletics at 16 years, 6 months and 22 days of age in the first game of a doubleheader against the Washington Senators. Curry had one hit in four at bats against Walter Johnson.

BIRTHDAYS TODAY

Richard (Dick) Barnett, 64, former basketball player, born Gary, IN, Oct 2, 1936.
John Neuman Cook, 43, golfer, born Toledo, OH, Oct 2, 1957.
Thomas Muster, 33, tennis player, born Leibnitz, Austria, Oct 2, 1967.
Jana Novotna, 32, tennis player, born Brno, Czechoslovakia, Oct 2, 1968.
Mark Robert Rypien, 38, former football player, born Calgary, Alberta, Canada, Oct 2, 1962.
Matthew Lovick (Matt) Walbeck, 31, baseball player, born Sacramento, CA, Oct 2, 1969.
Maurice Morning (Maury) Wills, 68, former baseball manager and player, born Washington, DC, Oct 2, 1932.

OCTOBER 3 — TUESDAY
Day 277 — 89 Remaining

BEVENS'S NEAR NO-HITTER: ANNIVERSARY. Oct 3, 1947. New York Yankees pitcher Floyd ("Bill") Bevens carried a no-hitter into the ninth inning of Game 4 of the World Series against the Brooklyn Dodgers. With two out and runners on first and second as the result of walks, pinch hitter Harry ("Cookie") Lavagetto doubled off the right-field wall at Ebbets Field. Two runs scored, the no-hitter evaporated and the Yankees lost the game.

BILLIE JEAN KING HAS $100,000 YEAR: ANNIVERSARY. Oct 3, 1971. Billie Jean King won the Virginia Slims Thunderbird tournament at Phoenix to become the first woman tennis player to win more than $100,000 in prize money in a single year.

BRETT WINS BATTING TITLES IN THREE DECADES: 10th ANNIVERSARY. Oct 3, 1990. George Brett of the Kansas City Royals went 1-for-1 to finish the season with a .329 average, good enough to win his third American League batting title. Brett also won in 1976 and 1980, one title in three different decades.

CLARKE, FRED: BIRTH ANNIVERSARY. Oct 3, 1872. Fred Clifford Clarke, Baseball Hall of Fame outfielder and manager, born at Winterset, IA. Clarke batted .315 for the Louisville Colonels and Pittsburgh Pirates (1894–1915). He managed the Pirates to four National League pennants, five second-place finishes and the World Series title in 1909. Inducted into the Hall of Fame in 1951. Died at Winfield, KS, Aug 14, 1960.

FIRST NFL GAME: 80th ANNIVERSARY. Oct 3, 1920. The Dayton Triangles defeated the Columbus Panhandles, 14–0, in the first game played in the American Professional Football Association. The APFA became the National Football League in 1922, but this game is considered the NFL's first game. Lou Partlow of Dayton scored what is regarded as the NFL's first touchdown.

GIANTS BEAT DODGERS IN PLAY-OFF: ANNIVERSARY. Oct 3, 1962. The San Francisco Giants came from behind to defeat the Los Angeles Dodgers, 5–4, in the deciding game of their three-game National League play-off. The Giants scored four runs in the ninth inning to advance to the World Series, where they lost to the New York Yankees, four games to three.

MAJOR LEAGUE BASEBALL DIVISION SERIES BEGIN. Oct 3 (tentative). Sites TBA. Major league baseball opens postseason play with the start of four Division Series. The National League and the American League each qualify four teams for the play-offs, the winners of the East, Central and West Divisions and the wild-card, the second-place team with the best record. The Division Series match these four teams in a best-three-of-five format, with the winners moving on to the League Championship Series.

ROBINSON NAMED BASEBALL'S FIRST BLACK MAJOR LEAGUE MANAGER: ANNIVERSARY. Oct 3, 1974. The only major league player selected MVP in both the American and National Leagues, Frank Robinson was hired by the Cleveland Indians as baseball's first black major league manager. During his playing career, Robinson represented the American League in four World Series playing for the Baltimore Orioles, led the Cincinnati Reds to a National League pennant and hit 586 home runs in 21 years of play.

RUNYON, DAMON: 120th BIRTH ANNIVERSARY. Oct 3, 1880. Alfred Damon Runyon, sportswriter and author, born at Manhattan, KS. Runyon began his newspaper career in the West and made his way to New York in 1911. He covered baseball and other sports, emphasizing the human-interest details that went beyond traditional straight reporting. Runyon's syndicated work in sports and other topics made him one of the best-known writers in the country. He also wrote short stories, some of which formed the basis for the musical *Guys and Dolls*. Given the J.G. Taylor Spink Award in 1967. Died at New York, NY, Dec 10, 1946.

"THE SHOT HEARD ROUND THE WORLD": ANNIVERSARY. Oct 3, 1951. Bobby Thomson hit a three-run home run with one out in the bottom of the ninth inning off Ralph Branca to give the New York Giants a 5–4 victory over the Brooklyn Dodgers in the deciding game of the 1951 National League play-off. The Giants entered the ninth trailing, 4–1. Whitey Lockman drove in one run, and then Thomson came to bat with runners on second and third. The home run has gone down in baseball legend as "The Shot Heard Round the World." The Giants' comeback in the pennant race to tie the Dodgers at the end of the regular season is known as "The Miracle of Coogan's Bluff."

US WOMEN'S MID-AMATEUR (GOLF) CHAMPIONSHIP. Oct 3–8. Big Canyon Country Club, Newport Beach, CA. For info: US Golf Assn, Golf House, Far Hills, NJ 07931. Phone: (908) 234-2300. Fax: (908) 234-9687. E-mail: usga@usga.org. Web: www.usga.org.

WHIRLAWAY PASSES $500,000 MARK: ANNIVERSARY. Oct 3, 1942. Whirlaway, horse racing's Triple Crown winner in 1941, won the 1942 running of the Jockey Club Gold Cup and became the first horse to win more than $500,000 in career earnings.

WORLD FOOTBALL LEAGUE FORMED: ANNIVERSARY. Oct 3, 1973. The World Football League was formed as a challenge to the National Football League, but it played less than two full seasons before folding.

BIRTHDAYS TODAY

Wilfredo Nieva (Wil) Cordero, 29, baseball player, born Mayaguez, Puerto Rico, Oct 3, 1971.

Frederick Steven (Fred) Couples, 41, golfer, born Seattle, WA, Oct 3, 1959.

Dennis Lee Eckersley, 46, former baseball player, born Oakland, CA, Oct 3, 1954.

Darrin Glen Fletcher, 34, baseball player, born Elmhurst, IL, Oct 3, 1966.

Neale Fraser, 67, former tennis player, born Melbourne, Victoria, Australia, Oct 3, 1933.

David Mark (Dave) Winfield, 49, former baseball player, born St. Paul, MN, Oct 3, 1951.

October 2000	S	M	T	W	T	F	S
	1	2	3	4	5	6	7
	8	9	10	11	12	13	14
	15	16	17	18	19	20	21
	22	23	24	25	26	27	28
	29	30	31				

OCTOBER 4 — WEDNESDAY
Day 278 — 88 Remaining

WORLD SERIES CHAMPIONS THIS DATE
1955   Brooklyn Dodgers

BROOKLYN WINS ONLY WORLD SERIES: 45th ANNIVERSARY. Oct 4, 1955. Left-hander Johnny Podres pitched a 2–0 shutout against the New York Yankees to give the Brooklyn Dodgers their only World Series championship. Before this seven-game triumph, the Dodgers had lost the Series in 1920, 1941, 1947, 1949, 1952 and 1953. The Dodgers left Brooklyn for Los Angeles after the 1957 season.

FIRST US OPEN GOLF CHAMPIONSHIP: 105th ANNIVERSARY. Oct 4, 1895. Horace Rawlins won the first US Open Golf Championship, contested at the Newport Golf Club at Newport, RI. Rawlins shot 173 over 36 holes to defeat Willie Dunn by 2 strokes.

INDIANS WIN PLAY-OFF: ANNIVERSARY. Oct 4, 1948. The Cleveland Indians defeated the Boston Red Sox, 8–3, in a one-game play-off to decide the American League pennant. The Indians used the pitching of Gene Bearden and the hitting of player-manager Lou Boudreau to advance to the World Series against the Boston Braves.

KELLY, JOHNNY: BIRTH ANNIVERSARY. Oct 4, 1889. John Brendan (Johnny) Kelly, Olympic gold medal rower, born at Philadelphia, PA. The son of working-class Irish immigrants, Kelly started his own construction company and became a millionaire. He began rowing in 1909 and compiled an impressive record, including three Olympic gold medals. His son, John, Jr, became a champion rower as well. His daughter Grace became Princess of Monaco. Died at Philadelphia, June 20, 1960.

LEAGUE CHAMPIONSHIP SERIES BEGIN: ANNIVERSARY. Oct 4, 1969. Following the inauguration of divisional play, teams from the National League and the American League opened competition in the first League Championship Series. The New York Mets beat the Atlanta Braves, 9–5, in the opening game of the NLCS. The Baltimore Orioles defeated the Minnesota Twins, 4–3, in 12 innings, in the first ALCS game.

LONGEST NFL INTERCEPTION: ANNIVERSARY. Oct 4, 1998. Defensive back Louis Oliver of the Miami Dolphins tied an NFL record by returning an interception 103 yards for a touchdown in a 37–10 win over the Buffalo Bills. For Oliver it was the first touchdown he had ever scored—in high school, college or professional football.

"MR HOCKEY" SKATES AT 69: ANNIVERSARY. Oct 4, 1997. Gordie Howe, known as "Mr Hockey," for his incredibly long and productive career in the National Hockey League and the World Hockey Association, skated one shift for the Detroit Vipers in their International Hockey League opening game. Howe, who at 69 became the only hockey player to compete in six decades, was on the ice for 47 seconds. He did not touch the puck.

OLIN, STEVE: 35th BIRTH ANNIVERSARY. Oct 4, 1965. Steven Robert (Steve) Olin, baseball player, born at Portland, OR. Olin pitched four seasons with the Cleveland Indians as a reliever. Died in a boating accident at Orlando, FL, Mar 22, 1993.

CHASE'S SPORTSQUOTE OF THE DAY
"I'd rather ride the buses managing in Triple A than be a lawyer."—Tony LaRussa, baseball manager and attorney

BIRTHDAYS TODAY

Michael David (Mike) Adamle, 51, broadcaster and former football player, born Kent, OH, Oct 4, 1949.
Frank Peter Joseph Crosetti, 90, former baseball player, born San Francisco, CA, Oct 4, 1910.
Anita L. DeFrantz, 48, Olympics executive and former rower, born Philadelphia, PA, Oct 4, 1952.
A.C. Green, Jr, 37, basketball player, born Portland, OR, Oct 4, 1963.
Robert Lee (Sam) Huff, 66, Pro Football Hall of Fame linebacker, born Edna Gas, WV, Oct 4, 1934.
Anthony (Tony) La Russa, Jr, 56, baseball manager and former player, born Tampa, FL, Oct 4, 1944.
Ryan Darrell McNeil, 30, football player, born Ft Pierce, FL, Oct 4, 1970.
Roger Allen Pavlik, 33, baseball player, born Houston, TX, Oct 4, 1967.
James Francis (Jimy) Williams, 57, baseball manager and former player, born Santa Maria, CA, Oct 4, 1943.

OCTOBER 5 — THURSDAY
Day 279 — 87 Remaining

WORLD SERIES CHAMPIONS THIS DATE
1942   St. Louis Cardinals
1953   New York Yankees

BAGBY, JIM: BIRTH ANNIVERSARY. Oct 5, 1889. James Charles Jacob Bagby, Sr, baseball player and umpire, born at Barnett, GA. Bagby pitched the Cleveland Indians to the American League pennant in 1920, winning 31 games. He hit the first World Series home run by a pitcher in Game 5 of the 1920 Series against the Brooklyn Dodgers. Died at Marietta, GA, July 28, 1954.

CHADWICK, HENRY: BIRTH ANNIVERSARY. Oct 5, 1824. Henry Chadwick, Baseball Hall of Fame sportswriter and innovator, born at Exeter, Devon, England. Known as the "Father of Baseball" and later as "Father Chadwick," he wrote voluminously about baseball, popularizing the game and protecting its integrity. He perfected the newspaper box score, served on the rules committee and devised the method of scoring games still in use. Inducted into the Hall of Fame in 1938. Died at New York, NY, Apr 20, 1908.

MICKEY OWEN'S DROPPED THIRD STRIKE: ANNIVERSARY. Oct 5, 1941. In the fourth game of the World Series between the Brooklyn Dodgers and the New York Yankees, Dodgers catcher Mickey Owen let a third strike get away from him in the ninth inning. The miscue allowed batter Tommy Henrich to reach first base safely, after which the Yankees went on to score four runs and win the game, 7–4. The victory gave New York a lead of three games to one. They won the Series in five games.

NFL'S 10,000th REGULAR-SEASON GAME: ANNIVERSARY. Oct 5, 1997. The Seattle Seahawks defeated the Tennessee Oilers, 16–13, in the National Football League's 10,000th regular-season game. Entering Week 6 of the 1997 season, the NFL had played 9,992 regular-season games. Seven games kicked off at 1 PM {ET}, to bring the total to 9,999. Thus, the first of the four games beginning at 4 PM {ET}, to conclude was deemed to be Game No. 10,000. The Seahawks-Oilers contest ended minutes before the other three games: the New York Jets at the Indianapolis Colts, the Minnesota Vikings at the Arizona Cardinals and the San Diego Chargers at the Oakland Raiders.

ROBINSON WINS 324th GAME: 15th ANNIVERSARY. Oct 5, 1985. The Grambling Tigers defeated Prairie View A&M, 27–7, to give coach Eddie Robinson the 324th victory of his coaching career. With the win, Robinson became college football's all-time winningest coach, surpassing Paul ("Bear") Bryant.

BIRTHDAYS TODAY

Raymond Lester ("Trace") Armstrong, 35, football player, born Bethesda, MD, Oct 5, 1965.
Dennis DeWayne Bird, 34, former football player, born Oklahoma City, OK, Oct 5, 1966.
Rex Everett Chapman, 33, basketball player, born Bowling Green, KY, Oct 5, 1967.
Laura Davies, 37, golfer, born Coventry, England, Oct 5, 1963.
Grant Henry Hill, 28, basketball player, born Dallas, TX, Oct 5, 1972.
Mario Lemieux, 35, former hockey player, born Montreal, Quebec, Canada, Oct 5, 1965.
Patrick Roy, 35, hockey player, born Quebec City, Quebec, Canada, Oct 5, 1965.
Rey Francisco Sanchez, 33, baseball player, born Rio Pedras, Puerto Rico, Oct 5, 1967.

OCTOBER 6 — FRIDAY
Day 280 — 86 Remaining

WORLD SERIES CHAMPIONS THIS DATE	
1936	New York Yankees
1941	New York Yankees
1947	New York Yankees
1963	Los Angeles Dodgers

IDAHO STATE DRAFT HORSE INTERNATIONAL. Oct 6–8. Sandpoint, ID. Three days of contests and exhibits as draft horses from the US and Canada show what can be done with a lot of horsepower and a whole lot of heart. The setting is near the mountains along Lake Pond Oreille. Est attendance: 7,000. For info: Sandpoint Chamber of Commerce, Box 928, Sandpoint, ID 83864. Phone: (208) 263-0887. Fax: (208) 265-5289. E-mail: chamber @sandpoint.net. Web: www.sandpoint.org/chamber.

MOODY, HELEN WILLS: 95th BIRTH ANNIVERSARY. Oct 6, 1905. Helen Wills Moody, tennis player, born at Centerville, CA. Perhaps the greatest American tennis player, Wills Moody won 31 major titles, including Wimbledon eight times and the US championship seven times. From August 1926 through 1935, she did not lose a

October 2000	S	M	T	W	T	F	S
	1	2	3	4	5	6	7
	8	9	10	11	12	13	14
	15	16	17	18	19	20	21
	22	23	24	25	26	27	28
	29	30	31				

match nor even a single set. She led a reclusive life after retiring, but she painted and wrote mystery novels and her autobiography. Died at Carmel, CA, Jan 1, 1998.

NATIONAL HOCKEY LEAGUE REGULAR SEASON OPENS. Oct 6 (tentative). The National Hockey League opens its 84th regular season leading to the Stanley Cup play-offs and the Stanley Cup Finals. Each of the league's 30 teams (including the Columbus Blue Jackets and the Minnesota Wild, expansion franchises) plays an 82-game schedule. The teams are arranged into two conferences of 15 teams each, with three divisions in each conference. The three division winners in each conference plus the next five best teams, regardless of division, will qualify for postseason play. For info: Natl Hockey League, 1251 Avenue of the Americas, 47th Floor, New York, NY 10020. Phone: (212) 789-2000. Fax: (212) 789-2020. Web: www.nhl.com.

NIEKRO WINS 300 GAMES: 15th ANNIVERSARY. Oct 6, 1985. Pitcher Phil Niekro of the New York Yankees won the 300th game of his career, shutting out the Toronto Blue Jays, 8–0, on the last day of the regular season. Niekro finished his career in 1987 with 318 wins.

PADGETT MAKES UNASSISTED TRIPLE PLAY: ANNIVERSARY. Oct 6, 1923. Shortstop Ernie Padgett of the Boston Braves recorded the fourth unassisted triple play in major league history. In the 4th inning of the second game of a doubleheader against the Philadelphia Phillies, Padgett caught a line drive hit by Walter Holke, stepped on second to double Cotton Tierney and tagged Cliff Lee before he could return to first.

RUTH HITS THREE SERIES HOME RUNS: ANNIVERSARY. Oct 6, 1926. Babe Ruth hit three home runs in the fourth game of the World Series against the St. Louis Cardinals. The Yankees won the game, 10–5, but the Cardinals won the Series in seven games.

SCOTLAND: SOLHEIM CUP. Oct 6–8. Loch Lomond Golf Club, Scotland. This biennial, transatlantic team match-play competition for women, begun in 1990, features the 12 best US-born golfers from the LPGA and the 12 best European-born players from the European Ladies Professional Golf Association (ELPGA). For info: LPGA, 100 International Golf Dr, Daytona Beach, FL 32124. Phone: (904) 274-6200. Fax: (904) 274-1099. Web: www.lpga .com.

SPECIAL OLYMPICS NEW YORK FALL GAMES. Oct 6–8. Binghamton, NY. About 700 athletes with mental retardation compete in soccer, softball, cross-country, golf, cycling and equestrian. For info: New York Special Olympics, Inc, 504 Balltown Rd, Schenectady, NY 12304-2290. Phone: (518) 388-0790. Fax: (518) 388-0795. E-mail: bmosberg@nyso.org.

US OPEN STOCK DOG CHAMPIONSHIP. Oct 6–8. Hubert Bailey Farm, Dawsonville, GA. In the foothills of the Appalachian Mountains, handlers from across the country will work both sheep and cattle. Also a petting zoo for children. Annually, in October. Est attendance: 3,000. For info: Dawson County Chamber of Commerce, PO Box 299, Dawsonville, GA 30534. Phone: (706) 265-6278. Fax: (706) 265-6279. E-mail: info@dawson.org. Web: www.dawson.org.

BIRTHDAYS TODAY

Dennis Ray ("Oil Can") Boyd, 41, former baseball player, born Meridian, MS, Oct 6, 1959.

Angelo Dominic ("Archi") Cianfrocco, 34, baseball player, born Rome, NY, Oct 6, 1966.

Anthony Kevin (Tony) Dungy, 45, football coach and former player, born Jackson, MI, Oct 6, 1955.

Gerald Wayne (Jerry) Grote, 58, former baseball player, born San Antonio, TX, Oct 6, 1942.

Rebecca Lobo, 27, basketball player, born Hartford, CT, Oct 6, 1973.

Darren Christopher Oliver, 30, baseball player, born Kansas City, MO, Oct 6, 1970.

OCTOBER 7 — SATURDAY

Day 281 — 85 Remaining

WORLD SERIES CHAMPIONS THIS DATE	
1933	New York Giants
1935	Detroit Tigers
1950	New York Yankees
1952	New York Yankees

ABC/WIBC FESTIVAL OF BOWLING. Oct 7–Dec 17 (tentative). Reno, NV. One-of-a-kind bowling event open to all ABC and WIBC members giving them opportunities to participate in 15 different bowling formats as often as desired. There are mixed men and women events, an event for beginning bowlers, a family event, a Baker format event, regular bowling events and senior events. For info: Michael Deering, American Bowling Congress, 5301 S 76th St, Greendale, WI 53129-0500. Phone: (414) 423-3309. Fax: (414) 421-3013.

AETNA US HEALTHCARE GREATER HARTFORD MARATHON. Oct 7. Hartford, CT. Marathon, half-marathon, marathon relay, 5K and kids' 1K. 5,000 runners. Est attendance: 15,000. For info: Beth Shluger, Hartford Marathon Foundation, Inc, 119 Hebron Ave, Glastonbury, CT 06033. Phone: (860) 652-8866. E-mail: eatnrun@erols.com. Web: www.hartfordmarathon.com.

CIRCLE CITY CLASSIC. Oct 7. RCA Dome, Indianapolis, IN. Bowl-style football game between teams from two predominantly black universities is preceded by several days of related activities, including concerts, the Coronation, the College Fair and a parade. Est attendance: 62,000. For info: Indiana Sports Corp, 201 S Capitol Ave, Ste 1200, Indianapolis, IN 46225. Phone: (317) 237-5000. Fax: (317) 237-5041. E-mail: isc@indianasportscorp.com. Web: www.indianasportscorp.com.

COUNTRY FAIR ON THE SQUARE AND "ALL CAR SHOW." Oct 7–8. Downtown Square, Gainesville, TX. More than 100 vintage cars, classic cars, street rods and pickups, all makes and models on display. Entertainment, quilt show, food, arts display, children's activities and more. Annually, the first Saturday and Sunday in October. Est attendance: 5,000. For info: Gainesville Area Chamber of Commerce, PO Box 518, Gainesville, TX 76240. Phone: (940) 665-2831. Fax: (940) 665-2833.

FIRST FEMALE GLOBETROTTER: 15th ANNIVERSARY. Oct 7, 1985. Lynette Woodard, captain of the gold-medal-winning US basketball team at the 1984 Olympics, was selected to be the first woman to play for the Harlem Globetrotters.

GEORGIA TECH BEATS CUMBERLAND: ANNIVERSARY. Oct 7, 1916. Georgia Tech University defeated Cumberland, 222–0, in the most lopsided college football game of all time.

KLEIN, CHUCK: BIRTH ANNIVERSARY. Oct 7, 1904. Charles Herbert (Chuck) Klein, Baseball Hall of Fame outfielder, born at Indianapolis, IN. Klein was the leading National League slugger around 1930 when hitting statistics were quite astronomical. He won the NL Triple Crown in 1933. Inducted into the Hall of Fame in 1980. Died at Indianapolis, Mar 28, 1958.

MEYER, LOUIS: DEATH ANNIVERSARY. Oct 7, 1994. Louis Meyer, auto racer, born at New York, NY, July 1904. Meyer became the first three-time winner of the Indianapolis 500, capturing that race in 1928, 1933 and 1936. He also finished second once and fourth twice. After World War II, he was co-owner of the Offenhauser engine business, whose engines won every Indianapolis 500 from 1947 through 1964. Died at Las Vegas, NV.

PAYTON SETS TWO RECORDS: ANNIVERSARY. Oct 7, 1984. Running back Walter Payton of the Chicago Bears broke two records held by Jim Brown in the same game. He passed the mark of 12,312 career rushing yards and rushed for 100 yards or more for the 58th time in his career as the Bears beat the New Orleans Saints, 20–7.

RUN TO READ. Oct 7. Central Library, Tulsa, OK. Annual 8K road race and 1-mile fun run benefiting Tulsa City-County Library's Ruth G. Hardman Adult Literacy Service. Annually, the first Saturday in October. Est attendance: 700. For info: Paula McKay, Spec Events Coord, Tulsa City-County Library System, 400 Civic Center, Tulsa, OK 74103. Phone: (918) 596-7901. Fax: (918) 596-7900.

SCOTTISH FESTIVAL AND HIGHLAND GAMES. Oct 7. Fairgrounds, Goshen, CT. Competition and demonstrations in Scottish athletic games such as caber toss, etc. Also clan tents, pipe bands, dancing, Scottish food and imports; continuous entertainment. Annually, the first Saturday in October. Est attendance: 7,000. For info: St. Andrew's Soc of Connecticut, PO Box 1195, Litchfield, CT 06759. Phone: (203) 366-0777.

VON DER AHE, CHRIS: BIRTH ANNIVERSARY. Oct 7, 1851. Christian Frederick Wilhelm (Chris) Von der Ahe, baseball executive, born at Hille, Germany. A brewer and a flamboyant showman, Von der Ahe owned the champion St. Louis Browns of the American Association in the 1880s. He conceived of the notion that beer should be sold in ballparks. Died at St. Louis, MO, June 7, 1913.

WALKER, FLEET: BIRTH ANNIVERSARY. Oct 7, 1856. Moses Fleetwood Walker, baseball player, born at Mt Pleasant, OH. Walker played major league baseball for the 1884 Toledo team in the American Association. He was the last black American to play in the majors before baseball imposed its color line. Died at Cleveland, OH, May 11, 1924.

WALKING WEEKEND. Oct 7–9. Northeastern Connecticut. More than 50 guided historic, cultural and recreational walks through the Quinebaug-Shetucket Rivers Valley National Heritage Corridor. Est attendance: 5,000. For info: Northeast Connecticut Visitors District, PO Box 598, Putnam, CT 06260. Phone: (860) 928-1228. Fax: (860) 928-4720.

WALKTOBERFEST. Oct 7–8. (Dates may vary by location.) Each October thousands of Americans participate in the American Diabetes Association's annual walk-a-thon to raise money to help find a cure for diabetes and to provide information and resources to improve the lives of all people affected by the disease. Walks are held in communities across America, combining fun and fitness with the chance to help people with diabetes. For info: Communications Dept, American Diabetes Assn, Natl HQ, 1660 Duke St, Alexandria, VA 22314. Phone: (800) 254-WALK.

BIRTHDAYS TODAY

Frank Conrad (Frankie) Baumholtz, 82, former baseball player, born Midvale, OH, Oct 7, 1918.

James Scott (Jim) Bruske, 36, baseball player, born East St. Louis, IL, Oct 7, 1964.

Richard Anthony (Rich) DeLucia, 36, baseball player, born Reading, PA, Oct 7, 1964.

Richard Manuel (Dick) Jauron, 50, football coach and former player, born Swampscott, MA, Oct 7, 1950.

Johnnie James Morton, 29, football player, born Inglewood, CA, Oct 7, 1971.

Brian Louis Allen Sutter, 44, hockey coach and former player, born Viking, Alberta, Canada, Oct 7, 1956.

OCTOBER 8 — SUNDAY
Day 282 — 84 Remaining

WORLD SERIES CHAMPIONS THIS DATE

1919	Cincinnati Reds
1922	New York Giants
1927	New York Yankees
1930	Philadelphia Athletics
1939	New York Yankees
1940	Cincinnati Reds
1959	Los Angeles Dodgers

BANKOH MOLOKAI HOE. Oct 8. Molokai to Oahu, HI. 49th annual men's 40.8-mile Molokai-to-Oahu championship six-person outrigger canoe race. Nearly 110 teams of the best outrigger canoe paddlers from around the world compete for the championship title. Spectators gather on the beach to watch the finish at Ft DeRussy Beach, Waikiki, when the teams are laden with leis. Est attendance: 4,000. For media info: Carol Hogan/Ocean Promotion, (808) 325-7400 or Linda Chinn, Bank of Hawaii, (808) 537-8658. For race info: Joan Malama, (808) 261-6615. E-mail: oceanpro@interpac.net.

BUSH, DONIE: BIRTH ANNIVERSARY. Oct 8, 1887. Owen Joseph ("Donie") Bush, baseball player and manager, born at Indianapolis, IN. Bush was an American League shortstop known for his hustle. He managed several clubs in the majors and the minors, spending 65 years in baseball. Died at Indianapolis, Mar 28, 1972.

October	S	M	T	W	T	F	S
2000	1	2	3	4	5	6	7
	8	9	10	11	12	13	14
	15	16	17	18	19	20	21
	22	23	24	25	26	27	28
	29	30	31				

CANADA: VALLEY HARVEST MARATHON. Oct 8. Kentville, Nova Scotia. For info: Steve Moores, RR #1, Wolfville, NS, Canada B0P 1X0. Phone: (902) 542-1867. E-mail: moores@glinx.com.

CURTIS, MARGARET: BIRTH ANNIVERSARY. Oct 8, 1883. Margaret Curtis, golfer and tennis player, born at Boston, MA. Curtis won three women's amateur national golf championships in 1907, 1911 and 1912. She teamed with Evelyn Sears to win the 1908 women's tennis national doubles title. She played golf well into her 70s. The Curtis Cup, contested biennially between teams of amateur women golfers from the US and Great Britain, was initiated by Curtis and her sister Harriott in 1932. Died at Boston, Dec 25, 1965.

DON LARSEN'S PERFECT GAME: ANNIVERSARY. Oct 8, 1956. Don Larsen of the New York Yankees pitched the only perfect game in World Series history. He defeated the Brooklyn Dodgers, 2–0, in Game 5. Pinch hitter Dale Mitchell, batting for Dodgers pitcher Sal Maglie, was called out on strikes for the last out.

GRAND NATIONAL AND WORLD CHAMPIONSHIP MORGAN HORSE SHOW. Oct 8–15. Oklahoma State Fairgrounds, Oklahoma City, OK. Morgan horses that have qualified at 2000 shows convene to vie for the title of World Champion. Annually, in October. Est attendance: 10,000. For info: Grand Natl and World Chmpshp Morgan Show, American Morgan Horse Assn, PO Box 960, Shelburne, VT 05482-0960. Phone: (802) 985-4944. Fax: (802) 985-8897. E-mail: info@morganhorse.com.

HEAD OF THE CONNECTICUT REGATTA. Oct 8. Connecticut River, Middletown, CT. Crew race regatta with 3,000 participants. Annually, the day before Columbus Day. Est attendance: 10,000. For info: Coord, Head of the Connecticut Regatta, PO Box 1, Middletown, CT 06422. Phone: (860) 346-1042 or (800) 486-3346. Fax: (860) 346-1043.

HUDSON HIGHLANDER VI. Oct 8. Bear Mountain, NY. An international field will compete in America's premier long-distance orienteering race, set at the metric marathon distance of 26.3 km. For info: Paul Bennett. Phone: (973) 642-8427. E-mail: pdbennett@juno.com.

MERKLE'S BONER RESOLVED: ANNIVERSARY. Oct 8, 1908. The Chicago Cubs defeated the New York Giants, 4–2, to win their third National League pennant in a row. The game was a replay of the Sept 23 game that ended in a disputed tie as umpire Hank O'Day called the Giants first baseman out for not touching second base on a hit by Al Bridwell that apparently scored the winning run. Cubs second baseman Johnny Evers called Merkle's mistake to the umpire's attention, and O'Day nullified the run. Both clubs protested, and league officials eventually ruled the game a tie.

MURTAUGH, DANNY: BIRTH ANNIVERSARY. Oct 8, 1917. Daniel Edward (Danny) Murtaugh, baseball player and manager, born at Chester, PA. Murtaugh had a limited career as a major league infielder but enjoyed great success as manager of the Pittsburgh Pirates. His teams won the World Series in 1960 and 1971. Died at Chester, Dec 2, 1976.

OATES SCORES 1,000th POINT: ANNIVERSARY. Oct 8, 1997. Center Adam Oates of the Washington Capitals scored three goals and two assists to move past the 1,000-mark in career NHL points. Oates finished the night with 1,004 points as Washington defeated the New York Islanders, 6–3.

RICKENBACKER, EDDIE: 110th BIRTH ANNIVERSARY. Oct 8, 1890. Edward Vernon (Eddie) Rickenbacker, auto racing pioneer, born at Columbus, OH. Besides his career in airplanes, "Captain Eddie" raced cars, once setting a land speed record at Daytona Beach, and founded the Rickenbacker Car Company in 1921. This racing enterprise developed four-wheel brakes, balloon tires and other improvements. He bought the Indianapolis Motor Speedway in 1927 and sold it to Tony Hulman in 1945. Died at Zurich, Switzerland, July 23, 1973.

SCOTLAND HIGHLAND FESTIVAL. Oct 8. Scotland, CT. 10th annual Scottish Highland games and festival includes heavy athletic competition, bagpipe bands, highland dancing, vendors, sheepdogs and folk music. Annually, the Sunday of Columbus Day weekend. Est attendance: 3,500. For info: Highland Festival Assn, PO Box 212, Scotland, CT 06264. Phone: (860) 423-1880.

CHASE'S SPORTSQUOTE OF THE DAY

"The million-to-one shot came in. Hell froze over. A month of Sundays hit the calendar. Don Larsen today pitched a no-hit, no-run, no-man-reaches-first game in a World Series."—Shirley Povich

---

BIRTHDAYS TODAY

Nathaniel Donnell (Donnie) Abraham, 27, football player, born Orangeburg, SC, Oct 8, 1973.
Matthew Nicolas (Matt) Biondi, 35, Olympic gold medal swimmer, born Moraga, CA, Oct 8, 1965.
William David (Billy) Conn, Jr, 83, former boxer and referee, born Pittsburgh, PA, Oct 8, 1917.
Bill Elliott, 45, auto racer, born Cumming, GA, Oct 8, 1955.
Michael Thomas (Mike) Morgan, 41, baseball player, born Tulare, CA, Oct 8, 1959.
David Robert (Dave) Phillips, 57, baseball umpire, born St. Louis, MO, Oct 8, 1943.
Rashaan Iman Salaam, 26, Heisman Trophy running back, born San Diego, CA, Oct 8, 1974.

OCTOBER 9 — MONDAY

Day 283 — 83 Remaining

WORLD SERIES CHAMPIONS THIS DATE

1928	New York Yankees
1934	St. Louis Cardinals
1938	New York Yankees
1944	St. Louis Cardinals
1949	New York Yankees
1958	New York Yankees
1961	New York Yankees
1966	Baltimore Orioles

CANADA: THANKSGIVING DAY. Oct 9. Annually, the second Monday in October.

COLUMBUS DAY. Oct 9. Public Law 90–363 sets observance of Columbus Day on the second Monday in October. Applicable to federal employees and to the District of Columbia, but observed also in most states on this day. Commemorates the landfall of Columbus in the New World, Oct 12, 1492.

DEAN SMITH RETIRES: ANNIVERSARY. Oct 9, 1997. Dean Smith abruptly retired as head basketball coach at the University of North Carolina just before the start of the 1997–98 season. In 36 years of coaching, Smith won 879 games, more than any other coach, and two NCAA championships, against only 254 losses. He was universally regarded as an exemplary practitioner of college athletics at its finest.

FIRST PGA CHAMPIONSHIP: ANNIVERSARY. Oct 9, 1916. The recently formed Professional Golfers' Association of America held its first championship at Siwanoy Country Club at Bronxville, NY. The trophy and the lion's share of the $2,580 purse, both offered by department store magnate Rodman Wanamaker, were won by British golfer Jim Barnes. After the next two championships were canceled by World War I, Barnes won again in 1919.

MARQUARD, RUBE: BIRTH ANNIVERSARY. Oct 9, 1889. Richard William ("Rube") Marquard, Baseball Hall of Fame pitcher, born at Cleveland, OH. Marquard was an excellent pitcher, winning 204 games over 18 years. He was nicknamed after Rube Waddell, another pitcher whom he resembled. Inducted into the Hall of Fame in 1971. Died at Pikesville, MD, June 1, 1980.

O'MALLEY, WALTER: BIRTH ANNIVERSARY. Oct 9, 1903. Walter Francis O'Malley, baseball executive, born at New York, NY. O'Malley, owner of the Brooklyn Dodgers when they left New York for Los Angeles for the 1958 season, is perhaps the most vilified man in baseball history. Nevertheless, he is responsible for expanding the sport to the West Coast. Died at Rochester, MN, Aug 9, 1979.

SEWELL, JOE: BIRTH ANNIVERSARY. Oct 9, 1898. Joseph Wheeler (Joe) Sewell, Baseball Hall of Fame shortstop, born at Titus, AL. Sewell joined the starting lineup of the Cleveland Indians on Aug 16, 1920, after Ray Chapman was fatally beaned. He struck out only 114 times in 7,132 at bats. Inducted into the Hall of Fame in 1977. Died at Mobile, AL, Mar 6, 1990.

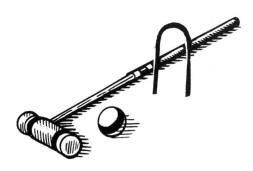

BIRTHDAYS TODAY

Kenneth (Kenny) Anderson, 30, basketball player, born New York, NY, Oct 9, 1970.
Joseph Anthony (Joe) Pepitone, 60, former baseball player, born New York, NY, Oct 9, 1940.
William Thomas (Bill) Pulsipher, 27, baseball player, born Ft Benning, GA, Oct 9, 1973.
Arnold D. (Arnie) Risen, 76, Basketball Hall of Fame center, born Williamstown, KY, Oct 9, 1924.
Michael (Mike) Singletary, 42, Pro Football Hall of Fame linebacker, born Houston, TX, Oct 9, 1958.
Annika Sorenstam, 30, golfer, born Stockholm, Sweden, Oct 9, 1970.

OCTOBER 10 — TUESDAY
Day 284 — 82 Remaining

WORLD SERIES CHAMPIONS THIS DATE

1924	Washington Senators
1926	St. Louis Cardinals
1931	St. Louis Cardinals
1937	New York Yankees
1945	Detroit Tigers
1951	New York Yankees
1956	New York Yankees
1957	Milwaukee Braves
1968	Detroit Tigers

ALEXANDER FANS LAZZERI: ANNIVERSARY. Oct 10, 1926. Veteran pitcher Grover Cleveland Alexander came out of the St. Louis Cardinals bullpen in the seventh inning of the seventh World Series game to strike out New York Yankees second baseman Tony Lazzeri with the bases loaded. The Cardinals held on to win the game, 3–2, as Babe Ruth was thrown out attempting to steal for the game's last out.

ARLINGTON INTERNATIONAL RACECOURSE CLOSES: ANNIVERSARY. Oct 10, 1997. Arlington International Racecourse at Arlington Heights, IL, ended its 1997 racing season with no racing dates scheduled for 1998. The track had lost an estimated $70 million in recent years, attributed mainly to competition from riverboat gambling. Arlington opened Oct 13, 1927, and became the first racecourse to host a stakes race with a million-dollar purse. The Arlington Million, run first in 1981, became the track's signature attraction.

BILLUPS, LEWIS: BIRTH ANNIVERSARY. Oct 10, 1963. Lewis Kenneth Billups, football player, born at Tampa, FL. Billups played at North Alabama and was drafted by the Cincinnati Bengals. His career was marred by legal troubles, including a year in jail for making threatening phone calls and allegations by a Seattle woman that Billups had sexually assaulted her. Died in a car crash at Orlando, FL, Apr 9, 1994.

JAPAN: HEALTH-SPORTS DAY. Oct 10. National holiday to encourage physical activity for building sound body and mind. Created in 1966 to commemorate the day of the opening of the XVIII Summer Olympic Games at Tokyo on Oct 10, 1964.

October 2000

S	M	T	W	T	F	S
1	2	3	4	5	6	7
8	9	10	11	12	13	14
15	16	17	18	19	20	21
22	23	24	25	26	27	28
29	30	31				

MAJOR LEAGUE BASEBALL LEAGUE CHAMPIONSHIP SERIES BEGIN. Oct 10 (tentative). Sites TBA. Major League Baseball launches the second round of postseason play, the League Championship Series. The two winners of the National League's Division Series meet in the best-four-of-seven NLCS. The two winners of the American League's Division Series meet in the best-four-of-seven ALCS. Winners move on to the World Series.

WELLS, WILLIE: 95th BIRTH ANNIVERSARY. Oct 10, 1905. Willie ("The Devil") Wells, Baseball Hall of Fame shortstop, born at Austin, TX. Wells is generally considered the greatest shortstop to play in the Negro Leagues. As manager of the Newark Eagles, he developed several players who became major leaguers. Inducted into the Hall of Fame in 1997. Died at Austin, Jan 21, 1989.

WORLD SERIES UNASSISTED TRIPLE PLAY: 80th ANNIVERSARY. Oct 10, 1920. The Cleveland Indians defeated the Brooklyn Dodgers, 8–1, in the fifth game of the 1920 World Series. The Indians' Elmer Smith hit the first grand slam in World Series play in the first inning, and winning pitcher Jim Bagby hit the first World Series homer by a pitcher in the fourth inning. But the most famous play in the game was the unassisted triple play recorded by Cleveland second baseman Bill Wambsganss in the fifth inning. Wamby caught a line drive hit by Clarence Mitchell, touched second to double off Pete Kilduff and tagged Otto Miller before he could return safely to first base.

BIRTHDAYS TODAY

Yinka Dare, 28, basketball player, born Kano, Nigeria, Oct 10, 1972.
Brett Lorenzo Favre, 31, football player, born Pass Christian, MS, Oct 10, 1969.
Derrick Wayne McKey, 34, basketball player, born Meridian, MS, Oct 10, 1966.
John Ulysses Mobley, 27, football player, born Chester, PA, Oct 10, 1973.
Chris Pronger, 26, hockey player, born Dryden, Ontario, Canada, Oct 10, 1974.
Fury Gene Tenace (born Fiore Gino Tennaci), 54, former baseball player, born Russelton, PA, Oct 10, 1946.
Alexei Zhitnik, 28, hockey player, born Kiev, USSR, Oct 10, 1972.

OCTOBER 11 — WEDNESDAY
Day 285 — 81 Remaining

WORLD SERIES CHAMPIONS THIS DATE

1913	Philadelphia Athletics
1918	Boston Red Sox
1943	New York Yankees
1948	Cleveland Indians

CHIP BECK SHOOTS 59: ANNIVERSARY. Oct 11, 1991. Playing at Sunrise Golf Club, Chip Beck shot 59 in the third round of the Las Vegas Invitational to equal Al Geiberger's record for lowest score in a single round of a PGA tournament. But he did not win the tournament. Andrew Magee did, defeating D.A. Weibring on the second hole of a sudden-death play-off.

CLARK, DUTCH: BIRTH ANNIVERSARY. Oct 11, 1906. Earl Harry ("Dutch") Clark, Pro Football Hall of Fame player and coach, born at Fowler, CO. Clark attended Northwestern briefly and then Colorado College, where he played football and became an All-American in 1929. He turned pro with the Portsmouth Spartans of the NFL and, after the team moved to Detroit and became the Lions, led the league in scoring three times. Clark later coached the Lions and the Cleveland Rams. Inducted into the Hall of Fame as a charter member in 1963. Died at Canon City, CO, Aug 5, 1978.

FIRST 100-YARD DASH UNDER 10 SECONDS: 110th ANNIVERSARY. Oct 11, 1890. John Owens ran the first 100-yard dash under 10 seconds at an AAU track meet at Washington. Owens's time was 9.8 seconds.

HOPPE, WILLIE: BIRTH ANNIVERSARY. Oct 11, 1887. William F. (Willie) Hoppe, billiards champion, born at Cornwall on the Hudson, NY. He won tournaments from age 18 until age 64. Died at Miami, FL, Feb 1, 1959.

MARSHALL, GEORGE PRESTON: BIRTH ANNIVERSARY. Oct 11, 1896. George Preston Marshall, Pro Football Hall of Fame executive, born at Grafton, WV. Marshall made a fortune in the laundry business and became part owner of the Boston Braves of the NFL in 1932. He bought the whole team, changed its name to the Redskins and moved it to Washington in 1937. The Redskins quickly became one of the league's most successful operations with Marshall leading the league in embracing television. He paid his players frugally, meddled in his coaches' decisions and promoted rules changes to encourage passing and field goals. Inducted into the Pro Football Hall of Fame as a charter member in 1963. Died at Washington, DC, Aug 9, 1969.

NATIONAL HOCKEY LEAGUE EXPANDS: ANNIVERSARY. Oct 11, 1967. The National Hockey League commenced the largest expansion in professional sports history, adding six new teams to the six existing teams. Five of the new teams—the Pittsburgh Penguins, Philadelphia Flyers, California Golden Seals, Minnesota North Stars and St. Louis Blues—made their debut on this date. The Los Angeles Kings played their first game on Oct 14.

BIRTHDAYS TODAY

Chidi Obioma Ahanotu, 30, football player, born Modesto, CA, Oct 11, 1970.

Jason Arnott, 26, hockey player, born Collingwood, Ontario, Canada, Oct 11, 1974.

Maria Esther Andion Bueno, 61, former tennis player, born Sao Paulo, Brazil, Oct 11, 1939.

Greggory William (Gregg) Olson, 34, baseball player, born Scribner, NE, Oct 11, 1966.

Cherokee Bryan Parks, 28, basketball player, born Huntington Beach, CA, Oct 11, 1972.

Dimitri Dell Young, 27, baseball player, born Vicksburg, MS, Oct 11, 1973.

Jon Steven (Steve) Young, 39, football player, born Salt Lake City, UT, Oct 11, 1961.

OCTOBER 12 — THURSDAY

Day 286 — 80 Remaining

WORLD SERIES CHAMPIONS THIS DATE

1907	Chicago Cubs
1916	Boston Red Sox
1920	Cleveland Indians
1967	St. Louis Cardinals

BIRD MAKES NBA DEBUT: ANNIVERSARY. Oct 12, 1979. After an All-American career at Indiana State, forward Larry Bird made his professional debut with the Boston Celtics. He scored 14 points and had five assists in 28 minutes as the Celtics beat the Houston Rockets, 114–108. Bird soon proved his ability to shoot, pass and rebound. He led the Celtics to 32 more victories than they had the previous season and won the league's Rookie of the Year Award.

CRONIN, JOE: BIRTH ANNIVERSARY. Oct 12, 1906. Joseph Edward (Joe) Cronin, Baseball Hall of Fame player, manager and executive, born at San Francisco, CA. Cronin played shortstop for Pittsburgh, Washington and the Boston Red Sox. He was a manager and became the first former player to be elected league president. Inducted into the Hall of Fame in 1959. Died at Osterville, MA, Sept 7, 1984.

FERRELL, RICK: 95th BIRTH ANNIVERSARY. Oct 12, 1905. Richard Benjamin (Rick) Ferrell, Baseball Hall of Fame catcher, born at Durham, NC. Ferrell caught 1,806 games in the American League, a record at the time. He hit .281 over 18 years and formed a strong battery with his brother Wes. Inducted into the Hall of Fame in 1984. Died at Bloomfield Hills, MI, July 27, 1995.

TENNESSEE SCORELESS STREAK: 60th ANNIVERSARY. Oct 12, 1940. The University of Tennessee football team defeated Tennessee-Chattanooga, 53–0, to extend its record streak of consecutive shutouts to 17 games. The streak started Nov 5, 1938, when the Vols beat the same team, and ended Oct 19, 1940, when Alabama scored 12 points but still lost, 27–12.

CHASE'S SPORTSQUOTE OF THE DAY

"The team that makes the fewest mistakes wins." —Robert Neyland, Tennessee football coach

---

BIRTHDAYS TODAY

Christopher Mark (Chris) Chandler, 35, football player, born Everett, WA, Oct 12, 1965.

Jean-Jacques (J.J.) Daigneault, 35, hockey player, born Montreal, Quebec, Canada, Oct 12, 1965.

Charles Sidney (Sid) Fernandez, 38, former baseball player, born Honolulu, HI, Oct 12, 1962.

Ned Jarrett, 68, broadcaster and former auto racer, born Neton, NC, Oct 12, 1932.

Todd Andrew Krygier, 35, hockey player, born Northville, MI, Oct 12, 1965.

Anthony Christopher (Tony) Kubek, 64, broadcaster and former baseball player, born Milwaukee, WI, Oct 12, 1936.

Leon Lett, Jr, 32, football player, born Mobile, AL, Oct 12, 1968.

Jose Antonio Valentin, 31, baseball player, born Manati, Puerto Rico, Feb 12, 1969.

Charlie Ward, Jr, 30, basketball player, born Thomasville, GA, Oct 12, 1970.

OCTOBER 13 — FRIDAY
Day 287 — 79 Remaining

WORLD SERIES CHAMPIONS THIS DATE

1903	Boston Pilgrims
1906	Chicago White Sox
1914	Boston Braves
1915	Boston Red Sox
1921	New York Giants
1960	Pittsburgh Pirates

BOSTON WINS FIRST WORLD SERIES: ANNIVERSARY. Oct 13, 1903. The Boston Pilgrims (later the Red Sox) won the first modern World Series, defeating the Pittsburgh Pirates, five games to three. The Pilgrims won Game 8, 3–0.

FIRST WORLD SERIES NIGHT GAME: ANNIVERSARY. Oct 13, 1971. The first night game in World Series history matched the Pittsburgh Pirates and the Baltimore Orioles. Pittsburgh beat Baltimore, 4–3, behind three hits by Roberto Clemente, to tie the Series at two games apiece.

MAZEROSKI WINS SERIES: 40th ANNIVERSARY. Oct 13, 1960. Second baseman Bill Mazeroski of the Pittsburgh Pirates led off the bottom of the ninth inning with a home run over the left-field wall to win Game 7 of the World Series against the New York Yankees, 10–9. Mazeroski hit the second pitch thrown to him by relief pitcher Ralph Terry. He was the first player to end a World Series with a homer in the bottom of the ninth.

SHAW, WILBUR: BIRTH ANNIVERSARY. Oct 13, 1902. Warren Wilbur Shaw, auto racer, born at Shelbyville, IN. Shaw was racing cars by age 18. An early crash led him to invent the crash helmet. After several years of frustration, he won the Indianapolis 500 three times, in 1937, 1939 and 1940, the first consecutive victories by one driver. He served as Indy's president and general manager after Tony Hulman bought the Speedway in 1945. Died at Ft Wayne, IN, Oct 30, 1954.

SOMERS, CHARLES: BIRTH ANNIVERSARY. Oct 13, 1868. Charles W. Somers, baseball executive, born at Newark, OH. Somers was one of the founders of the American League. As the league's vice president, he held financial interests in four teams to help keep them solvent in their early years. Died at Put-in-Bay, OH, June 29, 1934.

SOUTH DAKOTA RODEO ASSOCIATION CHAMPIONSHIP RODEO FINALS. Oct 13–15. Sioux Falls, SD. The best of the best. Top 12 cowboys and cowgirls in the state compete for $50,000 in prize money and year-end championship awards. Standard rodeo events plus rodeo dance at the Ramkota on Friday and Saturday nights. For info: Karen Knippling, South Dakota Rodeo Assn, HC 3, Box 28, Gann Valley, SD 57341. Phone: (605) 293-3460.

WADDELL, RUBE: BIRTH ANNIVERSARY. Oct 13, 1876. George Edward ("Rube") Waddell, Baseball Hall of Fame pitcher, born at Bradford, PA. Waddell is remembered as much for his carefree antics as for his excellent pitching. He won 191 games but never took the game too seriously. Inducted into the Hall of Fame in 1946. Died at San Antonio, TX, Apr 1, 1914.

October **2000**	S	M	T	W	T	F	S
	1	2	3	4	5	6	7
	8	9	10	11	12	13	14
	15	16	17	18	19	20	21
	22	23	24	25	26	27	28
	29	30	31				

BIRTHDAYS TODAY

Derek Ricardo Harper, 39, basketball player, born Elberton, GA, Oct 13, 1961.

Trevor William Hoffman, 33, baseball player, born Bellflower, CA, Oct 13, 1967.

Edwin Lee (Eddie) Mathews, 69, Baseball Hall of Fame third baseman, born Texarkana, TX, Oct 13, 1931.

Jermaine O'Neal, 22, basketball player, born Columbia, SC, Oct 13, 1978.

Paul Anthony Pierce, 23, basketball player, born Oakland, CA, Oct 13, 1977.

Jerry Lee Rice, 38, football player, born Starkville, MS, Oct 13, 1962.

Glenn Anton ("Doc") Rivers, 39, basketball coach and former player, born Maywood, IL, Oct 13, 1961.

OCTOBER 14 — SATURDAY
Day 288 — 78 Remaining

WORLD SERIES CHAMPIONS THIS DATE

1905	New York Giants
1908	Chicago Cubs
1929	Philadelphia Athletics
1965	Los Angeles Dodgers
1984	Detroit Tigers

ALL-SHUTOUT WORLD SERIES: 95th ANNIVERSARY. Oct 14, 1905. Christy Mathewson defeated the Philadelphia Athletics, 2–0, to win the World Series for the New York Giants in five games. All the games were shutouts, three by Mathewson and one each by New York's Joe McGinnity and Philadelphia's Chief Bender.

CHARLESTON, OSCAR: BIRTH ANNIVERSARY. Oct 14, 1896. Oscar McKinley Charleston, Baseball Hall of Fame outfielder and manager, born at Indianapolis, IN. Charleston was perhaps the best overall ballplayer in the Negro Leagues, drawing comparisons to Ty Cobb. He played with the great Homestead Grays and Pittsburgh Crawfords teams of the 1930s and managed as well. Inducted into the Hall of Fame in 1976. Died at Philadelphia, PA, Oct 6, 1954.

END OF LONGEST NFL LOSING STREAK: 55th ANNIVERSARY. Oct 14, 1945. The Chicago Cardinals (later the St. Louis, Phoenix and Arizona Cardinals) ended the longest losing streak in NFL history at 29 games by defeating the Chicago Bears, 16–7.

EWRY, RAY: BIRTH ANNIVERSARY. Oct 14, 1873. Raymond Clarence (Ray) Ewry, Olympic gold medal track and field athlete, born at Lafayette, IN. Ewry overcame polio as a child to win 10 Olympic gold medals, more than any other athlete. He won the standing broad jump and the standing high jump at the 1900, 1904, 1906 and 1908 games and added gold medals in the standing triple jump in 1900 and 1904. None of these events is contested today. Died at New York, NY, Sept 29, 1937.

GARTNER SCORES 500th GOAL: ANNIVERSARY. Oct 14, 1991. Right wing Mike Gartner of the New York Rangers scored the 500th regular-season goal of his National Hockey League career in a 5–3 loss to the Washington Capitals. Gartner, the 16th player to reach 500, finished his career with 708 goals.

STUHLDREHER, HARRY: BIRTH ANNIVERSARY. Oct 14, 1901. Harry A. Stuhldreher, football player, coach and executive, born at Massillon, OH. Stuhldreher called signals for Notre Dame's famed backfield, the Four Horsemen. After graduating in 1925, he played pro football and coached at Villanova and Wisconsin. Died at Pittsburgh, PA, Jan 26, 1965.

WORLD WRISTWRESTLING CHAMPIONSHIPS. Oct 14. Petaluma, CA. Nationally recognized event with more than 500 entrants vying for the title of World Wristwrestling Champion. Est attendance: 1,000. For info: Bill Soberanes, c/o *Argus Courier*, 830 Petaluma Blvd N, Petaluma, CA 94952. Phone: (707) 778-1430. Web: www.armwrestling.com.

BIRTHDAYS TODAY

Harry David Brecheen, 86, former baseball player, born Broken Bow, OK, Oct 14, 1914.

Midre Almeric Cummings, 29, baseball player, born St. Croix, Virgin Islands, Oct 14, 1971.

Beth Daniel, 44, LPGA Hall of Fame golfer, born Charleston, SC, Oct 14, 1956.

Joseph Elliott (Joe) Girardi, 36, baseball player, born Peoria, IL, Oct 14, 1964.

James Arthur (Jim) Jackson, 30, basketball player, born Toledo, OH, Oct 14, 1970.

Charles (Charlie) Joiner, Jr, 53, Pro Football Hall of Fame wide receiver, born Many, LA, Oct 14, 1947.

Patrick Franklin (Pat) Kelly, 33, baseball player, born Philadelphia, PA, Oct 14, 1967.

Derrick Andre Rodgers, 29, football player, born Cordova, TN, Oct 14, 1971.

Dwayne Kenneth Schintzius, 32, basketball player, born Brandon, FL, Oct 14, 1968.

Frank Wycheck, 29, football player, born Philadelphia, PA, Oct 14, 1971.

OCTOBER 15 — SUNDAY
Day 289 — 77 Remaining

WORLD SERIES CHAMPIONS THIS DATE

1917	Chicago White Sox
1923	New York Yankees
1925	Pittsburgh Pirates
1946	St. Louis Cardinals
1964	St. Louis Cardinals
1970	Baltimore Orioles

AMERICAN BOWLING CONGRESS–WOMEN'S INTERNATIONAL BOWLING CONGRESS FESTIVAL OF BOWLING. Oct 15–Nov 28. Reno, NV. Open competition for two-man, two-women teams, plus doubles and singles events. For info: Bowling, Inc, 5301 S 76th St, Greendale, WI 53129-1127. Phone: (414) 423-3456. Fax: (414) 421-3013.

CANADA: CANADIAN INTERNATIONAL MARATHON. Oct 15. Toronto, Ontario. Marathon, half-marathon, walk and corporate/school challenge. For info: 240 Heath St W, Ste 802, Toronto, ON, Canada M5P 3L5. Phone: (416) 972-1062. Fax: (416) 972-1238. E-mail: marathon@netcom.ca. Web: www.runtoronto.com.

FIRST BLACK COACH IN NBA: ANNIVERSARY. Oct 15, 1966. Bill Russell made his debut as the first black coach in the NBA as his Boston Celtics defeated the San Francisco Warriors, 121–113, at Boston Garden. Russell served as the Celtics' player-coach for three seasons and won two NBA titles.

GIBSON'S PINCH-HIT HOMER: ANNIVERSARY. Oct 15, 1988. Kirk Gibson hit a two-run, pinch-hit home run with two out in the bottom of the ninth inning to give the Los Angeles Dodgers a 5–4 win over the Oakland A's in the first game of the World Series. Gibson, hampered by a strained left knee, hobbled around the bases pumping his arm in jubilation. The Dodgers won the Series, four games to one.

HAWKEYE MEDICAL SUPPLY HOSPICE ROAD RACES. Oct 15. Iowa City, IA. Annual road race attracts top runners from throughout the country. Est attendance: 8,000. For info: Iowa City Road Races, Inc, PO Box 3148, Iowa City, IA 52244. Phone: (319) 338-8108 or (800) 722-3523. Fax: (319) 338-6822. E-mail: runicrr@aol.com.

LAND SPEED RECORD EXCEEDS SPEED OF SOUND: ANNIVERSARY. Oct 15, 1997. A British racing team, led by car owner Richard Noble and driver Andy Green, set a new land speed record of 763.035 miles per hour, exceeding the speed of sound. The feat was accomplished in the desert, 125 miles north of Reno, NV. Under the rules, the Thrust SSC team was required to make two supersonic runs in opposite directions within an hour. The jet-powered car ran at 759.333 mph on the first attempt and 766.109 on the second. The speed of sound, which varies according to weather and altitude, was this day calculated at 748.111 mph. Green had actually made two supersonic runs two days before, but a problem with a drag parachute delayed the team, and it took 61 minutes to make the second run.

LONGEST POSTSEASON GAME: ANNIVERSARY. Oct 15, 1986. Ray Knight of the New York Mets keyed a three-run rally in the ninth inning to tie the score in the sixth game of the National League Championship Series against the Houston Astros. The Mets won the game, 7–6, in 16 innings, to win the longest postseason game ever and the series as well.

MIKITA GETS 1,000th POINT: ANNIVERSARY. Oct 15, 1972. Center Stan Mikita of the Chicago Blackhawks scored the 1,000th point of his NHL career, gaining an assist in a 3–1 loss to the St. Louis Blues. Mikita finished his career with 1,467 points.

NFL STRIKE ENDS: ANNIVERSARY. Oct 15, 1987. The National Football League Players Association ordered its members to return to work without a contract, effectively ending a 24-day strike against the NFL. The players reported after the owners' deadline and were told they would not play or be paid for the upcoming Sunday's games.

ROMP IN THE SWAMP FUN WALK. Oct 15. Gordon Bubolz Nature Preserve, Appleton, WI. Choose to hike ¼-, 1½-, 2½- or 4-mile distances on the Preserve's beautiful trail system. Rest stops along the way. Prizes for the most money raised. Est attendance: 1,000. For info: Joann Engel, Office Mgr, 4815 N Lynndale Dr, Appleton, WI 54915. Phone: (920) 731-6041. Fax: (920) 731-9593. E-mail: bubolz@dataex.com.

SLAUGHTER SCORES FROM FIRST: ANNIVERSARY. Oct 15, 1946. Enos Slaughter of the St. Louis Cardinals scored from first base on a short double by Harry Walker to defeat the Boston Red Sox, 4–3, in the seventh game of the World Series.

SULLIVAN, JOHN L.: BIRTH ANNIVERSARY. Oct 15, 1858. John L. Sullivan, boxer, born at Roxbury, MA. "The Great John L." was one of America's first sports heroes. He captured the world's bare-knuckle heavyweight championship on Feb 7, 1882, and went six years without defending the title. He won the last bare-knuckle fight in 1889 and then lost the title to James J. Corbett in 1892. This was the first fight in which the boxers used gloves and were governed by the Marquess of Queensberry rules. Died at Abingdon, MA, Feb 2, 1918.

BIRTHDAYS TODAY

Fredrick Kristian (Fred) Hoiberg, 28, basketball player, born Lincoln, NE, Oct 15, 1972.
James Alvin (Jim) Palmer, 55, broadcaster and Baseball Hall of Fame pitcher, born New York, NY, Oct 15, 1945.
Roscoe Tanner, 49, former tennis player, born Lookout Mountain, TN, Oct 15, 1951.

OCTOBER 16 — MONDAY
Day 290 — 76 Remaining

WORLD SERIES CHAMPIONS THIS DATE	
1909	Pittsburgh Pirates
1912	Boston Red Sox
1962	New York Yankees
1969	New York Mets
1983	Baltimore Orioles

CAIN, BOB: BIRTH ANNIVERSARY. Oct 16, 1924. Robert Max (Bob) Cain, baseball player, born at Long-

ford, KS. Cain pitched in 140 major league games over five years, but he will be remembered for the four balls he threw to midget Eddie Gaedel on Aug 19, 1951. In one of St. Louis Browns owner Bill Veeck's most outrageous promotions, Gaedel came to bat to open the second game of a doubleheader against the Detroit Tigers. He walked and was banned from baseball the next day. Died at Cleveland, OH, Apr 7, 1997.

GOSLIN, GOOSE: 100th BIRTH ANNIVERSARY. Oct 16, 1900. Leon Allen ("Goose") Goslin, Baseball Hall of Fame outfielder, born at Salem, NJ. Goslin was an American League outfielder for 18 years, and he ranks high in many all-time offensive categories. He invented a zebra-striped bat to confuse pitchers, but it was ruled illegal. Inducted into the Hall of Fame in 1968. Died at Bridgetown, NJ, May 15, 1971.

HARRIDGE, WILL: BIRTH ANNIVERSARY. Oct 16, 1883. William (Will) Harridge, Baseball Hall of Fame executive, born at Chicago, IL. Harridge became president of the American League upon the death of Ernest Barnard in 1931. He had been private secretary to AL founder Ban Johnson. He resigned in 1958, having kept a fairly low profile. Inducted into the Hall of Fame in 1972. Died at Evanston, IL, Apr 9, 1971.

SMITH AND CARLOS GIVE BLACK POWER SALUTE: ANNIVERSARY. Oct 16, 1968. At the Mexico City Summer Olympics, American sprinters Tommie Smith and John Carlos, winners of the gold and bronze medals, respectively, in the 200-meter run, raised their black-gloved fists in a black power salute during the medal presentation to call attention to racism and poverty in the US. Two days later, the pair was suspended by the US Olympic Committee and sent home.

ULLMAN GETS 1,000th POINT: ANNIVERSARY. Oct 16, 1971. Center Norm Ullman of the Toronto Maple Leafs got the 1,000th point of his National Hockey League career, an assist in a 5–3 loss to the New York Rangers. Ullman finished his career with 1,229 points.

CHASE'S SPORTSQUOTE OF THE DAY
"Manute Bol is so skinny they save money on road trips. They just fax him from city to city."—Woody Allen

BIRTHDAYS TODAY

Melissa Louise Belote, 44, Olympic gold medal swimmer, born Washington, DC, Oct 16, 1956.
Manute Bol, 38, former basketball player, born Gogrial, Sudan, Oct 16, 1962.
David Albert (Dave) DeBusschere, 60, former baseball player, former basketball coach and executive, and Basketball Hall of Fame forward, born Detroit, MI, Oct 16, 1940.
Juan Alberto Gonzalez, 31, baseball player, born Vega Baja, Puerto Rico, Oct 16, 1969.
Paul Kariya, 26, hockey player, born Vancouver, British Columbia, Canada, Oct 16, 1974.
Darius Kasparaitis, 28, hockey player, born Elektrenai, USSR, Oct 16, 1972.
Jermaine Edward Lewis, 26, football player, born Lanham, MD, Oct 16, 1974.
James Timothy (Tim) McCarver, 59, broadcaster and former baseball player, born Memphis, TN, Oct 16, 1941.
Joseph Patrick (Joe) Murphy, 33, hockey player, born London, Ontario, Canada, Oct 16, 1967.
Kordell Stewart, 28, football player, born New Orleans, LA, Oct 16, 1972.
German Titov, 35, hockey player, born Moscow, USSR, Oct 16, 1965.

October 2000	S	M	T	W	T	F	S
	1	2	3	4	5	6	7
	8	9	10	11	12	13	14
	15	16	17	18	19	20	21
	22	23	24	25	26	27	28
	29	30	31				

OCTOBER 17 — TUESDAY

Day 291 — 75 Remaining

WORLD SERIES CHAMPIONS THIS DATE

1971	Pittsburgh Pirates
1974	Oakland Athletics
1978	New York Yankees
1979	Pittsburgh Pirates

ANDERSON, PAUL: BIRTH ANNIVERSARY. Oct 17, 1932. Paul Edward Anderson, Olympic gold medal weight lifter, born at Toccoa, GA. Anderson won the heavyweight world championship in 1955 and a gold medal at the 1956 Melbourne Olympics. He was renowned as the "World's Strongest Man" for his feats of strength, including a back lift of 6,270 pounds. In 1962 he opened the Paul Anderson Youth Home. Died at Vidalia, GA, Aug 15, 1994.

CHILE: COCA-COLA WORLD JUNIOR TRACK AND FIELD CHAMPIONSHIPS. Oct 17–22. Santiago, Chile. 8th competition. For info: Intl Amateur Athletic Federation, 17, rue Princesse Florestine, BP 359, 98007 Monte Carlo, Monaco. Phone: (377) 93-10-88-88. Fax: (377) 93-15-95-15. Web: www.iaaf.org.

CUMMINGS, CANDY: BIRTH ANNIVERSARY. Oct 17, 1848. William Arthur ("Candy") Cummings, Baseball Hall of Fame pitcher, born at Ware, MA. Cummings is generally regarded as the first pitcher to throw a curveball. He learned the technique, he said, sailing oyster shells. He played in baseball's amateur era and as a professional. Inducted into the Hall of Fame in 1939. Died at Toledo, OH, May 16, 1924.

EWING, BUCK: BIRTH ANNIVERSARY. Oct 17, 1859. William Buckingham (Buck) Ewing, Baseball Hall of Fame catcher, born at Hoagland, OH. Ewing was one of the best catchers of the 19th century and is credited by some with being the first to crouch immediately under the batter. Inducted into the Hall of Fame in 1939. Died at Cincinnati, OH, Oct 20, 1906.

KURRI SCORES 500th GOAL: ANNIVERSARY. Oct 17, 1992. Right wing Jari Kurri of the Los Angeles Kings became the 18th player in the National Hockey League to score 500 regular-season goals. He tallied into an empty net in an 8–6 victory over the Boston Bruins. Kurri ended his career with 601 goals.

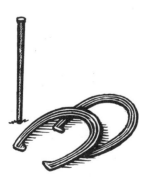

METS AND COLT .45s BORN: 40th ANNIVERSARY. Oct 17, 1960. The National League announced that expansion franchises were being awarded to the New York Metropolitan Baseball Club, Inc, headed by Mrs Joan Payson, and to a Houston group of investors led by Judge Roy Hofheinz. The two teams, later nicknamed the Mets and the Colt .45s, began play in the 1962 season.

WORLD SERIES EARTHQUAKE: ANNIVERSARY. Oct 17, 1989. Minutes before the start of Game 3 of the World Series between the Oakland A's and the San Francisco Giants, Candlestick Park and the Bay Area were rocked by an earthquake. The game was postponed and the Series delayed for 11 days.

BIRTHDAYS TODAY

Theodore Ernest (Ernie) Els, 31, golfer, born Johannesburg, South Africa, Oct 17, 1969.
Daniel John Willard (Danny) Ferry, 34, basketball player, born Hyattsville, MD, Oct 17, 1966.
Robert Craig ("Evel") Knievel, 62, former motorcycle stunt performer, born Butte, MT, Oct 17, 1938.
John Steven Mabry, 30, baseball player, born Wilmington, DE, Oct 17, 1970.

OCTOBER 18 — WEDNESDAY

Day 292 — 74 Remaining

WORLD SERIES CHAMPIONS THIS DATE

1977	New York Yankees

ADAMS, CHARLES FRANCIS: BIRTH ANNIVERSARY. Oct 18, 1876. Charles Francis Adams, Hockey Hall of Fame executive, born at Newport, VT. Adams secured a National Hockey League franchise for Boston in 1924 and named the team the Bruins. He used his substantial wealth, earned in the grocery business, to make the Bruins a success and to develop the league. His guarantee of $500,000 over four years for Bruins home games allowed construction of Boston Garden, opened in 1928. Adams also had an interest in horse racing, and he became a major stockholder in the Boston Braves. Inducted into the Hockey Hall of Fame in 1960. Died at Boston, MA, Oct 2, 1947.

AMERICAN BASKETBALL LEAGUE OPENS: ANNIVERSARY. Oct 18, 1996. The American Basketball League, a new professional league for women, opened its inaugural season with three games. The New England Blizzard defeated the Richmond Rage, 100–73, the Columbus Quest beat the Seattle Reign, 82–75, and the San Jose Lazers took the measure of the Atlanta Glory, 78–70. The Colorado Xplosion and the Portland Power were idle on the league's first night. Midway through its third season, the league folded.

BERRY, CHARLIE: BIRTH ANNIVERSARY. Oct 18, 1902. Charles Francis (Charlie) Berry, baseball player, baseball umpire and football official, born at Phillipsburg, NJ. Berry attended Lafayette College, where he played baseball and was an All-American football player. After graduation he played pro football and major league baseball. After retiring he became an NFL head linesman and an American League umpire, once calling a baseball doubleheader and an All-Star football game on the same day. Died at Evanston, IL, Sept 6, 1972.

MALARCHER, DAVE: BIRTH ANNIVERSARY. Oct 18, 1894. David Julius (Dave) Malarcher, baseball player and manager, born at Whitehall, LA. Malarcher played and managed in the Negro Leagues from 1920 through 1934. After retiring he became an accomplished poet. Died at Chicago, IL, May 11, 1982.

MEN'S SENIOR BASEBALL LEAGUE WORLD SERIES.
Oct 18–Nov 4. Various spring training facilities, Phoenix, AZ. The 13th annual national amateur hardball World Series for men 18+, 30+, 40+, 50+ and 60+. 310 teams expected in 2000. Est attendance: 5,000. For info: MSBL, One Huntington Quadrangle, Melville, NY 11797. Phone: (516) 753-6725. Fax: (516) 753-4031. E-mail: info@msbl national.com. Web: www.msblmnational.com.

RED GRANGE'S EPIC DAY: ANNIVERSARY. Oct 18, 1924. Harold ("Red") Grange of the University of Illinois helped his team dedicate its new football stadium with a 39–14 victory over the University of Michigan. Grange scored four touchdowns in the game's first 12 minutes on runs of 95, 67, 56 and 44 yards. He returned to the field later to score a fifth rushing touchdown and to throw a pass for a sixth.

REGGIE'S THREE SERIES HOME RUNS: ANNIVERSARY. Oct 18, 1977. Reggie Jackson hit three home runs in three consecutive at bats to lead the New York Yankees to a World Series championship over the Los Angeles Dodgers. Jackson's homers, all hit on the first pitch, came against Burt Hooton, Elias Sosa and Charlie Hough. They came in Game 6, won by New York, 8–4. Jackson hit two other home runs, in Games 4 and 5, to set a record for most homers in a six-game Series.

WORLD SINGLES DRIVING CHAMPIONSHIP. Oct 18–22. Hamilton Farm, Gladstone, NJ. World championship equestrian carriage-driving competition for single horses. For info: Gladstone Equestrian Assn, PO Box 119, Gladstone, NJ 07934. Phone: (908) 234-0151. Web: www.worldsingles.com.

CHASE'S SPORTSQUOTE OF THE DAY

"He was to football what Jack Dempsey was to boxing, what Babe Ruth was to baseball, and what Bobby Jones was to golf."—George Halas on Red Grange

---

BIRTHDAYS TODAY

Michael Keller (Mike) Ditka, 61, football coach and Pro Football Hall of Fame tight end, born Carnegie, PA, Oct 18, 1939.

Boyd Hamilton Dowler, 63, former football player, born Rock Springs, WY, Oct 18, 1937.

Alvis Forrest Gregg, 67, former football coach and Pro Football Hall of Fame tackle, born Birthright, TX, Oct 18, 1933.

Thomas ("Hit Man") Hearns, 42, former boxer, born Detroit, MI, Oct 18, 1958.

George Andrew Hendrick, 51, former baseball player, born Los Angeles, CA, Oct 18, 1949.

Willie Watterson Horton, 58, former baseball player, born Arno, VA, Oct 18, 1942.

Martina Navratilova (born Martina Subertova), 44, former tennis player, born Prague, Czechoslovakia, Oct 18, 1956.

Michael Stich, 32, tennis player, born Pinneburg, West Germany, Oct 18, 1968.

Bob Whitfield, Jr, 29, football player, born Carson, CA, Oct 18, 1971.

October 2000

S	M	T	W	T	F	S
1	2	3	4	5	6	7
8	9	10	11	12	13	14
15	16	17	18	19	20	21
22	23	24	25	26	27	28
29	30	31				

OCTOBER 19 — THURSDAY
Day 293 — 73 Remaining

AUSTRALIA: PARALYMPICS. Oct 18–29. Sydney, New South Wales. The Games of the 11th Paralympiad. 4,000 disabled athletes from 125 countries will compete in 582 events in 18 sports. Athletes are divided into six disability categories and then further classified according to their functional ability. The first Paralympics were contested at Rome in 1960. For info: Sydney Org Committee for the XXVII Olympic Games, Level 14, Maritime Centre, 207 Kent St, Sydney, NSW 2000, Australia. Phone: (61.2) 9297.2000. Fax: (61.2) 9297.2020. Web: www .sydney.olympic.org.

BROWN, THREE FINGER: BIRTH ANNIVERSARY. Oct 19, 1876. Mordecai Peter Centennial ("Three Finger") Brown, Baseball Hall of Fame pitcher, born at Nyesville, IN. Brown won 239 games in his 14-year career and five World Series games. His nickname came from a childhood injury that cost him one finger and misshaped others. Inducted into the Hall of Fame in 1949. Died at Terre Haute, IN, Feb 14, 1948.

EMPIRE STATE GOLDEN ARMS TOURNAMENT OF CHAMPIONS. Oct 19. Port Authority Bus Terminal, New York, NY. Winners of the New York Golden Arms Tournaments from each of the boroughs and Long Island compete in this classic arm-wrestling series finals. For info: New York Arm Wrestling Assn, Inc, 200-14 45th Dr, Bayside, NY 11361.

HOLMAN, NAT: BIRTH ANNIVERSARY. Oct 19, 1896. Nathan (Nat) Holman, Basketball Hall of Fame player and coach, born at New York, NY. Holman coached at CCNY and simultaneously played for several pro teams including the Original Celtics. As a pivot man, he devised the pivot play, giving the ball off to a cutting player, and the man-to-man defensive switch. His 1950 CCNY team was the only team to win both the NCAA title and the NIT in the same year, but its players were later disgraced by a cheating scandal. Inducted into the Hall of Fame in 1964. Died at New York, NY, Feb 12, 1995.

RICHARD SCORES 500th GOAL: ANNIVERSARY. Oct 19, 1957. Maurice ("Rocket") Richard of the Montreal Canadiens became the first player in National Hockey League history to score 500 regular-season goals when he tallied against the Chicago Blackhawks in a 3–1 Montreal victory. Richard finished his career with 544 goals and entered the Hockey Hall of Fame in 1961.

STASTNY GETS 1,000th POINT: ANNIVERSARY. Oct 19, 1989. Center Peter Stastny of the Quebec Nordiques got the 1,000th point of his National Hockey League career, a goal in a 5–3 win over the Chicago Blackhawks. Stastny finished his career with 1,239 points.

Santos (Sandy) Alomar, Sr, 57, former baseball player, born Salinas, Puerto Rico, Oct 19, 1943.

Timothy Wayne (Tim) Belcher, 39, baseball player, born Sparta, OH, Oct 19, 1961.

Evander Holyfield, 48, heavyweight champion boxer, born Atmore, AL, Oct 19, 1952.

Andre Wadsworth, 26, football player, born Miami, FL, Oct 19, 1974.

OCTOBER 20 — FRIDAY

Day 294 — 72 Remaining

WORLD SERIES CHAMPIONS THIS DATE

1982	St. Louis Cardinals
1988	Los Angeles Dodgers
1990	Cincinnati Reds

MANTLE, MICKEY: BIRTH ANNIVERSARY. Oct 20, 1931. Mickey Charles Mantle, Baseball Hall of Fame outfielder, born at Spavinaw, OK. Mantle replaced Joe DiMaggio in center field for the New York Yankees and grew to become the most beloved player of his era. His battle with liver cancer raised awareness for organ donation and alcoholism. Inducted into the Hall of Fame in 1974. Died at Dallas, TX, Aug 13, 1995.

MOSCOW SOCCER TRAGEDY: ANNIVERSARY. Oct 20, 1982. The world's worst soccer disaster occurred at Moscow when 340 fans were killed during a UEFA Cup match between the Spartak team from the Soviet Union and the Harlem team from Holland. Details of the tragedy, blaming police for forcing people into an open and icy staircase where many were crushed to death, were not published until nearly seven years later.

PRESIDENTS CUP. Oct 20–22. Robert Trent Jones Golf Club, Lake Manassas, VA. A biennial golf competition matching a team of US professionals against a team of professionals from the rest of the world, excluding Europe. The Presidents Cup was first contested in 1994. For info: PGA Tour, 12 TPC Blvd, Ponte Vedra Beach, FL 32082. Phone: (904) 285-3700.

SINKWICH, FRANK: 80th BIRTH ANNIVERSARY. Oct 20, 1920. Francis (Frank) Sinkwich, football player, born at McKees Rocks, PA. Sinkwich played halfback at the University of Georgia and won the 1942 Heisman Trophy. He played professionally and won the NFL's 1944 MVP Award, but his career was shortened by injury. Died at Athens, GA, Oct 22, 1990.

SPECIAL OLYMPICS MICHIGAN STATE SOCCER FINALS. Oct 20–21. Warren, MI. Olympic-style tournament for children and adults with mental retardation. For info: Special Olympics Michigan, Central Michigan Univ, Mt Pleasant, MI 48859. Phone: (800) 644-6404. Fax: (517) 774-3034. E-mail: M.K.Lindberg@cmich.edu. Web: www.somi.org.

Edmund Raymond ("Zeke") Bratkowski, 69, former football player, born Danville, IL, Oct 20, 1931.

William Dexter Coakley, 28, football player, born Charleston, SC, Oct 20, 1972.

Chad William Hennings, 35, football player, born Elberton, IA, Oct 20, 1965.

Keith Hernandez, 47, former baseball player, born San Francisco, CA, Oct 20, 1953.

Juan Antonio Marichal, 63, Baseball Hall of Fame pitcher, born Laguna Verde, Dominican Republic, Oct 20, 1937.

Herman Joseph Moore, 31, football player, born Danville, VA, Oct 20, 1969.

Raymond Earl (Ray) Rhodes, 50, football coach and former player, born Mexia, TX, Oct 20, 1950.

Lee Roy Selmon, 46, Pro Football Hall of Fame defensive end, born Eufaula, OK, Oct 20, 1954.

OCTOBER 21 — SATURDAY

Day 295 — 71 Remaining

WORLD SERIES CHAMPIONS THIS DATE

1973	Oakland Athletics
1976	Cincinnati Reds
1980	Philadelphia Phillies
1998	New York Yankees

BEVENS, BILL: BIRTH ANNIVERSARY. Oct 21, 1916. Floyd Clifford ("Bill") Bevens, baseball player, born at Hubbard, OR. Bevens nearly pitched the first no-hitter in World Series history, pitching for the New York Yankees against the Brooklyn Dodgers. In Game 4 of the 1947 Series, he carried his no-hitter into the ninth inning. With two out and two on, Cookie Lavagetto doubled home both runners, spoiling the no-hitter and winning the game, 3–2. Died at Salem, OR, Oct 26, 1991.

DRYER GETS TWO SAFETIES: ANNIVERSARY. Oct 21, 1973. Fred Dryer, defensive end for the Los Angeles Rams, became the first player in NFL history to score two safeties in the same game in the Rams' 24–7 victory over the Green Bay Packers.

FISK'S 12TH-INNING HOME RUN: 25th ANNIVERSARY. Oct 21, 1975. Catcher Carlton Fisk of the Boston Red Sox hit a home run in the 12th inning to defeat the Cincinnati Reds, 7–6, in the sixth game of the World Series. Fisk's dramatic homer forced a seventh game in what is generally considered one of the best World Series ever.

GREEN MOUNTAIN MARATHON. Oct 21. South Hero, VT. Marathon and half-marathon. For info: PO Box 527, Richmond, VT 05477. Phone: (802) 434-3228. E-mail: hatherton@pipeline.com.

HEAD OF THE CHARLES REGATTA. Oct 21–22. Charles River, Cambridge and Boston, MA. The largest rowing event. More than 5,600 male and female athletes compete in 20 events. Races begin at about 7:50 AM and last until 4:30 PM. Est attendance: 300,000. For info: Head of the Charles, PO Box 380052, Cambridge, MA 02238-0052. Phone: (617) 864-8415. Fax: (617) 225-2391. E-mail: regatta@hocr.org. Web: www.hocr.org.

INTERNATIONAL GOLD CUP. Oct 21. Great Meadow, The Plains, VA. A day of steeplechasing in the heart of Virginia's hunt country. Gates open at 10 AM for special events and activities. Corporate and chalet entertainment packages available. Conducted by the Virginia Gold Cup Association for benefit of free year-round use of Great Meadow for nonprofit community activities. Est attendance: 40,000. For info: Virginia Gold Cup Assn, PO Box 840, Warrenton, VA 20188. Phone: (540) 347-2612. Fax: (540) 349-1829. Web: www.vagoldcup.com.

PICCOLO, BRIAN: BIRTH ANNIVERSARY. Oct 21, 1943. Louis Brian Piccolo, football player, born at Pittsfield, MA. He played running back at Wake Forest and with the Chicago Bears. His interracial friendship with Gale Sayers earned him a certain fame, but at age 26 he was stricken with embryonal cell carcinoma, a virulent form of cancer that took his life seven months later. Died at New York, NY, June 16, 1970. His life became the subject of a book, *Brian Piccolo: A Short Season*, and a made-for-television movie, *Brian's Song*.

WORLD SERIES BEGINS. Oct 21 (tentative). Sites TBA. Winners of the National League Championship Series and the American League Championship Series meet in the World Series. The best-four-of-seven Series opens with two games in the home park of the American League team, followed by two games (and a third, if necessary) in the home park of the National League team. If needed, the Series returns to the American League park for Games 6 and 7.

BIRTHDAYS TODAY

Edward Charles ("Whitey") Ford, 72, Baseball Hall of Fame pitcher, born New York, NY, Oct 21, 1928.
Morris C. (Mo) Lewis, 31, football player, born Atlanta, GA, Oct 21, 1969.
William Ellis (Bill) Russell, 52, former baseball manager and player, born Pittsburg, KS, Oct 21, 1948.

OCTOBER 22 — SUNDAY
Day 296 — 70 Remaining

WORLD SERIES CHAMPIONS THIS DATE
1972	Oakland Athletics
1975	Cincinnati Reds

BECKMAN, JOHN: BIRTH ANNIVERSARY. Oct 22, 1895. John Beckman, Basketball Hall of Fame forward, born at New York, NY. Beckman was one of the game's first great stars even though he did not attend college. He played in early professional leagues before World War I and joined the Original Celtics after the war. Beckman was an outstanding scorer, especially from the foul line. He played until age 46 when the Original Celtics disbanded in 1941. Inducted into the Hall of Fame in 1959. Died at Miami, FL, June 22, 1968.

CARR, JOE: BIRTH ANNIVERSARY. Oct 22, 1880. Joseph F. (Joe) Carr, Pro Football Hall of Fame executive, born at Columbus, OH. Carr was a minor league baseball administrator, one of the founders of the 1925 American Basketball League and president of the American Professional Football Association (later the National Football League) from 1922 until his death. Carr stood for

an honest game that could be embraced by a wide public. Inducted into the Pro Football Hall of Fame as a charter member in 1963. Died at Columbus, May 20, 1939.

FIRST TELEVISED PRO FOOTBALL GAME: ANNIVERSARY. Oct 22, 1939. The Brooklyn Dodgers of the National Football League defeated the Philadelphia Eagles, 23–14, in the first televised pro football game, broadcast to about 1,000 homes in Brooklyn. The announcer was Allan ("Skip") Walz.

FOXX, JIMMIE: BIRTH ANNIVERSARY. Oct 22, 1907. James Emory (Jimmie) Foxx, Baseball Hall of Fame first baseman, born at Sudlersville, MD. Foxx was a ferocious batter who hit 58 home runs in 1932, two short of Babe Ruth's record. He managed a team in the All-American Girls Professional Baseball League. Inducted into the Hall of Fame in 1951. Died at Miami, FL, July 21, 1967.

LASALLE BANKS CHICAGO MARATHON. Oct 22. Grant Park, Chicago, IL. 23rd annual marathon (26.2 miles) and 10th annual 5K (3.1 miles). Marathon has a reputation for attracting an international field of top athletes and is ranked as one of the fastest in the world. Plus, a Breakfast Fun Run and a Youth Run. Annually, a Sunday in October. Est attendance: 800,000. For info: LaSalle Banks Chicago Marathon, PO Box 5709, Chicago, IL 60680-5709. Phone: (312) 904-9800. Fax: (312) 904-9820. Web: www.chicagomarathon.com.

WORLD FOOTBALL LEAGUE DISBANDS: 25th ANNIVERSARY. Oct 22, 1975. The World Football League, a 10-team enterprise struggling through its second season, suspended operations and disbanded prior to the 12th week of a 20-week schedule.

XTERRA CHAMPIONSHIP. Oct 22. Wailea, Maui, HI. Televised championship off-road triathlon. Includes 1.5K rough-water swim, 30K mountain bike race and 11K cross-country run. $30,000 pro purse. Est attendance: 5,000. For info: Team Unlimited, 1001 Bishop St, Pauahi Tower #880, Honolulu, HI 96813. Phone: (808) 521-4322. Fax: (808) 538-0314. E-mail: info@teamunlimited.com. Web: www.teamunlimited.com.

CHASE'S SPORTSQUOTE OF THE DAY

"He has muscles in his hair."—Yankees pitcher Lefty Gomez on Jimmie Foxx

BIRTHDAYS TODAY

Brian Anthony Boitano, 37, Olympic gold medal figure skater, born Mountain View, CA, Oct 22, 1963.
Slater Nelson Martin, Jr, 75, Basketball Hall of Fame guard, born Houston, TX, Oct 22, 1925.
Miroslav Satan, 26, hockey player, born Topolcany, Czechoslovakia, Oct 22, 1974.
Terry Yake, 32, hockey player, born New Westminster, British Columbia, Canada, Oct 22, 1968.

OCTOBER 23 — MONDAY
Day 297 — 69 Remaining

WORLD SERIES CHAMPIONS THIS DATE
1910	Philadelphia Athletics
1993	Toronto Blue Jays

BLACKWELL, EWELL: BIRTH ANNIVERSARY. Oct 23, 1922. Ewell Blackwell, baseball player, born at Fresno, CA. Known as "The Whip," Blackwell terrified right-handed batters with his fearsome sidearm delivery. He pitched in the majors for 10 seasons, threw a no-hitter in 1947 and played in six straight All-Star Games. Died at Hendersonville, NC, Oct 29, 1996.

October 2000

S	M	T	W	T	F	S
1	2	3	4	5	6	7
8	9	10	11	12	13	14
15	16	17	18	19	20	21
22	23	24	25	26	27	28
29	30	31				

CARTER HOME RUN WINS WORLD SERIES: ANNIVERSARY. Oct 23, 1993. Joe Carter of the Toronto Blue Jays hit a three-run homer off relief pitcher Mitch Williams of the Philadelphia Phillies with one out in the bottom of the ninth inning to win the World Series for Toronto. Carter's homer, coming after a walk to Rickey Henderson and a single by Paul Molitor, gave the Blue Jays an 8–6 win and a four-games-to-two Series triumph. Only once before, in 1960, had the World Series been ended by a home run in the bottom of the ninth.

HEISMAN, JOHN: BIRTH ANNIVERSARY. Oct 23, 1869. John William Heisman, football player, coach and administrator, born at Cleveland, OH. Heisman played football at Brown and Pennsylvania and began coaching at Oberlin. He moved to Akron, Oberlin again, Auburn, Clemson, Georgia Tech, Pennsylvania, Washington and Jefferson, and Rice. After his retirement, he became athletic director at the Downtown Athletic Club at New York. The club's award to the best college football player in the country was named in his honor posthumously. Died at New York, NY, Oct 3, 1936.

HULBERT, WILLIAM: BIRTH ANNIVERSARY. Oct 23, 1832. William Ambrose Hulbert, Baseball Hall of Fame executive, born at Burlington Flats, NY. Hulbert founded the National League in 1876 and exercised strong leadership during his term as president. He expelled clubs and players for conduct he thought would jeopardize the game. Inducted into the Hall of Fame in 1995. Died at Chicago, IL, Apr 10, 1882.

KINARD, BRUISER: BIRTH ANNIVERSARY. Oct 23, 1914. Frank ("Bruiser") Kinard, Pro Football Hall of Fame lineman, born at Pelahatchie, MS. Kinard was an outstanding two-way player who earned his nickname for his size and aggressiveness. He played at the University of Mississippi in the late 1930s and then professionally with the Brooklyn Dodgers (NFL) and the New York Yankees (AAFC). Inducted into the Hall of Fame as a charter member in 1963. Died at Jackson, MS, Sept 7, 1985.

BIRTHDAYS TODAY

James Paul David (Jim) Bunning, 69, US Senator and Baseball Hall of Fame pitcher, born Southgate, KY, Oct 23, 1931.

Gertrude Ederle, 94, swimmer, born New York, NY, Oct 23, 1906.

Douglas Richard (Doug) Flutie, 38, Heisman Trophy quarterback, born Manchester, MD, Oct 23, 1962.

Kevin Lerell Henry, 32, football player, born Mound Bayou, MS, Oct 23, 1968.

Alois Terry (Al) Leiter, 35, baseball player, born Toms River, NJ, Oct 23, 1965.

Tiffeny Carleen Milbrett, 28, soccer player, born Portland, OR, Oct 23, 1972.

Pele (born Edson Arantes do Nascimento), 60, former soccer player, born Tres Coracoes, Brazil, Oct 23, 1940.

Juan ("Chi-Chi") Rodriguez, 66, golfer, born Rio Piedras, Puerto Rico, Oct 23, 1934.

Michael John (Mike) Tomczak, 38, football player, born Calumet City, IL, Oct 23, 1962.

Keith Adam Van Horn, 25, basketball player, born Fullerton, CA, Oct 23, 1975.

OCTOBER 24 — TUESDAY
Day 298 — 68 Remaining

WORLD SERIES CHAMPIONS THIS DATE	
1992	Toronto Blue Jays

BLUEGE, OSSIE: 100th BIRTH ANNIVERSARY. Oct 24, 1900. Oswald Louis (Ossie) Bluege, baseball player, manager and executive, born at Chicago, IL. Bluege is the only man to have played on all three of the Washington Senators' World Series teams. He played 18 years in the majors, primarily as a third baseman, and managed the Senators from 1943 through 1947. Died at Edina, MN, Oct 14, 1985.

SOCKALEXIS, LOUIS: BIRTH ANNIVERSARY. Oct 24, 1871. Louis M. Sockalexis, baseball player, born at Old Town, ME. A Penobscot, Sockalexis is credited with being the first Native American to play major league baseball. He played for the Cleveland National League team in 1897–99, but his effect on that city was so strong that in 1914, its American League team was renamed the Indians in his honor. Died at Burlington, ME, Dec 24, 1913.

TORONTO TAKES SERIES TROPHY OUT OF US: ANNIVERSARY. Oct 24, 1992. The Toronto Blue Jays defeated the Atlanta Braves, 4–3, in 11 innings in Game 6 to become the first non-US-based team to win the World Series.

WORLD'S FIRST SOCCER CLUB: ANNIVERSARY. Oct 24, 1857. The world's first soccer club, the Sheffield Football Club at Sheffield, England, was founded. Six years later, the first soccer league, the Football Association of England, was founded.

BIRTHDAYS TODAY

Rafael Leonidas Belliard, 39, baseball player, born Puerto Nuevo Mao, Dominican Republic, Oct 24, 1961.

James Patrick (Jim) Brosnan, 71, author (*Pennant Race* and *The Long Season*) and former baseball player, born Cincinnati, OH, Oct 24, 1929.

Corey Dillon, 25, football player, born Seattle, WA, Oct 24, 1975.

Arthur Lee Rhodes, Jr, 31, baseball player, born Waco, TX, Oct 24, 1969.

Frank Paul (F.P.) Santangelo, 33, baseball player, born Livonia, MI, Oct 24, 1967.

Yelberton Abraham (Y.A.) Tittle, Jr, 74, Pro Football Hall of Fame quarterback, born Marshall, TX, Oct 24, 1926.

OCTOBER 25 — WEDNESDAY
Day 299 — 67 Remaining

WORLD SERIES CHAMPIONS THIS DATE
1987	Minnesota Twins

COOKE, JACK KENT: BIRTH ANNIVERSARY. Oct 25, 1912. Jack Kent Cooke, sports entrepreneur, born at Hamilton, Ontario, Canada. Cooke made his fortune, estimated at $825 million, in broadcasting, real estate and newspapers. He owned racehorses, the Los Angeles Lakers, the Los Angeles Kings and the Washington Redskins. He also built the Fabulous Forum at Inglewood, CA, and was at the time of his death finishing a new stadium for the Redskins in suburban Virginia. Crusty and flamboyant, he was married five times, once paying $49 million in a divorce settlement. Died at Washington, DC, Apr 6, 1997.

ELAM KICKS RECORD-TYING FIELD GOAL: ANNIVERSARY. Oct 25, 1998. Placekicker Jason Elam of the Denver Broncos kicked a 63-yard field goal in a game against the Jacksonville Jaguars, tying a record set by Tom Dempsey in 1970. Denver won, 37–24.

MARSHALL'S WRONG-WAY RUN: ANNIVERSARY. Oct 25, 1964. In a game between the Minnesota Vikings and the San Francisco 49ers, Minnesota defensive end Jim Marshall picked up a fumble by 49ers quarterback Billy Kilmer and ran 66 yards into the wrong end zone. His gaffe resulted in a safety, 2 points for San Francisco, but the Vikings still prevailed, 27–22.

MOOKIE'S GROUNDER THROUGH BUCKNER'S LEGS: ANNIVERSARY. Oct 25, 1986. The New York Mets won Game 6 of the World Series, 6–5, in 10 innings, over the Boston Red Sox. The Mets made a dramatic comeback in the last inning, scoring three runs after two were out. Twice down to their last strike, they bunched three singles, a wild pitch and a ground ball by Mookie Wilson that went through the legs of first baseman Bill Buckner to eke out the victory.

WOOD, SMOKY JOE: BIRTH ANNIVERSARY. Oct 25, 1889. Joe ("Smoky Joe") Wood, baseball player and coach, born at Kansas City, MO. Wood is regarded as one of the fastest pitchers of all time even though his career was cut short by a sore arm. After becoming an outfielder and then retiring, he coached baseball at Yale. Died at West Haven, CT, July 27, 1985.

CHASE'S SPORTSQUOTE OF THE DAY
"I would like to knock it on every green and two-putt, but that's not my style of play or my style of living." —Muffin Spencer-Devlin

BIRTHDAYS TODAY
Josef Beranek, 31, hockey player, born Litvinov, Czechoslovakia, Oct 25, 1969.
Robert William (Bobby) Brown, 76, former baseball executive and player, born Seattle, WA, Oct 25, 1924.
Kelly Wayne Chase, 33, hockey player, born Porcupine Plain, Saskatchewan, Canada, Oct 25, 1967.
Wendel Clark, 34, hockey player, born Kelvington, Saskatchewan, Canada, Oct 25, 1966.

October 2000
S	M	T	W	T	F	S
1	2	3	4	5	6	7
8	9	10	11	12	13	14
15	16	17	18	19	20	21
22	23	24	25	26	27	28
29	30	31				

David William (Dave) Cowens, 52, former basketball coach and Basketball Hall of Fame center, born Newport, KY, Oct 25, 1948.
Daniel Wayne (Danny) Darwin, 45, former baseball player, born Bonham, TX, Oct 25, 1955.
Daniel Mack (Dan) Gable, 52, Olympic gold medal wrestler, born Waterloo, IA, Oct 25, 1948.
Robert Montgomery (Bobby) Knight, 60, college basketball coach and former player, born Orrville, OH, Oct 25, 1940.
Robert Brown (Bobby) Thomson, 77, former baseball player, born Glasgow, Scotland, Oct 25, 1923.

OCTOBER 26 — THURSDAY
Day 300 — 66 Remaining

WORLD SERIES CHAMPIONS THIS DATE
1911	Philadelphia Athletics
1996	New York Yankees
1997	Florida Marlins

DENKINGER'S CONTROVERSIAL CALL: 15th ANNIVERSARY. Oct 26, 1985. The Kansas City Royals tied the World Series, three games to three, against the St. Louis Cardinals by winning Game 6, 2–1. A controversial call at first base by umpire Don Denkinger and a two-run single by Dane Iorg brought the Royals the win. Kansas City won the seventh game the next day, 11–0.

FORT LAUDERDALE INTERNATIONAL BOAT SHOW. Oct 26–30. Greater Ft Lauderdale/Broward County Convention Center. Everything from small boats to megayachts to boating equipment. For info: Greater Ft Lauderdale CVB, 1850 Eller Dr, Ste 303, Ft Lauderdale, FL 33316. Phone: (954) 765-4466.

FULKS, JOE: BIRTH ANNIVERSARY. Oct 26, 1921. Joseph (Joe) Fulks, Basketball Hall of Fame forward, born at Birmingham, KY. Fulks earned All-American honors at Murray State University in 1943 and developed the innovative jump shot, first using two hands and then gradually switching to one hand. After World War II, he was an outstanding scorer with the Philadelphia Warriors. On Feb 10, 1949, he scored 63 points in a game against the Indianapolis Jets, a league record at the time. Inducted into the Hall of Fame in 1977. Died at Eddyville, KY, Mar 21, 1976.

GLEASON, KID: BIRTH ANNIVERSARY. Oct 26, 1866. William J. ("Kid") Gleason, baseball player and manager, born at Camden, NJ. Gleason was a major league pitcher around the turn of the century. His career spanned 23 years, after which he coached and managed the Chicago White Sox, including the infamous 1919 "Black Sox." Died at Philadelphia, PA, Jan 2, 1933.

JOHNSON, JUDY: BIRTH ANNIVERSARY. Oct 26, 1899. William Julius (Judy) Johnson, Baseball Hall of Fame third baseman, born at Snow Hill, MD. Johnson was a defensive specialist who hit for a high average with occasional power. After retiring he scouted for several teams. Inducted into the Hall of Fame in 1975. Died at Wilmington, DE, June 14, 1989.

LEMIEUX SCORES 500th GOAL: 5th ANNIVERSARY. Oct 26, 1995. Center Mario Lemieux of the Pittsburgh Penguins became the 20th player in the National Hockey League to score 500 regular-season goals. He tallied against goalie Tommy Soderstrom of the New York Islanders in a 7–5 win. Lemieux finished his career with 601 goals and was inducted into the Hockey Hall of Fame in 1997.

SELEE, FRANK: BIRTH ANNIVERSARY. Oct 26, 1859. Frank Gibson Selee, Baseball Hall of Fame manager and executive, born at Amherst, NH. Selee guided the Boston National League team of the 1890s to five pennants in nine years, and then, after moving to Chicago, built the team that won three straight pennants in 1906, 1907 and 1908. Inducted into the Hall of Fame in 1999. Died at Denver, CO, July 5, 1909.

SHARKEY, JACK: BIRTH ANNIVERSARY. Oct 26, 1902. Jack Sharkey, boxer, born Joseph Paul Zukauskas at Binghamton, NY. Sharkey won the heavyweight championship on June 21, 1932, defeating Max Schmeling, and lost it a year later to Primo Carnera. After retirement, he became a referee and one of the world's top fly-casters. Died at Beverly, MA, Aug 17, 1994.

BIRTHDAYS TODAY

Jessie W. Armstead, 30, football player, born Dallas, TX, Oct 26, 1970.
Dudley Michael (Mike) Hargrove, 51, baseball manager and former player, born Perryton, TX, Oct 26, 1949.
Colbert Dale ("Toby") Harrah, 52, former baseball manager and player, born Sissonville, WV, Oct 26, 1948.
Gerald Wayne Martin, 35, football player, born Forrest City, AR, Oct 26, 1965.

OCTOBER 27 — FRIDAY
Day 301 — 65 Remaining

WORLD SERIES CHAMPIONS THIS DATE	
1985	Kansas City Royals
1986	New York Mets
1991	Minnesota Twins

GEORGE, BILL: 70th BIRTH ANNIVERSARY. Oct 27, 1930. William (Bill) George, Pro Football Hall of Fame linebacker, born at Waynesburg, PA. George played college football at Wake Forest and then was drafted by the Chicago Bears. Originally a middle guard, playing down on the line of scrimmage, George invented the position of middle linebacker, playing up and behind the line. Inducted into the Hall of Fame in 1974. Died in an automobile accident near Rockford, IL, Sept 30, 1982.

NATIONAL BASKETBALL ASSOCIATION REGULAR SEASON OPENS. Oct 27 (tentative). The National Basketball Association opens its 55th regular season leading to the play-offs and the NBA Finals. Each of the league's 29 teams plays an 82-game schedule. Eight teams from each of the two conferences qualify for the postseason.

For info: Natl Basketball Assn, Olympic Tower, 645 Fifth Ave, New York, NY 10022. Phone: (212) 826-7000. Web: www.nba.com/.

NATIONAL FINALS STEER ROPING. Oct 27–28. Lazy E Arena, Guthrie, OK. The World Championship and $90,000 are at stake as the top 15 steer ropers in the world compete. Est attendance: 12,000. For info: Lazy E Arena, Rt 5, Box 393, Guthrie, OK 73044. Phone: (405) 282-7433 or (800) 595-RIDE (7433). Fax: (405) 282-3785. E-mail: arena@lazye.net. Web: www.lazye.com.

CHASE'S SPORTSQUOTE OF THE DAY

"A laid-back crowd in San Diego. They're so laid back that they didn't even come."—Ralph Kiner

BIRTHDAYS TODAY

Elijah Jerry ("Pumpsie") Green, 67, former baseball player, born Oakland, CA, Oct 27, 1933.
John David Kasay, 31, football player, born Athens, GA, Oct 27, 1969.
Ralph McPherran Kiner, 78, broadcaster and Baseball Hall of Fame outfielder, born Santa Rita, NM, Oct 27, 1922.
Mary Terslegge Meagher, 36, Olympic gold medal swimmer, born Louisville, KY, Oct 27, 1964.
Brad William Radke, 28, baseball player, born Eau Claire, WI, Oct 27, 1972.
Leon Joseph ("Bip") Roberts, III, 37, baseball player, born Berkeley, CA, Oct 27, 1963.
William Kyle Rote, 73, former broadcaster and football player, born Bellevue, TX, Oct 27, 1927.
Sergei Samsonov, 22, hockey player, born Moscow, USSR, Oct 27, 1978.
Patty Sheehan, 44, LPGA Hall of Fame golfer, born Middlebury, VT, Oct 27, 1956.
Dick Trickle, 59, auto racer, born Wisconsin Rapids, WI, Oct 27, 1941.

OCTOBER 28 — SATURDAY
Day 302 — 64 Remaining

WORLD SERIES CHAMPIONS THIS DATE	
1981	Los Angeles Dodgers
1989	Oakland Athletics
1995	Atlanta Braves

BIG TEN CROSS COUNTRY CHAMPIONSHIP. Oct 28. University of Wisconsin, Madison, WI. For info: Big Ten Conference, 1500 W Higgins Rd, Park Ridge, IL 60068-6300. Phone: (847) 696-1010. Fax: (847) 696-1150. Web: www.bigten.org.

FIRST MEN'S FIELD HOCKEY GAME: ANNIVERSARY. Oct 28, 1928. The Westchester Field Hockey Club of Rye, NY, defeated the Germantown Cricket Club of Germantown, PA, 2–1, in the first organized men's field hockey game played in the US.

FRANCIS GETS 1,000th POINT: ANNIVERSARY. Oct 28, 1993. Center Ron Francis of the Pittsburgh Penguins got the 1,000th point of his National Hockey League career, a goal in a 7–3 loss to the Quebec Nordiques.

NBA HIRES WOMEN REFEREES: ANNIVERSARY. Oct 28, 1997. The National Basketball Association hired five new referees for the 1997–98 season, including the first two women ever. Dee Kantner and Violet Palmer both had extensive experience working women's college games and both worked exhibition games as a trial. Palmer got her first regular-season assignment on Oct 31 in Vancouver. Kantner worked her first game on Nov 5 at Philadelphia.

RICHMOND HIGHLAND GAMES AND CELTIC FESTIVAL. Oct 28–29 (tentative). Fairgrounds, Strawberry Hill, Richmond, VA. Celebration of Scottish and Celtic heritage featuring athletic competition, clan tents, pipe bands, sheepdog demonstrations; dogs, livestock and horses of the British Isles; fiddle, harp and Highland dance competitions; food, pubs and whiskey tasting; kilted and clan miles; storytelling and more. Est attendance: 200,000. For info: Clay Roberts, Richmond Highland Games and Celtic Fest at Strawberry Hill, PO Box 26805, Richmond, VA 23261. Phone: (804) 228-3238. Fax: (804) 228-3252. E-mail: equine@strawberryhill.com.

SECRETARIAT'S CAREER ENDS: ANNIVERSARY. Oct 28, 1973. Secretariat, the colt many considered the greatest thoroughbred racer of all time, concluded his career with a victory in the Canadian International Championship at Woodbine Race Course. His jockey on this occasion was Eddie Maple, substituting for the suspended Ron Turcotte.

CHASE'S SPORTSQUOTE OF THE DAY

"Whether it's delusion or not, I feel pretty much accepted—as much as a referee can be accepted. I don't feel singled out being a woman. From the fans, every once in a while you hear something gender specific, but you tolerate that from fans."—NBA referee Dee Kanter

---

BIRTHDAYS TODAY

Stephen Dennis (Steve) Atwater, 34, football player, born Chicago, IL, Oct 28, 1966.
Terrell Davis, 28, football player, born San Diego, CA, Oct 28, 1972.
Kevin Dineen, 37, hockey player, born Quebec City, Quebec, Canada, Oct 28, 1963.
Bert Tyrone Emanuel, 30, football player, born Kansas City, MO, Oct 28, 1970.
Juan Andres Guzman, 34, baseball player, born Santo Domingo, Dominican Republic, Oct 28, 1966.
Benoit Hogue, 34, hockey player, born Repentigny, Quebec, Canada, Oct 28, 1966.
William Bruce Jenner, 51, Olympic gold medal decathlete, born Mount Kisco, NY, Oct 28, 1949.
Bowie Kent Kuhn, 74, former commissioner of baseball, born Takoma Park, MD, Oct 28, 1926.
Leonard Randolph (Lenny) Wilkens, 63, Basketball Hall of Fame coach and guard, born New York, NY, Oct 28, 1937.
Randy Scott Wittman, 41, basketball coach and former player, born Indianapolis, IN, Oct 28, 1959.

OCTOBER 29 — SUNDAY
Day 303 — 63 Remaining

BROWNS BECOME ORIOLES: ANNIVERSARY. Oct 29, 1953. The sale of the St. Louis Browns from Bill Veeck to a group of Baltimore investors was completed, and the American League's most hapless team became the Orioles.

COLUMBUS MARATHON. Oct 29. Columbus, OH. For info: Columbus Marathon, 833 Eastwind Dr, Westerville, OH 43081. Phone: (614) 794-1566. E-mail: promo1@netwalk.com. Web: columbusmarathon.com.

October 2000	S	M	T	W	T	F	S
	1	2	3	4	5	6	7
	8	9	10	11	12	13	14
	15	16	17	18	19	20	21
	22	23	24	25	26	27	28
	29	30	31				

DAYLIGHT SAVING TIME ENDS; STANDARD TIME RESUMES. Oct 29–Apr 1, 2001. Standard Time resumes at 2 AM on the last Sunday in October in each time zone, as provided by the Uniform Time Act of 1966 (as amended in 1986 by Public Law 99–359). Many use the popular rule "spring forward, fall back" to remember which way to turn their clocks. (See also: "US: Daylight Saving Time Begins" Apr 2.)

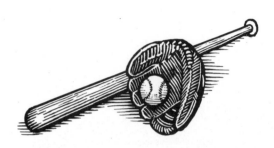

EBBETS, CHARLES: BIRTH ANNIVERSARY. Oct 29, 1859. Charles Hercules Ebbets, baseball executive, born at New York, NY. Ebbets bought into the Brooklyn baseball club in 1890 and became controlling owner in 1898. He sold 50 percent of the team to build Ebbets Field, the park whose enduring reputation has been the model for the new, old-fashioned parks constructed in recent years. Died at New York, Apr 18, 1925.

NBA ANNOUNCES ITS 50 GREATEST PLAYERS: ANNIVERSARY. Oct 29, 1996. The National Basketball Association got set to launch its 50th-anniversary season by announcing its 50 greatest players of all time. Ten of the 50 spent significant portions of their careers with the Boston Celtics.

BIRTHDAYS TODAY

Gustavo ("Karim") Garcia, 25, baseball player, born Ciudad Obregon, Mexico, Oct 29, 1975.
Joel Stuart Otto, 39, hockey player, born Elk River, MN, Oct 29, 1961.

OCTOBER 30 — MONDAY
Day 304 — 62 Remaining

ADCOCK, JOE: BIRTH ANNIVERSARY. Oct 30, 1927. Joseph Wilbur (Joe) Adcock, baseball player and manager, born at Coushatta, LA. Adcock starred at first base for the Milwaukee Braves in the 1950s. Although he once hit four home runs in a game, Adcock was most famous for ending pitcher Harvey Haddix's 1959 perfect game in the 13th inning. Died at Coushatta, May 3, 1999.

ALI REGAINS TITLE: ANNIVERSARY. Oct 30, 1974. Muhammad Ali became the first boxer to regain the heavyweight title by knocking out defending champion George Foreman in the eighth round of a fight at Kinshasa, Zaire.

ATLAS, CHARLES: BIRTH ANNIVERSARY. Oct 30, 1893. Charles Atlas, bodybuilder, born Angelo Siciliano at Acri, Calabria, Italy. Atlas created a popular mail-order bodybuilding course, pegged to his own youthful troubles as a "97-lb weakling." The legendary sand-kicking episode used later in advertising for his course occurred at Coney Island when a lifeguard kicked sand in Atlas's face and stole his girlfriend. Three generations of comic book fans read his advertisements. Died at Long Beach, NY, Dec 24, 1972.

BUCYK SCORES 500th GOAL: 25th ANNIVERSARY. Oct 30, 1975. Left wing Johnny Bucyk of the Boston Bruins scored the 500th regular-season goal of his career in a 3–2 victory over the St. Louis Blues. Bucyk, the 7th player in National Hockey League history to reach 500, finished his career with 556 goals and entered the Hockey Hall of Fame in 1981.

DAY, LEON: BIRTH ANNIVERSARY. Oct 30, 1916. Leon Day, Baseball Hall of Fame pitcher, outfielder and second baseman, born at Alexandria, VA. Day was a star in the Negro Leagues in the 1930s and 1940s. One week after being elected to the Hall of Fame and four months before his induction, he died at Baltimore, MD, Mar 13, 1995.

DELAHANTY, ED: BIRTH ANNIVERSARY. Oct 30, 1867. Edward James (Ed) Delahanty, Baseball Hall of Fame outfielder, born at Cleveland, OH. One of five brothers to play major league baseball, Delahanty starred with the Philadelphia team in the National League, compiling a .345 career batting average. His death was unusual. After being suspended in June 1903, he left his team at Detroit and boarded a train for New York. Drunk, he was put off by the conductor for disorderly conduct near Niagara Falls. He started walking along the tracks, fell through a bridge and plunged over the falls. Inducted into the Hall of Fame in 1945. Died at Niagara Falls, NY, July 2, 1903.

MBNA AMERICA® QUARTER HORSE RACING CHALLENGE. Oct 30. Los Alamitos Race Course, Orange County, CA. A purse and bonus awards program developed by AQHA to increase racing opportunities for older horses. For info: AQHA, PO Box 2000, Amarillo, TX 79168. Phone: (806) 376-4811. Fax: (806) 349-6409. Web: www.aqha.com.

TERRY, BILL: BIRTH ANNIVERSARY. Oct 30, 1898. William Harold (Bill) Terry, Baseball Hall of Fame first baseman and manager, born at Atlanta, GA. Terry was the last National League player to hit .400, batting .401 in 1930. He succeed John McGraw as manager of the New York Giants in 1932. Inducted into the Hall of Fame in 1954. Died at Jacksonville, FL, Jan 9, 1989.

BIRTHDAYS TODAY

Robert Randall (Bobby) Bragan, 83, former baseball manager and player, born Birmingham, AL, Oct 30, 1917.

Ty Hubert Detmer, 33, football player, born San Marcos, TX, Oct 30, 1967.

Ellis B. Johnson, 27, football player, born Wildwood, FL, Oct 30, 1973.

Diego Armando Maradona, 40, former soccer player, born Lanus, Argentina, Oct 30, 1960.

Mark Steven Portugal, 38, baseball player, born Los Angeles, CA, Oct 30, 1962.

Richard Albert (Dick) Vermeil, 64, football coach, born Calistoga, CA, Oct 30, 1936.

OCTOBER 31 — TUESDAY
Day 305 — 61 Remaining

ANTLEY WINS NINE RACES: ANNIVERSARY. Oct 31, 1987. Chris Antley became the first jockey to win nine thoroughbred races in a single day. He won four races in six tries at Aqueduct in the afternoon and five more in eight races at the Meadowlands at night.

FIRST BLACK PLAYS IN NBA GAME: 50th ANNIVERSARY. Oct 31, 1950. Earl Lloyd became the first black to play in an NBA game when he took the floor for the Washington Capitals at Rochester, NY. Lloyd was actually one of three blacks to become NBA players in the 1950 season, the others being Nat ("Sweetwater") Clifton, who was signed by the New York Knicks, and Chuck Cooper, who was drafted by the Boston Celtics (and debuted the night after Lloyd).

GIANT NFL TRADE COMPLETED: ANNIVERSARY. Oct 31, 1987. Running back Eric Dickerson signed a contract with the Indianapolis Colts to complete a complex, three-team NFL trade. The Colts got Dickerson from the Los Angeles Rams in exchange for one player and three draft choices. The Rams acquired an additional three draft picks and another player from the Buffalo Bills in exchange for the Colts' trading the rights to linebacker Cornelius Bennett to the Bills.

HUBBARD, CAL: 100th BIRTH ANNIVERSARY. Oct 31, 1900. Robert Cal Hubbard, Pro Football Hall of Fame tackle and Baseball Hall of Fame umpire, born at Keytesville, MO. Hubbard played college and professional football and is regarded as one of the game's greatest linemen. After a short coaching career, he became an American League umpire and later supervisor of umpires. Inducted into the Pro Football Hall of Fame as a charter member in 1963 and into the Baseball Hall of Fame in 1976. Died at Milan, MO, Oct 19, 1977.

KELTNER, KEN: BIRTH ANNIVERSARY. Oct 31, 1916. Kenneth Frederick (Ken) Keltner, baseball player, born at Milwaukee, WI. Keltner's two sterling plays at third base for the Cleveland Indians on July 17, 1941, helped end Joe DiMaggio's 56-game hitting streak. Died at Greenfield, WI, Dec 12, 1991.

BIRTHDAYS TODAY

Antonio Davis, 32, basketball player, born Oakland, CA, Oct 31, 1968.

Theodore ("Blue") Edwards, 35, basketball player, born Washington, DC, Oct 31, 1965.

Roger Kahn, 73, author (*The Boys of Summer, Good Enough to Dream, The Era* and *Memories of Summer*) and sportswriter, born New York, NY, Oct 31, 1927.

Frederick Stanley (Fred) McGriff, 37, baseball player, born Tampa, FL, Oct 31, 1963.

Edward Kenneth (Eddie) Taubensee, 32, baseball player, born Beeville, TX, Oct 31, 1968.

Stephen Christopher (Steve) Trachsel, 30, baseball player, born Oxnard, CA, Oct 31, 1970.

Joseph Henry (Joe) West, 48, baseball umpire, born Asheville, NC, Oct 31, 1952.

Lee Artis Woodall, 31, football player, born Carlisle, PA, Oct 31, 1969.

NOVEMBER 1 — WEDNESDAY
Day 306 — 60 Remaining

CHASE'S SPORTSQUOTE OF THE DAY

"Outlined against a blue-gray October sky, the Four Horsemen rode again."—Grantland Rice on the Notre Dame backfield he helped make famous

FIRST BAA GAME: ANNIVERSARY. Nov 1, 1946. The New York Knickerbockers defeated the Toronto Huskies, 68–66, in the first regular-season game ever played in the Basketball Association of America. (The BAA merged with the National Basketball League in 1949 to form the National Basketball Association.) For this inaugural contest, any fan taller than 6'8" Huskies center George Nostrand was admitted free.

HOCKEY MASK INTRODUCED: ANNIVERSARY. Nov 1, 1959. Tired of stopping hockey pucks with his face, Montreal Canadiens goalie Jacques Plante, having received another wound, reemerged from the locker room with seven new stitches—and a plastic face mask he had made from fiberglass and resin. Although Cliff Benedict had tried a leather mask back in the '20s and the idea didn't catch on then, after Plante wore his, goalies throughout the NHL began wearing protective plastic face shields as a matter of course.

MOORE, DAVEY: BIRTH ANNIVERSARY. Nov 1, 1933. Davey Moore, boxer, born at Lexington, KY. Moore won the world featherweight championship in 1959. He defended the title successfully several times, but on Mar 21, 1963, he was knocked out by Ultiminio ("Sugar") Ramos. An hour after the fight, he went into a coma and did not recover. Died at Los Angeles, CA, Mar 23, 1963.

NOTRE DAME USES FORWARD PASSES TO DEFEAT ARMY: ANNIVERSARY. Nov 1, 1913. In the first football game between two emerging gridiron powers, Notre Dame upset Army, 35–13, surprising the Cadets with an unprecedented barrage of forward passes. Quarterback Gus Dorais completed 14 of 17 passes for 243 yards. His frequent target was end Knute Rockne.

RICE, GRANTLAND: 120th BIRTH ANNIVERSARY. Nov 1, 1880. Henry Grantland Rice, sportswriter, born at Murfreesboro, TN. Rice played football and baseball at Vanderbilt, but after graduating in 1901, he quickly fell into sportswriting. He incorporated verse into his columns, the success of which got him to New York in 1911. Rice liked covering football best, but he also reveled in establishing nicknames, including the Four Horsemen, and promoting the careers of athletes. He wrote with great enthusiasm and helped create what many have called the Golden Age of Sports. Given the J.G. Taylor Spink Award in 1966. Died at New York, NY, July 13, 1954.

SEABISCUIT DEFEATS WAR ADMIRAL: ANNIVERSARY. Nov 1, 1938. In a special match race at Pimlico, Seabiscuit, ridden by George Wolff, defeated favored War Admiral before a crowd of 40,000. Seabiscuit captured the winner-take-all purse of $15,000.

Grantland Rice

BIRTHDAYS TODAY

Tahir ("Tie") Domi, 31, hockey player, born Windsor, Ontario, Canada, Nov 1, 1969.

Kent Douglas Graham, 32, football player, born Winfield, IL, Nov 1, 1968.

Theodore Paul (Ted) Hendricks, 53, Pro Football Hall of Fame linebacker, born Guatemala City, Guatemala, Nov 1, 1947.

Thomas Lee (Tom) Mack, 57, Pro Football Hall of Fame guard, born Cleveland, OH, Nov 1, 1943.

Gary Jim Player, 65, golfer, born Johannesburg, South Africa, Nov 1, 1935.

Fernando Anguamea Valenzuela, 40, former baseball player, born Navojoa, Sonora, Mexico, Nov 1, 1960.

November 2000	S	M	T	W	T	F	S
				1	2	3	4
	5	6	7	8	9	10	11
	12	13	14	15	16	17	18
	19	20	21	22	23	24	25
	26	27	28	29	30		

NOVEMBER 2 — THURSDAY
Day 307 — 59 Remaining

CAMPANIS, AL: BIRTH ANNIVERSARY. Nov 2, 1916. Alexander Sebastian (Al) Campanis, baseball executive and player, born Alessandro Campani at Kos, Greece. Campanis played only seven games in the major leagues, but he spent 44 years in the Los Angeles Dodgers organization as a minor league manager, scouting director, vice president of player personnel and general manager. He befriended Jackie Robinson and resolutely scouted and signed minority players, including Fernando Valenzuela. Yet, he was most remembered for a 1987 appearance on the television show "Nightline," during which he asserted that blacks "may not have some of the necessities to be, let's say, a field manager or a general manager." He apologized for these remarks, but they forced his resignation and retirement. Died at Fullerton, CA, June 21, 1998.

HAUGHTON, BILLY: BIRTH ANNIVERSARY. Nov 2, 1923. William Robert (Billy) Haughton, standardbred driver and trainer, born at Gloversville, NY. Haughton won nearly 4,900 races in his career. Along with Stanley Dancer, he dominated the New York trotting scene in the 1950s and then moved on to a national career. He suffered severe head injuries in a three-horse accident at Yonkers Raceway and died at Valhalla, NY, July 15, 1986.

JACKSON, TRAVIS: BIRTH ANNIVERSARY. Nov 2, 1903. Travis Calvin Jackson, Baseball Hall of Fame shortstop, born at Waldo, AR. Jackson played shortstop for the pennant-winning New York Giants teams of the 1920s and 1930s. Inducted into the Hall of Fame in 1982. Died at Waldo, July 27, 1987.

NATIONAL HORSE SHOW. Nov 2–5. Madison Square Garden, New York, NY. Hunters, Jumpers, Saddleseat, ASPCA-Maclay Medal Finals. Est attendance: 40,000. For info: Natl Horse Show, PO Box 2761, New York, NY 10116-2761. Phone: (516) 484-1865. Web: www.nhs.org.

NFL ATTENDANCE RECORD: ANNIVERSARY. Nov 2, 1958. The Chicago Bears and the Los Angeles Rams set an NFL single-game attendance record as 90,833 fans watched the Rams beat the Bears, 41–35, at the Los Angeles Coliseum.

RILEY WINS 800th GAME: ANNIVERSARY. Nov 2, 1996. Pat Riley became the ninth coach in professional basketball to win 800 games when his team, the Miami Heat, defeated the Indiana Pacers, 97–95.

VANDER MEER, JOHNNY: BIRTH ANNIVERSARY. Nov 2, 1914. John Samuel (Johnny) Vander Meer, baseball player, born at Prospect Park, NJ. Vander Meer is the only man to pitch consecutive no-hitters in the major leagues. On June 11, 1938, while a member of the Cincinnati Reds, he no-hit the Boston Bees. Four days later, pitching in the first night game played at Ebbets Field, he no-hit the Brooklyn Dodgers. He led the National League in strikeouts three times and won 15 or more games in five different seasons. Died at Tampa, FL, Oct 6, 1997.

BIRTHDAYS TODAY

James Leroy (Jim) Bakken, 60, former football player, born Madison, WI, Nov 2, 1940.
Kevin Patrick Gogan, 36, football player, born Pacifica, CA, Nov 2, 1964.
Larry Chatmon Little, 55, Pro Football Hall of Fame guard, born Groveland, GA, Nov 2, 1945.
Willie Dean McGee, 42, baseball player, born San Francisco, CA, Nov 2, 1958.
Orlando Luis Merced, 34, baseball player, born San Juan, Puerto Rico, Nov 2, 1966.

Thomas Marian (Tom) Paciorek, 54, broadcaster and former baseball player, born Detroit, MI, Nov 2, 1946.
Kenneth Robert (Ken) Rosewall, 66, former tennis player, born Sydney, New South Wales, Australia, Nov 2, 1934.
David Knapp (Dave) Stockton, 59, golfer, born San Bernardino, CA, Nov 2, 1941.

☆   ☆   ☆

NOVEMBER 3 — FRIDAY
Day 308 — 58 Remaining

BIG TEN FIELD HOCKEY CHAMPIONSHIP. Nov 3–5. University of Michigan, Ann Arbor, MI. For info: Big Ten Conference, 1500 W Higgins Rd, Park Ridge, IL 60068-6300. Phone: (847) 696-1010. Fax: (847) 696-1150. Web: www.bigten.org.

BIG TEN WOMEN'S SOCCER CHAMPIONSHIP. Nov 3–5. University of Iowa, Iowa City, IA. For info: Big Ten Conference, 1500 W Higgins Rd, Park Ridge, IL 60068-6300. Phone: (847) 696-1010. Fax: (847) 696-1150. Web: www.bigten.org.

FLEISCHER, NAT: BIRTH ANNIVERSARY. Nov 3, 1887. Nathaniel S. (Nat) Fleischer, sportswriter, born at New York, NY. Fleischer founded *The Ring* magazine in 1922, a publication generally regarded worldwide as "The Bible of Boxing." He served as editor and publisher, produced a record book and wrote more than 50 boxing biographies and histories. Died at New York, June 25, 1972.

LONGHORN WORLD CHAMPIONSHIP RODEO. Nov 3–5. LJVM Coliseum, Winston-Salem, NC. More than 200 cowboys and cowgirls compete in six professional contests ranging from bronc riding to bull riding for top prize money and world championship points. Featuring colorful opening pageantry and Big, Bad BONUS Bulls. 30th annual. Est attendance: 14,000. For info: W. Bruce Lehrke, Pres, Longhorn World Chmpshp Rodeo, Inc, PO Box 70159, Nashville, TN 37207. Phone: (615) 876-1016. Fax: (615) 876-4685. E-mail: lhrodeo@idt.net. Web: www.longhornrodeo.com.

NAGURSKI, BRONKO: BIRTH ANNIVERSARY. Nov 3, 1908. Bronislau ("Bronko") Nagurski, Pro Football Hall of Fame tackle and fullback, born at Rainy River, Ontario, Canada. He played football at the University of Minnesota, earning All-American honors at both positions, and for the Chicago Bears. After retiring from football, Nagurski wrestled professionally and operated a gas station. Inducted into the Hall of Fame as a charter member in 1963. Died at International Falls, MN, Jan 7, 1990.

NCAA WOMEN'S DIVISION III SOCCER CHAMPI-ONSHIP. Nov 3. First round. Sites TBA. For info: NCAA, PO Box 6222, Indianapolis, IN 46206-6222. Phone: (317) 917-6222. Fax: (317) 917-6888. Web: www.ncaa.org.

SHOEMAKER RETIRES: ANNIVERSARY. Nov 3, 1997. Bill Shoemaker, the winningest jockey in history and a successful trainer after his riding career ended, retired from horse racing at the conclusion of the Oak Tree meeting at the Santa Anita racetrack. Shoemaker rode 8,833 winners and won more than $41 million in purses. After his last ride on Feb 3, 1990, he turned to training. This second career was interrupted by an automobile accident in 1991 that left him paralyzed from the neck down. He returned to work after five months of rehabilitation and landed in the winner's circle just two days later.

WALSH INVITATIONAL RIFLE TOURNAMENT. Nov 3–5 (also Nov 10–13 and 17–19). Xavier University, Cincinnati, OH. To promote marksmanship and sportsmanship in the competitive spirit of collegiate athletics. International small-bore rifle and air rifle match open to all competitors. Recognized as "the largest indoor small-bore and air rifle match in the nation." Sponsor: Xavier University Athletic Department. Est attendance: 300. For info: Alan Joseph, O'Conner Sports Center, Dept of Athletics, Xavier Univ, 3800 Victory Pkwy, Cincinnati, OH 45207-6114. Phone: (513) 745-3413. Fax: (513) 745-4390.

BIRTHDAYS TODAY

Armando Benitez, 28, baseball player, born Ramon Santana, Dominican Republic, Nov 3, 1972.

Derrike Cope, 42, auto racer, born San Diego, CA, Nov 3, 1958.

Roy Stanley Emerson, 64, former tennis player, born Blackbutt, Queensland, Australia, Nov 3, 1936.

Dwight Michael ("Dewey") Evans, 49, former baseball player, born Santa Monica, CA, Nov 3, 1951.

Robert William Andrew (Bob) Feller, 82, Baseball Hall of Fame pitcher, born Van Meter, IA, Nov 3, 1918.

Larry Holmes, 51, former heavyweight champion boxer, born Cuthbert, GA, Nov 3, 1949.

Kenneth Dale (Ken) Holtzman, 55, former baseball player, born St. Louis, MO, Nov 3, 1950.

Edward Michael (Ed) Montague, 52, baseball umpire, born San Francisco, CA, Nov 3, 1948.

Paul John Quantrill, 32, baseball player, born London, Ontario, Canada, Nov 3, 1968.

Phillip Martin (Phil) Simms, 44, broadcaster and former football player, born Lebanon, KY, Nov 3, 1956.

NOVEMBER 4 — SATURDAY
Day 309 — 57 Remaining

BREEDERS' CUP CHAMPIONSHIP. Nov 4. Churchill Downs, Louisville, KY. Join the excitement of the 17th annual Breeders' Cup, the Super Bowl of horse racing. For info: Breeders Cup Ltd, PO Box 4230, Lexington, KY 40544. Phone: (606) 223-5444. Fax: (606) 223-3945. E-mail: breederscup@breederscup.com. Web: www.breederscup.com.

CANADA: FARMFAIR INTERNATIONAL. Nov 4–12. Northlands Park, Edmonton, Alberta. Canada's premiere celebration of Western-style living. The largest purebred livestock show and sale in Canada. Features traditional Western-style family entertainment, interactive exhibits, best-of-breed shows, purebred cattle sales, draft horse pulling and team cattle penning competitions and Alberta's only Western-themed trade and gift show. Est attendance: 50,000. For info: Cheryl Herchen, Northlands Park, PO Box 1480, Edmonton, AB, Canada T5J 2N5. Phone: (403) 471-7210 or (888) 800-PARK. Fax: (403) 471-8176. E-mail: npmarket@planet.eon.net. Web: www.northlands.com.

CONSIDINE, BOB: BIRTH ANNIVERSARY. Nov 4, 1906. Robert Bernard (Bob) Considine, sportswriter and author, born at Washington, DC. Considine parlayed some early success as a tennis player and a job as a federal government clerk into a career as a sportswriter. He covered baseball starting in 1933 and soon became a columnist for the Hearst newspapers. He branched out into politics and national affairs and served as a war correspondent during World War II. He wrote or co-authored more than 25 books, including the screenplay for *Pride of the Yankees*, the film biography of Lou Gehrig. Died at New York, NY, Sept 1, 1975.

DOUGLAS, BOB: BIRTH ANNIVERSARY. Nov 4, 1884. Robert L. (Bob) Douglas, Basketball Hall of Fame executive, born at St. Kitts, British West Indies. Douglas came to the US in 1888 and played basketball before founding the New York Renaissance, one of the game's greatest teams, in 1922. The Rens got their name from the Harlem Renaissance ballroom, where they played their home games, but they barnstormed extensively as well. Over 22 years, they won 2,381 games, including the 1931 World Professional Championship. The Rens were inducted into the Hall of Fame as a team in 1963. Douglas followed as an individual contributor in 1971. Died at New York, NY, July 16, 1979.

FIRST FREE AGENT DRAFT: ANNIVERSARY. Nov 4, 1976. Major League Baseball held its first draft of players who had declared themselves free agents. 24 players from 13 clubs were available for selection. Reggie Jackson eventually signed the most lucrative contract in this group, $2.9 million over five years, to play with the New York Yankees.

SPECIAL OLYMPICS VIRGINIA FALL TOURNAMENTS. Nov 4–5. Virginia Beach, VA. Nearly 500 athletes will compete in roller skating, soccer, unified bowling and volleyball. For info: Special Olympics Virginia, 3212 Skipwith Rd, Ste 100, Richmond, VA 23294. Phone: (804) 346-5544.

STEEPLECHASE AT CALLAWAY GARDENS. Nov 4. Pine Mountain, GA. A seven-race steeplechase meet where riders match their horses for speed and split-second timing over bush jumps. Box seating and infield tailgating spaces available. Est attendance: 12,000. For info: Steeplechase at Callaway Gardens, PO Box 2311, Columbus, GA 31902. Phone: (706) 324-6252. Fax: (706) 324-3651.

TORONTO GRANTED NBA FRANCHISE: ANNIVERSARY. Nov 4, 1993. The NBA Board of Governors accepted a recommendation from the Expansion Committee to award a franchise to a Toronto group headed by John Bitove, Jr. The team, later named the Raptors, began play in the 1995–96 season.

WORLD GOLF CHAMPIONSHIPS—STROKE PLAY. Nov 4–7. European site TBA. The third event in the first World Golf Championships, a new initiative created by the PGA Tours International Federation composed of the world's five leading golf tours (the PGA Tour, the European Tour, the Southern Africa PGA Tour, the PGA Tour of Australasia and the PGA Tour of Japan). The World Golf Championships will consist of three events, a match-play competition for 64 players in February, an invitational

November 2000	S	M	T	W	T	F	S
				1	2	3	4
	5	6	7	8	9	10	11
	12	13	14	15	16	17	18
	19	20	21	22	23	24	25
	26	27	28	29	30		

competition in August for all members of the last-named Presidents Cup and Ryder Cup teams and this stroke-play competition for approximately 60 of the top players in the world. For info: PGA Tour, 112 TPC Blvd, Ponte Vedra Beach, FL 32082. Phone: (904) 285-3700. Fax: (904) 285-2460.

BIRTHDAYS TODAY

Carlos Obed Baerga, 32, baseball player, born San Juan, Puerto Rico, Nov 4, 1968.

Eric Fichaud, 25, hockey player, born Montreal, Quebec, Canada, Nov 4, 1975.

Richard Morrow (Dick) Groat, 70, former baseball player, born Wilkinsburg, PA, Nov 4, 1930.

Eric Peter Karros, 33, baseball player, born Hackensack, NJ, Nov 4, 1967.

Steven (Steve) Mariucci, 45, football coach, born Iron Mountain, MI, Nov 4, 1955.

Orlando Lamar Pace, 25, football player, born Sandusky, OH, Nov 4, 1975.

NOVEMBER 5 — SUNDAY
Day 310 — 56 Remaining

AMERICAN QUARTER HORSE ASSOCIATION WORLD CHAMPIONSHIP SHOW. Nov 5–18. Oklahoma City, OK. Largest invitational world championship show. For info: AQHA, PO Box 200, Amarillo, TX 79168. Phone: (806) 376-4811. Fax: (806) 349-6409. Web: www.aqha .com.

AMERICAN SPORTS TRIVIA WEEK. Nov 5–11. Celebrates Americans' fascination with trivial information about sports, including baseball, football, basketball, hockey, auto racing and many more. From the publishers of *Super Bowl Trivia* and *World Series Trivia*. For info: Judy Colbert, Tuff Turtle Publishing, 1615 Parkridge Cir, #211, Crofton, MD 21114. Phone: (301) 858-0196. E-mail: jmcolbert@aol.com.

ENGLAND: LONDON TO BRIGHTON VETERAN CAR RUN. Nov 5. London. A 57-mile run for a maximum of 400 veteran cars, along the A23 road from Serpentine Row, Hyde Park, London, to Madiera Drive, Brighton, England. Celebrates the abolition in 1896 of the English law requiring that a man walk in front of motor vehicles carrying a red flag. Annually, the first Sunday in November. Est attendance: 1,000,000. For info: Motor Sports Assn Ltd, Events Dept, Slough, Riverside Park, Colnbrook, England SL3 0HG. Phone: (44) (175) 368-1736. Fax: (44) (175) 368-2938. E-mail: msa_mail@compuserve.com.

FIRST SHATTERED BACKBOARD: ANNIVERSARY. Nov 5, 1946. Chuck Connors of the Boston Celtics became the first NBA player to shatter a backboard, doing so during the pregame warm-up at Boston Garden. Connors also played major league baseball with the Brooklyn Dodgers and the Chicago Cubs and gained fame as star of the television series "The Rifleman."

NEALE, GREASY: BIRTH ANNIVERSARY. Nov 5, 1891. Alfred Earle ("Greasy") Neale, baseball player and Pro Football Hall of Fame player and coach, born at Parkersburg, WV. Neale, with his childhood nickname, played baseball and football at West Virginia Wesleyan. He spent eight seasons as a major league outfielder and coached at a variety of colleges. In 1941, he became head coach of the Philadelphia Eagles, winning two NFL titles. A football innovator, he is credited with devising an early version of the 4–3 defense. Inducted into the Hall of Fame in 1967. Died at Lake Worth, FL, Nov 1, 1973.

NEW YORK CITY MARATHON. Nov 5. New York, NY. 29,000 runners from all over the world gather to compete in the largest spectator event with more than two million spectators watching from the sidelines. For info: New York Road Runners Club, 9 E 89th St, New York, NY 10128. Phone: (212) 860-4455. Fax: (212) 860-9754. E-mail: membership@nyrrc.org. Web: www.nyrrc.org.

BIRTHDAYS TODAY

Sergei Berezin, 29, hockey player, born Voskresensk, USSR, Nov 5, 1971.

Todd Collins, 29, football player, born Walpole, MA, Nov 5, 1971.

Johnny David Damon, 27, baseball player, born Ft Riley, KS, Nov 5, 1973.

James Bremond (Jim) Evans, 54, baseball umpire, born Longview, TX, Nov 5, 1946.

Alvin Gentry, 46, basketball coach, born Shelby, NC, Nov 5, 1954.

Javier Torres (Javy) Lopez, 30, baseball player, born Ponce, Puerto Rico, Nov 5, 1970.

Jerry Darnell Stackhouse, 26, basketball player, born Kinston, NC, Nov 5, 1974.

William Theodore (Bill) Walton, III, 48, broadcaster and Basketball Hall of Fame center and forward, born La Mesa, CA, Nov 5, 1952.

Kellen Boswell Winslow, 43, Pro Football Hall of Fame tight end, born St. Louis, MO, Nov 5, 1957.

Alexei Yashin, 27, hockey player, born Sverdlovsk, USSR, Nov 5, 1973.

NOVEMBER 6 — MONDAY
Day 311 — 55 Remaining

AUSTRALIA: RECREATION DAY. Nov 6. Annually, the first Monday in November is observed as Recreation Day at Northern Tasmania, Australia.

CANZONERI, TONY: BIRTH ANNIVERSARY. Nov 6, 1908. Tony Canzoneri, boxer, born at Slidell, LA. At various times between 1928, when he was only 19, and 1936, Canzoneri held the featherweight, lightweight and junior welterweight titles. A popular fighter who dressed well and kept a cigar clutched between his teeth, Canzoneri later ran a restaurant, acted and led a dance band. Died at New York, NY, Dec 10, 1959.

JOHNSON, WALTER: BIRTH ANNIVERSARY. Nov 6, 1887. Walter Perry Johnson, Baseball Hall of Fame pitcher, born at Humboldt, KS. Johnson may well have been the best and the fastest pitcher of all time. He won 417 games, more than anyone else except Cy Young, and his nickname, the "Big Train," indicates the respect with which other players regarded his fastball. Inducted into the Hall of Fame as a charter member in 1936. Died at Washington, DC, Dec 10, 1946.

MAYS, REX: DEATH ANNIVERSARY. Nov 6, 1949. Rex Mays, auto racer, born at Glendale, CA, 1913. Mays won two national driving championships in his 18-year career, but his aggressive style often led to equipment failure. He held the pole position four times at the Indianapolis 500, finished second twice but never won the race. His deep concern for driver safety once led him to crash his car rather than hit another driver. Died in a crash at Del Mar, CA.

MESSIER SCORES 500th GOAL: 5th ANNIVERSARY. Nov 6, 1995. Center Mark Messier of the New York Rangers became the 21st player in the National Hockey League to score 500 regular-season goals. He tallied against goalie Rick Tabaracci of the Calgary Flames in a 4–2 win.

NAISMITH, JAMES: BIRTH ANNIVERSARY. Nov 6, 1861. James Naismith, inventor of basketball, born at Almonte, Ontario, Canada. Naismith invented basketball at the YMCA at Springfield, MA, as an indoor game to be played during the winter for exercise. He moved to Denver and then to the University of Kansas, but he never received recognition as the "Father of Basketball" until after his death. A minister and a physical educator, he shunned competitive athletics and had little to do with the development of the game he invented. Inducted into the Basketball Hall of Fame as a charter member in 1959. Died at Lawrence, KS, Nov 28, 1939.

NCAA WOMEN'S DIVISION III SOCCER CHAMPIONSHIP. Nov 6–7. Quarterfinals. Sites TBA. For info: NCAA, PO Box 6222, Indianapolis, IN 46206-6222. Phone: (317) 917-6222. Fax: (317) 917-6888. Web: www.ncaa.org.

NCAA WOMEN'S DIVISION III SOCCER CHAMPIONSHIP. Nov 6. Regionals. Sites TBA. For info: NCAA, PO Box 6222, Indianapolis, IN 46206-6222. Phone: (317) 917-6222. Fax: (317) 917-6888. Web: www.ncaa.org.

PGA ANNUAL MEETING. Nov 6–11. Charleston, SC. The 84th annual convention of the Professional Golfers' Association of America. For info: PGA of America, Box 109601, Palm Beach Gardens, FL 33410-9601. Phone: (561) 624-8495. Fax: (561) 624-8429.

SPINK, TAYLOR: BIRTH ANNIVERSARY. Nov 6, 1888. John George Taylor Spink, sports publisher, born at St. Louis, MO. Spink inherited management of *The Sporting News* upon the death of his father in 1914. He made the weekly newspaper into the "Bible of Baseball," a trade paper of indispensable value to all those connected with the game. Spink was a baseball insider; his publication not only reported on what had happened, but also advocated what should happen. First recipient of the J.G. Taylor Spink Award in 1962. Died at St. Louis, Dec 7, 1962.

BIRTHDAYS TODAY

Derrick Scott Alexander, 29, football player, born Detroit, MI, Nov 6, 1971.
John Robert Candelaria, 47, former baseball player, born New York, NY, Nov 6, 1953.
Chad David Curtis, 32, baseball player, born Marion, IN, Nov 6, 1968.
William Erik Kramer, 36, football player, born Encino, CA, Nov 6, 1964.

November 2000

S	M	T	W	T	F	S
			1	2	3	4
5	6	7	8	9	10	11
12	13	14	15	16	17	18
19	20	21	22	23	24	25
26	27	28	29	30		

NOVEMBER 7 — TUESDAY
Day 312 — 54 Remaining

CHASE'S SPORTSQUOTE OF THE DAY
"Giving Magic the basketball is like giving Hitler an army, Jesse James a gang, or Genghis Khan a horse. Devastation. Havoc."—sportswriter Jim Murray on Magic Johnson

BERENSON SCORES SIX GOALS: ANNIVERSARY. Nov 7, 1968. Center Gordon ("Red") Berenson of the St. Louis Blues scored six goals in a game against the Philadelphia Flyers to tie the record for most goals in a game set by Syd Howe of the Detroit Red Wings in 1944.

CARTER RELEASED: 15th ANNIVERSARY. Nov 7, 1985. Former middleweight boxer Rubin ("Hurricane") Carter was released from Rahway (NJ) State Prison after serving 19 years for a triple murder committed in a Paterson, NJ, bar in 1966. US District Court Judge J. Lee Sorokin ruled that prosecutors had violated the civil rights of Carter and a codefendant during their trials in 1967 and 1976.

ELECTION DAY. Nov 7. Many state and local government elections are held on this day, as well as presidential and congressional elections in the appropriate years. All US congressional seats and one-third of US senatorial seats are up for election in even-numbered years. Presidential elections are held in even-numbered years that can be divided equally by four. Annually, the first Tuesday after the first Monday in November.

MAGIC JOHNSON RETIRES: ANNIVERSARY. Nov 7, 1991. Earvin ("Magic") Johnson of the Los Angeles Lakers retired from basketball after announcing that he had tested positive for HIV. Despite his retirement, Johnson played in the 1992 NBA All-Star Game and in the 1992 Olympics as a member of the first US Dream Team. He coached the Lakers for part of the 1993–94 season and played part of the 1995–96 season before retiring again.

BIRTHDAYS TODAY

Valerie (Val) Ackerman, 41, basketball executive and former player, born Lakewood, NJ, Nov 7, 1959.
James Lee (Jim) Kaat, 62, broadcaster and former baseball player, born Zeeland, MI, Nov 7, 1938.
John Albert ("Buck") Martinez, 52, broadcaster and former baseball player, born Redding, CA, Nov 7, 1948.
Joseph Franklin (Joe) Niekro, 56, former baseball player, born Martins Ferry, OH, Nov 7, 1944.
Marc Rosset, 30, tennis player, born Geneva, Switzerland, Nov 7, 1970.
Richard Lee (Dick) Stuart, 68, former baseball player, born San Francisco, CA, Nov 7, 1932.

NOVEMBER 8 — WEDNESDAY
Day 313 — 53 Remaining

BIZARRE NBA GAME BEGINS: ANNIVERSARY. Nov 8, 1978. During a game between the Philadelphia 76ers and the New Jersey Nets, an official assessed three technical fouls against Nets coach Kevin Loughery and player Bernard King. The league office ruled that the official had acted in error and ordered the game replayed. It was, on Mar 23, 1979, and Philadelphia won, 137–133. On Feb 7, however, the 76ers had traded Ralph Simpson to New Jersey for Eric Money and Harvey Catchings. So these three wound up finishing the game as members of the teams they had originally opposed.

CANADA: CANADIAN FINALS RODEO. Nov 8–14. Northlands Coliseum, Edmonton, Alberta. It's always a wild ride as the top cowboys and cowgirls in the country compete for national titles and record prize money. One of the largest annual indoor sporting events in Canada. Each of the six performances features bull riding, bareback riding, saddle bronco riding, calf roping, steer wrestling and ladies' barrel racing. CFR's heart-stopping rodeo action sizzles with glittering Western pageantry and dynamic entertainment. CFR will also be accompanied by dozens of Western-related events during Be Seen in Jeans Week, an annual civic celebration. Est attendance: 81,000. For info: Cheryl Herchen, PR Supervisor, Northlands Park, Box 1480, Edmonton, AB, Canada T5J 2N5. Phone: (403) 471-7295. Fax: (403) 471-8176. E-mail: npmarket@planet.eon.net. Web: www.northlands.com.

HARRIS, BUCKY: BIRTH ANNIVERSARY. Nov 8, 1896. Stanley Raymond ("Bucky") Harris, Baseball Hall of Fame player and manager, born at Port Jervis, NY. Harris became manager of the Washington Senators when he was only 28. He wound up managing more major league games than anyone except Connie Mack and John McGraw. Inducted into the Hall of Fame in 1975. Died at Bethesda, MD, Nov 8, 1977.

HOUSLEY GETS 1,000th POINT: ANNIVERSARY. Nov 8, 1997. Defenseman Phil Housley of the Washington Capitals got the 1,000th point of his National Hockey League career, an assist in a 2–1 win over the Edmonton Oilers.

McGUIRE, FRANK: BIRTH ANNIVERSARY. Nov 8, 1916. Frank Joseph McGuire, Basketball Hall of Fame coach, born at New York, NY. McGuire coached successfully at both the college and pro levels. His 1952 St. John's team lost to Kansas in the NCAA title game. In 1957, his University of North Carolina team defeated Kansas and Wilt Chamberlain to win the NCAA title. He coached the Philadelphia Warriors in the NBA and then returned to the college ranks at the University of South Carolina. Inducted into the Hall of Fame in 1976. Died at Columbia, SC, Oct 11, 1994.

NFL RECORD FIELD GOAL: 30th ANNIVERSARY. Nov 8, 1970. Tom Dempsey of the New Orleans Saints set an NFL record by kicking a 63-yard field goal to give the Saints a 19–17 victory over the Detroit Lions.

NOTRE DAME TIES ARMY: ANNIVERSARY. Nov 8, 1946. The University of Notre Dame football team tied Army, 0–0, to snap West Point's 26-game winning streak.

RICHARD BECOMES NHL'S LEADING SCORER: ANNIVERSARY. Nov 8, 1952. Maurice ("Rocket") Richard of the Montreal Canadiens became the leading career goal scorer in the National Hockey League with his 325th goal in a 6–4 win over the Chicago Blackhawks.

BIRTHDAYS TODAY

Edgardo Antonio Alfonzo, 27, baseball player, born St. Teresa, Venezuela, Nov 8, 1973.
Jeffrey Michael (Jeff) Blauser, 35, baseball player, born Los Gatos, CA, Nov 8, 1965.
Brevin Knight, 25, basketball player, born Livingston, NJ, Nov 8, 1975.
Edward Emil (Ed) Kranepool, 56, former baseball player, born New York, NY, Nov 8, 1944.
Jose Antonio Offerman, 32, baseball player, born San Pedro de Macoris, Dominican Republic, Nov 8, 1968.
Henry Anderson Rodriguez, 33, baseball player, born Santo Domingo, Dominican Republic, Nov 8, 1967.

NOVEMBER 9 — THURSDAY
Day 314 — 52 Remaining

CHASE'S SPORTSQUOTE OF THE DAY
"I'll never make the mistake of being seventy again."
—Casey Stengel in announcing that the New York Yankees had "retired" him

BUCYK GETS 1,000th POINT: ANNIVERSARY. Nov 9, 1972. Left wing Johnny Bucyk of the Boston Bruins got the 1,000th point of his National Hockey League career, a goal in an 8–3 win over the Detroit Red Wings. Bucyk finished his career with 1,369 points.

CHADWICK, FLORENCE: BIRTH ANNIVERSARY. Nov 9, 1918. Florence May Chadwick, swimmer, born at San Diego, CA. Chadwick never won a national title and failed to qualify for the US Olympic team in 1936, but she won enduring fame by becoming the first woman to swim the English Channel in both directions. She swam from France to England on Aug 8, 1950, and from England to France a year later. She made other long-distance swims as well, including the Bristol Channel, the Catalina Island-to-California swim and the Strait of Gilbraltar. Died at San Diego, Mar 15, 1995.

GRAHAM, MOONLIGHT: BIRTH ANNIVERSARY. Nov 9, 1876. Archibald Wright ("Moonlight") Graham, baseball player, born at Fayetteville, NC. Graham's brief major league career (one game and no at bats) was fictionalized in *Field of Dreams*. Died at Chisholm, MN, Aug 25, 1965.

IKE BREAKS KNEECAP: ANNIVERSARY. Nov 9, 1912. West Point cadet Dwight D. Eisenhower broke his kneecap in a football game against Tufts University and gave up the sport forever. He did go on to prominence in other fields.

LIPSCOMB, BIG DADDY: BIRTH ANNIVERSARY. Nov 9, 1931. Gene Allen ("Big Daddy") Lipscomb, football player and wrestler, born at Detroit, MI. Lipscomb was known as "Big Daddy" because he could not remember his teammates' names and called everyone "Little Daddy." He made All-Pro three times with the Baltimore Colts (1957, 1958 and 1959) and was one of the first defensive linemen to develop a distinct on-field personality. He supplemented his football income by wrestling professionally. Died at Baltimore, MD, May 10, 1963.

YANKEES FIRE STENGEL: 40th ANNIVERSARY. Nov 9, 1960. The New York Yankees fired their manager, Casey Stengel, despite his having won 10 pennants and seven World Series in 12 years. Stengel returned to baseball in 1962 as first manager of the New York Mets.

BIRTHDAYS TODAY

Alice Coachman, 77, Olympic gold medal high jumper, born Albany, GA, Nov 9, 1923.

David Robert Duval, 29, golfer, born Jacksonville, FL, Nov 9, 1971.

Mark Lee Fields, 28, football player, born Los Angeles, CA, Nov 9, 1972.

Robert (Bob) Gibson, 65, Baseball Hall of Fame pitcher, born Omaha, NE, Nov 9, 1935.

Todd Gill, 35, hockey player, born Brockville, Ontario, Canada, Nov 9, 1965.

William Robert (Bill) Guerin, 30, hockey player, born Wilbraham, MA, Nov 9, 1970.

Dorrel Norman Elvert ("Whitey") Herzog, 69, former baseball manager, executive and player, born New Athens, IL, Nov 9, 1931.

Jimmy Davis Hitchcock, Jr, 29, football player, born Concord, NC, Nov 9, 1971.

Chad Wayne Ogea, 30, baseball player, born Lake Charles, LA, Nov 9, 1970.

Thomas Daniel (Tom) Weiskopf, 58, broadcaster and former golfer, born Massillon, OH, Nov 9, 1942.

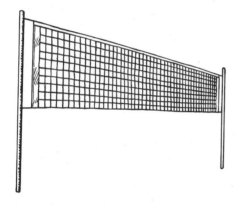

NOVEMBER 10 — FRIDAY
Day 315 — 51 Remaining

BIG TEN MEN'S SOCCER CHAMPIONSHIP. Nov 10–12. Ohio State University, Columbus, OH. For info: Big Ten Conference, 1500 W Higgins Rd, Park Ridge, IL 60068-6300. Phone: (847) 696-1010. Fax: (847) 696-1150. Web: www.bigten.org.

CASH, NORM: BIRTH ANNIVERSARY. Nov 10, 1934. Norman Dalton (Norm) Cash, baseball player, born at Justiceburg, TX. Cash won the American League batting title in 1961 and led the league in home runs. He hit .385 in the 1968 World Series. Died in a boating accident at Charlevoix, MI, Oct 12, 1986.

DODGE PRAIRIE CIRCUIT FINALS RODEO. Nov 10–11. Lazy E Arena, Guthrie, OK. The top 12 cowboys in each event from Oklahoma, Kansas and Nebraska compete for $60,000 and Circuit Championship titles. Est attendance: 15,000. For info: Lazy E Arena, Rt 5 Box 393, Guthrie, OK 73044. Phone: (405) 282-RIDE or (800) 595-RIDE. Fax: (405) 282-3785. E-mail: arena@lazye.com. Web: www.lazye.com.

November 2000

S	M	T	W	T	F	S
			1	2	3	4
5	6	7	8	9	10	11
12	13	14	15	16	17	18
19	20	21	22	23	24	25
26	27	28	29	30		

FIRST BREEDERS' CUP: ANNIVERSARY. Nov 10, 1984. The first Breeders' Cup day of Thoroughbred racing was held at Hollywood Park in California. Wild Again won the feature race, the $3 million Breeders' Cup Classic, beating Slew O' Gold and Gate Dancer.

HOWE SETS GOAL RECORD: ANNIVERSARY. Nov 10, 1963. Gordie Howe of the Detroit Red Wings scored the 545th goal of his career to surpass the mark held by Maurice Richard of the Montreal Canadiens.

WATERFOWL FESTIVAL (WITH GOOSE- AND DUCK-CALLING CHAMPIONSHIPS). Nov 10–12. Easton, MD. The World Championship Goose- and Regional Duck-Calling Contests take place during this three-day festival. Also includes retriever demonstrations, sporting clays tournament and decoy auction as well as wildlife exhibitors presenting wildlife art, carvings, sculpture, decoys, seminars and more. Annually, the second full weekend in November. Proceeds contributed to conservation. Est attendance: 18,000. For info: Waterfowl Festival, PO Box 929, Easton, MD 21601. Phone: (410) 822-4567. Fax: (410) 820-9286. E-mail: facts@waterfowlfest.org. Web: www.waterfowlfest.org.

BIRTHDAYS TODAY

Isaac Isidore Bruce, 28, football player, born Ft Lauderdale, FL, Nov 10, 1972.

Donald Eugene (Gene) Conley, 70, former baseball and basketball player, born Muskogee, OK, Nov 10, 1930.

Robert Leon ("Butch") Huskey, 29, baseball player, born Anadarko, OK, Nov 10, 1971.

Keith Virgil Lockhart, 36, baseball player, born Whittier, CA, Nov 10, 1964.

Larry Alton Parrish, 47, baseball manager and former player, born Winter Haven, FL, Nov 10, 1953.

Kenneth Scott (Kenny) Rogers, 36, baseball player, born Savannah, GA, Nov 10, 1964.

NOVEMBER 11 — SATURDAY
Day 316 — 50 Remaining

DAY, NED: BIRTH ANNIVERSARY. Nov 11, 1911. Edward P. (Ned) Day, bowler, born at Los Angeles, CA. Day was one of the first bowlers to tour, playing matches and giving exhibitions, including one at Harry Truman's White House. He was named Bowler of the Year in 1943 and 1944 and carried a 200 average over a 28-year career. Died at Milwaukee, WI, Nov 26, 1971.

DEBUT OF SPIKED SHOES: ANNIVERSARY. Nov 11, 1868. At a track meet at the Empire Skating Rink at New York City, William B. Curtis won the 75-yard dash wearing spiked shoes, the first athlete to do so.

DODD, BOBBY: BIRTH ANNIVERSARY. Nov 11, 1908. Robert Lee (Bobby) Dodd, football player, coach and administrator, born at Galax, VA. Dodd earned 16 letters in high school and played quarterback at the University of Tennessee. He coached at Georgia Tech from 1945 to 1967, and his teams won 9 of 13 bowl games. He developed the "belly series" offense and sought to motivate his players with lavish praise. Died at Atlanta, GA, June 21, 1988.

KNICKS' FIRST GAME AT MADISON SQUARE GARDEN: ANNIVERSARY. Nov 11, 1946. The New York Knickerbockers of the Basketball Association of America (predecessor of the NBA) played their first home game at Madison Square Garden. Before a crowd of 17,205, the Knicks lost in overtime to the Chicago Stags, 78–68. The halftime entertainment consisted of a fashion show and a brief exhibition basketball game between the New York Giants football team and members of the Original Celtics, basketball's legendary team from the 1920s.

MARANVILLE, RABBIT: BIRTH ANNIVERSARY. Nov 11, 1891. Walter James Vincent ("Rabbit") Maranville, Baseball Hall of Fame infielder, born at Springfield, MA. Maranville was a slick-fielding infielder who played with the 1914 "Miracle" Braves and enjoyed a 23-year career. He was known for his antics, on the field and off. Inducted into the Hall of Fame in 1954. Died at New York, NY, Jan 5, 1954.

SPECIAL OLYMPICS COLORADO FALL CLASSIC. Nov 11–12. Site TBA. Multisport competition for athletes with mental retardation. For info: Colorado Special Olympics, 600 17th St, Ste 910, Denver, CO 80202. Phone: (303) 592-1361. Fax: (303) 592-1364.

SPECIAL OLYMPICS CONNECTICUT UNIFIED SPORTS® CHAMPIONSHIPS. Nov 11–12. Hartford, CT. More than 700 athletes with mental retardation compete in volleyball, basketball, bowling, power lifting and adaptive sports. Unified Sports combines athletes with and without mental retardation on the same teams. For info: Special Olympics Connecticut, Inc, 2666-1 State St, Hamden, CT 06517-2232. Phone: (203) 230-1201. Fax: (203) 230-1202. Web: www.soct.org.

TRAYNOR, PIE: BIRTH ANNIVERSARY. Nov 11, 1899. Harold Joseph ("Pie") Traynor, Baseball Hall of Fame third baseman, born at Framingham, MA. Traynor is considered one of the greatest third basemen of all time. He was a superb hitter and an absolute genius with the glove. Inducted into the Hall of Fame in 1948. Died at Pittsburgh, PA, Mar 16, 1972.

VETERANS DAY. Nov 11. Celebrates the end of World War I and, by extension, the contributions and sacrifices of all veterans. For federal employees, when a holiday falls on a Saturday, it is observed on the preceding Friday.

BIRTHDAYS TODAY

Jacinto Damion Easley, 31, baseball player, born New York, NY, Nov 11, 1969.
Roberto Manuel Hernandez, 36, baseball player, born Santurce, Puerto Rico, Nov 11, 1964.
Reynaldo (Rey) Ordonez, 28, baseball player, born Havana, Cuba, Nov 11, 1972.
Frank Urban ("Fuzzy") Zoeller, 49, golfer, born New Albany, IN, Nov 11, 1951.

NOVEMBER 12 — SUNDAY
Day 317 — 49 Remaining

CHASE'S SPORTSQUOTE OF THE DAY

"I won over two hundred big league games, but no one today remembers that. When they think of me, I'm the guy who killed Chapman with a fastball."—Carl Mays

FIRST PROFESSIONAL FOOTBALL PLAYER: ANNIVERSARY. Nov 12, 1892. William ("Pudge") Heffelfinger became the first generally acknowledged professional football player when he was paid $25 for expenses and a cash bonus of $500. It was the cash bonus that made him professional. Scoring the winning touchdown for the Allegheny Athletic Association, he helped his team beat the Pittsburgh Athletic Club by a score of 4–0.

LANDIS NAMED COMMISSIONER: 80th ANNIVERSARY. Nov 12, 1920. In the wake of the growing scandal surrounding accusations that members of the Chicago White Sox conspired to fix the 1919 World Series, baseball owners appointed Federal Judge Kenesaw Mountain Landis the game's first commissioner with extremely broad powers. Landis replaced the National Commission, a three-man governing board, and served until his death in 1944.

LUCKMAN, SID: BIRTH ANNIVERSARY. Nov 21, 1916. Sidney (Sid) Luckman, Pro Football Hall of Fame quarterback, born at New York, NY. Luckman played football at Columbia and then starred as quarterback for the great Chicago Bears teams of the 1940s. Luckman's talents enabled coach George Halas to install a modern version of the T formation, emphasizing speed and deception instead of brute strength. Luckman led the NFL in touchdown passes three times and quarterbacked the Bears to four NFL titles, including their epic 73–0 thrashing of the Washington Redskins in 1940. Inducted into the Hall of Fame in 1965. Died at Aventura, FL, July 5, 1998.

MAYS, CARL: BIRTH ANNIVERSARY. Nov 12, 1893. Carl William Mays, baseball player, born at Liberty, KY. Mays was a submarine pitcher who started his career with the Boston Red Sox and was traded to the New York Yankees. In 1920, he hit Ray Chapman of the Cleveland Indians in the head with a pitched ball. Chapman died the next day. Died at El Cajon, CA, Apr 4, 1971.

SHULA WINS 100 IN 10: ANNIVERSARY. Nov 12, 1972. Don Shula of the Miami Dolphins became the first NFL coach to win 100 regular-season games in only 10 seasons as the Miami Dolphins defeated the New England Patriots, 52–0.

TRIPLE CROWN OF SURFING SERIES: EVENT 1— HAWAIIAN PRO. Nov 12–24. Alii Beach Park, Haleiwa, North Shore Oahu, HI. 18th annual. The Triple Crown Series is professional, big-wave surfing on Oahu's North Shore. Est attendance: 6,500. For media info: Jodi Young or Carol Hogan, (808) 325-7400. E-mail: oceanpro@inter pac.net. For contest info: Randy Rarick, (808) 638-7266.

WORLD HALF-MARATHON CHAMPIONSHIP. Nov 12. Site TBA. 9th competition. For info: Intl Amateur Athletic Federation, 17, rue Princesse Florestine, BP 359, 98007 Monte Carlo, Monaco. Phone: (377) 93-10-88-88. Fax: (377) 93015-95-15. Web: www.iaaf.org.

BIRTHDAYS TODAY

Steven Joseph (Steve) Bartkowski, 48, former football player, born Des Moines, IA, Nov 12, 1952.
Homer Giles Bush, 28, baseball player, born East St. Louis, IL, Nov 12, 1972.
Nadia Comaneci, 39, Olympic gold medal gymnast, born Onesti, Romania, Nov 12, 1961.
Gregory Carpenter (Greg) Gagne, 39, former baseball player, born Fall River, MA, Nov 12, 1961.
Tonya Harding, 30, former figure skater, born Portland, OR, Nov 12, 1970.
Kenneth Roy (Ken) Houston, 56, Pro Football Hall of Fame defensive back, born Lufkin, TX, Nov 12, 1944.
Jeffrey Scott (Jeff) Reed, 38, baseball player, born Joliet, IL, Nov 12, 1962.
Samuel (Sammy) Sosa, 32, baseball player, born San Pedro de Macoris, Dominican Republic, Nov 12, 1968.

NOVEMBER 13 — MONDAY

Day 318 — 48 Remaining

BILKO, STEVE: BIRTH ANNIVERSARY. Nov 13, 1928. Steven Thomas (Steve) Bilko, baseball player, born at Nanticoke, PA. Bilko was a phenomenal minor league slugger who never quite made it in the majors. In 1955, 1956 and 1957, he hit 37, 55 and 56 homers in the Pacific Coast League. Died at Wilkes-Barre, PA, Mar 7, 1978.

PETTIT SCORES 20,000 POINTS: ANNIVERSARY. Nov 13, 1964. Forward Bob Pettit of the St. Louis Hawks became the first player in NBA history to reach the 20,000-point mark when he scored 29 points in a 123–106 loss to the Cincinnati Royals.

SANDE, EARLE: BIRTH ANNIVERSARY. Nov 13, 1898. Earle Sande, jockey, born at Groton, SD. Sande began riding in the West and then moved east to become a professional jockey. Sande rode many of the best horses of his era, including Man O'War and Gallant Fox, a Triple Crown winner. He won the Kentucky Derby three times and the Belmont Stakes five times. Died at Jacksonville, OR, Aug 20, 1968.

BIRTHDAYS TODAY

Mark Fitzpatrick, 32, hockey player, born Toronto, Ontario, Canada, Nov 13, 1968.
Patrick George (Pat) Hentgen, 32, baseball player, born Detroit, MI, Nov 13, 1968.
Melvin Leon (Mel) Stottlemyre, Sr, 59, former baseball player, born Hazelton, MO, Nov 13, 1941.
Vincent Frank (Vinny) Testaverde, 37, football player, born New York, NY, Nov 13, 1963.

NOVEMBER 14 — TUESDAY

Day 319 — 47 Remaining

BIRTH OF AMERICAN LEAGUE: 100th ANNIVERSARY. Nov 14, 1900. Ban Johnson, president of baseball's minor Western League, announced his intention to upgrade its status to a major league and to change its name to the American League.

November *2000*	S	M	T	W	T	F	S
				1	2	3	4
	5	6	7	8	9	10	11
	12	13	14	15	16	17	18
	19	20	21	22	23	24	25
	26	27	28	29	30		

FIRST NFL 400-YARD GAME: ANNIVERSARY. Nov 14, 1943. Sid Luckman of the Chicago Bears became the first professional quarterback to pass for more than 400 yards in a single game, throwing for 433 yards and seven touchdowns as the Bears walloped the New York Giants, 56–7.

HULL GETS 1,000th POINT: ANNIVERSARY. Nov 14, 1998. Right wing Brett Hull of the Dallas Stars got the 1,000th point of his National Hockey League career, an assist in a 3–1 win over the Boston Bruins.

MARSHALL FOOTBALL TRAGEDY: 30th ANNIVERSARY. Nov 14, 1970. Forty-three members of the football team from Marshall University at Huntington, WV, were killed when a plane in which they were flying crashed at Kenova, WV.

SHULA GETS 325th WIN: ANNIVERSARY. Nov 14, 1993. Head Coach Don Shula of the Miami Dolphins won the 325th game of his career as the Dolphins defeated the Philadelphia Eagles, 19–14. The victory moved Shula past George Halas as the winningest coach in NFL history. Shula concluded his coaching career in 1995 with a record of 347 wins, 173 losses and 6 ties.

BIRTHDAYS TODAY

Robert Douglas (Bob) Christian, 32, football player, born St. Louis, MO, Nov 14, 1968.
Guillermo (Willie) Hernandez, 46, former baseball player, born Aguada, Puerto Rico, Nov 14, 1954.
Lawyer Milloy, 27, football player, born St. Louis, MO, Nov 14, 1973.
James Anthony (Jimmy) Piersall, 71, former baseball player, born Waterbury, CT, Nov 14, 1929.
Curtis Montague (Curt) Schilling, 34, baseball player, born Anchorage, AK, Nov 14, 1966.
Dana William Stubblefield, 30, football player, born Cleves, OH, Nov 14, 1970.
Aaron Matthew Taylor, 28, football player, born San Francisco, CA, Nov 14, 1972.

Phog Allen

NOVEMBER 15 — WEDNESDAY

Day 320 — 46 Remaining

CHASE'S SPORTSQUOTE OF THE DAY

"I lost the bloody match, but what a way to go."
—Martina Navratilova

ALLEN, PHOG: BIRTH ANNIVERSARY. Nov 15, 1885. Forrest Clare ("Phog") Allen, basketball player and Basketball Hall of Fame coach, born at Jamesport, MO. Allen met Dr. James Naismith, inventor of basketball, while

Allen was a student at the University of Kansas and Naismith was coaching there. Allen played for Naismith and then became a coach himself, primarily at his alma mater until 1956 when he was forced to retire. Over 46 years, his teams won 771 games and lost only 233. He wrote three books about the sport and was instrumental in having basketball added to the Olympic program in 1936. Inducted into the Hall of Fame in 1959. Died at Lawrence, KS, Sept 16, 1974.

BELL, GUS: BIRTH ANNIVERSARY. Nov 15, 1928. David Russell ("Gus") Bell, baseball player, born at Louisville, KY. Bell was nicknamed "Gus" by his parents in honor of former player Gus Mancuso. He played outfield for the Cincinnati Reds and several other teams in the 1950s and 1960s. His son, Buddy Bell, and his grandson, David Bell, both reached the majors as well. Died at Cincinnati, OH, May 7, 1995.

FIRST BLACK PROFESSIONAL HOCKEY PLAYER: 50th ANNIVERSARY. Nov 15, 1950. When Arthur Dorrington signed a contract to play hockey with the Atlantic City Seagulls of the Eastern Amateur League on Nov 15, 1950, he became the first black man to play organized hockey in the US. He played for the Seagulls during the 1950 and 1951 seasons.

NAVRATILOVA RETIRES: ANNIVERSARY. Nov 15, 1994. Ending her professional tennis career, Martina Navratilova played a losing first-round match against Gabriela Sabatini in the 1994 season-ending Virginia Slims tournament. Hardly a ripple was made in one of the most impressive records in tennis history. During 21 years of play, Navratilova chalked up a 1,443–211 singles match record and won 167 titles (the most ever for anyone, male or female). She recorded 18 Grand Slam singles titles, 31 Grand Slam women's doubles championships and six career Grand Slam mixed doubles championships.

PRESEASON NIT. Nov 15 (tentative). College basketball's premier preseason tournament begins with eight first-round games and four second-round games at campus locations. The semifinals and final are tentatively scheduled for Madison Square Garden in New York on Nov 22 and Nov 24. For info: Media Relations, Madison Square Garden, 2 Pennsylvania Plaza, New York, NY 10001. Phone: (212) 465-6000.

STERN NAMED NBA COMMISSIONER: ANNIVERSARY. Nov 15, 1983. David J. Stern was named the fourth commissioner of the NBA, effective Feb 1, 1984. He replaced Larry O'Brien, commissioner from 1975 to 1984.

13 PLAYERS FOUL OUT: ANNIVERSARY. Nov 15, 1952. In an NBA overtime game between the Baltimore Bullets and the Syracuse Nationals, a record 13 players, five Bullets and eight Nets, fouled out. The referees let some of the Syracuse players back into the game and called a technical foul every time one of them committed an additional personal foul. Baltimore won, 97–91.

Gregory C. (Greg) Anthony, 33, basketball player, born Las Vegas, NV, Nov 15, 1967.
Otis Armstrong, 50, former football player, born Chicago, IL, Nov 15, 1950.

NOVEMBER 16 — THURSDAY
Day 321 — 45 Remaining

BURKE, GLENN: BIRTH ANNIVERSARY. Nov 16, 1952. Glenn Lawrence Burke, baseball player, born at Oakland, CA. Burke spent four seasons in the majors (1976–79) with the Los Angeles Dodgers and the Oakland Athletics. He was the first former baseball player the cause of whose death was acknowledged as AIDS. Died at San Leandro, CA, May 30, 1995.

FIFTH DOWN: 60th ANNIVERSARY. Nov 16, 1940. Cornell University played Dartmouth College in football and came away with a victory. But the winning touchdown was scored on a fifth-down play, given to Cornell by referee's error. After the game, Cornell did what it called the honorable thing, surrendering the triumph.

NAIA MEN'S SOCCER CHAMPIONSHIP. Nov 16–21. New Mexico Soccer Tournament Complex, Bernalilo, NM. 12-team field competes for national championship. 42nd annual. Est attendance: 3,000. For info: Natl Assn of Intercollegiate Athletics, 6120 S Yale Ave, Ste 1450, Tulsa, OK 74136-4223. Phone: (918) 494-8828. Fax: (918) 494-8841. E-mail: khenry@naia.org. Web: www.naia.org.

NAIA WOMEN'S SOCCER CHAMPIONSHIP. Nov 16–21. St. Thomas University, Miami, FL. 12-team field competes for national championship. 17th annual. Est attendance: 3,000. For info: Natl Assn of Intercollegiate Athletics, 6120 S Yale Ave, Ste 1450, Tulsa, OK 74136-4223. Phone: (918) 494-8828. Fax: (918) 494-8841. E-mail: khenry@naia.org. Web: www.naia.org.

NOTRE DAME SNAPS OKLAHOMA'S STREAK: ANNIVERSARY. Nov 16, 1957. Notre Dame upset Oklahoma, 7–0, to snap the Sooners' NCAA record 48-game winning streak. Dick Lynch scored the game's only touchdown.

UNIVERSITY OF CHICAGO'S FIRST FOOTBALL VICTORY: ANNIVERSARY. Nov 16, 1892. The University of Chicago, which played to a 0–0 tie with Northwestern in its first-ever football game on the preceding Oct 22, won its first game for Coach Amos Alonzo Stagg, 10–4, against Illinois at Chicago. A founding member of the Big Ten, Chicago eliminated its football program for many years but now competes in the University Athletic Association against the likes of New York University, Emory and Washington University at St. Louis.

☆   ☆   ☆

Oksana Baiul, 23, Olympic gold medal figure skater, born Dnepropetrovsk, Ukraine, Nov 16, 1977.
Zina Lynna Garrison, 37, tennis player, born Houston, TX, Nov 16, 1963.
Dwight Eugene ("Doc") Gooden, 36, baseball player, born Tampa, FL, Nov 16, 1964.
Christopher Deane (Chris) Haney, 32, baseball player, born Baltimore, MD, Nov 16, 1968.
Terry Labonte, 44, auto racer, born Corpus Christi, TX, Nov 16, 1956.
Corey Allen Pavin, 41, golfer, born Oxnard, CA, Nov 16, 1959.

NOVEMBER 17 — FRIDAY
Day 322 — 44 Remaining

COLORADO RIVER CROSSING BALLOON FESTIVAL. Nov 17–19. Cibola High School, Yuma, AZ. 10th annual. 55 balloons. Sunrise balloon liftoffs, sunset balloon glow and fireworks. Entertainment, food, vendors. Free admission. Est attendance: 17,000. For info: Caballeros de Yuma, Inc, PO Box 5987, Yuma, AZ 85366. Phone: (520) 343-1715. Fax: (520) 783-1609. Web: www.caballeros.org.

ECKERT NAMED COMMISSIONER: 35th ANNIVERSARY. Nov 17, 1965. Baseball owners elected William D. ("Spike") Eckert Commissioner of Baseball to replace the retiring Ford Frick. Eckert, a retired Air Force general and comptroller of the Air Force, proved to be a poor choice. He was removed from office in 1969.

HEIDI GAME: ANNIVERSARY. Nov 17, 1968. NBC Television cut away from the broadcast of a football game between the Oakland Raiders and the New York Jets with several minutes remaining on the clock in order to begin a special production of *Heidi* on time. After the special began, the Raiders scored two touchdowns in the final minute to earn a 43–32 comeback victory. Football fans deluged NBC with telephone calls, and networks eventually decided to delay the start of regular programming if athletic events ran over their allotted time.

LONGHORN WORLD CHAMPIONSHIP RODEO FINALS. Nov 17–18. Municipal Auditorium, Nashville, TN. One of America's top 10 most-talented rodeos. $175,000 in purses and awards, including gold and silver trophy belt buckles, hand-carved trophy saddles, plus a full-size $30,000 pickup truck to the Top Hand. Featuring the top 72 contestants from more than 1,200 who competed in our preceding 2000 tour of Longhorn Rodeos across the country for championships of the year in six different world-class contests. Also colorful opening pageantry and Big, Bad BONUS Bulls. 35th annual. Est attendance: 30,000. For info: W. Bruce Lehke, Pres, Longhorn World Chmpshp Rodeo, Inc, PO Box 70159, Nashville, TN 37207. Phone: (615) 876-1016. Fax: (615) 876-4685. E-mail: lhrodeo@idt.net. Web: www.longhorn rodeo.com.

NFL STRIKE ENDS: ANNIVERSARY. Nov 17, 1982. NFL players, on strike for two months, ended their walkout, but the season, originally set for 16 games, had to be cut to 9 games. The regular play-off arrangement was also scrapped, replaced by a special Super Bowl Tournament involving the 16 teams with the best records.

SPECIAL OLYMPICS MICHIGAN STATE POLY HOCKEY FINALS. Nov 17–19. Lansing, MI. Olympic-style tournament for children and adults with mental retardation. For info: Special Olympics Michigan, Central Michigan Univ, Mt Pleasant, MI 48859. Phone: (800) 644-6404. Fax: (517) 774-3034. E-mail: M.K.Lindberg @cmich.edu. Web: www.somi.org.

SPECIAL OLYMPICS MISSOURI INDOOR CLASSIC. Nov 17–19. St. Joseph, MO. Olympic-style competition for children and adults with mental retardation. For info: Special Olympics Missouri, 520 Dix Rd, Ste C, Jefferson City, MO 65109. Phone: (573) 635-1660. Fax: (573) 635-8233. E-mail: hg@somo.org. Web: www.somo.org.

November 2000

S	M	T	W	T	F	S
			1	2	3	4
5	6	7	8	9	10	11
12	13	14	15	16	17	18
19	20	21	22	23	24	25
26	27	28	29	30		

WETHERED, JOYCE: BIRTH ANNIVERSARY. Nov 17, 1901. Joyce Wethered, golfer, born at Witley, Surrey, England. Wethered learned the game from her father and her brother Roger and went on to become the finest player of her day. She won the British Women's Amateur four times and after retiring played exhibitions for money. Her game won the admiration of golfers everywhere including Bobby Jones, who said he felt outclassed playing with her. Died at London, England, Nov 18, 1997.

BIRTHDAYS TODAY

Elvin Ernest Hayes, 55, Basketball Hall of Fame center, born Rayville, LA, Nov 17, 1945.

Elieser (Eli) Marrero, 27, baseball player, born Havana, Cuba, Nov 17, 1973.

Robert Bruce (Bob) Mathias, 70, former US Congressman and Olympic gold medal decathlete, born Tulare, CA, Nov 17, 1930.

George Thomas (Tom) Seaver, 56, broadcaster and Baseball Hall of Fame pitcher, born Fresno, CA, Nov 17, 1944.

Paul Anthony Sorrento, 35, baseball player, born Somerville, MA, Nov 17, 1965.

Mitchell Steven (Mitch) Williams, 36, former baseball player, born Santa Ana, CA, Nov 17, 1964.

NOVEMBER 18 — SATURDAY
Day 323 — 43 Remaining

COOMBS, JACK: BIRTH ANNIVERSARY. Nov 18, 1882. John Wesley (Jack) Coombs, baseball player, born at LeGrande, IA. Coombs was an outstanding pitcher for Connie Mack's Philadelphia Athletics, winning 31 games in 1910. He contracted typhoid fever in 1913 and pitched sparingly after that. Died at Palestine, TX, Apr 15, 1957.

NAIA MEN'S AND WOMEN'S CROSS-COUNTRY NATIONAL CHAMPIONSHIPS. Nov 18. University of Wisconsin—Parkside, Kenosha, WI. Men compete on an 8K course, and women compete on a 5K course, with the top 25 individual finishers in each championship receiving All-America honors. 45th annual men's, 20th annual women's. For info: Natl Assn of Intercollegiate Athletics, 6120 S Yale Ave, Tulsa, OK 74136-4223. Phone: (918) 494-8828. Fax: (918) 494-8841. E-mail: khenry@naia.org. Web: www.naia.org.

ST. JOHN, LYNN: BIRTH ANNIVERSARY. Nov 18, 1876. Lynn Wilbur St. John, Basketball Hall of Fame administrator, born at Union City, PA. St. John served on basketball's Joint Rules Committee from 1912 to 1937 and helped to bring the game under one set of playing rules. He was coach and athletic director at Ohio State University, where the basketball arena was named in his honor and helped organize the first Olympic basketball competition in 1936. Inducted into the Hall of Fame in 1962. Died at Columbus, OH, Sept 30, 1950.

SULLIVAN, JAMES: 140th BIRTH ANNIVERSARY. Nov 18, 1860. James Edward Sullivan, amateur sports promoter, born at New York, NY. Sullivan helped to establish the Amateur Athletic Union in 1888 to preserve pure amateurism. He also worked as president of the American Sports Publishing Company and edited Spalding's Athletic Library series. The Sullivan Memorial Trophy is presented annually in his honor to the best amateur athlete in the US. Died at New York, NY, Sept 16, 1914.

WORLD TOUR BEGINS: ANNIVERSARY. Nov 18, 1888. Albert G. Spalding's attempt to introduce baseball to the entire world began as he, the Chicago White Stockings and a group of all-star players set sail from San Francisco for Honolulu, the first stop on their round-the-world tour.

BIRTHDAYS TODAY

Alphonse Dante Bichette, 37, baseball player, born West Palm Beach, FL, Nov 18, 1963.

Samuel James (Sam) Cassell, 31, basketball player, born Baltimore, MD, Nov 18, 1969.

Thomas (Tom) Gordon, 33, baseball player, born Sebring, FL, Nov 18, 1967.

Raghib Ramadian ("Rocket") Ismail, 31, football player, born Elizabeth, NJ, Nov 18, 1969.

Seth Joyner, 36, football player, born Spring Valley, NY, Nov 18, 1964.

Gene William Mauch, 75, former baseball manager and player, born Salina, KS, Nov 18, 1925.

Harold Warren Moon, 44, football player, born Los Angeles, CA, Nov 18, 1956.

Mark Joseph Petkovsek, 35, baseball player, born Beaumont, TX, Nov 18, 1965.

Gary Antonian Sheffield, 32, baseball player, born Tampa, FL, Nov 18, 1968.

Allen Kenneth Watson, 30, baseball player, born New York, NY, Nov 18, 1970.

Jason Chandler Williams, 25, basketball player, born Belle, WV, Nov 18, 1975.

NOVEMBER 19 — SUNDAY

Day 324 — 42 Remaining

CAMPANELLA, ROY: BIRTH ANNIVERSARY. Nov 19, 1921. Roy Campanella, Baseball Hall of Fame catcher, born at Philadelphia, PA. One of the first black major leaguers and a star of one of baseball's greatest teams, the Brooklyn Dodgers' "Boys of Summer," Campy, as he was often called, was named the National League MVP three times in his 10 years of play, in 1951, 1953 and 1955. Campanella had his highest batting average in 1951 (.325), and in 1953 he established three single-season records for a catcher—most putouts (807), most home runs (41) and most runs batted in (142)—as well as having a batting average of .312. His career was cut short on Jan 28, 1958, when an automobile accident left him paralyzed. Campy gained even more fame after his accident as an inspiration and spokesman for people with disabilities. Inducted into the Hall of Fame in 1969. Died at Woodland Hills, CA, June 26, 1993.

CANADA: CANADIAN WESTERN AGRIBITION. Nov 19–26. Regina, Saskatchewan. Canada's premiere agricultural event is the world's largest indoor livestock show and marketplace. More than 4,000 cattle, sheep, swine and horses are brought to Agribition, plus pedigreed seed show and agricultural trade and technology show. Also, a variety of entertainment. Est attendance: 150,000. For info: Western Agribition, Box 3535, Regina, SK, Canada S4P 3J8. Phone: (306) 565-0565. E-mail: agribition @sk.sympatico.ca. Web: www.agribition.com.

NATIONAL GAME AND PUZZLE WEEK. Nov 19–25. To increase appreciation of games and puzzles while conserving the tradition of investing time with family and friends. Annually, the last week in November. For info: Frank Beres, Patch Products, PO Box 268, Beloit, WI 53512-0268. Phone: (608) 362-6896. Fax: (608) 362-8178. E-mail: patch@patchproducts.com. Web: www.patch products.com.

NOTRE DAME–MICHIGAN STATE TIE: ANNIVERSARY. Nov 19, 1966. In one of the more famous college football matchups between teams ranked No. 1 and No. 2, top-ranked Notre Dame tied second-ranked Michigan State, 10–10.

RYAN FIRST $1 MILLION PLAYER: ANNIVERSARY. Nov 19, 1979. Pitcher Nolan Ryan became the first baseball free agent to sign a contract for a salary of $1 million per year. Ryan moved from the California Angels to the Houston Astros.

SUNDAY, BILLY: BIRTH ANNIVERSARY. Nov 19, 1862. William Ashley (Billy) Sunday, baseball player, born at Ames, IA. Sunday was a major league outfielder in the 1880s before leaving the game to become an evangelist. Died at Chicago, IL, Nov 6, 1935.

ZAMBONI PROPOSAL: ANNIVERSARY. Nov 19, 1993. Alan Giarettino proposed marriage to Christy Stubblefield while she rode around the ice rink on the Zamboni during the intermission between the second and third periods of an East Coast Hockey League game at Huntington, WV. Stubblefield thought she had earned the ride by winning a contest. In truth, Giarettino had arranged the contest so that he could walk onto the ice during the ride, hand her a bouquet and drop to one knee. She said yes.

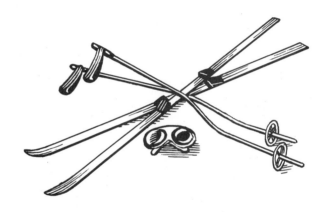

BIRTHDAYS TODAY

John Garfield ("Toby") Bailey, Jr, 25, basketball player, born Los Angeles, CA, Nov 19, 1975.

Robert Raymond (Bob) Boone, 53, former baseball manager and player, born San Diego, CA, Nov 19, 1947.

Gail Devers, 34, Olympic gold medal sprinter, born Seattle, WA, Nov 19, 1966.

Gary Thomas DiSarcina, 33, baseball player, born Malden, MA, Nov 19, 1967.

Jamir Malik Miller, 27, football player, born Philadelphia, PA, Nov 19, 1973.

Ahmad Rashad (born Bobby Moore), 51, broadcaster and former football player, born Portland, OR, Nov 19, 1949.

Kerri Strug, 23, Olympic gold medal gymnast, born Tucson, AZ, Nov 19, 1977.

Robert Edward (Ted) Turner, 62, baseball, basketball and cable TV executive, born Cincinnati, OH, Nov 19, 1938.

NOVEMBER 20 — MONDAY

Day 325 — 41 Remaining

CADORE, LEON: BIRTH ANNIVERSARY. Nov 20, 1890. Leon Joseph Cadore, baseball player, born at Chicago, IL. Cadore is most famous for pitching all 26 innings for the Brooklyn Dodgers in baseball's longest game, a 1–1 tie with the Boston Braves on May 1, 1920. Died at Spokane, WA, Mar 16, 1958.

CAL VS THE STANFORD BAND: ANNIVERSARY. Nov 20, 1982. The University of California football team defeated Stanford University, 25–20, on a most unusual last play. Stanford was ahead, 20–19, and had to kick off with only a few seconds left. The Cal players knew that if any of them were tackled, the game would be over. They began an unscripted series of five laterals that landed them in the end zone after they dodged all the Stanford players and the Stanford band which had rushed onto the field prematurely.

GREEN SETS CONSECUTIVE GAMES MARK: ANNIVERSARY. Nov 20, 1997. A.C. Green of the Dallas Mavericks set an NBA record for consecutive games played, 907, when he took the floor for the Mavericks' game against the Golden State Warriors. Green began his streak on Nov 19, 1986, when he played for the Los Angeles Lakers. It continued as he moved to the Phoenix Suns and then to the Mavericks. His accomplishment was noted with an elaborate halftime ceremony that included appearances by Randy Smith, the man whose record Green broke, and baseball's iron man, Cal Ripken.

GRIFFITH, CLARK: BIRTH ANNIVERSARY. Nov 20, 1869. Clark Calvin Griffith, Baseball Hall of Fame pitcher and executive, born at Stringtown, MO. Griffith pitched and managed the New York Highlanders (later the Yankees) and the Cincinnati Reds. He became owner of the Washington Senators and held the team until his death. Inducted into the Hall of Fame in 1946. Died at Washington, DC, Oct 27, 1955.

LANDIS, KENESAW: BIRTH ANNIVERSARY. Nov 20, 1866. Kenesaw Mountain Landis, Baseball Hall of Fame executive, born at Millville, OH. Landis, a federal judge, was named the first Commissioner of Baseball in 1920. He ruled with an absolutely firm hand and imposed his view of how baseball should operate upon owners and players alike. Inducted into the Hall of Fame in 1944. Died at Chicago, IL, Nov 25, 1944.

NCAA MEN'S AND WOMEN'S DIVISION I CROSS-COUNTRY CHAMPIONSHIPS. Nov 20. Finals. Iowa State University, Ames, IA. For info: NCAA, PO Box 6222, Indianapolis, IN 46206-6222. Phone: (317) 917-6222. Fax: (317) 917-6888. Web: www.ncaa.org.

BIRTHDAYS TODAY

Alejandro (Alex) Arias, 33, baseball player, born New York, NY, Nov 20, 1967.

Joey Galloway, 29, football player, born Bellaire, OH, Nov 20, 1971.

John William ("Jay") Johnstone, 55, former baseball player, born Manchester, CT, Nov 20, 1945.

Dwight Eugene Stephenson, 43, Pro Football Hall of Fame center, born Murfreesboro, NC, Nov 20, 1957.

Tra Thomas, 26, football player, born De Land, FL, Nov 20, 1974.

NOVEMBER 21 — TUESDAY
Day 326 — 40 Remaining

CARRS GREAT ALASKA SHOOTOUT. Nov 21–25. Sullivan Area, Anchorage, AK. Top NCAA basketball action as eight men's and four women's Division I teams from around the country compete. Est attendance: 48,000. For info: Univ of Alaska-Anchorage, Athletic Dept, 3211 Providence, Anchorage, AK 99508. Phone: (907) 786-1230. Fax: (907) 563-4565. E-mail: antlm@uaa.alaska.edu. Web: www.uaa.alaska.edu/athletic.

FRENCHMAN ROWS ACROSS PACIFIC: ANNIVERSARY. Nov 21, 1991: Gerard d'Aboville completed a four-month solo journey across the Pacific Ocean on Nov 21, 1991. D'Aboville began rowing across the Pacific on July 11 when he left Choshi, Japan. His journey ended at Ilwaco, WA.

LINDSTROM, FREDDIE: 95th BIRTH ANNIVERSARY. Nov 21, 1905. Frederick Charles (Freddie) Lindstrom, Baseball Hall of Fame third baseman and outfielder, born at Chicago, IL. Lindstrom played for the New York Giants in the 1920s and 1930s. In the 1924 World Series, a ground ball hit a pebble and bounced over his head, allowing the run that gave the championship to the Washington Senators. Inducted into the Hall of Fame in 1976. Died at Chicago, Oct 4, 1981.

NCAA WOMEN'S DIVISION III SOCCER CHAMPIONSHIP. Nov 21–22. Finals at a campus site TBA. For info: NCAA, PO Box 6222, Indianapolis, IN 46206-6222. Phone: (317) 917-6222. Fax: (317) 917-6888. Web: www.ncaa.org.

NEWCOMBE WINS FIRST CY YOUNG AWARD: ANNIVERSARY. Nov 21, 1956. Don Newcombe of the Brooklyn Dodgers won the first Cy Young award, given to the most outstanding pitcher in the major leagues. He added the National League MVP Award to his trophy case as well.

NFL RESUMES AFTER STRIKE: ANNIVERSARY. Nov 21, 1982. After a strike that commenced on Sept 23, the NFL resumed play, with the seven intervening weeks of the season having been canceled.

YANKEES BUY DiMAGGIO: ANNIVERSARY. Nov 21, 1934. The New York Yankees paid the San Francisco Seals $25,000 and four players for Joe DiMaggio. Despite DiMaggio's 61-game hitting streak in 1933 and his .341 batting average in 1934, the Yankees kept him with the Seals for 1935. He hit .398.

BIRTHDAYS TODAY

Troy Kenneth Aikman, 34, football player, born West Covina, CA, Nov 21, 1966.

George Kenneth (Ken) Griffey, Jr, 31, baseball player, born Donora, PA, Nov 21, 1969.

Danny Kanell, 27, football player, born Ft Lauderdale, FL, Nov 21, 1973.

November 2000	S	M	T	W	T	F	S
				1	2	3	4
	5	6	7	8	9	10	11
	12	13	14	15	16	17	18
	19	20	21	22	23	24	25
	26	27	28	29	30		

Vernon Earl ("The Pearl") Monroe, 56, Basketball Hall of Fame guard, born Philadelphia, PA, Nov 21, 1944.

Stanley Frank ("Stan the Man") Musial, 80, Baseball Hall of Fame outfielder and first baseman, born Donora, PA, Nov 21, 1920.

Olden Polynice, 36, basketball player, born Port-au-Prince, Haiti, Nov 21, 1964.

James Stephen (Jim) Ringo, 69, Pro Football Hall of Fame center, born Orange, NJ, Nov 21, 1931.

Michael Anthony Strahan, 29, football player, born Houston, TX, Nov 21, 1971.

NOVEMBER 22 — WEDNESDAY

Day 327 — 39 Remaining

BOSTOCK, LYMAN: 50th BIRTH ANNIVERSARY. Nov 22, 1950. Lyman Wesley Bostock, baseball player, born at Boston, MA. Bostock played four years in the major leagues before being fatally shot. Died at Denver, CO, Sept 16, 1968.

FIRST AFL DRAFT: ANNIVERSARY. Nov 22, 1959. The American Football League, set to begin play in 1960, held its first draft of college players. First-round choices of the eight teams included Gerhard Schwedes (Boston), Richie Lucas (Buffalo), Don Meredith (Dallas), Roger LeClerc (Denver), Billy Cannon (Houston), Monty Stickles (Los Angeles), Dale Hackbart (Minneapolis) and George Izo (New York).

GRETZKY SCORES 500th GOAL: ANNIVERSARY. Nov 22, 1986. Center Wayne Gretzky of the Edmonton Oilers scored the 500th goal of his National Hockey League career in only his 575th game, a 5–2 victory over the Vancouver Canucks. Gretzky became the 13th player in NHL history to reach 500.

LOWEST-SCORING NBA GAME: 50th ANNIVERSARY. Nov 22, 1950. The Fort Wayne Pistons used a stall tactic to defeat the Minneapolis Lakers, 19–18, in the lowest-scoring NBA game ever. The game drew a large crowd for 50-cent father-son night but was so boring that people were reading newspapers in the stands during play. The game led to the adoption of the 24-second clock in 1954.

BIRTHDAYS TODAY

Eric Andre Allen, 35, football player, born San Diego, CA, Nov 22, 1965.

Boris Franz Becker, 33, tennis player, born Leimen, Germany, Nov 22, 1967.

Selva Lewis (Lew) Burdette, 74, former baseball player, born Nitro, WV, Nov 22, 1926.

Harry Edwards, 58, sports sociologist, born St. Louis, MO, Nov 22, 1942.

Robert Thomas ("Butch") Goring, 51, hockey coach and former player, born St. Boniface, Manitoba, Canada.

Billie Jean Moffitt King, 57, former tennis player, born Long Beach, CA, Nov 22, 1943.

Ricardo Alberto (Ricky) Ledee, 27, baseball player, born Ponce, Puerto Rico, Nov 22, 1973.

Gregory Michael (Greg) Luzinski, 50, former baseball player, born Chicago, IL, Nov 22, 1950.

NOVEMBER 23 — THURSDAY

Day 328 — 38 Remaining

CHASE'S SPORTSQUOTE OF THE DAY

"Let's face it, baseball is show business."—Jack McKeon

ASHFORD, EMMETT: BIRTH ANNIVERSARY. Nov 23, 1914. Emmett Littleton Ashford, baseball umpire, born at Los Angeles, CA. Ashford was the first black to umpire a major league baseball game. Ashford began his pro career calling games in the minors in 1951 and went to the majors in 1966. He was noted for his flamboyant style when calling strikes and outs as well as for his dapper dress which included cufflinks with his uniform. Died at Marina del Rey, CA, Mar 1, 1980.

ATLANTA MARATHON AND ATLANTA HALF-MARATHON. Nov 23. Atlanta, GA. 26.2-mile and 13.1-mile races. Advance registration only, entry forms available in July. Send SASE. Est attendance: 8,000. For info: Atlanta Track Club, Atlanta Marathon, 3097 E Shadowlawn Ave, Atlanta, GA 30305. Race hot line (Atlanta area): (404) 262-RACE. Web: www.atlantatrackclub.org.

DAYTONA TURKEY RUN. Nov 23–25. Daytona International Speedway, Daytona Beach, FL. 27th annual car show of all makes of 1978 and older collector vehicles. Show includes display of classics, sports cars, muscle cars, race cars, and custom and special-interest vehicles on the speedway infield all three days, with a large swap meet of auto parts and accessories and car sales corral. Also crafts sale. Annually, Thanksgiving weekend. Est attendance: 70,000. For info: Rick D'Louhy, Exec Dir, Daytona Beach Racing and Recreational Facilities District, PO Box 1958, Daytona Beach, FL 32115-1958. Phone: (904) 255-7355. Web: www.carshows.org.

FIRST PLAY-BY-PLAY FOOTBALL GAME BROADCAST: ANNIVERSARY. Nov 23, 1919. The first play-by-play football game broadcast in the US took place on this day. Texas A&M blanked the University of Texas, 7–0.

FLUTIE'S "HAIL MARY" PASS: ANNIVERSARY. Nov 23, 1984. Quarterback Doug Flutie of Boston College passed for 472 yards and led the Eagles to a 47–45 upset of the Miami University Hurricanes. Flutie won the game with a desperation "Hail Mary" touchdown pass that end Gerald Phelan caught in the end zone.

SCOTLAND: SCOTTISH INTERNATIONAL BADMINTON CHAMPIONSHIP. Nov 23–26. Meadowbank Sports Centre, Edinburgh, Scotland. A European Badminton Union Grand Prix event. Est attendance: 5,000. For info: Scottish Badminton Union, Cockburn Centre, 40 Bogmoor Place, Scotland G51 4TQ. Phone: (44) (141) 445-1218. Fax: (44) (141) 425-1218.

THANKSGIVING DAY. Nov 23. Legal public holiday. (Public Law 90–363 sets Thanksgiving Day on the fourth Thursday in November.) Observed on this day in all states. Despite the wishes of cooks everywhere, Thanksgiving is a day for traditional football games at the professional, college and high school levels. The Detroit Lions and Dallas Cowboys host NFL games on this date.

BIRTHDAYS TODAY

Vincent Lamont (Vin) Baker, 29, basketball player, born Lake Wales, FL, Nov 23, 1971.

Saku Koivu, 26, hockey player, born Turku, Finland, Nov 23, 1974.

John Aloysius (Jack) McKeon, 70, baseball manager, born South Amboy, NJ, Nov 23, 1930.

Tony Parrish, 25, football player, born Huntington Beach, CA, Nov 23, 1975.

Dale Curtis Sveum, 37, baseball player, born Richmond, CA, Nov 23, 1963.

Luis Clemente Tiant, 60, former baseball player, born Marinao, Cuba, Nov 23, 1940.

George Harry Yardley, III, 72, Basketball Hall of Fame forward, born Hollywood, CA, Nov 23, 1928.

NOVEMBER 24 — FRIDAY
Day 329 — 37 Remaining

BURNS, GEORGE: BIRTH ANNIVERSARY. Nov 24, 1889. George Joseph Burns, baseball player, born at Utica, NY. Burns was an outfielder and not related to his contemporary, first baseman George Henry Burns. He wore a special cap and blue sunglasses to help him cope with the sun at the Polo Grounds. Died at Gloversville, NY, Aug 15, 1966.

FISH HOUSE PARADE. Nov 24. Aitkin, MN. 9th annual special parade of uniquely decorated fish houses used for ice fishing during the winter. Annually, the Friday after Thanksgiving. Est attendance: 5,000. For info: Carroll Kukowski, Exec Dir, Aitkin Area Chamber of Commerce, PO Box 127, Aitkin, MN 56431. Phone: (800) 526-8342. Fax: (218) 927-4494. E-mail: upnorth@aitkin.com. Web: aitkin.com.

McALLESTER THROWN FOR TOUCHDOWN: ANNIVERSARY. Nov 24, 1904. University of Tennessee fullback Sam McAllester was thrown for a touchdown to give the Volunteers a 7–0 victory over the University of Alabama. McAllester wore a special leather belt with handgrips sewn on the sides. His team engineered a 50-yard touchdown drive by repeatedly throwing him over the line of scrimmage, including one toss for the game's only touchdown. Football's rules were later changed to prohibit abetting the ballcarrier.

MEDWICK, DUCKY: BIRTH ANNIVERSARY. Nov 24, 1911. Joseph Michael ("Ducky") Medwick, Baseball Hall of Fame outfielder, born at Carteret, NJ. Medwick was a member of the St. Louis Cardinals' famous Gas House Gang and won the National League Triple Crown in 1937. His career batting average was .324. Inducted into the Hall of Fame in 1968. Died at St. Petersburg, FL, Mar 21, 1975.

PINEY CREEK SNOWSHOE RUN. Nov 24. Ski Cooper near Leadville, CO. The course consists of about four miles of unpacked, semi-packed and packed snow. Elevation: 10,500 feet. This race is the first in a series of many races held in the Leadville area. For info: Piney Creek Nordic Center, c/o Greater Leadville Area Chamber of Commerce, Leadville, CO 80461. Phone: (719) 486-1750 or (800) 933-3901. Fax: (719) 486-8478. E-mail: leadville@leadvilleusacom. Web: www.leadvilleusa.com.

November 2000

S	M	T	W	T	F	S
			1	2	3	4
5	6	7	8	9	10	11
12	13	14	15	16	17	18
19	20	21	22	23	24	25
26	27	28	29	30		

WORLD'S CHAMPIONSHIP DUCK-CALLING CONTEST AND WINGS OVER THE PRAIRIE FESTIVAL. Nov 24–25. Stuttgart, AR. Besides the championship competition, this festival also offers a fun shoot, 10K race, sporting collectibles, commercial exhibitors, Sportsman's Dinner and Dance, duck gumbo cook-off, carnival, arts and crafts booths and more. Annually, Thanksgiving weekend. Est attendance: 65,000. For info: Stuttgart Chamber of Commerce, 507 S Main, Stuttgart, AR 72160. Phone: (870) 673-1602. Fax: (870) 673-1604.

BIRTHDAYS TODAY

David (Dave) Bing, 57, Basketball Hall of Fame guard, born Washington, DC, Nov 24, 1943.

Robert Bartmess (Bob) Friend, 70, former baseball player, born Lafayette, IN, Nov 24, 1930.

David Andrew (Dave) Hansen, 32, baseball player, born Long Beach, CA, Nov 24, 1968.

John Henry Johnson, 71, Pro Football Hall of Fame fullback, born Waterproof, LA, Nov 24, 1929.

Stanley Paul (Stan) Jones, 69, Pro Football Hall of Fame guard, born Altoona, PA, Nov 24, 1931.

Robert Yale Lary, Jr, 70, Pro Football Hall of Fame defensive back, born Ft Worth, TX, Nov 24, 1930.

Albert Lee (Al) Martin, 33, baseball player, born West Covina, CA, Nov 24, 1967.

Larry Benard (Ben) McDonald, 33, baseball player, born Baton Rouge, LA, Nov 24, 1967.

Keith Primeau, 29, hockey player, born Toronto, Ontario, Canada, Nov 24, 1971.

Oscar Palmer Robertson, 62, Basketball Hall of Fame guard, born Charlotte, TN, Nov 24, 1938.

Rudolph (Rudy) Tomjanovich, 52, basketball coach and former player, born Hamtramck, MI, Nov 24, 1948.

Randy Lee Velarde, 38, baseball player, born Midland, TX, Nov 24, 1962.

NOVEMBER 25 — SATURDAY
Day 330 — 36 Remaining

CLARK HANDICAP. Nov 25. Churchill Downs, Louisville, KY. The nation's top handicap race following the Breeders' Cup. Est attendance: 25,000. For info: Churchill Downs, 700 Central Ave, Louisville, KY 40208. Phone: (502) 636-4400. Web: www.kentuckyderby.com.

DiMAGGIO, JOE: BIRTH ANNIVERSARY. Nov 25, 1914. Joseph Paul (Joe) DiMaggio, Baseball Hall of Fame outfielder, born at Martinez, CA. One of the most renowned ballplayers ever, "Joltin' Joe" starred for the New York Yankees from 1936 through 1951, losing three seasons to military service during World War II. He hit .325 with 361 home runs and 1,537 RBIs, played in 10 World Series and won the MVP Award three times. Graceful and economical, the "Yankee Clipper" was famous for rarely making a wrong move on the field and for his quiet dignity off it. His legacy includes a record 56-game hitting streak. After retirement, he was married for a short time to Marilyn Monroe. His stature as a baseball icon grew with the years even as he became more reclusive. Inducted into the Hall of Fame in 1955. Died at Hollywood, FL, Mar 8, 1999.

MATHESON, BOB: BIRTH ANNIVERSARY. Nov 25, 1944. Robert Edward (Bob) Matheson, football player, born at Boone, NC. Matheson played at Duke and was drafted in 1967 by the Cleveland Browns. After four seasons, he was traded to the Miami Dolphins, where he became an integral part of the famous "No Name" defense that helped win two Super Bowls. The Dolphins' "53" defense, utilizing Matheson as a linebacker, was named after his uniform number. Died at Durham, NC, Sept 5, 1994.

MINERAL COUNTY CHAMBER OF COMMERCE FISHERMEN'S HOLIDAY FISH DERBY. Nov 25. Walker Lake, NV. Trout fishing contest for cash and other prizes. Annually, the Saturday after Thanksgiving. For info: Mineral County Chamber of Commerce, PO Box 1635, Hawthorne, NV 89415. Phone: (775) 945-5896. Fax: (775) 945-1257.

NCAA DIVISION I-AA FOOTBALL CHAMPIONSHIP. Nov 25. First round. Sites TBA. For info: NCAA, PO Box 6222, Indianapolis, IN 46206-6222. Phone: (317) 917-6222. Fax: (317) 917-6888. Web: www.ncaa.org.

NO MAS, NO MAS: 20th ANNIVERSARY. Nov 25, 1980. Roberto Duran quit fighting with 16 seconds left in the eighth round, saying "No mas, no mas" (No more, no more), allowing ("Sugar") Ray Leonard to regain the WBC welterweight title.

BIRTHDAYS TODAY

Christopher D. (Cris) Carter, 35, football player, born Troy, OH, Nov 25, 1965.
Russell Earl ("Bucky") Dent (born Russell Earl O'Dey), 49, former baseball manager and player, born Savannah, GA, Nov 25, 1951.
Joe Jackson Gibbs, 60, auto racing executive, broadcaster and Pro Football Hall of Fame coach, born Mocksville, NC, Nov 25, 1940.
Bernie Joseph Kosar, Jr, 37, former football player, born Boardman, OH, Nov 25, 1963.
Leonard Edward (Lenny) Moore, 67, Pro Football Hall of Fame halfback, born Reading, PA, Nov 25, 1933.
Anthony Eugene Peeler, 31, basketball player, born Kansas City, MO, Nov 25, 1969.
Mark Anthony Whiten, 34, baseball player, born Pensacola, FL, Nov 25, 1966.

NOVEMBER 26 — SUNDAY
Day 331 — 35 Remaining

CHASE'S SPORTSQUOTE OF THE DAY

"I was the worst hitter ever. I never even broke a bat until last year. Then I was backing out of the garage."
—Lefty Gomez

DUFFY, HUGH: BIRTH ANNIVERSARY. Nov 26, 1866. Hugh Duffy, Baseball Hall of Fame outfielder, born at River Point, RI. Duffy had a 68-year career in baseball.

He starred for the Boston teams of the 1890s and hit .438 in 1894, the all-time record. After his retirement, he served as a manager, coach, executive and scout until his death. Inducted into the Hall of Fame in 1945. Died at Allston, MA, Oct 19, 1954.

GOMEZ, LEFTY: BIRTH ANNIVERSARY. Nov 26, 1908. Vernon Louis ("Lefty") Gomez, Baseball Hall of Fame pitcher, born at Rodeo, CA. Gomez was a star pitcher with the New York Yankees from 1930 to 1942. He won six World Series games without a defeat and was the winning pitcher in the first All-Star Game. Inducted into the Hall of Fame in 1972. Died at Greenbrae, CA, Feb 17, 1989.

RED GRANGE'S FIRST GAME AS A PROFESSIONAL: 75th ANNIVERSARY. Nov 26, 1925. After finishing his college football career at the University of Illinois, Harold ("Red") Grange, perhaps the most famous player of all time, played his first game as a professional. Wearing the uniform of the Chicago Bears, Grange was held to 35 yards rushing in a 0–0 tie against the Chicago Cardinals.

TRIPLE CROWN OF SURFING SERIES: EVENT 2-WORLD CUP OF SURFING. Nov 26–Dec 8. Sunset Beach, Haleiwa, North Shore, Oahu, HI. 18th annual. The Triple Crown of Surfing series is professional, big-wave surfing for men and women. Est attendance: 8,500. For media info: Jodi Young or Carol Hogan, (808) 325-7400. Fax: (808) 325-7400. E-mail: oceanpro@inter-pac.net. For contest info: Randy Rarick, (808) 638-7266.

BIRTHDAYS TODAY

Mario Antoine Elie, 37, basketball player, born New York, NY, Nov 26, 1963.
Charles Edward (Chuck) Finley, 38, baseball player, born Monroe, LA, Nov 26, 1962.
Dale Jarrett, 44, auto racer, born Newton, NC, Nov 26, 1956.
Shawn T. Kemp, 31, basketball player, born Elkhart, IN, Nov 26, 1969.
Chris Osgood, 28, hockey player, born Peace River, Alberta, Canada, Nov 26, 1972.
Arthur (Art) Shell, 54, former football coach and Pro Football Hall of Fame tackle, born Charleston, SC, Nov 26, 1946.
Jan Stenerud, 58, Pro Football Hall of Fame placekicker, born Fetsund, Norway, Nov 26, 1942.
Jeffrey Allen (Jeff) Torborg, 59, broadcaster and former baseball manager and player, born Plainfield, NJ, Nov 26, 1941.

NOVEMBER 27 — MONDAY
Day 332 — 34 Remaining

BUSH, BULLET JOE: BIRTH ANNIVERSARY. Nov 27, 1892. Leslie Ambrose ("Bullet Joe") Bush, baseball player, born at Brainerd, MN. Bush won 195 games as a pitcher in 17 major league seasons. He was a temperamental player who gave his managers difficulty, once screaming curses at Miller Huggins, who had ordered him to issue an intentional walk. Died at Ft Lauderdale, FL, Nov 1, 1974.

HOWE GETS 1,000th POINT: 40th ANNIVERSARY. Nov 27, 1960. Right wing Gordie Howe of the Detroit Red Wings became the first player in National Hockey League history to score 1,000 regular-season points by tallying an assist in a 2–0 Red Wings victory over the Toronto Maple Leafs. Howe finished his 26-year career with 1,850 points.

HUSING, TED: BIRTH ANNIVERSARY. Nov 27, 1901. Edward Britt (Ted) Husing, broadcaster, born at New York, NY. Husing moved from a job as varsity sports mascot at Columbia University to a career as a radio announcer where he gradually focused on sports. He made his mark doing college football games for the CBS network, using careful preparation, wide knowledge and precise speech to develop a national reputation. Died at Pasadena, CA, Aug 10, 1962.

McNALLY, JOHNNY BLOOD: BIRTH ANNIVERSARY. Nov 27, 1904. John Victor ("Johnny Blood") McNally, Pro Football Hall of Fame halfback, born at New Richmond, WI. McNally left Notre Dame over discipline code violations. Heading for a tryout with a semipro team, he adopted the name Johnny Blood, based on the Rudolf Valentino film *Blood and Sand*. He played 15 years in the NFL and led the Green Bay Packers to four titles. A flamboyant player who ignored team rules with abandon, he proved a disaster as a coach. Inducted into the Hall of Fame as a charter member in 1963. Died at Palm Springs, CA, Nov 28, 1965.

RAMADAN: THE ISLAMIC MONTH OF FASTING (YEAR 1421). Nov 27–Dec 27. Begins on Islamic lunar calendar date Ramadan 1, 1421. Ramadan, the ninth month of the Islamic calendar, is holy because it was during this month that the Holy Qur'an (Koran) was revealed. All adults of sound body and mind fast from dawn (before sunrise) until sunset to achieve spiritual and physical purification and self-discipline, abstaining from food, drink and intimate relations. It is a time for feeling a common bond with the poor and needy, a time for piety and prayer. Different methods for "anticipating" the visibility of the new moon crescent at Mecca are used by different Muslim sects or groups. US EST date may vary.

BIRTHDAYS TODAY

Larry Christopher Allen, 29, football player, born Los Angeles, CA, Nov 27, 1971.
Nickey Maxwell (Nick) Van Exel, 29, basketball player, born Kenosha, WI, Nov 27, 1971.

NOVEMBER 28 — TUESDAY
Day 333 — 33 Remaining

BILLIKENS WIN FIRST NCAA SOCCER TITLE: ANNIVERSARY. Nov 28, 1959. The St. Louis University Billikens won the first NCAA soccer championship, defeating the University of Bridgeport, 5–2.

PICARD, HENRY: BIRTH ANNIVERSARY. Nov 28, 1907. Henry B. Picard, golfer, born at Plymouth, MA. Picard won 30 tournaments, including the 1938 Masters and the 1939 PGA Championship. He was golf's leading money winner in 1941. Early in his career, he became the only golfer to defeat Walter Hagen in a play-off, doing so in the 1932 Carolina Open. Died at Charleston, SC, Apr 30, 1997.

TWO TDS ON RECOVERED FUMBLES: ANNIVERSARY. Nov 28, 1948. Dippy Evans of the Chicago Bears became the first player in NFL history to score two touchdowns on recovered fumbles in the same game as the Bears defeated the Washington Redskins, 48–13.

	S	M	T	W	T	F	S
November				1	2	3	4
2000	5	6	7	8	9	10	11
	12	13	14	15	16	17	18
	19	20	21	22	23	24	25
	26	27	28	29	30		

BIRTHDAYS TODAY

Pedro Julio Astacio, 31, baseball player, born Hato Mayor, Dominican Republic, Nov 28, 1969.
John David Burkett, 36, baseball player, born New Brighton, PA, Nov 28, 1964.
Dale Lavelle Carter, 31, football player, born Covington, GA, Nov 28, 1969.
Robert Allen (Robb) Nen, 31, baseball player, born San Pedro, CA, Nov 28, 1969.
John Sylvester (Johnny) Newman, Jr, 37, basketball player, born Danville, PA, Nov 28, 1963.
Todd Joseph Perry, 30, football player, born Elizabethtown, KY, Nov 28, 1970.
David Allen (Dave) Righetti, 42, former baseball player, born San Jose, CA, Nov 28, 1958.
Paul Dryden Warfield, 58, Pro Football Hall of Fame receiver, born Warren, OH, Nov 28, 1942.
Walter William (Walt) Weiss, Jr, 37, baseball player, born Tuxedo, NY, Nov 28, 1963.
Matthew Derrick (Matt) Williams, 35, baseball player, born Bishop, CA, Nov 28, 1965.

NOVEMBER 29 — WEDNESDAY
Day 334 — 32 Remaining

CHASE'S SPORTSQUOTE OF THE DAY

"This game is different from the rest. And if you lose you have the whole winter to think about it."—Red Blaik on the Army-Navy game

DETROIT'S FIRST THANKSGIVING GAME: ANNIVERSARY. Nov 29, 1934. The Detroit Lions played their first Thanksgiving Day game, the start of an NFL tradition, and lost to the Chicago Bears, 19–16.

FIRST ARMY-NAVY GAME: 110th ANNIVERSARY. Nov 29, 1890. Army played Navy for the first time in football, and Navy won, 24–0. Red Emrich scored four touchdowns (worth 4 points each) and kicked two field goals (worth 2 points each), and Moulton Johnson added the other touchdown to account for all the scoring.

LONGEST NFL INTERCEPTION: ANNIVERSARY. Nov 29, 1987. Safety Vencie Glenn of the San Diego Chargers set an NFL record by returning an intercepted pass 103 yards for a touchdown in the Chargers' 31–17 loss to the Denver Broncos.

NAIA WOMEN'S VOLLEYBALL CHAMPIONSHIP. Nov 29–Dec 3. Site TBA. 20 teams compete in a pool-play tournament to determine the national champion. 20th annual championship. Est attendance: 3,000. For info: Natl Assn of Intercollegiate Athletics, 6120 S Yale Ave, Ste 1450, Tulsa, OK 74136-4223. Phone: (918) 494-8828. Fax: (918) 494-8841. E-mail: khenry@naia.org. Web: www .naia.org.

ROBINSON COACHES FINAL GAME: ANNIVERSARY. Nov 29, 1997. Eddie Robinson ended his 56-year college football coaching career with a loss as Southern University beat his Grambling Tigers, 30–7, in the Bayou Classic. Robinson, who started coaching in 1941, compiled a record of 408–165–15. His teams won or shared 17 Southwestern Athletic Conference titles and eight black college national championships. Grambling's record in Robinson's last year was 3–8.

BIRTHDAYS TODAY

DeCovan Kadell ("Dee") Brown, 32, basketball player, born Jacksonville, FL, Nov 29, 1968.
Pavol Demitra, 26, hockey player, born Dubnica, Czechoslovakia, Nov 29, 1974.
Michael Anthony (Mike) Easler, 50, former baseball player, born Cleveland, OH, Nov 29, 1950.
William Ashley (Bill) Freehan, 59, former baseball player, born Detroit, MI, Nov 29, 1941.
Howard Michael Johnson, 40, former baseball player, born Clearwater, FL, Nov 29, 1960.
Kasey Keller, 31, soccer player, born Olympia, WA, Nov 29, 1969.
Jamal Mashburn, 28, basketball player, born New York, NY, Nov 29, 1972.
Saturnino Orestes Armas ("Minnie") Minoso, 78, former baseball player, born Havana, Cuba, Nov 29, 1922.
Vincent Edward (Vin) Scully, 73, Ford Frick Award broadcaster, born New York, NY, Nov 29, 1927.

NOVEMBER 30 — THURSDAY
Day 335 — 31 Remaining

NCAA WOMEN'S DIVISION I VOLLEYBALL CHAMPIONSHIP. Nov 30–Dec 3. First and second rounds. Sites TBA. For info: NCAA, PO Box 6222, Indianapolis, IN 46206-6222. Phone: (317) 917-6222. Fax: (317) 917-6888. Web: www.ncaa.org.

SMITH GETS 1,000th POINT: ANNIVERSARY. Nov 20, 1991. Center Bobby Smith of the Minnesota North Stars got the 1,000th point of his National Hockey League career, a goal in a 4–3 win over the Toronto Maple Leafs. Smith finished his career with 1,036 points.

BIRTHDAYS TODAY

Ray Durham, 29, baseball player, born Charlotte, NC, Nov 30, 1971.
Robert Otis Griffith, 30, football player, born Lanham, MD, Nov 30, 1970.
Vincent Edward ("Bo") Jackson, 38, former baseball player and Heisman Trophy running back, born Bessemer, AL, Nov 30, 1962.
Mark David Lewis, 31, baseball player, born Hamilton, OH, Nov 30, 1969.
Ivan ("Pudge") Rodriguez, 29, baseball player, born Vega Baja, Puerto Rico, Nov 30, 1971.
Robert Alan (Bob) Tewksbury, 40, former baseball player, born Concord, NH, Nov 30, 1960.
William Ernest (Bill) Walsh, 69, Pro Football Hall of Fame coach, born Los Angeles, CA, Nov 30, 1931.
Paul Douglas Westphal, 50, basketball coach and former player, born Torrance, CA, Nov 30, 1950.

DECEMBER 1 — FRIDAY
Day 336 — 30 Remaining

ALSTON, WALTER: BIRTH ANNIVERSARY. Dec 1, 1911. Walter Emmons Alston, baseball player and Baseball Hall of Fame manager, born at Venice, OH. Alston struck out in his only major league at bat, but he became one of the game's most successful managers. Working under a series of one-year contracts with the Brooklyn and Los Angeles Dodgers from 1954 through 1976, Alston won seven National League pennants and four World Series. Inducted into the Hall of Fame in 1983. Died at Oxford, OH, Oct 1, 1984.

BINGO'S BIRTHDAY MONTH. Dec 1–31. To celebrate the innovation and manufacture of the game of bingo in 1929 by Edwin S. Lowe. Today bingo, played as a charitable fund-raiser, brings in $5 billion annually. For info: Roger Snowden, Pres, Bingo Bugle, Inc, Box 527, Vashon, WA 98070. Phone: (800) 327-6437.

JAYHAWK SHOOTOUT. Dec 1–3. Coffeyville, KS. Kansas Jayhawk Community College Conference men's and women's basketball showcase. Est attendance: 10,000. For info: Jack McNickle, Coffeyville Community College, 400 W 11th St, Coffeyville, KS 67337. Phone: (316) 252-7105. Fax: (316) 252-7088. E-mail: deanc@raven.ccc.cc.ks.us. Web: www.ccc.cc.ks.us.

LAVAGETTO, COOKIE: BIRTH ANNIVERSARY. Dec 1, 1912. Harry Arthur ("Cookie") Lavagetto, baseball player and manager, born at Oakland, CA. Lavagetto was the first manager of the Minnesota Twins, but he is best remembered for breaking up Floyd Bevans's bid for a no-hitter in Game 4 of the 1947 World Series. Lavagetto doubled with two out in the bottom of the ninth inning, spoiling Bevans's effort and winning the game for the Brooklyn Dodgers. Died at Orinda, CA, Aug 10, 1990.

NATIONAL FINALS RODEO. Dec 1–10. Thomas and Mack Center, Las Vegas, NV. The National Finals Rodeo is the premier event in professional rodeo. Reserved for the top 15 contestants in seven events—bareback riding, steer wrestling, team roping, saddle bronc riding, calf roping, women's barrel racing and bull riding—the NFR brings together the best contestants, best livestock and best contract personnel in the industry. Est attendance: 175,000.

For info: Professional Rodeo Cowboys Assn, 101 Pro Rodeo Dr, Colorado Springs, CO 80919. Phone: (719) 593-8840 or (702) 739-3900 or for ticket info (800) 848-4615.

NICKLAUS PASSES $2 MILLION MARK: ANNIVERSARY. Dec 1, 1973. Jack Nicklaus won the Disney World Open to become the first golfer to earn more than $2 million in career winnings.

SPECIAL OLYMPICS MISSOURI GYMNASTICS CLASSIC. Dec 1–3. Springfield, MO. Olympic-style competition for children and adults with mental retardation. For info: Special Olympics Missouri, 520 Dix Rd, Ste C, Jefferson City, MO 65109. Phone: (573) 635-1660. Fax: (573) 635-8233. E-mail: hq@somo.org. Web: www.somo.org.

SPREWELL CHOKES COACH: ANNIVERSARY. Dec 1, 1997. Basketball player Latrell Sprewell of the Golden State Warriors, provoked, he said, by "a lot of verbal abuse," choked his coach, P.J. Carlesimo, at practice and threatened to kill him. The Warriors suspended Sprewell for 10 games and then terminated the remaining three years of Sprewell's $32 million, four-year contract, and the NBA suspended him for a year. The NBA Players Association filed a grievance on Sprewell's behalf, and on March 4, 1998, arbitrator John Feerick reinstated the contract and reduced the suspension to five months.

ZAMBONI MEDICAL ALERT: ANNIVERSARY. Dec 1, 1989. The Center for Disease Control revealed in the *Journal of the American Medical Association* that fumes from a Zamboni ice machine could make fans at a hockey game sick if the rink is not properly ventilated.

BIRTHDAYS TODAY

Carol Alt, 40, former *Sports Illustrated* swimsuit issue model, born New York, NY, Dec 1, 1960.

Morris Hiram ("Red") Badgro, 98, former baseball and football player, born Orilla, WA, Dec 1, 1902.

George Arthur Foster, 52, former baseball player, born Tuscaloosa, AL, Dec 1, 1948.

Martin Whitford (Marty) Marion, 83, former baseball manager and player, born Richburg, SC, Dec 1, 1917.

Calvin Coolidge Julius Caesar Tuskahoma (Cal) McLish, 75, former baseball player, born Anadarko, OK, Dec 1, 1925.

Gregory Winston (Greg) McMichael, 34, baseball player, born Knoxville, TN, Dec 1, 1966.

Kirk Wesley Rueter, 30, baseball player, born Centralia, IL, Dec 1, 1970.

Reginald Laverne (Reggie) Sanders, 33, baseball player, born Florence, SC, Dec 1, 1967.

Todd Edward Steussie, 30, football player, born Canoga Park, CA, Dec 1, 1970.

December 2000	S	M	T	W	T	F	S
						1	2
	3	4	5	6	7	8	9
	10	11	12	13	14	15	16
	17	18	19	20	21	22	23
	24	25	26	27	28	29	30
	31						

Lee Buck Trevino, 61, golfer, born Dallas, TX, Dec 1, 1939.

Larry Kenneth Walker, 34, baseball player, born Maple Ridge, British Columbia, Canada, Dec 1, 1966.

DECEMBER 2 — SATURDAY
Day 337 — 29 Remaining

ARMY-NAVY FOOTBALL GAME. Dec 2. PSINet Stadium, Baltimore, MD. The 101st game in one of college football's oldest traditional rivalries. Through 1998, Army led the series, 48–44, with 7 ties. Est attendance: 67,000.

BOARDWALK KENNEL CLUB DOG SHOW. Dec 2–3 (tentative). New Atlantic City Convention Center, Atlantic City, NJ. One of the largest all-breed dog shows in the country, with more than 2,200 entrants from across the US and Canada. 34th annual. Est attendance: 5,000. For info: Atlantic City Conv and Visitors Authority, 2314 Pacific Ave, Atlantic City, NJ 08401. Phone: (609) 449-7142.

DOLPHINS RUIN BEARS' UNDEFEATED SEASON: 15th ANNIVERSARY. Dec 2, 1985. The Miami Dolphins scored on their first five possessions and went on to defeat the Chicago Bears, 38–25. The Bears thus finished the regular season with a 15–1 record, and the Dolphins preserved their unique status as the only NFL team to go undefeated (17–0) in an entire season, a feat they accomplished in 1972.

NCAA DIVISION I-AA FOOTBALL CHAMPIONSHIP. Dec 2. Quarterfinals. Sites TBA. For info: NCAA, PO Box 6222, Indianapolis, IN 46206-6222. Phone: (317) 917-6222. Fax: (317) 917-6888. Web: www.ncaa.org.

WHITE, DEACON: BIRTH ANNIVERSARY. Dec 2, 1847. James Laurie ("Deacon") White, baseball player, born at Caton, NY. White was a catcher in the earliest days of professional baseball and was the first man to bat in the first game in baseball's first professional league. Died at Aurora, IL, July 7, 1939.

BIRTHDAYS TODAY

William Ferdie (Willie) Brown, 60, Pro Football Hall of Fame defensive back, born Yazoo City, MS, Dec 2, 1940.

Randy Gardner, 42, figure skater, born Marina del Rey, CA, Dec 2, 1958.

Darryl Andrew Kile, 32, baseball player, born Garden Grove, CA, Dec 2, 1968.

Mark Steven Kotsay, 25, baseball player, born Whittier, CA, Dec 2, 1975.

Otis James (O.J.) McDuffie, 31, football player, born Marion, OH, Dec 2, 1969.

Monica Seles, 27, tennis player, born Novi Sad, Yugoslavia, Dec 2, 1973.

Ronald (Ron) Sutter, 37, hockey player, born Viking, Alberta, Canada, Dec 2, 1963.

DECEMBER 3 — SUNDAY
Day 338 — 28 Remaining

DELAWARE MARATHON. Dec 3 (tentative). Middletown, DE. Marathon and marathon relays. For info: Marathon Sports, PO Box 398, Wilmington, DE 19899. Phone: (302) 654-6400. E-mail: waynek@mscal.com. Web: www.mscal.com.

BIRTHDAYS TODAY

Bobby Allison, 63, former auto racer, born Hueytown, AL, Dec 3, 1937.

Damon Scott Berryhill, 37, former baseball player, born South Laguna, CA, Dec 3, 1963.

Thomas Jesse (Tom) Fears, 77, former football coach and Pro Football Hall of Fame end, born Los Angeles, CA, Dec 3, 1923.

Darryl Quinn Hamilton, 37, baseball player, born Baton Rouge, LA, Dec 3, 1963.

Igor Larionov, 40, hockey player, born Voskresensk, USSR, Dec 3, 1960.

Rick Ravon Mears, 49, former auto racer, born Wichita, KS, Dec 3, 1951.

Katerina Witt, 35, Olympic gold medal figure skater, born Karl-Marx-Stadt, East Germany, Dec 3, 1965.

DECEMBER 4 — MONDAY
Day 339 — 27 Remaining

BLANCHARD FIRST JUNIOR TO WIN HEISMAN TROPHY: 55th ANNIVERSARY. Dec 4, 1945. Fullback Felix ("Doc") Blanchard of Army became the first junior to win the Heisman Trophy, emblematic of college football's best player. "Mr Inside" to teammate Glenn Davis's "Mr Outside," Blanchard also won the Sullivan Award, given to the country's best overall athlete.

BURKETT, JESSE: BIRTH ANNIVERSARY. Dec 4, 1868. Jesse Cail Burkett, Baseball Hall of Fame outfielder, born at Wheeling, WV. Burkett could pitch, but he was a superior hitter, compiling batting averages of more than .400 in 1895 and 1896. His nickname, "the Crab," came from his disposition on the field. Inducted into the Hall of Fame in 1946. Died at Worcester, MA, May 27, 1953.

FIRST BLACK NO. 1 NFL DRAFT CHOICE: ANNIVERSARY. Dec 4, 1961. Syracuse University halfback and Heisman Trophy winner Ernie Davis became the first African American to be selected first in the NFL draft when he was picked by the Washington Redskins.

GULICK, LUTHER: 135th BIRTH ANNIVERSARY. Dec 4, 1865. Luther Hasley Gulick, sports administrator, born at Honolulu, HI. A pioneer in the YMCA, Gulick designed the triangular logo symbolizing the physical, emotional and intellectual development that is still the Y's goal. While working at Springfield, MA, in 1891, Gulick persuaded Dr. James Naismith to devise an indoor game for use during the winter at the School for Christian Workers. The result was basketball. Inducted into the Basketball Hall of Fame in 1959. Died at South Casco, ME, Aug 13, 1918.

BIRTHDAYS TODAY

Helen M. Chase, 76, homemaker and now-retired chronicler of contemporary civilization as coeditor of *Chase's Annual Events*, born Whitehall, MI, Dec 4, 1924.

Alex Peter Delvecchio, 69, Hockey Hall of Fame center, born Ft William, Ontario, Canada, Dec 4, 1931.

Ted Johnson, 28, football player, born Alameda, CA, Dec 4, 1972.

Bernard King, 44, former basketball player, born New York, NY, Dec 4, 1956.

Lee Arthur Smith, 43, former baseball player, born Jamestown, LA, Dec 4, 1957.

Stanley Roger (Stan) Smith, 54, former tennis player, born Pasadena, CA, Dec 4, 1946.

Corliss Mondari Williamson, 27, basketball player, born Russellville, AR, Dec 4, 1973.

DECEMBER 5 — TUESDAY
Day 340 — 26 Remaining

INTERNATIONAL HOCKEY LEAGUE FOUNDED: 55th ANNIVERSARY. Dec 5, 1945. The IHL, founded at Windsor, Ontario, Canada, was designed to provide playing opportunities for Detroit–Windsor-area players returning home from service in World War II. Four teams played a 15-game schedule in 1945–46. Since that time, the IHL has become one of hockey's established minor leagues, with its franchises often serving as "farm teams" for National Hockey League teams.

PICKETT, BILL: 130th BIRTH ANNIVERSARY. Dec 5, 1870. Bill Pickett, rodeo cowboy, born at Williamson County, TX. Inventor of bulldogging, the modern rodeo event that involves wrestling a running steer to the ground. Died at Tulsa, OK, Apr 21, 1932.

WRIGLEY, PHILIP: BIRTH ANNIVERSARY. Dec 5, 1894. Philip Knight Wrigley, baseball executive, born at Chicago, IL. Wrigley inherited the Chicago Cubs upon his father's death in 1932. He and his family owned the team for 60 years until selling it to the Tribune Company in 1981. Died at Elkhart, WI, Apr 12, 1977.

BIRTHDAYS TODAY

Cornelius Clifford (Cliff) Floyd, 28, baseball player, born Chicago, IL, Dec 5, 1972.
Bobby Francis, 42, hockey coach and former player, born North Battleford, Saskatchewan, Canada, Dec 5, 1958.
James Arthur (Art) Monk, 43, former football player, born White Plains, NY, Dec 5, 1957.
James William (Jim) Plunkett, Jr, 53, Heisman Trophy quarterback, born San Jose, CA, Dec 5, 1947.
Jerry Lanston (Lanny) Wadkins, 51, golfer, born Richmond, VA, Dec 5, 1949.

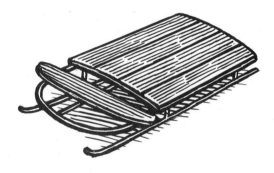

DECEMBER 6 — WEDNESDAY
Day 341 — 25 Remaining

CHASE'S SPORTSQUOTE OF THE DAY
"I demand respect on the field from managers and players. To me, that's 75 percent of umpiring."—Jocko Conlan

CONLAN, JOCKO: BIRTH ANNIVERSARY. Dec 6, 1899. John Bertrand ("Jocko") Conlan, baseball player and Baseball Hall of Fame umpire, born at Chicago, IL. Conlan played in the majors but made his reputation as one of the National League's most colorful umpires. He was particularly remembered for his run-ins with Leo Durocher. Inducted into the Hall of Fame in 1974. Died at Scottsdale, AZ, Apr 16, 1989.

December *2000*	S	M	T	W	T	F	S
						1	2
	3	4	5	6	7	8	9
	10	11	12	13	14	15	16
	17	18	19	20	21	22	23
	24	25	26	27	28	29	30
	31						

LAZZERI, TONY: BIRTH ANNIVERSARY. Dec 6, 1903. Anthony Michael (Tony) Lazzeri, Baseball Hall of Fame second baseman, born at San Francisco, CA. Lazzeri was the New York Yankees' regular second baseman from 1926 to 1937. He was a powerful clutch hitter who attracted many new Italian American fans to the game. Inducted into the Hall of Fame in 1991. Died at Millbrae, CA, Aug 6, 1946.

LITTLE, LOU: BIRTH ANNIVERSARY. Dec 6, 1893. Louis Lawrence (Lou) Little, football player and coach, born at Boston, MA. Little played football at the University of Pennsylvania and professionally, but he made his reputation as a college coach at Georgetown and Columbia. His 1933 Columbia team defeated highly favored Stanford in the 1934 Rose Bowl. He retired in 1957. Died at Delray Beach, FL, May 28, 1979.

NAVRATILOVA STREAK ENDS: ANNIVERSARY. Dec 6, 1984. The longest winning streak in the history of women's tennis came to an end when Helena Sukova defeated Martina Navratilova, who had won 74 matches in a row, starting Jan 15, 1974.

BIRTHDAYS TODAY

Robert Kevin Appier, 33, baseball player, born Lancaster, CA, Dec 6, 1967.
Lawrence Robert (Larry) Bowa, 55, former baseball manager and player, born Sacramento, CA, Dec 6, 1945.
Otto Everett Graham, Jr, 79, former football coach and Pro Football Hall of Fame quarterback, born Waukegan, IL, Dec 6, 1921.
Jelani Marwan McCoy, 23, basketball player, born Oakland, CA, Dec 6, 1977.
Andrew Richard (Andy) Robustelli, 75, former football executive and Pro Football Hall of Fame defensive end, born Stamford, CT, Dec 6, 1925.

DECEMBER 7 — THURSDAY
Day 342 — 24 Remaining

BROUN, HEYWOOD: BIRTH ANNIVERSARY. Dec 7, 1886. Heywood C. Broun, sportswriter, born at New York, NY. Broun dropped out of Harvard University to become a sportswriter and was highly regarded for his wit and his way with words. He covered politics, wrote theater reviews, published fiction and became a widely-read columnist. His son, Heywood Hale Broun, became a broadcaster. Given the J.G. Taylor Spink Award in 1970. Died at New York, Dec 18, 1939.

FISH, HAMILTON: BIRTH ANNIVERSARY. Dec 7, 1888. Hamilton Fish, football player, born at Garrison, NY. He played football at Harvard and was named to Walter Camp's 1908 and 1909 All-America teams. He also played basketball and soccer and graduated cum laude in 1910. After serving in the Army during World War I, he entered politics and sat in the House of Representatives from 1919 to 1945. Died at age 102 at Cold Spring, NY, Jan 18, 1991.

NCAA MEN'S DIVISION I SOCCER CHAMPIONSHIP. Dec 7–9. Finals. Ericsson Stadium, Charlotte, NC. For info: NCAA, PO Box 6222, Indianapolis, IN 46206-6222. Phone: (317) 917-6222. Fax: (317) 917-6888. Web: www.ncaa.org.

NCAA WOMEN'S DIVISION I VOLLEYBALL CHAMPIONSHIP. Dec 7–10. Regionals. Sites TBA. For info: NCAA, PO Box 6222, Indianapolis, IN 46206-6222. Phone: (317) 917-6222. Fax: (317) 917-6888. Web: www.ncaa.org.

ZASLOFSKY, MAX: 75th BIRTH ANNIVERSARY. Dec 7, 1925. Max Zaslofsky, basketball player and coach, born at New York, NY. Zaslofsky played for coach Joe Lapchick at St. John's University but joined the Chicago Stags of the BAA after just one year in college. He made the All-Star team four years running and was a leading scorer. After the formation of the NBA, he played with the New York Knicks, the Baltimore Bullets, the Milwaukee Hawks and the Ft Wayne Pistons. He favored the two-hand set shot over the jump shot and scored many of his baskets from beyond 30 feet. Died at New York, NY, Oct 15, 1985.

BIRTHDAYS TODAY

Robert ("Bo") Belinsky, 64, former baseball player, born New York, NY, Dec 7, 1936.

Johnny Lee Bench, 53, broadcaster and Baseball Hall of Fame catcher, born Oklahoma City, OK, Dec 7, 1947.

Larry Joe Bird, 44, basketball coach and Basketball Hall of Fame guard, born West Baden, IN, Dec 7, 1956.

Alexander (Alex) Johnson, 58, former baseball player, born Helena, AR, Dec 7, 1942.

Shane Lee Mack, 37, baseball player, born Los Angeles, CA, Dec 7, 1963.

Constantino (Tino) Martinez, 33, baseball player, born Tampa, FL, Dec 7, 1967.

Terrell Owens, 27, football player, born Alexander City, AL, Dec 7, 1973.

DECEMBER 8 — FRIDAY
Day 343 — 23 Remaining

AUSTIN, JIMMY: BIRTH ANNIVERSARY. Dec 8, 1879. James Philip (Jimmy) Austin, baseball player and manager, born at Swansea, Wales. Austin, third baseman for the St. Louis Browns, was part of the greatest baseball action photograph ever taken. The picture, taken on July 23, 1910, by Charles Martin Conlon, shows Ty Cobb, gritting his teeth and flashing his spikes, sliding into Austin on a steal of third. Died at Laguna Beach, CA, Mar 6, 1965.

BELMONT, AUGUST: BIRTH ANNIVERSARY. Dec 8, 1816. August Belmont, thoroughbred racehorse owner, born at Alzey, Rhenish Palatinate, Germany. Belmont was an agent for the Rothschilds when he came to the US in 1837. He organized August Belmont and Company, a financial institution, and amassed a large fortune. After the Civil War, he helped to revive horse racing, organized the American Jockey Club and founded the Belmont Stakes. Died at New York, NY, Nov 24, 1890.

FIRST PROFESSIONAL BASKETBALL GAME: ANNIVERSARY. Dec 8, 1898. The first professional basketball game was played between the Trenton Nationals and the Kensington Hancocks. This game marked the opening of the National League of Professional Basketball Teams, comprising six teams. Trenton went on to win the league championship with an 18–2 record.

HEXTALL SCORES GOAL: ANNIVERSARY. Dec 8, 1987. Ron Hextall of the Philadelphia Flyers became the first goalie in NHL history to shoot the puck into the opposing team's net in a 5–2 victory over the Boston Bruins. Billy Smith of the New York Islanders had been credited with a goal in 1979, but he was simply the last Islander to touch the puck before Colorado Rockies defenseman Rob Ramage accidentally put it into his own net.

NCAA DIVISION II FOOTBALL CHAMPIONSHIP. Dec 8. Final. Site TBA. For info: NCAA, PO Box 6222, Indianapolis, IN 46206-6222. Phone: (317) 917-6222. Fax: (317) 917-6888. Web: www.ncaa.org.

NFL'S MOST LOPSIDED VICTORY: 60th ANNIVERSARY. Dec 8, 1940. The Chicago Bears won the NFL championship by defeating the Washington Redskins, 73–0, the most one-sided victory in the league's title game.

SPECIAL OLYMPICS FLORIDA STATE INDOOR GAMES. Dec 8–9. Daytona Beach, FL. Olympic-style competition for children and adults with mental retardation. For info: Special Olympics Florida, 8 Broadway, Ste D, Kissimmee, FL 34741. Phone: (407) 870-2292. Fax: (407) 870-9810.

THOMPSON, HANK: 75th BIRTH ANNIVERSARY. Dec 8, 1925. Henry Curtis (Hank) Thompson, baseball player, born at Oklahoma City, OK. Thompson was the first black to play for both the St. Louis Browns and the New York Giants. Died at Fresno, CA, Sept 30, 1969.

BIRTHDAYS TODAY

Gordon Arthur ("Red") Berenson, 59, college hockey coach and former player, born Regina, Saskatchewan, Canada, Dec 8, 1939.

Stephen John (Steve) Elkington, 38, golfer, born Inverell, Australia, Dec 8, 1962.

Timothy John (Tim) Foli, 50, former baseball player, born Culver City, CA, Dec 8, 1950.

Jeffrey Scott (Jeff) George, 33, football player, born Indianapolis, IN, Dec 8, 1967.

Eino Anthony (Tony) Mayberry, 33, football player, born Wurzburg, West Germany, Dec 8, 1967.

Michael Cole (Mike) Mussina, 32, baseball player, born Williamsport, PA, Dec 8, 1968.

George Washington Rogers, Jr, 42, Heisman Trophy running back, born Duluth, GA, Dec 8, 1958.

DECEMBER 9 — SATURDAY
Day 344 — 22 Remaining

CHASE'S SPORTSQUOTE OF THE DAY

"I never set out to hurt anybody. Unless it was important, like a league game or something."—Dick Butkus

DICKERSON CRACKS 2,000-YARD MARK: ANNIVERSARY. Dec 9, 1984. Running back Eric Dickerson of the Los Angeles Rams became the second player to gain more than 2,000 yards rushing in a single season. Dickerson rushed for 215 yards in a game against the Chicago Bears to end the day at 2,006 yards. He ended the season with 2,105 yards.

HAZLE, HURRICANE: 70th BIRTH ANNIVERSARY. Dec 9, 1930. Robert Sidney ("Hurricane") Hazle, baseball player, born at Laurens, SC. Hazle joined the Milwaukee Braves from the minors in late July 1957. He hit .403 over 41 games to help the Braves win the National League pennant. Died at Columbia, SC, Apr 25, 1992.

KELLEY, JOE: BIRTH ANNIVERSARY. Dec 9, 1871. Joseph James (Joe) Kelley, Baseball Hall of Fame outfielder, born at Cambridge, MA. Kelley played for the great Baltimore Orioles teams of the 1890s. In 17 years, he hit .319. Inducted into the Hall of Fame in 1971. Died at Baltimore, MD, Aug 14, 1943.

NCAA DIVISION I-AA FOOTBALL CHAMPIONSHIP.
Dec 9. Semifinals. Sites TBA. For info: NCAA, PO Box
6222, Indianapolis, IN 46206-6222. Phone: (317) 917-
6222. Fax: (317) 917-6888. Web: www.ncaa.org.

NFL'S SNEAKERS GAME: ANNIVERSARY. Dec 9, 1934.
The New York Giants defeated the Chicago Bears, 30-13,
to win the NFL championship in a game that became
known as the "Sneakers Game." With the field at the Polo
Grounds covered by ice and the temperature at 9 degrees,
the Giants donned sneakers in the second half to gain
better traction. They scored 27 points in the fourth quarter to overcome a 13-3 deficit.

**TRIPLE CROWN OF SURFING SERIES: EVENT 3—
MOUNTAIN DEW GERRY LOPEZ.** Dec 9-21. Ehukai
Beach Park, Haleiwa, North Shore, Oahu, HI. 29th
annual. The Triple Crown of Surfing series is professional,
big-wave surfing on Oahu's North Shore. Est attendance:
12,500. For media info: Jodi Young or Carol Hogan, (808)
325-7400. E-mail: oceanpro@interpac.net. For contest
info: Randy Rarick (808) 638-7266.

BIRTHDAYS TODAY

Raymond Mitchell (Ray) Agnew, 33, football player, born
Winston-Salem, NC, Dec 9, 1967.
Richard Marvin (Dick) Butkus, 58, former broadcaster
and Pro Football Hall of Fame linebacker, born Chicago,
IL, Dec 9, 1942.
David D. ("Deacon") Jones, 62, Pro Football Hall of Fame
defensive end, born Eatonville, FL, Dec 9, 1938.
Thomas Oliver (Tom) Kite, Jr, 51, golfer, born Austin, TX,
Dec 9, 1949.
Petr Nedved, 29, hockey player, born Liberec, Czechoslo-
vakia, Dec 9, 1971.
Hartley Brent Price, 32, basketball player, born Shawnee,
OK, Dec 9, 1968.
James David (Jim) Riggleman, 48, baseball manager,
born Ft Dix, NJ, Dec 9, 1952.
Anthony Giacinto (Tony) Tarasco, 30, baseball player,
born New York, NY, Dec 9, 1970.

DECEMBER 10 — SUNDAY

Day 345 — 21 Remaining

**FIRST US HEAVYWEIGHT CHAMP DEFEATED IN
ENGLAND: 190th ANNIVERSARY.** Dec 10, 1810. Tom
Molyneaux, the first unofficial heavyweight champion
of the US, was a freed slave from Virginia. He was beaten
in the 40th round by Tom Cribb, the English champion,
in a boxing match at Copthall Common at London.

HARPER, JESSE: BIRTH ANNIVERSARY. Dec 10, 1883.
Jesse C. Harper, football player, coach and administrator, born at Pawpaw, IL. Harper played football at the
University of Chicago under the legendary Amos Alonzo
Stagg. He became head coach and athletic director at
Notre Dame in 1913 and plotted the famed upset of Army
utilizing the forward pass. At age 33, he retired to operate a cattle ranch, returning to Notre Dame for two years
after Rockne died in 1931. Died at Sitka, KS, July 31,
1961.

NORRIS, JIM: BIRTH ANNIVERSARY. Dec 10, 1879.
James D. (Jim) Norris, Sr, Hockey Hall of Fame executive
and sports promoter, born at St. Catherines, Ontario,
Canada. Norris made an enormous fortune in a variety
of businesses and invested heavily in indoor sports arenas, including Detroit's Olympia (and its team, renamed
the Red Wings) and New York's Madison Square Garden.
He built the Red Wings into an NHL power. Inducted into
the Hockey Hall of Fame in 1958. Died at Chicago, IL,
Dec 4, 1952.

OFF-TRACK, OFF-BEAT SNOWSHOE RACE. Dec 10 (tentative). Sugar Loafin' Campground near Leadville. This
classic snowshoe experience promises to live up to its reputation as one of the wildest, most fun and unique events
anywhere. Participants will cover more than six miles of
unknown terrain, all through deep snow. Registration
starts at the campground at 8:30 AM on race day. There
is a small fee. This is one of many showshoe races held
in the area. For info: Greater Leadville Area Chamber of
Commerce, PO Box 861, Leadville, CO 80461. Phone:
(719) 486-3581 or (800) 933-3901. Fax: (719) 486-8478.
E-mail: leadville@leadvilleusa.com. Web: www.leadville
usa.com.

BIRTHDAYS TODAY

Paul Andre Assenmacher, 40, baseball player, born Allen
Park, MI, Dec 10, 1960.
Robert Bowlby (Rob) Blake, 31, hockey player, born Sim-
coe, Ontario, Canada, Dec 10, 1969.
Richard Douglas (Doug) Henry, 37, baseball player, born
Sacramento, CA, Dec 10, 1963.
Norberto Edonal Martin, 34, baseball player, born Santo
Domingo, Dominican Republic, Dec 10, 1966.
Melquiades (Mel) Rojas, 34, baseball player, born Haina,
Dominican Republic, Dec 10, 1966.

DECEMBER 11 — MONDAY

Day 346 — 20 Remaining

**JOHN HENRY PASSES $4 MILLION MARK: ANNI-
VERSARY.** Dec 11, 1983. Thoroughbred John Henry
became the first racehorse to earn more than $4 million
when he won the Hollywood Turf Cup under jockey Chris
McCarron.

LAST AAFC GAME: ANNIVERSARY. Dec 11, 1949. The
Cleveland Browns defeated the San Francisco 49ers, 21-7,
to win the fourth and last championship game in the
All-America Football Conference. The Browns thereby
completed a four-season sweep of AAFC titles. Two days
before the final game, NFL Commissioner Bert Bell
announced that three AAFC teams—the Browns, the
49ers and the Baltimore Colts—would be admitted into
the senior league.

RADBOURNE, HOSS: BIRTH ANNIVERSARY. Dec 11,
1854. Charles Gardner ("Hoss") Radbourne, Baseball Hall
of Fame pitcher, born at Rochester, NY. Radbourne was
one of the most durable and successful pitchers of the
1880s. In 1884, he was credited with 59 complete-game
victories. Inducted into the Hall of Fame in 1939. Died
at Bloomington, IL, Feb 5, 1897.

December
2000

S	M	T	W	T	F	S
					1	2
3	4	5	6	7	8	9
10	11	12	13	14	15	16
17	18	19	20	21	22	23
24	25	26	27	28	29	30
31						

Julius Shareef Abdur-Rahim, 24, basketball player, born Marietta, GA, Dec 11, 1976.

Daniel Alfredsson, 28, hockey player, born Grums, Sweden, Dec 11, 1972.

Derek Nathaniel Bell, 32, baseball player, born Tampa, FL, Dec 11, 1968.

Jay Stuart Bell, 35, baseball player, born Pensacola, FL, Dec 11, 1965.

Dave Gagner, 36, hockey player, born Chatham, Ontario, Canada, Dec 11, 1964.

Thomas Sylvester Howard, 36, baseball player, born Middletown, OH, Dec 11, 1964.

DECEMBER 12 — TUESDAY
Day 347 — 19 Remaining

ARMSTRONG, HENRY: BIRTH ANNIVERSARY. Dec 12, 1912. Henry Armstrong, boxer, born Henry Jackson, Jr, at Columbus, MS. Armstrong was the first boxer to hold three world titles simultaneously. He won the featherweight title on Oct 29, 1937, the welterweight title on May 31, 1938, and the lightweight title three months later. Died at Los Angeles, CA, Oct 22, 1988.

GREAT SNOWPLOW PLAY: ANNIVERSARY. Dec 12, 1982. The New England Patriots defeated the Miami Dolphins, 3–0, in a driving snowstorm at Foxboro Stadium. The winning points came on a late field goal by John Smith, kicked after a snowplow came onto the field and cleared a spot for Smith and his holder.

HULL GETS 1,000th POINT: 30th ANNIVERSARY. Dec 12, 1970. Left wing Bobby Hull of the Chicago Blackhawks got the 1,000th point of his NHL career, an assist in the first period of a 5–3 victory over the Minnesota North Stars. Hull finished his career with 1,170 points.

SAYERS SCORES SIX TOUCHDOWNS: 35th ANNIVERSARY. Dec 12, 1965. Gale Sayers of the Chicago Bears tied an NFL record by scoring six touchdowns in the Bears' 61–20 win over the San Francisco 49ers. Sayers rushed for four scores, caught an 80-yard touchdown pass and returned a punt 85 yards. Previously, Ernie Nevers of the Chicago Cardinals had scored six touchdowns against the Chicago Bears in 1929, and Dub Jones of the Cleveland Browns had scored six against the Bears in 1951.

Tracy Ann Austin, 38, former tennis player, born Rolling Hills Estates, CA, Dec 12, 1962.

Leonard Ray Brown, Jr, 38, football player, born West Memphis, AR, Dec 12, 1962.

Robert Lee (Bob) Pettit, Jr, 68, Basketball Hall of Fame forward and center, born Baton Rouge, LA, Dec 12, 1932.

John Randle, 33, football player, born Hearne, TX, Dec 12, 1967.

Cathy Rigby, 48, actress and former gymnast, born Long Beach, CA, Dec 12, 1952.

David Andrew Szott, 33, football player, born Passaic, NJ, Dec 12, 1967.

Reinard Wilson, 27, football player, born Lake City, FL, Dec 12, 1973.

DECEMBER 13 — WEDNESDAY
Day 348 — 18 Remaining

JOHNSON, GUS: BIRTH ANNIVERSARY. Dec 13, 1938. Gus Johnson, Jr, basketball player, born at Akron, OH. Johnson played at the University of Akron, Boise Junior College and the University of Idaho. He was drafted by the Washington Bullets and helped make them a perennial contender for play-off honors. Johnson was the prototype of the power forward. He could score from the corner and was one of the first players to use the slam dunk. He finished his career with the Phoenix Suns. Died at Akron, OH, Apr 28, 1987.

MOORE, ARCHIE: BIRTH ANNIVERSARY. Dec 13, 1913. Archie Moore, boxer, born Archibald Lee Wright at Benoit, MS. One of the most colorful fighters ever, Moore boxed from the mid-1930s to 1963, holding the light-heavyweight title for a record nine years. For much of his career, he fought an average of once a month. Moore let an aura of celebrity surround him. He lied about his age, ate an unusual diet, married five times and spoke out on a variety of political and social issues. Died at San Diego, CA, Dec 9, 1998.

VUKOVICH, BILL: BIRTH ANNIVERSARY. Dec 13, 1918. William Vukovich, Sr, born William Vucerovich at Fresno, CA. Vukovich began racing midget cars in 1938 and picked up his career after World War II. Known as the "Mad Russian" for his hell-bent style, he won the 1953 Indianapolis 500 from the pole and the 1954 race as well. Ahead again in the 1955 race, he crashed on the 57th lap. Died at Indianapolis, IN, May 30, 1955.

Dale Anthony Berra, 44, former baseball player, born Ridgewood, NJ, Dec 13, 1956.

Lawrence Eugene (Larry) Doby, 76, Baseball Hall of Fame outfielder and former manager, born Camden, SC, Dec 13, 1924.

Carl Daniel Erskine, 74, former baseball player, born Anderson, IN, Dec 13, 1926.

Sergei Fedorov, 31, hockey player, born Pskov, USSR, Dec 13, 1969.

Robert Michael (Bob) Gainey, 47, hockey executive, former coach and Hockey Hall of Fame forward, born Peterborough, Ontario, Canada, Dec 13, 1953.

Ferguson Arthur Jenkins, 57, Baseball Hall of Fame pitcher, born Chatham, Ontario, Canada, Dec 13, 1943.

Michael Howard (Mike) Mordecai, 33, baseball player, born Birmingham, AL, Dec 13, 1967.

DECEMBER 14 — THURSDAY
Day 349 — 17 Remaining

CHASE'S SPORTSQUOTE OF THE DAY

"When you talk about Ernie Davis, you're treading on hallowed ground."—Coach Ben Schwartzwalder

BIRTH OF NASCAR: ANNIVERSARY. Dec 14, 1947. Part-time auto racer and full-time promoter Bill France, Sr, tried to bring some order to the chaotic world of stock car racing by opening a three-day meeting at the Streamline Hotel at Daytona Beach, FL, among several warring factions. The result of the meeting was the creation of NASCAR, the National Association of Stock Car Automobile Racing, the body that has governed the sport ever since.

DAVIS, ERNIE: BIRTH ANNIVERSARY. Dec 14, 1939. Ernest (Ernie) Davis, Heisman Trophy running back, born at New Salem, PA. Davis played football at Syracuse and won the Heisman Trophy in 1961. Drafted by the Washington Redskins and then traded to the Cleveland Browns, Davis never played pro football because he was stricken by leukemia. Died at Cleveland, OH, May 18, 1963.

DIONNE SCORES 500th GOAL: ANNIVERSARY. Dec 14, 1982. Marcel Dionne of the Los Angeles Kings became the 9th player in National Hockey League history to score 500 regular-season goals when he tallied in a 7–2 loss to the Washington Capitals. Dionne finished his career with 731 regular-season goals and was inducted into the Hockey Hall of Fame in 1992.

HEAT FINALLY WINS: ANNIVERSARY. Dec 14, 1988. The Miami Heat defeated the Los Angeles Clippers at Los Angeles to earn the first victory in the franchise's history. The Heat, in their first season, had gone 17 games without a win, an NBA record for most consecutive defeats at the start of a season.

KULWICKI, ALAN: BIRTH ANNIVERSARY. Dec 14, 1954. Alan Kulwicki, auto racer, born at Greenfield, WI. Kulwicki was NASCAR's Rookie of the Year in 1987 and Winston Cup champion in 1992. He won 24 NASCAR races in 207 starts. Died in a plane crash, Apr 1, 1993.

LONGEST US SOCCER GAME: 15th ANNIVERSARY. Dec 14, 1985. UCLA defeated American University, 1–0, with a goal in the eighth overtime period to win the NCAA soccer championship in the longest game in US college soccer history.

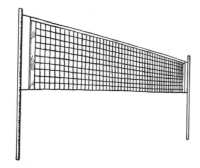

NCAA WOMEN'S DIVISION I VOLLEYBALL CHAMPIONSHIP. Dec 14–16. Finals. Richmond Coliseum, Richmond, VA. For info: NCAA, PO Box 6222, Indianapolis, IN 46206-6222. Phone: (317) 917-6222. Fax: (317) 917-6888. Web: www.ncaa.org.

BIRTHDAYS TODAY

Vijay Amritraj, 47, former tennis player, born Madras, India, Dec 14, 1953.

Craig Alan Biggio, 35, baseball player, born Smithtown, NY, Dec 14, 1965.

William Joseph (Bill) Buckner, 51, former baseball player, born Vallejo, CA, Dec 14, 1949.

Kenneth Wade (Ken) Hill, 35, baseball player, born Lynn, MA, Dec 14, 1965.

Anthony George Douglas Mason, 34, basketball player, born Miami, FL, Dec 14, 1966.

David Wayne Nilsson, 31, baseball player, born Brisbane, Queensland, Australia, Dec 14, 1969.

Bill Ranford, 34, hockey player, born Brandon, Manitoba, Canada, Dec 14, 1966.

Charles Louis (Charlie) Trippi, 78, Pro Football Hall of Fame halfback, born Pittston, PA, Dec 14, 1922.

December 2000

S	M	T	W	T	F	S
					1	2
3	4	5	6	7	8	9
10	11	12	13	14	15	16
17	18	19	20	21	22	23
24	25	26	27	28	29	30
31						

DECEMBER 15 — FRIDAY
Day 350 — 16 Remaining

BASEBALL'S MOST LOPSIDED TRADE: 100th ANNIVERSARY. Dec 15, 1900. In the most lopsided trade in baseball history, the New York Giants shipped pitcher Amos Rusie to the Cincinnati Reds for pitcher Christy Mathewson. Rusie won 245 games, all with the Giants and all before the trade; Mathewson won 373 games, all with the Giants and all after the trade.

DEMPSEY, JACK: BIRTH ANNIVERSARY. Dec 15, 1862. Jack ("Nonpareil") Dempsey, boxer, born at County Kildare, Ireland. Not the 20th-century heavyweight champ, this earlier Dempsey was the first fighter recognized as world middleweight champion. He won the newly created title on July 30, 1884, defeating George Fulljames. Died at Portland, OR, Nov 2, 1895.

HAWLEY RIDES 500th WINNER: ANNIVERSARY. Dec 15, 1973. Sandy Hawley became the first jockey to win 500 races in a single year when he rode Charlie Jr to victory in the third race at Laurel Race Course at Maryland.

HUNTER RULED A FREE AGENT: ANNIVERSARY. Dec 15, 1974. Pitcher Jim ("Catfish") Hunter was ruled a free agent by arbitrator Peter Seitz, who decided that Oakland A's owner Charley Finley had not fulfilled the terms set forth in Hunter's contract. Hunter later signed to play with the New York Yankees.

THIRD MADISON SQUARE GARDEN OPENS: 75th ANNIVERSARY. Dec 15, 1925. The Montreal Canadiens defeated the New York Americans, 3–1, as the third version of Madison Square Garden opened at New York. The game attracted more than 17,000 fans, including Mayor John F. Hylan, to what was then the world's largest ice hockey arena.

BIRTHDAYS TODAY

Stanley Raymond (Stan) Bahnsen, 56, former baseball player, born Council Bluffs, IA, Dec 15, 1944.

Nicholas Anthony (Nick) Buoniconti, 60, former football player, born Springfield, MA, Dec 15, 1940.

Rodney Scott Harrison, 28, football player, born Markham, IL, Dec 15, 1972.

Arthur Henry (Art) Howe, Jr, 54, baseball manager and former player, born Pittsburgh, PA, Dec 15, 1946.

James Richard (Jim) Leyland, 56, baseball manager, born Toledo, OH, Dec 15, 1944.

William Lewis (Billy) Shaw, 62, Pro Football Hall of Fame guard and center, born Natchez, MS, Dec 15, 1938.

Maurice Samuel (Mo) Vaughn, 33, baseball player, born Norwalk, CT, Dec 15, 1967.

Daniel (Dan) Williams, II, 31, football player, born Ypsilanti, MI, Dec 15, 1969.

DECEMBER 16 — SATURDAY
Day 351 — 15 Remaining

CHASE'S SPORTSQUOTE OF THE DAY
"When I was little, I was big."—William ("The Refrigerator") Perry

AMOS ALONZO STAGG BOWL (NCAA DIVISION III FOOTBALL CHAMPIONSHIP). Dec 16. Salem Stadium, Salem, VA. Est attendance: 8,000. For info: NCAA, 6201 College Blvd, Overland Park, KS 66211. Phone: (913) 339-1906.

JONES WINS FIRST SULLIVAN AWARD: 70th ANNIVERSARY. Dec 16, 1930. Golfer Bobby Jones won the first James E. Sullivan Award as the nation's best amateur athlete. The award was established by the Amateur

Athletic Union to honor its former president and is presented annually to the athlete who, "by his or her performance, example and influence as an amateur, has done the most during the year to advance the cause of sportsmanship."

NAIA FOOTBALL CHAMPIONSHIP. Dec 16. Savannah, TN. The final two teams from a 16-team field compete for the national championship. 45th annual. Est attendance: 7,000. For info: Natl Assn of Intercollegiate Athletics, 6120 S Yale Ave, Ste 1450, Tulsa, OK 74136-4223. Phone: (918) 494-8828. Fax: (918) 494-8841. E-mail: khenry@naia.org. Web: www.naia.org.

NCAA DIVISION I-AA FOOTBALL CHAMPIONSHIP. Dec 16. Final. Site TBA. For info: NCAA, PO Box 6222, Indianapolis, IN 46206-6222. Phone: (317) 917-6222. Fax: (317) 917-6888. Web: www.ncaa.org.

O.J. RUSHES FOR 2,003 YARDS: ANNIVERSARY. Dec 16, 1973. O.J. Simpson of the Buffalo Bills became the first running back to rush for more than 2,000 yards in a season, passing the milestone in a game against the New York Jets. Simpson ended the season with 2,003 yards, surpassing the previous record of 1,863 yards set by Jim Brown.

PARKER, BUDDY: BIRTH ANNIVERSARY. Dec 16, 1913. Raymond Klein ("Buddy") Parker, football player and coach, born at Kemp, TX. Parker played halfback at Centenary College and in 1934 kicked a field goal to upset Texas. He played with the Detroit Lions and the Cardinals for whom he was a player-coach. Named head coach of the Lions in 1951, he built a strong squad that won the NFL championship in 1952 and 1953. He resigned in 1957 and moved to the Pittsburgh Steelers with whom he enjoyed less success. He is generally credited with inventing the "two-minute offense." Died at Kaufman, TX, Mar 22, 1982.

BIRTHDAYS TODAY

Thomas Jefferson (Tom) Brookshier, 69, former broadcaster and football player, born Roswell, NM, Dec 16, 1931.

Christopher Carlos (Chris) Jones, 35, baseball player, born Utica, NY, Dec 16, 1965.

William Anthony ("The Refrigerator") Perry, 38, former football player, born Aiken, SC, Dec 16, 1962.

Clifford Ralph Robinson, 34, basketball player, born Buffalo, NY, Dec 16, 1966.

DECEMBER 17 — SUNDAY

Day 352 — 14 Remaining

FIRST NFL CHAMPIONSHIP GAME: ANNIVERSARY. Dec 17, 1933. The Chicago Bears won the National Football League's first championship game, defeating the New York Giants, 23–21. The Bears scored the winning touchdown on a pass-and-lateral play begun by Bronko Nagurski.

HAWAIIAN CHRISTMAS LOOONG DISTANCE INVITATIONAL ROUGH-H2O SWIM. Dec 17. Waikiki Beach, Honolulu, HI. 20th annual 7K (4.33-mile) swim across Waikiki Bay and return. Preregistration is required. Hawaii's longest open-ocean race. Est attendance: 90. For info: Jim Anderson, One Keahole Pl, #1607, Honolulu, HI 96825-3414. Fax: (808) 396-8868. E-mail: waikikijim@aol.com.

ORANGE BOWL INTERNATIONAL TENNIS CHAMPIONSHIPS. Dec 17–25 (tentative). Miami, FL. One of the top junior tournaments in the world. Past performers include Chris Evert, John McEnroe, Ivan Lendl, Bjorn Borg, Gabriela Sabatini, Mary Joe Fernandez, Boris Becker, Stefan Edberg and Jennifer Capriati. Est attendance: 10,000. For info: Orange Bowl Committee, 601 Brickell Key Dr, Ste 206, Miami, FL 33131. Phone: (305) 371-4600.

RIPKEN, CAL, SR: 65th BIRTH ANNIVERSARY. Dec 17, 1935. Calvin Edwin Ripken, Sr, baseball manager, born at Aberdeen, MD. Ripken spent 36 years in the Baltimore Orioles organization as a minor league player and manager, major league coach and manager and scout. He is the only man to manage two sons on the same major league team. Known to be gruff, wiry and blunt, Ripken brought a no-nonsense ethic to his work, deriving satisfaction from the results he achieved. Died at Baltimore, MD, Mar 25, 1999.

UNDERDOG DAY. Dec 17. To salute, before the year's end, all of the underdogs and unsung heroes—the number two people who contribute so much to the number one people we read about. (In the world of sports, today is the day to salute assistant coaches and trainers and cut men and outriders and ball boys and girls and caddies and all those who believe that winning is not everything.) For info: P. Moeller, Chief Underdog, Box 71, Clio, MI 48420-1042.

WRIGHT BROTHERS FIRST POWERED FLIGHT: ANNIVERSARY. Dec 17, 1903. Orville and Wilbur Wright, brothers, bicycle shop operators, inventors and aviation pioneers, after three years of experimentation with kites and gliders, achieved the first documented successful powered and controlled flights of an airplane. The flights, near Kitty Hawk, NC, piloted first by Orville and then by Wilbur, were sustained for less than one minute but represented man's first powered airplane flight and the beginning of a new form of transportation.

★ **WRIGHT BROTHERS DAY.** Dec 17. Presidential Proclamation always issued for Dec 17 since 1963 (PL88–209 of Dec 17, 1963). Issued twice earlier at congressional request in 1959 and 1961.

BIRTHDAYS TODAY

Craig Berube, 35, hockey player, born Calihoo, Alberta, Canada, Dec 17, 1965.

Tyrone Scott Braxton, 36, football player, born Madison, WI, Dec 17, 1964.

Vincent Damphousse, 33, hockey player, born Montreal, Quebec, Canada, Dec 17, 1967.

Earl Christopher Dotson, 30, football player, born Beaumont, TX, Dec 17, 1970.

Ken Hitchcock, 49, hockey coach, born Edmonton, Alberta, Canada, Dec 17, 1951.

Curtis John Pride, 32, baseball player, born Washington, DC, Dec 17, 1968.

Brian Marcee Williams, 28, football player, born Dallas, TX, Dec 17, 1972.

DECEMBER 18 — MONDAY
Day 353 — 13 Remaining

COBB, TY: BIRTH ANNIVERSARY. Dec 18, 1886. Tyrus Raymond (Ty) Cobb, Baseball Hall of Fame outfielder, born at Narrows, GA. Perhaps baseball's greatest player and perhaps its meanest, Cobb compiled a career batting average of .367, the best ever. He played 24 years and got more hits than any other player, until Pete Rose. Inducted into the Hall of Fame in 1936. Died at Atlanta, GA, July 17, 1961.

NFL'S INDOOR PLAY-OFF: ANNIVERSARY. Dec 18, 1932. The NFL held a postseason play-off game indoors, with the Chicago Bears defeating the Portsmouth (OH) Spartans, 9–0. The intended site of the game, Wrigley Field, was so frozen that officials moved the game to Chicago Stadium. The field was 80 yards long, and the goalposts were set on the goal lines instead of at the back of the end zones.

BIRTHDAYS TODAY

Scott Alan Bailes, 38, baseball player, born Chillicothe, OH, Dec 18, 1962.
William Allen (Willie) Blair, 35, baseball player, born Paintsville, KY, Dec 18, 1965.
Peter Boulware, 26, football player, born Columbia, SC, Dec 18, 1974.
G. Drew Coble, 53, baseball umpire, born Burlington, NC, Dec 18, 1947.
Charles Oakley, 37, basketball player, born Cleveland, OH, Dec 18, 1963.
Arantxa Sanchez Vicario, 29, tennis player, born Barcelona, Spain, Dec 18, 1971.
William Joseph (Bill) Skowron, 70, former baseball player, born Chicago, IL, Dec 18, 1930.

DECEMBER 19 — TUESDAY
Day 354 — 12 Remaining

CHASE'S SPORTSQUOTE OF THE DAY

"Bobby never lost a game in his life. Time just ran out on him."—Doak Walker on Bobby Layne

BARNEY, REX: BIRTH ANNIVESARY. Dec 19, 1924. Rex Edward Barney, baseball public address announcer and former baseball player, born at Omaha, NE. A fastball pitcher who had persistent trouble with his control, Barney nevertheless won 15 games in 1948 for the Brooklyn Dodgers and pitched a no-hitter against the New York Giants. After retiring, he was much beloved as the public address announcer for the Baltimore Orioles. He rewarded spectators who caught foul balls by saying, "Give that fan a contract," and he concluded every announcement with a dramatic "Thaaaank youuuu." Died at Baltimore, MD, Aug 12, 1997.

FIRST NHL GAMES: ANNIVERSARY. Dec 19, 1917. The National Hockey League opened its first season of play with two games. The Montreal Canadiens defeated the Ottawa Senators, 7–4, with Joe Malone scoring five goals, and the Montreal Wanderers beat the Toronto Arenas, 10–9, with Harry Hyland scoring five goals. Despite their victory, the Wanderers lasted only six games, withdrawing from the league when the Montreal Arena burned down.

FRICK, FORD: BIRTH ANNIVERSARY. Dec 19, 1894. Ford Christopher Frick, sportswriter and Baseball Hall of Fame executive, born at Wawaka, IN. Frick was a newspaperman who became Babe Ruth's ghostwriter, president of the National League and Commissioner of Baseball. He ruled in 1961 that Roger Maris's home run record would have to be categorized separately from Ruth's because the American League had lengthened its schedule from 154 to 162 games. Inducted into the Hall of Fame in 1970. Died at Bronxville, NY, Apr 8, 1978.

GRETZKY GETS 1,000th POINT: ANNIVERSARY. Dec 19, 1984. Wayne Gretzky of the Edmonton Oilers got the 1,000th point of his National Hockey League career, an assist in a 7–3 victory over the Los Angeles Kings.

HINKLE, TONY: BIRTH ANNIVERSARY. Dec 19, 1899. Paul D. ("Tony") Hinkle, football coach and Basketball Hall of Fame coach, born at Logansport, IN. Hinkle was one of the giants of the coaching profession, spending all five decades of his career at Butler University. His teams won more than 600 games, and more than 50 of his former players became coaches. Inducted into the Hall of Fame in 1965. Died at Indianapolis, IN, Sept 21, 1992.

LAYNE, BOBBY: BIRTH ANNIVERSARY. Dec 19, 1926. Robert Lawrence (Bobby) Layne, Pro Football Hall of Fame quarterback, born at Santa Ana, TX. Layne starred at the University of Texas before and after serving in the Merchant Marines during World War II. As a pro, he led the Detroit Lions to the NFL title in 1952, 1953 and 1957. His flamboyant leadership on the field was matched by a boisterous off-the-field lifestyle. Inducted into the Hall of Fame in 1967. Died at Lubbock, TX, Dec 1, 1986.

	S	M	T	W	T	F	S
December 2000						1	2
	3	4	5	6	7	8	9
	10	11	12	13	14	15	16
	17	18	19	20	21	22	23
	24	25	26	27	28	29	30
	31						

WOOLPERT, PHIL: 85th BIRTH ANNIVERSARY. Dec 19, 1915. Philipp D. (Phil) Woolpert, Basketball Hall of Fame coach, born at Danville, KY. Woolpert played at Loyola University of Los Angeles, graduating in 1940, and began coaching at St. Ignatius High School at San Francisco. In 1950 he moved to the University of San Francisco, where he put together one of the greatest college teams ever. Led by Bill Russell and KC Jones, the Dons won their last 26 games in 1954–55 and all 29 games in 1955–56. They won consecutive NCAA titles, too. Woolpert resigned in 1958–59 but later coached in the American Basketball League and at the University of San Diego. Inducted into the Hall of Fame in 1992. Died at Sequim, WA, May 5, 1987.

BIRTHDAYS TODAY

Santana N. Dotson, 31, football player, born New Orleans, LA, Dec 19, 1969.

Kristin Folkl, 25, basketball and volleyball player, born St. Louis, MO, Dec 19, 1975.

Thomas James (Tom) Gugliotta, 31, basketball player, born Huntington Station, NY, Dec 19, 1969.

Albert William (Al) Kaline, 66, Baseball Hall of Fame outfielder, born Baltimore, MD, Dec 19, 1934.

Lorie Kane, 36, golfer, born Prince Edward Island, Canada, Dec 19, 1964.

Luis Felipe Lopez, 26, basketball player, born Santo Domingo, Dominican Republic, Dec 19, 1974.

Randall Cornell McDaniel, 36, football player, born Phoenix, AZ, Dec 19, 1964.

Kevin Edward McHale, 43, basketball executive and former player, born Hibbing, MN, Dec 19, 1957.

Jason Steven ("Jake") Plummer, 26, football player, born Boise, ID, Dec 19, 1974.

Arvydas Sabonis, 36, basketball player, born Kaunas, Lithuania, USSR, Dec 19, 1964.

Warren Sapp, 28, football player, born Plymouth, FL, Dec 19, 1972.

Bryant Antoine Westbrook, 26, football player, born Charlotte, NC, Dec 19, 1974.

Reginald Howard (Reggie) White, 39, former football player, born Chattanooga, TN, Dec 19, 1961.

DECEMBER 20 — WEDNESDAY
Day 355 — 11 Remaining

CHASE'S SPORTSQUOTE OF THE DAY

"I'll never forget the day Merkle failed to touch second. He and I went back to our boarding house, and he never did have dinner that night, but just stayed in the room."
—teammate Larry Doyle

HARTNETT, GABBY: 100th BIRTH ANNIVERSARY. Dec 20, 1900. Charles Leo ("Gabby") Hartnett, Baseball Hall of Fame catcher, born at Woonsocket, RI. Hartnett was one of the game's outstanding catchers. His most famous moment was the "Homer in the Gloamin'," a late-season, late-inning home run that helped the Chicago Cubs win the 1938 National League pennant. Inducted into the Hall of Fame in 1955. Died at Park Ridge, IL, Dec 20, 1972.

HICKEY, EDDIE: BIRTH ANNIVERSARY. Dec 20, 1902. Edgar S. (Eddie) Hickey, basketball player and Basketball Hall of Fame coach, born at Reynolds, NE. Hickey played several sports at Creighton University and began coaching at Creighton Prep High School while still an undergraduate. He moved to the university in 1935 and became one of the country's most successful coaches. After nine years, he moved to St. Louis University, where

his Billikens won the 1948 NIT, and in 1958 to Marquette University. Over 37 years of coaching, he won 570 games against only 268 losses. Inducted into the Hall of Fame in 1978. Died at Mesa, AZ, Dec 5, 1980.

LAFLEUR SCORES 500th GOAL: ANNIVERSARY. Dec 20, 1983. Guy Lafleur of the Montreal Canadiens scored the 500th regular-season goal of his career in a 6–0 victory over the New York Rangers. Lafleur, the 10th National Hockey League player to reach 500, finished his career with 560 regular-season goals and was inducted into the Hockey Hall of Fame in 1988.

MERKLE, FRED: BIRTH ANNIVERSARY. Dec 20, 1888. Frederick Charles (Fred) Merkle, baseball player, born at Watertown, WI. Merkle will forever occupy a place in baseball history for his part in the events of Sept 23, 1908, when his team, the New York Giants, played the Chicago Cubs in a crucial game. Merkle was on first in the bottom of the ninth when the winning run apparently scored on a single. As was customary, he did not touch second base. Cubs second baseman Johnny Evers set off baseball's greatest dispute by demanding that Merkle be called out. Died at Daytona Beach, FL, Mar 2, 1956.

NBA GRANTS FRANCHISE TO SEATTLE: ANNIVERSARY. Dec 20, 1966. The NBA granted a franchise to Seattle for the 1967–68 season. The SuperSonics, as the team was nicknamed, were joined by the San Diego Clippers, to become the league's 11th and 12th teams.

POTVIN PASSES ORR: 15th ANNIVERSARY. Dec 20, 1985. Denis Potvin of the New York Islanders assisted on Mike Bossy's goal against the New York Rangers to earn the 916th point of his career, breaking Bobby Orr's NHL record for most career points by a defenseman.

RICHARD GETS 1,000th POINT: ANNIVERSARY. Dec 20, 1973. Henri Richard, the "Pocket Rocket," of the Montreal Canadiens, scored the 1,000th point of his NHL career, an assist in a 2–2 tie with the Buffalo Sabres. Richard finished his career with 1,046 points.

WIGHTMAN, HAZEL: BIRTH ANNIVERSARY. Dec 20, 1886. Hazel Virginia Hotchkiss Wightman, tennis player, born at Healdsburg, CA. Known as the "Queen Mother of Tennis," Wightman was a championship player, an instructor, a benefactor and the donor of the Wightman Cup, a trophy offered for competition between teams of women players from the US and England. Died at Chestnut Hill, MA, Dec 5, 1974.

BIRTHDAYS TODAY

Cecil Celester Cooper, 51, former baseball player, born Brenham, TX, Dec 20, 1949.

Jose DeLeon, 40, former baseball player, born Rancho Viejo, LaVega, Dominican Republic, Dec 20, 1960.

Oscar Charles Gamble, 51, former baseball player, born Ramer, AL, Dec 20, 1949.

Nathaniel (Nate) Newton, Jr, 39, football player, born Orlando, FL, Dec 20, 1961.

DECEMBER 21 — THURSDAY
Day 356 — 10 Remaining

GIBSON, JOSH: BIRTH ANNIVERSARY. Dec 21, 1912. Joshua (Josh) Gibson, Baseball Hall of Fame catcher, born at Buena Vista, GA. Gibson is regarded as the greatest slugger to play in the Negro Leagues and perhaps the greatest ballplayer ever. Gibson starred with the Pittsburgh Crawfords. His long home runs are the stuff of legend. Inducted into the Hall of Fame in 1972. Died at Pittsburgh, PA, Jan 20, 1947.

GRIFFITH-JOYNER, FLORENCE: BIRTH ANNIVERSARY. Dec 21, 1959. Delorez Florence Griffith-Joyner, Olympic gold medal track athlete, born at Los Angeles, CA. "Flo-Jo" revolutionized women's sprinting with her muscular speed and flamboyant fashion sense. She won three gold medals at the 1988 Summer Olympics and set several world records. She raced in spandex body suits and wore elaborately decorated fingernails, six inches long. Died at Mission Viejo, CA, Sept 21, 1998.

HAGEN, WALTER: BIRTH ANNIVERSARY. Dec 21, 1892. Walter Charles B. Hagen, golfer, born at Rochester, NY. Hagen won two US Opens, four British Opens and five PGA Championships. He was extraordinary in match play, including the Ryder Cup, because he was a master scrambler and absolutely unflappable. He was also a colorful showman who brought the game to the masses and helped to increase prize money. Died at Traverse City, MI, Oct 5, 1969.

ROSS, BARNEY: BIRTH ANNIVERSARY. Dec 21, 1909. Barney Ross, boxer, born Barnet David Rosofsky at New York, NY. Ross was the first boxer to hold two titles simultaneously. He won the lightweight crown in 1932 and the welterweight crown in 1934. He also won a Silver Star during World War II as a Marine. Died at Chicago, IL, Jan 18, 1967.

SANDERS JOINS 2,000-YARD CLUB: ANNIVERSARY. Dec 21, 1997. Barry Sanders of the Detroit Lions became the third player in NFL history to rush for more than 2,000 yards in a season when he gained 184 yards against the New York Jets. The Lions won, 13–10. He reached the 2,000-yard mark with a 2-yard run with just over two minutes left in the game. On the next play, he broke free for 53 yards, a gain that allowed the Lions to run out the clock and clinch a play-off berth. The other members of the 2,000-yard club are O.J. Simpson, who rushed for 2,003 yards in 1973, and Eric Dickerson, who ran for 2,105 yards in 1984.

WINTER. Dec 21–Mar 20, 2001. In the Northern Hemisphere winter begins today with the winter solstice, at 8:37 AM EST. Note that in the Southern Hemisphere today is the beginning of summer. Between Equator and the Arctic Circle the sunrise and sunset points on the horizon are farthest south for the year, and daylight length is minimum (ranging from 12 hours, 8 minutes, at the equator to zero at the Arctic Circle).

BIRTHDAYS TODAY

Michael Joseph (Mike) Alstott, 27, football player, born Joliet, IL, Dec 21, 1973.
Joaquin Andujar, 48, former baseball player, born San Pedro de Macoris, Dominican Republic, Dec 21, 1952.
Christine Marie (Chris) Evert, 46, broadcaster and former tennis player, born Ft Lauderdale, FL, Dec 21, 1954.
Thomas Anthony (Tom) Henke, 43, former baseball player, born Kansas City, MO, Dec 21, 1957.
David Arthur (Dave) Kingman, 52, former baseball player, born Pendleton, OR, Dec 21, 1948.
Terry Richard Mills, 33, basketball player, born Romulus, MI, Dec 21, 1967.
Charles Henry (Chuck) Smith, III, 31, football player, born Athens, GA, Dec 21, 1969.

December 2000	S	M	T	W	T	F	S
						1	2
	3	4	5	6	7	8	9
	10	11	12	13	14	15	16
	17	18	19	20	21	22	23
	24	25	26	27	28	29	30
	31						

Andrew James (Andy) Van Slyke, 40, former baseball player, born Utica, NY, Dec 21, 1960.
Karrie Webb, 26, golfer, born Ayr, Queensland, Australia, Dec 21, 1974.

DECEMBER 22 — FRIDAY
Day 357 — 9 Remaining

ABL CEASES OPERATIONS: ANNIVERSARY. Dec 22, 1998. The American Basketball League, one of two women's professional leagues, ceased operations midway through its third season. The league was unable to compete with the WNBA, backed by the financial power and marketing of the NBA.

BIRTH OF USGA: ANNIVERSARY. Dec 22, 1894. The United States Golf Association, the governing body for golf in the US, was founded at a meeting of representatives from five golf clubs.

BRUTON, BILLY: 75th BIRTH ANNIVERSARY. Dec 22, 1925. William Haron (Billy) Bruton, baseball player, born at Panola, AL. Bruton hit the first home run for the Milwaukee Braves in their debut game on Apr 14, 1953. He led the National League in stolen bases in 1953, 1954 and 1955. Died at Marshallton, DE, Dec 5, 1995.

COFFEY GETS 1,000th POINT: 10th ANNIVERSARY. Dec 22, 1990. Defenseman Paul Coffey of the Pittsburgh Penguins got the 1,000th point of his National Hockey League career, an assist in a 4–3 win over the New York Islanders.

ESPOSITO SCORES 500th GOAL: ANNIVERSARY. Dec 22, 1974. Center Phil Esposito of the Boston Bruins scored the 500th regular-season goal of his career in a 5–4 win over the Detroit Red Wings. Esposito thus became the 6th player in National Hockey League history to reach the 500-goal plateau. He finished his career with 717 regular-season goals and was inducted into the Hockey Hall of Fame in 1984.

HULL SCORES 500th GOAL: ANNIVERSARY. Dec 22, 1996. Right wing Brett Hull of the St. Louis Blues became the 24th player in the National Hockey League to score 500 regular-season goals. He tallied against goalie Stephane Fiset of the Los Angeles Kings in a 7–4 win.

MACK, CONNIE: BIRTH ANNIVERSARY. Dec 22, 1862. Connie Mack, Baseball Hall of Fame manager and executive, born Cornelius Alexander McGillicuddy at East Brookfield, MA. Mack was a major league catcher who became the original manager and a co-owner of the Philadelphia Athletics in 1901. He managed the team, always wearing street clothes and signaling to his players with a scorecard, through the 1950 season and retired after the 1953 season. The Mackmen often finished as also-rans, but his teams did win nine pennants and five World Series. Inducted into the Hall of Fame in 1937. Died at Germantown, PA, Feb 8, 1956.

BIRTHDAYS TODAY

Mateo (Matty) Alou, 62, former baseball player, born Haina, Dominican Republic, Dec 22, 1938.

Steven Norman (Steve) Carlton, 56, Baseball Hall of Fame pitcher, born Miami, FL, Dec 22, 1944.

Steven Patrick (Steve) Garvey, 52, former baseball player, born Tampa, FL, Dec 22, 1948.

William Ray Guy, 51, former football player, born Swainsboro, GA, Dec 22, 1949.

Michael Ray (Mike) Jackson, 36, baseball player, born Houston, TX, Dec 22, 1964.

Kirk Maltby, 28, hockey player, born Guelph, Ontario, Canada, Dec 22, 1972.

David Pearson, 66, former auto racer, born Spartanburg, SC, Dec 22, 1934.

Jan Stephenson, 49, golfer, born Sydney, Australia, Dec 22, 1951.

DECEMBER 23 — SATURDAY

Day 358 — 8 Remaining

FIRST JUDO DEMONSTRATION IN US: ANNIVERSARY. Dec 23, 1921. Jigoro Kano, a Japanese, gave the first demonstration of judo in the US at the New York Athletic Club. The crowd watched politely.

GILMOUR GETS 1,000th POINT: 5th ANNIVERSARY. Dec 23, 1995. Center Doug Gilmour of the Toronto Maple Leafs got the 1,000th point of his National Hockey League career, an assist in a 6–1 win over the Edmonton Oilers.

HUBBS, KEN: BIRTH ANNIVERSARY. Dec 23, 1941. Kenneth Douglass (Ken) Hubbs, baseball player, born at Riverside, CA. Hubbs was a fine defensive second baseman who won the National League Rookie of the Year Award and a Gold Glove Award in 1962. Died in a plane crash at Provo, UT, Feb 15, 1964.

IMMACULATE RECEPTION: ANNIVERSARY. Dec 23, 1972. The Pittsburgh Steelers defeated the Oakland Raiders, 13–7, in an AFC first-round play-off game. The Raiders were ahead, 7–6, with 22 seconds to play, and Pittsburgh had the ball on its own 40-yard line. Steelers quarterback Terry Bradshaw threw a desperation pass intended for John ("Frenchy") Fuqua. The ball deflected off an Oakland defender into the waiting arms of Franco Harris, who rumbled into the end zone for the winning score. The play has since been known as the "Immaculate Reception."

JACKSON WINS 500th GAME: ANNIVERSARY. Dec 23, 1997. Phil Jackson of the Chicago Bulls won the 500th game of his coaching career, as the Bulls defeated the Los Angeles Clippers, 94–89. Jackson got to 500 in his 682nd game, faster than any other coach in NBA history. He is the 20th coach to reach the 500 mark.

MORENZ SETS GOAL-SCORING RECORD: ANNIVERSARY. Dec 23, 1933. Howie Morenz of the Montreal Canadiens scored the 251st goal of his career to become the NHL's leading career scorer. Montreal beat Detroit, 3–0. Morenz ended his career with 270 goals.

BIRTHDAYS TODAY

Jack Raphael Ham, Jr, 52, Pro Football Hall of Fame linebacker, born Johnstown, PA, Dec 23, 1948.

James Joseph (Jim) Harbaugh, 37, football player, born Toledo, OH, Dec 23, 1963.

Paul Vernon Hornung, 65, broadcaster and Pro Football Hall of Fame running back, born Louisville, KY, Dec 23, 1935.

Jerome Martin (Jerry) Koosman, 58, former baseball player, born Appleton, MN, Dec 23, 1942.

Jerry Manuel, 47, baseball manager and former player, born Hahira, GA, Dec 23, 1953.

Robert Joseph (Bobby) Ross, 64, football coach, born Richmond, VA, Dec 23, 1936.

William Vernell (Willie) Wood, 64, Pro Football Hall of Fame safety, born Washington, DC, Dec 23, 1936.

☆ ☆ ☆

DECEMBER 24 — SUNDAY

Day 359 — 7 Remaining

BROWNS WIN NFL CHAMPIONSHIP: 50th ANNIVERSARY. Dec 24, 1950. The Cleveland Browns defeated the Los Angeles Rams, 30–28, to win the NFL championship. The Browns claimed the title in their first year in the league after the demise of the All-America Football Conference. The Rams, incidentally, had been the Cleveland Rams before they left for the West Coast after the 1945 season.

UNGER STARTS STREAK: ANNIVERSARY. Dec 24, 1968. Center Garry Unger played his first NHL game and thereby began a streak of 914 consecutive games played. Unger's feat stood as the NHL record until it was broken by Doug Jarvis in 1987.

BIRTHDAYS TODAY

John Francis D'Acquisto, 49, former baseball player, born San Diego, CA, Dec 24, 1951.

William McGarvey ("Bullet Bill") Dudley, 81, Pro Football Hall of Fame halfback, born Bluefield, VA, Dec 24, 1919.

DECEMBER 25 — MONDAY

Day 360 — 6 Remaining

CHAPMAN, BEN: BIRTH ANNIVERSARY. Dec 25, 1908. William Benjamin (Ben) Chapman, baseball player and manager, born at Nashville, TN. Chapman hit .302 over 15 seasons and was the first American League batter in the first All-Star Game (1933). He was a vocal opponent of Jackie Robinson's presence in the major leagues. Died at Hoover, AL, July 7, 1993.

CHEVROLET, LOUIS: BIRTH ANNIVERSARY. Dec 25, 1878. Louis Joseph Chevrolet, auto racing driver and engineer, born at LaChaux-de-Fonds, Switzerland. Chevrolet emigrated to Montreal in 1900 and moved to New York in 1902. He worked on early automobiles, drove in races and designed cars for the company that bore his name but which he did not own. His career was marked by a series of business failures and personal and family tragedies. Died at Detroit, MI, June 6, 1941.

CHRISTMAS. Dec 25. Christian festival commemorating the birth of Jesus of Nazareth. Most popular of Christian observances, Christmas, as a Feast of the Nativity, dates from the 4th century. Although Jesus's birth date is not known, the Western church selected Dec 25 for the feast, possibly to counteract the non-Christian festivals of that approximate date. Many customs from non-Christian festivals (Roman Saturnalia, Mithraic sun's birthday, Teutonic yule, Druidic and other winter solstice rites) have been adopted as part of the Christmas celebration (lights, mistletoe, holly and ivy, holiday tree, wassailing and gift giving, for example). Some Orthodox Churches celebrate Christmas on Jan 7 based on the "old calendar" (Julian). Theophany (recognition of the divinity of Jesus) is observed on this date and also on Jan 6, especially by the Eastern Orthodox Church.

FIRST INDOOR BASEBALL GAME: ANNIVERSARY. Dec 25, 1888. Long before the domed stadia of the late 20th century, a large building at the state fairgrounds at Philadelphia was the site of the first indoor baseball game. 2,000 spectators watched the Downtowners beat the Uptowners, 6–1.

FOX, NELLIE: BIRTH ANNIVERSARY. Dec 25, 1927. Jacob Nelson (Nellie) Fox, Baseball Hall of Fame second baseman, born at St. Thomas, PA. Fox is generally rated one of the greatest defensive second basemen of all time. He starred with the Chicago White Sox American League pennant winners in 1959 and was renowned as an exceptional fielder and a timely hitter. Inducted into the Hall of Fame in 1997. Died at Baltimore, MD, Dec 1, 1975.

GALVIN, PUD: 145th BIRTH ANNIVERSARY. Dec 25, 1855. James Francis ("Pud") Galvin, Baseball Hall of Fame pitcher, born at St. Louis, MO. Galvin was one of the outstanding pitchers of the 19th century. He won 361 games and pitched professional baseball's first perfect game in 1876. Inducted into the Hall of Fame in 1965. Died at Pittsburgh, PA, Mar 7, 1902.

JEEP ALOHA CHRISTMAS FOOTBALL CLASSICS. Dec 25. Aloha Stadium, Honolulu, HI. College football's only postseason doubleheader: the Jeep Oahu Bowl matching the fifth-place team from the PAC-10 versus an at-large team and the Jeep Aloha Bowl matching the fourth-place team from the PAC-10 versus (tentatively) the fourth-place team from the Big East. Est attendance: 50,000. For info: Jeep Aloha Christmas Football Classics, 1110 University Ave, Ste 403, Honolulu, HI 96826. Phone: (808) 947-4141. Fax: (808) 941-9911. E-mail: higames@aloha.net. Web: www.alohagames.com.

December 2000

S	M	T	W	T	F	S
					1	2
3	4	5	6	7	8	9
10	11	12	13	14	15	16
17	18	19	20	21	22	23
24	25	26	27	28	29	30
31						

KELLY TIRES BLUE-GRAY ALL-STAR FOOTBALL CLASSIC. Dec 25. Cramton Bowl, Montgomery, AL. College seniors from northern schools compete against their southern counterparts. Sponsors: Montgomery Lion's Club and Kelly Tires. Televised by ABC Sports, 12 noon EST. Est attendance: 22,000. For info: Charles W. Jones, Exec Dir, Box 94, Montgomery, AL 36101-0094. Phone: (334) 265-1266. Fax: (334) 265-5944.

TROUPPE, QUINCY: BIRTH ANNIVERSARY. Dec 25, 1912. Quincy Thomas Trouppe, baseball player and manager, born at Dublin, GA. Trouppe played and managed in the Negro Leagues for nearly a quarter century. He was a catcher and a switch-hitter. Died at St. Louis, MO, Aug 10, 1993.

BIRTHDAYS TODAY

Stu D. Barnes, 30, hockey player, born Edmonton, Alberta, Canada, Dec 25, 1970.

Lawrence Richard (Larry) Csonka, 54, Pro Football Hall of Fame running back, born Stow, OH, Dec 25, 1946.

Ned Franklin Garver, 75, former baseball player, born Ney, OH, Dec 25, 1925.

Rickey Henley Henderson, 42, baseball player, born Chicago, IL, Dec 25, 1958.

Gene William Lamont, 54, baseball manager and former player, born Rockford, IL, Dec 25, 1946.

Dimitri Mironov, 35, hockey player, born Moscow, USSR, Dec 25, 1965.

Chris Kealoha Naeole, 26, football player, born Kailua, HI, Dec 25, 1974.

Kenneth Michael (Ken) Stabler, 55, former football player, born Foley, AL, Dec 25, 1945.

DECEMBER 26 — TUESDAY
Day 361 — 5 Remaining

BULKELEY, MORGAN: BIRTH ANNIVERSARY. Dec 26, 1837. Morgan Gardner Bulkeley, Baseball Hall of Fame executive, born at East Haddam, CT. Bulkeley served as president of the National League for its first year, 1876. He was a figurehead faced with several troubling administrative problems. Inducted into the Hall of Fame in 1937. Died at Hartford, CT, Nov 6, 1922.

FIRST BLACK HEAVYWEIGHT CHAMPION: ANNIVERSARY. Dec 26, 1908. Jack Johnson became the first black man to win the heavyweight championship when he knocked out Tommy Burns in the 14th round of a fight at Sydney, Australia.

JESSE OWENS RACES A HORSE: ANNIVERSARY. Dec 26, 1936. Sprinter Jesse Owens, hero of the 1936 Berlin Olympics, raced against a horse at Havana, Cuba. Owens took on Julio McGraw in a 100-yard dash and won.

KWANZAA. Dec 26–Jan 1, 2001. American black family observance (since 1966) in recognition of traditional African harvest festivals. Stresses unity of the black family, with a communitywide harvest feast (karamu) on the seventh day. Kwanzaa means "first fruit" in Swahili. An optional observance to avoid commercialization of Christmas traditions.

MUSKEGON LUGE AND WINTER SPORTS COMPLEX OPENS FOR SEASON. Dec 26. Muskegon Winter Sports Complex, Muskegon, MI. Luge, cross-country ski trails and an ice rink open for the season, weather permitting (all are outdoors and affected by weather conditions; call ahead). Usually opens the day after Christmas. For info: Muskegon Sports Council, PO Box 5085, North Muskegon, MI 49445. Phone: (616) 744-9629. Luge Club phone: (616) 759-2201. Web: www.msports.org.

Susan Butcher, 46, sled dog racer, born Cambridge, MA, Dec 26, 1954.

Carroll Christopher (Chris) Chambliss, 52, former baseball player, born Dayton, OH, Dec 26, 1948.

Carlton Ernest Fisk, 53, former baseball player, born Bellows Falls, VT, Dec 26, 1947.

Jeffrey Wayne (Jeff) King, 36, baseball player, born Marion, IN, Dec 26, 1964.

Mario Mendoza, 50, former baseball player, born Chihuahua, Mexico, Dec 26, 1950.

Marcelo Rios, 25, tennis player, born Santiago, Chile, Dec 26, 1975.

Osborne Earl (Ozzie) Smith, 46, broadcaster and former baseball player, born Mobile, AL, Dec 26, 1954.

DECEMBER 27 — WEDNESDAY
Day 362 — 4 Remaining

CHASE'S SPORTSQUOTE OF THE DAY

"Never bet [against] anyone you meet on the first tee who has a deep suntan, a one-iron in his bag, and squinty eyes."—Dave Marr

CAYLEY, GEORGE: BIRTH ANNIVERSARY. Dec 27, 1773. Sir George Cayley, aviation pioneer, scientist and inventor, born at Scarborough, Yorkshire, England. Cayley was a theoretician who designed airplanes, helicopters and gliders. He is credited as the father of aerodynamics and he was the pilot of the world's first manned glider flight. Died at Brompton Hall, Yorkshire, Dec 15, 1857.

INSIGHT.COM BOWL. Dec 27 (tentative). Arizona Stadium, Tucson, AZ. Postseason college football game matching the fifth-place team from the Big 12 against either the second- or third-place team from the Big East or Notre Dame. Est attendance: 56,000. For info: Tucson Bowl Foundation, 120 S Ash Ave, Tempe, AZ 85281. Phone: (602) 350-0900. Fax: (602) 350-0915.

MARR, DAVE: BIRTH ANNIVERSARY. Dec 27, 1933. David (Dave) Marr, broadcaster and golfer, born at Houston, TX. The winner of the 1965 PGA Championship, Marr made a successful second career as a commentator on golf telecasts for ABC, the BBC and NBC. Died at Houston, Oct 5, 1997.

WARD, ARCH: BIRTH ANNIVERSARY. Dec 27, 1896. Arch Ward, sportswriter and promoter, born at Irwin, IL. As sports editor of the *Chicago Tribune*, Ward conceived of both the baseball All-Star Game and the College Football All-Star Game. He did not pretend in his writing and editing to any sort of objectivity, believing it his duty to promote the sports he was covering and to sell newspapers. Died at Chicago, IL, July 9, 1955.

Kevin Lars Constantine, 42, hockey coach, born International Falls, MN, Dec 27, 1958.

James Joseph (Jim) Leyritz, 37, baseball player, born Lakewood, OH, Dec 27, 1963.

Dean William Palmer, 32, baseball player, born Tallahassee, FL, Dec 27, 1968.

Bryan Anthony Smolinski, 29, hockey player, born Toledo, OH, Dec 27, 1971.

Charles Christopher Way, 28, football player, born Philadelphia, PA, Dec 27, 1972.

DECEMBER 28 — THURSDAY
Day 363 — 3 Remaining

BASKETBALL SHUTOUT: ANNIVERSARY. Dec 28, 1998. Oakridge High School at Arlington, TX, shut out Christway High School at Duncanville, TX, 103–0 in girls' basketball. Oakridge was ahead 37–0 after one quarter and 63–0 at the half. Christway missed all 23 field-goal attempts and two free throws.

BRIDGES, TOMMY: BIRTH ANNIVERSARY. Dec 28, 1906. Thomas Jefferson Davis (Tommy) Bridges, baseball player, born at Gordonsville, TN. Bridges won 194 games during 16 seasons with the Detroit Tigers (1930–46). He pitched three one-hitters and 33 shutouts. Died at Nashville, TN, Apr 19, 1968.

GREATEST NFL GAME: ANNIVERSARY. Dec 28, 1958. In what is generally considered the greatest game in NFL history, the Baltimore Colts defeated the New York Giants, 23–17, in overtime, to win the NFL championship. The Colts had the ball, third-down-and-goal, on the Giants' one-yard line when quarterback Johnny Unitas handed the ball to fullback Alan Ameche. The Wisconsin graduate and Heisman Trophy winner bulled into the end zone to conclude the first sudden-death NFL game.

LYONS, TED: 100th BIRTH ANNIVERSARY. Dec 28, 1900. Theodore Amar (Ted) Lyons, Baseball Hall of Fame pitcher, born at Lake Charles, LA. Lyons started for the Chicago White Sox from 1924 through 1942. He pitched well, much better than the rest of his team played, and developed a knuckleball after he hurt his arm in 1931. Inducted into the Hall of Fame in 1955. Died at Sulphur, LA, July 25, 1986.

Raymond Jean (Ray) Bourque, 40, hockey player, born Montreal, Quebec, Canada, Dec 28, 1960.

Hubert Myatt (Hubie) Green, III, 54, golfer, born Birmingham, AL, Dec 28, 1946.

Charles Ray Knight, 48, broadcaster, former baseball manager and player, born Albany, GA, Dec 28, 1952.

William Francis (Bill) Lee, 54, former baseball player, born Burbank, CA, Dec 28, 1946.

Rob Niedermayer, 26, hockey player, born Cassiar, British Columbia, Canada, Dec 28, 1974.

Melvin Ramos Nieves, 29, baseball player, born San Juan, Puerto Rico, Dec 28, 1971.

Patrick Rafter, 28, tennis player, born Mount Isa, Queensland, Australia, Dec 28, 1972.

Robert (Bobby) Taylor, 27, football player, born Houston, TX, Dec 28, 1973.

Stephen W. (Steve) Van Buren, 80, Pro Football Hall of Fame halfback, born La Ceiba, Honduras, Dec 28, 1920.

DECEMBER 29 — FRIDAY

Day 364 — 2 Remaining

ALL-COLLEGE BASKETBALL TOURNAMENT. Dec 29–30. Myriad Convention Center, Oklahoma City, OK. The oldest college basketball tournament in the world, outdating the NCAA, NAIA and NIT. Host school is Oklahoma University. Rest of field to be announced; 160 universities have competed. Annually, between Christmas and New Year's. Est attendance: 25,000. For info: Stanley Draper, Jr, OK City All Sports Assn, 100 W Main, Ste 285, Oklahoma City, OK 73102. Phone: (405) 236-5000. Fax: (405) 236-5008. Web: www.okcallsports.org.

CHICK-FIL-A PEACH BOWL. Dec 29 (tentative). Georgia Dome, Atlanta, GA. Postseason college football game matching the third pick from the Atlantic Coast Conference and the fifth pick from the Southeastern Conference. Sponsored by Chick-Fil-A. Est attendance: 71,000. For info: Peach Bowl, Inc, 235 International Blvd, Atlanta, GA 30303. Phone: (404) 586-8500. Fax: (404) 586-8508.

HAYES PUNCHES CLEMSON PLAYER: ANNIVERSARY. Dec 29, 1978. Ohio State University football coach Woody Hayes punched Charlie Bauman, a player from Clemson University, during Clemson's 19–15 victory in the Gator Bowl. Hayes was upset that the Buckeyes were losing, but OSU officials were upset, too. They fired Hayes for the incident.

MURRAY, JIM: BIRTH ANNIVERSARY. Dec 29, 1919. James Patrick (Jim) Murray, Jr, journalist, born at Hartford, CT. After a peripatetic career writing for several newspapers and magazines, Murray settled in as sports columnist for the *Los Angeles Times*. Despite serious eye problems, family tragedy and a decided lack of ego, he excelled at his craft, becoming one of only four sportswriters to win a Pulitzer Prize for general commentary. Given the J.G. Taylor Spink Award in 1987. Died at Los Angeles, CA, Aug 16, 1998.

NITSCHKE, RAY: BIRTH ANNIVERSARY. Dec 29, 1936. Raymond Ernest (Ray) Nitschke, Pro Football Hall of Fame linebacker, born at Elmwood Park, IL. Nitschke played for the Green Bay Packers from 1958 through 1972 and was the defensive anchor on teams that won five NFL titles, including two Super Bowls. He helped set the standard for punishing play at middle linebacker. Died at Naples, FL, Mar 8, 1998.

OSMANSKI, BILL: 85th BIRTH ANNIVERSARY. Dec 29, 1915. William (Bill) Osmanski, football player, born at Providence, RI. A graduate of Holy Cross, Osmanski was first-round draft choice of the Chicago Bears in 1939. He led the league in rushing as a rookie and scored the first touchdown in the Bears' legendary 73–0 defeat of the Washington Redskins in the 1940 NFL championship game. Died at Chicago, IL, Jan 1, 1997.

WILLARD, JESS: BIRTH ANNIVERSARY. Dec 29, 1881. Jess Willard, boxer, born at Pottawatomie County, KS. The towering Willard, 6'6¼" tall, took the heavyweight title from Jack Johnson in a fight at Havana, Cuba, on Apr 5, 1915. He defended his title only once in four years and then lost it to Jack Dempsey on July 4, 1919. Died at Los Angeles, CA, Dec 15, 1968.

December 2000

S	M	T	W	T	F	S
					1	2
3	4	5	6	7	8	9
10	11	12	13	14	15	16
17	18	19	20	21	22	23
24	25	26	27	28	29	30
31						

James Raleigh Mouton, 32, baseball player, born Denver, CO, Dec 29, 1968.

Darren Perry, 32, football player, born Chesapeake, VA, Dec 29, 1968.

Richmond Lockwood (Richie) Sexson, 26, baseball player, born Portland, OR, Dec 29, 1974.

Devon Markes White, 38, baseball player, born Kingston, Jamaica, Dec 29, 1962.

Jaret Samuel Wright, 25, baseball player, born Anaheim, CA, Dec 29, 1975.

DECEMBER 30 — SATURDAY

Day 365 — 1 Remaining

CULLIGAN HOLIDAY BOWL. Dec 30 (tentative). Qualcomm Stadium, San Diego, CA. Postseason college football game matching teams selected from the Pac-10 and Big 12. Est attendance: 100,000. For info: Mark Neville, Holiday Bowl, PO Box 601400, San Diego, CA 92160-1400. Phone: (619) 283-5808. Fax: (619) 281-7947. Web: www.holidaybowl.com.

GRETZKY GETS 50 IN 39: ANNIVERSARY. Dec 30, 1981. Center Wayne Gretzky of the Edmonton Oilers scored five goals to lead his team to a 7–5 win over the Philadelphia Flyers. His fifth goal, into an empty net, was his 50th of the year, scored in only 39 games.

NANCE, JIM: BIRTH ANNIVERSARY. Dec 30, 1942. James Solomon (Jim) Nance, football player, born at Indiana, PA. Nance played fullback at Syracuse University (1962–64) and for the Boston (later New England) Patriots, setting several AFL records. He finished his career with the New York Jets and the Memphis team in the short-lived World Football League. Died at Quincy, MA, June 16, 1992.

NATIONAL FOOTBALL LEAGUE WILD-CARD PLAYOFFS. Dec 30–31 (tentative). Sites TBA. Postseason play begins in the NFL with two games in the AFC and two games in the NFC. The three wild-card teams and the first-place team with the worst won-lost record in each conference square off in this first round. Winners advance to the divisional round next weekend. For info: NFL, 280 Park Ave, New York, NY 10017. Phone: (212) 450-2000. Fax: (212) 681-7573. Web: www.nfl.com.

WADE, MARGARET: BIRTH ANNIVERSARY. Dec 30, 1912. Margaret Wade, Basketball Hall of Fame coach, born at McCool, MS. Wade played basketball at Delta State Teachers College for three years, until administrators judged the game too strenuous for women. Players burned their uniforms in protest, but Delta State had no women's basketball team for 41 years. Wade turned to coaching, and in 1959 she returned to her alma mater, first to chair the physical education department and then, in 1973, to resurrect the basketball program. With Wade at the helm, Delta State won three straight AIAW championships, 1975–77. Inducted into the Hall of Fame in 1984. Died Feb 16, 1995.

BIRTHDAYS TODAY

BIRTHDAYS TODAY

Kerry Michael Collins, 28, football player, born West Lawn, PA, Dec 30, 1972.

Sean Marielle Higgins, 32, basketball player, born Los Angeles, CA, Dec 30, 1968.

Ben Johnson, 39, former track athlete, born Falmouth, Jamaica, Dec 30, 1961.

Sanford (Sandy) Koufax, 65, former broadcaster and Baseball Hall of Fame pitcher, born Brooklyn, NY, Dec 30, 1935.

Michelle McGann, 31, golfer, born West Palm Beach, FL, Dec 30, 1969.

Melvin Lacy (Mel) Renfro, 59, Pro Football Hall of Fame defensive back, born Houston, TX, Dec 30, 1941.

Frank Joseph Torre, 69, former baseball player, born New York, NY, Dec 30, 1931.

Kris Tschetter, 36, golfer, born Detroit, MI, Dec 30, 1964.

Eldrick ("Tiger") Woods, 25, golfer, born Cypress, CA, Dec 30, 1975.

DECEMBER 31 — SUNDAY

Day 366 — 0 Remaining

CONNOLLY, TOM: BIRTH ANNIVERSARY. Dec 31, 1870. Thomas Henry (Tom) Connolly, Sr, Baseball Hall of Fame umpire, born at Manchester, England. Connolly is regarded as the dean of American League umpires, working from 1901 to 1931, when he was named umpire in chief. He once went 10 seasons without ejecting anyone from a game. Inducted as the first umpire in the Hall of Fame in 1953. Died at Natick, MA, Apr 28, 1961.

JONES, BEN: BIRTH ANNIVERSARY. Dec 31, 1882. Benjamin Allyn (Ben) Jones, thoroughbred trainer, born at Parnell, MO. Jones saddled six Kentucky Derby winners, two of whom, Whirlaway and Citation, won the Triple Crown. He trained for Calumet Farms from 1939 until 1947, when he became the stable's general manager. Died at Lexington, KY, June 13, 1961.

KELLY, KING: BIRTH ANNIVERSARY. Dec 31, 1857. Michael Joseph ("King") Kelly, Baseball Hall of Fame catcher and outfielder, born at Troy, NY. Kelly was baseball's first superstar, his personality and behavior outdistancing his talents, which were themselves considerable. Kelly was an innovative player who took advantage of every situation. Inducted into the Hall of Fame in 1945. Died at Boston, MA, Nov 8, 1894.

NFL'S COLDEST TITLE GAME: ANNIVERSARY. Dec 31, 1967. The Green Bay Packers defeated the Dallas Cowboys, 21–17, to win the NFL championship. The game was played at Green Bay with the temperature at −14. Packers quarterback Bart Starr scored the winning touchdown on a quarterback sneak with 13 seconds left to play.

WELLS FARGO SUN BOWL. Dec 31 (tentative). Sun Bowl, El Paso, TX. Postseason college football game matching the third-place team from the PAC-10 against the fifth-place team from the Big Ten. For info: Wells Fargo Sun Bowl, 4100 Rio Bravo, Ste 303, El Paso, TX 79902. Phone: (915) 533-4416 or (800) 915-BOWL. Fax: (915) 533-0661. Web: www.sunbowl.org.

YOU'RE ALL DONE DAY. Dec 31. Acknowledge all that you have accomplished in the past year and savor the satisfaction of every time you crossed home plate, every touchdown you scored, every three-pointer you made, every time you put the puck in the net, every finish line you crossed or every time you gave your very best effort.

BIRTHDAYS TODAY

Richard Warren (Rick) Aguilera, 39, baseball player, born San Gabriel, CA, Dec 31, 1961.

Brent Robert Barry, 29, basketball player, born Roseville Park, NY, Dec 31, 1971.

Thomas Joseph (Tommy) Byrne, 81, former baseball player, born Baltimore, MD, Dec 31, 1919.

Tyrone Kennedy Corbin, 38, basketball player, born Columbia, SC, Dec 31, 1962.

Bradley William (Brad) Daluiso, 33, football player, born San Diego, CA, Dec 31, 1967.

Esteban Antonio Loaiza, 29, baseball player, born Tijuana, Mexico, Dec 31, 1971.

Hugh Edward McElhenny, 72, Pro Football Hall of Fame halfback, born Los Angeles, CA, Dec 31, 1928.

Joseph Heath Shuler, 29, football player, born Bryson City, NC, Dec 31, 1971.

Suntino Korleone Young, 22, basketball player, born Wichita, KS, Dec 31, 1978.

LEAGUE AND TEAM ADDRESSES

Major League Baseball

Commissioner's Office
245 Park Ave
New York, NY 10167
(212) 931-7800

American League
245 Park Ave
New York, NY 10167
(212) 931-7600

National League
245 Park Ave
New York, NY 10167
(212) 931-7700

AMERICAN LEAGUE
East Division
Baltimore Orioles
333 W Camden St
Baltimore, MD 21201
(410) 685-9800
Ticket info:
Oriole Park at Camden
    Yards (RS)
(410) 481-SEAT
Ft. Lauderdale Stadium (ST)
Ft. Lauderdale, FL
(954) 523-3309
(305) 358-5885

Boston Red Sox
4 Yawkey Way
Boston, MA 02215-3496
(617) 267-9440
Ticket info:
Fenway Park (RS)
(617) 267-1700
City of Palms Park (ST)
Ft. Myers, FL
(941) 334-4700

New York Yankees
Yankee Stadium
E 161 St and River Ave
Bronx, NY 10451
(718) 293-4300
Ticket info:
Yankee Stadium (RS)
(718) 293-6013
Legends Field (ST)
Tampa, FL
(813) 879-2244
(813) 287-8844

Tampa Bay Devil Rays
Tropicana Field
One Tropicana Dr
St. Petersburg, FL 33607
(727) 825-3137
Ticket info:
Tropicana Field
(727) 825-3250
Al Lang Stadium (ST)
St. Petersburg, FL 33705
(813) 825-3250

(RS) = Regular Season
(ST) = Spring Training

Toronto Blue Jays
One Blue Jays Way
Ste 3200
Toronto, ON M5V 1J1
(416) 341-1000
Ticket info:
Sky Dome (RS)
(416) 341-1000
Dunedin Stadium at Grant
    Field (ST)
Dunedin, FL
(813) 733-0429
(800) 707-8269

Central Division
Chicago White Sox
333 W 35th St
Chicago, IL 60616
(312) 674-1000
Ticket info:
Comiskey Park (RS)
(312) 674-1000
Tucson Electric Park (ST)
Tucson, AZ
(888) 683-3900

Cleveland Indians
2401 Ontario St
Cleveland, OH 44115
(216) 420-4200
Ticket info:
Jacobs Field (RS)
(216) 241-8888
Chain O'Lakes (ST)
Winter Haven, FL
(813) 293-3900

Detroit Tigers
Tiger Stadium
Detroit, MI 48216
(313) 962-4000
Ticket info:
Tiger Stadium (RS)
(313) 963-2050
Joker Marchant
    Stadium (ST)
Lakeland, FL
(941) 603-6278

Kansas City Royals
PO Box 419969
Kansas City, MO 64141-
    6969
(816) 921-8000
Ticket info:
Kauffman Stadium (RS)
(816) 921-8000
Baseball City Stadium (ST)
Davenport, FL
(941) 424-2500

Minnesota Twins
34 Kirby Puckett Place
Minneapolis, MN 55415
(612) 375-1366
Ticket info:
Metrodome (RS)
(800) 33-TWINS
Lee County Sports
    Complex (ST)
Ft. Myers, FL
(800) 338-9467

West Division
Anaheim Angels
2000 Gene Autry Way
Anaheim, CA 92806
(714) 940-2000
Ticket info:
Edison International Field
    of Anaheim
(714) 663-9000
Diablo Stadium (ST)
Tempe, AZ
(602) 254-3300

Oakland Athletics
7677 Oakport St, Ste 200
Oakland, CA 94621
(510) 638-4900
Ticket info:
Network Associates
    Coliseum (RS)
(510) 638-4627
Phoenix Stadium (ST)
Phoenix, AZ
(602) 392-0074

Seattle Mariners
PO Box 4100
83 King St
Seattle, WA 98104
(206) 346-4000
Ticket info:
SAFECO Field(RS)
(206) 622-4487
Peoria Stadium (ST)
Peoria, AZ
(602) 784-4444

Texas Rangers
1000 Ballpark Way
Arlington, TX 76011
(817) 273-5222
Ticket info:
The Ballpark in Arlington
    (RS)
(817) 273-5100
Charlotte County Stadium
    (ST)
Port Charlotte, FL
(941) 625-9500

NATIONAL LEAGUE
East Division
Atlanta Braves
PO Box 4064
Atlanta, GA 30302
(404) 522-7630
Ticket info:
Turner Field (RS)
(404) 249-6400
Disney's Wide World of
    Sports Baseball Stadium
    (ST)
Kissimmee, FL
(407) 839-3900
(407) 939-1418

Florida Marlins
2267 NW 199th St
Miami, FL 33056
(305) 626-7400
Ticket info:
Pro Player Stadium (RS)
(305) 350-5050
Space Coast Stadium (ST)
Melbourne, FL
(407) 633-9200

Montreal Expos
4549 Pierre-de-Coubertin
    Ave
Montreal, QC H1V 3N7
(514) 790-1245
Ticket info:
Olympic Stadium (RS)
(800) GO-EXPOS
Roger Dean Stadium (ST)
Jupiter, FL
(561) 775-1818

New York Mets
123-10 Roosevelt Ave
Flushing, NY 11368-1699
(718) 507-6387
Ticket info:
Shea Stadium (RS)
(718) 507-8499
Thomas J. White Stadium
    (ST)
Port St. Lucie, FL
(561) 871-2115

Philadelphia Phillies
PO Box 7575
Philadelphia, PA 19101
(215) 463-6000
Ticket info:
Veterans Stadium (RS)
(215) 463-1000
Jack Russell Stadium (ST)
Clearwater, FL
(727) 442-8496
(215) 463-1000

Central Division

Chicago Cubs
1060 W Addison St
Chicago, IL 60613-4397
(312) 404-2827
Ticket info:
Wrigley Field (RS)
(312) 404-2827
HoHoKam Park (ST)
Mesa, AZ
(800) 638-4253

Cincinnati Reds
100 Cinergy Field
Cincinnati, OH 45202
(513) 421-4510
Ticket info:
Cinergy Field (RS)
(513) 421-7337
(800) 829-5353
Ed Smith Stadium (ST)
Sarasota, FL
(941) 954-4101

Houston Astros
PO Box 288
Houston, TX 77001-0288
(713) 799-9500
Ticket info:
The Astrodome (RS)
(713) 799-9567
Osceola County Stadium (ST)
Kissimmee, FL
(407) 839-3900

Milwaukee Brewers
County Stadium
PO Box 3099
Milwaukee, WI 53201-3099
(414) 933-4114
Ticket info:
County Stadium (RS)
(414) 933-9000
Maryvale Baseball Park (ST)
Maryvale, AZ
(602) 784-4444

Pittsburgh Pirates
600 Stadium Circle
Pittsburgh, PA 15212
(412) 323-5000
Ticket info:
Three Rivers Stadium (RS)
(800) BUY-BUCS
McKechnie Field (ST)
Bradenton, FL
(941) 748-4610

St. Louis Cardinals
250 Stadium Plaza
St. Louis, MO 63102
(314) 421-3060
Ticket info:
Busch Stadium (RS)
(314) 421-2400
Roger Dean Stadium (ST)
Jupiter, FL
(561) 966-3304

West Division

Arizona Diamondbacks
401 E Jefferson
Phoenix, AZ 85003
(602) 514-8500
Ticket info:
Bank One Ballpark (RS)
(602) 514-8400
Tucson Electric Park (ST)
Tucson, AZ
(800) 638-4253
(520) 434-1111

Colorado Rockies
2001 Blake St
Denver, CO 80205-2000
(303) 292-2000
Ticket info:
Coors Field (RS)
(800) 388-7625
Hi Corbett Field (ST)
Tucson, AZ
(800) 388-ROCK

Los Angeles Dodgers
1000 Elysian Park Ave
Los Angeles, CA 90012
(213) 224-1500
Ticket info:
Dodger Stadium (RS)
(213) 224-1448
Holman Stadium (ST)
Vero Beach, FL
(561) 569-6858

San Diego Padres
PO Box 2000
San Diego, CA 92112-2000
(619) 881-6500
Ticket info:
Qualcomm Stadium
(888) 723-7379
Peoria Stadium (ST)
Peoria, AZ
(602) 878-4337

San Francisco Giants
3Com Park at Candlestick Point
San Francisco, CA 94124
(415) 468-3700
Ticket info:
3Com Park (RS)
(415) 468-3700
Scottsdale Stadium (ST)
Scottsdale, AZ
(602) 990-7972

National Football League

National Football League
280 Park Ave
New York, NY 10017
(212) 450-2000

AMERICAN FOOTBALL CONFERENCE
Eastern Division
Buffalo Bills
One Bills Dr
Orchard Park, NY 14127
(716) 648-1800
Ticket info:
Rich Stadium
(716) 649-0015

Indianapolis Colts
PO Box 535000
Indianapolis, IN 46253
(317) 297-2658
Ticket info:
RCA Dome
(317) 297-7000

Miami Dolphins
7500 SW 30th St
Davie, FL 33314
(954) 452-7000
Ticket info:
Pro Player Stadium
(305) 620-2578

New England Patriots
60 Washington St
Foxboro, MA 02035
(508) 543-8200
Ticket info:
Foxboro Stadium
(508) 543-1776

New York Jets
1000 Fulton Ave
Hempstead, NY 11550
(516) 560-8100
Ticket info:
Giants Stadium
(516) 560-8200

Central Division
Baltimore Ravens
11001 Owings Mills Blvd
Owings Mills, MD 21117
(410) 654-6200
Ticket info:
TBA
(410) 261-RAVE

Cincinnati Bengals
One Bengals Dr
Cincinnati, OH 45204
(513) 621-3550
Ticket info:
Cinergy Field
(513) 621-3550

Jacksonville Jaguars
One ALLTEL Stadium Place
Jacksonville, FL 32202
(904) 633-6000
Ticket info:
ALLTEL Stadium
(904) 633-2000

Pittsburgh Steelers
300 Stadium Circle
Pittsburgh, PA 15212
(412) 323-0300
Ticket info:
Three Rivers Stadium
(412) 323-1200

Tennessee Titans
Baptist Sports Park
7640 Highway 70 S
Nashville, TN 37221
(615) 673-1500
Ticket info:
TBA
(615) 673-7600

Western Division
Denver Broncos
13655 Broncos Pkwy
Englewood, CO 80112
(303) 649-9000
Ticket info:
Mile High Stadium
(303) 433-7466

Kansas City Chiefs
One Arrowhead Dr
Kansas City, MO 64129
(816) 924-9300
Ticket info:
Arrowhead Stadium
(816) 924-9400

Oakland Raiders
1220 Harbor Bay Pkwy
Alameda, CA 94502
(510) 864-5000
Ticket info:
Oakland-Alameda County
  Coliseum
(800) 949-2626

San Diego Chargers
PO Box 609609
San Diego, CA 92160-9609
(619) 874-4500
Ticket info:
Qualcomm Stadium
(619) 280-2121

Seattle Seahawks
11220 NE 53rd St
Kirkland, WA 98033
(425) 827-9777
Ticket info:
Kingdome
(206) 682-2800

**NATIONAL FOOTBALL
CONFERENCE
Eastern Division**
Arizona Cardinals
PO Box 888
Phoenix, AZ 85001-0888
(602) 379-0101
Ticket info:
Sun Devil Stadium
(602) 379-0102

Dallas Cowboys
One Cowboys Pkwy
Irving, TX 75063
(972) 556-9900
Ticket info:
Texas Stadium
(972) 579-5000

New York Giants
East Rutherford, NJ 07073
(201) 935-8111
Ticket info:
Giants Stadium
(201) 935-8222

Philadelphia Eagles
3501 S Broad St
Philadelphia, PA 19148
(215) 463-2500
Ticket info:
Veterans Stadium
(215) 463-5500

Washington Redskins
PO Box 17247
Dulles International
  Airport
Washington, DC 20041
(703) 478-8900
Ticket info:
Jack Kent Cooke Stadium
(301) 276-6050

Central Division
Chicago Bears
Halas Hall at Conway Park
1000 Football Dr
Lake Forest, IL 60045
(847) 295-6600
Ticket info:
Soldier Field
(847) 615-2327

Detroit Lions
1200 Featherstone Rd
Pontiac, MI 48342
(248) 335-4131
Ticket info:
Pontiac Silverdome
(248) 335-4151

Green Bay Packers
PO Box 10628
Green Bay, WI 54307-0628
(920) 496-5700
Ticket info:
Lambeau Field
(920) 496-5719

Minnesota Vikings
9520 Viking Dr
Eden Prairie, MN 55344
(612) 828-6500
Ticket info:
Metrodome
(612) 333-8828

Tampa Bay Buccaneers
One Buccaneer Pl
Tampa, FL 33607
(813) 870-2700
Ticket info:
Houlihan's Stadium
(813) 879-2827

Western Division
Atlanta Falcons
One Falcon Place
Suwanee, GA 30024
(404) 945-1111
Ticket info:
Georgia Dome
(404) 223-8444

Carolina Panthers
800 S Mint St
Charlotte, NC 28202-1502
(704) 358-7000
Ticket info:
Ericsson Stadium
(704) 358-7800

New Orleans Saints
5800 Airline Highway
Metairie, LA 70003
(504) 733-0255
Ticket info:
Louisiana Superdome
(504) 731-1700

St. Louis Rams
1 Rams Way
St. Louis, MO 63045
(314) 982-7267
Ticket info:
Trans World Dome
(314) 425-8830

San Francisco 49ers
4949 Centennial Blvd
Santa Clara, CA 95054-
  1229
(408) 562-4949
Ticket info:
3Com Park at Candlestick
  Point
(415) 468-2249

National Basketball Association

National Basketball
  Association
Olympic Tower
645 Fifth Ave
New York, NY 10022
(212) 407-8000

New Jersey Office
450 Harmon Meadow Blvd
Secaucus, NJ 07094
(201) 865-1500

**EASTERN CONFERENCE
Atlantic Division**
Boston Celtics
151 Merrimac St
Boston, MA 02114
(617) 523-6050
Ticket info:
FleetCenter
(617) 523-3030

Miami Heat
SunTrust International
  Center
One SE 3rd Ave, Ste 2300
Miami, FL 33131
(305) 577-4328
Ticket info:
Miami Arena
(305) 577-4328

New Jersey Nets
Nets Champion Center
390 Murray Hill Pkwy
East Rutherford, NJ 07073
(201) 935-8888
Ticket info:
Continental Airlines Arena
(201) 935-8888

New York Knicks
Two Pennsylvania Plaza
New York, NY 10121-0091
(212) 465-6000
Ticket info:
Madison Square Garden
(212) 465-JUMP

Orlando Magic
Two Magic Place
8701 Maitland Summit
   Blvd.
Orlando, FL 32810
(407) 649-3200
Ticket info:
Orlando Arena
(800) 338-0005

Philadelphia 76ers
3601 S. Broad St.
Philadelphia, PA 19148
(215) 339-7600
Ticket info:
First Union Center
(215) 339-7676

Washington Wizards
718 7th St NW
Washington DC 20004
(202) 661-5000
Ticket info:
MCI Center
(202) 481-SEAT

Central Division
Atlanta Hawks
One CNN Center
Ste 405, South Tower
Atlanta, GA 30303
(404) 827-3800
Ticket info:
The Omni
(800) 326-4000

Charlotte Hornets
100 Hive Dr
Charlotte, NC 28217
(704) 357-0252
Ticket info:
Charlotte Coliseum
(704) 522-6500

Chicago Bulls
1901 W Madison St
Chicago, IL 60612
(312) 455-4000
Ticket info:
United Center
(312) 559-1212

Cleveland Cavaliers
1 Center Court
Cleveland, OH 44115-4001
(216) 420-2000
Ticket info:
Gund Arena
(216) 420-2200
(800) 332-2287

Detroit Pistons
Two Championship Dr
Auburn Hills, MI 48326
(248) 377-0100
Ticket info:
The Palace of Auburn Hills
(248) 377-0100

Indiana Pacers
300 E Market St
Indianapolis, IN 46204
(317) 263-2100
Ticket info:
Market Square Arena
(317) 239-5151

Milwaukee Bucks
1001 N Fourth St
Milwaukee, WI 53203-1312
(414) 227-0500
Ticket info:
Bradley Center
(414) 276-4545

Toronto Raptors
20 Bay St, Ste 1702
Toronto, ON M5J 2N8
(416) 214-2255
Ticket info:
Air Canada Centre
(416) 366-3865

WESTERN CONFERENCE
Midwest Division
Dallas Mavericks
777 Sports St
Dallas, TX 75207
(214) 748-1808
Ticket info:
Reunion Arena
(972) 988-DUNK

Denver Nuggets
1635 Clay St
Denver, CO 80204
(303) 893-6700
Ticket info:
McNichols Sports Arena
(303) 893-6700

Houston Rockets
Two Greenway Plaza,
   Ste 400
Houston, TX 77046-3865
(713) 627-3865
Ticket info:
The Summit
(713) 627-3865

Minnesota Timberwolves
600 First Ave N
Minneapolis, MN 55403
(612) 673-1600
Ticket info:
Target Center
(612) 673-1600

San Antonio Spurs
100 Montana St
San Antonio, TX 78203-
   1031
(210) 554-7700
Ticket info:
Alamodome
(210) 554-7787

Utah Jazz
301 West South Temple
Salt Lake City, UT 84101
(801) 325-2500
Ticket info:
Delta Center
(801) 325-2500

Vancouver Grizzlies
800 Griffiths Way
Vancouver, BC V6B 6G1
(604) 899-7400
Ticket info:
Bear Country at General
   Motors Place
(604) 899-4666

Pacific Division
Golden State Warriors
1011 Broadway
Oakland, CA 94607
(510) 986-2200
Ticket info:
Arena in Oakland
(510) 986-2222

Los Angeles Clippers
3939 S Figueroa St
Los Angeles, CA 90037
(213) 745-0400
Ticket info:
LA Memorial Sports Arena
Arrowhead Pond of
   Anaheim
(213) 745-0500

Los Angeles Lakers
3900 W Manchester Blvd
PO Box 10
Inglewood, CA 90306
(310) 419-3100
Ticket info:
The Great Western Forum
(310) 419-3100

Phoenix Suns
201 E Jefferson
Phoenix, AZ 85004
(602) 379-7900
Ticket info:
America West Arena
(602) 379-7867

Portland Trail Blazers
One Center Court, Ste 200
Portland, OR 97227
(503) 234-9291
Ticket info:
The Rose Garden
(503) 797-9600

Sacramento Kings
One Sports Pkwy
Sacramento, CA 95834
(916) 928-0000
Ticket info:
ARCO Arena
(916) 928-6900

Seattle Supersonics
190 Queen Anne Ave N,
   Ste 200
Seattle, WA 98109-9711
(206) 281-5800
Ticket info:
KeyArena
(206) 283-3865

National Hockey League

New York Office
1251 Ave of the Americas
47th Fl
New York, NY 10020
(212) 789-2000

Toronto Office
75 International Blvd
Ste 300
Rexdale, ON M9W 6L9
(416) 798-0809

Montreal Office
1800 McGill College Ave
Ste 2600
Montreal, QC H3A 3J6
(514) 288-9220

EASTERN CONFERENCE
Atlantic Division
New Jersey Devils
PO Box 504
East Rutherford, NJ 07073
(201) 935-6050

New York Islanders
Nassau Veterans Memorial
Coliseum
Uniondale, NY 11553
(516) 794-4100

New York Rangers
2 Pennsylvania Plaza
New York, NY 10121
(212) 465-6486

Philadelphia Flyers
First Union Center
3601 S. Broad St.
Philadelphia, PA 19148
(215) 465-4500

Pittsburgh Penguins
66 Mario Lemieux Place
Civic Arena
Pittsburgh, PA 15219
(412) 642-1300

Northeast Division
Boston Bruins
1 FleetCenter, Ste 250
Boston, MA 02114-1303
(617) 624-1900

Buffalo Sabres
Marine Midland Arena
One Seymour Knox III Plaza
Buffalo, NY 14203
(716) 855-4100

Montreal Canadiens
1260 rue de la Gauchetiere
Ouest
Montreal, QC H3B 5E8
(514) 932-2582

Ottawa Senators
1000 Paladium Dr
Kanata, ON K2V 1A5
(613) 599-0250

Southeast Division
Atlanta Thrashers
One CNN Tower
13th S Tower
Atlanta, GA 30303
(404) 827-3394

Carolina Hurricanes
5000 Aerial Center, Ste 100
Morrisville, NC 27560
(919) 467-PUCK

Florida Panthers
100 North East Third Ave
2nd Fl
Fort Lauderdale, FL 33301
(954) 768-1900

Tampa Bay Lightning
401 Channelside Dr
Tampa, FL 33602
(813) 229-2658

Washington Capitals
601 F St NW
Washington, DC 20004
(202) 628-3200

WESTERN CONFERENCE
Central Division
Chicago Blackhawks
1901 W Madison St
Chicago, IL 60612
(312) 455-7000

Detroit Red Wings
600 Civic Center Dr
Detroit, MI 48226
(313) 296-7544

Nashville Predators
501 Broadway
Nashville, TN 37215
(615) 770-2300

St. Louis Blues
1401 Clark St
St. Louis, MO 63103
(314) 622-2500

Toronto Maple Leafs
60 Carlton St
Toronto, ON M5B 1L1
(416) 977-1641

Northwest Division
Calgary Flames
PO Box 1540
Station M
Calgary, AB T2P 3B9
(403) 777-2177

Colorado Avalanche
1635 Clay St
Denver, CO 80204
(303) 893-6700

Edmonton Oilers
Edmonton Coliseum
Edmonton, AB T5B 4M9
(403) 414-4000

Vancouver Canucks
800 Griffiths Way
Vancouver, BC V6B 6G1
(604) 899-4600

Pacific Division
Mighty Ducks of Anaheim
2695 E Katella Ave
PO Box 61077
Anaheim, CA 92803-6177
(714) 940-2900

Dallas Stars
211 Cowboys Pkwy
Irving, TX 75063
(972) 868-2890

Los Angeles Kings
3900 W Manchester Blvd
Inglewood, CA 90305
(310) 419-3160

Phoenix Coyotes
Cellular One Ice Den
9375 E. Bell Road
Scottsdale, AZ 85260
(602) 473-5600

San Jose Sharks
525 W Santa Clara St
San Jose, CA 95113
(408) 287-7070

Beginning play in:

2000–2001

Columbus Blue Jackets
150 E Wilson Bridge Rd
Ste 239
Worthington, OH 43085
(614) 436-2418

2000–2001

Minnesota Wild
Piper Jaffray Plaza
444 Cedar St
Ste 2000
St. Paul, MN 55101
(612) 333-PUCK

SPORTS HALLS OF FAME

Baseball Hall of Fame

PLAYERS

Aaron, Henry, 1982
Alexander, Grover Cleveland, 1938
Anson, Cap, 1939
Aparicio, Luis, 1984
Appling, Luke, 1964
Ashburn, Richie, 1995
Averill, Earl, 1975
Baker, Home Run, 1955
Bancroft, Dave, 1971
Banks, Ernie, 1977
Beckley, Jake, 1971
Bell, Cool Papa, 1974
Bench, Johnny, 1989
Bender, Chief, 1953
Berra, Yogi, 1972
Bottomley, Jim, 1974
Boudreau, Lou, 1970
Bresnahan, Roger, 1945
Brett, George, 1999
Brock, Lou, 1985
Brouthers, Dan, 1945
Brown, Mordecai, 1949
Bunning, Jim, 1996
Burkett, Jesse, 1946
Campanella, Roy, 1969
Carew, Rod, 1991
Carey, Max, 1961
Carlton, Steve, 1994
Cepeda, Orlando, 1999
Chance, Frank, 1946
Charleston, Oscar, 1976
Chesbro, Jack, 1946
Clarke, Fred, 1945
Clarkson, John, 1963
Clemente, Roberto, 1973
Cobb, Ty, 1936
Cochrane, Mickey, 1947
Collins, Eddie, 1939
Collins, Jimmy, 1945
Combs, Earle, 1970
Comiskey, Charley, 1939
    (also a founder)
Connor, Roger, 1976
Coveleski, Stanley, 1969
Crawford, Sam, 1957
Cronin, Joe, 1956
Cummings, Candy, 1939
Cuyler, Kiki, 1968
Dandridge, Ray, 1987
Davis, George, 1998
Day, Leon, 1995
Dean, Dizzy, 1953
Delahanty, Ed, 1945
Dickey, Bill, 1954
Dihigo, Martin, 1977
DiMaggio, Joe, 1955
Doby, Larry, 1998
Doerr, Bobby, 1986
Drysdale, Don 1984
Duffy, Hugh, 1945
Evers, Johnny, 1946
Ewing, Buck, 1939
Faber, Red, 1964
Feller, Bob, 1962

Ferrell, Rick, 1984
Fingers, Rollie, 1992
Flick, Elmer, 1963
Ford, Whitey, 1974
Foster, Bill, 1996
Foster, Rube, 1981
Fox, Nellie, 1997
Foxx, Jimmie, 1951
Frisch, Frankie, 1947
Galvin, Pud, 1965
Gehrig, Lou, 1939
Gehringer, Charley, 1949
Gibson, Bob, 1981
Gibson, Josh, 1972
Gomez, Lefty, 1972
Goslin, Goose, 1968
Greenberg, Hank, 1956
Grimes, Burleigh, 1964
Grove, Lefty, 1947
Hafey, Chick, 1971
Haines, Jesse, 1970
Hamilton, Billy, 1961
Hartnett, Gabby, 1955
Heilmann, Harry, 1952
Herman, Billy, 1975
Hooper, Harry, 1971
Hornsby, Rogers, 1942
Hoyt, Waite, 1969
Hubbell, Carl, 1947
Hunter, Catfish, 1987
Irvin, Monte, 1973
Jackson, Reggie, 1993
Jackson, Travis, 1982
Jenkins, Ferguson, 1991
Jennings, Hugh, 1945
Johnson, Judy, 1975
Johnson, Walter, 1936
Joss, Addie, 1978
Kaline, Al, 1980
Keefe, Tim, 1964
Keeler, Willie, 1939
Kell, George, 1983
Kelley, Joe, 1971
Kelly, George, 1973
Kelly, Mike, 1945
Killebrew, Harmon, 1984
Kiner, Ralph, 1975
Klein, Chuck, 1980
Koufax, Sandy, 1972
Lajoie, Nap, 1937
Lazzeri, Tony, 1991
Lemon, Bob, 1976
Leonard, Buck, 1972
Lindstrom, Fred, 1976
Lloyd, John Henry, 1977
Lombardi, Ernie, 1986
Lyons, Ted, 1955
Mantle, Mickey, 1974
Manush, Heinie, 1964
Maranville, Rabbit, 1954
Marichal, Juan, 1983
Marquard, Rube, 1971
Mathews, Eddie, 1978
Mathewson, Christy, 1936
Mays, Willie, 1979

McCarthy, Tommy, 1946
McCovey, Willie, 1986
McGinnity, Joe, 1946
Medwick, Joe, 1968
Mize, Johnny, 1981
Morgan, Joe, 1990
Musial, Stan, 1969
Newhouser, Hal, 1992
Nichols, Kid, 1949
Niekro, Phil, 1997
O'Rourke Jim, 1945
Ott, Mel, 1951
Paige, Satchel, 1971
Palmer, Jim, 1990
Pennock, Herb, 1948
Perry, Gaylord, 1991
Plank, Eddie, 1946
Radbourn, Hoss, 1939
Reese, Pee Wee, 1984
Rice, Sam, 1963
Rixey, Eppa, 1963
Rizzuto, Phil, 1994
Roberts, Robin, 1976
Robinson, Brooks, 1983
Robinson, Frank, 1982
Robinson, Jackie, 1962
Rogan, Bullet Joe, 1998
Roush, Edd, 1962
Ruffing, Red, 1967
Rusie, Amos, 1977
Ruth, Babe, 1936
Ryan, Nolan, 1999
Schalk, Ray, 1955
Schmidt, Mike, 1995
Schoendienst, Red, 1989
Seaver, Tom, 1992
Sewell, Joe, 1977
Simmons, Al, 1953
Sisler, George, 1939
Slaughter, Enos, 1985
Snider, Duke, 1980
Spahn, Warren, 1973
Spalding, Al, 1939
Speaker, Tris, 1937
Stargell, Willie, 1988
Sutton, Don, 1998
Terry, Bill, 1954
Thompson, Sam, 1974
Tinker, Joe, 1946
Vance, Dazzy, 1955
Vaughan, Arky, 1985
Waddell, Rube, 1946
Wagner, Honus, 1936
Wallace, Bobby, 1953
Walsh, Ed, 1946
Waner, Lloyd, 1967
Waner, Paul, 1952
Ward, John Montgomery, 1964
Welch, Mickey, 1973
Wells, Willie, 1997
Wheat, Zack, 1959
Wilhelm, Hoyt, 1985
Williams, Billy, 1987
Williams, Joe, 1999
Williams, Ted, 1966

Willis, Vic, 1995
Wilson, Hack, 1979
Wynn, Early, 1972
Yastrzemski, Carl, 1989
Young, Cy, 1937
Youngs, Ross, 1972
Yount, Robin, 1999

MANAGERS

Alston, Walter, 1983
Durocher, Leo, 1994
Griffith, Clark, 1946
Hanlon, Ned, 1996
Harris, Bucky, 1975
Huggins, Miller, 1964
Lasorda, Tommy, 1997
Lopez, Al, 1977
Mack, Connie, 1937
McCarthy, Joe, 1957
McGraw, John, 1937
McKechnie, Bill, 1962
Robinson, Wilbert, 1945
Selee, Frank, 1999
Stengel, Casey, 1966
Weaver, Earl, 1996
Wright, George, 1937
Wright, Harry, 1953

UMPIRES

Barlick, Al, 1989
Chylak, Nestor, 1999
Conlan, Jocko, 1974
Connolly, Tommy, 1953
Evans, Billy, 1973
Hubbard, Cal, 1976
Klem, Bill, 1953
McGowan, Bill, 1992

EXECUTIVES

Barrow, Ed, 1953
Bulkeley, Morgan, 1937
Chandler, Happy, 1982
Frick, Ford, 1970
Giles, Warren, 1979
Harridge, Will, 1972
Johnson, Ban, 1937
Landis, Kenesaw, 1944
MacPhail, Larry, 1978
MacPhail, Lee, 1998
Rickey, Branch, 1967
Veeck, Bill, 1991
Weiss, George, 1971
Yawkey, Tom, 1980

ORGANIZERS

Cartwright, Alexander, 1938
Chadwick, Henry, 1938

FOUNDERS

Comiskey, Charley, 1939
    (also a player)
Hulbert, William, 1995

Pro Football Hall of Fame

Adderley, Herb, 1980
Alworth, Lance, 1978
Atkins, Doug, 1982
Badgro, Morris (Red), 1981
Barney, Lem, 1992
Battles, Cliff, 1968
Baugh, Sammy, 1963
Bednarik, Chuck, 1967
Bell, Bert, 1963
Bell, Bobby, 1983
Berry, Raymond, 1973
Bidwill, Charles W., 1967
Biletnikoff, Fred, 1988
Blanda, George, 1981
Blount, Mel, 1989
Bradshaw, Terry, 1989
Brown, Jim, 1971
Brown, Paul, 1967
Brown, Roosevelt, 1975
Brown, Willie, 1984
Buchanan, Buck, 1990
Butkus, Dick, 1979
Campbell, Earl, 1991
Canadeo, Tony, 1974
Carr, Joe, 1963
Chamberlin, Guy, 1965
Christiansen, Jack, 1970
Clark, Dutch, 1963
Connor, George, 1975
Conzelman, Jimmy, 1964
Creekmur, Lou, 1996
Csonka, Larry, 1987
Davis, Al, 1992
Davis, Willie, 1981
Dawson, Len, 1987
Dickerson, Eric, 1999
Dierdorf, Dan, 1996
Ditka, Mike, 1988
Donovan, Art, 1968
Dorsett, Tony, 1994
Driscoll, Paddy, 1965
Dudley, Bill, 1966
Edwards, Turk, 1969
Ewbank, Weeb, 1978
Fears, Tom, 1970
Finks, Jim, 1995
Flaherty, Ray, 1976
Ford, Len, 1976
Fortmann, Danny, 1965
Fouts, Dan, 1993
Gatski, Frank, 1985
George, Bill, 1974
Gibbs, Joe, 1996

Gifford, Frank, 1977
Gillman, Sid, 1983
Graham, Otto, 1965
Grange, Red, 1963
Grant, Bud, 1994
Greene, Joe, 1987
Gregg, Forrest, 1977
Griese, Bob, 1990
Groza, Lou, 1974
Guyon, Joe, 1966
Halas, George, 1963
Ham, Jack, 1988
Hannah, John, 1991
Harris, Franco, 1990
Haynes, Mike, 1997
Healey, Ed, 1964
Hein, Mel, 1963
Hendricks, Ted, 1990
Henry, Wilbur, 1963
Herber, Arnie, 1966
Hewitt, Bill, 1971
Hinkle, Clarke, 1964
Hirsch, Elroy (Crazy Legs), 1968
Hornung, Paul, 1986
Houston, Ken, 1986
Hubbard, Cal, 1963
Huff, Sam, 1982
Hunt, Lamar, 1972
Hutson, Don, 1963
Johnson, Jimmy, 1994
Johnson, John Henry, 1987
Joiner, Charlie, 1996
Jones, Deacon, 1980
Jones, Stan, 1991
Jordan, Henry, 1995
Jurgensen, Sonny, 1983
Kelly, Leroy, 1994
Kiesling, Walter, 1966
Kinard, Frank (Bruiser), 1971
Krause, Paul, 1998
Lambeau, Curly, 1963
Lambert, Jack, 1990
Landry, Tom, 1990
Lane, Dick (Night Train), 1974
Langer, Jim, 1987
Lanier, Willie, 1986
Largent, Steve, 1995
Lary, Yale, 1979
Lavelli, Dante, 1975
Layne, Bobby, 1967

Leemans, Tuffy, 1978
Lilly, Bob, 1980
Little, Larry, 1993
Lombardi, Vince, 1971
Luckman, Sid, 1965
Lyman, Roy (Link), 1964
Mack, Tom, 1999
Mackey, John, 1992
Mara, Tim, 1963
Mara, Wellington, 1997
Marchetti, Gino, 1972
Marshall, George Preston, 1963
Matson, Ollie, 1972
Maynard, Don, 1987
McAfee, George, 1966
McCormack, Mike, 1984
McDonald, Tommy, 1998
McElhenny, Hugh, 1970
McNally, Johnny (Blood), 1963
Michalske, August (Mike), 1964
Millner, Wayne, 1968
Mitchell, Bobby, 1983
Mix, Ron, 1979
Moore, Lenny, 1975
Motley, Marion, 1968
Munoz, Anthony, 1998
Musso, George, 1982
Nagurski, Bronko, 1963
Namath, Joe, 1985
Neale, Earle (Greasy), 1969
Nevers, Ernie, 1963
Newsome, Ozzie, 1999
Nitschke, Ray, 1978
Noll, Chuck, 1993
Nomellini, Leo, 1969
Olsen, Merlin, 1982
Otto, Jim, 1980
Owen, Steve, 1966
Page, Alan, 1988
Parker, Clarence (Ace), 1972
Parker, Jim, 1973
Payton, Walter, 1993
Perry, Joe, 1969
Pihos, Pete, 1970
Ray, Hugh (Shorty), 1966
Reeves, Daniel F., 1967
Renfro, Mel, 1996
Riggins, John, 1992
Ringo, Jim, 1981

Robustelli, Andy, 1971
Rooney, Arthur J., 1964
Rozelle, Pete, 1985
Sayers, Gale, 1977
Schmidt, Joe, 1973
Schramm, Tex, 1991
Selmon, Lee Roy, 1995
Shaw, Billy, 1999
Shell, Art, 1989
Shula, Don, 1997
Simpson, O.J., 1985
Singletary, Mike, 1998
Smith, Jackie, 1994
St. Clair, Bob, 1990
Starr, Bart, 1977
Staubach, Roger, 1985
Stautner, Ernie, 1969
Stenerud, Jan, 1991
Stephenson, Dwight, 1998
Strong, Ken, 1967
Stydahar, Joe, 1967
Tarkenton, Fran, 1986
Taylor, Charley, 1984
Taylor, Jim, 1976
Taylor, Lawrence, 1999
Thorpe, Jim, 1963
Tittle, Y.A., 1971
Trafton, George, 1964
Trippi, Charlie, 1968
Tunnell, Emlen, 1967
Turner, Clyde (Bulldog), 1966
Unitas, John, 1979
Upshaw, Gene, 1987
Van Brocklin, Norm, 1971
Van Buren, Steve, 1965
Walker, Doak, 1986
Walsh, Bill, 1993
Warfield, Paul, 1983
Waterfield, Bob, 1965
Webster, Mike, 1997
Weinmeister, Arnie, 1984
White, Randy, 1994
Willis, Bill, 1977
Wilson, Larry, 1978
Winslow, Kellen, 1995
Wojciechowicz, Alex, 1968
Wood, Willie, 1989

Naismith Memorial Basketball Hall of Fame

PLAYERS
Abdul-Jabbar, Kareem, 1995
Archibald, Tiny, 1991
Arizin, Paul, 1977
Barlow, Tom, 1980
Barry, Rick, 1987
Baylor, Elgin, 1976
Beckman, John, 1972
Bellamy, Walt, 1993
Belov, Sergei, 1992

Bing, Dave, 1990
Bird, Larry, 1998
Blazejowski, Carol, 1994
Borgmann, Bennie, 1961
Bradley, Bill, 1982
Brennan, Joseph, 1974
Cervi, Al, 1984
Chamberlain, Wilt, 1978
Cooper, Chuck, 1976
Cosic, Kresimir, 1996
Cousy, Bob, 1970

Cowens, Dave, 1991
Crawford, Joan, 1997
Cunningham, Billy, 1986
Curry, Denise, 1997
Davies, Bob, 1969
DeBernardi, Forrest, 1961
DeBusschere, Dave, 1982
Dehnert, Dutch, 1968
Donovan, Anne, 1995
Endacott, Paul, 1971
English, Alex, 1997

Erving, Julius, 1993
Foster, Bud, 1964
Frazier, Walt, 1987
Friedman, Marty, 1971
Fulks, Joe, 1977
Gale, Laddie, 1976
Gallatin, Harry, 1991
Gates, William, 1989
Gervin, George, 1996
Gola, Tom, 1975
Goodrich, Gail, 1996

Greer, Hal, 1981
Gruenig, Ace, 1963
Hagan, Cliff, 1977
Hanson, Victor, 1960
Harris, Lusia, 1992
Havlicek, John, 1983
Hawkins, Connie, 1992
Hayes, Elvin, 1990
Haynes, Marques, 1998
Heinsohn, Tommy, 1986
Holman, Nat, 1964
Houbregs, Bob, 1987
Howell, Bailey, 1997
Hyatt, Chuck, 1959
Issel, Dan, 1993
Jeannette, Buddy, 1994
Johnson, William, 1976
Johnston, Neil, 1990
Jones, K.C., 1989
Jones, Sam, 1983
Krause, Moose, 1975
Kurland, Bob, 1961
Lanier, Bob, 1992
Lapchick, Joe, 1966
Lieberman-Cline, Nancy, 1996
Lovellette, Clyde, 1988
Lucas, Jerry, 1979
Luisetti, Hank, 1959
McCracken, Branch, 1960
McCracken, Jack, 1962
McDermott, Bobby, 1988
McHale, Kevin, 1999
Macauley, Ed, 1960
Maravich, Pete, 1987
Martin, Slater, 1981
McGuire, Dick, 1993
Meyers, Ann, 1993
Mikan, George, 1959
Mikkelsen, Vern, 1995
Miller, Cheryl, 1995
Monroe, Earl, 1990
Murphy, Calvin, 1993
Murphy, Stretch, 1960
Page, Pat, 1962
Pettit, Bob, 1970
Phillip, Andy, 1961
Pollard, Jim, 1977
Ramsey, Frank, 1981
Reed, Willis, 1981
Risen, Arnie, 1998
Robertson, Oscar, 1979

Roosma, John, 1961
Russell, Bill, 1974
Russell, Honey, 1964
Schayes, Dolph, 1972
Schmidt, Ernest, 1973
Schommer, John, 1959
Sedran, Barney, 1962
Semenova, Juliana, 1993
Sharman, Bill, 1975
Steinmetz, Christian, 1961
Thompson, Cat, 1962
Thompson, David, 1996
Thurmond, Nate, 1984
Twyman, Jack, 1982
Unseld, Wes, 1988
Vandivier, Fuzzy, 1974
Wachter, Ed, 1961
Walton, Bill, 1993
Wanzer, Bobby, 1987
West, Jerry, 1979
White, Nera, 1992
Wilkens, Lenny, 1989
Wooden, John, 1960
Yardley, George, 1996

COACHES
Anderson, Harold, 1984
Auerbach, Red, 1968
Barry, Sam, 1978
Blood, Ernest, 1960
Cann, Howard, 1967
Carlson, Clifford, 1959
Carnesecca, Lou, 1992
Carnevale, Ben, 1969
Carril, Pete, 1997
Case, Everett, 1981
Conradt, Jody, 1998
Crum, Denny, 1994
Daly, Chuck, 1994
Dean, Everett, 1966
Diaz-Miguel, Antonio, 1997
Diddle, Ed, 1971
Drake, Bruce, 1972
Gaines, Clarence, 1981
Gardner, Jack, 1983
Gill, Slats, 1967
Gomelsky, Alexandr, 1967
Hannum, Alex, 1998
Harshman, Marv, 1984
Haskins, Don, 1997

Hickey, Eddie, 1978
Hobson, Howard, 1965
Holzman, Red, 1986
Iba, Henry, 1968
Julian, Doggie, 1967
Keaney, Frank, 1960
Keogan, George, 1961
Knight, Bob, 1991
Kundla, John, 1995
Lambert, Ward, 1960
Litwack, Harry, 1975
Loeffler, Kenny, 1964
Lonborg, Dutch, 1972
McCutchan, Arad, 1980
McGuire, Al, 1992
McGuire, Frank, 1976
Meanwell, Walter, 1959
Meyer, Ray, 1978
Miller, Ralph, 1988
Moore, Billie, 1999
Nikolic, Aleksandar, 1998
Ramsay, Jack, 1992
Rubini, Cesare, 1994
Rupp, Adolph, 1968
Sachs, Leonard, 1961
Shelton, Everett, 1979
Smith, Dean, 1982
Taylor, Fred, 1985
Teague, Bertha, 1984
Thompson, John, 1999
Wade, Margaret, 1984
Watts, Stanley, 1985
Wilkens, Lenny, 1998
Wooden, John, 1972
Woolpert, Phil, 1992

CONTRIBUTORS
Abbott, Senda, 1984
Allen, Phog, 1959
Bee, Clair, 1967
Brown, Walter, 1965
Bunn, John, 1964
Douglas, Bob, 1971
Duer, Al, 1981
Fagan, Clifford, 1983
Fisher, Harry, 1973
Fleisher, Larry, 1991
Gottlieb, Eddie, 1971
Gulick, Luther, 1959
Harrison, Luther, 1979
Hepp, Ferenc, 1980
Hickox, Ed, 1959

Hinkle, Tony, 1965
Irish, Ned, 1964
Jones, William, 1964
Kennedy, Walter, 1980
Liston, Emil, 1974
McLendon, John, 1978
Mokray, Bill, 1965
Morgan, Ralph, 1959
Morgenweck, Frank, 1962
Naismith, James, 1959
Newell, Pete, 1978
O'Brien, John, 1961
O'Brien, Larry, 1991
Olsen, Harold, 1959
Podoloff, Maurice, 1973
Porter, H.V., 1960
Reid, William, 1963
Ripley, Elmer, 1972
St. John, Lynn, 1962
Saperstein, Abe, 1970
Schabinger, Arthur, 1961
Stagg, Amos Alonzo, 1959
Stankovich, Boris, 1991
Steitz, Ed, 1983
Taylor, Chuck, 1968
Tower, Oswald, 1959
Trester, Arthur, 1961
Wells, Clifford, 1971
Wilke, Lou, 1982
Zollner, Fred, 1999

REFEREES
Enright, Jim, 1978
Hepbron, George, 1960
Hoyt, George, 1961
Kennedy, Matthew, 1959
Leith, Lloyd, 1982
Mihalik, Zigmund, 1986
Nucatola, John, 1977
Quigley, Ernest, 1961
Shirley, Dallas, 1979
Strom, Earl, 1995
Tobey, David, 1961
Walsh, David, 1961

TEAMS
First Team, 1959
Original Celtics, 1959
Buffalo Germans, 1961
Renaissance, 1963

Hockey Hall of Fame

PLAYERS
Abel, Sid, 1969
Adams, Jack, 1959
Apps, Syl, 1961
Armstrong, George, 1975
Bailey, Ace, 1975
Bain, Dan, 1945
Baker, Hobey, 1945
Barber, Bill, 1990
Barry, Marty, 1965
Bathgate, Andy, 1978
Bauer, Bobby, 1996

Beliveau, Jean, 1972
Benedict, Clint, 1965
Bentley, Doug, 1964
Bentley, Max, 1966
Blake, Toe, 1966
Boivin, Leo, 1986
Boon, Dickie, 1952
Bossy, Mike, 1991
Bouchard, Butch, 1966
Boucher, Frank, 1958
Boucher, George, 1960
Bower, Johnny, 1976

Bowie, Russell, 1945
Brimsek, Frank, 1966
Broadbent, Punch, 1962
Broda, Turk, 1967
Bucyk, John, 1981
Burch, Billy, 1974
Cameron, Harry, 1962
Cheevers, Gerry, 1985
Clancy, King, 1958
Clapper, Dit, 1947
Clarke, Bobby, 1987
Cleghorn, Sprague, 1958

Colville, Neil, 1967
Conacher, Charlie, 1961
Conacher, Lionel, 1994
Conacher, Roy, 1998
Connell, Alex, 1958
Cook, Bill, 1952
Cook, Bun, 1995
Coulter, Art, 1974
Cournoyer, Yvan, 1982
Cowley, Bill, 1968
Crawford, Rusty, 1962
Darragh, Jack, 1962

Davidson, Scotty, 1950
Day, Hap, 1961
Delvecchio, Alex, 1977
Denneny, Cy, 1959
Dionne, Marcel, 1992
Drillon, Gord, 1975
Drinkwater, Graham, 1950
Dryden, Ken, 1983
Dumart, Woody, 1992
Dunderdale, Tommy, 1974
Durnan, Bill, 1964
Dutton, Red, 1958
Dye, Babe, 1970
Esposito, Phil, 1984
Esposito, Tony, 1988
Farrell, Arthur, 1965
Flaman, Fern, 1990
Foyston, Frank, 1958
Fredrickson, Frank, 1958
Gadsby, Bill, 1970
Gainey, Bob, 1992
Gardiner, Chuck, 1945
Gardiner, Herb, 1958
Gardner, Jimmy, 1962
Geoffrion, Bernie, 1972
Gerard, Eddie, 1945
Giacomin, Eddie, 1987
Gilbert, Rod, 1982
Gilmour, Billy, 1962
Goheen, Moose, 1952
Goodfellow, Ebbie, 1963
Goulet, Michel, 1998
Grant, Mike, 1950
Green, Shorty, 1962
Griffis, Si, 1950
Hainsworth, George, 1961
Hall, Glenn, 1975
Hall, Joe, 1961
Harvey, Doug, 1973
Hay, George, 1958
Hern, Riley, 1962
Hextall, Bryan, 1969
Holmes, Hap, 1972
Hooper, Tom, 1962
Horner, Red, 1965
Horton, Tim, 1977
Howe, Gordie, 1972
Howe, Syd, 1965
Howell, Harry, 1979
Hull, Bobby, 1983
Hutton, Bouse, 1962
Hyland, Harry, 1962
Irvin, Dick, 1958
Jackson, Busher, 1971
Johnson, Ching, 1958
Johnson, Moose, 1952
Johnson, Tom, 1970
Joliat, Aurel, 1947
Keats, Duke, 1958
Kelly, Red, 1969
Kennedy, Ted, 1966
Keon, Dave, 1986
Lach, Elmer, 1966
Lafleur, Guy, 1988
Lalonde, Newsy, 1950
Laperriere, Jacques, 1987
Lapointe, Guy, 1993
Laprade, Edgar, 1993
Laviolette, Jack, 1962

Lehman, Hughie, 1958
Lemaire, Jacques, 1984
Lemieux, Mario, 1997
LeSueur, Percy, 1961
Lewis, Herbie, 1989
Lindsay, Ted, 1966
Lumley, Harry, 1980
MacKay, Mickey, 1952
Mahovlich, Frank, 1981
Malone, Joe, 1950
Mantha, Sylvio, 1960
Marshall, Jack, 1965
Maxwell, Fred, 1962
McDonald, Lanny, 1992
McGee, Frank, 1945
McGimsie, Billy, 1962
McNamara, George, 1958
Mikita, Stan, 1983
Moore, Dickie, 1974
Moran, Paddy, 1958
Morenz, Howie, 1945
Mosienko, Bill, 1965
Nighbor, Frank, 1947
Noble, Reg, 1962
O'Connor, Buddy, 1988
Oliver, Harry, 1967
Olmstead, Bert, 1985
Orr, Bobby, 1979
Parent, Bernie, 1984
Park, Brad, 1988
Patrick, Lester, 1947
Patrick, Lynn, 1980
Perreault, Gilbert, 1990
Phillips, Tommy, 1945
Pilote, Pierre, 1975
Pitre, Didier, 1962
Plante, Jacques, 1978
Potvin, Denis, 1991
Pratt, Babe, 1966
Primeau, Joe, 1963
Pronovost, Marcel, 1978
Pulford, Bob, 1991
Pulford, Harvey, 1945
Quackenbush, Bill, 1976
Rankin, Frank, 1961
Ratelle, Jean, 1985
Rayner, Chuck, 1973
Reardon, Ken, 1966
Richard, Henri, 1979
Richard, Maurice, 1961
Richardson, George, 1950
Roberts, Gordon, 1971
Robinson, Larry, 1995
Ross, Art, 1945
Russell, Blair, 1965
Russell, Ernie, 1965
Ruttan, Jack, 1962
Salming, Borje, 1996
Savard, Serge, 1986
Sawchuk, Terry, 1971
Scanlan, Fred, 1965
Schmidt, Milt, 1961
Schriner, Sweeney, 1962
Seibert, Earl, 1963
Seibert, Oliver, 1961
Shore, Eddie, 1947
Shutt, Steve, 1993
Siebert, Babe, 1964
Simpson, Joe, 1962
Sittler, Darryl, 1989
Smith, Alf, 1962

Smith, Billy, 1993
Smith, Clint, 1991
Smith, Hooley, 1972
Smith, Tommy, 1973
Stanley, Allan, 1981
Stanley, Barney, 1962
Stastny, Peter, 1998
Stewart, Jack, 1964
Stewart, Nels, 1962
Stuart, Bruce, 1961
Stuart, Hod, 1945
Taylor, Cyclone, 1947
Thompson, Tiny, 1959
Tretiak, Vladislav, 1989
Trihey, Harry, 1950
Trottier, Bryan, 1997
Ullman, Norm, 1982
Vezina, Georges, 1945
Walker, Jack, 1960
Walsh, Marty, 1962
Watson, Harry E., 1962
Watson, Harry P., 1994
Weiland, Cooney, 1971
Westwick, Harry, 1962
Whitcroft, Frederick, 1962
Wilson, Gord, 1962
Worsley, Gump, 1980
Worters, Roy, 1969

BUILDERS
Adams, Charles F., 1960
Adams, Weston W., 1972
Ahearn, Frank, 1962
Ahearne, Bunny, 1977
Allan, Sir Montagu, 1945
Allen, Keith, 1992
Arbour, Al, 1996
Ballard, Harold, 1977
Bauer, Father David, 1989
Bickell, J.P., 1978
Bowman, Scottie, 1991
Brown, George V., 1961
Brown, Walter A., 1962
Buckland, Frank, 1975
Butterfield, Jack, 1980
Calder, Frank, 1947
Campbell, Angus, 1964
Campbell, Clarence, 1966
Cattarinich, Joseph, 1977
Dandurand, Leo, 1963
Dilio, Frank, 1964
Dudley, George, 1958
Dunn, Jimmy, 1968
Eagleson, Alan, 1982
Francis, Emile, 1982
Gibson, Jack, 1976
Gorman, Tommy, 1963
Griffiths, Frank, 1993
Hanley, Bill, 1986
Hay, Charles, 1974
Hendy, Jim, 1968
Hewitt, Foster, 1965
Hewitt, William, 1947
Hume, Fred, 1962
Imlach, Punch, 1984
Ivan, Tommy, 1974
Jennings, Bill, 1975
Johnson, Bob, 1992
Juckes, Gordon, 1979

Kilpatrick, General J.R., 1960
Knox, Seymour III, 1993
Leader, Al, 1969
LeBel, Bob, 1970
Lockhart, Tommy, 1965
Loicq, Paul, 1961
Mariucci, John, 1985
Mathers, Frank, 1992
McLaughlin, Major Frederic, 1963
Milford, Jake, 1984
Molson, Senator Hartland De Montarville, 1973
Murray, Msgr. Athol, 1998
Nelson, Francis, 1947
Norris, Bruce, 1969
Norris, James, 1958
Norris, James D., 1962
Northey, William, 1947
O'Brien, J. Ambrose, 1962
O'Neil, Brian, 1994
Page, Fred, 1993
Patrick, Frank, 1958
Pickard, Allan, 1958
Pilous, Rudy, 1985
Poile, Bud, 1990
Pollock, Sam, 1978
Raymond, Senator Donat, 1958
Robertson, John Ross, 1947
Robinson, Claude, 1947
Ross, Philip, 1976
Sabetzki, Gunther, 1995
Sather, Glen, 1997
Selke, Frank, 1960
Sinden, Harry, 1983
Smith, Frank, 1962
Smyth, Conn, 1958
Snider, Ed, 1988
Stanley of Preston, Lord, 1945
Sutherland, Captain James, 1947
Tarasov, Anatoli, 1974
Torrey, Bill, 1995
Turner, Lloyd, 1958
Tutt, Thayer, 1978
Voss, Carl, 1974
Waghorne, Fred, 1961
Wirtz, Arthur, 1971
Wirtz, Bill, 1976
Ziegler, John, 1987

REFEREES/LINESMEN
Armstrong, Neil, 1991
Ashley, John, 1981
Chadwick, Bill, 1964
D'Amico, John, 1993
Elliott, Chaucer, 1961
Hayes, George, 1988
Hewitson, Bobby, 1963
Ion, Mickey, 1961
Pavelich, Marty, 1987
Rodden, Mike, 1962
Smeaton, Cooper, 1961
Storey, Red, 1967
Udvari, Frank, 1973

World Golf Hall of Fame

MEN
Anderson, Willie, 1975
Armour, Tommy, 1976
Ball, John Jr, 1977
Ballesteros, Seve, 1999
Barnes, Jim, 1989
Boros, Julius, 1982
Braid, James, 1976
Casper, Billy, 1978
Cooper, Lighthouse
    Harry, 1992
Cotton, Henry, 1980
Demaret, Jimmy, 1983
DeVincenzo, Roberto,
    1989
Evans, Chick, 1975
Faldo, Nick, 1997
Floyd, Ray, 1989
Guldahl, Ralph, 1981
Hagen, Walter, 1974
Hilton, Harold, 1978
Hogan, Ben, 1974

Irwin, Hale, 1992
Jones, Bobby, 1974
Little, Lawson, 1980
Littler, Gene, 1990
Locke, Bobby, 1977
Mangrum, Lloyd, 1999
Middlecoff, Cary, 1986
Miller, Johnny, 1998
Morris, Tom Jr, 1975
Morris, Tom Sr, 1976
Nelson, Byron, 1974
Nicklaus, Jack, 1974
Ouimet, Francis, 1974
Palmer, Arnold, 1974
Player, Gary, 1974
Runyan, Paul, 1990
Sarazen, Gene, 1974
Smith, Horton, 1990
Snead, Sam, 1974
Taylor, John H, 1975
Thomson, Peter, 1988
Travers, Jerry, 1976

Travis, Walter, 1979
Trevino, Lee, 1981
Vardon, Harry, 1974
Watson, Tom, 1988

WOMEN
Alcott, Amy, 1999
Berg, Patty, 1974
Bradley, Pat, 1991
Carner, JoAnne, 1985
Daniel, Beth, 2000
Haynie, Sandra, 1977
Howe, Dorothy C.H., 1978
Jameson, Betty, 1951
King, Betsy, 1995
Lopez, Nancy, 1989
Mann, Carol, 1977
Rawls, Betsy, 1987
Sheehan, Patty, 1993
Shore, Dinah, 1994
Suggs, Louise, 1979

Vare, Glenna Collett,
    1975
Wethered, Joyce, 1975
Whitworth, Kathy, 1982
Wright, Mickey, 1976
Zaharias, Babe
    Didrikson, 1974

CONTRIBUTORS
Campbell, William, 1990
Corcoran, Fred, 1975
Crosby, Bing, 1978
Dey, Joe, 1975
Graffis, Herb, 1977
Harlow, Robert, 1988
Hope, Bob, 1983
Jones, Robert Trent, 1987
Roberts, Clifford, 1978
Rodriguez, Chi Chi, 1992
Ross, Donald, 1977
Tufts, Richard, 1992

LPGA Hall of Fame

PLAYERS
Alcott, Amy, 1999
Berg, Patty, 1951
Bradley, Pat, 1991
Carner, JoAnne, 1982
Daniel, Beth, 2000

Haynie, Sandra, 1977
Jameson, Betty, 1951
King, Betsy, 1995
Lopez, Nancy, 1987
Mann, Carol, 1977
Rawls, Betsy, 1960

Sheehan, Patty, 1993
Suggs, Louise, 1951
Whitworth, Kathy, 1975
Wright, Mickey, 1964
Zaharias, Babe
    Didrikson, 1951

CONTRIBUTOR
Shore, Dinah, 1994

ANNUAL SPORTS AWARD WINNERS

Associated Press Athlete of the Year

YEAR	MALE
1931	Pepper Martin, baseball
1932	Gene Sarazen, golf
1933	Carl Hubbell, baseball
1934	Dizzy Dean, baseball
1935	Joe Louis, boxing
1936	Jesse Owens, track
1937	Don Budge, tennis
1938	Don Budge, tennis
1939	Nile Kinnick, football
1940	Tom Harmon, football
1941	Joe DiMaggio, baseball
1942	Frank Sinkwich, football
1943	Gunder Haegg, track
1944	Byron Nelson, golf
1945	Byron Nelson, golf
1946	Glenn Davis, football
1947	Johnny Lujack, football
1948	Lou Boudreau, baseball
1949	Leon Hart, football
1950	Jim Konstanty, baseball
1951	Dick Kazmaier, football
1952	Bob Mathias, track
1953	Ben Hogan, golf
1954	Willie Mays, baseball
1955	Hopalong Cassady, football
1956	Mickey Mantle, baseball
1957	Ted Williams, baseball
1958	Herb Elliot, track
1959	Ingemar Johansson, boxing
1960	Rafer Johnson, track
1961	Roger Maris, baseball
1962	Maury Wills, baseball
1963	Sandy Koufax, baseball
1964	Don Schollander, swimming
1965	Sandy Koufax, baseball
1966	Frank Robinson, baseball
1967	Carl Yastrzemski, baseball
1968	Denny McLain, baseball
1969	Tom Seaver, baseball
1970	George Blanda, football
1971	Lee Trevino, golf
1972	Mark Spitz, swimming
1973	O.J. Simpson, football
1974	Muhammad Ali, boxing
1975	Fred Lynn, baseball
1976	Bruce Jenner, track
1977	Steve Cauthen, horse racing
1978	Ron Guidry, baseball
1979	Willie Stargell, baseball
1980	US Olympic hockey team
1981	John McEnroe, tennis
1982	Wayne Gretzky, hockey
1983	Carl Lewis, track
1984	Carl Lewis, track
1985	Dwight Gooden, baseball
1986	Larry Bird, basketball
1987	Ben Johnson, track
1988	Orel Hershiser, baseball
1989	Joe Montana, football
1990	Joe Montana, football
1991	Michael Jordan, basketball
1992	Michael Jordan, basketball
1993	Michael Jordan, basketball
1994	George Foreman, boxing
1995	Cal Ripken, baseball
1996	Michael Johnson, track
1997	Tiger Woods, golf
1998	Mark McGwire, baseball

YEAR	FEMALE
1931	Helene Madison, swimming
1932	Babe Didrikson, track
1933	Helen Jacobs, tennis
1934	Virginia Van Wie, golf
1935	Helen Wills Moody, tennis
1936	Helen Stephens, track
1937	Katherine Rawls, swimming
1937	Patty Berg, golf
1939	Alice Marble, tennis
1940	Alice Marble, tennis
1941	Betty Hicks Newell, golf
1942	Gloria Callen, swimming
1943	Patty Berg, golf
1944	Ann Curtis, swimming
1945	Babe Didrikson Zaharias, golf
1946	Babe Didrikson Zaharias, golf
1947	Babe Didrikson Zaharias, golf
1948	Fanny Blankers-Koen, track
1949	Marlene Bauer, golf
1950	Babe Didrikson Zaharias, golf
1951	Maureen Connolly, tennis
1952	Maureen Connolly, tennis
1953	Maureen Connolly, tennis
1954	Babe Didrikson Zaharias, golf
1955	Patty Berg, golf
1956	Pat McCormick, diving
1957	Althea Gibson, tennis
1958	Althea Gibson, tennis
1959	Maria Bueno, tennis
1960	Wilma Rudolph, track
1961	Wilma Rudolph, track
1962	Dawn Fraser, swimming
1963	Mickey Wright, golf
1964	Mickey Wright, golf
1965	Kathy Whitworth, golf
1966	Kathy Whitworth, golf
1967	Billie Jean King, tennis
1968	Peggy Fleming, skating
1969	Debbie Meyer, swimming
1970	Chi Cheng, track
1971	Evonne Goolagong, tennis
1972	Olga Korbut, gymnastics
1973	Billie Jean King, tennis
1974	Chris Evert, tennis
1975	Chris Evert, tennis
1976	Nadia Comaneci, gymnastics
1977	Chris Evert, tennis
1978	Nancy Lopez, golf
1979	Tracy Austin, tennis
1980	Chris Evert Lloyd, tennis
1981	Tracy Austin, tennis
1982	Mary Decker Tabb, track
1983	Martina Navratilova, tennis
1984	Mary Lou Retton, gymnastics
1985	Nancy Lopez, golf
1986	Martina Navratilova, tennis
1987	Jackie Joyner-Kersee, track
1988	Florence Griffith Joyner, track
1989	Steffi Graf, tennis
1990	Beth Daniel, golf
1991	Monica Seles, tennis
1992	Monica Seles, tennis
1993	Sheryl Swoopes, basketball
1994	Bonnie Blair, speed skating
1995	Rebecca Lobo, basketball
1996	Amy Van Dyken, swimming
1997	Martina Hingis, tennis
1998	Se Ri Pak, golf

James E. Sullivan Memorial Award

YEAR	WINNER
1930	Bobby Jones, golf
1931	Barney Berlinger, track
1932	Jim Bausch, track
1933	Glenn Cunningham, track
1934	Bill Bonthron, track
1935	Lawson Little, golf
1936	Glenn Morris, track
1937	Don Budge, tennis
1938	Don Lash, track
1939	Joe Burk, rowing
1940	Greg Rice, track
1941	Leslie MacMitchell, track
1942	Cornelius Warmerdam, track
1943	Gilbert Dodds, track
1944	Ann Curtis, swimming
1945	Doc Blanchard, football
1946	Arnold Tucker, football
1947	John B. Kelly, Jr, rowing
1948	Bob Mathias, track
1949	Dick Button, skating
1950	Fred Wilt, track
1951	Bob Richards, track
1952	Horace Ashenfelter, track
1953	Sammy Lee, diving
1954	Mal Whitfield, track
1955	Harrison Dillard, track
1956	Pat McCormick, diving
1957	Bobby Morrow, track
1958	Glenn Davis, track
1959	Parry O'Brien, track
1960	Rafer Johnson, track
1961	Wilma Rudolph, track

☆ Chase's 2000 SPORTS Calendar of Events ☆

YEAR	WINNER
1962	James Beatty, track
1963	John Pennel, track
1964	Don Schollander, swimming
1965	Bill Bradley, basketball
1966	Jim Ryun, track
1967	Randy Matson, track
1968	Debbie Meyer, swimming
1969	Bill Toomey, track
1970	John Kinsella, swimming
1971	Mark Spitz, swimming
1972	Frank Shorter, track
1973	Bill Walton, basketball
1974	Rick Wohlhuter, track
1975	Tim Shaw, swimming
1976	Bruce Jenner, track
1977	John Naber, swimming
1978	Tracy Caulkins, swimming
1979	Kurt Thomas, gymnastics
1980	Eric Heiden, speed skating
1981	Carl Lewis, track
1982	Mary Decker, track
1983	Edwin Moses, track
1984	Greg Louganis, diving
1985	Joan Benoit Samuelson, track
1986	Jackie Joyner-Kersee, track
1987	Jim Abbott, baseball
1988	Florence Griffith Joyner, track
1989	Janet Evans, swimming
1990	John Smith, wrestling
1991	Mike Powell, track
1992	Bonnie Blair, speed skating
1993	Charlie Ward, football
1994	Dan Jansen, speed skating
1995	Bruce Baumgartner, wrestling
1996	Michael Johnson, track
1997	Peyton Manning, football
1998	Chamique Holdsclaw, basketball

The Sporting News Sportsman of the Year

YEAR	WINNER
1968	Denny McLain, baseball
1969	Tom Seaver, baseball
1970	John Wooden, basketball
1971	Lee Trevino, golf
1972	Charles O. Finley, baseball
1973	O.J. Simpson, football
1974	Lou Brock, baseball
1975	Archie Griffin, football
1976	Larry O'Brien, basketball
1977	Steve Cauthen, horse racing
1978	Ron Guidry, baseball
1979	Willie Stargell, baseball
1980	George Brett, baseball
1981	Wayne Gretzky, hockey
1982	Whitey Herzog, baseball
1983	Bowie Kuhn, baseball
1984	Peter Ueberroth, Los Angeles Oympics
1985	Pete Rose, baseball
1986	Larry Bird, basketball
1987	no award
1988	Jackie Joyner-Kersee, track
1989	Joe Montana, football
1990	Nolan Ryan, baseball
1991	Michael Jordan, basketball
1992	Mike Krzyzewski, basketball
1993	Cito Gaston and Pat Gillick, baseball
1994	Emmitt Smith, football
1995	Cal Ripken, baseball
1996	Joe Torre, baseball
1997	Mark McGwire, baseball
1998	Mark McGwire, baseball and Sammy Sosa, baseball

Sports Illustrated Sportsman of the Year

YEAR	WINNER
1954	Roger Bannister, track
1955	Johnny Podres, baseball
1956	Bobby Morrow, track
1957	Stan Musial, baseball
1958	Rafer Johnson, track
1959	Ingemar Johansson, boxing
1960	Arnold Palmer, golf
1961	Jerry Lucas, basketball
1962	Terry Baker, football
1963	Pete Rozelle, football
1964	Ken Venturi, golf
1965	Sandy Koufax, baseball
1966	Jim Ryun, track
1967	Carl Yastrzemski, baseball
1968	Bill Russell, basketball
1969	Tom Seaver, baseball
1970	Bobby Orr, hockey
1971	Lee Trevino, golf
1972	Billie Jean King, tennis John Wooden, basketball
1973	Jackie Stewart, auto racing
1974	Muhammad Ali, boxing
1975	Pete Rose, baseball
1976	Chris Evert, tennis
1977	Steve Cauthen, horse racing
1978	Jack Nicklaus, golf
1979	Terry Bradshaw, football Willie Stargell, baseball
1980	US Olympic hockey team
1981	Sugar Ray Leonard, boxing
1982	Wayne Gretzky, hockey
1983	Mary Decker, track
1984	Mary Lou Retton, gymnastics Edwin Moses, track
1985	Kareem Abdul-Jabbar, basketball
1986	Joe Paterno, football
1987	"8 Athletes Who Care": Bob Bourne, hockey Kip Keino, track Judi Brown King, track
	Dale Murphy, baseball
	Chip Rives, football
	Patty Sheehan, golf
	Rory Sparrow, basketball
	Reggie Williams, football
1988	Orel Hershiser, baseball
1989	Greg LeMond, cycling
1990	Joe Montana, football
1991	Michael Jordan, basketball
1992	Arthur Ashe, tennis
1993	Don Shula, football
1994	Bonnie Blair, speed skating Johan Olav Koss, speed skating
1995	Cal Ripken, baseball
1996	Tiger Woods, golf
1997	Dean Smith, basketball
1998	Mark McGwire and Sammy Sosa, baseball

Heisman Trophy

YEAR	WINNER
1935	Jay Berwanger, Chicago, QB
1936	Larry Kelley, Yale, E
1937	Clint Frank, Yale, HB
1938	Davey O'Brien, TCU, QB
1939	Nile Kinnick, Iowa, HB
1940	Tom Harmon, Michigan, HB
1941	Bruce Smith, Minnesota, HB
1942	Frank Sinkwich, Georgia, TB
1943	Angelo Bertelli, Notre Dame, QB
1944	Les Horvath, Ohio State, TB-QB
1945	Doc Blanchard, Army, FB
1946	Glenn Davis, Army, HB
1947	Johnny Lujack, Notre Dame, QB
1948	Doak Walker, SMU, HB
1949	Leon Hart, Notre Dame, E
1950	Vic Janowicz, Ohio State, HB
1951	Dick Kazmaier, Princeton, TB

YEAR	WINNER
1952	Billy Vessels, Oklahoma, HB
1953	Johnny Lattner, Notre Dame, HB
1954	Alan Ameche, Wisconsin, FB
1955	Howard Cassady, Ohio State, HB
1956	Paul Hornung, Notre Dame, QB
1957	John David Crow, Texas A&M, HB
1958	Pete Dawkins, Army, HB
1959	Billy Cannon, LSU, HB
1960	Joe Bellino, Navy, QB
1961	Ernie Davis, Syracuse, HB
1962	Terry Baker, Oregon State, QB
1963	Roger Staubach, Navy, QB
1964	John Huarte, Notre Dame, QB
1965	Mike Garrett, USC, HB
1966	Steve Spurrier, Florida, QB
1967	Gary Beban, UCLA, QB
1968	O.J. Simpson, USC, HB
1969	Steve Owens, Oklahoma, HB
1970	Jim Plunkett, Stanford, QB
1971	Pat Sullivan, Auburn, QB
1972	Johnny Rodgers, Nebraska, FL
1973	John Cappelletti, Penn State, RB
1974	Archie Griffin, Ohio State, RB
1975	Archie Griffin, Ohio State, RB
1976	Tony Dorsett, Pittsburgh, RB
1977	Earl Campbell, Texas, RB
1978	Billy Sims, Oklahoma, RB
1979	Charles White, USC, RB
1980	George Rogers, South Carolina, RB
1981	Marcus Allen, USC, RB
1982	Herschel Walker, Georgia, RB
1983	Mike Rozier, Nebraska, RB
1984	Doug Flutie, Boston College, QB
1985	Bo Jackson, Auburn, RB
1986	Vinny Testaverde, Miami (FL), QB
1987	Tim Brown, Notre Dame, WR
1988	Barry Sanders, Oklahoma State, RB
1989	Andre Ware, Houston, QB
1990	Ty Detmer, BYU, QB
1991	Desmond Howard, Michigan, WR
1992	Gino Torretta, Miami (FL), QB
1993	Charlie Ward, Florida State, QB
1994	Rashaan Salaam, Colorado, RB
1995	Eddie George, Ohio State, RB
1996	Danny Wuerffel, Florida, QB
1997	Charles Woodson, Michigan, DB/WR
1998	Ricky Williams, Texas, RB

CHAMPIONSHIPS: TEAM AND INDIVIDUAL

World Series

YEAR	WINNER	LOSER	GAMES	YEAR	WINNER	LOSER	GAMES
1903	Boston AL	Pittsburgh NL	5–3	1951	New York AL	New York NL	4–2
1904	No series played			1952	New York AL	Brooklyn NL	4–3
1905	New York NL	Philadelphia AL	4–1	1953	New York AL	Brooklyn NL	4–2
1906	Chicago AL	Chicago NL	4–2	1954	New York NL	Cleveland AL	4–0
1907	Chicago NL	Detroit AL	4–0*	1955	Brooklyn NL	New York AL	4–3
1908	Chicago NL	Detroit AL	4–1	1956	New York AL	Brooklyn NL	4–3
1909	Pittsburgh NL	Detroit AL	4–3	1957	Milwaukee NL	New York AL	4–3
1910	Philadelphia AL	Chicago NL	4–1	1958	New York AL	Milwaukee NL	4–3
1911	Philadelphia AL	New York NL	4–2	1959	Los Angeles NL	Chicago AL	4–2
1912	Boston AL	New York NL	4–3*	1960	Pittsburgh NL	New York AL	4–3
1913	Philadelphia AL	New York NL	4–1	1961	New York AL	Cincinnati NL	4–1
1914	Boston NL	Philadelphia AL	4–0	1962	New York AL	San Francisco NL	4–3
1915	Boston AL	Philadelphia NL	4–1	1963	Los Angeles NL	New York AL	4–0
1916	Boston AL	Brooklyn NL	4–1	1964	St. Louis NL	New York AL	4–3
1917	Chicago AL	New York NL	4–2	1965	Los Angeles NL	Minnesota AL	4–3
1918	Boston AL	Chicago NL	4–2	1966	Baltimore AL	Los Angeles NL	4–0
1919	Cincinnati NL	Chicago AL	5–3	1967	St. Louis NL	Boston AL	4–3
1920	Cleveland AL	Brooklyn NL	5–2	1968	Detroit AL	St. Louis NL	4–3
1921	New York NL	New York AL	5–3	1969	New York NL	Baltimore AL	4–1
1922	New York NL	New York AL	4–0*	1970	Baltimore AL	Cincinnati NL	4–1
1923	New York AL	New York NL	4–2	1971	Pittsburgh NL	Baltimore AL	4–3
1924	Washington AL	New York NL	4–3	1972	Oakland AL	Cincinnati NL	4–3
1925	Pittsburgh NL	Washington AL	4–3	1973	Oakland AL	New York NL	4–3
1926	St. Louis NL	New York AL	4–3	1974	Oakland AL	Los Angeles NL	4–1
1927	New York AL	Pittsburgh NL	4–0	1975	Cincinnati NL	Boston AL	4–3
1928	New York AL	St. Louis NL	4–0	1976	Cincinnati NL	New York AL	4–0
1929	Philadelphia AL	Chicago NL	4–1	1977	New York AL	Los Angeles NL	4–2
1930	Philadelphia AL	St. Louis NL	4–2	1978	New York AL	Los Angeles NL	4–2
1931	St. Louis NL	Philadelphia AL	4–3	1979	Pittsburgh NL	Baltimore AL	4–3
1932	New York AL	Chicago NL	4–0	1980	Philadelphia NL	Kansas City AL	4–2
1933	New York NL	Washington AL	4–1	1981	Los Angeles NL	New York AL	4–2
1934	St. Louis NL	Detroit AL	4–3	1982	St. Louis NL	Milwaukee AL	4–3
1935	Detroit AL	Chicago NL	4–2	1983	Baltimore AL	Philadelphia NL	4–1
1936	New York AL	New York NL	4–2	1984	Detroit AL	San Diego NL	4–1
1937	New York AL	New York NL	4–1	1985	Kansas City AL	St. Louis NL	4–3
1938	New York AL	Chicago NL	4–0	1986	New York NL	Boston AL	4–3
1939	New York AL	Cincinnati NL	4–0	1987	Minnesota AL	St. Louis NL	4–3
1940	Cincinnati NL	Detroit AL	4–3	1988	Los Angeles NL	Oakland AL	4–1
1941	New York AL	Brooklyn NL	4–1	1989	Oakland AL	San Francisco NL	4–0
1942	St. Louis NL	New York AL	5–1	1990	Cincinnati NL	Oakland AL	4–0
1943	New York AL	St. Louis NL	4–1	1991	Minnesota AL	Atlanta NL	4–3
1944	St. Louis NL	St. Louis AL	4–2	1992	Toronto AL	Atlanta NL	4–2
1945	Detroit AL	Chicago NL	4–3	1993	Toronto AL	Philadelphia NL	4–2
1946	St. Louis NL	Boston AL	4–3	1994	Series canceled		
1947	New York AL	Brooklyn NL	4–3	1995	Atlanta NL	Cleveland AL	4–2
1948	Cleveland AL	Boston NL	4–2	1996	New York AL	Atlanta NL	4–2
1949	New York AL	Brooklyn NL	4–1	1997	Florida NL	Cleveland AL	4–3
1950	New York AL	Philadelphia NL	4–0	1998	New York AL	San Diego NL	4–0

* One tie

Super Bowl

GAME	DATE	PLACE	WINNER	LOSER	SCORE
I	January 15, 1967	Los Angeles	Green Bay NFL	Kansas City AFL	35–10
II	January 14, 1968	Miami	Green Bay NFL	Oakland AFL	33–14
III	January 12, 1969	Miami	New York AFL	Baltimore NFL	16–7
IV	January 11, 1970	New Orleans	Kansas City AFL	Minnesota NFL	23–7
V	January 17, 1971	Miami	Baltimore AFC	Dallas NFC	16–13
VI	January 16, 1972	New Orleans	Dallas NFC	Miami AFC	24–3
VII	January 14, 1973	Los Angeles	Miami AFC	Washington NFC	14–7
VIII	January 13, 1974	Houston	Miami AFC	Minnesota NFC	24–7
IX	January 12, 1975	New Orleans	Pittsburgh AFC	Minnesota NFC	16–6
X	January 18, 1976	Miami	Pittsburgh AFC	Dallas NFC	21–17
XI	January 9, 1977	Pasadena	Oakland AFC	Minnesota NFC	32–14
XII	January 15, 1978	New Orleans	Dallas NFC	Denver AFC	27–10
XIII	January 21, 1979	Miami	Pittsburgh AFC	Dallas NFC	35–31
XIV	January 20, 1980	Pasadena	Pittsburgh AFC	Los Angeles NFC	31–19
XV	January 25, 1981	New Orleans	Oakland AFC	Philadelphia NFC	27–10
XVI	January 24, 1982	Pontiac, MI	San Francisco NFC	Cincinnati AFC	26–21
XVII	January 30, 1983	Pasadena	Washington NFC	Miami AFC	27–17
XVIII	January 22, 1984	Tampa	Los Angeles AFC	Washington NFC	38–9
XIX	January 20, 1985	Stanford, CA	San Francisco NFC	Miami AFC	38–16
XX	January 26, 1986	New Orleans	Chicago NFC	New England AFC	46–10
XXI	January 25, 1987	Pasadena	New York NFC	Denver AFC	39–20
XXII	January 31, 1988	San Diego	Washington NFC	Denver AFC	42–10
XXIII	January 22, 1989	Miami	San Francisco NFC	Cincinnati AFC	20–16
XXIV	January 28, 1990	New Orleans	San Francisco NFC	Denver AFC	55–10
XXV	January 27, 1991	Tampa	New York NFC	Buffalo AFC	20–19
XXVI	January 26, 1992	Minneapolis	Washington NFC	Buffalo AFC	37–24
XXVII	January 31, 1993	Pasadena	Dallas NFC	Buffalo AFC	52–17
XXVIII	January 30, 1994	Atlanta	Dallas NFC	Buffalo AFC	30–13
XXIX	January 29, 1995	Miami	San Francisco NFC	San Diego AFC	49–26
XXX	January 28, 1996	Tempe, AZ	Dallas NFC	Pittsburgh AFC	27–17
XXXI	January 26, 1997	New Orleans	Green Bay NFC	New England AFC	35–21
XXXII	January 25, 1998	San Diego	Denver AFC	Green Bay NFC	31–24
XXXIII	January 31, 1999	Miami	Denver AFC	Atlanta NFC	34–19

College Football National Championship

Selected by: the Helms Athletic Foundation (1883–1935); the Dickinson System (1924–40); the Associated Press (1936–   ); United Press (1950–57); International News Service (1952–57); United Press International (1958–90); the Football Writers Association of America (1954–   ); the National Football Foundation and Hall of Fame (1959–   ); *USA Today*/CNN (1991–96); and *USA Today*/ESPN (1997–   ). In 1991, the American Football Coaches Association switched its poll from UPI to *USA Today*/CNN.

YEAR	TEAM				
1883	Yale	1899	Harvard	1916	Pittsburgh
1884	Yale	1900	Yale	1917	Georgia Tech
1885	Princeton	1901	Michigan	1918	Pittsburgh
1886	Yale	1902	Michigan	1919	Harvard
1887	Yale	1903	Princeton	1920	California
1888	Yale	1904	Penn	1921	Cornell
1889	Princeton	1905	Chicago	1922	Cornell
1890	Harvard	1906	Princeton	1923	Illinois
1891	Yale	1907	Yale	1924	Notre Dame
1892	Yale	1908	Penn	1925	Alabama (H)
1893	Princeton	1909	Yale		Dartmouth (D)
1894	Yale	1910	Harvard	1926	Alabama (H)
1895	Penn	1911	Princeton		Stanford (D)
1896	Princeton	1912	Harvard	1927	Illinois
1897	Penn	1913	Harvard	1928	Georgia Tech (H)
1898	Harvard	1914	Army		USC (D)
		1915	Cornell	1929	Notre Dame

YEAR	TEAM
1930	Notre Dame
1931	USC
1932	USC (H)
	Michigan (D)
1933	Michigan
1934	Minnesota
1935	Minnesota (H)
	SMU (D)
1936	Minnesota
1937	Pittsburgh
1938	TCU
1939	Texas A&M
1940	Minnesota
1941	Minnesota
1942	Ohio State
1943	Notre Dame
1944	Army
1945	Army
1946	Notre Dame
1947	Notre Dame
1948	Michigan
1949	Notre Dame
1950	Oklahoma
1951	Tennessee
1952	Michigan State (AP, UP)
	Georgia Tech (INS)
1953	Maryland
1954	Ohio State (AP, INS)
	UCLA (UP, FW)
1955	Oklahoma
1956	Oklahoma
1957	Auburn (AP)
	Ohio State (UP, FW, INS)
1958	LSU (AP, UPI)
	Iowa (FW)
1959	Syracuse
1960	Minnesota (AP, UPI, NFF)
	Mississippi (FW)
1961	Alabama (AP, UPI, NFF)
	Ohio State (FW)
1962	USC
1963	Texas
1964	Alabama (AP, UPI)
	Arkansas (FW)
	Notre Dame (NFF)
1965	Alabama (AP, FW—tie)
	Michigan State (UPI, NFF, FW—tie)
1966	Notre Dame (AP, UPI, FW, NFF—tie)
	Michigan State (NFF—tie)
1967	USC
1968	Ohio State
1969	Texas
1970	Nebraska (AP, FW)
	Texas (UPI, NFF—tie)
	Ohio State (NFF—tie)
1971	Nebraska
1972	USC
1973	Notre Dame (AP, FW, NFF)
	Alabama (UPI)
1974	Oklahoma (AP)
	USC (UPI, FW, NFF)
1975	Oklahoma
1976	Pittsburgh
1977	Notre Dame
1978	Alabama (AP, FW, NFF)
	USC (UPI)
1979	Alabama
1980	Georgia
1981	Clemson
1982	Penn State
1983	Miami, FL
1984	Brigham Young
1985	Oklahoma
1986	Penn State
1987	Miami, FL
1988	Notre Dame
1989	Miami, FL
1990	Colorado (AP, FW, NFF)
	Georgia Tech (UPI)
1991	Miami, FL (AP)
	Washington (USA, FW, NFF)
1992	Alabama
1993	Florida State
1994	Nebraska
1995	Nebraska
1996	Florida
1997	Michigan (AP, FW, NFF)
	Nebraska (USA)
1998	Tennessee

(H) = Helms Athletic Foundation
(D) = Dickinson System
(AP) = Associated Press
(UP) = United Press International
(INS) = International News Service

(UPI) = United Press International
(FW) = Football Writers Association of America
(NFF) = National Football Foundation
(USA) = *USA Today*

NBA Championship

SEASON	WINNER	LOSER	GAMES
1946–1947	Philadelphia Warriors	Chicago Stags	4–1
1947–1948	Baltimore Bullets	Philadelphia Warriors	4–2
1948–1949	Minneapolis Lakers	Washington Capitols	4–2
1949–1950	Minneapolis Lakers	Syracuse Nationals	4–2
1950–1951	Rochester Royals	New York Knicks	4–3
1951–1952	Minneapolis Lakers	New York Knicks	4–3
1952–1953	Minneapolis Lakers	New York Knicks	4–1
1953–1954	Minneapolis Lakers	Syracuse Nationals	4–3
1954–1955	Syracuse Nationals	Ft. Wayne Pistons	4–3
1955–1956	Philadelphia Warriors	Ft. Wayne Pistons	4–1
1956–1957	Boston Celtics	St. Louis Hawks	4–3
1957–1958	St. Louis Hawks	Boston Celtics	4–2
1958–1959	Boston Celtics	Minneapolis Lakers	4–0
1959–1960	Boston Celtics	St. Louis Hawks	4–3
1960–1961	Boston Celtics	St. Louis Hawks	4–1
1961–1962	Boston Celtics	Los Angeles Lakers	4–3
1962–1963	Boston Celtics	Los Angeles Lakers	4–2
1963–1964	Boston Celtics	San Francisco Warriors	4–1
1964–1965	Boston Celtics	Los Angeles Lakers	4–1
1965–1966	Boston Celtics	Los Angeles Lakers	4–3

SEASON	WINNER	LOSER	GAMES
1966–1967	Philadelphia 76ers	San Francisco Warriors	4–2
1967–1968	Boston Celtics	Los Angeles Lakers	4–2
1968–1969	Boston Celtics	Los Angeles Lakers	4–3
1969–1970	New York Knicks	Los Angeles Lakers	4–3
1970–1971	Milwaukee Bucks	Baltimore Bullets	4–0
1971–1972	Los Angeles Lakers	New York Knicks	4–1
1972–1973	New York Knicks	Los Angeles Lakers	4–1
1973–1974	Boston Celtics	Milwaukee Bucks	4–3
1974–1975	Golden State Warriors	Washington Bullets	4–0
1975–1976	Boston Celtics	Phoenix Suns	4–2
1976–1977	Portland Trail Blazers	Philadelphia 76ers	4–2
1977–1978	Washington Bullets	Seattle SuperSonics	4–3
1978–1979	Seattle SuperSonics	Washington Bullets	4–1
1979–1980	Los Angeles Lakers	Philadelphia 76ers	4–2
1980–1981	Boston Celtics	Houston Rockets	4–2
1981–1982	Los Angeles Lakers	Philadelphia 76ers	4–2
1982–1983	Philadelphia 76ers	Los Angeles Lakers	4–0
1983–1984	Boston Celtics	Los Angeles Lakers	4–3
1984–1985	Los Angeles Lakers	Boston Celtics	4–2
1985–1986	Boston Celtics	Houston Rockets	4–2
1986–1987	Los Angeles Lakers	Boston Celtics	4–2
1987–1988	Los Angeles Lakers	Detroit Pistons	4–3
1988–1989	Detroit Pistons	Los Angeles Lakers	4–0
1989–1990	Detroit Pistons	Portland Trail Blazers	4–1
1990–1991	Chicago Bulls	Los Angeles Lakers	4–1
1991–1992	Chicago Bulls	Portland Trail Blazers	4–2
1992–1993	Chicago Bulls	Phoenix Suns	4–2
1993–1994	Houston Rockets	New York Knicks	4–3
1994–1995	Houston Rockets	Orlando Magic	4–0
1995–1996	Chicago Bulls	Seattle SuperSonics	4–2
1996–1997	Chicago Bulls	Utah Jazz	4–2
1997–1998	Chicago Bulls	Utah Jazz	4–2
1998–1999	San Antonio Spurs	New York Knicks	4–1

NCAA Men's Basketball National Tournament

YEAR	WINNER	RUNNER-UP	SCORE	THIRD PLACE*	
1939	Oregon	Ohio State	46–33	Oklahoma	Villanova
1940	Indiana	Kansas	60–42	Duquesne	USC
1941	Wisconsin	Washington State	39–34	Arkansas	Pittsburgh
1942	Stanford	Dartmouth	53–38	Colorado	Kentucky
1943	Wyoming	Georgetown	46–34	DePaul	Texas
1944	Utah	Dartmouth	42–40 (OT)	Iowa State	Ohio State
1945	Oklahoma A&M	NYU	49–45	Arkansas	Ohio State

YEAR	WINNER	RUNNER-UP	SCORE	THIRD PLACE*	FOURTH PLACE*
1946	Oklahoma A&M	North Carolina	43–40	Ohio State	California
1947	Holy Cross	Oklahoma	58–47	Texas	CCNY
1948	Kentucky	Baylor	58–42	Holy Cross	Kansas State
1949	Kentucky	Oklahoma A&M	46–36	Illinois	Oregon State
1950	CCNY	Bradley	71–68	NC State	Baylor
1951	Kentucky	Kansas State	68–58	Illinois	Oklahoma A&M
1952	Kansas	St. John's	80–63	Illinois	Santa Clara
1953	Indiana	Kansas	69–68	Washington	LSU
1954	La Salle	Bradley	92–76	Penn State	USC
1955	San Francisco	La Salle	77–63	Colorado	Iowa
1956	San Francisco	Iowa	83–71	Temple	SMU

YEAR	WINNER	RUNNER-UP	SCORE	THIRD PLACE*	FOURTH PLACE*
1957	North Carolina	Kansas	54–53 (3OT)	San Francisco	Michigan State
1958	Kentucky	Seattle	84–72	Temple	Kansas State
1959	California	West Virginia	71–70	Cincinnati	Louisville
1960	Ohio State	California	75–55	Cincinnati	NYU
1961	Cincinnati	Ohio State	70–65 (OT)	St. Joseph's (PA)	Utah
1962	Cincinnati	Ohio State	71–59	Wake Forest	UCLA
1963	Loyola (IL)	Cincinnati	60–58 (OT)	Duke	Oregon State
1964	UCLA	Duke	98–83	Michigan	Kansas State
1965	UCLA	Michigan	91–80	Princeton	Wichita State
1966	Texas Western	Kentucky	72–65	Duke	Utah
1967	UCLA	Dayton	79–64	Houston	North Carolina
1968	UCLA	North Carolina	78–55	Ohio State	Houston
1969	UCLA	Purdue	92–72	Drake	North Carolina
1970	UCLA	Jacksonville	80–69	New Mexico State	St. Bonaventure
1971	UCLA	Villanova	68–62	Western Kentucky	Kansas
1972	UCLA	Florida State	81–76	North Carolina	Louisville
1973	UCLA	Memphis State	87–66	Indiana	Providence
1974	NC State	Marquette	76–64	UCLA	Kansas
1975	UCLA	Kentucky	92–85	Louisville	Syracuse
1976	Indiana	Michigan	86–68	UCLA	Rutgers
1977	Marquette	North Carolina	67–59	UNLV	NC-Charlotte
1978	Kentucky	Duke	94–88	Arkansas	Notre Dame
1979	Michigan State	Indiana State	75–64	DePaul	Penn
1980	Louisville	UCLA	59–54	Purdue	Iowa
1981	Indiana	North Carolina	63–50	Virginia	LSU

				THIRD PLACE*	
1982	North Carolina	Georgetown	63–62	Houston	Louisville
1983	NC State	Houston	54–52	Georgia	Louisville
1984	Georgetown	Houston	84–75	Kentucky	Virginia
1985	Villanova	Georgetown	66–64	Memphis State	St. John's
1986	Louisville	Duke	72–69	Kansas	LSU
1987	Indiana	Syracuse	74–73	Providence	UNLV
1988	Kansas	Oklahoma	83–79	Arizona	Duke
1989	Michigan	Seton Hall	80–79 (OT)	Duke	Illinois
1990	UNLV	Duke	103–73	Arkansas	Georgia Tech
1991	Duke	Kansas	72–65	North Carolina	UNLV
1992	Duke	Michigan	71–51	Cincinnati	Indiana
1993	North Carolina	Michigan	77–71	Kansas	Kentucky
1994	Arkansas	Duke	77–72	Arizona	Florida
1995	UCLA	Arkansas	89–78	North Carolina	Oklahoma State
1996	Kentucky	Syracuse	76–67	Massachusetts	Mississippi State
1997	Arizona	Kentucky	84–79 (OT)	Minnesota	North Carolina
1998	Kentucky	Utah	78–69	Stanford	North Carolina
1999	Connecticut	Duke	77–74	Ohio State	Michigan State

*In the years 1939–1945 and 1982 through the present, no competition was held between the two teams eliminated in the national semifinals. In the intervening years, 1946–1981, such a game was played.

NCAA Women's Basketball National Tournament

YEAR	WINNER	RUNNER-UP	SCORE	THIRD PLACE*	
1982	Louisiana Tech	Cheyney State	76–62	Maryland	Tennessee
1983	USC	Louisiana Tech	69–67	Georgia	Old Dominion
1984	USC	Tennessee	72–61	Cheyney State	Louisiana Tech
1985	Old Dominion	Georgia	70–65	NE Louisiana	Western Kentucky
1986	Texas	USC	97–81	Tennessee	Western Kentucky
1987	Tennessee	Louisiana Tech	67–44	Long Beach State	Texas
1988	Louisiana Tech	Auburn	56–54	Long Beach State	Tennessee
1989	Tennessee	Auburn	76–60	Louisiana Tech	Maryland
1990	Stanford	Tennessee	88–81	Louisiana Tech	Virginia
1991	Tennessee	Virginia	70–67 (OT)	Connecticut	Stanford
1992	Stanford	Western Kentucky	78–62	SW Missouri State	Virginia
1993	Texas Tech	Ohio State	84–82	Iowa	Vanderbilt
1994	North Carolina	Louisiana Tech	60–59	Alabama	Purdue
1995	Connecticut	Tennessee	70–64	Georgia	Stanford
1996	Tennessee	Georgia	83–65	Connecticut	Stanford
1997	Tennessee	Old Dominion	68–59	Stanford	Notre Dame
1998	Tennessee	Louisiana Tech	93–75	NC State	Arkansas
1999	Purdue	Duke	62–45	Georgia	Louisiana Tech

*There is no consolation game between losers in the semifinals.

College Basketball National Invitation Tournament

YEAR	WINNER	RUNNER-UP	SCORE
1938	Temple	Colorado	60–36
1939	Long Island U (Brooklyn)	Loyola (IL)	44–32
1940	Colorado	Duquesne	51–40
1941	Long Island U (Brooklyn)	Ohio	56–42
1942	West Virginia	Western Kentucky	47–45
1943	St. John's	Toledo	48–27
1944	St. John's	DePaul	47–39
1945	DePaul	Bowling Green	71–54
1946	Kentucky	Rhode Island	46–45
1947	Utah	Kentucky	49–45
1948	Saint Louis	New York University	65–52
1949	San Francisco	Loyola (IL)	48–47
1950	CCNY	Bradley	69–61
1951	Brigham Young	Dayton	62–43
1952	La Salle	Dayton	75–64
1953	Seton Hall	St. John's	58–46
1954	Holy Cross	Duquesne	71–62
1955	Duquesne	Dayton	70–58
1956	Louisville	Dayton	93–80
1957	Bradley	Memphis State	84–83
1958	Xavier	Dayton	78–74 (OT)
1959	St. John's	Bradley	76–71 (OT)
1960	Bradley	Providence	88–72
1961	Providence	Saint Louis	62–59
1962	Dayton	St. John's	73–67
1963	Providence	Canisius	81–66
1964	Bradley	New Mexico	86–54
1965	St. John's	Villanova	55–51
1966	Brigham Young	New York University	97–84

* Overtime

YEAR	WINNER	RUNNER-UP	SCORE
1967	Southern Illinois	Marquette	71–56
1968	Dayton	Kansas	61–48
1969	Temple	Boston College	89–76
1970	Marquette	St. John's	65–53
1971	North Carolina	Georgia Tech	84–66
1972	Maryland	Niagara	100–69
1973	Virginia Tech	Notre Dame	92–91 (OT)
1974	Purdue	Utah	97–81
1975	Princeton	Providence	80–69
1976	Kentucky	North Carolina-Charlotte	71–67
1977	St. Bonaventure	Houston	94–91
1978	Texas	North Carolina State	101–93
1979	Indiana	Purdue	53–52
1980	Virginia	Minnesota	58–55
1981	Tulsa	Syracuse	86–84 (OT)
1982	Bradley	Purdue	67–58
1983	Fresno State	DePaul	69–60
1984	Michigan	Notre Dame	83–63
1985	UCLA	Indiana	65–62
1986	Ohio State	Wyoming	73–63
1987	Southern Mississippi	La Salle	84–80
1988	Connecticut	Ohio State	72–67
1989	St. John's	Saint Louis	73–65
1990	Vanderbilt	Saint Louis	74–72
1991	Stanford	Oklahoma	78–72
1992	Virginia	Notre Dame	81–76 (OT)
1993	Minnesota	Georgetown	62–61
1994	Villanova	Vanderbilt	80–73
1995	Virginia Tech	Marquette	65–64 (OT)
1996	Nebraska	St. Joseph's	60–54
1997	Michigan	Florida State	82–73
1998	Minnesota	Penn State	79–72
1999	California	Clemson	61–60

Stanley Cup

SEASON	WINNER
1892–1893	Montreal Amateur Athletic Assn
1893–1894	Montreal Amateur Athletic Assn
1894–1895	Montreal Victorias
1895–1896	(Feb 1896) Winnipeg Victorias
1895–1896	(Dec 1896) Montreal Victorias
1896–1897	Montreal Victorias
1897–1898	Montreal Victorias
1898–1899	Montreal Shamrocks
1899–1900	Montreal Shamrocks
1900–1901	Winnipeg Victorias
1901–1902	Montreal Amateur Athletic Assn
1902–1903	Ottawa Silver Seven
1903–1904	Ottawa Silver Seven
1904–1905	Ottawa Silver Seven
1905–1906	Montreal Wanderers
1906–1907	(Jan 1907) Kenora Thistles
1906–1907	(Mar 1907) Montreal Wanderers
1907–1908	Montreal Wanderers
1908–1909	Ottawa Senators
1909–1910	Montreal Wanderers
1910–1911	Ottawa Senators
1911–1912	Quebec Bulldogs
1912–1913	Quebec Bulldogs
1913–1914	Toronto Blueshirts
1914–1915	Vancouver Millionaires
1915–1916	Montreal Canadiens
1916–1917	Seattle Metropolitans
1917–1918	Toronto Arenas
1918–1919	canceled*
1919–1920	Ottawa Senators
1920–1921	Ottawa Senators
1921–1922	Toronto St. Patricks
1922–1923	Ottawa Senators
1923–1924	Montreal Canadiens
1924–1925	Victoria Cougars
1925–1926	Montreal Maroons
1926–1927	Ottawa Senators
1927–1928	New York Rangers
1928–1929	Boston Bruins
1929–1930	Montreal Canadiens
1930–1931	Montreal Canadiens
1931–1932	Toronto Maple Leafs
1932–1933	New York Rangers

*Competition was canceled after five games because of a flu epidemic.

SEASON	WINNER		
1933–1934	Chicago Black Hawks	1966–1967	Toronto Maple Leafs
1934–1935	Montreal Maroons	1967–1968	Montreal Canadiens
1935–1936	Detroit Red Wings	1968–1969	Montreal Canadiens
1936–1937	Detroit Red Wings	1969–1970	Boston Bruins
1937–1938	Chicago Black Hawks	1970–1971	Montreal Canadiens
1938–1939	Boston Bruins	1971–1972	Boston Bruins
1939–1940	New York Rangers	1972–1973	Montreal Canadiens
1940–1941	Boston Bruins	1973–1974	Philadelphia Flyers
1941–1942	Toronto Maple Leafs	1974–1975	Philadelphia Flyers
1942–1943	Detroit Red Wings	1975–1976	Montreal Canadiens
1943–1944	Montreal Canadiens	1976–1977	Montreal Canadiens
1944–1945	Toronto Maple Leafs	1977–1978	Montreal Canadiens
1945–1946	Montreal Canadiens	1978–1979	Montreal Canadiens
1946–1947	Toronto Maple Leafs	1979–1980	New York Islanders
1947–1948	Toronto Maple Leafs	1980–1981	New York Islanders
1948–1949	Toronto Maple Leafs	1981–1982	New York Islanders
1949–1950	Detroit Red Wings	1982–1983	New York Islanders
1950–1951	Toronto Maple Leafs	1983–1984	Edmonton Oilers
1951–1952	Detroit Red Wings	1984–1985	Edmonton Oilers
1952–1953	Montreal Canadiens	1985–1986	Montreal Canadiens
1953–1954	Detroit Red Wings	1986–1987	Edmonton Oilers
1954–1955	Detroit Red Wings	1987–1988	Edmonton Oilers
1955–1956	Montreal Canadiens	1988–1989	Calgary Flames
1956–1957	Montreal Canadiens	1989–1990	Edmonton Oilers
1957–1958	Montreal Canadiens	1990–1991	Pittsburgh Penguins
1958–1959	Montreal Canadiens	1991–1992	Pittsburgh Penguins
1959–1960	Montreal Canadiens	1992–1993	Montreal Canadiens
1960–1961	Chicago Black Hawks	1993–1994	New York Rangers
1961–1962	Toronto Maple Leafs	1994–1995	New Jersey Devils
1962–1963	Toronto Maple Leafs	1995–1996	Colorado Avalanche
1963–1964	Toronto Maple Leafs	1996–1997	Detroit Red Wings
1964–1965	Montreal Canadiens	1997–1998	Detroit Red Wings
1965–1966	Montreal Canadiens	1998–1999	Dallas Stars

The Masters

YEAR	WINNER	SCORE	YEAR	WINNER	SCORE	YEAR	WINNER	SCORE
1934	Horton Smith	284	1956	Jack Burke, Jr	289	1978	Gary Player	277
1935	Gene Sarazen	282*	1957	Doug Ford	283	1979	Fuzzy Zoeller	280*
1936	Horton Smith	285	1958	Arnold Palmer	284	1980	Seve Ballesteros	275
1937	Byron Nelson	283	1959	Art Wall, Jr	284	1981	Tom Watson	280
1938	Henry Picard	285	1960	Arnold Palmer	282	1982	Craig Stadler	284*
1939	Ralph Guldahl	279	1961	Gary Player	280	1983	Seve Ballesteros	280
1940	Jimmy Demaret	280	1962	Arnold Palmer	280*	1984	Ben Crenshaw	277
1941	Craig Wood	280	1963	Jack Nicklaus	286	1985	Bernhard Langer	282
1942	Byron Nelson	280*	1964	Arnold Palmer	276	1986	Jack Nicklaus	279
1943	not held		1965	Jack Nicklaus	271	1987	Larry Mize	285*
1944	not held		1966	Jack Nicklaus	288*	1988	Sandy Lyle	281
1945	not held		1967	Gay Brewer, Jr	280	1989	Nick Faldo	283*
1946	Herman Keiser	282	1968	Bob Goalby	277	1990	Nick Faldo	278*
1947	Jimmy Demaret	281	1969	George Archer	281	1991	Ian Woosnam	277
1948	Claude Harmon	279	1970	Billy Casper	279*	1992	Fred Couples	275
1949	Sam Snead	282	1971	Charles Coody	279	1993	Bernhard Langer	277
1950	Jimmy Demaret	283	1972	Jack Nicklaus	286	1994	Jose Maria Olazabal	279
1951	Ben Hogan	280	1973	Tommy Aaron	283	1995	Ben Crenshaw	274
1952	Sam Snead	286	1974	Gary Player	278	1996	Nick Faldo	276
1953	Ben Hogan	274	1975	Jack Nicklaus	276	1997	Tiger Woods	270
1954	Sam Snead	289*	1976	Ray Floyd	271	1998	Mark O'Meara	279
1955	Cary Middlecoff	279	1977	Tom Watson	276	1999	Jose Maria Olazabal	280

*Won playoff

US Open (Golf)

YEAR	MEN'S CHAMPION
1895	Horace Rawlins
1896	James Foulis
1897	Joe Lloyd
1898	Fred Herd
1899	Willie Smith
1900	Harry Vardon
1901	Willie Anderson
1902	Laurie Auchterlonie
1903	Willie Anderson
1904	Willie Anderson
1905	Willie Anderson
1906	Alex Smith
1907	Alec Ross
1908	Fred McLeod
1909	George Sargent
1910	Alex Smith
1911	John McDermott
1912	John McDermott
1913	Francis Ouimet*
1914	Walter Hagen
1915	John Travers*
1916	Chick Evans*
1917	not held
1918	not held
1919	Walter Hagen
1920	Ted Ray
1921	Jim Barnes
1922	Gene Sarazen
1923	Bobby Jones*
1924	Cyril Walker
1925	Willie Macfarlane
1926	Bobby Jones*
1927	Tommy Armour
1928	Johnny Farrell
1929	Bobby Jones*
1930	Bobby Jones*
1931	Billy Burke
1932	Gene Sarazen
1933	Johnny Goodman*
1934	Olin Dutra
1935	Sam Parks, Jr
1936	Tony Manero
1937	Ralph Guldahl
1938	Ralph Guldahl
1939	Byron Nelson
1940	Lawson Little
1941	Craig Wood
1942	not held
1943	not held
1944	not held
1945	not held
1946	Lloyd Mangrum
1947	Lew Worsham
1948	Ben Hogan

1949	Cary Middlecoff
1950	Ben Hogan
1951	Ben Hogan
1952	Julius Boros
1953	Ben Hogan
1954	Ed Furgol
1955	Jack Fleck
1956	Cary Middlecoff
1957	Dick Mayer
1958	Tommy Bolt
1959	Billy Casper
1960	Arnold Palmer
1961	Gene Littler
1962	Jack Nicklaus
1963	Julius Boros
1964	Ken Venturi
1965	Gary Player
1966	Billy Casper
1967	Jack Nicklaus
1968	Lee Trevino
1969	Orville Moody
1970	Tony Jacklin
1971	Lee Trevino
1972	Jack Nicklaus
1973	Johnny Miller
1974	Hale Irwin
1975	Lou Graham
1976	Jerry Pate
1977	Hubert Green
1978	Andy North
1979	Hale Irwin
1980	Jack Nicklaus
1981	David Graham
1982	Tom Watson
1983	Larry Nelson
1984	Fuzzy Zoeller
1985	Andy North
1986	Ray Floyd
1987	Scott Simpson
1988	Curtis Strange
1989	Curtis Strange
1990	Hale Irwin
1991	Payne Stewart
1992	Tom Kite
1993	Lee Janzen
1994	Ernie Els
1995	Corey Pavin
1996	Steve Jones
1997	Ernie Els
1998	Lee Janzen
1999	Payne Stewart

YEAR	WOMEN'S CHAMPION
1946	Patty Berg
1947	Betty Jameson
1948	Babe Zaharias
1949	Louise Suggs
1950	Babe Zaharias
1951	Betsy Rawls
1952	Louise Suggs
1953	Betsy Rawls
1954	Babe Zaharias
1955	Fay Crocker
1956	Kathy Cornelius
1957	Betsy Rawls
1958	Mickey Wright
1959	Mickey Wright
1960	Betsy Rawls
1961	Mickey Wright
1962	Murle Lindstrom
1963	Mary Mills
1964	Mickey Wright
1965	Carol Mann
1966	Sandra Spuzich
1967	Catherine Lacoste*
1968	Susie M. Berning
1969	Donna Caponi
1970	Donna Caponi
1971	JoAnne Carner
1972	Susie M. Berning
1973	Susie M. Berning
1974	Sandra Haynie
1975	Sandra Palmer
1976	JoAnne Carner
1977	Hollis Stacy
1978	Hollis Stacy
1979	Jerilyn Britz
1980	Amy Alcott
1981	Pat Bradley
1982	Janet Anderson
1983	Jan Stephenson
1984	Hollis Stacy
1985	Kathy Baker
1986	Jane Geddes
1987	Laura Davies
1988	Liselotte Neumann
1989	Betsy King
1990	Betsy King
1991	Meg Mallon
1992	Patty Sheehan
1993	Lauri Merten
1994	Patty Sheehan
1995	Annika Sorenstam
1996	Annika Sorenstam
1997	Alison Nicholas
1998	Se Ri Pak
1999	Juli Inkster

* Amateur

US Open (Tennis)

YEAR	MEN'S CHAMPION
1881	Richard Sears
1882	Richard Sears
1883	Richard Sears
1884	Richard Sears
1885	Richard Sears
1886	Richard Sears
1887	Richard Sears
1888	Henry Slocum, Jr
1889	Henry Slocum, Jr
1890	Oliver Campbell
1891	Oliver Campbell
1892	Oliver Campbell
1893	Robert Wrenn
1894	Robert Wrenn
1895	Fred Hovey
1896	Robert Wrenn
1897	Robert Wrenn
1898	Malcolm Whitman
1899	Malcolm Whitman
1900	Malcolm Whitman
1901	Bill Larned
1902	Bill Larned
1903	Laurie Doherty
1904	Holcombe Ward
1905	Beals Wright
1906	Bill Clothier
1907	Bill Larned
1908	Bill Larned
1909	Bill Larned
1910	Bill Larned
1911	Bill Larned
1912	Maurice McLoughlin
1913	Maurice McLoughlin
1914	Dick Williams
1915	Bill Johnston
1916	Dick Williams
1917	Lindley Murray
1918	Lindley Murray
1919	Bill Johnston
1920	Bill Tilden
1921	Bill Tilden
1922	Bill Tilden
1923	Bill Tilden
1924	Bill Tilden
1925	Bill Tilden
1926	Rene Lacoste
1927	Rene Lacoste
1928	Henri Cochet
1929	Bill Tilden
1930	John Doeg
1931	Ellsworth Vines
1932	Ellsworth Vines
1933	Fred Perry
1934	Fred Perry
1935	Wilmer Allison
1936	Fred Perry
1937	Don Budge
1938	Don Budge
1939	Bobby Riggs

YEAR	
1940	Don McNeill
1941	Bobby Riggs
1942	Fred Schroeder
1943	Joe Hunt
1944	Frank Parker
1945	Frank Parker
1946	Jack Kramer
1947	Jack Kramer
1948	Pancho Gonzales
1949	Pancho Gonzales
1950	Arthur Larsen
1951	Frank Sedgman
1952	Frank Sedgman
1953	Tony Trabert
1954	Vic Seixas
1955	Tony Trabert
1956	Ken Rosewall
1957	Mal Anderson
1958	Ashley Cooper
1959	Neale Fraser
1960	Neale Fraser
1961	Roy Emerson
1962	Rod Laver
1963	Rafael Osuna
1964	Roy Emerson
1965	Manuel Santana
1966	Fred Stolle
1967	John Newcombe
1968	Arthur Ashe (Amateur)*
	Arthur Ashe (Open)*
1969	Stan Smith (Amateur)*
	Rod Laver (Open)*
1970	Ken Rosewall
1971	Stan Smith
1972	Ilie Nastase
1973	John Newcombe
1974	Jimmy Connors
1975	Manuel Orantes
1976	Jimmy Connors
1977	Guillermo Vilas
1978	Jimmy Connors
1979	John McEnroe
1980	John McEnroe
1981	John McEnroe
1982	Jimmy Connors
1983	Jimmy Connors
1984	John McEnroe
1985	Ivan Lendl
1986	Ivan Lendl
1987	Ivan Lendl
1988	Mats Wilander
1989	Boris Becker
1990	Pete Sampras
1991	Stefan Edberg
1992	Stefan Edberg
1993	Pete Sampras
1994	Andre Agassi
1995	Pete Sampras
1996	Pete Sampras
1997	Patrick Rafter
1998	Patrick Rafter

YEAR	WOMEN'S CHAMPION
1887	Ellen Hansell
1888	Bertha Townsend
1889	Bertha Townsend
1890	Ellen Roosevelt
1891	Mabel Cahill
1892	Mabel Cahill
1893	Aline Terry

YEAR	
1894	Helen Hellwig
1895	Juliette Atkinson
1896	Elizabeth Moore
1897	Juliette Atkinson
1898	Juliette Atkinson
1899	Marion Jones
1900	Myrtle McAteer
1901	Elizabeth Moore
1902	Marion Jones
1903	Elizabeth Moore
1904	May Sutton
1905	Elizabeth Moore
1906	Helen Homans
1907	Evelyn Sears
1908	Maud B. Wallach
1909	Hazel Hotchkiss
1910	Hazel Hotchkiss
1911	Hazel Hotchkiss
1912	Mary Browne
1913	Mary Browne
1914	Mary Browne
1915	Molla Bjurstedt
1916	Molla Bjurstedt
1917	Molla Bjurstedt
1918	Molla Bjurstedt
1919	Hazel Wightman
1920	Molla Mallory
1921	Molla Mallory
1922	Molla Mallory
1923	Helen Wills
1924	Helen Wills
1925	Helen Wills
1926	Molla Mallory
1927	Helen Wills
1928	Helen Wills
1929	Helen Wills
1930	Betty Nuthall
1931	Helen Moody
1932	Helen Jacobs
1933	Helen Jacobs
1934	Helen Jacobs
1935	Helen Jacobs
1936	Alice Marble
1937	Anita Lizana
1938	Alice Marble
1939	Alice Marble
1940	Alice Marble
1941	Sarah Cooke
1942	Pauline Betz
1943	Pauline Betz
1944	Pauline Betz
1945	Sarah Cooke
1946	Pauline Betz
1947	Louise Brough
1948	Margaret duPont
1949	Margaret duPont
1950	Margaret duPont
1951	Maureen Connolly
1952	Maureen Connolly
1953	Maureen Connolly
1954	Doris Hart
1955	Doris Hart
1956	Shirley Fry
1957	Althea Gibson
1958	Althea Gibson
1959	Maria Bueno
1960	Darlene Hard
1961	Darlene Hard
1962	Margaret Smith
1963	Maria Bueno

*This was an amateur-only tournament from its inception through 1967. In 1968 and 1969, there were both amateur and open competitions. Since 1970 it has been an open tournament.

YEAR	WOMEN'S CHAMPION
1964	Maria Bueno
1965	Margaret Smith
1966	Maria Bueno
1967	Billie Jean King
1968	Margaret Court (Amateur)*
	Virginia Wade (Open)*
1969	Margaret Court (Amateur)*
	Margaret Court (Open)*
1970	Margaret Court
1971	Billie Jean King
1972	Billie Jean King
1973	Margaret Court
1974	Billie Jean King
1975	Chris Evert
1976	Chris Evert
1977	Chris Evert
1978	Chris Evert
1979	Tracy Austin
1980	Chris Evert Lloyd
1981	Tracy Austin
1982	Chris Evert Lloyd
1983	Martina Navratilova
1984	Martina Navratilova
1985	Hana Mandlikova
1986	Martina Navratilova
1987	Martina Navratilova
1988	Steffi Graf
1989	Steffi Graf
1990	Gabriela Sabatini
1991	Monica Seles
1992	Monica Seles
1993	Steffi Graf
1994	Arantxa Sanchez Vicario
1995	Steffi Graf
1996	Steffi Graf
1997	Martina Hingis
1998	Lindsay Davenport

Soccer's World Cup

YEAR	WINNER	RUNNER-UP	SCORE	HOST COUNTRY
1930	Uruguay	Argentina	4–2	Uruguay
1934	Italy	Czechoslovakia	2–1 (OT)	Italy
1938	Italy	Hungary	4–2	France
1942	canceled			
1946	canceled			
1950	Uruguay	Brazil	2–1	Brazil
1954	West Germany	Hungary	3–2	Switzerland
1958	Brazil	Sweden	5–2	Sweden
1962	Brazil	Czechoslovakia	3–1	Chile
1966	England	West Germany	4–2 (OT)	England
1970	Brazil	Italy	4–1	Mexico
1974	West Germany	Holland	2–1	West Germany
1978	Argentina	Holland	3–1 (OT)	Argentina
1982	Italy	West Germany	3–1	Spain
1986	Argentina	West Germany	3–2	Mexico
1990	West Germany	Argentina	1–0	Italy
1994	Brazil	Italy	0–0*	United States
1998	France	Brazil	3–0	France
2002				South Korea

*Tied 0–0 after 30 minutes of overtime; Brazil won on penalty kicks, 3–2.

Heavyweight Boxing Champions

BOXER	YEAR	
John L. Sullivan	1885–1892	
James J. Corbett	1892–1897	
Bob Fitzsimmons	1897–1899	
James J. Jeffries	1899–1905	
Marvin Hart	1905–1906	
Tommy Burns	1906–1908	
Jack Johnson	1908–1915	
Jess Willard	1915–1919	
Jack Dempsey	1919–1926	
Gene Tunney	1926–1928	
Max Schmeling	1930–1932	
Jack Sharkey	1932–1933	
Primo Carnera	1933–1934	
Max Baer	1934–1935	
James J. Braddock	1935–1937	
Joe Louis	1937–1949	
Ezzard Charles	1949–1951	
Jersey Joe Walcott	1951–1952	
Rocky Marciano	1952–1956	
Floyd Patterson	1960–1962	
Sonny Liston	1962–1964	
Cassius Clay (Muhammad Ali)	1964–1970	
Ernie Terrell	1965–1967	(WBA)
Joe Frazier	1968–1970	(NYSAC)
Jimmy Ellis	1968–1970	(WBA)
Joe Frazier	1970–1973	
George Foreman	1973–1974	
Muhammad Ali	1974–1978	
Leon Spinks	1978	
Ken Norton	1978	(WBC)
Larry Holmes	1978–1980	(WBC)
Muhammad Ali	1978–1979	

☆ Chase's 2000 SPORTS Calendar of Events ☆

BOXER	YEAR		James Smith	1986–1987	(WBA)
John Tate	1979–1980	(WBA)	Tony Tucker	1987	(IBF)
Mike Weaver	1980–1982	(WBA)	Mike Tyson	1987–1990	
Larry Holmes	1980–1985		Buster Douglas	1990	
Michael Dokes	1982–1983	(WBA)	Evander Holyfield	1990–1992	
Gerrie Coetzee	1983–1984	(WBA)	Riddock Bowe	1992–1993	(WBA, IBF)
Tim Witherspoon	1984	(WBC)	Lennox Lewis	1992–1994	(WBC)
Pinklon Thomas	1984–1986	(WBC)	Evander Holyfield	1993–1994	(WBA, IBF)
Greg Page	1984–1985	(WBA)	Michael Moorer	1994	(WBA, IBF)
Michael Spinks	1985–1987		Oliver McCall	1994–1995	(WBC)
Tim Witherspoon	1986	(WBA)	George Foreman	1994–1995	(WBA, IBF)
Trevor Berbick	1986	(WBC)	Bruce Seldon	1995–1996	(WBA)
Mike Tyson	1986–1987	(WBC)	George Foreman	1995	(IBF)
			Frank Bruno	1995–1996	(WBC)
			Mike Tyson	1996	(WBC)
			Michael Moorer	1996–1997	(IBF)
			Mike Tyson	1996	(WBA)
			Evander Holyfield	1996–	(WBA)
			Lennox Lewis	1997–	(WBC)
			Evander Holyfield	1997–	(IBF)

WBA = World Boxing Association
NYSAC = New York State Athletic Commission
WBC = World Boxing Council
IBF = International Boxing Federation

Kentucky Derby

YEAR	WINNER							
1875	Aristides	1906	Sir Huon	1938	Lawrin	1970	Dust Commander
1876	Vagrant	1907	Pink Star	1939	Johnstown	1971	Canonero II
1877	Baden-Baden	1908	Stone Street	1940	Gallahadion	1972	Riva Ridge
1878	Day Star	1909	Wintergreen	1941	Whirlaway	1973	Secretariat
1879	Lord Murphy	1910	Donau	1942	Shut Out	1974	Cannonade
1880	Fonso	1911	Meridian	1943	Count Fleet	1975	Foolish Pleasure
1881	Hindoo	1912	Worth	1944	Pensive	1976	Bold Forbes
1882	Apollo	1913	Donerail	1945	Hoop, Jr	1977	Seattle Slew
1883	Leonatus	1914	Old Rosebud	1946	Assault	1978	Affirmed
1884	Buchanan	1915	Regret	1947	Jet Pilot	1979	Spectacular Bid
1885	Joe Cotton	1916	George Smith	1948	Citation	1980	Genuine Risk
1886	Ben Ali	1917	Omar Khayyam	1949	Ponder	1981	Pleasant Colony
1887	Montrose	1918	Exterminator	1950	Middleground	1982	Gato Del Sol
1888	MacBeth II	1919	Sir Barton	1951	Count Turf	1983	Sunny's Halo
1889	Spokane	1920	Paul Jones	1952	Hill Gail	1984	Swale
1890	Riley	1921	Behave Yourself	1953	Dark Star	1985	Spend A Buck
1891	Kingman	1922	Morvich	1954	Determine	1986	Ferdinand
1892	Azra	1923	Zev	1955	Swaps	1987	Alysheba
1893	Lookout	1924	Black Gold	1956	Needles	1988	Winning Colors
1894	Chant	1925	Flying Ebony	1957	Iron Liege	1989	Sunday Silence
1895	Halma	1926	Bubbling Over	1958	Tim Tam	1990	Unbridled
1896	Ben Brush	1927	Whiskery	1959	Tomy Lee	1991	Strike the Gold
1897	Typhoon II	1928	Reigh Count	1960	Venetian Way	1992	Lil E. Tee
1898	Plaudit	1929	Clyde Van Dusen	1961	Carry Back	1993	Sea Hero
1899	Manuel	1930	Gallant Fox	1962	Decidedly	1994	Go For Gin
1900	Lieutenant Gibson	1931	Twenty Grand	1963	Chateaugay	1995	Thunder Gulch
1901	His Eminence	1932	Burgoo King	1964	Northern Dancer	1996	Grindstone
1902	Alan-a-Dale	1933	Brokers Tip	1965	Lucky Debonair	1997	Silver Charm
1903	Judge Himes	1934	Cavalcade	1966	Kauai King	1998	Real Quiet
1904	Elwood	1935	Omaha	1967	Proud Clarion	1999	Charismatic
1905	Agile	1936	Bold Venture	1968	Forward Pass		
		1937	War Admiral	1969	Majestic Prince		

Triple Crown Winners

YEAR	HORSE	JOCKEY			
1919	Sir Barton	Johnny Loftus	1943	Count Fleet	Johnny Longden
1930	Gallant Fox	Earl Sande	1946	Assault	Warren Mehrtens
1935	Omaha	Willie Saunders	1948	Citation	Eddie Arcaro
1937	War Admiral	Charley Kurtsinger	1973	Secretariat	Ron Turcotte
1941	Whirlaway	Eddie Arcaro	1977	Seattle Slew	Jean Cruguet
			1978	Affirmed	Steve Cauthen

Indianapolis 500

YEAR	WINNER	MPH	NOTES	YEAR	WINNER	MPH	NOTES
1911	Ray Harroun	74.602		1956	Pat Flaherty	128.490	
1912	Joe Dawson	78.719		1957	Sam Hanks	135.601	
1913	Jules Goux	75.933		1958	Jimmy Bryan	133.791	
1914	Rene Thomas	82.474		1959	Rodger Ward	135.857	
1915	Ralph DePalma	89.840		1960	Jim Rathmann	138.767	
1916	Dario Resta	84.001	(scheduled for 300 miles)	1961	A.J. Foyt	139.130	
				1962	Rodger Ward	140.293	
1917	not held			1963	Parnelli Jones	143.137	
1918	not held			1964	A.J. Foyt	147.350	
1919	Howdy Wilcox	88.050		1965	Jim Clark	150.686	
1920	Gaston Chevrolet	88.618		1966	Graham Hill	144.317	
1921	Tommy Milton	89.621		1967	A.J. Foyt	151.207	
1922	Jimmy Murphy	94.484		1968	Bobby Unser	152.882	
1923	Tommy Milton	90.954		1969	Mario Andretti	156.867	
1924	L.L. Corum & Joe Boyer	98.234		1970	Al Unser	155.749	
1925	Peter DePaolo	101.127		1971	Al Unser	157.735	
1926	Frank Lockhart	95.904	(400 miles; rain)	1972	Mark Donohue	162.962	
				1973	Gordon Johncock	159.036	(332.5 miles; rain)
1927	George Souders	97.545		1974	Johnny Rutherford	158.589	
1928	Louie Meyer	99.482		1975	Bobby Unser	149.213	(435 miles; rain)
1929	Ray Keech	97.585					
1930	Billy Arnold	100.448		1976	Johnny Rutherford	148.725	
1931	Louis Schneider	96.629		1977	A.J. Foyt	161.331	
1932	Fred Frame	104.144		1978	Al Unser	161.363	
1933	Louie Meyer	104.162		1979	Rick Mears	158.899	
1934	Bill Cummings	104.863		1980	Johnny Rutherford	142.862	
1935	Kelly Petillo	106.240		1981	Bobby Unser	139.084	(penalty placing him second overruled by USAC)
1936	Louie Meyer	109.069					
1937	Wilbur Shaw	113.580					
1938	Floyd Roberts	117.200					
1939	Wilbur Shaw	115.035		1982	Gordon Johncock	162.029	
1940	Wilbur Shaw	114.277		1983	Tom Sneva	162.117	
1941	Floyd Davis & Mauri Rose	115.117		1984	Rick Mears	163.612	
				1985	Danny Sullivan	152.982	
1942	not held			1986	Bobby Rahal	170.722	
1943	not held			1987	Al Unser	162.175	
1944	not held			1988	Rick Mears	149.809	
1945	not held			1989	Emerson Fittipaldi	167.581	
1946	George Robson	114.820		1990	Arie Luyendyk	185.981	
1947	Mauri Rose	116.338		1991	Rick Mears	176.457	
1948	Mauri Rose	119.814		1992	Al Unser, Jr	134.477	
1949	Bill Holland	121.327		1993	Emerson Fittipaldi	157.207	
1950	Johnnie Parsons	124.002	(345 miles; rain)	1994	Al Unser, Jr	160.872	
				1995	Jacques Villeneuve	153.616	
1951	Lee Wallard	126.244		1996	Buddy Lazier	147.956	
1952	Troy Ruttman	128.922		1997	Arie Luyendyk	145.827	
1953	Bill Vukovich	128.740		1998	Eddie Cheever	145.155	
1954	Bill Vukovich	130.840		1999	Kenny Brack	153.176	
1955	Bob Sweikert	128.213					

Winston Cup

YEAR	WINNER								
1949	Red Byron	1961	Ned Jarrett	1974	Richard Petty	1987	Dale Earnhardt
1950	Bill Rexford	1962	Joe Weatherly	1975	Richard Petty	1988	Bill Elliott
1951	Herb Thomas	1963	Joe Weatherly	1976	Cale Yarborough	1989	Rusty Wallace
1952	Tim Flock	1964	Richard Petty	1977	Cale Yarborough	1990	Dale Earnhardt
1953	Herb Thomas	1965	Ned Jarrett	1978	Cale Yarborough	1991	Dale Earnhardt
1954	Lee Petty	1966	David Pearson	1979	Richard Petty	1992	Alan Kulwicki
1955	Tim Flock	1967	Richard Petty	1980	Dale Earnhardt	1993	Dale Earnhardt
1956	Buck Baker	1968	David Pearson	1981	Darrell Waltrip	1994	Dale Earnhardt
1957	Buck Baker	1969	David Pearson	1982	Darrell Waltrip	1995	Jeff Gordon
1958	Lee Petty	1970	Bobby Isaac	1983	Bobby Allison	1996	Terry Labonte
1959	Lee Petty	1971	Richard Petty	1984	Terry Labonte	1997	Jeff Gordon
1960	Rex White	1972	Richard Petty	1985	Darrell Waltrip	1998	Jeff Gordon
		1973	Benny Parsons	1986	Dale Earnhardt		

The America's Cup

YEAR	WINNER	COUNTRY
Schooners and J-Class Boats		
1851	America	USA
1870	Magic	USA
1871	Columbia and Sappho	USA
1876	Madeleine	USA
1881	Mischief	USA
1885	Puritan	USA
1886	Mayflower	USA
1887	Volunteer	USA
1893	Vigilant	USA
1895	Defender	USA
1899	Columbia	USA
1901	Columbia	USA
1903	Reliance	USA
1920	Resolute	USA
1930	Enterprise	USA
1934	Rainbow	USA
1937	Ranger	USA

YEAR	WINNER	COUNTRY
12-Meter Boats		
1958	Columbia	USA
1962	Weatherly	USA
1964	Constellation	USA
1967	Intrepid	USA
1970	Intrepid	USA
1974	Courageous	USA
1977	Courageous	USA
1980	Freedom	USA
1983	Australia II	Australia
1987	Stars & Stripes	USA
60-ft Catamaran vs 133-ft Monohull		
1988	Stars & Stripes	USA
75-ft International America's Cup Class		
1992	America3	USA
1995	Black Magic I	New Zealand

ODDS AND ENDS

Commissioners and Presidents

BASEBALL

Commissioner	Year
Kenesaw Mountain Landis	1920–1944
Albert (Happy) Chandler	1945–1951
Ford C. Frick	1951–1965
William Eckert	1965–1968
Bowie Kuhn	1969–1984
Peter Ueberroth	1984–1989
A. Bartlett Giamatti	1989
Fay Vincent	1989–1992
Allan H. (Bud) Selig	1992–

President, National League	Year
Morgan G. Bulkeley	1876
William A. Hulbert	1877–1882
A.G. Mills	1883–1884
Nicholas Young	1885–1902
Henry Pulliam	1903–1909
Thomas J. Lynch	1910–1913
John K. Tener	1914–1918
John A. Heydler	1918–1934
Ford C. Frick	1935–1951
Warren Giles	1951–1969
Charles (Chub) Feeney	1970–1986
A. Bartlett Giamatti	1987–1989
William White	1989–1994
Leonard Coleman	1994–

President, American League	Year
Byron Bancroft (Ban) Johnson	1901–1927
Ernest Barnard	1927–1931
William Harridge	1931–1959
Joe Cronin	1959–1973
Lee McPhail	1974–1983
Dr. Robert Brown	1984–1994
Gene Budig	1994–

NATIONAL FOOTBALL LEAGUE

President	Year
Jim Thorpe	1920
Joe Carr	1921–1939
Carl Storck	1939–1941

Commissioner	Year
Elmer Layden	1941–1946
Bert Bell	1946–1959
Austin Gunsel (acting)	1959–1960
Alvin (Pete) Rozelle	1960–1989
Paul Tagliabue	1989–

NATIONAL BASKETBALL COMMISSIONER

Commissioner	Year
Maurice Podoloff	1949–1963
Walter Kennedy	1963–1975
Lawrence O'Brien	1975–1984
David Stern	1984–

NATIONAL HOCKEY LEAGUE

President	Year
Frank Calder	1917–1943
Mervyn (Red) Dutton	1943–1946
Clarence Campbell	1946–1977
John A. Ziegler, Jr	1977–1992
Gil Stein	1992–1993

Commissioner	Year
Gary B. Bettman	1993–

NCAA

Executive Director	Year
Walter Byers	1951–1988
Richard Schultz	1988–1993
Cedric Dempsey	1993–

Baseball's Work Stoppages

YEAR	WORK STOPPAGE	LENGTH	DATES	BASIC ISSUE
1972	Strike	13 days	Apr 1–13	pensions
1973	Lockout	17 days	Feb 8–25	salary arbitration
1976	Lockout	17 days	Mar 1–17	free agency
1980	Strike	8 days	Apr 1–8	free agent compensation
1981	Strike	50 days	June 12–July 31	free agent compensation
1985	Strike	2 days	Aug 6–7	salary arbitration
1990	Lockout	32 days	Feb 15–Mar 18	salary arbitration and salary cap
1994–1995	Strike	234 days	Aug 12, 1994–Apr 2, 1995	salary cap and revenue sharing

Sites of the Modern Olympic Games

YEAR	SUMMER GAMES	WINTER GAMES
1896	Athens, Greece	
1900	Paris, France	
1904	St. Louis, MO, USA	
1906	Athens, Greece (unofficial)	
1908	London, England	
1912	Stockholm, Sweden	
1916	Berlin, Germany (canceled)	
1920	Antwerp, Belgium	
1924	Paris, France	Chamonix, France
1928	Amsterdam, Holland	St. Moritz, Switzerland
1932	Los Angeles, CA, USA	Lake Placid, NY, USA
1936	Berlin, Germany	Garmisch-Partenkirchen, Germany
1940	Tokyo, Japan (canceled)	Sapporo, Japan (canceled)
1944	London, England (canceled)	Cortina d'Ampezzo, Italy (canceled)
1948	London, England	St. Moritz, Switzerland
1952	Helsinki, Finland	Oslo, Norway
1956	Melbourne, Australia	Cortina d'Ampezzo, Italy
1960	Rome, Italy	Squaw Valley, CA, USA
1964	Tokyo, Japan	Innsbruck, Austria
1968	Mexico City, Mexico	Grenoble, France
1972	Munich, West Germany	Sapporo, Japan
1976	Montreal, Quebec, Canada	Innsbruck, Austria
1980	Moscow, USSR	Lake Placid, NY, USA
1984	Los Angeles, CA, USA	Sarajevo, Yugoslavia
1988	Seoul, South Korea	Calgary, Alberta, Canada
1992	Barcelona, Spain	Albertville, France
1994	————————	Lillehammer, Norway
1996	Atlanta, GA, USA	————————
1998	————————	Nagano, Japan
2000	Sydney, Australia	————————
2002	————————	Salt Lake City, UT, USA
2004	Athens, Greece	————————
2006	————————	Turin, Italy

DIRECTORY OF SPORTS ORGANIZATIONS

AIR HOCKEY
US Air Hockey Assn
Boulder, CO 80306
(303) 444-9164

AIR SPORTS
Balloon Federation of
America
112 E Salem
Indianola, IA 50125
(515) 961-8809
(515) 961-3537 FAX

US Parachute Assn
1440 Duke St
Alexandria, VA 22314
(703) 836-3495
(703) 836-2843 FAX

ARCHERY
Natl Archery Assn
One Olympic Plaza
Colorado Springs, CO 80909
(719) 578-4576
(719) 632-4733 FAX

Natl Field Archery Assn
31407 Outer I-10
Redlands, CA 92373
(909) 794-2133
(909) 794-8512 FAX

ARM WRESTLING
American Arm Wrestling
Assn
PO Box 79
Scranton, PA 18504
(717) 342-4984
(717) 342-1368 FAX

Intl Federation of Arm
Wrestling/IFAW
4219 Burbank Blvd
Burbank, CA 91505
(818) 953-2222
(818) 953-2220 FAX

New York Arm Wrestling
Assn/IFAW
PO Box 770-323
Woodside, NY 11377
(718) 544-4592
(718) 261-8111 FAX

AUTO SPORTS
All-American Soap Box Derby
PO Box 7233
Akron, OH 44306
(330) 733-8723
(330) 733-1370 FAX

Championship Auto Racing
Teams (CART)
755 W Big Beaver Rd, Ste 800
Troy, MI 48084
(810) 362-8800
(810) 362-8810 FAX
Schedule available in August

Indianapolis Motor Speedway
Corp
4790 W 16th St
Indianapolis, IN 46222
(317) 481-8500
(317) 248-6759 FAX

Pep Boys Indy Racing League
4565 W 16th St
Indianapolis, IN 46222
(317) 484-6526
(317) 484-6525 FAX
Schedule available in January

Intl Hot Rod Assn
Hwy 11E
Bristol, TN 37620
(423) 764-1164
(423) 764-4460 FAX

Intl Kart Federation
4650 Arrow Hwy, Ste C7
Montclair, CA 91763
(909) 625-5497
(909) 621-6019 FAX

Intl Race of Champions, Inc
(IROC)
45 Park Rd
Tinton Falls, NJ 07724
(908) 542-4762
(908) 542-2122 FAX

Natl Assn for Stock Car Auto
Racing (NASCAR)
1801 W Intl Speedway Blvd
Daytona Beach, FL 32114
(904) 253-0611
(904) 252-8804 FAX
Schedule available in
December

Natl Hot Rod Assn/NHRA
2035 Financial Way
Glendora, CA 91741-0750
(818) 914-4761
(818) 914-5481 FAX

Short Course Off-Rd Drivers
Assn/SODA
7839 W North Ave
Wauwatosa, WI 53213
(414) 452-SODA

Sports Car Club of
America/SCCA
9033 E Easter Place
Englewood, CO 80112
(303) 694-7222
(303) 694-7391 FAX

US Auto Club
4910 W 16th St
Indianapolis Speedway, IN
46224
(317) 247-5151
(317) 247-0123 FAX

Western Racing Assn
4385 Mentone Ave
Culver City, CA 90232
(310) 839-5023

World of Outlaws
624 Krona Dr, Ste 115
Plano, TX 75074
(214) 424-2202
(214) 423-3930 FAX

BADMINTON
USA Badminton Assn
One Olympic Plaza
Colorado Springs, CO 80909
(719) 578-4808
(719) 578-4507 FAX

BASEBALL
**(NL and AL
are on page 280)**

Professional
Appalachian League
283 Deerchase Circle
Statesville, NC 28677
(704) 873-5300
(704) 873-4333 FAX
Schedule available in October

Arizona Fall League
10201 S 51st St, Ste 230
Phoenix, AZ 85044
(602) 496-6700
(602) 496-6384 FAX

Arizona League
PO Box 4941
Scottsdale, AZ 85261-4941
(602) 483-8224
(602) 443-3450
Schedule available in June

Atlantic League
31 Turner Lane
Westchester, PA 19380
(610) 696-8662
(610) 696-8667 FAX

California League/A
2380 S Bascom Ave, Ste 200
Campbell, CA 95008
(408) 379-8038
(408) 369-1409 FAX
Schedule available in
December

Carolina League/A
PO Box 9503
Greensboro, NC 27429
(910) 691-9030
(910) 691-9070 FAX
Schedule available in
November

Eastern League/AA
PO Box 9711
Portland, ME 04104
(207) 761-2700
(207) 761-7064 FAX
Schedule available in
December

Florida State League/A
PO Box 349
Daytona Beach, FL 32115
(904) 252-7479
(904) 252-7495 FAX
Schedule available in
December

Frontier Professional Baseball,
Inc
PO Box 2662
Zanesville, OH 43702
(614) 452-7400
(614) 452-2999 FAX
Schedule available in
December

Gulf Coast League
1503 Clower Creek Dr, H-262
Sarasota, FL 34231
(941) 966-6407
(941) 966-6872 FAX

Intl League/AAA
55 S High St, Ste 202
Dublin, OH 43017
(614) 791-9300
(614) 791-9009 FAX
Schedule available in January
or February

Mexican League
Angel Pola No. 16
Col. Periodista
C.P. 11220
Mexico
(525) 557-10-07
(525) 557-14-08 FAX

Midwest League/A
PO Box 936
Beloit, WI 53512-0936
(608) 364-1188
(608) 364-1913 FAX
Schedule available between
November and February

New York–Pennsylvania
League/A
1629 Oneida St
Utica, NY 13501
(315) 733-8036
(315) 797-7403 FAX
Schedule available in March

Northern League
524 S Duke St
Durham, NC 27701
(919) 956-8150
(919) 683-2693 FAX
Schedule available in
    December

Northwest League/A
PO Box 4941
Scottsdale, AZ 85261
(602) 483-8224
(602) 493-3450 FAX
Schedule available in October

Pacific Coast League/AAA
(see below)
Schedule available in January

Pioneer League/A
812 W 30th St
Spokane, WA 99203
(509) 456-7615
(509) 456-0136 FAX
Schedule available in
    December

South Atlantic League/A
504 Crescent Hill
Kings Mountain, NC 28086
(704) 739-3466
(704) 739-1974
Schedule available in
    December

Southern League/AA
1 Depot St, Ste 300
Marietta, GA 30060
(404) 428-4749
(404) 428-4849 FAX
Schedule available in
    December

Texas League/AA
2442 Facet Oak
San Antonio, TX 78232
(210) 545-5297
(210) 545-5298 FAX
Schedule available in October

Texas-Louisiana League
2801 N. 3rd St.
Abilene, TX 79601
(915) 677-4501
(915) 677-4215 FAX
Schedule available in
    February

Pacific Coast League/AAA
1631 Mesa Ave
Colorado Springs, Co 80906
(719) 636-3399
(719) 636-1199 FAX

Western Baseball League
426 Broadway
    Ste 208
Chico, CA 95928
(530) 897-6125
(530) 897-6124 FAX

**Other Baseball
Organizations**
All-American Women's
    Baseball League
80 Fifth Ave, Ste 1506
New York, NY 10011
(212) 741-4668
(212) 741-5285 FAX

American Amateur Baseball
    Congress
118-119 Redfield Plaza
Marshall, MI 49068
(616) 781-2002
(616) 781-2060 FAX

American Legion Baseball
700 N Pennsylvania
Indianapolis, IN 46204
(317) 630-1213
(317) 630-1369 FAX

American Women's Baseball
    Assn, Inc
PO Box 1639
Chicago, IL 60690-1639
(312) 404-0932

Babe Ruth Baseball &
    Softball
PO Box 5000
1770 Brunswick Pike
Trenton, NJ 08638
(609) 695-1434
(609) 695-2505 FAX

Baseball Canada/Canadian
    Federation of Amateur
    Baseball
1600 James Naismith Dr
Gloucester, ON
Canada K1B 5N4
(613) 748-5606
(613) 748-5767 FAX

Dixie Baseball, Inc
101 Forest Ave
PO Box 193
Montgomery, AL 36106
(334) 241-2300
(334) 241-2301 FAX

Little League Baseball Inc
PO Box 3485
Williamsport, PA 17701
(717) 326-1921
(717) 326-1074 FAX

Natl Amateur Baseball
    Federation
PO Box 705
Bowie, MD 20718
(301) 262-5005
(301) 262-5005 FAX

Natl Baseball Congress
300 S Sycamore
Wichita, KS 67213
(316) 267-3372
(316) 267-3382 FAX

Pony Baseball and Softball
300 Clare Dr
Washington, PA 15301
(412) 225-1060
(412) 225-9852 FAX

USA Baseball
3400 E. Camino Campestre
Tucson, AZ 85716
(520) 327-9700
(520) 327-9221 FAX

BASKETBALL
(NBA is on page 282)
Continental Basketball Assn
Two Arizona Center
400 N Fifth St, Ste 1425
Phoenix, AZ 85004
(602) 254-6677
(602) 258-9985 FAX
Schedule available in June

Biddy Basketball
4711 Bancroft Dr
New Orleans, LA 70122
(504) 288-5128

Harlem Globetrotters
400 E Van Buren, Ste 300
Phoenix, AZ 85004
(602) 258-0000
(602) 253-5612 FAX
Schedule for top 50 major
    cities available in August;
    schedule for smaller cities
    available in November

Natl Wheelchair Basketball
    Assn
1100 Blythe Blvd
Charlotte, NC 28217
(704) 355-1064

US Basketball League
46 Quirk Rd
Milford, CT 06460
(203) 877-9508
(800) THE-USBL
(203) 878-8109 FAX

Women's National Basketball
    Assn
645 Fifth Ave
New York, NY 10022
(212) 688-9622
(212) 750-9622 FAX

BIATHLON
US Biathlon Assn
29 Ethan Allen Ave.
Colchester, VT 05446
(802) 654-7833
(802) 654-7816

BILLIARDS
Billiard Congress of America
910 23rd Ave
Coralville, IA 52241-1221
(319) 351-2112
(319) 351-7767 FAX

Professional Billiards Tour
    Assn
4412 Commercial Way
Spring Hill, FL 34606
(352) 596-7808
(352) 596-7441 FAX

Women's Professional Billiard
    Assn
1411 Pierce St
Sioux City, IA 51105
(712) 252-4789
(712) 252-4799 FAX

BOATING
US Offshore Racing Assn
18 N Franklin Blvd
Pleasantville, NJ 08232
(609) 383-3700
(609) 383-9501 FAX

Sail America
850 Aquidneck Ave.
    B-4
Middletown, RI 02542-7201
(401) 841-0900
(401) 847-2044 FAX
(410) 849-0220
(410) 847-4535 FAX

BOBSLEDDING
US Bobsled & Skeleton
    Federation, Inc
PO Box 828
Lake Placid, NY 12946
(518) 523-1842
(518) 523-9491 FAX

BOCCE
Intl Bocce Assn
400 Rutger St
PO Box 170
Utica, NY 13503-0170
(315) 733-9611

BOWLING
American Bowling Congress
5201 S 76th St
Greendale, WI 53129
(414) 421-6400
(414) 421-1194 FAX

Ladies Pro Bowlers Tour
7171 Cherryvale Blvd
Rockford, IL 61112
(815) 332-5756
(815) 332-9636 FAX

Professional Bowlers Assn of
    America
1720 Merriman Rd
Akron, OH 44313
(216) 836-5568
(216) 836-2107 FAX

USA Bowling
5201 S 76th St
Greendale, WI 52129
(414) 421-4700
(414) 421-1301 FAX

Women's Intl Bowling
    Congress, Inc
5301 S 76th St
Greendale, WI 52129
(414) 421-9000
(414) 421-4420 FAX

BOXING
Golden Gloves Assn of
    America, Inc
8801 Princess Jeanne NE
Albuquerque, NM 87112
(505) 298-8042
(595) 298-1191 FAX

US Amateur Boxing, Inc/USA
    Boxing
One Olympic Plaza
Colorado Springs, CO 80909
(719) 579-4506
(719) 632-3426 FAX

CANOEING/KAYAKING
US Canoe & Kayak Team
421 Old Military Rd
Lake Placid, NY 12946
(518) 523-1855
(518) 523-3767 FAX

CROQUET
US Croquet Assn
11588-B Polo Club Road
Wellington, FL 33414
(407) 753-9141
(407) 753-8801 FAX

CURLING
US Curling Assn
1100 Centerpoint Dr
Stevens Point, WI 54481
(715) 344-1199
(715) 344-6885 FAX

US Women's Curling Assn
PO Box 244
Hartland, WI 53029

CYCLING
American Bicycle Assn/ABA
9831 S 51st St, Ste D135
Phoenix, AZ 85044
(602) 961-1903
(602) 961-1842 FAX

American Motorcyclist Assn
33 Collegeview Ave
Westerville, OH 43081
(614) 891-2425
(800) AMA-JOIN
(614) 891-5012 FAX

League of American Bicyclists
1612 K St NW Ste 401
Washington DC 20006
(202) 822-1333
(202) 822-1314 (FAX)

Natl Bicycle League, Inc
3958 Brown Park Dr, Ste D
Hilliard, OH 43026
(614) 777-1625
(614) 777-1680 FAX

Ultra Marathon Cycling Assn
2761 N Marengo Ave
Altadena, CA 91001
(806) 499-3210
(806) 499-3210 FAX

US Cycling
One Olympic Plaza
Colorado Springs, CO 80909
(719) 578-4581
(719) 578-4628 FAX

DARTS
American Darts Organization
230 N Crescent Way #K
Anaheim, CA 92801
(714) 254-0212
(714) 254-0214 FAX

EQUESTRIAN
American Grandprix Assn
840 Natl City Bank Bldg
Cleveland, OH 44114
(216) 781-2050
(216) 781-5333 FAX

American Horse Shows Assn,
    Inc
220 E 42nd St, Ste 409
New York, NY 10017-5876
(212) 972-2472
(212) 983-7286 FAX

Breeders' Cup Ltd
2525 Harrodsburg Rd, 5th Fl
Lexington, KY 40544
(606) 223-5444
(606) 223-3945 FAX

US Combined Training Assn
515 Old Waterford Rd, NW
Leesburg, VA 20176
(703) 779-0440
(703) 779-0550 FAX

US Dressage Federation, Inc
7700 A St, PO Box 6669
Lincoln, NE 68506-0669
(402) 434-8550
(402) 434-8570 FAX

US Equestrian Team
Pottersville Rd
Gladstone, NJ 07934
(908) 234-1251
(908) 234-9417 FAX

US Polo Assn
4059 Iron Works Pike
Lexington, KY 40511
(606) 255-0593
(606) 231-9738 FAX

US Trotting Assn
750 Michigan Ave
Columbus, OH 43215-1191
(614) 224-2291
(614) 224-4575 FAX

EXERCISE/FITNESS
US Powerlifting Federation,
    Inc
PO Box 650
Roy, UT 84067
(801) 776-3628

US Weightlifting Federation
One Olympic Plaza
Colorado Springs, CO 80909
(719) 578-4508
(719) 578-4741 FAX

FENCING
US Fencing Assn
One Olympic Plaza
Colorado Springs, CO 80909
(719) 578-4511
(719) 632-5737 FAX

FIELD HOCKEY
US Field Hockey Assn
One Olympic Plaza
Colorado Springs, CO 80909
(719) 578-4567
(719) 632-0979 FAX

FISHING
Bassing America Corp.
16901 N Dallas Pkwy, Ste 107
Dallas, TX 75248
(972) 380-2656
(800) 972-3369
(972) 380-2621 FAX

US Fishing Assn, Inc
16901 N Dallas Pkwy, Ste 107
Dallas, TX 75248
(972) 713-6207
(972) 380-2621 FAX

FOOTBALL
(NFL is on page 281)
Arena Football
75 E Wacker Dr, Ste 400
Chicago, IL 60601
(312) 332-5510
(312) 332-5540 FAX

Canadian Football League
110 Eglinton Ave W
Toronto, ON
Canada M4R 1A3
(416) 322-9650
(416) 322-9651 FAX
Schedule available in March

NFL Europe
280 Park Ave
New York, NY 10017
(212) 450-2000
(212) 681-7577 FAX

FRISBEE
US Disc Sports Assn
855 Tunjunga Valley Rd
Sunland, CA 91040
(818) 353-6339

World Flying Disc Federation
200 Linden
Ft. Collins, CO 80524
(303) 484-6932
(303) 490-2714 FAX

GOLF
Futures Golf Tour
909 W Main St
Avon Park, FL 33825
(941) 453-4455
(941) 453-4466 FAX

Hooters Professional Golf Tour
202 Commerce Dr
Peachtree City, GA 30269
(770) 486-8687
(800) 992-8748
(770) 486-1055 FAX

Ladies' Professional Golf Assn
100 International Golf Dr
Daytona Beach, FL 32124
(904) 274-6200
(904) 274-1099 FAX

Minigolf Sport Assn of
    America
PO Box 32353
Jacksonville, FL 32237
(904) 781-GOLF
(904) 781-4843 FAX

Natl Assn of Left-Handed
    Golfers
6488 Shawnee Ct
Independence, KY 41051
(800) 844-NALG

PGA Tour
112 TPC Blvd, Sawgrass
Ponte Vedra Beach, FL 32082
(904) 285-3700
(904) 285-7913 FAX
Schedule available in October

PGA of America
100 Ave of the Champions
PO Box 109601
Palm Beach Gardens, FL
    33410
(407) 624-8400
(407) 624-8452 FAX

US Blind Golfers Assn
160 Lago Vista Blvd
Casselberry, FL 32707
(407) 332-0700

US Golf Assn
PO Box 708
Far Hills, NJ 07931-0708
(908) 234-2300
(908) 234-9687 FAX

GYMNASTICS
USA Gymnastics
Pan American Plaza
201 S Capitol Ave, Ste 300
Indianapolis, IN 46225
(317) 237-5050
(317) 237-5069 FAX

HANDBALL
US Handball Assn
2333 N Tucson Blvd
Tucson, AZ 85716-2726
(520) 795-0434
(520) 795-0465

ICE HOCKEY
(NHL is on page 284)
American Hockey League
425 Union St
W Springfield, MA 01089
(413) 781-2030
(413) 733-4767 FAX
Schedule available in
September

Central Hockey League
222 E Ohio St, Ste 820
Indianapolis, IN 46204
(317) 916-0555
(317) 916-0563 FAX
Schedule available in August

East Coast Hockey League
125 Village Blvd
Princeton, NJ 08450
(609) 452-0770
(609) 452-7147 FAX
Schedule available in August

Intl Hockey League
1577 N Woodward Ave,
Ste 212
Bloomfield Hills, MI 48304
(810) 258-0580
(810) 258-0940 FAX

USA Hockey, Inc
1775 Bob Johnson Dr
Colorado Springs, CO 80906
(719) 576-8724
(719) 538-7838 FAX

US Figure Skating Assn
20 First St
Colorado Springs, CO 80906
(719) 635-5200
(719) 635-9548 FAX

US Intl Speedskating Assn
PO Box 16157
Rocky River, OH 44116
(216) 899-0128
(216) 899-0109 FAX

IN-LINE SKATING
Intl In-Line Skating Assn
3720 Farragut Ave, Ste 400
Kensington, MD 20895
(301) 942-9770
(301) 942-9771 FAX

LACROSSE
National Lacrosse League
One Seymour H Knox III
Plaza
Buffalo, NY 14203-3096
(716) 855-4511
(716) 855-4003 FAX

US Lacrosse
113 W. University Pkwy
Baltimore, MD 21210
(410) 235-6882
(410) 366-6735

US Intercollegiate Lacrosse
Assn
4501 N Charles St
Baltimore, MD 21239
(410) 617-2773
(410) 617-2008 FAX

US Women's Lacrosse Assn
48 Boulder Brick Rd
Wellesley, MA 02181
(617) 235-7903

LUGE
US Luge Assn
35 Church St
Lake Placid, NY 12946
(518) 523-2071
(518) 523-4106 FAX

MARTIAL ARTS
US Judo, Inc
One Olympic Plaza, Ste 202
Colorado Springs, CO 80909
(719) 578-4730
(719) 578-4733 FAX

US Taekwondo Union
One Olympic Plaza
Colorado Springs, CO 80909
(719) 578-4632
(719) 578-4642 FAX

USA Karate Federation
1300 Kenmore Blvd
Akron, OH 44314
(216) 753-3114
(216) 753-6967 FAX

ORIENTEERING
US Orienteering Federation
PO Box 1444
Forest Park, GA 30051
(404) 363-2110
(404) 363-2110 FAX

PENTATHLON
US Modern Pentathlon Assn
530 McCullough Ave, Ste 619
San Antonio, TX 78215
(210) 246-3000
(210) 246-3096 FAX

RACQUETBALL
US Racquetball Assn
1685 W Uintah St
Colorado Springs, CO 80904-
2921
(719) 635-5396
(719) 635-0685 FAX

Women's Professional
Racquetball Assn
PO Box 17633
Anaheim, CA 92817-7633
(714) 281-0241
(714) 281-2410 FAX

RODEO
Intl Pro Rodeo Assn, Inc
2304 Exchange Ave
Oklahoma City, OK 73148
(405) 235-6540
(405) 235-6577 FAX

Longhorn World
Championship Rodeo, Inc
3679 Knight Rd
Whites Creek, TN 37189
(615) 876-1016
(615) 876-4685 FAX

Natl High School Rodeo Assn,
Inc
11178 N Huron, #7
Denver, CO 80234
(303) 452-0820
(303) 452-0912 FAX

Natl Intercollegiate Rodeo
Assn
2316 Eastgate N, Ste 160
Walla Walla, WA 99362
(509) 529-4402
(509) 525-1090 FAX

ROLLER HOCKEY
Roller Hockey International
13070 Fawn Hill Dr
Grass Valley, CA 95945
(916) 272-7825
(916) 272-7858 FAX

ROLLER SKATING
US Amateur Confederation of
Roller Skating
4730 South St
Lincoln, NE 68506
(402) 483-7551
(402) 483-1465 FAX

US Rowing Assn
201 S Capitol Ave, Ste 400
Indianapolis, IN 46225
(317) 237-5656
(317) 237-5646 FAX

RUGBY
USA Rugby
3595 E Fountain Blvd
Colorado Springs, CO 80910
(719) 637-1022
(719) 637-1315 FAX

USA Rugby-East, Inc
2312 Hillbeck
Columbia, SC 29210
(803) 254-4561
(803) 798-2137 FAX

SHOOTING
Amateur Trapshooting Assn
601 W Natl Rd
Vandalia, OH 45377
(513) 898-4638
(513) 898-5472 FAX

USA Shooting
One Olympic Plaza
Colorado Springs, CO 80909
(719) 578-4670
(719) 635-7989 FAX

Natl Rifle Assn
11250 Waples Mill Rd
Fairfax, VA 22030-7400
(703) 267-1000
(703) 267-3971 FAX

Natl Skeet Shooting Assn
5931 Roft Rd
San Antonio, TX 78253
(210) 688-3371
(210) 688-3014 FAX

SKIING/SNOWBOARDING
US Skiing
1500 Kearns Blvd, Bldg F
Park City, UT 84060
(801) 649-9090
(801) 649-3613 FAX

SLED DOG RACING
US Sled Dog Sports Federation
1848 A Commercenter E
San Bernardino, CA 92408
(714) 889-1000
(909) 884-0015 FAX

SOCCER
Major League Soccer/MLS
110 E 42nd St, 10th Fl
New York, NY 10017
(212) 450-1200
(212) 450-1300 FAX

Natl Professional Soccer
League/NPSL
115 Dewalt Ave, NW
Canton, OH 44702
(330) 455-4625
(330) 455-3885 FAX

US Amateur Soccer Assn,
Inc/USASA
7800 River Rd
North Bergen, NJ 07047
(201) 861-6277
(201) 861-6341 FAX

US Soccer Federation
1801-181 S Prairie Ave
Chicago, IL 60616
(312) 808-1300
(312) 808-1301 FAX

US Youth Soccer Assn
899 Presidential Dr, Ste 117
Richardson, TX 75081
(214) 235-4499
(800) 4SO-CCER
(214) 235-4480 FAX

SOFTBALL
Intl Softball Congress, Inc
6007 E Hillcrest Circle
Anaheim Hills, CA 92807
(714) 998-5694
(714) 282-7902 FAX

Natl Wheelchair Softball Assn
1616 Todd Ct
Hastings, MN 55033
(612) 437-1792

Senior Softball–USA, Inc
7052 Riverside Blvd
Sacramento, CA 95831
(916) 393-8566
(916) 393-8350 FAX

US Slo-Pitch Softball Assn
3935 S Crater Rd
Petersburg, VA 23804
(804) 732-4099
(804) 732-1704 FAX

USA Softball
2801 NE 50th St
Oklahoma City, OK 73111
(405) 424-5266
(405) 424-3855 FAX

Women's Professional
    Fastpitch
90 Madison St, Ste 200
Denver, CO 80202
(303) 316-7800
(303) 316-2779 FAX

SQUASH
US Squash Racquets Assn
PO Box 1216
Bala-Cynwyd, PA 19004-1216
(610) 667-4006
(610) 667-6539 FAX

SURFING
Assn of Surfing Professionals
17942 Sky Park Circle
4401/HJ
Irvine, CA 92714
(714) 851-2774
(714) 851-2773 FAX

Professional Surfing Assn of
    America
530 Sixth St
Hermosa Beach, CA 90254
(310) 372-0414
(310) 372-7457 FAX

Triple Crown, Inc
2525 Dale St, #1102
Honolulu, HI 96826
(808) 946-8097
(808) 946-8097 FAX

US Surfing Federation
350 Jericho Turnpike
Jericho, NY 11753
(516) 935-0400
(516) 942-4705 FAX

SWIMMING/DIVING
US Diving, Inc
201 S Capitol Ave, Ste 430
Indianapolis, IN 46225
(317) 237-5252
(317) 237-5257 FAX

US Swimming, Inc
One Olympic Plaza
Colorado Springs, CO 80909
(719) 578-4578
(719) 578-4669 FAX

US Synchronized Swimming
Pan American Plaza
201 S Capitol Ave, Ste 510
Indianapolis, IN 46225
(317) 237-5700
(317) 237-5705 FAX

TABLE TENNIS
USA Table Tennis
One Olympic Plaza
Colorado Springs, CO 80909
(719) 578-4583
(719) 632-6971 FAX

TEAM HANDBALL
US Team Handball Federation
1903 Powers Ferry Rd, Ste 230
Atlanta, GA 30339
(770) 956-7660
(770) 956-7976 FAX

TENNIS
ATP Tour
200 ATP Tour Blvd
Ponte Vedra Beach, FL 32082
(904) 285-8000
(904) 285-5966 FAX

Natl Fdtn of Wheelchair
    Tennis
940 Calle Amanecer, Ste B
San Clemente, CA 92672
(714) 361-6811

US Tennis Assn/USTA
70 W Red Oak Lane
White Plains, NY 10604
(914) 696-7000
(914) 696-7167 FAX

World Team Tennis Inc
445 N Wells, Ste 404
Chicago, IL 60610
(312) 245-5300
(312) 245-5321 FAX

WTA Tour
1266 E Main St, 4th Pl
Stamford, CT 06902-3546
(203) 978-1740
(203) 978-1702 FAX

TRACK & FIELD
USA Track & Field
One RCA Dome, Ste 140
Indianapolis, IN 46225
(317) 261-0500
(317) 261-0481 FAX

TRIATHLON
USA Triathlon
3595 E Fountain Blvd, F-1
Colorado Springs, CO 80910
(719) 597-9090
(800) TRI-1USA
(719) 597-2121 FAX

VOLLEYBALL
Assn of Volleyball
    Professionals
330 Washington Blvd, Ste 600
Marina del Rey, CA 90292
(310) 577-0775
(310) 577-0777 FAX

Natl Volleyball Association
1001 Mission St
S Pasadena, CA 91030
(800) 682-6820
(800) 5-SPIKER FAX

USA Volleyball
3595 E Fountain Blvd, Ste I-2
Colorado Springs, CO 80910-
    1740
(719) 637-8300
(719) 597-6307 FAX

Women's Professional
    Volleyball Assn
840 Apollo St, Ste 205
El Segunda, CA 90245
(310) 726-0700
(310) 726-0719 FAX

WATER POLO
US Water Polo, Inc
1685 W Uintah
Colorado Springs, CO 80904-
    2921
(719) 695-5396
(719) 635-0685 FAX

WATER SKIING
American Water Ski Assn
799 Overlook Dr
Winter Haven, FL 33884
(813) 324-4341
(800) 533-AWSA
(813) 325-8259 FAX

WRESTLING
USA Wrestling
6155 Lehman Dr
Colorado Springs, CO 80918
(719) 598-8181
(719) 598-9440 FAX

USA Wrestling–Women's
    Wrestling Committee
15418 S 24th St
Phoenix, AZ 85044
(602) 759-4096

MULTI-SPORT
ORGANIZATIONS
Amateur Athletic Union of
    the US
The Walt Disney World Resort
PO Box 1000
Lake Buena Vista, FL 32800-
    1000
(407) 363-6170
(407) 363-6171 FAX

Athletes in Action
5778 State Route 350
Oregonia, OH 45054
(573) 933-2421
(573) 933-2422 FAX

Black Coaches Assn
PO Box J
Des Moines, IA 50311
(515) 327-1248

Fellowship of Christian
    Athletes
8701 Leeds Rd
Kansas City, MO 64129
(816) 921-0909

Natl Assn of Sports Officials
2017 Lathrop Ave
Racine, WI 53405
(414) 632-5448
(414) 632-5460 FAX

Natl Fed of State High School
    Assns
11724 NW Plaza Circle
Kansas City, MO 64195-0626
(816) 464-5400
(816) 464-5571 FAX

Special Olympics Intl
1325 G St NW, Ste 500
Washington, DC 20005-4709
(202) 628-3630
(202) 824-0200 FAX

US Olympic Committee
One Olympic Plaza
Colorado Springs, CO 80909
(719) 632-5551
(719) 578-4654 FAX

ALPHABETICAL INDEX

Events are generally listed under key words; many broad categories have been created, including African-American, Agriculture, Animals, Archery, Automobiles, Aviation, Badminton, Baseball, Basketball, Bicycle, Boats, Bowling, Boxing, Children, Curling, Dance, Darts, Fishing, Football, Games, Golf, Gun Shows and Shooting Events, Health and Welfare, Hockey (Ice), Horses, Horse-shoes, Hunting, Journalism, Kites, Motorcycle, Olympics, Parades, Polo, Rodeo, Running, Skiing, Soccer, Softball, Super Bowl, Surfing, Swimming and Diving, Television, Tennis, Track and Field, Triathlon, Volleyball, Walking, Women and many more. Events that can be attended are also listed under the states or countries where they are to be held. This index indicates only the initial date for each event; see the chronology for inclusive dates of events lasting more than one day.

Stern Named NBA Commissioner: Anniv, **Nov 15**
Stokes, Maurice: Birth Anniv, **June 17**
Tatum, Goose: Birth Anniv, **May 3**
Taylor, Chuck: Birth Anniv, **June 24**
Temple Wins First NIT: Anniv, **Mar 16**
Texas Western Wins NCAA Crown: Anniv, **Mar 19**
13 Players Foul Out: Anniv, **Nov 15**
Three-Point Field Goal: Anniv, **Apr 2**
Toronto Granted NBA Franchise: Anniv, **Nov 4**
24-Second Clock: Anniv, **Apr 23**
12-Foot Basket Experiment: Anniv, **Mar 7**
Twins Drafted: Anniv, **Apr 26**
UCLA Sets Record: Anniv, **Jan 27**
UCLA Streak Snapped: Anniv, **Jan 19**
Underhand Free-Throw Shooting Tourn (Winfield, IL), **Sept 9**
US Loses Olympic Game: Anniv, **Sept 10**
Vancouver Joins NBA: Anniv, **Apr 27**
Villanova Upsets Georgetown: Anniv, **Apr 1**
Wade, Margaret: Birth Anniv, **Dec 30**
Whoopers and Hoopers Invitational Bask Tourn (Hastings, NE), **Mar 17**
Wilkens Double Milestone: Anniv, **Jan 19**
Wilkens Winningest Coach: Anniv, **Jan 6**
Wilkens Wins 800th Game: Anniv, **Mar 15**
Wilkens Wins 1,000th Game: Anniv, **Mar 1**
Wilt Retires Without Fouling Out: Anniv, **Mar 28**
Wilt Scores 100: Anniv, **Mar 2**
WNBA Inaugural Season: Anniv, **June 21**
Wooden's Last Title: Anniv, **Mar 31**
Woolpert, Phil: Birth Anniv, **Dec 19**
Yardley Scores 2,000: Anniv, **Mar 9**
Zaslofsky, Max: Birth Anniv, **Dec 7**
Bassen, Bob: Birth, **May 6**
Bastille Day Moonlight Golf Tourn (Washington, DC), **July 14**
Bathtub Race, Great Intl World Chmpshp, & Nanaimo Marine Fest (Nanaimo, BC, Canada), **July 20**
Battie, Tony: Birth, **Feb 11**
Battles, Cliff: Birth Anniv, **May 1**
Bauer, Hank: Birth, **July 31**
Baugh, Sammy: Birth, **Mar 17**
Baumann, Frank: Birth, **July 1**
Baumgartner, Ken: Birth, **Mar 11**
Baumholtz, Frankie: Birth, **Oct 7**
Bautista, Danny: Birth, **May 24**
Bay Country Boat Show (Hollywood, MD), **Apr 8**
Baylor, Don: Birth, **June 28**
Baylor, Elgin: Birth, **Sept 16**
BC Sr Games (Kelowna, BC, Canada), **Sept 6**
BC Summer Games (Victoria, BC, Canada), **July 27**
BC Winter Games (Quesnel, BC, Canada), **Feb 24**
Bean, Andy: Birth, **Mar 13**
Beanpot Tourn (Boston, MA), **Feb 7**
Bearden, Gene: Birth, **Sept 5**
Beargrease Sled Dog Marathon (Duluth, MN), **Feb 5**
Bearnarth, Larry: Birth, **Sept 11**
Beartooth Run (Red Lodge, MT), **June 24**
Beattie, Jim: Birth, **July 4**
Beaumont, Ginger: Birth Anniv, **July 23**
Beck, Rod: Birth, **Aug 3**
Becker, Boris: Birth, **Nov 22**
Becker, Rich: Birth, **Feb 1**
Beckley, Jake: Birth Anniv, **Aug 4**
Beckman, John: Birth Anniv, **Oct 22**
Bednarik, Chuck: Birth, **May 1**
Bee, Clair: Birth Anniv, **Mar 2**
Belanger, Mark: Birth Anniv, **June 8**
Belcher, Tim: Birth, **Oct 19**
Belfour, Ed: Birth, **Apr 21**
Belinda, Stan: Birth, **Aug 6**
Belinsky, Bo: Birth, **Dec 7**
Bell, Bobby: Birth, **June 17**
Bell, Buddy: Birth, **Aug 27**
Bell, Cool Papa: Birth Anniv, **May 17**
Bell, David: Birth, **Sept 14**
Bell, Derek: Birth, **Dec 11**
Bell, Gus: Birth Anniv, **Nov 15**
Bell, Jay: Birth, **Dec 11**

Bellamy, Walt: Birth, **July 24**
Belle, Albert: Birth, **Aug 25**
Belliard, Rafael: Birth, **Oct 24**
Bellino, Joe: Birth, **Mar 13**
Bellows, Brian: Birth, **Sept 1**
Belmont, August: Birth Anniv, **Dec 8**
Belmont Stakes (Elmont, NY), **June 10**
Belote, Melissa: Birth, **Oct 16**
Beman, Deane: Birth, **Apr 22**
Benard, Marvin: Birth, **Jan 20**
Bench, Johnny: Birth, **Dec 7**
Bender, Chief: Birth Anniv, **May 5**
Benes, Alan: Birth, **Jan 21**
Benes, Andy: Birth, **Aug 20**
Benitez, Armando: Birth, **Nov 3**
Benitez, Wilfred: Birth, **Sept 12**
Bennett, Cornelius: Birth, **Aug 25**
Benoit, David: Birth, **May 9**
Beranek, Josef: Birth, **Oct 25**
Berard, Bryan: Birth, **Mar 5**
Berardino, Johnny: Birth Anniv, **May 1**
Bere, Jason: Birth, **May 26**
Berenson, Red: Birth, **Dec 8**
Berenson, Senda: Birth Anniv, **Mar 19**
Berezin, Sergei: Birth, **Nov 5**
Berg, Moe: Birth Anniv, **Mar 2**
Berg, Patty: Birth, **Feb 13**
Bergman, Sean: Birth, **Apr 11**
Bering Sea Ice Golf Classic (Nome, AK), **Mar 18**
Bermuda
   Bank of Butterfield Marathon (Hamilton), **Jan 16**
Berra, Dale: Birth, **Dec 13**
Berra, Yogi: Birth, **May 12**
Berroa, Geronimo: Birth, **Mar 18**
Berry, Charlie: Birth Anniv, **Oct 18**
Berry, Raymond: Birth, **Feb 27**
Berry, Sean: Birth, **Mar 22**
Berryhill, Damon: Birth, **Dec 3**
Bertuzzi, Todd: Birth, **Feb 2**
Berube, Craig: Birth, **Dec 17**
Best, Travis: Birth, **July 12**
Bettenhausen, Tony: Birth Anniv, **Sept 12**
Bettis, Jerome: Birth, **Feb 16**
Beuerlein, Steve: Birth, **Mar 7**
Beukeboom, Jeff: Birth, **Mar 28**
Bevacqua, Kurt: Birth, **Jan 23**
Bevens, Bill: Birth Anniv, **Oct 21**
Biakabutuka, Tim: Birth, **Jan 24**
Biancalana, Buddy: Birth, **Feb 2**
Bias, Len: Death Anniv, **June 19**
Biathlon: Amicalola Fitness Fest (Dawsonville, GA), **May 27**
Bibby, Mike: Birth, **May 13**
Bichette, Dante: Birth, **Nov 18**
Bicycle
   Amicalola Fitness Fest (Dawsonville, GA), **May 27**
   Big Mac Shoreline Spring Scenic Tour (Mackinaw City, MI), **June 10**
   Bike Month, Natl, **May 1**
   Bike Van Buren (Van Buren County, IA), **Aug 19**
   Black Hills Trek (Black Hills, SD) **June 2**
   Boston-Montreal-Boston 2000 (Boston, MA, to Montreal, QC, Canada), **Aug 17**
   Cardinal Road Race (Roanoke, VA), **May 28**
   Chili Challenge Off-Road Bike Race (Angel Fire, NM), **Aug 26**
   Connecticut River Ride (Hartford, CT), **Aug 12**
   Enchanted Circle Century Bike Tour (Red River, NM), **Sept 9**
   First Six-Day Bike Race: Anniv, **Feb 17**
   Giants Ridge Mountain Bike Fest (Biwabik, MN), **Aug 19**
   Great Peanut Tour (Skippers, VA), **Sept 7**
   Great Texas Mosquito Fest Competitions (Clute, TX), **July 27**
   Hotter-N-Hell Hundred (Wichita Falls, TX), **Aug 25**
   JCBC Century Ride (Junction City and Ft Riley, KS), **Sept 10**
   Leadville Trail 100 Bike Race (Leadville, CO), **Aug 12**
   Lemond Wins Tour de France: Anniv, **July 27**

Magic Circle Bike Challenge (Willcox, AZ), **Sept 2**
Mudder's Day Off-Road Challenge (Rhinelander, WI), **May 14**
Natl Bike to Work Day, **May 16**
Perry's "BRR" (Bike Ride to Rippey) (Perry, IA), **Feb 5**
Pole, Pedal, Paddle (Bend, OR), **May 20**
Pole, Pedal, Paddle (Jackson, WY), **Apr 1**
Possum Pedal 100 Bicycle Ride/Race (Graham, TX), **Mar 25**
Register's Bicycle Ride Across Iowa (Des Moines, IA), **July 23**
ROC Hillclimb Time Trail Bike Race (Roanoke, VA), **May 27**
Saturn Fest Cup Bike Race (Roanoke, VA), **May 29**
Six Gap Century & Three Gap Fifty Ride (Dahlonega, GA), **Sept 24**
Southern Ontario Cycling Rally (Southern ON, Canada), **May 20**
The BiQue Ride (Toronto, ON/Montreal, QC, Canada), **July 8**
Tour de Cure, **Apr 1**
Tour Du Canada (Vancouver, BC/St. John's, NF, Canada), **June 27**
Tour of Somerville (Somerville, NJ), **May 29**
Vermont 50-Mile Mountain Bike and Run (Brownsville, VT), **Oct 1**
Walk & Roll Chicago (Chicago, IL), **May 21**
Wheel to Weston (Kansas City and Weston, MO), **June 18**
Bidwill, Charles: Birth Anniv, **Sept 16**
Bierman, Bernie: Birth Anniv, **Mar 11**
Big East Baseball Tourn (Site TBA), **May 17**
Big East Men's Basketball Tourn (New York, NY), **Mar 8**
Big East Men's/Women's Indoor Track/Field Chmpshp (Syracuse, NY), **Feb 19**
Big East Men's/Women's Outdoor Track/Field Chmpshp (Piscataway, NJ), **May 5**
Big East Men's/Women's Swim/Div Chmpshp (Uniondale, NY), **Feb 24**
Big East Men's/Women's Tennis Chmpshp (Coral Gables, FL), **Apr 20**
Big East Softball Tourn (Chestnut Hill, MA), **May 5**
Big East Women's Basketball Tourn (Storrs, CT), **Mar 4**
Big Mac Shoreline Spring Scenic Tour (Mackinaw City, MI), **June 10**
Big Sky State Games (Billings, MT), **July 14**
Big Sur Marathon (Carmel, CA), **Apr 30**
Big Ten Baseball Tourn, **May 18**
Big Ten Cross Country Chmpshp (Madison, WI), **Oct 28**
Big Ten Field Hockey Chmpshp (Ann Arbor, MI), **Nov 3**
Big Ten Men's Basketball Tourn (Chicago, IL), **Mar 9**
Big Ten Men's Golf Chmpshp (West Lafayette, IN), **May 12**
Big Ten Men's Gymnastics Chmpshps (East Lansing, MI), **Mar 17**
Big Ten Men's Indoor Track/Field Chmpshp (Bloomington, IN), **Feb 26**
Big Ten Men's Soccer Chmpshp (Columbus, OH), **Nov 10**
Big Ten Men's Swim/Div Chmpshp (Ann Arbor, MI), **Feb 24**
Big Ten Men's Tennis Chmpshp (Bloomington, IN), **Apr 27**
Big Ten Men's/Women's Outdoor Track/Field Chmpshp (Iowa City, IA), **May 19**
Big Ten Softball Tourn (Site TBA), **May 12**
Big Ten Women's Basketball Tourn (Indianapolis, IN), **Mar 3**
Big Ten Women's Golf Chmpshp (Madison, WI), **Apr 28**
Big Ten Women's Gymnastics Chmpshps (State College, PA), **Mar 18**
Big Ten Women's Indoor Track/Field Chmpshp (Minneapolis, MN), **Feb 26**
Big Ten Women's Soccer Chmpshp (Iowa City, IA), **Nov 3**
Big Ten Women's Swim/Div Chmpshp (Indianapolis, IN), **Feb 17**

Canada (cont'd)——Children

Kosar, Bernie, Jr: Birth, Nov 25
Kotsay, Mark: Birth, Dec 2
Koufax, Sandy: Birth, Dec 30
Kournikova, Anna: Birth, June 7
Kovalev, Alexei: Birth, Feb 24
Kozlov, Slava: Birth, May 3
Kramer, Erik: Birth, Nov 6
Kramer, Jack: Birth, Aug 1
Kramer, Jerry: Birth, Jan 23
Kranepool, Ed: Birth, Nov 8
Krause, Paul: Birth, Feb 19
Kravchuk, Igor: Birth, Sept 13
Kreuter, Chad: Birth, Aug 26
Krivda, Rick: Birth, Jan 19
Krone, Julie: Birth, July 24
Krygier, Todd: Birth, Oct 12
Kubek, Tony: Birth, Oct 12
Kuczynski, Bert: Birth Anniv, Jan 8
Kuhn, Bowie: Birth, Oct 28
Kuiper, Duane: Birth, June 19
Kukoc, Toni: Birth, Sept 18
Kulwicki, Alan: Birth Anniv, Dec 14
Kupchak, Mitch: Birth, May 24
Kwan, Michelle: Birth, July 7
Kwanzaa, Dec 26
La Russa, Tony, Jr: Birth, Oct 4
Labine, Clem: Birth, Aug 6
Labonte, Terry: Birth, Nov 16
Labor Day, Sept 4
Lachemann, Marcel: Birth, June 13
Lachemann, Rene: Birth, May 4
Lacoste, Rene: Birth Anniv, July 2
Lacrosse
  ACC Men's Chmpshp (College Park, MD),
    Apr 21
  ACC Women's Chmpshp (College Park, MD),
    Apr 22
  Lee-Jackson Classic (Lexington, VA), **May 6**
  NCAA Men's Div I Chmpshp (Finals) (College
    Park, MD), **May 27**
  NCAA Men's Div III Chmpshp (College Park,
    MD), **May 28**
  NCAA Women's Chmpshp (Finals) (Ewing
    Township, NJ), **May 19**
  NCAA Women's Chmpshp (First round at
    sites TBA), **May 10**
  NCAA Women's Chmpshp (Quarterfinals at
    sites TBA), **May 13**
  NCAA Women's Div III Chmpshp (Finals at
    site TBA), **May 20**
  NCAA Women's Div III Chmpshp (First round
    at sites TBA), **May 10**
  NCAA Women's Div III Chmpshp
    (Quarterfinals at sites TBA), **May 14**
  NJCAA Men's Invtl Chmpshp (Arnold, MD),
    May 13
Laettner, Christian: Birth, Aug 17
Lafleur, Guy: Birth, Sept 20
LaFrentz, Raef: Birth, May 29
Laimbeer, Bill, Jr: Birth, May 19
Lajoie, Nap: Birth Anniv, Sept 5
Lake Champlain Balloon Festival (New
  Haven, VT), June 2
Lake Placid Horse Show (Lake Placid, NY),
  June 28
Lake Winnebago Sturgeon Season (Fond du
  Lac, WI), Feb 12
Lake, Carnell: Birth, July 15
Lakestride Half-Marathon (Ludington, MI),
  June 17
Lalas, Alexi: Birth, June 1
Lambeau, Curly: Birth Anniv, Apr 9
Lambert, Jack: Birth, July 8
Lamonica, Daryle: Birth, July 17
Lamont, Gene: Birth, Dec 25
LaMotta, Jake: Birth, July 10
Landis, Kenesaw: Birth Anniv, Nov 20
Landrith, Hobie: Birth, Mar 16
Landry, Tom: Birth, Sept 11
Lane, Frank: Birth Anniv, Feb 1
Lane, Night Train: Birth, Apr 16
Lang, Andrew, Jr: Birth, June 29
Lang, Kenard: Birth, Jan 31
Langer, Jim: Birth, May 16
Langston, Mark: Birth, Aug 20
Lanier, Bob, Jr: Birth, Sept 10
Lanier, Willie: Birth, Aug 21

Lankford, Ray: Birth, June 5
Lansford, Carney: Birth, Feb 7
Lapchick, Joe: Birth Anniv, Apr 12
Lardner, Ring: Birth Anniv, Mar 6
Largent, Steve: Birth, Sept 28
Larionov, Igor: Birth, Dec 3
Larkin, Barry: Birth, Apr 28
Larsen, Don: Birth, Aug 7
Lary, Frank: Birth, Apr 10
Lary, Yale, Jr: Birth, Nov 24
Las Vegas Intl Marathon (Las Vegas, NV),
  Feb 6
LaSalle Banks Chicago Marathon (Chicago,
  IL), Oct 22
Lasorda, Tommy: Birth, Sept 22
Latham, Arlie: Birth Anniv, Mar 15
Lau, Charlie: Birth Anniv, Apr 12
Laukkanen, Janne: Birth, Mar 19
Lavagetto, Cookie: Birth Anniv, Dec 1
Lavelli, Dante: Birth, Feb 23
Laver, Rod: Birth, Aug 9
Law, Ty: Birth, Feb 10
Law, Vernon: Birth, Mar 12
Lawn Mower Race, Sta-Bil Natl Chmpshp
  (Mendota, IL), Sept 2
Layden, Elmer: Birth Anniv, May 4
Layne, Bobby: Birth Anniv, Dec 19
Lazzeri, Tony: Birth Anniv, Dec 6
Leadville Mosquito Marathon (Leadville,
  CO), July 15
Leadville Trail 100 Bike Race (Leadville, CO),
  Aug 12
Leadville Trail 100—10K (Leadville, CO),
  Aug 13
Leadville Trail 100 Ultramarathon (Leadville,
  CO), Aug 19
Leahy, Frank: Birth Anniv, Aug 27
Leahy, Pat: Birth, Mar 19
Leap Year Day, Feb 29
Leavenworth River Fest (Leavenworth, KS),
  Sept 9
LeClair, John: Birth, July 5
Ledee, Ricky: Birth, Nov 22
Ledesma, Aaron: Birth, June 3
Lee, Amp: Birth, Oct 1
Lee, Bill: Birth, Dec 28
Lee, Derrek: Birth, Sept 6
Lee-Jackson Lacrosse Classic (Lexington,
  VA), May 6
Lee, Sammy: Birth, Aug 1
Lee, Travis: Birth, May 26
Leetch, Brian: Birth, Mar 3
LeFlore, Ron: Birth, June 16
Lehtinen, Jere: Birth, June 24
Leiter, Al: Birth, Oct 23
Leiter, Mark: Birth, Apr 13
Lemaire, Jacques: Birth, Sept 7
Lemieux, Claude: Birth, July 16
Lemieux, Mario: Birth, Oct 5
Lemon, Bob: Birth, Sept 22
Lemon, Meadowlark: Birth, Apr 25
LeMond, Greg: Birth, June 26
Lenard, Voshon: Birth, May 14
Lendl, Ivan: Birth, Mar 7
Lenexa Freedom Run (Lenexa, KS), July 4
Lenglen, Suzanne: Birth Anniv, Mar 24
Leonard, Benny: Birth Anniv, Apr 7
Leonard, Buck: Birth Anniv, Sept 8
Leonard, Dennis: Birth, May 8
Leonard, Justin: Birth, June 15
Leonard, Sugar Ray: Birth, May 17
Leschyshyn, Curtis: Birth, Sept 21
Leskanic, Curtis: Birth, Apr 2
Lesnevich, Gus: Birth Anniv, Feb 22
Lett, Leon, Jr: Birth, Oct 12
Levens, Dorsey: Birth, May 21
Levinsky, Battling: Birth Anniv, June 10
Lewis, Carl: Birth, July 1
Lewis, Darren: Birth, Aug 28
Lewis, Jermaine: Birth, Oct 16
Lewis, Mark: Birth, Nov 30
Lewis, Mo: Birth, Oct 21
Lewis, Ray: Birth, May 15
Lewis, Strangler: Birth Anniv, June 30
Leyland, Jim: Birth, Dec 15
Leyritz, Jim: Birth, Dec 27
Licking PRCA Rodeo (Licking, MO), June 1

Lidstrom, Nicklas: Birth, Apr 28
Lieb, Fred: Birth Anniv, Mar 15
Lieberman-Cline, Nancy: Birth, July 1
Lierberthal, Mike: Birth, Jan 18
Ligtenberg, Kerry: Birth, May 11
Lilly, Bob: Birth, July 26
Lilly, Kristine: Birth, July 22
Lima, Jose: Birth, Sept 30
Linden, Trevor: Birth, Apr 11
Lindros, Eric: Birth, Feb 28
Lindsay, Everett: Birth, Sept 18
Lindstrom, Freddie: Birth Anniv, Nov 21
Lipinski, Tara: Birth, June 10
Lipscomb, Big Daddy: Birth Anniv, Nov 9
Listach, Pat: Birth, Sept 12
Lister, Alton: Birth, Oct 1
Liston, Sonny: Birth Anniv, May 8
Little Brown Jug (Delaware, OH), Sept 21
Little 500 (Anderson, IN), May 27
Little, Larry: Birth, Nov 2
Little League Baseball Week, Natl (Pres
  Proc), June 12
Little League Baseball World Series
  (Williamsport, PA), Aug 21
Little, Lou: Birth Anniv, Dec 6
Lizard Race, World's Greatest (Lovington,
  NM), July 4
Lloyd, Graeme: Birth, Apr 9
Lloyd, Pop: Birth Anniv, Apr 25
Loaiza, Esteban: Birth, Dec 31
Lobo, Rebecca: Birth, Oct 6
Lobster Race and Oyster Parade (Aiken,
  SC), May 5
Lockhart, Keith: Birth, Nov 10
Lofton, James: Birth, July 5
Lofton, Kenny: Birth, May 31
Lohaus, Brad: Birth, Sept 29
Lombardi, Ernie: Birth Anniv, Apr 6
Lombardi, Vince: Birth Anniv, June 11
Lonborg, Jim: Birth, Apr 16
London/Brighton Veteran Car Run (London,
  England), Nov 5
London Intl Boat Show (London, England),
  Jan 6
Lone Star Paper Chase (Amarillo, TX),
  May 27
Long, Howie: Birth, Jan 6
Longest Dam Run (Glasgow, MT), June 24
Longhorn World Chmpshp Rodeo (Auburn
  Hills, MI), Feb 18
Longhorn World Chmpshp Rodeo (Cape
  Girardeau, MO), Feb 25
Longhorn World Chmpshp Rodeo
  (Chattanooga, TN), Feb 4
Longhorn World Chmpshp Rodeo
  (Cincinnati, OH), Feb 11
Longhorn World Chmpshp Rodeo
  (Columbus, OH), Mar 17
Longhorn World Chmpshp Rodeo
  (Greenville, SC), Mar 10
Longhorn World Chmpshp Rodeo
  (Huntsville, AL), Mar 3
Longhorn World Chmpshp Rodeo (Little
  Rock, AR), Mar 24
Longhorn World Chmpshp Rodeo (Tulsa,
  OK), Jan 20
Longhorn World Chmpshp Rodeo (Winston-
  Salem, NC), Nov 3
Longhorn World Chmpshp Rodeo Finals
  (Nashville, TN), Nov 17
Longley, Luc: Birth, Jan 19
Longs Peak Scottish Highland Fest (Estes
  Park, CO), Sept 7
Lopes, Davey: Birth, May 3
Lopez, Al: Birth, Aug 20
Lopez, Felipe: Birth, Dec 19
Lopez, Hector: Birth, July 9
Lopez, Javy: Birth, Nov 5
Lopez, Nancy: Birth, Jan 6
Lopiano, Donna: Birth, Sept 11
Loretta, Mark: Birth, Aug 14
Los Angeles Marathon Quality of Life Expo
  (Los Angeles, CA), Mar 11
Lost Dutchman Days (Apache Junction, AZ),
  Feb 25
Lott, Ronnie: Birth, May 8
Loudd, Rommie: Birth Anniv, June 8

NCAA Women's Div I Swim/Div Chmpshps (Finals) (Indianapolis, IN), **Mar 16**
NCAA Women's Div I Swim/Div Chmpshps (Regionals) (various), **Mar 10**
NCAA Women's Div I Tennis Chmpshps (Finals) (Malibu, CA), **May 18**
NCAA Women's Div I Tennis Chmpshps (Regionals at sites TBA), **May 12**
NCAA Women's Div I Volleyball Chmpshps (Finals) (Richmond, VA), **Dec 14**
NCAA Women's Div I Volleyball Chmpshps (1st/2nd rounds at sites TBA), **Nov 30**
NCAA Women's Div I Volleyball Chmpshps (Regionals at sites TBA), **Dec 7**
NCAA Women's Div II Basketball Tourn (Finals at site TBA), **Mar 22**
NCAA Women's Div II Basketball Tourn (Regionals at sites TBA), **Mar 9**
NCAA Women's Div II Tennis Chmpshps (Finals at site TBA), **May 12**
NCAA Women's Div II/III Golf Chmpshps (Site TBA), **May 16**
NCAA Women's Div III Lacrosse Chmpshps (Finals at site TBA), **May 20**
NCAA Women's Div III Lacrosse Chmpshps (1st round at sites TBA), **May 10**
NCAA Women's Div III Lacrosse Chmpshps (Quarterfinals at sites TBA), **May 14**
NCAA Women's Div III Soccer Chmpshps (Finals at site TBA), **Nov 21**
NCAA Women's Div III Soccer Chmpshps (1st round at sites TBA), **Nov 3**
NCAA Women's Div III Soccer Chmpshps (Quarterfinals at sites TBA), **Nov 6**
NCAA Women's Div III Soccer Chmpshps (Regionals at sites TBA), **Nov 6**
NCAA Women's Div III Swim/Div Chmpshps (Finals) (Atlanta, GA), **Mar 9**
NCAA Women's Div III Tennis Chmpshps (Finals at site TBA), **May 9**
NCAA Women's Gymnastics Chmpshps (Finals at site TBA), **Apr 13**
NCAA Women's Gymnastics Chmpshps (Regionals), **Apr 1**
NCAA Women's Lacrosse Chmpshps (Finals) (Ewing Township, NJ), **May 19**
NCAA Women's Lacrosse Chmpshps (1st round at sites TBA), **May 10**
NCAA Women's Lacrosse Chmpshps (Quarterfinals at sites TBA), **May 13**
Ndur, Rumun: Birth, **July 7**
Nebraska
All-Canada Show (Omaha), **Feb 7**
Big 12 Wrestling Chmpshps (Lincoln), **Mar 4**
College World Series (Finals) (Omaha), **June 9**
Cornhusker State Summer Games (Omaha), **July 8**
Cornhusker State Winter Games (Omaha), **Feb 4**
Exeter Road Rally (Exeter), **Aug 13**
Kass Kounty King Korn Karnival (Plattsmouth), **Sept 7**
Mighty Mo 5K Run/Walk (South Sioux City), **June 17**
NAIA Men's/Women's Indoor Track/Field Chmpshps (Lincoln), **Mar 2**
NCAA Div I Baseball Tourn (Omaha), **June 9**
Nebraska's Big Rodeo (Burwell), **July 27**
Nebraskaland Days/Buffalo Bill Rodeo (North Platte), **June 9**
Oregon Trail Rodeo (Hastings), **Sept 2**
River City Roundup (Omaha), **Sept 22**
Special Olympics Nebraska Summer Games (Omaha), **May 31**
Whoopers and Hoopers Invitational Bask Tourn (Hastings), **Mar 17**
Neagle, Denny, Jr: Birth, **Sept 13**
Neale, Greasy: Birth Anniv, **Nov 5**
Nedved, Petr: Birth, **Dec 7**
Neely, Jess: Birth Anniv, **Jan 4**
Neilson, Roger: Birth, **June 16**
Nelson, Battling: Birth Anniv, **June 5**
Nelson, Cindy: Birth, **Aug 19**
Nelson, Don: Birth, **May 15**
Nelson, Lindsey: Birth Anniv, **May 25**
Nemchinov, Sergei: Birth, **Jan 14**

Nen, Robb: Birth, **Nov 28**
Netherlands
FIS Roller Skiing World Chmpshps (Rotterdam), **Aug 31**
Neudecker, Jerry: Birth Anniv, **Aug 13**
Neumann, Liselotte: Birth, **May 20**
Nevada
ABC-WIBC Fest of Bowling (Reno), **Oct 7**
ABC-WIBC Fest of Bowling (Reno), **Oct 15**
ABC-WIBC Sr Chmpshps (Reno), **May 27**
Bullnanza (Reno), **Sept 8**
Coyote Chase (Wellington), **June 17**
ESPY Awards (Las Vegas), **Feb 14**
Las Vegas Intl Marathon (Las Vegas), **Feb 6**
Mineral County Chamber of Commerce Fish Holiday Fish Derby (Walker Lake), **Nov 25**
Mountain Pacific Sports Federation Men's/Women's Indoor Track/Field Chmpshp (Reno), **Feb 25**
Mountain West Chmpshp (Las Vegas), **May 17**
Mountain West Men's/Women's Basketball Chmpshps (Las Vegas), **Mar 8**
Mountain West Women's Tennis Chmpshp (Las Vegas), **Apr 27**
Natl Finals Rodeo (Las Vegas), **Dec 1**
Reno Rodeo (Reno), **June 17**
Walker Lake Fish Derby (Walker Lake), **Feb 12**
WIBC Annual Mtg (Reno), **May 1**
WIBC Chmpshp Tourn (Reno), **Mar 11**
WIBC Queen's Tourn (Reno), **May 22**
Nevers, Ernie: Birth Anniv, **June 11**
Nevin, Phil: Birth, **Jan 19**
New Chicago Boat, RV and Outdoors Show (Chicago, IL), **Jan 26**
New England Sled Dog Races (Rangeley, ME), **Mar 4**
New England Volleyball Series, **May 6**
New Hampshire
Audi Mount Washington Hillclimb (Gorham), **June 23**
New Hampshire Highland Games (Lincoln), **Sept 15**
New Haven Labor Day Road Race (New Haven, CT), **Sept 4**
New Jersey
Antique Auto Show (Millville), **July 29**
Atlantic City Classic Car Show and Auction (Atlantic City), **Feb 5**
Atlantic City Intl Power Boat Show (Atlantic City), **Feb 2**
Big East Men's/Women's Outdoor Track/Field Chmpshp (Piscataway), **May 5**
Blue Claw Crab Craft Show & Crab Race (Harvey Cedars), **Aug 19**
Boardwalk Kennel Club Dog Show (Atlantic City), **Dec 2**
Corvette Show (Millville), **Sept 10**
Flemington Speedway Racing Season (Flemington), **May 1**
Gladstone Driving Event (Gladstone), **Aug 29**
Hambletonian Fest (East Rutherford), **July 29**
Hey Rube Get A Tube (Pt Pleasant), **Sept 17**
Natl Atlantic City Archery Classic (Atlantic City), **Apr 15**
NCAA Women's Lacrosse Chmpshp (Finals) (Ewing Township), **May 19**
Ocean County Decoy/Gun Show (Tuckerton), **Sept 23**
Sail Expo (Atlantic City), **Jan 20**
South Jersey Canoe/Kayak Classic (Lakewood), **June 3**
Toms River Wildfowl Art & Decoy Show (Brick), **Feb 5**
Tour of Somerville (Somerville), **May 29**
US Amateur (Golf) Chmpshp (Springfield), **Aug 21**
USET Fest of Champions (Gladstone), **June 25**
World Singles Driving Chmpshp (Gladstone), **Oct 18**
New Mexico
American Bowling Congress Convention (Albuquerque), **Mar 13**
American Bowling Congress Masters Tourn (Albuquerque), **May 2**

American Bowling Congress/Sandia Casino Chmshp Tourn (Albuquerque), **Feb 12**
Chili Challenge Off-Road Bike Race (Angel Fire), **Aug 26**
Enchanted Circle Century Bike Tour (Red River), **Sept 9**
Farmington Invtl Balloon Fest (Farmington), **May 27**
Golden Aspen Motorcycle Rally (Ruidoso), **Sept 20**
Great American Duck Race (Deming), **Aug 19**
Kite Flite (Alamogordo), **Apr 1**
Mountain West Men's Tennis Chmpshp (Las Cruces), **Apr 20**
NAIA Men's Soccer Chmpshp (Bernalilo), **Nov 16**
NCAA Men's Div I Basketball Tourn (Regional) (Albuquerque), **Mar 23**
Show of Wheels (Lovington), **Jan 29**
Taos Marathon (Taos), **June 4**
World Shovel Race Chmpshp (Angel Fire), **Feb 4**
World's Greatest Lizard Race (Lovington), **July 4**
New Orleans Boat Show (New Orleans, LA), Feb 9
New Year's Day, Jan 1
New York
Belmont Stakes (Elmont), **June 10**
Big East Men's Basketball Tourn (New York), **Mar 8**
Big East Men's/Women's Indoor Track/Field Chmpshp (Syracuse), **Feb 19**
Big East Men's/Women's Swim/Div Chmpshp (Uniondale), **Feb 24**
Capital District Scottish Games (Altamont), **Sept 2**
Empire State Golden Arms Tourn of Champions (New York), **Oct 19**
Friendship Fest (Buffalo/Ft Erie, ON, Canada), **July 1**
Golden Arms Tourn (Bronx), **July 4**
Golden Arms Tourn (Brooklyn), **June 4**
Golden Arms Tourn (Elmont), **Aug 20**
Golden Arms Tourn (Elmont), **May 7**
Golden Arms Tourn (Hicksville), **June 6**
Golden Arms Tourn (New York), **Sept 24**
Golden Arms Tourn (New York), **May 14**
Golden Arms Tourn (New York), **May 25**
Golden Arms Tourn (Staten Island), **Aug 13**
Hampton Classic Horse Show (Bridgehampton), **Aug 27**
Hershey's Kisses Figure Skating Challenge (Utica), **Apr 11**
HITS Catskills (Ellenville), **May 24**
Hudson Highlander VI (Bear Mountain), **Oct 8**
I Love New York Horse Show (Lake Placid), **July 5**
Isuzu Ironman USA Lake Placid (Lake Placid), **July 30**
Lake Placid Horse Show (Lake Placid), **June 28**
Macy's Fishing Contest in Prospect Park (Brooklyn), **July 7**
Millrose Games (New York), **Feb 4**
Natl Horse Show (New York), **Nov 2**
Natl Invitation Tourn (New York), **Mar 15**
NCAA Div I Hockey Chmpshp (Regional) (Albany), **Mar 24**
NCAA Men's Div I Basketball Tourn (1st/2nd rounds) (Buffalo, **Mar 16**
NCAA Men's Div I Basketball Tourn (Regional) (Syracuse), **Mar 23**
NCAA Men's/Women's Div II Swim/Div Chmpshps (Buffalo), **Mar 8**
New York City Marathon (New York), **Nov 5**
New York Natl Boat Show (New York), **Jan 8**
NFL Draft (New York), **Apr 15**
NJCAA Div III Baseball Chmpshp (Batavia), **May 20**
NJCAA Div III Men's Chmpshps (Delhi), **Mar 9**
NJCAA Div III Women's Basketball Chmpshp (Corning), **Mar 9**
NJCAA Men's Ice Hockey Chmpshp (Buffalo), **Mar 10**

Raymond Stampede (Raymond, AB, Canada), **June 30**

Red Lodge Home of Champions Rodeo (Red Lodge, MT), **July 2**

Red River Rodeo (Wichita Falls, TX), **June 7**

Reno Rodeo (Reno, NV), **June 17**

River City Roundup (Omaha, NE), **Sept 22**

Snake River Stampede (Nampa, ID), **July 18**

South Dakota Rodeo Assn Chmpshp Finals (Sioux Falls, SD), **Oct 13**

Southwestern Expo Livestock Show/Rodeo (Ft Worth, TX), **Jan 21**

Texas Ranch Roundup (Wichita Falls, TX), **Aug 18**

Timed Event Chmpshp of the World (Guthrie, OK), **Mar 10**

Twin Falls County Fair and Rodeo (Filer, ID), **Aug 30**

Wall Regional High School Rodeo (Wall, SD), **June 3**

Wonago World Chmpshp Rodeo (Milwaukee, WI), **June 16**

World's Oldest Continuous PRCA Rodeo (Payson, AZ), **Aug 17**

Rodgers, Derrick: Birth, Oct 14
Rodgers, Johnny: Birth, July 5
Rodman, Dennis: Birth, May 13
Rodriguez, Alex: Birth, July 27
Rodriguez, Chi-Chi: Birth, Oct 23
Rodriguez, Henry: Birth, Nov 8
Rodriguez, Ivan: Birth, Nov 30
Roe, Preacher: Birth, Feb 26
Roe, Rocky: Birth, Aug 16
Roenick, Jeremy: Birth, Jan 17
Rogan, Bullet Joe: Birth Anniv, July 28
Rogers, George, Jr: Birth, Dec 8
Rogers, Kenny: Birth, Nov 10
Rogue River Jet Boat Marathon (Gold Beach, OR), June 3
Rojas, Mel: Birth, Dec 10
Rolen, Scott: Birth, Apr 4
Rolex 24 (Daytona, FL), Feb 5
Roller Derby Begins: Anniv, Aug 13
Roller Skating Month, Natl, Oct 1
Roller Skiing: FIS World Chmpshps (Rotterdam, The Netherlands), Aug 31
Romanowski, Bill: Birth, Apr 2
Romp in the Swamp Fun Walk (Appleton, WI), Oct 15
Rooney, Art: Birth Anniv, Jan 27
Rose Bowl (Pasadena, CA), Jan 1
Rose, Jalen: Birth, Jan 20
Rose, Mauri: Birth Anniv, May 26
Rose, Pete: Birth, Apr 14
Roseboro, John: Birth, May 13
Rosen, Al: Birth, Feb 29
Rosenbloom, Slapsie Maxie: Birth Anniv, Sept 6
Rosewall, Ken: Birth, Nov 2
Ross, Barney: Birth Anniv, Dec 21
Ross, Bobby: Birth, Dec 23
Rosset, Marc: Birth, Nov 7
Rote, Kyle: Birth, Oct 27
Rothschild, Larry: Birth, Mar 12
Rowing
  Great Plains Chmpshps (Topeka, KS), Apr 29
  Head of the Charles Regatta (Cambridge and Boston, MA), Oct 21
  Head of the River Race (London, England), Mar 18
  Oxford vs Cambridge Boat Race (London, England), Apr 1
Roy, Patrick: Birth, Oct 5
Royal Ascot (Ascot, Berkshire, England), June 20
Royal Scottish Auto Club Rally (Scotland), June 8
Royal Windsor Horse Show (Windsor), May 11
Rozelle, Pete: Birth Anniv, Mar 1
Rubik, Erno: Birth, July 13
Rucinsky, Martin: Birth, Mar 11
Rucker, Johnny: Birth Anniv, Jan 15
Rudd, Dwayne: Birth, Feb 3
Rudd, Ricky: Birth, Sept 12
Rudolph, Wilma: Birth Anniv, June 23
Rueter, Kirk: Birth, Dec 1

Ruff, Lindy: Birth, Feb 17
Rugby
  Cape Fear 7s Tourn (Wilmington, NC), July 1
Run for Jodi Huisentruit (Iowa City, IA), June 3
Run of the Charles Canoe and Kayak Race (Boston, MA), Apr 30
Run to Read (Tulsa, OK), Oct 7
Running
  AEP/Fest Classic Run (Roanoke, VA), **June 3**
  Aetna US Healthcare Greater Hartford Marathon (Hartford, CT), **Oct 7**
  Amicalola Fitness Fest (Dawsonville, GA), **May 27**
  Annapolis Run (Annapolis, MD), **Aug 27**
  Anvil Mountain Run (Nome, AK), **July 4**
  Anvil Mt 59-Minute, 37-Second Challenge (Nome, AK), **Sept 14**
  AT&T Wireless Services Kokopelli Trail Marathon (Grand Junction, CO), **Sept 23**
  Atlanta Marathon and Half-Marathon (Atlanta, GA), **Nov 23**
  Avon Running–Hartford (West Hartford, CT), **July 8**
  Bank of Butterfield Bermuda Marathon (Hamilton, Bermuda), **Jan 15**
  Bare Buns Fun Run (Kaniksu Ranch, WA), **July 30**
  Beartooth Run (Red Lodge, MT), **June 24**
  Big Sur Marathon (Carmel, CA), **Apr 30**
  Bolder Boulder 10K (Boulder, CO), **May 29**
  Boston Marathon (Boston, MA), **Apr 17**
  Briggs & Stratton/Al's Run & Walk (Milwaukee, WI), **Sept 23**
  Calgary Herald Stampede Run-Off (Calgary, AB, Canada), **July 2**
  Canadian Intl Marathon (Toronto, ON, Canada), **Oct 15**
  Capital City Marathon (Tallahassee, FL), **Jan 16**
  Carolina Marathon (Columbia, SC), **Feb 26**
  Chaptico Classic (Chaptico, MD), **Aug 26**
  Charleston Distance Run (Charleston, WV), **Sept 2**
  Charlotte Observer Marathon Festival (Charlotte, NC), **Apr 15**
  Charlottetown Parks & Recreation/Atlantic Superstore Island Marathon (Charlottetown, PE, Canada), **Sept 24**
  Cheetah Run (Cincinnati, OH), **Sept 3**
  City of Los Angeles Marathon (Los Angeles, CA), **Mar 5**
  Columbus Marathon (Columbus, OH), **Oct 29**
  Coyote Chase (Wellington, NV), **June 17**
  Crater Lake Rim Runs and Marathon (Klamath Falls, OR), **Aug 12**
  Crim Fest of Races (Flint, MI), **Aug 24**
  Days of Marathon: Anniv, **Sept 2**
  Delaware Marathon (Middletown, DE), **Dec 3**
  Easter Beach Run (Daytona Beach, FL), **Apr 23**
  Equinox Marathon (Fairbanks, AK), **Sept 16**
  Examiner Bay to Breakers Race (San Francisco, CA), **May 21**
  First New York City Marathon: Anniv, **Sept 13**
  Forest of Nisene Marks Run (Aptos, CA), **June 3**
  Fox, Terry: Birth Anniv, **July 28**
  Freeze for Food 10K Race/5K Run/Walk (Madison, WI), **Jan 22**
  Ft Wayne Hoosier Marathon (Ft Wayne, IN), **June 10**
  Governor's Bay Bridge Run (Annapolis, MD), **May 7**
  Governor's Cup (Helena, MT), **June 3**
  Great Texas Mosquito Fest Competitions (Clute, TX), **July 27**
  Green Mountain Marathon (South Hero, VT), **Oct 21**
  Groundhog Run (Kansas City, MO), **Feb 6**
  Hangover Handicap Run (Klamath Falls, OR), **Jan 1**
  Hawkeye Medical Supply Hospice Road Races (Iowa City, IA), **Oct 15**
  Heroes Madison Marathon (Madison, WI), **May 28**

Hog Capital of the World Fest (Kewanee, IL), **Sept 1**
Jimmy Stewart Relay Marathon (Los Angeles, CA), **Apr 9**
Journeys Marathon (Eagle River, WI), **May 13**
Key Bank Vermont City Marathon (Burlington, VT), **May 28**
Lakestride Half-Marathon (Ludington, MI), **June 17**
Las Vegas Intl Marathon (Las Vegas, NV), **Feb 6**
LaSalle Banks Chicago Marathon (Chicago, IL), **Oct 22**
Leadville Mosquito Marathon (Leadville, CO), **July 15**
Leadville Trail 100—10K (Leadville, CO), **Aug 13**
Leadville Trail 100 Ultramarathon (Leadville, CO), **Aug 19**
Lenexa Freedom Run (Lenexa, KS), **July 4**
Lone Star Paper Chase (Amarillo, TX), **May 27**
Longest Dam Run (Glasgow, MT), **June 24**
Mackinaw City Fudge Classic (Mackinaw City, MI), **June 17**
Marathon by the Sea (St. John, NB, Canada), **Aug 20**
Maui Marathon (Kahului, HI), **Mar 19**
Mayor's Midnight Sun Marathon (Anchorage, AK), **June 17**
Methodist Health Care Houston Marathon (Houston, TX), **Jan 16**
Mighty Mo 5K Run/Walk (South Sioux City, NE), **June 17**
Motorola Austin Marathon (Austin, TX), **Feb 20**
Mount Marathon Race (Seward, AK), **July 4**
Myrtle Beach Marathon (Myrtle Beach, SC), **Feb 19**
Nanisivik Midnight Sun Marathon/Road Races (Nanisivik, NT, Canada), **July 1**
Nantucket Marathon (Nantucket, MA), **Mar 4**
New Haven Labor Day Road Race (New Haven, CT), **Sept 4**
New York City Marathon (New York, NY), **Nov 5**
Nokia Sugar Bowl Mardi Gras Marathon (New Orleans, LA), **Feb 6**
Paavo Nurmi Marathon (Upson, WI), **Aug 12**
Peachtree Junior (Atlanta, GA), **June 3**
Peachtree Road Race (Atlanta, GA), **July 4**
Pole, Pedal, Paddle (Bend, OR), **May 20**
Rose Ruiz Fraud: Anniv, **Apr 21**
Run for Jodi Huisentruit (Iowa City, IA), **June 3**
Run to Read (Tulsa, OK), **Oct 7**
Running and Fitness Week, **May 14**
St. George Marathon (St. George, UT), **Oct 1**
Saint Patrick's Day Run, McGuire's (Pensacola, FL), **Mar 11**
San Diego Marathon (San Diego, CA), **Jan 16**
Shamrock Sportsfest Marathon (Virginia Beach, VA), **Mar 17**
Sunburst Marathon (South Bend, IN), **June 10**
Sutter Home Napa Valley Marathon (Calistoga, CA), **Mar 5**
Taos Marathon (Taos, NM), **June 4**
300 Oaks Race (Greenwood, MS), **Sept 16**
Trail's End Marathon (Oregon coast), **Apr 1**
Tropical Triathlon (Lake Worth, FL), **Sept 3**
Turquoise Lake 20K Road/Trail Run (Leadville, CO), **June 3**
UPMC Health System/City of Pittsburgh Marathon (Pittsburgh, PA), **May 7**
Valley Harvest Marathon (Kentville, NS, Canada), **Oct 8**
Vancouver Intl Marathon (Vancouver, BC, Canada), **May 7**
Vermont 100-Mile Endurance Run (South Woodstock, VT), **July 14**
Waitz Wins Marathon: Anniv, **Aug 7**
Whooping Crane Run (Rockport, TX), **Apr 22**
World Half-Marathon Chmpshp (Site TBA), **Nov 12**
Wrong Way Marathoner: Anniv, **July 24**
Wyoming Marathon (Laramie, WY), **May 28**

Simms, Phil: Birth, Nov 3
Simon, Chris: Birth, Jan 30
Simpkins, Dickey: Birth, Apr 6
Simplot Games (Pocatello, ID), Feb 17
Simpson, O.J.: Birth, July 9
Simpson, Scott: Birth, Sept 17
Sinclair, Michael: Birth, Jan 31
Singh, Vijay: Birth, Feb 22
Singletary, Mike: Birth, Oct 9
Singleton, Ken: Birth, June 10
Sinkwich, Frank: Birth Anniv, Oct 20
Siragusa, Tony: Birth, May 14
Sisler, George: Birth Anniv, Mar 24
Six Gap Century & Three Gap Fifty Bike
   Ride (Dahlonega, GA), Sept 24
Skandia Life Cowes Week (Cowes, Isle of
   Wight, England), July 29
Ski-Joring Finals, Natl (Red Lodge, MT),
   Mar 11
Skiing
   American Birkebeiner (Cable to Hayward, WI),
     Feb 26
   Aspen/Snowmass Winterskol (Snowmass
     Village, CO), Jan 21
   First Security Boulder Mountain Tour (Sun
     Valley, ID), Feb 5
   FIS Alpine Jr World Chmpshp (Le Relais,
     Stoneham and Mount Ste. Anne, Canada),
     Feb 19
   FIS Nordic Jr World Chmpshp (Strbske Pleso,
     Slovakia), Jan 25
   FIS Skiflying World Chmpshp (Vikersund,
     Norway), Feb 10
   Fraser, Gretchen: Birth Anniv, Feb 11
   Johnson Bank of Hayward Kortelopet
     (Hayward, WI), Feb 26
   Johnson Wins Olympic Downhill: Anniv,
     Feb 16
   Kidd and Heuga Win Medals: Anniv, Feb 8
   Klammer Wins Downhill: Anniv, Feb 5
   Mahre Brothers Win Medals: Anniv, Feb 19
   Mahre Wins Third World Cup: Anniv, Mar 7
   Matti Nykanen's Triple: Anniv, Feb 24
   McKinney Wins World Cup: Anniv, Mar 1
   Natl Ski-Joring Finals (Red Lodge, MT),
     Mar 11
   NCAA Men's/Women's Chmpshps (Park City,
     UT), Mar 8
   Paul Bunyan Sled Dog Races, Skijoring and
     Mutt Races (Bemidji, MN), Jan 15
   Pole, Pedal, Paddle (Bend, OR), May 20
   Pole, Pedal, Paddle (Jackson, WY), Apr 1
   Roffe Wins Alpine Medal: Anniv, Feb 6
   Salomon Elite Sprints (Hayward, WI), Feb 24
   Snowfest (Tahoe City, CA), Mar 3
   Snowflake Intl Ski Jump Tourn (Westby, WI),
     Feb 12
   Special Olympics Virginia Winter Games—
     Skiing (Wintergreen, VA), Jan 10
   Swiss Miss Barnebirkie (Hayward, WI),
     Feb 24
   Werner, Buddy: Birth Anniv, Feb 26
Skowron, Bill: Birth, Dec 18
Skrudland, Brian: Birth, July 31
Slade, Chris: Birth, Jan 30
Slaney, Mary Decker: Birth, Aug 4
Slaughter, Enos: Birth, Apr 27
Sled Dog
   American Dog Derby (Ashton, ID), Feb 18
   Anchorage Fur Rendezvous (Anchorage, AK),
     Feb 11
   Beargrease Sled Dog Marathon (Duluth, MN),
     Feb 5
   Christmas Mt Village Winter Carnival and Sled
     Dog Pull (Wisconsin Dells, WI), Feb 5
   Festival du Voyageur (Winnipeg, MB,
     Canada), Feb 11
   Iditarod Sled Dog Race (Anchorage, AK),
     Mar 4
   Mackinaw Mush Sled Dog Race (Mackinaw
     City, MI), Feb 5
   Minden Sled Dog Derby (Minden, ON,
     Canada), Jan 16
   New England Sled Dog Races (Rangeley,
     ME), Mar 4
   Northern Exposure/Menominee Ice Challenge
     in Shawano (Shawano, WI), Jan 14

Open North American Chmpshp Race
   (Fairbanks, AK), Mar 17
Paul Bunyan Sled Dog Races, Skijoring and
   Mutt Races (Bemidji, MN), Jan 15
Race to the Sky (Helena, MT), Feb 11
Trig's Klondike Days (Eagle River, WI),
   Feb 26
UP 200 Sled-Dog Chmpshp (Marquette and
   Escanaba, MI), Feb 16
Yukon Quest 1,000-Mile Race (Fairbanks, AK,
   to Whitehorse, YT, Canada), Feb 12
Slegr, Jiri: Birth, May 30
Sloan, Jerry: Birth, Mar 28
Sloan, Tod: Birth Anniv, Aug 10
Slocumb, Heathcliff: Birth, June 7
Slovakia
   FIS Nordic Jr World Ski Chmpshp (Strbske
     Pleso), Jan 25
Slow-Pitch Softball Tourn (Williamsport),
   July 7
Small Craft Weekend (Mystic, CT), June 3
Smehlik, Richard: Birth, Jan 23
Smiley, John: Birth, Mar 17
Smith, Antowain: Birth, Mar 14
Smith, Bruce: Birth, June 18
Smith, Bubba: Birth, Feb 28
Smith, Chuck: Birth, Dec 21
Smith, Emmitt: Birth, May 15
Smith, Horton: Birth Anniv, May 22
Smith, Jackie: Birth, Feb 23
Smith, Jimmy, Jr: Birth, Feb 9
Smith, Kevin: Birth, Apr 7
Smith, Lee: Birth, Dec 4
Smith, Mark: Birth, Aug 28
Smith Mountain Lake State Park Triathlon
   (Smith Mountain Lake State Park, VA),
   May 13
Smith, Ozzie: Birth, Dec 26
Smith, Red: Birth Anniv, Sept 25
Smith, Robert: Birth, Mar 4
Smith, Rod: Birth, Mar 12
Smith, Stan: Birth, Dec 4
Smith, Steve: Birth, Mar 31
Smithsonian Kite Festival (Washington, DC),
   Mar 25
Smits, Rik: Birth, Aug 23
Smolinski, Bryan: Birth, Dec 27
Smoltz, John: Birth, May 15
Snake River Stampede (Nampa, ID), July 18
Snead, Sam: Birth, May 27
Snell, Matt: Birth, Aug 18
Snider, Duke: Birth, Sept 19
Sno'fly: First Kite Fly of the Year
   (Kalamazoo, MI), Jan 1
Snow Shovel Riding Contest (Economy, PA),
   Jan 15
Snow, Garth: Birth, July 28
Snow, J.T., Jr: Birth, Feb 26
Snow, Jack: Birth, Jan 25
Snowfest (Tahoe City, CA), Mar 3
Snowflake Intl Ski Jump Tourn (Westby, WI),
   Feb 12
Snowmobile
   Aspen/Snowmass Winterskol (Snowmass
     Village, CO), Jan 21
   Snowmobile Derby, Chmpshp (Eagle River,
     WI), Jan 20
   Trek Over the Top Destination Tok (Dawson
     City, YT, Canada), Feb 18
   World Chmpshp Watercross (Grantsburg, WI),
     July 14
Soap Box Derby, All-American (Akron, OH),
   July 29
Soap Box Derby Winner Disqualified: Anniv,
   Aug 20
Sobek, Joe: Birth Anniv, Apr 5
Soccer
   Big Ten Men's Chmpshps (Columbus, OH),
     Nov 10
   Big Ten Women's Chmpshps (Iowa City, IA),
     Nov 3
   Billikens Win First NCAA Soccer Title: Anniv,
     Nov 28
   Death of Escobar: Anniv, July 2
   Longest US Soccer Game: Anniv, Dec 14
   Major League Soccer Debuts: Anniv, Apr 6
   Moscow Soccer Tragedy: Anniv, Oct 20

   NAIA Men's Chmpshps (Bernalilo, NM),
     Nov 16
   NAIA Women's Chmpshps (Miami, FL),
     Nov 16
   NCAA Men's Div I Chmpshps (Finals)
     (Charlotte, NC), Dec 7
   NCAA Women's Div III Chmpshps (Finals at
     site TBA), Nov 21
   NCAA Women's Div III Chmpshps (1st round
     at sites TBA), Nov 3
   NCAA Women's Div III Chmpshp
     (Quarterfinals at sites TBA), Nov 6
   NCAA Women's Div III Chmpshps (Regionals
     at sites TBA), Nov 6
   Pele Plays Final Game: Anniv, Oct 1
   Schwan's USA Cup 2000 (Blaine, MN),
     July 16
   Soccer Tragedy: Anniv, May 29
   Special Olympics Michigan State Finals
     (Warren, MI), Oct 20
   US Women Win First Olympic Title: Anniv,
     Aug 1
   World Cup Held in US: Anniv, June 17
   World's First Soccer Club: Anniv, Oct 24
Sockalexis, Louis: Birth Anniv, Oct 24
Soden, Arthur: Birth Anniv, Apr 23
Soderstrom, Tommy: Birth, July 17
Softball
   ACC Tourn (Chapel Hill, NC), Apr 29
   ASA Boys' 18-and-Under Fast Pitch Natl
     Chmpshp (Oviedo, FL), Aug 7
   ASA Boys' Fast Pitch Natl Chmpshp (Sioux
     City, IA), July 27
   ASA Boys' Slow Pitch Natl Chmpshp
     (Anniston, AL), Aug 10
   ASA Boys' Slow Pitch Natl Chmpshp (Ft
     Payne, AL), Aug 2
   ASA Coed Class A Slow Pitch Natl Chmpshp
     (Midland, TX), Aug 24
   ASA Coed Major Slow Pitch Natl Chmpshp
     (Phoenix, AZ), Sept 1
   ASA Girls' 10-and-Under Fast Pitch Natl
     Chmpshp (Stockton, CA), Aug 8
   ASA Girls' 10-and-Under Slow Pitch Natl
     Chmpshp (Columbus, GA), Aug 10
   ASA Girls' 12-and-Under A Fast Pitch Natl
     Chmpshp (Bloomington, IN), Aug 10
   ASA Girls' 12-and-Under Slow Pitch Natl
     Chmpshp (Gadsden, AL), Aug 9
   ASA Girls' 14-and-Under A Fast Pitch Natl
     Chmpshp (Panama City, FL), Aug 9
   ASA Girls' 14-and-Under Slow Pitch Natl
     Chmpshp (Hattiesburg, MS), Aug 10
   ASA Girls' 16-and-Under A Fast Pitch Natl
     Chmpshp (Garland, TX), Aug 10
   ASA Girls' 16-and-Under Slow Pitch Natl
     Chmpshp (Tupelo, MS), Aug 10
   ASA Girls' 18-and-Under A Fast Pitch Natl
     Chmpshp (Normal, IL), Aug 8
   ASA Girls' 18-and-Under Slow Pitch Natl
     Chmpshp (Albany, GA), Aug 10
   ASA Girls' Gold 18-and-Under Fast Pitch Natl
     Chmpshp (St. Louis, MO), July 31
   ASA Men's Class A Church Slow Pitch Natl
     Chmpshp (Mobile, AL), Sept 1
   ASA Men's Class A Fast Pitch Natl Chmpshp
     (College Station, TX), Aug 30
   ASA Men's Class A Industrial Slow Pitch Natl
     Chmpshp (Dothan, AL), Sept 1
   ASA Men's Class A Modified Pitch Natl
     Chmpshp (Fond du Lac, WI), Aug 31
   ASA Men's Class A 16-Inch Slow Pitch Natl
     Chmpshp (Chandler, AZ), Sept 1
   ASA Men's Class A Slow Pitch Natl Chmpshp
     (Lancaster, CA), Sept 1
   ASA Men's Class B Fast Pitch Natl Chmpshp
     (Springfield, MO), Aug 30
   ASA Men's Class B Slow Pitch Natl Chmpshp
     (Lakeland, FL), Sept 22
   ASA Men's Class C Fast Pitch Natl Chmpshp
     (Aurora, CO), Aug 30
   ASA Men's Class C Slow Pitch Natl Chmpshp
     (Marietta, GA), Sept 22
   ASA Men's Class D Slow Pitch Natl Chmpshp
     (Montgomery, AL), Sept 22
   ASA Men's Major Church Slow Pitch Natl
     Chmpshp (Dothan, AL), Sept 1

Waddell, Rube: Birth Anniv, Oct 13
Wade, Margaret: Birth Anniv, Dec 30
Wade, Virginia: Birth, July 10
Wadkins, Lanny: Birth, Dec 5
Wadsworth, Andre: Birth, Oct 19
Wagner, Billy: Birth, June 25
Wagner, Honus: Birth Anniv, Feb 24
Wagner, Leon: Birth, May 13
Waikiki Roughwater Swim (Honolulu, HI), Sept 4
Waitz, Grete: Birth, Oct 1
Wakefield, Tim: Birth, Aug 2
Walbeck, Matt: Birth, Oct 2
Walcott, Jersey Joe: Birth Anniv, Jan 31
Walk & Roll Chicago (Chicago, IL), May 21
Walker, Antoine: Birth, Aug 12
Walker, Doak: Birth Anniv, Jan 1
Walker, Fleet: Birth Anniv, Oct 7
Walker, Herschel: Birth, Mar 3
Walker Lake Fish Derby (Walker Lake, NV), Feb 12
Walker, Larry: Birth, Dec 1
Walker, Samaki: Birth, Feb 25
Walking
  Briggs & Stratton/Al's Run & Walk (Milwaukee, WI), **Sept 23**
  Chaptico Classic (Chaptico, MD), **Aug 26**
  Custer State Park Seasonal Volksmarch (Custer, SD), **May 20**
  Freeze for Food 10K Race/5K Run/Walk (Madison, WI), **Jan 22**
  Mackinac Bridge Walk (St. Ignace to Mackinaw City, MI), **Sept 4**
  March of Dimes WalkAmerica, **Apr 29**
  Mighty Mo 5K Run/Walk (South Sioux City, NE), **June 17**
  Romp in the Swamp Fun Walk (Appleton, WI), **Oct 15**
  Run for Jodi Huisentruit (Iowa City, IA), **June 3**
  300 Oaks Race (Greenwood, MS), **Sept 16**
  Walking Weekend (Quinebaug-Shetucket Natl Heritage Corridor, CT), **Oct 7**
  Walktoberfest, **Oct 7**
  YMCA Spring Has Sprung 5K (Kingston, NY), **Apr 9**
Wall Regional High School Rodeo (Wall, SD), **June 3**
Wallace, John: Birth, Feb 9
Wallace, Rasheed: Birth, Sept 17
Wallace, Rusty: Birth, Aug 14
Walls, Wesley: Birth, Feb 26
Walsh, Bill: Birth, Nov 30
Walsh, Ed: Birth Anniv, May 14
Walsh Invitational Rifle Tourn (Cincinnati, OH), Nov 3
Walters, Rex: Birth, Mar 12
Walton, Bill: Birth, Nov 5
Walton, Isaac: Birth Anniv, Aug 9
Waltrip, Darrell: Birth, Feb 5
Waner, Lloyd: Birth Anniv, Mar 16
Waner, Paul: Birth Anniv, Apr 16
Warbirds in Action Air Show (Shafter, CA), **Apr 22**
Ward, Arch: Birth Anniv, Dec 27
Ward, Charlie, Jr: Birth, Oct 12
Ward, Monte: Birth Anniv, Mar 3
Warfield, Paul: Birth, Nov 28
Wargo, Tom: Birth, Sept 16
Warner, Pop: Birth Anniv, Apr 5
Washburn, Ray: Birth, May 31
Washington
  Bare Buns Fun Run (Kaniksu Ranch), **July 30**
  Corvette and High Performance Summer Meet (Puyallup), **June 23**
  Corvette and High Performance Winter Meet (Puyallup), **Feb 12**
  Everett Salty Sea Days (Everett), **June 1**
  PAC-10 Men's Swim Chmpshps (Federal Way), **Mar 2**
  Play Tacoma Days (Tacoma), **July 1**
  Seattle Boat Show (Seattle), **Jan 21**
Washington, District of Columbia
  Bastille Day Moonlight Golf Tourn, **July 14**
  Smithsonian Kite Festival, **Mar 25**
  White House Easter Egg Roll, **Apr 24**

Youth Hockey Tier I Natl Chmpshp (12 and under), **Apr 7**
Youth Hockey Tier I Natl Chmpshp (17 and under), **Apr 7**
Washington, Kenny: Birth Anniv, Aug 31
Washington, Ted: Birth, Apr 13
Water Ski Days (Lake City, MN), June 23
Waterfield, Bob: Birth Anniv, July 26
Waterfowl Festival (Easton, MD), Nov 10
Watermelon Seed-Spitting and Speed-Eating Chmpshp (Pardeeville, WI), Sept 10
Watermelon Thump (Luling, TX), June 22
Watson, Allen: Birth, Nov 18
Watson, Bob: Birth, Apr 10
Watson, Tom: Birth, Sept 4
Watters, Ricky: Birth, Apr 7
Way, Charles: Birth, Dec 27
Weatherspoon, Clarence: Birth, Sept 8
Weaver, Buck: Birth Anniv, Aug 18
Webb, Karrie: Birth, Dec 21
Webb, Richmond: Birth, Jan 11
Webb, Spud: Birth, July 13
Webber, Chris: Birth, Mar 1
Webster County Woodchopping Fest (Webster Springs, WV), May 20
Weight Lifting: USA Olympic Team Trials (New Orleans, LA), June 17
Weight, Doug: Birth, Jan 21
Weiskopf, Tom: Birth, Nov 9
Weiss, Walt, Jr: Birth, Nov 28
Weissmuller, Johnny: Birth Anniv, June 2
Wells, Bonzi: Birth, Sept 20
Wells, David: Birth, May 20
Wells Fargo Sun Bowl (El Paso, TX), Dec 31
Wells, Willie: Birth Anniv, Oct 10
Werblin, Sonny: Birth Anniv, Mar 17
Werner, Buddy: Birth Anniv, Feb 26
West Virginia
  Charleston Distance Run (Charleston), **Sept 2**
  Head-of-the-Mon-River Horseshoe Tourn (Fairmont), **May 27**
  Webster County Woodchopping Fest (Webster Springs), **May 20**
West, David: Birth, Sept 1
West, Doug: Birth, May 27
West, Jerry: Birth, May 28
West, Joe: Birth, Oct 31
Westbrook, Bryant: Birth, Dec 19
Western Stock Show and Rodeo, Natl (Denver, CO), Jan 8
Westminster Kennel Club Dog Show (New York, NY), Feb 14
Westphal, Paul: Birth, Nov 30
Wethered, Joyce: Birth Anniv, Nov 17
Wetteland, John: Birth, Aug 21
Wheat, Zack: Birth Anniv, May 23
Wheatley, Tyrone: Birth, Jan 19
Wheel to Weston (Kansas City and Weston, MO), June 18
Whitaker, Pernell: Birth, Jan 2
White, Bill: Birth, Jan 28
White, Deacon: Birth Anniv, Dec 2
White, Devon: Birth, Dec 29
White House Easter Egg Roll (Washington, DC), Apr 24
White, Jahidi: Birth, Feb 19
White, Randy: Birth, Jan 15
White, Reggie: Birth, Dec 19
White, Rondell: Birth, Feb 23
White, Sol: Birth Anniv, June 12
Whiten, Mark: Birth, Nov 25
Whitfield, Bob, Jr: Birth, Oct 18
Whitman, Walt: Birth Anniv, May 31
Whitworth, Kathy: Birth, Sept 27
Whoopers and Hoopers Invitational Bask Tourn (Hastings, NE), Mar 17
Whooping Crane Run (Rockport, TX), Apr 22
WICC Greatest Bluefish Tourn (Long Island Sound, CT and NY), Aug 26
Widger, Chris: Birth, May 21
Wiegert, Zach: Birth, Aug 16
Wightman, Hazel: Birth Anniv, Dec 20
Wildflower Triathlon Fest (Lake San Antonio, CA), May 5
Wildlife and Western Art Expo (Lakeland, FL), Mar 10
Wilhelm, Hoyt: Birth, July 26

Wilkens, Lenny: Birth, Oct 28
Wilkes, Jamaal: Birth, May 2
Wilkinson, Bud: Birth Anniv, Apr 23
Wilkinson, Dan: Birth, Mar 13
Wilkinson, J.L.: Death Anniv, Apr 21
Willard, Jess: Birth Anniv, Dec 29
Williams, Aeneas: Birth, Jan 29
Williams, Archie: Birth Anniv, May 1
Williams, Bernie: Birth, Sept 13
Williams, Billy: Birth, June 15
Williams, Brian: Birth, Dec 17
Williams, Buck: Birth, Mar 8
Williams, Darryl: Birth, Jan 8
Williams, Dan: Birth, Dec 15
Williams, Dick: Birth, May 7
Williams, Erik: Birth, Sept 7
Williams, Esther: Birth, Aug 8
Williams, Hot Rod: Birth, Aug 9
Williams, Jason: Birth, Nov 18
Williams, Jayson: Birth, Feb 22
Williams, Jimy: Birth, Oct 4
Williams, Lefty: Birth Anniv, Mar 9
Williams, Matt: Birth, Nov 28
Williams, Mitch: Birth, Nov 17
Williams, Scott: Birth, Mar 21
Williams, Serena: Birth, Sept 26
Williams, Ted: Birth, Aug 30
Williams, Venus: Birth, June 17
Williams, Wally, Jr: Birth, Feb 19
Williamson, Corliss: Birth, Dec 4
Williamson, Fred: Birth, Mar 5
Willis, Kevin: Birth, Sept 6
Wills, Bump: Birth, July 27
Wills, Maury: Birth, Oct 2
Wilson, Dan: Birth, Mar 25
Wilson, Hack: Birth Anniv, Apr 26
Wilson, Larry: Birth, Mar 24
Wilson, Mookie: Birth, Feb 9
Wilson, Paul: Birth, Mar 28
Wilson, Reinard: Birth, Dec 12
Wilson, Ron: Birth, May 28
Wimbledon (London, England), June 26
Winfield, Dave: Birth, Oct 3
Wingfield, Dontonio: Birth, June 23
Winslow, Kellen: Birth, Nov 5
Winter Begins, Dec 21
Winter Festivals and Celebrations
  Aspen/Snowmass Winterskol (Snowmass Village, CO), **Jan 21**
  Badger State Winter Games (Wausau, WI), **Feb 4**
  BC Winter Games (Quesnel, BC, Canada), **Feb 24**
  Bracebridge Winter Carnival (Bracebridge, ON, Canada), **Feb 11**
  Calgary Winter Fest (Calgary, AB, Canada), **Feb 11**
  Christmas Mt Village Winter Carnival and Sled Dog Pull (Wisconsin Dells, WI), **Feb 5**
  Frosty Frolics (Bancroft, ON, Canada), **Feb 19**
  Goodwill Games (Lake Placid, NY), **Feb 17**
  Gravity Games (Mammoth Lakes, CA), **Jan 20**
  Iowa Games Sports Fest (Dubuque, IA), **Feb 4**
  McCall Winter Carnival (McCall, ID), **Jan 28**
  Northern BC Winter Games (Ft St. John, BC, Canada), **Feb 4**
  Ontario Winter Carnival Bon Soo (Sault Ste Marie, ON, Canada), **Jan 28**
  Penguin Plunge (Jamestown, RI), **Jan 1**
  Perchville USA (East Tawas, MI), **Feb 4**
  Perry's "BRR" (Bike Ride to Rippey) (Perry, IA), **Feb 5**
  Polar Bear Swim (Sheboygan, WI), **Jan 1**
  Saint Paul Winter Carnival (St. Paul, MN), **Jan 28**
  Sandpoint Winter Carnival (Sandpoint, ID), **Jan 19**
  Snowfest (Tahoe City, CA), **Mar 3**
  Snowmobile Derby, Chmpshp (Eagle River, WI), **Jan 20**
  Tip-Up Town USA (Houghton Lake, MI), **Jan 14**
  Winter Carnival (Red Lodge, MT), **Mar 3**
  Winter Games of Oregon (Mt Hood), **Mar 3**

Women (cont'd)——Zuppke

Yes! Please send me additional copies of **Chase's 2000 Calendar of Events** and **2000 Chase's Sports Calendar of Events**.

Ship to _____

Address _____

_____

City, State, Zip _____

Phone (___) _____

Please send me _____ copies of the 2000 edition of
CHASE'S CALENDAR OF EVENTS at $59.95 each ISBN 0-8092-2776-2 $_____

and _____ copies of the 2000 edition of

CHASE'S SPORTS CALENDAR OF EVENTS at $29.95 each ISBN 0-8092-2600-6 $_____

Add applicable sales tax in AL, CA, FL, IL, NC, NJ, NY, OH, PA, TX, WA $_____

Shipping & Handling: Add $5.00 for the first copy,
$3.50 for each additional copy $_____

                                                               Total $_____

☐ Check or money order enclosed payable to: NTC/Contemporary Publishing Group, Inc.

Charge my   ☐ Visa   ☐ MasterCard   ☐ American Express   ☐ Discover Card

Acct. # _____ Exp. Date ____ / ____

X _____
              Signature (if charging to bankcard)

Name (please print) _____

STANDING ORDER AUTHORIZATION

To make sure that I receive each year's new edition, please accept this Standing Order
Authorization to ship me _____ copies of *Chase's Calendar of Events* and
_____ copies of *Chase's Sports Calendar of Events*, beginning with the 2001 edition.
Bill me at the address shown at the top of this order form. I understand that I may cancel
my Standing Order at any time.

X _____
              Signature   Date

_____ (___) _____
Name (please print)   Phone

GUARANTEE: Any book you order is unconditionally guaranteed and may be returned
within 10 days of receipt for full refund.

9437

Mail to: **NTC/Contemporary Publishing Group, Inc., Dept. C**
4255 W Touhy Ave
Lincolnwood, IL 60721-1975